The Palgrave Handbook of Learning for Transformation

"An exciting injection of fresh ideas and insights into a field that risks becoming 'stuck' and moribund! The editors of this Handbook bring together a remarkable and impressive set of international scholars and practitioners representing a wide range of geographical, disciplinary, and cultural perspectives in the field of transformative learning. Using the metaphor of 'provocation' as a lens and a world-wide pandemic as a backdrop, they challenge us as practitioners and scholars to re-envision our work and. Illuminating long-standing tensions and issues in the field, they bring new understandings to the meaning and practice of transformative learning, effectively blurring the lines between theory and practice and scholars and practitioners. Reflecting on this emerging future, the editors and authors invite us to use this moment and these provocations and propositions to transform ourselves, our worlds, and the field itself."

—John M. Dirkx, *Professor and Mildred B. Erickson Distinguished Chair (Emeritus) at Higher, Adult and Lifelong Education, Michigan State University, U.S.A.*

"When Tony Blair in 1997 was elected as British prime minister a reporter asked him what would be the three most important topics of his future policy. The famous reply was: 'education, education, education!' - and so Blair very soon started what became a consequent top-down streamlining and control of British schooling, which has certainly not resulted in any better and more versatile learning. The basis of this was a rather primitive understanding of human learning as a direct transfer of what is taught. The most consequent contrast to this is the concept and idea of transformative learning as introduced by Jack Mezirow in 1978 and later further developed in many ways. The present book can be seen as the most extensive publication of the interpretation and further development of this much more fruitful and forward-looking concept and approach of learning."

—Knud Illeris, *Professor Emeritus at Roskilde University, Denmark*

Aliki Nicolaides · Saskia Eschenbacher ·
Petra T. Buergelt · Yabome Gilpin-Jackson ·
Marguerite Welch · Mitsunori Misawa
Editors

The Palgrave Handbook of Learning for Transformation

palgrave
macmillan

Editors
Aliki Nicolaides
University of Georgia
Athens, GA, USA

Petra T. Buergelt
University of Canberra
Bruce, ACT, Australia

Marguerite Welch
Saint Mary's College of California
Moraga, CA, USA

Saskia Eschenbacher
Adult Learning & Counseling
Akkon University of Applied Sciences
for Human Sciences
Berlin, Germany

Yabome Gilpin-Jackson
SLD Consulting
Port Coquitlam, BC, Canada

Mitsunori Misawa
University of Tennessee
Knoxville, TN, USA

ISBN 978-3-030-84693-0   ISBN 978-3-030-84694-7   (eBook)
https://doi.org/10.1007/978-3-030-84694-7

© The Editor(s) (if applicable) and The Author(s), under exclusive license to Springer Nature Switzerland AG 2022
This work is subject to copyright. All rights are solely and exclusively licensed by the Publisher, whether the whole or part of the material is concerned, specifically the rights of translation, reprinting, reuse of illustrations, recitation, broadcasting, reproduction on microfilms or in any other physical way, and transmission or information storage and retrieval, electronic adaptation, computer software, or by similar or dissimilar methodology now known or hereafter developed.
The use of general descriptive names, registered names, trademarks, service marks, etc. in this publication does not imply, even in the absence of a specific statement, that such names are exempt from the relevant protective laws and regulations and therefore free for general use.
The publisher, the authors and the editors are safe to assume that the advice and information in this book are believed to be true and accurate at the date of publication. Neither the publisher nor the authors or the editors give a warranty, expressed or implied, with respect to the material contained herein or for any errors or omissions that may have been made. The publisher remains neutral with regard to jurisdictional claims in published maps and institutional affiliations.

Cover credit: ©Etan Pavavalung

This Palgrave Macmillan imprint is published by the registered company Springer Nature Switzerland AG
The registered company address is: Gewerbestrasse 11, 6330 Cham, Switzerland

FOREWORD BY VICTORIA J. MARSICK, ELIZABETH KASL AND KAREN E. WATKINS

We are honored to invite you into this Handbook in this Foreword. We trust you will find a strong and compelling vision of passages to transformation in these pages.

LOOKING BACK, LOOKING FORWARD

To situate our look forward, we begin by looking back. This Handbook has its roots in a discourse that blossomed in the adult education literature in the 1970s when Jack Mezirow began his quest to develop a comprehensive theory of adult learning. Our purpose here is to mark his effort to craft theory unbounded by disciplinary knowledge silos. Mezirow explains this effort:

> Psychologists interested in adult learning often find themselves trapped within the framework of particular theories and paradigms.... Philosophers, linguists, sociologists, and political scientists also have legitimate interests in adult learning, but each group has a different frame of reference and a different vocabulary for interpreting the phenomenon. Few efforts have been made to develop a synthesis of the different theories that educators of adults can use. (1991, p. xi)

Over the years, adult educators have continued to expand the breadth of disciplines that inform our understanding of learning that transforms (Anand et al., 2020; Taylor, 2008).

v

vi FOREWORD BY VICTORIA J. MARSICK, ELIZABETH KASL ...

This Handbook is the next milestone in that quest. Readers will broaden their horizons as they consider transformation from multiple perspectives—some that will be familiar, others that will be new. Handbook editors use the metaphor of "passageways" to entice readers into a pursuit of knowledge gleaned from crossing borders and possibly dissolving them:

> Our guiding metaphor in creating this Handbook is *passageways....* A passage points to two directions—backwards to the space one is leaving and forward to the space one is approaching.... Our intention is to invite the reader to "pass through," that is, to leave the familiar space that currently defines the territory of transformative learning and turn toward something new....

So what might readers expect as they pass through?

We note that "trans" is a Latin prefix meaning "across," "beyond," or "on the other side of." A few "trans" words describe the passageways that beckon readers.

- Transform: change in composition, structure, character, or condition
- Transition: process or period of changing from one state or condition to another
- Transcend: to go farther, rise above, or go beyond the limits of
- Transdisciplinary: integrating disciplines, transcending traditional boundaries

In planning the Handbook, editors called authors to reach for new horizons in conceptualizing transformative learning and transformation. They embodied this call with their first tentative title, which was "Trans*****." We applaud this invitation to find new configurations. A passageway is a liminal space—a space of limitless possibility as the passersby considers multiple possibilities in search of new understanding.

Creating Spaces of Possibility

Complexity science encourages us to see the way learning—especially transformational learning—allows us to emerge from the chaos of multiple perspectives with a new coherence (Juarrero, in Watkins et al., 2021). This occurs in part because of the sense making we do through the interconnected networks we are part of (Siemens, in Watkins et al., 2021). This Handbook creates a space of possibility (Juarrero, in Watkins et al., 2021) for a new coherence around the meaning of transformation to emerge.

In the spirit of seeking new horizons and new coherence, especially for our tribe of adult education scholar-practitioners, we reached out to people who are not adult educators and asked them about their vision of transformation.

Taking advantage of our common experience with one of the most dramatic moments in the past century, we used the concrete example of the global pandemic as a point of departure for thinking about transformation. Polling friends, family, and colleagues from different walks of life, we asked:

1. When you think about transformation of individuals, groups, systems, and/or communities post COVID-19, how would you characterize this emerging transformation?
2. What example comes to mind to illustrate your thinking about transformation?

People commented on the ways in which they have learned to live with uncertainty and the need to pivot on a dime, their need for connection and how they have found ways to attain this, the differential experiences of the poor and marginalized, and some of the fundamental changes in work environments that have impacted them.

Our respondents thought about the personal transformations triggered by the pandemic and shared what this meant to them, especially the way we are rediscovering our common humanity in our little corners of the world.

> it is a discovery of other aspects of the colleagues we have been used to know for how they deal with academic issues or for their ideas, but not for their creativity or for their personal interests and tastes. We are discovering and sharing family histories; we are entering each other's kitchens; we are encountering the others in new and different terms...—Maura Striano, University of Naples Federico II
> The view outside my window has become more important to me. It is truly my window on the world.—Nancy Dixon

viii FOREWORD BY VICTORIA J. MARSICK, ELIZABETH KASL ...

They thought about this as a global phenomenon:

> Lost and found. Found and lost. There have been other cataclysmic events in human history - yet the closest I can find to this is the spread of smallpox among indigenous peoples in the Americas - where entire cultures were wiped out (Aztecs and the Inca). While this disease will likely not destroy mankind - it is changing cultures throughout the world. The ambiguity that comes from this cultural assault combined with other transformative activities (generational shifts, technological shifts) will be merged into the transformed culture on some level. My question is 'Will the ambiguity lead to an awakening to our human mortality and the invasive nature of our activities?' And if so, what will our collective response be?—Jill Jinks
> I believe we are becoming more aware of the connections we share globally; more aware of work-life balance; more aware of the free-doms/empowerment we have that we sacrifice to organizations when we go "to work" at an office 40+ hours/week.—No name

So the ambiguity and liminal state of unknowing has reminded us of our global interconnectedness as well as the sacrifices we have taken for granted as part of working. These reflections have led to some changes of values and perspective.

> I think the biggest transformation has been one of perspective. Things that we previously took for granted as being available (public interactions, social gatherings, being able to visit a dying loved one in the hospital) are no longer a given. We have to re-think our decisions and actions pre-Covid and look at them in the new reality of what life is like now, or might be in the future. We also, as individual or groups, have to weigh the risks associated with each social activity against the possibility that we, friends/family, or strangers may be negatively affected by our actions if we are unknowingly contagious. This forces us to consider ourselves and others in ways we might not have considered previously. This change in perspective includes major life decisions, such as career trajectory (is my occupation pandemic-proof?) or more subtle ones (what do I get out of eating at a restaurant and is it worth it?).—Bonnie Marsick Decker
> Covid has propelled us out of many of our routines. While some of business as usual has just moved to virtual, taking more time, in other ways it has given us a chance to step out of our habits and routinized patterns to question the ways we have worked in the past and wonder about better ways to work. I think Covid has also given us an opportunity to stop and think about what really is important to us, sometimes raising some

uncomfortable questions. To be transformed as people or organizations or cultures, we will need to be willing to openly pursue even those uncomfortable questions. What is worth doing? What's the best way to work? How can we stay connected--really connected?—Betsy Aylin

These reflections describe the individual and potentially global perspective changes we may experience but do not alter our understanding of transformation. A couple of other comments hint of a deeper shift in transformation.

I was thinking about sexual development—an ongoing process over one's lifetime - as one of the most astounding series of transformations—the processes of coming to understand, and often repeatedly re-understand/re-define who you are as a sexual being and as a romantic partner. Some aspects of these transformations are guided by biological changes over which you have no control, while others, if they happen, are the result of much more intentional reflection - figuring out who you are, who you want to be, what you want from relationships, and what your relationship is to both your community and societal norms, to list just a few examples. These constitute so many moments of disorientation about things that are core to your existence and identity - discovering feelings you didn't know you had; discovering subconscious or suppressed desires, goals, agendas and past experiences; questioning your values; and discovering things you do and don't like about yourself and your interactions with others at both individual and community levels. As I think about all those moments of disorientation, it strikes me that there's something of a spectrum that may be useful in thinking through transformation - on one end are aspects of transformation that involve reflection and willful action and on the other end are things that will simply happen regardless of intention or intended action.—Adam Neaman
I think more and more people are experiencing world events (the pandemic, climate change & infrastructure failings, racial and society polarization and fracturing) that leave them feeling over their heads with complexity and a sense of overwhelm. Old ways of knowing and being are not working so some of us hunker down and cling to what we know and others of us feel the draw of opening up and surrender. I honestly am in a state of unknowing about what comes next -- how we will individually and collectively adapt to this emerging demand to evolve ... If transformation requires a liminal state of "unknowing" then this is where we are right now.—Renee Rogers

These reflections look at the difference in our experiences of transformation when the trigger is outside of our control vs. when we learn through personal reflection and also speak to the complexity and uncertainty of our experience of world events. We are in a liminal state of unknowing, what Ann Pendleton-Jullian (in Watkins et al., 2021) describes as working at the periphery.

Pendleton-Jullian's concept of work at the periphery calls for exploring many different avenues of meaning without closure of any options. This allows us to push ourselves into the liminal space beyond the bounds of our usual habits of mind. She opens and keeps open multiple lines of inquiry. These different "looks" at a situation invite the curious side of the brain to "sense breaking" to enable new orders of sense making. Keeping our attention on multiple lines of inquiry at the same time demands that the mind embrace and live with paradox and contradictions. We do not resolve our perplexity by choosing one direction over another; rather we remain in this state of perplexity, live in this dynamic tension, and in so doing, enable emergence of radically new "spaces." This Handbook is an excellent example of pursuing multiple passageways toward an emerging vision of transformation as yet undiscovered—still just a little out of reach.

Passing the Torch

We started this Foreword by noting the growth and variety in the scholarship of transformative learning. Yet, we also note that the research has been constricted by the homogeneity of the scholars theorizing and researching transformative learning. To date, our scholarship is dominated by the experiences of Western, Educated, Industrialized, Rich, and Democratic or (WEIRD) populations (Muthukrishna, et al., 2020). Ironically, transformative learning calls for opening up boundaries, inviting diversity, engaging in perspective taking, and revising beliefs and assumptions to grow views and mindsets. But the lack of diversity in the community of transformative learning scholars—and the potential negative messages that lack of diversity sends to the community's members—is a contradiction to the theory.

Some efforts have been made over time to transform the community of transformative learners in order to welcome and value work from many different disciplines, cultural traditions, races, ethnicities, and socioeconomic disparities—without much noticeable impact. Hoping to make progress with walking the talk of inclusion, organizers for the 2018 transformation learning conference chose the conference theme, "Building Transformative Community: Exacting Possibility in Today's Times."

Among the steps organizers took to further their goal was an action research study focused on inclusion. Twenty-two stakeholders—scholars, conference organizers, leaders, and community members—were asked how easy or difficult it is for a new person to become a member of the community and what barriers stand in the way of inclusiveness. Results indicated that as recently as the previous conference in 2016, creating a culture of inclusion continued to be a problem. One interviewee reported: "At the Tacoma conference, it broke my heart when this young African American woman, a first timer, stood up in the final session and said, 'I don't feel welcome here. I don't see people who look like me. I just don't feel comfortable, and I don't feel included.'" An African-American scholar who had researched transformative learning in an African-American community did not feel her work was valued because the community "didn't grab it." Most interviewees in the convenience sample reported that a big barrier to inclusion was the perception of an "insider" group whose members did not seek to extend their boundaries.

The 2018 conference sought multiple ways to invite participation of diverse members to change the conference's culture toward inclusion. For example, in a compelling and moving plenary session, a panel of scholars and practitioners shared their personal stories of transformative learning related to structural racism and microaggressions (Welch et al., 2020). An Inclusion Committee infused the conference with activities and guidelines to support engagement. One of these activities was the communal creation of a sand painting. Bert Benally, Dine artist from the Navajo Nation, facilitated this process "where participants can together identify an area causing disharmony in and find a symbol of the problem and another symbol or representation to correct that problem" (Welch et al., 2018, p. 52). These are examples of many efforts to draw in and value diversity of voices and perspectives.

This Handbook grew out of the groundwork laid in the 2018 conference. The editors have taken up the mantle of reinventing the way members in our community organize ourselves, our collective work, and our impulse toward a culture of greater inclusiveness. The Handbook is itself designed to open up new perspectives.

Mezirow grounded his view of transformative learning in rational discourse which embraced diversity of thought by advocating examination of assumptions in order to re-draw our collective understanding of ourselves and our worlds. The Editors of this Handbook invite us to a different way of sense making and sense breaking. They ask us to enter the liminal space of these passageways and to live in the tension of conflicting viewpoints while we seek to midwife emergence—as the authors we meet in these pages work at the periphery to open up different avenues of meaning making.

We pass the torch to these exciting new voices of transformative learning who are making sense of new generations of thought and practice in describing our shared complex world. Perhaps they will dis[RUPT][1] old ways of seeing the world and invite us to a new journey of transformation.

Victoria J. Marsick
Professor of Adult Learning &
Leadership, Teachers College
Columbia University
New York City, USA

Elizabeth Kasl
Independent Scholar
California, USA

Karen E. Watkins
Professor of Learning,
Leadership & Organization
Development
University of Georgia
Athens, USA

References

Anand, T. S., Anand, S. V., Welch, M., Marsick, V. J., & Langer, A. (2020). Overview of transformative learning theory I: Theory and its evolution. *Reflective Practice, 21*(6), 732–743.

Mezirow, J. D. (1991). *Transformative dimensions of adult learning.* Jossey-Bass.

[1] Rapid, Unpredictable, Paradoxical, Tangled—from the Center for Creative Leadership??

Muthukrishna, M., Bell, A. V., Henrich, J., Curtin, C. M., Gedranovich, A., McInerney, J., & Thue, B. (2020). Beyond Western, Educated, Industrial, Rich, and Democratic (WEIRD) psychology: Measuring and mapping scales of cultural and psychological distance. *Psychological Science, 31*(6), 678–701.

Taylor, E. W. (2008). Transformative learning theory. *New Directions for Adult and Continuing Education, 2008*(119), 5–15.

Watkins, K., Nicolaides, A., & Herr, N. (2021, January 29). *Learning through complexity: Exploring the intersection of complexity science and informal and incidental learning* [Webinar]. The University of Georgia. https://uoutu.be/USmWilo-Hnc.

Welch, M. A., Akasha, A. K. A., Saunders, P., Buerglet, P. T., Gilpin-Jackson, Y., Ferguson, J., & Marsick, V. J. (2020). Your story, our story: The transformative power of life narratives. *Reflective Practice, 21*(6), 861–876.

Welch, M. A., Marsick, V. J., & Holt, D. (Eds.) (2018). *Building transformative community: Exacting possibility in today's times.* Teachers College, Columbia University.

Foreword by Ahreum Lim

If anyone asks me how it was to work on this colossal project with 6 editors and 103 authors who share different cultural backgrounds, live in different time zones, and most importantly, whom I have never met before in a human form, I would suggest them to imagine a kid who comes to the swimming pool for the first time after graduating from a beginner's class. Imagine that the kid, who is just holding on her kickboard in the water, gets to watch a bunch of grown-ups swimming beyond the lane lines, without any kickboards freely. Surprisingly, they are gentle enough to let her join in and be one of the cool gangs, teaching her how to swim freely. Initially, the kid feels feel terrified, as it feels like starting a new way of living in the water. She doesn't want to look like a beginner ... although she is. Thus, she tries her best to let herself float in the water, even though she has no idea of what she is doing. Often, fear kicks in, when water suddenly gets up her nose, and she feels as if she is drowning. However, the generous helpers coach her to paddle harder, push the water harder, and find a balance of her own. Essentially, they are teaching her to get a sense of what it means to glide in the water somehow. Swimming closely with them is teaching her how to swim.

The analogy beautifully sketches my working experience with this team of utmost diversity as well as the Handbook itself. Six editors who wanted to create a portal toward a newer theory of transformation invited 103 authors who are sympathetic with their audacity to join the team. We had countless email exchanges. The editorial team held regular—more than

xvi FOREWORD BY AHREUM LIM

20—two-hour-long Zoom meetings that glued us together during the long global pandemic, with a twenty-minute-long check-in that summed up our past weeks of agony, joy, relief, and excitement, followed by a lively conversation over the chapters, reviews, and editorial feedback, for one sole purpose: creating a handbook that vitalizes the learning for transformation theory.

The goal is to let the readers swim beyond the lane lines. However, the way in which the editors open up the portal for the readers to escape from their comfort zone is inclusive, yet with discretion. Despite the rooted discipline of the theory, transformative learning invites epistemology beyond one discipline. Often the smorgasbord approach endangers the theory by making it a theory of everything, which would hinder rigor and dwindle faith in the theory. This Handbook refuses it deliberately. Instead, the Handbook offers a space that braids the lines of thought that are generated in different disciplines and/or contexts with different theoretical underpinnings, under the common scholarly interest in the quest for the transformation. Thus, their portal is rather exclusive, opening up the passage only for those who are committed to the field of transformation. Meanwhile, the authors offer this Handbook as a new provocation, one that surfaces the unheard voices, underexplored theories, and unprecedented methodologies of transformation, to make the portal inclusive.

However, this book is not only about challenging the normative practice. The editors do not want to throw you in the water without any protection. Reading this book, each provocation may feel as if the editors are holding your hand, watching you glide through water in a distance, coaching you on your stroke, or finally letting you swim on wherever you want. The chapters curated per provocation let the help emerge. In *Provocation 1: The Many Turns of Transformation*, the authors theoretically examine transformative learning theory and further discuss how their understanding departs from and beyond Mezirow's transformative learning. The theoretical root of transformative learning may make you feel a bit safe pedaling through the known water. In *Provocation 2: Generating Conditions for Transformation*, the authors present inquiry on how to facilitate transformation in different conditions. The practices that the authors suggest will give you sense on how to swim in the current. In *Provocation 3: (Un)known Discourses of Transformation*, the authors trouble the condition. You feel as if the water that you are swimming in is not still but constantly shifting. The unsurfaced discourses on transformation may let you sit in a happy confusion that may lead you to reimagine the theory and transformation. The chapters in *Provocation 4: Challenges and Emerging Future of Transformation* embody the reimagination. Through Provocations 3 and 4 you might learn how to swim against the current while finding joy in it.

As a doctoral student who has not yet emerged into the world of academia, my honest impression-of working with the editors, who are brave enough to welcome new thoughts, methods, and inquiries outside of the boundary, was disorienting yet tantalizing. Observing the way they slide through disciplinary boundaries, which I have been taught to be firmly established, made me think of the potency of the theory of transformation. The lively dialogue that I joined as a manager of the team, and the way in which these passionate scholars with different disciplinary focuses formed a dialogic space and allowed themselves to stay comfortable during the difficult dialogues, led me to feel their commitment as stewards of the concept of transformation. For me, this whole process of editing, managing, and participating is a part of my training to swim into deeper water.

I believe this book, which is an intertwining of theory, stewardship, and companionship—a passageway that connects the legacy of a living theory with current and real tumultuous conditions that invite new inquiries about transformation—intends to be disorienting, complex, and indeterminate. I also believe that this book is worth diving into as the authors and editors not only catch the current, but also are brave enough to trouble the currents. My advice for you, the reader, is to take a deep breath, and bravely dive into the water. Just jump in—when you come up for air, you may discover that you have come far from the land you were hesitant to leave.

Ahreum Lim
The University of Georgia
Athens, USA

The Fragrant Mountain Winds

We all feel helpless, clueless as to how to face the challenges ahead. Ever since the devastation of Typhoon Morakot that led to forced evacuation from our native tribes, we have been at a loss, unable to adapt to our relocated life in the resettlement centers and the permanent housing estates on the Makazayazaya Farm. What uses does it have to live in permanent housing without any lands? Our ancestral lands abound in rice, and the mountain winds are imbued with fragrance.

"The Fragrant Mountain Winds" refers to the lives of the tribespeople who survived the disaster. The havoc wreaked by Typhoon Morakot posed the greatest challenge in centuries upon the Tavadran (Dashe) tribe in Sandimen Township, Pingtung County. Having endured a long migration from their ancestral lands in the mountains, across Ailiao River, to the so-called permanent housing on the Makazayazaya Farm, the indigenous communities struggle to adapt to their new life in resettlement. They learn to cope with displacement, adjustment, and the reconstruction of their souls and spirits amidst changes in their living space and surrounding environment. Since Typhoon Morakot struck, the people of the Tavadran tribe have been confronted with a deep sense of unease and resignation triggered by migration, adjustment, and the loss of roots and lands. After they relocated to resettlement camps and permanent housing, someone in the tribe passed away almost every month. Some tribal elders explained, "our spirits reside in the mountains, so we have to return to the ancestral lands," expressing their profound attachment to and nostalgia for their montane native lands. "The Fragrant Mountain Winds" strives to pass on the unique resilience and optimism of the indigenous peoples in the face of disasters and migration over the centuries. Through the eyes, words, and wisdom of the elders, it seeks to manifest the soul and spirit of their homeland, while conveying their strength and dreams of rebuilding a new home.

Etan Pavavalung

Etan Pavavalung, Paiwan artist was born into the Tavadran tribe of Dashe village, Sandimen town in Pingtung County in Taiwan. He grew up in the renowned Pulima artisan family and was immersed in Paiwan life where traditional arts and culture are showcased everywhere. This environment would also set the tone for his future art creations. When studying at the Yushan Theological College and Seminary and the Tainan Theological College and Seminary, Etan was inspired to contemplate on philosophy and religious art. Besides writing poems and prose, he is also the director of several documentaries excelling at imagery poetry. Moreover, Etan has also been learning and keeping records on the Paiwanese mouth-blown and nose flutes, which led to the Ministry of Culture designating him as a cultural ambassador of the traditional performing arts. His innovative art form, "Trace Layer Carve Paint," has become the signature feature of his artwork. Etan's creative art is deeply embedded in his subjectivity about his Indigenous culture and his reflections on society and the ecosystem. During the "Return Our Lands" and "Regain Our Names" Indigenous movements in the 1990s, Etan took the lily flower, the token of his tribe's spirit, and started represented the lily on posters and T-shirts in the hope of strengthening identity. He now excels at presenting the multiple cultural imagery and depictions of the Indigenous Taiwan lily. Through personified visual movements, he creates harmony between humanity and the natural ecosystem. The aesthetic concept behind his mother culture, "Vecik" (lines, patterns, and words), nourishes his exploration in arts performance. In 2009, Etan took gravers to be his pens and wood board as his canvas and created "Trace Layer Carve Paint" as his anchor in terms of technique and form in the visual arts. "Trace Layer Carve Paint" shows the "trace" that the creator leaves on nature and the earth, and the civilized texture that is piled up in the "layers" of Aboriginal stone slab houses in Taiwan. Etan "carves" down deep into the cultural spirit, "paints" and widens artistic possibilities.

CONTENTS

1 The Many Turns of Transformation Creating New
   Vocabularies for Transformative Learning   1
   Aliki Nicolaides and Saskia Eschenbacher

Part I Provocation 1: The Many Turns of
        Transformation

2 Transformative Learning and Critical Theory: Making
   Connections with Habermas, Honneth, and Negt   25
   Ted Fleming

3 Reconsidering the Roots of Transformative
   Education: Habermas and Mezirow   45
   Saskia Eschenbacher and Peter Levine

4 The Pulse of Freedom and Transformative Learning:
   Winding Paths, Blind Alleys, and New Horizons   59
   Fergal Finnegan

5 The Transformation of the Reader   75
   Effrosyni Kostara

6 Mapping the Terrain: Analytic Tools for Future
   Thinking About Transformation   91
   Chad Hoggan

xxi

xxii CONTENTS

7 **A Practice-Based View of Transformative Learning: An Exploratory Study on the Practical Creativity** 109
Alessandra Romano, Francesca Bracci, and Victoria J. Marsick

8 **One of the Doors: Exploring Contemplative Practices for Transformative Sustainability Education** 129
Heather Burns, Nora Stoelting, Julie Wilcox, and Chantal Krystiniak

9 **Transformative Learning and Black Spirituality** 147
Maureen Ann Miller and Karen E. Watkins

10 **Transformative Learning and Sociomateriality** 165
Claudio Melacarne and Loretta Fabbri

11 **Developmental Reflexivity with Power and Emotion: Action Research Transformations for Generative Conflict** 181
Hilary Bradbury

12 **Transformative Pilgrimage Learning and the Big Questions in the COVID-19 Era—Love, Death, and Legacy: Implications for Lifelong Learning and Nursing Education** 199
Elizabeth J. Tisdell and Ann L. Swartz

13 **Washing the Dead Bed, from Poem to Digital Story** 217
Janet Ferguson and Massimo Lambert

14 **Transforming Individual to Structural Thinking About Race** 241
Stephen Brookfield

Part II Provocation 2: Generating Conditions for Transformation

15 **Transforming First Nations Individual and Community Realities: Reflections on a Decolonizing Higher Education Project** 257
Roz Walker and Rob McPhee

CONTENTS xxiii

16 Fostering Reorienting Connections via Ecological Practices 279
Mark Hathaway

17 Revitalizing Reflection in Teacher Education: A Digital Tool for Reflection as a Gentle Trigger for Transformation 301
Kaisu Mälkki, Marita Mäkinen, and Joni Forsell

18 Women in the Workplace: Negotiating Influence as a Leader 333
Beth Fisher-Yoshida

19 A Deliberately Developmental Organization: A New Organizational Space for Inclusion 347
Chang-kyu Kwon

20 The Power of Women Learning Together: Transcending the Bounds of a Transformative Leadership Development Program 363
Alexandra B. Cox, Kara L. Fresk, Carla A. Dennis, Emily J. Saunders, and Kristy L. Walker

21 The Role of Senior Management in Organizational Transformation 381
Nitasha Ramparsad

22 Liberating a Transformative Imagination: Leadership Learning at the Burren Leadership Retreat 395
Mary A. Stacey and Reilly L. Dow

23 Integral We-Spaces for Racial Equity: Loving Fiercely Across Our Differences 411
Placida V. Gallegos, Akasha Saunders, Steven A. Schapiro, and Carol Wishcamper

24 Listening for Transformation: Discovering Third Space and Connection Using a Listening Protocol 429
Laurie Anderson Sathe, Tes Cotter Zakrzewski, Anne-Liisa Longmore, Alessandra Romano, Deborah Kramlich, Janette Brunstein, Ed Cunliff, and Victoria J. Marsick

xxiv CONTENTS

25 Curating the Imagination: Perspective
Transformations and the Feminist Exhibition 447
Darlene E. Clover

26 Creating a Sense of Belonging: Enabling
Transformative Learning Through Participatory
Action Research in an Ubuntu Paradigm 469
Maren Seehawer, Sipho N. Nuntsu,
Farasten Mashozhera, Abongile Ludwane,
and Margaret Speckman

Part III   Provocation 3: (Un)known Discourses of
Transformation

27 More Than Harmony: Transformational Teaching
and Learning in Canada in an Age of Reconciliation 485
David Newhouse, Phil Abbott, Jason Fenno,
Mara Heiber, Gabriel Maracle, Robin Quantick,
and Heather Shpuniarsky

28 The Witness Blanket: Responsibility Through
an Ongoing Journey of Transformation 503
Carey Newman and Catherine Etmanski

29 Reflections on Transformation: Stories from Southern
Africa 521
Moyra Keane, Constance Khupe, and Vongai Mpofu

30 Pedagogy for Transformative Learning
in Post-colonial Contexts 537
Sal Muthayan

31 Transformation as Resistance 555
Bill Ashcroft

32 Transformative Learning as a Passageway
to Social Justice in Higher Education: An Asian
American and Pacific Islander (AAPI) Perspective
on Anti-Bullyist Practice in a North American Context 571
Mitsunori Misawa

CONTENTS xxv

33 Informal Transformative Learning Experiences from Humanitarian Emergencies and Other Life Events and Transitions 591
Paul Akpomuje, Tajudeen Ade Akinsooto, and Olutoyin Mejiuni

34 Dialogic and Noncoercive Learning for Transformational Change: A Systems Approach 611
Fodé Beaudet

35 In Service to My Community: Exploring Oppression and Internalized Racism 627
Taj Johns

36 Imaginative Perspectives on Transformative Learning 645
Randee Lipson Lawrence

37 Perspective Transformation in Interfaith Dialogue: A Six-Step Process 659
Elizabeth M. Pope

38 The Interpenetration of Individual and Collective Transformation: A Framework for Development, Collective Intelligence, and Emergence 677
Abigail Lynam, Geoff Fitch, Tamara Androsoff, and John Wood

Part IV Provocation 4 : Challenges and Emerging Future of Transformation

39 Power of Questions: Transformation in Complex Systems 699
Glenda H. Eoyang

40 Emotions, Affective Neuroscience, and Changing One's Mind 717
Kathleen Taylor and Catherine Marienau

41 *Living* Transformation: The Alchemy of Change in an Epochal Shift 733
Elizabeth A. Lange

xxvi CONTENTS

42 Learning, Experience and the Societal Unconscious: Combining a Materialistic Theory and a Dialectic Methodology 751
Henning Salling Olesen

43 Transformative Learning and Microradicalization 769
Dante Caramellino, Claudio Melacarne, and Benjamin Ducol

44 Evaluation as a Pathway to Transformation Lessons from Sustainable Development 785
Scott G. Chaplowe, Adam Hejnowicz, and Marlene Laeubli Loud

45 Restoring the Transformative Bridge: Remembering and Regenerating Our Western Transformative Ancient Traditions to Solve the Riddle of Our Existential Crisis 809
Petra T. Buergelt and Douglas Paton

46 The Embodying of Transformative Learning 831
Christina Schlattner

47 Transformation and the Language We Use 847
Linden West

48 Lessons from Utopia: Reflections on *Peak Transformative Experiences* in a University Studio in Auroville, India 863
Bem Le Hunte, Katie Ross, Suryamayi Clarence-Smith, and Aditi Rosegger

49 Could Transformative Learning Involve Youth? 883
Alexis Kokkos

50 Between Smoke and Crystal: The Practice of *In-Transformation* 897
Sarah J. Owusu

51 Conclusion Chapter: Propositions at the Threshold of Transformation 913
Yabome Gilpin-Jackson and Marguerite Welch

Index 939

Notes on Contributors

Phil Abbott is a Course Instructor in the Chanie Wenjack School of Indigenous Studies at Trent University. He also works as a Manager with Katimavik, a National Youth empowerment organization, to incorporate Truth and Reconciliation learning into the programs. Phil's Research interests include settler colonialism, historical consciousness, and history education.

Tajudeen Ade Akinsooto is a Lecturer in the Department of Adult Education and Lifelong Learning, Obafemi Awolowo University, Nigeria. He holds an M.A. and Ph.D. in Adult Education. His research interest is in adult informal learning within diverse contexts such as the workplace, life events, and transitions.

Paul Akpomuje teaches in the Department of Adult Education and Lifelong Learning, Obafemi Awolowo University, Nigeria. He holds an M.A. and Ph.D. in Adult Education. He is interested in the gender dimensions of adult education and informal learning, within diverse spectrum of contexts, including the military, emergencies, community, and the workplace.

Dr. Laurie Anderson Sathe's research interest is in a holistic transformative pedagogy that integrates the mind, body, and spirit in the learning process, the richness and discoveries available through narrative and listening theories/methodologies and their application to teaching, healing, and connection.

NOTES ON CONTRIBUTORS

Tamara Androsoff Grad. Dip Psychotherapy, is Program Director and Faculty for the GTC South Pacific Program. Tamara lives in Auckland, New Zealand and is a registered psychotherapist with over 20 years of experience in facilitating change in individuals, couples, and groups.

Bill Ashcroft is a renowned critic and founding exponent of postcolonial theory. He is Author and co-author of twenty-one books and over 200 articles and chapters, variously translated into six languages. He is Emeritus Professor at the University of NSW and a fellow of the Australian Academy of the Humanities.

Fodé Beaudet, M.A., CTDP is a Senior Learning Advisor at the Canadian Foreign Service Institute, Global Affairs Canada. He designs and facilitates multi-stakeholder initiatives, participatory methodologies approaches as well as collaboration projects to strengthen intercultural effectiveness. He serves as a Director-at-Large for the Institute for Performance and Learning.

Francesca Bracci is Associate Professor at University of Florence. She holds a Ph.D. in Adult Learning and Leadership from Catholic University of Milan and Teachers College, Columbia University. Her research focuses on collaborative research methodologies and practice-based approaches to the study of learning and change in organizations, communities, and adults.

Hilary Bradbury, Ph.D. is Curator at ActionResearchPlus. She is a scholar-practitioner focused on the human and organizational dimensions of creating healthy communities. Formally a Professor of Organizational Development she now supports educational institutions in transforming their knowledge creation work to respond to the social-ecological crisis of our times.

Stephen Brookfield is Distinguished Scholar at Antioch University and Adjunct Professor at Teachers College, Columbia University. He is interested in how adults learn to uncover and challenge dominant ideologies. His most recent book (co-authored with Mary Hess) is *Becoming a White Antiracist: A Practical Guide for Educators, Leaders and Activists* (Stylus, 2021).

Janette Brunstein is a Professor and Researcher with the Stricto Sensu Post-Graduation Program in Business Administration, Universidade Presbiteriana Mackenzie, Brazil. She is also Provost for Undergraduate Education at the same University. Her work is focused on education, learning, and development of competences for sustainability in the academic and organizational environment.

Petra T. Buergelt, Ph.D. is an Associate Professor at the University of Canberra. She is an interdisciplinary, award-winning researcher, and ally. Petra has deep adoptive and cultural ties with several Indigenous tribes in Australia and Taiwan. Petra also serves as Executive Member of the Collaborative Indigenous Research Collaborative and the International Transformative Learning Association Leadership Circle.

Dr. Heather Burns is an Associate Professor and Director of the Leadership for Sustainability Education (LSE) graduate program at Portland State University. Her scholarship focuses on sustainability pedagogy and leadership, including the roles of contemplative inquiry, spiritual ecology, and whole person learning in transformative change.

Dante Caramellino has been executive of the Presidency of the Council of Ministers (Italy) and now he works for nonprofit organizations in the field of prevention of radicalisms, international cooperation, and security affairs. He collaborates with many institutions for planning and design transformative educational practices.

Scott G. Chaplowe is an evaluation and strategy specialist with over 20 years' experience working with organizations seeking sustainable solutions for social and environmental challenges. He has authored publications and engages in forums at the intersection of evaluation and sustainable development, including the International Evaluation Academy, EVALSDGs, and Blue Marble Evaluation.

Suryamayi Clarence-Smith is a Postdoctoral Researcher, Educator, Facilitator, and Activist focused on prefigurative and utopian practice, based in the intentional community Auroville. As a fellow at the Sri Aurobindo International Institute of Educational Research and co-founder of the Auroville Research Platform, she holds a Ph.D. in Development Studies (University of Sussex).

Darlene E. Clover is a Professor of Adult Education at the University of Victoria, Canada. Her areas of teaching and research include feminist adult education, arts-based research and teaching methods, and museums and art galleries. She is currently co-editing a book entitled *Feminism, Adult Education and Creative Possibility: Imaginative Responses*.

Alexandra B. Cox, Ph.D. is an Assistant Clinical Professor in learning, leadership, and organization development at the University of Georgia. Her research and practice focus on adult learning and development, coaching, and building adults' capacities to meet the demands of work and life.

Ed Cunliff is a Professor of Adult and Higher Education at the University of Central Oklahoma, USA. Ed has worked in social services, health care and higher education. As Assistant Vice-President in Academic Affairs he was part of UCO's entrance into transformative learning as a central focus. His current learning and research activities include: transformative learning, authentic leadership, and MBE (mind, brain, education).

Carla A. Dennis, Ph.D. is the Director of administrative services and communications within University Housing at the University of Georgia. Her approach to leadership centers on creating sustaining teams and developing processes, where continual growth and development is encouraged and supported.

Reilly L. Dow is a Listener, Artist, and Scribe based. Since 2008, she has supported clients internationally by creating visual artifacts in the room or during virtual gatherings to invite inquiry, depth, and relationship. She is fascinated by group dialogue and collective learning, and holds a Master's degree in Interdisciplinary Studies.

Benjamin Ducol, Ph.D. is Scientific advisor at the Centre for the Prevention of Radicalization Leading to Violence (CPRLV) and Associate professor at the School of Criminology of the Université de Montréal. His research focuses on violent extremism, radicalization processes, and issues of prevention of radicalization leading to violence.

Glenda H. Eoyang, Ph.D., HSDP is the Executive Director of the Human Systems Dynamics Institute. Since 1986, she has applied principles of complexity science to practice in self-organizing human systems at all scales—from individual learning to global health.

NOTES ON CONTRIBUTORS xxxi

Saskia Eschenbacher, Ph.D. is Professor of Adult Learning and Counseling at Akkon University of Applied Human Sciences, Berlin, also a Convenor of the ESREA Network on Transformative Processes in Education. She has been a Researcher and Visiting Professor at New York University and Teachers College Columbia University, New York.

Catherine Etmanski is a Professor and Director of the School of Leadership Studies at Royal Roads University. Through her mother, she is British, Irish-American, New York Dutch, and United Empire Loyalist. Through her father, she is Kashubian from Poland and Scottish from Clan MacDonald of Clanranald.

Loretta Fabbri, Ph.D. is Full Professor of Transformative Methodologies at University of Siena and she is Vice Head of the Department of Education, Human Sciences and Intercultural Communication, (University of Siena). Her research is focused on Theory and Methods of Transformative Learning, Community of practices and qualitative research.

Jason Fenno is a Ph.D. Candidate at the Chanie Wenjack School for Indigenous Studies at Trent University. Jason holds an M.A. in Police Studies from the University of Regina and a B.A. in Justice from the University of Alaska Fairbanks. His research is focused on Northern Indigenous resurgence in the Far North of Canada.

Janet Ferguson, Ph.D. is an Independent Scholar, Adjunct Lecturer, and Story-worker. She provides consulting and advisory services to educational, public sector, and nonprofit organizations.

Fergal Finnegan is a Lecturer at Maynooth University, Ireland, where he co-directs the Doctorate in Higher and Adult Education and the Ph.D. in Adult and Community Education program. He is a co-convenor of the ESREA Active Democratic Citizenship and Adult Learning network and Co-editor of the *Journal of Transformative Education*.

Dr. Beth Fisher-Yoshida is a President and CEO of Fisher Yoshida International, LLC, which develops initiatives that strengthen clients' core negotiation skills and effectiveness and also a Professor of Professional Practice and Academic Director of the Master of Science in Negotiation and Conflict Resolution program at Columbia University.

Geoff Fitch is a Founder and Faculty at Pacific Integral and has been Creative Leader, Coach, and Educator for over 30 years. He holds Masters of Transpersonal Psychology from the Institute of Transpersonal Psychology and B.S. in Computer Science, magna cum laude, from Boston University.

Ted Fleming, B.Sc., M.A., Ed.D. (Columbia) is Faculty Member at Teachers College, formerly Associate Professor, Maynooth University. He is External Advisor to UNESCO funded Learning City, Larissa, Greece. Currently works on International Expert Panel advising the Irish Government National Manpower Agency about including student voice in the further education sector.

Joni Forsell, M.Ed. is a University Instructor at the Faculty of Education and Culture, Tampere University. In addition to teaching and facilitating learning in teacher education for those with immigrant background, he is involved in curriculum work and educational research.

Kara L. Fresk, Ph.D. is an organizational effectiveness strategist and leadership coach. Her work and her leadership approach is grounded in establishing structures and creating conditions for learning and growth.

Placida V. Gallegos works as an organization development consultant supporting the creation of healthier, more inclusive cultures where people can contribute their individual and cultural strengths. Recent publications include chapters in *Diversity Resistance in Organizations*, (Thomas, Ed.) and in *Diversity at Work: The Practice of Inclusion* (Ferdman and Dean, Eds.).

Dr. Yabome Gilpin-Jackson (she/her) is a scholar-practitioner in Human & Organization Development with research and professional awards in Canada, UK, and the USA. She is an Executive Leader, Consultant, and Educator across the private, public, and nonprofit sectors. She is Adjunct/Sessional Faculty at Simon Fraser University, Concordia University, and elsewhere.

Mark Hathaway was the 2018 recipient of the Patricia Cranton Distinguished Dissertation Award by the International Transformative Learning Association. He is a Sessional Lecturer in the School of the Environment, University of Toronto and a Faculty Member of the Earth Charter Center for Education for Sustainable Development.

Mara Heiber is an Assistant Professor at Trent University. Her research interests include Indigenous-settler relations and how identity impacts individual choices in terms of engaging with decolonizing frameworks.

Adam Hejnowicz, Ph.D. is a Research Associate in the Living Deltas Hub, Newcastle University, a Visiting Researcher at the University of York, and a Member of Centre for the Evaluation of Complexity Across the Nexus. His applied, policy-facing, and transdisciplinary research concerns the sustainability and governance of complex social-ecological systems.

Chad Hoggan is an Associate Professor of Adult, Workforce, and Continuing Professional Education at North Carolina State University and co-editor of the *Journal of Transformative Education*. His research revolves around the possibilities for dramatic change in adulthood.

Bem Le Hunte is the founding Course Director of the Bachelor of Creative Intelligence and Innovation at the University of Technology Sydney, a transdisciplinary, multi-award-winning degree, combining with 25 different disciplines to tackle complex challenges. She is also a critically acclaimed novelist, and researches creativity and approaches to transformative learning.

Taj Johns, Ph.D. is a Writer, Educator, and Artist whose creativity influences her teaching philosophy. Transforming one's educational experiences, she uses creativity to teach cultural diversity, intrapersonal leadership skills plus values and ethics. She is an Adjunct Professor at St. Mary's College in California.

Moyra Keane, Ph.D. is an Associate Professor at the University of Johannesburg and an Educational Developer and Research consultant for a number of universities. She teaches mainly postgraduate courses and presents workshops on Research Writing; Research Methodology; Postgraduate Supervision, Coaching, and Mindfulness. One of her research areas is Indigenous knowledge.

Constance Khupe, Ph.D. is a Student Advisor in the Faculty of Health Sciences at the University of the Witwatersrand in South Africa. A first-in-family graduate, Constance has a passion for supporting students in transition. Her research interest lies in indigenous knowledge systems and indigenous research methodology.

xxxiv   NOTES ON CONTRIBUTORS

Alexis Kokkos is Emeritus Professor of Adult Education at the Hellenic Open University, and Member of the Leadership Circle of the International Transformative Learning Association. His research and education practice are focused on the involvement of transformative learning in everyday teaching, as well as on the exploration of art toward perspective transformation.

Effrosyni Kostara, Ph.D. is an Adjunct Lecturer in the National and Kapodistrian University of Athens and the Hellenic Open University. She is specialized in teaching methodology and teachers' training. Her research focuses on the importance of critical reflection in adult education through the use of classical texts.

Deborah Kramlich is a visiting Postdoctoral Research Associate at Payap University as well as an English teacher at the Christliche Deutsche Schule both in Chiang Mai, Thailand. Dr. Kramlich is interested in using cultural humility and cultural safety to reframe pedagogy for the particular needs of the multicultural classroom. Her research interests include: transformative learning, multiculturalism, interculturalism, and design research.

Chantal Krystiniak is the 4-H program coordinator for Washington State University Extension in Clark County. She graduated with my Masters in Educational Leadership and Policy from the Leadership for Sustainability Education Program at Portland State University in 2020. She is passionate about regenerative education and transformative justice.

Chang-kyu Kwon, Ph.D. is an Assistant Professor of Human Resource Development at Oakland University. His research focuses on creating an inclusive workplace culture where individuals with marginalized identities can bring their whole selves.

Massimo Lambert is a geographer with a passion for arboriculture, carpentry, local politics, and storytelling. His freelance work has ranged from making maps depicting natural and political histories, providing technical support for digital storytelling projects. He lives in Oakland, California.

Elizabeth A. Lange, Ph.D. is Honorary and Adjunct Fellow at the Institute for Sustainable Futures, University of Technology Sydney, Australia. Her research focuses on transformative learning, sustainability education, and transcultural learning. She works extensively in the wider community through public speaking, workshops, and facilitation. You can find her at https://elizabethlange.ca.

Randee Lipson Lawrence, Ed.D. served on the Adult Education graduate faculty at National Louis University until her retirement in 2015 and currently teaches online courses and mentors student research at Yorkville University and Teachers College Columbia University. Her research interests span around holistic learning and arts-based research.

Peter Levine is an Associate Dean and the Lincoln Filene Professor of Citizenship & Public Affairs in Tufts University's Tisch College of Civic Life. Trained as a philosopher, Levine has spent most of his career conducting applied empirical research and organizing professional efforts related to civic life in the USA.

Anne-Liisa Longmore is the Dean of the Pilon School of Business at Sheridan College in Mississauga Ontario, Canada. She also was a Professor of Leadership and an Educational Development Consultant within Sheridan's Centre for Teaching and Learning.

Marlene Laeubli Loud (D.Phil.) is a Consultant and Trainer in public sector evaluation. Her experience includes both "doing" and "managing" commissioned evaluations. She has a keen theoretical and practical interest in evaluation utilization and edited with John Mayne the book, *Enhancing Evaluation Use: Insights from Internal Evaluation Units* (2014, Sage).

Abongile Ludwane is a Science Teacher at Nathaniel Nyaluza High School in Makhanda, South Africa and as passionate about teaching as about learning. Thus she pursues a Master's degree while also working as a part-time lecturer at Rhodes University.

Abigail Lynam is Faculty for Fielding Graduate University's Ph.D. in Human and Organizational Development where she teaches at the intersection of personal and systems transformation, with a particular emphasis on adult development and social change leadership. She is also Faculty for Pacific Integral's Generating Transformative Change program in Seattle and Ethiopia.

Marita Mäkinen, Ph.D. is a Professor of Education (Teacher Education) at the Faculty of Education and Culture, Tampere University, Finland.

xxxvi NOTES ON CONTRIBUTORS

Her research interests include (transforming) teacher education, inclusive education, student engagement, and pedagogy of multiliteracies.

Kaisu Mälkki, Ph.D. is a University Lecturer at the Faculty of Education and Culture, Tampere University, Finland. She has developed the theory of reflection and edge-emotions as well as digital tools to support critical reflection. Research focuses: critical reflection, transformative learning, co-creative pedagogies, systemic higher education development, sustainable and reflective working cultures, and well-being in teaching and learning.

Gabriel Maracle is a Ph.D. Candidate in the Chanie Wenjack School of Indigenous Studies at Trent University. He holds a Masters in Canadian and Indigenous Studies from Trent University and a Masters in Religion and Public Life from Carleton University. His research is focused on the healing journey of incarcerated Indigenous men working to achieve successful community reintegration.

Catherine Marienau, Ph.D. is Professor Emerita, DePaul University, School for New Learning: Faculty Mentor, Instructor, and Administrator in individualized graduate programs; Director, Center to Advance Education for Adults and Community Engagement Network. She currently coaches, consults, and writes in neuroscience and adult learning, women and aging, and women and holistic health.

Victoria J. Marsick is Professor of Adult Learning & Leadership at Columbia University, Teachers College where she directs academic programs in Adult Learning and Leadership. She holds a Ph.D. in Adult Education from the University of California, Berkeley, and an M.P.A. in International Public Administration from Syracuse University. Victoria's research examines naturally occurring, informal learning at work—including team and organizational learning; action learning; and transformative learning.

Farasten Mashozhera looks back at 30 years of teaching experience in his home country Zimbabwe and South Africa. Besides his passion for teaching, Farasten has a strong interest for plants, nature and agriculture and has worked on farms. He is the acting principal of Graham-stown Adventist Primary school, while also pursuing a Ph.D. at Rhodes University on the value of integrating food gardens in teaching and learning.

Rob McPhee is the Deputy Chief Executive Officer of the Kimberly Aboriginal Medical Services (KAMS). He is a Lecturer in the Indigenous Community Management and Development Program at Curtin, a Lecturer at the University of Western Australia, and also a Senior Adviser in community relations and Indigenous affairs to the oil and gas industry.

Olutoyin Mejiuni is a Professor of Adult Education and Women Studies in the Department of Adult Education and Lifelong Learning, Obafemi Awolowo University, Ile-Ife, Nigeria. She authored and co-edited, respectively, the books entitled: *Women and Power: Education, Religion and Identity* and *Measuring and Analyzing Informal Learning in the Digital Age.*

Claudio Melacarne, Ph.D. is Associate professor at University of Siena. He is the Coordinator of the Ph.D. Program in "Learning and Innovation in Social and Work Contexts". He works as consultant in the area of professional development and adult and continuing education with profit and no-profit organizations.

Maureen Ann Miller, Ph.D. is a Graduate of Learning, Leadership, and Organizational Development in the College of Education at the University of Georgia. Maureen's scholarly interests include transformative learning, Black spirituality, and leadership.

Mitsunori Misawa, Ph.D. is currently Associate Professor of Adult Learning in the Educational Psychology and Research program and Associate Department Head in the Department of Educational Psychology and Counseling at the University of Tennessee, Knoxville. Dr. Misawa's scholarly interests include bullying in adulthood, social justice, professionalism, leadership, mentoring, and qualitative research.

Vongai Mpofu, Ph.D. is a Lecturer in the Department of Science and Mathematics at Bindura University of Science Education in Zimbabwe. She coordinates and teaches on secondary school science teacher programs and supervises Ph.D. students. Her main research interests are including STEM Education, Indigenous Knowledge and School science/chemistry and indigenous qualitative research.

Sal Muthayan holds a Ph.D. from University of British Columbia and heads curriculum design at the National School of Government, South Africa, where she explores innovative and decolonizing methodologies to develop leadership programs that enable transformative learning for public servants responsible for bringing social justice to the former Apartheid state.

David Newhouse (Onondaga) is Onondaga from the Six Nations of the Grand River community near Brantford, Ontario. He is Professor of Indigenous Studies at Trent University in the Chanie Wenjack School for Indigenous Studies. He is the Co-chair of the SSHRC Indigenous Advisory Circle and the Science Officer for the CIHR Indigenous Peoples Health Research competitions. His research interests focus on the emergence of modern Indigenous society.

Carey Newman (Hayalthkin'geme) is a multi-disciplinary Artist and Master Carver. Through his father he is Kwagiulth from the Kukwekum, Giiksam, and WaWalaby'ie clans of Fort Rupert, and Sto:Lo from Cheam along the upper Fraser Valley. Through his mother he is English, Irish, and Scottish.

Aliki Nicolaides, Ed.D. is Associate Professor of Adult Learning and Leadership at the University of Georgia in the program of Learning, Leadership & Organization Development. She is also a founding steward and current Director of the International Transformative Learning Association. She seeks to optimize vital developmental conditions for self and society to learn and evolve.

Sipho N. Nuntsu has been a Teacher for almost 25 years and is currently the principle of a primary school in Eastern Cape province, South Africa. While teaching being his passion, Sipho is also a dedicated student and busy writing his Master Thesis on focusing on traditional practices and beliefs about food in a grade 6 township class.

Sarah J. Owusu is an award-winning Organisation Development practitioner and innovation specialist with a track-record of leading transformational change. She is co-founder of InkDot, a boutique consultancy focused on helping organizations build their innovation capability. She is passionate about uplifting African voices and perspectives through writing, storytelling, and dialogue.

Douglas Paton, Ph.D. is a Professor at CDU (Australia), an Expert Advisor on Community Resilience with WHO, and worked with UNESCO and the UN Office of Disaster Risk Reduction on disaster risk reduction policy. He develops and tests theories of community resilience and has published 23 books, 132 book chapters, and 190 peer-reviewed journal articles.

Elizabeth M. Pope is an Assistant Professor of Educational Research at the University of West Georgia. She is a qualitative research methodologist. Her research interests include adult and transformative learning through interfaith encounters, conversation analysis of interfaith dialogue, and teaching and learning qualitative research methods.

Robin Quantick is an Assistant Professor at the Trent University, Chanie Wenjack School for Indigenous Studies. Dr. Quantick holds an M.Ed. from Queen's University and a Ph.D. in Indigenous Studies from Trent University. His research is focused on the work of Elders and Elder led healing circles/programs in Canadian federal prisons.

Nitasha Ramparsad is Professor and Director of the Leadership Programmes at the National School of Government; and a Research Associate at the Durban University of Technology, Research Focus Area: Gender Justice, Health and Human Development in South Africa. She designs and delivers innovative and transformative learning experiences in the area of leadership, and oversees student research.

Alessandra Romano is an Assistant Professor with a tenure track position at University of Siena. She holds a Ph.D. in Adult Learning from University of Naples "Federico II" in co-tutorship with Teachers College, Columbia University. She is a Member of the Editorial Board of the Journal *Educational Reflective Practices*.

Aditi Rosegger is a Doctoral Researcher at the Institute for Sustainable Futures, University of Technology Sydney and is currently based in Auroville. Her transdisciplinary action research engages with transformative narratives for sustainable water governance in the context of Auroville's lived philosophy of experimentation, transformation, and lifelong learning.

Katie Ross, Ph.D. is curious and passionate about transformative sustainability learning in formal education and in lifelong learning. As a research director within the Institute for Sustainable Futures at the University of Technology Sydney, she collaboratively imagines, designs and delivers innovative, collective learning experiences for meaningful change.

xl   NOTES ON CONTRIBUTORS

Henning Salling Olesen is Professor, Former pro-/rector Roskilde University. Honorary Doctor Tampere University. Engaged in collaborative research with trade unions since 1970s. Founder of interdisciplinary doctoral school for lifelong learning and education research. Chair for European Society for Research in the Education of Adults 1998–2013. Founding member of the International Research Group for Psychosocietal Research. Advisory Professor for doctoral studies at East China Normal University, Shanghai.

Akasha Saunders, Ph.D. is a Pilgrim, Educator, and Developmental Coach with over 10 years of professional experience. He brings a constructive and intercultural developmental approach to cultivating spaces for people to grow and experience liberation. He lives in Grenada with his partner, their teenage son, and very protective cockapoo dog.

Emily Saunders is Senior Manager of training and development at the University of Georgia. Her specialties are leadership and career development, and she has a special passion for women's leadership development.

Steven A. Schapiro focuses his teaching and writing on transformative learning for social justice. He is co-editor of *Innovations in Transformative Learning: Space, Culture and the Arts*. His work has appeared in the *Adult Education Quarterly*, the *Journal of Transformative Education*, the *Handbook of Transformative Learning*, and *Teaching for Social Justice and Diversity*.

Christina Schlattner, M.A. is CEO of New Alchemy Communications. She consults with businesses, nonprofits, and First Nations on transformative learning for team, leadership, and project development. She also teaches coaches and experts to incorporate transformative learning into their courses for lasting change and impact.

Maren Seehawer is a Senior Lecturer at the Norwegian School of Theology Religion and Society where she coordinates and teaches an undergraduate one-year program in the social sciences. Her research focuses on decolonizing knowledge production and education systems with a Ph.D. project on the integration of indigenous knowledges in South African science education.

Heather Shpuniarsky is a Member of the faculty at the Chanie Wenjack School for Indigenous Studies at Trent University. In her teaching responsibilities, she teaches Indigenous Studies foundations courses and upper year courses around governance, Canadian nation-state relations with Indigenous nations and peoples via the media.

Margaret Speckman has had different occupations such as working in a bank or in retail, which have all taught her something important about life, but her true passion is teaching. She likes to challenge and to develop herself academically and is currently pursuing a post graduate diploma in education Management at Nelson Mandela University, hoping to proceed to studying psychology as there is a great need for school psychologists in South African Schools.

Mary A. Stacey, M.A. is Founder of the Burren Leadership Retreat and Context Consulting, an international leadership Advisor, Innovator of leadership development, and university Teacher. She works co-creatively with industry leaders and artists who are making bold inquiries and taking systemic action on behalf of future generations.

Nora Stoelting is pursuing a dual masters in Leadership for Sustainability Education and Urban and Regional Planning at Portland State. She is passionate about the intersections between community building, transformative learning, and orienting toward the process of creating an equitable, sustainable future.

Ann L. Swartz, D.Ed., MSN, CRNP was Nursing Program Coordinator and Faculty for the Second Degree Nursing Program at Penn State University—Harrisburg. In February 2021 she achieved certification as an ANFT Forest Therapy Guide, then retired from academia. She continues to live her life as pilgrimage.

Kathleen Taylor, Ph.D. is Professor, Doctoral Program in Educational Leadership, Saint Mary's College of California, and Former Fulbright Scholar. She currently mentors mid-career professionals, consults internationally, facilitates workshops, and writes/blogs about applications of affective neuroscience to adult development and learning in formal and informal settings, and in promoting open-mindedness and social justice.

Elizabeth J. Tisdell is Distinguished Professor of Lifelong Learning and Adult Education at Penn State University—Harrisburg, the Division Chair of Health and Professional Studies, and Professor-in-Charge of Lifelong Learning and Adult Education Graduate Programs. She is passionately committed to living life as pilgrimage and to help others do the same.

xlii   NOTES ON CONTRIBUTORS

Kristy L. Walker is the Associate Director of business and human resources within University Housing at the University of Georgia. Her work focuses on a utilizing progressive business practices, leadership and concepts to best serve a dynamic staff and student population.

Roz Walker, Ph.D. is a Principal Research Fellow at the University of Western Australia. She is involved in research and evaluation to transform diverse services, enhance workforce cultural competence, and promote system level change to improve Aboriginal health, mental health, and social and emotional well-being outcomes for individuals and communities.

Dr. Karen E. Watkins is Professor of Learning, Leadership and Organizational Development in the College of Education at the University of Georgia. Karen's scholarly interests include organizational learning assessment, informal and incidental learning, and action science. She is on the Board of Trustees of the Geneva Learning Foundation in Switzerland.

Marguerite Welch, Ph.D. is Program Director and Faculty for the M.A. in Leadership Program at Saint Mary's College of California. She designs and facilitates innovative and transformative learning experiences in the areas of building cross-cultural capacity, online learning, leadership, and student research.

Linden West is Professor at Canterbury Christ Church University. His books include *Distress in the City*; *Beyond Fragments*; and, with Laura Formenti, *Transforming Perspectives in Lifelong Learning and Adult Education*, which won the Houle prize for outstanding literature. Linden was recently inducted into the Adult Education Hall of Fame.

Julie Wilcox, M.S. is a Program Specialist for the Oregon Center for Career Development in Childhood Care and Education at Portland State University. She supports leadership and professional development programs for educators to achieve high quality early education for children and youth.

Carol Wishcamper has decades of leadership experience in the education and nonprofit sectors and extensive training in Gestalt, Integral theory, Spiral Dynamics, Complex Adaptive Systems, and meditative and embodied practices. She recently Co-Chaired the Maine Wabanaki Child Welfare Truth and Reconciliation Commission, designed to promote inter-generational and intercultural healing.

Dr. John Wood is a Psychologist, Facilitator, and Coach specializing in leadership and team development. He has 35 years of experience in the field, and an interest in adult development and personal transformation. He is a Member of the faculty for Pacific Integral and has been self-employed for 26 years based in Australia.

Tes Cotter Zakrzewski Director of Learning Innovation & Technology, Wentworth Institute of Technology, USA has worked in global financial services and higher education. Dr. Zakrzewski is a passionate Educator and Practitioner dedicated to excellence in teaching and learning. Research interests include: dialogue and reflective practice, experiential and informal learning, transfer of learning, and organizational development.

LIST OF FIGURES

Fig. 7.1	Creativity as a performative socio-situated practice (*Source* Personal Elaboration of the Authors, inspired by Glăveanu [2011]	121
Fig. 8.1	The tree of contemplative practices	136
Fig. 11.1	Stages of developmenting toward co-creation	190
Fig. 16.1	Connie's Meditation Journal	285
Fig. 16.2	Jonathan's Meditation Journal	287
Fig. 16.3	Irene's Meditation Journal	291
Fig. 16.4	Anna's Meditation Journal	296
Fig. 16.5	Connie's Meditation Journal	297
Fig. 17.1	Teacher reflection field of research	302
Fig. 17.2	Transformative stance as systemic frame for pedagogic activity	305
Fig. 17.3	Theory of edge emotions	307
Fig. 17.4	Edge emotions theory expanded based on findings	324
Fig. 17.5	Transformative-oriented reflection	326
Fig. 17.6	Transformative teaching stance revisited	327
Fig. 22.1	The retreat as imaginal space	401
Fig. 22.2	Leadership needed now	407
Fig. 23.1	Integral we-spaces for racial equity (SOLFIRE Relational Institute)	420
Fig. 24.1	Top 40 mentions	437
Fig. 25.1	Clothesline	454
Fig. 25.2	Image from Zenith Digest	456
Fig. 25.3	Qwetminak on her Knees	457

Fig. 25.4	Bedroom Installation	458
Fig. 25.5	We Stage the Battle for Injustice	459
Fig. 25.6	Chief Justice Kokum (Grandmother) Raven	460
Fig. 28.1	The Witness Blanket on display at CMHR. Shared stewardship of Carey Newman and the Canadian Museum for Human Rights (Photograph by Jessical Sigurdson/CMHR)	507
Fig. 29.1	Accumulative learning purposes (*Source* Adapted from Malcolm 2000)	523
Fig. 37.1	The process of transformation within interfaith dialogue	663
Fig. 38.1	STAGES model (O'Fallon & Barta, 2018)	681
Fig. 38.2	I/We model: four phases	684
Fig. 38.3	I/We model	693
Fig. 40.1	Adapted from Kasl and Yorks (2012, p. 508) and Heron (1999, p. 46)	726
Fig. 44.1	Illustrative mapping of SDG interconnectedness (Courtesy of Eurostat, 2019)	792
Fig. 44.2	Cartoon by Julie Smith (Courtesy of the IFRC, 2011, p. 26)	794
Fig. 44.3	SDG (2, 3, 7, & 14) Interactions (Figure provided courtesy of International Council for Science, 2017)	796
Fig. 44.4	Linear Intervention Design (Figure courtesy of Chaplowe, 2017)	798
Fig. 44.5	Complexity adaptive intervention design (Figure courtesy of IFRC, 2010; Chaplowe, 2017)	800
Fig. 48.1	First engagement with "Kolam" practice in an Auroville workshop (Photo K. Ross)	871
Fig. 50.1	Smoke-crystal conceptual framework for transformation praxis	907
Fig. 51.1	Geographic countries of residence of handbook contributors	918
Fig. 51.2	Disciplinary representation of handbook chapters	919

LIST OF TABLES

Table 7.1	Participant demographics	114
Table 10.1	Comparative card of foundational constructs	174
Table 10.2	Connection and differences	175
Table 13.1	Questions and the following observations and comments	221
Table 13.2	Washing the Dead Bed – Digital Story—https://youtu.be/-QluWHV9g-s	222
Table 17.1	Reflections on emotions	318
Table 22.1	Participant reflections on the retreat experience	400
Table 24.1	Accessible transformative listening protocol	435
Table 33.1	Informal transformative learning model: iconic experiences, transformative learning, perspectives on transformation and the focus of change and action	604
Table 44.1	Illustrative conventional vs. transformational practices	803
Table 48.1	Characteristics of peak transformative experiences adopted in this chapter	869

CHAPTER 1

The Many Turns of Transformation Creating New Vocabularies for Transformative Learning

Aliki Nicolaides and Saskia Eschenbacher

METAPHOR AND META-LENS: ENVISIONING THE HANDBOOK OF LEARNING FOR TRANSFORMATION

Passageways is our guiding metaphor in creating this Handbook. As editors, we embrace this metaphor for its twofold advantage: First, a passage points in two directions—backward to the space one is leaving, and forward to the space one is approaching. Second, a passage is passed through. Our intention is to invite the reader to "pass through," that is,

---

A. Nicolaides (✉)
Department of Lifelong Education, Administration and Policy, University of Georgia, Athens, GA, USA
e-mail: alikin@uga.edu

S. Eschenbacher
Department of Adult Learning and Counseling, Akkon University of Applied Human Sciences, Berlin, Germany
e-mail: saskia.eschenbacher@akkon-hochschule.de

© The Author(s), under exclusive license to Springer Nature Switzerland AG 2022
A. Nicolaides et al. (eds.), *The Palgrave Handbook of Learning for Transformation*, https://doi.org/10.1007/978-3-030-84694-7_1

1

to leave the familiar space that currently defines the territory of transformative learning and turn toward something new. We envision our exploration of the phenomena of transformation as passageways because we believe our turn toward new spaces will foster a more inclusive and in-depth discourse about transformative learning.

The metaphor of passageways has an additional dimension. It allows us to ground our inquiry in a multidisciplinary understanding of adult education and the multifaceted nature of transformation. While scholar-practitioners generally perceive that the roots of adult education are multidisciplinary, drawing strength from the perspectives of indigenous knowledges, climate activism, democratic civilizing approaches, and arts-based inquiry, we envision a multidisciplinary approach that connects these disciplines without the necessity of leaving any one discipline behind in order to foster further theory development. Exploring the phenomenon of transformation as a shared space of possibility among various disciplines is itself a passageway. It allows us to move among, between, and within disciplines and fields of inquiry. In that sense, our metaphor of passageways is more fluid than static, putting the concept of movement at its heart.

Looking at the phenomenon of transformation through the lens of Rorty's (1989) philosophy helps shed some light on the vision of our Handbook. Of particular interest is Rorty's (1989) argument for "changing vocabularies" instead of relying on "final vocabularies." His invitation involves creating new vocabularies instead of extending existing ones—and therefore a new language that can serve as a meta-lens for our Handbook. In our attempt to make space for new discourses about transformative learning through the phenomenon of transformation, we[1] find his ethic of invention particularly helpful. We see his work as one possible example among others to grasp the passageways this Handbook seeks to offer. It is open to infinite possibilities and examples, in working toward a new discourse on transformation.

Even though we choose Rorty's ideas here, we keep the mystery of the unknown alive, as we do not know what passageways authors (and readers) will go down as this Handbook unfolds. As a set of ideas, it

---

[1] We, refers to the co-editorial team members. Aliki Nicolaides, Saskia Eschenbacher, Petra T. Buergelt, Yabome Gilpin-Jackson, Mitsu Misawa & Marguerite Welch. This chapter was written by Aliki Nicolaides and Saskia Eschenbacher in consultation with the co-editorial team.

helps us to keep the conversation about transformative learning going, as it is an infinite conversation.

What makes Rorty's philosophy interesting for us? So interesting that we select two of his ideas as a meta-lens for this Handbook? Reflecting on Rorty (1989)'s work allows us not only to find new answers to familiar questions but also to pose new, unfamiliar questions. By asking new questions, we are able to explore unexplored passageways, to establish new discourses, and to create new vocabularies about transformative dimensions of adult learning. In short: It is an example of the sort of passageways to new vocabularies itself that the Handbook is intended to generate. Here is why we think two of his ideas might be helpful to describe the passageways of transition in which we locate ourselves:

- Rorty (1989) embraces an "ethic of invention" (Bernstein, 2016) and invites us to look at the world in new, unfamiliar ways and opens up the possibility of transforming ourselves. This ethic of invention might help in our quest for learning to transform the very structures out of which we live and transform in order to become something new (Eschenbacher, 2018).
- Rorty's (1989) ironist idea of changing vocabularies stresses the freedom we have to create new ways of looking at the world, new ways of being in the world, or as Rorty might say, to create new vocabularies. His ideas are reflected in our intention as editors to create new ways of researching, understanding, and practicing transformative learning. This is not so much a Handbook in the traditional sense of describing the current state of the field or indeed where transformative learning has been (historically). It is instead interested in creating new vocabularies, new possibilities for the future of transformative learning.

Rorty (1989) stresses the contingent nature of our way of being as one vocabulary among others. He helps us become aware of the fact that there are always other possibilities that can be explored and that one is not trapped by one way of looking at the world or being in the world that is forced on us, but that we are free to create new vocabularies and to transform our guiding assumptions (Eschenbacher, 2018). Reflecting on Rorty's ideas gives us the opportunity to explore new passageways. His attempt "to liberate us from the dead weight of past vocabularies and open up space for the imaginative creation of new vocabularies" (Bernstein, 2016, p. 52) is itself a passageway for us in creating the aforementioned new ways of researching, understanding, and practicing transformative learning.

It is an invitation to leave the (mental) home of the discourse on transformative learning. Working with a theory in progress, we need to leave this home; the continuous movement within and beyond the boundaries of "our" disciplines (and familiar discourses) is integral, if we want to give rise to new insights and explore a part of the unknown.

As editors, we have reflected on the language and the vocabulary that are currently employed about the discourse of transformative learning in attempting to generate new insights. With Rorty, we ask: "Does our use of these words get in the way of our use of those other words?" (p. 12). We decided to study the *phenomenon of transformation,* instead of *transformative learning,* as a passageway that might allow us to explore as yet unfamiliar territories. "This is a question about whether our use of tools is inefficient, not a question about whether our beliefs are contradictory" (p. 12). In our attempt to hold the mystery of the unknown and not limit the diverse passageways authors would explore, we decided to employ a different vocabulary centered on the phenomenon of transformation. We remain curious about what new discourses and passageways will evolve from this Handbook, knowing "(a)ll we can do is work with the final vocabulary we have, while keeping our ears open for hints about how it might be expanded or revised" (Rorty, 1989, p. 197). In our case, the phenomenon of transformation is a final vocabulary that is open to be changed and renew itself.

PROVOCATIONS AND PASSAGEWAYS: JOURNEYING THE HANDBOOK

The Handbook is structured along these four entangled provocations: multiple perspectives on transformation; generating conditions for transformation; (un)known discourses on transformation; and challenges and emerging futures for transformation. The invitation is to move between, through, and within the provocations pulling at threads that stay with you—the reader—as you explore the passageways that connect and depart from each provocation. Every reader will take a different journey. A new, transformed starting point for exploring yet unfamiliar passageways will set our final chapter. We see this as an invitation to keep journeying, to move beyond what is known and unknown about the phenomenon of transformation. It is an invitation to reflect within the boundaries we have drawn while questioning and crossing them at the same time. In that sense, our metaphor of passageways remains fluid, as we see our Handbook as a passageway itself, into new discourses that are not yet imagined.

The phenomenon of transformation is multifaceted, and there are variations in meaning across disciplines. However, common to all disciplines is the understanding that transformation denotes "significant change." For the purposes of this Handbook, we return to classical Greek for a definition. *Metamorphosis* (μεταμόρφωσις) is the connection between two words: meta (after, or going beyond in a definitive way) + morphe (form) (Merriam-Webster., n.d.-a). The meaning of metamorphosis is a change in form or structure, a special change that transcends the form from within the form itself. *Form*, in our view, includes meaning structures and frames of reference that are most commonly related to the process of transformative learning, while we also recognize form as structure, relationship, systems, cosmologies, conflicts, landscapes, and materiality transformation unsettles common sense assumptions and opens new possibilities for forms of action (Gergen, 1994).

Transformative learning portrays the phenomenon of transformation through the lens of adult learning. While the phenomenon of transformation is not limited to the field of adult education, adult learning is not always transformative. Mezirow (1991) developed his theory of transformative learning by conceptualizing the transformative dimensions of adult learning. Exploring the phenomenon of transformation may help us gain deeper insight into various transformational dimensions of adult learning and therefore expand our current understanding of transformative learning. This Handbook is not only an invitation to search for a passageway that allows the theory of transformative learning to renew itself as a theory in progress (Mezirow, 2000); the Handbook is itself a passageway, as we have noted earlier, into new territory spaces of possibility. As editors, we are intentionally making many new turns— toward, away, within, and through familiar and unfamiliar discourses of transformative learning to become curious about the phenomenon of transformation.

This opening chapter takes up the idea of passageways. We (1) contextualize it between the familiar discourse on transformative learning and unfamiliar new questions and urgencies that arise from the current global challenges we are facing. This sets the stage for another passageway (2) as we explore a web of discourses on problems and concerns of the space we are about to leave, the familiar discourses on transformative learning. It allows us (3) to connect through yet other passageways the problems and concerns of current discourses to transformative learning theory's reflexive-understanding as a theory in progress, one that evolves and has evolved continually. We finally leave familiar common ground by exploring possible new passageways, paving ways (4) toward new languages that illuminate the phenomena of transformation disrupting the known territories of transformative learning. As passageways evoke images of pioneers, we inquire about our chosen path: What is unfolding as we turn toward and through new passageways of transformation and what new questions emerge in these new spaces that are beyond familiar common ground? Journeying through these passageways also means a willingness to remain curious about what we do not know lies ahead and beyond our current understandings of transformative learning.

Passageway 1: Making a Turn into a New Passageway and New Spaces for Inquiry About Transformation

In the globalized twenty-first century, many of our old cultural and social norms, traditions, mores, ways of knowing, and being in the world are undergoing profound and unpredictable shifts. To some extent, we have to learn that the world as we presently experience it denies us what we need in order to find a direction for learning and being in the world. This Handbook emerged in the middle of a world in crisis, fighting COVID-19, the upheavals of structural and systemic racism, and the struggle to transform these structures through movements such as Black Lives Matter, and the climate crisis are undeniable and inescapable. Regarding these existential experiences of crisis and the resistance and immunities to constructively re-work these crises into opportunities, we explore the territory between familiar discourses on transformative learning and unfamiliar new questions and urgencies that arise from the current global challenges we are facing.

What motivates our efforts to create this Handbook and to learn is our desire for (self)knowledge and finding new ways to live our way through transformation. In that sense, our Handbook can be an opportunity to quest after a more coherent, deeper knowledge about the struggles we are currently facing while also exploring ways to move into new ways of living transformation. We put the quest for transformative learning and transformation itself at risk: Is transformation possible? How do we humble ourselves to turn toward a new passageway for transformation to take hold in these liquid times?

Zygmunt Bauman (2013; see also Bauman et al., 2016, p. 89) states that we currently "find ourselves in a time of 'interregnum' when the old ways of doing things no longer work, the old learned or inherited modes of life are no longer suitable...but when the new ways of tackling the challenges and new modes of life better suited to the new conditions have not as yet been invented, put in place and set in operation." This "liquid modernity" that Bauman describes fundamentally requires that individuals become flexible and adaptable in order to meet the challenges and opportunities of the modern world which is itself fluid and rapidly changing, offering no enduring truths or conditions for living (Bauman, 2013; Jarvis, 2011; Nicolaides, 2015). Hoggan et al., (2017, p. 12) show how the phenomenon of liquid modernity precipitates the need for perspective transformation "there is considerable evidence of a decisive shift in modern society toward detraditionalization, highly individualized, and fluid societies in which a specific form of reflexive action, the change and transformation of the self, is highly valued" and has become an essential ingredient to operating successfully in the post-modern world. This shift from "solid" to "liquid"

> requires individuals to make sense of their fragmented lives by being flexible, adaptable, and constantly ready and willing to change tactics, to abandon commitments and loyalties without regret; and to act in a moment, as failure to act brings greater insecurity- such demands place adults 'at the threshold of ambiguity, to turn towards the unknown. (Nicolaides, 2015, p. 180)

A global pandemic, climate crisis, civic unrest, political polarization, and luminous inequities across societies have emerged out of the shadows into clear view. The global context is ripe for transformative learning and yet the promise for transformation is not yet evident in the collective actions of people. As we write this chapter, the Chauvin trail is underway in Minneapolis while protests in Brooklyn Center rage on at the continuous shooting of Black and brown people (The New York Times, 2021). Inequities are real; turning away from them, sweeping them under the rug, is not as easily done when the pandemic is fast moving and variants

8   A. NICOLAIDES AND S. ESCHENBACHER

are increasing spread in some places such as India and Brazil, and where severity varies with richer nations doing better than poor nations.

In other words, individuals living in these times of liquid modernity find themselves in a series of crises that are simultaneously personal, societal, and environmental. All of us, members of the global context, are increasingly being asked to address these crises as both personal opportunities for transformative development and growth and societal transformation (Hoggan et al., 2017; Jarvis, 2011; Nicolaides, 2015). Where we once were able to construct relatively stable selves with at least somewhat fixed answers to the most important questions in life, we now engage in a "continual search for meaning, a need to make sense of the changes and the empty spaces we perceive both within ourselves and our world" (Dirkx, 1997, p. 78; Dirkx et al., 2006). It is therefore more important than ever that we, as individuals, groups, organizations, and societies, develop the capacity for new expansions to learning in order for us to navigate this environment of increasing volatility, uncertainty, complexity, and ambiguity (Bennett & Lemoine, 2014; Dirkx, 1997; Nicolaides, 2015), and to explore new passageways to transformation as a way forward. This "struggle for meaning, the need to feel and be authentic with ourselves and with one another, and to realize a more just social order is the focus of several strands of research and theory referred to as transformational theories of adult learning" (Dirkx, 1997, p. 79), is the territory we seek to explore and uncover new passageways for transformation.

The Liquid Context in This Moment

The authors of this chapter and the co-editors of this Handbook are undergoing a transformation as we learn and are living our way through a global pandemic, felt and materialized differently across the parts of the world, we each live in. While the pandemic rages around the world and in our lives in discreet and overt ways, the social fabric that felt so real and solid has become liquid beneath us. The structural racism and protests spread globally involving more people of privilege than ever before were an opening towards transformation, yet we wonder if a transformation is taking hold? In the United States, beliefs about racism and support for the racial and social justice, such as the Black Lives Matter movement, were amplified while at the same time diminished once people in the United States began to pay attention to different things such as summer travel and vaccinations on the horizon. Though our individual consciousness, as members of the editorial team, was heightened with regard to the possibility of death that COVID-19 signaled, and it influenced our collective consciousness related to the illuminated prevalence of structural racism and pervasive poverty, this awareness, enacted in different ways, nudged us further into possible passageways of transformation. We spend hours together on Zoom listening, connecting, and continuing to work to make sense of the pandemic while also making progress on the completion of this Handbook. We paused to notice that we adapted to the disquiet of these times by working harder while at the same time feeling the struggle of our individual needs to remain safe. We collectively grew in our awareness of how bushfires in Australia complexified an already complex pandemic reality; how conservative political views took to the streets of Germany and France; how polarization widened the American political divide; discourses on inclusion remain exclusive; political divides are increasingly visible around the world. We are all living this moment together and not the same. How we live through the liquid of this time into a territory that holds us, individually and collectively, to become aware, conscious of the new spaces for greater justice that includes all of societies diversity, is itself a passageway that we are currently in the middle of. We intentionally ask: Do we transform, or are we transformed by the forces that pull us underneath the familiar territory of our consciousness? How willing are we to be pulled into the unknown? These inquiries turn out attention toward another passageway.

Passageway 2: Problems and Concerns Within the Field of Transformative Learning Theory

We explore a web of discourses on problems and concerns of the space we are about to leave, the familiar discourse on transformative learning. While learning has many aspects and as many theories, adult educator Illeris (2018) argues in his comprehensive history of learning theories that there are four primary types of learning: cumulative, assimilative, accommodative, and transformative. Transformative learning was first described as such by Jack Mezirow in the 1970s and 1980s. In the intervening years, transformative learning has become one of the most popular, influential, and important theories in adult education (Hoggan, 2016; Hoggan et al., 2017; Illeris, 2014a, 2014b; Jarvis, 2011; Newman, 2012a, 2012b, 2014; Taylor, 2008; Taylor & Cranton, 2013). This work and its subsequent critiques and elaborations have enriched, broadened, and further developed the theory of transformative learning from its inception well into the twenty-first century and have led to multiple lines of inquiry—passageways—within transformational learning (Taylor, 2008). There are many essential differences among the various threads of transformative learning theory, on everything from the definition of transformative learning, its aims and goals, its desired outcomes, its processes, and its usefulness in pedagogy and in practice (Dirkx, 1997; Dirkx, et al, 2006; Hoggan, 2016; Hoggan et al., 2017; Illeris, 2014a, 2014b; Jarvis, 2011; Mezirow, 2008; Newman, 2012a, 2012b, 2014; Taylor, 2008; Taylor & Cranton, 2013). There are also major differences relating to "the emphasis on either personal or emancipatory transformation, the emphasis on either individual or social change, the role of culture in transformative learning," among other things (Taylor, 2008, p. 7). While in some ways these differences may be important to the development of theory and to furthering research into creating the conditions for transformative learning to take place, these different approaches have also led to some substantial problems and concerns raised by many theorists in the field.

At the beginning of the twenty-first century, theorists were warning that the language around transformative learning had become so diffuse that the theory was in danger of losing its distinct ideas and specific meaning (Brookfield, 2000; Kegan, 2000). We will take up this idea later in our quest for a new language on transformation. This concern was echoed by Michael Newman (2012a, p. 37) when he introduced his "mutinous thought" that because of the lack of clarity in defining what transformative learning is, what the outcomes of transformative learning are or ought to be, and what separates transformative learning from other types of learning that "perhaps there is no such thing as transformative learning; perhaps there is just good learning." In their response to Newman's mutinous thought, Cranton and Kasl (2012, p. 394) agreed that there was a need for a unified "theoretical belief system about what transformative learning is and how we facilitate it" but that unified theory has not yet emerged. In his response to Newman's original article, John Dirkx agreed that Newman was correct in citing "the proliferation of widely disparate and uneven ways in which transformative learning has been interpreted and used" as valid criticism of the field (Dirkx, 2012, p. 399). He went on to argue that:

Gaining new information, learning a new skill, developing a new or different attitude, or even acquiring a new role or occupation may reflect effective learning experiences, but they do not alone indicate the kinds of experiences intended by serious scholars of transformative learning...This lack of theoretical discipline has almost certainly undermined the credibility of the concept itself and further blurred its meaning. (Dirkx, 2012, p. 401)

Newman (2012b, p. 409), somewhat ungenerously, replied in his own response that while he appreciated that Mezirow "injected intellectual rigor into a flagging field and has kept our attention ever since" he felt that Mezirow had been "worrying away at his theory like a terrier at a rug, tugging at it here, adjusting its position there, and making the rest of us not quite sure of our footing." Illeris (2014a, p. 575) writes that if scholars in the field cannot agree on a commonly held definition of what transformative learning is and of what form transforms their disagreement will "undermine the whole idea and issue of transformative learning both theoretically and practically" and that the fracturing of the field will "develop into a source of uncertainty and disagreement that can erode the concept so much that it becomes meaningless." However, despite the warnings, admonitions, and general agreement that the field is in danger of losing its meaning, there remains a lack of consensus into most aspects of transformative learning theory and how it operates.

Passageway 3: Transformative learning—A theory in continuous progress

While most scholars in the field maintain that transformative learning is fundamentally different from other types of learning, there is still no general agreement on the fundamental aspects of transformative learning theory. To connect through yet another passageway the problems and concerns to transformative learning theory's self-understanding as a theory in progress, one that evolves and has evolved continually is a liquid state that we wish to embrace as a flow into new passageways. For example, Illeris (2014b, p. 150) writes that we are now in a "situation in which, although the issue of transformative learning is more in demand and more celebrated than ever, there is basic conceptual uncertainty and even confusion as to what this term actually includes, covers, and implies"

12 A. NICOLAIDES AND S. ESCHENBACHER

and that there is a "lack of a clear and immediately understandable definition that can separate transformative from non-transformative learning." Though there are differing perspectives about what transforms, there is a continued interest in the phenomenon of transformation through processes of adult learning. Mezirow (1978) first defined transformative learning as a process of

> perspective transformation involving a structural change in the way we see ourselves and our relationships. If the culture permits, we move toward perspectives which are more inclusive, discriminating and integrative of experience. We move away from uncritical, organic relationships toward contractual relationships with others, institutions and society. (p. 100)

Since then, debate continues to bring distinction to facets of transformative learning that have dominated much of the literature in adult education and specifically transformative learning as a theory of adult learning (Taylor, 2008). Patricia Cranton (2006) in her book *Understanding and Promoting Transformative Learning* grouped transformative learning by scholarship in terms of their multidisciplinary influence that includes, connected knowing (Belenky & Stanton, 2000; Tisdell, 2000); social change (Brookfield, 2000; Collard & Law, 1989; Cunningham, 1992; Hart, 1990; Torres, 2003); group and organizational learning (Kasl & Ellias, 2000; Watkins & Marsick, 1993; Yorks & Marsick, 2000); ecological view (Gunnlaugson, 2003; Hathaway, 2017; O'Sullivan, 2003); and the extrarational approach (Boyd, 1989; Boyd & Myers, 1988; Dirkx, 1997; Herman, 2003). These groupings illustrate the appeal of the concept of transformative learning to describe the kind of significant individual change that each of these lenses fosters through adult learning.

In spite of the appeal of transformative learning across these perspectives, essential features that result in transformative learning have not been evolved to show a theory in progress. In Mezirow's view, critical refection, critical self-reflection, and conscientization (Freire, 2018) are essential to transformative learning. As are development and growth to Daloz (1999) and Kegan (2000), individuation to Boyd (1988), categories of consciousness as described by Gunnlaugson (2007) and edge emotions for Mälkki (2010, 2019). These authors represent variations on subject of reflection and the fluid nature of essential features that may lead to transformation. In his *Transformative Dimensions of Adult Learning*,

1 THE MANY TURNS OF TRANSFORMATION ... 13

Mezirow (1991) described three key distinctions to reflection: content (what is the problem?), process (how did this problem come about?), and premise (why is this problem a problem?). It is only premise reflection—that challenged the very basis of the problem at hand—that has the potential to promote a perspective transformation (for a more detailed and recent analysis of these three distinctions, see Kitchenham, 2008).

Kegan (2000) posed the provocative inquiry "What form transforms?" and brought distinction to "Learning aimed at changes in not only *what* we know but changes in *how* we know...come closer to the etymological meaning of education ('leading out'). Trans-*form*-ative learning put the form itself at risk of change" (pp. 48–49). This articulation of what entails transformative learning aligns with Mezirow's premise reflection and draws from Dirkx (1997) who offers that

> transformative learning also involves very personal and imaginative ways of knowing, grounded in a more intuitive and emotional sense of our experiences...Unlike the analytic, reflective, and rational processes of transformation described by Mezirow, learning through soul fosters self-knowledge through symbolic, imagistic, and contemplative means.

This understanding transcends the rational cognitive emphasis that is central to content, process, and premise reflection. O'Sullivan (2002) integrates all three reflective distinctions and a qualitative depth of experience of human and non-human relatedness as the ground for transformation. Per Sullivan, transformative learning

> involves experiencing a deep, structural shift in the basic premises of thought, feelings, and actions. It is a shift of consciousness that dramatically alters our way of being in the world. Such a shift involves our understanding of ourselves and our self-locations; our relationships with other humans and with the natural world; our understanding of relations of power in interlocking structures of class, race, and gender; our body awareness; our visions of alternative approaches to living; our sense of possibilities for social justice and peace and personal joy. (p. 11)

While Jarvis (2011) very carefully integrates all three forms of reflection and relatedness in his description of transformative learning, the combination of processes throughout a lifetime whereby the whole person - body (genetic, physical, and biological), and mind (knowledge, skills, attitudes, values, emotions, meaning, beliefs, and senses)— experiences social situations, the content of which is then transformed cognitively, emotively, or practically (or through any combination) and integrated into the individual person's biography resulting in a continually changing (or more experienced) person. (p. 22)

In 2008, Mezirow revised his description of transformative learning to "the process by which we transform problematic frames of reference (mindsets, habits of mind, meaning perspectives) - sets of assumptions and expectations - to make them more inclusive, discriminating, open, reflective, and emotionally able to change" (p. 42). This evolution of Mezirow's thinking illustrates the permeability and influence of multiple disciplinary perspectives on Mezirow's continued articulation of transformative learning as Taylor (2008) describes, "they include the psychocritical and accept the influences of the psychoanalytical, psychodevelopmental, social emancipatory, neurobiological, cultural-spiritual, race-centric, and planetary" (p. 7).

However, though the understanding of transformative learning continued to evolve through the influence of multiple disciplinary perspectives, the epistemology and ontology of the theory itself have not undergone a transformation; that is, it has not evolved. We notice that efforts to unify the theory and to shift the conversation from variations on transformative learning to return to theorize about transformative learning is beginning to shape new ways of conceiving transformative learning theory. Hoggan (2016) asserts that "transformative learning is a metatheory under which individual theories aggregate. Transformative learning refers to the processes that result in significant and irreversible changes in the way a person experiences, conceptualizes, and interacts with the world" (p. 71).

Passageway 4: The Need for New a Language that Illuminates the Phenomenon of Transformation

We finally leave familiar common ground by exploring a possible new passageway, paving the way toward a new language that illuminates the phenomenon of transformation by a disruption of the known territory of transformative learning. As the majority of scholarship and practice is still focused on answering the same questions over and over again, a sense of "stuckness" has become a commonplace concern among scholars of transformative learning (Illeris, 2014a, 2014b; Malkki & Green, 2014). There is a real danger that transformative learning theory will become "reified" because the theory itself rarely undergoes explicit scrutiny of its premises (Malkki & Green, 2014). Taylor and Cranton (2013, p. 34) have argued that much of the research had become redundant not only because researchers keep asking the same questions but also because "transformative learning no longer transforms itself."

Taylor and Cranton (2013) identify two main reasons for this redundancy. First, many scholars rely on reading literature reviews that summarize theoretical developments and research findings instead of consulting the original primary sources, which means they are missing out on opportunities to discover the nuances and subtleties of the foundational thinkers and what the original researchers have learned. This lack of rigor impacts newer researchers' and theorists' ability to frame and integrate their work with the work that has come before them and to critique that work in their own studies. The second factor that accounts for redundancy in empirical work about transformative learning, according to Taylor and Cranton, is the lack of variety in research methodology. Most of the current research on transformative learning uses the similar qualitative interview-based methodology, which has dominated the empirical studies in the literature. Encouraging and exploring different research methodologies, such as "arts-based research, narrative inquiry, action research, and participatory action research" would refresh the dominant inquiry of processes of transformative learning and open up multidisciplinary and transdisciplinary research that would renew the theory on its continuous evolving path (p. 43).

Our second reason for calling our readers to a passageway that can lead to a new language of transformative learning is that the current state of our language is too fractured to serve us well. This is problematic if we consider that this fracturing has often stymied forward progress of the development of the theory and that the circular nature of revisiting the same arguments about definitions and outcomes has in some ways led to stagnation that has prevented the debates from moving on to other, as yet unaddressed or understudied, questions (Malkki & Green, 2014; Taylor, 2008; Taylor & Cranton, 2013). Our Handbook consciously turns away from both the fracturing and the efforts to cohere a unified theory of transformative learning. Our aim is to open up new passageways that consciously inquire into the visible and growing insistence across epistemologies and ontologies throughout cultures and living theories, that transformation is both a private and public (Rorty, 1989) response as care for our shared commons.

Our felt disquiet regarding the current discourses on transformative learning is partly reflected in this lack of a clear distinction between the phenomenon of change and the phenomenon of transformation (Brookfield, 2000; Eschenbacher, 2018; Newman, 2012b). Adult education is concerned with both; transformative learning, however, is grounded in the phenomenon of transformation (Brookfield, 2000; Mezirow, 1991). At the same time, discourses on transformative learning often employ a language of change instead of a language of transformation. Why should we employ the latter? How is a change in form or structure different from a change in content? Where are these phenomena touching each other, where are they distinct from each other? Despite the similarities, one may ask if these differences are gradual or if *transformation* is essentially different from *change*? What is the benefit of getting a more nuanced understanding of transformation as a special form of change that transfigures the form itself from within the form? Moving through this passageway of transfiguration, how does this fluid movement lead to changes regarding the pedagogy, research, and practice of transformation?

Mezirow (1991) differentiates four forms of learning on a conceptual level (elaborating existing (1) frames of reference, (2) learning new frames of reference, (3) transforming points of view, and (4) transforming habits of mind, while only two of them are transformative (transforming points of view (3) and habits of mind (4)). His distinction remains somehow blurry. This lack of basic conceptual clarity is not limited to Mezirow's notion of transformative learning (see Illeris, 2014b). Both Kegan (2000) and Brookfield (2000) criticize the body of transformative learning for its conceptual looseness and its lack of a clear understanding of the transformative dimension of adult learning. We believe that both aspects inhibit further development of the theory and practice of transformative learning. Therefore, we see a need to address the aforementioned conceptual uncertainty (Illeris, 2014b). One way of doing so is to explore the very phenomenon of transformation as a passageway that enacts the transformation that is central to transformative learning, but is not limited to the field of inquiry for adult educators. The field of adult education is one of the multiple disciplines concerned with transformation. This field strives to develop comprehensive theory about adult learning, which includes but is not limited to transformative learning. The particular interest in learning offered by the discipline of adult education leads us to ask: How is our understanding of transformation enhanced when we view it through the lens of learning?

A WORLD IN CRISIS: A QUEST FOR TRANSFORMATION?

Translating the phenomenon of transformation into the field of adult education, creating a new vocabulary has "connotations of an epiphanic, or apocalyptic, cognitive event—a shift in the tectonic plates of one's assumptive clusters" (Brookfield, 2000, p. 139). The multiple dilemmas we are currently facing (i.e., pandemic, racism, climate change) announce the tectonic shifts that reveal how we have misunderstood formerly unproblematic notions of how we should live for ourselves and together. The immunity and resistance to transform our way of being and living together in the midst of crisis also reveal our inability to change. We may need to humble ourselves? Is our transformation possible so that new possibilities for societal coherence may emerge? What are passageways that may lead us to a new discourse on transformation? What are ways through this dilemma? The existing vocabulary, what Mezirow (e.g., 1991, 2012) describes as the frame of reference and Kegan refers to as the very form itself, is at risk (Kegan, 2000, p. 49). This applies to our thinking about transformation—the form as well as the premises and the content of our quest for understanding how far from transformation we are, while at the same time how near possibilities for new vocabularies that transform exist. Rorty's concept of a vocabulary is one answer to Kegan's question "What form transforms?" (Kegan, 2000).

Rorty (1989)'s care for transformation helps us shed new light on discourses of transformative learning within the field of adult education; it sharpens our view on the task and goal of adult educators. His ideas are reflected in our intention as editors of this Handbook, aiming at creating new ways of researching, understanding, and practicing transformative learning. Working with Rorty's philosophy is just one example of how we can learn more about transformative dimensions of adult learning by exploring the phenomenon of transformation by turning toward distinct and related fields. Reflecting on his work illustrates how we can use the phenomenon of transformation as a passageway, connecting existing discourses on transformative learning with new, unfamiliar discourses and employing a new vocabulary.

This Handbook emerged in a world in the middle of multiple crises—who are we now is a potent inquiry. The purpose of this Handbook is to catalyze a more complex inquiry into transformation. We did not expect to find ourselves in the middle of a civilization-wide transformation that has forced us to look at transformation from the inside. We all know someone who got sick or died or lost their job as a result of COVID-19. The New York Times published a special issue on transformation and how the pandemic has birthed an awakening for many Americans (https://www.nytimes.com/interactive/2021/04/05/us/coronavirus-pandemic.html?searchResultPosition=1). Are we awake? How have we been transformed from the place we stand? This civilization-wide transformation has been forced upon us and many of us chose it, surrendering to its potency to bring us into new spaces of possibility and ways of becoming. How we have transformed will be an inquiry that remains with us for the coming months and years ahead. For some, the reflection of what, if anything, has transformed is just beginning. In spite of the appeal of transformation, there is more evidence of stagnation and less evidence of generativity (i.e., as we finalize this Handbook, as vaccinations mount in some of the world's wealthiest countries and people cautiously envision life after the pandemic, the crisis in South America and India is taking an alarming turn for the worse). What would new vocabularies include that would trouble how to transform ourselves, our communities, our fields of research, our ways of living together, and our attempt of co-creating a new, more just society. What new, unfamiliar passageways can we see emerging?

The Handbook's simple inquiry is: Why do we quest for transformation? What draws so many disciplines and their hope for the influence of transformation on people, workplace, communities, environment, and society? How do we move through transformation, with humility, and, transform?

References

Bauman, Z. (2013). *Liquid modernity*. Polity Press.
Bauman, Z., Jacobsen, M. H., & Tester, K. (2016). *What use is sociology?: Conversations with Michael Hviid Jacobsen and Keith Tester*. John Wiley & Sons.

1 THE MANY TURNS OF TRANSFORMATION ...   19

Bennett, N., & Lemoine, G.J. (2014, February). *What VUCA really means for you*. Harvard Business Review, https://hbr.org/2014/01/what-vuca-really-means-for-you

Belenky, M. F., & Stanton, A. (2000). Inequality, development, and connected knowing. In J. Mezirow, & Associates (Eds.), *Learning as transformation: Critical perspectives on a theory in progress* (pp. 71–102). Jossey-Bass.

Bernstein, R. J. (2016). *Ironic life*. Polity Press.

Boyd, R. D. (1989). Facilitating personal transformation in small groups. *Small Group Behavior, 20*(4), 459–474. https://doi.org/10.1177/104649649021 4006

Boyd, R. D., & Myers, J. G. (1988). Transformative education. *International Journal of Lifelong Education, 7*(4), 261–284. https://doi.org/10.1080/026 0137880070403

Brookfield, S. (2000). Transformative learning as ideology critique. In J. Mezirow, & Associates (Eds.), *Learning as transformation. Critical perspectives on a theory in progress* (pp. 125–148). Jossey-Bass.

Cranton, P. (2006). *Understanding and promoting transformative learning: A guide to theory and practice* (1st ed.). Stylus Publishing.

Cranton, P., & Kasl, E. (2012). A response to Michael Newman's "Calling transformative learning into question: Some mutinous thoughts." *Adult Education Quarterly, 62*(4), 393–398. https://doi.org/10.1177/0741713612456418

Collard, S., & Law, M. (1989). The limits of perspective transformation: A critique of Mezirow's theory. *Adult Education Quarterly, 39*(2), 99–107. https://doi.org/10.1177/0001848189039002004

Cunningham, P. (1992). From Freire to feminism: The North American experience with critical pedagogy. *Adult Education Quarterly, 42*(3), 180–191. https://doi.org/10.1177/074171369204200306

Dirkx, J. M. (1997). Nurturing soul in adult learning. *New Directions for Adult and Continuing Education, 1997*(74), 79–88. https://doi.org/10.1002/ace. 7409

Dirkx, J. M., Mezirow, J., & Cranton, P. (2006). Musings and reflections on the meaning, context, and process of transformative learning: A dialogue between John M. Dirkx and Jack Mezirow. *Journal of Transformative Education, 4*(2), 123–139. https://doi.org/10.1177/1541344606287503

Dirkx, J. M. (2012). Self-formation and transformative learning: A response to "Calling transformative learning into question: Some mutinous thoughts", by Michael Newman. *Adult Education Quarterly, 62*(4), 399–405. https://doi. org/10.1177/0741713612456420

Daloz, L. A. (1999). *Mentor*. Jossey-Bass.

Eschenbacher, S. (2018). Drawing lines and crossing borders: Transformation theory and Richard Rorty's philosophy. *Journal of Transformative Education, 17*(3), 251–268. https://doi.org/10.1177/1541344618805960

20 A. NICOLAIDES AND S. ESCHENBACHER

Freire, P. (2018). *Pedagogy of the oppressed: 50th anniversary edition*. (M. B. Ramos, Trans.). Bloomsbury Academic Publishing. (Original work published 1968).

Gergen, K. J. (1994). *Towards transformation in social knowledge*. Sage.

Gunnlaugson, O. (2003). Toward an integral education for the ecozoic era: A case study in transforming the global learning community of Holma College of Integral Studies. *Journal of Transformative Education, 2*(4), 313–335. https://doi.org/10.1177/1541344604267197

Gunnlaugson, O. (2007). Shedding light on the underlying forms of transformative learning theory. Introducing three distinct categories of consciousness. *Journal of Transformative Education, 5*(2), 134–151. https://doi.org/10.1177/1541344607303526

Hart, M. (1990). Critical theory and beyond: Further perspectives on emancipatory education. *Adult Education Quarterly, 40*(3), 125–138. https://doi.org/10.1177/0001848190040003001

Hathaway, M. D. (2017). Activating hope in the midst of crisis: Emotions, transformative learning, and "the work that reconnects." *Journal of Transformative Education, 15*(4), 296–314. https://doi.org/10.1177/1541344616680350

Herman, L. (2003, October 23–25). Engaging the disturbing images of evil [Conference Session]. In C. A. Wiessner, S. R. Meyer, N. Pfhal, & P. Neaman (Eds.), *Transformative learning in action: Building bridges across contexts and disciplines*. 5th International Conference on Transformative Learning. https://st4.ning.com/topology/rest/1.0/file/get/2865643287?profile=original

Hoggan, C. (2016). Transformative learning as a metatheory: Definition, criteria, and typology. *Adult Education Quarterly, 66*(1), 57–75. https://doi.org/10.1177/0741713615611216

Hoggan, C., Mälkki, K., & Finnegan, F. (2017). Developing the theory of perspective transformation: Continuity, intersubjectivity, and emancipatory praxis. *Adult Education Quarterly, 67*(1), 48–64. https://doi.org/10.1177/0741713616674076

Illeris, K. (2014). Transformative learning re-defined: As changes in elements of the identity. *International Journal of Lifelong Education, 33*(5), 573–586. https://doi.org/10.1080/02601370.2014.917128

Illeris, K. (2014). Transformative learning and identity. *Journal of Transformative Education, 12*(2), 148–163. https://doi.org/10.1177/1541344614548423

Illeris, K. (2018). An overview of the history of learning theory. *European Journal of Education, 53*(1), 86–101. https://doi.org/10.1111/ejed.12265

Jarvis, P. (2011, May 28–29). *The transformative potential of learning in situations of crisis* [Keynote speech]. 9th International Conference on Transformative Learning. http://storage.ning.com/topology/rest/1.0/file/get/2865639417?profile=original

1 THE MANY TURNS OF TRANSFORMATION ... 21

Kasl, E., & Elias, D. (2000). Creating new habits of mind in small groups. In J. Mezirow (Ed.), *Learning as transformation. Critical perspectives on a theory in progress* (pp. 229–252). Jossey-Bass.

Kegan, R. (2000). What 'form' transforms? In J. Mezirow (Ed.), *Learning as transformation: Critical perspectives on a theory in progress*. Jossey-Bass.

Kitchenham, A. (2008). The evolution of John (sic) Mezirow's transformative learning theory. *Journal of Transformative Education, 6*(2), 104–123.

Mälkki, K. (2010). Building on Mezirow's theory of transformative learning: Theorizing the challenges to reflection. *Journal of Transformative Education, 8*(1), 42–62. https://doi.org/10.1177/1541344611403315

Mälkki, K., & Green, L. (2014). Navigational aids: The phenomenology of transformative learning. *Journal of Transformative Education, 12*(1), 5–24. https://doi.org/10.1177/1541344614541171

Mälkki, K. (2019). Coming to grips with edge-emotions: The gateway to critical reflection and transformative learning. In T. Fleming, A. Kokkos, & F. Finnegan (Eds.), *European perspectives on transformation theory* (pp. 59–73). Palgrave Macmillan.

Mezirow, J. (1991). *Transformative dimensions of adult learning*. Jossey-Bass.

Mezirow, J. (1978). Perspective transformation. *Adult Education, 28*(2), 100–110. https://doi.org/10.1177/074171367802800202

Mezirow & Associates. (2000). *Learning as transformation: Critical perspectives on a theory in progress*. Jossey-Bass.

Mezirow, J. (2008). An overview on transformative learning. In P. Sutherland & J. Crowther (Eds.), *Lifelong learning* (pp. 40–54). Routledge.

New York Times. (2021, April 21). *How George Floyd died, and what happened next*. New York Times. https://www.nytimes.com/article/george-floyd.html

Newman, M. (2012). Calling transformative learning into question: Some mutinous thoughts. *Adult Education Quarterly, 62*(1), 36–55. https://doi.org/10.1177/0741713610392768

Newman, M. (2012). Michael Newman's final comments in the forum on his article "Calling transformative learning into question: Some mutinous thoughts." *Adult Education Quarterly, 62*(4), 406–411. https://doi.org/10.1177/0741713612456421

Newman, M. (2014). Transformative learning: Mutinous thoughts revisited. *Adult Education Quarterly, 64*(4), 345–355. https://doi.org/10.1177/074 1713614543173

Nicolaides, A. (2015). Generative learning: Adults learning within ambiguity. *Adult Education Quarterly, 65*(3), 179–195. https://doi.org/10.1177/074 1713614568887

O'Sullivan, E., Morrell, A., & O'Connor, M. (Eds.). (2002). *Expanding the boundaries of transformative learning*. Palgrave Press.

O'Sullivan, E. (2003, October 23–25). *The ecological terrain of transformative learning: A vision statement.* [Conference session]. 5th International Conference on Transformative Learning. https://st4.ning.com/topology/rest/1.0/file/get/2865643287?profile=original

Rorty, R. (1989). *Contingency, irony, and solidarity.* Cambridge University Press.

Taylor, E. W. (2008). Transformative learning theory. *New Directions for Adult and Continuing Education, 2008*(119), 5–15. https://doi.org/10.1002/ace.301

Taylor, E. W., & Cranton, P. (2013). A theory in progress?: Issues in transformative learning theory. *European Journal for Research on the Education and Learning of Adults, 4*(1), 35–47. https://doi.org/10.3384/rela.2000-7426.rela5000

Torres, C. A. (2003). *Paulo Freire, education and transformative social justice learning.* [Conference session]. 5th International Conference on Transformative Learning. https://st4.ning.com/topology/rest/1.0/file/get/2865643287?profile=original

Tisdell, E. (2000). Spirituality and emancipatory adult education in women adult educators for social change. *Adult Education Quarterly, 50*(4), 308–335. https://doi.org/10.1177/074171360005000404

Watkins, K., & Marsick, V. J. (1993). *Sculpting the learning organization: Lessons in the art and science of systemic change.* Jossey-Bass.

Yorks, L., & Marsick, V. J. (2000). Organizational learning and transformation. In J. Mezirow & Associates (Eds.), *Learning as transformation. Critical perspectives on a theory in progress* (pp. 253–281). Jossey-Bass.

PART I

Provocation 1: The Many Turns of Transformation

CHAPTER 2

Transformative Learning and Critical Theory: Making Connections with Habermas, Honneth, and Negt

Ted Fleming

Since the theory of transformative learning was published (Mezirow, 1978; Mezirow & Marsick, 1978), a significant body of scholarship and research has been developed and the theory merits its title as a living theory in progress (Mezirow, 2000). Mezirow borrowed concepts from Jürgen Habermas in order to build a theoretical base (Mezirow, 1981). With recent iterations of critical theory by Honneth and Negt, this chapter explores the potential of their ideas for developing a critical theory of transformative learning—one that would avoid becoming rather conventional and politically neutral.

Collard and Law (1989) and Clarke and Wilson (1991) critiqued transformation theory as overly concerned with individual change. Newman (1994) forcefully argued that Mezirow was not concerned with equalizing

---

T. Fleming (✉)
Teachers College Columbia University, New York City, USA
e-mail: ejf2129@tc.columbia.edu

© The Author(s), under exclusive license to Springer Nature   25
Switzerland AG 2022
A. Nicolaides et al. (eds.), *The Palgrave Handbook of Learning for Transformation*, https://doi.org/10.1007/978-3-030-84694-7_2

26 T. FLEMING

power relations in society and stripped the theory of its potential for social transformation. Hart (1990), Cunningham (1992), and Tennant (1993) make similar critiques. More recently, Hoggan et al. (2017) identify a certain "stuckness" in the theory as critiques are often repeated without adding to the debate (p. 49). All reinforce the idea that the missing social dimension in transformative learning remains problematic. Collard and Law (1989), who were students at the time, acknowledged Mezirow's comments on their work (p. 99). Such studies have always prompted debates, clarifications, and further development of the theory particularly by Mezirow (HYPERLINK "sps:refid::bib35|bib37|bib38|bib40") who emphasized the connection between transformation and social action while (Mezirow, 1953, 1997) always made a distinction between fostering critically reflective learning and social action.

In order to develop a critical theory of adult learning, Mezirow (1981) utilized key ideas of Habermas. Though Mezirow's approach was imaginative and original, critiques emerge from his selective borrowing from Habermas. In a problematic argument, Mezirow (1981) states that:

> As educators, we need not concern ourselves with the philosophical question of whether Habermas has succeeded in establishing the epistemological status of the primary knowledge-constitutive interests with categorically distinct object domains, types of experience and corresponding forms of inquiry. (p. 72)

This also led Mezirow to not fully utilize other useful ideas from Habermas including the demise of the public sphere and the capacity of civil society as a location for decolonizing the lifeworld. As a result, critiques gained traction and this hindered the ability to address them.

This chapter is based on the idea that critiques may stand or fall but should not be (re)asserted without rethinking the critical theory foundations and potentials that are partially but not comprehensively exploited by transformative learning—and its critics. Allies in this study are Jürgen Habermas, Axel Honneth, and Oskar Negt who help build a more complete critical theory of transformative learning.

FRANKFURT SCHOOL: HABERMAS, HONNETH, NEGT

The Institute for Social Research, usually called the Frankfurt School, was formed at the Goethe University of Frankfurt in the 1920s. It engages in an interdisciplinary research study of how capitalism and injustices in society can be explained and ways sought to take emancipatory actions. Philosophy, sociology, and psychology were explored as interdisciplinary contributions by Horkheimer, Adorno, and Marcuse—who with Fromm, Benjamin, and others developed a body of scholarship that included an integrated psychoanalytic analysis. One could only understand oppression by analyzing both social systems and their dialectic relationship with the unconscious. This classical project of critical theory evolved with varying but parallel trajectories by Habermas, Honneth, and Negt. All are interested in social justice, reason, truth, and democracy and agree that philosophy aims at the "practical transformation of the existing social conditions" (Habermas, 1981, p. 469).

Jürgen Habermas (2008) is the most widely known member of the Frankfurt School who wrote that "the public sphere as a space of reasoned communicative exchanges is the issue that has concerned me all my life" (pp. 12–13). He proposes that any decision in society must be deliberated on freely and equally by all without hindrance or exclusion by social inequalities. He argues that reasoned discourse about the good life is possible, practicable, and epistemologically legitimate.

Axel Honneth is Director of the Frankfurt School and Professor at Columbia University, New York. He reorients critical theory by interpreting the communicative turn of Habermas as a recognition turn (Honneth, 1995). Damaged recognition motivates social change—rather than distorted communication. For Honneth (2009), critical theorists, in spite of their differences, agree that the living conditions of modern capitalist societies produce social practices, attitudes, or personality structures that result in a pathological distortion of our capacities for reason ... They always aim at exploring the social causes of a pathology of human rationality (p. vii).

He reinterpreted oppression as a form of misrecognition and emancipation could be achieved through the struggle for recognition (Fleming, 2016). His reimagined emancipatory philosophy foregrounds a theory of recognition and intersubjectivity as crucial mooring points for critical theory.

Oskar Negt studied with Horkheimer and Adorno, was assistant to Habermas in 1962, and is a prominent scholar at Leibniz University Hannover that Illeris (2002) asserts is an "extension of the Frankfurt School" (p. 147). With a long history of involvement in critical and emancipatory worker education, he rethinks the role of experience making it

28   T. FLEMING

central to his pedagogical agenda. He may be unique in European critical theory, certainly as a Frankfurt scholar, to have published his autobiography (Negt, 2016, 2019). These Frankfurt School scholars help progress Mezirow's theory of transformative learning.

MEZIROW AND HABERMAS

Transformation theory relies on Habermas (1971) for understanding domains of learning (instrumental, communicative, and emancipatory), critical reflection, and discourse. These give transformation theory a firm theoretical base and Mezirow (1981) proposes that transformation theory is a critical theory of adult learning.

Domains of Learning

In addition to instrumental and communicative learning, Mezirow (1991) added emancipatory learning to form distinct learning domains. Emancipatory learning involves becoming aware of problematic underlying assumptions in either instrumental or communicative learning. Emancipation (Mezirow, 1991) is from "libidinal, institutional or environmental forces which limit our options and rational control over our lives but have been taken for granted as beyond human control" (p. 87). For Honneth (1995), the emancipatory interest is the struggle for recognition, and for Negt, it is discovered through the experiences of workers (Negt & Kluge, 1993).

Critical Reflection

For Habermas (1971), critical self-reflection is not just philosophical speculation but a form of rationality, equal in status to the reason of sciences (logic) and humanities (hermeneutics). When Mezirow borrowed these ideas, he (unknowingly?) placed the intersubjective basis for critical reflection at the center of transformative learning. His thinking (1971) was grounded in the work of Blumer and G. H. Mead who are important sources of ideas on the intersubjective nature of learning and development. The idea that learning is individual, as argued by critics of transformation theory, seems to be also contrary to the Habermas view that psychoanalysis is an intersubjectively practiced form of self-reflection.

Discourse

In discourse, every member is free to engage and the only force at play is the force of the better argument and is the kind of discussion that characterizes democracy. Habermas idealistically outlines rules for such discourse and Mezirow (2000) adopted them saying that participants in the discussions involving transformative learning must also have:

> full accurate and complete information; freedom from coercion and distorting self-deception; openness to alternative points of view; empathy and concern about how others think and feel; the ability to weigh evidence and assess arguments objectively; greater awareness of the context of ideas and, more critically, reflectiveness of assumptions, including their own; an equal opportunity to participate in the various roles of discourse; willingness to seek understanding and agreement and to accept a resulting best judgement as a test of validity until new perspectives, evidence or arguments are encountered and validated through discourse as yielding a better judgement. (pp. 13–14)

Like critical reflection, discourse demands a great deal from participants, including emotional maturity, empathy, self-awareness, an ability not to be adversarial, and an ability to hold different and apparently contradictory thoughts concurrently. It also emphasizes consensus building—not always possible in real life (Mezirow, 2000, p. 11). Whether these are requirements for or an outcome of transformative learning is not always clear! Other concepts are important in further iterations of transformation theory.

Lifeworld

The lifeworld is a pool of intuitive knowledge about the objective, social, and intersubjective world, employed, usually without thinking, in order to establish and sustain interactions. According to Mezirow (1991), it is "a vast inventory of unquestioned assumptions and shared cultural convictions, including codes, norms, roles, social practices, psychological patterns of dealing with others and individual skills" (p. 69). For Habermas (1987), knowledge stored in the lifeworld is deeply sedimented and normally unproblematic in everyday life (p. 126). As if anticipating transformative learning, Habermas asserts that as soon as the lifeworld becomes problematic it loses its role as a background certainty

30   T. FLEMING

and becomes subject to discursive examination. Transformation theory indicates that the lifeworld is transformed (Mezirow, 1991, p. 69).

Communicative action or conducting free open democratic discourse involves exactly the conditions necessary for transformative learning. Full free participation in critical and reflective discourse is viewed by Mezirow as a core activity of transformative learning and is indeed a human right (Mezirow et al., 1990, p. 11). It is these connections that suggest transformation theory is already a critical theory.

Intersubjectivity

Mezirow (1994) insists that transformation theory has a social dimension:

> Perspective transformation does necessitate a critique of alienating social forms when one is addressing socio-linguistic codes, which include social norms, language codes, ideologies, philosophies, theories. This process may obviously lead to collective action. However, a critique of social organizations may be of limited utility when one addresses either psychological or epistemic codes. (p. 228)

Discourse and transformative learning require intersubjectivity. Habermas (1992) states that the rational potential in linguistic practice is based on sound intersubjectivity that is a "glimmer of symmetrical relations marked by free, reciprocal recognition" (p. 145). Communicative action, discourse, and critical reflection are firmly grounded in the mutuality of intersubjectivity.

Habermas (2008) states that the "public domain of the jointly inhabited interior of our lifeworld is at once inside and outside" (p. 14) and the "barrier between inner and outer is not just a filtering by an osmotic membrane" (p. 15). The inside/outside dichotomy is misleading. He (2008) continues:

> Even in expressions of its most personal feelings and its most intimate excitations, an ostensibly private consciousness thrives on the impulses it receives from the cultural network of public, symbolically expressed, and intersubjectively shared categories, thoughts and meanings. (p. 15)

It is difficult to imagine a stronger statement of the false dichotomy of individual and social, public, and private that seems to inform the critiques that transformative learning is individualistic. It is difficult to disconnect

2 TRANSFORMATIVE LEARNING AND CRITICAL THEORY ... 31

an individual's transformative learning from the social dimension. In this, transformative learning is closely allied to critical theory. Transformation theory holds that effective learners in an emancipatory, participative, democratic society—a learning society—become a community of cultural critics and social activists (Mezirow, 1995) and the dichotomy of individual and society is transcended by an epistemology of intersubjectivity. Transformation theory asserts that the dichotomy between individual and social development is a spurious one for educators. These ideas from Habermas lead us to conclude that transformation theory is grounded in and infused with a sense of the social. Collard and Law (1989) may be correct when they critique Mezirow's inability to fuse the interactionist legacy in his thinking with "ideas from Habermas" (p. 100).

Habermas is a neglected contributor to how we understand learning in society. In addition to writing (1970) on the role of universities in society he adopted as a basic theorem that "subjects capable of speech and action, who can be affected by reasons, can learn – and in the long run even, 'cannot not learn'" (2003, p. 8). He (1975) holds that

> the fundamental mechanism for social evolution in general is to be found in an automatic inability not to learn. Not learning, but not-learning is the phenomenon that calls for explanation at the socio-cultural level of development. Therein lies, if you will, the rationality of man. (p. 15)

We learn by growing into the symbolic structures of our lifeworlds. A society learns by taking on the evolutionary challenges caused by the failure of the available steering capacities (Habermas, 1991) and new problem-solving capacities are always a result of new problematic situations. For Habermas (2003), the task of epistemology is to "explain the learning process, complex, *from the very beginning*, that sets in when the expectations that guide our actions are problematized" (p. 13). The disorienting dilemmas of transformative learning are suggested here.

Habermas relates adult learning to his vision of a democratic society and calls democracy an adult learning project (Habermas, 1987) as he associates democracy with free and unrestrained communication. Habermas (1979) continues: "I can imagine the attempt to arrange a society democratically only as a self-controlled learning process" (p. 186). By implication, transformative learning becomes a democracy project. This echoes Dewey's (1943) understanding of school as "a miniature

32   T. FLEMING

community, an embryonic society" (p. 18). Habermas (1987) also postulates an adult learning crisis in modern society, arguing that adults are not sufficiently prepared for what is central to his vision of a democratic society, namely participation in public discourse.

Subsequent iterations of critical theory build on this and identify recognition (rather than distorted communications) as the pathology of capitalism. As we grow and develop the

> deeper the process of individuation shapes the inner life of a person, the deeper she becomes entangled towards the outside,... in an even denser and more fragile network of relationships of reciprocal recognition. (Habermas, 2008, p. 16)

Axel Honneth is our ally realizing this recognition turn hinted at by Habermas.

HONNETH'S CRITICAL THEORY

Axel Honneth (2009) continues the Frankfurt School's social critique by asserting that the living conditions of

> Modern capitalist societies produce social practices, attitudes, or personality structures that result in a pathological distortion of our capacities for reason.... They [critical theorists] always aim at exploring the social causes of a pathology of human rationality. (p. vii)

He reorients critical theory by interpreting the distorted communications of Habermas as misrecognitions. He brings to the fore a theory of intersubjectivity and the struggle for recognition (1995) as key ideas for critical theory today. He (1995) argues that

> the reproduction of social life is governed by the imperative of mutual recognition, because one can develop a practical relation-to-self only when one has learned to view oneself, from the normative perspective of one's partners in interaction, as their social addressee. (p. 92)

Central to Honneth's (1995) work is a clear statement of intersubjectivity and this "relationship to oneself ... is not a matter of a solitary ego appraising itself, but an intersubjective process, in which one's attitude towards oneself emerges in one's encounter with the other's attitude towards oneself" (p. xii).

The struggle for recognition, based on the need for self-esteem and the experience of disrespect, explains social development. The experience of disrespect triggers actions motivated by feelings of indignation and injustices (Honneth, 2014a). Internal (psychic) conflicts resulting from inadequate recognition drive social change. In this way, the social and personal are connected. The antidote to being too individualistic lies in Honneth's critical theory of the struggle for recognition. Recognition and mutual acceptance explicitly underpin the communicative action of Habermas as well as critical reflection for transformative learning. Discourse is built on mutual recognition and intersubjectivity (Honneth, 1995). This moves the debate about critical reflection away from the perceived highly cognitive and rational interest of Habermas toward an expanded theory of recognition and intersubjectivity. This has the potential to resolve the problem in transformation theory as to whether learning is an individual or social phenomenon.

From Recognition to Emancipation

Honneth (2014a) also reorients critical theory beyond recognition to focus on freedom. In order to realize social freedom, individuals must be able to view each other's freedom as a condition for their own. Members of society are defined as free by their ability to enhance and initiate mutual recognition. Honneth's vision of democracy involves not only the political sphere but emancipated democratic families and socialized markets. For Honneth (2014a), the realization of freedom in any one of these areas depends on its realization in the others as democratic citizens, emancipated families, and ethical markets "mutually influence each other, because the properties of one cannot be realized without the other two" (p. 331). Everything is connected. Individual freedom cannot be realized if one is not involved in the "we" of democratic will formation where the same weight is afforded to the contributions of all citizens (Honneth, 2014b). Individual and social freedoms are connected—not in some vague or superficial way but essentially. One cannot be fully free in some individual way alone but only when individual and social emancipation are connected. This has clear implications for the ways in which critiques have attempted to disconnect individual learning from social learning.

This immediately suggests a softening of the highly rational and demanding concept of critical reflection and a rethinking of transformation theory. Recognition is a precondition for rational discourse. As long as transformative learning is strongly associated with Habermas, it may well remain overly rational in its presentation. It needs to be grounded more firmly in the intersubjectivity of Honneth's critical theory. This does not imply that these ideas are absent in Habermas. They are not. They seem to be more easily identified and accessible in Honneth.

Honneth and Transformative Learning

Transformation theory can now be reframed so that rational discourse is seen as based on an interpersonal process of recognition that builds self-confidence, self-respect, and self-esteem. The idea that learning is either individual or social can be reframed. This implies that transformative learning is best supported by interactions that are respectful but that also explicitly recognize the unique worth of each individual along with the aspirations that prompt their struggles for recognition. Transformative learning escapes the charge of being overly rational.

Struggles for recognition can also be reinterpreted as disorienting dilemmas—the first step toward transformative learning. Dilemmas involve whether to stay in a world circumscribed by experiences of misrecognition or respond to struggles for recognition and acknowledgment through addressing perplexities that prompt learning.

Transformative learning also involves making connections between individual problems and broader social issues. Personal problems are closely and necessarily connected to broader social issues. This is an epistemologically essential step in interpreting the world that cannot be understood properly without connecting personal and social perspectives.

As Honneth allows us to reinterpret the work of Mezirow, we rephrase Freire's "pedagogy of the oppressed" as "pedagogy of the misrecognized." But a living theory cannot remain static and survive. The critical theory of Oskar Negt allows us to reimagine these ideas again in the search for a critical theory of transformative learning.

Oskar Negt

Negt is a prolific writer on philosophy, sociology, and organization theory and is equally active in journalism and the media (Langston, 2020). He collaborates with Alexander Kluge, an award-winning movie/TV producer (Kluge, 2020). Negt's main interests are work as a source of identity and dignity (in the face of injustices); critical pedagogy for adults and schools (as a source of social theory, emancipatory learning, and action); and politics. Oskar Negt shares the concerns of Habermas and Honneth and says that "Democracy is the only politically conceived social order that has to be learned, over and over, every day, into old age" as a "process of education and learning" (Kluge & Negt, 2014, p. 452).

Negt (2008) is one of the few critical theorists who explicitly addresses adult education and is active in worker education (Langston, 2020). His focus is on the experiences of workers as the starting point for learning and teaching. The experience of workers (Kluge & Negt, 2014) is a source of social recognition and identity but is infused with the contradictions of capitalist society. This experience is a source of "resistance to capitalism" (p. 31). His concept of exemplary learning uses these experiences of workers along with a sociological imagination to understand these issues and foster social action to alter the condition of workers (and learners). Stollman (in Kluge & Negt, 2014) writes that "the rallying cry for Negt and Kluge's work is no longer 'Workers of the world, unite!' but rather 'Experiences of the world, unite!'" (p. 464).

He suggests how the experiences of learners might be utilized in teaching (Kluge & Negt, 2014; Negt & Kluge, 1993) and makes use of a range of materials and pedagogical techniques to enhance the critical intelligence of students (Negt & Kluge, 1993, p. 106). He is acutely aware that political and social change is difficult and involves what Kluge refers to in his recent book title (quoting Weber) as a slow and powerful "drilling through hard boards" (Kluge, 2017).

Negt and Transformative Learning

Negt's work on experience is important for constructing a critical theory of transformative learning that starts with a disorienting dilemma. This is an experience of disorientation, of fear maybe, or anxiety and of identifying one's problem with broader social issues. Negt (Illeris, 2002) expands Dewey's understanding of experience on which Mezirow relied so heavily.

Dewey (1966) defines education as "that reconstruction or reorganization of experience which adds to the meaning of experience, and which increases ability to direct the course of subsequent experience" (p. 76) and included "organizing, restructuring and transforming" experience (p. 50). For Dewey, experience has two dimensions. First, experience is in continuity with previous experience. In pursuing meaning we modify or integrate new experience with previous experiences. For Mezirow (1978), "a meaning perspective refers to the structure of cultural assumptions within which one's new experience is assimilated to—and transformed by—one's past experience" (p. 101). Second, experience is in interaction with one's broader environment. Experience is created by interacting with the environment (Dewey, 1963, p. 43). Learning involves becoming aware of these interactions and continuities (Dewey, 1966, pp. 76–77) and how they too are themselves distorted processes open to misinterpretation. Frames of reference help interpret experience and dysfunctional frames of reference distort our experience. In fact, misrecognitions distort meaning schemes.

Dewey (1933) was clearly against the dualisms of Western philosophy and its Cartesian habit of thinking in terms of "either/or"—for example with respect to mind/body or fact/value. The problem for Dewey, having rejected dualism as a habit of thought, was how to connect the interactions and continuities that formed habits of cognition. He typically connected these conflicting polarities of Cartesian thought with an "and." He emphasized this in a number of book titles (*Democracy and Education*, etc.). But there is a further and more critical iteration of these connections beyond the anti-dualism of Dewey and the pragmatists (e.g., Pierce and James). It is worth noting how strongly Mezirow relied on Dewey's (1933, p. 16) concept of habit of mind or of expectation.

Mezirow probably allowed the dialectical understanding of experience escape his grasp. Dewey accepted dialectical understandings in a number of areas of his philosophy (ethics, art, and methodology) and his reliance on Hegel, though clear, is complicated by how these ideas evolved over time especially in dialogue with other Hegelians. Dewey's (1966, p. 272) understanding of education for growth was enhanced by his accepting that the process was dialectical. Learning and experience are dialectical.

This may have been a missed opportunity for Mezirow (and transformative learning theory) to grasp the full contextualized understanding as outlined by Hegel.

Negt reframes experience and says that the continuities and interactions are dialectical. This has implications for transformative learning. Mezirow (1978, p. 101) hardly hints that this interaction between one's current experience and one's previous experience is dialectical. The internal process of the individual and the environment is also dialectical. This fundamentally alters our understanding of transformative learning theory. The familiar phases of transformative learning must now be reinterpreted. The accommodations and assimilations referred to by Hoggan et al., (2017, p. 51) miss the dialectical aspects of experience. This dialectical turn avoids the "stuckness" of false dichotomies involving the social and personal and is a different version of "stuckness" in transformation theory to that mentioned by Hoggan et al., (2017, pp. 50–54).

Transformative learning also involves connecting one's individual experience with broader social issues and this connection is also dialectical. Critiques of transformation theory focus on the way the social dimension of learning is misconstrued. We can now define this problem differently. Individual problems are connected dialectically with broader social issues. The political is personal—dialectically. This makes understanding one's problems or dilemmas and the search for solutions more complex than previously understood and are not properly understood unless they are seen as dialectical. Connecting with broader social issues is not just an interesting add-on, but an essential dimension of understanding one's experiences. Indeed, without this dialectical dimension, the connections are misconstrued. I now propose that the actions one takes, as a result of the final phase of the transformative learning process, should be a dialectically interconnected set of personal and social actions. Praxis is always dialectical.

This reconstruction is a consequence of Mezirow's approach to thinkers whose ideas were useful for his project. He was aware that Dewey's understanding of critical reflection was problematic for understanding an adult version of critical reflection and he ignored Dewey's reliance on Hegel. Negt's work is particularly helpful for illuminating aspects of Mezirow's work that have been uncritically conceptualized. Mezirow borrowed selectively.

These are not entirely new ideas in European education studies. Salling Olesen is credited by Knud Illeris (2002) with borrowing these ideas from

38 T. FLEMING

Negt in 1989. Negt, more than any other critical theorist associated with the Frankfurt School, builds an education theory around these ideas. Even if learners are not aware of these connections, real understandings are only fully revealed when they are interpreted as dialectic. Quoting Hegel, Negt and Kluge (1993) write that:

> The dialectical movement, which consciousness performs on itself, both on its knowledge as well as on its object, in so far as the new, true object emerges from consciousness from this movement is in fact what is known as experience. (p. 5)

Negt's contribution to adult education includes concepts such as exemplary learning and societal competencies that he worked out in the context of emancipatory trade union and worker education. The links with the concept of sociological imagination of C Wright Mills are clear. Negt (1971) emphasizes the promise of Mills interdisciplinary method that illuminates "structural relationships between individual life histories, immediate interests, wishes, hopes and historical events" (p. 28).

Negt (1971) goes beyond the teaching of skills and competences and emphasizes the important pedagogical idea of understanding "workers existence as a social problem" (p. 4). He involves workers in analyzing and interpreting their social situation in order to understand the causes of their current situation and inform actions to change it. Negt focusses on developing an emancipatory theory of worker education and a corresponding teaching manual. His social theory is grounded in the experiences of workers. This involves an exercise in sociological imagination so that both lived experiences of learners and the possibilities that may emerge are reimagined. He calls this exemplary learning, learning that is connected to the interests of learners; that connects the experiences of learners with broader social issues and is relevant for their emancipation (Negt, 1971, p. 97). This is a rare excursion into adult learning theory by a Frankfurt School scholar (1971).

Learning is more than accumulating knowledge. It is a collective journey of self-determination leading to political and emancipatory actions. Unlike transformative learning, Negt supports a curriculum or list of competences that are essential for exemplary learning. The topics taught, or competences as Negt (2010) calls them, are these six: identity competence; historical competence; social justice (or awareness) competence; technological competence; ecological competence; and economic competence (pp. 218–234). This curriculum links the learners' individual experiences with broader social issues; investigates and explores the interconnections in order to see how individual experiences and structural issues are connected dialectically. Along with dialectical thinking, this meta-learning is fundamental to exemplary learning (Negt, 1993, p. 661).

This leads to a systematic theory and practice of worker education (adult education) and closely approximates to transformative learning. It involves thinking independently, dialectically, systemically, with sociological imagination, utilizing critical reflection and democratic participation. This extends transformation theory into social and political arenas in ways not found in transformative learning's traditionally tame and politically neutral stance.

Negt takes adult education beyond the concepts of personal growth and development that may in practice lead to fitting into the social structures of the current world. He outlines how experience itself is modified by social structures (Illeris, 2002, p. 151). Negt and Kluge (1993) say that "experience is the most important thing that workers actually produce" (p. xlviii). Illeris (2002) states this well: "The working class can break through the distortion of immediate experiences, experience the structural conditions for their experiential development, and then fight to change these conditions" (p. 152). The experience of workers is the best route to understanding the social system as it is. Illeris insightfully (but only in passing) connects these ideas with Mezirow's theory.

Olesen (1989) and Wildemeersch (1992) have been aware for these ideas for some time. Olesen (1989), quoting Negt, sees "experience as a collective process because when we experience as individuals we also do so through a socially structured consciousness" (p. 8) and again "the socialized individual cannot experience individually" (p. 68). The individual is always multiple, or as Brecht writes: "the self is always plural" or individual (cited in Kluge & Negt, 2014, p. 45). These connections extend the links between the central role of experience in transformative learning and critical theory—a theory with a dialectic core.

Using literature, especially science fiction, satire, fragments of literature, film, and documentaries, Negt encourages the dangerous thoughts of critical intelligence. In a book title Kluge calls this pedagogy "learning processes with a deadly outcome" (Kluge, 1996).

Conclusion

As the ongoing project of contributing to a critical theory of transformative learning commenced by Mezirow (1981), we identify a number of strands of critical theory that contribute to this project. Some of these Mezirow creatively utilized, and others he ignored. In both instances, the full potential of the ideas was not identified so that critiques could be addressed. Transformation theory and critical theory continue to evolve and the task continues of researching the possibility of further connections, whether through Habermas, Honneth, Negt, or indeed others so that a fuller iteration of a living theory of transformative learning might unfold to meet the increasingly challenging learning needs of individuals, communities, and society.

All the authors discussed here have pedagogical orientations. Mezirow has a pedagogy of transformation; Habermas a pedagogy of rationality; Honneth a pedagogy of recognition and emancipation; and Negt a pedagogy of dialectical experience. The case could be made to switch these around and associate these concepts with the different authors. For instance, transformation theory might become a pedagogy of democracy, rationality, and intersubjectivity; a pedagogy of recognition and emancipation; and a pedagogy of dialectical experience. It might even, if is to remain a critical theory of adult learning, become a pedagogy of dialectical and dangerous thinking.

References

Clark, C., & Wilson, A. (1991). Context and rationality in Mezirow's theory of transformational learning. *Adult Education Quarterly, 41*(2), 75–91.

Collard, S., & Law, M. (1989). The limits of perspective transformation. *Adult Education Quarterly, 39*(2), 99–107.

Cunningham, P. M. (1992). From Freire to feminism: The North American experience with critical pedagogy. *Adult Education Quarterly, 42*(3), 180–191.

Dewey, J. (1933). *How we think*. Regnery.

Dewey, J. (1943). *The school and society*. University of Chicago Press.

Dewey, J. (1963). *Experience and education*. Macmillan.

Dewey, J. (1966). *Democracy and education*. The Free Press.

Fleming, T. (2016). Reclaiming the emancipatory potential of adult education: Honneth's critical theory and the struggle for recognition. *European Journal for Research on the Education and Learning of Adults, 7*(1), 13–24.

Habermas, J. (1970). Towards a rational society: Student protest, science and politics. Beacon Press.

Habermas, J. (1971). *Knowledge and human interests*. Beacon Press.

Habermas, J. (1975). *Legitimation crisis*. Beacon Press.

Habermas, J. (1979). Communication and the evolution of society. Beacon Press.

Habermas, J. (1981). *Kleine Politische schriften I-IV* [Short political writings]. Suhrkamp.

Habermas, J. (1987). The theory of communicative action, Lifeworld and system: A critique of functionalist reason, volume 2. Beacon Press.

Habermas, J. (1991). Toward a reconstruction of historical materialism. In J. Habermas (Ed.), *Communication and the evolution of society* (pp. 130–177). Beacon Press.

Habermas J. (1992). *Postmetaphysical thinking*. Polity.

Habermas, J. (2003). Introduction: Realism after the linguistic turn. In J. Habermas (Ed.), *Truth and justification* (pp. 1–49). MIT Press.

Habermas, J. (2008). *Between naturalism and religion*. Polity.

Hart, M. (1990). Critical theory and beyond: Further perspectives on emancipatory education. *Adult Education Quarterly, 40*(3), 125–138.

Hoggan, C., Mälkki, K., & Finnegan, F. (2017). Developing the theory of perspective transformation: Continuity, intersubjectivity and emancipatory praxis. *Adult Education Quarterly, 67*(1), 48–64.

Honneth, A. (1995). *The struggle for recognition: The moral grammar of social conflicts*. MIT Press.

Honneth, A. (2009). *Pathologies of reason: On the legacy of critical theory*. Columbia University Press.

Honneth, A. (2014a). *Freedom's right: The social foundations of democratic life*. Polity.

Honneth, A. (2014b). *The I in we: Studies in the theory of recognition*. Polity.

Illeris, K. (2002). *The three dimensions of learning: Contemporary learning theory in the tension field between the cognitive, the emotional and the social*. Krieger.

Kluge, A. (1996). *Learning processes with a deadly outcome*. Duke University Press.

Kluge, A. (2017). *Drilling through hard boards: 133 Political stories*. University of Chicago Press.

Kluge, A. (2020). *Alexander Kluge: Homepage*. https://www.kluge-alexander.de/. Accessed July 10, 2020.

Kluge, A., & Negt, O. (2014). *History and obstinacy*. Zone Books.

Langston, R. (2020). *Dark matter: A guide to Alexander Kluge and Oskar Negt*. Verso.

Mezirow, J. (1953). Youth awakens a sleeping town. *Adult Leadership, 1*(9), 6–8.

Mezirow, J. (1971). Towards a theory of practice. *Adult Education Journal, XX, 1*(3), 135–147.

42   T. FLEMING

Mezirow, J. (1978). Perspective transformation. *Adult Education Quarterly, 28*(2), 100–110.

Mezirow, J. (1981). Towards a critical theory of adult education. *Adult Education Quarterly, 32*(1), 3–24.

Mezirow, J. (1991). *Transformative dimensions of adult learning.* Jossey-Bass.

Mezirow, J. (1994). Understanding transformation theory. *Adult Education Quarterly, 44,* 222–232.

Mezirow, J. (1995). Transformation theory of adult learning. In M. Welton (Ed.), *In defense of the lifeworld* (pp. 39–70). SUNY Press.

Mezirow, J. (1996). Contemporary paradigms of learning. *Adult Education Quarterly, 46*(3), 158–172.

Mezirow, J. (1997). Transformation theory out of context. *Adult Education Quarterly, 48*(1), 60–62.

Mezirow, J. (2000). Learning to think like an adult: Core concepts of transformation theory. In J. Mezirow, & Associates (Eds.), *Learning as transformation: Critical perspectives on a theory in progress* (pp. 3–33). Jossey-Bass.

Mezirow, J., & Associates. (1990). *Fostering critical reflection in adulthood.* Jossey-Bass.

Mezirow, J., & Marsick, V. (1978). Education for perspective transformation: Women's re-entry programs in community colleges. Teachers College.

Negt, O. (1971). *Soziologische Phantasie und exemplarisches Lernen: Zur Theorie und Praxis der Arbeiterbildung,* [Sociological imagination and exemplary learning: On the theory and practice of workers' education]. Europäische Verlagsanstalt.

Negt, O. (1993). Wir brauchen ein zweite gesamtdeutsche Bildungsreform [We need a civic all-German educational reform]. *Gewerkschaftliche Monatshefte, 11,* 657–666.

Negt, O. (2008). Adult education and European identity. *Policy Futures in Education, 6*(6), 744–756.

Negt, O. (2010). *Der politische Mensch: Demokratie als Lebensform* [The political person: democracy as a way of life]. Steidl Verlag.

Negt, O. (2016). *Überlebensglück. Eine autobiographische Spurensuche* [Survivor's happiness/luck: An autobiographical search for traces]. Steidl Verlag.

Negt, O. (2019). *Erfahrungsspuren. Eine autobiographische Denkreise* [Traces of experience: An autobiographical thought-journey]. Steidl Verlag.

Negt, O., & Kluge, A. (1993). Public sphere and experience: Analysis of the bourgeois and proletarian public sphere. University of Minnesota Press.

Newman, M. (1994). Defining the enemy: Adult education in social action. Stewart Victor Publishing.

Olesen, H. S. (1989). *Adult education and everyday life.* Adult Education Research Group.

Tennant, M. (1993). Perspective transformation and adult development. *Adult Education Quarterly, 44*(1), 34–42.

Wildemeersch, D. (1992). Ambiguities of experiential learning and critical pedagogy. In D. Wildemeersch & T. Jansen (Eds.), *Adult education, experiential learning and social change: The postmodern challenge* (pp. 19–34). VUGA.

CHAPTER 3

Reconsidering the Roots of Transformative Education: Habermas and Mezirow

Saskia Eschenbacher and Peter Levine

TRANSFORMATION IN MEZIROW'S THEORY

"Civil society has the dual function of ensuring that those who exercise power do not abuse it and of transforming the system to regenerate more democratic practices" (Fleming, 2018, p. 9). Proceeding from this notion of civil society, the call for transformation, for more democratic practices, provides the starting point for a theory of learning that is concerned with fostering democratic practices by challenging taken-for-granted ways of (co-)creating society. As "an approach to teaching based on promoting change, where educators challenge learners to critically question and assess the integrity of their deeply held assumptions about how they relate

S. Eschenbacher (✉)
Akkon University of Applied Human Sciences, Berlin, Germany
e-mail: saskia.eschenbacher@akkon-hochschule.de

P. Levine
Tisch College of Civic Life, Tufts University, Medford, MA, USA
e-mail: Peter.Levine@tufts.edu

© The Author(s), under exclusive license to Springer Nature Switzerland AG 2022
A. Nicolaides et al. (eds.), *The Palgrave Handbook of Learning for Transformation*, https://doi.org/10.1007/978-3-030-84694-7_3

45

to the world around them" (Mezirow & Taylor, 2009, p. xi), trans-formative learning theory seeks to assist adult learners in their attempt to liberate themselves from assumptions that limit their way of being and living. Mezirow outlined the process of perspective transformation where learners came to a new, transformed understanding of themselves, including their self-concept and identity. They were able to liberate themselves from the governing ideas and social norms regarding sex-stereotypical roles (Mezirow, 1978a). This process of liberation emerged through the women's movement: Learners came to understand how the public breaks into the private by gaining a deeper understanding of the relationship between personal problems and public issues, where "women's experiences became de-privatized" (Hart, 1990b, p. 56).

Where does the idea of transforming one's way of being and living come from? The process of perspective transformation is historically rooted in social movements, more precisely the women's movement (e.g., Mezirow, 1978a, 1978b, 1990a). In the course of Mezirow's investigation for factors that impede or facilitate the progress of re-entry programs for women—supporting them to pursue a degree or a job after an extended hiatus—he came to identify a structural re-organization of women's relationship to themselves and the world around them (Mezirow, 1978a). It is the intersection of the women's move-ment and adult education—through re-entry programs—that gave rise to the development of Mezirow's theory of transformation (Baumgartner, 2012).

The heart of the theory "refers to the process by which we trans-form our taken for-granted frames of reference" (Mezirow, 2000, p. 7). Instead of acting under assumptions that have been uncritically assimi-lated (as ideas, beliefs, and norms) from others, adults need to learn how to negotiate and act on their own purposes, meanings, and values. The phenomenon of transformation central to this way of learning sets out the idea of a perspective transformation (Mezirow, 1991, p. 167),

> the process of becoming critically aware of how and why our assump-tions have come to constrain the way we perceive, understand, and feel about our world; changing these structures of habitual expectation to make possible a more inclusive, discriminating, and integrative perspective; and, finally, making choices or otherwise acting upon these new understandings.

The meaning perspective to be transformed is also described as a frame of reference which constitutes itself out of experiences (Mezirow, 2012, p. 82),

> the structure of assumptions and expectations through which we filter sense impressions. It involves cognitive, affective, and conative dimensions. It selectively shapes and delimits perception, cognition, feelings, and disposition by predisposing our intentions, expectations, and purposes. It provides the context for making meaning.

Transforming this perspective is an "epiphanic, or apocalyptic, cognitive event—a shift in the tectonic plates of one's assumptive clusters" (Brookfield, 2000, p. 139). The phenomenon of transformation is therefore very different from the idea of change. Mezirow (1991, pp. 168–169) differentiates 10 phases within the process of perspective transformation, starting with a (1) disorienting dilemma which sets the stage for (2) an exploration of feelings like guilt or shame that arise in the wake of the crisis or dilemma. In a third step (3) learners critically assess and reflect their guiding assumptions underlying their current meaning perspective. What follows is (4) the realization that one's personal problem is shared and (sometimes) a public issue: The public breaks into the private sphere and learners realize that others have negotiated and undergone similar changes and challenges. In the next phase (5) learners explore alternative ways of being and living in terms of relationships, roles, and actions. This phase is complemented by another phase, where (6) learners plan (new) courses of action and (7) acquire new knowledge in order to put these courses of action into practice. In the aftermath of (8) learners trying out these new roles (provisionally), they (9) build (self-) confidence and competence and (10) re-integrate into their lives, employing a new, transformed (meaning) perspective.

Mezirow's theory of transformative learning "is directed at the intersection of the individual and social" (Tennant, 1993, p. 36). This becomes apparent in Mezirow's description of the transformation leaner, who "comes to identify her personal problem as a common one and a public issue" (Mezirow, 1978a, p. 15), as described in phase four. This tension between individually experienced problems and structural, public issues calls for both, individual and collective action, whereas the choice of social action resides at the same time with the learner. Mezirow (1989) sees collective and social transformation as a separate entity from individual transformation. The phenomenon of perspective transformation is located within the individual, not within society (Tennant, 1993), "the site of change—as well as agency—is envisaged primarily in terms of the transformation of the inner mental landscape of an individual learner which may, or may not, have broader social consequences" (Finnegan, 2019, p. 48). Finnegan (2019) argues that even though Mezirow's theory of transformative learning is concerned with the individual, it is not an individualistic theory, as Mezirow puts an emphasis on intersubjective learning through discourse.

Habermas' Account of Transformation

Mezirow acknowledges Habermas as a major influence, and Habermas, like Mezirow, presents a theory of transformation.

Habermas developed as an intellectual in the Frankfurt School and led it after 1964. The first generation of the Frankfurt School was certainly committed to social transformation. Most founders of the School sought dramatic transformation through revolution rather than the gradual amelioration promised by social democrats (Benjamin, 1968, p. 260). Not only did these thinkers decry the social and economic system of their time, but they viewed human personalities as distorted and limited by capitalism. They combined Marxian analysis of large-scale social forces with a Freudian account of neurosis to paint a portrait of both people and societies in dire need of transformation.

In contrast to certain orthodox forms of Marxism, the founders of the Frankfurt School believed that culture was not merely a consequence of economic realities but could influence the course of history. For example, propagandistic mass culture and ideology could persuade the working class to support capitalism or even fascism. As Raymond Geuss (1981) writes,

> The very heart of the critical theory of society is the criticism of ideology. Their ideology is what prevents the agents in the society from correctly perceiving their true situation and real interests; if they are to free themselves from social repression, the agents must rid themselves of ideological illusion. (pp. 2–3)

Therefore, transformation must address culture, not just politics and economics.

The first generation of the Frankfurt School saw all mass communication in a capitalist society as ideology. Their main recommendation was to reveal this fact as a kind of "talking cure" that might free the working class of its neuroses. But their culture-critique proved ineffective and it missed, Habermas felt, the positive "potentials" of discourse and communication in capitalist democracies (Habermas, 1987, p. 381).

One of Habermas' core insights is that discourse can either be strategic (aiming to make another person believe and act as you want) or communicative (aiming to persuade another person on the basis of good arguments, and perhaps to change your own view if other arguments prove better). In small groups, people can act communicatively, exchanging arguments and reasons. In this way, they can challenge the assumptions of their respective lifeworlds. A *lifeworld* is a "reservoir of taken-for-granteds, of unshaken convictions that participants in communication draw upon in cooperative processes of interpretation" (Habermas, 1987, p. 124). We each need a lifeworld; it is the content or material that gives any life its significance and uniqueness. However, we can—and should—test our assumptions in discourse with other people, adjusting them or replacing them one by one whenever our fellow citizens offer valid criticisms.

In this way, ordinary discourse can be transformative. Some critics take Habermas to task for assuming that this kind of face-to-face deliberation is all we need to improve both society and our inner lives (e.g., Young, 2001 p. 690). Habermas does analyze discussions in ideal settings in order to yield insights about the logic of communication (e.g., Habermas, 1975, pp. 110, 108). But it is a mistake to think that his social prescription is to create many ideal settings for discussion. He offers a much more realistic and thorough social critique. Borrowing from Max Weber, Habermas argues that modernity is characterized by "systems" (particularly markets and states) that employ people in specialized social roles (Habermas, 1987, pp. 301–404). Systems use efficient means to pursue fixed aims: profit in the case of businesses, power and control for governments. They are therefore biased toward instrumental rather than communicative action. They threaten to swamp the spontaneous and free discussions of small groups with mass communications—commercial advertising, state propaganda, and popular culture—all aimed at manipulating people to do what the systems want from them.

One solution that Habermas proposes is a properly organized democratic constitution that protects freedom of speech and establishes an

50   S. ESCHENBACHER AND P. LEVINE

accountable legislature as a space for true deliberation (Habermas, 1985). Another (related) solution is a vibrant public sphere composed of publications, associations, and venues of discussion (Habermas, 1964, and many subsequent works). The public sphere is always at risk of being colonized by market and governmental systems, but it is not a myth. People genuinely improve what they believe and value by participating in the public spheres of modern societies, even if newspapers belong to businesses and libraries are bureaucracies.

Finally, Habermas endorses social movements that challenge the assumptions of their societies and compel discussion. He sees them as popular forces that arise in civil society to challenge institutional inertia and prevent the colonization of the lifeworld (Fleming, 2018). He ends his magisterial two-volume work, *Theory of Communicative Action*, with a positive account of the social movements of his day, including feminism and the anti-nuclear movement. In the Theory of Communicative Action, Habermas talks very little about civil discussions among peers but concludes with an invocation of squatters and protesters in the streets. The widespread interpretation of Habermas as a proponent of rational deliberation is therefore misleading (Levine, 2018).

WHAT MEZIROW LEARNED FROM HABERMAS

In order to further identify the overlooked resources of Habermas' works, we need to first take a look into the ideas and concepts that Mezirow incorporated into his theory of transformative learning (for an extended critical analysis, see Eschenbacher, 2018).

Mezirow adopts Habermas' idea to distinguish between instrumental, communicative, and emancipatory interest and interprets them as domains of learning: "A key proposition of transformative learning theory recognizes the validity of Habermas's fundamental distinction between instrumental and communicative learning" (Mezirow, 2003, p. 59). Following Habermas, the third interest, the emancipatory interest, has a derived status as distinguished from the other two domains (Habermas, 1971). It pertains to critical theory as a scientific field. Mezirow (1981) conceptualizes Habermas' third knowledge domain as the learning involved in perspective transformation. He later sets Habermas' distinction aside, which adds to the confusion: "Although Habermas suggests a third learning domain, emancipation, transformation theory redefines this as the transformation process that pertains in both instrumental and communicative learning domains" (Mezirow, 2012, p. 78). Apart from this confusion, Mezirow develops a theory of adult learning that opens up a new path for educators by differentiating different domains of learning. Whereas an instrumental view of learning was dominant in the field of adult learning (Dirkx, 1998), Mezirow's emphasis on transforming existing ways of knowing and learning, and generating more democratic practices, put adult education in a position to initiate and catalyze processes of transformation within the individual learner and society as a whole.

Habermas' adult learning crisis and the call for transformation are reflected in Mezirow's democratic vision of society and the necessity of developing a theory that enables adults to live in and co-create a society of which they are a part, and to deliberate decision-making processes that are deeply relevant for exploring alternatives on how to live life. It is not surprising that this process of deliberation and decision-making is at the core of transformation theory. As we have seen earlier, the theory is concerned with a learning process that enables adults to act on their own purposes and meanings instead of acting under the guiding assumptions acquired from others uncritically.

The theory aims on enabling adults to own their lives in the sense of being better able to take control in a (social) responsible way by making one's own decisions (Mezirow, 2000). Therefore, Mezirow (1991) incorporates Habermas' () idea of rational discourse to promote learning transformatively by exchanging arguments and puts it at the heart of the theory. Central to Habermas' notion of discourse is that all participating have equal access and an opportunity to debate. Transformative learning theory's grounding in Habermas' work is not surprising, although his reliance on Habermas' notion of discourse, ideal speech conditions, and domains of learning were not part of the initial study. Women were hindered to deliberate decisions or engage in the question what their lives should or could look like.

Discourse as the forum where one learns transformatively also needs enabling conditions, to assure the kind of perspective transformation Mezirow was looking for. This led him to ultimately implement Habermas' conception of an ideal speech situation, as a key element within transformative learning theory (e.g., Mezirow, 1991), although within the context of adult learning, the ideal speech situation is "theoretically based, with little support from empirical research" (Taylor, 1997, p. 54). This is unfortunate insofar as Mezirow ties fostering transformative learning up with promoting an ideal speech situation to ground his theory in a democratic vision but leaves the educator without further guidance in his writings.

The intertwined relationship between generating more democratic practices and learning transformatively becomes also apparent in the emphasis on critical (Brookfield, 2005), as Mezirow (2000) aims at expanding the learners' ability to reason and to engage in discourse. Furthermore, Finnegan (2019) points to Mezirow's interest in supporting a democratic learning culture: "Mezirow could not be clearer that he is interested in supporting democratic movements and progressive social change—but they are not foregrounded in a systematic way" (p. 47). This lack of a systematic framework opens up another opportunity to reflect on Habermas' work against transformative learning theory's background, as an yet overlooked resource.

Others have argued for a dual agenda that emerges from the theory's grounding in Habermas' work. We learn from Fleming (2002) that this agenda "involves the strengthening of the lifeworld against colonization by the system, and it involves taking into the system a commitment to fostering critical reflection, critical learning, and supporting discursive understanding" (p. 13). Transformative education, following Mezirow and his application of Habermas, has then "a clear mandate to work in the seams and at the boundaries of systems to humanize and transform them so that they operate in the interests of all" (Fleming, 2018, p. 9). The call for transformation in the public sphere is reflected in the commitment of adult educators to "encourage the opening of public spheres of discourse" as Mezirow (1990b, p. 375) puts it, and in Habermas' notion of discourse itself, which clearly belongs to the public sphere (Rorty, 1989, for an extended analysis, see Eschenbacher, 2019 and Eschenbacher & Fleming, 2020).

To return to transformation theory's agenda, the lifeworld should be strengthened against the system, but how can that be translated into learning transformatively? The proximity to Habermas' notion of lifeworld becomes clear in Mezirow's conceptualization as being "made up of a vast inventory of unquestioned assumptions and shared cultural convictions, including codes, norms, roles, social practices, psychological patterns of dealing with others, and individual skills" (Mezirow, 1991, p. 69). Consequently, the lifeworld can be strengthened by being transformed within transformative learning theory. Fleming (2002) suggests we think of a frame of reference or meaning perspective as a way to define the lifeworld, being constituted through personality, social, and cultural dimensions. The phenomenon of perspective transformation involves a process where we are "rethinking deeply held, and often distorted beliefs, about who we are and our lifeworld" (Finnegan, 2019, p. 46), when we defend our freedom and ultimately liberate our "colonized meaning perspective" (Hart, 1990b, p. 52).

This process of transformation is in need of the other, a community, providing a safe (enough) space for assessing the ground of one's guiding assumptions, and experiencing a tectonic shift in one's assumptive clusters (Brookfield, 2000). This kind of learning needs others, likeminded learners, serving as "critical mirrors who highlight our assumptions for us and reflect them back to us in unfamiliar, surprising, and disturbing ways" (Brookfield, 2000, p. 146). Following Mezirow, Brookfield (2012) argues that learning transformatively is about freeing oneself from reified forms of thought (ideology), which implies for him the necessity to change—or transform—the very structures that produce and maintain these reified forms of thought. The tension one encounters here is that the very process of transforming an individual's meaning perspective while it is simultaneously permeated by structural issues and society itself (Hart, 1990a). Vice versa, Heaney and Horton (1990) argue that transformative education—from a Freireian perspective—is only emancipatory when it becomes reflected in political institutions, such as when laws become institutionalized; which Mezirow would most probably agree with.

What Else Should Transformative Learning Take from Habermas?

Mezirow shares the "transformative, metamorphosing impulse" (Brookfield, 2012, p. 131) of critical theory. However, Mezirow has been criticized for a "selective interpretation and adaption of Habermas" (Collard & Law, 1989, p. 102) that ultimately led him to "neglect the radical impetus behind Habermas' writings" (Hart, 1990a, p. 125). Mezirow "never fully adopted the critical theory of Habermas and this may have given traction to some of the critiques of transformative learning theory" (Fleming, 2018, p. 1).

Mezirow chose some Habermasian ideas as core concepts within his theory (mainly the different cognitive interests as domains of learning and the idea of discourse and its enabling conditions) but he ignored the role of social movements and democratization.

We would recommend that the field of transformative learning give more attention to social movements. Here are some vital research questions that have interested Habermas and that are addressed in the literature on social movements but that could benefit from the perspective of transformative learning theory: Does social movement participation transform individuals (McAdam, 1990)? How do differences among social movements change their transformational effects on individuals? For example, does the organizational structure of a movement matter? Are highly decentralized movements more or less transformational than those that are led by charismatic figures? Have social movements changed in fundamental ways, or have their defining features persisted over time (Offe, 1985; Tilly & Wood 2020)? Can online movements transform people more or less well than face-to-face varieties? Can social movements change institutions to allow more transformational learning? Or do social movements tend to conclude by making modest changes in institutions, allowing Habermasian "systems" to reproduce themselves? How can social movements avoid the traps of bureaucratization and co-optation? Are social movements being routinized and losing their transformational potential (Crozat et al., 1997)?

Relatedly, we recommend that transformative learning theory pay more attention to large-scale sociology—to the systems that have always concerned Habermas (Fleming, 2002). How are opportunities for transformative learning affected by the overall structure of a given society, and especially by the roles and relationships among the state, the market, civil society, and lifeworlds? If these relationships are not satisfactory for transformational learning, how can we change them (Brookfield, 2012)? One approach to such change is social movement activism, but it is not the only option. Political parties, elections, and legal and constitutional reform efforts are also relevant.

Transformational Learning and Civic Studies

Both of us have been involved in the development of a new field—or at least a new intellectual network—called Civic Studies (Forstenzer, 2019; Levine, & Sołtan, 2014; Schröder, 2018). Its goal is to reorient the study of society and social change from questions like, "What is justice?" "What should the government do?" and "How does the society work?" to a question that puts group agency at its core: "What should we do?" That question combines values (normative judgments and arguments)

3 RECONSIDERING THE ROOTS OF TRANSFORMATIVE EDUCATION ... 55

with empirical analysis of the situation and strategic choices. It generates additional questions, such as: "How should we organize ourselves into effective and durable groups?" "How should we address disagreement about values?" and "How should we detect and resolve unjust exclusions from the group that forms a 'we'?" These questions have pragmatic significance for people who want to improve or even transform the world; they also pose theoretically complex challenges that require research and inquiry.

The focus on group agency is essential to Civic Studies, which posits that individuals are too weak and too cognitively and ethically limited to transform the world. Civic Studies intends to expand scholars' attention from individual ethics, on one hand, and the analysis of impersonal social forces, on the other, to encompass groups of people who think and work together intentionally.

If transformational learning theory pays more attention to social movements and to large-scale sociological issues, it will move closer to Civic Studies. For its part, Civic Studies should learn from and absorb Mezirow's insights about personal transformation. Transformative learning has not yet been a strong enough theme in Civic Studies, which has been mostly about how to organize groups and discuss values. We see much potential in the combination of these two fields.

REFERENCES

Baumgartner, L. M. (2012). Mezirow's theory of transformative learning from 1975 to present. In E. W. Taylor & P. Cranton (Eds.), *The handbook of transformative learning: Theory, research, and practice* (pp. 99–115). Jossey-Bass.

Benjamin, W. (1968). Theses on the philosophy of history. In W. Benjamin, Illuminations (Ed.), *Hannan Arendt* (H. Zohn, Trans.). Schocken.

Brookfield, S. D. (2000). Transformative learning as ideology critique. In J. Mezirow (Ed.), *Learning as transformation: Critical perspectives on a theory in progress* (pp. 125–148). Jossey-Bass.

Brookfield, S. D. (2005). Learning democratic reason: The adult education project of Jürgen Habermas. *Teachers College Record, 107*(6), 1127–1168.

Brookfield, S. D. (2012). Critical theory and transformative learning. In E. W. Taylor & P. Cranton (Eds.), *The handbook of transformative learning: Theory, research, and practice* (pp. 131–146). Jossey-Bass.

Collard, S., & Law, M. (1989). The limits of perspective transformation: A critique of Mezirow's theory. *Adult Education Quarterly, 39*(2), 99–107.

56 S. ESCHENBACHER AND P. LEVINE

Crozat, M., Hipsher, P. L., Katzenstein, M. F., Keck, M. E., Klandermans, B., Kubik, J., & Reiter, H. (1997). *The social movement society: Contentious politics for a new century*. Rowman & Littlefield Publishers.

Dirkx, J. M. (1998). Transformative learning theory in the practice of adult education: An overview. *PAAACE Journal of Lifelong Learning, 7*, 1–14.

Eschenbacher, S. (2018). *Transformatives Lernen im Erwachsenenalter: Kritische Überlegungen zur Theorie Jack Mezirows*. Peter Lang.

Eschenbacher, S. (2019). Drawing lines and crossing borders: Transformation theory and Richard Rorty's philosophy. *Journal of Transformative Education, 17*(3), 251–268.

Eschenbacher, S., & Fleming, T. (2020). Transformative dimensions of lifelong learning: Mezirow, Rorty and COVID-19. *International Review of Education, 66*(5–6), 1–16.

Finnegan, F. (2019). Freedom is a very fine thing: Individual and collective forms of emancipation in transformative learning. In T. Fleming, A. Kokkos, & F. Finnegan (Eds.), *European perspectives on transformation theory* (pp. 43–57). Palgrave Macmillan.

Fleming, T. (2002). Habermas on civil society, lifeworld and system: Unearthing the social in transformation theory. *Teachers College Record*, 1–15.

Fleming, T. (2018). Critical theory and transformative learning: Rethinking the radical intent of Mezirow's theory. *International Journal of Adult Vocational Education and Technology, 9*(3), 1–13.

Forstenzer, J. (2019). *Deweyan experimentalism and the problem of method in political philosophy*. Routledge.

Geuss, R. (1981). *The idea of a critical theory: Habermas and the Frankfurt School* (Modern European Philosophy). Cambridge University Press.

Habermas, J. (1964). Öffentlichkeit (Ein Lexikonartikel) in Fischer Lexikon, Frankfurt/Main, 220–26. Reprinted in English: The public sphere: an encyclopaedia article, in New German Critique, 3 (1974).

Habermas, J. (1974). The public sphere: An encyclopedia article (1964). *New German Critique, 3*, 49–55.

Habermas, J. (1971). *Knowledge and human interest*. Beacon Press.

Habermas, J. (1975), *Legitimation crisis* (T. McCarthy Trans.), Beacon Press.

Habermas, J. (1984). *The theory of communicative action* (vol. 1). Beacon Press.

Habermas, J. (1985). Civil disobedience: Litmus test for the democratic constitutional state. *Berkeley Journal of Sociology, 30*(1985), 95–116.

Habermas, J. (1987). *The theory of communicative action* (vol. 2). Beacon Press.

Hart, M. U. (1990). Critical theory and beyond: Further perspectives on emancipatory education. *Adult Education Quarterly, 40*(3), 125–138.

Hart, M. U. (1990). Liberation through consciousness raising. In J. Mezirow (Ed.), *Fostering critical reflection in adulthood: A guide to transformative and emancipatory learning* (pp. 47–73). Jossey-Bass.

3 RECONSIDERING THE ROOTS OF TRANSFORMATIVE EDUCATION ... 57

Heaney, T. W., & Horton, A. I. (1990). Reflective engagement for social change. In J. Mezirow (Ed.), *Fostering critical reflection in adulthood: A guide to transformative and emancipatory learning* (pp. 74–98). Jossey-Bass.

Levine, P., & Sołtan, K. S. (2014). Civic studies: approaches to the emerging field. In P. Levine, & K. S. Soltan (Eds.), *Civic Studies: Bringing Theory to Practice*. Bringing Theory to Practice.

Levine, P. (2018). Habermas with a whiff of tear gas: Nonviolent campaigns and deliberation in an era of authoritarianism. *Journal of Public Deliberation, 14*(2). https://doi.org/10.16997/jdd.306

McAdam, D. (1990). *Freedom summer*. Oxford University Press.

Mezirow, J. (1978). *Education for perspective transformation: Women's re-entry programs in community colleges*. Columbia University Press.

Mezirow, J. (1978). Perspective transformation. *Adult Education, 28*(2), 100–110.

Mezirow, J. (1981). A critical theory of adult learning and education. *Adult Education, 32*(1), 3–24.

Mezirow, J. (1989). Transformation theory and social action: A response to Collard and Law. *Adult Education Quarterly, 39*(3), 169–175.

Mezirow, J. (1990). How critical reflection triggers transformative learning. In J. Mezirow (Ed.), *Fostering critical reflection in adulthood: A guide to transformative and emancipatory learning* (pp. 1–20). Jossey-Bass.

Mezirow, J. (1990). Conclusion: Toward transformative learning and emancipatory education. In J. Mezirow (Ed.), *Fostering critical reflection in adulthood: A guide to transformative and emancipatory learning* (pp. 334–376). Jossey-Bass.

Mezirow, J. (1991). *Transformative dimensions of adult learning*. Jossey-Bass.

Mezirow, J. (2000). Learning to think like an adult: Core concepts of transformation theory. In J. Mezirow (Ed.), *Learning as transformation: Critical perspectives on a theory in progress* (pp. 3–33). Jossey-Bass.

Mezirow, J. (2003). Transformative learning as discourse. *Journal of Transformative Education, 1*(1), 58–63.

Mezirow, J. (2012). Learning to think like an adult: Core concepts of transformation theory. In E. W. Taylor & P. Cranton (Eds.), *The handbook of transformative learning: Theory, research, and practice* (pp. 73–95). Jossey-Bass.

Mezirow, J., & Taylor, E. W. (2009). Preface. In J. Mezirow & E. W. Taylor (Eds.), *Transformative learning in practice: Insights from community, workplace, and higher education* (pp. xi–xiv). Jossey-Bass.

Offe, C. (1985). New social movements: Challenging the boundaries of institutional politics. *Social Research, 52*(4), 817–868.

Rorty, R. (1989). *Contingency, irony, and solidarity*. Cambridge University.

Schröder, N. (2018). A civic studies perspective on European citizens: In search for potential in the conflict surrounding TTIP. *European Politics and Society, 19*(1), 120–145.

Taylor, E. W. (1997). Building upon the theoretical debate: A critical review of the empirical studies of Mezirow's transformative learning theory. *Adult Education Quarterly, 48*(1), 34–59.

Tennant, M. C. (1993). Perspective transformation and adult development. *Adult Education Quarterly, 44*(1), 34–42.

Tilly, C., & Wood, L. J. (2020). *Social movements, 1768–2008.* Routledge.

Young, I. M. (2001). Activist challenges to deliberative democracy. *Political Theory, 29*(5), 670–690.

CHAPTER 4

The Pulse of Freedom and Transformative Learning: Winding Paths, Blind Alleys, and New Horizons

Fergal Finnegan

INTRODUCTION

One of the most significant lines of division in the field of transformative education research relates to what should be used as the primary unit of analysis for thinking about and fostering emancipatory learning processes. The decision, explicit or implicit, to concern oneself mainly with individuals or primarily society in analysis is highly consequential and remains an enduring line of division among scholars of transformative education and learning. I want in this chapter to argue that this line of division is based on a false dichotomy which frequently leads to unproductive debate and unnecessary confusion. To paraphrase the US novelist Thomas Pynchon (1973/2000) if we begin by asking the wrong questions, then

F. Finnegan (✉)
Department of Adult and Community Education, Maynooth University, National University of Ireland, Maynooth, Ireland
e-mail: fergal.finnegan@mu.ie

© The Author(s), under exclusive license to Springer Nature Switzerland AG 2022
A. Nicolaides et al. (eds.), *The Palgrave Handbook of Learning for Transformation*, https://doi.org/10.1007/978-3-030-84694-7_4

60   F. FINNEGAN

the answers do not matter. The key contention of the chapter is that to advance this debate we need to be able to conceptualize learning and transformation in relation to emancipatory desires, interests, and experiences in a dialectical and nuanced manner (Eschenbacher, 2019; Hoggan et al., 2017; Fleming et al., 2019). This chapter will outline one way of thinking relationally about persons in society through a reconstructive critique of the work of Jack Mezirow. In the first part, I will offer a novel way of framing and contextualizing Mezirow and transformative adult education through a critical realist understanding of emancipation and reflexive agency. This will be followed by a summary of the most common criticisms of Mezirow's work as a social and emancipatory theory of learning. In the next and most detailed part of the chapter, I examine how Mezirow approaches reflexive agency, freedom, and emancipation.

All of these strands: the critical realist conceptualization of freedom and agency; the discussion of Mezirow's contribution to adult learning theory; the summary of critiques of his work; the detailed exploration of Mezirow's approach to emancipation and reflexivity are woven together at the end of the chapter. The purpose of the piece is to present an explicitly differentiated conception of transformative learning which can account for, and help foster, individual and collective forms of emancipatory agency.

Reflexive Agency, Freedom, and Transformative Learning

This chapter is an essay which has the aim of clearing some conceptual ground in relation to the way freedom and emancipation are understood in transformative learning and education. While I will not link this directly to case studies or life stories, it is important to note that the arguments are based on extensive empirical research with non-traditional students[1] and graduates in universities in Ireland and across Europe (Finnegan et al., 2014, 2019). This research employed a range of methods but

---

[1] Non-traditional students is a rather open and somewhat flawed term to denote student groups who come from groups that have been, and often continue to be, underrepresented in third-level education, such as mature students, working-class students, and students from ethnic minorities. The term is used in European higher education research to explore the extent to which traditional institutions are adapting and facilitating access for these student groups.

4 THE PULSE OF FREEDOM AND TRANSFORMATIVE LEARNING ...   61

biographical[2] interviews were the most important element of this work. Participants gave open, in-depth accounts of their educational experiences and how this fitted, or did not fit, with the rest of their life.[3] A significant portion of the fieldwork comprised of longitudinal interviews with students as they entered into, went through, and came out of university into the labor market. To a very striking degree, when people spoke of important transitions, shifts, and transformations in their lives, it was linked to the desire for greater reflexive agency and freedom. Participants in this research reported very significant, deep, and transformative learning experiences, but the structural limits and institutional blocks to such learning were equally apparent in these accounts. Making sense of this, and the way this was achieved or hampered, has led me to reflect on emancipation and education (Finnegan, 2019). This, combined with my engagement with adult education literature, relational sociology, social movement research, and critical theory, has led me to develop a differentiated theory of transformative learning which explores the pulse of freedom on different scales. This research underpins the reading of Mezirow offered in this chapter.

Let me then say a little more about how learning, reflexive agency, and freedom are understood in general terms. Reflexivity is seen as the exercise of the ordinary ability to reflect on ourselves "in relation to our contexts and vice versa" (Archer, 2007, p. 4). But as Mezirow (1991) notes, critical reflection has varying levels of depth, and it is the capacity to reflect on our assumptions that is most transformative (I will say more about this below). This insight can be usefully supplemented by Gregory Bateson's (2000) account of the five levels of learning (0, I, II, III, IV) each of which is defined by an increasing of level of complexity, depth of reflexivity, and crucially for the discussion here scope. The simplest form (0) involves a response to stimulus but with no real learning, and the highest (IV) is a perhaps wholly ideal type of learning, which completely transcends the paradigms within which learning happens. The intermediate levels of II and III are the ones which are most pertinent to thinking about scope: II relates to changes in the process of learning and III to changes in the system of sets of alternatives from which we chose.

[2] See Merrill and West (2009) for useful methodological overview of the biographical approach.

[3] Approximately 200 interviews in Ireland and 1300 interviews across Europe were collected across one national and three transnational projects see (Finnegan et al., 2014).

How might the depth and scope of critically reflective learning be connected to emancipation? As the British philosopher Roy Bhaskar (1994, 2011, 1979) notes, we pursue freedom based on knowledge of our interests, the cultivation of the disposition to act for freedom, and the (re)discovery of sources of agency (Bhaskar, 1994, 2011). In other words, we move toward and into freedom through reflexive action. Emancipation here is viewed as a social process, a type of movement, which always involves learning and the development of reflexive agency of varying sorts. Reflexive agency lays the basis for various forms of emancipation which "is defined as the transformation from unwanted, unneeded and/or oppressive structures or states or affairs to wanted, needed and/or liberating ones" (Bhaskar, 1994, p. 145). This definition will be important for the discussion later in this chapter for two reasons. It can be used to envisage emancipatory processes on different scales enacted by individuals and by diverse collective bodies. Also, the description of *freedom* as the movement from unwanted to wanted determinations alerts us to the fact that the exercise freedom is always structured and context bound. This is a simple but important proposition which is at odds with the widely diffused, highly ideological, and ultimately impossible notion that freedom means unconstrained individual choice.

From this perspective, the basic desire for freedom and the complex development of powers of self-determination are rooted in the search for human flourishing (Bhaskar, 1994). Human flourishing depends on the exercise and enhancement of individual and collective powers of various sorts. Flourishing is necessarily a social and relational matter as well. This means any discussion of freedom and reflexive agency also brings us to consider questions about the just distribution and proper use of resources (Sen, 1999), and to consider how institutions and practices can be altered or developed to minimize harm and avoid unnecessary suffering (Wright, 2010). From this perspective, freedom cannot be deepened without achieving greater equality in the distribution of goods, patterns of social recognition, and modes of political participation (Fraser, 2013).

This latter point about participation is crucial—this is something that requires a type of learning for democracy. Emancipation in support of human flourishing depends on enlarging our powers of rational thought and increased lucidity about what structures society and shapes our life choices (Freire, 1972; Mezirow, 1991). As individuals, as members of organizations and institutions, as participants in social movements, reflexive agency depends on developing shared rational and accurate interpretations of structures, states, and affairs which are corrigible, exploratory, and open (Bhaskar, 1994; Castoriadis, 1987; Freire, 1972; see also Mezirow, 1991). It also requires reform and experiment in how reflexive agency is institutionalized in decision-making processes in education, communities, workplaces, regions, and larger polities (Castoriadis, 1987). The scope of transformative learning is therefore linked to the capacity to embed reflexive participatory processes in social life.

The Paths to Freedom: False Dichotomies and Premature Resolutions in Transformative Learning Theory Research

From this critical realist and egalitarian perspective, the field of transformative education and a great deal of adult education can be described as a collective effort to elaborate an approach to education and learning in which reflexive agency for freedom is viewed as a central concern, goal, and problematic. The challenge then is to puzzle out how we elaborate institutions, cultures, and practices which allow people to take full ownership over learning and the production of knowledge so they can become more reflexively agentic in their lives and can participate in a living democracy (Rubenson, 2011; see also Finnegan, 2016; Finnegan & Grummell, 2019).

As we know, within adult education and transformative education, there are multiple, overlapping but also somewhat conflicting accounts of how to foster reflexive agency and how we might describe emancipatory interests and desires (e.g., critical pedagogy, andragogy, cultural historical activity theory, progressivism, and so forth). Mezirow's work is a major intervention and contribution to this scholarship, and remains one of the most elaborated, ambitious, and influential attempts to theorize reflexive agency in relation to adult learning.

The basic premises of Mezirow's work have already been outlined in Chapters 2 and 3. As I mentioned briefly in the previous section, I am especially interested in Mezirow's description of the varying depths at which critical reflection operates. Furthermore, one of Mezirow's fundamental concerns is how such critical reflection can support greater agency and this runs as a golden thread through the various iterations of his theory of transformative learning (Mezirow, 1978, 1981, 1990, 1991,

64   F. FINNEGAN

1998, 2000, 2003, 2007; Mezirow, et al., 1990). Of particular importance, he argues, is the developing of the capacity to reflect on our taken-for-granted assumptions in order to act in more insightful, discriminating, and rational ways. Mezirow's work is of exceptional importance in conceptualizing critical reflection and explaining why deep forms of critical reflection on assumptions (1998) are so vital in the present era.

I will explore some of these ideas in further detail below. Before I do so it should be said that the adequacy of Mezirow's work as a social and emancipatory theory of learning has repeatedly been called into question (Collard & Law, 1989; Hart, 1990; Inglis, 1997; Newman, 2012; Tennant, 1993; less directly Cunningham, 1998). Within this body, there are three substantive claims. They are: (1) Mezirow "lacks a coherent and comprehensive theory of social change" (Collard & Law, 1989, p. 102) and does not give sufficient attention to social movements, (2) that Mezirow is too strongly focussed on individual agency (Inglis, 1997), and (3) that his work is sociologically "thin" and lacks clarity in terms of political vision and analysis (Inglis, 1997; Newman, 2012).

To my mind, these arguments are well-founded and convincing. However, when we review these debates retrospectively, we encounter an interesting paradox; despite three decades of thoughtful and able critique accompanied by a good deal of heated exchange and promising dialogue (Mezirow, 1989, 1997, *inter alia*), the results have been somewhat disappointing. While there have been noteworthy efforts to unearth the social and emancipatory dimensions of transformative learning by scholars such as my colleague Ted Fleming (e.g., 2002) and Stephen Brookfield (e.g., 2000), we have seen relatively little development of these ideas within transformative learning research generally, and there is little evidence of shared research agenda on these matters (Cranton & Taylor, 2012; Hoggan et al., 2017).[4] Certainly, if one reviews the proceedings of the *International Lifelong Learning Conference* and the journals which are central to the field such *as Adult Education Quarterly* and the *Journal of Transformative Education*, it is striking how little work there has been which seeks to explicitly move beyond these early debates. There is a clear tendency of researchers to use either/or ways of thinking (Freire versus

---

[4] This is especially striking when we compare it with the critiques and debates which argued for a holistic and less rationalistic approach to transformative learning (Dirkx, 2008; Yorks & Kasl, 2002; etc.) and have largely succeeded in going beyond critique toward a modified and elaborated version of transformative learning.

Mezirow, modernism versus postmodernism, individual versus collective transformative processes, etc.) or more typically to disregard what critics of Mezirow have said and assume the theory is already sufficient as a social and emancipatory theory of learning.

BLIND ALLEYS AND HIDDEN PASSAGEWAYS: THINKING WITH AND AGAINST MEZIROW

The Social and Political Dimensions of Transformative Learning

One might offer a variety of explanations for why these critiques of the social and political dimensions of Mezirow's ideas in the 1990s have had so little effect on the field as a whole. I think it can in part be ascribed to a certain amount of polemical excess about the supposed deficiency of these ideas. While the social, political, and emancipatory dimensions of the theory are uneven and undeveloped, they are certainly not absent. Mezirow's understanding of learning and reflexive agency is not asocial and is based on a creative theoretical synthesis which seeks to link theories of personal and social freedom. In fact, as Mark Tennant (1993, p. 36) has observed, the theory is explicitly "directed at the intersection of the individual and social." This orientation is evident from very early on in the development of transformative learning theory where Mezirow (1978) draws liberally on the insights of humanism and andragogy alongside psychological and psychoanalytical theories of human development, and combines them with Freirean critical pedagogy and an interest in the learning taking place in and through feminist movements. In fact, Mezirow self-consciously shuttled between social and individual points of reference throughout his career (Mezirow, 1978, 1981, 1990, 1991, 1998, 2000, 2003, 2007). For Mezirow (2007), personal and social freedom and human and community development are intricately bound up with each other. This "persons in society" framework underpins what he says about socialization and the formation of meaning perspectives (Mezirow, 1991).

Reflexive Agency and Freedom in Mezirow

In order to suggest how we might advance this critique in a new direction let us first look at how Mezirow understands reflexive agency and freedom in more detail. According to Mezirow, critical reflection requires a type of

66 F. FINNEGAN

epistemic break from the givenness of the world and requires us to take some distance from our routinized understanding of ourselves and the events and processes which shape us. In this way, we can begin to grasp:

> how we are caught in our own history and are reliving it. We learn to become critically aware of the cultural and psychological assumptions that have influenced the way we see ourselves and our relationship and the way we pattern our lives. (1978, p. 101)

Following further engagement with critical theory, three years later Mezirow chose to describe this movement toward freedom through critical reflection in the following terms:

> Emancipation is from libidinal, institutional or environmental forces which limit our options and rational control over our lives but have been taken for granted as beyond human control. Insights gained through critical self-awareness are emancipatory in the sense that at least one can recognize the correct reasons for his or her problem. (1981, p. 5)

This conception of the process and aims of deep critical reflection was developed further through the 1980s, through further engagement with the work of Habermas, and was given a full systematic expression in Mezirow's (1991) in *Transformative Dimensions of Adult Learning* which engaging in egalitarian and democratic discourse with other people is described as a vital aspect of stepping back from our assumptions.

According to Mezirow, deep reflection on assumptions always results in some type of action, however small (Bloom et al., 2015). Deep reflexivity is inextricably bound to an enhanced capacity for agency. Action is described by Mezirow in a range of registers drawing on diverse sets of theories from the existentialist inflected proposition that it is the "choosing, the deciding, that is crucial for personal development" (1978, p. 105) to discussions of the importance of taking action in pursuit of social justice (1991, 2000).

Freedom is not discussed in a systematic fashion by Mezirow[5] but the movement away from constraint and a discovery of powers of autonomy—what I called reflexive agency for freedom and flourishing in the first part

---

[5] It is a type of synthetic notion combines notion of freedom from classic liberalism (J.S. Mill), Kantian notions of autonomy, and more radical notions of social freedom linked to civil rights, popular education, and community development.

of this chapter—is undoubtedly central in transformative learning theory. Mezirow (1991, 2007) discusses freedom in personal terms, the breaking of what William Blake (1977, p. 143) memorably called "mind forg'd manacles" but also as the shaking off of unaccountable authority and the weight of dead traditions.

Against the claims of some of his critics, we can say that Mezirow does offer a socially situated and intersubjective theory of reflexive agency in which empowerment and emancipation are foregrounded. Crucially, Mezirow's theory is sensitized to small and large acts of freedom. However, his critics are right to point to the limits of his work: Mezirow pays scant attention to the necessity of constraint or to the social forces and structures that actively hinder or block agentic reflexivity. In these respects, the gaps in Mezirow's work are very significant and I think they can only be overcome by transformative learning researchers actively seeking to foster a much more developed sociological imagination by looking toward other disciplines and research traditions (Mills, 1959; see Finnegan, 2011, 2014).

Bracketing the Social, Foregrounding the Individual

Looking beyond transformative learning to re-evaluate and develop it in a new direction is especially necessary because of two other recurrent features of Mezirow's theory. First, while the fundamental building blocks of the theory are rooted in persons in society perspective, there is nevertheless a tendency to foreground the individual in transformative processes in the presentation of his ideas. As I have noted elsewhere (Finnegan, 2019), Mezirow's theory is especially dense and elaborated in the examining critical reflection in the remaking of an individual's assumptive world. To explicate this clearly, Mezirow largely brackets off social processes. The dynamic, layered, and conflictual nature of transformative learning within social processes is underplayed in order to offer a tidy and clear conceptualization. Diagrams in *Transformative Dimensions of Adult Learning* reinforce this as they invite the reader to treat the social context as background to the foregrounded individual's reconstruction of assumptions (see, for example, 1991, p. 67 versions of which were used by Mezirow from the 1970s onward).

I am convinced this bracketing is linked to the avowed purpose of Mezirow (1978, 1991, 1997, 1998) to develop a comprehensive theory

68   F. FINNEGAN

of adult learning which is relevant to, and resonates with adult education, researchers and practitioners from diverse settings and backgrounds. Mezirow repeatedly notes the importance of the principles of democracy, freedom, and equality as well as the need for critical social analysis in transformative learning but these matters are then left aside to provide an ideal-type description of a transformative learning process which can be readily linked to practices embedded in varying political and institutional contexts.

As with a great deal of adult education theory, there is a strong humanist and phenomenological orientation in Mezirow's work which celebrates agency. This orientation along with the mode of explication discussed above means the theory cannot fully trace the interplay of structure and agency and fails to account for the depth and power of certain social structures (e.g., the gendered division of labor, classed patterns of ownership, institutional racism, etc.).

Social Action, Personal Transformation, and Freedom in Mezirow

This ambition to develop a comprehensive theory of learning of, and for, adult education is also linked to the second issue I want to highlight in this part of the essay—the way collective agency and individual agency are viewed in relation to each to other. Mezirow (1991, 1997, 2000) consistently argues that reflexive agency takes many forms, and while he believes the capacity of an individual to reflect on their own assumptions is supportive of participatory democracy and emancipatory social action, these things cannot be treated as the sole focus or privileged end goal adult education.[6] Thus, critical pedagogy and popular education which foreground social transformation are for Mezirow only one particular form of transformative learning—a subset of transformative learning in fact—which is given no more or less value than other forms (1998).

Mezirow (1997) explains this position in some detail in his response to Tom Inglis' (1997) critique of his work and it is worth quoting at some length:

---

[6] Mezirow is also at pains to stress (1990) his opposition to any form of indoctrination in adult education but I think his concern with indoctrination is a straw man argument. An opposition to indoctrination was shared by key radical adult educators (Freire, 1972; Horton et al., 1990). The key fault line here is I think the emancipatory value of certain forms of political knowledge (see Hart, 1990).

4 THE PULSE OF FREEDOM AND TRANSFORMATIVE LEARNING ...   69

social movements come and go. What makes them possible is cultural change, meaning transforming prevailing cultural paradigms or collective frames of reference. This involves *cultural action* to build ways of thinking that make social movements and other forms of social action possible. This process is one of critical reflection on assumptions upon which conventional understanding and action are based, validating reflective understandings through discursive inquiry, and taking reflective action. In the case of changing social frames of reference, this means finding others who share your reflective insights with whom to act to effect cultural changes—in families, communities, workplaces, and on a national or global scale. Every adult educator engaged in fostering transformative learning is engaged in the process of cultural action. So is every learner who acts upon his or her transformative insights with others to effect changes in previously taken-for-granted frames of reference. Some adult educators, in some situations, will also be able to help learners learn how to take direct social or political action.

I think this set of propositions has not been responded to properly by radical critics of Mezirow. Many advocates of critical pedagogy and post-structuralist theorists of power treat politics in an almost metaphysical way. Power permeates every aspect of being; it is everywhere and nowhere. While I think Mezirow's account is flawed, for reasons I will elaborate upon forthwith, I think he is quite right to highlight the multiplicity of forms of learning in everyday life and the wide variety of life projects that call for reflexive agency. A keen alertness to the subtleties of power and a theory of social reproduction and social change is, I think, absolutely necessary for transformative education, but nonetheless many, many aspects of life (adapting to chronic illness, dealing with aging, learning about and from child rearing, etc.) are poorly described in the first instance by theories of oppression, let alone notions of will to power. A sensitivity to such needs in educational research and pedagogy is especially important in a period in which many researchers have discerned a new "reflexive imperative" in modern life (e.g., Archer, 2007) where on a day-to-day basis we need to be reflexive in order to make our way in the world. I am convinced Mezirow's realistic appraisal of the variety of learning projects and the era in which we live is part of the reason Mezirow's work continues to have explanatory value in several important respects.

My contention then is that we need a theory of transformative learning that pays attention to the power of reflexive agency on an individual level.

70   F. FINNEGAN

However, and this is linked to arguments made above already, Mezirow account is too one-sided. It is a mistake to treat collective agency as a simple scaled-up aggregate version of what happens at an individual level. Research on social movements and emancipatory social change (e.g., Cox & Mullan, 2001; Eley, 2002; Tilly, 2004; Zibechi, 2012) points to the complexities and specific characteristics and modalities of these emancipatory processes, including as learning spaces (Choudry, 2015; Freire, 1972). Mezirow's analysis of this is very undeveloped indeed and at times even simplistic.

New Horizons?

We are now in the position to bring the various parts of the arguments made across the chapter together. At the start of this piece, I made the case that emancipation is best understood as the replacement of unwanted determinations with wanted determinations through the exercise of reflexive agency in support of human flourishing. I also argued that from this perspective Mezirow's work is of enormous importance because of the contribution he makes to thinking about the varying depths of critical reflection and the importance of deep reflection on assumptions in projects of autonomy and freedom. His theory also speaks directly to the tasks and needs of a reflexive era. However, the social and political dimensions of Mezirow's theory of transformative learning are unevenly worked through and in many respects theoretically undeveloped. As a result, the theory does not offer a realistic and sufficiently nuanced framework for analyzing the scope or social impact of various transformative learning processes. These are long-standing criticisms of Mezirow's work. However, the tendency in the research field to either dichotomize between social and individual transformation or, on the other hand, view them as identical phenomena has meant these weaknesses are overlooked by many and exaggerated by others.

Moving beyond this situation requires a sustained and systematic rethinking of emancipatory transformative learning theory in at least two respects. These are: (1) developing a more tightly conceptualized notion of freedom within transformative learning and (2) working toward an explicitly differentiated and multidimensional theory of transformative learning processes. As transformative researchers and educators, I believe we need a theory which is alert to the scope and depth of various forms of critical reflection and which can differentiate between various modes

4 THE PULSE OF FREEDOM AND TRANSFORMATIVE LEARNING ...   71

of agency and their impact on self and context. To this end has outlined a conceptual framework which integrates the insights of Mezirow (1991) within a critical realist account of emancipatory education (Bhaskar, 1994; Bateson, 2000; Castoriadis, 1987; Fraser, 2013; Freire, 1972; see also Engeström, 1987).

How might such a conceptualization be applied concretely? To offer a topical example let me turn to the COVID-19 pandemic. We can readily identify how this has sparked critical reflection at varying depths and how such reflections are intimately connected to questions of reflexive agency, freedom, and human flourishing. It has prompted a great number of us to reflect on media reports and the veracity and value of the information we receive from others; it has also led to widespread reflection on the soundness of particular public health measures and strategies. At a deeper level, the gravity of the situation has undoubtedly led innumerable people to reflect deeply on their assumptions about health, well-being, the organization of society, and humans' relationship with the environment. Some of these transformative, and potentially transformative, processes are by their nature highly individual responses to social events (thinking about experiences of grief and care in a pandemic), albeit with important social dimensions. Others (e.g., getting to grips with the assumptions that have led to the increasing incidence of zoonoses in contemporary capitalism, or tackling the assumptions that underpin vaccine "nationalism") are mainly social and political concerns. Crucially, in the latter examples reflexive agency on an individual level is important, but to lead to genuinely transformative emancipatory outcomes this will require collective forms of reflexive agency capable of reforming institutions. For social, political, and intellectual reasons, we need to be able to think across such reflective processes and to make links between them, but also to distinguish between levels of scope and impact as they pertain to emancipation.

This way of thinking about emancipation and transformative learning is a departure point rather than a destination. What I hope is that a number of transformative learning researchers can come together to approach these questions and themes in a corrigible, open, and collective way. Developing this further would entail empirically investigating the complex ways biographical change and shifts in self-understanding, significant group experiences, institutional experiments, social movement activity, and large-scale social change are linked or distinct and how these modes of reflexive agency interfere and collide with each other in the struggle for freedom.

REFERENCES

Archer, M. S. (2007). *Making our way in the world: Human reflexivity and social mobility.* Cambridge University Press.

Bateson, G. (2000). *Steps to an ecology of mind.* University of Chicago Press.

Bhaskar, R. (1979). *The possibility of naturalism: A philosophical critique of the contemporary human sciences.* Humanities Press.

Bhaskar, R. (2011). *Reclaiming reality: A critical introduction to contemporary philosophy.* Routledge.

Bhaskar, R. (1994). *Plato etc: The problems of philosophy and their resolution.* Verso.

Blake, W. (1977). *The complete poems.* Penguin.

Bloom, N., Gordon, J., & Mezirow, J. (2015). *Jack Mezirow on transformative learning: Conversations at home with Jack Mezirow* [Video]. Timeframe Digital Communications. https://www.youtube.com/watch?v=iEuctPHsre4

Brookfield, S. D. (2000). Transformative learning as ideology critique. In J. Mezirow & Associates (Eds.), *Learning as transformation: Critical perspectives on a theory in progress* (pp. 125–148). Jossey-Bass.

Castoriadis, C. (1987). *The imaginary institution of society.* MIT Press.

Choudry, A. (2015). *Learning activism: The intellectual life of contemporary social movements.* Toronto University Press.

Collard, S., & Law, M. (1989). The limits of perspective transformation: A critique of Mezirow's theory. *Adult Education Quarterly, 392,* 99–107.

Cox, L., & Mullan, C. (2001). *Social movements never died: Community politics and the social economy in the Irish Republic* [Paper presentation]. International Sociological Association/British Sociological Association Social Movements Conference, Manchester.

Cranton, P., & Taylor, E. W. (2012). Transformative learning theory: Seeking a more unified theory. In E. W. Taylor, P. Cranton & Associates (Eds.), *The handbook of transformative learning: Theory, research and practice* (pp. 3–20). Jossey-Bass.

Cunningham, P. M. (1998). The social dimension of transformative learning. *PAACE Journal of Lifelong Learning, 7,* 15–28.

Dirkx, J. (2008). The meaning and role of emotions in adult learning. *New Directions for Adult and Continuing Education, 120,* 7–18.

Eley, G. (2002). *Forging democracy: The history of the left in Europe, 1850–2000.* Oxford University Press.

Engeström, Y. (1987). *Learning by expanding: An activity-theoretical approach to developmental research.* Helsinki Orienta-Konsultit.

Eschenbacher, S. (2019). *Regaining balance: Transformative learning theory between individual transformation and social action* [Paper presentation]. ESREA 9th Triennial European Research Conference Adult education research and practice between the welfare state and neoliberalism, Belgrade University.

Finnegan, F. (2011). *Learning as transformation or adaptation? Thinking with and against Mezirow and Bourdieu*. International Transformative Learning Conference: In a Time of Crisis: Individual and Collective Challenges, Athens.

Finnegan, F. (2014). Embodied experience, transformative learning and the production of space. In A. Nicolaides & D. Holt (Eds.), *Spaces of transformation and transformation of space*. Proceedings of the 11th International Transformative Learning Conference, Teachers College Columbia University.

Finnegan, F. (2016). The future is unwritten: Democratic adult education against and beyond neoliberalism. *The Adult Learner*, 46–58.

Finnegan, F. (2019). "Freedom is a very fine thing": Individual and collective forms of emancipation in transformative learning. In T. Fleming, A. Kokkos, & F. Finnegan (Eds.), *European perspectives on transformation theory*. Palgrave Macmillan.

Finnegan, F., & Grummell, B. (Eds.). (2019). *Power and possibility: Adult education in a diverse and complex world*. Sense/Brill.

Finnegan, F., Merrill, B., & Thunborg, C. (Eds.) (2014). *Student voices on inequalities in European higher education: Challenges for policy and practice in a time of change*. Routledge.

Finnegan, F., Valadas, S., O'Neill, J., Fragoso, A., & Paulos, L. (2019). The search for security in precarious times: Non-traditional graduates perspectives on higher education and employment. *International Journal of Lifelong Education, 38*(2), 157–170.

Fleming, T. (2002). Habermas on civil society, lifeworld and system: Unearthing the social in transformation theory. *Teachers College Record*, 1–17.

Fleming, T., Kokkos, A., & Finnegan, F. (Eds.). (2019). *European perspectives on transformation theory*. Palgrave Macmillan.

Fraser, N. (2013). *Fortunes of feminism: From state-managed capitalism to neoliberal crisis*. Verso.

Freire, P. (1972). *Pedagogy of the oppressed*. Penguin.

Hart, M. (1990). Critical theory and beyond: Further perspectives on emancipatory education. *Adult Education Quarterly, 40*, 125–138.

Hoggan, C., Mälkki, K., & Finnegan, F. (2017). Developing the theory of perspective transformation: Continuity, intersubjectivity, and emancipatory praxis. *Adult Education Quarterly, 67*(1), 48–64.

Horton, M., Freire, P., Bell, B., Gaventa, J., & Peters, J. M. (1990). *We make the road by walking: Conversations on education and social change*. Temple University Press.

Inglis, T. (1997). Empowerment and emancipation. *Adult Education Quarterly, 48*, 3–17.

74   F. FINNEGAN

Merrill, B., & West, L. (2009). *Using biographical methods in social research*. Sage.

Mezirow, J. (1978). Perspective transformation. *Adult Education Quarterly, 28*(2), 100–110.

Mezirow, J. (1981). A critical theory of adult learning and education. *Adult Education Quarterly, 321*, 3–24.

Mezirow, J. (1989). Transformative learning and social action: A response to Collard and Law. *Adult Education Quarterly, 393*, 169–175.

Mezirow, J. (1990). Toward transformative learning and emancipatory education. In J. Mezirow & Associates (Eds.), *Fostering critical reflection in adulthood* (pp. 354–375). Jossey-Bass.

Mezirow, J. (1991). *Transformative dimensions of adult learning*. Jossey-Bass.

Mezirow, J. (1997). Transformative learning and social action: A response to Inglis. *Adult Education Quarterly, 49*(1), 70–72.

Mezirow, J. (1998). On critical reflection. *Adult Education Quarterly, 48*(3), 185–199.

Mezirow, J. (2000). Learning to think like an adult: Core concepts of transformation theory. In J. Mezirow & Associates (Eds.), *Learning as transformation: Critical perspectives on a theory in progress* (pp. 3–34). Jossey-Bass.

Mezirow, J. (2003). Transformative learning as discourse. *Journal of Transformative Education, 11*, 58–63.

Mezirow, J. (2007). Adult education and empowerment for individual and community development. In T. Fleming, D. McCormack, B. Connolly, & A. Ryan (Eds.), *Radical learning for liberation* (pp. 5–14). MACE.

Mezirow, J. et al. (1990). *Fostering critical reflection in adulthood: A guide to transformative and emancipatory learning*. Jossey-Bass.

Mills, C. W. (1959). *The sociological imagination*. Oxford University Press.

Newman, M. (2012). Calling transformative learning into question: Some mutinous thoughts. *Adult Education Quarterly, 62*, 36.

Pynchon, T. (1973/2000). *Gravity's rainbow*. Penguin Books.

Rubenson, K. (2011). The field of adult education: An overview. In K. Rubenson (Ed.), *Adult learning and education* (pp. 3–14). Academic Press/Elsevier.

Sen, A. (1999). *Development as freedom*. Oxford University Press.

Tennant, M. (1993). Perspective transformation and adult development. *Adult Education Quarterly, 44*, 34–42.

Tilly, C. (2004). *Social movements, 1768–2004*. Paradigm.

Wright, E. O. (2010). *Envisioning real utopias*. Verso.

Yorks, L., & Kasl, E. (2002). Toward a theory and practice for whole-person learning: Reconceptualizing experience and the role of affect. *Adult Education Quarterly, 25*(3), 176–192.

Zibechi, R. (2012). *Territories in resistance*. AK Press.

CHAPTER 5

The Transformation of the Reader

Effrosyni Kostara

INTRODUCTION

In order to study Mezirow's Transformation Theory one may initially refer to his fundamental work *Transformative Dimensions of Adult Learning* (1991), where he describes in detail the foundations of his theory. Additionally, collective volumes he edited and several articles and papers he authored constitute valuable sources. Throughout his whole work, the disorientating dilemma, the first among the ten phases (Mezirow, 1991, p. 168), is acknowledged as the defining moment for the activation of transformational processes. Nevertheless, he refers only twice to literary works as the cause of the disorientating dilemmas, without further analyzing the reasons or the way these affect readers (Mezirow, 1991, p. 168; 1994, p. 229).

A disorienting dilemma that begins the process of transformation also can result from an eye-opening discussion, book, poem, or painting.

E. Kostara (✉)
Hellenic Open University, Patras, Greece
e-mail: kostara.effrosyni@ac.eap.gr

© The Author(s), under exclusive license to Springer Nature Switzerland AG 2022
A. Nicolaides et al. (eds.), *The Palgrave Handbook of Learning for Transformation*, https://doi.org/10.1007/978-3-030-84694-7_5

One may or may not become critically aware of his or her premises in looking at an artwork or in reading a novel or a textbook or in seeing a play.

In addition, he seems to acknowledge the power that literature could wield in the context of his theory by the fact that in the collective volume he edited, entitled *Fostering Critical Reflection in Adulthood—A Guide to Transformative and Emancipatory Learning* (1990), Mezirow invites Greene (1990) to author a chapter about the transformational power of literature, where she connects the importance of literature with his theory. At the same time, Mezirow, in his article *On Critical Reflection* (1998), presents Greene's (1990) view of the process of reflective learning, according to which the teaching of literature, when approached critically, leads to emancipatory thinking.

According to the aforementioned, Greene's chapter proves to be the only extended and probably accurate source for the scholars in order to understand how Mezirow viewed the role of literature in the context of his theory. According to Greene, literature gives readers the opportunity, through their imagination, to meet different life stories and as a result to release themselves from traditional and stereotypical ways of thinking. They have the opportunity to meet assumptions and values quite different from their own. Imagination is for Greene an alternative way of thinking that can bring about transformation of distorted assumptions and lead both to personal awakening and social transformation.

It is worth noting that Mezirow as well fully recognized the contribution of imagination in the transformative process and considers it an important element:

> Imagination is indispensable to understanding the unknown. We imagine alternative ways of seeing and interpreting. The more reflective and open to the perspectives of others we are, the richer our imagination of alternative contexts for understanding will be. (Mezirow, 1991, p. 83)

The transformative potential of stories, with emphasis on storytelling, is also mentioned by Hoggan (2009) who notes that:

> Stories can take many forms: from journaling, short stories, narratives, poetry, and novels to movies, theatrical productions, and role playing. They can be fiction or nonfiction, one's own work or the creative writing of someone else. Through story, ideas are given meaning and relevance

as they bring abstract concepts into concrete and personal terms. This personal connection has the potential to lead to transformational experiences because it touches the soul, the spirit, the emotion of being. (p. 51)

As a result, while scholars put considerable emphasis on the exploitation of literature and stories as a means of activating the imagination and causing transformation, there is no targeted approach, on a theoretical basis, concerning the value of the literary work itself, its inherent characteristics and the way it could be exploited in practice, with the aim to provoke a disorientating dilemma and, consequently, engage the readers in a process of critical thinking on their stereotypical and dysfunctional perceptions.

Literature's Transformative Power

The aim of the first section of this chapter is to present some of the inherent characteristics of literature, which, responding to core elements or prerequisites of transformative learning, could potentially activate intellectual processes leading to it. It should be noted that, since they constitute inherent features of literature, the educator's physical presence is not presupposed, and, therefore, neither is the reading of the work in the strict context of the educational act, in order to activate potentially transformative processes. However, it is clear that an educator who is familiarized with literature and reading could, by using it as an educational tool, serve as a catalyst and mediator by accelerating intellectual and, in particular, reflective processes, which students would need more time to activate on their own.

Among the core elements that characterize works of high aesthetic value and especially literature, (1) the strong presence and emergence of truth and reality, (2) the activation of senses, (3) the autonomy, (4) the simultaneous presence of the aesthetically not acceptable and non-beautified alongside the beautiful and the ideal, (5) the challenge for change, (6) the shocking feelings, as well as (7) the mental exercise of the reader, are the ones that stand out (Bruns, 2011; Roche, 2004; Schwarz, 2008). These elements shall be outlined subsequently, aiming in this way to highlight, on the one hand, how close literature is to real life, thus affecting the readers and contributing to their intellectual and emotional evolution, and, on the other hand, whether these inherent features of literature can be detected in key functions of transformative learning, such as critical thinking, disorientating dilemma, evoking intense feelings as an object of cognitive examination, dysfunctional perceptions, etc.

Truth

Through its heroes and myths, literature talks about both nature and human in an ideal way, yet more profoundly true and sincere than reality, remaining inextricably linked with it. Without imitating reality, literature describes something that could happen. There lies its power. By pondering on the ideas and values expressed in the works, we actually reflect on a superior world, an ultimate and ideal world, wherein enduring and permanent truths are revived, which are transferable through the work of art across cultures and from one era to the following. After reading the work and viewing another real world, turning to a complex and problematic reality, the one around us, we are now able to see its negative features, by attempting to change it. At the same time, the work has raised complex questions, which, although often left without answers, constitute a stimulus in the search for the essence and meaning of things for the reader. In addition, literature is able through its concepts and heroes to illustrate the forgotten, distant, and marginalized, what reality hides from us even though it exists, urging us to acknowledge its value and, therefore, criticize our time and its mistakes which have concealed the whole truth up until now (Roche, 2004, pp. 17–23).

Using the terms of transformative learning, although the real world as it is revealed through the work of literature exists, it is yet impossible for us to behold in our daily life in the way it is shaped and defined by norms and rules that family, society, and politics have established, and, thus, concealed from us. The frames of reference and our points of view have been established with these norms as a reference point (Mezirow, 1991). Nevertheless, by conflicting with the existing reality the truth of the work, may be the first rupture, a cause for reflection on everything we took for granted. At the same time, the existence of the marginalized and the forgotten can only be accepted through the reading of perceptions and the recognition of roles that we ignored up until now. Thus, the readers' critical attitude is activated, even when it is limited to a simple awareness of the existence of an alternative view, and also, potentially, along with their questioning attitude and the possibility of experiencing a minor, disorientating dilemma, if the text is so revealing that it expresses truths regarding the world and the self, overlooked by the readers.

Sensuousness

A work of literature has the power to elicit a number of intellectual, psychological, and aesthetic reactions from us. In this sense, it is a real and complete experience, in the context of which readers see, listen, think, and feel. Therefore, by reading a text, their emotional wealth is activated and also their appreciation of the text itself is developed both structurally and morphologically. When participating in the reading act, readers imagine what it would be like to live somebody else's life, who, if the circumstances and situations changed, could be them. Therefore, otherness is right before them, so close yet so far away from them (Bohlin, 2005, p. 27; Roche, 2004, pp. 24–30).

The possibility provided to the readers, through reading the work, to undergo a complete and intense experience constitutes in itself an opportunity for transformation. The critical consideration of everything they study activates strong and often conflicting feelings which they may mentally process at a second stage. The attempt to understand their feelings and to critically approach them may constitute another opportunity to unveil dysfunctional perceptions, which surfaced, through the work, in the sphere of the conscious and were the deeper cause of these feelings. Close to this idea is Mälkki's view on the rational approach of feelings within the context of transformative learning (Mälkki, 2010, 2019). Additionally, this awareness and interpretation of uncomfortable feelings could fall into Mezirow's second phase of the transformation process (Mezirow, 1991, p. 168).

Autonomy

What makes art, and more specifically literature, distinct is its separation from reality, being at the same time, as we have seen, inextricably linked with it. This disconnection concerns the fact that art is independent from the reader's self and its needs. It does not pertain to the reader's calculations, wishes, instincts, and the practicality of daily life. Independent from external motives, it transfers readers through imagination beyond what is real, to other eras and worlds. Through its autonomy, literature ultimately serves a moral goal. Acting as a counterweight to reality and as a counterexample, it reveals its fragmentary and disorderly nature, emphasizes rationality, reasoning, and objectivity and finally delimits recipients and readers morally and emotionally. Outside the narrow boundaries of reality, the artist may experiment, risk-free, with new perceptions, which finally, if proven sufficient, will be showcased and recommended to the reader.

Therefore, readers are provided with the opportunity to engage in a dialogue with the work, and indirectly with themselves as well, since they are provided with the potential to think and express themselves through the work, and talk with the heroes in an environment of safety and neutrality. The distance of the work from their real lives creates a liberation context wherein readers shall be able to view more clearly and illuminate their own lives and perceptions (Bohlin, 2005, p. 27).

At the same time, readers shall transition through literature to a level superior than that of their own selves. Through the stories of others, their experiences and culture, they broaden their perception of life and the world. Coming into contact with distinct things, they abandon the egoistic and biased tendencies and move toward what is real and objective. A reader by associating themself with literary heroes engages with and shares common values and interests, that belong to the wider community, thus the reader participates in a collective thought. This triggers reflection on the existing beliefs and preconception, which in turn enables the reader to perceive their personal identity more clearly. They are able to distinguish themselves through the others, they become aware of themselves, they reflect on themselves and evolve. Finally, they realize that they are part of a totality and that they should act within the totality rather than being disconnected from it (Bruns, 2011, pp. 18–21; Schwarz, 2008, p. 38).

This process could prove extremely valuable both for the individual and society. This sharing of thoughts, feelings, and ideas, as well as the recognition that the individual is part of a totality, could constitute the first step for social transformation; the reader thinks and acts not only according to their personal interests. They undertake a new role within the society (element which falls into Mezirow's fifth phase of the transformation process) (Mezirow, 1991, p. 168) and as a result they could initiate social change.

5 THE TRANSFORMATION OF THE READER 81

The Role of the Ugly

As a depiction of reality even in an idealized form, art can only integrate the horrible and the ugly into its components. In order to feature depth and truth, a nice work should, apart from the pure and clean, be orientated toward elements such as evil, isolation, pain, hunger, and death. Furthermore, in order to select the truly good, one should include and be able to recognize among the available choices the evil, as a possibility which has to be overcome or transformed. Within the context of transformative learning, the dysfunctional and painful assumptions of the individual hold the role of the ugly that should be recognized and transformed. Once more, the realization of these dysfunctional assumptions, and the negative feelings they provoke, constitute elements of Mezirow's second phase among the ten phases of transformation (1991, p. 168).

Call for Change

The contribution of literature is amplified by the fact that it highlights the individual's power. It is common for heroes in works of literature to finally manage to change the world through their actions and decisions. Readers are, therefore, encouraged to fight and act. Moreover, the special virtues of the hero that led him to change are highlighted, such as self-sacrifice, faith, or solidarity, and the reader is called upon to cultivate them. Nevertheless, even when the hero fails to change situations, literature urges the readers to take a reflective approach for a better understanding of how the world functions. Again, through the hero's change, the reader potentially prepares their own personal change. The hero's actions transform the evolution of their story. Respectively, the reader has to act and transform their personal skills and values in order to change their life story. The reader is getting ready to undertake a new role, falling into the eighth phase of the transformation process (Mezirow, 1991, p. 168).

Impact (or a Disorienting Dilemma)

The reader's encounter with a narration that disturbs the serenity and pre-existing perception of things while reading a story may have a massive impact, parallel to a disorienting dilemma in the jargon of transformative learning. The case of ancient tragedy is rather characteristic, since, through tragic revelations and horrible events, it would shake the

82   E. KOSTARA

certainty and erroneous perceptions of both the heroes and the audience. Through this disorienting dilemma, readers demolish established perceptions, develop others and, in the end, are led to knowledge. When they realize something new about their own self through the hero's experience, in essence they feel that they are not alone, and their experiences are acknowledged (Bruns, 2011, p. 18).

Reading as a Mental Exercise

Finally, it is worth referring, except for the context, to the structure of the literary text, which also challenges the reader mentally. Being a complex process, literature reading requires readers to recall, regain, and reflect on experiences and knowledge of the past to construct on everything mentioned in the text. In the context of this process, the readers are required to distinguish between opinions and facts, realize the literal meaning of everything that the author describes, and also decode the underlying messages. Additionally, to identify the causal relationship between events and reflections, in order to interpret consequences, events, continuities, choices, by identifying and determining the essential features of the text (Tung & Chang, 2009).

These complex mental processes which are carried out by the readers in the context of reading a work activate, on the one hand, their critical thinking as a purely mental skill, and on the other hand, as already demonstrated above, a reflective and self-reflective attitude which, with continuous practice, may constitute a new way of perception and consideration of experiences, facts, and perceptions of themselves and the others.

In conclusion, it could be derived that, according to its inherent characteristics described above, literature has the potential to become a transformation means both for the individual and the educator. Nevertheless, by focusing on an educational act which aims to activate transformative processes, it becomes clear that the educator, apart from choosing literature itself as an educational tool, will also have to choose the appropriate works that could contribute more systematically toward transformative learning.

The content and theme of the works to be studied should provide stimuli for critical approach and alternative view of various and different attitudes to life and perceptions, which should ideally derive from the widest time and geographical scope possible, highlighting in this way their resilience, dynamic, and value within space and throughout time. The study of stories and characters from different times and cultures, which should revolve around common topics in different ways of approaching as far as possible, would be an exercise of critical reflection for the readers on social, political, and moral issues which may often be linked to distorted and dysfunctional sociolinguistic and moral-ethical habits of mind (Mezirow, 2000, p. 17) within the context of transformative learning.

Therefore, the selected works which would focus, for example, on the position of woman and the role of both genders, the experience of loss, exile, or migration, the struggles of social groups, who often lived and still live isolated, for acceptance and acknowledgment, the preservation and evolution of ideas such as democracy and freedom, all seen under the light of a different era and culture every time, could awaken the readers and acquaint them with a new, totally different world that they may have overlooked. This act of acknowledging the different could serve as the transformative disorientating dilemma of phase one.

To that end, as advocated hereinafter, the educational, though not solely, exploitation of literature in light of the theory of World Literature could respond.

The Theory of World Literature

Johann von Goethe was the first to elaborate on the concept of *World Literature* (*Weltliteratur*). World Literature refers to literary works that are translated into multiple languages and circulated to an audience outside their country of origin. From Goethe's time onward, World Literature has often been seen in one or more of three ways: as *classics*, as *masterpieces*, and as *windows on the world* (Damrosch, 2009, pp. 1–11; Puchner, 2017).

Classics mostly refer to Greek and Latin literature. *Masterpieces* would be recognized almost as soon as they would be published and would circulate in translation. The writer of a masterpiece could come from quite modest origins. Classics are mostly acknowledged as masterpieces (Damrosch, 2009, p. 5).

However, apart from reading World Literature as classics (e.g., Homer's *Odyssey*) and masterpieces (e.g., Dostoevsky's *Crime and Punishment*), since the mid-1990s, there has been a great emphasis on the view of World Literature as a *set of windows on the world* (Damrosch,

2009, p. 5). Through this dimension of World Literature, the emphasis is put on the exploitation of works which are not creations, as in the two previous dimensions, by a few privileged male and White authors from Western countries, but additionally by men and women authors who come from a non-western culture and reflect it in their work, thus making the presence of literature more inclusive. Regardless of whether they may be characterized as masterpieces, they are works that highlight more marginal, determined by their own cultural context, mainstream voices, with a special emphasis on women authors. This is the dimension we will adopt for the rational of the present chapter.

Through World Literature readers direct their attention to otherness and to aspects of it which are highlighted through the selected works. This is the otherness they try to understand through reading, and also to accept. In contrast to the usual practice, the aim of the World Literature approach is for readers to be able to overcome the mind's tendency to assimilate the other into the familiar and the commonplace. It is exactly the process which takes place during the disorienting dilemma. Individuals fail to assimilate their experiences to their established frames of reference and as a result are involved in a situation of disorientation. This disorientation is the one that World Literature aims to challenge. Engaging in reading, readers are required to identify the elements that don't make sense at first reading, to identify alternative views about the topic under study, as they are formed in space and time, and finally to compare them with their own personal assumptions. By knowing the different, readers implicitly know that they don't know, and, at the same time, they realize the obsolete nature of their own perceptions and of their cultural features in contrast to what they read. Social and geographical position of the readers is the main cause of these outdated perceptions and assumptions, which is reversed when they come into contact with new cultures and civilizations (Cooppan, 2009, pp. 38–42; Longxi, 2009, pp. 62–66, 70–71).

Goethe himself defines the basic aim of World Literature, as a way to give the nations the opportunity not to think alike but to understand each other in a way that would lead them to learn how to live together and tolerate one another (Cooppan, 2001, p. 18). The recognition, acceptance, and understanding of the alternative view are among the basic goals of transformative learning as well and the means for the desirable expansion of readers' frames of reference.

Reading about common experiences from the perspective of different cultures provides readers with the opportunity, irrespective of their race and ethnicity, especially if they participate in a structured educational process, to share freely their opinions and experiences, which were unable to share until then, through the different characters of every work. Issues of violence, discrimination, and marginalization are proven to be common, resulting in the readers finally realizing that they are closer than they thought.

This globalization of literary works and their study involves the development of a relational thinking in which although we experience the local, this becomes simultaneously part of the global. Placing a text alongside another from different tradition and time offers the opportunity to change the way we see things and the premises through which we interpret what we see (Cooppan, 2001, pp. 26, 32). This premise is fundamental when reading literature as means for transformative learning.

Readers are involved in a process of discourse both with the heroes and the author. Its characteristics bring it close to what Mezirow defines as reflective dialogue. Between the literary work and the reader, an environment is created where readers are free to hear and comprehend alternative ideas. The reader participates actively without feeling the need to act as a leader. A cognitive and emotional relationship is built (Mezirow, 2000). Through this process of discourse with alternative views and cultures, democracy is enhanced and social cohesion is developed, with society to become more tolerant and inclusive: Citizens think more critically and finally acquire an ability to occupy cultural positions different from their own (Komar, 2009, pp. 103, 107–109).

World Literature in Practice

According to what was presented in the two previous sections concerning the inherent characteristics of literature and the World Literature theory as a perspective from which it could be exploited, it can be seen that works of literature may constitute an exquisite tool in the hands of an educator. Especially in the context of a curriculum which aims at activating transformative processes, the selection of the appropriate excerpts and their systematic approach on the part of the training group could prove to be rather effective.

For example, an educator who would like to work with students on issues concerning the role of women and stereotypes related to it could use works of literature by women authors, mostly autobiographical ones. However, attempting, in this endeavor, to give a more intercultural character in order to integrate alternative perspectives, they could exploit works, the authors, and content which are not strictly part of a western context. Hereby, is a selection of works according to the theory of World Literature. Among them, we identify both masterpieces and classical works, which all constitute a set of windows on the world.

The Golden Notebook, a novel by Nobel Prize-winning author Doris Lessing, shows up the dangers and difficulties that women encounter if they try to live a free life in a man's world (Walter, 2014). *The Bluest Eye,* a novel by Nobel Prize-winning author Toni Morrison, tells the tragic story of Pecola Breedlove, an African American girl who equates beauty and social acceptance with whiteness; she therefore longs to have "the bluest eye," i.e., the feature which together with blond hair and white skin make a woman beautiful. Regarding the rights and also the stereotypes against women, data may be also drawn from the autobiographical work by Rigoberta Menchú, *I, Rigoberta Menchú: An Indian Woman in Guatemala.* The book records the detail of everyday Indian life. Rigoberta vividly describes both the religious and superstitious beliefs of her community and her personal response to feminist and socialist ideas. Needless to say, among the excerpts to be exploited, excerpts of the classics could be incorporated, such as excerpts from the ancient Greek tragedy *Medea* or *Helen* by Euripides, where once again many ideas are expressed, concerning the role and power of women in the context of *oikos.* This selection gives readers the opportunity to recognize women's voices being uttered in different periods and within different cultures.

Ideally, the students should read the whole work. Since this is not always possible, the educator has to choose on their own the excerpts, which they should later approach through a process of reflective discourse. At the same time, targeted questions can be used and also short essays assigned. The intercultural element as well as the historical context of the heroes and the authors themselves should not remain untapped, as they constitute major factors in themselves, both in the shaping and consolidation of stereotypes, and in challenging them when they are approached critically and in comparison with what applies in other cultures and eras.

By using questions, regarding, for example, the opinions expressed in the excerpt, the feelings of the heroes and also those of the readers, the obstacles and difficulties the heroes face, their common experiences and their differences as well, the response of society to these, and also by using experiential techniques, such as role-playing, the students will be able to express their opinions, assume the role and experience the feelings and obstacles of the heroines, and see and listen to the inner thoughts and experiences of people who, in their daily context, are likely to live isolated, not having the opportunity to express themselves freely. At the same time, the selection of texts from the totality of World Literature is likely to give voice to members of the training group who come from different cultures and perhaps have remained silent so far. Thus, an opportunity arises to highlight the fact that often experiences and perceptions may not only separate people, but also unite them. Once again, the process of reflective discourse is activated. This time the discourse is held among the participants within an environment of empathy, openness, freedom, and acceptance (Mezirow, 2000).

Epilogue

Mezirow's Transformation Theory is more relevant than ever in the current reality. Nevertheless, his work does not contain references as to the practical way that the students could be involved in a transformative process within the context of educational act. Especially as far as exploiting literature, his mentions were extremely limited apart from what Greene's work has to offer.

Nonetheless, in view of the above, literature could constitute an appropriate educational tool with the objective to, on the one hand, pose a disorientating dilemma for the readers, and on the other hand, engage them in a process of critical thinking and reflection leading to the transformation of stereotypical perceptions. The transformative power of literature, however, may also be activated irrespective of the educational context, by the reading act itself, as a result of the inherent features of the literary work.

World Literature could integrate even more perspectives into the critical consideration of views and perceptions. Moreover, in the context of a multicultural environment, it could be the right occasion for the members with a different cultural background, who usually remain silent, to express themselves.

88   E. KOSTARA

REFERENCES

Bohlin, K. (2005). *Teaching character education through literature: Awakening the moral imagination in secondary classrooms.* Routledge.

Bruns, C. V. (2011). *Why literature?* Continuum Publishing Corporation.

Cooppan, V. (2001). World literature and global theory: Comparative literature for the new millennium. *Globalism & Theory, 9*(1/2), 15–43.

Cooppan, V. (2009). The ethics of world literature: Reading others, reading otherwise. In D. Damrosch (Ed.), *Teaching world literature* (pp. 34–43). The Modern Language Association of America.

Damrosch, D. (Ed.) (2009). *Teaching world literature.* The Modern Language Association of America.

Greene, M. (1990). Realizing literature's emancipatory potential. In J. Mezirow & Associates (Eds.), *Fostering critical reflection in adulthood* (pp. 251–288). Jossey-Bass.

Hoggan, C. (2009). The power of story: Metaphors, literature, and creative writing. In C. Hoggan, S. Simpson, & H. Stuckey (Eds.), *Creative expression in transformative learning: Tools and techniques for educators of adults* (pp. 51–74). Krieger Publishing Company.

Komar, K. (2009). Teaching world literature in a microcosm of the world. In D. Damrosch (Ed.), *Teaching world literature* (pp. 101–109). Modern Language Association of America.

Longxi, Z. (2009). What is literature? Reading across cultures. In D. Damrosch (Ed.), *Teaching world literature* (pp. 61–72). Modern Language Association of America.

Mälkki, K. (2010). Building on Mezirow's theory of transformative learning: Theorizing the challenges to reflection. *Journal of Transformative Education, 8*(1), 42–62.

Mälkki, K. (2019). Coming to grips with edge-emotions: The gateway to critical reflection and transformative learning. In T. Fleming, A. Kokkos, & F. Finnegan (Eds.), *European perspectives on transformative learning* (pp. 59–73). Palgrave Macmillan.

Mezirow, J. (1991). *Transformative dimensions of adult learning.* Jossey-Bass.

Mezirow, J. (1994). Understanding transformation theory. *Adult Education Quarterly, 44*(4), 222–232.

Mezirow, J. (1998). On critical reflection. *Adult Education Quarterly, 48*, 185–198.

Mezirow. J. (2000). Learning to think like an adult: Core Concepts of transformative theory. In J. Mezirow & Associates (Eds.), *Learning as transformation: Critical perspectives on a theory in progress* (pp. 3–33). Jossey-Bass.

Puchner, M. (2017). *The written world: The power of stories to shape people, history, civilization.* Random House.

Roche, M. (2004). *Why literature matters in the 21st century*. Yale University Press.

Schwarz, D. (2008). *In defense of reading: Teaching literature in the twenty-first century*. Chichester.

Tung, C.-A., & Chang, S.-Y. (2009). Developing critical thinking through literature reading. *Journal of Humanities and Social Sciences, 19*, 287–317.

Walter, N. (2014). Doris Lessing: An unusual feminist. *Independent*. Retrieved November 8, 2020 from https://www.independent.co.uk/news/people/profiles/doris-lessing-unusual-feminist-9266166.html

CHAPTER 6

Mapping the Terrain: Analytic Tools for Future Thinking About Transformation

Chad Hoggan

People have the capacity to change. Such change is easy to see in children as they develop in terms of maturity and cognitive ability, but it is often less visible, and almost certainly less frequent, in adulthood. In fact, some argue that humans are set in their ways by the time they become adults. This view is embedded in such cultural idioms as "You cannot teach an old dog new tricks" and "A leopard cannot change its spots." An alternative view is that there is always the possibility for important, substantial change, a phenomenon often loosely described as transformation. The belief in the potential for transformation inspires, and arguably is the raison d'être, for many who work in professions involving adult education, most visibly perhaps in literacy, counseling, pastoral care, community development, or social change.

C. Hoggan (✉)
Department of Leadership, Policy and Human Development, North Carolina State University, Raleigh, NC, USA
e-mail: cdhoggan@ncsu.edu

© The Author(s), under exclusive license to Springer Nature Switzerland AG 2022
A. Nicolaides et al. (eds.), *The Palgrave Handbook of Learning for Transformation*, https://doi.org/10.1007/978-3-030-84694-7_6

What does it mean, though, to say that adults can change, especially if by that we mean they can change in dramatic, significant, momentous ways? How are they different after this change? What does the change process look like? How is such an event initiated? What are its prerequisites? How do educators appropriately facilitate such change?

One attempt to answer these questions that really captured the attention and imagination of adult education scholars and practitioners was Mezirow's theory of perspective transformation, or as it was later called, transformative learning theory (1978, 1991, 2009). Although the theoretical work that Mezirow provided is valuable, its greater significance is that it instigated over 30 years of scholarship focused on this idea of humans' potential for transformation. The interest that scholars have shown in transformative learning demonstrates a yearning for concepts, language, and theoretical justifications with which to ponder, discuss, and design for this aspect of learning.

However, because Mezirow offered the seminal conception of transformative learning, scholars tend to position their work in relation to his theory rather than in relation to the most relevant issues or to a broader range of theories. In so doing, all the inevitable idiosyncrasies, limitations, and lacunae of a single perspective come to dominate the larger body of scholarship. Seminal theories can thus have the unintended consequence of acting as tethers which limit future conceptions of the phenomenon they purport to understand. Being first does not necessarily mean that a theory is best suited to being central to all future theories.

Rather than positioning Mezirow at the center of the theory, thus marginalizing all other approaches around his seminal work, this chapter proposes a metatheoretical approach. The distinction between theory and metatheory lies in their different purposes. Mezirow claimed to have developed a theory, a "body of inductively formulated generalizations by which the behavior of adults in educational situations may be understood and predicted" (Mezirow, 1971, p. 135). In this sense, a theory describes premises and interactions of learning phenomena, which provide a rationale to explain, design, support, and/or evaluate learning. A metatheory, on the other hand, does not offer such specifics about the phenomenon. Rather, it brings together disparate theories that address a particular phenomenon, thus providing insights that cut across multiple theoretical perspectives. By studying, analyzing, and comparing the sources, assumptions, contexts, uses, and implications (Wallis, 2010, p. 76) of a variety of theories attempting to explain similar phenomena, "we gain the opportunity to understand and integrate theories across disciplinary boundaries" (p. 75).

Those insights often take the form of conceptual and analytic tools derived from an analysis of several different theories. For instance, one tool might be the creation of a common vocabulary such that scholarship from different disciplines can more easily be brought into dialogue with each other. Also important for the metatheory of transformative learning, is that it can offer frameworks within which potential theories, approaches, or descriptions of the transformative aspects of learning can be positioned relative to each other (rather than relative to Mezirow) based on such criteria as, for instance, the nature of the transformative change they seek to describe or the contexts in which they are most relevant.

This idea for a "metatheoretical discourse" was first proposed by Gunnlaugson (2008). He described existing literature as "first wave," in that it offered specific perspectives on what transformation is and how it happens, and he called for "second wave" scholarship that would integrate these specific theories. Such integration, however, is not the only value of metatheory. Rather, the main value is to provide insights from across the range of different theories.

In order to productively move forward in providing such insights (i.e., concepts, language, and theoretical understandings) for the transformative possibilities of learning, this chapter provides several analytic tools that may be useful. It begins by providing a definition of transformative learning as a metatheory, as well as criteria to describe how, in what ways, and to what extent a particular learning phenomenon is transformative. Next, this chapter presents several analytic tools developed through metatheoretical analysis and which may be useful for future scholarly work around transformative learning. The chapter concludes with some cautionary considerations about the normativity inherent in any desired transformational outcome and provides three orientations toward (ways of thinking about) transformative learning.

Core Concepts of the Metatheory of Transformative Learning

What determines whether, or to what extent, a learning experience is transformative? This is an important question because the purpose and value of metatheory is to gain insights from across different perspectives. And, although various theoretical lenses will produce different conceptions of transformation, they are at least connected by the claim that transformation is happening. However, if there are no agreed upon criteria about what transformation is, then any resulting cross-analysis will have no shared basis and therefore be meaningless.

Some scholars have argued that all learning changes people in some ways, and therefore no learning is uniquely transformational (e.g., Newman, 2012). To these scholars, there would be no value in studying transformative learning and therefore no need to have criteria by which to clarify whether, or to what extent, or in what ways learning is transformational. The multitude of scholars who have been writing about transformative learning over the last 30 years seem to disagree; they believe that there are indeed "transformative dimensions of learning" (Mezirow, 1991), and that it is important to understand how and why learning can be transformational. Nothing as complex as learning can be cleanly dichotomized (i.e., either transformative or not transformative), and it seems logical that a particular learning experience can have "transformative dimensions" without necessarily completely transforming the learner (Hoggan, 2019). In naming his book *Transformative Dimensions of Adult Learning*, Mezirow (1991) implies that one important consideration is not necessarily whether a learning event is transformational, but rather that many learning events will have transformational dimensions (or characteristics) to them. This is an important distinction, as it creates space to talk about learning events that do not immediately transform the whole person, but that nevertheless have certain qualities that are transformational in nature. In light of these considerations, it is necessary for the metatheory to have parameters, definitions, and further concepts so that scholars interested in transformation can exercise clarity in their thinking, writing, and practice.

To address this need, I draw on a metatheoretical project which analyzed 206 articles addressing transformative learning that were published between 2003 and 2014 (see Hoggan [2016b] for details of the study). Based on this analysis, the definition of transformative learning as a metatheory was created: "Transformative learning refers to processes that result in significant and irreversible changes in the way a person experiences, conceptualizes, and interacts with the world" (Hoggan, 2016a, p. 71). This definition establishes parameters around the phenomena that the metatheory of transformative learning is intended to address. The descriptors highlight the fact that the change resulting from transformative learning is holistic. There is a change in thinking ("conceptualizes"), e.g., how one views the world, how one knows and interacts with knowledge. There are also changes in how a person exists in the world ("experiences"), e.g., how one feels on a moment-to-moment basis in various situations, how one reacts viscerally, how one perceives herself in relation to others or to the world in general. And, of course, there is a change in behavior ("interacts"), whether that is knee-jerk reactions to stimuli or purposeful engagement in new activities.

For this discussion, it is helpful to offer concrete examples to illustrate the need for scholars to address transformative learning in terms of these parameters. For instance, one Web site's description of transformative learning demonstrates some common ambiguities around transformative learning. It claims that transformative learning "can be anything from an adult who transforms their ability to spread their opinion after learning how to use social networks and the Internet to a person who has a transformative experience on the way they view life due to a traumatic experience" (VALAMIS, 2020). To my mind, these two examples differ markedly. In the former, the learner becomes better able to communicate. This is indeed something useful to learn, but based on this description alone, it does not seem to qualify as being transformative. In contrast, the latter example intuitively seems likely to be transformative. One can imagine a person going through the diagnosis, treatments, and recovery from cancer, with all of its inherent psychosocial challenges, and emerging from that experience with a completely different view of herself, new priorities, greater appreciation for life, and similar fundamental changes (Hoggan, 2014; Stanton et al., 2006). To complicate this comparison, it is conceivable that finally being able to communicate one's ideas might indeed have a ripple effect that culminates in transformation for the learner; and conversely, it is often the case that cancer survivors are not significantly different afterward (Stanton et al., 2006). The descriptors in the definition of transformative learning provide conceptual parameters that can be used to name and discuss why and to what extent each of these is or is not accurately described as a transformation.

The first parameter asserts that changes must be significant and irreversible. In inquiring about the significance of a learning outcome, the definition means that in order for a learning experience to be considered transformative, the change would have to be beyond superficial. How, then, can we be more specific about the degree of change necessary to claim it was transformative? Two criteria offered are that the significant learning outcomes have depth and breadth (Hoggan, 2016a).

Depth refers to the degree of change; a learning outcome has depth when its effects on the learner are substantial. For instance, many students study critical thinking skills in their college classrooms. For students who already know and use such skills, the learning likely will not have substantial impact (depth) because the new learning does not change their thinking habits very much. Similarly, those students who learn about critical thinking but do not really employ those skills in their own thinking will not experience substantial impact. However, for those students who had never really questioned the rationale of knowledge claims, its sources and justifications, and who begin to exercise more criticality rather than passivity in their interaction with knowledge claims, the learning in the classroom for them may indeed have a substantial impact. Evaluating depth of learning in this way is tricky, as it does not necessarily mean that something was learned well (e.g., the students who already practice critical thinking skills can easily score well on an exam, but the learning will not impact them very much because they already practice it). Rather, it means that the learning caused an important shift in some relevant domain for the learner.

At the level of metatheory, in requiring a sufficient degree of change in order for a learning experience to be considered transformative, it is difficult to point to a specific measure of change. However, such measures are possible for individual theories. For instance, the Subject-Object Interview (SOI) is an assessment method designed to evaluate someone according to Kegan's model of epistemological development (1994). A pre- and post-assessment using the SOI could show with exact scores how a learner changed according to this model, and the difference of those scores could be used to evaluate the extent to which a person's development had progressed (or, in terms of this criterion, the depth of the change).

The criterion of significance also includes the need for breadth. Breadth refers to the expansiveness of the change on the learner's life, especially in terms of the different contexts in which the change has substantial impact. The idea here is that learning is often contextual: Some learning only affects the context in which it took place, and other learning affects many or all of the person's life contexts. Returning to the example of critical thinking, students may learn how to think critically in a college classroom, and they may develop the habit of using those newly learned skills in that context, but that does not mean that they have transformed. What might point to a transformation, however, is if those critical thinking skills became habitually used in all the contexts of the students' lives: when reading the newspaper, watching a documentary, talking with work colleagues or neighbors, and so forth.

As another example, if a person changes his way of being in a relationship (e.g., the way of participating in, being present in, viewing, and treating that relationship), the question would still arise whether that change only affected one relationship or most/all of his relationships. It would not make sense to claim that a person was transformed simply on the basis that he changed his way of being with his best friend. However, if a person changed his ways of being such that it affected all his relationships, it would be much more justifiable to describe it in terms of a transformation. As above, there is no clean demarcation between "transformative" or "not transformative," but clearly the greater the number of contexts affected, the more transformative the learning seems to have been.

The third part of the definition, irreversibility, insists that there must be relative stability, that temporary change cannot rightly be called a transformation. As with the other criteria, this is not cleanly demarcated. To change one's ways of being in relationship with others for, say, a month, and then returning to previous patterns and habits, is not a transformation; it is a temporary foray into new possibilities. For transformation, the changes would need to be stable. And yet, former norms and habits may still emerge occasionally, especially when prompted by stress or contextual triggers. There is a difference between occasional relapses of former ways of being and reverting to old norms. So again, the demarcation line is fuzzy. Also, irreversible change does not mean stagnation, as possibilities for further change always exist. Nevertheless, the criterion of relative stability requires that change is not simply temporary.

Analytic Tools for the Metatheory of Transformative Learning

There are two types of metatheoretical work: synthetic and analytic (Wallace, 1992). Synthetic metatheory organizes existing literature into categories. These classification systems help readers understand how various theories within the metatheory relate to each other. In the case of transformative learning, these systems have been offered by Clark (1993),

Dirkx (1998), and Taylor (2008). These systems provide categories within which specific theories of transformation fit. For instance, Taylor (2008) proposes that theories of transformation currently in the literature can be organized into the following categories based on underlying disciplinary perspectives and/or premises about what prompts transformation and how it occurs: Cultural-Spiritual, Neurobiological, Planetary, Psychoanalytic, Psychocritical, Psychodevelopmental, Race-centric, and Social-Emancipatory.

A second type of metatheory work is analytic. Analytic metatheory provides categories of components common among (or at least applicable to) multiple underlying theories. One helpful set of conceptual tools emanating from this type of work is the "Disorienting Index" (Ensign, 2019a). Based on an analysis of 256 peer-reviewed articles on transformative learning, Ensign developed an eight-point classification system by which disorienting events (i.e., initiating events of the transformation process) can be described.

- Acuteness (acute/epochal or not)
- Seclusion (alone or not)
- Origin (externally or internally generated)
- Familiarity (prior experience or not)
- Affect (negative affect or not)
- Setting (educational setting or not)
- Place (new location or not)
- Locus of Control (voluntary or involuntary)

This study provides insights and benefits illustrative of the value of metatheoretical work. Prior to the advent of the Disorientation Index, all types of disorientation were described under the same broad umbrella and often referred to as a "Disorienting Dilemma." Ensign's study revealed that not all disorienting experiences are negative or dilemmas that are thrust upon us; some are, in fact, positively disorienting and sometimes even sought out by the learner. It provides a more nuanced understanding of the experiences occurring in this important introductory phase of the transformation process. It also moves us toward a better understanding of how we might conceptualize the unique and individual contexts of transformative learning (i.e., there are thousands of possible combinations of these eight dimensions that create unique and individual context profiles).

Additionally, because most approaches to transformative learning agree that a disorienting experience is the initiating circumstance for transformative learning, the Disorientation Index unites these research streams with a common vocabulary, and the identification of eight dimensions of disorientation, via extensive qualitative and foundational research, positions our field for further exploration and validation of these dimensions. The Disorientation Index is also useful as an analytical tool for practitioners to better facilitate transformative learning processes (Ensign, 2019b).

Another set of conceptual tools developed by analytic metatheory work is the Typology of Transformative Learning Outcomes (Hoggan, 2016b), derived from the same study as the definition of transformative learning (described above). Whereas Ensign's system describes instigators of the transformation process, Hoggan describes the outcomes of it. This typology is intended to provide categories of change so that scholars are prompted to consider the multifaceted outcomes of (transformational) learning. According to this typology, the outcomes of any particular learning experience can be described by the combination of specific ways in which a person's (or group's or society's) ways of conceptualizing, experiencing, and interacting with the world have changed. Following are the six broad categories comprising the typology, along with examples of more specific types of outcomes within each of them.

- Worldview
    - Change in assumptions, beliefs, values, expectations
    - New interpretations of previous experiences
    - More comprehensive or complex worldview
- Self
    - Change in sense of self-in-relation to others or the world
    - Change in identity/view of self
    - Change in sense of empowerment
    - Increased self-knowledge
    - Change in personal narrative
    - New meaning/purpose in life
- Epistemology
    - More discriminating epistemological habits

- Utilizing extra-rational ways of knowing
- Becoming more open-minded

- Ontology

  - Change in moment-to-moment affective experience of life
  - Change in habitual tendencies and dispositions
  - Increased mindfulness
  - Change in attributes (e.g., more patient, compassionate, hopeful)

- Behavior

  - New behaviors, consistent with new perspectives
  - New skills, necessary for other changes to occur

- Capacity

  - Higher level of cognitive development
  - Higher order of consciousness
  - Greater sense of connection to something greater than oneself

This typology is intended to prompt scholars to create precise portrayals of transformational change and to consider possible outcomes that they may otherwise have neglected. It presupposes that any learning experience can be described as a combination of many specific outcomes. (Space limitations preclude a detailed demonstration here, but Schroeder et al., 2020, is an example of using this typology to structure, understand, and present learning outcomes.) On a final note, these learning outcomes, although arguably transformative in nature, do not necessarily mean that a learner experiencing one or more was them was transformed. They could also be used to describe any learning outcome or even to describe how a person (or group) is making meaning of the world. In order for the outcome to be transformative learning, the criteria of depth, breadth, and relative stability would still apply.

Considerations Concerning Normativity

A question that sometimes arises is whether a distinction should exist between the word "transformation" and the term "transformative learning," as if the word "learning" implies that there must be a positive outcome. Although it may be important to consider transformative outcomes in terms of the degree to which they are positive or negative, helpful or not helpful, or even hurtful (and to whom), such an evaluation is always and necessarily from a normative perspective. For instance, consider the long-standing debate on the issue of educational objectives.

> It is one thing to recognize the right (and responsibility) of parents to educate their children as members of a family, quite another to claim that this right of familial education extends to a right of parents to insulate their children from exposure to ways of life or thinking that conflict with their own. ... A state makes choice possible by teaching its future citizens respect for opposing points of view and ways of life. It makes choice meaningful by equipping children with the intellectual skills necessary to evaluate ways of life different from that of their parents. History suggests that without state provision or regulation of education, children will be taught neither mutual respect among persons nor rational deliberation among ways of life. (Gutmann, 1987, pp. 29, 30–31)

Considering this debate in the context of college classrooms, a humanities professor may hope that her teaching will help students become more open-minded and accepting of difference, with perhaps more relativistic views. This educator might be thinking in terms of developing more civic- or equity-minded citizens. In contrast, the parents of some of these college students may perceive such changes in their children as a real harm to their children. These parents might be thinking in terms of wanting their children to "turn out right" according to their (the parents') values and traditions. It is problematic to assume that one's vision for appropriate, good, or helpful transformations is de facto good or correct in everyone's eyes. Therefore, great care needs to be taken to reflect on the values and ideologies that inform one's view of what a positive transformation should look like. The following subsections present some reflections on and implications of this theme.

Three Orientations of Transformative Learning as an Educational Goal

This section seeks to make explicit the (often tacit) ways that scholars and practitioners think about the implementation of transformative learning. It provides important clarification about what is meant by transformative learning by presenting a classification system that describes three orientations for implementing transformative learning: prescriptive, process-oriented, and adaptive (Hoggan & Kloubert, 2020). Based on these orientations, three corresponding conceptualizations of transformative learning are derived.

Transformative Learning as Prescriptive

The first orientation to transformative learning as an educational goal is prescriptive, meaning that the educator determines how learners need to transform and then designs pedagogies to initiate and lead to that particular transformation. The educator decides, for instance, the worldview that learners need to adopt, the epistemology that must be learned and habitually used, and so forth. In essence, it assumes the educator knows the fundamental deficits that need to be corrected in learners. As is hopefully obvious from this description, this orientation can be highly problematic. It very easily can be disrespectful towards learners as autonomous agents, treat learners as objects needing to change for the benefit of others' purposes, and/or presuppose that the educator has the moral right to decide how learners should change in ways that could have dramatic consequences in their lives. As Mezirow (1989) noted, it can resemble indoctrination rather than emancipation. This is not to say that a prescriptive approach is never ethical or appropriate. Imagine an educational program that promises in its advertisements to transform participants through immersive experiences in a "third world" country, or learning to practice mindfulness, or ... in military boot camp. These programs all would have a prescriptive approach to implementing transformative learning, but those intended outcomes are at least advertised and known beforehand by potential participants. Purposively trying to transform other people is always problematic enough that educators should be both reflective and transparent about their goals.

For the purpose of analyzing or theorizing about transformation, however, a prescriptive orientation toward implementing transformative learning converts to a (very helpful) approach to studying transformation. In essence, it focuses scholars' attention on exactly how learners are different after a so-called transformative experience, and only then does it seek to understand the processes, contexts, and other factors that led to such outcomes. The two additional orientations presented below, although different in important ways from this first one, nevertheless are

6 MAPPING THE TERRAIN: ANALYTIC TOOLS FOR FUTURE THINKING ... 103

still based on this understanding that the ultimate criterion for describing a learning experience as transformative is the outcome of that experience; i.e., how learners are actually different afterward. Despite this commonality, the following two additional orientations provide important nuances to understanding how transformative learning is conceptualized as an educational goal.

Transformative Learning as Process-Oriented

A second orientation toward the implementation of transformative learning focuses on processes that hold the potential for long-term changes (Hoggan & Kloubert, 2020). An example of this orientation is Mezirow's (1991) description of education for perspective transformation. In it, he advocated for specific processes; i.e., critical dialogue and critical reflection. He did not advocate for specific worldviews these processes would lead to (which would have been a prescriptive approach), but rather that developing the skill and habit of using these processes would lead to improved ways of thinking and being in the world (i.e., meaning perspectives that were more discriminating, inclusive, permeable, open, and discerning). This orientation points to an important distinction between: (1) striving for a particular set of views, thought processes, and behaviors (prescriptive); and (2) promoting processes of thinking and being that are deemed to be good and that hold within them potentialities for long-term change (process-oriented).

This orientation allows a scholar to talk about aspects of a learning experience that hold the potential for long-term change. It was explicitly used in reporting on a research study describing the effects of using fictional short stories as a pedagogy in college courses:

> Although we do not expect the reading of one short story to foster transformative learning, we do expect that it has the potential to set up some of the processes that may lead to transformative learning (e.g., creating a disorienting dilemma, leading to critical reflection, or looking at oneself or the world through a new lens). (Hoggan & Cranton, 2015, p. 9)

In the above article, the authors argue that pedagogies, and the learning experiences they create, can be described in terms of the transformative potential they have and the types of long-term change they point to. Such pedagogies might include teaching the skills and promoting the

104   C. HOGGAN

habits of, for instance: thinking critically, practicing empathy, exploring alternatives, questioning taken-for-granted norms, and so forth. The idea behind this perspective is that if a person learns one or more of these skills and develops the habit of using them, then over time those habits will presumably lead to profound changes in how they experience, conceptualize, and interact with the world. Planting the metaphorical seeds of transformation is indeed one form that transformative education takes.

Transformative Learning as Adaptive

A third way that learning can be considered transformative is by seeing it as an adaption to a dramatically new or changed context. Recognizing that certain situations demand transformative change is important, and implementing transformative learning from this perspective, i.e., an adaptive approach, signals to people working in those situations that particular forms of support and facilitation of learning (i.e., those designed to help learners navigate transformational learning challenges) are necessary (Hoggan & Kloubert, 2020).

This orientation recognizes that there are situations that are likely to cause major challenges, disruptions, or disorientations for a person (e.g., death of a loved one, divorce, illness, job layoff or termination, birth of children), and that these situations inherently hold the potential for transformative learning. An example of such an adaptive approach was used in a study of breast cancer survivorship. The approach recognized that the overall experience of having breast cancer (with its diagnosis, treatment, and recovery, and especially the psychosocial challenges that accompanied these experiences) as a situation producing extremely difficult challenges, the reaction to which holds the potential for transformation.

> In trying to understand the learning and growth experiences of the participants in this study, it became apparent that in the particular context in which the women lived and the particularities of cancer as a context-changing series of events, both played a central role in shaping the form that their process took and the eventual outcomes of it. (Hoggan, 2014, p. 201)

This study showed that the lived reality of battling breast cancer prompted deep learning and change as the participants were forced to confront physical, mental, and emotional challenges that they perceived to be, at times, unbearable. The study also found that the approaches used to deal with these challenges led to and shaped the eventual transformative outcomes; e.g., a participant who focused on accepting the difficulties of life (rather than predetermining how life was supposed to be) eventually saw this focus become a habit she employed consistently in her life.

Not all breast cancer survivors emerge from the experience having worked through especially problematic issues in a way that benefits the rest of their lives; challenges do not always yield positive benefits. Nevertheless, the context is inherently transformative, and educators who focus on supporting learners specifically in these challenges, and scholars who focus on contexts and situations that are likely to cause such challenges, are taking an adaptive approach to implementing transformative learning.

Summary of Analytic Tools

Definition:

Transformative learning refers to processes that result in significant and irreversible changes in the way a person experiences, conceptualizes, and interacts with the world.

Criteria:

Depth, Breadth, Relative Stability.

Disorienting Index:

Acuteness, Seclusion, Origin, Familiarity, Affect, Setting, Place, Locus of Control.

Typology of Transformative Learning Outcomes:

Self, Worldview, Epistemology, Ontology, Behavior, Capacity.

Orientations towards Transformative Learning:

Prescriptive, Process-oriented, Adaptive.

Conclusion

As with all human sciences, the task for those who research and theorize about transformative change is to understand and convey truths that take the form of human meaning rather than physical form (Bateson, 1972/2000; Gadamer, 1975/2019). As Bateson explains: "The conservative laws for energy and matter concern substance rather than form. But mental processes, ideas, communication, organization, differentiation, pattern, and so on, are matters of form rather than substance" (1972/2000, p. xxxii), and the task of studying form involves ordering, patterning, classifying, and naming (pp. xxx–xxxi).

Further, the task of researching and theorizing form or meaning, especially as it relates to transformative change, has few conceptual tools that are not inextricably linked with a particular theory (e.g., Mezirow's meaning perspectives, Jung's model of the psyche, Kegan's orders of mind). These conceptual tools emanating from a particular theory assume a priori the underlying explanation behind a given instance of change. Theory-specific conceptual tools are not very helpful in situations where the learning phenomena do not align closely with those theoretical explanations. More important, clinging to vocabulary and concepts of a particular theoretical explanation makes it difficult to examine and discuss change across multiple disciplinary and theoretical orientations. As this book is intended to explore possibilities for understanding transformative change more broadly, the conceptual tools described in this chapter, from a metatheory perspective, are offered in hopes that they will be a useful starting point.

References

Bateson, G. (1972/2000). *Steps to an ecology of mind*. The University of Chicago Press.

Clark, C. M. (1993). Transformational learning. *New Directions for Adult and Continuing Education, 57*, 47–56.

Dirkx, J. M. (1998). Transformative learning theory in the practice of adult education: An overview. *PAACE Journal of Lifelong Learning, 7*, 1–14.

Ensign, T. G. (2019a). *The seed of transformation: A disorientation index* [Doctoral dissertation, Pepperdine University]. Digital Commons: https://digitalcommons.pepperdine.edu/cgi/viewcontent.cgi?article=2055&context=etd

Ensign, T. G. (2019b). Triggers of transformative learning in global leadership development: The Disorientation Index. In *Advances in Global Leadership* (Vol. 12, pp. 125–150). Emerald Publishing Limited. https://doi.org/10.1108/S1535-120320190000012008

Gadamer, H. G. (1975/2019). *Truth and method* (J. Weinsheimer & D. Marshall, Trans.). Bloomsbury Academic.

Gunnlaugson, O. (2008). Metatheoretical prospects for the field of transformative learning. *Journal of Transformative Education, 6*(2), 124–135.

Gutmann, A. (1987). *Democratic education.* Princeton University Press.

Hoggan, C. (2014). Lessons from breast cancer survivors: The interplay between context, epistemology and change. *Adult Education Quarterly, 64*(3), 191–205. https://doi.org/10.1177/0741713614523666

Hoggan, C. (2016). Transformative learning as a metatheory: Definition, criteria, and typology. *Adult Education Quarterly, 66*(1), 57–75. https://doi.org/10.1177/0741713615611216

Hoggan, C. (2016). A typology of transformation: Reviewing the transformative learning literature. *Studies in the Education of Adults, 48*(1), 65–82.

Hoggan, C. (2019). Foxes and hedgehogs: The value of transformation (and any other) theory. *Journal of Transformative Education, 17*(4), 295–298.

Hoggan, C., & Cranton, P. (2015). Promoting transformative learning through reading fiction. *Journal of Transformative Education, 13*(1), 6–25. https://doi.org/10.1177/1541344614561864

Hoggan, C., & Kloubert, T. (2020). Transformative learning in theory and practice. *Adult Education Quarterly, 70*(3), 295–307.

Kegan, R. (1994). *In over our heads: The mental demands of modern life.* Harvard University Press.

Mezirow, J. (1971). Toward a theory of practice. *Adult Education, 21*, 135–147.

Mezirow, J. (1978). *Education for perspective transformation: Women's re-entry programs in community colleges.* Columbia University.

Mezirow, J. (1989). Transformation theory and social action: A response to Collard and Law. *Adult Education Quarterly, 39*(3), 169–175.

Mezirow, J. (1991). *Transformative dimensions of adult learning.* Jossey-Bass.

Mezirow, J. (2009). Transformative learning theory. In J. Mezirow, E. W. Taylor & Associates (Eds.), *Transformative learning in practice: Insights from community, workplace, and higher education* (pp. 18–32). Jossey-Bass.

Newman, M. (2012). Calling transformative learning into question: Some mutinous thoughts. *Adult Education Quarterly, 62*, 36–55. https://doi.org/10.1177/0741713610392768

Schroeder, S., Currin, E., Washington, E., Curcio, R., & Lundgren, L. (2020). "Like, share, comment", and learn: Transformative learning in online anti-Trump resistance communities. *Adult Education Quarterly, 70*(2), 119–139. https://doi.org/10.1177/0741713619884270

Stanton, A., Bower, J. E., & Low, C. A. (2006). Posttraumatic growth after cancer. In L. G. Calhoun & R. G. Tedeschi (Eds.), *Handbook of posttraumatic growth: Research and practice* (pp. 138–175). Lawrence Erlbaum.

Taylor, E. W. (2008). Transformative learning theory. *New Directions for Adult and Continuing Education, 2008*(119), 5–15.

VALAMIS. (2020). *Transformative learning.* https://www.valamis.com/hub/transformative-learning

Wallace, W. (1992). Metatheory, conceptual standardization and the future of sociology. In G. Ritzer (Ed.), *Metatheorizing* (pp. 53–68). Sage.

Wallis, S. (2010). Toward a science of metatheory. *Integral Review: A Transdisciplinary and Transcultural Journal for New Thought, Research, and Praxis, 6*(3), 73–120.

CHAPTER 7

A Practice-Based View of Transformative Learning: An Exploratory Study on the Practical Creativity

Alessandra Romano, Francesca Bracci, and Victoria J. Marsick

THE ISSUE

This research analyzes transformative learning in relationship to workplace education, intertwining it with the theoretical frameworks of informal and incidental learning (Watkins & Marsick, 2020), and practice-based

---

Declaration of Conflicting Interests: The authors declared no potential conflicts of interest with respect to the research, authorship, and/or publication of this article.

A. Romano
Department of Social, Political and Cognitive Sciences, University of Siena, Siena, Italy
e-mail: alessandra.romano2@unisi.it

F. Bracci (✉)
Department of Education, Languages, Intercultures, Literatures and

© The Author(s), under exclusive license to Springer Nature Switzerland AG 2022
A. Nicolaides et al. (eds.), *The Palgrave Handbook of Learning for Transformation*, https://doi.org/10.1007/978-3-030-84694-7_7

109

studies (Gherardi, 2019). Our purpose is to examine the contribution that a practice-based view of transformative learning offers to the study of creativity (Bracci et al., 2021). We are interested in detecting how and under what conditions professionals in a wide-range of fields can learn and practice to design and realize innovative creative products. The ability to develop innovative products can be a source of competitive advantage for companies; the generation of ideas for new products, or creativity, is the first step in this innovation process (Thompson, 2018). In order to expand our understanding about how to cultivate practices of creativity, the strategic aspects we analyzed and valorized are the comprehension, identification, and development of learning and knowledge situated in material work practice.

The chapter is structured as follows: First, a comprehensive theoretical framework on transformative learning and practice-based studies is outlined. Second, the research design and methodology are described, followed by data analysis. Third, the emerging findings are presented. The chapter sums up with discussion and reflective conclusions.

Theoretical Frameworks

A Practice-Based View

The conceptual framework is nurtured by the growing breadth of eclectic contributions on transformative learning theory (Marsick & Watkins, 2018; Mezirow & Associates, 2000), hybridized with studies on creativity and practices within the field of adult education and workplace learning, including practice-based studies on community (Wenger et al., 2002), situated learning (Suchman, 2000), socio-materialism (Gherardi, 2019), and practical creativity as sociocultural participation (Glăveanu, 2011; Nohl, 2015; Sennett, 2008).

Psychology, University of Florence, Florence, Italy
e-mail: francesca.bracci@unifi.it

V. J. Marsick
Department of Organization & Leadership, Teachers College, Columbia University, New York, NY, USA
e-mail: marsick@tc.columbia.edu

Transformative learning is informed by how, and the level at which, we question, reflect upon, and converse about experiences in order to develop and grow (Eschenbacher & Fleming, 2020). Mezirow's perspective transformation highlights the necessity to create a critical awareness of how perspectives and guiding assumptions limit our ways of living, working, and being in the world (Eschenbacher & Fleming, 2020). Despite the accusation of being a primarily rational-based and individual-based theory of development, perspective transformation does not reinforce an exclusively individualistic approach to learning, as Mezirow himself put emphasis on "intersubjective learning through discourse" (Eschenbacher & Fleming, 2020, p. 5). Intersubjective learning refers to any learning process that happens between people who communicate and act in order to support or understand each other (ibid., p. 5).

Expanding this position, our focus is on the type of intersubjective, inter-corporeal, and inter-material learning that happens through and in practices (Nohl, 2015). Several voices including Tisdell (2012) and Taylor & Snyder (2012), Marsick and Neaman (2018) have emphasized the need to widen the approaches to transformative learning from a variety of practical perspectives. Our effort is to provide a practice-based view of transformative learning theory, paying specific attention to the inter-practices material domain in which people are pushed to question their familiar and prior assumptions and to experiment with new practical schemes of action (Nohl, 2015).

A practice-based view of transformative learning is distinctive in that it:

- emphasizes that behind all the apparently durable features of our world, from routine activities to formal organizations, there is some type of productive and reproductive work. This proposition transforms the way in which we conceive of social order and conceptualize the apparent stability of the social world (the nature of social structures—in sociological jargon, as a socio-material product);
- forces us to rethink the role of agents, materials, and structures (e.g., creative, the created, the designer, the artifacts, etc.);
- foregrounds the importance of the body and objects in workplace and social practices;
- highlights the nature of situated knowledge and practice-oriented discourse;

- reaffirms the centrality of personal interests and of the constructs of power and positionality in human and non-human relationships (Bracci et al., 2021; Nicolini, 2012).

A practice-based approach promotes a non-dualistic account of learners and context bound up in the dynamic unity of practice. Central are interactions with others, situated communication, the construction of situations, the relationship with the physical environment and the objects in it, and, above all, the principle that these elements are held together and express a logic of practice contextual to the situation (Gherardi, 2009; Sandberg & Tsoukas, 2011). Theories of practice locate the source of significant patterns in how conduct is enacted, performed, or produced (Gherardi, 2019). They offer a socio-material viewpoint in which agency is distributed between humans and non-humans and in which the entanglement among the social world, organizational routines, and materiality can be subjected to inquiry.

A practice-based lens offers viewpoints that are amenable to constructing a deeper interpretation of transformative learning theory. In practice-based accounts, participation in social practices is a key to understanding learning (Hodge, 2014). Transformative learning is portrayed as a process by which an adult discovers determinants of his/her/their/its thoughts, feelings, and actions that have been at work unconsciously. This discovery is made possible through the dysfunction of assumptions that have been shaping an individual's experience resulting in a disorienting dilemma. In the wake of this experience, the learner may engage in self-examination and critical reflection on assumptions, a path in which the person can come to realize the limitations of key assumptions and potentially revise them. The assimilation of initial meaning perspectives corresponds to an "inbound" trajectory of membership of a large-social and community practice (Hodge, 2014). In the same context, a disorienting dilemma, self-examination, and critical assessment of prior assumptions can be conceived as the "outbound" trajectory identified by a practice-based approach (Wenger, 1998). If we translate the practice-based approach to transformative learning, transforming meaning perspectives is not only a cognitive act of revision and change of meaning schemes, but also an act of transformation of tacit and implicit structures of thinking that is derived from the practices, and that conceptually returns to practices. Transformative learning thus can be seen as an intentional break with one community of practice along with socialization into the practices of a new community—which leads Hodge (2014) to assert that transformative learning functions as a way of engaging in inter-practice thinking.

A practice-based approach could represent one of the future strands of research for expanding transformative learning theory beyond the cognitive and rational positions. While the interconnected relationship of transformative learning theory, the arts, and expressive ways of knowing is an established realm of inquiry (Lawrence, 2014), few studies have focused on practice-based learning and its domain on practical creativity as a reflective process situated in material practices. A common misconception holds, that the best way to encourage people's creativity is simply to get out of the way and let them be creative. Although it's certainly true that individuals might be naturally curious and inquisitive, the fabrication of innovative and creative products is located in inter-material practices of learning, doing, reflecting, and transforming (Resnick, 2018). This process is not a "suddenly insightful" one-shot moment, but looks more like a transformational process within an iterative cycle of informal reflective learning (Nohl, 2015).

Against this backdrop, the next paragraphs draw insights from an interpretative case study on practice-based material creativity in order to depict new perspectives on transformative learning theory.

THE STUDY DESIGN

Drawing on key literature themes, we adopted an exploratory case study in, the interpretative tradition, involving 20 professionals expert in creativity practices. Table 7.1 synthesizes graphically the composition of the sample of 20 participants: their number, their ages, and professional roles. In order to de-identify participants, respondents are conventionally categorized as P1, P2, P3, etc.

The researchers chose an interpretive case study approach because of its advantages "in creating novel and profound insights and its focus on examining the rich social, cultural, material and political influences in an organisational context" (Naidoo, 2019, p. 259). The unit of analysis in our study is the individual respondent, e.g., a person who had an experience of relevance to the study (Myers, 2017).

The research questions were:

1. How do practices of creativity and innovation take shape?

114 A. ROMANO ET AL.

Table 7.1 Participant demographics

Professional role	Participants	Code number and age range
Creative directors	$n = 5$	**P1** = 37 years old; **P2** = 38 years old; **P3** = 40 years old; **P4** = 47 years old; **P5** = 55 years old
CEO of innovative enterprises in the media and tech field	$n = 4$	**P6** = 39 years old; **P7** = 42 years old **P8** = 54 years old; **P9** = 63 years old
Fashion graphic designers	$n = 2$	**P10** = 34 years old; **P11** = 38 years old
Human resource senior manager	$n = 2$	**P12** = 45 years old; **P13** = 48 years old
Career developer	$n = 2$	**P14** = 32 years old; **P15** = 40 years old
Social media specialist	$n = 5$	**P16** = 33 years old; **P17** = 39 years old; **P18** = 41 years old; **P19** = 43 years old; **P20** = 47 years old

Source Study data summarized by the authors

2. How and under what conditions do creative professionals produce objects, artifacts, and products that are considered innovative?
3. How can adult learners be supported in developing core competences required to think, create, and realize creative and innovative products?

We used a purposive sampling technique that included snowballing methods to recruit a heterogeneous group of practitioners in the field of creative professions and highly innovative service companies as participants in this study. We based the rationale for our material focus on creative practices on practice-based studies (Gherardi, 2019) indicating that the sociomaterial approach would allow us to focus on what people do in practice, not what on they say. We purposefully included a wide range of practitioners considered as "creative workers" with different ages/backgrounds/genders across a variety of organizations and companies that are considered "leaders" in producing innovative services and products. We expected this sampling methodology to afford us maximum opportunities for in-depth analysis of creative practices of practitioners from different backgrounds, ages, and workplaces, as well as having a variety of professional experiences (Gherardi, 2019).

Relevance to the research questions was prioritized in sampling rather than representativeness of the broader population of those engaging in creativity practices as the criterion for the selection of cases (Creswell, 2015). All participants were informed about the context and the object of the study. A semi-structured interview guideline (Rosenthal, 2004, pp. 48–53) was developed, in order to conduct guided in-depth interviews. One qualitative in-depth semi-structured interview was conducted with each of the 20 participants with probes intended to gain deep insights by allowing flexible answers and follow-up questions, while still ensuring comparability among the different actors. The interviewees were, initially, asked to freely give an account of their professional histories from the beginning to the present. Only thereafter did the interviewer pose questions to request that the interviewee narrate parts of his/her work in practice, drawing out detailed and rich descriptions of how to produce creative and innovative products.

The interviews lasted between 60 and 180 minutes depending on the communicativeness of the interviewees. Given the "narrative drives and constraints" that "propel the narrator to (a) go into details, (b) close the gestalt, and (c) assess the relevance and to condense" during his or her account (Schütze, 2014, p. 229), such in-depth semi-structured interviews have demonstrated a high validity as concerns the participant's professional practical experience (though not necessarily regarding historical facts).

The interviews were then transcribed and interpreted following the principles of the qualitative thematic analysis prescribed by Creswell (2015). In the first step, the content was summarized; the second step served to reconstruct the manner in which the interviewees tackled the topics of their professional experience, usually not explicated by themselves but implied as a means of sense-making while describing practices in their narrations. Hence, this second interpretative step focused on the material aspects of everyday practices, that is, on the tacit "orientations" within which problems were solved, innovative artifacts and products were produced, and on "*what can be innovative*" was perceived (Bohnsack, 2014, pp. 221–222).

Special attention was given to those among the 20 interviews where the professional orientations changed over time. Such a transformation of practice orientations reflects conceptually Mezirow's notion of a change of "meaning perspective" and underscores the tacit and practical aspects of "thought, feeling and will" (Mezirow, 1978, p. 105). Most important, the actors in fact may not even explicitly know that what they went through, essentially, was a transformative learning process or at least the beginning of one. As researchers, we reinterpreted the acts or changes described in their stories—ex post facto—as processes of transformation (Kroth & Cranton, 2014).

The reconstruction of implicit orientations was facilitated by comparing various professional accounts with one another to elucidate the specific ways in which, for example, material and collaborative practices were transformed, and the perspectives on innovation and creativity changed over time (Nohl, 2015). The focus was on practice domains in their workplaces that can be considered transformative because they challenge familiar and taken-for-granted trajectories, embedded in their work and in the way they work, draw out different ways of thinking, and thus help them to look at a situation from diverse perspectives (Hodge, 2014; Nohl, 2015). These comparative analyses among actors involved also helped identify common patterns across different professional narrations and different domains of practice involved. Most importantly, the core elements of these transformative practices were then captured in the emerging findings section.

Additional anecdotal data were gathered also through ethnographic observations carried out in three of the human resource managers' organizations, and via formal and informal discussions among researchers and involved practitioners. These anecdotal data were used to triangulate the sources of information and validate insights and categories emerging from the analysis of the interviews. The issue at stake was to define an approach able to make explicit and formalize the competence profiles of professionals whose expertise and commitment contributed to creating the excellence representing the distinctive hallmark of their organizations and companies. We explored the interrelationship between competence and practice, considering them as "mutually dependent constructs, constantly negotiated through practising" (Bjørkeng et al., 2009, p. 154). The proprietary know-how, guarded in professional practices and constantly renewed through practical creativity, is intended as a process establishing connections in action between the material and immaterial elements that constitute a practice so that they are bound together within a form (Sennett, 2008). We followed a narrative approach as the main entrance to practice-based transformation of perspectives, since our aim was to illustrate how ongoing "practicing creativity" rests on methods that enact changing realities. The scope was to furnish narratives of the processes through which creative products are constructed (Gherardi, 2019).

Emerging Findings. Creativity as a Performative, Ecologically Embedded, and Collaborative Practice

We discuss findings based on preliminary analysis. We limited the discussions of the findings only to categories that are relevant to the research questions as well as workplaces and education that prioritize creativity and innovation. We seek to offer insights for practitioners and adult educators as to what types of accompanying learning paths they might want to facilitate or construct to increase the performative potential of work practices. Findings also offer discernments of potential methodological repertories to embed in educational and training programs with the aim of cultivating practical creativity.

Creativity as a Socio-Material Practice

One of the first emerging outcomes was to frame creativity as situated and embedded practice, as well as the result of material collaboration and transfer of knowledge, models, and skills. This is quite novel if we consider that the strong contemporary belief is that creativity is the result of action or thinking by an individual considered a "genius." Through a practice-based lens, creativeness, instead, is seen not contained solely in the psyches of particular individuals, but also, in the objects, techniques, and materials that those individuals manipulate to produce ideas or objects that materialize creativity. When asked about how they produce an innovative product, participants pointed to the possibility of materially "doing" and "re-doing" things as well as the opportunity to collaborate with colleagues from other sectors.

The unit of inquiry, then, encompasses the analysis of these performative acts in terms of main actors, learning processes within the entire realm of material practices through which a creative product finds its shape. "When I make things, I don't know when my body ends and material starts, or when material ends and my body starts. They are one thing" (creative director, 37 years old). Each product is created within a vast nexus of material practices, also referred to as knots, networks, sites, configurations, bricolage, assemblages, and prototypes (Gherardi, 2019). "Every piece is a collective undertaking, and a plethora of people have contributed" (graphic designer, 41 years old). The activity of "creative design and fabricating" is one of the most illustrative forms of admixed both cultural and social participation: it entails engaging with extant cultural and material artifacts to produce new material artifacts, employing culture to generate new and unexpected ways to use materials, ideas, media, stuff, and technologies (Gherardi, 2019; Resnick, 2018). We can assume the term "creating-in-practice" to move away from the mental and individual image of creativity to consider it as an enactment. To convey a preliminary idea of how creative practice is here analyzed as creating-in-practice, we may say that creativity can be seen and analyzed as an activity, rather than as a mental skill; it emerges from the context of its production and is anchored by/in material supports in that context. We may also say that creativity is both an individual and collective activity; that it is an activity situated in working practices of people who try to convey in practice a potential idea; and that, therefore, practical creativity is contextual as opposed to being decontextualized and mental.

Another key-concept emerging is the formativeness and re-formativeness that denotes the process by which objects, products, artistic work acquire from within a practice. Form-and-reformativeness also qualifies a specific learning process realized through a doing that, while it does, reinvents "the way of doing."

> How does practical creativity work? How do we give rise to the form of artistic products? Well, there's no one answer. Forming and creating requires a relationship with materiality. It is not a mere ideational process that you can carry out in front of the screen of your computer. Creating means forming a material, a product, in example a prototype. Creativity is the process whereby artistic and innovative products take form and become realized: is not in the idea before doing, is both the work practices that bring to the birth those products and the accomplished pieces that those products assume in the process of creation—creative director, age 47.

As the creative director expresses below, it is not a matter of sudden and brilliant inspiration, but rather of following a series of suggestions that arise from the formative activity itself and prompt the mixing of characteristics that make the product so unique. It is more an experiment with materiality and learning that occurs in this situation:

I had to do some work for the Academy, I wanted to take something, for decoration, I wanted to make a project and I needed something transparent but solid ... So, I tried out some things for this project and then I looked for some transparent varnishes, and resin was ok. I don't remember when and how... but I made this block of resin. I had to create some movement in this block, and I began to do some tests, fine, fine... and then I searched for a different resin, here and there, I experimented a bit, then I found these special resins used for flooring, among other things. You try things, you experiment, you get information... nobody teaches you how to use resin for a show or which resin is sensitive to damp, and so on... you try them out. We create a lot of things, very different things, in the sense that we don't repeat things in series, we make things felt in gut, we make them feeling, touching, experimenting, tasting the material and its potential—fashion graphic designer, age 38.

This material approach to creativity does not at all neatly separate learning from doing (they are typically described as coincident), knowing from creating, and, as the responses of our participants pointed out, creating-in-practice contains at the same time the creation and the acquisition of knowledge, and the enactment of this creative learning.

Socio-Material Approach, Creativity, and Transformative Learning

What can this socio-material approach add to transformative learning theory? Creative practice is a socio-material learning process because: (a) the set of skills and types of knowledge that practitioners possess are developed through iterative cycles of imagination, inquiry, experimentation, testing, and validation; (b) this iterative cycle is carried out in collaborative practices; and (c) creativity exists only in relation to an established ensemble of cultural norms, material practices, and products that nourish the iterative learning process and integrate its "outcomes." Material creation, in this way, is seen,

> as a collaborative process of working with a shared object and growing through the process. To solve complex and unforeseen problems, at the edge of our competence, we have to create, extend, play and build shared products and services—career developer, 40 years old.

The situated collaborative practices described by participants diverge from other routine social practices in that they usually take place in the fluid settings designed for the furtherance of innovation and knowledge. Rather than merely relying on mundane habits or repeated meaning schemes (that may be also needed some days), such practices are aimed at solving emergent undefined problems, creating, testing, and validating new schemes of action, and constantly pursuing novelty and innovation.

> That there's no one way to do creative things, because I believe that it is not through a prescriptive and routinized path that one can learn how to produce high-quality and innovative services"—graphic designer, 41 years old.

Colleagues can play a crucial role in fostering, encouraging, guiding, and supporting creative learning:

> There is a constant interplay between making new things in the world and making new ideas in your head. As you make new things, and get feedback from others (and from yourself), you can revise, modify, and improve your ideas. And based on these new ideas, you are inspired to make new things—social media specialist, age 39.

The process goes on and on, with making and learning reinforcing one another in a never-ending spiral (Resnick, 2018).

> Creativity does not mean being struck by a divine lightning bolt. It means to have a clear objective, to test a project, to have motivation to be open to feedback from other viewpoints, to cultivate passion. Creativity draws out from a very specific hard work, which combines curiosity-driven exploration, with playful experimenting and systematic inquiry. It is a typical distortion of the belief that innovative ideas come up as stunning insights, but actually they are the outcomes of an iterative cycle of imagination, vision, designing, testing, collaboration and reflection upon all the process —social media specialist, age 39.

This last point deserves particular attention since it postulates more than an interconnection—we would use the expression of "entanglement"—among creativity, culture, practice (Gherardi, 2019). Practice is vital for the existence of creativity and creativity is vital for culture transformation and practices development.

Figure 7.1 synthesizes a framework for creativity as a socio-material-practical learning process that brings together "self" and "others"—peers, practitioners, possible target of clients—the "existing" and the "new," the "culture" and the "practices," and captures the intricate entanglement of all of them in the form of creative activity.

Several important aspects of the creative process are illustrated in Fig. 7.1 that identifies creativity as a situated-practical-learning process:

1. creative acts are simultaneously forms of externalization of prior culturally assumed schemes and of material expression;
2. "creation" is always an emerging performance, integrated in pre-existing cultural ensembles but capable of bringing about new possibilities which professionals are required to re-view in order to re-create both *within,* and *coherently with,* the new framing that emerges;

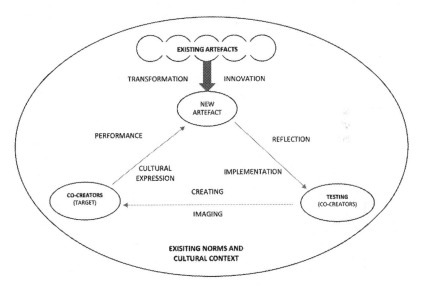

Fig. 7.1 Creativity as a performative socio-situated practice (*Source* Personal Elaboration of the Authors, inspired by Glăveanu [2011])

3. creators and professionals collaborate in multiple and dynamic ways in the creation of the creative product, in testing it, and in reflecting *on* and *upon* the process.

> When you make something in the world, it becomes an external representation of ideas in your head. It enables you to play with your ideas and to gain a better understanding of the possibilities and limitations of your ideas. Why didn't it work the way I expected? I wonder what would happen if I changed this piece of it?—CEO, 42 years old.

This perspective enriches our understanding of what is called here "externalization" of prior culturally assumed schemes that are more dialectic and intertwined in creative thinking, acting, reflecting (Glăveanu, 2011).

> Creation never spurs from nowhere, with no roots and no help from others. If I have to design a bag, I need to talk with the artisans that will fabricate the bag, with the material responsible for understanding what materials or leather will fit with my idea, I need as a minimum some dialogue and exchange—CEO, 39 years old.

Key to our discovery is that collaborative practices in workplaces catalyze divergent thinking, creativity, and potential for situated transformations. By giving an external shared form and shape to their ideas, professionals also provide opportunities for other people to play with their projects and give suggestions based on them. The dual process of performing creativity, and of being recognized as so doing, is thus an ongoing negotiation between the creative practitioner, perceived as performer, and their peers, acting as target and co-creators (both internal and external) (Hjorth et al., 2018). Such creative "entre-relating" succeeds when:

> the audience of the innovative products perceive an organization, its processes, players and products, able to fully enact their values, preferences, and practices—CEO, 39 years old.
>
> If you need to produce a bag, or if you are asked to design a service or a product, you need to pose yourself questions as: How can I make it more useful for more people? Who will use this bag? What are their needs?—fashion graphic designer, 38 years old.

IMPLICATIONS FOR AN EDUCATION TO CREATIVE AND CRITICAL THINKING

The entanglement among creativity, practice, learning, and culture proposed in the present chapter has several important methodological implications. We desire to outline here only one of the major contributions—innovative ways of researching and fostering creative and critical thinking in education.

It is widely accepted that at the heart of any long-term strategy to prepare people for the jobs they will want to occupy in the future, we need to have a much more intentional approach to supporting creative learning and antidisciplinary research throughout our education systems (Schmidt et al., 2016, p. 155).[1] The limited capabilities of educational institutions and traditional teaching methods to adequately prepare new generations for the uncertainties and potentialities of a rapidly changing working life are widely recognized.

How can we help such students as they move through university and beyond, continue to learn in the kind of professional activities that are informed by a practice-based approach, so that they are supported in becoming creative thinkers? A possible enacted response to this challenge is to provide students with problem-based methods and high complexity scenarios. To solve ambiguous and partially unforeseen problems at the edge of their creative competences, where students have to fabricate, extend, test, and build shared artifacts, which translate in practice their evolving knowledge, understanding, imagination, and reflection (Lehtinen et al., 2014). The key challenge is not how to "teach creativity" to future professionals, but rather how to create a fertile environment in which their learning and creativity can take root, grow, and flourish. A practice-collaborative informed approach to the education of creativity operates with a different set of assumptions and tools than those commonly used in education today. It encourages active engagement with cultural resources, the exercise of joint activity in the production of new

---

[1] Antidisciplinary research is a construct proposed to define working in spaces that simply do not fit into any existing academic discipline—a specific field of study with its own particular words, frameworks, and methods" in order to engage people "interested in disruptive ideas, the people who can see future sooner than others (Ito, 2016). In this chapter, we use the expression "antidisciplinary research" to refer to the cross-disciplinary and trans-disciplinary approach devoted to the cultivation of future creative and innovative professionals.

artifacts, and collective-ideas-sharing with small but incremental changes as well as the modelling through an iterative cycle of practicing, testing, reflecting, and communicating.

We assume that working in high uncertainty contexts, with the need for bringing innovation in content, processes, and materials, in some ways had to force our interviewees to cope with ambiguity as central to their job—"identifying the common in the contradictory, tolerating the anxiety implicit in paradox, searching for synthesis and reframing" (Mezirow et al., 2012, p. 80, in Eschenbacher & Fleming, 2020, p. 5). Those elements could have challenged their habitual automatic unconscious mechanisms of self-actualization, and motivate them to go beyond their comfort zone.

The proposal to create a shared repertoire of practices that foster innovation-creating processes can represent a useful resource, both for leveraging past experience and for creating new knowledge—assuming that it is used as a process that is constantly managed, updated, renewed, and extended. Such a repertoire cannot be considered or used as a set of decontextualized teaching techniques or strategies to be applied arbitrarily without an appreciation for their deep connection to the larger theoretical frameworks of transformative learning and to the purposes of teaching for change (Taylor & Cranton, 2012). Understood in the latter context, however, it can offer suggestions and methodological trajectories to assist future practitioners (and researchers) in carrying out coordinated inquiries, cross-fertilizing their knowledge, and hybridizing across multiple domains of knowledge (Lehtinen et al., 2014). In broad overview, innovation-creating processes may involve deliberate efforts toward spanning boundaries of prevailing prior knowledge by creating novel often far-reaching networking linkages to experts, organizations, and communities representing heterogeneous domains of knowledge, competences, and experiences.

CONCLUSIONS

The influence of practice-based studies (Wenger et al., 2002) on creativity studies in the workplace requires going beyond the present conventional research differentiation of the individual from the collective in examining learning processes and embracing an integrative sociomaterialistic approach. Within those frameworks, workplace learning is understood to involve not just human change but interconnections of humans and their actions with rules, tools and texts, as well as cultural, and material environments. Such interactions are often embodied, not even involving conscious cognitive activity while, at the same time, they are also embedded in everyday practices, actions, and conversations (Fenwick, 2008).

The practice-based view of transformative learning theory that we have partially captured through our study may shed light on the argument that entails augmenting the possible construing of meaning perspectives to include representations of the often tacit understandings that structure social practices and the process of meaning perspective transformation, itself, as a movement from one social practice into another, or of spanning different social and community practices to produce creative thinking (Hodge, 2014). It prompts investigating the methodological implications of this depiction of the learning process as situated in the system of ongoing practices in ways that are relational, mediated by artifacts, and always rooted in a context of interaction. To sum up, this perspective has four main features:

a. It is oriented toward processes, or what people do in action;
b. It involves an interest in the social aspects of learning, placing processes of knowing and creating not solely in the mind of the individual but also in the emerging entanglement of social practices and relationships with other individuals;
c. It acknowledges that the collaborative practices leverage what individuals bring to this entanglement as they co-create in social practices;
d. It sees knowledge as situated in a spatio-temporal context, anchored in materiality, mediated by what has happened in the past and has been learned from experience but also by the contact with other systems of practices capable to break the attachment to this consolidated knowledge, to open views of things from a different perspective that enables a new framing/re-framing of the situations.

The discussion articulated herein has for sure some limits. The empirical investigation at hand, albeit being based on interviews with actors of different genders, educational backgrounds, and ages who are engaged in various topical terrains, nevertheless works with a snowball-determined sample that implicitly cannot exclude bias. Nor, having been aggregated from a population rather homogenous in many ways, can the sample typology, although covering positionalities such as age, gender, and education, be considered representative of the many populations with different life experiences, e.g., as ethnic minorities (Johnson-Bailey, 2012), or from other societies (Taylor & Snyder, 2012, pp. 42–44). Future research needs to explore whether and how creativity could be supported in training activities in formal contexts. Moreover, the field of study in practice-based approach to transformative learning, undoubtedly in the early stages of an ongoing performance, surely contains vastly more questions still unexplored than answers: How and under what conditions, for example, might it be possible to deliberate critical reflection in collaborative practices? How do transformational processes actually occur? What role, if any, have prior consolidated assumptions on transformational practices in confining our thinking? Those are only few of the open-ended questions that need to be investigated in the future.

Despite, or precisely because of these limitations, the hope is that the empirical results discussed inspire further empirical research and new theoretical reflections on transformative learning, by drawing out complementarities between transformative theory and a practice-based approach.

References

Bjørkeng, K., Clegg, S., & Pitsis, T. (2009). Becoming (a) practice. *Management Learning, 40*(2), 145–159.

Bohnsack, R. (2014). Documentary method. In U. Flick (Ed.), *SAGE handbook of analyzing qualitative data* (pp. 217–223). Thousand Oaks, CA: Sage.

Bracci, F., Romano, A., Marsick, V. J., & Melacarne, C. (2021). Toward a shared repertoire of methods and practices of fostering transformative learning: initial reflections. *Nuova Secondaria Ricerca, 1,* 286–306.

Creswell, J. (2015). *Educational research: Planning, conducting, and evaluating quantitative and qualitative research.* Pearson.

Eschenbacher, S., & Fleming, T. (2020). Transformative dimensions of lifelong learning: Mezirow, Rorty and COVID-19. *International Review of Education, 25,* 1–16. https://doi.org/10.1007/s11159-020-09859-6. Epub ahead of print. PMID: 33012842; PMCID: PMC7517743.

Fenwick, T. (2008). Workplace learning: Emerging trends and new perspectives. *New Directions for Adult and Continuing Education, 119,* 17–26.

Gherardi, S. (2009). Introduction: The critical power of the 'practice lens.' *Management Learning, 40*(2), 115–128. https://doi.org/10.1177/135050 7608101225

Gherardi, S. (2019). *How to conduct a practice-based study. Problems and methods* (2nd ed.). Edward Elgar Publishing.

Glăveanu, V. P. (2011). Creativity as cultural participation. *Journal for the Theory of Social Behaviour, 41*(1), 48–67.

Hjorth, D., Strati, A., Drakopoulou Dodd, S., & Weik, E. (2018). Organizational creativity, play and entrepreneurship: Introduction and framing. *Organization Studies, 39*(2–3), 155–168. https://doi.org/10.1177/0170840617752748

Hodge, S. (2014). Transformative learning as an "inter-practice" phenomenon. *Adult Education Quarterly, 64*, 165–181.

Ito, J. (2016). Design and science. *Journal of Design and Science.* https://doi.org/10.21428/f4c68887

Johnson-Bailey, J. (2012). Positionality and transformative learning. In E. W. Taylor & P. Cranton (Eds.), *The handbook of transformative learning* (pp. 260–273). Jossey-Bass.

Kroth, M., & Cranton, P. (2014). *Stories of transformative learning.* Springer.

Lawrence, R. L. (2014). Artful learning: Holistic curriculum development for mind, body, heart and spirit. In V. C. Wang, & V. C. Bryan (Eds.), *Andragogical and pedagogical methods for curriculum and program development* (pp. 299–322). Hershey, PA: IGI Global.

Lehtinen, E., Hakkarainen, K., & Palonen, T. (2014). Understanding learning for the professions: How theories of learning explain coping with rapid change. In S. Billett, C. Harteis, & H. Grubern (Eds.), *International handbook of research in professional practice-based learning* (pp. 199–224). Springer.

Marsick, V. J., & Neaman, A. (2018). Adult informal learning. In N. Kahnwald & V. Täubig (Eds.), *Informelles Lernen* (pp. 53–72). Springer.

Marsick, V. J., & Watkins, K. E. (2018). An update on informal and incidental learning theory. In E. Scully-Russ, A. Nicolaides, V. J. Marsick, & K. E. Watkins (Eds.), *Update on informal and incidental learning theory* (pp. 9–12). New Directions in Adult and Continuing Education, No. 159, Wiley, pp. 9–20.

Mezirow, J. (1978). Perspective transformation. *Adult Education Quarterly, 28*, 100–110.

Mezirow, J., & Associates. (2000). *Learning as transformation: Critical perspective on a theory in progress.* Jossey-Bass.

Mezirow, J., Taylor, E., & Associates. (2012). *Transformative learning in practice: Insights from community, workplace, and higher education.* Jossey-Bass.

Myers, M. D. (2017). Coming of age: Interpretive research in information systems: An overview. *Journal of Information Technology, 13*(4), 233–234.

Naidoo, R. (2019). Guidelines for designing an interpretive case study for business and management doctoral students. In A. Stacey (Ed.), *18th European Conference on research methodology for business and management studies* (pp. 256–263). Wits Business School Johannesburg.

Nicolini, D. (2012). *Practice theory, work, and organization: An introduction.* Oxford University Press.

Nohl, A.-M. (2015). Typical phases of transformative learning: A practice-based model. *Adult Education Quarterly, 65*(1), 35–49. https://doi.org/10.1177/0741713614558582

Resnick, M. (2018). *Come i bambini. Immagina, crea, gioca e condividi. Coltivare la creatività con il Lifelong Kindergarten del MIT.* Trento: Erickson.

Rosenthal, G. (2004). Biographical research. In C. Seale, G. Gobo, J. F. Gubrium, & D. Silverman (Eds.), *Qualitative research practice* (pp. 48–64). Sage. https://nbn-resolving.org/urn:nbn:de:0168-ssoar-56725

Sandberg, J., & Tsoukas, H. (2011). Grasping the logic of practice: Theorizing through practical rationality. *Academy of Management Review, 36*, 338–360.

Schmidt, J. P., Resnick, M., & Ito, J. (2016). Creative learning and the future of work. In D. Nordfors, V. Cerf, & M. Senges (Eds.), *Disrupting unemployment. Reflection on a sustainable, middle class economic recovery* (pp. 147–155). Ewing Marion Kauffman Foundation.

Schütze, F. (2014). Autobiographical accounts of war experiences: An outline for the analysis of topically focused autobiographical texts. *Qualitative Sociology Review, 10*, 224–283. http://www.qualitativesociologyreview.org/ENG/arc hive_eng.php

Sennett, R. (2008). *The craftsman.* Yale University Press.

Suchman, L. (2000). Embodied practices of engineering work. *Mind, Culture, and Activity, 7*(1–2), 4–18.

Taylor, E., & Cranton, P. (Eds.). (2012). *The handbook of transformative learning: Theory, research, and practice.* Jossey-Bass.

Taylor, E. W., & Snyder, M. J. (2012). A critical review of research on transformative learning theory, 2006–2010. In E. W. Taylor & P. Cranton (Eds.), *Handbook of transformative learning theory* (pp. 37–54). San Francisco, CA: Jossey-Bass.

Thompson, N. (2018). Imagination and creativity in organizations. *Organization Studies, 39*, 229–250.

Tisdell, E. (2012). Themes and variations in transformative learning: Interdisciplinary perspectives on forms that transform. In E. Taylor & P. Cranton (Eds.), *A handbook of transformative learning.* Jossey-Bass.

Watkins, K. E., & Marsick, V. J. (2020). Informal and incidental learning in the time of Covid-19. *Advances in Developing Human Resources, 23*, 88–96.

Wenger, E. (1998). *Communities of practice. Learning, meaning and identity.* Cambridge University Press.

Wenger, E., McDermott, R. A., & Snyder, W. (2002). *Cultivating communities of practice: A guide to managing knowledge.* Harvard Business Press.

CHAPTER 8

One of the Doors: Exploring Contemplative Practices for Transformative Sustainability Education

Heather Burns, Nora Stoelting, Julie Wilcox, and Chantal Krystiniak

INTRODUCTION (HEATHER)

I am sitting in a circle with 9 graduate students, surrounded by elder fir trees, sipping tea made from plants recently harvested in this forest; cedar tips, thimbleberry leaves, oxalis. The autumn light is filtering down to the

---

From a line in the Mary Oliver (2012) poem Today: "Stillness. One of the doors into the temple."

H. Burns (✉)
Leadership for Sustainability Education, Portland State University, Portland, OR, USA
e-mail: hburns@pdx.edu

N. Stoelting · J. Wilcox · C. Krystiniak
College of Education, Portland State University, Portland, OR, USA

© The Author(s), under exclusive license to Springer Nature Switzerland AG 2022
A. Nicolaides et al. (eds.), *The Palgrave Handbook of Learning for Transformation*, https://doi.org/10.1007/978-3-030-84694-7_8

lush forest floor where we are sitting quietly with sword ferns, Oregon grape, and vanilla leaf. Nuthatches are calling to one another and water from a nearby creek is chortling a soft song. As the forest therapy guide and instructor of this forest therapy graduate course, I am facilitating our closing "tea ceremony" in which we share our reflections after a few hours of forest bathing, a practice of intentionally engaging in mindful and sensual invitations in the forest. These invitations have included tuning in to our senses of hearing, smelling, tasting, and feeling, walking mindfully and slowly through the forest, having conversations with trees, making artistic offerings of found objects, beholding plants, and finding "sit spots" (Clifford, 2018). This forest therapy course is an exercise in transformative sustainability education (TSE), seeking to engage learners in (their often buried) relationship with the living earth and each other in meaningful and embodied ways. This experiential course provides an opportunity for learners to mindfully explore who they are within a web of relationships with the more than human world, and in doing so to expand their felt understanding of what it means to be engaged in healing and transformative work. My students are in graduate school, preparing to be sustainability educators and leaders. This is to say they are learning to be transformative educators who engage in collaborative leadership for change, systemic justice, and holistic ways of being and doing. Leadership for Sustainability Education (LSE) alum are innovative educators and leaders who are creating systemic and sustainable change in organizations such as non-profits, local governments, school systems, higher education, and businesses. In their learning and preparation process, they need real embodied experiences that foster transformative sustainability learning. As we sit and sip tea together, we co-create meaning from our forest experience. We talk about what it means to hold space for connection, presence, and compassion. We listen to each other mindfully and from our hearts. We offer back to the living earth our gratitude and appreciation in reciprocation of our learning.

Forest therapy is one of many contemplative practices that we engage with in the LSE graduate program at Portland State University in Portland, Oregon. In grappling with what it means to participate in the systemic, holistic, transformative sustainability learning that our world so desperately needs, we have come to understand that our teaching and learning must move away from dominant frameworks of learning and embody the kinds of changes we are hoping to create. In the

LSE program we have been exploring TSE, or ways to bring a relational, holistic, emergent, and transformative approach to sustainability education.

TSE draws from and forms a productive edge with both the field of transformative learning and sustainability education, expanding both with new onto-epistemological perspectives that offer transformative and regenerative opportunities. In doing so TSE invites us to stretch into new learning spaces of healing, reconnection, and sustainable change, what Eisenstein (2013) calls "the space between, and birth into the new." Yet, despite these opportunities, the theory of TSE is somewhat new and as Lange (2018) notes, "has not yet been explicitly theorized." As such, this chapter first seeks to further theorize and explain TSE, drawing on recent work at this theoretical edge. We then discuss contemplative pedagogies and how these can support TSE. Finally, the co-authors and I highlight several contemplative pedagogies that are present in the LSE graduate program and share personal stories that link these pedagogies to TSE.

Transformative Sustainability Education

While still a theory in development, TSE emerges with and from other strands of transformative learning theory, such as that attributed to O'Sullivan which combines ecology, spirituality, and sustainability while touching on the integration of cognition, consciousness studies, critique, and creativity (Tisdell, 2012). As a theory TSE moves beyond the modernist lens within which much of transformative learning theory is located, bringing together strands of knowledge from quantum physics, indigenous knowledge, and living systems theory to understand transformation as a nonlinear relational practice of unlearning, healing, and reconnecting (Burns, 2018; Lange, 2018; O'Neil, 2018; Selby & Kagawa, 2018; Williams, 2018).

Rooted in quantum science and an ecological worldview, TSE is centered in a relational ontology, or a way of being and knowing in which everything/one is related and interconnected (Lange, 2018). TSE is essentially an ontological change in how humans and the world relate (O'Neil, 2018). This ontological shift involves a (perhaps disorienting) unlearning of a dominant worldview that is unsustainable and no longer tenable. TSE acknowledges and dismantles the modernist mechanistic worldview that fuels the current global spiral of ecological and cultural destruction. This dominant ontology is rooted in separation; modernist assumptions of a dualistic, linear, mechanistic, individualistic reality in which predictability, and control and separation are paramount. We are separated mind from body and spirit. We are individuals separated from other humans. We are separated from what we are learning. We are separated from the living earth and from the natural processes and flows of energy that sustain all life.

TSE shifts beyond the dominant paradigm of learning that is situated in Cartesian science and these modernist assumptions. The relational learning process of unlearning, healing, and reconnecting includes cultivating both holistic awareness and engagement. To unlearn we observe and become aware of the dominant paradigm, how it shapes our world, and how we have been conditioned to believe in and participate in destructive dominant systems of separation and oppression such as corporate capitalism, patriarchy, and white supremacy. At the same time, we engage in holistic and relational learning processes that honor our emotions, our spirits, and our bodily senses, and re-awaken our relationships with each other and the earth.

In this way TSE is learning *as* sustainability. Learning *as* sustainability is a shift toward learning as change; a dynamic, emergent, and transformative process (Sterling, 2002). We change how we learn and as we learn we change. TSE is a relational way of knowing and learning that acknowledges our entanglement with the living earth as related reciprocal beings, and embraces reality as nonlinear, emergent, and constantly changing (Burns, 2018). Within this ontology, consciousness, agency, and intelligence is the nature of all beings, not just human beings. This is also an Indigenous Life-World perspective, in which all beings "are embedded in a unifying energy of consciousness with the potential to attune with every other life form in the universe. Society is constituted not just by human to human relationships, but from the … interrelations between humans, other animals, plant, mineral and spirit worlds" (Williams, 2018). This understanding of learning as relational and interconnected is healing and restorative.

In a world where everything is embedded in everything else and in which flow, movement, and process are the norm, knowledge is provisional and uncertain (Selby, 2002). TSE embraces the constancy of change, honors disequilibrium, and validates subjectivity as an essential source of knowledge, since the learner and what is being learned both change as they interact. TSE is therefore a highly relational, dynamic, and fractal learning process, in which there are ways of knowing and learning

8 ONE OF THE DOORS: EXPLORING CONTEMPLATIVE PRACTICES ...   133

that are not limited to an autonomous human brain (Lange, 2018). Since relationship is all there is to reality (Wheatley, 2006), sustainability learning takes place within a network of relationships, within a contextual experience. Learning that is rooted in relationship and quantum interconnection is an empathetic, embodied, spiritual, and slow process (Selby, 2002) that reconnects us to our intuitions, bodies, and to the places where we eat, breathe, move, and work. This kind of learning provides opportunities for increased awareness and attunement to the rhythms of the earth body and the deep oneness and interconnectedness that we are all part of.

In a world full of injustice and disconnection, TSE supports a transformative learning process of unlearning dominant paradigms and embracing reciprocal and interconnected ways of knowing and being. In doing so, TSE brings healing and re-connection to the relationships between humans and the rest of the living world (Lange, 2018), transforming our ways of knowing and being. TSE is thus a relational healing process of dynamic change or learning *as* sustainability in which we are unlearning our unsustainability and reconnecting to our entanglement with the living world (O'Neil, 2018; Selby & Kagawa, 2018). TSE offers transformative potential by both challenging unsustainable worldviews and systems and by offering new paradigms and pathways for living and being. TSE is thus a powerful theory and practice as we seek to create more just, holistic, and sustainable ecosystems and communities.

Heather's Story of Engagement with Transformative Learning

My own process in becoming a transformative sustainability educator has emerged from my specific lived experience as a learner, teacher, and scholar. Offering insights into this process may serve to contextualize TSE in a more personal way. I initially encountered transformative learning theory through a modernist lens, with its underlying assumptions of autonomous individualism, and change as a linear process of personal improvement, growth, and empowerment (Mezirow, 1991). Attracted to this potential for making change, I embraced transformative learning theory early in my career as an educator. I have since been engaged in exploring various aspects of transformative learning theory that in my own teaching practice have greatly expanded and braided together over the years. For example, because of my transformative learning experience as a college student studying in Central America in the early 90s, I have

134　H. BURNS ET AL.

sought to facilitate identity and worldview shifts by creating disorienting dilemmas for students through experiential community-based learning activities and travel experiences (Cranton, 2002; Kolb, 1984). Because of my experience of growing up in a conservative patriarchal community and through my study of feminism, feminist pedagogy, globalization, and neoliberalism, I have emphasized systems of oppression and emancipatory pedagogy in my teaching (Freire, 1970/2000). Because of my experimentation with art therapy, the study of dreams, training as a reiki practitioner, and experience as a meditator and yogi, I have explored the use of art, image, symbol, movement, and other emotional and extra-rational perception as a way to awaken learners to their own transformative potential and relationship with a connected consciousness (Dirkx, 1998). My own connection to the earth through wilderness experiences, development of an ecological and spiritual identity, training as a forest therapist, practice of permaculture and ecological design, and study of quantum science and deep ecology have led me to emphasize relationships, spirituality, and interbeing in my sustainability teaching (Capra, 2002; Lange, 2012; O'Sullivan, 2008). In my practice as a transformative sustainability educator I continue to weave together all of these strands of transformative learning, rooting these practices in a critique of dominant systems and a relational ontology in which deep interconnection and interbeing are central to learning and change. In this process, I have often turned to contemplative pedagogies to explore *how* to more effectively integrate a holistic and relational approach to TSE.

CONTEMPLATIVE PEDAGOGIES

Contemplative practice is characterized by grounded presence, openness, holding space for silence, presence, and awareness (Barbezat & Bush, 2014). These practices often provide a respite or antidote to the fragmentation, alienation, superficiality, and fast pace of modern life (Eaton et al., 2017). These modern challenges are very present in systems of higher education, and perhaps even more so when learning is focused on complex and sticky issues of unsustainability such as systemic racism, globalization, and climate change. Suffering related to social and ecological injustice has increasingly become part of the classroom experience (Berila, 2016). Contemplative practices and pedagogies can thus support learners and educators as we face the overwhelming emotions that come with increased awareness of complex and intense sustainability issues in our world (Eaton et al., 2017). Contemplative pedagogies support the development of insight, creativity, concentration, and deep inquiry and have a variety of objectives including building focus and mental stability, deepening learning, connecting to others, developing personal meaning, and caring for the soul (Barbezat & Bush, 2014; Berila, 2016). All of these objectives can support sustainability learning and in particular transformative sustainability learning in which learners deepen their knowledge and understanding from a relational perspective.

Contemplative pedagogies include elements of introspection and reflection that allow learners to develop self-awareness and emotional regulation and to engage in what they are learning in a personal way (Eaton et al., 2017; Neff, 2011). Mindfulness, the process of becoming more self-aware, is a primary catalyst for transformation (Berila, 2016). Contemplative pedagogies, rooted in what bell hooks refers to as "engaged pedagogy," also emphasize well-being and welcome various ways of knowing and learning including somatic, affective, and ethical dimensions (Berila, 2016; Eaton et al., 2017). In particular, somatic or physical ways of knowing such as learning through the senses, trusting intuition, and deep awareness of the body are not often included in academic settings that typically privilege the mind and in doing so perpetuate a destructive dualistic approach to mind and body. Learning through and with the body opens our connection to learning relationally and with our emotions (Pyles & Adam, 2016). Learning to cultivate compassion, wonder, gratitude, and love are all important elements of learning in a context in which bad news is the norm, and despair, hopelessness, and grief are very present (Eaton et al., 2017). Learning to hold difficult emotions related to unlearning dominant systems, while also cultivating resiliency, supports holistic and transformative sustainability learning. Intentionally cultivating learning through the body, emotions, or spirit can support relational learning as we connect to our own consciousness, to other humans we are learning with, and to the more than human beings and the living earth.

Contemplative practices can take a variety of forms including relational practices such as deep listening, storytelling, council circles, music, and dialogue. These practices can also take the form of movement such as walking meditation, yoga, and Qigong, or stillness such as guided meditation, silence, and self-compassion. The tree of contemplative practices provides a visual summary of these and many other contemplative practices including ritual, activist, generative, and creative practices that can support holistic teaching and learning (CMind, 2014) (see Fig. 8.1).

Contemplative practices can support transformative sustainability learning by providing space for the disorientation of unlearning. Simultaneously, contemplative practices create space for relational learning that honors the physical, emotional, spiritual, and intellectual selves. When engaging in contemplative practices together, within a learning community, we deepen our capacity to show up in ways that are focused,

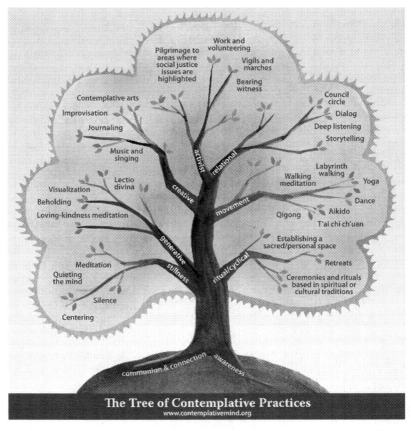

Fig. 8.1 The tree of contemplative practices

attentive, critical, creative, and compassionate. Practicing contemplative practices together also allows opportunities for co-developing insight through shared experience, deepening and co-creating learning that is soulful and meaningful (Barbezat & Bush, 2014).

I approach all of my teaching and course design with transformative learning as a central intention, and seek to design learning experiences that create opportunities for holistic relational learning. Indeed, in a recent study of LSE alumni, nearly all participants said that the program had been transformative for them (Burns & Schneider, 2019). I seek to invite whole selves into relational learning spaces in which learning is co-created through relationship and interconnection. In this process I also seek to offer opportunities for unlearning, healing, and re-connection with the living earth. In doing this, contemplative pedagogies have been a wonderful tool for supporting the development of TSE.

The following are some of the contemplative practices that I include in my teaching to foster TSE. Following my description of each contemplative practice is a personal narrative written by a recent graduate of the LSE program. These powerful stories shed light on the impact of these contemplative practices and highlight some of the relational and healing aspects of transformative sustainability learning.

Opening Circle

Over time I have developed an opening circle ritual that I use in all my classes. The opening circle is a way to build relationships and to signal the importance of relational learning in the TSE classroom. The opening circle begins with participants standing or sitting in a circle and greeting one another. We take a few breaths and just acknowledge each other's presence as we begin tuning in to the energy of the group. As the facilitator, I give an overview of our class plan/agenda for the day (also written on the board) and ask if there are any questions or comments. I then pose a check-in question or two that each person can choose to answer (or pass if they don't want to participate). The check-in question is often personal and seeks to solicit a whole person response, going beyond perfunctory or insignificant interactions. For example, I might ask: How is your heart today? What have you been learning about yourself in the context of this course? or What is a challenge and a joy that you are experiencing?

I have found that the check-in question is most powerful when it is personal and connected to the learning theme that we are focusing on during the class session. We check in either by going around the circle in order, by engaging a popcorn-style approach (people answer as they are ready), or by having each person invite another person to share. The check-in is followed by a mindfulness activity that I facilitate. This usually includes some mindfulness meditation focused on breathing, and often some body awareness meditation or self-compassion meditation. We follow this activity with some facilitated body movement. I rely on the gentle warm-up of the shadow yoga practice I have trained in as an accessible and useful movement practice. We continue to breathe mindfully but often laugh and carry a light and playful attitude during the movement portion of opening circle. Once the movement is done, we gently transition from opening circle into our first learning activity. In the following story, Nora discusses how opening circle helped her unlearn some of her dominant assumptions about learning, and shares how she has embraced relational connection as a central aspect of all learning spaces.

Nora's Story

Contemplation rests at the heart of the LSE program. This shows up in a multitude of ways including journaling, centering observation, prioritizing self and community care, and listening to nature. Contemplative pedagogy challenges the dominant culture, which encourages us to move faster, do more, be better, buy more—leading us to feel generally inadequate and dissatisfied. School is, of course, influenced heavily by dominant culture. The message of "not enough" shows up in school through standardized tests, compartmentalization of disciplines, and power dynamics between teacher and student. Through my time in LSE I have observed how the dominant culture has conditioned my approach to learning. Contemplative pedagogy has given me the time and space to notice this, and to grow from it—to see huge personal value in ways of learning that I had merely dipped my toes in before. The opening circle has been a particularly profound tool that has impacted how I learn in LSE classes, and beyond.

Prior to graduate school, my feelings walking into classrooms have generally been neutral, uncertain, nervous, occasionally excited. In graduate school, my feelings walking into classrooms have been energized, welcomed, loved, supported, and alive. Walking into class now feels like a coming home. The container of LSE classes is beautifully crafted to invite students to bring their whole selves. This starts with opening circle—a time for us to remember that we have a physical self, emotional self, intellectual self, and spiritual self that all get to show up to our learning. Though the dominant system might teach us that bringing our whole selves slows down our learning, I have experienced the profound ways it has enhanced my learning experience. Learning is deep and communal when we open up class in this way. We stretch, we breathe, we pause, we embrace moments of stillness, we welcome moments of movement, we organize our bodies in a circle—a beautiful metaphor for nonlinear process.

The question of "how are you?" often posed in opening circle is such a simple and common question, yet rarely do we take the time to contemplate it and answer truthfully. In addition to breathing and stretching, opening circle is a chance to check in. It is common to move through our days so speedily, we forget why we are even moving in the first place. The simple question of "how are you" in opening circle is transformative because it pushes back on emotional stoicism and fast-paced answers. Opening circle is slow. It is mindful. It is connective. I take my time answering the "how are you" question in opening circle because I know it can have so much meaning, and is often glossed over in everyday conversation, missing many opportunities for connection. Beyond "how are you?" we are often also invited to answer a question related to the topic of the class to begin to open our minds to learning. These questions side by side serve as a bridge between our personal experiences and moving into the collective experience of the classroom.

Opening circle has been transformative in the way I show up to class. The container of LSE classes, largely influenced by opening circles, has had a huge impact on the energy and aliveness I feel in the classroom. It has also changed the ways I facilitate and organize groups outside of class. I have had the pleasure of facilitating experiences for work, friends, group projects, and summer camps where I have used opening circle as a gathering tool. I have found that it encourages vulnerability, mindfulness, and growth. There is transformative power in gathering intentionally with any group at the beginning because it sets the stage for the whole experience. Contemplation in the classroom is beautiful because it encourages learning that is rich, alive, reflective, and ever evolving.

Cultivating a Personal Spiritual Practice

In the course that I teach, Spiritual Leadership for Sustainable Change, I ask students to develop a personal spiritual practice with which they can engage most days for the duration of the course. This assignment is intended to encourage students to embody and practice spirituality and to engage in a spiritual practice that is personally supportive. The practice can be anything students feel they want to pursue related to spirituality and the assignment is self-graded. For this assignment students have chosen to engage in yoga, walking meditation, sitting and listening to birds, morning journaling, prayer, dance, and more. In giving this assignment, I hope to convey the importance of cultivating a relationship with the energetic whole, a spiritual connection that is often rooted in embodiment, presence, and relationship. Students reflect on their learning from this assignment and often comment that they feel more connected, alive, and grounded as a result. In the following story, Julie shares how starting a practice of mindfulness meditation allowed her to notice and begin to unlearn her constant focus on the future, and to re-connect with her joy and gratitude situated in the present moment. This was a healing learning process as she embraced reconnection through presence.

Julie's Story

Before coursework in Spiritual Leadership for Sustainable Change, I understood spirituality and religion to be inextricably linked. My upbringing and early education were steeped heavily in the Christian tradition. I left the church early in adulthood and with it, I left behind concern for spiritual practice. For a very long time thereafter, I ignored vital connections between mind, body, and spirit. Committing to a contemplative practice during the Spiritual Leadership for Sustainable Change course felt foreign and uncomfortable. When I began to practice meditation, I had no idea how much my spirit was in need of rejuvenation, compassion, and care or how transformational the practice of meditation would be in bringing a calm and centered flow to my life.

My first few attempts at meditation were discouraging, to say the least. Immediately a sort of mantra developed in my head in which I asked over and over, "Am I doing this right?" Since then, I have found a lot of people have had this same experience. However, for me, this highlighted how loud and intense my inner dialogue of perfectionism had become.

8 ONE OF THE DOORS: EXPLORING CONTEMPLATIVE PRACTICES ...   141

In order to continue to meditate or to even try to develop a practice, I needed to accept that learning a spiritual practice is a process. At the time it felt uncomfortable, but it was important to me to open both my mind and my heart to the learning experience. Once I accepted that this was not going to be a perfect process, I began to have fleeting moments of fully embodied presence during meditation. This experience may sound simple, but this was a building block for transformation.

When I wasn't questioning my technique or the validity of my practice, my mind would often wander to all of the things I thought I should be doing instead of meditating. Long ago, I learned to allow the responsibilities of work, school, relationships, and the ups and downs of life to supersede care for myself or my spirit. Yet, the idea beginning to unfold through meditation was that spiritual practices are simply ways to care for my spirit. This was a new and much needed avenue of self-care and meditation began to feel rejuvenating and healing. Regardless of how distracted I was with the busyness of life, I noticed that I simply felt better after meditating.

With time and meditation practice, I learned to recognize when my mind had strayed to the demands of my life. I began to acknowledge these thoughts, to be with them for a time, and then let them go. Slowly, the fleeting moments of embodied presence became more enduring. During the day I noticed that, somewhat unconsciously, I began to react to stressful situations with centered, mindful breaths. Meditation techniques at night helped soothe my busy head and improved my sleep patterns.

The biggest transformation from mediation came as I began to understand that I was living my life in a projection of the future, rather than the present. I was constantly planning and anticipating the next step, the next meeting, the next career move, the next meal, the next school paper, even the next time I could relax. I came to realize that by living in the future, I had successfully avoided the pain, stress, and anxiety of the present. In turn, this avoidance also meant I was bypassing the joy, beauty, and deep connections of the present. This understanding changed everything for me.

My meditation practice is still not perfect today, and that is okay. I have days when I care for my spirit better than others. At times, I get caught up in what I think will happen tomorrow rather than experiencing the openness of the present, though I find myself living in the future less and less. Through meditation, a calm presence has crept into my heart and into my spirit, which I can only describe as gratitude. I have come into myself and recognize that for me, embodied gratitude is the most authentic expression of love and joy. I now understand that I can be thankful for experiences in the past and excited for experiences in the future. Yet, my truest gratitude is experienced in the beauty of this moment right now.

Practicing Self-Compassion

I have been incorporating the exploration and practice of self-compassion into several of my courses because of its healing potential. I first understood this potential in my own life as I learned to practice self-compassion and wanted to share these practices with students. I have noticed that my students, who as graduate students in sustainability education tend to be high achievers and extremely active change-makers, are often very hard on themselves. Like many of us, they hold themselves to high standards and their private self-talk is full of negative and berating messages that they would never impart on anyone else. Self-compassion practices are a good fit for my students as these practices can alleviate stress and anxiety, can increase focus and confidence, as well as kindness and caring (Neff, 2011; Neff & Davidson, 2016; Neff et al., 2005). As we seek unlearn destructive patterns and bring healing to our world, we can also recognize the fractal, interconnected nature of relationships and the importance of self-compassion and self-care as earth-compassion and earth-care. In learning how to bring self-compassion to our inner lives, we also bring compassion into who we are and the work we are doing in the world. I am grateful to the extensive work of Kristin Neff and Chris Germer (2018) whose book, *The Mindful Self-Compassion Workbook,* has become assigned reading in our program. I often bring self-compassion exercises into opening circle and include them as reading and homework assignments as I have noticed that self-compassion can be a powerful way to engage in sustainability learning. Chantal's story highlights how she is unlearning a dominant pattern of being self-critical and is engaging in healing through increased self-care and awareness. This awareness and care has transformed her sense of purpose and relationships with others.

Chantal's Story

Learning to embody self-compassion is a new journey for me. I first accepted the challenge to practice self-compassion in a graduate course called Spiritual Leadership for Sustainable Change. Throughout the course I explored the interconnected elements of common humanity, self-kindness, and mindfulness while learning to confront why I am hardest on myself and how to welcome self-compassion into my life. Engaging with self-compassion practices in graduate school has supported my work to enact sustainable and regenerative change by learning how to deeply connect with myself and others. I feel most aligned with my ability to relate to others and my sense of purpose when I spend meaningful time observing and interacting with nature. Connecting to nature helps me ground in my values of relating to others with empathy and compassion. In the same way, my sense of purpose continues to be shaped through mindfully tuning into the rhythms of my heart, body, and mind to fully feel the complex emotions that arise daily.

Beginning my self-compassion practice felt unnatural, it went against everything that I thought I knew about motivating myself. I was, and still am, my biggest critic. I resisted engaging with the parts of myself that were aching to be acknowledged. Over time, I have discovered that I return to myself when I am in nature. I have found metaphors for self-compassion and healing through spending time in the forest. For instance, I recognize the strength and resiliency of the trees and reflect on how I embody the same qualities. Self-compassion has become a part of my everyday life. It sustains my energy for the hard work that I engage in to carry out transformative change for the health of all human and more than human beings.

The process of engaging with a self-compassion practice is emergent. My practice emerges and shapes as I listen to what I need daily. I have found that through heightening my self-awareness I am able to better relate to others. My relationships have been transformed through being true to myself and authentic with others. Mindfulness allows me to focus all my senses on what is happening around me. Practicing presence and intention has helped me care for myself so that I have the energy and ability to care for others. I have learned that when I give myself love, care, and kindness I am able to radiate that to others.

In the same way, my sense of purpose has been transformed through moving toward what feels right within my heart and distancing myself from what does not align with what I want in my life. One area that I focus on that has enabled me to grow and find meaning in my life is addressing my ego and shadow within. I have become more loving toward myself by confronting my inner darkness and noticing others face the same insecurities. I connect more with others when I show myself the grace that I would want people in my life to show me. Showing myself and others compassion, empathy, and understanding helps in the collective effort to create a safer world for all. The work to be my best self continues as I stay committed to my self-compassion practice that empowers me to embrace change and deeply connect with myself and others.

Conclusion

As we explore contemplative practices as part of TSE in our graduate program, we are drawn into a connected and relational learning process. We work to unlearn destructive patterns and ways of being that separate us from each other and the living earth. We learn together with other learners, and we learn to connect to the more than human world of consciousness and energetic presence. We slow down, we get into our bodies, emotions, and spirits, relying on our whole selves to help us learn in interconnected ways. We often look to stillness, as the poet Mary Oliver (2012) suggests, as one of the doors into the temple. While the temple may be somewhat different for each learner, as sustainability educators and leaders we are attempting to embody the temples of peace, justice, and relatedness.

Through a variety of contemplative practices, we are drawn into reverence for the complexity of relationships and beauty in the world that we are part of and completely connected to. In cultivating this reverence for connectedness and relationship, we begin to understand that our work as sustainability educators and leaders is not to each individually control, fight, and struggle for a better world, but to learn to be part of the living world, to be in harmony and flow with the energies of healing and connectedness, to learn to let go and to lean into interbeing. In doing so we find that more, not less, learning happens and work gets done. We find that we can live with more harmony, peace, and purpose and that this sense of peace and purpose extends beyond us to all we are related to. Tightly woven into the web of interconnectedness, what we experience in a transformative learning process is also noticed and felt throughout the web. This kind of sustainability learning is a process that isn't over at the end of an academic term but spirals out over time and into all our relationships. Although there is much to still learn about TSE, we continue to be inspired and in awe of this transformative learning process as we lean into its' power and potential.

REFERENCES

Barbezat, D., & Bush, M. (2014). *Contemplative practices in higher education*. Jossey-Bass.

Berila, B. (2016). *Integrating mindfulness into anti-oppression pedagogy*. Routledge.

Burns, H. (2018). Thematic analysis: Transformative sustainability education. *Journal of Transformative Education, 16*(4). https://doi.org/10.1177/1541344618796996

Burns, H., & Schneider, M. (2019). Insights from alumni: A grounded theory study of a graduate program in sustainability leadership. *Sustainability, 11*(19). https://doi.org/10.3390/su11195223

Capra, F. (2002). *The hidden connections*. Anchor Books.

Clifford, A. (2018). *Your guide to forest bathing: Experience the healing power of nature*. Conari Press.

CMind. (2014). *The tree of contemplative practices* [Illustration]. The Center for Contemplative Mind in Society. http://www.contemplativemind.org/practices/tree

Cranton, P. (2002). Teaching for transformation. *New Directions for Adult and Continuing Education, 93*, 63–72.

Dirkx, J. (1998). Transformative learning theory in the practice of adult education: An overview. *PAACE Journal of Lifelong Learning, 7*, 1–14.

Eaton, M., Hughes, H., & MacGregor, J. (2017). *Contemplative approaches to sustainability in higher education*. Routledge.

Eisenstein, C. (2013). *The more beautiful world our hearts know is possible*. North Atlantic Books.

Freire, P. (1970/2000). *Pedagogy of the oppressed*. Continuum.

Kolb, D. (1984). *Experiential learning: Experience as the source of learning and development*. Prentice-Hall.

Lange, E. (2012). Transforming transformative learning through sustainability and the new science. In E. Taylor & P. Cranton (Eds.), *The handbook of transformative learning* (pp. 195–211). Jossey-Bass.

Lange, E. (2018). Transforming transformative education through ontologies of relationality. *Journal of Transformative Education, 16*(4). https://doi.org/10.1177/1541344618786452

Mezirow, J. (1991). *Transformative dimensions of adult learning*. Jossey-Bass.

Neff, K. (2011). *Self-compassion: The proven power of being kind to yourself*. HarperCollins.

Neff, K., & Davidson, O. (2016). Self-compassion: Embracing suffering with kindness. In I. Ivtzan & T. Lomas (Eds.), *Mindfulness in positive psychology* (pp. 37–50). Routledge.

Neff, K., & Germer, C. (2018). *The mindful self-compassion workbook*. Guilford Press.

Neff, K., Hseih, Y., & Dejitthirat, K. (2005). Self-compassion, achievement goals, and coping with academic failure. *Self and Identity, 4*, 263–287.

Oliver, M. (2012). *A thousand mornings.* Penguin Group.

O'Neil, J. (2018). Transformative sustainability learning within a material-discursive ontology. *Journal of Transformative Education, 16*(4). https://doi.org/10.1177/1541344618792823

O'Sullivan, E. (2008). Finding our way in the great work. *Journal of Transformative Education, 6*(1), 27–32.

Pyles, L., & Adam, G. (2016). *Holistic engagement: Transforming social work education in the 21st century.* Oxford University Press.

Selby, D. (2002). The signature of the whole: Radical interconnectedness and its implications for global and environmental education. In E. O'Sullivan, A. Morrell, & M. A. O'Connor (Eds.), *Expanding the boundaries of transformative learning* (pp. 77–93). Palgrave.

Selby, D., & Kagawa, F. (2018). Teetering on the brink: Subversive and restorative learning in times of climate turmoil and disaster. *Journal of Transformative Education, 16*(4). https://doi.org/10.1177/1541344618782441

Sterling, S. (2002). *Sustainable education: Re-visioning learning and change.* Green Books.

Tisdell, E. (2012). Themes and variations of transformational learning. In E. Taylor, P. Cranton, & Associates (Eds.), *The handbook of transformative learning* (pp. 21–36). Jossey-Bass.

Wheatley, M. (2006). *Leadership and the new science.* Berrett-Koehler.

Williams, L. (2018). Transformative sustainability education and empowerment practice on indigenous lands: Part one. *Journal of Transformative Education, 16*(4). https://doi.org/10.1177/1541344618789363

CHAPTER 9

Transformative Learning and Black Spirituality

Maureen Ann Miller and Karen E. Watkins

INTRODUCTION

There is a growing interest in spirituality in the practice of adult education and specifically transformative learning scholarship (Mikaelian, 2018; Tolliver & Tisdell, 2006). Race-centric scholarship on transformative learning is a recent development, often focused on the African or African American experience (Dei, 2002; Johnson-Bailey & Alfred, 2006; Taylor, 2017). However, there is still a poor representation of empirical studies on transformative learning within the context of Black spirituality.

I locate this discourse within the framework of race-centric scholarship and examine Black spirituality as a significant player in the transformative

M. A. Miller (✉)
University of Georgia, Athens, GA, USA

K. E. Watkins
Department of Lifelong Education, Administration & Policy, University of Georgia, Athens, GA, USA
e-mail: kwatkins@uga.edu

© The Author(s), under exclusive license to Springer Nature Switzerland AG 2022
A. Nicolaides et al. (eds.), *The Palgrave Handbook of Learning for Transformation*, https://doi.org/10.1007/978-3-030-84694-7_9

147

learning experience. This chapter examines the findings of a qualitative research study on transformative learning and Black spirituality. The purpose of the study was to explore how a group of Black church lay leaders interpreted and responded to their transformative learning experiences in a leadership development program and the possible role of Black spirituality in their meaning making. The study asked, "What role, if any, did Black spirituality play in their perspective transformation?" The chapter will discuss the findings related to this question in six major sections: context, literature review, research design, critical incidents, discussion, and conclusion.

Context

The context of this study was a one-year church leadership development program. The goal was to create an educative space that provided theological knowledge and simultaneously challenged and fostered examination of underlying assumptions. The pedagogical structure was based on Mezirow's (1978) transformative learning theory and guided by Cranton's (2002) seven steps to set up a learning environment for transformation.

The curriculum incorporated a critical theological approach. The goal was to create a disorienting dilemma between the person's previously held assumptions or home theology, and the current emerging understanding of the literature (Cranton, 2002; Mezirow, 1978). The core principle of the pedagogical design was to create and maintain a safe holding environment (Kegan, 1994), providing ample support and challenges for developmental growth. The pedagogy included critical friend feedback (Costa & Kallick, 1993), journaling (Boud, 2001), Gestalt art (Bourgault du Coudray, 2020), and critical reflective practices (Brookfield, 2000; Cranton, 2002; Schon, 1984).

Besides the curriculum, the cultural context was also significant. Mezirow (2000) concurred culture impacts meaning making. "The who, what, when, where, why, and how of learning may be only understood as situated in a specific cultural context" (p. 7). In this study, the ethnic background and church institutionalization of the participants were important considerations. The ethnicity of the students was predominantly African American and Afro Caribbean. Further, all participants were affiliated with interdenominational churches with roots in the historically Black Pentecostal movement.

The participants referred to their religious context as "Black Pentecostalism" throughout their narratives. There is no one type of modern-day Black Pentecostal church, but there are numerous churches with links to the Azusa Street revival in 1906. Such denominations include Church of God in Christ (COGIC), Pentecostal Assemblies of the World (PAW), and Charismatic churches (1960s). The Holiness movement of the nineteenth century, emphasizing piety and stoical living, eventually became intertwined with the Pentecostal movement. Hence, the Pentecostal Holiness church emerged (Alexander & Yong, 2011). Overall, African Americans have been at the helm of the Pentecostal movement, forging the worship and music, and shaping the theological landscape. Participants in this study had roots in either Black Pentecostal Holiness churches or the Church of God, headquartered in Tennessee. The Church of God began in 1886 as a breakaway from the Baptist movement and later began to follow the doctrine of sanctification and the holiness movement.

There has been some relaxation of the standards of piety in the neo-Pentecostal churches, but very little has changed in worship styles or theology (Alexander & Yong, 2011). In essence, Black spirituality is a way of life from birth to death (Appiah, 2005). There are deep rooted values, notably regarding commitment to church attendance, the role of the pastor, and worship styles. Church attendance is an accepted way of life for those steeped in Black church culture and is disproportionately higher among African Americans than White Protestant Americans (Wiggins, 2005). Black church pastors perceive themselves as playing more of a social and political role in their communities than White pastors (Cohall & Cooper, 2010). The pastor has a strong authoritative role in the faith community and plays a dominant role as the locus of authority for biblical knowledge (Appiah, 2005). This is even more pronounced in the interdenominational context in which the pastor is typically the founder and progenitor of the church's doctrine and praxis. In the traditional Black church ethic, there is a tacit understanding of authoritarianism and loss of voice as worshippers may not critically question interpretations, methodologies, ideologies, and/or doctrine. There is a "devoicing" and "internalized devoicing" in the hegemonic relationships in the Black church (Appiah, 2005).

Worship is another distinguishing characteristic of the Black church in both North America and the Caribbean (Erskine, 2014; Herskovits, 1943, 1990). Whether slave or free, Blacks brought their African worship

150 M. A. MILLER AND K. E. WATKINS

to Christianity. Along with their own songs of hope known as "Negro Spirituals," clapping hands, dancing, and crying aloud were customary. The religious dance called "ring shout" or "running sperichils" was widespread (Frazier & Lincoln, 1974; Raboteau, 1980). In traditional Black churches, variations of the shout and spirited worship are still actively practiced. These deep historical values are significant considerations in an examination of the ontology and epistemology of Black lay church leaders. The cultural and spiritual context affects not only what they know, but what they value, and how they construct meaning.

LITERATURE REVIEW

Until recently, spirituality was given limited attention in the adult education literature outside of religious education studies. Formerly, adult learning was understood primarily as a cognitive process. Now, adult learning is regarded as multi-dimensional, involving the body, emotions, spirit, and mind (Merriam, 2008). There is a growing body of literature acknowledging the role of spirituality in adult education (Merriam & Ntseane, 2008; Mikaelian, 2018; Richards, 2019; Roberts, 2009). A concept of spirituality informing this study is the interconnectedness between spirituality and cultural identity (Charaniya, 2012; Tisdell & Tolliver, 2003; Tolliver & Tisdell, 2002, 2006). Spiritual and cultural identity are interwoven (Tisdell, 2008). Individuals give expression to their experiences and construct meaning through the lens of culture—symbols, values, rituals, and images (Tisdell & Tolliver, 2003). Similarly, these elements are at the core of how spiritual knowing is interpreted and expressed (Fowler, 1981). Therefore, spirituality can have an important role to play in culturally relevant education (Tisdell & Tolliver, 2003).

There is a general trend in the adult education literature of distancing spirituality from any religious commitment and toward more holistic learning. This study is informed by the understanding of spirituality as the conscious honoring of and connection to the Life-force (Tolliver & Tisdell, 2002, 2006). Further, Tisdell and Tolliver (2003) proposed seven assumptions about spirituality and education, four of which are relevant to this study: (1) it is a conscious honoring of and connection to the Life-force that is occurring through everything; (2) since the Life-force is always present, people's spirituality is always present in the learning environment; (3) spirituality is about how people make meaning, and about experiences that contribute to their wholeness of life; and (4) it is how

9 TRANSFORMATIVE LEARNING AND BLACK SPIRITUALITY   151

people construct knowledge through unconscious images, symbols, and music.

While there is a deficit of empirical research on adult learning within a Black spiritual context, three studies—Mattis (2002), Merriam and Ntseane (2008), and Salinas et al. (2018)—showed the interweaving of culture, spirituality, and adult learning. Mattis (2002) interviewed ten African American women to determine how they used spirituality to cope and construct meaning in times of adversity. Participants reported a strong reliance on the Transcendent in times of adversity as the source of knowledge, identity, guidance, and compass for character and moral principles. Merriam and Ntseane's (2008) qualitative study in Botswana examined how the culture shaped the transformative learning process. Using Mezirow's transformative learning theory as a guide, the researchers interviewed twelve participants who acknowledged having an experience that significantly changed their view of themselves or their perspectives. The findings showed participants constructed meaning of their experiences within their cultural contexts of spirituality, gender roles, and community responsibilities and relationships. The researchers noted participants' interpretation was guided by a "spiritual system" operating parallel to their faith tradition (Merriam & Ntseane, 2008, p. 89). Similarly, the Salinas et al. (2018) study on *The Role of Spirituality for Black Male Community College Students,* showed an affinity toward cultural understandings of spirituality. The study using semi-structured and group interviews included twelve Black and Latino college males. Like the African American women in Mattis' (2002) study, the Black male students had a high awareness of their spirituality as a source of self-identity. They relied on their spirituality as a source of courage in times of challenge and had a strong reliance on their spirituality for guidance and a sense of purpose. As with the Botswanan participants, the Black men's learning experiences were intertwined with strong ties to their spirituality, community, and family.

Conceptual Framework

The goal of this constructivist study was to understand not only the outcome of the transformative experiences, but to explore how, if at all, their spirituality shaped their meaning making process. Mezirow's (1978) theory of perspective transformation guided our understanding of the meaning construction of the participants. Mezirow (1978) described

152   M. A. MILLER AND K. E. WATKINS

perspective transformation as "involving a structural change in the way in which we see ourselves and our relationships" (p. 100). Over the years, a plethora of understandings of transformative learning has emerged, often nuanced by disciplinary approaches.

RESEARCH DESIGN

This study used a qualitative research methodology (Creswell, 2007; Patton, 2002), framed from an interpretive paradigm and a constructivist epistemology. Data collection consisted of semi-structured interviews using the Critical Incident Technique (CIT; Flanagan, 1954). The purpose was to understand how participants interpreted their transformative learning experiences and to examine how they constructed meaning during such incidents. Qualitative critical incident was deemed the best method due to its strength in capturing both incidents that evidence the phenomena of interest and the participants reasoning or meaning making about the incident. Therefore, every activity during the interview process was intentionally designed to invite the participant to tell their story in as much detail as possible (Kain, 2004). Participants had to have completed all courses and successfully graduated from the program. Incidents were participants' experiences of perspective transformation. A constructivist narrative approach to CIT (Ellinger & Watkins, 1998) allowed the researcher to capture both context and meaning from the perspective of the respondent.

The interview questions sought significant incidents of perspective transformation (Kain, 2004). Questions included "Think about a time when your perspective of God, yourself, or others changed as a result of the program; tell me what happened, who was involved, and what was the outcome." There was no limit to the number of incidents a participant could describe. The probing technique was used to obtain "rich thick descriptions" of each incident (Denzin & Lincoln, 1994). Interviews were conducted with nine graduates of the program who acknowledged experiencing some type of perspective change and who volunteered to participate in the study. The sample included six females and three males.

The analytical approach selected for this study was narrative analysis. Narrative analysis was used successfully in similar research studies (Watkins, et al., 2018). This study used Ollerenshaw and Creswell's (2002) method of analyzing stories through restorying or retelling. Restorying is a process of gathering stories, analyzing them for key elements such as time, place, plot, and scene, and rewriting the story to place it within a chronological sequence (Ollerenshaw & Creswell, 2002). Often the participant's stories do not follow a logical sequence. Hence, the researcher provides a "causal link" among the fragments, including rich detail about the context or setting of the incident (p. 332).

Researchers Subjective Location

As a clergy woman and educator, Miller is located in and committed to adult development and growth. Miller approached this study as a Black Jamaican female, educator, clergy, and a naturalized American citizen, with an interdenominational faith praxis. Watkins is an adult educator, scholar of adult learning, and expert in qualitative critical incident techniques.

FINDINGS: CRITICAL INCIDENTS

Participants recalled incidents of disorienting dilemmas related to their faith symbols and practices (Fowler, 1981) and described their meaning making process as they grappled with the disorienting dilemma during their transformative learning experience. Participants reported negotiating their interpretations of four major symbols of Black Pentecostalism: (1) the sacred text, (2) authority of the pulpit voice, (3) rules of piety, and (4) spiritual worship. Each of these symbols is presented below with supporting data from the critical incidents of transformation identified and narrated by the participants. The words of the participants are identified in italics.

Negotiating the Non-negotiable Sacred Text

When Mary[1] became aware of diverse literary voices in the biblical text as a result of the course on biblical exegesis, she struggled to reconcile the paradox of the human yet divine authorship of the sacred text. Mary did not recall when or how she came back around to accepting the sacred text as holy after her disorienting dilemma, but she reframed her perspective

---

[1] All names are pseudonyms. Biblical names were selected that best fit the nature of the incidents.

to make sense of the dichotomy. For Mary, transformation was changing the way she received the sacred text.

> We were reading two parallel stories that said the exact opposite of each other. I remember so clearly; it was about David taking the census. To my amazement, one narrative said God incited David and the other said Satan incited David to take the census. I said, 'Wait, was it God or was it Satan?' For the first time, I began to see human perspectives behind the text. I came from a nondenominational church, but we had a Pentecostal background. So, we were taught the Bible is written by God. If I questioned anything in it, the response was basically, 'Because God said it' and 'This is just what the book says. So, we're just going to do what the book says.' But something happened to me that day when I read these parallel stories. It was challenging to move from the idea that this is a book written by God, to accept it is a book written by human beings with opinions. It just had me questioning. Is everything in here real? Should I believe all of that? … And where does that leave me? That definitely shook everything in me because, with the Christian faith, the Bible is our everything. And so now I was put into a situation where I didn't know if I should believe everything in the book. What should I do with this new information? So, everything I thought I knew was ripped apart. I don't know how, but somehow it brought me back into understanding that although this book is written by humans, it is sanctioned by God. I think God wanted us to see ourselves in it …, and [if] it was just all divine, we would never achieve what it says, or be able to relate or grasp it.—Mary

Likewise, Joshua recalled struggling with placing confidence in a text with human authorship. He reframed his meaning making in another course to accept the sacredness of the writings again. Below he explicated how he resolved the anomaly.

> On the second class, we were introduced to the two creation stories in Genesis by two different sources. We were learning how to identify their voices in the texts and how they tell the same story differently. I had never heard there were two creation stories or different sources. I struggled with it. How do I know the stories are accurate? How could redactors just add or re-arrange it? Can I believe what's in here? I think what brought it all back together for me was when we got to the New Testament and there were stories that were similar in the synoptic gospels but yet focused on different aspects of the event. I realized these writings were recordings of ordinary people's testament of what happened and how they saw it. I

9 TRANSFORMATIVE LEARNING AND BLACK SPIRITUALITY   155

found confidence in seeing the stories were very similar although handed down from different sources. So the fact that they were so closely similar, gave me confidence that these things really happened.—Joshua

Negotiating the Authority of the Pulpit Voice

The authority of the preacher is a hallmark of Black spirituality (Wimbush, 2000) and in the Black church context, the preacher and the denomination are the authoritative voices. Therefore, participants had to reinterpret this symbol of the faith in light of their new knowledge. Deborah described the dynamic of the pulpit–congregant relationship.

> We go to church on Sunday mornings and we expect the preacher to tell us everything. And I was one of those people. Prior to this, I had never gone back to see, is this really true ... I've spent the majority of my Christian life just being churched and being a listener. I never really had the urge to check things for myself .... And so, this awakened me to realize there are things we've been taught but we never really went back to inquire ... We've been taught just to do things as part of the tradition, but it doesn't mean it's for today or that we are following the original meaning or intention for it ... But I recognize now that I do have to do my due diligence in searching scripture for myself and not just accept everything that someone says from the pulpit. I recognize the intentions are good, but they are giving their interpretation ... I am now more attentive to what's being taught, and I research what I hear to see if it's correct or makes sense to me ... I'm not just being led, so to speak. —Deborah

Ruth and Leah found a way to integrate their new knowledge and growth with honoring the pulpit voice. They focused on getting something out of it anyway. Ruth elucidates,

> I remember the first time we looked at one of the popular texts we love to quote and realized we had taken it out of context. It didn't mean what we thought. I felt like, what?! Was I taught wrong? I don't want to go that far, but is it ignorance? Why don't they know this? Why is it being taught like this to us? ... I came to a point where I realized I don't have to make those definite judgments like they were wrong because it could be a number of things and it's okay. I just think it's culture, education, class, it's just a whole bunch of factors, but they're still doing the best they can.—Ruth

I try not to think they're right or wrong. When something is preached that I now know is taken out of context, I tell myself, 'just focus on the main point'.—Leah

Negotiating Piety

The third pillar of Black Pentecostalism participants grappled with during their critical incidents was symbols of piety. Ruth summarized her assumptions, *"You have to be a perfect Christian and you have to dot all your I's, cross all your T's and everything is supposed to go perfect."* Mary narrated how she felt pressured to hide her tattoos when she went to church and coloring her hair was a major step toward redefining piety. When Joshua declared, *"I stepped out of the religious box,"* he was referring to letting go of embeddedness to institutional standards of piety from his upbringing in the Black Pentecostal Holiness church. He admitted, *"And to be honest … I've been so strict on what we shouldn't be wearing."* Ruth reframed her perception of the Old Testament laws as standards of piety for her life. Instead of *"rules, rules, rules,"* she saw the commandments as guidelines for life which she could selectively choose to apply.

One significant area of transformation for Paul was his perception of the Transcendent as judgmental and an enactor of rules. He became aware of how this previously taken for granted assumption had affected him and his relationship with his family. He explained,

> I used to see God as a judgmental God, a harsh God, a hard God, and if I don't pray, if I don't read the Bible, God's going to cut me off. So I used to put pressure on myself, always trying to appease and keep God from being angry with me. It was so bad that even when I went on vacation, I would search for a church to attend on Sunday. I felt God would be upset with me if I missed church. I began to see this did not match what I was seeing in the stories. So I grabbed hold of this new God I never knew; I began to see God as gracious and merciful. Now I live my life knowing God forgives me of whatever I've done wrong. I can rest knowing that God's love is unconditional.—Paul

Paul later explained how his relationship with his daughter changed because of his new way of seeing and being.

> From that moment I was a changed person. I realized my perspective of God as a harsh judge had affected my relationships with others. I was very

9 TRANSFORMATIVE LEARNING AND BLACK SPIRITUALITY 157

judgmental. I would pressure my wife and family to do what I thought was the only way to serve God.—Paul

Negotiating Worship

High spirited worship is a hallmark of Black spirituality. Throughout their narratives, participants referenced the primacy placed on spiritual worship and exuberant preaching styles in the Black Pentecostal church. Exuberant worship defined one's level of spirituality. Anna commented, "*We're taught that if you don't jump and shout, then something is wrong.*" Anna recalled her own struggle:

I was sitting in my seat and everyone around me was dancing and shouting and someone asked me, "What trouble did you get into?" She asked because I wasn't shouting or jumping ... One thing that changed [for me] is how I worship at church. That's something I struggled with for a long time because I've always felt it should not be about my emotions, but we're taught that if you don't jump and shout then something is wrong ... So, I think that I have changed in a way that's more beneficial to me because sometimes I would do things just to please everybody else .... Yes, there's a place to dance and shout ... I will dance and shout when I want to, but not because other people think I should.—Anna

Milcah explained further:

From the Black church standpoint, it's a lot of whooping and hollering that we're used to. And I come from a Pentecostal background. So it's like once you hear, "God is good all the time" and "you were called for a purpose for such a time as this," you start shouting. But what is the text about? Who was the intended audience? What can the text tell me? So, now I read with my brain turned on and listen to the Holy Spirit. Then I can shout because I have understanding.—Milcah

Interestingly, neither Milcah nor Anna chose to let go of the worship style. Milcah did not abandon this hallmark of her faith but integrated the more substantive understanding with the dance: "*So, now I read with my brain turned on .... Then I can shout because I have understanding.*" Similarly, Anna integrated her new perspective with the dance. "*Yes, there's a place to dance and shout .... I will dance and shout when I want to, but*" *not because other people think I should."* The core of Anna's struggle was not demonstrative worship; it was about her freedom to choose.

DISCUSSION

The findings showed negotiating four symbols of Black spirituality was a significant part of the participants' perspective transformative experience and created new understandings of freedom. Black spirituality represented the culture, mythos, praxis, and doctrine of Black Pentecostalism. The symbols represented the frames of reference through which new experience and knowledge were filtered. The symbols of Black spirituality were a way of life (Appiah, 2005).

Life-Force

The reported critical incidents showed that participants viewed God as the ultimate architect from the beginning; a life-force that was present and involved (Tisdell & Tolliver, 2003; Tolliver & Tisdell, 2002, 2006). Similarly, participants saw their lives as grounded in relatedness to God. There was a tacit understanding God was to be revered. These findings are congruent with prior empirical studies on Black spirituality (Mattis, 2002; Merriam & Ntseane, 2008; Salinas et al., 2018).

The participants' transformative learning experiences included reexamining meaning perspectives rooted in Black Pentecostalism regarding the sacred text, the authority of pulpit voices, forms of piety, and demonstrative worship. While participants reported incidents of new perspectives concerning these pillars of the faith, their meaning making centered on holding on to these symbols and reintegrating the new perspectives into their current contexts (Fowler, 1981). Thus, this is an interesting example of transformative learning in that perspectives changed, deepened, and a new level of awareness emerged; yet core symbols of Black spirituality were preserved. Faith development theorist James Fowler (1981) supports this finding in his discussion of "centers of value" that consciously or unconsciously have great worth to us and give our lives meaning (p. 276). Fowler (1981) elucidated the significance of symbols and images during transformative learning. It is a process of holding on, letting go, and renegotiating symbols with which we have aligned ourselves and find meaning.

9 TRANSFORMATIVE LEARNING AND BLACK SPIRITUALITY 159

Reframing Perspectives

When participants encountered an anomaly with a core pillar of Black spirituality, they engaged in a process of reframing to preserve the sanctity of the pillar. There was a conscious or unconscious understanding that certain symbols of their faith would not be altered. Certain pillars, such as the sacredness of scriptures and exuberant worship, were indelibly etched. A part of the participants' process of meaning making included reframing their perspective to accommodate the new knowledge while re-establishing the validity of the symbol. When an experience is too threatening or strange, the learner makes a new interpretation that reinforces the existing frame of reference (Mezirow & Associates, 1990). In Merriam and Ntseane's (2008) study, participants interpreted their transformative experience within the confines of their spiritual systems, community and familial traditions. Similarly, the participants in this study demonstrated a contextually bounded transformation.

Mezirow and Associates (1990) included reframing in the reflection phase. Mezirow (2000) discussed two types of reframing, objective (critical reflection on the assumption of others) and subjective (critical reflection of one's own assumptions). Neither description correlated with the participants' experiences in this study. Instead, we saw a blend of both types in the nature of their reflections. There is robust data in the study to support the integrated process of reframing as an alternate step in perspective transformation.

New Sense of Freedom

Perspective transformation includes epistemological and ontological processes in which knowers experience enlargement in their identities and in how they are being in the world (Charaniya, 2012; Lange, 2004). Participants in this study identified experiencing more freedom as one of the hallmarks of their experience of perspective transformation. Being free to ask questions about texts or to independently choose how to carry out their faith were some of the liberatory actions described by participants. Participants indicated a deep desire to be liberated from restraining structures and to make an impact in a wider world.

Conclusion

Participants in this study reported critical incidents of perspective transformation and described how negotiating key communal symbols of Black spirituality played a key role in their transformative learning experience. The study demonstrates Black spirituality is a nuanced cultural context, affecting not only how individuals view themselves and the Transcendent, but how they learn, grow, and construct meaning. The mythos, symbols, and values played a significant role in how the Black lay leaders constructed meaning during their experiences of perspective transformation. While the participants hailed their expanded freedom to question or to choose, there was an unconscious commitment to key symbols. Further, the study supports that transformative learning engages the whole person (Dirkx, 2012; Tisdell, 2000), including one's spirituality which transcends religion. The study highlights spirituality is not homogenous and further delineation in future scholarship on the spiritual dimensions in transformative learning is required. The study posits Black spirituality is much more than a style of worship; it is cultural and spiritual, with its own interpretive lenses and an active influence on adult learning experiences. Finally, although the study focused on a Judeo-Christian context, there are implications for future research on Black spirituality in other religious and non-religious contexts.

References

Alexander, E., & Yong, A. (2011). *Afro-Pentecostalism: Black Pentecostal and charismatic Christianity in history and culture.* New York University Press.

Appiah, K. (2005). *The ethics of identity.* Princeton University Press.

Boud, D. (2001). Using journal writing to enhance reflective practice. *New Directions for Adult and Continuing Education, 2001*(90), 9–18.

Bourgault du Coudray, C. (2020). Theory and praxis in experiential education: Some insights from Gestalt therapy. *Journal of Experiential Education, 43*(2), 156–170.

Brookfield, S. D. (2000). The concept of critically reflective practice. In A. L. Wilson & E. R. Hayes (Eds.), *Handbook of adult and continuing education* (pp. 33–49). San Francisco, CA: Jossey-Bass.

Charaniya, N. K. (2012). Cultural-spiritual perspective of transformative learning. In E. W. Taylor & P. Cranton (Eds.), *The handbook of transformative learning: Theory, research, and practice* (pp. 231–244). Jossey-Bass.

Cohall, K. G., & Cooper, B. S. (2010). Educating American Baptist pastors: A national survey of church leaders. *Journal of Research on Christian Education, 19*(1), 27–55.

Costa, A. L., & Kallick, B. (1993). Through the lens of a critical friend. *Educational Leadership, 51,* 49–49.

Cranton, P. (2002). Teaching for transformation. *New Directions for Adult and Continuing Education, 2002*(93), 63–72.

Creswell, J. W. (2007). *Qualitative inquiry and research design: Choosing among five approaches* (2nd ed.). Sage.

Dei, G. J. S. (2002). Spiritual knowing and transformative learning. In *Expanding the boundaries of transformative learning* (pp. 121–133). Palgrave Macmillan.

Denzin, N. K., & Lincoln, Y. S. (1994). Introduction: Entering the field of qualitative research. In N. K. Denzin & Y. S. Lincoln (Eds.), *Handbook of qualitative research* (pp. 1–17). Sage.

Dirkx, J. M. (2012). Nurturing soul work: A Jungian approach to transformative learning. In E. W. Taylor & P. Cranton (Eds.), *The handbook of transformative learning: Theory, research, and practice* (pp. 116–130). Jossey-Bass.

Ellinger, A., & Watkins, K. (1998). *Updating the critical incident technique after 45 years.* In Proceedings of the Academy of HRD 1998 Annual Conference. Academy of HRD.

Erskine, N. L. (2014). *Plantation church: How African American religion was born in Caribbean slavery.* Oxford University Press.

Flanagan, J. C. (1954). The critical incident technique. *Psychological Bulletin, 51*(4), 327–358.

Fowler, J. W. (1981). *Stages of faith: The psychology of human development and the quest for meaning.* Harper

Frazier, E. F., & Lincoln, C. E. (1974). *The Negro church in America.* Schocken Books.

Herskovits, M. J. (1943). The Negro in Bahia, Brazil: A problem in method. *American Sociological Review, 8,* 394–404.

Herskovits, M. J. (1990). *The myth of the Negro past.* Beacon Press. (Original work published 1941).

Johnson-Bailey, J., & Alfred, M. (2006). Transformational Teaching and the practices of black women adult educators. *New Directions for Adult and Continuing Education, 2006*(109), 49–58.

Kain, D. L. (2004). Owning significance: The critical incident technique in research. In K. deMarrais & S. D. Lapan (Eds.), *Foundations for research: Methods of inquiry in education and the social sciences* (pp. 69–86). Lawrence Erlbaum Associates.

Kegan, R. (1994). *In over our heads: The mental demands of modern life.* Harvard University Press.

162 M. A. MILLER AND K. E. WATKINS

Lange, E. A. (2004). Transformative and restorative learning: A vital dialectic for sustainable societies. *Adult Education Quarterly, 54*(2), 121–139.

Mattis, J. S. (2002). Religion and spirituality in the meaning-making and coping experiences African American women: A qualitative analysis. *Psychology of Women Quarterly, 26*(4), 309–321.

Merriam, S. B. (2008). Adult learning theory for the twenty-first century. *New Directions for Adult and Continuing Education, 2008*(119), 93–98.

Merriam, S. B., & Ntseane, G. (2008). Transformational learning in Botswana: How culture shapes the process. *Adult Education Quarterly, 58*(3), 183–197.

Mezirow, J. (1978). Perspective transformation. *Adult Education, 28*(2), 100–110.

Mezirow, J. (2000). Learning to think like an adult: Core concepts of transformational theory. In J. Mezirow (Ed.), *Learning as transformation: Critical perspectives on a theory in progress* (pp. 3–33). Jossey-Bass.

Mezirow, J., & Associates (Eds.). (1990). *Fostering critical reflection in adulthood*. Jossey-Bass.

Mikaelian, M. (2018). The transformative learning experiences of southern California church-based small group members. *Christian Education Journal, 15*(2), 171–188.

Ollerenshaw, J. A., & Creswell, J. W. (2002). Narrative research: A comparison of two restorying data analysis approaches. *Qualitative Inquiry, 8*(3), 329–347. https://doi.org/10.1177/10778004008003008

Patton, M. Q. (2002). *Qualitative research and evaluation methods* (3rd ed.). Sage.

Raboteau, A. J. (1980). *Slave religion: The "invisible institution" in the antebellum South*. Oxford University Press.

Richards, K. M. (2019). *The role of spirituality in women's doctoral journeys: A portraiture study* (Order No. 13856211) (Doctoral dissertation). Northern Illinois University. ProQuest Dissertations & Theses Global.

Roberts, N. A. (2009). *The role of spirituality in transformative learning* (Order No. 3377924) (Doctoral dissertation). Florida International University. ProQuest Dissertations & Theses Global.

Salinas, C., Jr., Elliott, K., Allen, K., McEwan, D., King, C., & Boldon, C. (2018). The role of spirituality for black male community college students. *Community College Journal of Research and Practice, 42*(7–8), 504–518.

Schon, D. A. (1984). *The reflective practitioner: How professionals think in action* (Vol. 5126). Basic Books.

Taylor, E. W. (2017). Transformative learning theory. In *Transformative learning meets bildung* (pp. 17–29). Brill Sense.

Tisdell, E. J. (2000). Spirituality and emancipatory adult education in women adult educators for social change. *Adult Education Quarterly, 50*(4), 308–335.

Tisdell, E. J. (2008). Spirituality and adult learning. *New Directions for Adult and Continuing Education, 2008*(119), 27–36.

Tisdell, E. J., & Tolliver, D. E. (2003). Claiming a sacred face: The role of spirituality and cultural identity in transformative adult higher education. *Journal of Transformative Education, 1*(4), 368–392.

Tolliver, D., & Tisdell, E. J. (2002). Bridging across disciplines: Understanding the connections between cultural identity, spirituality and sociopolitical development in teaching for transformation. In J. M. Pettitt & R. P. Francis (Eds.), *Proceedings of the 43rd adult education research conference* (pp. 391–396). North Carolina State University.

Tolliver, D. E., & Tisdell, E. J. (2006). Engaging spirituality in the transformative higher education classroom. *New Directions for Adult and Continuing Education, 2006*(109), 37–47.

Watkins, K., Suh, B., Brenes-Dawsey, J., & Oliver, L. (2018). *Analyzing critical incident HRD data from multiple qualitative paradigms* (Paper). The 2018 Academy of Human Resource Development International Research Conference in the Americas, Richmond, VA. http://www.eventscribe.com/2018/AHRD/assets/handouts/636410.pdf

Wiggins, D. C. (2005). *Righteous content: Black women's perspectives of church and faith*. New York University Press.

Wimbush, V. (2000). *African Americans and the Bible*. Continuum Publishing Group.

CHAPTER 10

Transformative Learning and Sociomateriality

Claudio Melacarne and Loretta Fabbri

INTRODUCTION

This article aims to probe the theoretical and development potential of Transformative Learning Theory (Mezirow, 1991) and the Actor Network Theory (Fenwick, 2000), ANT, exploring possible intersections between two souls that appear contrasting, the transformative one with the primacy of meanings and the sociomaterial one with the primacy of the relationship between human life and artifacts, technologies, and objects.

The article mainly tries to show some perspective similarities between transformative learning theory and ANT, without any presumption to discuss a new great ontology, nor to replace either of them. Comparing theoretical or philosophical perspectives can be dangerous, especially

C. Melacarne (✉) · L. Fabbri
University of Siena, Siena, Italy
e-mail: claudio.melacarne@unisi.it

L. Fabbri
e-mail: loretta.fabbri@unisi.it

© The Author(s), under exclusive license to Springer Nature
Switzerland AG 2022
A. Nicolaides et al. (eds.), *The Palgrave Handbook of Learning
for Transformation*, https://doi.org/10.1007/978-3-030-84694-7_10

165

when we try to enclose the ideas or encapsulate them under a transcendent term, under a common umbrella category that we consider valid, to synthesize two theories that instead arise as peculiar expressions on a specific problem. As evidenced by the volume edited by Kokkos (2019) titled *Expanding Transformation Theory* you can open interesting and profitable ways to refresh and reinvigorate a theory as widespread as the transformative one.

We are convinced that seeking new connections, from the theoretical point of view, can provide us with new ideas to implement more effective educational practices and develop new research plans. While empirical studies allow us to describe, interpret, and transform a phenomenon through experience, theory

> is indispensable for the *conceptualisation of the phenomenon* one wishes to investigate. While researchers may wish to study learning, it is only after they have engaged with the question how one wishes to conceptualise learning—for example, as information processing, as behavioural change, as acquisition, as participation, as social practice—that they can make decisions about what the phenomena are they should focus on and how one might go about in doing so (the question of design, methodology and methods). (Biesta et al., 2014, p. 6)

In the analysis of the sources, some exclusions are therefore necessary, given the limited scope of the work. It could be interesting to incorporate references to the evolution of feminist debate and gender studies (Bray, 2007), the work of Knorr-Cetina (1997) on object relations in professional knowledge, and the studies on power (Hearn & Michelson, 2006).

In the next paragraphs, we will explore the two theories, and after, we will analyze some key points of both theories, trying to evidence some impact for empirical research, educational practices, and theory of education.

TRANSFORMATIVE LEARNING

Mezirow (1991) is clear about the evolution of theories of adult learning, often bent by behaviorist approaches and unwilling to value the way people categorize the world. From this premise his theory is thus explicitly placed within the framework of constructivist studies and defines, as early as in the introduction of his first volume, learning as a transformation of meaning making. This is an important position because it clarifies that from the point of view of transformative learning theory there is no contrast between what subjects think and what they do, between the meanings they attribute to things and their behavior. However, there is a priority. In order to change the way, we live in the world we must first transform the way we interpret it. It is an important connection between Mezirow (1996) and the axis of the idea of consciousness of Freire. At the same time, Mezirow develops a theoretical system that draws on Habermas and in particular on the theory of communicative action. Starting from this idea, Mezirow describes adult learning as a dialectical process that aims to understand the meaning that is generated by a context. Transformative learning thus adopts those concepts coming from the Frankfurt School, in particular the Habermassian theorization of critical self-reflection: The validation of acquisitions is a fundamental prerequisite for emancipation from conditioning that must support every area of human knowledge; the technical premises of empirical verification of environmental data; and communication procedures geared to understanding the social world. Learning in emancipatory terms means acquiring awareness of how our history and biography have expressed themselves in our relationship with ourselves, in our assumptions about learning and the nature and use of knowledge, as well as in our social roles and expectations, and in the repressed feelings that influence.

Echoing Kelly (1991)'s theory of personal constructs, Mezirow also emphasizes the importance of the fundamental roles fulfilled by the frame of reference acquired by an individual, through which meaning is built. Finally, the red thread of all his work is the epistemological matrix of Dewey (1938) intertwined with previous perspectives, which allows him to describe the dynamics with which adults learn to negotiate and validate meanings through a thoughtful process that allows them to critically process the experience. It is the emancipatory interest that must sustain learning in adulthood, feeding the explanation and the evaluation of the premises on which the learning is built. The key construct of transformative learning theory is identified in the word "transformation" and how it unfolds in a particular investigation. Thus, the investigation of thought on cultural, epistemological, and psychological constraints allows the transition from pre-reflective thought to reflective thought. Therefore, the logic that sustains the tension of transformative learning is reflective rationality.

The reference to the literature on adult development leads Mezirow to underline the positions of those who question the assertions that describe the concept of socialization as a dynamic and inexorable process that leads to maturity. Some sociological studies, especially those by ethno-anthropologists, reject this concept. According to such research, the change would result from cultural contact, rather than from the transition to a higher evolutionary stage. It is a culture that can hinder or facilitate the development of self-awareness and the ability to perform symbolic representations. The ability to become aware of the self, to distinguish personal-psychological reactions from external events, to distinguish between one's thought or description of a thing and the thing itself are the skills necessary for decentralization, for decontextualization, the construction of identity. In these terms, the achievement of the ability to be part of increasingly complex systems of action emerges from a perspective of evolutionary learning and refers to a process of intentional learning.

It thus outlines an implicit idea of the self as a construct incorporating the idea of meaning. Meaning exists within ourselves, and the relationship that each subject has with the world is a function of their previous personal experiences. Through socialization, the subjective self is constructed in a unique way from the biographical point of view. It is this point of view that provides a set of interpretative rules to give meaning to everyday life.

To the extent that we realize that our perception of reality has been conditioned by cultural constraints and prior circumstances, rather than by a view of history as an impersonal account of the past and by a stadial development, reflection becomes the most influential way of drawing meaning from experience, because it is defined as the central dynamic of intentional learning and verification of validity that is carried out through rational dynamics.

It is a reflection that allows an enlightened action that focuses on the explication of the meaning of an experience or the reinterpretation of that meaning. Reflection becomes an intrinsic element of learning that allows the recovery and rational analysis of one's own experience, in a process of explanation and critical review of those assumptions on which knowledge is structured and justified. Transformative learning theory is based on the assumption that learning is the result of a process of elaboration of knowledge, carried out in light of codes and interpretative criteria acquired in previous experiences, reproduced mostly uncritically.

Transformative learning is learning nourished by reflective rationality that, in verifying the validity of its interpretative models, builds the basis for a more integrative knowledge of experience, open to possible and alternative visions, free from pre-reflective, tacit, and crystallized distortions. Learning implies the ability and willingness to elaborate, transform, increase existing interpretations, or to build new ones through the transformation of dysfunctional patterns or perspectives through four phases:

- extension of meaning schemes;
- creation of new patterns of meaning;
- the transformation of old patterns; and
- change in outlook.

Transformative learning lays the foundation for a more integrative knowledge of experience; alternative revisions to epistemological, cultural, and psychological assumptions that previously seemed obvious, immutable, and all the more tacit.

Mezirow (1995) suggests a hierarchy of learning processes that can help outline possible validation steps of experiences. Understanding new situations may require different categories from those previously relied upon. In this case, the reflexive dynamics can create the conditions for a redefinition of the meaning schemes that, while remaining compatible with the perspective that contains them, are improved. In this case the experience is reread, revisited, and otherwise problematized, remaining in tune with the previous interpretative orientation. Therefore, transformation is not always necessary or appropriate.

Actually, transformative learning theory is expanding its boundaries beyond adult learning research. Yorks and Kasl (2002) explore a more integrated learning model of transformative learning theory, while Taylor (2008) recognizes five perspectives of transformative learning theory: psychoanalytical, psychodevelopmental, social-emancipatory, neurobiological, and cultural-spiritual (Taylor, 2008, p. 10). Other researches have connected transformative learning theory to the theory of the communities of practice, to the performative methodologies, to the coaching practices, to the studies on organizations, complexity, and social change (Melacarne, 2019).

170 C. MELACARNE AND L. FABBRI

So, transformative learning theory has seen in recent decades an important evolution passing from its initial elaboration (Mezirow, 1978, 1991), to an important reinterpretation made by its founder (Mezirow & Taylor, 2009), until the emergence of a third iteration in which transformative learning theory has also been reread in light of studies from different streams of research (Taylor, 2007).

ACTOR NETWORK THEORY

Sociomaterial approaches, such as those generated by ANT (Law & Hassard, 1999), Theory of Systems of Activity (Engeström, 2009), or Theory of Complexity (Varela et al., 1991), have assumed increasing importance in recent years, both theoretically and methodologically. From a sociomaterial perspective the theoretical problem is this: "in some definitions, the term workplace learning has been limited to individual change, with organizational learning reserved for groups. However, the problem with this division is that many recent perspectives of learning in work refuse to separate the individual from the collective in examining learning processes" (Fenwick, 2008, p. 19).

Fenwick argues that sociomaterial studies start from those theories that we might call post-human, stating that matter is a fundamental variable in the constitution and recognition of all phenomena, as well as their relationship with people and the way they change and learn. The sociomaterial perspectives question the dichotomous readings and the binary modalities with which the research has categorized the events, differentiating them between individual/organization, subject/object, knower/known. She said that

> often these notions of participation are confined to human interactions, focusing on social relations and cultural forces and the ways in which humans 'use' tools or move through contexts.' In such conceptualizations, the very processes of materialization that designate these different entities and their possibilities for interaction become obscured. (Fenwick, 2010, p. 107)

Within the sociomaterial framework, ANT is an approach that has evolved mainly within social studies and technological sciences that today, for the same scholars of ANT, looks more like a sensibility than a real theory (Fenwick, 2000). It is the synthesis of many widespread traditions that have evolved in such ways that sometimes betray its original principles.

Developing in the field of epistemology, sociology, and engineering, authors such as Latour (1999), Callon (2005), and Law (1991) have contributed from different perspectives to the generation of ANT combining a constructivist perspective, a semiotic material method, and an extension of social understanding, by focusing on networks of human and non-human actors. Their work is relevant because they have tried to overcome essentialist perspectives, often concentrated in drawing causal lines between phenomena, but also to develop a theory capable of mapping relationships that are simultaneously material and semiotic, thus also recognizing the action of the "no human," their power to transform society. They thus introduce the idea that there is no opposition between subject and reality, nor an earlier or later stage in which the acts of generating knowledge are consumed. While distinguishing itself from the studies of Lave and Wenger (1991), ANT shares with these the idea that knowledge is emerging and situated, embodied in practices that are born, grow, and dissolve over time.

ANT is based on performative ontology rather than on representative epistemology (Barad, 2003). In this sense, we can say that the plane of meanings, the way in which people shape the world through their own language, is not pre-existent to an external reality but is comprehensible within the relationship situated and in which they manifest themselves. This distinctive feature introduces a challenging theme for adult education research, because the understanding of learning processes or educational practices does not pass from the study of individual knowledge-building processes, but by how knowledge is produced in the interaction between human and non-human, between learners and technologies for example, or between learners and social rules, or between worker and material artifacts that build the field of work. This is a relational epistemology.

The goal of ANT is to trace the process through which the elements that make up a situation (people, meanings, materials, technologies, rules, etc.) come together and succeed in resisting together and configuring themselves as a stable network. These networks produce energies, force and generate knowledge, identities, rules, routines, behaviors, new technologies and tools, regulatory regimes, reforms, diseases, and so on. The networks are not a static phenomenon and for this reason the knowledge embedded into them changes over time. Unlike a "pure" structuralist perspective, in ANT analysis there is no distinction between human or social structure. What we observe is bounded by symmetric relations. Objects, nature, technology, and humans influence and mobilize networks that include tools, knowledge, institutions, policies, and identities. The processes that manifest themselves within a network thus become acts of translation and precarious stabilization. This is why qualitative research is the most used in studies based on this theory. Micro-negotiations make dynamic translations, and the processes of mobilization of knowledge can generate practices of inclusion and exclusion, differences in power management, and the dynamics of maintaining status and role. In this regard, Hughes Thomas' study describes the technological changes that have taken place on a large scale and show that technology cannot be understood without being part of a cultural context (Bijker et al., 1987). In the same year Callon (1986) reported the case of the scientific and economic controversy caused by the decline of the scallop population in the bay of St. Brieuc and told of the attempts of three biologists to develop a strategy for conservation of this marine population. In reporting the case it described and expanded the concept of translation, suggesting a new way of reading social phenomena as processes that arise from the bottom of interactions rather than from procedures.

Thus, objects are fluid; they are quasi-objects produced by nets that do not behave as stable and clear but that hide real "black boxes" of knowledge (Edwards et al., 2015). ANT considers the generation of knowledge a joint exercise of relational strategies within networks that are scattered in space and time.

ANT studies are particularly useful for tracing how phenomena arise, develop, and end up as an inseparable unit. It can show how people are invited or excluded from knowledge-building processes, how some connections work and others don't, and how connections can be strengthened to become stable and durable, connecting to other networks and things, accepting compromises, and inhabiting border areas where the value of the relationship is established by people and objects.

In addition, ANT focuses on the practices of articulation, moments and spaces in which a connection is generated and mechanisms are revealed, through which people engage to persuade, coerce, seduce, resist, and compromise with each other, as they unite and negotiate. ANT allows the revelation of the contradictions and the complexity with which people and artifacts generate alliances and networks together, revealing that each can connect with others in such a way that they are intentionally blocked, or can pretend to connect, partially connect, or feel disconnected and excluded even when they are connected.

An important contribution of ANT is in emphasizing the need to include in analysis and research plans the study of human activity understood as the study of material actions and contexts of action. In this perspective, it is not the meanings alone that take on a value, not even the attention to actions alone. For example, unlike the Theory of the System of Activity (Engeström, 2009), where human activity is an activity of translation and transfer of material/structural constraints—artifacts, rules, roles, budget—and intangible/cultural constraints—in local systems of meaning, in ANT networks of management of decision-making power, professional, and organizational culture—are understandable if placed in the relationship between subjects and objects. It is the objects and concepts that mediate the interaction between individuals, which allow the building of alliances and networks of relationships, so much so that Blok and Jensen (2011) describe this passage as a real paradigm shift from epistemology and representation to practical ontology and performativity.

ANALYSIS

Our intention is to try to expand and to integrate the transformative learning construct through the analysis of the connections between two perspectives not immediately close to each other; we used the results of the metatheory analysis of Hoggan (2016) to find comparison and analysis categories. Through a careful review of the literature, Hoggan tries to circumscribe some distinctive features of the transformative learning construct and formalizes three distinctive criteria: depth, breadth, and relative stability. Transformative learning therefore implies a profound revision of assumptions by changing the overall system with which the learner interprets all their past experience, present and future, in a stable and lasting way. In conducting this work, Hoggan also makes explicit some categories that emerge transversally to the debate on transformative learning (Mezirow & Taylor, 2009). It's these constructs that we're going to use to reread both traditions. Thus we assume that both theories while transforming over time, express: a vision of the world, a vision of the self, an epistemology, an ontology, the idea of behavior and ability.

We used a card (Table 10.1) to analytically explain our reflections that we will share in narrative form in the conclusion, describing the gains that we believe can be achieved by this reading.

174 C. MELACARNE AND L. FABBRI

Table 10.1 Comparative card of foundational constructs

	Identity		Knowledge		Action	
Theory	Self	Worldview	Ontology	Epistemology	Behavior	Capacity
TLT						
ANT						

Transformative learning theory and ANT are born in different contexts, but both consider relationships, acts of producing meanings, and power, the three key concepts to understand how people learn. ANT uses the idea of translation rather than transformation, a key concept in the tradition of transformative learning studies. The concept of translation refers in fact to the idea that knowledge is produced within the interaction between people and things, and that this is not necessarily oriented toward an evolution of thought or practices in the critical and emancipative sense. The idea of transformation necessarily embodies for Mezirow (1978) the condition of a profound change in the ways in which meaning is generated, as in an act of emancipation from one's own learning history. Transformative learning theory is more focused on creating meaningful processes and the role of past learning in shaping interpretation in the present.

In addition, ANT stresses the materiality of the experience and stresses that the learning process is connected and integrated into standards, technologies, and artifacts. It adds that evolution and change are determined not only by some form of an intentional act of people, but that there are the things in the world that condition change. They condition it with respect to how these things (technologies, documents, procedures, books, objects of use, etc.) were built and designed (Norman, 2013). ANT allows us to rethink transformative learning in connection with the materiality of experience, because "material things are performative: they act, together with other types of things and forces, to exclude, invite and regulate particular forms of participation" (Fenwick & Edwards, 2010, p. 7).

This tradition should be developed with recent sociomaterialist studies and in particular with research that has sought to link the theory of ANT education with that of adults (Fenwick, 2000). By understanding the interconnections between transformative learning theory and ANT

10 TRANSFORMATIVE LEARNING AND SOCIOMATERIALITY   175

(Table 10.2), we can expand the concept of transformation, so that the change cannot be interpreted in a dichotomous way, exclusively as an individual process or, on the other hand, as a social process. Transformation is the set of integrated processes in which people and contexts, employers and employees, human and non-human actors, interact and simultaneously create the conditions for transformation.

Table 10.2 Connection and differences

	Identity		Knowledge		Action	
Theory	Self	Worldview	Ontology	Epistemology	Behavior	Capacity
TLT	The construction of the Self is historically and socially conditioned. The meaning that the learner attaches to events is central	Social contexts anticipate the construction of personal meanings	There is a distinction between personal and social knowledge, between history and contingent situation. The ontological unit of analysis is the thoughtful act of the learner	Knowledge is produced through diversified reflexive acts, the most important of which is critical reflection	Behavior is the outcome of a set of meaningful expectations built by the learner in the course of his or her life	This focus is on the ability to self-destruct one's own learning process through the ability to critical reflection
ANT	The construction of the self is distribute within a context between things and meanings. The idea of translation and situativity is central	Social contexts are defined in the interaction between humans and non-humans. There is no meaning or thing preceding the act of knowing	There is no distinction between human and non-human. The ontological unit of analysis is interaction	Knowledge is an act of translation, that is, of situation negotiation, of which is the most useful knowledge to reach a goal that is emerging from practice	Behavior is the result of a contingent solution between people and things and takes value in its realization in a specific context	The focus is on the agency of the context, that is, the possibility of conditioning the course of events by humans and non-humans

CONCLUSION

Both transformative learning theory and ANT have experienced a profound revision of their initial theoretical assumptions, in favor of multidisciplinary readings and applications in different fields of science and professional applicability. For Law (1999) there is nothing strange about this process and, more than a factor of weakness and theoretical robustness, he sees this shift of a theory, from its original formulation to its redefinition, as an evolutionary process to appreciate positively, as "only dead theories and dead practices celebrate their identity" (Law, 1999, p. 10).

From this reading emerge at least three key points to develop research practices inspired by transformative learning theory and ANT: (a) consider artifacts, technologies, and standards in transformative learning research; (b) do research with the network/communities and not for them; and (c) rethink transformative learning as social actions rather than as an individual process.

Transformative learning processes in everyday life or in organizations involve radical changes in the way people have meaning and behavior. Mezirow's work (1991) describes this process in a constructivist context as a transformation of perspectives. This transformation is the process of becoming critically aware of how and why people use a specific frame of reference. Within a reflective perspective the objective of the training processes is, above all, to explain the nature and role of these interpretative structures and to identify the type of rationality necessary to modify them if they are distorted, are not appropriate to new contexts of action, or in any case limiting new and more fruitful interpretations of experience. To learn in adulthood requires the willingness to revise meanings about experience, through the criticism of unexamined premises that have supported and justified previous interpretations. The task of education is to accompany communities toward a double reading:

- one that has as its object the mental schemes, the interpretative categories that act as a symbolic matrix of practical activities, behaviors, ways of thinking, and the judgments of the actors. In this case, the emphasis is placed on the transformative potential of a subject epistemologically able to give meaning to the world in which it lives and to validate the criteria with which it builds and manages its knowledge;

10 TRANSFORMATIVE LEARNING AND SOCIOMATERIALITY

- one that allows us to recognize that every activity of thought is first and foremost a social activity, mediated by artifacts, by relationships, by belonging to local histories and knowledge, by the division of work that emerges as an aspect of working action. It is a type of reading that, starting from the construct of a system of activity, ascribes knowledge, competence, criteria for the attribution of meaning within the dynamics of a materially connoted system. Knowledge in action has to do not only with a mental nature, but also with material nature, historically determined.

The perspective of a double reading allows the enhancement of complementarity of different approaches to the analysis of practices. There emerges a form of analysis that calls into question the recognition of subjects as builders of reality, of a materially connoted reality.

The transformative learning construct and ANT contribute to the theme of practice as a system of material activity in which knowledge is not separated from doing, and learning is themed as a social activity and not just as a cognitive activity. Knowledge is the result of a contextualized or situated activity, where there are not only representations, ideas, thoughts, but also an intricate world of phenomena and processes that are only partially explored by transformative learning theory and its evolutions. The adoption of these perspectives problematizes and moves toward overcoming the distinction between knowledge and experience, between theoretical and practical thought. Practical is not opposed to theoretical, but is that culturally mediated thought, located in frameworks of historically and culturally determined activities.

Using transformative learning theory and ANT jointly could expand our knowledge of adult learning processes and educational practices in three directions:

1. Empirical research: Consider the unit of analysis as the relationship between individuals and the material world of things. How can we promote transformations or emancipatory processes if we do not consider the material limits of the context? Sociomateriality encourages transformative learning theory traditions to move in a third direction; not only individual transformation, not only social transformation, but also transformation of the relationship between individual and things, rules, roles, artifacts, and technology.

2. Educational practices: ANT and transformative learning theory suggest that educators of adults pay attention to the context in which people live and work, considering that that context is not only an individual or social construction. It is a network of human and non-human actors, so the transformational processes are not only a transformation of meanings of a person, a group, or a culture organization. To transform, in this hybrid connection from transformative learning theory and ANT, means to change the material environment as well;
3. Theory of education: ANT could open a new area of interest in the field of comparative research. In the tradition of sociomaterial studies, it could be interesting have a look to the links with the System of Activity Theory or the tradition in feminists and race studies, or the study on power in social sciences. ANT expands transformative learning theory in the direction of a more inclusive and complex understanding of the limits of a constructivist perspective, often individualistic, where the power of the material world is not considered. Sociomateriality stresses transformative learning theory in some points at least: the connections of the ontology of the sign and the ontology of things, the idea of transformation as situated revolutionary phenom of an environment, the occidental matrix within which this theory was born, and the capacity of this framework to intercept another point of view from over the world.

References

Barad, K. (2003). Posthumanist performativity: Toward an understanding of how matter comes to matter. *Journal of Women in Culture and Society, 28*(3), 801–831.

Biesta, G. J. J., Allan, J., & Edwards, R. G. (Eds.). (2014). *Making a difference in theory: The theory question in education and the education question in theory.* Routledge.

Bijker, W. E., Hughes T. P. & Pinch, T. (Eds.). (1987). *The social construction of technological systems.* MIT Press.

Blok, A., & Jensen, T. E. (2011). *Bruno Latour—Hybrid thoughts in a hybrid world.* Routledge.

Bray, F. (2007). Gender and technology. *Annual Review of Anthropology, 36,* 37–53.

Callon, M. (1986). Some elements of a sociology of translation: Domestication of the scallops and the fishermen of Saint Brieuc Bay. In J. Law (Ed.), *Power, action and belief: A new sociology of knowledge?* (pp. 196–233). Routledge.

Callon, M. (2005). Peripheral vision: Economic markets as calculative collective devices. *Organization Studies, 26*(8), 1229–1250. https://doi.org/10.1177/0170840605056393.

Dewey, J. (1938). *Logic: The theory of inquiry.* Holt.

Edwards, R., Fenwick, T., & Sawchuk, P. (2015). *Emerging approaches to educational research: Tracing the socio-material.* Routledge.

Engeström, Y. (2009). The future of activity theory: A rough draft. In A. Sannino, H. Daniels, & K. D. Gutierrez (Eds.), *Learning and expanding with activity theory* (pp. 302–328). Cambridge University Press.

Fenwick, T. J. (2000). Expanding conceptions of experiential learning: A review of the five contemporary perspectives on cognition. *Adult Education Quarterly, 50*(4), 243–272.

Fenwick, T. (2008). Workplace learning: Emerging trends and new perspectives. *New Directions for Adult and Continuing Education, 119,* 17–26.

Fenwick, T., & Edwards, R. (2010). *Actor-network theory in educational research.* Routledge.

Hearn, M., & Michelson, G. (2006). *Rethinking work: Time, space and discourse.* Cambridge University Press.

Hoggan, C. D. (2016). Transformative learning as a metatheory: Definition, criteria, and typology. *Adult Education Quarterly, 66*(1), 57–75.

Kelly, G. A. (1991). *The psychology of personal constructs.* Taylor & Frances/Routledge.

Knorr-Cetina, K. (1997). Sociality with objects: Social relations in postsocial knowledge societies. *Theory Culture and Society, 14,* 1–30.

Kokkos, A. (Ed.). (2019). *Expanding transformation theory: Affinities between Jack Mezirow and emancipatory educationalists.* Routledge.

Latour, B. (1999). *Pandora's hope: Essays on the reality of science studies.* Harvard University Press.

Lave, J., & Wenger, E. (1991). *Situated learning: Legitimate peripheral participation.* Cambridge University Press.

Law, J. (1991). Power, discretion and strategy. In J. Law (Ed.), *A sociology of monsters? Essays on power, technology and domination* (pp. 165–191). Routledge.

Law, J. (1999). After ANT: Topology, naming and complexity. In J. Law & J. Hassard (Eds.), *Actor network theory and after* (pp. 1–14). Blackwell.

Law, J., & Hassard, J. (1999). *Actor network theory and after.* Blackwell.

Melacarne, C. (2019). The theory and practice of evaluating transformative learning processes. In T. Fleming, A. Kokkos, & F. Finnegan (Eds.), *European perspectives on transformation theory* (pp. 193–206). Palgrave Macmillan. https://doi.org/10.1007/978-3-030-19159-7_13.

Mezirow, J. (1978). Perspective transformation. *Adult Education Quarterly, 28,* 100–110.

Mezirow, J. (1991). *Transformative dimensions of adult learning.* Jossey-Bass.

Mezirow, J. (1995). Transformation theory of adult learning. In M. Welton (Ed.), *In defense of the lifeworld: Critical perspectives on adult learning* (pp. 37–90). State University of New York Press.

Mezirow, J. (1996). Contemporary paradigms of learning. *Adult Education Quarterly, 46,* 158–172.

Mezirow, J., & Taylor, E. (Eds.) (2009). *Transformative learning in practice: Insights from community, workplace, and higher education.* Jossey-Bass.

Norman, D. A. (2013). *Design of everyday things.* Basic Books/MIT Press.

Taylor, E. W. (2007). An update of transformative learning theory: A critical review of the empirical research (1999–2005). *International Journal of Lifelong Education, 26*(2), 173–191.

Taylor, E. W. (2008). Transformative learning theory. *New Direction for Adult and Continuing Education, 119,* 5–15.

Varela, F. J., Thompson, E., & Rosch, E. (1991). *The embodied mind: Cognitive science and human experience.* MIT Press.

Yorks, L., & Kasl, E. (2002). Toward a theory and practice for whole-person learning: Reconceptualizing experience and the role of affect. *Adult Education Quarterly, 52*(3), 176–192.

CHAPTER 11

Developmental Reflexivity with Power and Emotion: Action Research Transformations for Generative Conflict

Hilary Bradbury

Power without love is reckless and abusive, and love without power is sentimental and anemic.—Rev. Dr. Martin Luther King
The practice of love is the most powerful antidote to the politics of domination.—bell hooks

Conflict can be a vehicle, even an opportunity, for community transformation (Larrea, 2019). This chapter builds on and extends action researchers' efforts in change (Bradbury, 2015; Greenwood & Lewin, 2009; Reason & Bradbury, 2009; Stringer & Ortiz, 2020), by drawing on constructivist adult development theory (Cook-Greuter, 2010; Garvey Berger, 2006; Torbert & Associates, 2004). Capacity for successful collaboration requires reflexivity because change that involves conflict includes

---

H. Bradbury (✉)
AR+ | Action Research Plus Foundation, International, Portland, USA
e-mail: hilary@hilarybradbury.net

© The Author(s), under exclusive license to Springer Nature Switzerland AG 2022
A. Nicolaides et al. (eds.), *The Palgrave Handbook of Learning for Transformation*, https://doi.org/10.1007/978-3-030-84694-7_11

dynamics of power and emotion. The resulting stage model, makes a contribution to action researching transformations because it centers capacity building for reflexivity in support of collaboration.

"Where power is, there is no love; where love is, no power" goes the famous quote from Carl Jung. In this formulation, power was seen primarily as a coercive force (Blau, 1964). In recent decades, however, more nuanced approaches to power have arrived through a reappraisal of power as more than simply domination (Foucault, 1977). Early female pragmatists are also being rediscovered for their successful experiments that brought life to the inquiry of living together better, e.g., Jane Addams (1910), Hull House Community, and Mary Parker Follett's (1942) conceptualization of organizing through reciprocal relations. A refreshed reconsideration of the practice of power appears particularly timely as plural claims to power are rising in our increasingly complex, diverse, and postmodernist cultures. For example, #MeToo, a feminist social movement to end sexual harassment, re-ignited globally in September 2018, and #Black Lives Matter (#BLM), a race justice movement to end police violence and race discrimination, re-ignited in May 2020. Through these movements inherited patriarchal/supremacist structures are being delegitimized as we stretch toward the practice of "beloved community" as outlined in the work of bell hooks and Martin Luther King.

The chapter proceeds with a brief review of Action Research for Transformations, followed by three brief learning histories. A learning history is to action research what a case history is to other fields (Gearty et al., 2013); its purpose is to describe notable results just enough to engage stakeholders in conversation about their own transformation. The three learning histories are of communities that move from inquiry (colloquium) to conflict, within which there are alternations between repressive silence and hurtful name calling (colosseum). An adult developmental stage theory of power and emotion is presented. The possibility of transformation of conflict is introduced as a three stage model. Throughout, transformative inquiry is understood to require responsible thinking (Mezirow, 1997). However, in action research (Bradbury, 2015), transformative inquiry aims to foster creative action within the very systems that previously inhibited well-being. Transformation requires reflexivity that includes but goes beyond cognitive reappraisal of those involved about how they enable and inhibit community well-being. Reflexivity involves creative experiments with others to move toward desired futures.

Reflexivity is therefore a transformative process of inquiry in action; the inner work of those involved manifests in improved outer circumstances. Reflexivity is a developmental relational process. It involves experimenting with others in creating something new that starts with thinking about our own underlying patterns of values and world views. In the discussion of the learning histories presented there is therefore a focus on reflexivity and right timing for intervention. The learning approach that integrates reflexive inquiry with action for transformations is referred to as Action Research Transformations.

ACTION RESEARCH TRANSFORMATIONS

Action Research Transformations, or ART (Bradbury et al., 2019), is a contemporary expression of Action Research (Reason & Bradbury, 2009), a paradigm which has grown from pragmatist and constructivist roots (Dewey, 1938; Habermas, 1981; James, 1907). Operating increasingly with a social constructivist lens (Berger & Luckmann, 1966), and embracing concern for emancipation (Freire, 1996) has shaped its contemporary expressions (Bradbury, 2015). Like all action research, ART brings attention to designing creative experiments with stakeholders. ART, however, explicitly intends positive transformation toward a more life sustaining society and invites agents of transformation to see themselves also as subjects of transformation, (Bradbury et al., 2019). This means "turning the camera around" on oneself and making our subjectivity an object of inquiry (Kegan, 1998) so that we can better know our positive and negative impacts on community. ART is informed by developmental integration of personal, relational, and systems perspectives concerning the practice of power (Bradbury & Torbert, 2016). Reflexive work of this type cannot be accomplished alone. It requires supportive community, i.e., a group context that is experienced as a learning space, or oasis (Arieli & Friedman, 2013), for experiential and experimental transformation of all involved.

ART, a form of pragmatic social learning in the tradition of Addams and Parker Follett, serves self and community transformations through scaffolding capacity for developmental reflexivity. Rather than avoiding inter-subjective complexity or seeing it as outside the domain of scholarly inquiry, power, emotion, and subjective meaning making are treated as opportunities for inquiry and transformation of our inherited systems (Larrea et al., 2021). As such ART is a complement to the work of

184   H. BRADBURY

conventional science which excels at precise descriptions of reality but is unable to offer much by way of supporting the transformations now needed in our context of compounding eco-social crises.

THREE LEARNING HISTORIES

Consider three North American learning communities: (1) A 20-year-old meditation community (50 active participants, average age 40+ , most of whom are in the helping professions), (2) A five-year-old professional scholar–practitioner community (50 active participants, average age 40+ , most of whom are executives and leaders in the helping professionals), and (3) A two-week executive residency within a two-year professional school program (50 active participants, average age 35+ , most of whom are executives and leaders in the helping professionals). In each there is a gender balance and low-to-medium levels of ethnic diversity. All three share normative contemporary Western organizational values that emphasize dialogue, albeit with low tolerance for expressions of conflict and almost total absence of appreciation for aversive emotions such as hostility, anger, or envy, which also feature in organizational life (Bion, 1970).

RELATING WITH POWER AND EMOTION

From a developmental point of view, all three learning communities are forms of developmental hierarchy, akin to a functional family. In each a recognized teacher(s) convenes and leads the community in explicit support of the developmental growth of the participants. While there is an explicit commitment to equalitarian participation, this co-exists within a conventional but not explicitly recognized patriarchal power structure. Power is therefore structurally centralized. In all cases varying degrees of developmental maturity are present among the member participants. The author was involved in all three, mainly as an active participant, but also sometimes in a design/teaching role. I now adopt a first-person voice and note that what I write is partial in the multiple senses of the term in that I may overlook some details that others would emphasize and vice versa. I have asked for an integrated feedback from other participants, including the leaders.

Given my partial lens I start the learning histories with a personal reflection to signal where my partiality steers my attention. I am interested in understanding what happened; not as an end in itself but to the

11 DEVELOPMENTAL REFLEXIVITY WITH POWER ... 185

degree that understanding may inform how to improve similar circumstances in the future. In other words, I hope that my reflection can aid reflexivity and support similar for others.

PERSONAL REFLECTION

My attention is called foremost by the explosive colosseum moments. In these I experienced bullying, both finding myself sometimes on the receiving end in face-to-face and social media interactions, as well as witnessing similar of others. I felt emotionally wounded which demanded immediate attention, only later allowing more spaciousness for cognitive formulations. In the latter my attention was called to perceptions of power dynamics and surprise by how much power I was perceived as having.

First, I had to allow the hurt. Even that was not simple. In an atmosphere where emotional expression was deemed unacceptable by a vocal minority—for its being a defensive form of fragility that blocks learning (DiAngelo, 2018)—I mostly acknowledged the ugliness of the bullying I experienced to my journal and to an intimate partner. Doing so allowed me to consider the impact of trauma among all of us who had a stake in these communities, and how both those bullying and those bullied, likely included a varying degree of unhealed wounding in our backgrounds.

Then I wondered why I had failed to notice that I was perceived as a power holder. This led me to wonder if I had become too enchanted by a younger disempowered identity who, in exploring, for example, glass ceiling experiences, and teaching and theorizing about nuances of power, had failed to notice how much privilege I had gathered along the way. Certainly my proximity to leadership in these communities conferred an ambiguous form of power. As a professional woman and educated immigrant. I simultaneously enjoy the resources associated with my education/economic status in combination with being white, yet embodied as a female immigrant (albeit English speaking).

Looking deeper at the ambiguity of access to resources and privilege was an opportunity for bridging across multiple perceptions of identities (Hurtado, 1989). Looking both within myself and bridging to others, I became more sensitized to differences and similarities. Deeper inquiry into the connection between my apparent oblivion of my own power and the bullying it incited became a space for inquiry at my own developmental edge for maturing my practice of leadership. My awareness and practice with power can even serve in moving from "power-over" to "power-with." A key inquiry, therefore, from which this writing also arises, concerns the sharing of power—both structurally and in interpersonal practice—in a way that works for more involved.

I now sketch the outlines of the three learning histories before introducing a phenology of power and emotion, based on the findings of adult development theory, with which to guide transformative practice.

COLLOQUIUM BECOMES COLOSSEUM

What had been enthusiastic regular meetings over years turned, in each of the three learning communities, toward major disruption with a final blow-up episode that caused each community to stop meeting. All disruptions transpired within the foment of #MeToo and #BLM. The leaders were accused of sexual, and in one case, racial harassment. To oversimplify, conflict arose between group members who criticized the leaders for harassing and disempowering members, and this conflict quickly extended to those close to the leaders, escalating into an us/them situation. Where once there had been total absence of difficult emotions now were mostly expressions of upset and near total absence of positive regard between polarized factions. As community members struggled to talk together, social media (email lists, Facebook, etc.) was used by some to denounce leaders and those close to them.

In all cases the presumptive offending teachers apologized publicly. Dialogue circles were invited. The dialogues, however, seemed to produce only more distress, which found expression outside the circles, with people resorting to newly forming ingroups and using electronic communication. There was little successful inquiry about what may have actually happened, e.g., whether sexual or racial predation had actually occurred was never agreed upon. Was offering a hug a form of sexual harassment? Does having white skin automatically make a person racist? Seismic cultural shifts happening in the larger social environment associated with #MeToo and #BLM made what may have been even simple assessments that much more difficult. There seemed little space for nuance.

In the end two communities closed down entirely; the university reorganized the residency members so thoroughly that few students ever met again.

Turning to Constructivist Adult Developmental Theory

Adult development describes a journey of the ego (Cook-Greuter, 2010), led by cognition (Kegan, 1998), of increasing capacity to deal with complexity, especially of the kind that threatens a personal sense of security. It is a non-linear journey taking in more perspectives and becoming capable in the face of complexity. In this adult development describes a maturing of capacity for meaning making and action taking, replete with fallback to early stages (McCallum, 2008). In our capacity to make sense of and respond in a learning-full way to complexity we learn also to see ourselves more fully. We see who we are, warts and all, so to speak.

Adult constructivist developmental theory implications are important for agents of transformation. Because ART involves a developmental journey overtly concerned with transformation, the insights of adult development appear to expand ARTists' possible resources for transformation of conflict. Key is seeing that what's "out there" is actually "in here." Adult development theory meeting with ART therefore offers the possibility of scaffolding psychological resources while also turning the camera around on ourselves in service to self and others development in the community. As suggested in the personal reflection above, issues of power and emotion are figural.

Developmental Stages of Control, Autonomy, and Co-Creativity

The theory is often used to describe important aspects of human life, e.g., human knowledge (Piaget, 1967), religious devotion (Fowler, 1981), leadership development (Torbert & Associates, 2004). Power and emotion similarly are arguably perceived and used differently at different developmental stages of ego and cognitive maturity. In discussing the stages I highlight aspects of relevance to conflict transformation. Important to note is that later stages carry all previous stages within them as a possible repertoire of response.

Early and Maturing Stages of Self-Protective Control

Ego first develops around age two when we sense ourselves as small and helpless. We focus on concrete things in the outer, empirical world; we operate with a short time horizon. Emotional self-control is haphazard

188   H. BRADBURY

and the emotion of fear is both salient but not conscious. At this stage, self-awareness is not yet available. Psychologically, this is an environment of coercion/manipulation, or avoiding coercion, albeit for the lucky ones at least, playing out in pastel colored nurseries. Feminist theory (Belenky et al., 1986) points out that for women (and perhaps all people whose agency has been suppressed), the earliest self-protective stage is more often a period of silent avoidance and hiding out rather than aggressive acting out, which tends to be a more masculine trait. Regardless however of whether aggressive or silent in form, the typical child (and more relevant to our discussion, the anxious inner child of all of us in conflict) is invested in controlling self, others, and context. At the next controlling stage, we can see a softer charming power and emotion at work, typically coming into being in the action logic of young teenagers. Attention remains external and now focused peer ingroup's standards while striving to avoid conflict and conform loyally, but distancing from the outgroup of others. Disapproval of the ingroup becomes a serious punishment. While a leap beyond aggression and muteness of the earlier stage, this soft power is also anchored in unilateral control of the other, albeit with face-saving public good cheer by those involved in what amounts to manipulation. We may say that this earliest stage became the predominant one for a majority of in the communities in conflict. This was a kind of fallback as participants associated with an ingroup whose boundary was defined by not being the other "bad" group. Capacity to spring back to their more everyday stages of sensemaking and acting was different for individuals involved.

Early and Maturing Stages of Autonomous Power and Emotion

In later adolescence and in large part as a result of access to education, critical thinking becomes available and with it what Torbert (2004) calls "expert" action logic. At this stage, people have become interested in problem solving based on a new rational-analytic logic. While this is a fundamentally critical orientation toward self and others, no longer about control but autonomy, the new critical thinker accepts feedback only from objective craft masters. Principled in a dogmatic and perfectionistic way, they choose efficiency over effectiveness and value decisions based on merit. This type of autonomous, analytic power, and emotion predominates in our schools, academia, and bureaucracies, evidenced by reliance on objectivity measures. While moving beyond the limitations of soft power which has aimed to simply keep the peace, this type of unilateral power and emotion may take the guise of admiration and respect. This is the center of gravity for most educated people in our society as it is the goal of Piaget (1967) inspired education which aims to foster critical thinking skills before people leave high school. We may say that this has been the predominant everyday stage for the operation of the community before the conflict arose. While non-violent, it is a stage of binary thinking that lacks nuance driven by mostly unacknowledged and self-constrictive anxiety, e.g., either the leaders are racist-sexist or not.

Next we see the beginnings of more collaboration. This allows for an expression of power with more relationally engaging emotion (interest, admiration, friendliness) that offer the true beginning of capacity for doing ART. This is when more pragmatic achiever power and emotion allow us become engaged with others, giving and receiving feedback. This pragmatic power and emotion frees up energies, encourages more feedback, amplifying admiration and positive emotions to focus attention toward a desired goal around which to align. The possibility of creating something new—of being pragmatic together—rather than being stymied by reacting, ruminating, or controlling opens up. Access to pragmatic power and emotion is a foundational capacity for an ARTist.

Early and Maturing Stages of Power and Emotion as Expressed in Cocreativity

Mutually transforming power and emotion may come on line as achievers notice and explore the value of having feedback and mutuality and therefore inviting stakeholders to a co-created process. As plural voices are appreciated (not just tolerated), more complexity is understood, and so too more people become engaged. Simultaneously there is more disruption; an increasingly pluralistic process is always more messy. Still, those able to withstand the destabilization, while holding the intention for transformation—which necessitates clarity of individual and shared intention—find that surrendering to the complexity and reorienting within it can open up a new and more spacious communicative space (Wicks & Reason, 2009) in which something better can happen.

According to the adult constructivist development theory, power and emotion become increasingly mutuality seeking over time. It's important to note that, in spite being a stage theory, adult development is non-linear and that maturity includes fall back to earlier stages.

Fallback

The useful concept of fallback names a temporary loss of perspective and capacities to grapple with complexity (Livesay, 2013; McCallum, 2008). It gives language to when we are not at our everyday best for a period of time. In fallback we are not capable of making sense, and not capable of feeling or acting, or behaving in the way that we would were we to have our center-of-gravity way of making sense of the world and our place in it. Therefore, in fallback access to holding complexity (e.g., my reality, and yours, and what we share may be different) and individuals at various stages of awareness of their own motivations may alternate between avoiding and or externalizing unexamined projections. In other words fallback happens and can be corrected for; springing forward is therefore also happening.

Given the stage development that is non-linear, I will use the ecological term *phenology* to offer a graphic of how power and emotion interweave. Phenology refers to the fact that plants bloom, seed, flower, etc. at an appropriate time within their environment, e.g., a too-early bloom may mean a flower will perish in unseasonable burst of cold. Figure 11.1 includes primary theorists and different stage names, as well as power and emotion orientation related to the stages. Note that emotion and power start separately and then interweave over time. If we allow that conflict is an entirely normal human experience, then the phenology of conflict

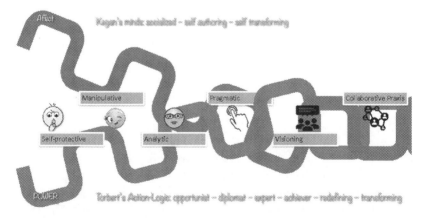

Fig. 11.1 Stages of developmenting toward co-creation

transformation may clarify which reflexivity practices are constructive and when. These will be discussed in the next section.

STAGES OF REFLEXIVITY PRACTICE

The following insights may benefit those who see themselves as both agents and subjects of transformation.

1. Having an overview of the adult development theory from which the stages of power and emotion arise, helps bring a perspective of caring. We see how learning community participants are maturing, but also where we've come from (imagine our fraught two-year-old!) and how we therefore struggle, each in our unique way, to grow and learn. The stages allow us appreciate the human ego with its many expressions and therefore those moments when we don't have as big a perspective or as much capacity to respond to the complexity all around us. Reflexivity efforts start with tuning into our experience when reactivity rears up. None of us has capacity to grapple well with reactivity all the time, and some of us may not have yet gained those capacities, or perhaps simply can't access them in a given circumstance. In other words, first and foremost the stages allow us to bring compassion to self and one other.

2. Reflexively is enhanced by enriching our definitions of power and emotion. . The feminist pragmatist Mary Parker Follett used the term "power-with." The term alone immediately suggests we can deduce multiple forms of power beyond the simple the idea that power exists only to dominate. The following operational definitions brought nuance to my experience of power and emotion. They are informed by social theorist Foucault's (1977) idea that power is pervasive and always transgressing its own containment. Also by Damasio's (1994) who reminds us how important the emotional anchors of cognition are these definitions suggest that power-over is associated with the earliest stages of ego when attention is externalized and that more mutuality is available at later stages.

   - Power over: I/we can make this person do something they don't want.

- Power under: This person can make me/us do something I don't want.
- Power within: I/we feel self-expressed. I/we feel myself as a powerful presence. Purposeful.
- Power with: We/I are equals. I/we feel positive/creative momentum together.

Likewise qualities of inquiry and emotion can be made more operational. The following definitions may be helpful to reflexivity efforts:

- Inquiry I/we reflected on/discussed/asked questions about the experience.
- Self-contractive emotion: fear, hopelessness
- Relational enhancing emotion, goodwill, love, admiration, respect, attraction, curiosity, engagement, and open heartedness.

These definitions not only help enrich vocabulary for discussing power and emotion, more importantly they invite more close-up investigation of key moments of conflict thereby turning conflict into an opportunity for learning at our developmental edge.

3. Tackling fallback. Unfortunately for the human ego, there is the least psychological resourcing when it's most needed, namely when reactivity arises in conflict. Yet a previous stage must be successfully managed for the next stage to ensue. Looking, then, at the earliest stages, we see that feeling self-protective is associated with externalizing activities. This suggests—perhaps for want of anything else to try!—that acknowledging external facts could help both validate personal tensions and normalize upset. Focusing on what's external means there can be no hints (yet) of personal responsibility; simply suggesting that "we are all grappling with complex issues" can offer a more spacious container in which the constricted self/selves of the community can be held. Referring to any known, external circumstances alongside reminders of existing community norms of behavior may be helpful. Relevant to the learning communities described was that we were sitting within the societally shared context of #MeToo and #BLM. It therefore becomes possible to mention that difficult issues are alive in our wider society. Many

communities are suffering, as in "we are not alone with our struggles." The key here is the word almost impersonal use of the pronoun "we" which operates both to deflect attention away from personal responsibility while simultaneously maintaining a sense of community within a larger context in which many communities are suffering.

4. The value of dialogue circles cannot be presumed. The stages help explain why in each community the dialogue circles had little value; they were premature. In all cases they were called during a stage when little authentic inquiry was possible and when competing narratives (e.g., what is harassment) simply could not be resolved. Dialogue circles belong to a later stage when analysis—making what has been so conflictual a matter of inquiry.

    a. Analytic power: Assuming minimal agreements and a little spaciousness has been established, there can be space to continue into meaningful inquiry. Conventional tools for group learning processes can be effective. Recall that early stages allow little nuance of right/wrong thinking and so care to evaluate impacts/actions rather than people's intentions may be most clearly assessed. Generally the more distant from self the inquiry starts, the easier it is for those who are struggling with powerful emotions. Cognitive inquiry is easier to embrace as if emotions are not present. While emotions are also present, they may be best considered uncontainable. Emotions can be acknowledged. Inquiry, however, likely needs to be superficial at first. Understanding that people suffer with prior impact of trauma warns us to go slow.

    b. Individuals will spring back to their optimal maturity at a different paces. Agents of transformation are invited to step into uncomfortable inquiry about power structures that until recently had gone unremarked upon. Doing this will bridge the most potentially reactive stage of the conflict into something more proactive. It will also determine whether the community can survive and even thrive. It is to be expected that reactivity will raise its head from time to time. With the ambiguous energies of ingroup/outgroup at this stage. Sometimes a cycle of apology must be completed alone and without expectation of reciprocity.

Yet relational reciprocity is required if there is to be a community (Parker Follett, 1942).

5. A pragmatic stage appears at mid point when constructive solutions can be discussed. In the three learning histories above, we see that structural issues—not the least which is the very practice and meaning of leadership—are indeed key to understanding the fragility of the communities. A pragmatic inquiry would be to ask how might each participant arise with their contribution to shared leadership. The original leaders of the communities must decide transparently how much power to share. A true experimental approach will establish a mechanism for honest evaluation of the experiments—assuming that many will be skeptical that change can happen. At this stage of community, dialogue can become a truly positive force for community as the energy to really listen and learn has come (back) online, through which relational reciprocity provides a new foundation for proceeding.

6. Stages beyond pragmatic power are referred to as post-conventional stages of development, implying—and encouraging—capacity and comfort with discarding conventions if they are considered unhelpful. Fewer people arrive ready for these later stages. The theory of constructivist adult development tells us that around 20% of people may be able to design and work easily within such a community (Cook-Greuter, 2010). However, there is reason to believe that if designed by those who are able, a greater number of people can step up into the enabling structures. Co-creative solutions in a movement toward co-creative praxis become possible over time. Indeed, the very process of engaging the conflict likely makes space for deeper inquiry, at least for some participants. The use of elements from psychodrama, or techniques of theater, though unconventional, may be used effectively at this stage. They also build levity and relational positivity which the phenology suggests correlates with more use of power-with. For example, dramatical gestures can quickly express what emotions are being felt by participants in a circle—and allow them to be safely discharged—eventually even with humor as ego begins to relax and wonder why they'd been so upset in the first place! Naturally, the more a community practices with such skillful means, the more likely it may tolerate doing so under boiling point conditions of conflict. This in turn allows for

deeper and nuanced inquiry in the socially serious matters of how to redistribute power in a polyvocal community.

7. For those who want to, or can, go deeper into transformative stages, a next round of reflection might include the question of how does the conflict remind us of previous traumatic events we've known. Answers to this need may not need to be shared, but can give great insight on why the interaction caused so much emotionally reactive protest. Somatic race educator, Resmaa Menakem (2017), suggests that trauma decontextualized in an individual looks like the individual's personality. And trauma decontextualized in a community looks like its culture. The suggestion here is that the body and its holding patterns, say tense shoulders, leaping to making others wrong, are a legacy of the past and unless and until this legacy is appreciated the past will interfere and confuse actual experience in the present. Therefore, simply (not at all simplistically) turning to personal and community wounding starts to bring healing from the transmutation of reactivity. However, this relational reflexivity implies somatic work, not individual cognitive reflection at a safe distance. The advantage it offers is access to a more liberated sense of what the Self and or community culture is capable of. This reflexive capacity building is cultivation of self as a space for community transformation. Giving space to such somatic restoration together means taking a bigger step into community within which a deeper resilience for conflict and new capacity for co-creativity arises.

Conclusion

Creating and co-creating the opportunity to reimagine and take experimental steps with envisioning power/emotion anew may be a key requirement of those interested in capacity building toward mutuality and experimentation in service of a more life enhancing, partnership-based society. I am hopeful that those who are similarly engaged with the new social movements about rights and or post-colonial restorative justice efforts, and who want to privilege pragmatist-constructive voices and experiments, might join in systematic inquiries with others on how to build resilience for conflict transformation.

A new dialogue on power is arriving in our classrooms and communities in general and our ART experiments. We must assume that learning spaces will repeatedly enjoy conflict in which most of us revert to early action logics. This is not bad news. It offers the opportunity for human society to evolve. Making sure to grow leaders who share leadership is all the more important, and therefore, having spaces in which we develop ourselves and our leadership skills is critical. For this to happen we must turn toward, not away, from conflict. Simultaneously we must turn toward our inner landscapes and do our transformative learning together. To undertake these apparently paradoxical moves is to grapple with complexity; it is to mature our ego. The human species is capable of this. We have been burdened by the (surprisingly common!) practice of avoiding conflict when we can use conflict to develop new relational *répertoires*. In this we imagine new systems of relating beyond binary power/no power or equalitarian consensus. For those interested in bringing research and action together in response to the escalating social-ecological crises of our time, we may realize that how we work with conflict is especially important. Indeed turning to conflict is not new as much as it's re-finding ourselves within our larger ecosystem and within which conflicts over resources are more peacefully transmuted and by a vast majority of living beings, except humans. As such developmental reflexivity of ART may be considered a valuable complement to knowledge creation as old hierarchies fall and more of us are called to respond to eco-social crises.

If I have succeeded with this writing it is to suggest future pathways for inquiry and experiment. To a modest degree this chapter has already served as an entree into scaffolding generativity from conflict, while at the same time it has afforded me some conceptual handrails as a leader in a new learning community that has not (yet!) experienced much conflict.

Ever tried, ever failed, never mind, try again, fail better.—Samuel Beckett

REFERENCES

Addams, J. (1910). *Hull house community*. MacMillan Press.

Arieli, D., & Friedman, J. (2013). Negotiating reality: Conflict transformation in natural spaces of encounter. *The Journal of Applied Behavioral Science, 49*(3), 308–332.

Berger, P. L., & Luckmann, T. (1966). *The social construction of reality: A Treatise in the sociology of knowledge*. Doubleday.

Belenky, M. F., Clinchy, B., Goldberger, N., & Tarule, J. (1986). *Women's ways of knowing. The development of self, voice, and mind.* BasicBooks, Inc.

Bion, W. (1970). *Attention and interpretation.* Rowman and Littlefield.

Blau, P. (1964). *Exchange and power in social life.* Routledge.

Bradbury, H., & Torbert, W. (2016). *Eros/power: Love in the spirit of inquiry.* Integral Publishers.

Bradbury, H. (Ed.). (2015). *The handbook of action research: Participative inquiry and practice* (3rd ed.). Sage.

Bradbury, H., Waddell, S., O' Brien, K., Apgar, M., Teehankee, B., & Fazey, I. (2019). A call to Action Research for Transformations (ART): The times demand it [Editorial]. *Action Research, 19*(1), 1–11.

Cook-Greuter, S. (2010). *Post autonomous ego development* [Dissertation]. Integral Publishers.

Damasio, A. R. (1994). *Descartes error: Emotion, reason and the human brain.* Putnam.

Dana, D. (2018). *The polyvagal theory in therapy.* WW Norton.

Dewey, J. (1938). *Experience and education.* Collier.

DiAngelo, R. (2018). *White fragility.* Beacon Press.

Eisler, R. (2007). *The real wealth of nations: Creating a caring economics.* Berrett-Koehler.

Foucault, M. (1977). *Discipline and punish* (T. Sheridan, Trans.). (Original work published 1975)

Fowler, J. (1981). *Stages of faith: The psychology of human development and the quest for meaning.* Harper Collins.

Freire, P. (1996). *Pedagogy of the oppressed.* Penguin.

Garvey Berger, J. (2006). Thriving in a complex world. New Frontiers Press.

Gearty, M., Bradbury-Huang, H., & Reason, P. (2013). The sustainable learning history. *Management Learning, 46*(1), 44–66.

Greenwood, D., & Lewin, M. (2009). *Introduction to action research.* Sage.

Habermas, J. (1981). *Theory of communicative action, volume one: Reason and the rationalization of society* (T. A. McCarthy, Trans.). Beacon Press.

Hurtado, A. (1989). Common grounds and crossroads: Race, ethnicity, and class in women's lives. *Signs, 14*(4), 833–855.

James, W. (1907). *Pragmatism.* Harvard University Press.

Kegan, R. (1998). *In over our heads: The mental demands of modern life.* Harvard University Press.

Larrea, M., Bradbury, H., & Bandarian, X. (2021). Action research and politics: power, love and inquiry in political transformations. *International Journal of Action Research.* Forthcoming.

Larrea, M. (2019). We are not third parties: Exploring conflict between action researchers and stakeholders as the engine of transformation. *Action Research (london), 19*(1), 110–125.

Livesay, V. (2013). *Exploring the paradoxical role and experience of fallback in developmental theory* [Doctoral dissertation]. University of San Diego.

Macy, J. (1998). *& Young Brown, M.* Practices to reconnect our lives our world. New Society Publishers.

McCallum, D. C., Jr. (2008). *Exploring the implications of a hidden diversity in Group Relations Conference learning: A developmental perspective [Doctoral dissertation].* Columbia University.

Menakem, R. (2017). *My grandmother's hands.* Central Recovery Press.

Mezirow, J. (1997). Transformative learning: Theory to practice. *New directions for adult and continuing education,* 5–11. Jossey-Bass.

Parker Follett, M. (1942). *Dynamic administration: The collected papers.* Harper.

Piaget, J. (1967/1971). *Biology and knowledge: An essay on the relations between organic regulations and cognitive processes* (B. Walsh, Trans.). University of Chicago Press.

Reason, P., & Bradbury, H. (Eds.). (2009). *The handbook of action research: Participative inquiry and practice.* Sage.

Rorty, R. (1979). *Philosophy and the mirror of nature.* Princeton University Press.

Stringer, E., & Ortiz, A. (2020). *Action research* (5th ed.). Sage.

Torbert, W. R. & Associates (2004). *Action inquiry: The secret of timely and transforming leadership.* Berrett-Kohler Publications.

Wicks, G. P., & Reason, P. (2009). Initiating action research: Challenges and paradoxes of opening communicative space. *Action Research, 7*(3), 1–10.

CHAPTER 12

Transformative Pilgrimage Learning and the Big Questions in the COVID-19 Era—Love, Death, and Legacy: Implications for Lifelong Learning and Nursing Education

Elizabeth J. Tisdell and Ann L. Swartz

It is Fall 2020. Our worlds have been turned upside down by COVID-19, and as educators, we have moved to teaching over Zoom. We are aging and seasoned academics (both well into our 60s), and think not only of what is useful to our students, many of whom also have clinical responsibilities as health care workers, but our age and COVID-19 together also make us think more about the Big Questions of life: love, death,

---

E. J. Tisdell · A. L. Swartz (✉)
Penn State University—Harrisburg, Middletown, PA, USA
e-mail: als25@psu.edu

E. J. Tisdell
e-mail: ejt11@psu.edu

© The Author(s), under exclusive license to Springer Nature   199
Switzerland AG 2022
A. Nicolaides et al. (eds.), *The Palgrave Handbook of Learning for Transformation*, https://doi.org/10.1007/978-3-030-84694-7_12

and legacy. These questions have largely been ignored in transformative learning as conceptualized by Mezirow (1991) and those who draw on his work as contributed in the 2012 *Handbook of Transformative Learning* (Taylor & Cranton, 2012). We have been teaching in academia for 20–30 years, after earlier careers—Libby (Tisdell) in pastoral ministry, and Ann (Swartz), in Army nursing. How does transformative learning offer insight to our ongoing life's work within and beyond higher education, and how can the notion of transformative pilgrimage learning offer insight to transformative learning theory and practice for educators, health care providers, and our students? This is the purpose of this chapter: to explore the notion of Transformative Pilgrimage Learning (TPL) and what it means in the COVID-19 era for dealing with a few of life's great challenges: love, death, and legacy. Libby has explored TPL as related to these Big Questions (Tisdell, 2020a), elsewhere; but here we do so in the context of our relationship and in the COVID-19 era. Writing this chapter together is a developmental "spiraling back" and moving forward in our pilgrimage relationship.

In order to set the context, first, we begin by discussing some of our background related to the notion of TPL and provide some general information about how it connects to our lives and to teaching of adults, primarily health professionals, in higher education. There is a collaborative element that is autoethnographic (Blalock & Akehi, 2017). Second, we discuss how TPL connects to our responsibility as educators, and to the BIG questions of life—particularly love, death, and legacy. Finally, we offer some tentative conclusions.

Transformative Pilgrimage Learning: Background Context and Components

It's July 2009. I've arrived in Ireland for my sabbatical, leaving the US and my 89-year- old father in ill health. I'm a little worried about going but he pushed me forward. I've had many discussions with Ann and her daughter, Mira, about pilgrimage, and Mira's fascination with Croagh Patrick, and her study of pilgrimage as a master's project. She's such an inspiration! They invite me to join them at the beginning of my sabbatical to do the 22-mile pilgrimage journey from Ballintubber Abbey in County Mayo on to the sacred mountain Croagh Patrick on Reek Sunday. I'm honored to be invited: I meet them at Galway Airport.—Libby Tisdell

12 TRANSFORMATIVE PILGRIMAGE LEARNING ... 201

Our first collective activity as trio is boot shopping, because I have just 'lost my sole' in the Irish wilderness, scouting our upcoming pilgrimage. Mira and I are five years into a relationship with the holy mountain site that began when it beckoned to her from afar and we made our first trip together. The mountain has called her back for two summers of archaeology and research, and now engages her brother, Alec, as her hiking companion. We bid him farewell and join Libby for our special, first time engagement with the long ancient pilgrimage at Lammas, the Tochar Phadraig. This is just the beginning of our few weeks of women's journey to sacred sites from all historical eras, guided by Mira's folklore and anthropology knowledge discussed in her thesis about pilgrimage and identity construction (Johnson, 2011). It is also flamed by my love of history and Libby's study of spirituality. We are on an adventure. I have no idea that exactly one year hence I will be diagnosed with breast cancer, and this pilgrimage experience will take on additional meaning as rehearsal in perseverance. "Think like a goat," I tell myself as the rain beats against me under dark skies and I lose my footing in the muddy scree of the steep climb.—Ann Swartz

We begin with these little vignettes as part of the background story of pilgrimage and transformative pilgrimage learning (TPL), because this is where the concept of TPL began. Spirituality is a significant part of each of our lives, and for both of us as educators it was difficult to think about our own experiences of transformative learning simply as the process of dealing with a disorienting dilemma and ultimately critically reflecting on our assumptions and coming into a transformed worldview as Mezirow (1991) describes. Indeed, most of our deepest transformative experiences had also been significant spiritual experiences. We pondered and discussed Robert Kegan's (2000) key question often cited in transformative learning discussions: "What form transforms?" Disorienting dilemmas certainly have the power to transform, but those that had a spiritual (and often embodied) component were the most transforming. Pilgrimages are such experiences, as we learned when the two of us, with Mira leading the way, performed the Croagh Patrick pilgrimage. We wrote about our experiences together and presented a paper on it at the Adult Education Research Conference the following year (Johnson et al., 2010).

In the years since then we continued discussions of the connection of spirituality to teaching and learning, and edited a sourcebook together on wisdom (Tisdell & Swartz, 2011) which was an extension of these discussions, though we didn't tie it to pilgrimage. Writing and editing together was a helpful distraction during Ann's cancer treatment. The book focused on wisdom's connections to spirituality and culture, integrating perspectives on adult embodied learning. Having a decade of our independent experiences built on pilgrimage, we are grateful to spiral back together to discuss them and how they inform our theorizing of TPL.

A Deeper Understandings of Pilgrimage with Age and Experience

Life always happens as we age, and the more we age, the more encounters there are for potential transformative learning experiences, some welcome and some not. We discuss our independent journey with these that eventually sowed the seeds for what we discuss as TPL.

Libby Tisdell

The Croagh Patrick pilgrimage was particularly powerful for me not only because of being of Irish-Catholic descent, but also because it set the context for how I dealt with my father's death four months later. In fact it is nearly impossible for me to think of the Croagh Patrick journey without thinking of my dad and his death, and how he lived much of his life as pilgrimage. So, in the aftermath of a divorce late in 2011, I wanted to walk my way into a new sense of being and decided to walk the 500-mile pilgrimage journey of the Camino de Santiago from St. Jean Pied de Ports in the South of France across Spain to Santiago. Taking inspiration from the memories of Croagh Patrick and guided by one of my favorite secular texts, *We Make the Road by Walking* (Horton & Freire, 1990), and one of my favorite sacred texts—the 7th beatitude of Jesus (Matthew 5:9) "Blessed are the peace-makers," which more literally means (according to Douglas-Klotz, 1990) "Blessed are they who plant peace in every step"—off I went. I dedicated myself to trying to do just that.

I have discussed in detail elsewhere what I learned from this nearly 6-week pilgrimage undertaken in the summer of 2012 (Tisdell, 2017). Of the most significant was how to deal with pain, from meditating on the phrase from the Gospel story of Jesus healing the paralytic "pick up your mat and walk" until it became manageable by walking through it to the other side. This meditation on pain helped me further understand embodied learning and its potential connection in some instances to spirituality. Second was the mystery of light and shadow, and how the sunflowers, as heliotropes turn their faces toward the light. Third was the power of meditative walking itself, which helped me realize that while I had spent a lot of time thinking about the nature of wisdom I hadn't spent much time contemplating the wisdom of nature.

There were many lessons I learned on the Camino, including the power of group singing and daily ritual to help me greater attune to the sacred. The overall effect of these learnings is that I am still metaphorically walking the Camino, because through these pilgrimage learning experiences, I have come to see the possibility of living life as pilgrimage (see Tisdell, 2020a for further discussion). As a result of such experiences, not the least of which is walking the journey to the edge of the veil in 2014 with a close friend who died of cancer, in the past year I have come full circle and did a unit of Clinical Pastoral Education working as a hospital chaplain, work that I will continue to do into my retirement. All of these experiences have ultimately to do with love, death, and legacy.

Ann Swartz
Love, legacy, and death infuse my decision to co-author this chapter. I want to honor my daughter, respect my dissertation advisor/colleague, and adhere to strict boundaries because Mira is not here. She sacrificed the opportunity to present her young scholarship in Portugal to care for me during chemotherapy. So many cords are tied to my notions of pilgrimage. The significant frame that I carried forward from *Tochar Phadraig* was the embodied experience that allowed me to transcend time and space to the place where I resonated with ancestors. I had always wondered why my Pennsylvania colonial ancestors, Catholic, Presbyterian, and Quaker had left such a beautiful place, and the places that came before. Pilgrimage offered a way to explore my question. Just like the environmental educators whose transformation Kovan and Dirkx (2003) described, the experience "called me awake." Since our first Croagh Patrick climb in 2004, we have returned as growing family. The spirit of pilgrimage continues to guide family travel. Past, present, and future, we make our legacy together.

The years that followed our 2009 pilgrimage were defined by my cancer treatment, my father's decline and death, my mother's constant caring, and my children's gifts and sacrifices in support of all of us. Throughout, my parents continued taking care of their community, the land, sharing their wisdom. With my brothers and their families, all of us lived a climb as rigorous, and as marked with sacred moments as the Croagh Patrick path. I cherish the suppers when neither my father nor I could eat, following our afternoons of reading history together, discussing

Thomas Jefferson's Bible, exchanging family stories, and watching old westerns. Just as he and his faith had always shown us how to live, he also taught us how to die. He knew how to identify what truly matters, big questions if you will; how to discern his sacred. When he died, all aspects of my life were open for questioning. I eliminated, for at least one year, everything that didn't contribute meaningfully to my life. I wanted physical movement and new ways to bring healing. My spiritual practice became very private without formal religion.

My learning: The land is wise. If we listen, self-awareness can grow. Trust intuition and when met with resistance, move on. That is not your econiche. Self-awareness helps us know how to care for others, human and other-than-human. Sometimes there is no light to turn to. We must learn to love the dark and create light by making connections that allow movement to continue.

The Components of Transformative Pilgrimage Learning

So what is it that we mean by TPL, and how is it distinct from transformative learning? As has been discussed in detail elsewhere (Tisdell, 2017, 2020a, b), TPL is a more specific form of transformative learning in that it has to do with literal pilgrimage with its particular components, namely the sense of sacred place, the sense of movement, and its connection to the body, and to the spiritual world that is often deeply rooted to or brings us back to nature. Many aspects of these have been hinted at above. Other authors have noted similar aspects of pilgrimage (Cousineau, 1998; Morinis, 1992) writing that pilgrimage has both physical and spiritual components, and/or that the embodied dimension of pilgrimage is key to the learning and cannot be separated from the spiritual; indeed, as Scriven (2014) notes "pilgrimage is a transformative event" (p. 252).

In considering how TPL connects with the transformative learning world as Mezirow (1991) originally conceptualized, we can draw some parallels and differences between Mezirow's conceptualization of transformative learning and Cousineau's discussion of pilgrimage (See, Tisdell, 2017 for detail). Mezirow (1991) specifically focuses on learning and notes 10 phases of transformative learning. Cousineau (1998) does not focus on learning, but rather on spiritual pilgrimage in light of seven stages, namely: the longing (to move into a new way of being); the call (listening to one's inner longing to make a change); the departure (the preparation and actual leaving); the pilgrim's way (the journey itself); the labyrinth (following one's inner journey as well as the outward walk or movement); the arrival (at a particular physical place); and the coming home (the return and the sense of integration.).

Cousineau (1998) describes these stages literally but there are metaphorical parallels in the parenthetical remarks above. It becomes clear that there are aspects to these stages that are parallel to Mezirow's (1991) 10 phases but Cousineau's have more of a spiritual twist. The call and longing are somewhat parallel to the disorienting dilemma, whereas Mezirow's "planning a course of action" is akin to the departure stage. Mezirow's "trying on new roles" perhaps is parallel to Cousineau's pilgrim way and labyrinth stages. Finally Cousineau's coming home and its integration is akin to Mezirow's transformed perspective. Most significantly in clarifying the difference, there is no sense of spirituality in Mezirow's conception of transformative learning, which is central to Cousineau's understanding of pilgrimage, as is the notion of physical movement. In sum, Mezirow's focus is learning; by contrast, the focus of pilgrimage is the spiritual dimension as connected to (physical) movement, embodiment, and nature.

The spiritual dimension is particularly evident in Cousineau's discussion of the labyrinth stage, which may have implications for the notion of TPL as connected to an overall perspective of "life as pilgrimage." Cousineau merges this idea of movement on the physical pilgrimage itself with the inner journey of one's soul. He likens this to having a sense of "following an invisible thread" and quotes Artress: "for by following an invisible thread we connect to the Source, the Sacred" (p. 150). One does not necessarily have to engage in a serious physical pilgrimage to a sacred site to cultivate a sense of life as pilgrimage. But having done so makes it even more possible. Further, such experiences practiced often and taken together sometimes help people feel like they are "following the invisible thread" of their life journey back to the Sacred Source. This indeed is part of what makes it possible to live life as pilgrimage.

Ann's contribution to the scholarship of transformative learning through pilgrimage was our original presentation (Johnson, et al., 2010) where she noted the salience of transformative learning's planetary thread (Selby in O'Sullivan, 2001) to explain her experience. This has not changed. Coming now to consideration of Libby's recent scholarship, she notes the difference between her own familial experience of pilgrimage grounded in repeated connection with a place, and Libby's extended experience walking alone, but with others, a specific well-known path at a turning point in her life. These differences may be meaningful.

Bringing her historical ancestral perspective to analysis of the two modes described above, transformative learning and TPL, Ann points out the need to merge the literature of the genealogies supporting each model. This understanding of lineage becomes important for building new theoretical connections to transformative learning literature, for instance, to healthcare disciplines. Mezirow's transformative learning arguably arose from complex systems thinking about change (Swartz & Sprow, 2010), while Cousineau's phases reflect the anthropological scholarship of mythic transformation (Campbell, 1949) and liminality in ritual process (Turner, 1969) born from van Gennep's (1909) study of rites of passage. The richness of this lineage should not be lost. As Cousineau (1998) provides an expansive coverage of pilgrimage in multiple cultures and religions, the appeal to Libby is clear. Cousineau is harmonious with work on spirituality and culture in transformative learning (Charaniya, 2012; Tisdell & Tolliver, 2003). A primary implication of TPL for transformative learning might be to dig deeply into its theoretical and philosophical ancestry, then turn to its own edges and notice the richness.

Libby has documented her ideas about living life as pilgrimage and the meaning of this for life's big questions (Tisdell, 2020a, b). Ann's companion view resonates with life dedicated to health professions practice. If life is viewed as pilgrimage, a type of hero's journey (Campbell, 1949) in one giant arc of leaving home to pursue an ideal, then perhaps the period of professional activity, within discipline, is a great period of liminality, with shifts in and out of varying degrees of creative productivity. Re-entry and reintegration phase constitutes legacy, what our transformed form has to offer the community, and is obligated to now share. Within the larger arc there are shorter enactments of ritual, at intervals, and at major rites of passage when we find ourselves intersecting with death, an inevitable and predictably unpredictable life process, and love, a choice we make or do not make, over and over again. Both big issues involve major change; both are inevitably embodied actions and experiences of transformation. Pilgrimage is useful framework because at its core, pilgrimage is rooted in the sacred.

TPL and Responsibility in the Covid-19 Era

Through a slowly emerging network of connections that arose by living into pilgrimage, I have found a nature attentive community where I understand myself as very broadly practicing community health nursing. More specifically, I carry the intention to promote health, and if my licensed skills are needed I share them. As an invited young Elder, I have been exposed to their decolonization work and my understanding of working with youth is being transformed as I function with a group of women Elders during COVID-19, on Zoom, facilitating grief, using story and ritual to foster movement through our shared hero's journey. We are a multi-ethnic international group with an underlying appreciation for the sacred. It is a treasure to experience the unique wisdom of each woman and appreciate how we weave our threads together to form the basket of wisdom that can hold the youth. My nursing students share similar griefs of lost ceremonies and wondering what comes next, and we work together to remember the wisdom of their Elders, share the music that helps us persevere, and encourage each other to get outside and move. At this point in time, this is my professional and community legacy. This is where I meet my responsibility.—Ann Swartz

In being committed to living life as pilgrimage, I begin each day with a heart rhythm meditation practice. Since the beginning of COVID-19 in March I've been leading these meditations over Zoom for my Unitarian Church three times per week; after all if I'm going to engage in such a practice, I might as well do it with others. It's now mid-October, and I always ask what folks want to focus on at the beginning. This morning someone said "more sanity for the world during the next few weeks" (during the election season), and we meditate on what it might mean to breathe into "God-consciousness/higher self-consciousness." I focus on imagining the Lifeforce of "God consciousness" to flow through us like Living Water— of inspiration and sanity. I'm reminded of the beautiful fall colors and the autumn sun on the waters of the creek from my walk with the dogs early this morning. I focus on the magic of my own breath, and also ponder George Floyd's last words of "I can't breathe." What is my legacy? What is my responsibility?—Libby Tisdell

These vignettes focus on the sense of responsibility we feel in trying to live life as pilgrimage in the COVID-19 era. This affects how each of us view teaching in our respective disciplines of lifelong learning and adult education (Libby) and nursing (Ann) and how we live our lives. Hence, we return again to speaking in different voices.

TPL and Responsible Practice in Lifelong Learning and Adult Education (Libby)

The roots of the field of Lifelong Learning and Adult Education are to a large extent in working for social justice, which is why the book *We Make the Road by Walking* (Horton & Freire, 1990) is so significant to me. Further, as one who is committed to living life as pilgrimage and engages in a daily meditation practice focused on heart and breath, what should my response be when the world witnessed the senseless killing of a black man whose last words are "I can't breathe"? What is my responsibility? Surely it's greater than to simply keep meditating; rather it's meditation that leads to action.

Creating an Engaged Classroom Community

Last summer I was teaching a graduate class of 15 students, "Mindfulness and Meditation, Embodied Learning, and Health" over Zoom (due to COVID-19). Race, gender, and class are dealt with to some extent in all my classes; as such there were readings dealing with cultural humility (Velott & Sprow Forte, 2019), race, and mindfulness. George Floyd was killed two days before the particular session on cultural humility. The question in many people's minds is what should our response be to these overt and unnecessary acts of racism and murder? That was the crux of our discussion in my class that night where we talked about these issues of cultural humility and the potential connection between meditation and working toward racial justice (King, 2018; Magee, 2019). One of the three Black students was crying during the discussion, but was grateful that this was a part of the readings for the course, and commented on the serendipitous nature of these readings on that particular day. This particular group of students from different political persuasions, most from the health and medical professions, over the next couple of months developed a bond like I have experienced only occasionally in a classroom, as we created and engaged in a teaching/learning community together. We named the elephant in the room—the elephant of racism. We also opened our hearts and breathed into it as we meditated together; it created a special bond, and individuals took action in different ways.

Some students would say the class was transformative as they engaged in multiple ways of knowing even over Zoom, and they took what they learned into their clinical and educational practice. Creating meditative space that also deals with the difficult issues of racism and social justice is and was part of my action. Sawatsky (2017) discusses such actions of naming hard things as learning to "dance with elephants." I see it as my responsibility as an educator at this time in history to be an elephant dancer, to help students name the elephant, and to draw on multiple ways of knowing as they live their way into taking action and dancing with the elephant. I learned so much with them and from them, about the power of engaging multiple ways of knowing, including meditation, that helps give people courage to deal with difficult subjects. This is my responsibility in living life as pilgrimage: to dance with more elephants!

Lifelong Learning, Love, Death, and Legacy

The field of Lifelong Learning and Adult Education is not just about what happens in classrooms. Most transformative learning experiences happen while we are living our lives, not while we are in classrooms. My experiences of TPL have given me the courage to take what I have learned from trying to intentionally live my life as pilgrimage in the past decade and to bring some of those learnings into the classroom, or at the bedside as a chaplain, or to nonformal education settings. Many of these experiences have been about love, and death, and the intermingling of the two, though these are topics that have been little dealt with in transformative learning, but have been so present in our narratives above.

People keep asking me when I'm retiring. I think about it but I totally love my students and I don't think of them as students but rather as co-learners on the journey. I learn so much from them as I have from Ann and Mira and so many others. From Ann I've learned not only about TPL, but also about complexity science, and about trauma and embodied learning, which ultimately paved the way for healing from some of my own trauma through Yoga and meditation. I have supervised more than 50 dissertations in my academic career, and many have to do with transformative learning, and I've forged important relationships with many of these amazing lifelong learners. This is part of my legacy, but it's not all of it. I've learned much from sitting at the bedside of dying family members, friends, and patients in my chaplaincy. I've learned so much from love in its varied forms—from friends, lovers, and loves lost. And I've learned so much more from falling in love again and having the magic of the legacy of unexpected grandchildren. This too is legacy. But quite literally at the heart of it all is trying to create greater heart capacity, to be able to dance

210   E. J. TISDELL AND A. L. SWARTZ

with more elephants, hold more love, more pain, and more suffering, and to have the courage to take action that leads to greater justice, and further TPL. For me, key to cultivating such learning is meditation on heart and breath, creating sacred rituals, spending time in nature, and continuing to walk my way into a new sense of being. This is how I see trying to live life as pilgrimage; surely it has a place in the field of Lifelong Learning and Adult Education.

TPL and Responsible Practice in Nursing Education (Ann)

Earning my terminal degree in Adult Education resonated with a personal desire to educate nurses for action in their independent function as advocates rather than more traditional emphasis on our dependent functions. My doctoral education grounded the Clinical Action Pedagogy (Swartz, 2012) that guides my teaching. From simple to complex, using embodied learning to compare subjective and objective views of body, nurses coming into being are supported. Cultural humility and appreciation of differences are a thread throughout the primarily clinical program. Teaching for self-awareness brings this thread to life. Our local nursing curriculum delivery has been purposely shaped as rite of passage, therefore understandable as pilgrimage. Students, faculty, and staff together, we are building a legacy, creating the next generation of nurses who will care for our people.

Creating an Engaged Classroom Community

By design, I teach each cohort in every semester. Every class begins with embodied engagement, then check-in to identify issues and offer each other support. When COVID-19 arrived in spring 2020, we were half-way through the program and had learned in my classes through simulation about pandemics and interpersonal violence as public health issues with connections to disparities. As we went virtual, we continued with disaster simulations, community health education, and a family scrapbook project that is always transformative. This year it was especially so as our cohorts now include international medical graduates and have become very ethnically diverse. The sense of radical jump to a higher level of being seen and heard was palpable. In summer, we were together for mental health nursing and found it useful to reflect on dynamics of past pandemics such as denial, then seeking answers and attributing blame, abandonment of patients, abandonment of family members, and forgetting lessons learned (Eghigian, 2020; Knoll, 2020). We shared our ongoing community assessments and individual actions. Many students recognized media distortions and presented their personal actions to teach their networks, especially the most vulnerable, evidence-based self-care and how to access care. We validated each other's efforts at this local level to mitigate any sense of helplessness. This was a useful vessel for holding all of us when the violence began. A few students shared anti-racism resources from a professional association. I shared the way my extended inter-racial family was intensifying and sharing our research into slave ancestry with its centuries of secrets, and how this emotional work felt like a way to build resilience in our younger generations who thought they had no story. That choice to love, past divorces for many of us, reinforced our capability and intention to survive.

What was striking to me about "I can't breathe" was the way it became so broadly meaningful to so many people at exactly the time that all of us could no longer breathe without thinking about breathing. The most natural of automatic bodily actions, necessary for life, now requiring thoughtful prevention in order that the necessary not become deadly. We talked about this in class, and about the basic human fear of being confined, trapped. Concurrently, what emerged among students was a mighty sense of need to return to the clinical setting, no matter what. They were bored and impatient with virtual clinical. Faculty proved much more reticent and set the stage for some conflict fueled by the death, violence, and uncertainties in our outside world as they tugged very close to home.

I was reminded of the transformative journey of my dissertation research, begun 15 years ago and mentored by Libby, studying nurses learning through fear and trauma. Fear is exactly what we had to teach with and through, in summer 2020, in the most exquisite time for becoming a nurse. We discerned the location of our sacred by looking to nursing's past, and those who were able and willing took students back to the hospital in any way we could arrange. As nurses we need connection and courage to transcend fear of our own death; to choose to love strangers who do not always appreciate us, and love the human race that sometimes seems unlovable; to walk among dangers with no promise of happy ending, just because it needs to be done, we can do it, and we would appreciate if someone took that walk for us. It is easy to understand this journey as pilgrimage.

Nursing Education, Love, Death, and Legacy

Although Registered Nurses (RNs) may trace our long history back to ancient healers, we know that "modern" nursing arose from hospitals, armed conflict, and the transformative embrace of germ theory. Nursing's big questions are well documented: professional autonomy, working conditions, relationships with other health professionals, appropriate knowledge for licensure, gender, class, and race (Baer et al., 2001). These workplace factors when perceived beyond one's control are the source of burnout. An enduring nursing response is to infuse our work with ritual. Without a sacred element, our actions might be mere routines. In *Nurses' Work: The Sacred and the Profane*, inspired by van Gennep (1909) and Turner (1969), nursing scholar Wolf (1988) described her ethnographic study of an inpatient nursing unit. The sacred rituals that allowed nurses to negotiate the profane realities of their responsibilities were post-mortem care, medication administration, medical aseptic practices, and change-of-shift reporting. Any experienced RN reads this list with a smile of recognition and a tug at the heart.

People might assume nurses are comfortable with death and dying. I made that assumption until I began to teach. I learned from my students that many nurses are uncomfortable with death and lifeless bodies, despite rituals. On my first day of work as an 18-year-old nurse's aide, I was assigned to care for a woman as she died. No instructions, no one checking in; a traditional nursing hero's journey without the rite of passage. I did what came to mind, what I would have wanted someone to do for me. I looked in her eyes when they were open, held her hand, and read her the 23rd psalm, many times. Without talking, I knew her. I was so grateful for the familiar verses that calmed both of us. Her kind eyes helped me through her death. I had discerned what was my sacred at that time.

Continually throughout every nursing career, there are questions: Why do I want to do this? What do I have to offer? Why am I exposing myself so deeply to others' illness, sadness, trauma, families, grief, joy, loss, and triumphs? The answer is usually some form of love, of a decision to commit to ongoing connection, presence, engagement, and action no matter what. That is the decision of love, with its many attendant emotions, both positive and negative. Nurses do what they do because they can, it has to be done, they love helping people, they love the puzzle and challenge, because they are called. If sacred were not deeply embedded in the profound connections with human life that are nursing practice, the profanities of the experience could engulf. In their classic essay, *Nursing as Metaphor*, Fagin and Diers (1983) explain discomfort often arises in social settings in the presence of a nurse, because we know people and bodies so intimately and are present and involved during life's most basic rites of passage. We hold each other and our stories that cannot be told.

A satisfied and fulfilling career in nursing is transformative pilgrimage. We make the journey and are changed forever. A big question about legacy for nursing education today, in the era of COVID-19, is how do we maintain our sacred cord to our past? How do we move forward with our students, with the courage nurses have always mustered, in a world that seems, to some, much more dangerous than the one in which they trained and practiced? The students are teaching us about courage and how to nurse in the twenty-first century. What wisdom do we have to offer? Where are the commitments of our love decisions placed, and where do we stand in relation to our own deaths? Can we be the unselfish Elders who hold while listening and inviting the youthful voices to speak? Can we dream the future with them?

Conclusion

Life brings major changes that can transform us, particularly if we engage thoughtfully with others to make meaning rather than reacting automatically. Must we wait for the catastrophic? Is it only life's huge decisions that matter enough to transform us? A clear message from pilgrimage experience is that we can choose the long, unpredictable journey of transformation, personally and pedagogically. While the previous assumptions learned from family and culture may be barriers to personal transformation and action for good of the whole, (Mezirow, 1991), sometimes those assumptions fuel our finest fires, when fed with intention and openness to the sacred present in the world around us. We must be wise enough to discern our sacred.

So what does all this mean, and what conclusions can we draw about TPL and transformative learning? To be sure, most of the people that we know are most changed by what Mezirow called "epochal" transformative learning experiences, experiences of love and death that change our fundamental sense of identity. Literal pilgrimage experiences have done that, in that they helped us know how strong we really are and what we are made of, and have implications for lifelong learning. So have significant experiences of walking the journey of death with those we deeply love, or those we connect deeply with in their final days or hours of life when we have had the courage to stay in spite of our fear. Such experiences allow us to stay in spite of fear in other difficult conversations, where we learn to dance with the elephant in the room and encourage our students, mentors, and mentees to do the same. It's by blending head with deep heart, to spend time seeking the wisdom of nature at work as our bodies tread lightly on the earth, and remembering to breathe deeply, and to help free others who cry out "I can't breathe." This is part of the task of lifelong learning and of nursing us all back to life in the COVID-19 era. And it's also to claim important sacred rituals of well-being, such as turning our faces toward the sun like the heliotropic sunflowers do, or learning to make fire in the dark, while contemplating the mystery of light in shadow, not with embarrassment, but with sacred knowing that we can offer as options to our students and other lifelong learners. Indeed, this is part of our legacy, and we offer it with deep gratitude and deep love. While our formal teaching careers will end, all of us are always teaching and learning from each other, whether we know it or not. Living life as pilgrimage means that we try to do so with intention and celebrate it with glory and gratitude.

References

Baer, E. D., D'Antiono, P., Rinker, S. & Lynaugh, J. E. (Eds.). (2001). *Enduring issues in American nursing*. Springer.

Blalock, A. E., & Akehi, M. (2017). Collaborative autoethnography as a pathway for transformative learning. *Journal of Transformative Education, 16*(2), 89–107.

Campbell, J. (1949). *The hero with a thousand faces*. Pantheon.

Charaniya, N. (2012). Cultural-spiritual perspective of transformational learning. In E. W. Taylor & P. Cranton (Eds.), *The handbook of transformational learning: Theory, research and practice* (pp. 231–244). Jossey-Bass.

Cousineau, P. (1998). *The art of pilgrimage*. Conari Press.

Douglas-Klotz, N. (1990). *Prayers of the cosmos*. Harper.

Eghigian, G. (2020, May 8). The Spanish Flu pandemic and mental health: A historical perspective. *Psychiatric Times, 37*(5). https://www.psychiatrictimes.com/view/spanish-flu-pandemic-and-mental-health-historical-perspective.

Fagin, C., & Diers, D. (1983). Nursing as metaphor. *New England Journal of Medicine, 309*, 116–117.

Horton, M., & Freire, P. (1990). *We make the road by walking*. Temple University Press.

Johnson, M. (2011). *The Croagh Patrick pilgrimage: Identity construction and spiritual experience at Ireland's holy mountain* [Unpublished Master's thesis]. University of Oregon.

Johnson, M., Swartz, A., & Tisdell, E. (2010). An Irish spiritual pilgrimage and the potential for transformation. In Proceedings of the 48th Annual Adult Education Research Conference, 212–218. Sacramento State University.

Kovan, J. T., & Dirkx, J. M. (2003). 'Being called awake': The role of transformative learning in the lives of environmental activists. *Adult Education Quarterly, 53*(2), 99–118.

Kegan, R. (2000). What form transforms? In J. Mezirow (Ed.), *Learning as transformation* (pp. 35–70). Jossey-Bass.

King, R. (2018). *Mindful of race*. Sounds True.

Knoll, J. L. (2020, March 30). Panic and pandemics: The return of the absurd. *Psychiatric Times*. https://www.psychiatrictimes.com/view/panic-and-pandemics-return-absurd.

MaGee, R. J. (2019). *The inner work of racial justice: Healing ourselves and our communities through mindfulness*. Tarcher Perigee/Random House.

Mezirow, J. (1991). *Transformative dimensions of adult learning*. Jossey-Bass.

Morinis, A. (1992). Introduction: The territory of the anthropology of pilgrimage. In A. Morinis (Ed.), *Sacred journeys: The anthropology of pilgrimage* (pp. 1–28). Greenwood.

Sawatsky, J. (2017). *Dancing with elephants*. Red Canoe Press.

Selby, D. et al. (2001). The signature of the whole. In E. O'Sullivan (Ed.), *Expanding the boundaries of transformative learning* (pp. 77–93). Palgrave.

Scriven, R. (2014). Geographies of pilgrimage. *Geography Compass, 8*, 249–261.

Swartz, A., & Sprow, K. (2010). Is complexity science embedded in transformative learning? In P. Gandy, S. Tieszen, C. Taylor-Hunt, D. Flowers, & V. Sheared (Eds.), *Proceedings of the 51st Adult Education Research Conference*. Sacramento State University.

Swartz, A. (2012). Embodied learning and patient education: From nurses' self-awareness to patient self-caring. In R. L. Lawrence (Ed.), *Bodies of Knowledge: Embodied Learning in Adult Education: New Directions for Adult and Continuing Education*, no. 134 (pp. 15–24). Wiley.

Taylor, E., & Cranton, P. (Eds). (2012). *The handbook of transformative learning*. Jossey-Bass.

Tisdell, E. (2012). Themes and variations in transformative learning: Interdisciplinary perspectives on forms that transform. In E. Taylor & P. Cranton (Eds.), *The handbook of transformative learning* (pp. 21–36). Jossey-Bass.

Tisdell, E. (2017). Transformative pilgrimage learning and spirituality on the Camino de Santiago. In A. Laros, T. Fuhr, & E. Taylor (Eds.), *Transformative learning meets Bildung* (pp. 341–352). Sense Publishing.

Tisdell, E. (2020a). The pulpit and the pew: Transformative teaching and learning and making sense of spiritual and religious experience: A Covid-19 view. In C. A. Lemke (Ed.), *Public sphere and religion. Entangled relations in history, education and society* (pp. 172–197). Olms-Wiedmann.

Tisdell, E. (2020b). Re-searching spirituality and culture: Transformative pilgrimage learning and living answers into big questions. *Journal for the Study of Spirituality, 10*(1), 1–11.

Tisdell, E., & Swartz, A. (Eds.). (2011). *Adult education and the pursuit of wisdom: New directions for adult and continuing education*, no. 131. Jossey-Bass.

Tisdell, E., & Tolliver, E. (2003). Claiming a sacred face: The role of spirituality and cultural identity in transformative adult higher education. *Journal of Transformative Education, 1*(4), 368–392.

Turner, V. (1969). *The ritual process: Structure and anti-structure.* Aldine.

van Gennep, A. (1909). *The rites of passage.* Routledge and Kegan Paul.

Velott, D., & Sprow Forte, K. (2019). Toward health equity: Mindfulness and cultural humility. *New Directions for Adult and Continuing Education, 161*, 57–66.

Wolf, Z. R. (1988). *Nurses' work, the sacred and the profane.* University of Pennsylvania Press.

CHAPTER 13

Washing the Dead Bed, from Poem to Digital Story

Janet Ferguson and Massimo Lambert

BACKGROUND

In July 2017, I witnessed "Washing the Dead Bed," a Tobago Heritage festival ceremony (Small, 2011). In response, I wrote a reflective poem and then set it aside for three years. Recently, with the support of Massimo Lambert (videographer) and Robert Yeates (audio-technician), we converted the poem into a digital story. In summary, my aim in this paper is to explore the refractive and illuminative capacity of digital storytelling by signposting the soulful, spiritual, and community connections required to navigate the complexity of my late life learning as an Afro-Caribbean (Tobagonian) woman. Much like a cartographer, I want to map the transformational terrain of the poem and reveal the

J. Ferguson (✉)
Boaz Island, Bermuda

M. Lambert
Oakland, CA, USA

© The Author(s), under exclusive license to Springer Nature
Switzerland AG 2022
A. Nicolaides et al. (eds.), *The Palgrave Handbook of Learning for Transformation*, https://doi.org/10.1007/978-3-030-84694-7_13

217

dynamic interaction of place, history, community through personal and participatory story-making.

The initial writing of the poem coincided with a number of significant life events. These upheavals included dramatic changes in my personal lifestyle, heightened career and family demands, cross-jurisdictional caregiving responsibilities, and the loss of older family members including my mother.

The experiences of uncertainty, loss, and grief triggered a period of introspection and experimentation with creative expressive forms and rituals drawn from my Caribbean heritage. Bolton and Delderfield (2018) notes that reflective writing is the mirror in which we recognize and work with our "other" selves. In this instance, my mirror was the poem *Washing the Dead Bed.*

Bourdieue (1984) cited by Field (2012) notes the salience of "dispositions" and the disciplinary role of "habitus." We are bound by the socio-cultural context of our biographies and sustained by constantly reworked "positioning narratives." The poem Washing the Dead Bed explores the impact of disengagement with habitus and the overwhelming sense of personal negligence and consequent displacement.

These mid-life feelings of disconnection are not unusual. In response to a widespread recognition of the twenty-first-century shift in longevity patterns, Bateson (2011) describes the "third age" and documents the challenges of navigating life after 55. Waxman (2016) rejects one-off time bound constructions of "mid-life crisis" and suggests instead the idea of a sustained middlescence life period of multiple challenges requiring skillful navigation. Conley and Rauth (2020) ask us to consider this mid-life period as an opportunity-rich life stage extending from 45 to 65.

There is an adult education history of drawing on narrative and the autobiographical for learning. Yet we should distinguish sharing narratives, from story-work and the participative practices that explore meaning, challenge assumptions, and reveal transformative possibilities (Chlopczyk, 2018a). Swarts in Chlopczyk (2018b) explains that storying distills memory in ways that facilitate the recognition of the instructive moments of lived experience.

In *Identity and Lifelong Learning, Becoming Through Lived Experience,* Motulsky et al. (2020) demonstrate the timely convergence of lifelong learning, identity formation, and narrativity. This is preceded by a sustained adult learning narrative turn stretching all the way back to learning biographies (Dominice, 2000), life history inquiry (Biesta et al., 2011), and adult learning biographical research practices (Merrill & West, 2009). This has taken adult learning out of classrooms and into everyday life.

Bhat (2019) describes her transformative encounter with Storycenter's Stories of Home workshop. She explains that the hands-on learning experience included: "identifying a story, writing a highly focused story script, audio recording the script, selecting images, creating and editing the storyboard and producing a short digital film."

Storycenter, the founding home of digital storytelling, insists that digital story-work must be self-revelatory and insightful; stories are personal and written in the first-person voice. Digital stories are no more than three hundred words and reflect a commitment to aesthetic values (Lambert & Hessler, 2020). Digital story-work has much in common with Mezirow's (1991) transformative learning model in so far as both practices aim to facilitate the emergence of insight based on altered perspectives and consequent shifts in meaning making (Lambert & Hessler, 2017).

Methodology

This paper describes the curation of a digital story. The story-center practice model anticipates a group work process somewhat similar to Freire's (2013) "conscientization" cultural circles. While I wrote the poem, Massimo (videographer) and Robert (audio-technician) participated in the curation and assembly of the digital story. Massimo in his role as videographer and co-creator has been an integral part of shaping the digital story.

This paper offers snapshots of the poem to digital story conversion experience through the lends of Cranton's (2016, p. 25) three-dimensional content, process, and premise reflective model.

A multi-voiced elaboration of the process dimension is created by drawing on Formenti and West's (2018) delightful application of Bateson's concept of metalogue. This allows Massimo (ML) and I (JF) to share samples of the things we thought about and said to each other as we worked together in the story-making space.

The Cranton (2016, p. 25) and Formenti and West (2018, p. 27) combination is outlined here:

220   J. FERGUSON AND M. LAMBERT

- Content

    What image/audio is used?
    What is the context of the image/audio use?

- Process

    How and why, are these choices made?
    What do you see?
    How does what you see shape your seeing?
    How did you come to think and answer like that?
    What are your assumptions?
    What do you believe? Who are you?

- Premise

    What is the underlying meaning or interpretative analysis?
    Washing the Dead Bed – Digital Story
    https://youtu.be/-QluWHV9g-s

Afterthoughts

Upon witnessing the Washing of the Dead Bed, I experienced a sense of release; something that needed to be said had been expressed. Back then, I had no idea of how digital story-making and reflective writing about the experience could reveal new insights.

This reflection is multi-layered; the poem, the digital story, and an exposition based on Cranton's (2016) reflective model have surfaced a constellation of stories that were not previously visible or available.

The lens provided by the content, process, and premise dimensions of the reflective schema has revealed the ways in which the particularities of my socio-cultural context had shaped the poem. The digital story-making work brought these to the surface.

For me a poem is an authentic expressive outpouring, a narrative exploration of the landscape of identity that paints images with words. In this instance, digital story-making brought to light a bricolage of hitherto unseen narratives.

This doubling back and deepening of awareness revealed the multi-layered socio-cultural context that informed the writing of the poem.

Digital storytelling enables us to convert powerful moments in our lives into creative multimedia expressions of truth and insight. Poetic reflection, an inherent quality of this kind of story-making, distills memory and narrative and consequently brings a transformational lens to the practice of learning from experience.

Massimo Lambert (videographer), Robert Yeates (audio-technician), and I (the writer) created this digital story. Along the way we engaged in spirited exchanges that included significant questions and observations. As Massimo and I worked on the poem resolving the issues of the geographical distance (he lives in California, I was "CoVid sheltering in place" in Tobago), editing the poem so that it was concise enough for a digital story, and engaging Robbie the audio-technician, we were also building relationships across generational, cultural, and gender differences.

Most importantly, through our collaborative engagement, we were shifting each other's perspectives and broadening our understandings of the world (Table 13.1).

In closing storytelling, an emerging genre, is a unique feature of late-modernity, an admixture of creativity and digital technology inspired by the human compulsion to share lived experiences by telling stories (Table 13.2):

Table 13.1 Questions and the following observations and comments

Questions...	*Observations and comments*
• Do we have too many images that are getting in the way of telling the story?	• *In digital storytelling, less images tell more. Let's aim for 15 images (MLM)*
• Which ones should we remove, when we love them all? (JF)	• *This beautiful moving water river video I like, I'm keeping it, even if it does nothing for the story. [eventually it was edited out] It's your story you decide"! (MLM)*
• Can Zoom keep us connected across the complex math of East coast/West coast/Caribbean time zones?(JF)	• *How bad is the bad audio? Can we find studio quality audio technology in the middle of a CoVid shut down? (JF)*
• Do we need copyright to use family pictures, especially if all those people are dead? (JF)	• *Incredible, this feels like 2017 all over again and I never recognized that this is a "transplanted" West African ritual (JF)*
• Why are we laying on this Yoruba chant, I liked the quiet, sombre reflective tone? (MLM)	• *Here is a Tobago "wake" video: This is how we celebrate life in the midst of death, vibrant music is present in everything we do! (JF)*

Table 13.2 Washing the Dead Bed – Digital Story—https://youtu.be/-QluWHV9g-s

Content
Image: Blue Hole Park, Bermuda
Audio: none
Notes
Bermuda, my home away from home for more than 30 years, is a British colonial territory, settled in 1609
While they are associated with stagnation and flooding mangroves hold the potential for vibrant plant and animal life

Premise
Dirkx (2001) explains that images help learners "connect the knowable conscious world to the unknowable or the unconscious"
Images facilitate subliminal levels of story-work by providing metaphors that take our sensorial awareness beyond the boundaries of everyday discursive terrains. This broadens and deepens the interface of reflective engagement
This image" highlights the complex micro-systems that simultaneously represent possibilities of stagnation and re-generation

Process
(MLM) Initially, we planned on using a short video of a stream to begin the story. I was tenaciously attached to it. When we switched to this image as an opener, it made the story more cohesive, connecting with the motif of in-between, liminal spaces of the land and mind; shorelines and memories
(JF) Massimo settled on this image and we agreed that it conveyed the tone and register of the opening movement of the poem
(JF) Mangroves provoke wariness and a sense of foreboding; mangroves and swamps figure prominently in Caribbean and African folklore and mythology as places of mystery and hidden secrets. They are also sacred threshold spaces

Content

Image: Roxborough Cocoa Estate, Tobago
I did not walk the huddled squat of bow-legged cocoa
I did not tread
the veins of molted leaves
did not hear the sigh
of windblown bamboo

Notes

From 1866–1920 Trinidad and & Tobago was the world's third largest cocoa producer (Bekele, 2004)
Cocoa cultivation provided employment entrepreneurial opportunities for early generations of no longer enslaved people (Craig-James, 2008)
Cocoa's decline pushed islanders out of the region in search of opportunities
Migration is a salient feature of the Caribbean socio-historical landscape (Faure, 2018)
In the Arrivants, a poetic trilogy, poet-historian, Brathwaite celebrates Caribbean identity formation in the context of forced and voluntary migrations (Samakande, 2018)

"Regret and remorse can be either paralyzing or inspiring" (Bateson, 2011, p. 199)

Process

(JF) We chose this image to strengthen the opening lines of the poem
(JF) For me this image of "decline and abandonment" triggers a visceral connection with the shock waves of the sudden decline of the cocoa industry
(JF) I "see" the long shadow of the vagaries of imperial history. My great-grandfather was a cocoa farmer circa 1890 to the 1930s. Three generations of his descendants including myself have migrated

Premise

This tactile journey through a narrative of regret is achieved by combining sound and images in ways that engage "imaginal knowing" (Heron, 1992)
White (2007), a narrative therapist, suggests that story-work fosters the recognition of the "landscape of identity". Our stories raise questions about absences and presences
In my absence what has been neglected, what has been lost?
Digital storytelling curates images and sounds in ways that bring our backstories forward

(continued)

Table 13.2 (continued)

Content
Image: Main Ridge Forest, Tobago Recognized as Crown Reserve in 1776 The Main Ridge Forest Reserve; retrieved (01/12/2021)
Audio:
I did not see the first light crawl
along the dew-dropped canopy
did not rub blue marbled soap
on a rippled washboard
I did not wash
the bed of the dead
Notes
TOBAGO RITUALS Mere Myths or Meaningful Practices?
"Washing the dead bed is also an important ritual. Women take the clothes of the dead down to the river wash in an effort to prevent the spirit of the dead from returning to haunt the living. Washing of the dead's clothes must be conducted where the river meet[s] the sea"
https://tobagorituals.wordpress.com/death/

Citing Canu (2013), Karangi, (2019) notes the defining influence of African cosmology on both diaspora and continental Africans. He explains: "African cosmology is the way Africans perceive, conceive and contemplate their universe; the lens through which they see reality, which affects their value systems and attitudinal orientations" (Karangi, 2019, p. 1)

Process

(JF) Initially, we used multiple images of the river and nearby areas. We agreed that the flowing river images were too literal; they cluttered the narrative and overtold less important aspects of the story

(JF) Effective digital storytelling depends on a delicate minimalist curation of images, words and audio

(MLM) While the text conveys the author's inability to 'See', the image juxtaposes it with clarity, though blurry. This effect intends to remind the viewer that it was always there, though unseen

(JF) The image of the forest canopy conveys a sublimated sense of shame grounded in disconnection and regret

Content

Image: Sugar Works of the Roxborough Estate, Parish St. Mary's, Tobago

Audio:
last night
the full moon vanished
my mother called my name out loud
old women sang
one thousand verses
a steady stream
of poured libations
Background audio: Yoruba chant

Premise

"Washing the Dead Bed" is a ritual practice that has survived enslavement. This endurance illustrates multi-generational resistance to cultural erasure and the retention of Afro-centric practices that demonstrate an adherence to African cosmology

For me migration and disconnection with the island's day-to-day practices of collective and personal resilience reduced my opportunities for generative engagement and vigorous expressions of personal agency. The challenge of navigating midlife changes alongside this "coming apart" coalesced into a tangle of seething undercurrents of regret Story-work can be the transformative space in which we work with feelings of disconnection, re-framing experience through the illuminative lens of digital story-making

Spiritual Baptist

Forde (2019, p. 18), describes the Spiritual Baptist "mourning" ritual: "'The spiritual world is best explored in the mourning ritual. During this long rite of seclusion, sensory deprivation, fasting and praying, ritual candidates conduct a journey to one or more of the nations or to other spiritual places'"

(continued)

Table 13.2 (continued)

Process	Premise
(JF) Music strengthens the somatic resonance of the ritual. African cosmology affirms life in the presence of death. We discussed grief and ritual practices across cultures (MLM) This image induced claustrophobia at first, leading me to choose slow, ominous music. The ensuing discussion about Tobagonian wakes catalyzed questions about funerals, and death and the overlap of grief and joy between	The dreamscape of the poem's second movement draws on the Spiritual Baptist discerning practice of "moaning"; the introspective journey undertaken by initiates Digital story-making journeys can facilitate aesthetic movement along familiar socio-cultural pathways of reflection and inquiry Principled and authentic story-work respects the particularities of the stories, the storytellers and the socio-cultural context
Content Image: Lambeau River, Lower Scarborough Tobago Audio: crayfish listened to the alligator's stories river currents crossed and wet the sea **Notes** As a child I repeatedly heard the proverb "when the crayfish tells you the alligator's belly has scales, you must believe it." The general meaning of that proverb is that ecosystems are defined by interdependent relationships "Bronfenbrenner's Ecological systems theory suggests that "people are nested in and are an inseparable part of their community. People develop within these intertwined organizational, community, home and personal settings that are joined formally or informally to create a system or ecology in which they are shaped and, in turn can influence" (Bennett & Grant, 2016, p. 2)	 At the turn of the nineteenth century my great-grandfather owned the properties that bordered both sides of this river's entrance to the sea

Process

(JF) Familiar image evokes memories of my early childhood morning walks, the sound of my grandfather's hip-holstered leather machete swinging against his trousered thigh

(JF) I see myself, gazing into the water listening to wild duck calls and thinking about my uncle's late evening hunting and fishing outings

Content

Image: River mouth - Speyside Village, Tobago
Audio:
salt wrestled spirits
drifted away at high tide
dawn spat into the open mouth
of faced backwards buckets
drummed dance lines shook
bent low, never spilled a drop
Background audio: Yoruba chant fades

Notes

In his ethnographic description of the ritual Small (2011, p. 18) notes "The spectacle may differ with every community or culture but indeed the element of bereavement as performance remains universal"

Premise

The slave trade forcibly removed people from Africa in order to provide slave labor in the Caribbean and the Americas (Rodney, 1973). Water is the reminder of our transatlantic journey

How did those who have gone before move beyond survival? How did my great-grandfather, a black man born one generation after slavery manage to achieve economic autonomy?

If he were here now, what would I want to ask him across time and generations? What can I, as his great-granddaughter, learn and carry forward from him?

(continued)

Table 13.2 (continued)

Process	Premise
(JF) The river mouth is a cleansing image We agreed on the placement of this image, it repeats the water trope while simultaneously signaling possibilities beyond the horizon while highlighting connectivity (MLM) The river mouth represents space where two worlds collide; the river as a finite, familiar village, the sea as an infinite border. In the context of the story, it represents memories as well, West African traditions kept alive over centuries of harsh colonialism	This final image on the dream sequence draws on an African cosmology that affirms life in the face of death. Singing and dancing emphasizes the capacity of the living to carry on in spite of loss and grief These acts of practicing and yearning for African connections ensures a rejection of the Eurocentric "othering", the central feature of the colonial project For those who have experienced the impact of colonialism this provides a liberating transcendence of the sense of shame and inadequacy fostered by relationships of subordination (Samakande, 2018)
Content Image: Cafe picture - Books & Books, Coral Gables Miami Audio: all the while I was seated in a cafe designer sunglasses cream panama hat my hand folded morning paper set the world down in four rectangled window panes all tucked neatly at the elbow morning coffee on a lace metallic table	
Note The Panama hat was a migration status symbol flaunted by migrant returnees visiting from Aruba, Panama and other regional jurisdictions where seasonal employment was readily available	

Process

(JF) It was difficult to settle on this single image. Much of the poem's original script in this section was removed. This included a description of cafe life and the surrounding area. We agreed that these details cluttered the 'digital story". They were distracting and undermined the movement of the action
Digital stories are limited to 300 words
(MLM) Initially, I found this image to be dull, and resisted using it for an entire stanza. In retrospect, that is its purpose. This moment in the text is about absence. The emptiness of the cafe allows the imagination to follow the poem, placing its objects on the tables

Premise

This is the loitering spot for the marginalized voyeur who belongs everywhere and nowhere. The life affirming dance associated with the ritual "Washing of the Dead Bed" is replaced by "the café" as a universal trope of disconnection
We can move beyond a singular story of Caribbean migration and displacement to the universal themes of marginalization and anomie
As mature adults it is possible hold the position of "marooned migrant" irrespective of our nationality or origins
Despite navigating an assortment of challenges we can find ourselves at mid-life cut off from re-vitalizing community networks and rituals; ill-equipped for encountering late modernity

(continued)

Table 13.2 (continued)

Content

Image -Bermuda Banana doll made by Ronnie Chameau (Bermudian dollmaker) for the Lifelong Learning Centre, Bermuda College (2018)
Audio:
a Banana woman
with indigo eyes
read my spooned espresso grounds
Drawing on folk memory the image is a combination of two Trinidad and Tobago folklore figures:
the Douen, "a mythical figure that lives in swamps and near rivers"
the Lajabless, "a devil woman who comes out at night to prey on unsuspecting men"

Process

(JF) In selecting this image from my collection of photos I was not thinking about mythical figures. I was reluctant to use a specific figure for fear of being too literal by matching words and images

(MLM) The banana woman doll conjures up spirits, reminding me of Pueblo Kachina dolls from the American Southwest and Corn husk dolls from Oaxaca

Content

Image: 100 year old cup and saucer
Audio:
from the bottom of a blue rimmed cup

Note

Place here: about Tobago history - plantation economics, indigo, cotton, sugar, cocoa, cash crops "as wealthy as Tobago planter"

Premise

The "banana woman with indigo eyes" is the disrupter of the voyeuristic distancing described in the previous café scene. She is an outsider. Much like an adult education practitioner/digital story facilitator, her role is the practice of "helpful disruption" (Newman, 2006) describes the difficulty of finding a simple explanation of the facilitative and instructional role of adult educators

Block and Markowitz (2012) in their field-book liken" process" consultants to fairground fortune tellers who vanish at the end of the fair

Formenti (Formenti and West, 2019) explains her turn from the practice of psychology to adult education by noting the developmental and emancipatory promise of adult learning theory and practice

(continued)

Table 13.2 (continued)

Process	Premise
(JF) This is the last cup of my Grandmother's personal "espresso collection", she purchased more than 100 years ago from a door-to-door salesman (JF)The image of a cup that brings together the colonial histories of Caribbean sugar, cocoa, and coffee. These Cash crops were sources of extracted wealth that contributed to the growth of cities in France, England and Spain	The banana woman with indigo eyes reads "the [coffee] grounds". Her presence sign-posts the convergence of normally separated spheres As migrants, as women, and as members of marginalized minorities we often exist in spaces in which we are defined by oppressive and subordinating relationships What kinds of questions do we have sitting at the bottom of our blue-rimmed cups? Who reads our [coffee] grounds?
Content Image: - image of blowing curtain *"spirit passing"* Audio: you are lost" she said "they are looking for you" the spirits called your name out loud and you must go **Note** In a world which casually recognizes the ability of the spirits to slip imperceptibly between the material and the spiritual realms a moving curtain is a gentle reminder of the eve- present protection and guidance of the ancestors	

Process

(JF) The curtain blowing, open door image reminds me of belief systems that affirms the existence of a multi-dimensional world in which we are never alone, the spirits are always in attendance; we remain connected to the ancestors

(JF) We had no difficulty selecting and agreeing on this image. It works well and conveys everything we want to tell by showing (MLM) This image shows the wind as a vehicle for spirits, ancestors that bring themselves to us in dreams. It shows a shared, transcultural understanding of spirits presenting themselves in doorways, visitors unseen

Premise

This is an exploration of ancestral presence within the context of an intergenerational acknowledgement of African cosmology
The assertion "you are lost" is underpinned by a subtext of rescue and recovery. Hence "the spirits called your name out loud" is an irrevocable confirmation of "belonging"
We can relate to ancestral presence if we set aside reliance on the objective measurement of time and privilege the more fluid interpretation of the temporality of experience
Participants and witnesses are in the past and the present simultaneously; knowledge is transmitted across dissolved boundaries of linear time and space; participatory engagement and movement within this performative space of an act of coming to know

Content

Image: Convict bath house, Hospital Island, Bermuda
Audio:
It is midnight
I have walked backwards
into the forest

Note

Walking in the Forest
"If you were to meet Mama Dio in the forest and wish to escape her, take off your left shoe, turn it upside down and immediately leave the scene, walking backwards until you reach home"
Triniview Our Folklore is Predominantly of African Origin
http://www.triniview.com/TnT/Folklore.htm

(continued)

Table 13.2 (continued)

Process	Premise
(JF) Images of convict bath house ...walking feet Massimo was able to produce an image of a journey to re-connection—with illustrative action steps (MLM) This image invokes a spiritual gateway, or portal. In the context of the story, it symbolizes an evolution from questioning to understanding. With its transition to color, the image conveys a new day, bridging the circle between midnight dreams and dawn revelations	This solid, walled and bricked representation of achievement in the context of measured time is presented alongside the temporality of the experience of "walking backwards into the forest" A respectful and mindful entry into "the unknown" honors community memory while affirming an African cosmology defined by the tropes of "creole" resistance and African retention While admitting the absence of a universal definition of transformation Nerstrom (2014) confirms the value of accommodating somatic, affective and spiritual interpretations alongside rational cognitive interpretations of transformative learning
Content Image: Lambeau Village, Milford Road- eroding shoreline adjacent to the river Audio: I am looking for the river mouth That is looking for the sea I am listening for the drum That listens for the song of women And hears the crayfish tell the alligator's secrets	

Process

(JF) An active shoreline that contrasts with the mangrove swamps at the opening of the digital story

(JF) We can see movement and change

(MLM) The choice to overlay a transparent image of Janet's ancestors over the image of the sea contrasts with the previous overlay in the cocoa house, and coincides with Janet's reflection on feeling a deep release after writing the poem

Premise

There is movement towards a different way of being characterized by an open readiness to sensitively encounter a landscape that previously provoked feelings of disconnection; guided by the recent transformative encounter there is an acute awareness of what to listen for, how it can be heard and what it means

Nerstrom (2014, p. 327) replaces Mezirow's ten-phase model of transformative learning with a non-sequential four-phased schema

Her emergent approach emphasizes "becoming":

"Adopting and acting upon a new perspective, we view ourselves and others through a more encompassing lens. Transformative learning becomes a new experience leading to openness for it to occur again" Nerstrom (2014, p. 328)

Content

Image: stone cairns built in my grandparents' yard
Audio: my heart is open,
I am ready
to wash the bed
of the dead

Note

Throughout the Covid "shelter in place" lockdown. On my best days, I built four cairns

(continued)

Table 13.2 (continued)

Process	Premise
(JF) Enduring stones that predate my existence. They convey a pervasive sense of timelessness (MLM) The cairns were a serendipitous conclusion to the story. Initially we discussed using the image of Janet's family members, but it felt too literal, and was limited by the quality of the images, and glare. The image of cairns, symbolic of ancestors, were a much more powerful choice	The poem ends on a note of surrender and reconciliation completing the transformative movement from disconnection to re-integration The cairns are similar to shrines encountered along the banks of local rivers often left after ritual spiritual baths. Perhaps the impulse to build cairns is an expression of my subliminal link to the island's cosmology of Afro-retentions informed by defining patterns of resistance and resilience Reflection on the making of the digital-story brought this significant middlessence navigation trope forward

"It is an ancient Mariner,
And he stoppeth one of three.
'By thy long grey beard and glittering eye,
Now wherefore stopp'st thou me?"

—Rime of the Ancient Mariner, Coleridge

REFERENCES

Baldwin, C. (2007). *Storycatcher: Making sense of our lives through the power & practice of story*. New World Library.

Bateson, M. C. (2011). *Composing a further life: The age of active wisdom*. Vintage

Bekele, F. L. (2004). The history of cocoa production in Trinidad and Tobago. In *Proceedings of the APASTT Seminar – Exhibition Entitled Revitalisation of the Trinidad & Tobago Cocoa Industry, 20 September 2003* (pp. 4–12). St. Augustine, Trinidad.

Bennett, J., & Grant, N. (2016). Using an ecomap as a tool for qualitative data collection in organizations *New Horizons in Adult Education & Human Resource Development, 28*(2), 1–13. https://doi.org/10.1002/nha3.20134

Bhat, M. (2019). *Empowering immigrant and refugee women through digital storytelling*. Ms. https://msmagazine.com/2019/10/14/empowering-migrant-women-through-digital-storytelling/

Biesta, G., Field, J., Hodkinson, P., Macleod, F., & Goodson, I. (2011) *Improving learning through the lifecourse: Learning lives*. Routledge.

Block, P., & Markowitz, A. (2012). *The flawless consulting fieldbook and companion*. Pfeiffer.

Bolton, G., & Delderfield, R. (2018). *Reflective practice: Writing and professional development*. Sage.

Bourdieue, P. (1979/1984). *Distinction a social critique of the judgement of taste*. Harvard University Press.

Braithwaite, E. K. (1973). *The Arrivants: A new world trilogy*. Oxford University Press.

Campbell, J. (2008). *The hero with a thousand faces*. New World Library.

Conley, C., & Rauth, I. (2020). *The emergence of long life learning*. https://www.researchgate.net/publication/344407283_The_Emergence_of_Long_Life_Learning

Cranton, P. (2016). *Understanding and promoting transformative learning*. Stylus Publishing.

238   J. FERGUSON AND M. LAMBERT

Chlopczyk, J. (2018a, Summer). Why storytelling, why now? Circling around a Buzzword. Re-authoring futures, *CON-TEXTS*, Beyond Storytelling Conference Reader, Hamburg, p. 26. https://www.beyondstorytelling.com/s/rea der-final-print.pd

Chlopczyk. J. (2018b, Summer). Across the Ocean—A conversation with Chené Swart about re-authoring futures. Re-authoring futures, *CON-TEXTS*, Beyond Storytelling Conference Reader, Hamburg, p. 6. https://www.bey ondstorytelling.com/s/reader-final-print.pd

Craig-James, S. (2008). *The changing society of Tobago 1838–1938—A fractured whole* (Vol. II, 1900–1938). CornerStone Press

Coleridge, S. (1992). *The rime of the ancient mariner.* Dover Publications.

Conley, C. & Rauth, I. (2020). *The emergence of longlife learning* (White Paper). https://www.researchgate.net/publication/344407283_The_Emerge nce_of_Long_Life_Learning

Dirkx J. M. (2001). Images, transformative learning and the work of the soul. *Adult Learning, Contestations, Invitations, and Explorations, Spirituality in Adult Learning, 12*(3).

Dirkx, J. M., Espinoza, B. D., & Schlegel, S. (2018). *Critical reflection and imaginative engagement: Towards an integrated theory of transformative learning* (Paper presentation). Adult Education Research Conference, Vancouver, Canada. https://newprairiepress.org/aerc/2018/papers/4

Dirkx, J. (2008). The Meaning and Role of Emotions. *New Directions for Adult and Continuing Education* (120), 7–78.

Dominice, P. (2000). *Learning from our lives: Using educational biographies with adults.* Jossey Bass

Erlach C., & Müller M. (2020). Stories: What organizations are made of. In C. Erlach & M. Müller (Eds.), *Narrative organizations making companies future proof by working with stories.* Springer.

Faure, A. (2018). *Migratory patterns in the Caribbean: Impacts and perspectives for Caribbean countries.* http://www.open-diplomacy.eu/blog/migratory-pat terns-in-the-caribbean-impacts-and-perspectives-for-caribbean

Field, J. (2012). Learning from our lives. In P. Jarvis (Ed.), *Routledge international handbook of lifelong learning* (pp. 176–183). Routledge.

Maarit, F. (2019). The Spiritual Baptist religion. *Caribbean Quarterly, 65*(2), 212–240. https://doi.org/10.1080/00086495.2019.1606991

Formenti, L., & West, L. (2018). *Transforming perspectives in lifelong learning and adult education.* Palgrave Macmillan.

Friere, P. (2013). *Education for critical consciousness.* Bloomsbury

Heron, J. (1992). *Feeling and personhood: Psychology in another key.* Sage.

Hessler, B., & Lambert, J. (2017). Threshold concepts in digital storytelling: Naming what we know About storywork. In G. Jamisson, P. Hardy, Y.

Nordkvelle, & H. Pleasants (Eds.), *Digital storytelling in higher education, international perspectives* (pp. 19–21). Palgrave Macmillan.

Karangi, M. (2019). *African cosmology.* Retrieved on January 1, 2021 from https://www.researchgate.net/publication/336445595_AFRICAN_C OSMOLOGY

Lambert, J., & Hessler, B. (2020). *Digital storytelling storywork for urgent times.* Digital Diner Press.

Nerstrom, N. (2014). *An emerging model for transformative learning* (Paper presentation). Adult Education Research Conference, Vancouver, Canada. https://newprairiepress.org/aerc/2014/papers/55

Merrill, B., & West, L. (2009). *Using biographical methods in social research.* Sage.

Mezirow, J. (1991). *Transformative dimensions of adult learning.* Jossey-Bass.

Motulsky, S. L., Gammel, J. A., & Rutstein-Riley, A. (2020). *Identity and life-long learning, becoming through lived experience.* Information Age Publishing. Retrieved January 12, 2021 from https://nationaltrust.tt/location/the-main-ridge-forest-reserve/

Newman, M. (2006). Throwing out the balance with the bathwater. In *The encyclopedia of pedagogy and informal education.* Retrieved January 14, 2021 from https://infed.org/mobi/adult-education-throwing-out-the-balance-with-the-bathwater/

O'Neal, J. J. (n.d.). *Tobago rituals. Mere myths or meaningful practices?* https://tobagorituals.wordpress.com/death/

Samakande, E. (2018). *The transnational griot Afro-Caribbean culture: Discussing the search for identity in Edward Kamau Brathwaite's the arrivants: A new world trilogy.* https://www.academia.edu/38133033/BRA THWAITE_PRESENTATION_pdf

Small, D. (2011). *The heritage festival—A study of cultural authenticity and festival tourism with specific reference to the washing of the dead bed ritual of Charlotteville* (Undergraduate thesis). University of West Indies.

Rodney, W. (1973). *How Europe underdeveloped Africa.* Bogle-L'Ouverture.

Triniview.com (n.d.). *Our folklore is predominantly of African origin.* http://www.triniview.com/TnT/Folklore.htm

Turner, V. (2017). *The ritual process structure and anti-structure* (Foreword by R. D. Abrahams). Routledge, Taylor & Francis Group.

Waxman, B. (2016). *The middlescence manifesto: Igniting the passion of midlife.* The Middlescence Factor

White, M. (2007). *Maps of narrative practice.* W. W. Norton.

Wiley Online Library. (2018). *Terrestrial species adapted to sea dispersal: Differences in propagule dispersal of two Caribbean mangroves.* https://onlinelibrary.wiley.com/doi/abs/10.1111/mec.14894

CHAPTER 14

Transforming Individual to Structural Thinking About Race

Stephen Brookfield

The perspectives we use to make sense of the world around us inevitably frame our actions. When it comes to understanding actions around race and identity, the ideology of white supremacy has, understandably, been a major focus of attention. White supremacy as an ideology is built on the notion that Whites should automatically and naturally be in positions of power and authority. This is because Whites are presumed to exhibit supposedly higher intelligence and to possess the ability to use logic, reason, and analysis to make calm and objective decisions. Under white supremacy, people of color, on the other hand, are viewed as too emotional, unpredictable, and prone to losing control very easily. White supremacy uses their presumed irrationality and propensity to act violently as a justification for conflating leadership with whiteness.

This ideology is learned from an early age. When viewed through the lens of white supremacy and what Feagin (2013) calls the white racial frame, the same behaviors are assigned very different meanings based on

S. Brookfield (✉)
Antioch University, Culver City, CA, USA

© The Author(s), under exclusive license to Springer Nature   241
Switzerland AG 2022
A. Nicolaides et al. (eds.), *The Palgrave Handbook of Learning for Transformation*, https://doi.org/10.1007/978-3-030-84694-7_14

the racial identity of the person concerned. For example, an admission of error or owning up to a mistake is seen as a refreshingly honest display of openness and vulnerability by a White person, but as evidence of incompetence and affirmative action gone wrong in a person of color. Standing up and speaking strongly in support of your ideas is much more likely to be taken as evidence of admirable commitment in Whites, but seen as pushing an agenda or being "uppity" in people of color. Displaying emotion and shedding tears is viewed as an indicator of deep authenticity in Whites, but a sign of psychological instability in people of color.

Replacing an individualist perspective with one that now interprets racism as a structural phenomenon involves understanding that white supremacy is embedded in, and learned from, institutional policies, practices, and protocols. This constitutes a transformative cognitive shift that has great ramifications for how we dismantle racism. No longer do we focus only on intrapersonal anti-racism. Instead, we devote significant time and energy to changing institutional structures and collective habits. Our attention shifts to the importance of collective efforts as we come to realize that individual and collective liberation are inseparable (Crass, 2013). Learning to think structurally is an example of a fundamental shift in our meaning perspective of how we understand racism and white supremacy functions and how best to combat these.

The Ideology of Individualism

Individualism as a dominant ideology in the United States comprises a set of beliefs and practices that help keep a blatantly unequal system in place. It comprises two core beliefs. The first is that we live on a roughly level playing field and that anyone can make what they want of their life by dint of their own perseverance and hard work. When parents tell their children that they can be anything they want to be, this seems an optimistic and motivational message. It inspires children to visualize alternative futures. It inspires dreams and underscores the Horatio Alger mythology that anyone can lift themselves up by their boot straps, pull their socks up, and soar out into the world as a dynamic entrepreneur.

The second core belief is that we are in control of our individual destinies, captains of our souls. What we make of our lives is believed to be a result of the personal decisions we take at the significant turning points we all experience. The feelings, instincts, and intuitions that govern our actions are believed to be unique to us alone. Together they constitute our particular identity, the sole actor who maneuvers through the terrain of an individual life. At some deep level, we see ourselves as disconnected from the settings, locations, and people that surround us as we choose our particular path.

This individualist emphasis is an enduring, deeply rooted, and extremely powerful element of the American psyche, particularly for Whites. It's bound up with notions of individual liberty, the flag, freedom of speech, and Lady Liberty waving in generations of hopeful immigrants and giving them the chance to make better lives for themselves. Archetypal figures such as the cowboy, the frontier settler, even the venture capitalist embody the notion that anyone can be President or the CEO of a global corporation.

Of course, this is a white lie in that life chances are irrevocably tied to racial identity. So if you are White, then the chances that you will be able to aspire to and create wealth are higher. The myth of individualism uses Black exceptionalism—the successes of individuals of color from President Obama to Michael Jordan or Kanye West—to prove its truth. "Look at all these successful Black politicians, media moguls and billionaire sports stars—they prove that anyone can be wildly successful irrespective of their race!"

Individualism and Racism

An individualistic understanding of racism interprets it as a personal choice. White people are judged to be able to decide on a day by day basis whether or not they will behave in a racist way. When racism is perceived as a series of individual judgments and actions—today I was racist but yesterday I was not—then combatting racism becomes seen as a matter of personal fortitude. Whites can make a resolution to be on high alert for their own enactment of racial microaggressions, can vow to monitor their implicit biases, and strive to cut out racist jokes, tropes, and stereotypes. Viewed this way, Whites like myself can convince ourselves that real progress is being made, one person at a time.

I don't want to dismiss these individual kinds of efforts as naïve. I take them very seriously and try to work on myself in all the ways just described. But I'm also aware that seeing anti-racism as a matter of personal resolve obscures the systemic nature of the phenomenon. Individual acts of racism are the personal enactments of structural reality.

White supremacy as an ideology and system ensures the continuing dominance of one racial group by portraying its exercise of control as an uncontestable empirical truth. If you are imbued with this ideology, then the fact that Whites end up in positions of power and authority is not the result of systemic oppression, but just the way things are. The continuing disenfranchisement and marginalization of people of color are not seen as being linked to school district funding mechanisms, the specific design of intelligence tests, or redlining housing policies. The disproportionate levels of infant mortality or poor health care among communities of color are rarely tied to the fact that members of those communities have to piece together a minimum wage from two or three part-time jobs, none of which carry health benefits. The school to prison pipeline is not connected to the criminalization of blackness and brownness.

An anti-racist identity must focus on understanding racism as structural and systemic, and on a commitment to taking collective action to change those structures and systems. Working on your own racist habits, inclinations, and biases is important and necessary, but it is only the beginning of a fully realized anti-racist identity. We must move from the personal to the collective, from the individual to the systemic. We must contribute to building movements, commit to furthering institutional and community initiatives that address inequity, and focus our energies on changing policies and structures. People come and go but structures and policies endure unless some collective effort disrupts them. In short, we need to think structurally, not individually.

In their analysis of the structural roots of implicit bias, Daumeyer et al. (2017) argue that, "a model of implicit bias that situates its expression on situational factors, then, should be more acceptable to individuals" (p. 258). I have observed this to be the case when working with Whites to unearth learned racism. It seems that when biases, microaggressions and racist stereotypes are understood as socially and culturally learned rather than as originating in individual psyches, there is less embarrassment to owning up to them. If teachers and leaders disclose how they learned to think structurally and explain that a white supremacist view of the world comes from passing through structures and systems, then this can legitimize others going public with their own learned racism. When teachers and leaders present how learning racism was as a normal part of their enculturation and socialization, then it often makes it easier for people to talk about how it's manifested in their own lives. I often say that to grow up in a racist world and not to have learned racist conditioning

14 TRANSFORMING INDIVIDUAL ... 245

would be very strange. So I try to normalize racism by presenting it not as a shameful personal moral defect but as a natural outcome of living every day in racist systems and structures.

Beginning with Story: The Brain Fart

I advocate starting most work on developing a White anti-racist identity with some kind of personal narrative or story that is analyzed using a structural frame. When teaching structural thinking, people are encouraged to work backward from a particular event and to see how specific actions are structurally framed.

The following is an example of a story I use to lead participants into structural thinking.

I was running what I thought was an effective student discussion one day in a university graduate class that was overwhelmingly White and mostly female. I considered the discussion successful because it seemed that everybody was participating in roughly equal measure.

About thirty minutes into the class, I raised a particular issue and asked everyone to contribute their thinking on the topic. A couple of students hesitantly ventured their initial thoughts and I practiced my usual waiting time until eventually everyone had spoken. The contributions were focused and thoughtful and I was pleased by the way the students had brought a variety of perspectives to the issue.

I began summarizing the main themes that I thought had emerged from the comments and I started to differentiate the contradictory views that I felt had been expressed.

Suddenly a White woman participant, Jenn, raised her hand.

"Excuse me, we haven't heard from Mia," she said.

Mia was a young Asian American woman and the thought that I had overlooked her was immediately embarrassing to me.

"I'm really sorry about that Mia," I said. "I don't know how that happened. My apologies, I don't know how I missed you. Can we hear from you what you're thinking about?"

Mia made her contribution and shortly afterward we took a mid-class break.

I was still bothered and feeling embarrassed by my not noticing that Mia hadn't spoken and as I brewed up some tea in my office close to the classroom I started to go over what had just happened.

246   S. BROOKFIELD

It became obvious to me almost immediately that this was a classic example of a microaggression. Microaggressions occur when members of the dominant culture act unwittingly in ways that diminish, demean, and marginalize members of minority groups. These actions are so subtle that the receivers are often left wondering "Did that really happen?" or "Am I making too much of something? Am I imagining this?"

When challenged on their actions, those committing microaggressions usually respond by saying the person identifying the aggression is being too sensitive, making a mountain out of a molehill, or just misunderstanding what was said or meant. Members of the dominant culture then usually jump in to excuse and explain away the aggression, saying that it was a slip of the tongue, came out the wrong way, and that no harm was meant. This is often accompanied by character witness testimonials of how the aggressor doesn't have a racist bone in their body, is a good person, and cares for all students.

The class resumed after break and I began by speaking about what had happened when I had overlooked Mia.

"I want to thank Jenn for bringing to my attention the fact that I completely overlooked Mia in class. What you've just witnessed is a classic example of a racial microaggression. I had no intent to exclude Mia from the discussion and no awareness of that happening. Yet when I thanked you all for contributing and began to summarize your comments I completely overlooked a woman of color. Microaggressions are the small acts of exclusion that Whites often enact against people of color. They're not deliberate or intentional and they happen with no wish to harm someone else. But that's what happened when I didn't notice that Mia hadn't spoken and I went into my summary."

Almost immediately, the only White male member of the group, John, spoke up.

"You know Dr. Brookfield I think you're being way too hard on yourself. You just had a forgetful moment. Not every action has to do with race. Sometimes you're just tired. You just had a brain fart. I don't think you should blame yourself. If we take this to the extreme we're never going to be able to do or say anything without being thought of as racist."

I thought it was beautifully ironic that John's response captured a dynamic of microaggressions that I hadn't previously talked about. His comments illustrated precisely how members of the dominant culture jump in to save others who they feel are being unjustly accused. I, not

Mia, had been the one to name my own microaggression, and yet John had felt compelled to jump in and save me from myself.

I told John that he had just exemplified a very predictable dynamic that happens of Whites trying to excuse other Whites who are called on their microaggressions.

John seemed offended by my comments. "Well, it's obvious I can't say anything in this course without being called a racist!" he exclaimed. "This is clearly not a safe space for me so I'm just going to shut up."

Just then Mia spoke up.

"This is not the first time this has happened to me," she said, her voice quavering. "In every class I've been in at this institution I feel I've been systematically ignored. It's like people don't see me or think I'm in the room."

CODING THE STORY

Here's how I get students to connect a story such as The Brain Fart to thinking structurally about race.

I hand out a written version of the story and ask people to spend five minutes carefully reading it. They are told to answer the three questions below:

- What events or actions in the story demonstrate the presence of white supremacy as an ideology or set of practices?
- How is the specific location of the story affected by wider structures, systems, and forces?
- Whose interests inside and outside the specific location of the story are served or harmed by the events described?

After completing their responses to the questions, people share their responses in small groups. The whole workshop, class, or meeting then reconvenes and we hear what people have talked about.

Here's how the discussion of The Brain Fart might go.

- What events or actions in the story demonstrate the presence of white supremacy as both an ideology or set of practices?

Since the story is about a racial microaggression, it's pretty predictable that people will point out how my forgetting to include Mia is an example of white supremacy in action. They'll also recognize that Jenn's interruption represented a challenge both to white supremacy and to patriarchy. My initial apology when reacting to Jenn's pointing out my ignoring Mia is often interpreted as a typically white blindness to the effect of one's actions. At this point, people may cite the notion of white fragility (DiAngelo, 2018).

John's intervention to excuse and save me is also cited as an example of white supremacy at play. By excusing my ignoring Mia, John is trying to advance the idea that race had little significance in the situation, and that this was a one-off event and not any form of systemic exclusion. John's announcing that he now doesn't feel safe in the course and that he's going to withdraw from subsequent conversations is also an exemplar of whiteness. Whites, unlike people of color, are able to choose when they wish to engage with race.

- How is the specific location of the story affected by wider structures, systems, and forces?

The story takes place in a specific classroom and it is easy to assume that this constitutes more or less a self-contained universe. But I hope that participants will dig deeper.

The first point of analysis is usually the college. People ask about the college's mission statement, its funding, and the health of student enrolments. They ask about the degree to which the class itself exemplifies or contradicts the mission statement. I usually mention the influence of market forces. I teach in a private institution, so the logic of capitalism is clearly at play. My institution is tuition driven, and it's clear that an overwhelming concern of leadership is to attract the maximum number of students.

I ask people to ponder what influence, if any, the concern to attract tuition revenue might have on the conduct of the class. Have I created a problem by making John decide he doesn't wish to participate any more in the course? Could this lead to him dropping out and the subsequent loss of tuition revenue? What will be the financial consequences of my teaching about microaggressions? If communities of color become aware this is happening, would it cause more students of color to apply to the university? Or, would this work be opposed by alumni as too radical and not in keeping with the university's traditions and identity?

It's likely that I'll then ask participants to consider how traditions are shaped and institutional identities defined. This brings into play the levers and influences behind the scenes such as the Board of Trustees. Students tend to think that power in colleges resides in the senior leadership team comprised of the President, Provost, and Dean's Council. In fact, the body ultimately responsible for setting policy, defining goals, and assessing compliance with the mission is the Board of Trustees.

Knowing this, I get people to go to the college's web site and look up the composition of the board. What kind of occupations or interests are represented in the board's membership? Typically, board members are recruited because they can ensure the financial stability of the college by attracting possible donors. Hence, many of them hold prominent positions as CEOs or CFOs in major corporations, banks, and investment firms. I suggest that participants employ online search engines to find out about the racial mix of the board and ask what it means for the direction of the university to be set and monitored by a group composed of mostly White, business representatives.

- Whose interests inside and outside the specific location of the story are served or harmed by the events described?

Here participants have to shift their frame of analysis to considering asymmetries of power. People often say that it's obvious that Mia's interests are served because she got the opportunity to contribute, and that John's interests are harmed because he felt Stephen had silenced him.

When this analysis is expressed, I ask participants to go back and read the story again. I explain that I want them to think about the framing of this story within a system of white supremacy and emphasize that, like all dominant ideologies, white supremacy is designed to be self-sustaining. In other words, it's set up to keep white power and white normativity in place and viewed as the natural state of things. White supremacy protects itself by appearing to be unremarkable, a form of common sense. For me this suggests a reading of the story that's directly opposite to the one just described.

Sometimes, the reminder of the construct of white supremacy means that people now talk about Mia and John in different ways. Mia is seen as someone who has a history of being silenced by being ignored. People quote the fact that she tells the class that being overlooked is her typical experience at the university.

John's situation is now seen as more complicated. Although people still argue he has been harmed by my intervention and acknowledge his feeling that he is now in an unsafe environment, his decision to remove himself from the discussion is now sometimes positioned as an act of white privilege. John is privileged because he can simply turn away from the reality of race and choose not to think about what it means in a racist world. He has been granted the option of denying reality without much harm accruing to him. This, of course, is the direct opposite to the experience of people of color who are robbed of the choice of ignoring the daily realities of racism and white supremacy.

Doing a Power Analysis

The next stage is to ask people to conduct a power analysis of the story. I want them to be aware of how power dynamics are embedded in specific events. Although the story focuses on one class in one institution at one particular moment, the interactions described are shaped by wider asymmetries of power.

To help students do this, I give a brief typology of three different kinds of power. I discuss what these terms mean and give examples of them in action.

- Repressive power—power used to constrain options, limit freedom, or maintain the status quo. This could be as simple as a supervisor telling someone not to make trouble by bringing up a contentious issue, or as explosive as paramilitary forces beating up or killing protesters on the street.
- Emancipatory power—power experienced as motivating or galvanizing and that fuels activism and the desire for change. This could be a supervisor asking an employee "How can I help you do your best work?" to Black Lives Matter members mobilizing quickly for a day of protest immediately after a police killing.
- Disciplinary power—power that people exert on themselves to make sure they don't transgress too far against the powers that be. An

example might be arguing for more institutional diversity and inclusion efforts but stopping short of lobbying for a direct focus on uncovering white supremacy at the institution.

I then ask the participants to reread the story on their own and identify (a) the kinds of power they see being exercised in the story and (b) the wider systems, structures, and ideologies that support the exercise of each kind of power. They then compile their responses in small groups and the whole class reconvenes.

Repressive Power

I am usually identified as the chief enactor of repressive power. This is because people see my overlooking of Mia as an example of how systems embody white normativity and patriarchy. As the instructor, I have the weight of institutional authority behind his actions. That means it takes an act of courage to stand up to me and point out my disregarding of a woman of color. I am often identified as enacting patriarchy, the idea that because men are assumed to think more logically, rationally, and objectively they should be in charge of making decisions for the collective.

John is also sometimes cited as exercising repressive power because he has removed himself from any further discussion of racial issues. On the face of it, this seems like a withdrawing or giving up of power. However, in removing himself from the conversation, he is denying other students the chance to learn how he experiences and enacts white supremacy. After all, the experts on how white supremacy and patriarchy are learned and internalized are White people. By not contributing to future discussions, John is blocking the other students' opportunity to understand better how dominant ideologies operate to determine Whites' behavior.

Emancipatory Power

Because she spoke up to address Stephen's overlooking of Mia, Jenn is typically cited as the chief enactor of emancipatory power. Her intervention caused me to ask Mia to express her opinion on the matter at hand. It also prompted me to reflect on the incident during the break and to come back and initiate a conversation on microaggressions.

Sometimes, people get into a deep conversation about the problematic notion of a White person "liberating" a person of color, and the colonial legacy that embodies. Was it condescending of Jenn to intervene, thereby robbing Mia of the chance to speak up for herself? Did it perpetuate the "savior" mentality, where Whites take on the responsibility to liberate people of color from oppression? Or, was Jenn using her white privilege in a responsible way to bring the exercise of white supremacy to the attention of a powerful White male? After all, she could make the challenge to my authority without the risk of being accused of playing the race card, whereas I could have dismissed Mia as seeing a racial motive where none existed.

Disciplinary Power

Disciplinary power is power exercised by someone on themself, to ensure they keep their conduct within acceptable tramlines and norms. In this instance, Mia is usually identified as the enactor of disciplinary power. She has learned to stay quiet when she is overlooked or ignored either because she has learned that's how the world works or because she has suffered the consequences of speaking up for herself. Maybe her peers have told her that challenging a White professor for sins of omission will bring down a punishment on her. Possibly, her elders have instilled in her a cultural reverence of authority and told her it is disrespectful to criticize a teacher. Maybe her complaints in the past have been dismissed or not believed. Perhaps she is just exhausted from having to confront all the microaggressions and institutional racism she has experienced.

As people talk about Mia's choice to remain silent, the very notion of choice becomes examined. When you know you will be dismissed or punished for an action, what kind of free choice really exists? Participants ponder whether staying silent was a conscious decision on Mia's part informed by her past experience of criticizing authority, or whether it was a deeply internalized response that she had little awareness of. Perhaps this represented the way she had been taught to move through her life.

The discussion can then branch into different directions. Sometimes, people focus on the way that Asian American culture and the Confucian tradition instill the notion of good conduct as listening respectfully to elders and automatically attributing wisdom to their actions and decisions. When that happens we talk about the way that cultural upbringing frames so many interactions in communities and organizations. If we focus on Mia learning that to survive she needs to stay silent when she is over-looked, then we are back to acknowledging the influence of patriarchy and white supremacy. If the discussion goes in this latter direction then we talk about the racial and gender composition of influential bodies such as congress, the presidency, the military, multinational banking, the judiciary, and corporate America. Female participants tend to bring numerous examples of being systematically marginalized or ignored in the male dominated institutions or organizations where they have worked.

Final Comment

Thinking structurally is a transformative cognitive move in developing an anti-racist White identity. Moving away from an individualist ideology means that we come to understand our own learned racism not as an inherent moral flaw but as a very predictable result of growing up subject to quietly effective white supremacist conditioning. Viewing our own racist acts and inclinations as structurally determined helps move people past an extended fixation on their guilt and shame. It is easy to spend all your time focused on your past sins and embarrassing naiveté and to be mortified by the casual racism you've enacted. This obsession with white guilt is a dead end. Thinking structurally lifts you out of that extended fixation on your flaws and moves you more quickly to activism.

A structural perspective inevitably emphasizes the humanly created nature of white supremacy. Anything that has been created by humans can be dismantled and replaced by them. Of course, doing this will be a long and difficult process that will require collective effort. Many anti-racist trainings focus on changing individual behavior and becoming less influenced by implicit biases and racial stereotypes. Although those things are important starting points, real, and substantive, change will only come when structures, systems, and policies are fundamentally altered or replaced. And that will only happen if people work in political parties and social movements. In his way, thinking structurally is the mental kick-starter to collective action.

References

Crass, C. (2013). *Towards collective liberation: Anti-racist organizing, feminist praxis, and movement building strategy.* PM Press

Daumeyer, N. M., Rucker, J. M., & Richeson, J. A. (2017). Thinking structurally about implicit bias: Some peril, lots of promise. *Psychological Inquiry, 28*(4), 258–261.

DiAngelo, R. (2018). *White fragility: Why it's so hard for white people to talk about racism.* Beacon Press.

Feagin, J. R. (2013). *The white racial frame: Centuries of racial framing and counter framing* (2nd ed.). Routledge.

PART II

Provocation 2: Generating Conditions for Transformation

CHAPTER 15

Transforming First Nations Individual and Community Realities: Reflections on a Decolonizing Higher Education Project

Roz Walker and Rob McPhee

INTRODUCTION

This chapter encompasses several areas of inquiry and contributions across provocations I, II, III which frame this Handbook. Drawing on the transformative learning approaches which influenced the development and implementation of the Indigenous Community Management and Development Program (ICMDP) and the emerging Indigenous ontologies of transformation, we describe how Indigenous knowledges and practices have helped to transform individual, community, and broader social and political realities. Evidence of transformative possibilities and the enactment of the discourse of empowerment and self-determination are

R. Walker (✉)
University of Western Australia, Perth, WA, Australia
e-mail: roz.walker@uwa.edu.au

R. McPhee
Danila Dilba Health Service, Darwin, NT, Australia

© The Author(s), under exclusive license to Springer Nature Switzerland AG 2022
A. Nicolaides et al. (eds.), *The Palgrave Handbook of Learning for Transformation*, https://doi.org/10.1007/978-3-030-84694-7_15

257

provided through ICMDP graduate voices and experiences of incorporating Indigenous terms of reference (ITR) and navigating the cultural interface to improve their own and their family and community lives. It draws on Roz Walker's (RW's) PhD dissertation, titled *Transformative Strategies in Indigenous Education: Decolonization and Positive Social Change* (2004), documenting her reflections and experience in this highly innovative and emancipatory curriculum development project, and Rob McPhee's (RM's) experience and reflections of his transformative journey as a student (1995–1997), teacher and program coordinator (1998–2007), and their theoretical observations of and actions in navigating the social and political context of Indigenous education within Australia.

The challenge was to develop curriculum strategies that are genuinely transformative, empowering, and contribute to decolonization and positive social change. We describe the development and implementation of a transformative curriculum project and pedagogy by a group of Aboriginal and non-Aboriginal educators and scholars at CAS between 1989 and 2007. While the goals, aims, and principles of the program have endured it continues to successfully evolve to respond to the shifts in Indigenous education, social policies and community circumstances.

Background—Positioning Indigenous People in Australia

There are currently an estimated 798,400 Indigenous people living in Australia, 5% of whom live in New South Wales, Queensland, and Western Australia, comprising 3.3% of the total Australian population. Approximately 66% live in remote, very remote, or regional areas and 33% live in metropolitan cities. The Indigenous population is relatively young, with a median age of 20.3 years, compared to 37.8 years for the non-Indigenous population. Indigenous Australians are both geographically and culturally diverse comprising hundreds of groups with their own distinctive languages, histories, and cultural traditions. With the exception of year 12 completions, the government has failed to close the gap for Indigenous people on most key indicators including health and social and emotional well-being (SEWB), employment, housing, and economic status (AIHW, 2018).

Positioning Ourselves in This Transformative Project

This chapter positions the ICMDP and the staff and students within various sites of struggle within the university and the broader social and political context of contemporary Indigenous education. It outlines the theoretical frameworks, discourses, and methodological approaches utilized in developing and refining the ICMDP. We acknowledge the political and ethical issues/moral imperatives of voice, representation, and power relations in terms of RW's position as a non-Indigenous researcher, academic coordinator, participant, and observer within the process and privilege/center RM's perspectives as an Indigenous student, graduate, lecturer, and program coordinator as he traversed each of these passageways. Both authors experienced profound personal and professional transformation, deeply committed to decolonizing the disciplines and political structures, policies, programs, and professional practices impacting Indigenous people's lives. RW became involved with the initial program development at the beginning of 1987 and was appointed as the North West Field Support Coordinator from its commencement in 1989, beginning her own transformative journey. The position involved liaison and negotiation with Indigenous organizations, communities, and government stakeholders throughout the Pilbara and Kimberley, promoting this radical new Indigenous program, as well as providing advocacy and academic support for students. In July 1990, RW moved back to Perth and was appointed Academic Coordinator to assist Darlene Oxenham, the Indigenous Program Coordinator, to develop the program implementation, monitoring, and evaluation systems and ongoing curriculum refinement. RW remained in this role until the end of 1995.

Over the past 30 years there have been significant developments in theorizing about the complexities around decolonizing and transforming education (Dei, 2008; Green, 2009; McKinley & Barney, 2010; McKinley & Smith, 2019; Nakata et al., 2012; Sarra, 2012; Tuck & Yang, 2012). Some of these authors question whether non-Indigenous people can participate in such projects, what qualities they need and whether they can genuinely engage in critically reflexive decolonizing practice given the ever-present risks of resorting to dominant discourses and worldviews.

The chapter highlights our dilemmas and those of many ICMDP colleagues as we attempted to "navigate, redeploy and out maneuver the often treacherous and deceptively alluring and commonsensical discursive formations and culturalist assumptions around equality of access and outcomes that inform contemporary Indigenous higher education" (Walker, p. 1).

Policy Context in Indigenous Education

Attempts by Indigenous academics and their allies to gain recognition of Indigenous rights and interests in all spheres of education have achieved only limited success in quite specific areas (McConaghy, 2000; Nakata, 2002; Walker, 2000). The legacies of colonization still pervade the curriculum and pedagogy disrupting family and community structures and impacting adversely on access to education and employment (Walker, 2000). These enduring consequences of colonization and its continuing effect upon Indigenous Peoples include transgenerational impacts of the Stolen Generations policies which systematically and forcibly removed Indigenous people from families and traditional country (Dudgeon et al., 2014), disrupting Indigenous ways of knowing, being, and doing (Martin & Mirraboopa, 2003). Colonial policies have also contributed to the social and economic disadvantage experienced by Indigenous Peoples which have in turn affected their SEWB and educational attainment.

According to Rose, in Gillan, Mellor and Krakouer (2017) Indigenous policy over the last 50 years.

> has become cluttered with concepts and positions challenging the education profession, yet among this clanging discord of multiple voices, the Indigenous voice, whose cadence is clear and consistent with the Uluru Statement, coming from standing on solid ground, has not changed. (15, p. iv)

In that time there have been significant contributions by Indigenous leaders and peak bodies to Indigenous policies to bring about significant reform. The principles and goals of Indigenous self-determination underpinning the 1989 National Aboriginal Education Policy validated the development and implementation of the ICMDP and are reinforced in the 1999 *Coolangatta* Statement (1999), which asserts the inalienable right of Indigenous Australians to an education which incorporates their knowledges, values, culture, and spirituality.

However, as the review by Gillan et al. (2017) suggests, despite these policy commitments few improvements in Indigenous education outcomes have occurred (Gillian et al., 2017). Only a small percentage of Indigenous year 12 students tertiary achieved entry results—affirming the importance of the alternative entry strategy offered by the ICMDP that recognizes and values Indigenous knowledges and experiences as legitimate. We also created flexible structures, with consistent, creative interpretations of academic policies regarding entry, advanced standing, and recognition of prior learning, to transform the academy.

Transformative Learning Approaches

In this section, we define the elements and practices that provide the program's strategic decolonizing and transformative potential along with the various discourses and assumptions that influenced our thinking and everyday practice.

The enduring legacies of colonialism make it problematic to situate Indigenous education within a post-colonialist context (Moreton-Robinson, 1998). For many Indigenous academics, "post-colonialism has become a strategy for reinscribing or reauthorizing the privileges of non-Indigenous academics because [it] has been defined in ways that can still leave out Indigenous People's ways of knowing and interests" (Walker, 2004, p. 3). In order to challenge the pervasive colonialism and culturalism that underpins extant policy discourses and practices in Indigenous education we drew on feminism (Lather, 1991), cultural theorists (Bhabba, 1994; Giroux, 1985, 1993; Mezirow, 2003), and Indigenous standpoints (Nakata, 1997; Oxenham, 1999; Rigney, 1997), and the intersectionality of culture and gender (Moreton-Robinson, 1998). We engaged with postcolonial discourses "as a tactic to serve Indigenous interests and disrupt existing knowledge/power relations' (Nakata) and scientific culturalism" (McConaghy, 2000, p. 269).

The ICMDP curriculum, strategies, and pedagogical practices—teaching, learning, and assessment processes described below—have enabled both staff and students to reframe postcolonial and poststructuralist discourse(s) to serve Indigenous interests and to positively and productively change "extant and implicit knowledge/power relations" (Walker, 2004).

The ICMDP creatively challenged curriculum standards and expectations built on Western theoretical and philosophical ideologies and regimes of truth (Foucault, 1977) in order to promote Indigenous interests and priorities. We worked tactically with key aspects of critical emancipatory discourses/theories of relevance to positive social change within Indigenous higher education to inform our learning approach (Foucault, 1979). Drawing on Foucault (1979) we established a range of critically reflexive processes to enable students to understand the philosophical and political underpinnings of colonialism and liberalism, and their interconnectedness to the discourses, practices, and roles played by policymakers and program providers in the government agencies and bureaucracies in which students worked (Foucault, 1979; Walker, 2004). Students learned skills and strategies to interrogate a range of policies that revealed government's responsibility to, assumptions about, and representations of Indigenous people as "citizens" in Australia's contemporary social democracy (McPhee & Walker, 2001). Students were able to use this language back at government when attempting to effect positive changes in their work and community settings.

Reflecting upon the emancipatory, transformative nature of the ICMDP, and its potential to achieve genuine improvements for students and their communities evoked a range of emotional, social, and intellectual complexities for ICMDP staff along the journey. Nevertheless, we deployed several key transformative strategies that enable/d staff and students to contribute to decolonization and positive social change in contemporary Australia. As Bernard-Donals (1994) states, "the ways in which humans change their social composition, and more imperatively, their material conditions of existence, must be elaborated for a useful theory of social change" (Bernard-Donals, 1994, p. 113, cited in Walker, 2004, p. 5).

The key transformative, decolonizing strategies of the ICMDP included: (1) developing a competency-based curriculum; (2) the concept/construct of the ICMD Practitioner as a distinctive, legitimate role to facilitate empowerment; (3) the theorization and enactment of ITR; and (4) the identification of specific skills, tools (e.g., critical reflection) and knowledges to negotiate the cultural interface to bring about positive personal and social change (Walker, 2004). ITR involved "a set of principles, core values and a process for applying a framework to determine an Indigenous viewpoint on an issue in an Indigenous context" (Oxenham, 1999, p. 4).

Developing a Competency-Based Curriculum

The ICMDP competencies for Indigenous community management and development practitioners were incorporated within a multi-disciplinary framework, informed by relevant extant literature (Crawford, 1989; Howard, 1988; HRSCAA, 1989, 1990; Kelly & Sewell, 1989; Stringer, 1987); policy reviews, the national competency framework, and Australian Standards Framework (NTB, 1991). Competencies were also informed and validated by collecting and analyzing student voices and experiences in study block, workshop, and field support course evaluations, informal employer feedback and verbal and written reports from field support staff, tutors and mentors working with students in their work and community settings (Walker, 2004). These sources informed the ongoing program development and refinement enabling us to make "more explicit the critical and transformative strategies in the ongoing program together with the necessary skills, values and attributes to be an *effective, conscious and ethical practitioner*" (ICMDP, 1993, emphasis added).

Drawing on a range of theories and policy reviews in the literature, we identified the knowledge, understandings, attributes, values, and skills required in the respective discipline areas of community management and community development to navigate the tensions across the different discipline areas (HRSCAA, ; Kelly & Sewell, 1989). We articulated the competencies and elements necessary for students to work effectively and culturally responsively across these competing disciplines. Navigating through the competencies and making sense of the competency statements encompassed within a complex theoretical framework proved to be a powerful and transformative learning process for students as RM's reflection 20 years on attests (see p. 21).

The skills and capacity needed by students to recognize and work with the complexities in making decisions, implementing programs and services, planning projects and activities, and determining Indigenous identified futures at the cultural interface were incorporated within the ICMDP teaching and assessment processes. Throughout 1993 we reviewed the relevance and cultural appropriateness of different learning theories and processes to meet the diverse learning needs, aspirations, and priorities of students across Australia.

The program encompassed adult and self-directed learning principles; recognition and respect for the distinctive knowledge and understandings required to be an effective ICMDP practitioner working at the cultural interface; and a belief that learning is more effective when relevant to the student's workplace and community reality. Principles of individual and collective empowerment and positive social change provided "the basis for both the design and delivery of the course, the roles carried out by staff, and the teaching and assessment approaches used in the ongoing development of the course" (ICMDP, 1993).

We drew on critical, traditional liberal/humanist, instrumental, and Indigenous learning theories to inform the design, structure, and teaching within the ICMDP courses (Walker, 2004). These theoretical paradigms challenge the cultural politics within the university as well as the dominant values and standards imposed on students in their specific work and community contexts, enabling them to work developmentally with their communities to determine their own directions to promote Indigenous interests. Students were able to critically reflect upon their own and others values, beliefs, attitudes, and experiences; and, to enact, evaluate, and if necessary reframe their ideas and decisions in an ongoing action reflection cycle using Community Participatory Action Research (CPAR). They were provided with tools of critical reflection and skills to negotiate their own learning needs within their specific work and community settings within a coherent theoretical framework of community development, empowerment, and self-determination and clearly explicated set of goals in which to situate and give meaning to their learning (Walker, 2004). The curriculum/pedagogy enabled students to understand how learning theories and processes contributed to Indigenous self-determination and empowerment, agency, and control.

Between 1994 and 1995 the ICMDP curriculum was further refined to enhance student's competency, abilities, and capacity to work within existing institutional constraints to effect positive changes to benefit Indigenous people within the wider social and political system that had historically disenfranchised their families and communities. By 1995, a coherent Indigenized curriculum framework was established, mapping the concepts, skills, attributes, and competencies of the ICMD practitioner, as well as the learning and assessment sites across the three years of the course.

Curriculum Design

The ICMDP adopted a competency-based curriculum design and delivery. This approach enabled Indigenous students to obtain the necessary skills and knowledge to more effectively operate in a range of community and organizational settings. Founded on the principles and goals of self-determination, empowerment, social justice, and Indigenous rights, the ICMDP program design is highly innovative, flexible, individualized, and culturally appropriate. The course is operated on a block release basis to maximize students' time in their workplace and community settings and minimize disruption to family, community, and work. The culturally appropriate curriculum content and processes are designed to meet and demonstrate academic and professional standards for a wide range of employer groups as well as the needs, priorities, and aspirations of geographically and culturally diverse student groups.

The study blocks enable students to integrate their own knowledge, understanding and experiences with newly learned skills and knowledge within an interdisciplinary framework of community management and community development. Students gain new understandings, formulate their own grounded theories, and establish a practice framework (a code of ethics, principles, and practices), to work developmentally to empower the groups they are working with to identify issues and factors adversely impacting them as well as the strategies to address them.

Indigenous education theories are integrated with and inform and decolonize management theories and practices, community development processes, and policy development and implementation issues. Students completing the Bachelor of Applied Science engage in an evaluative research project in their final year, using culturally relevant approaches and Indigenous criteria to improve existing practice, processes, and outcomes of policies, programs, and projects developed and implemented in Indigenous settings. Most crucially, in the first year students participate in picture building and analysis of the ways in which historical, social, political, and economic factors have impacted/influenced contemporary Indigenous society. As evident in RM's reflection (p. needs to be changed to the handbook number), this analysis can prove to be a truly pivotal moment in transforming individual student's lives in highly productive and sustained ways.

Incorporating Indigenous Knowledges and Practices

Indigenous knowledges and practices, new articulations, and emerging ontologies of transformation (Provocations II) are evident in the ICMDP curriculum and pedagogy. The program acknowledges the existing knowledge, skills and understandings, and experience of Indigenous students, which enhance their competency working in management, administrative, leadership, and community development positions. Indigenous knowledges and experiences are combined with the new knowledges, skills, and attributes and self-understanding required to assume roles in Indigenous organizations and communities. Through this synthesis of ideas, students are empowered to facilitate/negotiate more effective, culturally appropriate processes and practices in their work and communities.

The goals of Indigenous self-determination and positive social change are embedded in both the learning processes and outcomes of the ICMDP (McPhee et al., 1998; Walker, 2000; Wilson, 2001). Students incorporate Indigenous Terms of Reference, knowledges, and standpoints within their engagement and negotiations with dominant discourses. This is a positive, decolonizing, and transformative process requiring the recognition and legitimation of the indissoluble qualities of Indigenous rights. "Importantly, acknowledgement of Indigenous rights is an essential requisite for students to achieve productive or transformative outcomes as opposed to simply disrupting or resisting assimilationist elements" (Walker, 2004, p. 120). Recognition of these rights, grounded in a human rights framework within the ICMDP, is/was both empowering and transformative, enabling students to convey and strive for a re-imagined future within their individual and collective practice (Foucault, 1979).

Discourses for Enacting Transformation

The adoption of a rights-based discourse in the ICMDP to address the unacceptable inequities and disadvantage experienced by Indigenous people is a potent and emergent force for transformation (Walker, 2004) as RM's reflection in this section attests (Provocations III). The ICMDP curriculum and pedagogy was premised on the fact that,

> Redressing the negative effects of Australia's colonial history on the social and material condition of Indigenous people, the majority of whom are disadvantaged in relation to the non-Indigenous population, creates a moral imperative to integrate discourses of decolonization, social change, and cultural affirmation in Indigenous education (Walker, 2004, p. 23)

Establishing processes for students to enact transformation we drew on the discourses of Foucault (1977), Bhabha (1994), and Giroux (1985, 1993) that reveal how uncertainty, ambivalence, contradictions, and instabilities in the dominant ideological structures provide the possibility for transformation (Walker, 2004). We also drew on the theories and strategies of Indigenous authors (Martin & Mirraboopa, 2003; Moreton-Robinson, 1998; Nakata, 1997, 2002) to explore the role of education in social change generally and the limits and possibilities of Indigenous education in transformation.

It was important that as teachers committed to decolonizing the curriculum we were cognizant of how colonial discourses, policies and practices, and legacies continued to impact upon the everyday lives of Indigenous Peoples and to recognize our moral responsibility as well as our power and privilege in helping redress and transform this situation. The overall curriculum framework was geared toward interrupting "the legitimating formations that inscribe and prescribe 'epistemic authority' and 'disciplinary capacity' which serve to restrict the transformative and development potential of Indigenous education" (McConaghy, 2000, pp. 1–16).

A key focus of the course was/is about strengthening and acknowledging Indigenous identity and facilitating empowerment and capacity building at individual and collective levels through an array of teaching strategies. In the study blocks students examine the mechanisms of power and privilege and unquestioned dominant viewpoints and discourses operating within the broader historical, social, and political context. As a group they discuss and theorize about the actualities, possibilities, and potential constraints in transforming and decolonizing policies and practices locally and nationally in Australia. Through these processes, students attain levels of conscientization necessary to bring about positive social change.

The ongoing curriculum development and implementation processes revealed and reaffirmed Indigenous ontologies. Culturally specific study blocks and workshops were developed to facilitate these transformative learning processes and outcomes by students and to provide them with a new way of looking at the world. As evident in RM's reflection these processes enabled students to more effectively identify and understand what was happening around them, at individual, family, and community levels and why. Their individual growth included changes to their own, and their family's lives, and the ability to use this conscientization process (Freire, 1973; Smith, 1999) to further empower themselves, their families, and communities to transcend and transform aspects of their lives.

The ICMDP enabled students to address a multitude of complex and challenging issues impacting on their own, their families', and their communities' SEWB. For many students, it was the beginning of their individual and collective empowerment and healing journeys. Student's community projects incorporated the interrelated concepts of self-determination, capacity building, empowerment, and healing which Smith (1999) identifies as essential elements for a decolonizing Indigenous research and practice (Dudgeon et al., 2020).

Significantly, students evaluated their own situations and the effectiveness of their activities in bringing about positive social change using CPAR. This process facilitated individual and community conscientization (Freire, 1973) through their individual and collective community identification of the historical, socio-political, and cultural issues and factors operating at local, regional, state, and national levels which served to hinder or strengthen the possibility for transformation (Walker, 2000). These processes enable the development of community-based practices, policies, and programs for addressing the social and cultural determinants impacting their lives. The use of CPAR contributed to generating a strength-based Indigenous epistemology and ontology.

More recent work led by Indigenous academic and psychologist Pat Dudgeon and colleagues using the same principles and processes that informed the ICMDP, in the development of the National Empowerment Program has "demonstrated how the principles of interconnectedness and collectivism, underpin the distinctive ontologies of SEWB, shaping how individual stories are experienced, expressed, framed, and understood" (Cajete, 1994, p. 31). The research and evaluation underpinning the program development utilized Indigenous Research Methodologies within a broader Indigenous paradigm which has since been articulated as a distinctive Aboriginal Participatory Action Research (APAR) (Dudgeon et al., 2020) that has evolved from the principles underpinning PAR (Freire, 1973). The principles of APAR provide culturally safe spaces to ensure that individuals could share their stories. Further the process of "sharing of these stories in groups was important in building and 'restorying' relationships and networks of support, and strengthening individual, families, and communities" (Cajete, 1994, p. 31).

Similarly, ICMDP students were/are required to share their oral histories and evaluations of their organization and community-led projects which enable further knowledge exchange and conversations, ongoing analyses, and more comprehensive understandings to promote greater advocacy for governmental and wider community accountability to address Indigenous identified needs and priorities.

Reflecting on My Journey of Transformation—Becoming an ICMD Practitioner

Growing up in Australia I was constantly reminded about the accomplishments of the settlers who for over 200 years overcame immense adversity while taming the wild frontiers of the harsh Australian landscape. I was taught that our history was one of hardship, starting from the long and dangerous journeys of the fleets carrying men who risked their lives to come to the new land either as explorers, entrepreneurs, or convicts. They arrived at a barren and empty land and through strength and grit, created the luckiest country in the world. We celebrate the battlers, the diggers, and most of Australia's states, cities, roads, and landscapes are named in honor of the important individuals from the mother country or new arrivals who traversed our landscape. The mention of Aboriginal people in the history I was taught was minimal, set in the margins, and often portrayed as a life of indifference, misery, dysfunction, and laziness.

It was 1995 and I was 21 years old when I started as a student in the Indigenous Community Management and Development Program (ICMDP). At this point in my life, I understood my Aboriginal heritage, I had been exposed to some basic information about Aboriginality but I was completely confused about what being an Aboriginal person in Australian society truly meant. I was confused about where I stood. Was I Aboriginal? Was I Australian? Was I both? What did that mean? While I didn't think about these questions consciously at the time, I look back and know that I was confused, trying to navigate what my personal family and individual history meant for me and where I was going. What was my purpose? I had a good job, I was doing ok but what was I really trying to achieve in my work?

My first study block in the ICMDP was exciting but also confronting. There were more than 50 Aboriginal and Torres Strait Islander people from across Australia crammed into the classroom at Curtin University. During that first study block, I had no idea about the journey I was about to go on, how it would transform me and the relationships, bonds, and respect that we would build between students and staff, not only over the 3 years of the course, but for the rest of my life.

On reflection, it was the first year of the course that I consider to have had the most significant impact on me. I attended two workshops that were focused on history, culture, identity, and Aboriginal ways of working. I remember one of the lecturers at the time, talking about the Roman Empire, the religious wars, the British Empire, and the things that were happening in the world leading up to the first fleet leaving England for Australia. My eyes were wide open, I was taking it all in. I had never understood what colonization was and what it was motivated by. I had never heard the stories about how this had been going on for centuries and how power and wealth had been challenged and fought for across the globe for millennia. I had never understood the power of controlling land and the political and economic motivations for England setting sail to Australia. Suddenly, the unsettling feeling I had inside myself about who I was and what my purpose was, was starting to transform.

What was different about what I was learning was that I was starting to see history through the eyes of Aboriginal and Torres Strait Islander people. We went way back to the Dreaming, we explored the cultural, social, economic, and political complexity of the hundreds of Aboriginal groups and languages spread across Australia. We talked about the values systems, the lore, the way our societies were organized and thrived. We started to unpack the events that occurred from the moment of the arrival of the first fleet and most importantly, I could see how there were two clear perspectives of what had happened from that moment on—one seen through the eyes of Aboriginal people and the other seen through the eyes of the colonizer.

Unfortunately, the history that was familiar to me was the colonial history of Australia. The history that I learnt through the ICMDP was one about colonization/invasion—dispossession—protection—assimilation—self-determination and more recently reconciliation.

It was a completely new lens to the history of Australia. It helped me understand my own family background. I started to ask questions of my old people about where we were from, what our histories were, and how I had got to where I was. The laws and policies we studied through the course suddenly reflected my own personal history.

My great grandparents had been removed from their families and placed in a mission in Queensland (QLD) where they met, married, and had children. My great grandfather was "bonded" from one Presbyterian mission in QLD to another in Western Australia (WA). All of this was sanctioned by the QLD and WA Aborigine Protection Boards; the same institutions and legislation that I had read about through my course. While it was confronting, it was also liberating. I now knew my history and how it was connected to countless numbers of other Aboriginal and Torres Strait Islander people across Australia.

Understanding the issues my community faced and where they stemmed from made me angry at first. But the benefit of the ICMDP was that it didn't leave us students sitting in that wallow of hurt, rather it challenged us to do something about it. It motivated me to do whatever I could to fight against the injustice, hurt, and trauma countless families had experienced.

Over the remaining years of the course, I was exposed to various practical and tactical tools to channel my energy. I was taught about policy, about the Australian political system, about how power manifests itself in Australian politics and lives. I was given access to skills in writing submissions, in doing budgets, managing staff, and developing community-led projects to address disadvantage. I was shown how to look at an issue from the perspective of the community, to privilege community voices, to draw on culture to strengthen community. I was taught how to critically reflect on my own values, my own assumptions and biases, and question where these were coming from and how they enabled or hampered community empowerment. I was shown how to evaluate the impact and outcomes of community actions and programs, how to improve and strengthen the work we were doing.

By the end of the course, I had not only changed as a result of the new knowledge and skills I had gained, but I felt like I had gone through a process of personal transformation; by better understanding myself, my purpose and how I must do what I can to bring about social and political justice and equality for Aboriginal and Torres Strait Islander people. The lens through which I now viewed the world was permanently altered and my thoughts, actions, and beliefs reflect this.

Since completing the Program over 20 years ago, I have continued to access and further build upon the foundational knowledges, skills, and understandings acquired in the course. I continue to critically reflect on my purpose as I am exposed to and respond, to changes in the social and political environment. As a country, the burden of impact on Aboriginal and Torres Strait Islander people is not only ours but is a reflection on our nation as a whole and one that we must all work toward redressing.

Conclusion

While intellectuals contest theories, representations, and standpoints, appropriate curriculum approaches and pedagogy, and while policymakers debate the reasons for persistent poor academic outcomes over the past 50 years, Gillan et al. (2017) demonstrate that Indigenous People continue to experience unacceptable levels of disadvantage and social marginalization which impacts on their SEWB and their social and economic and political status in Australia.

On a positive note, since the course commenced in 1989, over 1,000 students have graduated from the ICMDP. The majority of graduates hold senior positions in Aboriginal community controlled and government organizations across Australia. Many have been instrumental in transforming community lives, influencing policy changes, and enhancing programs and services.

We have drawn on RW's thesis and RM's reflections on his journey in the course to share our experiences and perspectives at several time points while working at an Indigenous Centre dedicated to developing a unique transformative curriculum project and pedagogy to not just improve Indigenous education outcomes, but to transform the lives of Indigenous individuals, families, and communities and the Aboriginal community controlled organizations that support them.

Throughout the program's development we drew on Indigenous literature that emphasizes the critical importance of restorying history, privileging Indigenous knowledges, ontologies, and epistemologies about learning, connecting with culture and identity, and engaging in healing to promote individual, collective and cultural reclamation and social transformation (Cajete, 2019; McKinley & Barney, 2011; Smith, 1999). These Indigenous perspectives enabled us to rearticulate and crystalize a decolonized notion of transformation that extends and departs in important and powerful ways from those proposed in dominant Western theories of transformation (Foucault, 1977; Freire, 1970, 1973). A key difference underpinning Indigenous conceptualizations of individual, collective, and social transformation in the ICMDP includes acknowledging and redressing the adverse and ongoing transgenerational impacts and legacies of colonization. These key theories underpinning the ICDMP curriculum and pedagogy are strongly echoed in recent Indigenous writings about transformative theories in education and social change (Cajete, 2019; McKinley & Barney, 2011; Morgan, 2019; Smith, 1999; Smith & Smith, 2019).

Throughout this chapter, we have brought together Western and Indigenous knowledge systems and theories regarding emancipatory education, individual agency, race, class, and gender relations and their interplay with various levels and spheres of the institutional state apparatus to implement decolonizing strategies to support the positive transformation of individual, family, and community lives.

The ICMDP curriculum and pedagogy serve to operationalize the urgent and necessary task identified by Indigenous intellectuals and practitioners to reveal how dominant agendas continue to obstruct Indigenous peoples (and their allies) attempts to decolonize the languages, discourses, and practices in and through education in Australia (Grogan & Oxenham, 1992; Hart & Whatman, 1998; Watson, 1985). This chapter has described the key theories, strategies, and defining moments in creating and engaging with a critical transformative curriculum and pedagogy specific to Indigenous Australians over the past 30 years.

We have highlighted the need to build Indigenous-led collaborations between students and communities to influence policy and programs and bring about positive social and structural/system level changes to improve the social realities for Indigenous individuals, families, and communities (Howard, 1988). Further research will provide much needed evidence of the transformative and beneficial links between using APAR and decolonizing strategies and discourses and Indigenous ontologies of SEWB (Dudgeon et al., 2020) which underpinned the courses at the Centre for Aboriginal Studies.

References

Australian Institute of Health and Welfare (2018). *Closing the Gap targets: 2017 analysis of progress and key drivers of change*. Cat. no. IHW 193. AIHW

Bernard-Donals, M. F. (1994). *Mikhail Bakhtin: Between phenomenology and Marxism*. Cambridge University Press

Bhabba, H. K. (1994). *The location of culture*. Routledge.

Bhabha, H. (1995). Cultural diversity and cultural difference. In B. Ashcroft, G. Griffiths, & H. Tiffin (Eds.), *The empire writes back*. Routledge.

274 R. WALKER AND R. McPHEE

Cajete, G. (1994). *Look to the mountain: An ecology of indigenous education.* Kivaki Press.

Cajete, G. A. (2019). Envisioning indigenous education: Applying insights from indigenous views of teaching and learning. In E. A. McKinley & L. T. Smith (Eds.), *Handbook of indigenous education* (pp. 823–845). Springer. https://doi.org/10.1007/978-981-10-3899-0_43

Code, L. (1995). *Rhetorical space: Essays on gendered locations.* Routledge.

Coolangatta Statement. (1999). *World Indigenous Peoples Conference – Education.*

Crawford, F. (1989). *Jarlinardi ways, whitefellas working in Aboriginal communities.* Curtin University of Technology.

Dei, G. J. S. (2008). Indigenous knowledge studies and the next generation: Pedagogical possibilities for anti-colonial education. *The Australian Journal of Indigenous Education, 37*(S1), 5–13. https://doi.org/10.1375/s13260111 00000326

Dudgeon, P., Bray, A., Darlaston-Jones, D., & Walker, R. (2020). *Aboriginal participatory action research: An indigenous research methodology strengthening decolonization and social and emotional wellbeing* (Discussion Paper and Literature Review). Lowitja Institute.

Dudgeon, P., Wright, M., Paradies, Y., Garvey D., & Walker, I. (2014). The social and cultural and political context. In P. Dudgeon, H. Milroy, & R. Walker (Eds.), *Working together: Aboriginal and Torres Strait Islander mental health and wellbeing principles and practice* (pp. 3, 24). Australian Government.

Foucault, M. (1977). Politics and the study of discourse. *Ideology and Consciousness, 3,* 7–26.

Foucault, M. (1979). Governmentality. *Ideology and Consciousness, 9,* 5–21.

Freire, P. (1970). *Pedagogy of the oppressed.* Bloomsbury Academic.

Freire, P. (1973). *Education for critical consciousness.* Continuum.

Gillan, K. P., Mellor, S., & Krakouer, J. (2017). *The case for urgency: Advocating for indigenous voice in education.* Australian Council for Educational Research.

Giroux, H. (1985). Critical pedagogy, cultural politics and the discourse of experience. *Journal of Education, 167*(2), 22–41.

Giroux, H. A. (1988). Border pedagogy in the age of postmodernism. *Journal of Education, 170*(3), 162–181. https://doi.org/10.1177/002205748817 000310

Giroux, H. A. (1993). *Curriculum discourse as postmodernist critical practice.* Deakin University Press.

Greene, M. (2009). In search of a critical pedagogy. In A. Darder, M. H. Baltodano, & R. D. Torres (Eds.), *The critical pedagogy reader* (pp. 84–96). Routledge.

Grogan, G., & Oxenham, D. (1992). A case study in curriculum development: Quiet revolutionary approaches. In C. White (Ed.), *Towards 2000: Maintaining the momentum, National Aboriginal and Torres Strait Islander Higher Education Conference* (pp. 78–83).

Hart, V., & Whatman, S. (1998). Decolonizing the concept of knowledge (Paper presentation). In *Transformation in Higher Education, HERDSA Annual International Conference*.

House of Representatives Standing Committee on Aboriginal Affairs (HRSCAA). (1989). *A chance for the future. Training in skills for Aboriginal Torres Strait Island community management and development.* AGPS Press.

House of Representatives Standing Committee on Aboriginal Affairs (HRSCAA). (1990). *Our future, our selves: Aboriginal and Torres Strait Islander community control, management and resources.* AGPS Press.

Howard, S. (1988). *Competency based design of curriculum* (Discussion paper for Curtin University Course Advisory Committee).

Indigenous Community Management and Development Program (ICMDP). (1993). *Course review notes.* Centre for Aboriginal Studies.

Kelly, A., & Sewell, S. (1989). *With head, heart and hand.* Booralong.

Lather, P. (1991). *Getting smart: Feminist research and pedagogy with/in the postmodern.* Routledge.

Martin, K., & Mirraboopa, B. (2003). Ways of knowing, being and doing: A theoretical framework and methods for indigenous and indigenist re-search. *Journal of Australian Studies, 27*(76), 203–214. https://doi.org/10.1080/14443050309387838

McConaghy, C. (2000). *Rethinking indigenous education: Culturalism, colonialism and the politics of knowing.* Post Pressed.

McKinley E. A., & Smith. L.T. (2019). *Handbook on indigenous education.* Springer.

McKinley, E., & Barney, K. (2010). Transformative learning in first year indigenous Australian studies: Posing problems, asking questions and achieving change. A Practice Report. *The International Journal of the First Year in Higher Education, 1*(1). https://doi.org/10.5204/intjfyhe.v1i1.27

McKinley, E., & Barney. (2011). Teaching and learning for social justice: An approach to transformative education in indigenous Australian studies. In *Talking back, talking forward: Journeys in transforming indigenous educational practice* (pp. 117–128).

McPhee, R., & Walker, R. (2001). Citizens for new world: Education for negotiating and transforming social realities. In *The Eighth International Literacy and Education Research Network Conference on Learning Learning for the Future*.

McPhee, R., Greville, H., & Wilson, E. (1998). Educating for self determination: A look at the indigenous community management and development program. *Northern Radius, 5*(2).

Mezirow, J. (2003). Transformative learning as discourse. *Journal of Transformative Education, 1*(1), 58–63. https://doi.org/10.1177/1541344460325 2172

Moreton-Robinson, A. (1998). When the object speaks, a postcolonial encounter: Anthropological representations and Aboriginal women's self-presentations. *Discourse: Studies in the Cultural Politics of Education, 19*(3), 275–289. https://doi.org/10.1080/0159630980190302

Morgan, B. (2019). Beyond the guest paradigm: Eurocentric education and Aboriginal peoples in NSW. In E. A. McKinley & L. T. Smith (Eds.), *Handbook of indigenous education*. Springer. https://doi.org/10.1007/978-981-10-3899-0_43

Nakata, M. (1997). *The cultural interface: An exploration of the intersection of Western knowledge systems and Torres Strait Islander positions and experiences* (Unpublished PhD Thesis). James Cook University.

Nakata, M. (2002). Indigenous knowledge and the cultural interface: Underlying issues at the intersection of knowledge and information systems. *IFLA Journal, 28*(5–6), 281–291. https://doi.org/10.1177/034003520202 800513

Nakata, M., Nakata, V., Keech, S., & Bolt, R. (2012). Decolonial goals and pedagogies for indigenous studies. *Decolonization: Indigeneity, Education and Society, 1*(1), 20.

National Training Board (NTB). (1991). *National competency standards: Policy and guidelines*. NTB.

Oxenham, D. (1999). *Aboriginal terms of reference: The concept at the Centre for Aboriginal Studies*. Curtin Indigenous Research Centre.

Rigney. Lester Irabinna. (1997). *Internationalisation of an indigenous anti-colonial cultural critique of research methodologies: A guide to indigenist research methodology and its principles*. Flinders University of South Australia.

Sarra, C. (2012). *Strong and smart: Towards a pedagogy for emancipation: Education for first peoples*. Routledge.

Smith, L. T. (1999). *Decolonizing methodologies: Research and indigenous peoples*. Zed Books.

Smith, G. H., & Smith, L. T. (2019). Doing indigenous work: Decolonizing and transforming the academy. *Handbook of Indigenous Education*, 1075–1101. https://doi.org/10.1007/978-981-10-3899-0_69

Stringer, E. (1987). *Report on training: For Aboriginal people* (Unpublished Report). Centre for Aboriginal Studies, Western Australian Institute of Technology.

Tuck, E., & Yang, K. W. (2012). Decolonization is not a metaphor. *Decolonization: Indigeneity, Education and Society, 1*(1), 1–40.

Walker, R. (2000). *Indigenous performance in Western Australia universities: Reframing retention and success.* Evaluations and Investigations Programme, DETYA.

Walker, R. (2004). *Transformative strategies in indigenous education: Decolonization and positive social change* (PhD dissertation, pp. 1–291). University of Western Australia.

Watson, L. (1985). The establishment of Aboriginal terms of reference in a tertiary institution. In *Aborigines and Islanders in Higher Education: The Need for Institutional Change National Conference.*

Wilson, E. (2001). *Narrative analysis of ICMDP student/practitioners', community in diversity: Reinventing liberatory practice* (PhD dissertation). University of Western Australia.

CHAPTER 16

Fostering Reorienting Connections via Ecological Practices

Mark Hathaway

Is it not ludicrous to … speak to other organisms and elements as though they could understand? Certainly not, if such is the simplest way to open our ears toward those others, compelling us to listen, with all our senses, for the reply of the things.

To be sure, the valleys and the oaks do not speak in words. But neither do humans speak only in words. We speak with our whole bodies, deploying a language of gesture, tone, and rhythm that animates all our discourse.

—David Abram (2005, p. 189)

M. Hathaway (✉)
School of the Environment, University of Toronto, Toronto, ON, Canada
e-mail: mark.hathaway@utoronto.ca

Earth Charter Center for Education for Sustainable Development, San José, Costa Rica

© The Author(s), under exclusive license to Springer Nature Switzerland AG 2022
A. Nicolaides et al. (eds.), *The Palgrave Handbook of Learning for Transformation*, https://doi.org/10.1007/978-3-030-84694-7_16

279

280 M. HATHAWAY

Many of us have at times experienced a sense of profound connection with the more-than-human world. It may happen when we are children playing outdoors—wandering deep in the woods, sitting in a tree in our backyard, or playing on a vacant urban lot. Later in life, we may experience such connections walking by the seashore, climbing a steep mountain path, sitting by a rushing river, or encountering a bloom of flowers in the desert. In such moments, we may be enveloped by a deep sense of awe, gratitude, joy, or love. These times often transform us forever by helping us experience ourselves as part of a greater community of life and inculcating a sense of care for other beings. The changes such experiences bring about in us may be gradual and subtle, or sudden and deep (Hathaway, 2018), but they may indeed shift us toward an ecological consciousness that dramatically alters "our way of being in the world" (O'Sullivan, 2002, p. 11).

These experiences—which I refer to as reorienting connections (Hathaway, 2018)—both resemble and differ from the disorienting dilemmas described by Mezirow (1978, 2000) as the initial impetus for transformative learning. Disorienting dilemmas engender cognitive dissonance that stimulates deeper self-examination, leading one to reassess basic assumptions and values that result in more inclusive frames of reference (Kennedy-Reid, 2012). While reorienting connections may lead to self-reflection and shifts—not only in frames of reference, but in consciousness itself—they are seldom accompanied by the feelings of shame, anger, guilt, or fear that Mezirow describes. Moreover, the shifts in consciousness do not appear to depend on critical self-examination, although reflection may deepen—or at least, help articulate—the transformations experienced (Hathaway, 2018).

Reorienting connections may foster transformative "learning toward an ecological consciousness," enabling persons to overcome an "instrumental consciousness" which perceives the world as a mere storehouse of raw materials and move toward an intersubjective worldview rooted in a "wider sense of connection with all the powers of the world" (O'Sullivan & Taylor, 2004, pp. 11, 13). The world is no longer perceived as a mere "collection of objects," but rather as a "a communion of subjects," a living Earth community (Berry, 1999, p. 82). For this to occur, we must learn "*our way into* seeing, acting, and understanding" so that we can "survive the despair of our current condition" and "create an expansive, life-giving vision" which engages the human spirit and fosters ecological values such as connection, generosity, reciprocity, mutuality, and celebration (O'Sullivan & Taylor, 2004, p. 3, emphasis in original). One way to encourage such a vision and foster a sense of connection with other beings may be to nurture self-transcendent emotions like compassion, gratitude, and awe which "help individuals form enduring commitments to kin, nonkin, and social collectives" (Stellar et al., 2017, p. 6)—and with the more-than-human world.

In a study of over 30 educators and activists conducted by Hathaway (2018), countless stories of deeply transformative encounters with other beings, including ants, shrimp, spiders, bees, eagles, rhinos, deer, groundhogs, horses, maple trees, giant redwoods, and even stones emerged. Many participants also recounted joyful experiences of playing outdoors as children or being filled with awe while immersed in the beauty of nature. Often, these experiences led to deep feelings of wonder, reverence, gratitude, and empathy that built a sense of connection with the more-than-human world. The analysis of the stories suggested that—while disorienting dilemmas related to the ecological crisis often contribute to transformative learning—experiences of awe, gratitude, beauty, and intersubjective connection with other beings—or reorienting connections—appear to play an even greater role in the emergence of ecological consciousness. Indeed, these experiences were mentioned more frequently and with greater elaboration and emphasis than experiences which would correspond more closely to disorienting dilemmas. Similarly, Chawla's (1999) work on significant life experiences suggests that positive experiences of natural areas play a larger role in fostering pro-environmental commitment than the disorienting dilemmas that accompany experiences of pollution or habitat loss.

Over the course of this chapter, the experience and transformative potential of these reorienting connections will be explored by considering a case study involving undergraduate students engaging in a series of ecological practices designed to foster a sense of connection with the more-than-human world. After describing the study and some of the key theoretical underpinnings of the practices, the chapter considers a sample of student experiences, grouped by similarity. After examining some of the reported transformations and benefits experienced, some possible implications for transformative learning theory are considered.

REORIENTING CONNECTIONS IN PRACTICE

Is it possible to foster experiences of reorienting connections? To see how such connections might be cultivated in practice, I gave students in a third-year ecological worldviews class at the University of Toronto the option of engaging in outdoor, meditative practices based on Sewall's skill of ecological perception (1995, 1999) and related insights from ecophenomenology (Abram, 1997, 2005). The students who chose this option had to keep a journal and write brief reflection papers as a course assignment.

The students began their practices with an orientation in late September in a local park. I led the students in an elemental breaths meditation—based on a traditional practice by Sufi teacher Hazrat Inayat Khan—that fosters a sense of connection with earth, water, fire, and air through time, emphasizing the interdependence of all life. I then led the students in a walking meditation—based on both Sufi and Buddhist practices—to help cultivate a dynamic perception of connection with breath and the ground we walk upon. Finally, each student engaged individually in intersubjective meditation; each student sought out at least one other-than-human being they were drawn to and used all their senses to perceive what that being was communicating or teaching them.

In designing the practice of intersubjective meditation, I drew on ecopsychologist Laura Sewall's skill of ecological perception (1995, 1999). Based on research on neuroplasticity that demonstrates that new brain synapses are cultivated via the use of focused attention and ongoing practice, Sewall (1995, p. 204) proposes a "devotional practice" to foster ecological perception with five dimensions:

- Learning to attend: Being mindful, paying attention to beauty, form, color, and texture;
- Learning to perceive relationships and context: Seeing a being in-relation-to-others;
- Developing perceptual flexibility: Perceiving a being's journey through time and space as well as patterns;
- Learning to perceive depth and meaning: Understanding how the story of another entwines with other stories; and
- Using the imagination to extend our perception, empathize with other beings, and envision new possibilities.

Over the course of six weeks, students were expected to engage in the meditative practices taught in the orientation session at least five times for at least half an hour each session. While students were invited to use all the practices, greater emphasis was placed on intersubjective meditation. Since, Toronto has many parks—many located in ravines and accessible by public transit—most students engaged in their practices in urban settings, albeit some did so on weekend trips out of town. Many students chose to spend more than half an hour per session or to engage in additional sessions. Students kept a journal to reflect on their experience and were encouraged to include photos, drawings, or natural objects.

After receiving ethics approval from the University of Toronto and after students had completed the course, I requested permission from students to analyze their journals and reflection papers. In total, 34 students from two different academic years granted me permission, the large majority (28) being women. While formal demographic data was not collected, most participants were in their early 20s and were reflective of the University of Toronto's cultural diversity

Experiences of Reorienting Connections

The journals and reflection papers were analyzed using a qualitative methodology informed by an organic approach which integrates thematic narrative, phenomenological and relational approaches to inquiry (Anderson & Braud, 2011). I then employed Sewall's (1995, 1999) dimensions of ecological perception to group selected reflections—not to impose a theory upon a diverse set of experiences—but rather to organize these in a coherent manner which might illuminate how reorienting connections are experienced in practice.

Learning to Attend: Connecting with Other Beings

In the orientation session, I suggested that it could be helpful to begin by taking time to still the mind and open the senses. At first, many students found this difficult—often noting problems with concentration or disconnecting from technology. Mary,[1] for example, noted that simply

---

[1] All names used here are pseudonyms.

paying attention in nature was a novel experience—normally she would be listening to music or talking to another person.

Over time, most students found that their ability to practice simple awareness of their surroundings improved and that they were able to enter more fully into mindfulness. Irene, for example, notes that "Concentrating on the present moment, I extended my attention to the sensations of the grass and wind against my body; the sounds of leaves rustling and birds calling; and the smells of moist earth and wood. I then slowly paced around imagining the sources and interactivity of the sensations I perceived."

When practicing mindfulness, participants often began to notice one particular being. Mary first observed ants climbing through the grass and went on to imagine "the world from the ant's perspective." Jonathan, after listening to the sounds around him and feeling the warmth of the sun, opened his eyes to see a hawk flying high above: "The entire time I watched it, it maybe flapped its wings a handful of times but somehow stayed high up in the air, using the wind in combination with its open wings to glide." Reading his journal, I felt drawn into the sky as he watches the hawk circling, hunting for prey.

Matthew heard a "choir of crickets" and began to pay attention to their singing, trying "to listen to different crickets individually and then collectively." Each had "a unique chirp" with different tempos, "but together they combined into a melodic tune." Then he noticed the breeze in the trees and how that sound blended with the cricket song. He watched "the wind interact with each of the trees as it blew through, knocking leaves off on its way and stirring up leaves that had been laid to rest on the forest floor" and finishes his reflection noting: "The forest felt so much more alive today. I'm not sure if it was the breeze, the sun, the leaves, or a combination, but whatever it was made me feel much more connected to nature. I sat there taking it in, like a patron at a play."

Anna and Connie both decided to try meditation at night, opening themselves to new ways of perceiving. Anna notes, "My senses were heightened as they compensated for the lack of sight. I heard the shuffling of nocturnal creatures and smelt the dampness of the earth." Connie visited a tree she had known since childhood and recalls seeing this tree "through the eyes of my younger self." She approached the tree, leaves, and acorns crunching underfoot, and hugged it, feeling the dampness and the scratchy texture of the bark. "Through my skin, I imagine the hundred-year-old cells within the trunk, the core *soul* of this tree.

I wonder what it has seen over the years?" She smelled the tree and pondered the many creatures inhabiting its boughs and felt a deep sense of friendship with it as she stared through its branches to the stars above (Fig. 16.1).

Amelia took a walk in a local park and decided to veer off onto a nearly hidden path. She found a secluded spot and began her meditation, sitting in silence as she closed her eyes and focused on her breathing. "When I opened my eyes a very strange sensation came over me—that I was

Fig. 16.1 Connie's Meditation Journal

invisible." After several minutes passed, "My hypothesis was confirmed. Squirrels and birds began to scurry and hop past me as if I was not there, or rather that I was there but was a natural part of their home backdrop." While being silent, still, and aware, she felt that she had been accepted by the animals and this makes her feel at one with the woods. Awareness and stillness bear fruit in a deep sense of connection with other beings.

Perceiving Relationships and Intersubjectivity

For several students, the elemental breaths exercise served as a gateway into an experience of interconnection and communion with the more-than-human world. Jacob, for example, remarked, "My mind has been broadened through the inhalation and exhalation of the air, which intimately connects my body with the natural world." Meditation on the four elements—earth, water, fire, and air—reminded him how "humans are inseparable from nature." Lily found that the breathing exercise served as "a portal to peace," enabling her to open her senses and "realize that ... I am made up of stardust that is billions of years old" and that breathing itself connects her with living beings through time and space, helping her "build a sacred bond with the non-human world."

Engaging in intersubjective meditation, Elizabeth noted that initially she was unable to approach another organism without attaching a name and preconceptions to it. An important shift came when she was able to perceive a being in-relation-to-others. "Just as the tree provides a place for a bird to build its nest, it provides those on the ground with shade, and its entire ecosystem with life-supporting oxygen." Lily observed a bee pollinating a flower and receiving nectar in return. She noted that, together, they live in a relationship of mutually beneficial reciprocity and this filled her with a sense of Earth as an interconnected, living community. After watching a beetle on a piece of wood, Jack came to see the truth expressed by Abram (2014, p. viii) who writes that when we perceive "the biosphere in this manner, not as an inert collection of passive and determinate objects but as a community of animate material agencies ..., we straightaway begin to feel ourselves as members of this community."

Kimberley wrote, "I learned that the landscape developed its own stories and if I paid close enough attention, I would be able to hear those stories" and that even the rocks themselves could speak. Indeed, Jonathan experienced just that at Furnace Falls as he contemplated the rock beneath him and pondered its history through time as well as the "why" of being a rock (Fig. 16.2).

At the same time, the ecological meditations may also lead to an awareness of *disconnection* from the more-than-human world—something that may more closely resemble a disorienting dilemma. Erica wrote that, as an environmental studies student, she had thought that she was very connected to the natural world, "but these practices helped me to feel I am not as connected as I thought." Similarly, Miriam wrote that, as she engaged in the practices, she realized that her relationship with the

Fig. 16.2 Jonathan's Meditation Journal

288 M. HATHAWAY

more-than-human world had previously been quite superficial and that she needed, not only to study nature in a more theoretical or detached manner, but also to immerse herself in it and experience it.

Developing Perceptual Flexibility Across Time and Space

Jonathan's experience of the rock at Furnace Falls and Amelia's contemplation of the life of her beloved tree both reveal how ecological meditations can lead to a deeper sense of time and story, as does the observation of Lily that the complex elements in our bodies that were born in a supernova explosion mean that we are literally, living and breathing stardust.

Similarly, Matthew observed a single, yellow leaf in a dry riverbed, and he began to ponder "the fate of this leaf," imagining "it decomposing, transforming into a series of smaller pieces until the pieces were too small to be seen", and how these would become food for other organisms. "I thought how altruistic and beautiful this cycle was: death provides life. It clicked in at this moment that we all were really part of a dynamic and intricate web of life." Likewise, Pamela observed an "erratic" boulder deposited by a long-past ice age and was transported back to a time when the world was covered by a thick sheet of ice and long-lost creatures inhabited the Earth.

Other journeys through time were more personal, connecting back to childhood experiences. Gazing up at the stars during her night-time meditation, Anna recalled stargazing with her father as a child. Amelia remembered visiting the tree as her childhood self, while Erica—on seeing a frog—recollects how she would catch frogs as a child and reflected, "It makes me wonder if my childhood was a time that I was more connected with nature. Or am I still connected with nature, but just don't have the time to realize it?".

Other students learned new ways of perceiving by engaging in the practices. Miriam, for example, wrote that, instead of merely trying to observe squirrels, she endeavored to connect with them and listen to what they might be trying to teach her. In so doing, she realized the difference between coming to know something by confronting or dissecting it and knowing something from the inside-out, by empathically attempting to become (or identify with) the other being.

In her meditation practice, Irene began to notice "patterns and connections ..., such as the reciprocal calls among birds, and the freezing response of squirrels to sudden noises" and that "perceiving the world as fragmented objects suppresses their underlying connectivity and precludes humans from experiencing nature as an interdependent community of beings."

Perceiving Depth and Meaning: An Animate World

In a brief reading that I shared with students, Abram (2005, p. 189) speaks of how, "in its oldest form, prayer consists simply in speaking *to* the world" and asks whether we can "also speak to these powers, and listen for their replies." In practicing intersubjective meditation, I invited students to not only seek to learn from other beings, but also to approach them as potential teachers who can communicate and share wisdom with us.

Connie seems to have experienced this while watching a seagull swimming in Lake Ontario. "I thought about emotional language. I listened carefully to the noises the seagull was making. I thought I could sense some distress in his calls." She goes on to comment that, even though we may speak different languages, we can understand other beings insofar as we share the same emotions.

Priscilla experienced communication from a shrub she encounters alone on a barren, muddy patch of ground. In watching it struggle with shriveled, bug-eaten leaves, she felt that it was struggling hard in harsh conditions and that it had somehow succeeded where no other plant has survived. "I think it was trying to communicate that you can continue to grow despite harsh conditions if you keep trying. It also teaches me to persevere at anything I may attempt."

Jacob reflected that these practices have opened him to experience a relationship between humans and nature that is more active and reciprocal than he had anticipated: "I watch the leaves 'waving' to each other; I hear the trees 'whispering.'" Jacob then noted that his interactions with the more-than-human world are meaningful and that he is never truly alone in nature. Moreover, "the relationship is animated because the interaction between humans and nature is dynamic and continuous."

Imagination, Empathy, and Creativity

As Sewall (1995) notes, imagination may play a key role in extending our perception, both to encompass wider time scales and by imagining, for example, that other beings—even trees and stones—are watching us. Perhaps more importantly, imagination enables us to put ourselves into the place of another, very different being. Even if we may not be able to fully experience the sensations or perceptions of other living entities, the very attempt to imagine these may cultivate empathy and compassion for others. Indeed, our brains contain "mirror neurons" that fire in sympathy with the feelings we perceive or imagine in others (Lakoff & Johnson, 1999).

While sitting on the grass, Gwen imagined the diverse species living there, even though she could not perceive them directly: "My senses were extended, and all barriers were shattered. I felt united with mother nature." Mary attempted to see "the world from an ant's perspective" as she watched them climbing on blades of grass. As Connie meditated in the tree, she imagined "the hundred-year-old cells within the trunk" and sensed the tree's soul. Irene contemplated the fate of two acorns—one that is eaten by a squirrel and another that grows into an oak tree—to ponder whether each had served their purpose, even if in very different ways. The use of imagination is also evident in Kimberley hearing stories in the landscape and Jonathon journeying with a rock through time (Fig. 16.3).

Transformations and Benefits

Analyzing the journals and reflections of the students, it is evident that many were able to experience a more ecological form of perceiving the world, similar to what Sewall (1995, 1999) envisions when she writes of the skill of ecological perception. It is more difficult, particularly in this time-limited study, to evaluate whether deeper, more lasting transformations resulted; yet many students did report changes in their perspective and worldview as a result of engaging in the ecological practices.

Mary, for example, spoke of a shift from a more abstract or theoretical ecological worldview to one that she actually experienced through "direct contact with nature" that enabled her "senses to become more attuned" while Petra spoke of "visceral learning that cannot be replicated in the classroom."

Phoebe observed that the ecological practices shifted her perspectives because she needed "to routinely seek a relationship with nature that did not revolve" around her own immediate desires or goals; she began to perceive herself as "less of an isolated agent" and more as "a part of an

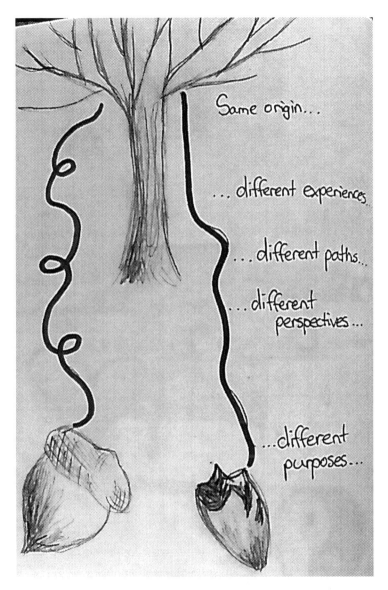

Fig. 16.3 Irene's Meditation Journal

interconnected system of cyclical processes" that were less goal oriented. Previously, her concern for ecological issues had been based primarily on analysis, but now it had extended "to include a more emotional attachment" and feelings of growing interrelatedness. Noreen seems to have experienced something similar, which she articulates by quoting Fox (1984, p. 196), musing that perhaps "by subtracting your own self-centred and self-serving thoughts from the world, you come to realize that the other is none other than yourself." Debbie likewise writes that her sense of self had broadened, enabling her to experience her "relation with the universe."

Alicia began to see "the world in a very new light" as she "became more aware of the inherent beauty within it, how we connect to it and how we depend on it." Priscilla noticed a change in herself when, during walking meditation, a bug crawled onto her arm: "Normally I would have flicked it off of me, but it didn't bother me anymore. I let it crawl around until it decided to be on its way and flew off." Lily noted, "I saw a friend in the animals, the wisdom handed down to me by my departed grandparents in the trees, and [a] home in the forest." Through her practices, she began to experience "the land as a living community rather than property" where even the abiotic elements are animate and deserve respect. Moreover, she began to experience that "the Earth itself as a whole indeed has a soul, the anima mundi."

Amy noted, "my ecological worldview indeed changed" and that "being with natural living things and the beauty of it makes me feel like I'm a part of this life." She reflected that her process of transformation affirms Sewall's observation that "our worldview is constituted by our predominant experience" (1999, p. 244). Interacting with the more-than-human world on a regular basis—rather than simply with human-made artifacts—changed the focus of her perception and that, in turn, changed the way she experienced the world to one as a communion of subjects with whom she is in relationship. Gwen similarly observed, "When we change the way we perceive the world around us, we simultaneously change the way we react to this world." The following sections describe in more depth the nature of some of the changes and shifts experienced.

16 FOSTERING REORIENTING CONNECTIONS ... 293

Communication, Reciprocity, and Animacy

A first shift that some students reported was toward a sense of deep connectivity in which the world is experienced as a living—even sentient—communion of beings. This shift is also marked by a sense of reciprocity where other beings communicate with, support, and provide guidance to humans. Noreen learned that "the trees and wind are excellent listeners and always seem to know what I'm thinking, as they know when a sympathetic rustle is appropriate." Ariana stared at a tree and began to feel it revealing itself to her: "It was a windy day so the branches and leaves were constantly moving, as though they were dancing to the crisping sounds of the leaves." Looking at the other trees, she realized how different they were from each other and perceives that each has its own story, just as each human person does.

Connie experienced a reciprocal relationship with the wind as she breathes, blowing through her with each inhalation and then returning with each exhalation: "A relationship of sharing: Maybe wind is really just everyone and everything breathing in and out together. Touching everything with our own winds." Later, she wrote that her long familiarity with many of the places she visited helped reinforce a sense of connectivity to the point where she came "to see their animate qualities" and experienced a kind of "reciprocal dialogue" with them.

Shifts in Spirituality

Several students also noted a change in how they experienced their spirituality. Karen, for example, observed that as a woman of faith, she often converses with God in nature and feels a "natural instinct to praise the Creator." Yet, as she entered more deeply into the ecological practices, she found herself relating more directly to other-than-human beings: "I noticed myself talking directly to the wonders around me, asking questions such as 'how did you get here, what is your story, what have you seen?'" particularly "in the presence of an older entity, such as a tree or a boulder." Petra similarly remarked that she resonated with Abram's (2005, p. 189) idea of prayer being a way of "speaking to the world, rather than solely about the world" insofar as she felt "most attuned to the Earth's life forces" when outdoors "rather than in a church or a classroom." Judy, whose faith integrates elements of both Christianity and Islam, felt these practices reconnected her with experiences she had with several First Nations communities, particularly the teaching to be mindful of "all my relations." Rather than marking a shift away from a belief in a Creator, these changes seemed to mark a new perception of the intrinsic value of all life—i.e., creation is to be appreciated and loved, not only because it is the work of the Creator, but because each being is a relative who has value in and of itself.

Love and Care

Alicia found herself falling "in love with the Earth," simply by interacting with other beings and by becoming more attentive to them. This, in turn, motivated her to "start making more choices in [her] life that would create positive change" both personally and "in the larger picture." Gwen similarly observed that the emotional connection she now feels with her surroundings motivates her to protect the Earth: "When some form of attachment is formed, future actions will be in compliance with this attachment." Because of this sense of interconnection, "we come to realize that triggering harm on other beings will only generate collective loss."

Overcoming Anxiety

Many students noted that the ecological practices helped them to overcome anxiety, improve mood, and find peace. Paul noted that the practices "functioned as a calming technique, while offering the chance to step away from the material world, away from cell phones, laptops, and televisions" and helping him gain a greater sense of focus in his life. Mo reflected that the practices helped him put problems in perspective and "gain a sense of calm understanding" because he now realized that he is "part of a bigger whole, that everyone has problems, and that in time they don't matter quite as much." Contemplating the life story of a tree, for example, helped him to see his own life from a broader and more inclusive perspective. Alicia found that the practices helped her to deal with devastating experiences in her life and "find out who I am and what I really want." Matthew discovered that he was able to free himself from anxiety and toxic feelings and increase his confidence in his future plans. Not only, then, did these practices help motivate caring actions, they also seem to have helped participants find a sense of focus and empowerment for moving forward in life.

Fostering Creativity

A final benefit of the ecological practices is reflected in the wide variety of photographs, drawings, collected leaves, and poetry included in the journals. For instance, Mary writes a poem:

The wind is strong,
So long-lasting and powerful.
But its presence,
Is an afterthought.
The whipping, the lashing, the force,
The terror and the strife.
Feel the strength,
The needs required,
Nature is in us,
We are one.

Anna shared how she is drawn to let her pen "just move without thinking of anything specific" (Fig. 16.4).

Connie notes the importance of creative expressions including "free-hand sketching, gathering of vibrant foliage, and even singing" which contributed to her overall enjoyment of the meditation experience. She noted that art amplifies the visceral quality of the practices which includes "physical contact with the mystifying touch of bark from different trees and the striking cold of stream water" (Fig. 16.5).

The role of Reflection: Journaling

While the practice of meditation tended to foster a more intuitive and emotional mode of learning, reflection and analysis also played a role, particularly through journaling. Irene wrote that creating a physical record of her experiences helped give "visible life to the connections" she developed with the more-than-human world while Karen wrote that journaling helped "amplify" her sense of connection. Kimberley noted that writing helped her "reflect and see what changes I could make to deepen my connection with nature the next time I went outdoors" while Petra found that writing helped her more clearly perceive a deepening in her meditation practice over time. Mary found that writing enabled her to make sense of her thoughts while Karen noted that journaling helped her find deeper meanings in her experiences.

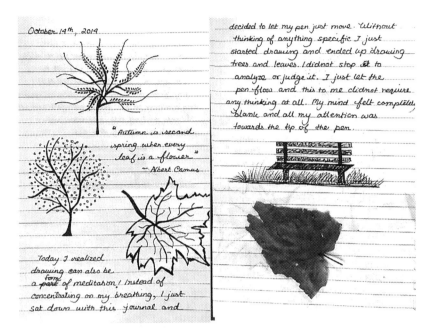

Fig. 16.4 Anna's Meditation Journal

While journaling was generally helpful, others found that the expectation of writing may have hindered them from entering fully into the meditative experience. Pamela, for example, noted: "Many times I struggled to translate my feelings, emotions, and thoughts onto paper" which in turn caused stress during meditation. "I had to nit-pick in my mind the most important things I was experiencing–which was distracting to the overall activity."

Shifting or Deepening?

While some students reported a significant transformation in their worldview and perceptions of the more-than-human world, others seem to have experienced instead a deepening of a worldview that they already had. Several observed that five sessions spent outdoors were a rather limited timeframe, although most noticed a deepening over that short time. As

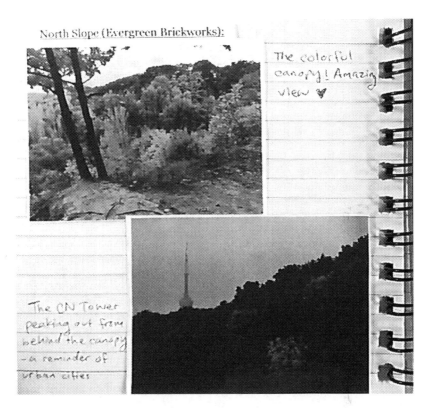

Fig. 16.5 Connie's Meditation Journal

Mo noted, "doing five practices did not have a dramatic effect. I definitely felt more connected to nature after doing the practices, but that feeling did not last long after I went back to my daily routine." To be truly effective, he noted, his practice would have to become part of his daily life.

Others, perhaps, felt a deeper change. Amy remarked that she indeed had experienced a transformation in her worldview and others—as we have seen—similarly speak of more long-lasting shifts. Several were motivated to continue these practices after the course ended. Gwen, for example, remarks that "meditation has become a way of life" for her while Jack notes that engaging with the more-than-human world is like playing an instrument: "Eventually, you lose your ability to play if you do not

298   M. HATHAWAY

practice. I believe that we may lose our ability to appreciate nature if we do not spend time with it and reflect on it." This coincides with Sewall's (1999) assertion that, to change the neural ensembles that enable new perceptions to arise requires, not only attention, but ongoing practice.

CONCLUSION

O'Sullivan (2002, p. 1) defines transformative learning as "a deep, structural shift in the basic premises of thought, feelings, and actions" that "dramatically and irreversibly alters our way of being in the world." Since this study was time-limited, the duration and depth of the transformations the students experienced is difficult to ascertain. Yet, it seems apparent that many experienced a taste of ecological consciousness and a "wider sense of connection with all the powers of the world" that fostered new perceptual abilities (O'Sullivan & Taylor, 2004, p. 3).

For most, this process of experiencing reorienting connections seems to have been gradual, marked by a myriad of subtle, and at times, more marked shifts rather than by dramatic epiphanies. At least some of the transformations described, however, seem to have been both significant and potentially long-lasting. Drawing on systems theory, Hathaway (2018) observes that transformative learning is often marked by a kind of punctuated equilibrium in which many smaller changes eventually reach a tipping point, leading to a more dramatic shift in how we perceive and act. Often, it is only in looking back over life events that their true significance and impact becomes apparent.

Almost all the shifts reported by the students—with the possible exception of the awareness of disconnection—seem to differ from Mezirow's classic description of disorienting dilemmas. Rather than feelings of shame, fear, anger, or guilt, the shifts were accompanied by self-transcendent emotions like love, compassion, wonder, mutuality, appreciation for beauty, and a sense of connection or an expanded self.

There are good reasons to hope that these shifts in perception and consciousness may, over time, also bear fruit in concrete action for sustainability. Several large-scale studies over the past two decades indicate that an emotional sense of connectedness to the more-than-human world is associated with pro-ecological behaviors such as resisting consumerism, participating in environmental organizations, using public transit, and buying sustainably produced foods (Mayer & Frantz, 2004; Nisbet, et al., 2009). One of the students who engaged in the ecological practices,

Phoebe, affirms the insight that an affective sense of connection may be key to reorienting transformations, noting that logic alone seems insufficient to convince people to adopt sustainable lifestyles or take action: "Perhaps the fostering of a more emotional ... relationship with nature is the vital change needed in order to motivate more meaningful change in behavior."

References

Abram, D. (1997). *The spell of the sensuous: Perception and language in a more-than-human world* (1st Vintage Books ed.). Vintage Books.

Abram, D. (2005). Between the body and the breathing Earth: A reply to Ted Toadvine. *Environmental Ethics, 27*(2), 171–190.

Abram, D. (2014). On wild ethics. In D. A. Vakoch & F. Castrillón (Eds.), *Ecopsychology, phenomenology, and the environment* (pp. vii–ix). Springer.

Anderson, R., & Braud, W. (2011). *Transforming self and others through research: Transpersonal research methods and skills for the human sciences and humanities.* SUNY Press.

Berry, T. (1999). *The great work: Our way into the future.* Bell Tower.

Chawla, L. (1999). Life paths into effective environmental action. *The Journal of Environmental Education, 31*(1), 15–26.

Fox, W. (1984). Deep ecology: A new philosophy of our time? *The Ecologist, 14*(5–6), 194–204.

Hathaway, M. (2018). *Cultivating ecological wisdom: Worldviews, transformative learning, and engagement for sustainability* (Doctor of Philosophy Dissertation). University of Toronto, Canada.

Kennedy-Reid, S. K. (2012). *Exploring the habitus: A phenomenological study of transformative learning processes* (Doctoral Dissertation). The George Washington University, Washington, DC.

Lakoff, G., & Johnson, M. (1999). *Philosophy in the flesh: The embodied mind and its challenge to Western thought.* Basic Books.

Mayer, F. S., & Frantz, C. M. (2004). The connectedness to nature scale: A measure of individuals' feeling in community with nature. *Journal of Environmental Psychology, 24*(4), 503–515.

Mezirow, J. (1978). Perspective transformation. *Adult Education Quarterly, 28*(2), 100–110.

Mezirow, J. (2000). Learning to think like an adult. In J. Mezirow & Associates (Eds.), *Learning as transformation: Critical perspectives on a theory in progress* (1st ed., pp. 3–34). Jossey-Bass.

Nisbet, E. K., Zelenski, J. M., & Murphy, S. A. (2009). The nature relatedness scale: Linking individuals' connection with nature to environmental concern and behavior. *Environment and Behavior, 41*(5), 715–740.

O'Sullivan, E. V. (2002). The project and vision of transformative learning. In E. V. O'Sullivan, A. Morrell, & M. A. O'Connor (Eds.), *Expanding the boundaries of transformative learning: Essays on theory and praxis* (pp. 1–12). Palgrave Macmillan.

O'Sullivan, E. V., & Taylor, M. M. (2004). Glimpses of ecological consciousness. In E. V. O'Sullivan & M. M. Taylor (Eds.), *Learning toward an ecological consciousness: Selected transformative practices* (pp. 5–23). Palgrave Macmillan.

Sewall, L. (1995). The skill of ecological perception. In M. Gomes, A. Kanner, & T. Roszak (Eds.), *Ecopsychology: Restoring the earth, healing the mind* (pp. 201–215). Sierra Club Books.

Sewall, L. (1999). *Sight and sensibility: The ecopsychology of perception.* J.P. Tarcher/Putnam.

Stellar, J. E., Gordon, A. M., Piff, P. K., Cordaro, D., Anderson, C. L., Bai, Y., ... Keltner, D. (2017). Self-transcendent emotions and their social functions: Compassion, gratitude, and awe bind us to others through prosociality. *Emotion Review: Journal of the International Society for Research on Emotion, 9*(3), 200–207.

CHAPTER 17

Revitalizing Reflection in Teacher Education: A Digital Tool for Reflection as a Gentle Trigger for Transformation

Kaisu Mälkki, Marita Mäkinen, and Joni Forsell

Teacher reflection, which has attracted substantial attention in the teacher education literature over the past few decades (e.g., Beauchamp, 2015; Loughran, 2010; Tripp, 2010; Williams, 2020), is considered a crucial element of teacher professional development, giving teachers a means to understand their school practices (e.g., Avalos, 2011; Cochran-Smith et al., 2008). Accordingly, the goal for teacher education programs to equip preservice teachers with a teacher as "reflective practitioner" stance

---

K. Mälkki (✉) · M. Mäkinen · J. Forsell
Faculty of Education and Culture, Tampere University, Tampere, Finland
e-mail: kaisu.malkki@tuni.fi

M. Mäkinen
e-mail: marita.makinen@tuni.fi

J. Forsell
e-mail: joni.forsell@tuni.fi

© The Author(s), under exclusive license to Springer Nature Switzerland AG 2022
A. Nicolaides et al. (eds.), *The Palgrave Handbook of Learning for Transformation*, https://doi.org/10.1007/978-3-030-84694-7_17

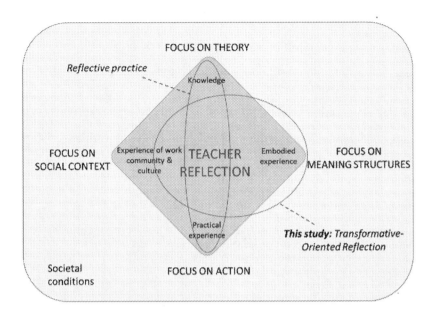

Fig. 17.1 Teacher reflection field of research

introduced by Schön (1983) is supported globally. However, obstacles to applying teacher reflection in research and practice hinder the successful implementation of reflective activities that support professional development (e.g., Beauchamp, 2015), many of them stemming from conceptual looseness (e.g., Atkinson, 2012; Collin et al., 2013; Korthagen, 2014). Furthermore, the teaching profession is highly intertwined with societal and cultural conditions that are historically variable (e.g., Darling-Hammond, 2006; McConn & Geetter, 2020; Zeicher et al., 2015). These relations are often overlooked when researching the processes of teacher reflection. This is an issue not only in terms of fostering student achievement and engagement in heterogenous school realities, but also in terms of teacher well-being and collective efficacy (Mäkinen, 2013).

We contend that the problematic nature of reflection in the teacher education field stems from associating reflection mainly with the consideration of concrete teaching practices. Our purpose in this chapter is to revitalize teacher reflection by studying the nature and process of reflection that focuses on meaning structures (Fig. 17.1). We investigate a new way to promote critical reflection for professional development using a recently developed digital tool called the "reflection facilitator" (RF) in initial teacher education program. Reflection is discussed in an integrated frame of teacher reflection studies and transformative learning theory research, two of the authors' long-term academic research topics. We focus on transformative-oriented reflection as a contextually specified interpretation of reflection within the theoretical framework of the transformative teaching stance (Mäkinen, 2013) that situates teacher reflection in its societal context. Consequently, we aim to redefine the concept of reflection in the interface between embodied experiencing and societal conditions by developing the theory of edge emotions (Mälkki, 2011).

Considering the theory of reflection more generally, we drew on the transformative learning theory research originated by Mezirow (e.g., 1991, 2000; Hoggan et al., 2017; Illeris, 2014; Taylor & Cranton, 2013). From this perspective, the practices that facilitate reflection should not socialize the student into reproducing pre-defined truths; instead, such practices should support the student's ability to deal with uncertainty and promote critical reflection regarding the structures of teacher education, with the aim of restoring praxis through collective discovery (Ashwin, 2014; Biesta, 2013; Eschenbacher & Fleming, 2020; Freire, 1972; Mezirow, 2000; Rainio et al., in press). That is, the facilitator— whether human or digital—should "make every effort to transfer their authority over the learning group to the group itself as soon as this is feasible" so that "they become collaborative learners" (Mezirow, 2000, pp. 30–31; also, Finnegan, 2019).

The aim of the current research is twofold. First, we focus on ways in which the empirical data, which are based on student experiences with the RF, indicate reflection and how the RF may facilitate reflection. Second, we aim to develop transformative-oriented reflection as a theoretical concept by focusing on the kinds of reflection that may foster a transformative teaching stance. More specifically, we inquire into the mechanisms by which transformative-oriented reflection may enhance teacher well-being in complex teaching environments.

Teacher Reflection in Societal Frame

Prevailing teacher reflection research focuses on developing practical instruments (e.g., Akbari et al., 2010; Pellegrino & Gerber, 2012) or mentoring behaviors to facilitate teachers' reflective practices to enhance teacher efficacy (e.g., Allas et al., 2020; Korthagen, 2014; Tripp, 2010) and on quantitatively investigating the correlations between diverse contextual variables and teacher reflection (e.g., Aliakbari et al., 2020). A more recent, complementary approach has been offered by studies focusing on the conditions that foster critical subjectivity for the teacher to support the teacher's work as both societally and pedagogically constructive, as well as personally sustainable (Behizadeh et al., 2019; Berghoff et al., 2011; Mäkinen, 2013; Parsons & Stephenson, 2005). In these studies, the societal conditions of the school practices are viewed as the starting point, while the ultimate goal of teacher reflection is to facilitate critical subjectivity to collaboratively transform school communities (Darling-Hammond, 2006; Mäkinen, 2013; Zeicher et al., 2015). Consequently, teacher reflection is situated in relation to the educational knowledge structures and learning theories adopted during initial teacher education, accompanied by the complex demands of the work in societal and cultural contexts (e.g., Behizadeh et al., 2019; Berghoff et al., 2011; Kramer, 2018; Mäkinen, 2013; Rainio et al., in press).

The transformative teaching stance employed in this study as the contextual frame for researching reflection stems from prior research on teachers' reflections on work experiences in an inclusive setting (Mäkinen, 2013). The transformative teaching stance (Fig. 17.1) is defined by four conceptual anchors that form a systemic framework for pedagogical activity: (1) the broader aim of teachers' work, that is, transforming the school into a "professional learning community" (DuFour, 2007); (2) systemic reflective orientation that is critical, open, curious, and sensitive, i.e., transformative-oriented reflection; (3) personally held values; and (4) the collective efficacy that teachers both are empowered by and contribute to, introduced originally by Bandura (1997) (Fig. 17.2).

According to the transformative teaching stance, teacher performance standards and teacher development goals are not pre-defined based on teacher education knowledge and practices, school policy, or pre-existing school practices. Instead, the systemic framing of the transformative stance involves taking a reflective approach to examining each of the four anchors and their societal contexts (also, Biesta, 2013; Freire, 1972). That is, neither the current knowledge nor the practices or personal understandings are infallible, and all the conditions for reflection are open for critical considerations. This construct may be seen to embody fallibilism (Holma & Hyytinen, 2015) as the underlying epistemic position. Consequently, the notion of dealing with uncertainty (Shulman, 2005) can be

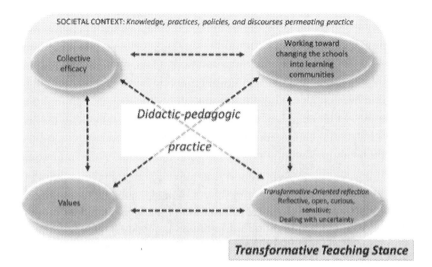

Fig. 17.2 Transformative stance as systemic frame for pedagogic activity

placed at the core of the framework (Rainio et al., in press). Similarly, the underlying premise of epistemological fallibilism may be seen to be expressed in the term transformative-oriented reflection: reflection within the framework of the transformative teaching stance (Mäkinen, 2013) is not assumed to be transformative as such but to intend or aspire to become transformative, necessitating critical assessments of the process and methods of reflection as well (see also Mezirow, 1991).

The framing of the transformative teaching stance may add further demands to the process of reflection that, based on previous research, is already considered challenging and even, at times, painful (e.g., Berger, 2004; Brookfield, 1994). Furthermore, it is not necessarily easy to remain optimistic when critically challenging dominant practices and ideologies (Brookfield, 2000). However, Mäkinen (2013, p. 58) maintained, based on her study, that teachers who embody a transformative teaching stance may be better off in terms of well-being (e.g., Behizadeh et al., 2019; Berghoff et al., 2011). Furthermore, Brookfield (2000) claimed that critical reflection aimed at transforming societal circumstances must be a collaborative process, undertaken only with the help of critical friends providing both alternative perspectives and emotional sustenance (e.g., Eschenbacher & Fleming, 2020; Finnegan, 2019). However, these studies do not offer an understanding of what this form of reflection is actually like, how it may bring about well-being, and how it is facilitated. We address these issues in this study.

NATURE OF REFLECTION WITHIN TRANSFORMATIVE LEARNING

Most studies on teacher reflection draw on the Deweyan theory of experience. However, Dewey's work has its limitations in terms of locating the reflective processes within societal perspectives. Mezirow's (1991, 2000) work shifts the focus of reflection from pragmatic action to the way societal context shapes our thinking and experiencing, while being limited to rational depiction of the process of reflection. Mälkki's theory of edge emotions integrates Mezirow's (1991, 2000) critical viewpoint and Dewey's (1938; see also Hoggan et al., 2017) naturalistic perspective on experience involving the dimensions of continuity and interaction. Mälkki (2010, 2011, 2019) explains the conditions necessary to become critically aware of the assumptions questioned while bringing focus to the experiential dimensions of thinking. Thereby critical reflection is situated in the embodied and contextual experience (e.g., Leigh & Bailey, 2013; Yorks & Kasl, 2002).

Mälkki's work is based on analyzing Mezirow's (1991, 2000) transformative learning theory and Damasio's (e.g., 1999; see Jordi, 2011) work on neuroscience indicating the intertwinement of emotion and cognition in the construction of consciousness. Mälkki (2011) suggested that biological emotions, functioning as a life-support system, make up the experiential dimensions of meaning perspectives: when we can manage our lives without problems, without experiencing significant challenges to our assumptions, values, social relations, and sense of belonging, we find ourselves settling into our comfort zone. In contrast, when our meaning perspectives are questioned, we experience unpleasant emotions—the so-called edge emotions—such as fear, anger, frustration, anxiety, and shame. Both the edge emotions and the comfort zone have their functions in supporting the continuity and coherence of our meaning perspectives (Mälkki, 2010, 2011, 2019), or experience, in Dewey's terms. The edge emotions signal a threat and orient us to automatically act so as to preserve the previously experienced balance. Despite the natural instinct to avoid unpleasant emotions through immediate and premature interpretation and action, we may learn to embrace them in order to access the questioned assumptions that gave rise to the edge emotions. Coping with edge emotions requires sensitivity, since it involves our innate embodied protection mechanisms, not an object that is rationally manageable (Mälkki, 2011) (Fig. 17.3).

While our reactions in conjunction with emotions have biological bases and functions, they are also socially and societally formed. This gives rise to collective comfort zones, where consensus exists on the assumption of what is acceptable within a given social setting (Mälkki, 2019). More specifically, we experience a sense of validation and acceptance based on shared values and assumptions, that is, affinities between meaning perspectives. Therefore, when we critically consider our personal assumptions, we invoke a risk to our social relations and sense of belonging (Brookfield, 1994).

Based on the theory of reflection and edge emotions, edge emotions and their innate resistance to reflection must be recognized and managed to facilitate reflection to reach an understanding of the assumptions questioned. When the edge emotions are not recognized and harnessed, it is likely that reflection remains within the comfort zone, thereby confirming the existing assumptions. In this case, the critical purpose of reflection

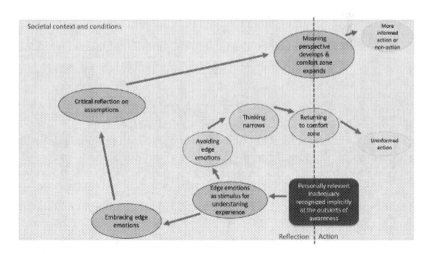

Fig. 17.3 Theory of edge emotions

is reversed, and moral and ethical perspectives remain limited. In all, the rational capacities of our thinking to make decisions, justify beliefs and behaviors, select information, and weigh evidence, for example, are bound to both the comfort zone and the edge emotions as part of human functionality (Mälkki, 2011). The depiction of the nature of reflection combining the essences of Dewey (1938), Mezirow (1991) and Mälkki (2011, 2019), forms the basis for both the empirical analysis and the RF tool that we consider next.

Reflection Facilitator (RF)

RF is an open-access digital audio recording that guides listeners step-by-step through a reflection process. The RF was designed to meet three objectives: (a) provide users with a conceptual understanding of the nature of the reflection process, (b) help users learn to embrace edge emotions as a pathway to reflection and learning (Mälkki, 2010, 2011, 2019), and (c) facilitate step-by-step support for users to guide them through reflecting on their experiences in an experiential manner.

The RF is general in nature, suitable for use by any adult or youth, but it can also address more specific tasks. For example, when the focus of an exercise, such as a course topic, must be narrowed, students can be instructed to choose the case for the exercise from their personal experiences regarding certain topics. The RF is suitable both for beginners and for people with more experience with reflecting, as it can deepen their reflective abilities and provide them with support for reflective practices, especially those related to challenging situations.

RESEARCH SITE AND METHODS

The study was conducted through Teacher's Professional Learning and Development, an advanced course (10 ECTS) included in a Finnish university-level teacher education program. Due to the COVID-19 pandemic in 2020, the one-semester course was carried out fully online through interactive webinars, small-group projects, collaborative media monitoring, and individual assignments that involved practice with the RF. Of the 49 students in the course, 44 gave their informed consent for their coursework to be used for research purposes. The students' written responses to an individual pre-assignment for the course, which they completed prior to engaging with the faculty or the course topics, form the main data for this study. Pre-assignment was not included in the course grading. The assignment involved doing the RF exercise and responding to questions online concerning the experiential exercise. The questions considered the experiences of the exercise, perceptions of the RF, their perspectives on the relevance of the RF both generally and in relation to professional growth, and their view of the relation between thinking and emotions in learning.

In addition to the data from preservice teachers, additional data for the study consisted of similar written reflections based on the RF by students from other fields and phases of study ($n = 530$), allowing for cross-validation of the findings.

Analysis

An inductive content analysis (Hsieh & Shannon, 2005), a method appropriate for studies that intend to develop theory, was used to articulate variations of participants' meaning making and varied ways of experiencing and interpreting their reflections on the RF-guided experience. The basic unit for analysis was defined as a sentence or a short notion in which a participant expressed their thoughts, emotions, or reflections related to RF experiences and professional development. In the first analysis phase, we investigated how the participants experienced the RF and what their reflections addressed. A theoretical anomaly that emerged in the inductive phase was then focused on from the perspective of thinking with theory (Jackson & Mazzei, 2012). This method utilizes data to think with and use theory to think about the data. We interpreted the data through the combined lens of Dewey's (1933, 1938), Mezirow's (1991, 2000), and Mälkki's (2010, 2011, 2019) frameworks, as described in the theoretical framework section, considering reflection as experiential, critical, and social. These theoretical bodies of knowledge were then used to construct empirically grounded theoretical explanations for the empirical anomaly revealed in the first phase.

Findings

The systematic and digitally guided approach to reflection as a concept and process was, for the students, a new way to support learning and professional development. The concept of edge emotions, as well, was new to them. Therefore, neither the knowledge structures presented during their teacher education studies nor the activities they underwent provided the students with previous experiences and expectations based on which they could have made definitive sense of the exercise and the experience of it within the lines of their existing meaning perspectives, as exemplified by the following data excerpt. (All quotes are translated from Finnish.)

> The idea of edge emotions and working with them was entirely new and exciting for me. To reflect on a negative situation or feeling in this way felt wonderfully safe and even motivating.

The student writings overall represented the kind of sincerity, openness, and lack of inhibition that the authors, based on their combined decades of experiences as academic instructors, have not commonly observed in academic writings. The accounts indicated a nuanced and dialectic approach to emotions whereby the emotions—or the exercise—were not judged as positive or negative, but both pleasant and unpleasant aspects of their experience were considered in an encompassing way.

> At first it was difficult to understand the purpose of the tool and what kind of situation I was supposed to address. When I engaged in the exercise, then I was able to concentrate and to immerse myself into the situation, even when it brought up strong emotions.

Perhaps the feelings of safety allowed them to move through the uncertainty of using the new tool, that is, they could move beyond reflectively observing the way their reflection process was facilitated by the RF to surrendering to being facilitated.

Letting go of reflective observation and surrendering to the facilitation of one's own reflection process could also be experienced as being coerced to give up one's existing meaning structures and values. However, the students seemed not to surrender unquestioningly to the facilitation; instead, the accounts indicated the students established a critical distance from the tool and the exercise. We may hypothesize some elements that supported the students in maintaining a critical distance to the exercise. One dimension of this may be the nature of the tool as a human-narrated open-access digital recording. That is, the facilitation was not prompted by a person in live interaction but by an external artifact, whereby input from the tool and the user's own experiences may be more easily disentangled.

The recording explicates both the purpose of the exercise and the theoretical underpinnings, thereby giving students the conceptual tools and framework necessary to develop an informed and personal relation to what they were doing and to what extent they wished to engage in reflection. Perhaps the free and open expressions in the written assignments and the nuanced grasp of their personal experiences indicated ownership of the reflection process. That is, while the facilitation provided by the RF was considered helpful and necessary for the reflection process, student accounts indicated they formed a personal relation to the reflection process that extended beyond the contexts of formal education, rather than experiencing the facilitation or the reflective exercise as a form of socialization within a given professional field.

This personal relationship with the reflection process was represented in the data by the students' explorations into meanings in lieu of taking the practices, standards, and goals of teacher education and the process and value of reflection for granted. Furthermore, in later discussions during the course, the students expressed interest in communicating with other students and teachers to share experiences regarding the exercise and their personal experiences with edge emotions.

The aim of the RF was to support critical reflection on one's meaning perspectives by scaffolding the re-experiencing of unpleasant emotions regarding a self-chosen situation that had remained perplexing to the student. As such, experiences of unpleasantness were expected to be documented in the student accounts. However, student accounts described the reflection experience as tender, pleasant, or intriguing, as the following data excerpts exemplify.

> The ending of the reflection exercise made it possible to be a truly human being. I can imagine, in my future profession, [employing this method to solve] a situation that I will be dealing with. The moment when the issue was considered separately but, in the end, through compassion, and it was allowed to form into oneself, was a touching experience that will help me in my own professional growth.
>
> It is also interesting, how easily one evades uncomfortable emotions or thoughts, although considering them openly and calmly is much more pleasant and more profitable also for the future.

Actually, this was a good day to complete the exercise, since I felt that today I hadn't succeeded in doing any of the tasks that I tried. The exercise created a sense of mercy on one's thinking.

In all, most students found the embracing of critical perspectives and working with unpleasant emotions during the experiential exercise to be pleasant and supportive of a gentler approach to themselves. The student writings indicated the students felt a renewed sense of acceptance and softness toward themselves. This is an unexpected finding that does not agree with the prevailing research evidence on the critical and painful nature of the reflection process. This paradox of gentleness and criticality is what we focus on in the next sections in which we investigate this theoretical dynamic based on the empirical data. First, we focus on the nature of meaning perspectives, and second, on the nature of embodied experience. Lastly, based on these two, we crystallize the responses to the research questions.

Gentleness and Criticality—The Nature of Meaning Perspectives and Reflection

The exercise involved considering a personally chosen perplexing practical situation, but the prevailing feature in the data was the students' reflecting on the nature of meaning perspectives and the process of reflection. In the following sections, these considerations are elaborated on, first, from an epistemological perspective, and second, from an ontological perspective, in order to disentangle the paradoxical dynamic of gentleness and criticality in the process of reflection.

The Nature of Meaning Perspectives and Reflection—Epistemic Perspective

Through their reflections, students identified habitual ways in their thinking: they not only considered the specific case that the exercise guided them to consider, but they also reflected on the assumptions that more generally guide their thinking, feeling, and acting. Moreover, the ways in which they interpret situations were not seen as self-evidently true or final but, instead, as thoughts to be reviewed and, based on further considerations, possibly reframed. These considerations may be seen as indicative of the epistemic position of fallibilism that "admits to the uncertainty of knowledge but does not end up with the relativist conclusion that all beliefs are equally valid" (Holma & Hyytinen, 2015, p. 9). This kind of epistemic framing can be considered a functional premise for understanding reflection as an open, ongoing process, as expressed in the following excerpts.

> The exercise confirmed the thought that the surrounding operating models and thought patterns are not carved in stone, but they can be questioned and developed if they feel wrong.
>
> [I experienced the exercise as] absolutely interesting! In my view it is important to explore one's own thought patterns more specifically, and during the process to learn more about their backgrounds and their effects in the long term.
>
> The following accounts represent a meta-level recognition that one's understanding of experience or external context may be limited, while these reflections appear to be grounded on working with a concrete personal experience during the exercise.
>
> I pondered that I sometimes easily create preconceptions about other people's thoughts. Because of those preconceptions, I might interpret situations and communication involving those people differently than they intended. In fact, I may not have ever actively aimed at working with these kinds of thought patterns on my own before.
>
> Perhaps the most central issue was that this kind of in-depth dealing with issues often helps to clarify that the situation/issue is not as bad as one perceives it to be. I have a bad habit of focusing on the worst and dwelling on that feeling. When the situations that evoke difficult feelings are more often dealt with, one might notice they are not such big failures after all.

These student writing excerpts demonstrate critically reflecting, rationally, through explicit considerations, on the way their understandings of their own experiences and external contexts are not necessarily rational and certain: they are based on pre-existing habitual ways of interpreting that may not be useful for making sense of the present experience.

Based on the data, we cannot know whether these reflections were generated by the experiential exercise or whether the exercise accompanied with the writing assignment merely allowed the students to bring in view, in a study context, something they already consciously considered or that had been in the back of their minds without being consciously contemplated. Furthermore, whether these reflections altered the way the students interpret and act in reality in the future is not known. However, instances of becoming aware of and questioning assumptions that orient thinking, feeling, and acting, as indications of critical reflection (Mälkki, 2011; Mezirow, 1991, 2000), were clearly present in the data.

Namely, the students did not merely focus on a specific situation and interpreting or fixing it. Rather, they pondered more general, underlying premises and patterns in their interpretations (stimulated by considering the specific case). Significantly, the pattern is not recognized as something that merely, rationally, needs to be changed since it has been revealed as inadequate. Instead, the pattern seems to be understood as something that calls for reflection while not necessarily being rationally fixable.

The Nature of Meaning Perspectives and Reflection—Ontological Perspective

In addition to the epistemic perspective of fallibilism, most student reflections indicated certain ontological positions regarding the nature of human rationality. They did not consider their meaning perspectives in the context of the ideal of rationality or "perfect" knowledge, practices, and policies stemming from their teacher education studies. Rather, they exhibited a more general understanding of rational abilities as human at their core; in other words, thinking processes do not always operate smoothly and logically; they tend to be complex and messy. Yet, rationality was not discarded either. On the contrary, the reflection process was portrayed as a vehicle for dealing with the inherent limitations of rationality in human thinking.

> I'm sure the tool is most useful when one recognizes some jumble in the brain or is stuck in some thought. Often, these kinds of recurring chains of thought are extremely difficult to stop, and this might be of help in that.
>
> The recording and the exercise got me, first and foremost, to stop and recognize that those situations that remain on the top of the mind and the edge emotions (disgusting feelings) that relate to them, which we naturally ignore by our customary and possibly limited action and thinking, are allowable and provide a key perspective to seeing the world with new eyes.

This kind of implicit assumption of the human context bounding rational processes—as opposed to assuming rational processes to be unbounded—may be seen as functional in terms of maintaining a reflective approach to considering one's experiences on a general basis: when the human mind is assumed to be unboundedly rational, any instance indicating a lack of rationality may prompt one to question the assumption of being a normal human, thereby evoking edge emotions (Mälkki, 2011) signaling a threat to our meaning perspectives. When unbounded rationality is assumed, the possible edge emotions may, however, not be recognized and embraced since the very perception of oneself experiencing edge emotions presents a threat—by challenging the assumption of thinking as entirely rational. Therefore, the edge emotions are likely to orient our interpretations implicitly to quickly restore the comfort zone where our assumptions no longer appear to be questioned (Mälkki, 2011). Thus, we would think we are rationally explaining the situation through reflection, whereas our interpretations and explanations may function in order to avoid dealing with the questioned assumptions.

In contrast, the assumption of human context for rationality may bring gentleness into reflective processes, thus paradoxically supporting criticality and rational thinking: When humanness is assumed as both context and condition for our rational thinking processes, the mere presence of edge emotions or the recognition of inadequate assumptions may not be experienced, to the same extent, as a threat to our meaning perspectives. Rather, the assumption of humanness, in this case, may provide a framework that enables the acceptance of flaws of rationality as natural elements of our human composition. Therefore, the amount of threat that the flaws of rationality invoke to our meaning perspectives may be significantly reduced.

Furthermore, unbounded rationality as the premise that becomes questioned in personal reflection may be experienced as representing a threat to one's sense of belonging or being accepted by others. This may be illustrated by the following fictional example: "I am the only one who is failing to fulfill the expectation of being unboundedly rational." In contrast, when the inadequacies of rational thinking are encountered within a framework of assuming humanness as the basis (i.e., human-bound rationality), the assumption of shared humanness may act as a source of support. This is illustrated by the following fictional example: "The challenges that I experience in this reflection process stem from our human nature and, hence, they tend to be challenges for anyone."

In this sense, the shifting of perspectives in critical reflection between considering one specific personal experience and more general premises that may prevail across varying contexts and persons may open access to a source of support in the social dimension of a sense of belonging and being accepted. That is, generating a conceptually higher perspective from which to approach the personal experience facilitates regaining a connection to others through shared humanness, as opposed to experiencing oneself as if in a "pocket of shame" where the acknowledged inadequacy is taken as a personal failure that separates one from the community of unboundedly rationally competent significant others. The following instance reflects this perspective.

> I gained a perspective that professionality is part of my everyday self and not a separate characteristic that emerges only at work or in class. Personal growth = professional growth.

The student departs from the assumption that the professional self is separate from the personal self, and in relation to this, departs from the assumption that personal growth is unrelated to professional growth. Thus, for the student, the processes of reflection that reveal personal habits of relying on unquestioned assumptions appear to contribute to professional learning. This may be seen as creating a sense of connection not only to people in general, referring to the shared human basis, but also to the specific professional community the student aspires to be part of by entering the field. Thus, paradoxically, exploring one's personal experiences with a critical view may support not only the development of meaning perspectives but also one's sense of belonging and acceptance in one's professional community.

The Nature of Meaning Perspective and Reflection—A Combined Perspective

The considerations discussed thus far involved epistemological and ontological perspectives that bring out understanding of the dynamics of gentleness and criticality with regard to reflection. In contrast to naive realism or relativism that assume the truth to be ready-made or that all beliefs are equally valid, respectively, the epistemic assumption of fallibilism (Holma & Hyytinen, 2015) may be a necessary premise for reflection to be understood as a process that is open, ongoing, and critical. From the ontological perspective, when the process of reflection, or more generally, our rational abilities, are assumed to be unboundedly rational, the process of reflection may end up intolerably painful, demanding, and even scary: instead of viewing edge emotions as a gateway to reflection, they are experienced as a threat to be avoided. Further, we may feel threatened by any instance indicating a lack of rationality in ourselves or when the limits of rationality are shown where we expected the situation to be solved rationally. In contrast, gentleness may be seen to result, on one hand, when the extent of the threat is lessened by (critically) questioning the assumption of unbounded rationality while positioning rational abilities within the human context in connection with gaining ownership of the edge emotions that emerge when our assumptions are questioned. On the other hand, the experience of gentleness may stem from experiencing social support for the private experiences of critical reflection through the assumption of shared humanness.

Gentleness and Criticality—Reflection Anchored into Embodied Experience

In addition to the considerations on the nature of meaning structures and how to exist and work with them, based on the data, another aspect integral to further disentangling the dynamics of criticality and gentleness in the process of reflection is the embodied experience. The students seemed to critically consider taken-for-granted assumptions (of their own or of others) so as to explicate their current understandings in conjunction with, or stimulated by, the exercise where they, themselves, personally and privately, were experiencing the reflection process as an embodied practice, involving emotions. That is, the embodied experience as a phenomenological anchor to these reflections was the context for these critical considerations, rather than, for example, an experience involving emotions being something that are talked about or observed in others but not personally experienced. They seemed to reflect as if from the inside out, embodying the embodiment of their reflections.

Criticality as Departing from Taken-for-Granted Assumptions Concerning Emotions

The student accounts involved reflecting on emotions, that is, how the nature of emotions is understood and how to exist and work with them. The criticality regarding the nature of emotions was indicated by reflectively departing from a belief or assumption they used to take for granted (Table 17.1).

The instances exemplified in the excerpts in Table 17.1 concerning the nature of emotions involve students describing their thoughts or current relation to something by departing from something else. This "something

318   K. MÄLKKI ET AL.

Table 17.1   Reflections on emotions

Example from data	*Assumption departed from*
I learned how you can deal with difficult issues gently, without feeling bad and difficult	• Difficult issues cannot be dealt with gently
I experienced that I shut off certain emotions or feel ashamed of them, but it is important to take them out and recognize what in my own life generates them. What gives rise to this emotion, and what thinking and action does it evoke in me?	• Certain emotions should be suppressed • Certain emotions are shameful
[I learned] that situations that evoke difficult emotions and remain in the mind should be dealt with before they stay and form a big chunk in the head and trigger a prolonged feeling of failure...	• Uncomfortable emotions should not be embraced. They should only be considered after prolonged presence of a feeling of uncomfortableness and failure
After completing the exercise, the idea that stood out to me was that no one emotion is more or less valuable than another. Feelings should not be feared; it is good to face them openly and deal with the "more uncomfortable" feelings. In this way, it is possible to get past the bottleneck of limitations and thereby expand one's own way of thinking	• Emotions can be valued from the perspective of whether they are justified or good or bad • Emotions are scary • Uncomfortable emotions should not be embraced
I learned, that exploring and especially accepting one's own emotions and feelings helps in the development of thinking and in learning. For example, it is important that one does not judge and assess one's emotions too much	• Exploring/accepting emotions is unrelated to learning and the development of thinking • Emotions can be valued from the perspective of whether they are justified or good or bad
When I develop my professional identity, I often move on a very analytical and cognitive level. The exercise sparked ponderings on the messages and impact of embodied sensations and emotions and their implications for teaching and professional growth. Reflection need not always involve thoughtful and conscious and brain-level pondering, but also in a professional sense, reflecting on emotions and feelings is important and meaningful	• Reflection regarding professional identity is cognitive and analytical in nature • Embodied emotions and experiences do not have implications for teaching and professional growth

else" seems, in some cases, to be their habitual way of responding, something that they have previously learned to take for granted. In other cases, this "something else" seems to be what goes on "out there," what "many people" may think. We elaborated this departure through two dimensions that represent ontological and epistemic perspectives, respectively, as follows:

First, a prevailing feature in student accounts was critically departing from assumptions concerning emotions as controllable or shameful or as disturbing to one's life, actions, and thinking. This can indicate departing from the assumption that emotions can and should be entirely rationally managed (as merely an object of rationality). The premise of unbounded rationality, as argued in the previous section, would sketch a highly demanding mirror to making meaning of one's human experiences. Instead, the student accounts, through criticality, indicate a gentler approach toward emotions—they take them as accepted parts of being human, thereby suppressing or judging the emotions would mean suppressing or judging their ontological human nature.

Second, while the assumption of emotions as entirely rationally manageable is being questioned, the emotions are not considered from the opposite perspective, that they should be accepted and cherished as they are. Rather, the critical perspective also considers emotions: The students demonstrate that emotions should not be merely left to run free but need further considerations. That is, the initial interpretation of the emotion(s) is seen as something that calls for reflection, rather than being assumed to represent self-evidently a valid meaning making to one's experience. Emotions, epistemologically, are seen as not necessarily understood, based on the taken-for-granted assumptions. Thus, the embodied experienced emotions are both the object of one's thinking and the experiential basis for discerning the limitations to one's thinking. That is, the rational analysis can aim to understand emotions, but the analysis is likely to be fallible. The justification for the validity of one's interpretation stems not only from epistemological criteria defined from outside the experience, but also from phenomenological criteria regarding the extent to which aspects of internal experiences are allowed to "be seen" by one's own interpretation. Further, the limitations to one's thinking may stem from what one has previously socially learned, or what one experiences to be actively embraced by others, thus affecting what (i.e., what portion) of emotions falls within the scope of the interpretation, and, respectively, what remains outside, even potentially evoking edge emotions if aimed to make sense.

Inviting in Disintegrated Aspect of Experience

Along with disentangling the process of reflection in theoretical fashion through student reflections, the experiential or embodied basis must be noted. That is, the student accounts indicated that they experienced emotions related to the re-working of their interpretations of the perplexing event they considered in the exercise. In other words, they were observing the ways in which emotions and interpretations were intertwined in situ, in their direct experiencing. Based on the data, we cannot know whether the experiential exercise and the writing assignment caused the insights or whether the experiential exercise and the writing assignment together offered the space to bring in view and explicate in an academic context something that was already a tacit or explicit understanding for the student.

Therefore, the RF accompanied with the writing assignment may have provided the students with an alternative social context for framing their experiences that supported appreciating and tapping into their private and personal experiencing. Yet, the writing assignment did not ask participants to specifically report anything concerning, for example, the case they chose or the inadequate assumptions they may have identified. Rather, the questions were more general, thus allowing the students themselves to choose the level and amount of information they wished to write concerning the exercise. Furthermore, the students carried out the exercise as a home assignment, and they were encouraged to choose an environment that best suited them. Thus, the RF seemed to support the students in tuning into the experiential, human aspects of their interpreting and experience within an academic study context and its theoretical frames, while the ownership of the process of reflection was preserved for the students themselves.

In this sense, whether the reflections were caused by the exercise or whether the exercise merely invited in aspects to be experienced that they had not previously considered within the academic context does not appear crucial to know regarding the focus of this study. Instead, it was essential that the exercise supported integrating professional studies with the human aspects of experience. That is, in many student reflections, they seemed to move rather seamlessly between the private and the professional, in other words, between private experiencing, identifying their personal habitual ways of interpreting based on unquestioned assumptions, and general considerations on humans or emotions, for example, and in general what it means to be professional.

> It helped me to understand that everyone encounters difficult issues in their profession and professional growth. Dealing with those emotions gently helps to accept one's own professionality.
> In this way one can develop better professionally all the time. The exercise teaches us to see all situations as experiences and situations where one may learn about oneself.

The central mechanism by which the RF fosters reflection seems to be supporting the integration of aspects of experience that have previously remained separate. The starting point in the exercise was the student's freely chosen event that had remained perplexing. From a theoretical viewpoint, the fact that this situation has remained perplexing indicates aspects of the experience remaining disintegrated, without being integrated into their meaning perspectives and (thereby) comfort zone. According to Mezirow (2000, p. 3), we have an urgent human need "to understand the meaning of our experience, to integrate it with what we know to avoid the threat of chaos." The perplexity of the "perplexing situation" can be seen to stem from edge emotions that signal the threat of chaos (Mälkki, 2011), that is, of our meaning perspectives appearing insufficient to make sense of the experience or to form the continuity between past, present, and future (Dewey, 1938) that is innately humanly needed. The perplexity of the past situation may bring an implicit worry of the future since we experience our meaning-making processes as inadequate, as fictionally exemplified: "If we cannot make sense of something that happens presently or happened in the past, how can we trust that we can manage the future of uncertain events?" Thus, one dimension of the renewed sense of gentleness toward oneself in connection with using the RF may be about this implicit worry being released, substituted with an implicit sense of confidence in one's ability to come to terms with future uncertain events, as exemplified by the following fictional quote: "Since I was able to learn in order to deal with something that didn't readily fit with my existing understandings, I may be able to deal also with future experiences that do not fall within the scope of my expectations and existing understandings."

Reviewing Parameters of Collective Comfort Zone as Support for Integrating Experience

While the process of reflection is individual by nature, the issue of integrating what used to be disintegrated brings in view the social roots of meaning perspectives brought forth by Mezirow (1991). That is, meaning perspectives can be viewed as individual compilations of shared resources of beliefs. Meaning perspectives are adopted through socialization, interaction, education, language, and so on (Mezirow, 1991). Thus, when working on our "private" meaning perspectives, we are, in fact, simultaneously working with the social roots of those assumptions, beliefs, and values that have come to comprise our worldview and sense of self. An ultimate example of this is what Brookfield (1994) called the experience of cultural suicide whereby reflection may, in extreme cases, result in disconnecting us from the communities that used to sustain us. Consequently, the disintegration can be seen to have a social origin: The social context in which we have learned to interpret our experiences in certain ways may not have provided us with concepts or validation to allow certain experiences to be more fully integrated. Thus, what one brings about in private reflection may be seen as a step away from the social givens one has adopted. Moreover, the collective comfort zone (Mälkki, 2019) in any given social context can be seen as an anchor keeping both the collective and personal meaning perspectives intact, similar to any tradition that both feeds forward and stabilizes.

From this viewpoint, what is portrayed in the personal reflection data is not unrelated to the collective comfort zones of certain contexts, such as teacher education. The RF may have provided the students with an alternative discursive space in which they were not, in fact, reflecting alone, as if personally having to pioneer new paths of meaning into the subjectively experienced collective comfort zones that have governed their previous meaning making regarding these specific topics. Namely, the RF can provide social support that holds space for users to safely learn to perceive and navigate social givens from both their personal meaning perspectives and those that "other people" may uphold.

In this way, the alternative social context provided by the RF may have provided the students with alternative parameters of collective comfort zones to be subjectively experienced as the definers of the social space where they expect to feel accepted with their "meaning perspectives under construction."

The exercise was very useful and gave concrete methods to deepen one's own reflection. I, myself, am, so to speak, a 'heavy reflector' and analyze my own actions. From this exercise I gained more tools and words and explanations for those feelings that I earlier felt evoked by reflection. Now I understand those uncomfortable emotions that reflection has sometimes evoked in me. I understand them better and also why some of my earlier reflections may not have been successful. The exercise gave me confidence to go to the uncomfortable zone and to deepen reflection, it actually requires that I have the courage to face edge emotions (at least in the right mind-state) and that uncomfortableness and perplexing sense indicate that an update for one's thought patterns is available. An exercise that sparks hope and inspires.

Essentially, when this alternative context was experienced by the students as an alternative that resonates with, or supports tapping into, their authentic experiencing, it allowed them to become aware of certain previous (subjectively experienced) parameters of collective comfort zones that they had taken for granted.

DISCUSSION

Our purpose in this chapter was to give substance to the concept of transformative-oriented reflection through theoretically oriented empirical analyses based on a guided reflection process. The RF method for guided reflection was designed to address problems highlighted in previous research (e.g., Atkinson, 2012; Collin et al., 2013; Korthagen, 2014) regarding teacher reflection. Based on the findings, the RF offered a new approach to facilitating reflection that depends on the following: (a) allowing space for the innate human need for reflection to come into play in the academic setting; (b) offering the guidance and support necessary to support the challenging process of reflection while the learners themselves sustain ownership of the process, and; (c) offering concepts to assist with understanding and working with the unpleasant emotions one may already experience, personally and professionally. Although both the exercise and the theory of edge emotions were, for most participating students, entirely new, already during the first exercise session they gained ownership of the process of dealing with edge emotions and found a renewed sense of gentleness to support critical reflection and professional development. These empirical findings represented a theoretical anomaly that called for theoretical developments to broaden perspectives in order to understand how this was possible through reflection that can be challenging and even painful, as shown in previous research (e.g., Berger, 2004; Brookfield, 1994; Mälkki, 2011).

Next, we summarize the theoretical developments on edge emotions that emerged from the findings that enabled the development of a conceptual structure to transformative-oriented reflection within the frame of the transformative teaching stance. Also discussed are the mechanisms through which transformative-oriented reflection can contribute to the well-being of teachers in complex work contexts (Fig. 17.4).

The theory of edge emotions was expanded based on the findings. First, the edge emotions can be defined as biological emotions that arise when our meaning perspectives are questioned (Mälkki, 2011) that indicate the need to integrate disintegrated experience. This is equivalent to the innate human need to understand our experiences, mentioned by Mezirow (2000). This need involves a pre-existing source of motivation for reflection.

Second, the challenges of working with edge emotions can be individual or societal. Working with edge emotions is individually challenging since it aims to intervene with the coherence-producing process of continuity and the shared assumptions that offer us our sense of social acceptance (Mälkki, 2011). Based on this study, we suggest further that

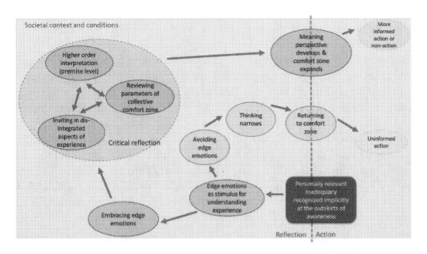

Fig. 17.4 Edge emotions theory expanded based on findings

societal and social dimensions may either increase or decrease this load factor of working with edge emotions: Subjectively experienced societal parameters of collective comfort zones tend to inhibit us from personally inviting in, to our embodied experiencing, aspects of experiences that are unaligned with what is perceived as normal and acceptable.

Third, the ways in which working with edge emotions may generate critical reflection and, thereby, broader perspectives and interpretations, are interrelated with inviting in disintegrated aspects of experience and reviewing parameters of the collective comfort zone. That is, higher order interpretation may emerge when the tensions between these three aspects are lessened. This may be induced, on one hand, by providing alternative societal parameters for the collective comfort zone that broaden the social space within which the individual may integrate their experiences. On the other hand, the tensions between the aspects may be lessened by opening up to the embodied experience of edge emotions that offers a gateway to experiencing, and thereby inviting in, the disintegrated experience.

Learning to work with edge emotions may be supported by fallibilism as an epistemological stance and an ontological understanding of human-bounded rationality and shared humanness. At the same time, learning to work with edge emotions may support adopting the epistemological stance of fallibilism and the ontological understanding of human-bound rationality and shared humanness.

The prevailing teacher reflection model anchoring on the notion of reflective practice focuses mainly on reflecting on didactic or pedagogic practices, while ignoring the perspective of reflecting on meaning structures. Based on the findings, we redefine transformative-oriented reflection as a specific form of meaning making involving working with and gaining ownership of edge emotions (Fig. 17.5). The notion of transformative-oriented reflection theoretically integrates Dewey's (1938) principles of continuity and interaction and the further developed theory of edge emotions, while explicating the context for these involving embodied experience and societal context, as well as dealing with uncertainty and integrating disintegrated aspects of experience.

Transformative-oriented reflection fosters the ability to deal with uncertainty in oneself and in one's surroundings and the ability to remain open and sensitive to contextual and societal challenges present in a teacher's work by working with edge emotions. This may, in turn, foster well-being as part of the transformative teaching stance (Mäkinen,

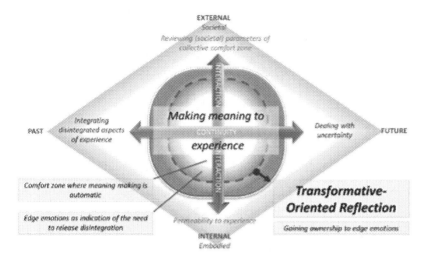

Fig. 17.5 Transformative-oriented reflection

2013), since it releases disintegration by integrating aspects of experience, fosters the critical review of collective givens, and generates more informed interpretations, thereby also supporting reflection on personal values. Furthermore, through the underlying assumptions of fallibilism and shared humanness, indicated by the notion of working with edge emotions, transformative-oriented reflection fosters the ability to connect to others as a source of intellectual and emotional support in the collective effort to transform the school. That is, transformative-oriented reflection may not only enable one to tolerate and deal with uncertainty but also to draw on it in order to bring about transformation both in the social context and in one's meaning structures. This further elucidates on the elements integral to developing schools as professional learning communities (e.g., DuFour, 2007).

Based on redefining the notion of transformative-oriented reflection, we introduce a framework for the transformative teaching stance (Fig. 17.6).

The transformative teaching stance involves considering teachers' work in a societal context. We hypothesize that the development of the transformative teaching stance may be supported by transformative-oriented

17 REVITALIZING REFLECTION IN TEACHER EDUCATION: A DIGITAL ...

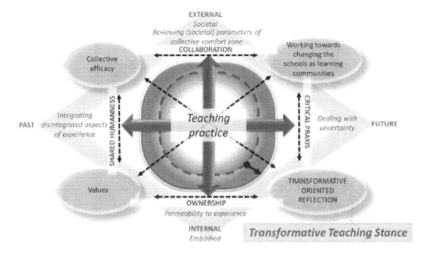

Fig. 17.6 Transformative teaching stance revisited

reflection that integrates both societal and embodied aspects, to complement practice-oriented reflection. This kind of view on reflection offers a new approach to supporting preservice teacher reflection that draws on the students' everyday experiences and tacit understandings of the process of reflection, thereby facilitating a sense of ownership of reflection also in professional contexts.

Further research is needed to examine the development process of the transformative teaching stance (Mäkinen, 2013) and how to facilitate this long-term process in teacher education programs. Also schools as professional learning communities (DuFour, 2007) need to be considered as sources of societal parameters of collective comfort zones. Furthermore, longitudinal research is needed on the use of the RF as support for reflection practices and the ways in which individual reflection processes and dialogical processes can be fruitfully combined. An interesting venue for further research is to explore the possibilities of RF to support reflection in diverse, specifically targeted disciplinary teaching contexts.

References

Akbari, R., Behzadpoor, F., Dadvand, B., & Modares, T. (2010). Development of English language teaching reflection inventory. *Science Direct, 38*(2), 211–227. https://doi.org/10.1016/j.system.2010.03.003

Aliakbari, M., Khany, R., & Adibpou, M. (2020). EFL teachers' reflective practice, job satisfaction, and school context variables: Exploring possible relationships. *TESOL Journal, 11*(1), 1–20.

Allas, R., Leijen, Ä., & Toom, A. (2020). Guided reflection procedure as a method to facilitate student teachers' perception of their teaching to support the construction of practical knowledge. *Teachers and Teaching, 26*(2), 166–192. https://doi.org/10.1080/13540602.2020.1758053

Ashwin, P. (2014). Knowledge, curriculum and student understanding in higher education. *Higher Education, 67*, 123–126. https://doi.org/10.1007/s10734-014-9715-3

Atkinson, B. (2012). Rethinking reflection: Teachers' critiques. *The Teacher Educator, 47*(3), 175–194.

Avalos, B. (2011). Teacher professional development in *Teaching and Teacher Education* over ten years. *Teaching and Teacher Education, 27*(1), 10–20. https://doi.org/10.1016/j.tate.2010.08.007

Bandura, A. (1997). *Self-efficacy: The exercise of control*. Freeman.

Beauchamp, C. (2015). Reflection in teacher education: Issues emerging from a review of current literature. *Reflective Practice, 16*(1), 123–141. https://doi.org/10.1080/14623943.2014.982525

Behizadeh, N., Thomas, C., & Cross, S. (2019). Reframing for social justice: The influence of critical friendship groups on preservice teachers' reflective practice. *Journal of Teacher Education, 70*(3), 280–296. https://doi.org/10.1177/0022487117737306

Berger, J. (2004). Dancing on the threshold of meaning: Recognizing and understanding the growing edge. *Journal of Transformative Education, 2*(4), 336–351. https://doi.org/10.1177/1541344604267697

Berghoff, B., Blackwell, S., & Wisehart, R. (2011). Using critical reflection to improve urban teacher preparation: A collaborative inquiry of three teacher educators. *Perspectives on Urban Education, 8*(2), 19–28.

Biesta, G. (2013). Interrupting the politics of learning. *Power and Education, 5*(1), 4–15. https://doi.org/10.2304/power.2013.5.1.4

Brookfield, S. D. (2000). Transformative learning as ideology critique. In J. Mezirow & Associates (Eds.), *Learning as transformation: Critical perspectives on a theory in progress* (pp. 125–148). Jossey-Bass.

Brookfield, S. D. (1994). Tales from the dark side: A phenomenography of adult critical reflection. *International Journal of Lifelong Education, 13*(3), 203–216. https://doi.org/10.1080/0260137940130303

17 REVITALIZING REFLECTION IN TEACHER EDUCATION: A DIGITAL ... 329

Cochran-Smith, M., Feiman-Nemsar, S., & McIntyre, D. J. (2008). *Handbook of research on teacher education: Enduring questions in changing contexts* (3rd ed.). Routledge, Taylor & Francis Group and the Association of Teacher Education.

Collin, S., Karsenti, T., & Komis, V. (2013). Reflective practice in initial teacher training: Critiques and perspectives. *Reflective Practice: International and Multidisciplinary Perspectives, 14*(1), 104–117.

Damasio, A. R. (1999). *The feeling of what happens: The body and emotion in the making of consciousness.* Hart Court Brace.

Darling-Hammond, L. (2006). Constructing 21st-century teacher education. *Journal of Teacher Education, 57*(2), 1–15.

Dewey, J. (1933). *How we think: A restatement of the relation of reflective thinking to the education process.* D.C. Heath and company.

Dewey, J. (1938). *Experience and education.* Simon and Schuster.

DuFour, R. (2007). Professional learning communities: A bandwagon, an idea worth considering, or our best hope for high levels of learning? *Middle School Journal, 39*(1), 408.

Eschenbacher, S., & Fleming, T. (2020). Transformative dimensions of lifelong learning: Mezirow, Rorty and COVID-19. *International Review of Education, 66*(5–6, 1–16). https://doi.org/10.1007/s11159-020-09859-6

Finnegan, F. (2019). "Freedom is a very fine thing": Individual and collective forms of emancipation in transformative learning. In T. Fleming, A. Kokkos, & F. Finnegan (Eds.), *European perspectives on transformation theory* (pp. 43–57). Palgrave Macmillan. http://doi-org-443.webvpn.fjmu.edu.cn/10.1007/978-3-030-19159-7_4.R

Freire, P. (1972). *Pedagogy of the oppressed.* The Continuum International Publishing Group.

Hoggan, C., Mälkki, K., & Finnegan, F. (2017). Developing the theory of perspective transformation: Continuity, intersubjectivity, and emancipatory praxis. *Adult Education Quarterly, 67*(1), 48–64. https://doi.org/10.1177/0741713616674076

Holma, K., & Hyytinen, H. (2015). The philosophy of personal epistemology. *Theory and Research in Education, 13*(3), 334–350. https://doi.org/10.1177/1477878515606608

Hsieh, H.-F., & Shannon, S. E. (2005). Three approaches to qualitative content analysis. *Qualitative Health Research, 15*(9), 1277–1288.

Illeris, K. (2014). *Transformative learning and identity.* Routledge.

Jackson, A. Y., & Mazzei, L. A. (2012). *Thinking with theory in qualitative research: Viewing data across multiple perspectives.* Routledge.

Jordi, R. (2011). Reframing the concept of reflection: Consciousness, experiential learning, and reflective learning practices. *Adult Education Quarterly, 61*(2), 181–197. https://doi.org/10.1177/0741713610380439

330 K. MÄLKKI ET AL.

Korthagen, F. A. J. (2014). Promoting core reflection in teacher education: Deepening professional growth. In L. Orland-Barak & C. J. Craig (Eds.), *International teacher education: Promising pedagogies* (Part A; pp. 73–89). Emerald.

Kramer, M. (2018). Promoting teachers' agency: Reflective practice as transformative disposition. *Reflective Practice, 19*(2), 211–224. https://doi.org/10.1080/14623943.2018.1437405

Leigh, J., & Bailey, R. (2013). Reflection, reflective practice and embodied reflective practice, body. *Movement and Dance in Psychotherapy, 8*(3), 160–171. https://doi.org/10.1080/17432979.2013.797498

Loughran, J. (2010). Reflection through collaborative action research and inquiry. In N. Lyons (Ed.), *Handbook of reflection and reflective inquiry: Mapping a way of knowing for professional reflective inquiry* (pp. 399–413). Springer.

Mäkinen, M. (2013). Becoming engaged in inclusive practices: Narrative reflections as descriptors of teachers' work engagement in inclusive schools. *Teaching and Teacher Education, 35*, 51–61. https://doi.org/10.1016/j.tate.2013.05.005

Mälkki, K. (2011). *Theorizing the nature of reflection* (Doctoral dissertation, Institute of Behavioural Sciences, University of Helsinki). Studies in Educational Sciences 238. http://urn.fi/URN:ISBN:978-952-10-6982-6

Mälkki, K. (2019). Coming to grips with edge-emotions. The gateway to critical reflection and transformative learning. In T. Fleming, A. Kokkos, & F. Finnegan (Eds.), *European perspectives on transformative learning* (pp. 59–73). Palgrave Macmillan. https://doi.org/10.1007/978-3-030-19159-7_5

Mälkki, K. (2010). Building on Mezirow's theory of transformative learning: Theorizing the challenges to reflection. *Journal of Transformative Education, 8*(1), 42–62. https://doi.org/10.1177/1541344611403315

McConn, M. L., & Geetter, D. (2020). Liminal states of disorienting dilemmas: Two case studies of English teacher candidates. *Journal of Transformative Education, 18*(3), 231–250. https://doi.org/10.1177/1541344620909444

Mezirow, J. (2000). Learning to think like an adult. Core concepts of transformation theory. In J. Mezirow & Associates (Eds.), *Learning as transformation. Critical perspectives on a theory in progress* (pp. 3–33). Jossey-Bass.

Mezirow, J. (1991). *Transformative dimensions of adult learning*. Jossey-Bass.

Parsons, M., & Stephenson, M. (2005). Developing reflective practice in student teachers: Collaboration and critical partnerships. *Teachers and Teaching, 11*(1), 95–116. https://doi.org/10.1080/1354060042000337110

Pellegrino, A. M., & Gerber, B. L. (2012). Teacher reflection through video-recording analysis. *Georgia Educational Researcher, 9*(1), 1–20. https://doi.org/10.20429/ger.2012.090101

Rainio, A., Mälkki, K., Mäkinen, M. & Talvio, M. (in press). The stranger in us: Embracing heterogeneity and ambivalent ways of being in classrooms. In M. Talvio & K. Lonka (Eds.), *International approaches to promoting social and emotional learning in schools: A framework for developing teaching strategy.* Routledge.

Schön, D. A. (1983). *The reflective practitioner: How professionals think in action.* Basic Books Inc.

Shulman, L. S. (2005). Pedagogies of uncertainty. *Liberal Education, 91*(2), 18–25.

Taylor, E. W., & Cranton, P. (2013). A theory in progress? Issues in transformative learning theory. *European Journal of Research on the Education and Learning of Adults, 4*(1), 33–47. https://doi.org/10.3384/rela.2000-7426. rela5000

Tripp, T. (2010). *The influence of video analysis on teaching* (Doctoral dissertation, David O. McKay School of Education)]. Theses and Dissertations. 2562. https://scholarsarchive.byu.edu/etd/2562

Williams, A. T. (2020). Growing student teachers' reflective practice: Explorations of an approach to video-stimulated reflection. *Reflective Practice, 21*(5), 699–711. https://doi.org/10.1080/14623943.2020.1798917

Yorks, L., & Kasl, E. (2002). Toward a theory and practice for whole-person learning: Reconceptualizing experience and the role of affect. *Adult Education Quarterly, 25*(3), 176–192. https://doi.org/10.1177/07417136020523002

Zeicher, K., Payne, K., & Brayko, K. (2015). Democratizing Teacher Education. *Journal of Teacher Education, 66*(2), 122–135. https://doi.org/10.1177/0022487114560908

CHAPTER 18

Women in the Workplace: Negotiating Influence as a Leader

Beth Fisher-Yoshida

INTRODUCTION

Success in an organizational context is partly achieved by being able to read the room and know the rules of engagement for that context. Some people may call it being politically savvy. You can also think of it as marketing or presentation of self (Goffman, 1959) in how you appear to others. It is important to be able to communicate in ways that are considered to be contributing value to the organization and demonstrating that you are both an asset and someone who can be depended on to get the job done.

However, as important as it is for you to be able to read the room, it is equally critical to understand that people in the room are reading

---

B. Fisher-Yoshida (✉)
Columbia University, New York, NY, USA
e-mail: bf2017@columbia.edu

Cliffside Park, NJ, USA

© The Author(s), under exclusive license to Springer Nature Switzerland AG 2022
A. Nicolaides et al. (eds.), *The Palgrave Handbook of Learning for Transformation*, https://doi.org/10.1007/978-3-030-84694-7_18

333

you as well. Gender, race, ethnicity, and other factors play a role in influencing how people are perceived, and in many cases these traits cause women and minorities to need to prove their competence more often than other groups in an organizational context (McKinsey, 2019). Some of these situational assessments are not as obvious as others and more subtle means of discrimination can be referred to as microaggressions that accumulate over time influencing how candidates are determined to be ready for advancement (Sue et al., 2019). *Microaggressions* can be thought of as daily indignities that are intentional or unintentional, and that can have negative effects on a person's self-esteem and health.

The form of how these subtle microaggressions may play out in the workplace can be categorized as gender microassaults, gender microinsults, or gender microinvalidations (Capodilupo et al., 2010). *Gender microassaults* can be thought of as the old-fashioned way you picture sexism, by the making of overt rude comments and name-calling. *Gender microinsults* are when women are consistently overlooked, as when women and men attend and participate in meetings, but only the men's contributions are positively acknowledged. *Gender microinvalidations* are when male colleagues may bond on shared activities and do not invite women to attend assuming they will not be interested (Capodilupo et al., 2010). These can play a role in how women are perceived as leaders and for being eligible candidates considered for advancement.

ORGANIZATIONAL CONTEXT

As you move up the ladder in an organization, the scope of the work and responsibilities becomes broader, more strategic, and less operational. It can be a challenge to let go of what you did on the frontlines to take a more strategic view of the larger organization. When you perform well in a certain context and then are promoted, you need to be cognizant of the success measures in this new role and context. In many cases, your strengths that worked in your favor and enabled you to be noticed and promoted in the first place may not be as valued in this new role. You need to discover the measures of success in this new context and role (Fisher-Yoshida, 2022).

In any event, once you discover what is needed to perform well, you will still need to communicate about the performance in order to demonstrate your worth, connect with others, and contribute to the well-being of the organization. It is not enough to only do good work because it may not be noticed or understood in the way that you want it to be, and that could cause judgment against you about how much effort you exerted. This very act of not communicating about the work accomplished can sometimes work against women because women have been known to be better at advocating for others rather than themselves (Amanatullah & Tinsley, 2013). Women may assume the work completed to be part of the job and that drawing attention to it would be bragging. In negotiation terminology, this translates into women being more comfortable creating value for others, rather than claiming value for themselves when conditions are favoring more stereotypical male behaviors in a negotiation context (Kray et al., 2004). In addition, organizations tend to recognize leadership behaviors typically associated with a stereotypical male version of a leader and overlook women in the process of identifying talent for advancement (Ely et al., 2011).

Taking all of this into account, you can see that it can be challenging for women to succeed according to rules that were made by men, and the expected behaviors that are more male-oriented. In some cases there is backlash for women adhering to these male-oriented behaviors, which is acting outside the norm (Amanatullah & Tinsley, 2013), creating the need for conditions that are favorable to women's ways of succeeding. Adler and Osland (2016) found that it is more frequent for women than men to create their own entrepreneurial businesses or run a family business partly due to these larger organizational challenges. In addition, women more often than men, lead social enterprises. A message here is that women are being creative in expanding the pie, so to speak, so that in addition to competing with men on the playing fields men established, they are also branching out to other fields where they can find opportunities for success, utilizing their innate and socially constructed behaviors.

Working with Narrative

The role of narrative and the stories you tell about yourself have an influence on your self-esteem and how you "show up" to others. Czarniawska (2004) differentiates narrative as a sequence of chronological events, while a story is an emplotted narrative. A plot develops in a narrative when there is a change in state or equilibrium and there is an explanation offered to make sense of the series of chronological events. These stories and plots are culturally influenced because the sense making that takes place needs to be contextually situated to promote a shared understanding of the narrative. A narrative for a woman in an organization can be a chronological ordering of events from recruitment to current ranking, while the process of advancement, with its benefits and challenges, is the story she carries.

The stories you have about selfdevelop over the years from a variety of life experiences and social contexts. Stories with moral implications are communicated to you by your families, communities, education, media, and more. This tells you the way you should be in the world, what you should initiate, what you should follow, and what you should expect. You are usually not aware of the stories by which you live until you are confronted with a competing narrative, as in going to a different culture and seeing the norms are different. This causes you to become aware of the assumptions you hold (Brookfield, 2011) about the way food should be served in a restaurant, how you are supposed to greet people at their homes, and what leadership looks like in an organizational context. It is in the space of recognizing your tacitly held assumptions that transformative learning can take place (Taylor, 2009).

When you operate on autopilot you engage in ways that are familiar and habitual and are reflections of your deeply embedded belief systems and the stories of how you see the world. This can have an effect on how you see gender in the workplace, and if you are not aware of the assumptions you make then implicit biases can be operating. "One impact may be that we may perceive and rate a female leader's performance lower than it actually is due to our unquestioned bias" (Hansen, 2020). This is partly due to the attributions you may unconsciously be assigning to women in the workplace based on male-dominant organizations developing "formal structure and informal norms around gendered notions of work and behavior" (Kolb & Porter, 2015, p. xxvi).

You learn about yourself and develop a keener sense of self-awareness by paying more attention to the stories you tell and how you tell them. This is critical as women advance into leadership roles as their self-talk and narrative about what it means to be a good leader and whether they qualify, can influence how they behave and are perceived as leaders. In some cases, women may sabotage themselves from succeeding based on the stories they tell themselves, which come from the social contexts in which they grew up and currently live and work.

Likewise, it is important in learning about others to hear about their life experiences through the stories they tell about who they are and how they interact with others. As you listen to their stories, there are many processes you can use to deconstruct the parts that make the whole: How they tell the story; how you raise questions in response to listening; and then in this relational process, how the original narratives are rendered (Schaafsma & Vinz, 2011). It is in these renderings that change takes place, and this can be in the form of a coaching relationship.

Role of Communication and Stories

Narratives are known for capturing the lived and told experiences, and perhaps identifying gaps between the two sets of stories that may not be congruent (Cresswell & Poth, 2018). These stories are also better understood when the context is known, as the meaning making process is more enhanced considering these situational boundaries. This is especially relevant when you need to take into consideration the sociocultural context of where these stories originate and take place (Merriam & Tisdell, 2016). This is where the plot development shifts a chronological narrative or retelling of events into a story with a plot that reflects both personal and social origins.

When you use stories as part of work in qualitative research or with clients, a good starting place is asking a general question that is open and broad to allow the space for the client to tell the story the way she wants it to be told. From there you can mutually explore the many factors that created the story, and work toward identifying the aspects of the story that work well and are supportive and constructive, and the parts that get in the way of the client living a meaningful and rewarding life. Asking clarifying questions and going beyond the told story provides an opportunity for the client to expand in areas she may have just brushed the surface of in telling. An example of this could be, "Earlier in the story you were mentioning the meeting you had with Person A. Could you describe that in more detail, for example, how did you prepare for this meeting, what were you expecting, what did you do in response to his reaction?"

Another model that provides for a deeper and more expansive dive into stories is the LUUUUTT model of the Coordinated Management of Meaning (CMM) (Pearce, 2007). The acronym stands for stories lived, untold stories, unheard stories, unknown stories, untellable stories, stories told, and the process of storytelling (Pearce, 2007). This model expands the typical framing of stories lived and told that is characteristic of narrative inquiry.

CMM is a communication theory and practice that takes a communication perspective and follows the premise that you make the social worlds within which you live through your communication. A question often asked from a CMM perspective is, "What are we making?" This is very meaningful because you see that communication is not just a means to an end, but rather a meaning making process in itself. The quality of how you talk creates the quality of your social worlds (Penman & Jensen, 2019). Taking a communication perspective means you look at communication and not through it. In looking at communication you are identifying the patterns, where they lead you, and what they are creating.

Therefore, it is very empowering when you realize that the stories you tell yourself and about yourself create what happens next. It means that you have a stronger sense of agency than what you may have originally realized, because if you create your narratives, then, likewise, you have the ability to change those narratives to better serve you.

Of course, there are many social influences that shape the narratives you carry, and these narratives are longstanding and deeply embedded. It is not just a matter of declaring that you want to tell a different story. You need to construct the story and create a new habit of thinking, feeling, and communicating that is more reflective of the belief system you want to embrace. As this new learning begins to take hold, you need to integrate these new habits into your story of self to construct a coherent narrative (Siegel, 2007). You need newer versions of your story to create change, and this is done by creating renewed iterations of your narrative through an intentional and conscious process (Hansen, 2020).

COACHING: ADVANCING IN AN ORGANIZATION

This case study is an illustration of a woman coaching client who was being considered for a promotion. For a working definition of coaching, you can say that "Executive coaching is an experiential, individualized, leadership development process that builds a leader's capability to achieve short and long-term organizational goals" (Ennis in Stern, 2004, p. 154). In my experience as an executive coach, organizations typically engage executive coaches for a variety of reasons, with one of the most popular being to advance those identified as high-potential contributors. Sometimes the high potentials need to have an intensive customized program to advance them more quickly in certain aspects because of an imminent promotion or transfer. In other cases, it could be because they need to be more well-rounded, and a customized coaching engagement provides more directed learning. This is not unique to women, rather, it is available to anyone considered a high potential that the organization deems is worth investing in because they will continue to add value.

Case Study: Marlee

There were many strengths this particular coaching client, Marlee, brought to the organization, and she had several advocates. However, there were also reservations that while she was good at what she did, there were feelings of uncertainty that she would be able to rise to the occasion to a role with broader responsibilities. She worked in finance and the promotion would give her a broader portfolio, larger budget, and an increase in team members reporting to her.

Naturally, being in finance you need to have good detail orientation and be able to back up your work with lots of facts, evidence, and numbers to support your recommendations. However, all of this backup information does not need to be included in how you communicate your findings. It can be there in an appendix, for example, to call upon should more proof be needed as support. Being able to translate these findings into a strategic communication that can be understood by those who are not finance or detail oriented, are not concerned with all the evidence, and are more concerned with the narrative of how this fits into the bigger strategic plan, is critical. It is not the same skill or orientation, and often when you are stronger in one of those skills you need to intentionally develop other ones.

The coaching engagement started with a series of exercises to give Marlee more insights into her own style, character, strengths, and where she could develop further. It came as no surprise that she was strong in detail orientation, very conscientious, and not assertive. She was also not strong in her interpersonal skills, and it was making sense to Marlee that she was very good at her job in finance because of her strengths, but that her career would be stymied if she did not develop other ways to be savvy and demonstrate her value contributions to those who needed to recognize them in a way they would be able to see them.

While these insights provided Marlee with the information she needed to make the difference in her presentation of self and information, her

340 B. FISHER-YOSHIDA

deeply ingrained behaviors and work ethic prevented her from being able to embrace them. For Marlee, her belief was that in order to demonstrate her worth she needed to share all of the evidence that led her to the final numbers and overall budget. It was very challenging for her to present the budget narrative without getting in the weeds, and it was frustrating to whom she was presenting because they did not think in this level of detail and wanted the big picture summary. The messaging was clear that unless she was able to connect with upper management on this level she would be passed over this round for a promotion.

Marlee's Narrative

The narrative Marlee had looping in her head was that she needed to be thorough, and that sharing anything less was being shallow and not demonstrating her competence. She was very motivated to want to make a difference and also challenged because it turned all of her preconceived and habitual thinking upside down (Mezirow, 2000). She needed to use deductive communication rather than inductive communication, which was her comfort zone. Marlee wanted to take everyone on her journey with her as to how she arrived at the numbers and budget narrative, but they wanted to start at the destination with some evidence of how she got there. They did not have the patience for the whole journey and in their minds it was not adding value for them to know.

This also meant Marlee had to change the narrative in her head about who she is as a professional and how she demonstrates competence and adding value. She needed to separate the worth she brought in how she did the work from how she communicated about it. This may seem like an easy or simple shift to make, but if you had built the past 20+ years of your career on performing in a certain manner, and your self-esteem as a professional was built on this narrative, it is very difficult to change those patterns. Her identity was attached to this version of her narrative. All of her internal predictions about what should be and the ways she should perform were being challenged with these new demands and information (Feldman Barrett, 2017). It felt as though the very foundation her career was built on was being shattered, and it increased her feelings of confusion and of not being grounded.

Of course, that was not the case. She was being recognized for her past accomplishments by even being considered for a promotion; she just needed to modify some of the ways she interacted and communicated with others, in order to move to the next level of her career. The challenge here, bigger than learning new skills, was the self-talk that Marlee had about who she was as a professional. She prided herself on her great work ethic, that involved being thorough, and now she was being asked to communicate about her work in ways that she felt did not reflect the amount of effort she put into her work. This confusion was generating emotional reactions, and she had some doubts of her ability (Feldman Barrett, 2017).

For Marlee, this was a shift in her worldview about what it means to be professional. Shifting to new ways of communication required her to change the narrative in her mind about what being professional and being a leader meant. She was grappling with being authentic and being effective, and now the ways she had previously defined and acted on those terms were not congruent (Sparrowe, 2005). This caused dissonance in Marlee. "Self-awareness, self-regulation, and consistency thus are central to contemporary perspectives on authentic leadership" (p. 423), and Marlee was feeling a disconnect among those three characteristics.

Cognitively, she understood very well what was expected of her to succeed, but emotionally she was not comfortable with this new way of being in the workplace. It went against what she had built her career on up to this point, or so she believed. Dissonance may not be an enjoyable state of being, but it does provide a foundation for receptivity to transformative learning (Mezirow, 2009).

MARLEE'S TRANSFORMATIVE LEARNING

Through the process of coaching and critically reflecting on her identity, her relationships, and the organizational context within which she was working, Marlee experienced transformative learning as defined by the characteristics of *psycho-developmental* framing (Taylor, 2017). Specifically, Marlee had a new way of understanding and making meaning of her value contributions to the workplace from her own sense of identity, and not just the behavioral modifications she made in how she demonstrated her competence. This was a significant shift for her because all the ways in which she had been rewarded in her career were linked to her expertise in detail orientation and accuracy in finance. Now she was being asked to continue to have those qualities, but to not share them the way she had before, and instead to tailor her messages in ways that did not explicitly showcase these strengths and the work she did behind the scenes. This

B. FISHER-YOSHIDA

was an identity crisis for Marlee and disorienting her to the point of her feeling incapable of knowing how to move forward (Mezirow, 2000). She felt trapped in her old narrative paradigm.

Types of Transformation

Moons (2016) identified four categories necessary for transformation to occur in a short amount of time through a coaching engagement that includes: "understanding of a 'shift in the room'; setting the scene; working in the reflective space; the happening of the 'shift in the room'" (p. 50). Moons (2016) goes on to say that the terminology "shift in the room" she later changed to "transformational shift" because the transformation was incremental and happened over time (Mezirow, 2009).

For Marlee, understanding the shift in the room happened when she realized that even though she thought she was delivering her best quality work, the needs of the people to whom she was reporting required that the information be presented in a different format. This was a level of other-awareness that shifted her perspective from her needs to the needs of others.

The second category, setting the scene, is about establishing a trusting relationship between the coach and coachee, and creating a safe space for the coaching to occur. This was not very challenging to do because Marlee was very motivated to engage in this coaching process. She has two direct bosses, one for the individual organization within the larger conglomerate, who was very supportive of Marlee advancing. The other boss was for her finance function, and he was more unsure of Marlee being able to handle the nuances beyond finance that would come with a promotion. This helped clarify for Marlee who she needed to appeal to in order for her to be able to advance to this new position.

Working in the reflective space, the third category, is about the coach being responsive to the person being coached and noticing what is happening and deciding what comes next. In Marlee's case, it was about asking different types of questions to prompt Marlee to uncover some of her implicit assumptions about performance and the people with whom she was working and deciding what needed to be done once these were surfaced. Brookfield (2011) uses a three-level typology of assumptions, paradigmatic, prescriptive and causal, that he surfaces through his critical thinking process. Asking questions to uncover the assumptions in the first place is necessary for Brookfield's process; this begins with identifying assumptions.

One very strongly embedded assumption Marlee held was that she should do more of what she was good at in order to demonstrate competence. Brookfield (2011) would classify this as a paradigmatic assumption in that Marlee's belief system led her to assume her challenges were in demonstrating competency and so every action was geared toward proving her competence. She would, therefore, provide more data, more evidence of number crunching, and more details to show the thoroughness of her work. The big "ah-ha" moment for her was in recognizing that it was not a question of her competence, because those in her workplace had confidence in her capabilities. It was in the delivery of the key points necessary to be valuable for strategic decision-making that was the issue. This was a necessary realization because it now opened the way for her to modify her behavior from a place of deeper understanding of the dynamics.

Once Marlee made this realization, the fourth category of noticing, the happening of the shift in the room, was apparent. Marlee slowed down her process so that instead of working on autopilot to continue providing more data, she was much more thoughtful about what needed to take place. This did not happen smoothly; it took time to shift to this new way of thinking. At first, Marlee was stuck in not knowing what to do next because all of her previous resources and practices were in the frame of providing data to prove competence (Pearce, 1989). The *resources* referred to here would be the abilities and approaches on which she had based her previous assumptions. The *practices* would be the ways in which she acted on those resources. The motivation for wanting to make this shift in how she communicated to demonstrate advancement in performance reflects that "a realm of moral obligation is a defining feature of communication" (Penman & Jensen, 2019, p. 36). Marlee felt the moral reasoning inherent in making these adjustments as a constructively contributing member of the organization.

COACHING PROCESS

The coaching engagement allowed for a few important developments to take place. First, it provided a structured and relational process by which Marlee was able to learn more about herself, her values, how she defined success, and to reflect on different levels of meaning she interpreted in her interactions with others. This affected how she understood the feedback she received. Instead of continuing to feel confounded by what she perceived as mixed messages, she identified the underlying needs of the people providing the feedback and how that related to her need to demonstrate competence. She was able to flex her style to present information in ways in which she could be valued without losing her sense of identity and self-respect.

A second way is that having a coach as a conversation partner, gave her the language to expand her worldview on what it means to be successful in the workplace. This was transformational for her because she realized she did not need to work as hard as she had been in the areas where she was not getting positive reinforcement. Instead, she was able to shift her energy so that she put extra effort into modifying her presentation of information that was more customized to her audience, even though it was not her preferred style (Fisher-Yoshida & Yoshida, 2016). This shift and transformation came about as a result of making explicit the underlying paradigmatic assumptions by which Marlee was operating and developing more resources and new practices for her to effectively demonstrate that shift.

The third way, which also encapsulated other ways of transformation, is that she learned practices that she could use on her own to continue her journey to becoming more adaptable in the workplace. This further shifted her identity from a fixed framing to a more agile one as she relaxed her boundaries of defining success for herself. It developed a stronger sense of agency in Marlee and revised her self-narrative to being one who is not only competent, but also who is able to demonstrate that competency.

CONCLUSION

There are many ways to be successful in organizations and identifying your unique contribution is important. Equally important is how you talk about your strengths and contributions, because it affects your behavior and how you demonstrate your value added. Women are learning more strategies for how to advocate for themselves and claim value, which is not as strong a traditional social conditioning as advocating for others and creating value has been.

As you change the narrative that describes who you are and how you add value, which is deeply connected to your identity, shifts in worldview take place. These shifts transform your identify and how you make meaning in your life and work. These transformations take courage, and it is beneficial to have a conversation partner in the role of a coach who is able to guide you in the process, provide feedback and reflection, and support you in entertaining alternative perspectives and ways of seeing the world.

REFERENCES

Adler, N. J., & Osland, J. S. (2016, August 10). Women leading globally: What we know, thought we knew, and need to know about leadership in the 21st century. In *Advances in global leadership* (pp. 15–16). https://doi.org/10.1108/S1535-120320160000009003

Amanatullah, E. T., & Tinsley, C. H. (2013). Ask and ye shall receive? How gender and status moderate negotiation success. *Negotiation and Conflict Management Research, 6*(4), 253–272.

Brookfield, S. A. (2011). *Teaching for critical thinking: Tools and techniques to help students question their assumptions.* Jossey-Bass.

Capodilupo, C. M., Nadal, K. L., Corman, L., Hamit, S., Lyons, O. B., & Weinberg, A. (2010). The manifestation of gender microaggressions. In D. W. Sue (Ed.), *Microaggressions and marginality: Manifestation, Dynamics, and Impact.* Wiley.

Cresswell, J. W., & Poth, C. N. (2018). *Qualitative inquiry and research design: Choosing among five approaches* (4th ed.). Sage.

Czarniawska, B. (2004). *Narratives in social science research.* Sage.

Ely, R. J., Insead, H. I., & Kolb, D. M. (2011). Taking gender into account: Theory and design for women's leadership development programs. *Academy of Management Learning & Education, 10*(3), 474–493.

Feldman Barrett, L. (2017). *How emotions are made: The secret life of the brain.* Houghton Mifflin Harcourt.

Fisher-Yoshida, B. (2022). In search of a shared narrative of leadership. In G. Perruci (Ed.), *The study and practice of global leadership.* ILA Building Leadership Bridges Series. Emerald Publishing.

Fisher-Yoshida, B., & Yoshida, R. (2016). Transformative learning and its relevance to coaching. In S. Grief, et al. (Eds.), *Handbook of key concepts for coaching.* Springer.

Goffman, E. (1959). *The presentation of self in everyday life.* Anchor Books.

Hansen, H. (2020). *Narrative change: How changing the story can transform society, business, and ourselves.* Columbia University Press.

Kolb, D. M., & Porter, J. L. (2015). *Negotiating at work: Turning small wins into big gains*. Jossey-Bass.

Kray, L. J., Reb, J., Galinsky, A. D., & Thompson, L. (2004). Stereotype reactance at the bargaining table: The effect of stereotype activation and power on claiming and creating value. *Personality and Social Psychology Bulletin, 30*(4), 399–411.

McKinsey & Company and Lean In. (2019). *Women in the workplace 2019*. https://wiw-report.s3.amazonaws.com/Women_in_the_Workplace_2019.pdf

Merriam, S. B., & Tisdell, E. J. (2016). *Qualitative research: A guide to design and implementation* (4th ed.). Jossey-Bass.

Mezirow, J. (2000). Learning to think like an adult: Core concepts of transformation theory. In J. Mezirow & Associates (Eds.), *Learning as transformation: Critical perspectives on a theory in progress*. Jossey-Bass.

Mezirow, J. (2009). Transformative learning theory. In J. Mezirow & E. W. Taylor (Eds.), *Transformative learning in practice: Insights from community, workplace, and higher education* (pp. 18–31). Jossey-Bass.

Moons, J. (2016, June). A shift in the room—Myth or magic? How do coaches create transformational shifts in a short period of time? *International Journal of Evidence Based Coaching and Mentoring*. Special Issue No. 10.

Pearce, W. B. (1989). *Communication and the human condition*. Southern Illinois University Press.

Pearce, W. B. (2007). *Making social worlds: A communication perspective*. Blackwell.

Penman, R., & Jensen, A. (2019). *Making better social worlds: Inspiration from the theory of the coordinated management of meaning*. CMM Institute Press.

Schaafsma, D., & Vinz, R. (2011). *Narrative inquiry: Approaches to language and literacy research*. Teachers College Press.

Siegel, D. J. (2007). *The mindful brain: Reflection and attunement in the cultivation of well-being*. Norton.

Sparrowe, R. T. (2005). Authentic leadership and the narrative self. *The Leadership Quarterly, 16*(2005), 419–439.

Stern, L. R. (2004). Executive coaching: A working definition. *Consulting Psychology Journal: Practice and Research, 56*(3), 154–162.

Sue, D. W., Alsaidi, S., Awad, M. N., Glaeser, E., & Calle, C. Z. (2019). Disarming racial microaggressions: Microintervention strategies for targets, white allies, and bystanders. *American Psychologist, 74*(1), 128–142.

Taylor, E. W. (2009). Fostering transformative learning. In J. Mezirow & E. W. Taylor (Eds.), *Transformative learning in practice: Insights from community, workplace, and higher education* (pp. 3–17). Jossey-Bass.

Taylor, E. W. (2017). Transformative learning theory. In A. Laros, T. Fuhr, & E. W. Taylor (Eds.), *Transformative learning meets Bildung: An international exchange* (pp. 17–29). Sense Publishers.

CHAPTER 19

A Deliberately Developmental Organization: A New Organizational Space for Inclusion

Chang-kyu Kwon

INTRODUCTION

Today's world is characterized as being VUCA—volatile, uncertain, complex, and ambiguous. In this new environment, it is almost impossible to conceptualize and predict reality with accuracy. Sociologist Zygmunt Bauman (2013) described such a fluid and unreliable characteristic of the present conditions of the world in which we live as "liquid modernity." As such, transformative learning, which has long been practiced as a useful method for individual growth and development, is gaining greater relevance than ever before, calling us to critically reexamine assumed ways of knowing, doing, and being, and potentially change them to better adapt to constantly evolving circumstances (Mezirow, 2003).

However, in today's highly interconnected world, there is also an increasing need for various social actors—individuals, organizations,

C. Kwon (✉)
Department of Organizational Leadership, Oakland University, Rochester, MI, USA
e-mail: ckwon@oakland.edu

© The Author(s), under exclusive license to Springer Nature Switzerland AG 2022
A. Nicolaides et al. (eds.), *The Palgrave Handbook of Learning for Transformation*, https://doi.org/10.1007/978-3-030-84694-7_19

347

communities, nations, and so on—to learn collaboratively and find innovative ways to meet the demands of the upcoming society. Racial discrimination, inequalities in education and health, unemployment, and climate change are just a few examples of the kinds of complex issues that humanity is currently faced with. As Bohm (1996) suggested over twenty years ago, what seems vital for contemporary leaders of all kinds in these challenging times is perhaps their ability to create spaces for authentic inquiry and dialog: Where all stakeholders can come together with no predetermined or fixed purpose, agenda, or interest, rather than to problem solve in a siloed manner. Only by creating such free and empty spaces for all can the possibilities of generating something new emerge (Nicolaides, 2015). Scharmer and Kaufer (2013) described this evolutionary unfolding process as "learning from the emerging future," which demands the radical opening of both one's mind (cognitive boundaries) and heart (relational boundaries).

As an academic, my ongoing inquiry has been centered around creating organizational conditions for deep relational learning (Cunliffe, 2016) and understanding how diversity is experienced in such a context (Bouten-Pinto, 2016). Aligned with the findings of Lambrechts et al. (2008), my research has shown that high quality relationships cultivated within a generative learning space hold the potential for transcending power differentials deriving from a variety of human differences (Kwon, 2019, 2020; Kwon & Nicolaides, 2017, 2019). I believe that this line of research is particularly timely and promising in thinking about new ways of leading and organizing diversity in a VUCA world. Therefore, my purpose in this chapter is to present Robert Kegan's theory and practice of Deliberately Developmental Organization (DDO) as an alternative organizational space for inclusion, where the diversity of perspective that comes from all members of the organization becomes a live source of continuous transformative learning. To accomplish this goal, I will begin by discussing current diversity and inclusion practices in organizations and by stating the organizing principles on which these practices are based. Then, I will provide the core tenets of DDO and explain how they are distinct from how conventional organizations work. Finally, I will endeavor to make the case of how this new space of organizing contributes to developing a workplace culture that is inclusive of diversity.

Current Diversity and Inclusion Practices in Organizations

Diversity and inclusion is one of the most attended topics in the management of contemporary organizations and is causing more leaders to recognize the benefits of having diversity and its strategic role in the success of the organization. According to results of interviews conducted with eleven CEOs known for making a public commitment to diversity, managers care about diversity because it helps them secure top human resources from diverse talent pools, create a culture that learns from diverse perspectives, and understand diverse customer bases (Johnson, 2017). Simply said, the purpose of most of these change initiatives, if not all, is to establish a business case for inclusion, through which organizations can enhance their competitive advantage. In discussing the historical development of diversity and inclusion practices, Thomas and Ely (1996) proposed this form of inclusion to be called the "learning and effectiveness paradigm," where achieving organizational goals through increased creativity and innovation derived from people with diverse skills and knowledge is at the heart of inclusion. Dass and Parker (1999) argued that when organizations respond to diversity challenges in such a proactive way, inclusion strategies are systematically incorporated at all levels and parts of the organization.

However, critical diversity scholars have been skeptical about this strictly managerial view on diversity that essentializes human differences (Hoobler, 2005; Noon, 2007). Their central argument is that in mainstream diversity research, individual identities are conceptualized as fixed and stable, overlooking historically determined structural power differentials that are prevalent in organizations. Moreover, this positivistic approach to diversity is limited in its ability to explain the notion of intersectionality and the ongoing agency exercised by individuals in resisting a dominant culture that marginalizes them. A recent study conducted by Dashper (2019) is a perfect example that illustrates the limitations of traditional diversity programs in addressing deep-seated issues of inequality in the workplace. Her analysis of interview data gathered from a total of 30 mentors and mentees participating in a women's mentoring program in the female-dominant events industry found that the program reproduced effects of masculine hegemony, despite the original intent to tackle persisting gender inequality. Specifically, the participants' attitudes were ambivalent, and often contradictory, in that they attributed the cause of their discriminatory experiences to themselves personally and sought support from senior male leaders as a form of authorization in continuing the program. The findings of this study are surprising because they demonstrate how strong existing masculine norms and values are, even in the industry that is relatively favorable to women. In a similar vein, Janssens and Zanoni (2014) contended that an approach that taps into structural factors of inequality is needed, rather than individual-focused programs or policies aimed at reducing personal biases.

What is more problematic, in a fundamental sense, is that a business case approach to inclusion can paradoxically serve as its own reason for excluding diversity. While diversity was positively reframed to be worthy of inclusion, it may no longer be prioritized when it is determined not to be contributing to organizational bottom lines, or when the organization is faced with economic downturn. Recently, during the COVID-19 crisis, we have observed numerous incidents of societal fallback toward intolerance, non-inclusivity, and even violence and hate crimes against members of underrepresented communities. In most organizations dictated by the neoliberal economic principle of profit maximization, it is reasonable to anticipate that efforts for diversity and inclusion may, at any point, experience difficulties in gaining continued support inside and outside the organization. According to one survey conducted by McKinsey and Co, after the COVID-19 outbreak, 27% of diversity and inclusion leaders reported that their organizations had stopped all or most of their diversity and inclusion initiatives due to the pandemic (Dolan et al., 2020).

Nevertheless, the vision for creating diverse, equitable, and inclusive organizations for all should, and will never, stop. At this point, before proceeding to present Robert Kegan's Deliberately Developmental Organization (DDO), it should be made clear that the inclusion of diversity in organizations can be discussed at two levels. The first is concerned with the issue of how to make the process of entering organizations inclusive. In other words, how do organizations recruit and hire qualified individuals from diverse groups and build a diverse workforce? The second is concerned with the issue of how to make the culture of organizations inclusive, which is the case I aim to make through a DDO. Once having a diverse workforce, how do organizations ensure that its diverse voices and perspectives are truly heard across the system? My intent in this chapter is not to say that organizations need to focus on one or the other, but to showcase how cultural transformation toward greater inclusivity may be possible in organizations by deliberately incorporating various developmental principles into everyday work operation. This also leads to my broader definition of diversity that includes but transcends demographic differences in a traditional sense.

Jennifer Brown, an award-winning speaker, consultant, and diversity and inclusion author, wrote in her recent book that the biggest challenge in making truly welcoming and inclusive workplaces lies in how contemporary organizations are structured (Brown, 2016). She asserted that an organizational hierarchy legitimizing top-down, command-and-control leadership that suppresses employees being vocal about their perspectives must be transformed into a new form of organizing; so that workplaces become more motivating, engaging, and fulfilling for everyone, including employees from marginalized groups. It is not a coincidence that she cited companies such as Zappos and Patagonia, whose innovative non-hierarchical management practices were the subject of inquiry for Laloux (2014): A futurist management scholar who has not studied or written specifically about issues of diversity and inclusion. Zanoni et al. (2010) similarly stated that "we plea for diversity studies that actively search for new, emancipating forms of organizing" (p. 19). In my own scholarship, I call this move a paradigm shift (Kwon & Nicolaides, 2017) because, in this new space of organizing, there would no longer be separation between majority and minority (Kwon & Nicolaides, 2019). Here, the practice of inclusion is expanded from bringing employees at the margins to the center, to enabling everyone with a variety of needs, perspectives, and experiences to openly participate with all of who they are. How do we create such an organizational culture of inclusivity where employees from marginalized groups are not reduced to parts for organizational performance, but are accepted as themselves, and organizational performance is achieved as a consequence? What are the benefits of such a whole-person approach to inclusion, as distinct from a business case approach to inclusion? In the remainder of this chapter, I will further explore these questions using Kegan's theory and practice of DDO.

What Is a Deliberately Developmental Organization?

Robert Kegan is a retired adult development psychologist at the Harvard Graduate School of Education. Since his first publication, *The Evolving*

Self in 1982, Kegan has made a tremendous influence on the transformative learning community through his development and writing of constructive-developmental theory. His work is primarily about the lifelong journey of human development: more specifically, how the meaning making capacity of adults grows and evolves within purposefully cultivated relational spaces of support and challenge (Kegan, 1982, 1994). According to the theory, there are three distinct stages of mind in adulthood: a socialized mind, a self-authoring mind, and a self-transforming mind.

People at the stage of a socialized mind tend to be dependent when interacting with others. Their action is overly influenced by others' perspectives and external circumstances. Meeting the norms and expectations of the groups, institutions, or society that they belong to and think are of importance becomes a guide for their thinking and decisions. Growing into a self-authoring mind, people become more independent in their ways of knowing. They begin to have their own internal meaning making systems, through which the assessments or suggestions of others are organized according to self-determined philosophies and priorities. Taking into account personal needs, values, and desires in relation to those of others becomes available to self-authored people. People with a self-transforming mind acknowledge the interdependence of multiple individuals with distinct worldviews and identities. They recognize the limitations inherent in their own systems of thinking and continually seek for ways to grow their minds. They have the capacity to examine both self and others through a spirit of co-existence and manage the complexities and tensions existing in a larger system within which they are embedded.

The book, *An Everyone Culture: Becoming a Deliberately Developmental Organization*, that Kegan and his colleagues published in 2016 is an extended version of constructive-developmental theory in the organizational context. It discusses what organizations can do to create conditions in which their employees can continuously learn and grow; and as a result of such a developmental practice, how organizations can become more adaptive and productive in responding to the needs of the customers that they serve (Kegan & Lahey, 2016).

To briefly explain what a DDO looks like, it is comprised of three conceptual structures: edge, groove, and home. First, *edge* represents the height of a DDO's developmental aspiration. A DDO is organized around the simple but fundamental principle of helping its employees continuously learn, grow, and develop. This is an ontological value that all members of a DDO embrace and live with. In a DDO, development is understood qualitatively as the process of overcoming individual limitations, weaknesses and blind spots, and evolving to have the capacity to engage in complex thinking (Kegan & Lahey, 2009). This is distinct from the way most non-developmental organizations view development; for example, expanding the size of business or climbing up a corporate ladder. One might wonder how such a developmental approach to leading organizations meets the organizational need to perform and remain competitive. However, it is not the case that a DDO exists only to support employees. DDOs are strictly business-driven, in addition to being developmental. DDOs do not see performance and development as either/or. For DDOs, profits are an outcome of their systematized practice of encouraging and even rewarding people to continuously work on becoming better versions of themselves.

Next, *groove* represents the breadth of a DDO's developmental practice. One common way in which development takes place in a DDO is through feedback. By actively and systematically exchanging feedback in daily work contexts, people can constantly gain new perspectives, personally and professionally. This allows them to be aware of their areas of improvement and learn from them. Additionally, through a system of regular job rotation, people are provided with ongoing developmental opportunities to expand their scope and ability to take on more complex and challenging work. While gaining mastery and expertise is considered to be an indicator of one's success in traditional organizations, once such a thing happens in a DDO, people are expected to engage in new experiences that step outside their comfort zones so that their growth continues. Fundamentally, all of these practices are enabled within a psychologically safe environment (Edmondson, 1999; Kahn, 1990). People strive to express their whole selves (as distinct from partial selves), feel comfortable about conflicts or disagreements, and trust that doing so is much more developmental and effective in the long run than hiding one's deep thoughts and acting differently.

Finally, *home* represents the depth of a DDO's developmental community. In a DDO, ranks and titles are not tied to the traditional notion of power: Leaders are instead equally subject to feedback and changing their ways of knowing, doing, and being, which truly makes a DDO a developmental community. This is a radical shift in the way leaders bring themselves to work. Typically, the norm is that command and control are necessary for effective people management and that leaders must have clear future directions for organizations. Employees are taught, implicitly or explicitly, not to question and to simply follow the instructions of leaders. However in a DDO, everyone becomes a teacher and a learner. Everyone, from entry-level employees to senior leaders, all have things to say, and all perspectives are received as valid ones. In a sense, a DDO becomes a strong, trustworthy holding environment where everyone can feel comfortable being vulnerable and learning from such experiences.

In short, what DDOs practice is the intentional design of themselves in a way that fosters continuous transformative learning, allowing for the realization of the full potential of both individuals and organizations. At an individual level, people can constantly learn new ways of doing things, relating with others, and engaging in organizations. Employees are supported while growing from a socialized mind to a self-authoring mind with an ability to speak up and share feedback independently to others. Leaders are challenged to grow from a self-authoring mind to a self-transforming mind by constantly being reflective of the limits of their ways of knowing and are also challenged to seek opportunities for mutual growth and development. At an organizational level, the cultivation and spread of a developmental culture enable ongoing inquiry, dialog, and reflection for transformative learning, which leads to greater creativity and innovation.

Leveraging Three Lessons from Deliberately Developmental Organizations

How does this new space of organizing contribute to the evolving discourse of diversity, equity, and inclusion in organizations? The perspective I take and aim to feature here is a novel one, given few applications have been made with a constructive-developmental framework and issues of diversity or social justice. For example, Eberly et al. (2007) examined student teachers' dispositions toward racial diversity and argued for the need to help them gain more complex and systemic perspectives so that they can grow into more culturally sensitive educators of the future. Drago-Severson and Blum-Destefano (2017) provided a more neutral and concrete theoretical analysis regarding how the different developmental-orientations of social justice teachers and leaders may impact the quality of their engagement and interventions in practice. Additionally, Bridwell's (2013) study demonstrated that individuals from groups often regarded as marginalized based on race, class, and gender can equally experience the epistemological growths posited by constructive-developmental theory; however, its focus was not on the participants' understanding of or attitude toward diversity. As the theory and some of the studies discussed above imply, adults with more complex ways of knowing tend to be capable of recognizing differences as legitimate, and are willing to engage in ongoing inquiry in relationships with others to support and promote mutual growth and development. Yet, little is known about how to foster this sense of connectedness and the deep relational learning that derives from it in organizational, and more specifically, workplace contexts. Below are three points as to how a DDO makes a case for inclusion along with supporting data gleaned from previous research; the goal of which was to understand the experiences of employees with disabilities working for DDOs (Kwon, 2019).

First, a DDO culture promotes the development of all employees through the intentional and ongoing utilization of diverse perspectives. Considering the evidence of inequality perpetuation in organizations, making it harder for less privileged individuals to break down discriminatory practices and succeed professionally (Van Dijk et al., 2020), a DDO offers unique insights into how to systematically provide growth experiences for all of its employees, within existing work contexts and without having to spend extra money. Incorporating developmental principles into everyday work operation (as described in the earlier section) is not only equitable but also cost-effective in today's competitive talent war. If organizations can put the same energy into helping people become the best versions of themselves, instead of competing to recruit and hire the best people, it would be much more sustainable in securing capable human resources (Kegan et al., 2014). In a DDO, there is a strong belief in the potential of all human beings, and the belief that unleashing that potential is the organization's first and foremost mission. It is unlikely that a development in one's perspective will occur without being exposed to and challenged by the diverse experiences of people coming from diverse backgrounds; therefore, a DDO sees human diversity as a valuable asset for ongoing learning that the organization can rely on for long-term success. In sum, DDOs innovatively and equitably engage with the issue of employee development, while building a culture that is genuinely inclusive of diverse perspectives. Below is a quote from an employee with a spinal cord injury describing a developmental culture of his company.

356   C. KWON

> Everyone is encouraged to share their point of view and not only are they encouraged to speak up and say, oh well, this is going on, they are always asking questions like, what do you think about this? And then they can give their point of view and be completely honest without worrying about any kind of repercussions or anything.

He continued to explain how, as a result of his company's developmental culture, he was able to become more skilled in his work.

> I would say in my job here, the parts that I make, some of them are simple, some are easy, but there are very difficult ones too. And the ones that are very difficult, you have to scrap so much to get one out of them. And because I just started, it was a challenge because I had to be at a certain level in my profession and I had to get there somehow. So, I spent a lot of time learning and fixing mistakes and trying to get around it. And learning a skill is very hard but I was able to learn that skill and improve, have more finesse with it. And now I got to the point where every time I send a part to QC, that it passes.

As shown above, in a DDO, the interviewee was able to continually push the boundaries of his ability and become more capable at what he does, which is distinct from the lower expectations typically placed on people with disabilities to grow and develop as equally competent professionals like other non-disabled colleagues.

Second, an open and honest DDO culture for transformative learning creates a work environment in which employees can become compassionate to each other's weaknesses. In a DDO, there is a shared understanding that everyone cannot be perfect all the time. This is a revolutionary shift in the way employees are viewed in the workplace, in contrast to the traditional expectation for them to constantly demonstrate competences. Instead of covering up what they lack or do not know, employees support each other's growth and development as well as work on personal challenges. Such a practice demands the welcoming of a whole self and creates a sense of vulnerability deriving from overcoming one's limitations. Yet, it is through this radically open and safe-to-fail environment that employees in a DDO can form an ongoing, real-time learning community (Kwon et al., 2020; Torbert, 2004). Suppose what this developmentally oriented culture would be like for employees from marginalized groups. In traditional organizations, they have been socialized to conform to the dominant norms and values of the organization (Alvesson & Willmott, 2002). Expressing their deep identities, thoughts, and values have been perceived to be deviant from the image of an ideal worker. However, a DDO culture respects all of its employees from both dominant and non-dominant groups as persons and professionals, so that everyone can bring their best selves to work. Below is a quote from an employee with an anxiety disorder illustrating how the acceptance of his full self enhanced his work experiences in a DDO.

> People didn't treat me any different once I explained to them. You're still (name) and every once in a while you get into your feelings. Every once in a while you have your feelings but it's okay. That's cool. We'll hit the rest button. Let's go home. Give time to yourself. You come back the next day and you're fine. And that's really worth my day. Most people would be like, no you got issues man, he's not the right fit. We need to go another route to fit our team or whatever. I got accepted from all around.

The comment above shows well the developmental culture that seeks to support, rather than to punish one's different ability. Through the spirit of deep care and compassion available in a DDO, the interviewee was not expected to fit into the dominant culture but to be himself, which made him to be able to testify that he was accepted all around.

Third, a non-hierarchical DDO culture creates a sense of mutuality and egalitarianism among employees. The idea that all members of the organization, regardless of rank or title, have an equal voice that can practically be reflected in improving work processes and outcomes is engaging for everyone, but particularly empowering for employees from marginalized groups. Recognizing that efforts to increase the representation of employees from marginalized groups across all levels of the organization do not guarantee that their perspectives are fully heard and utilized, the developmental principles practiced in a DDO naturally make it a workplace where diverse perspectives are open for transformative learning. The commitment of leaders to equally participate in the process of mutual inquiry and learning—taking risks to be challenged and experience vulnerability—signals that people development is an essential part of a DDO and that it is indeed safe to make mistakes and learn from them, in relationships with anyone in the organization (Brown, 2018). This modeling of leaders to engage in transformative learning is a crucial condition for the employees of a DDO to become stronger together. Becoming stronger here means growing to be adaptive, creative, and innovative, but more importantly, maturing into humble individuals who are respectful of people different from themselves and who recognize the relational nature of human beings (Cunliffe, 2016). In a DDO, the full understanding of who someone is demands the perspectives of others, and thus people are always in relationships, supporting each other's sometimes painful but productive processes of uncovering their potential. Below is a quote from an employee with multiple sclerosis explaining a sense of connectedness generated from the practice of mutual learning.

> It allows me to be less hard on myself and that's really where the personal development aspect comes in. I am just a girl who essentially stumbled in off the street into this company last year. I was doing my best but it still felt very much out of my league, whereas the woman I was talking to used to be the CEO of a corporation and has been coaching for twenty years and is smart and good at what she does and knows this world. We're relating to each other as equals because in many ways we are equals, and so it reminded me that we are all in the same boat. I am not the only one that has these particular feelings and that we all could deal with the feelings better and perhaps learn from them. So yes, that is freeing.

This is a good illustration of how the genuine commitment to continuous learning as a whole can enable a deep connection among employees beyond their knowledge, experience, and status in organizations.

To summarize, a DDO is organized around the collective yearning for continuous learning, growth, and development. Its interest is in finding ways to facilitate individual transformative learning as a catalyst for organizational growth and development. A DDO intentionally cultivates an organizational culture and structure in which employees can form mutual and trustworthy relationships and safely explore the unknown dimensions of themselves, others, their work, and the system that they are part of on an ongoing basis. Employees invite all of who they are—their deep thoughts, feelings, needs, and desires—as a subject for reflection and learning, which makes a DDO a space for whole-person inclusion (Yorks & Kasl, 2002). This new space of organizing for continuous learning and growth does not leave anyone behind from equal developmental opportunities, helps everyone feel comfortable being who they are and be connected with each other in a way that transcends superficial differences. Of anything else, leaders' capacity to show up and lead with vulnerability seems to be one of the most crucial conditions in which these developmental principles can be systematized and embedded in everyday work operation (Brown, 2018). Although a DDO does not provide specific insights into how to enhance the representation of employees from marginalized groups in a demographic sense, it is an innovative example of how to create an organizational culture that constantly evolves to become more diverse, equitable, and inclusive for all.

CONCLUSION

In this chapter, I endeavored to make the case of a Deliberately Developmental Organization (DDO) as an alternative organizational space for inclusion. A DDO's developmental aspiration, practice, and community together make it a place where diverse perspectives are welcomed and embraced for the continued growth and development of all employees, and the organization as a whole. People are connected at a deeper level through the authentic sharing of themselves, enabling a greater understanding toward the experiences of employees from marginalized groups. Leaders' willingness to engage in mutual learning cultivates a spirit of relationality from which new meanings of diversity are constructed, deconstructed, and reconstructed on an ongoing basis. Such a developmentally oriented, whole-person approach to inclusion radically departs from a traditional, and yet still dominant, business-case approach to inclusion that views diversity as a subject for management. However, this conversation is not merely about how to differently include diversity. The new space of organizing created by a DDO centers around the principles of adult learning and development, and because of the fluidity and emergence derived from ongoing interactions of diverse perspectives; it is most adaptive, generative, and co-creative in meeting the unprecedented challenges of today's complex and rapidly changing world.

REFERENCES

Alvesson, M., & Willmott, H. (2002). Identity regulation as organizational control: Producing the appropriate individual. *Journal of Management Studies, 39*(5), 619–644. https://doi.org/10.1111/1467-6486.00305

Bauman, Z. (2013). *Liquid times: Living in an age of uncertainty*. Polity.

Bohm, D. (1996). *On dialogue*. Routledge.

Bouten-Pinto, C. (2016). Reflexivity in managing diversity: A pracademic perspective. *Equality, Diversity and Inclusion, 35*(2), 136–153. https://doi.org/10.1108/edi-10-2013-0087

Bridwell, S. D. (2013). A constructive-developmental perspective on the transformative learning of adults marginalized by race, class, and gender. *Adult*

Education Quarterly, 63(2), 127–146. https://doi.org/10.1177/074171361 2447854

Brown, B. (2018). *Dare to lead: Brave work, tough conversations, whole hearts.* Random House.

Brown, J. (2016). *Inclusion: Diversity, the new workplace & the will to change.* Publish Your Purpose Press.

Cunliffe, A. L. (2016). "On becoming a critically reflexive practitioner" redux: What does it mean to be reflexive? *Journal of Management Education, 40*(6), 740–746. https://doi.org/10.1177/1052562916668919

Dashper, K. (2019). Challenging the gendered rhetoric of success? The limitations of women-only mentoring for tackling gender inequality in the workplace. *Gender, Work & Organization, 26*(4), 541–557. https://doi.org/10.1111/gwao.12262

Dass, P., & Parker, B. (1999). Strategies for managing human resource diversity: From resistance to learning. *Academy of Management Perspectives, 13*(2), 68–80. https://doi.org/10.4324/9781315252025-25

Dolan, K., Hunt, V., Prince, S., & Sancier-Sultan, S. (2020, May 19). *Diversity during COVID-19 still matters.* McKinsey & Company. https://www.mck insey.com/featured-insights/diversity-and-inclusion/diversity-still-matters

Drago-Severson, E., & Blum-Destefano, J. (2017). The self in social justice: A developmental lens on race, identity, and transformation. *Harvard Educational Review, 87*(4), 457–481. https://doi.org/10.17763/1943-5045-87.4.457

Eberly, J. L., Rand, M. K., & O'Connor, T. (2007). Analyzing teachers' dispositions towards diversity: Using adult development theory. *Multicultural Education, 14*(4), 31–36. https://eric.ed.gov/?id=EJ774717

Edmondson, A. (1999). Psychological safety and learning behavior in work teams. *Administrative Science Quarterly, 44*(2), 350–383. https://doi.org/10.2307/2666999

Hoobler, J. M. (2005). Lip service to multiculturalism: Docile bodies of the modern organization. *Journal of Management Inquiry, 14*(1), 49–56. https://doi.org/10.1177/1056492604270798

Janssens, M., & Zanoni, P. (2014). Alternative diversity management: Organizational practices fostering ethnic equality at work. *Scandinavian Journal of Management, 30*(3), 313–331. https://doi.org/10.1016/j.scaman.2013.12.006

Johnson, S. K. (2017). What 11 CEOs have learned about championing diversity. *Harvard Business Review.* Retrieved from https://hbr.org/2017/08/what-11-ceos-have-learned-about-championing-diversity on August 17, 2017.

Kahn, W. A. (1990). Psychological conditions of personal engagement and disengagement at work. *Academy of Management Journal, 33*(4), 692–724. https://doi.org/10.5465/256287

19 A DELIBERATELY DEVELOPMENTAL ORGANIZATION: A NEW ...   361

Kegan, R. (1982). *The evolving self: Problem and process in human development.* Harvard University Press.

Kegan, R. (1994). *In over our heads: The mental demands of modern life.* Harvard University Press.

Kegan, R., & Lahey, L. L. (2009). *Immunity to change: How to overcome it and unlock potential in yourself and your organization.* Harvard Business Press.

Kegan, R., & Lahey, L. L. (2016). *An everyone culture: Becoming a deliberately developmental organization.* Harvard Business Press.

Kegan, R., Lahey, L., Fleming, A., Miller, M., & Markus, I. (2014). *The deliberately developmental organization.* Way to Grow, Inc.

Kwon, C. (2019). *Exploring the possibility of an alternative organizational space for disability inclusion* (Unpublished doctoral dissertation). University of Georgia.

Kwon, C. (2020). Resisting ableism in deliberately developmental organizations: A discursive analysis of the identity work of employees with disabilities. *Human Resource Development Quarterly, 2020*(1), 1–18. https://doi.org/ 10.1002/hrdq.21412

Kwon, C., Han, S., & Nicolaides, A. (2020). The impact of psychological safety on transformative learning in the workplace: A quantitative study. *Journal of Workplace Learning, 32*(7), 533–547. https://doi.org/10.1108/JWL-04-2020-0057

Kwon, C., & Nicolaides, A. (2017). Managing diversity through triple-loop learning: A call for paradigm shift. *Human Resource Development Review, 16*(1), 85–99.

Kwon, C., & Nicolaides, A. (2019). Reconceptualizing social movement learning in HRD: An evolutionary perspective. *Advances in Developing Human Resources, 21*(2), 267–279.

Laloux, F. (2014). *Reinventing organizations: A guide to creating organizations inspired by the next stage of human consciousness.* Nelson Parker.

Lambrechts, F., Martens, H., & Grieten, S. (2008). Building high quality relationships during organizational change: Transcending differences in a generative learning process. *International Journal of Diversity in Organizations, Communities and Nations, 8*(3), 93–102. https://doi.org/10.18848/ 1447-9532/cgp/v08i03/39590

Mezirow, J. (2003). Transformative learning as discourse. *Journal of Transformative Education, 1*(1), 58–63. https://doi.org/10.1177/154134460325 2172

Nicolaides, A. (2015). Generative learning: Adults learning within ambiguity. *Adult Education Quarterly, 65*(3), 179–195. https://doi.org/10.1177/074 1713614568887

Noon, M. (2007). The fatal flaws of diversity and the business case for ethnic minorities. *Work, Employment and Society, 21*(4), 773–784. https://doi.org/10.1177/0950017007082886

Scharmer, O., & Kaufer, L. (2013). *Leading from the emerging future: From ego-system to eco-system economies.* Berrett-Koehler Publishers.

Thomas, D. A., & Ely, R. (1996). Making differences matter: A new paradigm for managing diversity. *Harvard Business Review, 74*(5), 79–90.

Torbert, W. R. (2004). *Action inquiry: The secret of timely and transforming leadership.* Berrett-Koehler.

Van Dijk, H., Kooij, D., Karanika-Murray, M., De Vos, A., & Meyer, B. (2020). Meritocracy a myth? A multilevel perspective of how social inequality accumulates through work. *Organizational Psychology Review, 10*(4), 1–30. https://doi.org/10.1177/2041386620930063

Yorks, L., & Kasl, E. (2002). Toward a theory and practice for whole-person learning: Reconceptualizing experience and the role of affect. *Adult Education Quarterly, 52*(3), 176–192. https://doi.org/10.1177/0741713602052003002

Zanoni, P., Janssens, M., Benschop, Y., & Nkomo, S. (2010). Unpacking diversity, grasping inequality: Rethinking difference through critical perspectives. *Organization, 17*(1), 9–29. https://doi.org/10.1177/1350508409350344

CHAPTER 20

The Power of Women Learning Together: Transcending the Bounds of a Transformative Leadership Development Program

Alexandra B. Cox, Kara L. Fresk, Carla A. Dennis, Emily J. Saunders, and Kristy L. Walker

INTRODUCTION

In a world facing new challenges minute by minute, the need for effective leadership has never felt greater. No individual, organization, or system

---

A. B. Cox (✉) · C. A. Dennis · E. J. Saunders · K. L. Walker
University of Georgia, Athens, GA, USA
e-mail: alliecox@uga.edu

C. A. Dennis
e-mail: cadennis@uga.edu

E. J. Saunders
e-mail: esaunder@uga.edu

K. L. Walker
e-mail: klwalker@uga.edu

© The Author(s), under exclusive license to Springer Nature
Switzerland AG 2022
A. Nicolaides et al. (eds.), *The Palgrave Handbook of Learning for Transformation*, https://doi.org/10.1007/978-3-030-84694-7_20

363

can deny the world is changing faster than we can keep up, from social unrest over racial injustice, to uneven and inadequate political responses to the pandemic, to a globe that is past the point of crisis regarding climate change. Responding to twenty-first century life forces us to lead from where we are—whether we lead ourselves, our families, our communities, or our organizations. Leadership programs within organizations are a critical support structure to encourage and build this response capacity among human beings.

In 2015, the University of Georgia launched a Women's Leadership Initiative to address issues such as recruitment and hiring, career development, work-life balance, and leadership development among women students, faculty, and staff. To support this broader initiative, the human resources department created the Women's Staff Leadership Institute (WSLI), a one-year, cohort-based transformative learning program designed for women staff to help them enhance the individual capacities necessary for leading through the complexities of higher education. In 2019, the first two cohorts of the WSLI recognized a need to continue their learning and growth together beyond their initial WSLI experience and commit to a greater purpose. They subsequently founded "The Collective," a new holding environment (Kegan, 1994) for women that seeks to create the conditions for support, development, and belonging.

The purpose of this case study is to present the transformative elements and outcomes of the WSLI, as well as the continued post-program growth of members of The Collective. As the five members of the steering committee for The Collective (the original WSLI curriculum designer/facilitator and four WSLI alumnae, one of whom has since become a co-facilitator), the coauthors' approach to writing this case study mirrors the evolution of our independent and mutual transformative learning experiences into The Collective. First, from a third-person perspective, we will present background on women's leadership development and the WSLI program curriculum. Then, from a first-person individual perspective, we will present and integrate our own narratives of transformative learning and evidence of our growing leadership capacity. Lastly, from a first-person collective perspective, we will conclude the case

---

K. L. Fresk
Collective Growth Endeavors, Athens, GA, USA
e-mail: kara@collectivegrowthendeavors.com

study by describing our current strategy and features of The Collective as an initiative that transcends the bounds of the original WSLI program and traditional approaches to leadership development.

BACKGROUND

Women are highly underrepresented in leadership roles in organizations across industry and government (Catalyst, 2020). In higher education institutions, women hold fewer leadership positions than men (Cook, 2012; Eagly & Carli, 2007), despite entering the professional and managerial ranks at the same rate as men for the last thirty years (Ely et al., 2011) and accounting for more than half of the college-educated workforce (Fry, 2019). At the highest levels of U.S. colleges and universities, thirty percent of presidents are women, an increase of just four percent since 2011, and the number of female members on higher education institutional governing boards has remained at or near thirty percent since 2000 (American Council on Education, 2017).

According to Zenger and Folkman (2019), it is "not a lack of capability but a dearth of opportunity" (p. 6) that is holding women back from assuming formal leadership positions. Furthermore, "when given those opportunities, women are just as likely to succeed in higher level positions as men" (Zenger & Folkman, 2019, p. 6). One popular strategy organizations use to narrow the gender gap is formal women's leadership development programs. These programs focus on individual development rather than system and structural changes to the organizational practices and are often an attempt at organizational succession planning to create a more diverse pipeline of qualified candidates for higher-level positions.

Women's Leadership Development

The challenges women face leading in the workplace are uniquely theirs. Modes of leadership typically used by men do not provide adequate examples of leadership for women, do not completely reflect women's organizational realities, and do not cultivate sustainable leadership behavior for women (Defrank-Cole et al., 2014; Ely et al., 2011). Typical leadership programs that build skills around male-centric behaviors such as assertiveness and powerfulness can be counterproductive and cause harm, victimizing women for their relational and collaborative approaches to leadership (Ely & Meyerson, 2000; Gherardi & Poggio, 2001; Mandell &

Pherwani, 2003). Programs that implicitly or explicitly equate leadership with behaviors typically attributed to men, and then educate and train women in these leadership behaviors, communicate to women that they are ill-suited for leadership roles (Ely et al., 2011). However, when participating in a women's-focused leadership program, women may experience a learning environment that advises, challenges, mentors, and affirms, while learning from a majority position (Brue & Brue, 2018; Debebe, 2011). "Leadership development programs geared specifically toward women are needed" (DeFrank-Cole et al., 2014, p. 52), and when designing women's leadership development programs, ones that simply deliver the same program to women that they do to men do not suffice (Martin & Meyerson, 1998).

The core of women's leadership development is identity work (Ely et al., 2011), particularly among emerging women leaders, who believe leadership is a mindset more so than a role (Brue & Brue, 2016). The cognitive process by which women construct their identities as leaders occurs at personal, relational, and collective levels (DeRue & Ashford, 2010; Ibarra et al., 2013; Lord & Hall, 2005) and is informed by their lived experiences, relationships, and how they are seen by others as a leader (Brue & Brue, 2018; DeRue & Ashford, 2010). Women develop their leadership identities through a process of mutual influence over time and within a shared context (Marchiondo et al., 2015). One such shared context for leadership identity construction are women's-only leadership programs. In their 2018 study of a workplace women's-only leadership program, Brue and Brue found that participants constructed new leadership identities during program participation on personal and social levels through experiences of validation, belonging, self-reflection, and being supported in their emerging leadership identities. After participating in the program, women were able to assume and retain their emerging leadership role identities (Brue & Brue, 2018).

Transformative Learning for Leadership Development

Typical leadership development focuses on competency development, characterized by delivering task-oriented knowledge and teaching behaviors expected of an effective leader (Petrie, 2014). Also known as "horizontal" development (Berger, 2012; Kegan, 1982, 1994), this skills-based approach to leadership development has value when encountering predictable, solvable problems under conditions of certainty and stability. Given the complex conditions and relational dynamics through which women construct their leadership identities, this approach fails to acknowledge the unique process needed by women to fully develop and embrace their self-concept as leaders (Brue & Brue, 2018; Carroll & Levy, 2010; Smith, 2016; Zahidi & Ibarra, 2010).

Developing one's capacity to lead, also known as "vertical development" (Berger, 2012; Kegan, 1982, 1994), happens through a process of transformative learning that cannot be transmitted from experts but rather must be earned for oneself (Mezirow, 1991, 2000; Petrie, 2014). In order to support women's emerging leadership role identities, women's leadership development curriculum must fully acknowledge the internal authorship required of such development (Carroll & Levy, 2010; Ely et al., 2011). To that end, transformative learning theory (Mezirow, 1991, 2000), constructive-developmental theory (Kegan, 1982, 1994), and women's development theory (Belenky et al., 1986; Gilligan, 1982) offer a framework to build curriculum that attends to identity development through complexity to support the practice of women's leadership.

Transformative learning theory (Mezirow, 1991, 2000) outlines a learning process in which an individual's perspective fundamentally shifts in order to reconcile a disorienting dilemma. Mezirow's theory describes how existing frames of reference expand, how new frames of reference become, how new habits of mind form, and how points of view change. This process of perspective change is adult growth and development; transformational learning "can contribute to the development of the self through reconfiguring the individual's way of knowing" (Drago-Severson, 2004, p. 19). Mezirow (1991) confirms, "this is what development means in adulthood...a strong case can be made for calling perspective transformation the central process of adult development" (p. 155). Transformative learning theory describes the learning process that may spur adult development.

Constructive-developmental theory (Kegan, 1982, 1994), describes how perspectives and mindsets transform. As a stage theory of development in the Piagetian tradition, constructive-developmental theory focuses on the underlying structure of adults' meaning making systems. Kegan posits five sequential stages of mind that represent how individuals construct their perceptions of reality through their experiences and interactions with the world around them. As people transition into later stages of meaning making, their perspectives evolve and their ability to successfully lead through complexity and ambiguity grows (Eigel & Kuhnert,

368 A. B. COX ET AL.

2005; Torbert, 2004). Together with transformative learning, these two mutually reinforcing theories support a curriculum to grow mindsets and prepare leaders for the twenty-first century.

Theories of women's development describe how women make meaning of their experiences, focusing on how women develop and exercise their voices (Belenky et al., 1986; Gilligan, 1982). In addition, the role others play in one's construction and reconstruction of the self is forefront for women; women's developmental theories include feminine features such as relational connectedness that challenge male-centric models of development (Belenky et al., 1986; Gilligan, 1982). "Intimacy goes along with identity, as the female comes to know herself as she is known, through her relationships with others" (Gilligan, 1982, p. 12). Women's perspectives range in a series of five epistemological categories from *silence*, a position in which women experience themselves as subject to the whims of external authority, to *constructed knowledge*, a position in which women experience themselves as creators of knowledge and value both subjective and objective strategies for knowing (Belenky et al., 1986). As women develop their authentic voices through categories of increasing cognitive complexity, they begin to develop the capacity to self-author their own leadership identity in relation with others (Brue & Brue, 2018; Kegan, 1994; Mantler, 2020).

When considering adult development programs, Belenky et al. (1986) urge educators to "help women develop their own authentic voices" by emphasizing "connection over separation, understanding and acceptance over assessment, and collaboration over debate" (p. 229). As the purpose of training and development programs is to "assist adults in creating the order of consciousness the modern world demands" (Kegan, 1994, p. 287), workplace education efforts must attend to the transformational elements that allow such development to occur.

WOMEN'S STAFF LEADERSHIP INSTITUTE

The WSLI program was designed using the theoretical framework of transformative learning, constructive-developmental theory, and women's development to develop women's leadership identities, build their leadership practice skills, and create a network of mentors and peers to act as a holding environment for their ongoing growth and development. The WSLI curriculum attends to these three dimensions in a series of ten, half-day sessions occurring approximately once a month throughout a year. Ten to twelve participants comprise the cohort each year.

Curriculum

The first aspect of the curriculum is career-building and leadership skills and includes topics such as negotiating, mentorship and sponsorship, and panel discussions with women administrators across the university. These sessions focus on horizontal development to build the competencies of women leaders. The second aspect of the curriculum is networking and relationship-building. Participants spend time nurturing their relationships with each other and, in some cases, with alumnae from other cohorts and the presenters from program sessions. The degree to which cohorts socialize with and among each other varies, but the intention behind this networking is twofold: to build a community of women across the organization and to foster trust and vulnerability within the cohort to engage deeply in the more transformative learning aspects of the curriculum.

The third aspect of the curriculum is leadership identity development, and these transformative elements of the curriculum encourage individual reflection and collective perspective-taking. Early sessions orient participants to women's leadership from an organizational and adult development lens, and as an introductory activity on the first day, participants share their personal stories through an exercise based on developmental action logics (Rooke & Torbert, 2005). This activity simultaneously begins to build community as participants open up to one another as well as sets the stage for the explorations of their own development. They continue reflecting and increasing their self-awareness by taking the Hogan assessment (Hogan, 2007), receiving a coaching session, and participating in an Immunity to Change (Kegan & Lahey, 2009) workshop. Another session on integrating personal values and professional goals encourages participants to reflect on what is most important to them in their careers.

The penultimate session focuses on navigating complexity in higher education and clarifies the difference between technical and adaptive challenges (Heifetz et al., 2009). To meet their adaptive challenges, participants learn a tool for collaborative learning called action learning sets (Revans, 1982). Action learning sets begin with a participant's adaptive challenge; then, the group works through a series of prompts and questions together to help uncover the participant's assumptions and discover new perspectives and ideas related to the situation. The goal is not to solve the participant's challenge, but rather to reorient her to the situation in a way that she can recognize potential blind spots and see new perspectives and possibilities. As participants practice this tool in the session, they are encouraged to use it as a strategy for continuing to meet after the formal end of the program of the first year. In effect, this creates a second year of learning and growing together in which the participants are responsible for self-directing as a group. Although optional, to date, almost all the members of each cohort continued meeting monthly for a second year of action learning.

Outcomes

Assessing the outcomes of a transformative learning curriculum such as the WSLI relies on external and internal measures. From an external programmatic perspective, after participating in the WSLI, individuals gained promotions both inside and outside the university; served the university in leadership roles on committees, task forces, and boards; formed and led professional groups across the university; participated in philanthropic support of women's leadership development; and nominated colleagues in their network for the WSLI. From an internal experiential perspective, focus group evaluation data show that participants' transformative learning experiences encompass themes of support and connection, career development, empowerment, and personal awareness. Beyond content offered in specific workshops, participants report that the program fosters a sense of relational closeness among their cohort members and encourages a reflective practice.

We, as coauthors, also have our own outcomes as a result of participating, and in some cases facilitating, the WSLI. As referenced in the introduction, the process of writing this chapter reflects our evolution from developing within a prescribed holding environment to creating our own. To bridge these states, we offer the following reflections of our transformative experiences.

From the Curriculum Creator and Current Co-facilitator

When I learned that our university administration was interested in developing a leadership program for women staff members, I asked my director if I could create the program. Leading this new initiative was definitely a stretch assignment, and it was also the first time I had said, "I want this," and hadn't hesitated. It was a moment of personal growth when I decided to speak up, be seen, and act on my own voice. That transformative moment of leadership gave way to many more, and I feel I am approaching another tipping point as I ask myself, "How can I allow others to change me? What will I lose, including parts of myself, and what will I gain?" Fortunately, I find myself being seen and held in this group of women who both gently and firmly show me the limits of my approach and my next growing edge.

From a 2017 Alumna and Current Co-facilitator

My immediate attraction to the Women's Staff Leadership Institute stemmed from the desire to learn new skills and leadership perspectives and share them with students and alumni to support their professional aspirations. It's almost shameful to admit I had given little thought to advancing my career aspirations at the time. As a mother of two young children, I was content in my current position and ambivalent about new leadership positions—especially those that might result in additional life complications. Hearing from successful administrators and other members of my cohort helped me imagine more ambitious career aspirations. Moving into a new role and now serving as a WSLI facilitator has exposed new growth edges. While I still struggle with confidence, I am more open to new challenges and willing to push myself and pull others along with me.

From a 2017 Alumna

During the Institute, I experienced honest conversations as the group worked together to explore our leadership identities. I didn't feel alone. I felt nurtured, and as I continued to shape my identity as a leader, I started to feel like I had a real story to tell. After the initial program, all alumnae of the first cohort committed to meet monthly to engage in action learning sets. I agreed to serve as one of our group's facilitators for these sessions and found myself learning how to question initial assumptions, feeling more comfortable with having candid conversations, and reframing concepts to challenge peers in an effort to assist with their inner growth. It was in these sessions that, as Brene Brown (2018) writes, I "rumbled with vulnerability" as a leader—leaning into it and staying within its messiest parts in order to approach a problem in a different way. During this process, I looked inwardly in ways I had not done previously, and I did it with the help and support of some amazing women.

From a 2018 Alumna

My journey with the Women's Staff Leadership Institute began under false pretenses. While my application stated that I was interested in "exploring the connections between my personal identities, strengths, and leadership style," my primary objective was to identify leadership strategies to execute. Further, I believed that leadership was a role to be performed solely in the context of the position I held. Fortunately, I did not receive the prescriptive set of leadership tools I was seeking. Instead, the WSLI prompted me to look inward and explore leadership as part of my identity. In my first year as an alumnus, I began to view leadership as transcendent to a performative role and central to my identity. I also began to experience dissonance between that identity and what it means in the context of a system created and reinforced by a traditionally male-oriented approach to leadership. Three years out, I am coming to realize that engaging in personal development alongside women committed to doing the same has created the conditions for all of us to individually and collectively lead in new and emerging ways.

From a 2018 Alumna

The WSLI has been (and continues to be) the environment that has allowed me to see myself on a necessary journey to explore what best serves the greater good. Part of my necessary journey happened when moments prior to expressing interest in serving on the steering committee for The Collective, I was extremely nervous about what I might be able to contribute. However, I felt compelled to challenge myself in an effort to share the type of leadership development I gained through WSLI. I remember how enlightening it was to hear varied perspectives and experiences throughout the first year of the program as well as the action learning sets in the second year. The group processing allowed for me to critically analyze my role at UGA and how I might be able to contribute to the university more broadly. Though we are in the beginning stages of The Collective, I am excited about being a part of an initiative that I view as truly necessary.

Through our experiences in the WSLI, we have discovered our voices, our leadership identities, and our next growing edges. These themes typify those many women find on their leadership path and are reflected in women's leadership development literature; however, we did not write these narratives in context of the literature nor with prior knowledge of the WSLI curriculum framework (with the exception of the co-facilitators). The learning described in our personal reflections confirms that the curriculum provided horizontal and vertical development and built capacities that exceeded the initial holding environment.

The powerful transformations we experienced during the first two years of the WSLI set the stage for our next developmental experience together. After transforming in individual ways, it was time to come together for an experience that could hold us in our collective transformation. The desire to continue learning and growing together had outgrown the bounds of the original WSLI curriculum, and a retreat marked the next turn in our group's evolution.

The Retreat

The first two cohorts of the WSLI gathered in the fall of 2019 for an alumnae retreat. Seventeen women convened around the inquiries, "What is our WSLI alumnae community's purpose," and "What larger contribution do we want to make for our institution, for our state, and for the greater good?" Two years of development and relationship-building in each cohort leading up to the retreat had built interior conditions for reflexivity and trust that galvanized a collective transformative experience.

With the support of an outside facilitator, we spent the first half of the retreat reflecting individually and connecting with each other. Individual journaling prompts on our values and contexts and "empathy walks" in pairs allowed us to progressively focus on discovering our own deep desires and commitments, in addition to focusing on each other's needs and commitments. Planned and spontaneous connection over food breaks and time spent outdoors on the retreat grounds built a greater sense of trust and community, inspiring us to inquire and share authentically. In sharing what was important and relevant to us as individuals rather than relating to one another through our professional roles, we were able to resist institutional projections and expectations and show up in new authentic ways without the pressure of titles or positions.

Through guided introspection and discussion prompts, we discovered our daily approach to leadership was preventing us from realizing our full potential as women leaders. Our organizational context, like most higher education institutions, is grounded in a traditional masculine approach to leadership. For most of us, deviating too far from that norm places us at risk of losing social and political capital, and therefore, efficacy as a leader. As a result, we continued leading from our previous paradigms with subtle modifications rather than fully embracing and operating in accord with our evolved leadership identities. In the retreat setting, a site two hours away from our normal workspaces and the conscious and unconscious reminders of our institutional power structures, we focused our energies on each other and stripped away the limiting beliefs that normally held us back in order to dream together and begin leading authentically. In conversation with one another about ourselves, we discovered the power of leading from a women's approach—an approach that places relational connectedness, interdependence, and belonging at its core.

Throughout the second half of the retreat, our community of women began to uncover a desire for a larger contribution: to share our sense of community and growth with other women. Through a guided inquiry where each of us was asked to share, "Who are we as a group?" and "How might our group serve the whole?" our group's mindset of maximizing individual leadership shifted to a mindset of building capacities of other women to lead themselves, their organizations, and their communities. In a particularly powerful moment, one of us asked the rest of the group, "What if UGA is us?" and we slowly recognized ourselves as the system. After that, the group began to listen to itself, let go of needing permission to act, and took on greater responsibility to act meaningfully on behalf of a larger purpose. We entered a generative state (Baudet et al., 2017; Nicolaides, 2015), where ideas, dreams, and possible ways to cultivate a greater community were put to paper. Through a process of integrating individual commitments and a collective sense of purpose, the seeds of a new vision, purpose, and scope for women's leadership development emerged.

The Collective

To support and realize this new vision, we collaboratively created a bigger container for our continued development. Called "The Collective," this holding environment (Kegan, 1994) seeks to incubate a new, multi-faceted, scalable structure for women's development that goes beyond the audience for the WSLI and embraces multiple perspectives and mindsets while also attending to conditions for our continued capacity-building—namely, conditions of support, development, and belonging. Although the WSLI curriculum was always intended to create conditions to move us from ripeness to readiness, foster connection, and build tolerance for the disorientation and discomfort that is required for transformative learning and development (Kegan, 1982, 1994; Mezirow, 1991, 2000), none of us, facilitators included, could have envisioned the ways we would eventually expand those conditions to further our development. Our recognized need for a more expansive developmental container and our subsequent creation of The Collective is perhaps the biggest surprise and greatest evidence of transformative learning in the WSLI curriculum.

Fully embracing the women's way of leading while at the retreat informed the vision for The Collective. We knew the structure we designed for The Collective needed to provide a space for transformational learning and individual development through collective development. We also knew it needed to attend to multiple stages of ripeness, readiness, and development, and incorporate an iterative component that allowed for continued reinforcement and expansion. Key highlights of the model we created include:

- Yearlong development opportunity for our women colleagues to engage in a curriculum that emphasizes individual and small group development supplemented by large group gatherings;
- continued development for WSLI alumnae as we engage in action learning through co-leadership of small women's groups and structured reflection about their experiences; and
- continued development for Collective facilitators as we engage in action learning through co-leadership of the small group leaders, large group gatherings, and action research about The Collective.

The vision of The Collective goes beyond basic connections, networking, and information sharing; it is a commitment to creating the conditions necessary to engage in open, safe dialogue.

Conclusion

When we look back on our experiences to date alongside our aspirations and plans for The Collective, we recognize that our group continues to evolve as we continue to grow as individual women leaders. The holding environment we created for ourselves to support our growth and development, and seek to create for others, has three overarching features. These features further the individual, relational, and collective dimensions posited in women's development practice (Ibarra et al., 2013) and reflect how they are operationalized in a group setting designed to foster transformative learning.

First, at the individual level, we continue to grow our leadership toward optimization over maximization. In a new growing edge, we desire to move beyond current states—of ourselves, of the curriculum, of one another, and of the organization. Rather than maximizing our capabilities to do more in a strategy typical of horizontal development, we seek to optimize our capacities to do better, a strategy typical of vertical development. Optimization requires that we no longer be subject to the roles and responsibilities women are socialized into performing in the workplace; it is in this recognition and reframing that we can author our own relationships to the organization that serve more mutual purposes. The women's approach to leadership honors this distinction and seeks to optimize individuals and The Collective.

Second, at the relational level, we continue to grow and develop through community. Our development happens in a container where women connect and build trust and eventually feel empowered to sit in their discomfort and take risks. This initial container was formed during the first year of the WSLI curriculum and grew the second year of the action learning sets. The subsequent two-day retreat provided a peak developmental experience so that we expanded our container and strengthened the environment of trust, vulnerability, and belonging. The creation of these robust conditions took time, but the consistent and intentional coming together in community has led to a dynamic holding environment that continues to adapt to our growing individual capacities.

Third, at the collective level, we continue to grow and develop through building collective intelligence. Collective intelligence describes the ability of individuals through multiple interactions in community to grow their capacity for interrupting old patterns and adapting to new situations (Baudet et al., 2017). Individuals enter a learning state where "each one of the members is deeply in touch with [herself], and, at the same time, something greater than [herself]. This state brings about, for a group, creative results that are beyond the competencies of each individual member" (Baudet et al., 2017, p. 27). As a space to bring our adaptive challenges and work through multiple perspectives and potential approaches, The Collective seeks to generate new learning for all its members—those that participate in the newly created program as well as the WSLI alumnae who facilitate it. This feature of The Collective is notable even in our approach to writing this chapter, as we have collaboratively written a piece that transcends any of our own capabilities to capture the experiences of both our individual and collective transformative learning.

Our approach honors the spirit of women's leadership we envision and promote—that is, a spirit of support, development, and belonging. By fostering the same conditions for growth and development through The Collective that we have experienced in our own transformative learning, we strive to build the capacities of women leaders at the University of Georgia, in the field of higher education, and across our communities.

REFERENCES

American Council on Education. (2017). *Women presidents.* https://www.ace acps.org/women-presidents/

Baudet, E., Baysselier, C., Christol, O., Genre-Jazelet, C., Grandclement, N., Pena, C., De Rauglaudre, L., & Thiriet, J. F. (2017). *Mastermind groups: Accelerators of success.* Dilts Strategy Group.

Belenky, M. F., Clinchy, B., Goldberger, N. R., & Tarule, J. M. (1986). *Women's ways of knowing: The development of self, voice, and mind.* Basic Books.

Berger, J. G. (2012). *Changing on the job: Developing leaders for a complex world.* Stanford University Press.

Brown, B. (2018). *Dare to lead: Brave work.* Random House.

Brue, K., & Brue, S. (2016). Experiences and outcomes of a women's leadership development program: A phenomenological investigation. *Journal of Leadership Education, 15*(3), 75–97.

Brue, K., & Brue, S. (2018). Leadership role identity construction in women's leadership development programs. *Journal of Leadership Education, 17*(1), 7–27.

Carroll, B., & Levy, L. (2010). Leadership development as identity construction. *Management Communication Quarterly, 24*(2), 211–231.

Catalyst. (2020). *Statistical overview of women in the workforce*. Catalyst. https://www.catalyst.org/research/women-in-the-workforce-global/

Cook, S. G. (2012). Women presidents: Now 26.4% but still underrepresented. *Women in Higher Education, 21*(5), 1–3.

Debebe, G. (2011). Creating a safe environment for women's leadership transformation. *Journal of Management Education, 35*(5), 679–712.

DeFrank-Cole, L., Latimer, M., Reed, M., & Wheatly, M. (2014). The women's leadership initiative: One university's attempt to empower females on campus. *Journal of Leadership Accountability and Ethics, 11*(1), 50–64.

DeRue, D. S., & Ashford, S. J. (2010). Who will lead and who will follow? A social process of leadership identity construction in organizations. *Academy of Management Review, 35*(4), 627–647.

Drago-Severson, E. (2004). *Becoming adult learners: Principles and practices for effective development*. Teachers College Press.

Eagly, A. H., & Carli, L. C. (2007). *Through the labyrinth: The truth about how women become leaders*. Harvard Business School Press.

Eigel, K., & Kuhnert, K. (2005). Authentic development: Leadership development level and executive effectiveness. *Monographs in Leadership and Management, 3*, 357–385.

Ely, R. J., Ibarra, H., & Kolb, D. M. (2011). Taking gender into account: Theory and design for women's leadership development programs. *Academy of Management Learning & Education, 10*(4), 474–493.

Ely, R. J., & Meyerson, D. E. (2000). Theories of gender in organization: A new approach to organizational analysis and change. *Research in Organizational Behavior, 22*, 103–151.

Fry, R. (2019, June 20). *U.S. women near milestone in the college-educated labor force*. Pew Research Center. https://pewrsr.ch/2ZEVQB3

Gherardi, S., & Poggio, B. (2001). Creating and recreating gender order in organizations. *Journal of World Business, 36*(3), 245–259.

Gilligan, C. (1982). *In a different voice*. Harvard University Press.

Heifetz, R., Grashow, A., & Linsky, M. (2009). *The practice of adaptive leadership*. Harvard Business Press.

Hogan, R. (2007). *Personality and the fate of organizations*. Psychology Press.

Ibarra, H., Ely, R., & Kolb, D. (2013). Women rising: The unseen barriers. *Harvard Business Review, 91*(9), 61–66.

Kegan, R. (1982). *The evolving self: Problems and process in human development*. Harvard University Press.

Kegan, R. (1994). *In over our heads: The mental demands of modern life*. Harvard University Press.

Kegan, R., & Lahey, L. L. (2009). *Immunity to change: How to overcome it and unlock the potential in yourself and your organization*. Harvard Business School Publishing Corporation.

Lord, R. G., & Hall, R. J. (2005). Identity, deep structure and the development of leadership skill. *Leadership Quarterly, 16*(4), 591–615.

Mandell, B., & Pherwani, S. (2003). Relationships between emotional intelligence and transformational leadership: A gender comparison. *Journal of Business and Psychology., 17*(3), 387–404.

Mantler, N. (2020). Women's Authentic Leadership Development (WALD). *Integral Review, 16*(1), 215–224.

Marchiondo, L. A., Myers, C. G., & Kopelman, S. (2015). The relational nature of leadership identity construction: How and when it influences perceived leadership and decision-making. *The Leadership Quarterly, 25*(5), 892–908.

Martin, J., & Meyerson, D. (1998). Women and power: Conformity, resistance, and dis-organized coaction. In R. Kramer & M. Neale (Eds.), *Power, politics, and influence* (pp. 311–348). Sage.

Mezirow, J. (1991). *Transformative dimensions of adult learning.* Jossey-Bass.

Mezirow, J. (2000). Learning to think like an adult: Core concepts of transformation theory. In J. Mezirow & Associates (Eds.), *Learning as transformation* (pp. 3–34). Jossey-Bass.

Nicolaides, A. (2015). Generative learning: Adults learning within ambiguity. *Adult Education Quarterly, 65*(3), 179–195.

Petrie, N. (2014). *Vertical leadership development—Part 1* [White paper]. Center for Creative Leadership. https://www.ccl.org/wp-content/uploads/2015/04/VerticalLeadersPart1.pdf

Revans, R. W. (1982). *The origin and growth of action learning.* Chartwell-Bratt.

Rooke, D., & Torbert, W. R. (2005). Seven transformations of leadership. *Harvard Business Review, 83*(4), 67–76.

Smith, L. R. (2016). *Growing together: The evolution of consciousness using collaborative developmental action inquiry* (Unpublished doctoral dissertation). University of Georgia, Athens.

Torbert, B., & Associates. (2004). *Action inquiry: The secret of timely and transforming leadership.* Berrett-Koehler.

Zahidi, S., & Ibarra, H. (2010). *The corporate gender gap report 2010.* World Economic Forum.

Zenger, J., & Folkman, J. (2019, June 25). Research: Women score higher than men in most leadership skills. *Harvard Business Review.* https://hbr.org/2019/06/research-women-score-higher-than-men-in-most-leadership-skills

CHAPTER 21

The Role of Senior Management in Organizational Transformation

Nitasha Ramparsad

THE CURRENT STATE OF ORGANIZATIONAL DYNAMICS IN 2020

There are various factors that affect the effective implementation of gender equality in South Africa. Some of the factors include digital divide, economic empowerment, gender relations, gender-based violence, poverty, women's access to political power, and women's mobility in the workplace (Bangani & Vyas-Doorgapersad, 2020). The feminist movements resulted in the notion of transformation that demands that gender-based aspects need integration in all government policies, programs, and projects. This approach is called the gender mainstreaming approach.

N. Ramparsad (✉)
Durban University of Technology, Durban, South Africa
e-mail: Nitasha.Ramparsad@thensg.gov.za

National School of Government, Pretoria, South Africa

Vega Art School, Johannesburg, South Africa

© The Author(s), under exclusive license to Springer Nature Switzerland AG 2022
A. Nicolaides et al. (eds.), *The Palgrave Handbook of Learning for Transformation*, https://doi.org/10.1007/978-3-030-84694-7_21

381

This chapter explores the use of gender mainstreaming as an approach to achieving gender equality in the South African workplace.

Compared to "regular" recessions, which affect men's employment more severely than women's employment, COVID-19 has had a direct impact on the employment drop which related to social distancing measures. This has a large impact on sectors with high female employment shares. In addition, closures of schools and daycare centers have massively increased childcare needs, which has a particularly large impact on working mothers. The effects of the crisis on working mothers are likely to be persistent (Alon et al., 2020). This observation is true for South Africa as we see many women in the informal labor market affected by the institution of lockdown. Childcare, which places a huge burden on women, has also changed under the conditions of COVID-19. Worldwide more than 1.5 billion children are out of school right now (UNESCO, 2020). This has dramatically increased the need for childcare. In addition, grandparent-provided childcare is now discouraged due to the higher mortality rate for the elderly, and given social distancing measures, sharing childcare with neighbors and friends is very limited also. Thus, most families have no choice but to watch their kids themselves. Based on the existing distribution of child care duties in most families, mothers are likely to be more affected than fathers. Single mothers, of which there are many in South Africa, and who are often in a disadvantaged economic position to begin with, will take the biggest hit.

Workers who lose jobs now forgo returns to experience and are likely to have less secure employment in the future (Jarosch, 2015). The consequences are not just limited to those who lose jobs, but also those who were about to enter the labor market for the first time (Altonji et al., 2016). Many businesses are now becoming much more aware of the childcare needs of their employees and respond by rapidly adopting more flexible work schedules and telecommuting options. Through learning by doing and changing norms, some of these changes are likely to prove persistent. As a result, in many places mothers and fathers alike will gain flexibility in meeting the combined demands of having a career and running a family. Since currently women are more exposed to these competing demands, they stand to benefit disproportionately (Alon et al., 2020).

There are changing dynamics of gender roles in the private space with many men taking up more labor in this space due to the current working from home mandatory arrangements for most organizations. Often, people will speak of ensuring equality by recognizing diversity. While this may seem a contradiction at first, the ethnic, religious, and sexual diversity of contemporary societies demands such a holistic approach. In order to treat individuals with equal respect, care, and attention, their diverse, individual needs must be taken into account.

Those people who strive for diversity in organizations emphasize the value of difference. A diverse workforce, for instance, will be much better equipped to meet the needs of their diverse customers or clients. Furthermore, the more valued each member of a workforce feels, the more productive they are likely to be. This chapter looks at the transformation process and the critical role of senior management. *Transformation* here refers to a marked change in form, nature, or appearance of the workplace (see www.dictionary.com).

Ethnicity (or race), religion, and sexuality are not the only factors to consider. Societies are also divided into groups of varying wealth (or class), age, physical ability or mental health and of course gender. While equality is often backed by anti-discrimination laws, in practice, it requires an ongoing commitment to diversity. This article stresses the need for equal access for men and women in the workplace, meaning that women and men must be provided with the correct capacity in terms of skills, human and financial resources to achieve their goals and be afforded the same opportunities and experiences. This, I argue, can be regulated through policies for equality rather than equity. The terms equity and equality are sometimes used interchangeably, which can lead to confusion because while these concepts are related, there are also important distinctions between them.

Understanding the Concepts

Equity, as we have seen, involves trying to understand and give people what they need to enjoy full, healthy lives. Equality, in contrast, aims to ensure that everyone gets the same things in order to enjoy full, healthy lives. Like equity, equality aims to promote fairness and justice, but it can only work if everyone starts from the same place and needs the same things. I believe this to be true for both men and women; single working mothers and single working fathers should be offered the same benefits (see Hassim, 1999, 2003). The same benefits should apply for maternity and paternity policies and men and women's work should be valued equally (see Alston, 2006).

Equality in the workplace is never a cut and dry process. This requires commitment from both management and from the human resources department. Essentially, equality in the workplace means that no person should experience or fear discrimination based on their gender, sex, age, race, etc. The laws are designed to open the door for complaints. Before anti-discrimination laws, complaining about discrimination in the workplace was only likely to cause further discrimination and even termination without cause. Now, victims are entitled to have their complaints taken seriously. Discrimination can present itself as a form of disparate treatment is a blatant form of discrimination where someone is treated less favorably because they are a member of a protected class.

There are several phases of the transformation process; however, it is important to narrow these to three key phases: the planning, implementation, and consolidation phases. The role and commitment of the executive staff across all management hierarchies are crucial for introducing and implementing a transformation strategy. In this respect, their main responsibility is to adopt both the formal and informal mechanisms by which they usually create accountability and strengthen commitment, in order to ensure that all staff members are dedicated to a transformed workplace.

Creating an Enabling Environment

Rathgeber (2006, p. 14) argues

> some agencies have regarded gender mainstreaming as a goal that can be achieved through the provision of appropriate training materials, guidelines and checklists for their staff. However, experience has shown that gender mainstreaming cannot be achieved without active involvement by senior managers. (2006, p. 14)

Rathgeber's experience is echoed in my own experience of implementing the gender mainstreaming initiatives within the South African State. This has by and large been a difficult task as the buy-in of senior management is key to the initiatives of any organization trying to mainstream gender. The lesson that emerged is that regardless of resource allocation for training and capacity building interventions, training is but one piece of a larger of a proverbial pie.

Globally, other governments have noted that organizational mechanisms must be developed in order for gender to be effectively mainstreamed. This shift is largely due to pressure from the United Nations (UN). Rai (2008, p. 75) states that:

> States' acceptance of the outcome of the world conferences on women, particularly the Beijing Platform For Action and the outcome document of the twenty-third special session of the Gender Assembly on Gender Equality, Development and Peace for the Twenty-First Century, has resulted in commitment to some form of institutional change.

Madrid (2009) adds to the debate by arguing that though much attention has been paid to gender equity, this issue has not been adequately addressed by countries seeming to be in compliance with the requirements of international treaties. Madrid therefore supports the notion that countries are complying with legalistic requirements for gender mainstreaming in a very limited manner thus rendering gender mainstreaming efforts ineffectual. Compliance is highlighted in this book as a major element in limiting gender mainstreaming initiatives.

Transformation must be led by senior management through a top-down approach. Senior management buy-in is not easy to attain and therefore must be lobbied by yourself as someone leading a transformation process, with the help of those who already believe in the message of gender equality and who currently have seats of power in your organization (see Hassim, 2003). In the absence of such allies, you will have to make the case for gender equality on your own by considering the following:

- demonstrate how gender mainstreaming contributes to better achieving the organization's mandate and goals (benefits of transformation mainstreaming);
- have concrete suggestions on how to introduce and implement transformation mainstreaming as a transformation strategy;
- understand possible concerns and constraints and consider how to address these in advance;
- find initial support from staff members in key positions (if none is forthcoming, revert to the other points provided here); and
- approach managers who are thought most likely to support the initiative first.

You must consider the strengths and weaknesses of the current status quo at your organization. Also think of the tangible and intangible barriers that exist to achieving gender equality. This will assist you in determining how to approach the planning phase. Undertake a SWOT (strengths, weaknesses, opportunities, threats) analysis before you commit to any sort of company action, whether you're exploring new initiatives, revamping internal policies, considering opportunities to pivot, or altering a plan midway through its execution.

Several factors in the SWOT analysis will inform how you approach your gender mainstreaming strategy for the achievement of gender equality in the workplace. Both internal and external factors are represented in the SWOT analysis.

The first two letters in the acronym, S (strengths) and W (weaknesses), refer to internal factors, which means the resources and experience readily available to you. Examples of areas typically considered include:

- financial resources (funding, sources of income, investment opportunities)
- physical resources (location, facilities, equipment)
- human resources (employees, volunteers, target audiences)
- access to natural resources, trademarks, patents, and copyrights
- current processes (employee programs, department hierarchies, software systems)

External factors influence and affect every company, organization, and individual. Whether these factors are connected directly or indirectly to an opportunity or threat, it is important to take note of and document each one. External factors typically reference things you (the reader) or your organization do not control, such as: market trends (new products and technology, shifts in audience needs); economic trends (local, national, and international financial trends); funding (donations, legislature, and other sources); demographics; relationships with suppliers, and partners; and political, environmental, and economic regulations.

Additional analytic tools to consider include PEST (political, economic, social, and technological), MOST (mission, objective, strategies, and tactics), and SCRS (strategy, current state, requirements, and solution) analyses.

In approaching the implementation of transformation mainstreaming for equality between men and women in the workplace, you, the reader, must consider the following key questions: Is promoting equality part of the organization's general focus? Does the organization have an official statement on their goal for equality and their strategy for pursuing transformation mainstreaming (this could also be part of your transformation strategy)? Is transformation mainstreaming integrated in the regulations of the organization and in both the formal and informal standard operating procedures? Do the executive staff members demonstrate their commitment to equality and the implementation of transformation mainstreaming, in both formal and informal ways? Do the executive staff members exercise their responsibility for the implementation of transformation mainstreaming, both by strengthening the commitment of all staff members and by adopting a gender equality perspective in their regular decision-making?

In your planning phase you must realistically calculate the possible resources needed both financial and human. It is the responsibility of an organization's management to provide the necessary resources. Furthermore, allocating sufficient resources is a strong signal of the management's commitment to implementing transformation mainstreaming. The workload of the mainstreaming support structure should be calculated. In organizations that already have transformation staff, it is mostly them who are given the responsibility for introducing gender mainstreaming. This assignment of new tasks should be accompanied by a corresponding increase in the amount of working time made available for this purpose. Considerations need to be made regarding whether or not this can be achieved by redistributing other tasks, by extending working hours, or by recruiting additional staff.

Some questions to consider when allocating both human and financial resources: Do the expertise exist for the allocated team who will be responsible for the implementation of the transformation strategy? Have senior managers been allocated to the core team for the implementation of the transformation projects? Are the financial resources allocated for introducing transformation realistically calculated and sufficient in order to ensure long-term success?

An organizational analysis is required through an audit. A transformation audit is a participatory method for conducting an organizational analysis. It is a guided process of self-assessment supported by experienced facilitators, who raise key issues, enhance awareness about norms and attitudes, and foster organizational learning. As audit is a sophisticated approach that addresses the cultural and informal aspects of an organization's operation in particular. It aims at building ownership and promoting commitment to transformation by involving as many staff as possible, for example, through a series of workshops and focus group meetings. This may be outsourced or undertaken by yourself. Consider the following elements when looking at your organization.

Transformation practitioners must engage senior management for their buy-in for any initiative to succeed. The success of this aspect will result in many operational projects finding momentum. The importance of values-based leadership for managers at senior level has also been stressed as a major component of the transformation strategy. Managers must see themselves as leaders who must embody the values set down for their organization. If you are able to succeed in at least beginning this process, then that in itself is a major accomplishment. Change is slow and realistic targets must be set in your action plan. The latter is the key to mainstreaming. Managers and employees at all levels must commit to these goals/targets in their performance agreements and relevant project plans to ensure that gender equality is met as an overall organizational goal.

Building an organizational culture that supports gender equity is critical to creating a gender-equitable workplace. Equity in a workplace means everyone receives fair treatment. There's a transparency to cause and effect, and everyone knows what to expect in terms of consequences and rewards. When equity exists, people have equal access to opportunities. It sets up an advantageous environment for both the employees and the employer. A supportive organizational culture helps to create and sustain an *authorizing environment* for change, meaning that senior managers will authorize and support the initiatives around organizational culture that encourages equity. A workplace culture that supports gender equity can be seen in organizations that are: aware of the importance of transformation and respectful; relationships and their current performance; ready to talk about inequality, gender stereotypes; and violence against women.

Critical Role of Performance Agreements

Performance management is perhaps one of the most common approaches for ensuring gender mainstreaming in an organization. As a human resource practitioner, performance management is one of the core duties one has to undertake. It is important however to attain senior management buy-in order mainstream the relevant performance indicators such as quotas for women and men at all levels of the organization; progressive policies such as sexual harassment policies as well as policies for working arrangements; this will ensure that mainstreaming occurs at all levels of an organization. Notably, senior management buy-in may be difficult to ascertain. However, the development of a management committee at your organization with key representatives at all levels will assist in circumventing this. This committee should be representative of employees at all levels with a specific focus on the inclusion of men. This is to ensure that gender equality is not relegated to being a women's issue and to ensure a fair representation of interests. This committee should be led by the highest office, namely the Chief Executive Office or head of department. The committee's duties include but are not limited to the overall management of interventions to assist with the mainstreaming of gender for gender equality at your organization. The proposals emanating from this committee must be presented at the executive management meetings to ensure that buy-in is received from the highest level.

Setting targets for gender equality in the workplace is a difficult exercise and requires much negotiation and influence. Targets are achievable, time-framed objectives which organizations can set on a regular basis to focus their efforts on achieving improved outcomes. They are an essential part of managing business performance and most organizations are familiar with a target setting process for financial and operating performance. Gender targets operate in much the same way by setting objectives around a key management area of focus, in this case, gender composition (see Clisby, 2005).

Nurturing a Supportive Workplace Community

In the age of information, it is important for you to understand the value of constant messaging and its relationship to sustainable gender equality campaigns. The notion of campaigns is explored in the physical and digital space. These initiatives are highlighted for their value in driving the goals of the Action Plans that will be developed for the entire organization. Campaigns are often synonymous with internal marketing. You will have to launch an internal marketing campaign. With an internal marketing strategy, employees are treated as "internal customers" who must be convinced of a company's vision and worth just as aggressively as "external customers" (Boyte, 2004).

Campaigns around gender equality are difficult to sustain and develop. You must therefore look at who the target audience is and understand what their barriers to receiving information may be. This will inform your strategy. You will have to decide on whether your campaign could be digital or perhaps a physical messaging campaign in the form of posters and leaflets in the office. The idea is to provide a targeted intervention for all employees to understand what gender equality is and why it is important. Your main aim is to align the goals and attitudes of employees toward equality. Given the nature of gender equality campaigns, you must expect resistance. Campaigns are not about information sharing and with gender equality, you are looking to change mindsets which have been entrenched quite literally since childhood. You already know your context but if not, and you feel that you want some confirmation please undertake a gender audit before embarking on the implementation of a gender equality campaign. Knowing your audience is ultimately the key to a successful gender equality campaign. Try mapping out the forces for and against what you want to happen. Draw a map of the problem—the people involved, the organizations, the organizations—work out exactly what the mechanisms are for the decisions you want to change.

The KISS principle is applicable for both internal and external campaigns. In this case, you want to communicate a clear message to your internal customers using the Keep it Simple Stupid (KISS) principle. Communicate only one thing at a time so as to get the message out. Use a simple unambiguous call to action, which requires no explanation. You need to follow the sequence: > awareness > alignment > engagement > action. Each stage will require careful consideration in order to achieve the overall result of employees motivating themselves to act. The campaign involves a deliberate series of revelations or communication exercises to take your employees from an assumed state of ignorance, through interest and then concern (components of awareness), into engagement (motivation), and finally into a state of satisfaction or reward. Showing a problem may lead to concern but in itself that won't lead to action. Gender equality as the ultimate outcome.

Framing your messages is perhaps the most important part of your campaign. Directly or indirectly, a campaign consists of persuading others not just that you are right but that you are so right that they must take some form of action. The simplest thing you can do to help your message

WHERE TO NOW?

It is necessary to recognize the workplace as a space that is charged with emotions, cultures, prejudices, etc. The workplace is not a gender-neutral space. As a transformation practitioner you are implementing a solution for transformation related to gender equality. This cannot be located on its own and therefore must also take into account other issues of diversity. Gender issues in an organization are not always visible, some are tacit and will need to be unearthed through undertaking a gender audit. A visible indicator could be, for example, the representation of women at levels of an organization. However, this is not an apt reflection of the gendered barriers. Sexual harassment may exist but may not be as visible due to fears around victimization.

Gender equality and ultimately transformation in your institution is everyone's responsibility (Hannan, 2000). The ultimate goal of using gender mainstreaming as a strategy is to achieve gender equality in the organization. You must undertake the phases of planning, implementation, and consolidation. The consolidation phase is ultimately the main goal wherein gender equality is part of all regular procedures. At this stage, there is no need to apply specific gender mainstreaming methods because gender equality has been merged into the organization's standard procedures. It is an unquestioned requirement, similar to other principles such as saving costs or working efficiently. Gender equality is sustainably anchored within an organization's culture. This is easier said than done but ultimately this is the stage which is the ultimate goal.

Promoting equal access opportunities for women is not equivalent to gender mainstreaming; however, it must be included as part of the overall activities to ensure equality in the workplace. Some quick wins that you can explore are:

1. Consider developing equal opportunity policies such as bursaries available to all employees regardless of age and/or vocation. Equal opportunities allow for a more equitable workplace.
2. Include a gender perspective in the organizational activities of your will result in fresh perspectives on procedures and working results.

3. Place a stronger focus on impacts and results. For example, taking into account differentiated statistics as well as knowledge about gender issues in the planning stages requires a research-based approach to thinking and acting.
4. Introduce new forms of cross-sectoral cooperation and networks within an administration system as well as cooperation between experts and researchers are stimulated. This can make working routines more interesting.

Notably, you must engage the seats of power in enabling your strategy for gender mainstreaming. Often, agents of change are those who already subscribe to the way of thinking that you are advocating. Use these agents of change in assisting you to mainstream your strategy in your organization. As a transformation practitioner, the onus is on you to develop the acceptance of gender mainstreaming as a strategy for transformation in your organization from the highest level. Gender mainstreaming is a top-down approach with senior management leading by example. Noting that the accountability for transformation lies at all levels of the organization, it is still very important for senior management to lead the process.

References

Alon, T., Doepke, M., Olmstead-Rumsey, J., & Tertilt, M. (2020). *The impact of COVID-19 on gender equality.* NBER. Accessed June 19, 2020 from https://www.nber.org/papers/w26947

Alston, M. (2006). Gender mainstreaming in practice: A view from rural Australia. *National Women's Studies Association Journal, 18*(2), 123–129.

Altonji, J. G., Kahn, L. B., & Speer, J. D. (2016). Cashier or consultant? Entry labor market conditions, field of study, and career Success. *Journal of Labor Economics, 34*(S1), S361–S401.

Bangani, A., & Vyas-Doorgapersad, S. (2020). The implementation of gender equality within the South African Public Service (1994–2019). *Africa's Public Service Delivery & Performance Review, 8*(10). https://doi.org/10.4102/aps dpr.v8i1.353

Boyte, H. (2004). Seeing like a democracy: South Africa's prospects for global leadership. *African Journal of Political Science, 9*(1), 104–124.

Clisby, S. (2005). Gender mainstreaming or just more male-streaming? *Gender & Development, 13*, 23–35.

Hannan, C. (2000, March 20–21). *From concept to action: Gender mainstreaming in operational activities* (Paper). Technical Review Meeting: Assessment of

Gender Mainstreaming and Empowerment of Women in Sub-Saharan Africa, UN Headquarters.

Hassim, S. (1999). From presence to power: Women's citizenship in a new democracy. *Agenda, 40*, 6–17.

Hassim, S. (2003). The gender pact and democratic consolidation: Institutionalising gender equality in the South African state. *Feminist Studies, 29*(3), 505–528.

Jarosch, G. (2020). *Searching for job security.* https://www.nber.org/papers/w28481. Accessed 12 November 2020.

Madrid, S. (2009, November 29–December 3). *Silence, fear and desire: Why Chile doesn't have a gender equity policy in education, and some lessons for Australia* (Paper). AARE Annual Conference, National Convention Centre, Canberra.

Rai, S. M. (2008). *The gender politics of development.* Zed Books.

Rathgeber, M. E. (2006). *Towards a gender action plan for the department of technical cooperation (TC) International Atomic Energy Agency (IAEA).* Report for the Department of Technical Cooperation, Mexico.

UNESCO. (2020). *Global Education Coaltion Report, 2020.* https://en.unesco.org/covid19/educationresponse/globalcoalition. Accessed 11 November 2020.

CHAPTER 22

Liberating a Transformative Imagination: Leadership Learning at the Burren Leadership Retreat

Mary A. Stacey and Reilly L. Dow

INTRODUCTION

In early 2020, a few weeks after COVID-19 lockdowns became widespread, a prominent business journal published a crisis management article titled *We Need Imagination Now More Than Ever* (Harvard Business Review, 2020). In the article, Reeves and Fuller framed the imagination as the "capacity to create, evolve, and exploit mental models of things or situations that don't yet exist" and "the crucial factor in seizing and creating new opportunities, and finding new paths to growth" (para. 2). The article takes us inside the industrial growth worldview (Macy,

---

M. A. Stacey (✉)
Burren Leadership Retreat/Context Consulting, Toronto, Canada
e-mail: mary.stacey@contextconsulting.com

R. L. Dow
Burren Leadership Retreat/Context Consulting, Mexico City, Mexico
e-mail: reilly@pinkfish.ca

© The Author(s), under exclusive license to Springer Nature 395
Switzerland AG 2022
A. Nicolaides et al. (eds.), *The Palgrave Handbook of Learning for Transformation*, https://doi.org/10.1007/978-3-030-84694-7_22

2009), which commodifies the imagination as a strategic tool best used to achieve short-term goals. It positions humans as a resource from which this commodity can be extracted, bringing to mind another view—that the linear, controlling, external mind will never even glimpse the gift that is the imagination (Fox, 2002; O'Donohue, 2003).

In these times of fragmentation, anxiety, and unprecedented possibilities, there is increasingly urgent recognition of the need to re-shape the human relationship with the natural world. It seems timely and essential to also recognize that the imagination is something other than a resource to be exploited. What if we re-claimed the imagination as a core human capacity, one that lives alongside E. O. Wilson's (1984) proposal that humans possess an innate biophilia, a love of that which, like us, is alive? Wilson placed the roots of biophilia in the most basic pressure of our evolutionary past: life requires life, to live. He recognized that humans are called to whatever alters and moves from one state of being to another. With this awareness, could we enter a field where the full potential of the imagination, in its relationship with transformation, might bring us into the community of life (Hirshfield, 2015; Wilson, 1984; Bateson, 1979)

True learning is connective and imaginative, and life increases in complexity through learning (Banishoeib, 2020; Omer, 2017). If we are disconnected from our imagination, we are disconnected from learning too (Galafassi, 2018). In today's complexity and uncertainty, we need to learn our way through life—individually and collectively—and do so in ways that are more attentive and fluent in noticing, responding, and living interdependently with the world around us. There is great potential in recognizing the imagination as a transformative capacity that is uniquely matched to these times.

This chapter is written from the authors' attempts to live in a true learning field—a place of not knowing—and to write about what we're noticing in it, to imagine our way through it, to become aware of what we're learning as we do, and to open ourselves to be transformed by it. We happily leave a knowing stance to those who have investigated the imagination across the ages and through diverse lenses. Instead, we share what we have glimpsed through our experience designing environments for leadership learning. We hope our offering will help catalyze a deeper, more complex inquiry into transformation, acknowledging its more subtle, less visible sources. Perhaps our perspective will be of service to those interested in re-claiming their relationship with imagination, and to others who wish to refine their design of learning spaces to support the emergence of a vibrant transformative imagination, with all it has to offer this contemporary moment.

THE IMAGINATION IN TRANSFORMATION

The imagination is of interest across a wide range of contemporary disciplines from psychology to anthropology, political science, education, and the arts (Galafassi, 2018), and it has long been held that creativity and imagination play a role in meaning making, transformative learning, and human development (Kegan & Lahey, 2009; Mezirow, 2000; Yeyinmen & Stacey, 2019; Stacey, 1998). We have explored these viewpoints and others that cohere with our experience as designers of leadership learning environments. If meaning making flows from different dimensions of awareness, it is imagination that helps us make meaning of our contexts, relationships, and experiences by supporting the integration of sense perceptions with memories and notions of possible futures (Mezirow, 2000; Simpson, 2006; Cranton, 1994). Imagination is not simply the ability to think up new things. Kant and others view imagination as an active part of human perception, with a capacity to organize perceptions into meaningful, coherent unities that are central to the creation of meaning (Galafassi, 2018). There is an imaginal core to human experience that functions as a bridge between the interior and exterior dimensions of personal reality as well as the individual and collective levels of social reality (Omer, 2017). In its creative expression, the imagination provides a way to tap into intergenerational knowledge to promote personal and collective transformations (Lawrence, 2005), where transformations are seen as fundamental changes in values, beliefs, and worldviews, lending often to non-linear, emergent changes across multiple scales and domains (Westley et al., 2011) and fundamental changes in meaning making structures underlying the systems that shape the world we live in (O'Brien, 2012; Westley et al., 2011). Galafassi (2018) offers that a transformative imagination has the capacity to support fundamentally new ways of seeing, feeling, encountering, and envisaging the world.

In the poetic tradition, imagination is a central integrative intelligence that can discern complex patterns that surround human beings. English poet-critic Samuel Coleridge made the distinction between the primary imagination as the site of our human journey and the secondary imagination which is related to creativity and has a role to play in refining the primary imagination (Fischer, 2019). When finely tuned, the imagination is able to reveal beauty that dwells between worlds and cannot be reached with known language or bare senses (Keats, 1817; Hebron, 2014; O'Donohue, 2003; D. Whyte, personal communication, 2019). This sense of the imagination's ability to form a central internal image that can make sense of all the images we're surrounded by lives alongside Vygotsky's view of the imagination as a process of resolving and connecting the fragmented, poorly coordinated experience of the world (Galafassi, 2018). Imagination both integrates and transforms our experience (Omer, 2017).

Zen Buddhist scholar Norman Fischer (2019) writes that the imagination doesn't measure, devise, or instrumentalize. Its nature is to open, mystify, delight, shock, inspire. It extends without limit; it leaps from the known to the unknown, soaring beyond facts to visions and intensities. Celtic scholar Matthew Fox (2002) writes that the imagination takes us to a place of elsewhere, to nothingness, to emptiness, to what is not yet, and therefore what still might be.

Fischer (2019) and Fox (2002), citing Irish poet, theologian, and philosopher John O'Donohue (2003), point to the same source and beneficiary of the intelligence that is the imagination: the soul. In the Celtic way of seeing the world, the soul is the place where the imagination lives, operating at a threshold where fact and possibility, light and dark, visible and invisible come together. From his Buddhist view, Fischer (2019) says all imaginative productions rise up from the unconscious longing to expand the soul—to transform it. Both Fischer and Fox seem to agree, from their grounded rather than new age perspectives, that the imagination is connected to a reality not fully accessible by the senses, to spirit, to "another world, but in this one" (Hutchison, 2010).

It takes a special turn of mind to grasp formless reality in its essential nature and to distinguish it from the figments of the imagination which, all the same, thrust themselves urgently on our attention with a certain semblance of reality (Goethe, 1819/1998).

If we intuit that the world is vaster than we can tangibly know, we can see that one aspect of the imagination's work is to open avenues we can follow into a less formed reality, into places beyond language, into another world. If the imagination has a goal, perhaps it is nothing less than liberation itself. Liberating us from the forces that hold us "here," the imagination transports us to a world that bears the mark of infinity (Fox, 2002).

Liberating a Transformative Imagination at the Burren Leadership Retreat

The Burren Leadership Retreat (The Retreat) is an annual gathering and growing community of globally minded leaders who are involved with systems change. Taking place in Ireland, the overarching aim of The Retreat is to evolve leadership for the sake of future generations, by supporting leaders to generatively expand themselves, their relationships, and the systems in which they lead. The participants are diverse, coming from different working contexts and cultures, and are aware of and deeply concerned about the today's urgent need for global systems transformation. While some might say that the world is facing a leadership crisis caused by a failure of imagination (Galafassi, 2018), it has been heartening to notice over the past seven years at The Retreat that transformative imagination is vibrantly alive, seeking the light of experience that can liberate it from the suppressive and reductionist forces of the industrial growth worldview dominant in our culture.

Imaginal Space

The Retreat participants, long past interest in competency-based programs, are called to join gatherings that have—what one has referred to as—unstructured structure. In evaluations, they note that The Retreat is itself a creative process and a psychologically safe, hospitable space where they experience shifts in their perspectives and emotional landscapes, and greater integration of mind, heart, and body. Table 22.1 includes post-Retreat reflections offered by participating leaders.

These reflections frame The Retreat as an intuitive place of possibilities, an imaginal space (Hutchison, 2010; Summa, 2017) with the potential to help participants come into a fresh relationship with the imagination as attentive and explorative, relational and connective, and unfolding between the world of sensory bodily lived experiences, the world of perceptions and ideas, and "another world in this one" (Galafassi, 2018; Hutchison, 2010). Most intriguing is the recurring feedback we receive about The Retreat being an alchemical space, hard to describe, that requires trust.

The four-day gathering unfolds at the intersection of artistic and leadership practice and is imbued with interwoven elements which do indeed seem to combine alchemically to meet each person in unique ways that are

400   M. A. STACEY AND R. L. DOW

Table 22.1   Participant reflections on the retreat experience

An alchemical experience, hard to articulate, that requires trust
The Retreat filled me with a centeredness and hope in the face of some of the most
challenging days in my country. The experience two years ago was deep and remains a
touchstone
I am in awe of your simply ingenious creative technique of unstructured structure, that
had me gleaning the most profound learning of the leadership style that is required in
our troubled world today
A transformative space, a creative place of risk taking where questions emerge, stories
are shared, and the power of the arts allow us to move beyond the rational
I couldn't have known, when looking for an 'at the edge' leadership development
experience, what an important chapter in my life the four days would be
An extraordinary experience of peace, beauty, challenge and exploration
This is a place without an agenda to change you but, at the same time, providing a
setting with poetry and music that invite you to consider your relationship with
yourself and others as a leader
It is a deep way to meet life and its conversation
I can see how much we're all carrying and how much we need to put down to reach
into the unknown, not knowing what we're reaching for
The poetry and music open you in very powerful ways to new feelings and insights
A deep way to get to the real meaning of leadership without masks, and a way to
recover our own creativity
I carry with me two very strong images: the call for leaders to be pilgrims and the call
to embody leadership so that it really flows
An inspiration I return to, whenever the spirit is flagging
Months later, I find wisdom emerging in my work that I didn't even realize I'd found

expansive and transforming. Artistic elements include poetry, music, and visual arts; biophilic elements include pilgrimages in nature and exposure to the vast, ancient landscape; and reflective elements include meditation and peer dialogue. Figure 22.1 illustrates the elements that interweave The Retreat's imaginal space.

The Arts and Artistic Expression

Art allows us to perceive from multiple perspectives simultaneously and helps us integrate the conscious and unconscious sense-making of our world. Art speaks in relationships, and a key role of the arts is to develop human sensibilities to the interconnectedness of life. We are in relationship to it and each other, in a mess of entangled, shifting impressions and associations. Art is, in that sense, alive, much like a pond or a forest (Bateson, 2016; Galafassi, 2018).

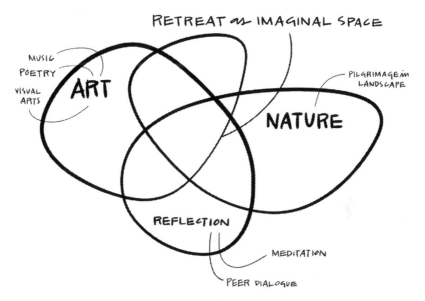

Fig. 22.1 The retreat as imaginal space[1]

Art experiences play an important role in refining our sensory system and nurturing imaginative capacities. They do this by offering people a focused opportunity to attend to qualities of sight, sound, taste, and touch and to directly experience things rather than just receiving a description. Art as a facilitator of experience helps give form to human feelings. It may help deal with ambiguity, loss and emotions, develop empathy, open up associative thinking (which is key for creativity), loosen up constrained and fixed categories of thinking, and give rise to uncommon connections (Galafassi, 2018, pp. 22–24).

At The Retreat, our Creative Arts Faculty complement the process with their offerings of poetry, music, and visual art. As working artists, these faculty have developed sophisticated ways of merging imagination and experience, creating worlds that invite people to think and feel within another conception of reality. They are experts in the craft of creating worlds (Galafassi, 2018).

---

[1] The Retreat as Imaginal Space Copyright 2021 Mary A. Stacey and Reilly L. Dow.

Hutchison (2010) says "the greater the poet, the more coherent we'll find the glimpses of other worlds scattered throughout their work" (para. 6). Poet Jane Hirshfield (2015) states that transformation occurs in poems in many ways, and at many levels of scale, we have not yet begun to explore:

> A poem is a cup of words filled past its brim, carrying meanings beyond its own measurable capacity. Poems are made of words that act beyond words' own perimeter because what is infinite in them is not in the poem, but what it unlocks in us. A good poem is a through-passage, words that leave poet, reader, and themselves ineradicably changed. (pp. 259–271)

She continues, creating an image that evokes the Burren landscape:

> Like water passing through limestone, a good poem reveals, entering and leaving altered whatever it meets. Poems do not need to reverse grief, or to undo or re-cast history to do their work of moving and change. By the human act of being with poetry in community with each other, we are opened and changed. Music and poetry bring hope and community, inscribing into our thirst for connection their particular, compassionate compact, the inseparability of our own lives and the lives of others, of all that exists. (Hirshfield, 2015 p. 264)

Master musician and Creative Arts Faculty member Martin Hayes speaks of the process of music making and the Irish music tradition that he brings to The Retreat, and the potential he senses there:

Looking at the process of music making can often provide us with useful insights and metaphors for the larger creative project of living our own lives. Understanding the creative process can help us stay open to inspiration and help us to live more creatively and courageously.

The dominant instruction I received from my mentors when first learning to play music was to play from the heart. This was the quality of musical expression that the older musicians of county Clare most valued. Being guided by our heart I later discovered requires acknowledging and accessing our own vulnerability. At its best, music can be a transformative heart opening experience that gives us access to other parts of our being that need to be heard and acknowledged.

For me, the ethos of openness and trust that underpins The Retreat makes it a setting that allows me to dig deep and express musically from that deepest place. I believe that with the help of music we can begin to integrate and trust more what our heart guidance can offer to our leadership process. To that end, my continuing ambition is to have music continue to deepen our encounters and help us connect at the heart level (M. Hayes, personal communication, January 13, 2021).

During The Retreat, participants enter the Studio for an afternoon of creative expression. Our Studio practice is designed to enhance perspective shifts through spontaneous imagination, which is often disregarded as inconsequential (Cassou & Cubley, 1995). The black canvas that participants encounter is a metaphor for the imaginal space created by The Retreat as a whole, and for the rich possibility alive in each of us and in the collective. Participants are invited to stand, each facing a fresh sheet at the wall, and ground in the body before making an unplanned, gestural mark with paint. This is the beginning of an active transformation of the surface—presence, not plan.

The moment before the gesture is essential. As Cassou and Cubley (1995) write, "the untouched surface has a special power, so much so it can often intimidate or momentarily paralyze us. ... *Let yourself rest in the void for a while* [emphasis added]" (pp. 58–59). There is a necessary polarity between listening—sensing from a place of silence—and making a move. Painting in this context provides a low-risk but intense set of conditions in which to move freely in this polarity. Inhale, exhale. We make a move; we observe what is becoming visible, sense into what may be possible, what the moment may be telling us; and we continue with the next move.

Describing the pair of blackboards used by artist Joseph Beuys in the 1970s during a series of workshops on art and the future of society, Gardiner (2017) writes: "At first glance, they are empty. A blank slate. There's nothing there. But look at them for a while, and they start to ask questions. What was written there 40 years ago, written and then erased? What happened to all those ideas for the improvement of society? Did any of them take root? Is the world a better place? And: What idea should we try next?" (para. 15). Past, present, and possibility live together when we recognize lineage, and the work of other artists and leaders over time (M. Hayes, & P. Ó Tuama, personal communication, August 24, 2020). The black surface holds the spoken and unspoken possibilities; the potential to become positive and negative space. It keeps a record even of those brushstrokes we did not make. Bird (2018) writes, "black represents vast possibility" adding, it is "old, wise, even seductive in its quiet" (para. 17).

The painting process asks us one of the same fundamental questions as leadership, as life: it is self, or is it source? (It must be both.) What is the inner source we can connect to and draw from when we are out in the world, no longer together in physical space of The Retreat? Is this the transformative imagination? At times, leaders must imagine community, imagine an invisible network of support and help in a hostile and uncertain environment, and the bodily memory of ways in which they have engaged together may carry forward imprints of these forms of support where needed.

Landscape Learning—Cultivating Biophilic Relationship

Beresford-Kroeger (2019) writes that "all imagination originates in nature" (p. 193). The Burren's craggy features and otherworldly magic are believed to have informed Tolkien's Lord of the Rings. Everywhere paradox and surprise are the norm. Uniquely on the planet Arctic, Mediterranean and Alpine plants grow side-by-side while acid and alkaline loving plants abide in close proximity. Grasses grow in the crevices of the limestone pavement, a natural underfloor heating system, and waters flow through labyrinthine underground caves.

In Celtic mythology, places such as the Burren are threshold spaces where the visible and invisible world come into their closest proximity (Gomes, 1996; Stacey & Dow, 2019). In such a thin place, "we lose our bearings, and find new ones ... we are jolted out of old ways of seeing the world" (Weiner, 2012, para. 3). Thin spaces transform us—or more accurately—they unmask us. We let go and become our essential, or more authentic selves (Weiner, 2012; Blanton, 2014). In hidden places, we have more chance of accessing what Thomas Merton called a hidden wholeness (Hare & LeBoutillier, 2017).

Shifts in environmental consciousness have been noted to emerge from the interplay between imagination and lived experiences of aesthetic sensorial and emotional encounters in with the natural world (Galafassi, 2018). As we step beyond the realm of the human and are released from narrow boundaries, the power of the landscape widens perspective and brings solace. We feel ourselves part of the community of life, one that is ever altering and changing. And we too are changed, for when the shape of the outer alters, the inner must shift to meet it, or we will be left in broken incoherence inside our own lives (Hirshfield, 2015, p. 271). We internalize the landscapes that have meaning to us.

The Retreat is hosted at the local college of art, where openings are facilitated not just by the nature of a center with an explicitly artistic purpose but by elemental ingredients of welcome, hospitality, and safety. Crossing the threshold of the seventeenth century tower house, on whose grounds the college is built, symbolically announces that there is permission to access liminal capacities of the imagination—the 'Tír na nÓg (the land of youth) of the Irish tradition.

Each day artists and leaders begin the day in a circle that invites listening, empathy, shared understanding, and creating bridges that unite whatever has been divided in and between us (Jones, 2006; Stacey & Dow, 2019). Participants let go of usual roles and status and sit as peers learning to become present in a group space, a field of authenticity where we can be liberated from shadows, projections, and other limiting constraints. Small group inquiry invites intimacy that allows vulnerability and discovery of possibilities for generative action (Stacey & Dow, 2019).

We've begun to see The Retreat as an imaginal space that invites subtle awareness of a threshold between the visible and invisible, the already and not yet, and, in the echo of the earlier participant reflections, with the ability to support and liberate the imagination as a transformative capacity that is, indeed, hard to describe, yet ripe with potential.

Gifts of a Transformative Imagination

Over time, we have seen patterns emerge from participant reflections, which have helped us to sense the gifts that can be received when imaginal space supports the emergence of a transformative imagination:

An inner spaciousness that helps participants become more able to work with the internal discomforts and complex emotions that were with them long before they arrived—grief, anxiety, anger—all emotions necessary for going through transformations (Galafassi, 2018).

A field of coherence in which individuals and the collective can host fragmentation through a witnessing capacity, and glimpse a harmonious unified whole, a dimension of reality beyond the senses; an underlying coherence, enfolding, unfolding, ever present (Bohm & Nichol, 2004; Maté & Hübl, 2019).

A sort of *innate optimism* that arises in all works of the imagination (Fox, 2002), which Solnit (2016) nuances as hope, "not a sunny everything-is-getting-better narrative. ... you could call it an account of complexities and uncertainties, with openings" (para. 6).

A gaze drawn to *the edges of things*—an ability to see new possibilities in what appeared fixed and framed, and to perceive relationships and interdependencies that were previously invisible (Bateson, 2016).

The wisdom of discernment, an ability to meet life where it is, in an expansive way, and to perceive the meaning and importance of signs it offers, while in the midst of multi-contextual, multi-layered environments.

With all of this, and from here, the awakened imagination offers leadership a more expanded and intuitive worldview, a web of belonging, and the inspiration and creativity to make new pathways by their own walking (Machado, 2003).

Summary—At the Edge

The transformative imagination is not a romanticization of child-like fantasy. It is an always moving, ever-expanding, and mature capacity which Fischer (2019) advocates we need to intentionally develop, given its necessity for human survival and thriving in times ahead. As designers of transformative learning environments, we continue our exploration in this field of practice while encouraging participants of The Retreat, during our annual gatherings and ongoing peer community learning experiences, to adapt what they encounter so as to deepen personal reflection and artistic expression, and to localize place-based biophilic experiences that can support them in cultivating ways of being that are, as illustrated in Fig. 22.2, fundamental to the kind of leadership we need today: deeply relational, imbued with artistry, and interdependent with all of life.

We hope that this chapter has helped to illuminate the risk that humans and the world we live in face if we continue to posit in leadership learning that the imagination is a resource to be exploited, and fail to re-claim and reveal a transformative imagination that can help us tap into the sources of learning, wisdom, and strength that lie within and around us (Brown, 2018).

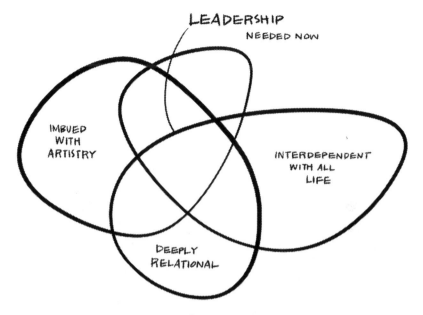

Fig. 22.2 Leadership needed now[2]

References

Banishoeib, F. (2020, April 9). The difference between problem solving and learning. *ReNew Business*. https://rnewb.com/blog/2020/4/7/the-difference-between-learning-and-problem-solving

Bateson, G. (1979). *Mind and nature: A necessary unity*. Dutton.

Bateson, N. (2016). *Small arcs of larger circles: Framing through other patterns*. Triarchy Press.

Beresford-Kroeger, D. (2019). *To speak for the trees: My life's journey from ancient Celtic wisdom to a healing vision of the forest*. Random House.

Bird, K. (2018, July 12). Ecosystem activation. Kelvy Bird. http://www.kelvybird.com/ecosystem-activation

Blanton, S. (2014, March 17). Thin places and the transforming presence of beauty. *On Being*. https://onbeing.org/blog/thin-places-and-the-transformative-presence-of-beauty/

Bohm, D., & Nichol, L. (2004). *On dialogue*. Routledge.

---

[2] Leadership Needed Now Copyright 2021 Mary A. Stacey and Reilly L. Dow.

408 M. A. STACEY AND R. L. DOW

Brown, M. (2018, July). Deep time and the moral imagination. *Deep Times.* https://journal.workthatreconnects.org/2018/07/20/deep-time-and-the-moral-imagination/

Cassou, M., & Cubley, S. (1995). *Life, paint, and passion: Reclaiming the magic of spontaneous expression.* Tarcher; Putnum.

Cranton, P. (1994). *Transformative learning.* Jossey-Bass.

Evans, H. (n.d.). Imagination and rigor in harmony. *Emic Focus.* https://emicfocus.com/imagination-and-rigor-in-harmony

Fischer, N. (2019). *The world could be otherwise: Imagination and the Bodhisattva path.* Shambhala Press.

Fox, M. (2002). *Creativity: Where divine and human meet.* Penguin Group.

Galafassi, D. (2018). *The transformative imagination: Re-imagining the world towards sustainability* [Doctoral dissertation]. Stockholm University. Digitala Vetenskapliga Arkivet. http://urn.kb.se/resolve?urn=urn:nbn:se:su:diva-152294

Gardiner, S. (2017, October 23). What a pair of empty blackboards can teach us about art and social change. *Smithsonian Magazine.* https://www.smithsonianmag.com/smithsonian-institution/what-pair-empty-blackboards-can-teach-us-about-art-social-change-180965304/

Goethe, J. W. (1998). *Maxims and Reflections* (E. Stopp, Trans.). Penguin Classics. (Original work published 1819).

Gomes, P. J. (1996). *Reading the Bible with the mind and heart.* Harper Collins.

Hare, S. Z., & LeBoutillier, M. (2017). *Thin places: Seeking courage to live in a divided world.* Prose Press.

Hebron, S. (2014, May 15). *John Keats and 'negative capability.'* British Library. https://www.bl.uk/romantics-and-victorians/articles/john-keats-and-negative-capability

Hirshfield, J. (2015). *Ten windows: How great poems transform the world.* Random House.

Hutchison, J. (2010, January 25). On imaginal space. *Joseph Hutchison.* https://www.jhwriter.com/on-imaginal-space/

Jones, M. (2006). *Artful leadership: Awakening the commons of the imagination.* Trafford Publishing.

Keats, J. (1817). To Benjamin Bailey. In S. Colvin (Ed.), *Letters of John Keats to his family and friends.* Project Gutenberg. http://www.gutenberg.org/files/35698/35698-h/35698-h.htm#Page_40

Kegan, R., & Lahey, L. (2009). *Immunity to change: How to overcome it and unlock potential in yourself and your organization.* Harvard Business Review Press.

Lawrence, R. L. (Ed.). (2005). Artistic ways of knowing: Expanded opportunities for teaching and learning [Special issue]. *New Directions for Adult and Continuing Education, 2005*(107).

Machado, A. (2003). *There is no road*. White Pine Press.

Macy, J. (2009, June 29). *The great turning*. Center for Ecoliteracy. https://www.ecoliteracy.org/article/great-turning

Maté, G., & Hübl, T. (2019) *Working with collective trauma: Gabor Maté & Thomas Hübl* [Video]. YouTube. https://www.youtube.com/watch?v=Fhl VIhjZj4k&list=PLwBxg78hmjPvZ_cuOBsoavKqw8Rm3qQSb&index=5& t=0s

Mezirow, J. (Ed.). (2000). *Learning as transformation: Critical perspectives on a theory in progress*. Jossey-Bass.

O'Brien, K. (2012). Global environmental change II: From adaptation to deliberate transformation. *Progress in Human Geography, 36*(5), 667–676.

O'Donohue, J. (2003). *Beauty: The invisible embrace*. Bantam Press.

Omer, A. (2017, July 18). Imagination, emergence, and the role of transformative learning in complexity leadership. *Enlivening Edge*. https://www.enlive ningedge.org/features/imagination-emergence-role-transformative-learning-complexity-leadership/

Reeves, M., & Fuller, J. (2020, April 10). We need imagination now more than ever. *Harvard Business Review*. https://hbr.org/2020/04/we-need-ima gination-now-more-than-ever

Simpson, S. (2006). *The role of the arts, imagination, and creativity in transformative learning: What is adult education's responsibility in facilitating this learning?* [Paper presentation]. Adult Education Research Conference, Minneapolis, MN, United States.

Solnit, R. (2016, July 15). 'Hope is an emplace of the unknown': Rebecca Solnit on living in dark times. *The Guardian*. https://www.theguardian. com/books/2016/jul/15/rebecca-solnit-hope-in-the-dark-new-essay-emb race-unknown

Stacey, M. (1998). *Constructivist learning environments for developing leadership capacity* [Unpublished master's thesis]. Royal Roads University.

Stacey, M., & Dow. R. (2019). *Interweaving U: Releasing potential for personal transformation and global systems change at the Burren Executive Leadership Retreat*. Trifoss Business Press.

Summa, M. (2017). Phenomenology of imaginal space. In M. T. Catena & F. Masi (Eds.), *The changing faces of space* (pp. 75–99).

Weiner, E. (2012, March 9). Where heaven and earth come closer. *The New York Times*. https://www.nytimes.com/2012/03/11/travel/thin-pla ces-where-we-are-jolted-out-of-old-ways-of-seeing-the-world.html

Westley, F., Olsson, P., Folke, C., Homer-Dixon, T., Vredenburg, H., Loorbach, D., Thompson, J., Nilsson, M., Lambin, E., Sendzimir, J., Banerjee, B., Galaz, V., & van der Leeuw, S. (2011). Tipping toward sustainability: Emerging pathways of transformation. *Ambio, 40*(7), 762–780. https://doi. org/10.1007/s13280-011-0186-9

Wilson, E. O. (1984). *Biophilia*. Harvard University Press.

Yeyinmen, K., & Stacey, M. (2019). Team coaching at scale: Creating conditions for the emergence of adaptive leadership cultures. In D. Clutterbuck, J. Gannon, S. Hayes, I. Iordanou, K. Lowe & D. MacKie (Eds.), *The practitioner's handbook of team coaching* (pp. 405–419). Routledge. https://doi.org/10.4324/9781351130554

CHAPTER 23

Integral We-Spaces for Racial Equity: Loving Fiercely Across Our Differences

Placida V. Gallegos, Akasha Saunders, Steven A. Schapiro, and Carol Wishcamper

INTRODUCTION: THE NEED IS GREAT

As we put the finishing touches on this chapter in January 2021, we do so amidst grave violence and polarization in the United States, where

---

P. V. Gallegos · S. A. Schapiro (✉)
Fielding Graduate University and Solfire Relational Institute, Cedar Crest, NM, USA
e-mail: steve@solfireinstitute.org

P. V. Gallegos
e-mail: placida@solfireinstitute.org

A. Saunders
St. George's University and Solfire Relational Institute, True Blue, Grenada
e-mail: akasha@solfireinstitute.org

C. Wishcamper
Solfire Relational Institute, Cedar Crest, NM, USA
e-mail: carol@solfireinstitute.org

© The Author(s), under exclusive license to Springer Nature Switzerland AG 2022
A. Nicolaides et al. (eds.), *The Palgrave Handbook of Learning for Transformation*, https://doi.org/10.1007/978-3-030-84694-7_23

411

three of us live, reinforcing the dire need for break-through ideas and practices to address racism and white supremacy. We are lost in a world we have never seen before heading toward a future that defies prediction. This moment calls us to step into our fullest humanity, which means bringing from the shadows our hidden biases, blind spots, and heartbreak. As change agents in our various professional roles, we have considerable frustration at the slow pace of societal change that has brought us to this pivotal historical moment. We ask ourselves why various policies like affirmative action and the diversity and inclusion efforts of organization development practitioners over the past 40 years have not borne more fruit. Why are we so polarized and unable to bridge across our differences in ways that produce significant transformation and realignment of power relations in our society? What have we been missing about our current state that has kept us from making more progress toward true racial equity? Why have we not yet realized our shared values and dreams of co-creating "beloved" multicultural communities?

In these times of unprecedented unrest and distress—from the global pandemic, to greater awareness of racial injustice, to increased polarization in societies around the world, to the accelerating climate crisis, to white supremacists storming the US Capital—our work as group facilitators and social justice educators is to provide solace, help make meaning, join in true partnership with a world that is suffering because of our difficulty daring to connect across our most pernicious group differences. The need is great. Many people are expressing readiness to join across racial, generational, ethnic, gender, religious, and class differences to counter inequitable power relations and structures and to heal divisiveness and suffering. Yet often the question that comes up is, "how"?

In answering that question, we explore the theory and practice of our emerging model for creating the conditions and spaces needed for deep engagement across difference, engagement that can lead to transformation in our understandings of our social identities, and to emergent practices for deconstructing white supremacy and patriarchy and "creating a world in which it is easier to love" (Freire, 1970). We see our model, We-Spaces for Equity, as a potentially valuable map to such a new world. But the map is not the territory, so we recognize the limitations of our thinking and practice and yet boldly step into the space we see as having potential for fostering greater capacity to engage meaningfully and intentionally across our differences. We explore how the application of the Integral AQAL Theory to this work can lead to individual, group, and structural transformation to foster a more just and equitable world. In describing *Why We Matters*, Terry Patten (2016) points to the potential of such an approach.

Our global crisis-opportunity is generating a context of urgency, capacity and potential that is fertile ground to sprout the seeds of radical transformation being sown in our We-Spaces. Perhaps our shared experience can interweave diversity that liberates our evolutionary urge to converge, and the intuitive system energy to pull it off ... We have only to do a good job of learning better ways of being us together, while intending innovations that turn evolutionary corners into emergent new territory. (p. 243).

As gestalt practitioners and designers of group learning events, we are humbly experimenting with ways for racially diverse groups of people to come together to move beyond predictable conflicts and typical ways of relating. Building upon the pioneering work of Otto Scharmer in his U-Lab methodology (2007), we are developing a design for diverse groups to address their hidden biases and barriers to full inclusion. In the convenings that we have called "Dare to Connect WE-Labs," we guide groups to build community and then push into the more difficult conversations possible in We-Spaces for Equity.

In describing our approach, we are challenged to find words and specific examples to give the reader a window into the ineffable. Words and concepts can only point the way toward lived experience. We invite you to suspend skepticism and bring radical imagination and embodied reading, allowing for the imaginal possibilities of We-Space. What if? If only? Perhaps it's possible to make contact across differences beyond current or past efforts.

Before we describe the scholarly and theoretical foundation of our practice, we want to offer an example from one of our sessions that demonstrates the generative possibilities of engaging proactively in collective learning that acknowledges our individual uniqueness but that is more focused on our intergroup relating. We convened one of our workshops in October 2019 at the famous Ghost Ranch conference center in New Mexico. People came from across the United States and from other countries to participate in the session. The largest demographic of the group was White women. At one point, one of our facilitators of color challenged them to move beyond the defensive moves of white fragility. One of the participants later reflected on this moment, remembering:

the invocation voiced by Placida in the spiral, "I need my White sisters to stand with me in their fierceness, not crumble from their shame." When she said this, something inside me shifted. I arrived. ...

This call to action resonated throughout the session where the White group met and struggled with how to more fully show up as allies to People of Color, both during the workshop and in their professional roles when they returned home. They encouraged each other to find their power and their voices and were able to push themselves and our group as a result. Following the workshop, the group self-organized and continued a self-directed year-long practice of reading, small group activities, and holding each other accountable for becoming more anti-racist allies. What began as a cross group conversation morphed into transformative change and development for many of these white women. This work continues beyond the life of the Ghost Ranch workshop and demonstrates the power of activating people to claim their identities and find their courage to grow and continuously lean into the deeper questions and issues. Little did they know that 2020 would become a crucible for national reckoning with race.

This project brings together four streams of transformative theory and practice with our work on transformative learning through group work and dialogue (Gallegos, 2014; Schapiro et al., 2012; Wasserman & Gallegos, 2009). These streams include gestalt group work (Nevins, 2014), social identity development (Quinones-Rosada, 2010; Wijeyesinghe & Jackson, 2012), and integral theory, including the AQAL model (Esbjorn-Hargens, 2010; Wilber, 2000) and the notion of We-Space (Gunnlaugsen & Brabant, 2016). An integration of these approaches to DEI work and to personal growth through group experience is necessary because used in isolation they often lead to either an accentuating of our individuality at the expense of our group identities, or to an essentialism of group identities that ignores both our common humanity and our individual differences.

We bring these streams together to create transformative learning experiences through which the body, mind, heart and, senses can tap into the widest and deepest imaginal possibilities to generate break-through ideas and practices for disrupting and evolving beyond our white and male supremacist culture, systems, and structures. In this "brave space" (Arao & Clemens, 2013), people are invited to embrace and maximize their differences and to connect with curiosity, courage, and love. We add to the integral conception of We-Space an emphasis on our social group identities. Such spaces are expansive enough to hold our differences and yet enable us to be our fullest autonomous selves within a collective and coherent whole. In our WE-Lab workshops, we value and encourage respectful conflict, engagement, dialogue, and radical honesty (Brown, 2017).

In our work, we draw on our diverse identities as a Chicana (Placida), an Afro-Caribbean man (Akasha), a white Jewish man (Steve), and a white Jewish woman (Carol) as we develop and model our own We-Space and capacity to love fiercely across our own differences. Seeing our differences as critical and valued resources rather than insignificant or problematic aspects of our relating, we strive to practice what we invite our participants to practice, elevating our differences by engaging in constructive conflict and creating brave space among us where we can be our fullest, individual selves while simultaneously elevating our collective intentions and connections. We dare to connect across our racial, ethnic, class, gender, religious, and individual differences and help our participants lean in courageously to theirs. Meaningful and inclusive collaboration requires effort, attention, and time. In our preparation for delivering workshops and processing during sessions, we practice deep listening and dialogue, which often challenges us to change.

For example, during our first five day workshop, we found ourselves, after an unsatisfying opening evening, struggling with what to do. Working long into the night, Akasha challenged us to rework our design, feeling that our BiPOC participants had been less visible and engaged during that opening session. While Steve was reluctant to let go of our plan and Carol encouraged us to stay open, we decided to center the leadership and perspectives of Akasha and Placida, who took the lead in moving us to a more emergent space, contrary to the norms of dominant white supremacist culture. We had to step away from habitual centering of whiteness in order to create a We-Space for us, and our participants, where all were on equal footing. We modified our design and were intentional about elevating, supporting, and centering the voices and experiences of People of Color while challenging the White people to stay engaged and contribute from a less dominant stance, with deeper empathy for those in marginalized identities. This led to powerful learning for both groups. Our parallel process of working on ourselves as designers while the group accelerated their capacity to engage with each other created a rich field experiment in resonance and collective learning.

OUR THEORIES OF CHANGE

Group Work and Dialogue: Transformative Learning in Relationship

The chapter titled "Group work and dialogue: Spaces and processes for transformative learning in relationship" (Schapiro et al., 2012) differentiates between three sometimes overlapping approaches to transformative group work, defined by their focus of change: individual growth and self-awareness; relational empathy across our group identities (e.g., race and gender); and critical systemic consciousness through awareness of systems of power and privilege. While differentiated in theory, in practice these approaches often overlap. Picturing a Venn diagram with three circles, the point at which the three circles/approaches overlap, is "the place where the most integrated and transformational experiences can occur ... it is at that nexus— where our individual, group, and systemic levels of consciousness come together—that we have the opportunity to change in the most profound ways" (p. 368). In what follows, we explore how to work in that "sweet spot" through the application of other theories and practices that can help to make that integration and deep transformation possible.

Gestalt Group Work and the Paradoxical Theory of Change

A key principle we draw upon is the paradoxical theory of change, a central tenet of gestalt theory, which holds that in order to move toward a different future state, we thoroughly ground ourselves in the current state. In other words, in order to move into the future in a more fully integrated way, we begin with the present and fully immerse ourselves in what is true for us right now. As first articulated by Beiser (1970):

> change occurs when one becomes what he [sic] is, not when he tries to become what he is not. ... change can occur when the patient abandons, at least for the moment, what he would like to become and attempts to be what he is. (p. 77)

In regard to racial justice work, this means that we must accept our implicitly racist biases, assumptions, and practices if we are to be able to move beyond them, including, for People of Color, our internalized racism. We must embrace our collective shadow as a society, uncovering cultural bias, distortions, rigidity, traumas, numbness, and "the pernicious stuff lodged within the thought systems and body that hampers the process of connections" (Murray, 2016, p. 209). Our belief is that when shadow is freed up, we see new connections more clearly. At the collective level, "shadow is what is not talked about, represented or enacted. Therefore, to heal the shadow is to speak a truth not previously consciously known to self and the rest of the group" (p. 210).

One example of recovering these collective shadows during our workshops comes when we ask people to bring forward some of their "ancestors" into the training space. We invite them to identify a person from their past from whom they draw inspiration. It was remarkable for people to both appreciate the lessons learned from their forbears while recognizing the racism and historical trauma experienced by and perpetrated by them. This is the shadow work of racism—the recognition that we were all given racist messages that have reinforced white dominance and the oppression of marginalized people. Our challenge is to appreciate that our ancestors did the best they could and that we inherited unconscious biases as a result. Purging ourselves of these requires active exploration and excavation of these messages, loving our ancestors fiercely and yet letting go of the racist baggage most of us received from them. Bringing these dynamics into the present and squarely facing them provides us with new energy in the moment to engage in new ways with people from other backgrounds.

This way of being allows us to work with the present reality, trusting that the path forward will emerge as we stay open to the here and now, which is another key principle that we draw from gestalt group work (Huckabay, 2014; Kepner, 2008). As Kepner explains:

> Gestalt group process ... is an attempt to create conditions for learning about what it means to be a member of a group ... so that the polarities and dilemmas of separateness and unity can be experienced ... Within the boundaries of that social system, phenomenological processes are occurring simultaneously on all three system levels: the intrapersonal level, the interpersonal level and the systems level ... which affects the way people in that system feel about themselves and each other, as well as the way they behave in that environment. (p. 3)

Utilizing the paradoxical theory of change, we invite a deeper awareness of the collective dynamics that keep us locked in intractable "wicked problems" (Camillus, 2008) of racism, white supremacy and structural inequities. In our work with diverse groups, we focus on what it means to be a member of an ethnoracial identity group (e.g., Black, Latinx, White, and Multi-racial), as manifest and experienced in the larger group (Gallegos & Ferdman, 2012). This requires that we acknowledge both our separateness and unity and the systems level implications of our racialized ways of being. In our workshops, we intentionally build brave containers where people can feel seen and acknowledged in their unique individuality while also accepting their membership in groups that have unequal power relations historically established to maintain patterns of domination and subordination. In the section that follows, we expand on this notion of how we understand our social identities.

Social Identity Development

Social identity refers to how one identifies with specific categories and groups to which one is assigned based on characteristics such as race, gender, age, and sexual orientation. As Quinones-Rosada (2010) puts it, these are "group identities based on differences that make a difference, on characteristics and on circumstances that are shared by groups of people ... based on ... realities that psychologically and materially matter in people's lives" (p. 4).

Social identity development refers to the ways in which one's identity regarding each of these group categories can develop over time as one becomes increasingly aware of their social construction, one's relationship to the power dynamics involved, and one's potential choices as to how one relates to this identity; for instance, what it means to be Black, White, or Latinx. Social identity development theory was initially articulated by Hardiman and Jackson (1997) and is used as one of the key conceptual frameworks in the approach to social justice education developed by them and their colleagues (Adams et al., 2007), an approach that we draw on in our work.

The model describes stages that people potentially go through as they become disembedded from their socialized identities and become more intentional as to how they relate to these identities. From a Mezirowian perspective (1991, 2000), these stage changes come about through a process of disorientation, reflection, and action as our present perspectives and frames of reference about, for example, our racial identity, no longer satisfactorily explain our experience, and we develop new ways of making meaning—and of thinking, being, and acting—in response. From a constructive-developmental and integral perspective, social identity is one of the lines of development that people may experience as various aspects of themselves that they are subject to become "objects" that they can reflect on and potentially change (Kegan, 1982); that is, ideas or ways of thinking that we have and that do not have us, and that we can therefore change. One must, for instance, accept one's identity as White before one can resist the socially dominant definition of whiteness and move to redefine it and practice authentic rather than performative allyship. In keeping with the paradoxical theory of change, one cannot become anti-racist without first understanding how one is being racist and supporting racist systems.

Integral AQAL and We-Space

We have found that the Integral AQAL and We-Space concepts provide useful frames for how to integrate and bring to a deeper level the group work and development perspectives on racial justice and equity described above. By bringing together DEI work with these integral perspectives, we believe that we are creating a way of working that transcends the limits of each on their own, infusing a deeper level of collective wisdom to the DEI work, while overcoming what has been a tendency toward spiritual bypassing (Masters, 2010) in the integral work; that is, a tendency to claim a collective form of consciousness that leaves behind the richness of our diversity, and obscures the differentials in power and privilege that remain under the surface. We question whether there can be such an authentic transcendence absent the willingness to acknowledge and address racism, bias and structural oppression that is baked into all our institutions and systems. Rather than avoiding or ignoring these, our work is an attempt to directly engage and shift these destructive patterns, opening the way for truly meaningful and "fierce love" across difference and fostering humanizing, heartful spaces that take into account structural and systemic oppression (Welch et al., 2020). As Quinones-Rosada (2010) argues, social identity development and awareness of racial injustice do not come automatically with higher forms of psychological development. While people at such stages have the capacity to disembed themselves from the socialized mind (Kegan, 1982) and unconscious white supremacist ways of thinking and being, such development does not happen without intentional focus and learning. Our work with groups is designed to bring such a focus (Fig. 23.1).

Our We-Spaces for Equity model is adapted from Ken Wilber's Integral AQAL theory. AQAL is an acronym for "all quadrants, all lines, all levels." Integral Theory describes four perspectives—subjective (inside), objective (outside), intersubjective (collective), and interobjective (systems)—that are used to understand any issue or aspect of reality. These perspectives also represent dimensions of identity—"I" (Upper Left/UL), "we" (Lower Left/LL), "it" (Upper Right/UR), and "its" (Lower Right/LR). Individuals have subjective or interior experiences as well as observable behaviors and characteristics, or exteriors. Additionally, and critical to our conceptualization of We-Space, individuals are members of groups, including social identity groups with interior or intersubjective cultural elements and exterior social systems, as described above. One of the uses of Integral Theory and its AQAL model is to present a form of

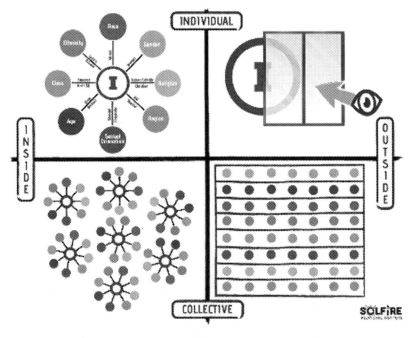

Fig. 23.1 Integral we-spaces for racial equity (SOLFIRE Relational Institute)

harmonization and integration of various perspectives. It is with this traditional application in mind that we have adopted and adapted AQAL for facilitating our We-Labs. Our work focuses on people's experiences in the lower left, or WE quadrant, informed by the other three perspectives. We are excited about the untapped potential of this quadrant including deeper consideration of racial subgroups and how they are deeply impacted by systemic racism.

In using and adapting the concept and practice of We-Space, we build upon the considerable body of work that has been developed in the integral community over the course of the last twenty years (Gunnlaugsen & Brabant, 2016) as a way of understanding and explaining what is possible as we develop and work with the collective wisdom that can be found in working in that WE or lower left quadrant. Patten (2018), in his book, *A New Republic of the Heart*, describes We-Space as:

> a relatively new term, used in the integral evolutionary community to describe an emerging set of practices to catalyze an intersubjective awakening of a higher order intelligence, in which 'we is smarter than me'. This is an inherent dimension of our being, as old as evolution, and vast in size and scope. It includes all human culture, especially what is implicit rather than explicit—in other words, everything that 'we all just know'. (p. 265)

He goes on to describe the powerful "shift from me to we" as

> a move into a level of experience in which we are not radically separate. This collective phenomenon mirrors the integral shift from thinking 'from the parts to the whole' to thinking 'from the whole to the parts and back again'. This is a new social orientation, particularly for postmodern Westerners who take great pride in their individuality. (p. 273)

In describing various practices that aim to develop and use We-Space, Patten also points out what he sees as the yet-unrealized potential to use these spaces to not only develop collective consciousness within our own groups of like-minded people from shared social and cultural identities, but also to communicate deeply across those divides.

> Other frontiers involve our racial and ethnic ... divides, and we will continue to learn to engage ethnic identity issues more frankly and fruitfully. It is crucial to learn to conduct generative conversations that cross

boundaries of race ..., conversations in which not only are all participants heard, but all learn and change and hear one another. (p. 268)

This is the frontier and missing piece in Integral and DEI practices that our work addresses. The overemphasis in Western culture on individualism and individual autonomy blinds theorists, practitioners, and participants from seeing more of what may be available in the lower left quadrant where We-Spaces reside. We wonder what might be possible if we could suspend our obsessive attachment to individuality and excessive rationality to feel our way into another way of connecting. What could we discover in our interactions if we learned to listen differently, to hold our histories differently, to amplify our sub-group identities, and really see their powerful, ubiquitous shaping influences on us? What kinds of skills, capacities, and practices do we need to thrive in the foreign territory of collective contact available in We-Spaces for Equity? These are the questions that we are living our way into as we work with groups to make radical contact, as we describe in more detail below.

WE-SPACES FOR EQUITY: CONNECTING AQAL AND DEI

Guiding assumptions that inform our work with groups include our belief that human beings strive to make meaning of the world and their place in it. In this way, we come to know ourselves more as we engage with other individuals and groups. We also believe that too little time and attention has been given to functional ways to engage across group differences. While many maintain that emphasizing differences only leads to conflict and hard feelings, we believe instead that under supportive conditions, differences are a source of deeper connection, learning, and innovation. Our bias is that when we maximize collective space, people learn a deeper practice to stay in We-Space and are able to focus intentionally on what is emerging from the collective. When we practice We-Spaces for Equity, we acknowledge and hold sacred the dignity of individuals and subgroups as part of a collective that loves publicly and fiercely across differences and moves toward greater connections that include rather than avoiding difficult conversations about racism, sexism, white supremacy, and power. These can be thought of as the sub-we's within the larger WE of the lower left quadrant; in other words, the subcultures that we are all members of interacting and maintaining contact at the collective rather than individual level.

Deriving from our developmental theory and practice about how adults learn and grow, and the streams of transformative theory and practice described above, we utilize a combination of modalities including experiential, contemplative and somatic presencing, time in nature, intentional relationship building, racially homogenous subgroups, intentional dialogue across groups, just in time conceptual frameworks, frequent practice opportunities with enough scaffolding to support experimentation, and brave enough space to make mistakes. We see the flow of the group's time together as building sequentially from simpler and more interpersonal connections in the early period to gradually accelerating levels of complexity in our interactions and topics, basically introducing the group to itself in each of the quadrants: as individuals, interpersonally, through intentional intergroup contact and collective experience. Our intention throughout is to build a container safe enough to support growth while still uncomfortable enough to help people stretch into new and untested behaviors and ways of relating. Mezirow's (1991) concept of "disorienting dilemmas" fits well with the context of this work as we intentionally create opportunities to disembed from current ways of knowing about ourselves, others, and our group memberships. The resulting disorientation, when well-supported, allows a fundamental reorienting toward more expansive ways of knowing self and other. As one of our participants thoughtfully reflected:

> I left the group awakened and exhausted, full and emptied out, connected and deeply craving solitude—a personal and collective alchemy of contradictions. The honest truth is that I know something powerful happened to me, I'm just still figuring out exactly what it was …

We also believe that building community is a critical prerequisite for deep and collective learning to occur. Rather than assuming one size fits all, we spend considerable time in the early life of the group setting ground rules, testing assumptions and introducing the group to itself along multiple dimensions, learning more about what individuals are bringing to the community. Our workshops, which have ranged from in-person retreats to multiple sessions in virtual spaces, are designed to intentionally take participants on a journey that builds from preliminary foundational contact into more challenging levels of knowing and being known, from simplicity of individuality toward complexity of intergroup and systemic awareness and experience.

As mentioned earlier, one of the early processes often includes making intimate contact with ancestors. This fundamental practice has proved to be important in grounding participants in the historical antecedents of our identities and experiences. Often bittersweet stories are shared and include examples of when we had been both victimized and perpetrators of victimization. We engage in the powerful invitation to bring those ancestors to the collective along with the request for direct messages from them to us as a community. Their offerings are often profound, personal, and yet deeply relevant to what we are challenged by today in our lives. Collectively, the group is able to experience our shared humanity while also attending to the vast diversity of regions, cultures, and personal experiences present in the group.

We-Lab

In our sessions during the WE-Lab, we intentionally support individuals to recognize and take in the implications of their group memberships, unchosen and socially constructed, yet powerfully determinant of our experiences, opportunities, joys, and heartbreak as human beings. Rather than pretending to be color blind or evolved beyond these differences, we intentionally amplify our awareness of our diversity, but do so in a loving community of mutuality and attention to power relations. Our notion is that once we become more aware of the impact of these powerful dynamics on our day-to-day experiences and actions, the greater chance we can disembed ourselves from systems of oppression and use ourselves as change agents and allies in even more impactful ways.

We-Space Dialogue Sessions

In addition to the content and process pieces of our design, we incorporate explicit We-Space community time in each session where the group is able to practice being in collective awareness, as a particular discipline and practice. Each of these periods focuses on different aspects of what the group is learning about itself but largely is unstructured allowing the collective voice of the whole to emerge. Our experiences parallel what Brabant and Diperna (2016) describe as:

> a deepening awareness and sensitivity to time, place, and culture. One can maintain contact with the local 'we' while simultaneously expanding the

horizon of awareness to larger and larger fields i.e. practitioners demonstrating this stage of we-intelligence gain the capacity to feel into the way that larger social issues such as race, gender, sexual orientation, and religious affiliation are influencing and shaping both individual perspectives as well as the overall group field itself. (p. 22)

Stretching the limits of past ways of relating across differences is sometimes profoundly disorienting and yet in the context of a supportive learning community, people are able to hold each other lovingly and, at times, critically. One participant was able to describe her fundamental transformation that allowed her to see her White identity in the context of larger systems at play and yet maintain contact with others who did not share that identity:

> I walked away with an embodied sense of how deeply people want to love and be loved across differences and to be part of a 'we' rather than 'me' and 'us vs. them'. I was moved by the power of that desire, built stronger from acts of sharing of love through our stories and affirming interactions with each other, to hold individuals and groups through hard conversations about white supremacy. I found capacity and language within myself to bring love more explicitly into anti-racism work moving forward.

In We-Space, we connect AQAL with DEI to look at our individual awareness as a person with social identities in the Upper Left of the AQAL. Using these identities, we help ourselves and others build awareness around the behaviors that reinforce a culture of dominance, such as white supremacy, classism, and various forms of oppression. What we are offering is a way to build capacity to access and deal with social identity issues at the group and systemic levels. We operate on the assumption that there is more in the collective space that we are not fully tapping into. Our We-Space approach is not just about a collection of individuals who contribute to the We. Each individual brings their social identities. We cannot have a full We-Space if we do not deal with the multiple We's within the larger We.

CONCLUSION

Our intention in this chapter has been to invite other scholar-practitioners into this grand experiment we have been conducting. Our We-Space practice builds on the good work of others but takes that work even further in service of these perilous times we find ourselves in as a society. Our call to action is for bold experimentation and humility at the same time. We are not claiming to have found the magic solution to these issues but we are also clearly tapping unto an underdeveloped resource. We are calling for deep collaboration and connectivity across our racial differences in a way that does not harmonize to maintain superficial contact but instead brings the full force and power of our differences together to strengthen, deepen, and make more authentic relating possible. Do you hear the call and are you willing to truly "dare to connect?".

REFERENCES

Adams, M., Bell, L. A., & Griffin, P. (Eds.). (2007). *Teaching for diversity and social justice*. Routledge.

Arao, B., & Clemens, K. (2013). From safe spaces to brave spaces: A new way to frame dialogue around diversity and social justice. In L. Landreman (Ed.), *The art of effective facilitation: Reflections from social justice educators*. Stylus.

Brabant, M., & DiPerna, D. (2016). Initial mapping and the eternal mystery of We-Space. In I. Gunnlaugsen & M. Brabant (Eds.), *Cohering the integral we-space: Engaging collective emergence, wisdom and healing in groups*. Integral Publishing House.

Brown, A. M. (2017). *Emergent strategy: Shaping change, shaping worlds*. AK Press.

Camillus, J. (2008). Strategy as a wicked problem. *Harvard Business Review, 86*, 98–101. Retrieved April 19, 2–18 from https://hbr.org/2008/05/strategy-as-a-wicked-problem

Esbjorn-Hargens, S. (2010). *Integral theory in action*. SUNY Press.

Freire. P. (1970). *Pedagogy of the oppressed*. eabury Press.

Gallegos, P. (2014.) The work of inclusive leadership: Fostering authentic relationships, modeling courage and humility. In B. Ferdman & B. Deane (Eds.), *Diversity at work: The practice of inclusion*. Jossey Bass.

Gallegos, P., & Ferdman, D. (2012). Latina and Latino ethnoracial identity orientations: A dynamic and developmental perspective. In C. L. Wijeyesinghe & B. W. Jackson (Eds.), *New perspectives on racial identity development* (2nd ed.). New York University Press.

Gunnlaugsen, I., & Brabant, M. (Eds.). (2016). *Cohering the integral we-space: Engaging collective emergence, wisdom and healing in groups*. Integral Publishing House.

Hardiman, R., & Jackson, B. W. (1997). Conceptual foundations for social justice courses. In M. Adams, M. L. A. Bell & P. Griffin (Eds.), *Teaching for diversity and social justice*. Routledge.

Huckabay, M. A. (2014). An overview of the theory and practice of gestalt group process. In E. Nevis (Ed.), *Gestalt therapy: Perspectives and applications*. CRC Press.

Kegan, R. (1982). *The evolving self*. Harvard University Press.

Kepner, E. (2008). Gestalt group process. In B. Feder & J. Frew (Eds.), *Beyond the hot seat revisited: Gestalt approaches to groups*. Gestalt Institute Press.

Masters, R. A. (2010). *Spiritual bypassing: When spirituality disconnects us from what really matters*. North Atlantic Books.

Mezirow, J. (1991). *Transformative dimensions of adult learning*. Jossey Bass.

Mezirow, J., & Associates. (2000). *Learning for transformation: A theory in process*. Jossey Bass

Murray, T. (2016). We-Space practice: Emerging themes in embodied contemplative design. In I. Gunnlaugsen & M. Brabant (Eds.), *Cohering the integral we-space: Engaging collective emergence, wisdom and healing in groups*. Integral Publishing House.

Nevins, E. (Ed.). (2014). Gestalt therapy: Perspectives and applications. *Gestalt Press*. https://doi.org/10.4324/9781315799001

Patten, T. (2016). Why we matters. In I. Gunnlaugsen & M. Brabant (Eds.), *Cohering the integral we-space: Engaging collective emergence, wisdom and healing in groups*. Integral Publishing House.

Patten, T. (2018). *A new republic of the heart: An ethos for revolutionaries*. North Atlantic Books.

Quinones-Rosada, R. (2010). Social identity development and integral theory. *Integral Leadership Review, X*, 5.

Schapiro, S. A., Wasserman, I., & Gallegos, P. (2012). Group work and dialogue: Spaces and processes for transformative learning in relationship. In E. Taylor, P. Cranton & Associates (Eds.), *The handbook of transformative learning*. Jossey Bass.

Scharmer, C. O. (2007). *Theory U: Leading from the future as it emerges*. Barret-Koehler.

Wasserman, I., & Gallegos, P. (2009). Engaging diversity: Disorienting dilemmas that transform identity. In B. Fisher-Yoshida, K. Geller & S. A. Schapiro (Eds.), *Innovations in transformative learning*. Peter Lang.

Welch, M. A., Akasha, Aka Pete Saunders, Buergelt, P. T., Gilpin-Jackson, Y., Ferguson, J. & Marsick, V. J. (2020). Your story, our story: the transformative power of life narratives. *Reflective Practice, 21*(6), 861–876. https://doi.org/10.1080/14623943.2020.1821633

Wijeyesinghe, C. & Jackson, B. (Eds.). (2012). *New perspectives on racial identity development: A theoretical and practical anthology*. New York University Press.

Wilber, K. A. (2000) *A theory of everything*. Shambala.

CHAPTER 24

Listening for Transformation: Discovering Third Space and Connection Using a Listening Protocol

Laurie Anderson Sathe, Tes Cotter Zakrzewski,
Anne-Liisa Longmore, Alessandra Romano,
Deborah Kramlich, Janette Brunstein, Ed Cunliff,
and Victoria J. Marsick

INTRODUCTION

We share the evolving story of a group of interdisciplinary global scholars', the Transformative Listening Collaborative, collective work and exploration of listening as a space for transformation. As we share our story, we also seek to cultivate a space within the context of this chapter

---

L. Anderson Sathe (✉)
St. Catherine University, Saint Paul, MN, USA
e-mail: landersonsathe@stkate.edu

T. C. Zakrzewski
Wentworth Institute of Technology, Boston, MA, USA

A.-L. Longmore
Sheridan College, Oakville, Canada

© The Author(s), under exclusive license to Springer Nature Switzerland AG 2022
A. Nicolaides et al. (eds.), *The Palgrave Handbook of Learning for Transformation*, https://doi.org/10.1007/978-3-030-84694-7_24

429

where the reader joins us in the process of continued exploration of listening not only as a space but as a third space in the quest to expand our notions of transformative learning. Specifically, we invite readers to join in the conversation and engage in the continued iterative development and research on the Transformative Listening Protocol (hereafter referred to as the Protocol) for transformative discovery.

This is a time of significant individual and global evolution, and we recognize that an important goal of transformative education is to create opportunities for people to become change agents, through connections and relationships across intersections of race, class, gender, ethnicity as well as cultural, national, generational, functional, or disciplinary boundaries. With a focus on social justice, equity and liberation, we see the need for empathy, understanding, deep relationships, and human connection as critical in today's world (Schwab, 2016).

Finding voice, telling stories, and generating new meanings are important components of transformation. Engaging in storytelling, and more specifically listening to another person, can play a key role in creating conditions to facilitate true and authentic connection, foster sense-making and deeper understanding of self and others (Lipari, 2014). The dialogic threshold space formed while listening to the story of another is what Bhabha (1994) describes as a third space through which narrative interpretation and understanding of the other emerges. In many interpersonal exchanges of storytelling, speech is often privileged over listening (Jacobs & Coghlan, 2005) with the role of listening often assumed but not always specifically addressed (Pery et al., 2020). Jacobs and Coghlan

---

A. Romano
University of Siena, Siena, Italy

D. Kramlich
Payap University, Chiang Mai, Thailand

J. Brunstein
Universidade Presbiteriana Mackenzie, São Paulo, Brazil

E. Cunliff
University of Central Oklahoma, Edmond, OK, USA

V. J. Marsick
Teachers College, Columbia University, New York, NY, USA

(2005) suggest, "by listening to another person, we acknowledge the other in his or her difference and thereby prepare the relational ground for intersubjective generation of new meanings" (p. 129). The interpersonal nature of storytelling in dyads is key and presupposes a storyteller and a story listener. To date, storytelling in dyads, and specifically research on listening in dyads, is underrepresented in the literature (Greene & Herbers, 2011; Joshi & Knight, 2014; Pery et al., 2020). We see transformative listening through story, with its focus on attention and presence, as a crucial condition for the formation of trust and connection, required for transformative learning that can promote connection, empathy, and understanding. With this premise, we co-created the Protocol that facilitates a process of reciprocal storytelling and story listening, connection, and possible transformation. Together with the reader, we seek to explore the potential for applying the Protocol in multiple contexts to create transformative spaces.

Our research addresses a specific gap in the literature which is to understand the experience of listening through story as a space for transformation in dyads (Imhof & Janusik, 2006; Pery et al., 2020). Our intended contribution over time is twofold: (1) To the theoretical discussion of the role of listening in transformative learning theory and (2) the practical/methodological iterative process of developing the Protocol to foster transformative listening in a wide range of settings and cultural environments.

Against this backdrop, in this chapter, we begin with *listening as a space for transformation*, telling the story of our collaborative, interdisciplinary research process in developing the Protocol and its theoretical framework. We also provide an emergent iterative prototype inquiry methodology for assessing or describing the Protocol and its application in a variety of contexts (Bogers & Horst, 2014). We move into *rediscovering third space for transformation* where we describe the themes that emerged and the nascent theory arising from the experience of using the Protocol. Finally, in *further listening*, we describe the possible implications of transformative listening for transformative learning theory as well as the implications for practitioners dedicated to facilitating purpose and meaning, equity and justice, and hope for a better world.

432 L. ANDERSON SATHE ET AL.

LISTENING AS A SPACE FOR TRANSFORMATION

The Transformative Listening Collaborative, an interdisciplinary research team, listened to a call or invitation to gather in the summer of 2017 over our shared passion for bridging divisions, creating connection and understanding across differences, and recognition of our shared humanity. What started as our participation in the International Day of Listening subcommittee for the 2018 Transformative Learning Conference became a dynamic group of scholars and practitioners exploring, learning, and listening together well beyond the experience of the conference. We came together with the common goal to foster dialogue in collaborative spaces in which all are welcome. As researchers and practitioners, each of us brought to our learning community different ways of being and knowing informed by our past experiences and discipline-specific paradigms. We draw from different disciplines and theoretical backgrounds that inform our worldviews and thus the development of the Protocol and our research.

During the process of developing the Protocol as a collaborative interdisciplinary team, each individual brought forward ideas framed by their respective areas of expertise and knowledge with the common goal of developing a tool to facilitate listening for transformation. Nagy Hesse-Biber and Leavy (2008) contend, "interdisciplinary research provides an opportunity for researchers to think outside disciplinary boundaries" (p. 2). In our experience, we found that each of us contributed to the creation of the Protocol, while leveraging and adapting our disciplinary perspectives as we learned with and from one another (Nagy Hesse-Biber & Leary, 2008). In this way, we created a holistic and iterative journey where all team members were heard and respected, and through our collective and generative experience, co-inquiry, and reflections, the Protocol was developed and an idea for a research study emerged (Heron, 1992).

At its core, our theoretical framework for the Protocol is framed by transformative learning theory and our intentions to understand and situate listening as an essential element of transformative learning. At the edges, and informing the core, are the multiple disciplinary perspectives and our lived experiences as researchers and practitioners. When we started we were very pragmatic in our process. Each researcher informed the process and the Protocol from our respective perspectives. The dialogue around our own underlying theories followed because we made assumptions about theoretical foundations which necessitated conversations about how we all approach transformative learning and also listening. We offer as part of our theoretical discovery intersections that were previously invisible to us. We invite readers to contribute their disciplinary perspectives and experiences to this sensemaking journey of listening.

Through this process of discovery, we see that the development of the Protocol was informed, in particular, by holistic transformative learning, narrative/storytelling, listening, and third space theories. Transformative learning theory, attributed to Jack Mezirow (1990), involves a change in one's perception of the world, or a part of the world, from one frame of reference to a new one. It is the application of this new or different frame that facilitates meaning making. The Protocol is founded in an holistic embodied framing of transformative learning recognizing both the cognitive rational and extra rational, reflective, imaginative, emotional, and social aspects of learning (Cranton & Roy, 2003). We saw storytelling as a way for people to be present and connect with one another's mind, body, and spirit. Indeed, adult learning, in the context of storytelling, deepens and transforms (Tyler & Swartz, 2012); promotes holistic attention and connection to oneself and another (Taylor & Cranton, 2012) and, we suggest, helps us connect with one another and find new meaning (Heron, 1992; Jacobs & Heracleous, 2005; Kofman & Senge, 1993; Wheatley, 2002).

Heron (1992) offers storytelling as a linguistic kind of presentational knowledge, where the pattern of a good story symbolizes what the listener feels is significant and meaningful about the structure of the story of their own, someone else's, or anyone's life—what Boje describes as mutually gifting stories (2020). Engaging in storytelling, and more specifically listening, can facilitate the creation of a space for transformative learning; and therefore, listening is at the center of the Protocol. The Protocol has a strong dyadic component, where two people engage in reciprocal storytelling that is associated with intimacy. Listening and speaking qualities are reciprocated or intertwined at the dyadic level, but only listening quality, and not speaking quality, predicts intimacy and consequently willingness to help (Kluger et al., 2019). "Storytelling or hearing stories told places us on a threshold between two worlds: the world of our physical sense experience and the world of the story—this phenomenon of straddling two sets of consciousness is a liminal space" (Curteis, 2010, p. 7) what Bhabha (1994) calls third space. We further suggest that listening invites us to quiet our inner voices and noise so we may hear what others are sharing and hear how we receive and respond to their stories (Isaacs, 1999).

The Protocol includes time and questions to reflect on the storytelling process. As supported by Tyler and Swartz (2012), "Key to this process [of transformation] is the ability of the listeners and the teller to engage in post-telling conversations that explore the stories in ways that clarify, deepen, enlarge, expose new facets, and experiment with new meaning." (p. 465).

TRANSFORMATIVE LISTENING PROTOCOL

We offer the Protocol as a process to create a learning space for reciprocal storytelling where deep transformative listening becomes possible. As researchers, we are particularly interested in the kinds of experiences participants have when engaging with others in reciprocal storytelling. We are curious to discover how participants' existing practices of listening help, or inhibit, their abilities to cultivate meaningful connections; if and how participants gain a deeper appreciation for the other person in their learning contexts; and, finally, if and how using the Protocol influences the learning space by enhancing participants' connections, relationships, bridging cultural differences, and/or contributing to sensemaking ability.

In designing the Protocol (Table #24.1 below), we applied an emergent iterative prototype inquiry method (Bogers & Horst, 2014). To date, the emerging prototype of the Protocol has been tested in various settings and cultures by seven researchers, with feedback provided by users and researchers informing further modifications of both the Protocol and its implementation. Given our assertion of the importance of lived experience in the transformative listening process, and the narrative foundation upon which this project is built, it was believed that an iterative process would provide authentic opportunities to gain insight, make sense of, and understand the experiences of participants. We believe the ongoing, iterative process of creating, developing the Protocol in diverse settings with participants, and engaging with participant and researcher reflective feedback allows for a continuing evolution of the Protocol (Table 24.1).

Participants were recruited using convenience sampling at each site (adults 18 or over) who were students in investigators' classrooms,

24 LISTENING FOR TRANSFORMATION: DISCOVERING ... 435

Table 24.1 Accessible transformative listening protocol

Accessible Transformative Listening Protocol
This activity was designed by the Transformative Listening Project in conjunction with the 2018 International Transformative Learning Conference, "Building Transformative Community: Enacting Possibility in Today's Times." It is meant to improve appreciative listening skills through sharing and responding to stories in pairs and in groups
1. Before the Story: Storyteller and Listener(s)
a. Take a deep breath and relax
b. Be fully present to the story and your body's responses
c. Listen to the story without judgment
2. Instructions for the Listening Activity
a. The Storyteller: describe an experience of yours in three to five minutes:
1. What and whom did you see? Hear? Smell? Feel? Taste? Sense?
2. What happened?
3. How did you feel during the experience? After the experience?
4. What made this experience important to you?
b. The Appreciative Listener(s): listen deeply as if you are there:
1. What and whom do you see? Hear? Smell? Feel? Taste? Sense?
2. What do you perceive is happening?
3. What are you feeling? What do you perceive the storyteller is feeling? iv. If your mind wanders or you find yourself wanting to ask questions, refocus on the story
c. The Appreciative Listener(s): after the story, share in three to five minutes:
1. What particularly stands out for you in the story
2. If listening stirs up feelings or memories you have had in your own experiences
3. What you appreciate about their sharing
d. The Storyteller: listen to the listener(s):
1. Is/are the listener(s) understanding you well?
2. How are the listener(s)' feelings alike or different from yours?
3. What new feelings or meanings are emerging for you?
e. The storyteller: reflect on and share what you are feeling or learning in three to five minutes:
1. What did you feel or learn when you were in the story?
2. Are listener comments leading to new feelings? Insights? Questions?
3. What are your "take-aways"?
f. The Appreciative Listener(s): listen again to the storyteller and other listeners and share in three to five minutes:
1. Is listening to their reflections leading you to new feelings? Insights? Questions?
2. What are your "take-aways"?
g. All: Afterward, sharing new feelings, insights, stories:
1. You can dialogue, e.g., share similar stories
2. Another person may tell a different story
3. Share reflections on how this process has helped you to tell stories and listen more effectively
4. Thank each other for sharing and listening

students and/or professionals (i.e., faculty, trainers, coaches, and facilitators) convened for the purpose of testing the Protocol and/or professional development in workshops, classrooms, symposiums, and conferences with varying size groups of participants. All participants were volunteers. No one who attended was excluded; however, anyone could voluntarily choose to leave or opt out of sharing post-experience feedback.

Once participants were recruited, facilitating the Protocol followed a consistent process applied in all settings and contexts:

1. Participants were informed about the context and history of the Protocol development. Participants were invited to find and/or assigned a partner.
2. Participants were invited to take a deep breath, relax, and become fully present to the storyteller and story.
3. Dyad partners were instructed to listen to one another tell a story/or experience without using the Protocol.
4. The process of using the Protocol was explained.
5. Participants were instructed to take turns being a storyteller and listener working through the Protocol step by step.
6. After each storytelling, the story teller and listener reflected on their feelings, meaning making, and insights.
7. After both participants shared their stories, they were invited to reflect on their experiences of using the Protocol and the impact it had on their perspectives of listening and storytelling by engaging in a debrief dialogue and/or reflective writing.

In some settings, a small group of participants shared stories around a circle. Some debriefs took place at the group level after individuals had a chance to reflect. On average, it took 60–90 minutes to facilitate the use of and reflection on the experience of using the Protocol. The anecdotal data was aggregated across all research sites using the Protocol.

The word cloud in Fig. 24.1 is representative of the themes that emerged from the data. Preliminary data themes suggest that for participants using the Protocol a third space was created where transformative listening took place and participants felt they were better able to meet others where they were, hear them, and gain a deeper appreciation for who they were while also feeling validated and being heard themselves.

Fig. 24.1 Top 40 mentions

In Boje's (2012) quantum storytelling, there are simultaneous stories happening with infinite possibilities. We found this to be true in our experience of international storytelling and listening. While the dyads may not have been in the same room, their experience was similar and synergistic. They are all interconnected through their connection to the Transformative Listening Collaborative. For example, during a faculty development session, participants found sharing of stories and use of the Protocol allowed them to suspend judgment and create a generative space where new ideas and possibilities emerged through the give and take of stories. Connections were created and differences could be explored in such a way that allowed new insights and frames of references to emerge and transformation in thinking. For example, Brazilian graduate and doctoral students found their narratives reinforced that the Protocol helped them put themselves in the storyteller's shoes and created some helpful, reliable empathy. Furthermore, participants shared that a positive shift in their perspectives of listening resulted through participating in the exercises in which the Protocol was used.

DISCOVERING THIRD SPACE
FOR CONNECTION AND TRANSFORMATION

What we saw emerge from the data was a third space, rediscovery of what Bhabha (1994) describes in other contexts. Key to our discovery is that listening through storytelling in dyads creates a third space as a catalyst for connection and the potential for transformative learning. We find support for our discovery in the literature on listening, storytelling, third space, and transformation and see this as adding to existing literature on transformative learning.

The use of the Protocol for listening created a bridge to help meet across differences and was a vehicle through which participants began the process of understanding one another and learning from/with one another. A Brazilian graduate student shared: "I asked questions to understand and to check if my understanding was correct, which I might not do if I did not have a Protocol." An International graduate management student in Italy found "A good listener is able to listen with the eyes of another, this means that listening to another is to listen to her/his needs."

We acknowledge that the current dialogue in the literature discusses the physiological process of listening, or more precisely hearing, and study of communication, and listening's place (or lack thereof) in it, and the mechanics of what is deemed effective listening, are beyond the scope of this chapter. However, we learned through use of the Protocol that listening is embodied, relational, and intersubjective (Lipari, 2014), and is learned and largely informed by culture (Imhof & Janusik, 2006; Isaacs, 1999; Lipari, 2014; Purdy, 2000). The notion of culture has been identified by some as a "difficult term to define, as it has many accepted meanings" (Jarvis, 2006). According to Jarvis (2006), a simplified definition for culture might be, "the totality of knowledge, beliefs, values, attitudes and norms and mores of a social grouping" (p. 8). According to Bruner (2010), cultures emerge and maintain their respective structures and boundaries through narrative. Indeed, Bruner (2010) posits, "narrative is rather an all-purpose vehicle. It not only shapes our ways of communicating with each other and our ways of experiencing the world, but it also gives form to what we imagine, to our sense of what is possible" (p. 46). The reality of our current uncertain and rapidly changing context in our lives, and thus our cultures are "perpetually open to improvisation" (Bruner, 2010, p. 46).

Culture, through our narrative, illuminates "the ways we have learned to listen, to impose or apply meaning to the world, [and] are very much a function of our mental models, of what we hold in our minds as truths" (Isaacs, 1999, p. 84). Participants found there was a significant difference between how they listened the first time they shared a story with one another without the Protocol and when they shared a story using the steps of the Protocol. For example, at an Academy of Management conference in 2019, participants who were scholars from different countries, some of whom met for the first time during the conference, shared they "felt more connected to the process" of listening; "our group had very connected conversations;" "the first conversation was better than most in the Academy, but the second was a true connection;" "the Protocol experience was more emotional, open, and connected;" "More vulnerable in sharing, trust;" and "Tension turned into softness, resentment into acceptance." In another example, a management graduate student in Italy said, "In my opinion, everyone needs to be listened to before being a good listener."

Polkinghorne (1988) describes that through story, our identities and self-concepts are intertwined as part of a narrative whole, as we hear how our stories unfold and intersect in the developing story of others. Story listening (Tyler & Swartz, 2012) which is different from active listening, allows space for care, compassion, trust, and authentic exploration to emerge. In an unfolding transformative story experience, one person's response can validate, affirm, or reflect the other's and may depend importantly on locating ourselves with each other or within each other's story to sustain a mutually supportive interchange (Gergen et al., 2001). Engaging in storytelling, and more specifically listening, can play a key role in creating spaces and facilitating connection. Some participants experienced a feeling of profound connection and communion, even though many of the dyads met for the first time using the Protocol.

An Academy of Management participant in 2020 shared their use of the Protocol in reciprocal storytelling was "emotional, we bonded in a way I didn't know was possible in such a short period of time." Isaacs (1999) calls this "koinonia...it means 'impersonal fellowship'. In this state people connect very intimately with one another, but not intrusively" (p. 103). Not only do people connect in this state, the co-created listening space allows for storyteller and story listener to move beyond the boundaries of one another and together imagine new possibilities (Lipari, 2014). Participants shared that using the Protocol provided a space through which they could meet the other where they are, be focused on the moment and be fully engaged. As they shared in listening to one another: they were not judging the storyteller; could feel the emotions of the story/experience being shared; and felt empathy and learned something new. Participants who shared their stories felt heard, validated, and connected with the listener, and the listener seemed "with them." Graduate students from Italy found the Protocol served as a catalyst for them to share personal stories, they were thankful for having the space where they felt free to be open and self-disclosing with each other. The Protocol was an effective tool to enhance the quality of listening to the other and self-awareness about their emotions to the other's story. The notion of a third space through which one may meet and learn about the other, establish trust, connection, and co-create meaning was a common theme among the majority of participants in all contexts in which the Protocol was tested. For example, Brazilian graduate students shared "when the storyteller exchanged positions with the listener, they have already built a trusting relationship." We propose it is the third space, cultivated through listening, that opens the door for transformation to occur. In Bhabha's view, it is in third space where narrative interpretation and understanding of the other emerges. The third space allows for a blurring of boundaries where cultural meanings are resignified and reconstituted (Kramsch & Uryu, 2012). One might consider third space as both a noun and a verb. As a noun, third space is a container, a bridge, a location betwixt and between two or more people, cultures, and identities coming together through story (Bhabha, 1994). Further, it is a hybrid space that "displaces the histories that constitute it, and sets up new structures" (Bhabha, as cited in Rutherford, 1990, p. 211).

We suggest, if the third space emerges and resides through the narrative or storytelling domain, listening is a critical component and catalyst to co-creating a sustainable third space. As a verb, third space is active energy co-created through the intersubjective communication of two or more people, constituted around and through encounters through story. This space can be framed as a container of sorts (Isaacs, 1999) where it is possible for listening and receiving to occur. The body, mind, and emotions are all holistically involved to set the stage for intersections, connections, and creative transformation to emerge (Isaacs, 1999). Pery et al. (2020) suggest the shared space generated through interpersonal exchanges holds the potential for those participating in these conversations to cultivate connections, co-create new meaning, and make discoveries about self and another. The context and the quality of listening create the energy in which the telling and listening of stories generates new understanding and insights not previously available (Tyler & Swartz, 2012). Participants shared they: came to understand the other person's perspective better, opening their hearts, minds, and thoughts to something different; bonded in a way they didn't know was possible; experienced a deeper level of connection, and felt emotional, open, and connected.

When considering the identities of two people engaged in conversation or storytelling, one might suggest that each person's identity may be viewed as being in a constant state of flux and flow, and informed by their encounters in third space with others (Bhabha, 1994). Our identities and our ways of viewing the world are transformed—shifting and changing through those intersecting moments as we listen. Connection does not arise just because of speaking, but because of listening. We become one when we listen together (Isaacs, 1999; Lipari, 2010).

Further Listening…future Implications

Seeking to understand something new or different requires one to suspend what is already understood—to reach out into the precipice of the unknown, be uncomfortable and release what is familiar (Lipari, 2014). As a group of scholars and practitioners, we continue to suspend our assumptions, be open to a diversity of views, and sit within the discomfort of not knowing. We offer this chapter as an opportunity for the reader to potentially be uncomfortable and release what is familiar by continuing to further explore transformative learning in their own contexts of storytelling, listening, and third space We encourage readers to continue to evolve the story with us and engage in the iterative development and research on the Protocol, and listening as a re-emerging force into transformative discovery and learning.

During this time of significant individual and global evolution, the importance of the goal of transformative education to create opportunities for people to become change agents across intersections of race, class, gender, ethnicity as well as cultural, national, generational, functional, or disciplinary boundaries cannot be overstated. Listening engages the whole person and provides opportunities for individual transformation where individual change may lead to community change and then to social change. We propose the following implications, questions, and possible areas for further exploration as catalysts for researchers and practitioners as they continue their quests to generate new understandings, facilitate empathy, understanding, connection, purpose and meaning, equity and justice, and hope for a better world.

In what ways might transformative listening through storytelling in dyads, and more specifically the Protocol, facilitate spaces in which transformative learning might occur? We invite dyads to practice embodied listening through the use of the Protocol to help create the conditions for connection across differences and development of a deeper understanding of self and others. In addition, dyads may learn to appreciate the complexity of the simple act of listening and to value listening as an everyday practice that can be developed. We offer the Protocol with the hopes of awakening an awareness of our interconnections and shared humanity.

How might developing authentic connections within dyads enhance listening, learning, and potential for transformation? How might further interdisciplinary collaborations drawing from diverse disciplines and cultures provide opportunities for new and unique perspectives for transformative listening and learning? We invite colleagues to lean in, listen, and further explore the role of listening for transformation. Nagy Hessey-Biber and Leavy (2008) eloquently share:

> neither the paradigm shifts nor the turn to interdisciplinary within academia have occurred in a vacuum. Rather social and political forces have shaped both the social world and our methods for learning about it. Entirely new paradigms have emerged as a result of the changing social world: examples include feminism, multiculturalism, queer studies, critical race theory, and third world perspectives. (p. 4)

Might there be an opportunity to engage with current political forces and bring listening out from the margins and create a space for transformative listening as a paradigm within the auspices of transformative learning theory?

Might we imagine listening and reciprocal storytelling anew, as a re-emerging force for holistic transformation, that holds the potential to transform a person's worldview through listening in dyads using the Transformative Listening Protocol? We encourage expansion of the concept of listening in dyads as a third space to foster the potential for transformation, as well as further exploration of the role of storytelling and listening in holistic transformative learning. Our chapter endeavors to expand the conversation on transformative learning by focusing on listening as an essential third space to transformation.

REFERENCES

Bhabha, H. K. (1994). In H. K. Bhabha (Ed.), *The location of culture*. Routledge.

Bogers, M., & Horst, W. (2014). Collaborative prototyping: Cross-fertilization of knowledge in prototype-driven problem solving. *Journal of Product Innovation Management, 31*(4), 744–764. https://doi.org/10.1111/jpim.12121

Boje, D. (2012). Reflections: What does quantum physics of storytelling mean for change management? *Journal of Change Management, 12*(3), 253–271.

Boje, D. (2020, December). Spirit & Storytelling. In S. Waddock (Facilitator), *Intellectual Shaman Conversation*. Series conducted by the International Humanistic Management Association.

Bruner, J. (2010). Narrative, culture and mind. In A. Nylund, D. Schiffrin, A. De Fina (Eds.), *Telling stories: Language, narrative, and social life* (pp. 45–50). United States: Georgetown University Press.

Cranton, P., & Roy, M. (2003). When the bottom falls out of the bucket: Toward a holistic perspective on transformational learning. *Journal of Transformative Education, 1*(2), 86–98.

Curteis, I. (2010). Storytelling: The hindrance of holding a raw egg—Storytelling and the liminal space. *Local-Global: Identity, Security, Community, 7*, 150–162. https://search.informit.com.au/documentSummary;dn=582430397202836;res=IELHSS

Gergen, K, J., McNamee, S., & Barrett, F. (2001). Toward transformative dialogue. *International Journal Of Public Administration, 21*(7–8), 697–707.

Heron, J. (1992). *Feeling and personhood: Psychology in another key*. Sage.

Imhof, M., & Janusik, L. A. (2006). Development and validation of the Imhof-Janusik listening concepts inventory to measure listening conceptualization differences between cultures. *Journal of Intercultural Communication, 35*(2), 79–98.

Isaacs, W. (1999). *Dialogue and the art of thinking together.* Currency and Doubleday.

Jacobs, C., & Coghlan, D. (2005). Sound from silence: On listening in organizational learning. *Human Relations, 58*(1), 115–138.

Jacobs, C., & Heracleous, L. (2005). Answers for questions to come: Reflective dialogue as an enabler of strategic innovation. *Journal of Organizational Change Management, 18*(4), 338–352. https://doi.org/10.1108/095348 10510607047

Jarvis, P. (2006). *Towards a comprehensive theory of human learning: Lifelong learning and the learning society (vol 1).* Routledge.

Joshi, A., & Knight, A. P. (2014). Who defers to whom and why? Dual pathways linking demographic differences and dyadic deference to team effectiveness. *Academy of Management Journal, 58*(1), 59–84. https://doi.org/10.5465/AMJ.2013.0718

Kluger, A. N., Elfenbein, H. A., Campagna, R. L., Eiskenkraft, N., Lehmann, M., Pery, S., Dirks, K. T., Hekman, D. R., & Malloy, T. E. (2019). Dyadic-level analyses in organizational behavior: The utility of the social relations model. *Proceedings of the Academy of Management Annual Meeting, Boston, MA, 2019*(1), 1.

Kofman, F., & Senge, P. (1993). Communities of commitment: The heart of learning organizations. *Organizational Dynamics, 22*(2), 5–23. http://dx.doi.org.ezproxy.lib.ucalgary.ca/10.1016/0090-2616(93)90050-B

Kramsch, C., & Uryu, M. (2012). Intercultural contact, hybridity, and third space. In J. Jackson (Ed.), *The Routledge handbook of language and intercultural communication.* Routledge.

Lipari, L. (2010). Listening, thinking, being. *Communication Theory, 20*(3), 348–362. https://doi.org/10.1111/j.1468-2885.2010.01366.x

Lipari, L. (2014). (Ed.). *Listening, thinking, being: Toward an ethic of attunement.* The Pennsylvania State University Press.

Mezirow, J. (1990). *Fostering critical reflection in adulthood: A guide to transformative and emancipatory learning.* Jossey-Bass.

Nagy Hesse-Biber, A., & Leavy, P. (2008). In A. Nagy Hesse-Biber & P. Leavy (Eds.), *Handbook of emergent methods.* Sage.

Pery, S., Doytch, G., & Kluger, A. N. (2020). Management and Leadership. In D. L. Worthington & G. D. Bodie (Eds.), *The Handbook of Listening* (pp. 163–180). Wiley & Sons. https://www.wiley.com/en-us/exportProduct/pdf/9781119554141

Polkinghorne, D. E. (1988). *Narrative knowing and the human sciences.* State University of New York Press.

Purdy, M. W. (2000). Listening, culture and structures of consciousness: Ways of studying listening. *International Journal of Listening, 14*(1), 47–68.

Rutherford, J. (1990). *Identity: Community, culture, difference*. Lawrence & Wishart. https://muse.jhu.edu/book/34784

Schwab, K. (2016). *The fourth industrial revolution*. World Economic Forum.

Taylor, E. W., & Cranton, P. (2012). *The handbook of transformative learning: Theory, research, and practice*. John Wiley & Sons.

Tyler, J. A., & Swartz, A. L. (2012). Storytelling and Transformative Listening. In E. W. Taylor & P. Cranton (Eds.), *The handbook of transformative learning: Theory, research, and practice*. Jossey Bass.

Wheatley. M. (2002). *Turning to one another: Simple conversations to restore hope to the future*. Berrett-Koehler.

CHAPTER 25

Curating the Imagination: Perspective Transformations and the Feminist Exhibition

Darlene E. Clover

INTRODUCTION

History knocked on your door, did you answer?
—Klein, 2014, p. 466.

Hoggan et al (2017) remind us of the strong "connection and inter-action between one's past, present and future" (p. 50). Central to connection and inter-action is how we story and represent the past and the present, and their implications for how people will see, know, and act in the future. When there exist major omissions, distortions, stereo-types, or misrepresentations in our narratives and visualizations, people can both consciously and unconsciously assimilate these as truths about society, others, and even themselves even when their experiences tell them otherwise. Stating this more pedagogically, "people will see what they are

D. E. Clover (✉)
University of Victoria, Victoria, Canada
e-mail: clover@uvic.ca

© The Author(s), under exclusive license to Springer Nature   447
Switzerland AG 2022
A. Nicolaides et al. (eds.), *The Palgrave Handbook of Learning for Transformation*, https://doi.org/10.1007/978-3-030-84694-7_25

being taught to see and remain blind to what they are being taught to ignore" (Cramer et al., 2018, p. 2).

For feminists such as Cramer et al. (2018), our stories and representations are always about power and particularly, the power to see, to hear, and to know. Who gets to be seen and who is "hidden from view" (p. 1)? Who gets to represent and imagine their experiences and ways of knowing, and who has these storied and presented for them? Criado-Perez (2019) argues that for the most part, what is produced, shown, and told about the "past, present and even the future has been marked—disfigured—by a female-shaped absent presence" (p. xi). This absent presence operates as a hidden curriculum to instill problematic gendered perceptions of men as knowers who perform actively, deeply, and intentionally on the world, and women as underdeveloped, shallow, passive *mise-en-scène*. These perceptions, whether conscious or otherwise, shore up a hierarchal binary matrix of masculinity and femininity that has profound epistemic and agential implications for women in all their diversity. We continue to perceive in adult education classrooms low levels of self-esteem and confidence, unhealthy obsessions with beauty and body image, an absence of historical memory and gender awareness, a restrictive sense of future possibility, and a distaste for or misunderstanding of the feminist political project of disruption and social transformation (e.g., Bierema, 2003; Clover et al., 2015).

As a feminist and arts-based adult educator, my strategy is to design pedagogical approaches that take up the power of stories and representations to bring about what Mezirow (1991) called perspective transformation(s). Central to perspective transformation is for me, the imagination and its power to disrupt normative gendered lines of sight thereby stimulating a critical-creative consciousness of seeing beyond what we are being taught, made, and allowed to see and to know about women.

In this chapter, I focus on a space of feminist transformative learning through the imagination, specifically, a multi-media, feminist research exhibition entitled *Disobedient Women: Defiance, Resilience and Creativity Past and Present* (Disobedient Women). The aim of curating this exhibition was to showcase women's diverse aesthetic and activist methods in the past and the present with the intent of expanding perspectives and understandings and encouraging action.

I begin my chapter with a discussion of the exhibition's impetus—the disorientating dilemmas—that brought about its existence. I then outline its theoretical and pedagogical foundations and civic engagement strategies. To bring the exhibition to life I highlight some of its stories and images before turning to some of the key outward transformative learnings shared by visitors through onsite comments cards. I also include a brief discussion of inward transformations in the form of my own perspective transformations through the act of curating Disobedient Women. Transformations occurred through memories, meaning making, new cross-cultural connection, feelings of hope, and the aesthetic inspiration to act. But the exhibition was also an uncomfortable awakening, a disruption to assumptions, and an impetus for critical self and social reflection. A central transformative learning component of a feminist exhibition is the imagination and its ability to comfort and connect, mobilize and enliven, and disrupt and awaken in the interests of gender justice and change.

Disorientating Dilemmas

Mezirow's (1991) theory of transformative learning revolves around the idea of the disorienting dilemma. For some, this is a moment of clarity, a sudden, realization, an "ah-ha" moment that changes one's perception of an issue, a situation, and so forth. Transformative learning is also taken up as a developmental process of questioning, revising, and validating perspectives in light of new information or experiences gained over time (e.g., Formenti & West, 2018; Hoggan et al., 2017; Scott, 1998; Taylor & Cranton, 2017).

Disobedient Women was a coming together of these two transformations. In 2008, I turned my research attention to the adult education strategies of museums and art galleries, placing an emphasis on their aesthetics, particularly, the stories and images of their displays and exhibitions. As my study progressed, I began to realize that few stories or images were "about me." Like many other visitors, and despite my deep feminist consciousness, I had simply taken for granted that what museum exhibitions told and showed me would be the truth, and that it would include all of humanity. I failed to see what was hiding in plain sight, namely a series of narratives and representations riddled with female omissions, misrepresentations, and stereotypes. As feminist and transformative learning scholars remind us, we are never free of the assumptions instilled through what Code (2003) calls the powerful patriarchal "epistemologies of mastery" that visualize and story the world in their own interests.

The startling moment, however, that propelled me into action was a narrative I heard on public radio upon my return to Canada from study leave in 2017. The Tory government was in the process of encouraging large- and small-scale celebrations to commemorate the creation of the nation in the upcoming Sesquicentenary of Canadian Federation. The announcer asked a key government representative to identity the most memorable moments in Canadian history. He began to unfurl a tale of masculine exceptionalism and heroism of discovery, cultural and epistemic conquest, righteous war, and ice hockey. Dumbfounded by the narrowness and deeply sexist and colonial subtexts of this narrative, not to mention its intersections with my exhibition study findings, I immediately called together a group of feminist and Indigenous professors, museum and art gallery educators and curators, artists, and graduate students to explore what we could do to interrupt this masculine narrative with a feminist tale. That tale became Disobedient Women exhibition.

THE EXHIBITION FOUNDATIONS

In her overview entitled *Transformation Theory in Adult Education in Canada*, Scott (1998, p. 179) argued that in order for our practices to be truly transformational we needed to ground them theoretically.

We grounded Disobedient Women firstly in feminist theory, understood as a means to fundamentally transform the world for all women (and men) who suffer the indignity, devaluation, oppression, and marginalization of the masculine gaze and its epistemologies of mastery that govern how we will know and see the world, each other and even, ourselves. We took to heart Ahmed's (2017) assertion that feminism "does not mean adopting a set of ideals or norms of conduct" (p. 1). Woman is not a stable category but a combination of intersectionalities of race, class, geography, sexuality, and so forth. Being complex and diverse, women will experience and respond to patriarchy and oppression differently, and so the stories we to tell need to be equally broad and representative of diversity. At the same time, it is critical to attend to similarities or what unites because gender injustice exists across the planet as a powerful force with many consequences including our own complicity as women in the smooth functioning of the epistemic and ideological agenda of patriarchal supremacy (e.g., Bierema, 2003; Criado-Perez, 2019; Clover et al., 2015).

A second theoretical grounding was the aesthetic imagination. The creation of the imagination, Haiven and Khashnabish (2014) remind us, "is an active process, not a steady state" (p. 7). The role of the aesthetic imagination is powerful when it works "to awaken, to disclose the ordinarily unseen, unheard and unexpected" (Greene, 1995, p. 28). Arts-based educators cultivate imaginary spaces so that "people can [find] a space for themselves ... form a presence" (p. 28) but equally, as Greene (2000, p. 21) reminds us, to break through the "inertia of habit" and challenge the taken-for-granted assumptions that limit our perspectives and our lives. For this reason, Mohanty (2012) speaks to the imagination as "the most subversive thing a pubic can have" (p. vii).

Feminist transformative learning was another framework, and for this, we chose to use a feminist exhibition. Benjamin (2014) refers to exhibitions as "plays of force" because they are designed specifically and intentionally to influence the public's perspectives on their particular topic or subject (p. 14). In other words, exhibitions do not simply mirror the world; they actively construct perspectives and ways of seeing and knowing. Exhibitions work because they are storytellers. A feminist exhibition is a storyteller that situates women's knowing and lives in the context of gendered social dynamics where they would have otherwise gone unnoticed. Women's knowing through exhibitions is storied nondiscursively (visual arts, objects, and images) and/or discursively (poetry, labels, texts). Feminists exhibitions are also a form of creative nonfiction that have the power to encourage new insights, heighten visitors' consciousness, and, potentially, encourage a sense of agency to engage with and in feminist struggle (Bartlett, 2016).

Another transformative element of large-scale feminist exhibitions is the power of immersion. Immersion is an experiential learning process which is both cognitive and emotional. By immersing, visitors in their creative nonfiction feminist exhibitions supply new information and encourage emotions and feelings. Immersion can produce feelings of safety and comfort, making one want to linger and learn; immersion can also cause discomfort when it brings us face to face with things that disrupt our confident status quo thinking.

ENACTING CIVIC ENGAGEMENT

> History that comes not from the lofty perspective of 'great men' is always difficult to perceive. Its protagonists are rarely documented; theirs is all too frequently the untold story...To term 'disobey' here is a byword for women's creative spirits.
> —Excerpt, Curatorial Statement

Civic engagement is, for many scholars, a central activity and goal of transformative learning (e.g., Formenti & West, 2018; Taylor & Cranton, 2017). For feminist adult educators, civic engagement centers on encouraging women to participate in the public sphere by becoming actors, makers, and shapers in a diversity of ways (e.g., Clover et al., 2015; English & Irving, 2015).

Our first civic engagement strategy was to create and disseminate widely a Call for Items through social media and to friends, colleagues, and organizations. An excerpt from the call reads:

We want to share the work of women (including hetero, lesbian, trans, non-binary, and two-spirited) who are outspoken activists, and have used things such as placards, quilts, pamphlets puppets, banners, posters, pins, vamps, masks, t-shirts, buttons, videos, drums, costumes, hats, and all other manner of artistic, creative, and/or interventionist arts. We also want to share the work of women (and organizations) who have made contributions to society beyond more normative practices of activism. These women have made bannock, drawn pictures, created photomontages, altered books, developed zines, sewed costumes, knitted sweaters, written poetry, made music, quilted, and undertaken many other activities aimed to maintain culture and peace, create community, speak out, and make change.

As noted in this excerpt, we wanted the participation of a diversity of women, and to showcase diverse activisms and creativities as together, they sketch the broadest picture of women's contributions to Canadian society over time.

Our second method of civic engagement was to commission artists (the present). From my own student and Maltwood Gallery connections we, selected seven activist-artists to create pieces for the exhibition around the theme of "disobedience." We chose disobedience deliberately, based on Bachelard's idea that "to disobey in order to take action is the byword of all creative spirits [and] the spark behind all knowledge" (cited in Flood & Grindon, 2015, p. 7). The works submitted as by-products and representations of disobedience ranged from paintings to videos, installations to puppets, protest buttons to posters. Building on this, we asked donors and artists to compose their own labels or descriptors. There were two reasons for this. The first is Cixous's (1976) argument that a woman must have the opportunity "to put herself into the text— as into the world and into history—by her own movement" (p. 875). Secondly, Marshment (1993) reminds us that until women represent themselves, "they will be subject to the definitions ... of others" (p. 23). We wanted these women to speak to their artworks or share their stories as they wanted them, and not as we the curators might story them.

A third civic engagement strategy was to identify some historical materials (the past). Archivists and librarians at the University of Victoria and the Royal British Columbia Museum were contacted for stories and images of women in their collections and they took up the task with enthusiasm, unearthing objects, newsletters, quilts, photos, and more. Donors, however, also augmented our historical work by lending us stories of courageous and daring women who are not likely to be found in the archives or at least not in disobedient form. For example, one PhD student submitted an image of her Nan, Anne "Nan" McKay. Nan was significant because she graduated in 1915 as the "first Metis woman" (exhibition label) to graduate from the University of Saskatchewan, and is much lauded and remembered for this. However, the chosen image for Nan shows her in a canoe with a female companion, proudly kissing that woman and illustrating her frank rejection of the gendered norms of the time. For this, she is neither lauded nor remembered in the university archives, we are told.

Our fourth practice of community engagement was to interview women in the community to get their stories and showcase their practices or works of art. Two examples are a local physician who had been for decades active in the anti-nuclear movement, and an Indigenous Elder who keeps her culture alive by knitting traditional sweaters and teaching the practice to youth. This also demonstrates our commitment to viewing feminism and activism broadly.

Another practice of civic engagement was a vertical clothesline (see Fig. 25.1) we created for visitors to pin up completed, onsite comment cards. This practice responds to Perry's (2012, p. 27) call for curatorial "strategies that facilitate active visitor participation" and Weiser's (2017)

Fig. 25.1 Clothesline

belief that exhibition stories become more meaningful to visitors when their ideas are slotted in to expand and build the story.

Finally, we curated the exhibition in two different locations. The exhibition began in a free municipal art gallery in central Victoria where it remained for three weeks in September. This location provided access for a diverse audience, including homeless and street involved people and tourists. The exhibition then moved to the University of Victoria Maltwood Legacy Gallery. The many on-campus students, faculty, alumnae, and visitors had access to the exhibition as the space was open and free to all. The exhibition was to remain from October 15 to December 15 at the Maltwood but it was held over to January 15 due to its popularity.

Stories and Narratives of Disobedient Women

As noted, the stories and images of the exhibition bring together the present with the past. Historical learning spaces are important, as Giroux

(2004, p. 68) reminded us, because they are "not about constructing a linear narrative but about blasting history open, rupturing its silences … [with] the legacy of the often unrepresentable or misrepresented." Feminist Hemmings (2011, p. 16) adds that "shuttle[ing] back and forth between the past and present" is in fact an excellent strategy to encourage a future that has yet to be imagined.

Although the exhibition was not in any chronological order, I begin with some historical pieces. In the archives, we identified photographs of the First Chinese Women's Auxiliary, circa 1900, and the story of Rosemary Brown, the first Black woman in the BC government. Despite this, her story is all but excluded from the provincial museum. We also unearthed copies of *Zenith Digest,* a newsletter edited by Trans-woman Stephanie Castle. Showcasing this newsletter was especially important because it illustrated that feminists had been focusing on trans issues since the 1960s (Fig. 25.2).

From diverse women contributors, we received many different types of items. One was a photographic collage commemorating International Women's Day. We also received numerous newspaper clippings of women enacting various forms of civil disobedience, including being arrested. Figure 25.3 below shows Qwetminak, a grassroots Lil'wat leader who was arrested and later convicted for criminal contempt of court for blocking the road to logging trucks attempting to enter without permission her nation's unceded territory. Her story tells us this was the first time in her otherwise law-abiding life that she had chosen to act out and speak out in the public sphere.

A feminist lawyer traveled by ferry from Vancouver to lend us bins of her life-long collection of phonographic records, protest tee-shirts, and feminist magazines, books, and posters. A graduate student-artist working on the project curated the materials in a diorama of a budding feminist's bedroom (see Fig. 25.4) based on this descriptor label by the donor:

Our formative years have a great influence on the music we listen to, the art we are drawn to, and how we choose to dress. For me, it was those years when I became a feminist, acutely aware of the injustices in the world around me. My bedroom became an extension of myself, and the ideas I was beginning to form as a young woman. I spent many hours reading, listening to music, and adorning my walls with posters, photos, and art. I read.

There were three other types of installations. One was the West Coast League of Lady Wrestlers, a group of diverse women who dress

Fig. 25.2 Image from Zenith Digest

in costume and wrestle with gender, social, and ecological issues (see Fig. 25.5). Another was dedicated to the Raging Grannies, a courageous group of older women who endeavor to raise awareness about diverse social justices through protests, direct action, and satirical songs. Materials ranged from a life size cut-out of a granny complete with feather boa, to books they had written, to the comical lyrics of songs they had produced. The installation also included a photograph of two grannies

25 CURATING THE IMAGINATION ... 457

Fig. 25.3 Qwetminak on her Knees

Fig. 25.4 Bedroom Installation

heading naked into a freezing lake to protest water pollution. The final installation was a bedside table loaded with bricks and dust as a metaphor of domesticity.

A number of artists submitted artworks created in the past but which they felt responded to the topic of disobedience. One was a photographic series by a group of Sikh feminists. Called *(Mis)Interpretation: Sikh Feminisms in Representation, Texts and Lived Realities*, this series aimed to decenter the notion of a normatively androcentric faith and visually introduce Sikh feminist thought and understanding. A second was a series of painting of Feminist Ravens (see Fig. 25.6) from Indigenous artist and law professor, Val Napoleon. The ravens are "tricksters," unconventional figures who

> teach us by being a troublemaker and by upsetting the log jams of unquestioned assumptions. She can also teach us with love, patience, and a wicked

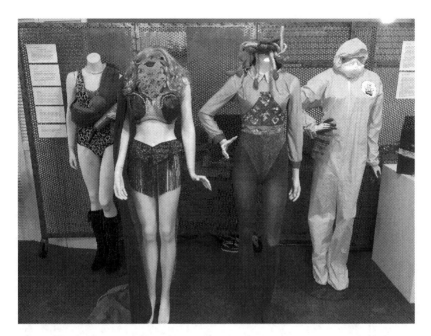

Fig. 25.5 We Stage the Battle for Injustice

sense of humour. She can create spaces for conversations and questions – that is her job as a trickster and as a feminist so that nothing is taken for granted and all interpretations are laid bare. (from the label)

To design the exhibition, we used the strategy of juxtaposition to make correlations, as noted above, between past and present. One object from the archives was piece of cloth containing a variety of protest buttons from a woman's organization active from the 1960s to the late 1990s. We juxtaposed this with a series of recent protest buttons made by a young artist-activist. While some of the issues had changed—child care and the pay gap were more prevalent in the past—the issues on both sets were eerily similar, illustrating visually, just why, as one visitor noted on a comment card, "the work for change just has to continue. We just have to keep at it."

Fig. 25.6 Chief Justice Kokum (Grandmother) Raven

The exhibition also contained three videos. One was a story about women told through slam poetry, another an animated illustration of defiance, and a third, a recording of panels from a conference on women, leadership and power. We were given two sets of hand puppets. One showcased global women leaders such as Wangari Maathai of the Greenbelt Movement, while the other was composed of female creatures from mythology.

Other items included activist quilts containing issues ranging from sexual exploitation to body image, and two brightly painted hard hats that accompanied a story entitled *Hammering in a Man's World* by a woman who had worked in the "masculine trades" for many years. The exhibition also included a book of poetry by Jill Carter, a woman who had found herself living on the streets but transformed herself into a passionate, creative, and committed advocate for women.

Outwardly: Perspective Transformations and the Visitors

> I am leaving here just so inspired [with] new energy. I will never forget what you have done for me.
> —Onsite comment

Three hundred and twenty-two visitors completed the onsite comment cards and placed them on the clothesline. In this section, I focus on comments that illustrate diverse perspective transformations and ideas for future actions.

For many visitors, Disobedient Women was a trip down memory lane, or as one comment stated,

> like being welcomed back to my past life." However, for others there was a transformation in how they now saw their historical selves, as illustrated in this comment: "I learned that I am part of herstory ... of this story ... I was a pioneer by establishing the first sexual assault center in Canada! I never saw myself like that before.

For other visitors, the exhibition offered a new meaning perspective on culture. For example, a self-identified Indigenous woman acknowledged that "few exhibitions have prompted me to alter my connection to my own culture." She went on to say that "as an Indigenous woman disconnected from my culture, it was particularly meaningful to see elements here that spoke to female's Indigenous strengths—sort of promising that I could become part of that too." This new vision and story of the past allowed her to imagine a possible future.

As we had hoped, many bridges were built by visitors between past and present, often spoken to as a new way of seeing: "I see now that we have both come a long way but not far enough. Continue the struggle!" This sentiment was similarly echoed in French: "*Plus ça change, plus c'est la même chose. La lutte pour l'égalité continue!*"[1] Another example of perspective transformation came from a woman who had spent time with the protest buttons displays. Her remark to me when I asked her what

---

[1] The more things change, the more they stay the same.

462   D. E. CLOVER

she was seeing was, "I never would have believed it. I thought equality was pretty much fixed. Geez."

There were many examples of transformative learning around the idea of activism. One visitor admitted to equating the term activism "with violence or that you are against something and you were angry." She stated, however, that Disobedient Women had "opened my eyes to why women act in public and the need for this." Her understandings were transformed as she realized as a result of the exhibition that women "do it to get things done. They do it because it is needed. They do it to change history." For another visitor, "this exhibition showed me how speaking out and choosing not to follow the rules can be liberating."

The second major transformation in understandings was around feminism. As an adult educator, and like many other feminists, I am very accustomed to, but also very weary of, hearing young women tell me that feminism is only about White women, is an outdated term, or is about man hating bitterness. You can imagine the elation when we came across comments such as, "I see now that many different women exist under 'feminism'. That is not what I had heard." Other comments drew attention to feminisms' creative and playful sides as well as political inventiveness. As one visitor wrote, "I learned that it [feminism] is fun and creative, inclusive and fierce and has a long legacy." Another comment from a young man registered astonishment at

> the amount of humour. I never thought of feminism like that. But the look on that woman's face as she was being hauled away by the cops, and the crazy quilts and those ravens, well this is just fun. Don't get me wrong this is serious stuff but it's pretty amazing don't you think?

What we see in these comments is Disobedient Women's ability to respond to Gregoricic's (2020) assertion that transformative learning is a process through which an individual enlarges "an existing frame of reference, learning a new frame of reference, transforming points of view and transforming habits of mind" (p. 181).

While the literature of transformative learning does not speak so much to hope, Paulo Freire (2014) argued passionately that in order to fundamental change the world adult educators needed to take seriously the power of instilling hope. For feminists, critical hope plays a key role in women being able to imagine and then fight for a different world (Clover et al., 2015). There were many instances of hope being generated throughout the comments such as: "This exhibition gives me hope and strength. It is amazing to see these 'bad-ass' women"; "I wasn't prepared for the hope I would find here ... for the future." Linked to this was the transformation of aesthetic agency. For example, as one visitor wrote, "Art has such political power. I never thought about my art together with politics. I can do this with my own art." In reference to the West Coast League of Lady Wrestlers, a woman student explained: "This is what struck me most. I am taking drama so I am thinking WOW, I can use my theatre skills to change the world!" What I see here is Hoggan et al., and and's (2017, p. 52) assertion that in transformative learning "the end of one change process"—in this case the end of her viewing the installation—"is often a stimulus for something new."

Inwardly: Perspective Transformations and the Curator

I learned, or perhaps even better said, felt many things during the time of Disobedient Women. In this section, I speak to two of the most poignant.

I was not a curator when I began this venture. My assumption in working with two galleries was that I would collect the content for the exhibition and they, the real curators, would, well, curate it. I was quickly disabused of this notion. What I came to realize is curators have the story in their head, and therefore, they must be the ones to tell the story. The "real" curators hang the quilts and paintings and even offer editorial suggestions, but they do not imagine the narrative into being because they do not know the story, so they cannot tell the tale. I also learned that curating the exhibition is not just about storytelling. There is an extraordinary amount of mathematics involved as you fit things into the limitations of cabinets or wall spaces. However, as I learned how to curate, as the images and stories in fact showed me what I needed to do, it was transformational. I was not a curator, but I identify as one now.

I actually cried the day we took the exhibition down. I had not realized the incredible sense of accomplishment it had given, nor how much I have invested in this project. I had spent hours with Disobedient Women, savoring its stories and images and talking with visitors. As it was coming down, and I experienced a very different disorientating dilemma. As a curator, however, I now accept that exhibitions such as this are ephemeral. They are something to be feasted upon in the moment, but they are not destined to last. I carry the exhibition in my heart but also, in the form of a zine which the students created for me.

Challenges

Although far fewer than I expected, there were some interesting and insightful challenges. One was working with municipal officials at the city center gallery. I had met with two female officials who were excited by the project and particularly, its feminist theme which one called "exciting and timely." They assured me of funding and other types of support. Although neither funding nor support materialized mere days before curation a memo did, stating "there can be no swearing, nudity or anything that is not family friendly and that includes feminism and its bias against men." This is a very deeply ingrained and problematic stereotype, what Mezirow (1991) would call a "psycho-cultural assumption [that is] untrue and inadequate and therefore in need of revision" (p. 6).

Linked to this were concerns expressed about men. One visitor queried if "a man visiting this exhibition would feel safe?" Many men did of course visit the exhibition and the question of safety is important. This also disregards the fact that literally thousands of exhibitions exclude women. But this does remind us, as Hoggan et al. (2017) argue, that we must stay "critically aware and explicit about the costs and consequences involved for leaners we aim to transform" (p. 53) and therefore, there can be pushback. As feminist adult educators suggest we must therefore strive to create safe and comfortable learning environments (e.g., English & Irving, 2015). However, the fundamental transformations required for gender justice call for practices of discomfort, for spaces that take people outside their comfort zones (Hoggan, et al., 2017; Mezirow, 1991). I believe the imaginative and immersive power of Disobedient Women walked this dynamic tension of comfort (memory, connection) on the one hand and the uncomfortable on other (realizing one's own perceptive limitations).

The third challenge was to the term "disobedient." One visitor argued, "The naming of women as 'disobedient' is undermining the whole initiative. 'Disobedient' is a word that casts shame and guilt. Difference should not be equated with disobedient." As Best (2016) reminds us, feminist exhibitions can be read as re-inscriptions of marginalization and victimhood. The second comment aligned the term with children: "An effective exhibition **BUT**! disobedient to whom? Like children?" And yet, as alluded to above, the *Oxford Dictionary* defines disobedience as "failure or refusal to obey rules or someone in authority" and notes that "disobedience to law is sometimes justified." It was this disobedience we chose to represent in the exhibition. However, the lesson is that words are never understood as simply neutral, their meanings are caught up and conditioned by our cultures, our pasts, and our lives.

FINAL THOUGHTS

We see things as we do because of what we expect them to look like. The expected is shaped by the stories and images of the past and the present, and these in turn condition what we will expect to see into the future. If our representations continue to show and tell a tale of women's subordination, as is still very much the case, they will have implications for women's "life dreams and what they believe they can achieve" (Bierema, 2003, p. 4). How do we re-imagine and re-represent women's lives in ways that are transformative, that challenge the taken for granted of a patriarchal norm? More specifically and returning to the quotation above by Klein, how, when a limiting narrative of history aimed to maintain the status quo knocks, do we answer?

We answered with the Disobedient Women exhibition. We did so because we believed that feminist exhibitions have the pedagogical ability to transform by opening up and challenging perspectives through creative nonfiction, presentational knowing, and the imagination. When we imagine into presentational form that which is not expected and therefore, unperceived, we challenge ourselves to see and to think differently, to make connections where none existed before, to feel a sense of hope and agency or even, discomfort. Feminist exhibitions such as Disobedient Women shape perspectives by interrupting normative patriarchal lines of sight and story lines. These interruptions unleash the imagination as an act of rebellion, resistance, and "the capacity to think critically, reflexively and innovatively" (Haiven & Khasnabish, 2014, p. 2). When we interrupt, we open up opportunities to change, to transform, and most importantly, to imagine the possible.

REFERENCES

Ahmed, S. (2017). *Living a feminist life*. Duke University Press.

466   D. E. CLOVER

Benjamin, W. (2014). The work of art in the age of its technological reproducibility. In L. Steeds (Ed.), *Exhibition* (pp. 26–35). Whitechapel Gallery.

Bartlett, A. (2016). Sites of feminist activism. Remembering Pine Gap. *Continuum: Journal of Media and Cultural Studies, 30*(3), 307–315.

Best, B. (2016). What is a feminist exhibition? *Considering Contemporary Australia: Women, Journal of Australian Studies, 40*(2), 190–202.

Bierema, L. (2003). The role of gender consciousness in challenging patriarchy. *International Journal for Lifelong Education, 22*(1), 3–12.

Cixous, H. (1976). The laugh of the Medusa. *Signs, 1*(4), 875–893.

Clover, D. E., Butterwick, S., & Collins, L. (Eds.). (2015). *Women, adult education and leadership in Canada*. Thompson Educational Publishing.

Code, L. (2003). *Ecological thinking: The politics of epistemic location*. Oxford University Press.

Criado Perez, C. (2019). *Invisible women: Data bias in a world designed by men*. Abrams Press.

Cramer, L., & Witcomb, A. (2018). Hidden from view? An analysis of the integration of women's history and women's voices in Australia's social history exhibitions. *International Journal of Heritage Studies.* https://doi.org/10.1080/13527258.2018.1475490

English, L., & Irving, C. (2015). *Feminism in community: Adult education for transformation*. Sense Publishing.

Flood, C., & Grindon, G. (2015). *Disobedient objects*. V&A Publishing.

Formenti, L., & West, L. (2018). *Transforming perspectives in lifelong learning and adult education: A dialogue*. Palgrave Macmillan. http://WorldCat.org.

Freire, P. (2014). *Pedagogy of hope*. Bloosmbury Press.

Giroux, H. (2004). Cultural studies, public pedagogy, and the responsibility of intellectuals. *Communication and Critical/cultural Studies, 1*(1), 59–79. https://doi.org/10.1080/1479142042000180926

Greene, M. (1995). *Releasing the imagination: Essays on education, the arts and social change*. San Francisco: Jossey-Bass Publishing.

Haiven, M., & Khasnabish, A. (2014). *The radical imagination*. Zed Books.

Hemmings, C. (2011). *Why stories matter: The political grammar of feminist theory*. Duke University Press.

Hoggan, C., Mälkki, K., & Finnegan, F. (2017). Developing the theory of perspective transformation: Continuity, intersubjectivity, and emancipatory praxis. *Adult Education Quarterly, 67*(1), 48–64.

Klein, N. (2014). *This changes everything*. Simon and Schuster.

Marshment, M. (1993). The picture is political: Representation of women in contemporary popular culture. In D. Richardson & V. Robinson (Eds.), *Thinking feminist* (pp. 123–150). The Guildford Press.

Mezirow, J. (1991). *Transformative dimensions of adult learning*. Jossey-Bass.

Mohanty, C. (2012). Series editor forward. In L. Manicom & S. Walters (Eds.), *Feminist popular education in transnational debates: Building pedagogies of possibility*. New York: Palgrave Macmillan.

Perry, D. (2012). *What makes learning fun?* AltaMira Press.

Scott, S. (1998). An overview of transformation theory in adult education. In S. Scott, B. Spencer & Alan Thomas (Eds.), *Learning for life: Canadian readings in adult education*. Toronto: Thompson Educational Publishing.

Taylor, E. W., & Cranton, P. (Eds.). (2017). The handbook of transformative learning: Theory, research, and practice. John Wiley & Sons, Inc.

Weiser, E. (2017). *Museum rhetoric: Building civic identity in national spaces*. The Pennsylvania State University Press.

CHAPTER 26

Creating a Sense of Belonging: Enabling Transformative Learning Through Participatory Action Research in an Ubuntu Paradigm

Maren Seehawer, Sipho N. Nuntsu, Farasten Mashozhera, Abongile Ludwane, and Margaret Speckman

INTRODUCTION

In this chapter, we share four South African science teachers' experiences with transformative learning through participatory action research (PAR). The chapter both provides insight into the nature of the teachers' transformation and discusses what enabled their transformative learning. The

M. Seehawer (✉)
Norwegian School of Theology Religion and Society, Oslo, Norway
e-mail: Maren.seehawer@mf.no

S. N. Nuntsu
Rhodes University, Grahamstown, South Africa

F. Mashozhera
Grahamstown Adventist Primary School, Grahamstown, South Africa

© The Author(s), under exclusive license to Springer Nature   469
Switzerland AG 2022
A. Nicolaides et al. (eds.), *The Palgrave Handbook of Learning for Transformation*, https://doi.org/10.1007/978-3-030-84694-7_26

five authors were part of a small team that explored the integration of Indigenous knowledges into South African science education. Abongile, Margaret, Sipho, and Farasten are science teachers in the South African city of Makhanda in Eastern Cape Province. Maren is a Norway-based researcher who initiated and facilitated the study.

The study was conducted in 2015 and can be contextualised into the struggle for educational transformation and decolonisation in post-apartheid South Africa. Despite acknowledging Indigenous knowledge systems as one of the curriculum's foundational principles (DBE,), the South African curriculum still witnesses colonial legacy and is very "Western" in content. For the duration of four months, our research team met for weekly 60–90 min workshops to explore the integration of Indigenous knowledges into some of the teachers' regular science classes. We followed the common action research phases of reflection, planning, action, and evaluation. During the first workshops, we thus reflected on, and discussed, questions and challenges regarding (the teaching of) Indigenous knowledges. During planning stage, the teachers planned one or several lessons that integrated Indigenous content with the Western science curriculum. The lessons were taught and evaluated in the action and evaluation phase, respectively (for a detailed discussion about research process and findings see Seehawer, 2018a; Seehawer & Breidlid, 2021). Methodologically, the study was guided by Paulo Freire's (1988, 1996) writing on collaborative research as well as by Indigenous research methodologies that conceptualise research as a space for personal transformation and growth (Lavallée, 2009). Freire (1988) conceptualises research as undertaken not on but with people who become co-researchers in a process that evolves as a dynamic movement between research and action. We briefly return to Freire below. The data used in this chapter stems from the audio-recorded and transcribed action research workshops, a semi-structured conversation between Maren and

---

A. Ludwane
Nathaniel Nyaluza High School, Grahamstown, South Africa

M. Speckman
George Dickerson Primary School, Grahamstown, South Africa

one of the co-researchers, as well as a collaborative presentation and evaluation meeting of our research in 2015. In addition, we draw on some of the co-author' reflections from 2020.

Ubuntu as a Framework for Transformation

This chapter builds on an understanding of transformation that derives from the Southern African paradigm of Ubuntu. This is done on the insight that when researching into decolonising and contextualising educational practice, our theoretical frameworks too, need to be decolonised and contextualised. Botswanan scholar Peggy Gabo Ntseane (2011) notes that Mezirow's theory of transformational learning "primarily addresses the *individual's* [emphasis added] capacity to use critical reflection and other rational processes to engage in making meaning" (p. 311). In the context of Southern Africa, however, realities continue to unfold in a *we-paradigm* (Van Stam, 2019), in which individuals exist through relating to others. Ntseane (2011) elaborates: "as a Motswana of a certain ethnic group, I know and believe that without these relationships I do not exist or there is no self or individual" (p. 312). In English language, this paradigm, Ubuntu, is often phrased as "I am, because we are," which stands in sharp contrast to the Cartesian "I think therefore I am." The latter centres around the rational individual, the former around community. While challenged by romanization, corruption and narrow interpretations, Ubuntu continues to be shared and appreciated by many peoples below the Sahara. Therefore, in a Southern African context, it is appropriate to consider "the role of support from other individuals, family, community, and overall cultural values in the process of transformational learning" (Ntseane, 2011, pp. 309–310).

Ubuntu addresses the core of being human. Conceptualised as "humble togetherness" (Swanson, 2009), it emphasises communality, caring for, and relating positively to, others. Framed as "humanness" (Ramose, 2009), Ubuntu contains both a dimension of being human through humble togetherness and a dimension of becoming human through "entering more and more deeply into community with others" (Shutte, 2001, in Metz & Gaie, 2010, p. 275). Humanness in the sense of Ubuntu is not anthropocentrism. On the contrary, it emphasises not only the interconnectedness among human beings, but also among humans and the surrounding environment and the universe, about which humans are just one part (Goduka, 2000; LenkaBula, 2008). Furthermore, interconnectedness has to be understood "in a holistic manner; physically, socially and spiritually. It also focuses on the development of the whole person; physical, mental, spiritual and social" (Mkabela, 2015, p. 287). It is both the infinitive state of becoming and "ceaseless unfolding" (Ramose, 2009, p. 308) and the "intertwinement [with others] that makes ubuntu transformative, as there is always more work to do together in shaping our future" (Cornell & Van Marle, 2015, p. 5).

In the quest toward becoming human, a common agenda for Ubuntu and Freirean PAR as a vehicle for transformative learning can be found (Seehawer, 2018b). Freire (1996), too, regards it as the people's "vocation" to "become more fully human" (p. 48). Freire's martial rhetoric about "regain[ing] humanity by cease[ing] to be things and fight[ing] as men and women" (p. 50) might sound add odds with Ubuntu terminology. Yet, Seehawer (2018b) argues that the Freirean liberation struggle eventually also aims at peaceful togetherness with the former oppressor: "the oppressed must not, in seeking to regain their humanity ... become in turn oppressors of the oppressors, but rather restorers of the humanity of both" (Freire, 1996, p. 16). In the next section, we give insights into the nature of the teachers' transformative learning.

From Challenges to Agency. Transforming Ourselves to Transform Our Educational Practice

Indigenous knowledges and practices are much alive in many South African homes. Yet, after centuries of subjugation, they have a status as inferior knowledges. As Abongile once put it: "When you go to an herbalist, you feel you go to a lesser qualified medical practitioner" (Workshop 4, August 12, 2015). The "colonisation of the mind" (Ngũgĩ, 1986), which regards the white man and his knowledge as the desirable norm, goes deep. It might have had an influence on our research process, too, as the team's focus was repeatedly drawn to the challenges concerning (the teaching of) Indigenous ways of knowing. A focus on challenges certainly makes sense, given that the current science curriculum, while rhetorically inviting knowledge integration, neither specifies any Indigenous content nor provides proper guidance of how to do so.[1] However, dwelling on what is challenging with Indigenous ways of knowing invites considering what Maori scholar Linda Tuhiwai Smith (1999) has written about the internalised connection between *Indigenous* and *problem*. "The 'Indigenous problem' ... a recurrent theme in all imperial and colonial attempts to deal with Indigenous peoples" (p. 94), became pervasive in public and academic discourses. So much research, both colonial and "post"-colonial, was devoted to "dealing with the Indigenous problem," that for many communities "the word research is believed to mean, quite literally, the continued construction of Indigenous peoples as the problem" (p. 96).

During the evaluation phase of the PAR, it was thus a rather surprising realisation that, after a four-month collaborative learning process, none of the initially identified challenges had proven to be a serious obstacle to integrating Indigenous knowledges into the teachers' science classes.[2] Rather, the teachers recognised their agency to address some of the challenges, such as the problem of Indigenous knowledges getting lost, through their own teaching (Seehawer, 2018a). "I think that is the main reason why we are here," Farasten observed during one of our final workshops, "for empowerment. We search for information, we implement, we share, so that we as educators become resource persons" (October 28, 2015). As a contribution to this chapter, Farasten underlines his emphasis on teacher's agency by formulating "A Call to Empowerment and Action". He states that

> the call to rethinking education locally, nationally and globally requires changing to a mind-set that is action-oriented. Teachers have a mandate to embrace the call. Everyone we come across has been in the classroom with the teacher, even people who are in jail; also they have been in the classroom with a teacher. Therefore, teachers have a bigger role to play when it

---

[1] The science curricula for grade four to nine state that "[t]eachers have the freedom to expand concepts and to design and organise learning experiences according to their own local circumstances," provided the selected examples of Indigenous knowledge "link directly to specific content in the Natural Sciences and Technology." Beyond this statement, hardly any Indigenous content is suggested in the curriculum (DBE, 2011a, p. 16; DBE, 2011a, p. 14).

[2] For a detailed account on which challenges our team identified as preventing teachers from integrating Indigenous knowledges into their teaching and how these challenges were overcome (see Seehawer, 2018a).

comes to what kind of society we want to live in. (personal communication, May 31, 2020)

Sipho describes his ongoing learning journey as a "project" from which "I did not turn back" (personal communication, May 21, 2020). Before becoming a part of our research team five years ago, he valued Indigenous ways of knowing, but "didn't have a plan or method how to integrate these knowledges into my science classes" (personal communication, May 21, 2020). Now he gladly lists the different ways in which he makes use of his agency both as a teacher and in his pursuit of academic learning:

> I started integrating Indigenous knowledges into my lessons; I started sending my learners to go out to their communities and come back with Indigenous knowledges which we then discuss in class; I started using expert community members as the custodians of Indigenous knowledges to present in my class about cultural beliefs and practices; I study in a Master of Educational sciences programme, where I focus on Indigenous knowledges and I am looking forward to pursuing my PhD from 2021 on knowledge integration and to collaborating with other scholars locally, continentally and globally. (personal communication, May 21, 2020)

Abongile recalls that she "used to feel like Indigenous knowledge, it's something very big, something that I cannot really incorporate in my lessons" (semi-structured conversation, November 9, 2015) but that participating on our weekly workshops "opened my mind. When it comes to Indigenous knowledge, I know my limitations," she reflected at the end of the PAR in 2015,

> so I felt like our research was something that was really going to challenge me to think out of the box. And it did just that! So much that I feel so sad that now we've come to the end, because, I was growing with the workshops that we had. So for me this research project came about as an opportunity to grow and even, at a later stage, even in my studies, maybe something that I can even look up for doing in my Masters or PhD. (semi-structured conversation, November 9, 2015)

For Abongile, a transformative moment was a team discussion on a study that incorporated local Indigenous knowledges into a grade 7 curriculum unit on HIV Aids (Schabort, 2011). In this study, students in an impoverished rural South African area engaged critically with their own prejudices when discovering the relevance of their Indigenous knowledge in that local plants and animals such as the protein-rich mopane worm, which they had been familiar with their whole lives, would provide a nutritious diet for HIV patients. Abongile calls this

> a great eye-opener, because I realised that it is important to ensure that learners appreciate what they have. In many cases you find that people want to associate good things with 'developed' places, urban areas, without realizing what they have right out in their own backyards. So what I want to install in my learners is that value of self-worth, of appreciating their own backgrounds. Some of our learners are coming from very poor backgrounds and they will think that there is nothing of value. But with my new understanding of Indigenous knowledge, I want to make them think out of the box, with regards to what they have within their community, within their homes. (research presentation, November 11, 2015)

For Farasten, Sipho, and Abongile, the changes in their understanding of their agency and mandates as teachers as well as the subject of this study, Indigenous ways of knowing, led to changes in their teaching practice. Based on this study's experience, we suggest that transforming ourselves is what enables us to transform our educational practice. In the next section, we focus on what enabled the teachers' transformative learning.

CREATING A SENSE OF BELONGING THROUGH COLLABORATIVE LEARNING

Our PAR project took place under real-life conditions. During the four months of research, all four teachers worked full-time and were under pressure to cover the curriculum and prepare their students for the upcoming end-of-year exams. Simultaneously, two of the teachers were pursuing a Master's and Honor's study programme respectively, another teacher had small children waiting at home, and one was nursing an elderly mother. One teacher did not receive any salary from the school for months, which resulted in much personal stress. At one point, xenophobic violence and shop lootings in the townships as well as student protests in the city centre stirred up the city's peace, and the research team members' peace of mind. To be able to research under these circumstances, it was vital to create a process that allowed space for these events within the research, rather than seeking to exclude them (Seehawer, 2018b). Ubuntu recognises that everything in life is connected and thus, research is not separable from life as such, but becomes a part of life. That way, the research contributes to the quest of holistic development of human beings. In line with this, Abongile noted that the community we had grown into during the course of the study "accommodated of us as people, not just as the research participants" (Workshop 15, November 11, 2015).

Our community emerged through the relations that gradually developed among the members of the research team. Growing bonds among the teachers became visible through supporting each other with learning materials and teaching advice or discovering unknown commonalities. Much to their joy, Sipho and Abongile realised that not only did they share the same hometown but even the same neighbourhood— and "Sipho even knows my aunt!" (Research evaluation, November 11, 2015). The teachers' relationships to Maren, the research facilitator, manifested themselves depending on the teachers' interests and situation in life. They included Maren visiting Margaret in her house and joining her at church, having conversations with Farasten between school lessons, and Abongile's and Maren's families picnicking together in the botanical garden. Most importantly, however, our weekly workshops as the core of the research also served as the core space for humble togetherness. Margaret remarked that through looking at peoples' strengths rather than weaknesses and through valuing "every person's contribution," the workshops "installed a sense of belonging" (Research evaluation, November 11, 2015), a site to which team members could turn even during periods of personal, professional, and political stress.

Perusing her transcript of the research evaluation meeting in 2015, Maren noted that almost all of the teachers' comments focused either on the relational dimension or on learning—and most of the time, the two were connected. For example, Abongile said about the research team: "we're a nice group to be. I learnt a lot from every person who was here; I got new friends" (Research evaluation, November 11, 2015). Margaret stated that she

> learnt a lot from everybody. And despite everything [the events outlined at the beginning of this section], they were still focused and wanted to help you and build the group and the team. We all have one mind and we all enjoyed the fruit of our work. (Research evaluation, November 11, 2015)

These comments embed the research in a context of interacting as whole persons rather than just participants. In such a setting, gaining new friends and gaining new knowledge are inseparable, but become part of the same quest towards shaping a common future by becoming more human though entering deeper into community with others. As Margaret said: "it was not about them, it's not about me, it's about what we achieved as a team" (Research evaluation, November 11, 2015).

Knowledge in the Ubuntu paradigm has been defined as "the codified essence of experience after communal discourse about its meaning" (Mucina, 2011, p. 1). Storytelling as an Ubuntu Research Method, Mucina (2011) explains:

> In traditional Ubuntu orality, the storyteller does not give an analysis of the story ... [but] leaves each listener to analyse the story, because he or she knows that each person will gain something different from it. Each listener will bring their experience to the analysis of the story. (pp. 8–9)

This was also the case in our team's meaning making. We were a diverse group regarding age, knowledge, interests, and life experiences that we brought to our collaborative research and we gained different insights from it. For example, for Abongile, the key message discussing the above-mentioned study in knowledge integration (Schabort, 2011), was the students' learning to value the local resources and local knowledge. Farasten, with his background in farming and interest in school food gardens, focused on the nutritious content of Indigenous foods that were described in the study. Maren understood the case as an example of dialogue between epistemologies, a theoretical concept she explored during the research (Seehawer & Breidlid, 2021). Thus, communal discourse or having "one mind," as Margaret called it, does not deny individual learning. Rather, the discussion and collaborative learning was what enabled individual learning. In the next section, we continue the discussion on what facilitated the teachers' transformative learning by moving to some more challenging aspects.

Transforming (Problematic) Relations

Research such as the study discussed in this chapter, is not free from ethical challenges, but needs to be situated within the tensions of power imbalances between researcher and researched. While writing convincingly about co-researching and co-learning in a manner that makes teacher and students "jointly responsible for a process in which all grow" (1996, p. 61), Freire remains vague about what actually qualifies a person to become such a researcher or teacher. Additionally, studies involving Western outsiders initiating research in Global South contexts, as was the case here, carry the baggage of research as an inseparable part of the colonial endeavour (Smith, 1999). Western research(ers) played a central role in imposing the colonisers' worldview and knowledge system that led to the colonisation of the mind.

Despite much reflection on her positionality and seeking to hand over power and co-lead the research with the teachers, Maren struggled to come to terms with the power attached to her role as an outsider researcher (Seehawer, 2018b). Six years after the initial research, she still wonders whether and on what premises Western outsiders may conduct research in the Global South. Yet it seems that Maren's role as a facilitator and the relationships that developed between her and the teachers were decisive for the success of the project. "It's not easy to do research of this nature. It was tough," Farasten said during the evaluation meeting. "We had other commitments and really, I was tired. But there in my mind, I said, [I will attend the next workshop] just for the sake of Maren" (November 11, 2015). "I think we all share those sentiments with Farasten", Abongile continued,

> because it was of your facilitation of the entire project, regardless of what ... You cared. ... It was challenging. Sometimes I didn't come [to our workshops] and I'd feel that I was behind of the group, but because of your encouragement, you made each person of the group feel like they had a valuable input. And that, I think, was what made us to want not to disappoint you, because you had so much faith in us. So you encouraged us, you helped to rebuild our self-confidence, so we really appreciate your leadership and your facilitation. (November 11, 2015)

Prior to the evaluation meeting, the team had collaboratively presented their research to an audience consisting of teacher colleagues, friends, and university staff. Thus, the conversation took place in the cheerful, relaxed, and enthusiastic spirit of having achieved a common goal. Margaret's accurate imitation of Maren trying to reach Sipho by phone when he was late to one of our workshops was met with hearty laughter and applause from the whole team. "I have been a bit annoying, haven't I," (November 11, 2015) Maren remarked, which resulted in more cheerfulness. It felt good to celebrate (the success of) our group and to laugh off the challenges of completing the research. A research, during which Maren sometimes moved beyond her comfort zone to motivate the teachers to continue their participation despite all their other obligations. Still the isiXhosa name the teachers awarded her at the end of the research was Thandeka, which means *lovable*.

Colonial history, a history that in many aspects is far from over, makes it challenging to write about caring (research) relations on the coloniser-colonised hyphen. Because of the danger of being (mis)read as a Westerner's move to innocence, Maren until now never publicly thematised the explicit acknowledgement she received as a facilitator of this study. She found it more appropriate to focus on those aspects of the research that remained problematic from a decolonial perspective (e.g. Keane, et al., 2017; Seehawer, 2018b). Two decades ago, Linda Tuhiwai Smith (1999) formulated questions for cross-cultural research contexts: "Who defined the research problem? For whom is the study worthy and relevant? Who says so? ... To whom is the researcher accountable?" (pp. 175–176). Considering such questions in order to address skewed power relations and colonising research practice is equally relevant today as it was twenty years ago. Yet, in a context of transformation and transformative learning, we might need to open up for the possibility that relationships in the sense of Ubuntu may—eventually—transform "colonial/coloniser relations" into "relations," in a common quest for shaping our common futures.

Conclusion

The collaborative transformative learning process presented in this chapter included the research team's gradual shift from focusing on challenges to recognising our agency as teachers and lifelong learners. Such transformation of ourselves enables us to transform our educational practice— and educational transformation is indeed needed in present-day South Africa, where there is often little connection between what teachers are presenting in the classroom and the knowledge and experience students bring to the school.

In conclusion, what made this transformative journey possible was a research process that involved us as whole persons rather than just being participants. Analysing our research process through the lens of Ubuntu, we found a connection between learning and relating positively to others. In fact, we experienced developing relations among and developing new or deeper knowledge as two sides of the same process: a shared quest towards shaping a common future by becoming more human through entering deeper into community with others.

REFERENCES

Cornell, D., & Van Marle, K. (2015). Ubuntu feminism: Tentative reflections. *Verbum et Ecclesia, 36*(2), Art. #1444, 8. https://doi.org/10.4102/ve.v36i2.1444

Department of Basic Education (DBE). (2011a). *Curriculum and assessment policy statement. Intermediate phase grades 4–6: Natural sciences and technology.* DBE.

Department of Basic Education (DBE). (2011b). *Curriculum and assessment policy statement. Natural sciences: Senior phase Grades 7–9.* DBE.

Freire, P. (1988). Creating alternative research methods: Learning to do it by doing it. In S. Kemmis, & R. McTaggart (Eds.), *The Action Research Reader* (pp. 269–274). Deakin University. (Original work published in 1982).

Freire, P. (1996). *Pedagogy of the oppressed.* Penguin Books. (Original work published in 1970).

Goduka, I. N. (2000). African/Indigenous philosophies: Legtimizing spiritually centred wisdoms within the academy. In P. Higgs, N. C. G. Vakalisa, T. V. Mda, & N. T. Assie-Lumumba (Eds.), *African voices in education* (pp. 63–83). Juta Academic.

Keane, M., Khupe, C., & Seehawer, M. (2017). Decolonising methodology: Who benefits from Indigenous knowledge research? *Educational Research for Social Change, 6*(1), 12–24. https://doi.org/10.17159/2221-4070/2017/v6i1a2

Lavallée, L. F. (2009). Practical application of an Indigenous research framework and two qualitative Indigenous research methods: Sharing Circles and Anishnaabe symbol-based reflection. *International Journal of Qualitative Methods, 8*(1), 21–40. https://doi.org/10.1177/160940690900800103

LenkaBula, P. (2008). Beyond anthropocentricity – Botho/Ubuntu and the quest for economic and ecological justice in Africa. *Religion & Theology, 15,* 375–394. https://doi.org/10.1163/157430108X376591

Metz, T., & Gaie, J. B. R. (2010). The African ethic of Ubuntu/Botho: Implications for re-search on morality. *Journal of Moral Education, 39,* 273–290. https://doi.org/10.1080/03057240.2010.497609

Mkabela, Q. N. (2015). Ubuntu as foundation for researching African Indigenous psychology. *Indilinga – African Journal of Indigenous Knowledge Systems, 4*, 284–291. http://journals.co.za/content/linga/14/2/EJC 183440

Mucina, D. D. (2011). Story as research methodology. *AlterNative: An International Journal of Indigenous Peoples, 7*(1), 1–14.

Ngũgĩ wa Thiong'o. (1986). *Decolonising the mind: The Politics of language in African literature.* James Currey. (Original work published in 1981).

Ntseane, P. G. (2011). Culturally sensitive transformational learning: Incorporating the Afrocentric paradigm and African feminism. *Adult Education Quarterly, 61*(4), 307–323. https://doi.org/10.1177/0741713610389781

Ramose, M. B. (2009). Ecology through Ubuntu. In M. F. Murove (Ed.), *African ethics: An anthology of comparative and applied ethics* (pp. 308–314). University of Kwazulu-Natal Press.

Schabort, F. A. (2011). *Can science education be empowering to girls in rural South Africa? Contextualizing science education through action research [Unpublished doctoral dissertation].* Norwegian University of Life Sciences.

Seehawer, M. (2018a). South African science teachers' strategies for integration of Indigenous and Western knowledges in their classes: Practical lessons in decolonisation. *Educational Research for Social Change, 7*, 91–110. https://doi.org/10.17159/2221-4070/2018/v7i0a7

Seehawer, M. K. (2018b). Decolonising research in a Sub-Saharan African context: Exploring Ubuntu as a foundation for research methodology, ethics and agenda. *International Journal of Social Research Methodology, 21*(4), 453–466. https://doi.org/10.1080/13645579.2018.1432404

Seehawer, M., & Breidlid, A. (2021). Dialogue between epistemologies as quality education. Integrating knowledges in in Sub-Saharan African classrooms to foster sustainability learning and contextually relevant education. *Social Sciences & Humanities Open, 4*(1). https://doi.org/10.1016/j.ssaho.2021.100200

Smith, L. T. (1999). *Decolonizing methodologies: Research and Indigenous peoples.* Zed Books.

Swanson, D. (2009). Where have all the fishes gone? Living Ubuntu as an ethics of research and pedagogical engagement. In D. Caracciolo, & A. M. Mungai (Eds.), *In the spirit of Ubuntu. Stories of teaching and research* (pp. 3–22). Sense Publishers.

van Stam G. (2019). Method of research in a We-Paradigm, lessons on living research in Africa. In P. Nielsen, & H. Kimaro (Eds.), *Information and communication technologies for development: Strengthening Southern-driven cooperation as a catalyst for ICT4D. ICT4D 2019. IFIP Advances in Information and Communication Technology, 552.* https://doi.org/10.1007/978-3-030-19115-3_7

PART III

Provocation 3: (Un)known Discourses of Transformation

CHAPTER 27

More Than Harmony: Transformational Teaching and Learning in Canada in an Age of Reconciliation

David Newhouse, Phil Abbott, Jason Fenno, Mara Heiber, Gabriel Maracle, Robin Quantick, and Heather Shpuniarsky

INTRODUCTION

In 2015, Canada launched a multi-generation national project of reconciliation between the original inhabitants and the settlers who have been arriving over the last three hundred years. Senator Murray Sinclair, the Chair of the Canadian Truth and Reconciliation Commission (TRC)

D. Newhouse (✉) · P. Abbott · J. Fenno · M. Heiber · G. Maracle ·
R. Quantick · H. Shpuniarsky
Chanie Wenjack School for Indigenous Studies, Trent University, Peterborough, ON, Canada
e-mail: dnewhouse@trentu.ca

P. Abbott
e-mail: pabbott@trentu.ca

J. Fenno
e-mail: jasonfenno@trentu.ca

© The Author(s), under exclusive license to Springer Nature
Switzerland AG 2022
A. Nicolaides et al. (eds.), *The Palgrave Handbook of Learning for Transformation*, https://doi.org/10.1007/978-3-030-84694-7_27

485

continuously states: "education got us into this mess. Education will get us out" (Truth and Reconciliation Commission, 2015). His statement affirms education's ability to transform individuals, institutions and societies. The promise of education is that it can transform the relationship between Indigenous peoples and Canada and foster a Canada that treats the original inhabitants with dignity and respect. The Final Report of the Truth and Reconciliation Commission (TRC) argues that for this to happen, "there has to be awareness of the past, acknowledgement of the harm that has been inflicted, atonement for the causes, and action to change behaviour" (2015).

This paper reflects on the efforts of a group of Indigenous and non-Indigenous university instructors to create a transformative education experience for students in a first-year Indigenous Studies course at Trent University in Peterborough, Canada. Our efforts are founded in Indigenous Knowledge (IK), the foundation of the Trent University Chanie Wenjack School for Indigenous Studies. The first-year Indigenous Studies course entitled *Foundations for Reconciliation* has an enrolment of 2000 students comprising about 55% of students entering first year. As of September 2018, all Trent students must take a one-semester course on Indigenous issues as a requirement for graduation. We had a captive audience, so to speak, and an excellent opportunity to see if we might create transformative experience for those who did not want to take the course. Consistent with the IK foundation of the Chanie Wenjack School, we based our teaching on Indigenous pedagogies of narrative story-telling and reflective exercises. As 95% of our students were non-Indigenous, we wondered if Indigenous pedagogies could foster a transformation of the attitudes, values and beliefs held by our students about Indigenous peoples and help them to find their place in the huge Canadian Reconciliation project. What we learned is the subject of this paper.

G. Maracle
e-mail: gabrielmaracle@trentu.ca

R. Quantick
e-mail: rquantick@trentu.ca

H. Shpuniarsky
e-mail: hshpunia@trentu.ca

Background

Over the decades, transformative teaching and learning has become a key concept in education, generating much discussion, theory and applications. Mezirow (1997) articulated a theory of transformation and defined it as "the process of effecting change in a frame of reference" (1997, p. 5). Through his work with adult education, Mezirow indicated that adults experience and understand the world based on their frames of reference. Adults become attached to these ideas and dismiss those ideas that do not fit our preconceived narratives. Transformative teaching and learning seek to upend understanding by guiding learners through a process to question their own assumptions. Through creating disorienting circumstances, students are asked to critically reflect on the new knowledge with the resulting impact often leading towards a shift in their worldview.

Transformative teaching and learning can encompass a variety of understandings (Hoggan, 2015). There is no one approach to transformative teaching and learning, as there are a number of overlapping concepts, including theorists who have tried to distill transformative learning into concepts and approaches. Stevens-Long et al. (2011) describe transformative learning as four intersecting theoretical perspectives based on: a cognitive-rational approach, a depth psychology approach, a structural-developmental approach, and a social emancipatory approach. Transformative learning is expanding one's awareness of socio-cultural reality through action, reflection and discourse; and the transformative education develops the realization of hegemonic social tendencies, socio-cultural freedom, and understanding ways to take constructive action (Stevens-Long et al., 2011; Walker, 2018, p. 26).

The lead instructor, David Newhouse, Onondaga,[1] grounds the course in Haudenosaunee educational philosophy:

The purpose of teaching is to foster good minds so that we may engage the world mindfully, with rationality and with full awareness of self as an interconnected being whose actions affect and are affected by others. We live as part of a web of life and education helps us to foster peace among all living things. We are educated when we understand ourselves,

---

[1] The Onondaga are one of the five original Indigenous nations of the Haudenosaunee Confederacy, commonly referred to as the Iroquois Confederacy. The other members of the original confederacy are Mohawk, Seneca, Oneida and Cayuga. It is common in Canada for Indigenous academics to identify their Indigenous national affiliation.

the nature of the world that we live within, what we might offer to it and can act to advance peace.

The teaching and learning approaches in Indigenous Studies are consistent with the social emancipatory approach to transformative learning. Williams and Brant (2019) suggest that transformative education resonates with Indigenous education pedagogies which aim to help the learner come to understand not just themselves but the broader context in which they live and how social forces influence and shape their individual and collective selves. The Trent Centre for Teaching and Learning defines Indigenous pedagogical approaches as "holistic in nature, focusing on the four interrelated dimensions of human development. A learner's academic or cognitive knowledge, self-awareness, emotional and spiritual growth are all equally valued, challenging dominant ideologies that specifically neglect the latter domain" (Hugeunin, 2020). Adopting an Indigenous pedagogical approach meant that as instructors we should pay attention to all four dimensions. We also adopted Indigenous pedagogical strategies: narrative, experiential and relational (Archibald, 2008).

Canadian universities responded to the TRC calls for action by developing Indigenization plans. A key feature of these plans has been the development of new programs and curricula intended to provide students with a broad understanding of Canadian colonialism and its impact upon Indigenous peoples, as well as Indigenous responses to colonialism.

The Chanie Wenjack School for Indigenous Studies at Trent University has been a Canadian leader in teaching about Indigenous people and issues for more than a half century. The school offers a range of programs from undergraduate diploma programs to PhD. In 2017, as a result of a report from the Senate Committee on Indigenous Education, Trent became the third university in Canada to implement an Indigenous Course Requirement (ICR): Every incoming undergraduate student, approximately 3600 students per year, must complete an ICR course as part of their undergraduate degree program. The Senate Committee argued that an understanding of Indigenous peoples' histories, cultures, aspirations and knowledge are important to a 21st Canada (Trent, 2017).

Learning about its colonial history, its impact on Indigenous peoples, and one's part in maintaining colonialism has not been a part of Canadian public-school (kindergarten-secondary) education. Most students see colonization as the actions of past generations and do not see how their actions in the present continue the actions of the past. However, as a study that examined attitudes, values and beliefs about reconciliation among Canadian youth (Environics, 2019) indicates, young people are aware of this history and are optimistic about reconciliation.

Cree-Métis Elder Michael Thrasher[2] uses the medicine circle[3] to describe the process of learning (Heart-Mind Online, 2020). He teaches us that learning is a cycle that moves from awareness to understanding to knowledge and then to wisdom. Our learning journey is guided by action, reflection, and feeling. For him, like many Indigenous Elders, transformational teaching is the process that moves us around the medicine circle from initial awareness to understanding, knowledge and awareness. Elder Thrasher tells stories and then asks you to interpret them. He encourages students to demonstrate their knowledge in practical actions. He teaches that you know something when you are able to take it inside of yourself and then express it in your words and, if appropriate, act upon it. This Elder, like many others, will not simply give you the answer. You must figure it out for yourself.

The ICR Challenge

Our challenge is to move our 2000 students around the Medicine Wheel: from awareness to understanding to knowledge and then to wisdom. The teaching group consists of 5 instructors and 16 teaching assistants, most of whom are non-Indigenous. More than 90% of our students have not taken an Indigenous Studies course before they arrive in our classrooms. Based upon our course surveys, 4 out of 5 of our students are non-Indigenous and 5% of our students are international students. At the start of the course, we asked why students enrolled and we found that most took the course to meet the ICR credit. Moreover, three out of four students told us they did not want to take the course and would not have enrolled were it not a requirement.

---

[2] Traditional Indigenous Elders are identified by the Indigenous national affiliation. Elders have been teachers within the Chanie Wenjack School since 1977. Their teachings are largely oral and not written down.

[3] The medicine wheel is a circle divided into four quadrants. Each quadrant is a different colour and represents an aspect of human beings: body, mind, emotions and spirit. All aspects of the medicine wheel are interconnected and inter-related. What affects one aspect affects all. The medicine wheel has emerged as an important Indigenous theoretical perspective.

Students also come to the class with an expectation of an Indigenous cultural and spiritual experience, that exams and tests will be mostly content recall, and that the course will be an easy credit. Students want us to tell them information through lectures and readings which they then give back to us. They also come to the class with stereotypes about Indigenous peoples that they have encountered through the news and entertainment media.

The challenge of achieving a transformative educational experience in an ICR setting is helping students to recognize that their learning affects all four aspects of the human being: mind, body, emotions and spirit. Students are presented with learning experiences that challenge conceptions of the country they grew up in, conceptions of themselves, and of Indigenous peoples; in some cases, it even challenges their spirituality and religion as they discover the impact of Christian missionaries and Indian Residential Schools. It can be an unsettling experience for many students to discover that their country has a history of colonization and that there continues to be colonial structures that drive our society, from which some of them benefit. Similarly, it can be unsettling for them to learn that Indigenous resistance is long-standing and widespread and based upon a desire to exercise self-determination. Students are unaware of the literature written by Indigenous leaders, setting out their ideas, critiques and analysis of Canada dating from the 1800s and continuing to the current time.

Our course is also significantly different from first-year social science offerings. We use a narrative approach (Archibald, 2008) presenting our material through the lens of story. Using the Thrasher medicine wheel approach, we start with creating an awareness through telling a story. Then, we help our students to move to understanding and knowledge by asking them to recall the main elements of the story (content recall), as well as express their own understanding and meaning of the story through reflective exercises. Finally, we ask them what they will do now that they know the story, moving them from knowledge to action. Our students are pre-occupied in a search for the "right answer" and not with acting upon the knowledge they have gained.

Elder Thrasher teaches that moving through the learning cycle takes time. We do not expect everybody will internalize their teachings from the first time they hear a narrative. For most of us we will need to hear the narrative several times before it becomes understanding, and we need to act upon it before it becomes knowledge. A few years ago, a student went to the school administrator to launch a complaint about an Anishinaabe[4] Elder who was leading a course on Anishinaabeg women's traditional knowledge. The student complained that the Elder told the same story over and over again and that she was learning nothing from the class. The administrator asked, "Can you tell the story?" And added, "When you can tell the story, then the Elder will say that you have started to learn. When you can tell what the story means to you, the Elder will say that you have learned."

In Elder Thrasher's view, transformative learning means that students can tell the story and figure out its meaning for themselves. They learn as much about themselves as they do about the world and Indigenous peoples. The story and its understanding become the basis for action. In the classroom environment, it turns out that Elders and transformative teachers have a lot in common. Both tell stories, both encourage students to understand the story, and both expect that students will be able to act upon their understanding of the story. In learning the story, the student has the possibility of transforming themselves and in acting upon the story, the possibility of transforming the world.

The ICR Journey

Foundations for Reconciliation is committed to transforming the consciousness of a diverse student population. Elder Thrasher teaches that reconciliation requires more than objective knowledge of the world but also an understanding of one's own values, attitudes and beliefs and how they are translated into action. The Final Report of the TRC (TRC, 2015) conceives of reconciliation as an active process that requires changes in societal structures and processes to create places of dignity and respect for Indigenous peoples. It sets out 94 recommendations, or calls to action, to emphasize the action component. Our overt pedagogical goal is to help students to gain knowledge and skills that enable them to undertake reconciliation efforts within their own communities. Elder Thrasher would say that we are moving our students around the Medicine Circle from awareness to understanding to knowledge.

---

[4] The Anishinaabe are the Indigenous peoples who reside in a large part of Ontario. The Michii Sagiig Anishinaabeg is the Indigenous nation of the Anishinaabe who reside in the area that Trent occupies.

We describe our approach to the course as anti-colonial (Dei & Kempf, 2006). By this we mean that Indigenous Knowledge, thought and perspectives are fundamental to both pedagogy and content. We use traditional Indigenous teachings such as: the Anishinaabe medicine circle, a teaching tool that reflects Anishinaabe understanding of human beings and society, interconnectedness and holism; the Anishinaabe Seven Grandfather/Grandmother teachings, ethics of love, respect, bravery, truth, honesty, humility, and wisdom; the Good Mind, a Haudenosaunee theory of the human mind; and Indigenous creation stories which serve as the foundation for expected human behaviours and relationships between all life forms. These teachings serve as interpretative frames for social phenomenon and history. Narrative rests at the heart of the course: we tell stories that bring Indigenous Knowledge, perspective and voices to the table.

What Did We Learn?

We used a team-teaching approach to course delivery; five faculty members and sixteen seminar leaders. The course teaching group consisted of both Indigenous and non-Indigenous faculty and graduate students. All of the graduate students were enrolled in the Indigenous Studies PhD Program at Trent; three of the non-Indigenous faculty were graduates of the program. All had significant engagement with local Anishinaabe Elders and were familiar with Indigenous pedagogies.

As a group, we met weekly throughout the term to discuss the progress of the course, student reaction to the material and pedagogy, our own classroom experiences focusing on the questions: What are we learning about our students? About ourselves? About teaching reconciliation? We framed our discussions as moving from awareness to understanding to knowledge and action. Wisdom escaped us at this stage of our learning.

Taking an Indigenous Knowledge approach to the course means more than just including material produced by Indigenous peoples and Indigenous perspectives. Elders like Michael Thrasher emphasize the importance of building good relationships with students and creating a respectful learning climate. Newhouse (2008) argues, based upon the Chanie Wenjack School's half-century of engagement with Elders and traditional Indigenous Knowledge, that an approach based in Indigenous Knowledges transforms both teacher and learner. As instructors, we were transformed by our experiences.

What we learned about increasing the possibility of creating a transformational learning experience for our students is grouped around four themes: Self as Teacher/Learner, Responsibility to Be Kind, Responsibility to Show Humility, and Stories Matter, Feelings Matter.

Self as Teacher/Learner

One of the fundamental aspects of traditional Indigenous teaching is understanding oneself, the source and limitations of one's knowledge, and how experience shapes our lives. Traditional Indigenous teachers like Cree Métis Michael Thrasher, or Anishinaabe Elder Shirley Williams, or Michii Sagiig Elder Doug Williams present themselves as constantly learning and offering only what they know in a spirit of humbleness. They are open about themselves, the limitations of their own knowledge and experiences. We presented ourselves in the same manner to our students, emphasizing our own learning journeys. As most of our students are non-Indigenous, it was also important for the non-Indigenous instructors and seminar leaders to share their own learning journeys, emphasizing how they came to teach the course. Doing so created a sense that transformational learning is possible.

Phil, a non-Indigenous course instructor and PhD candidate in the Indigenous Studies program states:

> I am a non-Indigenous educator and have been helping to teach the first year Indigenous Studies courses at Trent University for the past decade. Through this time, I have learned the importance of being open about my own learning/unlearning journey with students to address the uncomfortable realities that are raised in this process relearning history and connecting that to the current realities. In the first-year classes many students are just starting to peel back the layers of the colonial narratives of history they have been taught.

Mara, a non-Indigenous course instructor, seminar leader and a non-Indigenous graduate of the Indigenous Studies PhD program states:

> When I work with students in the ICR courses, I always remind them who I am. I am a settler and treaty person with responsibilities and relationships connected to those identities. I also talk about how each person needs to find their own relationship to the territory they call home and ask them

to keep thinking about their responsibility and relationship to that territory ... My openness about my learning and sharing who I am—Jewish, middle-class, urbanite, settler, White—creates a space of openness amongst the students to share their stories about where they come from and the challenges, they encounter with the course material.

Responsibility to Be Kind

Indigenous transformational teaching is only possible when it emerges from a place of kindness. The First Nations Health Authority in British Columbia invented the concept *lateral kindness* as a commitment based upon the teachings of Dene Elders: "Be considerate of others; treat people kindly; seek to know your Creator" (FNHA, 2017). The Health Authority argues that leaders and organizations seeking to create transformative change must embody this change. The Anishinaabe Seven Grandfather/Grandmother teachings include Zaagidiwin (Love) as one of the fundamental values governing all human behaviours.

We use these values to guide our behaviours towards our students, trying to translate them into actions that create a learning climate that respects the dignity of all members. We often turn to the teachings of an Anishinaabe Traditional Indigenous teacher, Victor McCoy, who worked with young Indigenous men who were incarcerated. Thousands of young Indigenous people's lives were changed through their encounters with him; he taught that kindness, and often tough love, was fundamental to transformational learning.

Jason, a seminar leader and non-Indigenous PhD candidate in the Indigenous Studies PhD program states:

> I approach my position as a non-Indigenous ally ... who acknowledges my privilege as a Caucasian male for this course by modeling respect, care, and humility in all my interactions with students ... I also make a point of thanking all of the students for attending INDG 1001H because their presence is a step in my mind on a pathway towards healing ... I believe that this small act provides a sense of humanity for all the students in my workshop.

Mara also adds:

> We treat everyone with respect and kindness, no matter the circumstances. We answer emails promptly. We support students talking with

other members of the team when they may not feel as safe with the person directly responsible for their workshop. We ask students for their stories when they want extensions on their papers; a good story (always) gets an extension.

Responsibility to Show Humility

One of the Seven Grandfather/Grandmother teachings[5] is Dbaaden-diziwin (Humility). To have humility is to see one as part of something greater than oneself and to recognize the equality of all living beings. Traditional teachers emphasize how much they do not know rather than how much they know. They are humble about their knowledge and about their ability to transform others. They know that learning is hard work; that it is a process that takes time, and that they cannot transform someone else. As a result, they practice kindness and patience and provide guidance rather than answers.

Each of the people who work in the ICR classroom understand that their efforts may not result in change or transformation now or ever but that there is always the possibility of transformation. Being open to the possibility requires humility.

Stories Matter, Feelings Matter

Thomas King, a Cherokee writer states in *Green Grass, Running Water* (1993): "There are no truths, Coyote. Only Stories" (p. 326). We live our stories and when we exchange our stories, transformational learning can happen. Traditional Indigenous teachers emphasize the importance of learning in ways that engage both thinking and feeling. The Haudenosaunee ideal of the *Good Mind* balances reason and emotion (Newhouse, 2008). Fostering a Good Mind requires that we cultivate our ability to see, hear, think, and feel. A powerful story engages all of these senses and can be transformative (Corson-Knowles, 2020).

Mara illustrates:

---

[5] The Seven Grandfather/Grandmother teachings: Humility, Bravery, Honesty, Wisdom, Truth, Respect and Love are the foundational moral values of Anishinaabe society. They are the values which are used most often as the basis for the behaviour of Indigenous teachers.

> When I work with students both in small groups and for those that come to spend time with me in office hours, I share stories I think will help them. Sometimes they are stories I have heard and sometimes they are my personal stories reflecting on how I dealt with something similar.

Story is an essential element for supporting a transformation to begin, for students and for the ongoing decolonization of Canada. We created the "Homelands Paper" to help students begin to think differently about their homes and the Indigenous peoples who live there. We ask all students to tell the story of their home nation or community, focusing on identifying the Indigenous presence through treaties and other agreements, Indigenous nations and organization and issues facing them. This research assignment provides students an opportunity to see aspects of their communities they have not seen before, to understand the ongoing impact of colonization on the community and their own lives and to see Indigenous peoples as actively striving to create good lives for themselves. The assignment is an opportunity for students to express their own story in their own words about their home nation or community in the context of colonization.

We encourage students to write the Homelands and other assignments from the first person and incorporate their own experiences and thoughts into their papers. Students begin to express their own emotional reactions to the narratives of history they are learning. We have found that through this process students come to a deeper understanding of the issues. Often, they express surprise at what they find, become upset at the ways in which Indigenous peoples have been treated by their communities, and are sometimes heartened by the optimism and actions of local Indigenous leaders. Elder Michael Thrasher teaches that moving from awareness to knowledge to understanding is not just an intellectual exercise but one that engages the emotions and spirit. This movement is facilitated through the use of story.

Students, like all of us, struggle with the material and its meaning in their lives. We ask them through statements of learning to tell us periodically what they are learning, and we ask them what they will do with the knowledge they have gained. We ask the students to tell us the story of their learning. We also ask students to tell us how they have helped others to learn, emphasizing that learning is meant to be shared and foster improved individual and collective lives. Students in their end of course comments tell us of their transformations:

Learning About My Ancestors and Trauma of My People is Hard Emotionally.

I entered this course with a somewhat negative mindset ... this course has changed my perspective ...

We didn't get told the history, we got told stories, and those stores taught us so much.

I took this course just because it was a requirement, but slowly as I moved towards the end of this term, I realized the importance of this course which actually helps me appreciate and respect the values and culture of Indigenous people. I also did a lot of new things, I had never done a PowerPoint presentation, a book review or made a video before, because of the course I got to do new things and develop new skills.

The Indigenous Knowledge Classroom

Indigenous Knowledge, Elders and Traditional Teaching are essential features of the Indigenous Knowledge classroom. The faculty of the Chanie Wenjack School at Trent includes several local Anishinaabe Elders who provide us with the lessons and inspiration that help us to foster transformation among our students. We define Indigenous Knowledge as that knowledge that is gained from a long-term inhabitation of a particular place. Indigenous studies programs in Canada have tended to ensure that they are informed first by the knowledge of local Indigenous Elders and then by Elders across the globe. In our case, the Elders who are part of our faculty are Anishinaabe and Haudenosaunee who have lived in the area for thousands of years.

Founding our teaching and learning on local Indigenous knowledge which includes Indigenous epistemologies, pedagogies and ways of knowing creates what we call an anti-colonial classroom. Taking an Indigenous knowledge approach means that we act from local Indigenous cultural premises. Formal openings and closings by Elders are standard practices for meetings within the Indigenous community. Accordingly, we start each class with an opening, often a traditional Indigenous song or short talk by an Indigenous Elder, often by video. We often use YouTube or Vimeo videos to bring students into a different world and tell them a story, not about culture, but about the ideas, theories and concepts that underlay culture. We tell a story of what happened not as a series of dates spread out over time, but as the expression of cultural ideas. The opening creates a liminal world where there is a possibility. And at the end, we have a formal closing, where we return students to the world they came from.

Robin, a non-Indigenous course instructor and graduate of the Indigenous Studies PhD program adds:

> My most important teacher has been a Mohawk Elder from Tyendinaga. Al Brant tells me that he 'works with one person at a time, from the inside out.' In describing his approach to responsibility, he positions himself, 'I hold a mirror up and wait for the person to find the courage to see ...' In my work I aspire to be the kind of teacher that Al Brant is: to have the patience and the humility to hold up the mirror and wait.

The Indigenous knowledge classroom is created through its framing by the opening and closing. Our anthropology colleagues will describe it as a liminal space. It is an invitation to surrender and open ourselves to the possibility of transformation (Seale, 2016). The opening is not a prayer in the Christian sense. It is a thanksgiving to all aspects of creation and an acknowledgement of the humanity and interconnectedness of student and teacher. The Indigenous knowledge classroom is not a space of protest; it is a sacred space that invites learning and creates the possibility of transformation, one person at a time.

CONCLUSIONS: WHAT WE HAVE LEARNED

Heather, a non-Indigenous course instructor and graduate of the Indigenous Studies PhD program speaks of her experience with Indigenous knowledge:

> In the teachings I have received from Elders and Traditional Knowledge holders, I have learned the importance of grounding my Indigenous studies classes in Indigenous Knowledges. They have helped me understand my responsibilities as a bridge builder and the importance of self-awareness. Once students are exposed to Indigenous knowledges, I have found they cannot help but be changed by it.

The TRC and their 94 Calls to Action (2015) have attempted to initiate a transformation in Canada, and this has been taken seriously by many post-secondary institutions. Part of this discussion is a conversation about the utility and effectiveness of Indigenous Course Requirements (ICRs). Our teaching group has also grappled with these questions.

Gaudry and Lorenz (2018) grappled with ICRs as transformation and the Indigenous scholars they interviewed saw potential in these courses to create meaningful change, not only in individual students, but within the larger landscape of Canada. Gaudry and Lorenz (2018) have stated that the most successful ICR "transforms student attitudes and encourages future learning" (2019, p. 163). They see the potential in these courses, while also admitting that student transformation is not guaranteed by the end of the course or at any time in the future. There are always students who merely set out to satisfy the base requirements, as well as those who are resistant and resentful of having to take the course. Our end-of-course surveys provide us with evidence that many students have a shift in awareness and positionality with respect to reconciliation in Canada.

Foundations of Reconciliation is a commitment to transforming the consciousness of a diverse student population of 2000 students. The goal is to provide students with the knowledge and skills that enable them to participate effectively in reconciliation efforts within their own communities.

Some of our students express frustration about the pedagogy of the course. While the course syllabus looks like other courses, its pedagogy is grounded in traditional Indigenous approaches to learning. They struggle with the content and the challenge to their self-conception. Gabriel, a Mohawk citizen, Indigenous Studies PhD candidate, and one of the seminar leaders speaks of the need for patience in the face of student frustration:

A good deal of the Elders I have had the pleasure of working with have been involved in the criminal justice system in one way or another. Elders who work with Indigenous youth going through the Indigenous restorative justice system, Elders who have worked as parole officers, Elders who have led Indigenous men's groups to stop domestic violence. My own father worked as a prison Elder for a number of years. He taught me that even the most angry, hateful people can be reached through kindness and patience. In fact, all of the Elders I have worked with have instilled in me that the fundamental in teaching is patience.

Transformative Teaching and Learning, from an Indigenous perspective, involves moving around the medicine wheel from awareness to understanding to knowledge and wisdom. The task of a teacher is to facilitate that movement through the creation of a transformational educational climate that supports the student's movement.

References

Archibald, J. (2008). *Indigenous storywork educating the heart, mind, body and spirit*. UBC Press.

Corson-Knowles, T. (2020). *Stories matter: Why stories are important to our lives and culture*. TCK Publishing. https://www.tckpublishing.com/stories-matter/

Dalai Lama Centre for Peace and Education. *Lessons from the medicine wheel: Learning is a cycle*. Heart Mind Online. https://heartmindonline.org/resour ces/lessons-from-the-medicine-wheel-learning-is-a-cycle

Dei, G. J. S., & Kempf, A. (Eds.). (2006). *Anti-colonialism and education: The politics of resistance* (Vol. 7). Sense Publishers.

Environics Institute for Survey Research and Canadian Roots Exchange. (2019). *Canadian youth reconciliation barometer 2019 final report*. https://www.env ironicsinstitute.org/docs/default-source/project-documents/youth-reconcili ation-barometer-2019/canadian-youth-reconciliation-barometer-2019---final-report.pdf?sfvrsn=6429b940_2

First Nations Health Authority. (2017). *Lateral kindness declaration of commitment*. http://fnhda.ca/wp-content/uploads/Lateral-Kindness-Declar ation-of-Commitment.pdf

Gaudry, A., & Lorenz, D. (2018). Decolonization for the masses? Grappling with Indigenous content requirements in the changing Canadian post-secondary environment. In W. K. Yang, L. T. Smith, & E. Tuck (Eds.), *Indigenous and decolonizing studies in education: Mapping the long view* (1st ed., pp. 159–174). Routledge.

Hoggan, C. D. (2015). Transformative learning as a metatheory. *Adult Education Quarterly, 66*(1), 57–75. https://doi.org/10.1177/074171361 5611216

Huguenin, M. (2020). *Indigenous pedagogy*. Trent Centre for Teaching and Learning. https://www.trentu.ca/teaching/research/indigenous-pedagogy

King, T. (1993). *Green grass, running water*. HarperCollins Publishers.

Mezirow, J. (1997). Transformative learning: Theory to practice. *New Directions for Adult and Continuing Education, 1997*(74), 5–12. https://doi.org/10. 1002/ace.740

Newhouse, D. (2008). Ganigonhi:oh: The hood mind meets the academy. *Canadian Journal of Native Education, 31*(1).

Seale, A. (2016). *The liminal space—Embracing the mystery and power of transition from what has been to what will be*. Center for Transfor-mational Presence. https://transformationalpresence.org/alan-seale-blog/lim inal-space-embracing-mystery-power-transition-will-2/

Senate Committee on Indigenous Education. (2017). *Preparing students for a 21st century Canada: The report of the special committee Indigenous education*. Trent University.

Stevens-Long, J., Schapiro, S. A., & McClintock, C. (2011). Passionate scholars. *Adult Education Quarterly, 62*(2), 180–198. https://doi.org/10.1177/074 1713611402046

Thrasher, M. (2020). *Lessons from the medicine wheel: Learning is a cycle.* https://heartmindonline.org/resources/lessons-from-the-medicine-wheel-learning-is-a-cycle

Truth and Reconciliation Commission of Canada. (2015). *Honouring the truth. Reconciling for the future. The Report of the Truth and Reconciliation Commission.* www.trc.ca

Walker, S. L. (2018). Development and validation of an instrument for assessing transformative learning: The Transformative Learning Environments Survey (TLES). *Journal of Transformative Learning, 51*(1), 23–46. https://jotl.uco.edu/index.php/jotl/article/view/200/137

Williams, K., & Brant, S. (2019). Good words, good food, good mind: Restoring Indigenous identities and ecologies through transformative learning. *Journal of Agriculture, Food Systems, and Community Development*, 1–14. https://doi.org/10.5304/jafscd.2019.09b.010

CHAPTER 28

The Witness Blanket: Responsibility Through an Ongoing Journey of Transformation

Carey Newman and Catherine Etmanski

This chapter explores several areas of transformative learning: the relationship between individual, collective, and structural transformation; the power of the arts in transformation; and how transformation is a lifelong, ongoing journey. To anchor this exploration, we draw upon the artist and master carver Carey Newman's ongoing journey of transformation, and explore how his individual and collective work has begun to transform Canadian consciousness through a monumental art installation titled *The Witness Blanket* (hereafter referred to as the "blanket," or "WB"). More recently, this collective transformation has also promoted legal-structural change through an innovative stewardship agreement detailing collective responsibility for the blanket.

C. Newman (✉)
University of Victoria, Victoria, BC, Canada
e-mail: careynewman@uvic.ca

C. Etmanski
Royal Roads University, Victoria, BC, Canada
e-mail: catherine.etmanski@royalroads.ca

© The Author(s), under exclusive license to Springer Nature Switzerland AG 2022
A. Nicolaides et al. (eds.), *The Palgrave Handbook of Learning for Transformation*, https://doi.org/10.1007/978-3-030-84694-7_28

503

Overview of Chapter

Adhering to Carey's Kwakwaka'wakw cultural tradition, we begin this chapter by locating ourselves and our ancestors in relationship to this work. We then provide a brief context of the WB, followed by an invitation to readers to share in the responsibility created by reading the stories in this chapter. From there we move into a discussion of the individual, collective, and structural elements of transformation connected to Carey's journey. We demonstrate how the individual is connected to ceremony, the collective is connected to art and ceremony, and the structural is connected to a specific stewardship agreement that draws from both and transforms our relationship with objects and each other through Kwakwaka'wakw worldviews. Through a focus on responsibility instead of rights, each ripple of transformation is connected to responsibility. We close with our own call to action, based on a sense of responsibility, deep enough to propel individual, collective, and structural change.

Locating Ourselves

'Yo!'Nugwa'am Carey Newman, He'man bak'wamxtla'yi' Hayalkang a me'. Through my father I am Kwakwaka'wakw from the Kukwak'am, Gixsam, and Wawalaba'yi clans of northern Vancouver Island, and Coast Salish from Cheam of the Sto:lo Nation along the upper Fraser Valley. Through my mother my ancestors are Settlers of English, Irish, and Scottish heritage.—Carey Newman

My name is Catherine Etmanski and I am a descendant of immigrants. My first known family members arrived from Scotland in 1772 in the lands now understood as Canada. They were settlers on Prince Edward Island. Through my mother, I am Irish-American, Dutch, and British. Through my father, I am Kashubian from Poland, and Scottish from Clan MacDonald of Clanranald. I have a deep curiosity for learning and research through the arts and a commitment to decolonization and reconciliation, within myself and in my identity as an educator.—Catherine Etmanski

In making the WB, Carey was determined that the process must reflect the goal, and he has tried to embody that ethos in all subsequent projects. His work is primarily about reconciliation, and at the core of that is transforming relationships, whether they be with people, land, objects, or knowledge. Our writing relationship is built upon that foundation and is connected to the responsibility of bearing witness.

This chapter builds upon three years of collaboration between us. That this collaborative relationship exists is part of the cascading effect of the ways in which the WB pulls people into action that we explore in this chapter. Each new action connected to the WB has the potential to—and does—lead to further action.

A quote that encapsulates our working relationship comes from Indigenous Australian activist groups: "If you have come here to help me, you are wasting your time. But if you have come because your liberation is bound up with mine, then let us work together."[1] It is this idea of working collaboratively toward a new world (structural change) and in solidarity for mutual liberation, emancipation, and freedom (interdependent individual change) that draws us, Carey and Catherine, together.

Context: The Witness Blanket

Canada's Truth and Reconciliation Commission (TRC, 2015) findings concluded that this country engaged in cultural genocide against the Indigenous peoples of this land. We quote the TRC at length here as it provides the necessary context for readers not familiar with Canada's colonial history:

> Cultural genocide is the destruction of those structures and practices that allow the group to continue as a group. States that engage in cultural genocide set out to destroy the political and social institutions of the targeted group. Land is seized, and populations are forcibly transferred and their movement is restricted. Languages are banned. Spiritual leaders are persecuted, spiritual practices are forbidden, and objects of spiritual value are confiscated and destroyed. And, most significantly to the issue at hand, families are disrupted to prevent the transmission of cultural values and identity from one generation to the next. In its dealing with Aboriginal people, Canada did all these things. (TRC, 2015, p. 1)

---

[1] This quote is often attributed to Dr. Lilla Watson, Australian Indigenous visual artist, activist and academic from Gangulu country in Central Queensland. The following source suggests that she prefers that the attribution for this quote go to the collective: http://unnecessaryevils.blogspot.com/2008/11/attributing-words.html.

State interventions into the lives of Indigenous people include violent acts of warfare, exposure to diseases, segregation and restriction of travel through a system of land reservations, forced sterilization, social policies that promoted the legal adoption of Indigenous children into white families, and, most prominently, the confinement of Indigenous children in government-sponsored schools run by churches, called "Indian[2] residential schools" (Ball, 2005). As described by the first Prime Minister of Canada, Sir John A MacDonald, in 1883: "Indian children should be withdrawn as much as possible from the parental influence...put them in central training industrial schools where they will acquire the habits and modes of thought of white men" (TRC, 2015, p. 2). This is not ancient history; the last Indian residential school closed in Lebret (Qu'Appelle), Saskatchewan in 1998 (National Centre for Truth and Reconciliation, n.d.; University of Regina, n.d.). The legacy of personal and concentric trauma that ripples through generations, legal discrimination, and other forms of systemic racism continues to this day. Revealing collective truths (Newman & Etmanski, 2019) about this context is part of the current era of truth and reconciliation in Canada.

It is within this context of reconciliation that Carey Newman, undertook his nationally celebrated work on the WB. As described in our earlier writing,

> the WB is a national monument of the Indian Residential School Era made of items collected from residential schools, churches, government buildings, and traditional structures across Canada. Through these tangible objects, it weaves together a comprehensive narrative of both survivor experience and the history of residential schools in Canada. Each item included in the WB has a multitude of stories attached to it. Carey not only designed the 40-foot multimedia installation, he was also the project manager. He attained the commission through a national call for proposals by the Truth and Reconciliation (TRC) Commission. (Newman & Etmanski, 2019, p. 235)

There are over 886 contributions in the WB, collected during a year-long cross-Canada, in-person engagement process and represented in the form of physical objects and images integrated into the installation. The full installation is 40 feet long, with a height of 10.5 feet. Readers can

---

[2] Indigenous peoples were incorrectly referred to as Indians by colonizers.

Fig. 28.1 The Witness Blanket on display at CMHR. Shared stewardship of Carey Newman and the Canadian Museum for Human Rights (Photograph by Jessical Sigurdson/CMHR)

learn more about the WB online at http://witnessblanket.ca/, by visiting it in person at the Canadian Museum for Human Rights (CMHR) in Winnipeg, by viewing the documentary (Newman & Graham, 2015), or by reading earlier works (Newman & Etmanski, 2019; Newman & Hudson, 2019) (Fig. 28.1).

Reading this Work

Storytelling is a central aspect of Indigenous pedagogy (Neeganagwedgin, 2020, p. 3). In this chapter, we have made the conscious decision to share a number of stories from Carey's life that he has identified as moments of transformation. For example, Carey's own childhood experience of abuse allowed him to hold space for the trauma and carry the weight of the stories embodied in many of the artifacts that make up the WB. All italicized sections below are Carey's first-person accounts.

We share these personal, catalytic moments in the spirit of learning, and in so doing make a request of you as the reader. Just as Carey learned through making the WB that he now carries responsibility to both the people who contributed and also to the stories and artifacts they shared, upon reading the stories in this chapter you, too, will share in that responsibility. We ask that you treat the stories with respect, honor the spirit and intention behind their inclusion here, and take action however you can within your sphere of influence.

Individual Transformation as a Lifelong Process

Looking at transformative learning as "an ongoing mythic journey of the soul" (Dirkx, 1998, p. 3), Dirkx called upon educators to pay attention to the "emotional and spiritual dimensions that are often associated with these profoundly meaningful experiences" (p. 4). Lawrence and Cranton (2015) referred to these pivotal periods of change as catalysts; they differentiated catalysts from disorienting dilemmas by stating that "a catalyst can be traumatic, a turning point in a process, epochal (dramatic) or incremental (gradual)" (p. 63). They suggested that these catalysts could be triggered by an external event or could be a more internal process within an individual's consciousness. They further suggested that "a series of everyday events could also lead to transformative learning" (Lawrence & Cranton, 2015, p. 63). Whatever the cause of the catalyst, they argued that "these events alone did not cause the transformation" leading to greater consciousness (Lawrence & Cranton, 2015, p. 65); rather, the seeds of transformation had already been planted, thus generating more of an ongoing process than a static and final, transformed state (Etmanski, 2018). Moreover, as Carey's stories exemplify, as we age and acquire new experience and perspective, we continue to learn from transformative moments long after they happen. In the same way that it is unrealistic to expect people to heal or move on from trauma when the conditions that caused it persist, neither can the process of transformation be complete. As we will demonstrate in the first story below, Carey was transformed by the same moment when he was nine and again at age 45. In this way, transformation is a lifelong process. The transformative nature of an experience can be revisited throughout one's lifetime. In the sections below, Carey has identified four stories of personal transformative experiences that relate to making the WB. These experiences are examples of the conditions that led to Carey's ability to undertake a project with as much emotional weight as the WB. Each experience contributed to a mindset and gave Carey the personal fortitude, sensitivity, and insight to make his way through the WB project. He believes that he would not have been mentally and emotionally prepared to do the work of making the blanket without these experiences. Just as Carey needed to look backwards before he could look forward, the experiences outlined below interweave and join the individual to collective transformation. Taken together, these four stories constitute some of the multiple passageways that lead to the structural transformation represented in his agreement with the CMHR.

Story 1, experiencing trauma: The strength to make the Witness Blanket

For most of my childhood, I was homeschooled, but my parents sent me to school in grade three so that I could compare my development to other children my age, rather than my older sister. That year, I experienced sexual abuse and betrayal of trust at the hands of my teacher. I identify this, not to focus on my childhood trauma, but rather, on what it has taught me later in life. At the time, I went to group counselling and as a nine-year-old, my way of coping was to tell myself and others that it wasn't that bad and carry on with life.

The shield I deployed remained intact for the better part of 35 years and is part of what enabled me to carry the emotional weight of the stories told by residential school Survivors during the WB project. But during the COVID-19 pandemic I found myself remembering and reliving that trauma over again. Eventually I realized the reason that I couldn't stuff it behind the same shield that had worked for so long was that I now experience it from a different perspective: as a parent. I kept thinking about how painful it must have been for my parents and the trauma that it might have triggered for my father, who is a residential school Survivor. Although for most my life I would have considered myself healed, when it comes to trauma there is no way to fully heal. As my life experience and perspective changed, my relationship with my past traumas has also changed. This enabled me to gain a deeper layer of insight to all the stories I heard during the making of the WB.

Through the creation of the WB, something that I have heard from multiple residential school Survivors is that they don't so much heal and move on as develop the skills to survive despite their trauma. This resonates with me, because three and a half decades after my own abuse, I am transformed and retransformed again by the same moment. As a father unable to imagine something happening to my daughter, I can no longer downplay the seriousness of my own experience. I am still developing new survivor skills, learning new things about myself, and deepening my understanding of the recovery process.—Carey Newman

The story above demonstrates two aspects of Carey's transformation. First, that later in life, he still found himself learning from the same experience; thus, it is a demonstration that transformative learning is a lifelong process, as described above, and that you can be transformed by the same instance more than once because as context changes, so does perspective. Secondly, working on a project like the WB and regularly hearing about often-horrific traumas inflicted upon children takes a significant emotional toll. Even with access to supports, several team members either left because of, or distanced themselves from, the heaviest parts of the project. The trauma Carey experienced as a child gave him the fortitude to carry the emotional weight of the WB.

While the previous story deals with experiencing trauma, the next three stories look at various ways that ceremony contributes to the process of transformation. Ceremony is widely used in diverse Indigenous communities. Robin Wall Kimmerer, who is an enrolled member of the Citizen Potawatomi Nation, has described the role of ceremony as clarifying intention, holding one accountable, and connecting our actions beyond the human realm (Kimmerer, 2013, p. 249). In the three examples below, Carey describes three ceremonies that supported his individual process of transformation. He begins by describing the vital role that witnesses play in ceremony, a role pivotal to naming the WB project (see Newman & Etmanski, 2019, for further description of the naming process).

Story 2, the role of witnessing in ceremony

Ceremony was integrated throughout the process of making the WB. From starting with ceremony to prepare myself and my team for undertaking a project with the emotional weight and scope as the WB, to following local protocol while visiting each of the traditional territories we entered, to caring for the spirit of each item we gathered, cultural traditions were woven throughout the process of making the WB and are present in the completed work. All these ceremonies, small or large, are part of acknowledging that there is something greater than the individual or the moment that we are in. That same gravity and intention extend into the role of witnessing. Each person who contributed in some way was considered a witness, and we gifted each of them as payment for taking up their responsibility to remember and share the story of the blanket. Ceremonies have contributed to the collective response to the WB and have also been important to my personal transformation. Ceremonies have also deepened the sense of responsibility to take action.—Carey Newman

Story 3, burning ceremony: Balancing out the good deeds ahead

My grandmother's memorial was the only time I have experienced what might be called a vision. Shortly after a powerful moment where hundreds of people drummed and sang her song, we performed a burning of belongings and food that my grandmother would need for her journeys in the next world. The cultural person performing the work cautioned us not to look directly into the fire, lest our spirits try to go with her, but emotional from the moment, I found myself staring into the flames. Through a blur of tears, I saw all my good and bad deeds as figures made from shadow and light, walking ahead of me, silently introducing me everywhere I went. It was a visualization of the energy or aura that surrounds a person. At the time I was reevaluating my life and undergoing substantial personal growth and the experience showed me that I needed to do more to balance out the good deeds that walk ahead of me. I think of that vision as a message from my grandmother.—Carey Newman

This experience prepared the way for Carey's transformation from an individual artist, working alone in his studio, mostly on artwork for commercial sale, to when he started working in community. Through a project called the Spirit Pole, he started looking outward and making more public and community-engaged artwork. This transition signified a shift in Carey's process "as a necessarily integrated process of individual and social transformation" (Stevens-Long et al., 2012, p. 185). This shift ultimately enabled him to envision and carry out his next major project, the WB, which included an engagement process with a nation-wide scale.

Story 4, bathing ceremony: Gaining clarity

During the lead up to the Spirit Pole tour in 2008, an Elder offered to guide me through a ceremony to prepare for a project that would see me take a twenty-foot totem through over fifty communities and share a hands-on experience of carving a totem with more than 11,500 people. The ceremony consisted of going to the river at sunrise, four mornings in a row. Each day I would brush myself with cedar boughs before submerging myself in the icy water four times. Like other traditional ceremonies in which I have participated, the act is simple while creating space for intentional thought and activating senses and/or altering physical state (e.g., fasting/hunger, sweat lodges/body temperature, smudge/smell of smoke, pipe ceremony/inhaling smoke). In this bathing ceremony, each day I felt a little more clarity about how to approach the coming challenge. By the fourth day, I surfaced with a better understanding about what was going to be most important for the success of the project —Carey Newman

Taken together, the ceremonies described above, along with the vital role of witnessing, operated on multiple levels to support Carey in his personal process of transformation. They enable him to tune into the deeper intention of supporting reconciliation through projects such as the WB. In particular, the burning and bathing ceremonies helped him uphold the sacredness and integrity of his work and maintain the energy and fortitude needed to sustain large-scale undertakings involving multiple objects, people, places, and emotionally heavy content. The act of witnessing—both through engagement with the WB and throughout the stewardship agreement ceremony with CMHR—also serves a larger role in collective transformation insofar as it holds others accountable to what they witness, which we explore next.

Art and Collective Transformation

From the very beginning, many people helped to make the WB into a reality and since it was completed, there have been multiple related projects. Among them are a national tour, a book, documentary film, a virtual reality model (under construction), a full-scale touring replica, and various other video and educational projects and resources. Most of these additional projects were proposed by people who have seen the WB somewhere along the way. As more and more related projects evolve, I have become curious about what it is that empowers those who are moved to action.

I believe the answer is connected to the witnessing described above. I have observed that the impetus to action occurs when a person's understanding moves from intellectual to personal. However, there are other layers related to collective truth (Newman & Etmanski, 2019) and emotional dissonance. Collective truth is found, not by interrogating the veracity of individual Survivors' recollections that may contain inconsistencies due to how time and trauma affect memory, but in considering them collectively, examining their relationship with one another, and looking at how they support each other. We might be able to dismiss individual claims, but when there are hundreds or—as is true with residential schools—tens of thousands of claims, isolated inconsistencies do not render the rest false. Rather, they can be accepted as reliable because the sheer volume of independent recollections—along with the geographical spread and time span they cover—serve to testify on behalf of one another and corroborate the basic and undeniable truth. Collective truth is co-created through these collective memories and in the case of the WB, collective truth is also found in the items from which it is made. Each piece is itself a witness that carries meaning not only through the stories of the person who gave it or the memories of what occurred within the institution it was collected from, but by its own presence, colors, textures and marks of age, contributes a tangible element that anchors the stories and memories.

Many Canadians were structurally denied from knowing about the genocide of Canadian colonialism (MacDonald, 2019) and grew up believing in a progressive and just Canada. When the WB shatters that reality by exposing the collective truth of residential schools, the result can be what I describe as emotional dissonance. Emotional dissonance can also occur when two related experiences are compared and the relative happiness from one's own memory magnifies the recognition of injustice for the other. Examples of this are in the WB documentary (Newman & Graham, 2015) where we ask viewers, "How would you feel if someone came and took your child?" and, "Did your school have a graveyard?" Sometimes this dissonance manifests as anger, rejection, or disbelief, but more often I have seen it in the form of tears. When looked at as disorientating dilemmas (Mezirow, 1991), or catalysts (Lawrence & Cranton, 2015) these moments of fracture open space for critical reflection and the possibility for transformation.

I have started to think of the WB as having its own small orbit, complete with a gravitational pull that draws people, including me, into action. Seeing the way the WB has inspired people to initiate related projects has given me insight into the power of art as a catalyst for change, a topic that has long been the focus of transformative educators (Brookfield, 2002) and critical theorists (Marcuse, 1978) alike. These are transformational realizations because they continue to inform the way that I approach both my life and my work. This, in particular, is the power of art in the process of transformation, because rather than being directive, like a lecture, or written words, it leads to a process of discovery or realization that requires critical self-reflection. The change begins within.

When something becomes personal it becomes important and once something is important, people are more likely to make the sacrifices necessary for transformation or change. So, perhaps the WB turns people to action, not only by a catalyst, emotional dissonance, or the responsibility connected to witnessing, but also the way that personal relatability to at least one of the many tangible objects or familiar stories that are part of the blanket, allows people to see how they are connected through their own memories and stories.

The concept of collective transformation is not well understood and is difficult to document (Buechner et al., 2020). However, we contend that the artistry of the WB itself begins to shift the understanding of those who experience it, prompting collective meaning making (Buechner et al., 2020) and sometimes leading to a shift in consciousness, particularly among non-Indigenous Canadians. Examples of spin-off projects that resulted from people viewing the WB include Canada-wide invitations to tour of the final installation, others stepping up to create both an interactive and a virtual reality version of the installation as well as a documentary film about how the WB was created, the innovative agreement with the Canadian Museum of Human Rights described below, and this chapter itself. Our perspective is that viewing the WB reaches people at an emotional and personal level, which compels them (us) to take further action. Aesthetically, it is a powerful and tragically beautiful piece, which can reach the heart through the symbolism of the multiple artifacts contained within. This occurs as people connect with the individual stories contained within the WB, as well as the scope represented by the entirety of the collection. The arts are already understood, bring to the surface pre-conscious or previously unarticulated concerns and desires (Davis-Manigaulte et al., 2006). As such, educators and others who feel an ethical commitment to reconciliation in Canada may deepen their understanding through interacting with the WB and feel motivated to generate further opportunities for themselves and others to learn in relationship with this important national monument. This gradual shift in individual consciousness is, in itself, part of the ongoing process of (re)conciliation—with each individual leading to a more collective transformation—in Canada.

Structural Transformation: Agreement with Canadian Museum for Human Rights (CMHR)

After touring the installation for over four years, Carey sought a permanent home for this WB. However, he knew that he did not want this to be a usual transaction with a museum. Since residential school Survivors and community members had entrusted him with their personal keepsakes and memories as part of the creation process, he understood that he had taken on a different level of responsibility.

Guided by lessons learned from moments of personal transformation and cultural teachings, as well as the experience of making the WB, rather than sell the rights to this artwork, he co-created a new form of agreement with the CMHR. Central to the agreement were innovative approaches to rights and responsibilities and the way in which the agreement was enacted through ceremony.

I have been taught to respect the materials I use, a concept embedded within the traditional teachings of respecting the past, honoring the present, and taking responsibility for the future. It also relates to my understanding of the Kwakwaka'wakw ways of awi'nakola: being one with the land, air, waters, and spirit world.

Recognizing that the WB was not mine to sell, instead of treating it as an inanimate asset, I took inspiration from how my ancestors thought of and treated our masks and Bighouses as living spirits. I therefore asked that we place all the legal rights associated with the agreement upon the WB. Instead of setting a transaction price, I asked if the museum would invest into the WB, the same amount of money that went into building it in the first place. This meant that we could do things like pay to restore and conserve the original blanket; make a replica to travel in its place; provide free access to a documentary that records the inspiration, making, and meaning of the WB; and eventually establish a legacy project.

I could no more give up responsibility than I could sell the WB, so instead we became partners in stewardship. Because we agreed that all rights rest with the artwork, rather than negotiating to protect and indemnify ourselves from every conceivable contingency, we were able to focus on shared responsibilities. By making the small change of focusing on responsibility instead of rights, our purposes aligned, and the negotiation became less positional. We were then able to develop a collaborative method for making decisions in the best interest of the WB and the stories it carries. We explicitly recognized that this was a living agreement, based in relationship not only with one another, but also with the artwork itself. This led us to make the commitment to maintain that relationship over time by sharing meals from time to time to discuss the shifting needs of the WB.

The meaning of language changes when read by different people in a different context or time. Knowing that not all of those who were part of establishing this agreement would be around to uphold our intentions in the future, I turned to my traditions once again. Taking up the oral tradition of passing important events, laws, and governance through generations by the telling and retelling of stories, we agreed that once we came to terms in a written contract, we would enact it through ceremony.

On October 16th, 2019, in a Bighouse named Kumugwe on the K'omoks First Nation, a traditional ceremony was held to uplift and animate the stewardship agreement between the CMHR and me. The words spoken there by former CMHR CEO, John Young, and by me were reflected upon by the witnesses called. We danced, we feasted, and together all those who were part of the ceremony now share the responsibility of looking after the WB. Through personnel changes at the CMHR, the strength of the agreement will now be tested.

Conclusion: From Individual to Collective to Structural

We are writing this chapter in a time where the climate crisis is upon us, a global pandemic is exacerbating pre-existing inequalities, and openly racist and misogynist leaders are granting permission to inflame further divisions. In Canada, everyday people are standing up for their rights and demanding immediate justice and action. These calls to action are echoed in the findings of the 2015 TRC, the 2019 National Inquiry into Missing and Murdered Indigenous Women, Girls, and 2SLGBTQQIA people, the #BlackLivesMatter movement, and many more global and local movements for equality and justice. The COVID-19 pandemic has demonstrated that leaders have the capacity to take bold and unprecedented actions. We know that change is possible. If ever there were an era where individual, collective, and structural transformation and reconciliation is needed, it is now.

Making explicit the interconnectedness of Carey's story and the story of the WB offers a model of how individual-collective-structural transformations interact to create transformative actions. Carey's individual transformative journey of trauma and a shift from commercial to more community-engaged artistic practice based on ceremony and cultural teachings created the conditions that enabled the making of the WB. Making the WB then led to Carey's understanding of responsibility to the collective over individual ownership rights. Furthermore, multiple factors spanning process, collective efforts, and the resulting art installation, as described above, moved others to action and hint at a more collective transformation of Canadian consciousness. Willingness to act enabled the structural change of the stewardship agreement. All aspects of transformation are informed and inspired by multiple, complex factors interacting over time. Taken together, these stories suggest to us that transformation is an ongoing and deeply integrated individual and collective process. This process of deepening responsibility is enriching for Carey as an individual and for the people drawn into the WB's orbit, including the work that we as co-authors are doing here. In Carey's words:

I have been reflecting on the interconnection between the maker and the material. Through the process of making the Witness Blanket, I have been transformed. As I took in other people's stories and took on an increasing sense of responsibility, I couldn't help but become a different person and take on a different perspective. In this way I become both the maker and the material.

This transformation through the creative process links back to responsibility. When I live and uphold those values of collective responsibility, seen through the lens of personal freedom or the Western concept of liberty, making an agreement like this might seem like a selfless act or even a burden. Yet, it is a reciprocal relationship, so if I truly uphold these traditional teachings, individual success is bound up with that of community, and I am made better by the contributions I make to the collective.

In the oral traditions that were observed as part of making and animating the unique agreement with the CMHR, each witness has an important responsibility. To ensure that spoken commitments and intentions are not forgotten, witnesses watch, listen, and then remember and retell what they learned. Carey learned through making the WB that he now carries responsibility to the people who contributed and also to the stories and artifacts they shared. In keeping with those intentions, we invite each of you to be a witness, to honor this knowledge by sharing it with others, because upon reading the stories in this chapter, you too now carry that responsibility.

References

Ball, J. (2005). "Nothing about us without us": Restorative research partnerships involving Indigenous children and communities in Canada. In A. Farrell

(Ed.), *Exploring ethical research with children* (pp. 81–96). Open University Press/McGraw Hill Education.

Brookfield, S. (2002). Reassessing subjectivity, criticality, and inclusivity: Marcuse's challenge to adult education. *Adult Education Quarterly, 52*(4), 265–280.

Buechner, B., Dirkx, J., Konvisser, Z. D., Myers, D., & Peleg-Baker, T. (2020). From liminality to communitas: The collective dimensions of transformative learning. *Journal of Transformative Education, 18*(2), 87–113.

Davis-Manigaulte, J., Yorks, L., & Kasl, E. (2006). Expressive ways of knowing and transformative learning. *New Directions for Adult and Continuing Education, 109*, 27–35.

Dirkx, J. (1998). Knowing the self through fantasy: Toward a mytho-poetic view of transformative learning. *Adult Education Research Conference*. https://new prairiepress.org/aerc/1998/papers/25/

Etmanski, C. (2018). Seeds and stories of transformation from the individual to the collective. *Journal of Transformative Education, 16*(2), 151–167. https://doi.org/10.1177/1541344617696973

Kimmerer, R. W. (2013). *Braiding sweetgrass: Indigenous wisdom, scientific knowledge, and the teachings of plants*. Milkweed.

Lawrence, R. L., & Cranton, P. (2015). *A novel idea: Researching transformative learning in fiction*. Sense.

MacDonald, D. B. (2019). *The sleeping giant awakens: Genocide, Indian residential schools, and the challenge of conciliation*. University of Toronto Press.

Marcuse, H. (1978). The aesthetic dimension: *Toward a critique of Marxist aesthetics* (rev. ed.). Fitzhenry & Whiteside.

Mezirow, J. (1991). *Transformative dimensions of adult learning*. Jossey-Bass.

National Centre for Truth and Reconciliation. (n.d.). *Interactive map*. University of Manitoba. https://nctr.ca/map.php

National Inquiry into Missing and Murdered Indigenous Women and Girls. (2019). *Reclaiming power and place: The final report of the national inquiry into missing and murdered Indigenous women and girls*. https://www.mmiwg-ffada.ca/final-report/

Neeganagwedgin, E. (2020). Indigenous systems of knowledge and transformative learning practices: Turning the gaze upside down. *Diaspora, Indigenous, and Minority Education, 14*(1), 1–13. https://doi.org/10.1080/15595692.2019.1652815

Newman, C. Hayalthkin'geme with Etmanski, C. (2019). Truthful engagement: Making the Witness Blanket, an ongoing process of reconciliation (Report from the field). *Engaged Scholar Journal, 5*(2), 235–243. https://esj.usask.ca/index.php/esj/article/view/68347/52079

Newman, C., & Graham, C. (Directors). (2015). *Picking up the pieces: The making of the Witness Blanket* [Documentary film]. Produced by C. Newman & Media One. Presented by Canadian Museum for Human Rights. https://humanrights.ca/story/picking-up-the-pieces-the-making-of-the-witness-blanket

Newman, C., & Hudson, C. (2019). *Picking up the pieces: Residential school memories and the making of the Witness Blanket*. Orca.

Stevens-Long, J., Schapiro, S. A., & McClintock, C. (2012). Passionate scholars: Transformative learning in doctoral education. *Adult Education Quarterly, 62*(2), 180–198. https://doi.org/10.1177/0741713611402046

Truth and Reconciliation Commission of Canada. (2015). *Honouring the truth, reconciling for the future: Summary of the final report of the Truth and Reconciliation Commission of Canada*. https://nctr.ca/assets/reports/Final%20Reports/Executive_Summary_English_Web.pdf

University of Regina. (n.d.). *Shattering the silence: The hidden history of Indian Residential Schools in Saskatchewan eBook*. Heart eBook resource for educators. University of Regina, Faculty of Education. https://www2.uregina.ca/education/saskindianresidentialschools/lebret-quappelle-indian-industrial-residential-school/

CHAPTER 29

Reflections on Transformation: Stories from Southern Africa

Moyra Keane, Constance Khupe, and Vongai Mpofu

INTRODUCTION

In this chapter we explore the meaning of transformation through our personal narratives of early learning in two different worlds geographically, physically, and paradigmatically. As three teachers, mothers, academics, and researchers, we each narrate our journey of starting out as children in South Africa (SA) and Zimbabwe respectively and coming to realize the power of living in more than one world. Our own journeys have also

---

M. Keane (✉)
University of Johannesburg, Johannesburg, South Africa
e-mail: moyrak@uj.ac.za

C. Khupe
University of the Witwatersrand, Johannesburg, South Africa
e-mail: constance.khupe@wits.ac.za

V. Mpofu
Bindura University of Science Education, Bindura, Zimbabwe
e-mail: vmpofu@buse.ac.zw

© The Author(s), under exclusive license to Springer Nature   521
Switzerland AG 2022
A. Nicolaides et al. (eds.), *The Palgrave Handbook of Learning for Transformation*, https://doi.org/10.1007/978-3-030-84694-7_29

522 M. KEANE ET AL.

made us more aware of the hazardous transitions students need to make in moving through different cultural and knowledge contexts. Collectively, our stories illustrate the right of passage from closed worlds to connected possibilities.

TRANSFORMATIVE LEARNING

Transformative learning includes emerging from closed worlds to expanded understandings and connections. Escaping from fixed and limiting, or biased views, requires not only "Border-crossing," as the eminent researcher Aikenhead (Aikenhead & Elliott, 2010) describes, but, in our experiences, a transcending of borders. Transformative learning starts with the individual and is shaped by our different environments. We move from within our own inner and outer context to a new position of understanding. In this, our learning moves us toward liberation from limiting perspectives.

> Liberatory learning cannot be standardised. It has to be situated, experimental, creative—action that creates the conditions for transformation by testing the means of transformation that can work here" (Shor & Freire, 1987, p. 26).

In formal education, learning purposes may be represented in three levels (Fig. 29.1).

Learning aims are often instrumental: for personal advancement, success, status, and employability. A humanistic aim includes broader self-development and caring for others. Transformative learning, builds on the other levels. It is holistic, open to states of un-knowing, able to acknowledge many ways of knowing, deepens insight into the interconnection and mystery of life. Stories may move through these levels and offer opportunities for interpretation and insight.

"What adults learn is fundamentally grounded in the way they think about themselves and their worlds, opening possibilities for transformation and creating dramatic shifts in one's consciousness" (Dirkx, 2001, p. 15). We look back at our life journeys and see how we transformed as we learnt, as new possibilities opened up. In post-colonial contexts, such as ours, the discourse of transformation is often associated with institutional structures. These structures may emphasize diversity and

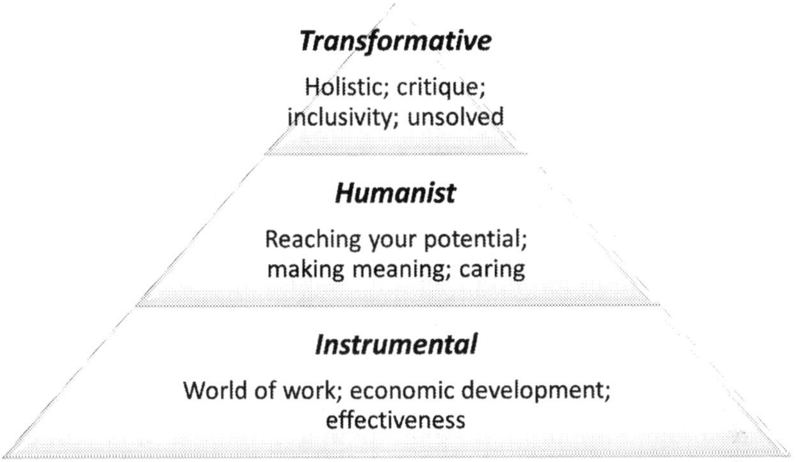

Transformative

Holistic; critique;
inclusivity; unsolved

Humanist

Reaching your potential;
making meaning; caring

Instrumental

World of work; economic development;
effectiveness

Fig. 29.1 Accumulative learning purposes (*Source* Adapted from Malcolm 2000)

inclusivity as the main feature of transformation. This aspect of transformation is, of course, necessary for social justice, redress, expanded opportunities for those previously excluded. However, we suggest that such institutional transformation needs to include a change in individuals, in their own perceptions and life journeys. The resultant learning, as Dirkx (2001) suggests, creates shifts in consciousness. Our view of transformation extends its meaning beyond simple "change" as an event, to the process of being intentional about seeing beyond ourselves and our comfort zones.

As Connely and Clandinin (1990) say, humans are storytelling beings who, individually and socially, lead storied lives. In *Things Fall Apart*, Chinua Achebe (1958) presents his main character, Okonkwo, as a self-made man. We view ourselves not as self-made, but as being shaped into who we are and who we are becoming through experiential and social journeys.

Through story we explore: What are the lessons to be learnt and the transformations still to come? How may transformation unfold? How may we contribute to learning transformations? Through story we gain a greater understanding of the world and each other. Stories provide a

524   M. KEANE ET AL.

healing rather than a factual truth. Stories allow for nuanced perspectives and interpretations (Allen, 2005; Blair, 2006). Stories contribute to learning (Gargiulo, 2006), and combine fact and fiction together with feeling (Mittins, 2010).

For children, the influence from adults (through story, for example, admonishing, disciplining, encouraging) provides, often well-remembered, critical incidents that shape their identity and a sense of agency. We transform. We often use this term as positive but our change could go either way, of course. Losing one's culture or identity could result in a contracted transformation into something diminished (Webb, 2015).

In sum: transformation may happen not just in form but in substance; not just at a level of knowing but of being; not just in policies but in lived experiences. In our own stories we share how our initial identities changed, expanded and became more connected. In the genre of narrative each of us presents a story of moving from one world to another—and in the process progressively transforming who we are.

OUR STORIES

Constance

As a young child, I remember my mother being a live-in domestic worker for a Dutch Reformed Church missionary couple. I therefore grew up under the custody of my grandmother and my mother's relatives in the tribal trust lands (as rural areas in Zimbabwe were called then). My grandmother had been widowed when I was four, and had headed her household since. As a subsistence farmer, she grew and processed all our food and drinks at home. She made millet-meals, peanut butter, dried vegetables, and brewed *mahewu*,[1] and *mukumbi*.[2] The grocery stores were a half-day trip away, and there was not always money for unnecessary food purchases. We had bread only when an odd relative from town visited, or at Christmas. But do not be tempted to make wrong conclusions: by the standards of our community, we were not poor at all.

---

[1] A non-alcoholic drink made from fermented millet meal.

[2] A beverage made from marula fruits. It can be made into either alcoholic or non-alcoholic drink.

I did not have modern pre-schooling; there was none to go to. Besides, it would be horrendous to walk any toddler on a 10 km round trip per day. My preschool was at my grandmother's feet as she did her household and farm tasks. I learnt mostly by observation (and some participation), for instance, while shooshing away hens when grandmother was grinding millet, shelling nuts; or raising a burning stick over the pot for her to see while she cooked at night. The best part of any day would be when she told me a story. Of course the stories were repeated, and that meant I would remember more, sing along better, and ready myself to retell the story to my friends.

Birth certificates and any other forms of identity were not a requirement in the village. Who needs a paper to certify your existence when the proof is there in person? For those parents who chose Western school for their children, there was no standard age to start school. The further you lived from school, the older you were likely to be when you started. My own test for readiness was an instruction to fling my right arm over my head and fully cover my left ear. I passed the test and I registered for first grade at the age of six. None of the learning I had from my grandmother was required at school. My first encounter with the English language was in first grade. We cheerfully sang and recited English rhymes, some of whose meanings we would only understand years later.

I used to visit my mother at her workplace during school holidays. She shared a tiny room with another servant girl. My mother's employers had no children—if they had, I never saw them—but they had a very large house. I was allowed only as far as the kitchen, and would sit on a little bench while my mother went about her servant duties. The lady of the house would frequently yell, "Varaidzo!" to which my mother would answer "Juffrou![3]" and hurry toward the caller. The lady would then say things in a language that I did not understand.

I was among the few who successfully squeezed through the bottleneck of Black education and attended secondary school at a renowned Catholic boarding school. Life there was very different from home, and that is where I got to meet people from outside of my culture. Prominent among these was the expatriate English language teacher who couldn't fathom how after eleven years of learning the language we still referred to woman as "he" and man as "she". I only learnt later at my teacher's

---

[3] Juffrou is the Afrikaans for Madam.

college that my home language was a hindrance to speaking English properly. This awareness helped me as a high school teacher of English language to understand my students' struggles better.

A complex mix of socioeconomic and political goings-on resulted in my family seeking economic refuge in South Africa. Compared to the experience in my home country at the time, I realized that I could more easily pursue doctoral studies in South Africa, and thus applied for admission with Wits School of Education. My scattered research ideas did not attract any of the supervisors in the School. I was therefore "advertised" further afield to colleagues in the Faculty of Science. Following a meeting to discuss my thoughts, Moyra (first author) and another colleague took on the challenge to mentor me through the research journey. I had my fair share of culture shock—especially having to learn to relate with supervisors on a first-name basis—especially considering that they were the same race as my mother's Juffrou. Moyra even cared beyond the research relationship to personal and family wellbeing. My husband once remarked, "I sometimes wonder if Moyra is your supervisor or your Aunt!".

My previous experience was that relationships in tertiary institutions were characterized by a clear pecking order, not too different from the army. A frequent question that came up in many of the research conversations with Moyra was, "Constance, what do you think?" In the early parts of my PhD journey, I genuinely thought the question was unnecessary. She was my supervisor and I was only a student, and in my experience, students were there to be seen and not necessarily to be heard. With time, I began to wonder if in more ways than one, my two decades of school and tertiary education had only taught me to follow.

Vongai's PhD research was in Indigenous plant healing, and our relationship stemmed from the similarity in research pursuits. Coming from the same country, our conversations often extended beyond our studies to more personal and family matters. Consistent with our Indigenous cultures, we found a new relationship by totem (Khupe, 2014, p. 6) in which Vongai is married into my clan. We are family.

My present job is in student academic advising. My university is cosmopolitan. Apart from formal training and ongoing professional development, the experiences in my life journey have also equipped me for student advising. Of even greater significance is what I continue to learn through interaction with my students.

Moyra

I grew up in a house of books and writing. My father was a journalist. Looking back, authors largely replaced real relationships. Every night a bed-time story; every birthday books for presents with messages on the opening page. My father read a book a day almost every day of his life (although he refused to read a book written by a woman). At the supper table he would lecture me and my brother on Marxist philosophy, or evolution, or the corruption of the Catholic church, while Mum would tell us to "Sit up straight." Fridays we had fish (one grandfather was Catholic) and once a week we had curry (Mum was born in Lucknow, India.) We had no Black friends or Afrikaans friends. I also had no cousins or extended family. Many things were not talked about. Current politics was one of them. We lived in a leafy suburb in apartheid Johannesburg. I never made my own bed or washed dishes—at least I dressed myself. My grandmother, who grew up in Puna before the British left, never dressed herself and had never even made a cup of tea until she was 30 years old and visited England. Much of my contained life perplexed me and I had no idea there were children who lived in other worlds.

At age four I was sent off to nursery school and ran home the same day. I told my mother I didn't go to school to play with dough and color-in. I needed to learn to read and write and find things out. Surprisingly she was amused and I didn't get punished. Arriving a few years later at "big school" was an equal disappointment.

I went to arguably one of the best schools in the world. Most of the girls' fathers were diplomats, government ministers or CEOs. (The mothers simply dressed well and had been to the same private girls' school.) My friends shopped in Paris and had parties at the country club. We got marks for deportment and the teachers checked the color of our underwear (really!). OK, I'm sure things have changed since then. But I spent my first year at university in post-private-school-culture shock. Three quarters of the way through the year I still hadn't found some of my lecture venues. (I didn't know how to ask a question without putting up my hand.) How is it that for the sum of a few Land Rovers the school gave me less poise, savvy, and motivation than the street kids I have worked with? I didn't make it through first year at university. That was the end of further education for me for about a decade. At age 27 I enrolled in a teachers' college. This was a little more like school and manageable. My 4-year old, longing to learn, started me on decades of study. As

I ventured into teaching it was the engagement with both children and older students that challenged and delighted me. Learning through books or lectures was one thing, but I have learned about other worlds mostly through students, communities, and mentors.

Apartheid had closed us in and schooling amounted to indoctrination. The planned curriculum was exclusively Western knowledge; the delivered curriculum was often Dickensian; and the hidden curriculum spoke to elitism, patriarchy, and Whiteness—and sometimes was not so hidden.

In this journey I came to experience the African concept and worldview of Ubuntu. I could give the oft-quoted translation "I am because you are" but rather, here is one of the lessons I had in Ubuntu: I was driving an old car on a rough remote road in Zambia on my way to the so-called Victoria Falls. A bolt dropped out of the chassis somewhere so the wheel went skew. (That was the extent of my mechanical knowledge in spite of a major in physics!) The car struggled up to a small dusty homestead of round huts and a couple of derelict cars under the thorn trees. An old man sat on a small stool in the yard while ragged children ran around chasing chickens with almost no feathers on them. The old man called some older children to scratch around and find a bolt for my car, which they did. Before leaving I wanted to give the family some money. They refused. I then offered some trays of fruit I had on the back seat—for the children. Again the old man refused: "You are a human being; I am a human being. How sad if we could not help one another." And so I drove off deeply humbled.

I remember only vaguely Constance, an ex-school principal, coming into my office to discuss her interest in doing a PhD. I remember better a year or two later her sitting in the car next to me during one of the eight hour drives back to Joburg from the remote rural village. As we spoke she took notes. I was faintly amused and thought, "What a diligent student." When we reached her house near the inner-city, her husband, Todd, met us in the street with his deep warm smile: "Ah! The academic tourists are back!" as he took the bags. His sweetness, support, and humor, keeping house while his wife was away, touched me. This is how families can be —a healing truth.

Vongai was a mature PhD student, an educator, scientist, and school principal. I was impressed by her work in Indigenous knowledge in Zimbabwe. I was also drawn to her quiet grace and natural authority. I asked her to take part in a study on coaching doctoral candidates. At a point in the recorded session the coach asked her what her role was as a PhD student in the supervision relationship. She responded: "I never thought I had a role. I was just a student under supervision. I thought that to be a supervisor means you have superior vision." This encounter prompted me to be more interested in the pedagogy of supervision and the power dynamics in the student-supervisor relationship. Awakenings often come from brief statements or encounters.

Vongai

I grew up in a house of multiple cultural practices: African Indigenous, Western, and modernized African. At primary school, I was my mother's and father's student. I was willing and ready to follow but was also groomed to lead through collective voices, cultural embracing, and sensitivity.

I never realized the different worlds of my life until I journeyed into my PhD in science education on Indigenous knowledge of plant healing and classroom science. I lived with my three cultures—and practiced them contextually. My three names Vongai, Tracey, and Kutsigira, all given at birth, reflect the specific practices I adopted in different contexts—school, city visits, and home. Vongai is an official name which is written in all my education certificates and identity documents. It is a Karanga dialect name of Shona language in Zimbabwe which in English means "be thankful." In this name Tracey, I imitated the White Western ways of life which I mostly used in urban settings on visits to my relatives who lived in Salisbury. Salisbury was the capital city of Rhodesia before 1980, the year in which Zimbabwe attained its independence. Tracey positioned me in the western ways of living. Kutsigira literarily means to support. It is family level name grounded in my family's ancestry ways of living. In the name Kutsigira, I took African cultural roles of a family aunt (Vatete). Vatete is a family post in Shona cultures. Thus, Kutsigira connotes the roles of a family pillar—the responsibilities I took up since my childhood. In Karanga families, Vatete is a female with roles and responsibilities of advising, counseling, and mediating among the family members. I grew up in a large family of the surviving seven siblings (three boys and four girls). We never at any time lived as only the seven biological siblings. My parents looked after our relatives from both the maternal and paternal side. We also lived with herd boys and maids who were just being treated as relatives.

My parents worked at a school about six kilometers from our rural home. My father was the school head and my mother a grade one and two teacher. I lived a good life, with enough food, expensive clothing, and occasional visits to town in my father's van. I lived in our house at school from Monday to Friday and spent weekends and holidays at our rural home.

At home, we engaged in life-sustaining activities: farming and animal rearing. Many people thronged to my rural homestead for help with different life problems. My father was a traditional healer and offered these services at our rural home. This was a practice only known within our village community. I kept it a secret in my interaction beyond our community for fear of being labeled primitive and a witch. Though many people, even from faraway places, received this Indigenous medical help, I often felt isolated at school because traditional healing practices were looked at as antichristian. My father was also a community leader who gave advice to village heads and chiefs. Community people visited our father to get advice on the education of their children beyond primary school.

Within my Western context of living, I dressed likewise, went to school and took up a science teaching career. However, I carried my traditional/Indigenous healing background as a secret wherever I went. The Indigenous medicine we practiced is rooted in African Indigenous worldviews. Regardless of context, I did not denounce Indigenous African culture as most of my peers did. This is because I knew traditional healing was useful and effective. I was living in it. I merely did not talk about it.

I attended an all-girls posh Catholic boarding school for my junior secondary education. I later completed secondary school at a day school in the mining town of Selukwe because the Catholic school was closed during the liberation struggle. At the Catholic school all preaching referred to African traditional healing as primitive and sinful. In school science, traditional ways of learning were never taught. They were given as examples of primitive non-scientific knowledge. I never contested this Indigenous knowledge subjugation. I merely realized that it was not for schooling. I taught secondary school science for several years. By then I lived in three separate worlds: the inner self that embraced traditional knowledge systems, the outer world that became part of the Western modern way of life, and the Afro-western way. I associated the language of Karanga with my traditional life in my rural village, and that of English with my professional life.

My parents instilled in me the desire to continue learning. I only realized on searching for a suitable PhD study area that addressing colonial ills of western-oriented science curricula in former western colonized nations, was a topical issue. One theme which recurred in my reading was that many African students struggle with the learning of scientific concepts because they represent a totally different culture. British colonialism amounted not only to cognitive imperialism and epistemic violence but also to assimilation. The Western curriculum excluded all aspects of my African culture. This sends a clear message that the world is White and that Western knowledge and ways of living are far superior to that of Indigenous Africans. Thus, my doing a PhD study at a university which was then White-dominated, and in a nation with an apartheid history, was my turning point. My transformation journey started with my settling on exploring the possibilities of integrating Indigenous knowledge of plant healing in school science curricula in Zimbabwe (See Mpofu, 2016). This PhD journey unfolded my cultural secrets through open talk, writing, and teaching.

One afternoon, as I was engrossed in my studies, I just thought of checking my student mail. In my in-box was a request from Moyra to take part in a study on coaching doctoral candidates. I met Moyra face-to-face for the first time before the session. We discussed my research. I realized that this area of study was similar to Constance's. I was not sure whether we could be friends, because she was White and me being Black. I later on realized that she was humble, accommodative, and persuasive. I liked these attributes so much that we continued engaging beyond academic levels. I was struggling with supervision and got to know about her scaffolding, teasing, and respectful approach to PhD supervision from Constance.

Constance was at an advanced stage of her study when I joined the university. We met as Zimbabwean students studying in a foreign nation. She inquired about my Mpofu surname and quickly said, "You are my sister-in-law because I am a Chihera." In Zimbabwe, Chihera is a common name given to all females belonging to the Eland clan. We clicked on the onset and found out that we shared many other things in common. We are family.

My PhD study made the knowledge and practice of Ubuntu more open and explicit. In the rural community where I grew up, all members are related through totems and marriage. Most survival activities such as working in fields and raising children in accordance to our cultural

532   M. KEANE ET AL.

values were done collectively. There is no concept of nuclear and extended family. All people of the same ancestral lineage belong to one big family. However, when growing up and starting high school the Ubuntu paradigm became overshadowed by the competitive western ways of living. The tensions between Western and African worlds created cultural shocks for me. I needed to continually switch between the school, church, and home ways of life. I began to spend more time in Western cultural spaces. Before my PhD I coped by using separatist strategies. I was Indigenous at home and Western in school. I now openly use the Indigenous, the Western and the blended lenses whenever appropriate. I have turned into an Indigenous scholar who wishes to contribute to the decolonization of education and the nurturing of Indigenous knowledge systems for the benefit of all races.

PATHS OF TRANSFORMATION

In the post-colonial context, transformation is often perceived as external to the individual. In our universities it is often viewed as an institutionalized drive to achieve decoloniality, to embrace the "other"—driven by the need for equity, or at least to comply with equity targets. We view transformation also from a personal change perspective, which is only visible to oneself when one pauses to reflect on the past. Narratives present a helpful lens through which transformation can be identified and understood. Our own learning experiences have given us an interest in not only the process of transformation and transformative learning, but in the ways that this may be facilitated. We also consider: transformation into what? What ontologies make us more human? Whose epistemologies count? The process of transformation begins with awareness, openness, and empathetic intention. The process may move to dialogue and critical reflection, questioning and becoming an agent of change on dominant ideologies.

Paths Unfold as We Walk Them

Much has been said about education for liberation over decades (Shor & Freire, 1987) in South America; and in Africa (Mbembe, 2019; Ngugi wa Thiong'o, 1986); and particularly about self and system transformation from colonized and colonizing to decoloniality (Breidlid, 2013;

Jansen, 2019; Seehawer, 2018). This is envisioned as education transformation ultimately for systemic change, but may also be individual, social, and spiritual (Dirkx, 2001). African knowledge centers on the notion of the archive, the repository of memories and stories of people (Mbembe, 2019). We contribute toward highlighting the place of the interconnected individual in the big-picture of systemic transformation.

In a Southern African context, there exists an ancient basis for relating, for being in the world and understanding our place without harming our social or natural ecosystems: Ubuntu. Ubuntu is deeply knowing we belong. While Ubuntu as an academic/philosophical construct can be learnt through literature (e.g. Gianan, 2010; Mabovula, 2011), some among us were born into it and it informed the core of who we are and how we relate. For decades this Indigenous knowledge has been under threat, marginalized, not part of the upwardly mobile pathway that the neoliberal Western education has designed. Suliman (1990, p. 162), thirty years ago, warned: "… [education may produce] literate people who may know how to read books … do not know the ways of nature; people who are alien in their own surroundings, unable to maintain a harmonious relationship with the fauna and flora around them, to respect the balance of give and take."

We are seeing the consequences of this failure in the violence, greed and confusion in the world. We are often too busy getting educated, educating others, and staying afloat in the chaos, that deeper questions of transformation can slip by. It is easier to ask, "Are students learning?" than to ask, "Does what they learn matter?" In all our stories we started in a narrow or compartmentalized world, as people usually do. The worldview we grow up in is part of our hidden curriculum. As children, we may be shaped by, and respond to our context. In our relating to others we may find out more about ourselves; indeed, find ourselves. Realizing this is part of our learning; making conscious and compassionate choices deepens our understanding of ourselves and the world (SEE Learning, Social Emotional & Ethical Learning, 2021[4]); carrying out our choices enables our transformation.

---

[4] SEE Learning' (Social Emotional & Ethical Learning). https://seelearning.emory.edu/node/5.

Worldview and Paradigm Shifts

Ogunniyi (2002) describes worldview as a thought system which determines to a large extent the habitual way in which one copes with experience. He also describes it as a way of knowing and living which is embedded in one's culture. Worldviews could be considered synonymous to paradigms. One worldview may be invisible or unimaginable to that of another, and there is likely to be accepted and assumed good practice in our teaching, intended outcomes, and processes that may be at odds with other cultural paradigm. As Bennett (2008, p. 2) explains: "Seeing ourselves as members of a world community, knowing that we share a future with others —requires not only intercultural experience but also the capacity to engage that experience trans-formatively." Thus, we see transformation as shifts from singular and narrowed paradigms to multiple paradigms that align with the progression of time and emerging life trends.

Through noticing worldviews, we are more able to think beyond them, connect with greater awareness, and teach more meaningfully. Through our stories we hope to show that having the ground of our assumptions challenged, we had some opportunities to examine our worldviews and the possibilities of owning a wider sense of belonging. We experience shifts in paradigms at both individual and group levels. Ese-osa Idahosa (2020) urges that we interrogate our interests, blind spots and positionality and through engagement, experience transformation. As Achile Mbembe writes: "… who among us can doubt that the moment has finally arrived for us to begin-from-ourselves." (2017, p. 7).

As one of our rural students in a participatory research project said "I see knowledge is everywhere." Others said: "Knowledge is available outside school." "We have learned to believe in ourselves… that what we think is important." Elders said: "Without respect there is no future. We need respect for the land, respect for work, respect in speaking and behaving, respect for elders, (Keane, 2008, p. 594). These wise words from our African elder indicate a path to transformation.

Conclusion

Our narratives may provoke the following questions: At what point did we transform? How much have we transformed? Our experiences have stretched over a few decades. Our transformation has not been once-off work. We have expanded views and changed perspectives, learned, unlearned, and relearned along the way. We have learnt and transformed through relationship—as we opened our worlds to others. Our transformation has sometimes been from inside-out, and at other times, from outside-in. We are transformation-in-progress.

REFERENCES

Achebe, C. (1958). *Things fall apart*. Heinemann.

Aikenhead, G. S., & Elliott, D. (2010). An emerging decolonizing science education in Canada. *Canadian Journal of Science, Mathematics and Technology Education, 10*(4), 321–338.

Allen, K. (2005). Organisational storytelling. *Franchising World*, November, 63–64.

Bennett, J. M. (2008). On becoming a global soul: A path to engagement during study abroad. In V. Savicki (Ed.), *Developing intercultural competence and transformation: Theory, research and application in international education* (pp. 13–31). Stylus Publishing.

Blair, M. (2006). Renewable energy: How story can revitalize your organization. *The Journal for Quality and Participation, 29*(1), 9–13.

Breidlid, A. (2013). *Education, indigenous knowledges, and development in the global south: Contesting knowledges for a sustainable future* (Vol. 82). Routledge.

Connelly, F. M., & Clandinin, D. J. (1990). Stories of experience and narrative inquiry. *Educational Researcher, 19*(5), 2–14.

Dirkx, J. M. (2001). Images, transformative learning and the work of soul. *Adult Learning, 12*(3), 15.

Ese-osaIdahosa, G. (2020). *Agency and social transformation in South African higher education*. Routledge.

Gargiulo, T. L. (2006). Power of stories. *The Journal for Quality and Participation, 29*(1), 5–8.

Gianan, N. A. (2010). Valuing the emergence of Ubuntu philosophy. *Cultura International Journal of Philosophy of Culture and Axiology, 7*(1), 86–96.

Keane, M. (2008). Science education and worldview. *Cultural Studies of Science Education, 3*(3), 587–621.

Khupe, C. (2014). *Indigenous knowledge and school science: Possibilities for integration* [Doctoral dissertation, University of the Witwatersrand, Johannesburg]. http://wiredspace.wits.ac.za/handle/10539/15109

Mabovula, N. N. (2011). The erosion of African communal values: A reappraisal of the African Ubuntu philosophy. *Inkanyiso: Journal of Humanities and Social Sciences*, 3(1), 38–47.

Malcolm. C. (2000). *Working together with science*, Gauteng Institute of Curriculum Development workshop, February, Johannesburg.

Mbembe, A. (2017). *Critique of black reason*. Wits University Press.

Mbembe, A. (2019). Future knowledges and their implications for the decolonisation project. In J. Jansen (Ed.), *Decolonisation in universities: The politics of knowledge* (pp. 239–254). NYU Press.

Mittins, M. (2010). *Corporate reputational elements reflected in organisational storytelling* [Unpublished MBA thesis, University of the Witwatersrand, Johannesburg]. http://wiredspace.wits.ac.za/handle/10539/9642

Mpofu, V. (2016). *Possibilities of integrating Indigenous knowledge into classroom science: The case of plant healing* [Doctoral dissertation, University of the Witwatersrand, Johannesburg]. http://wiredspace.wits.ac.za/handle/10539/20706

Ngugi wa Thiong'o (1986). *Decolonizing the Mind: The politics of language in African literature*. Heinemann.

Ogunniyi, M. B. (2002, January 22–26). *Border crossing and the contiguity learning hypothesis*. Paper presented at the 10th Annual Meeting of the South African Association for Research in Mathematics, Science and Technology Education, University of Natal, Durban.

SEE Learning. (2021). Social emotional and ethical learning. Retrieved from https://seelearning.emory.edu/ on January 13 2021.

Seehawer, M. K. (2018). Decolonising research in a Sub-Saharan African context: Exploring Ubuntu as a foundation for research methodology, ethics and agenda. *International Journal of Social Research Methodology*, 21(4), 453–466.

Shor, I., & Freire, P. (1987). *A pedagogy for liberation: Dialogues on transforming education*. New York: Greenwood Publishing Group.

Suliman, M. (1990). Sustainable development strategies. In B. Onimode, H. Sunmonu, H. Okullu, B. Turok, E. Maganya, M. Turok, & M. Suliman (Eds.), *Alternative development strategies for Africa* (Coalition for change, Vol. 1, pp. 141–165). Institute for African Alternatives.

Webb, S. (2015). Learning to be through migration: Transformation learning and the role of learning communities. *International Journal of Continuing Education & Lifelong Learning*, 8(1), 62–84.

CHAPTER 30

Pedagogy for Transformative Learning in Post-colonial Contexts

Sal Muthayan

INTRODUCTION

The disenchantment of the South African populace has been manifested by rampant protests related to the lack of jobs and basic services such as water, sanitation, and health. These protests, the result of rising poverty, unemployment, and inequality, when viewed together with the phenomenon of State capture,[1] indicate that, nearly three decades later, the government is failing to achieve Nelson Mandela's dream of a transformed rainbow society. Recent global pandemics have further exposed the gross inequities in our society. The protests may be viewed as the "new struggles for freedom ... aimed at liberating them from oppression by the inherited and imposed post-colonial African state" (Ndlovu-Gatsheni, 2012, p. 71).

[1] State capture here refers to systemic meta-corruption whereby private interests, in collaboration with politicians, assume control of State institutions to drain the public coffers to benefit themselves.

S. Muthayan (✉)
National School of Government, Pretoria, South Africa

© The Author(s), under exclusive license to Springer Nature Switzerland AG 2022
A. Nicolaides et al. (eds.), *The Palgrave Handbook of Learning for Transformation*, https://doi.org/10.1007/978-3-030-84694-7_30

537

Jonas (2019) admits the developmental state, which the post-Apartheid South Africa has vigorously pursued, remains elusive:

an ambitious project to create a developmental state to transform the apartheid economy has been hamstrung by the absence of the necessary coherence and capability, as well as the existence of patronage, corruption and state capture. (p. 2)

He warns of the "growing restlessness of our people who are not blind to the obscene inequality that abounds and who are losing hope in the vision of a future of shared prosperity" (p. 2).

Hence, the prescripts of the Constitution for improving the lives of the people, the fundamental contract of public servants, are not being realized. The significant investments in the capacity development of public servants over the three decades, to enable them to transform the public service, has not resulted in the desired transformation. Conventional training programs are not transformative as they are heavily content based, focusing on teaching policies and legislation with little attention paid to context. Freire refers to this approach as the "banking concept of education" (1970/2000, p. 73).

My function at the National School of Government (NSG)[2] has been to achieve transformative learning for public servants through the design of innovative curricula. I have found that the pedagogy of the Art of Facilitation program allows learners to co-create curriculum and imbues them with a sense of empowerment, altered frames of reference and awareness of the spheres of influence in which they can lead, instill hope and dream of new futures.

Rationale for Decolonizing and Transformative Pedagogy

Decolonizing Epistemologies—Whose Knowledge? Expert vs the People?

Research as we know it today, had its origins in the imperial project. Systems of knowledge were used to justify the exploitation of so-called sub-human races and the extraction of raw materials to benefit the Imperialist Centre (see Galtung, 1971). The knowledge of local peoples

---

[2] South African government institution responsible for capacity building public servants.

were denied and denigrated. Value was attached to Western culture and norms and post-colonial societies have continued to privilege these kinds of knowledge as expert knowledge, as scientific knowledge (Muthayan, 2008).

Yet, knowledge is not only the purview of experts such as academics, professionals, or famous people. Ordinary people also are purveyors of knowledge. According to Swart (2013), "Power relations benefit from our dependence on experts .... When we divide human beings into those who know and those who do not, we decide who can speak and who must remain silent ... teacher/ student; doctor/ patient; leader/ follower; *educated/ uneducated*" (emphasis added) (p. 25). The community workers in my programs have low levels of education but are engaging in the work of humanity.

Of relevance to my work are empirical research findings pointing to the importance of taking into account the participants' context and background as we design programs. Taylor (2007) for instance argues that "context may be the most important variable on transformative learning" hence the need to consider "sociocultural variables" such as "race, class, gender, sexual orientation and culture" (as cited in Gambrell, 2016, p. 3, 28). These variables are central to the co-creation of curriculum and the pedagogy of the Art of Facilitation program that I propose below.

Decolonizing methodologies frame the participatory and social justice work I have engaged in for decades now as critical feminist theory alone does not adequately provide me with the analytical tools to understand the complexities of post-colonial societies striving to become successful developmental states.

Why Transformative Learning?

Transformative knowledge as opposed to knowledge for individual progress, is needed to transform and rebuild post-colonial societies. As Taylor (2007) and Gambrell (2016) argue, transformative learning theory has progressed beyond Mezirow's initial conceptions. Some critics observe that Mezirow's theory "reflected White, Western values of individualism, self-direction and human agency, which is not the case for all cultures" (Gambrell, 2016, p. 2). Lange (2004) found that "transformation in fostering citizen action towards a sustainable society to be more

540 S. MUTHAYAN

than an epistemological change in worldview; it also involved an onto-logical shift, reflective of a need to act on the new perspective" gained through the learning experience (as cited in Taylor, 2007, p. 10).

In my work, cognitive dissonance and disorienting dilemmas attained through memory recall enable the participants to gain new perspectives on which they can act to bring about further change both within themselves and without. Gambrell (2016) explains that cognitive dissonance "occurs when an individual is confronted with an idea or experience that contradicts prior epistemological assumptions" leading to changes in one's frame of reference and hence "a paradigm shift," whereas, disorienting dilemmas refers to inner conflict arising from a major life transition, acute personal or social crisis leading to internal soul searching (pp. 4–5).

Pedagogy for Post-Colonial Contexts

The pedagogy I have developed for the Art of Facilitation is one that I have been using since the early 1990s while working in field of early childhood development and community development to empower marginalized communities who had suffered from the inhumanity of Apartheid. My thinking was influenced by the works of Fanon, Ngũgĩ wa Thiong'o, Nkrumah, and Achebe. Freire's "education for liberation" influenced my work with disenfranchised communities.

My introduction to Shamanism and my work in antiracist and gender bias training[3] in the 1990s inspired my "storytelling through regression" method which informs the Art of Facilitation pedagogy[4] discussed in this chapter. It is to commence any development process, be it a training session, development project, or conflict resolution process with the recall of the earliest childhood memories to affirm and celebrate participants' knowledges, histories and identities and exude the traumas experienced by them.

Because this pedagogy goes against the grain of the conventional courses, I had to introduce it incrementally to the NSG through the Lead Facilitator Development Program: Art of Facilitation (LFDP) (2016).

---

[3] Influenced by the work of Rani Parker, Washington DC.

[4] Acknowledgments to all groups I have worked with over the decades who taught me all I know.

The success of the program has been attested to by participant feedback. One participant, who arrived feeling hopeless amidst the dire challenges she and the community faced daily, said at the conclusion of the program: "I can fly."

This program has been adapted for public servants responsible for varying functions, e.g. HR managers across departments, senior managers in the National Treasury of South Africa and the Public Service Commission, community development workers, and traditional leaders.

Components of the Co-Created Curriculum

Due to limited space not all components of the pedagogy can be dealt with in this chapter. Instead, I will focus on the storytelling through regression component which is key to the transformative learning process. I also provide scenarios to show how the memory regression step may be altered for different audiences.

The co-created curriculum consists of the following components: (a) Learning Needs Analysis through storytelling; (b) approval of program design and content by participants; (c) participant review of draft curriculum; (d) beginning the learning program with storytelling; (e) design of new story: their new work projects and; (f) self- and peer assessment of their new projects intended to support change in the workplace/communities.

Co-Creating the Curriculum Through Storytelling

Storytelling creates a passageway between the old and new ways of knowing, being, and doing. Through storytelling the facilitator and participants co-create the curriculum, beginning with participants' old stories, usually from their childhood memory. They leave the program with new stories that constitute new plans, projects, knowledges, skills, and ways of being. There is an interconnectedness between the past and future based on work accomplished in the present. This leads to the transformative learning experience.

Storytelling is part of indigenous African traditions, a passageway for knowledge and information to be passed from one generation to the next spanning centuries. It is an approach that views all humans as knowledgeable and as experts in the life stories they tell. It is in this sense that I prefer the term storytelling to narrative methodology in this paper.

A participatory learning needs analysis (LNA) as opposed to a conventional "training needs analysis" by an outside expert, is conducted through storytelling that is a simpler but more evocative method in yielding thick data. The LNA elicits information on participants' actual or intended work project, their contexts, existing knowledges, challenges, successes, hopes, aspirations, and dreams. These contributions create the ontological and epistemological foundations on which the program was built.

Validating whether the learning assessment results are accurate prior to the design of learning materials such as handbooks or guides, may appear unnecessary and expensive but it results in relevant and impactful programs. The expense is justifiable when compared with costs of the plethora of programs that have not led to transformation.

Continued references by the facilitator to the initial stories, now displayed in the room shows the ongoing connectedness of emerging learning processes, enables further "unpacking," meaning making and "thickening." As the participants' experiences deepen, they continue contributing to the co-creation of the curriculum.

Co-creating the curriculum is about facilitating a process and being in the moment, the outcome is not a goal in itself but a process evoking transformation which is fluid and ongoing. By contrast, conventional program content is based on exit outcomes that become the end in themselves rather than a means to an end, Transformation.

TEN STEP STORYTELLING THROUGH REGRESSION METHOD

Below, I present the storytelling pedagogy and adaptations for differing scenarios I have dealt with. These are steps that the facilitator may follow. Kindly use a gentle tone and simple, brief instructions bearing in mind you are drawing upon the memory of the child within. For second language English speakers use either local languages or simple English.

This facilitator guided exercise, a visualization entailing memory recall, consists of the following ten steps: (1) safe container, (2) relaxation exercise; (3) memory recall through regression; (4) self-reflection; (5) cognitive dissonance—good and bad experiences, (6) emotions—identification of feelings, (7) writing out your story—cognitive and emotional intelligences, (8) peer-sharing, (9) interconnectedness of stories, and (10) affirmations—identities restored.

Step 1: Safe Container

A safe container refers to the designation of the classroom as a safe environment where confidentiality and mutual trust are established and agreed to by everyone present. It is agreed that sensitive information will remain confidential so everyone feels safe and comfortable to share openly. It is a space where everyone agrees to respect each other, listen attentively, not interrupt or make light of anyone and to only share if they are inclined to.

Step 2: Relaxation

For the relaxation exercise the participants are invited to be comfortable, put aside any thoughts and worries, focus on their breathing and relax their bodies, working from the soles of the feet to the head. The main significance of this is that the participants need to be calm, have clarity of mind brought on by deep breathing, and be open to what will flow when they access their childhood memories as this step constitutes the beginning of the visualization for memory recall.

The participants usually welcome this opportunity to relax and focus on themselves. For government officials, crises are a norm while for community workers there is no end to crises emanating from the trauma of poverty. This step is a passageway from their chaotic work environments to a process of self-reflection and self-awareness that is critical to transformative learning. It is about "letting go and letting come" because what comes is usually unexpected and can be traumatic. One participant commented, after the relaxation exercise, that she felt as if she had been to the spa, an unaffordable luxury for this group.

Step 3: Memory recall

This carefully guided step is a critical component of the storytelling method and may be adapted according to the aim of the particular learning program. The different adaptations will be discussed in the next section. This example is for facilitating on the topic of race/gender. In this step the participants are asked to recall their earliest childhood memory related to the topic, for example, their first awareness of their

544   S. MUTHAYAN

race/gender[5] and difference pertaining thereto. They must utilize all their sensory perceptions for the visualization as this enables what Yorks and Kasl (2006) refer to as "expressive ways of knowing," knowing that is accessed through their own "images, body sensation, and imagination" (p. 43).

By utilizing all their senses to re-conjure childhood localities, contexts, people, relationships, cultures, and communities they remember incidents in their past. On average, participants in my sessions have reverted to their memories of between 4 to 12 years old. This unveiling of their childhood identity re-awakens the value systems, identities, and cultural norms they grew up with. The intention is not just any memory nor is it a broad instruction to recall a traumatic event. Rather the context of the memory is prescribed, based on the topic of the program and linked to the curriculum content that is being co-created in this way.

Step 4. Self-Reflection

The work of self-transformation begins with opportunities to self-reflect. The participants must be given enough time to engage in quiet self-reflection. This also contributes to the decolonizing process. Fanon (1967) speaks about the need to decolonize as the need to self-negate, self-reflect before you can work as a collective toward achieving liberation.

Further opportunities for self-reflection are structured into the program through independent reflective tasks and "homework" which entail practicing communication and conflict resolution tools at home. A senior manager who had lost enthusiasm for his work and any belief that he could bring about change, shared how astonished his family was with the change they observed in him. Though he had attended several courses during his long career, the family claimed that they had never seen such enthusiasm for a program or experienced such profound conversations with him in the evenings. He claimed he was a transformed person, they claimed he was a transformed person. As the facilitator I could see the change compared to his disenchanted demeanor on the first day.

---

[5] I have used this method for a range of topics with different groups. First memory of: school, money, xenophobia, commitment to the poor communities, being informed that you would be the Traditional Leader of your people, etc.

Step 5. *Cognitive Dissonance—Good and Bad Experiences*

Cognitive dissonance, as noted above, is critical to the development of the human mind. But to progress from knowledge for the sake of knowledge to knowledge that contributes to social justice, emotions and feelings must be provoked. For learning to be transformative, there must be an integration of cognitive and emotional intelligences. By emotional intelligence I refer to self-awareness, good interpersonal skills, being cognizant of one's own feelings and emotions as well as that of others, and very importantly, displaying empathy toward others. Goleman (1997) contends that 80% of success is due not to pure intelligence but emotional intelligence.

In this step the participants reflect on good and bad experiences related to the topic, depending on the aim of the session. Deep personal reflections, for example, a traumatic childhood memory on racism, enable the mind, heart, and psyche to open. Through experiencing and expressing these emotions in the safe container, a dissonance is created leading to cognition. New learnings then land on receptive and engaging minds and hearts—decolonizing their minds and allowing transformative learning to take place.

Step 6: *Emotions—Identification of Feelings*

In this step, the participants are asked to reflect upon their feelings and think of a word that best describes these feelings. The effect of feeling and identifying emotions associated with past experiences is both affirming for positive experiences and therapeutic for negative experiences.[6] It provides an opportunity to speak openly about trauma that many have never spoken about. They can celebrate their identity and successes and exude their pain and suffering in an empathetic environment and confidential space.

A sense of ownership and renewed interest in their work can ensue only after these individuals have experienced a sense of release. Gilpin-Jackson (2020) refers to this process as:

---

[6] Commonly expressed feelings include: happy, proud, excited, sad, hurt, surprised, angry, worried, fear, guilt, depressed.

Resonance—a moment of awakening, through personal stories, that opens space or creates an opportunity for transformative learning... .the stories from your life that deeply connect you to who you are today and to the work you do in the world (job or otherwise)" (p. 3)

Step 7: Writing Out Your Story—Cognitive and Emotional Intelligences

Writing is a creative process that can contribute to the consolidation of new knowledges through both the cognitive and emotional processes. It is healing, therapeutic and leads to self-discovery. In this exercise they write down the story which instills a sense of pride in their pasts. Thereafter, they identify and write "out" the feeling which serves as the title of the story and a way of exhaling any negativity. As they write, they should avoid interaction so as to remain engaged in deep self-reflection. The process of writing separates them from the problem itself. Prior to this process, the participants and the dire conditions they face were merged.

Step 8: Peer-sharing

In this step, the facilitator invites the participants to share their stories with peers in trios which allows them to bear witness to and acknowledge each other's successes and commiserate with their challenges. This creates a community of empathy, safety, support, validation, and solidarity because there is resonance in common experiences, histories, contexts, and feelings. Swart (2013) speaks of a "community of concern" (p. 16).

It is important to assure them that they do not have to share if they do not want to. The peers must be reminded to listen with respect and to not interrupt the speaker. The facilitator should listen attentively to the stories as this informs the curriculum for the program. The methodology enables me to work with large groups of 30 to 50 as if each one is receiving my personal attention. Peer-sharing creates more co-facilitators. Eventually, everyone wants to share because they find it affirming and cathartic to share.

Step 9: Interconnectedness of Stories

The concept of interconnectedness has become important as we place more emphasis on our common humanity, our planet, and the universe.

It encompasses all aspects of our lives. Bringing their attention to our interconnectivity as human beings, the similarity of some stories and how storytelling is connected to indigenous ways of being, ancient African traditions, I point out that stories do not only come from books written in the West but also from small local communities like theirs.

I explain the interconnectivity of their stories with the curriculum content and how throughout the program we will revert to their stories thereby creating an interconnectedness between the old and new knowledge to find new ways to solve our problems as a collective. We discuss how our stories are passageways from our pasts to our futures.

This process animates them and they value the training because it is continuously about them and the wealth of knowledge they have to offer. This realization is empowering: Hope is restored and power is taken back. They now have a different relation with the challenges that previously subsumed them. Gilpin-Jackson (2020) found that through memory recall participants experience "a deep sense of social consciousness that they ascribed to a heightened sense of our human connectedness" (p. 23).

Step 10: Affirmations—Identities Restored

Affirming them and underscoring the richness of their contributions by inviting them to display their work prominently around the room establishes the worthiness of themselves, their childhood, their contexts, their cultures, their languages, their relationships, their families, their lifestyles, even if underprivileged and impoverished. It is a celebration of their identity—stories give them voice. I am careful not to correct or rephrase their authentic words, being respectful of their ownership of their stories and explaining that only they can author these stories because no one else knows more about your story than you. Gilpin-Jackson (2020) aptly pronounces on this process: "for any issue worth addressing in life, it must first be acknowledged as important. Therefore, the reality of the existence of trauma must first be acknowledged head-on, before it can be engaged for transformation" (p. 40).

ADAPTION OF STEP 3B: MEMORY RECALL FOR DIFFERENT SCENARIOS

As noted, Step 3b above may be adapted for different contexts where the learning intention or topic may differ. The following five scenarios

548   S. MUTHAYAN

are examples of how I have adapted step 3b above for different kinds of programs and participants. Steps 3a, c, d remain as elucidated above.

Scenario 1: Trauma Debriefing

For this scenario, Step 3 remains as captured above. The memory recall requires the earliest childhood memory on trauma incidents. It requires the facilitator to be able to handle trauma with sensitivity.

My experience is that many people, especially Black people, have memories fraught with trauma resulting from their oppression during the Apartheid era. Most, if not every, Black person has experienced humiliation and denigration, regardless of their station in life, simply because of the legalized and institutionalized system of racism during that period. In addition, they deal with the trauma of poverty on a daily basis. Gilpin-Jackson's groundbreaking work on trauma and "resonance" resonates with my findings that "Resonance moments can occur in the midst of trauma and post-traumatic stress, and when they do, they open up the possibility for transformative learning" (2020, p. 41).

In a trauma debriefing session[7] with community workers, 19 questions around different kinds of trauma were posed and participants were invited to cross a line along the floor if they had experienced any of those kinds of trauma. One man crossed the line 19 times for: incarceration; beatings; being disabled as a result of police shooting; losing family to political violence; job loss; starvation; and rape of a relative. A woman shared how her brain injury, goes back 40 years to when her abusive husband struck her with a panga. These are just two examples of trauma related to race, gender, and disability. Another spoke of flashbacks related to a child rape incident she had helped with. They had never shared these stories previously. Each participant in the group of 50 had a story to tell indicating that they encounter the "faces of poverty"[8] on a daily basis. How can they support their communities if they themselves need trauma debriefing? We taught them to debrief each other and community members they work with.

---

[7] Gratitude to Diann Le Roux, counselling psychologist and professional coach, who assisted with the trauma debriefing component.

[8] Term I used to describe their work with poor people whose plight is invisible to the rest of society.

Scenario 2: For Trainers and Development Facilitators

The initial Art of Facilitation, the LFDP, was designed to professionalize trainers who deliver the NSG programs. It aims to address the shortcomings of conventional learning programs by transforming trainers, focused on the transmission of content through slide presentations ("death by slides"[9]), into facilitators leading development through transformative learning processes. Hence the title Lead Facilitator Development Program, which promotes a shift from: teaching content to facilitating a process; changing others to changing self; new management theory to a social justice approach and; from assessments by portfolios to developmental assessment through self and peer assessment of new projects.

Adaptation of Step 3b for Scenario 2

This audience may be asked to recall the earliest memory of school beginning with a good experience in the classroom. Once they have had time to do this, ask them to repeat the process with a bad classroom recall.

This exercise reveals the good and bad qualities for teachers which provides insights and norms for the kind of facilitator we need to aspire toward. This awareness through recall may also help prevent the bad experience from becoming their way of teaching.

Scenario 3: For a Technical Subject—Financial Management or Budgeting

While many education experts support participatory and experiential approaches, they often believe that technical subjects, like science and finance, cannot be facilitated in this way. Instead, these courses are often content-based or information giving, for example, intended to "teach" public servants relevant government legislation and policies. I customized the Art of Facilitation for a group of skeptical senior managers from the National Treasury, which turned out to be so successful that the group requested further training for a larger cohort of participants.

[9] Phrase I coined for the LFDP to describe conventional trainers' heavy reliance on slide presentations capturing content mainly.

550   S. MUTHAYAN

Adaptation of Step 3b for Scenario 3
For this context, the participants were invited to recall the first time they became aware of or had an experience with money. I found the participants relating stories of being asked by their parents to shop for bread or milk. Instead, they bought candy and ran out of money for the bread. One participant then sat on the pavement weeping, afraid to go home and face the consequences. Another bought bread but lost the change while playing and was severely rebuked when he returned home. Yet another shared how he had admired the wealthy shopkeeper and aspired to become one someday. He had heard that you need to grow your money. So when he received a shiny coin from his uncle he buried it in the ground, watered it daily, waiting for his money to "grow." Even though he was a person of status now as a senior public servant, his evocation of the sadness he felt as a child when the money didn't grow was palpable in the room. He indicated it was the first time he had shared this story.

This exercise revealed the disparities of the different races in the group. The first experience of money for minority groups, such as Whites, Indians, and Coloreds,[10] were of piggy banks[11] whereas for Black African participants there simply was no spare money to save.

The stories from this group led us directly to the principles of the legislation, for example, unauthorized expenditure; wasteful expenditure; irregular expenditure; inefficient management of funds, etc. This made for robust discussions on the legislation, corruption, and consequence management.

Scenario 4: The Art of Facilitating Participatory Community Engagement

Designed for voluntary community workers (retired nurses) and community development workers,[12] the aim is to improve their capacity to work in participatory ways with the community to promote socioeconomic development.

---

[10] This official term denoting people of mixed race is being contested at this time.

[11] Piggy boxes or money boxes were common among children of more privileged race groups as a way to save pennies.

[12] Employed by government to interface directly with communities.

The opportunity to facilitate their self-empowerment and self-transformation afforded me a direct line in working toward improving the conditions of local communities. I would express how honored I was to work with them and say, "When I touch you, I am one person away from reaching the poorest of poor person."

Adaptation of Step 3b for Scenario 4
The community workers are requested to reflect on their community work over the years and to recall one of their greatest achievements, a success story. This should be repeated with a recall of one of the greatest challenges experienced. While all the groups I have worked with praised the pedagogy, this group was exuberant, empowered, and expressed gratitude for the opportunity to learn in this way. In subsequent sessions they reported on successes they had achieved since implementing their new learnings. One of them said, "I am a transformed person. The experience truly changed my life."

Scenario 5: The Art of Facilitating Socio-economic Development for Traditional Leaders

This program targeted traditional leaders who are custodians of two key assets of the country, land, and people. This program aimed to build their capacity to work together with their rural communities to build economic projects such as citrus/nut farming, goat husbandry, poultry farms, and mining.

Adaption of Step 3b for Scenario 5
I commenced with a consultative session to establish rapport and trust, conscious of special protocols required, aware of my gender and race as a woman of Indian descent among indigenous African royalty. The next process was a learning needs analysis workshop, beginning with the regression exercise which was hugely successful. I asked them to go back to their earliest memory of when they first realized or became aware that they would become King/ Queen someday.

They relished the opportunity to relate the story of the moment they first learned they would become leaders of their people and how they felt upon hearing this. They indicated that they had never related this before. This encouraged them to reflect deeply about leadership, commitment, and accountability to rural communities. The program that they

552   S. MUTHAYAN

co-designed, fostered greater camaraderie among the peers as it is not common for them to share the socioeconomic challenges, and successes they face in their respective kingdoms.

Facilitating Development is an Art

A key ingredient of the Art of Facilitation is the facilitator who guides the transformative learning process. The facilitator must be authentic, demonstrate a genuine interest in the participants and their stories and evoke deep mutual trust and respect for each other and the learning process. They must recognize the participants as knowledgeable, co-facilitators. While most senior public servants hold two university qualifications, this may not be the case with community workers and many traditional leaders. Muthayan (2008) advises, "Don't mistake a lack of education for ignorance—they know where they want to go" (p. 189). Facilitators may adopt this pedagogy to empower communities to find their own solutions to the challenges they face.

CONCLUSION

My aim is not to eschew the value of conventional didactic pedagogies but rather to argue that alternate, experiential, and expressive modes, such as storytelling in the Art of Facilitation, are valuable complementary practices. Storytelling is not a respite from the "real thing," an ice-breaker or energizer but a means to authentic transformative learning (Yorks & Kasl, 2006, p. 44).

The Art of Facilitation pedagogy, serves to decolonize and empower the participants. It is consistent with John Heron's (1992) theory of person and his conceptualization of whole-person epistemology (pp. 192–204). It brings "into awareness tacit and subconscious forms of knowing" that deepen the group's propensity, through the peer-sharing, "to engage one another's worldviews at profound levels of mutual respect, trust, and authentic understanding" (Yorks & Kasl, 2006, pp. 45, 61).

Storytelling allows learners to co-create curriculum for custom-made learning programs that respond to and are relevant to their specific development needs and contexts. The ensuing learning is transformative and may empower those responsible for the transformation of these post-colonial societies, i.e., public servants, to honor their Constitutional obligations and address more effectively the challenges of poverty, unemployment, and inequality. Transformative learning may provide not only the necessary "coherence and capability," the absence of which is lamented by Jonas (2019) above, but an improved sense of commitment to stem the tide of state capture and utilize these resources for the provision of basic services to the people.

In post-colonial societies there is a disjuncture between who we were, who we are and who we can or want to be. The majority of Black African people grew up in rural villages or segregated ghettoized townships. Their childhoods were embedded in indigenous cultures and values within a broader colonial context that devalued their identities and supplanted their precolonial histories with colonial histories. The segregated apartheid schooling system cemented their identity as the inferior subservient other. Later in the world of work, they continued to experience this loss of identity as the post-colonial system reifies the colonial arrangements. Within the public service there exists a tyranny of discourses which both crystallizes and obscures the post-colonial intents to perpetuate the colonial arrangements.

The dominant narrative of public servants includes deficit and negative terms such as "inefficient," "corrupt," "failure," "lack of …," "lazy," and so forth. Newcomers enter with enthusiasm that gives way to feeling demoralized, hopeless and trapped. Swart (2013) speaks of the "problem stories" that become powerful, leading to individuals feeling stuck (p. 3). Individuals and entire communities can take their identity of victimhood from these negative stories which render them dysfunctional. The Art of Facilitation is about the "resonance" afforded through the memory regression, signaling the "powerful moment(s) when people begin to integrate their past experiences, even traumatic ones and shift out of despair or hopelessness towards narratives of transformation" (Gilpin-Jackson, 2020, p. 4).

Programs drawing on the Art of Facilitation pedagogy, can contribute to the decolonizing work that still needs to be undertaken in post-colonial societies that continue to experience the denigration of the people's knowledges, value systems and ways of being. Storytelling creates a passageway from colonization to liberation and must be seen in the context of Fanon's work in allowing participants opportunities for subjective experiences: the deep self-reflection that precedes the authentic liberation of communities. Transformation.

References

Fanon, F. (1967). *Toward the African revolution* (H. Chevalier, Trans.). Grove.

Freire, P. (2000). *Pedagogy of the oppressed* (M. B. Ramos, Trans., 30th anniversary ed.). Continuum. (Original work published in 1970).

Galtung, J. (1971). A structural theory of imperialism. *Journal of Peace Research, 8*(2), 81–117.

Gambrell, J. A. (2016). Beyond personal transformation: Engaging students as agents for social change. *Journal of Multicultural Affairs, 1*(2), 1–35.

Gilpin-Jackson, Y. (2020). *Transformation after trauma: The power of resonance.* Peter Lang.

Goleman, D. (1997). *Emotional intelligence: Why it can matter more than IQ.* Bantam.

Heron, J. (1992). *Feeling and personhood: Psychology in another key.* Sage.

Jonas, M. (2019). *After dawn hope after state capture.* Picador Africa.

Muthayan, S. (2008). Decolonising research practices at South African universities. In A. A. Abdi & G. Richardson (Eds.), *Decolonizing democratic education* (pp. 183–193). Sense.

National School of Government, South Africa. (2016). *Lead facilitator development programme.* National School of Government.

Scott, G. G. (1991). *Shamanism and personal mastery.* New York: Paragon.

Scharmer, C. O. (2007). *Theory U: Leading from the future as it emerges.* Cambridge, USA: Society for Organisational Learning.

Ndlovu-Gatsheni, S. (2012). Fiftieth anniversary of decolonization in Africa: A moment of celebration or critical reflection? *Third World Quarterly, 33*(1), 71–89. https://doi.org/10.1080/01436597.2012.627236

Swart, C. (2013). *Re-authoring the world. The narrative lens and practices for organizations, communities and individuals.* Knowres.

Taylor, E. W. (2007). Transformative learning theory New directions for adult and continuing education. *Third Update on Adult Learning Theory, 119,* 5–15. https://doi.org/10.1002/ace.30

Yorks, L., & Kasl, E. (2006). I know more than I can say: A taxonomy for using expressive ways of knowing to foster transformative learning. *Journal of Transformative Education, 4*(5). doi: https://doi.org/10.1177/154134460 5283151.

CHAPTER 31

Transformation as Resistance

Bill Ashcroft

These two words—resistance and transformation—appear to be antonyms. *Resistance* refers to the application of force to prevent pressure, *transformation* is the process of movement and change. Colonial occupation attempted to transform, develop, or change the colonized culture by a strategy of civilizing violence and the colonial response is usually seen as resistance against that force. We tend to think of transformation as a consequence, something that happens to the subject, but transformation can be dynamic and intentional. It is important to recognize, then, that the term *postcolonial transformation* refers not to the transformation of colonial society by imperial power, but the opposite—the transformation of the discourses and technologies of power by the colonized. Such major discourses as literature, history, the representation of place, and ultimately modernity itself have been transformed by the active intervention of postcolonial artists and writers. This transformative dynamic reconfigures what we understand by "postcolonial resistance."

B. Ashcroft (✉)
University of NSW, Sydney, NSW, Australia
e-mail: b.ashcroft@unsw.edu.au

© The Author(s), under exclusive license to Springer Nature Switzerland AG 2022
A. Nicolaides et al. (eds.), *The Palgrave Handbook of Learning for Transformation*, https://doi.org/10.1007/978-3-030-84694-7_31

Resistance has become a much-used word in postcolonial discourse, and indeed, in all discussion of "Third World" politics, invariably connoting the imagery of conflict. This has much to do with the generally violent nature of colonial incursion. But we might well ask whether armed or ideological rebellion, or even active insurgency, is the only possible meaning of resistance, and, more importantly, whether the history of colonial rebellion leaves in its wake a rhetoric of opposition emptied of any capacity for social change. What does it really mean to *resist*? If we think of resistance as any form of defense by which an invader is kept out, then subtle and sometimes even unspoken forms of social and cultural resistance have been much more common. It is these subtle and more widespread forms of resistance, forms of avoidance and evasion that are most interesting because they are most difficult for imperial powers to combat. Undoubtedly the most effective form of resistance has been the transformation of the forces of oppression.

How then did postcolonial resistance develop as a process of transformation? Paradoxically, it began with the British determination to teach English to Indian elites, to create a class of "mimic men." The founding moment of this move was Lord Macaulay's Minute to Parliament in 1835. This document, Gauri Viswanathan (1987) tells us, signified the rise to prominence of the Anglicists over the Orientalists in the British administration of India. The Charter Act of 1813, devolving responsibility for Indian education on the colonial administration, led to a struggle between the two approaches, ultimately resolved by Macaulay's Minute, in which we find stated not just the assumptions of the Anglicists, but the profoundly universalist assumptions of English national culture itself. "We must educate a people who cannot at present be educated by means of their mother-tongue," says Macaulay, with breathtaking confidence, that because English "stands pre-eminent even among the languages of the west" (1835, pp. 349–350) the advancement of any colonized people could only occur under its auspices, and it was on English literature that the burden of imparting civilized values was to rest. This strategy worked so well as a form of cultural studies because English literature "all but effaced the sordid history of colonialist expropriation, material exploitation and class and race oppression behind European world dominance" (Viswanathan, 1987, p. 22). Consequently, English literature became a prominent agent of colonial control, indeed, it can be said that English literary study really began in earnest even in Britain once its function as a discipline of cultural indoctrination had been established, and its ability to "civilize" the lower classes had thus been triumphantly revealed.

But what the administrators of colonial education could never have anticipated was that the English language and the literature used to inculcate British culture provided the colonized with the tools of resistance. This resistance proceeded subtly as colonized peoples transformed the language into a vehicle of self-representation and wrote their own literature in English to interpolate and transform the edifice of English literature itself. So the very tools the empire used to inculcate the colonized with Western culture were transformed into tools with which the non-European culture was given a global voice.

Transforming English

The first stage of this strategy was the transformation of the English language into a culturally relevant vehicle. This was achieved by appropriating the language to the grammatical and syntactical forms of the mother tongue, and the best place to do this and disseminate it was literary writing. Such writing became, in effect, an ethnography of the writer's own culture. The simplest of these techniques is the glossing of individual words, such as "he took him into his obi (hut)." But a more common technique is that of including untranslated vernacular words. Refusing to translate words not only registers a sense of cultural distinctiveness but also forces the reader into an active engagement with the vernacular culture. Other forms of linguistic transformation include the development of an "interlanguage" by fusing the linguistic structures of English and mother tongue. But perhaps the most common method of inscribing cultural mobility is the technique of switching between two or more codes, particularly in the literatures of the Caribbean "creole continuum" (See for e.g., Bickerton, 1973; D'Costa, 1983, 1984; Le Page, 1969; Le Page & DeCamp, 1960). The techniques employed by the polydialectical writer include variable orthography to make dialect more accessible, double glossing, and code switching to act as an interweaving interpretative mode, and syntactic fusion. All these are common ways of installing cultural distinctiveness in the writing (See Ashcroft et al., 1989, pp. 39–77).

These strategies open up what may be called a *metonymic gap*— the cultural gap formed when writers (in particular) transform English according to the needs of their source culture (Ashcroft, 2008, p. 174).

558   B. ASHCROFT

Such variations become synecdochic of the writer's culture—the part that stands for the whole—rather than representations of the world, as the colonizing language might. Thus the transformed language "stands for" the colonized culture in a metonymic way, and its very resistance to interpretation constructs a gap between the writer's culture and the colonial culture. Being constructed, this gap is very different from the gaps that might emerge in a translation. The local writer is thus able to represent his or her world to the colonizer (and others) in a version of the metropolitan language, and at the same time, to signal and emphasize a difference from it. In effect, the writer is saying "I am using your language so that you will understand my world, but you will also know by the differences in the way I use it that you cannot share my experience."

When writers transform the English language, then, they are engaged in a political and cultural act, an act that assertively occupies what Homi Bhabha calls the "Third Space of Enunciation." The difference is that this Third Space characterizes language itself. Edward Kamau Brathwaite, Caribbean poet and critic, describes local appropriations of English by the term "Nation Language," giving us an excellent insight into the ways in which the character of language, not just the orthography and grammar, can be transformed: "English it may be in terms of some of its lexical features. But in its contours, its rhythm and timbre, its sound explosions, it is not English" (Brathwaite, 1984, p. 13).

Transforming English Literature

The transformation of language was the beginning of this process because English became a medium of literary expression, producing literary works that interpolated the discipline of English literature and effectively transformed it by broadening its reach. Macaulay's Minute shows how deeply English literature is rooted in the cultural relationships established by British imperialism. The ideological function of English was re-confirmed in all postcolonial societies, in very different pedagogic situations. Literature, by definition, excluded local writing. Mathew Arnold's glowingly humanist credo "nothing human is alien to me"[1] only operates by incorporating an extensive array of quite specific exclusions; for you cannot

---

[1] This is a quote from the Roman poet Terence from the play "Heauton Timorumenos": "Homo sum, humani nihil a me alienum puto," or "I am human, and I think nothing human is alien to me".

have a Culture that is Ugandan, Australian, or Jamaican. The matter was put succinctly by Edmund Gosse, commenting on Robert Louis Stephenson's return to Samoa: "The fact seems to be that it is very nice to live in Samoa, but not healthy to write there. Within a three-mile radius of Charing Cross is the literary atmosphere, I suspect" (Gosse, 1891, p. 375). This bias assumed the status of an ideology—one that became absorbed by colonial cultural production itself: colonials also often believed that the margin of empire was not the place to write literature.

Postcolonial writers tend to recognize the way in which intellectual endeavor is compromised and contained by State power as it is mediated through intellectual work. Bringing to mind Adorno's thesis of the state production of culture, Edward Said says:

> To a great extent culture, cultural formations, and intellectuals exist by virtue of a very interesting network of relationships with the State's almost absolute power. (1983, p. 169)

This is a set of relationships about which all contemporary left criticism, according to Said, and indeed all literary study, remains stunningly silent.

As Said goes on to point out, even if we want to claim that "culture" as aesthetic production subsists on its own, according to an art-for-art's sake theory, no one is prepared to show how that independence was gained nor, more importantly, how it was maintained.

The postcolonial writer is very attuned to the fact that this work is "occurring at some place at some time in a mapped-out and permissible terrain" (p. 169) because the reality of place, the reality of publishing requirements, markets, form some of the defining conditions of its production, and the ideological containment produces the tension against which it must constantly test itself. However, because "containment" by the State is far from absolute, being negotiated at many levels by an access to and appropriation of global culture, the transformation of English literature by postcolonial writers demonstrates the broader agency of global subjects to interpolate structures of power. The resilience of postcolonial production in its appropriation of imperial forms for local identity construction, is, as we shall see, a model for the local engagement with global culture.

560 B. ASHCROFT

Transforming History

The transformation of imperial language and literature is a key transformation because it is focused on the critical issue of cultural representation. But postcolonial societies made many other responses to imperial discourse. When we consider the extensive ways in which the West came to control global reality we can see that language and the technologies of writing were instrumental in perpetuating the modes of this dominance. The engagement with geography, history and a wide-ranging array of dominant epistemological discourses demonstrates a remarkable facility in colonized people to use the modes of these discourses against imperial power, transforming them in ways that have been both profound and lasting.

Historiography has been one of the most influential Eurocentric constructions of subjectivity. As Ashis Nandy puts it, "Today the whole world wants to enter History," because "Historical consciousness now owns the globe...Though millions of people continue to stay outside history, millions have, since the days of Marx, dutifully migrated to the empire of history to become its loyal subjects." (1995, p. 46) When colonial societies are historicized they are brought into history, brought into the discourse of "modernity" as a function of imperial control—mapped, named, organized, legislated, inscribed. But at the same time they are kept at History's margins, implanting the joint sense of loss and desire. Being inscribed into History is to be made modern because History and European modernity go hand in hand. History is that which keeps the colonized locked into the embrace of empire with its promise of modernity and nationality (see Chakrabarty, 1992, p. 19).

By interpolating history through literary and other non-empirical texts, postcolonial narratives of historical experience reveal the fundamentally fabricated nature of history itself but more pertinently the different historical experience of the colonized. Postcolonial histories began to give rise to various counter-narratives that took the view of the colonized, but such narratives may also contest the disciplinary boundaries of history as well. Wilson Harris believes that "a philosophy of history may well lie buried in the arts of the imagination" (Harris, 1970, pp. 24–5). For Harris such imaginative arts extend beyond the literary to include the discourse of the limbo dance or of vodun, all examples of the creativity of "stratagems available to Caribbean man in the dilemmas of history which surround him" (p. 25).

There are various ways in which the colonized can respond to the imperial function of history: they may acquiesce with its historical narrative; they may interject a different perspective into the discipline of history; they may interpolate history in a way that reveals its assumptions and limitations; or they may offer a different more rhetorical version of history (White, 1982, p. 120). The simplest is *acquiescence*, a characteristic of those colonial histories which ask no questions at all about historical method, and which accede to the idea of colony as an outpost of civilization, an "empirical record" of the movement of civilized values into the wilderness of an "undiscovered wasteland."

But there are a number of transformative responses to historical method, the simplest of which is *interpolation*, in which the basic premises of historical narrative are accepted, but a contrary narrative, which claims to offer a more immediate or "truer" picture of postcolonial life, a record of those experiences omitted from imperial history, is inserted into the historical record. A good example of this is Ayi Kwai Armah who is better known for his earlier novels such as *The Beautyful Ones are Not Yet Born* (1968), *Fragments* (1970) and *Why are We so Blessed?* (1972)— all deeply pessimistic about the post-independence African regimes. Yet that dystopian view of the present betrayal of Africa by its leaders is closely connected to the utopianism that emerges in his work (1977, 2002, 2006). *Two Thousand Seasons* (1973, 2000) is an example of an allegorical re-writing of African history in which a pluralized communal voice recounts the experiences of his people over a period of one thousand years.

Re-telling the history of slavery as this novel does is one form of historical recuperation, which offers the vision of a different future, but Armah is even more interested in engaging the discourse of western history and he does this by adopting the revisionist history of Cheikh-Anta Diop. Diop's book, *Nations Nègres et Culture* (1974), is a passionate attempt to show that ancient Egyptian civilization was in fact a Black African achievement, and thus to prove that the west owed its enlightenment not to Greece but to Africa. The concept of Pharaohnic Africa was taken up wholeheartedly by Armah in *KMT* (2002, pronounced "Kemet") and *Osiris Rising* (1995, 2008), extending his re-imagining of African history into a vision of the subversive and politically repressed reality of African Egypt in African culture. This method is fundamentally a political contestation of European imperial power. But it is one that works through, in

562   B. ASHCROFT

the interstices of, in the fringes of rather than in simple opposition to history.

Where at least one of Armah's purposes was to interpolate world history with a narrative of the pharaohnic past, Ben Okri manages, in the Famished Road trilogy (1991, 1998), to achieve the sense of a different kind of history in the language itself, as well as his narrative. His representation of a fantastically expanded world of experience conceives the rich horizon of African reality, an *imaginaire* that constantly resists the temptation of the Western reader to appropriate it into a familiar landscape. Thus, Okri does in narrative what many examples of transformed language do in postcolonial writing—communicating and resisting at the same time. This leads to a language that overlaps magical realism, a language of excess and accretion, a layering of experience in which the border between the real and spirit world is dissolved.

Transforming Colonial Space

There is a growing perception among human geographers that space is not "simply there" but is the product of social actors: "space, and by implication scale, are both material and discursive categories that are 'constructed' or 'produced' by social processes and the intervention of human agents" (Sheppard & McMaster, 2004, p. 15). These social processes are also critical in the production of place. The issues surrounding the concept of place: how it is conceived, how it differs from space or location, how it enters into and produces cultural consciousness, how it becomes the horizon of identity, are some of the most difficult and debated in postcolonial experience. Where is one's place? What happens to the concept of "home" when home is colonized, when the very ways of conceiving home, of talking about it, writing about it, remembering it, begin to occur through the medium of the colonizer's way of seeing the world? The Eurocentric control of space, through its ocularcentrism, its cartography, its development of perspective, its modes of surveillance, and above all, through its language, has been one of the most difficult forms of cultural control faced by postcolonial societies. Resistance to dominant assumptions about spatial location and the identity of place has occurred most generally in the way in which such space has been inhabited.

The Western construction of global space has become a given for contemporary representations of place and remains the inevitable context in which those local representations must occur. In effect, the discourse of place operates within the same set of power relations that affect other forms of postcolonial transformation, and indeed, becomes one of their most contested sites. The Mercator Atlas was a key instrument in that re-organization of space and time, which characterized the great historical and discursive shift of European modernity. The most far-reaching impact of this re-organization upon colonized societies was the severance of the traditional links between time, space, and place within modern consciousness. This is not only because many pre-colonial societies were categorized as "pre-modern," and have therefore experienced very great social and cultural disruptions through colonization, but because all postcolonial societies, indeed all societies today, are subject to global representations of time and space, which have little reference to locality. A radical disruption of the experience of place was also made by the colonial imposition of the concept of private property, which in Australia for instance, saw one's place as that which was bordered and fenced sealed off from the "Absolute Dark" of Aboriginal country (Malouf, 1993).

What becomes apparent in postcolonial artists and writers is that place is much more than the land. The theory of place does not propose a simple separation between the place named and described in language, and some "real" place inaccessible to it, but rather indicates that in some sense place is language, something in constant flux, a discourse in process. Place is never simply location, nor is it static, a cultural memory which colonization buries. For, like culture itself, place is in a continual and dynamic state of formation, a process intimately bound up with the culture and the identity of its inhabitants. Above all place, like space, is a result of habitation, a consequence of the ways in which people inhabit space, particularly that conception of space as universal and uncontestable that is constructed for them by imperial discourse. The transformation of imperial conceptions of place, and of imperial technologies of spatial representation, has often occurred successfully through imaginative acts of resistance in the creative representations of place. Such place forms itself out of the densely woven web of language, memory, and cultural practice and keeps being formed by the process of living.

Perspective

While there are far more aspects to the perception and representation of space than can be addressed here, the prominence of perspective in Western seeing offers a strategic reference point. The "discovery" of perspective during the Renaissance, the invention of the perspectival method, was a huge and crucial shift in European spatial perception, and became so embedded and naturalized that visual perspective became the only and "true" way to see. This construction of the method of perspectival perception offers a clear example of the development of a discourse. That which we take for granted today as the way the world really is visual, is the result of a highly codified method that grew out of Renaissance theories about the separation of the individual subject from the world. The discourse of space is one which we enter as we enter ideology. So complete is the success of the perspectival method that this is the way we (westerners, and increasingly, all cultures) understand what the world looks like.

The perspectival concept of space, the sense of static extension and the isolation of the viewer from the scene, the separation of subject and object, are all characteristic of European painters' views of colonial space. In most cases, colonial painters find in the open spaces of many of the colonized places, a spatial extension, a horizon of uninhabited land, which provides a ready opportunity to impose the priority of perspective, indeed the priority of visual space itself over any other indigenous modes of spatial perception. But the view of space in many colonized cultures hinges of the presence of the subject in the scene, a reversal of the principle of perspective. For instance, in Aboriginal societies, place is traditionally not a visual construct at all in the perspectival tradition, neither a measurable space nor even a topographical system but a tangible location of one's own dreaming, an extension of one's own being.

The most strategic place to transform the dominance of perspective was in art. Perspective was invented in Renaissance art. It is in art that the transformation of colonial space occurs, and Aboriginal art offers an important model for the transformation of the perspectival view. This art is metonymic and symbolic rather than representational in function, and deeply implicated in the performance of religious obligations. Animal and abstract forms are drawn for their sacred significance because, like oral language, they embody rather than represent the power of the things they signify. The Aboriginal paints on things and on the body itself, rather than paint the perception of things because the individual's art is an activity that expresses the community's participation in this power. Sometimes paintings may seem to follow the principles of a map but the elements are organized in terms of ritual power and inhering relationships rather than in terms of spatial extension. On the other hand, the art of the White settlers in Australia appears to be obsessed with landscape, and especially with the task of inventing the spatial representation of a landscape as a way of "indigenizing" place. Such passion for the visual space, with its Gothic overtones of vastness and hostility, is evident in the literature as well, but it is in the landscape that we find the most striking visual metaphor for a sense of cultural uniqueness which the settler society constructs as a sign of its distinctiveness from imperial culture.

The Aboriginal has no need to paint the landscape in traditional artistic activity because the land as a visual space is nameless. What matters are those named features into which the Dreaming ancestors metamorphosed when they completed their travels on the nameless plane of the original universe. By relationship with these beings the land is a function of the Aboriginal's own being, an embodiment which is expressed in art, and in dance. As Galarrwuy Yunipingu says:

> When aboriginal people get together we put the land into action. When I perform, the land is within me, and I am the only one who can move, land doesn't, so I represent the land when I dance. (Yunipingu, 1980. pp. 13–14)

The idea of not owning the land but in some sense being owned by it, is a way of seeing the world that is so different from the materiality and commodification of imperial discourse, that effective protection of one's place is radically disabled when that new system—perspectival vision—becomes the dominant one as European spatial representations are inscribed upon the palimpsest of place. Aboriginal art offers a different way of seeing that has made a global impact.

Transforming Modernity

Perhaps the most profound postcolonial transformation has been that of modernity itself, or more specifically, our growing recognition of the multiplicity of modernity. This transformation occurred in three ways: the role of Indigenous art in the emergence of European modernism; the appropriation and transformation of Western modernity through creative adaptation; and the emergence of non-Western, and particularly Indigenous modernities through the engagement with imperial power.

The Origins of Modernism

The story begins with the pivotal role of the artworks of the colonized in the emergence of European modernism. The discovery of cultures whose aesthetic practices and cultural models were radically disruptive of the prevailing European assumptions forced Europeans to realize that their culture was only one among a plurality of alternative ways of conceiving of reality and organizing its representations in art and social practice. Central to this realization was the encounter with African culture after the scramble for Africa in the 1880s and 90 s. An alternative view of the world emerged from the collection of African masks, carvings, and jewelry that were seized and expatriated to Europe and generally stored away in the basements of the new museums of ethnology and anthropology. When placed on display in the early decades of the next century, the art was to inspire the modernists and encourage them in their attempts to create the images of an alternative and radically "unrealistic" art. Universalist claims of taste and function for art were subverted as these alternative cultural artifacts transformed contemporary art. The colonial inspiration of European modernism transformed European modernity in a specific and strategic case, one that began to show the transcultural effects of colonial occupation.

Creative Adaptation

In many cases the transformation of modernity followed the pattern of the transformation of language and literature, which can be taken as a metonym for the creative adaptation of Western modernity. A common assumption is that European modernity swept over the world like a wave. Achille Mbembe claims that colonization and the modern went hand in hand: "Like Islam and Christianity, colonization is a universalizing project. Its ultimate aim is to inscribe the colonized in the space of modernity" (Mbembe, 2002, p. 634). But if colonization was a universalizing project, did it succeed? Did it "inscribe" the colonized in the space of modernity, and if so was that a "wave-like" engulfment, a cultural disorientation, or did the colonized take hold of the pen and inscribe themselves in that space in a curious act of defiance modeled by postcolonial writers?

Despite the ambivalence toward both colonial culture and its literature, transformation was a particularly enterprising form of resistance that utilized the technologies of European modernity without being engulfed by them. Postcolonial literature therefore stands as a metonym for the creative adaptation of non-Western modernities: they are a specific practice, an enterprise engaged by agents who locate themselves in a discourse in a resistant, counter-discursive way through the transformation of dominant technologies. They are a specific example of how individual subjects could "change the world that is changing them" (Berman, 1982, p. 16). This doesn't mean that they act independently of the forces acting upon them, but they act. Whereas *development*—the acultural theory of modernization—acts to force the local into globally normative patterns, *transformation* shows that those patterns are adjusted to and by the requirements of local values and needs. Subsequently, the features of these alternative modernities may be re-circulated globally in various ways.

Indigenous Modernities

Perhaps the most significant transformation of our understanding of modernity has been the growing recognition of the development of non-Western modernities quite distinct from the direct influence of the West. This is not so much a transformation of modernity as a transformation of our understanding of the diversity of modernity. In many cases, the originating moment in non-Western modernities was coeval with that of the West rather than inherited. This was not limited to Indigenous peoples but to the entire non-European world. David Carter argues, for instance, that one cannot "speak simply of the arrival of modernism in Australia." The Australian reactions are not made directly to such modernists as Eliot, Joyce, Picasso, or Freud, but they are "multiple artistic, intellectual and political responses to communist revolution, world war, economic depression and the threat of fascism" (1984, p. 160).

In many cases the colonized saw colonial invasion as a process of creating a binary between primitive and modern and Indigenous societies regularly produced their own modernities as reactions to rather than copies of the imperial arm of European modernity. The flourishing of Indigenous art is one example of the emergence of modernity as the product of cultural tension. Stephen Muecke suggests that.

> This modernity is quite distinct from European modernisation processes since it developed its own forms, later including modernist and postmodernist aesthetics. (Muecke, 2004, p. 155)

As Pamela Scully points out, "like modernity, indigeneity was and is as much about self-representation and self-presentation as about lineage or parentage or place. (Scully, 2012, p. 591). Far from being merely "primitives" Indigenous people have crafted versions of their own indigeneity in a system of representational transformation. The character of Indigenous modernity lies precisely in this capacity for engagement and transformation.

The "Indigenous modern" may seem to be an oxymoron, but it is a phrase that should be as acceptable as "modern Australian." We take the Indigenous modern as an inclusive category of the contemporaneous, and hence as part of an argument for implementing fully serviced and responsibility-bearing citizenship for Aboriginal people. How can one be seen to be a fully participating citizen if one is deemed to be either from a radically incommensurable traditional culture, or a perpetually disadvantaged urban one? At the very simplest, being modern means having a range of inventive responses to the contemporary world (p. 158).

The identification of Indigenous modernities transforms modernity in particular ways: it contests the assumption that European modernity engulfed the world like a wave; it refutes the myth of "belatedness" which sees "traditional" or "pre-modern" societies "catching up" with the West in a process of delayed influence; it refutes the idea that European modernity is global, inevitable and unavoidable; it refutes the "acultural" theory of modernity that sees it severed from culture, place and time; and it refutes the idea that there is only one modernity, despite the undoubted colonizing power of capitalism.

Conclusion

The message of postcolonial engagements with imperial power is that transformation can be a consequence of concerted political action. Whereas the discourse of development has acted to transform the non-Western world, that world has shown, through the example of postcolonial creative producers, that power and its technologies can be transformed by active political engagement. This is more than decolonization. By transforming the technologies of power—language, literature, and history, conceptions of space and place, and ultimately modernity itself—postcolonial writers have begun to transform the landscape of power.

Such action stands as a model for the power of dominated and oppressed classes on a global scale. The range of strategies, the tenacity, and the practical assertiveness of the apparently powerless are striking. When we project our analysis onto a global screen we find that the capacity, the agency, the inventiveness of postcolonial transformation helps us to explain something about the ways in which local communities resist absorption and transform global culture itself. In the end the transformative energy of postcolonial societies, tells us about the present because it is overwhelmingly concerned with the future.

References

Ashcroft, B. (2008). *Caliban's Voice: the Transformation of English in Post-Colonial Literatures*. Routledge.

Armah, A. K. (1973). *Two thousand seasons*. Per Ankh. 2003.

Armah, A. K. (1977). *The Healers*. Per Ankh. 2000.

Armah, A. K. (2002). *KMT: In the house of life*. Per Ankh.

Armah, A. K. (2006). *The eloquence of scribes*. Per Ankh.

Ashcroft, B., Griffiths, G., & Tiffin, H. (1989). *The Empire Writes Back: Theory and Practice in Post-colonial Literatures*. Routledge.

Berman, M. (1982). *All that is solid melts into air: The experience of modernity*. Verso.

Bickerton, D. (1973). On the nature of a Creole continuum. *Language, 49*(3).

Brathwaite, E. K. (1984). *A history of the voice*. New Beacon.

Carter, D. (1984). Modernism and Australian literature. *World Literature Written in English, 24*(1), 158–169.

Chakrabarty, D. (1992). Postcoloniality and the artifice of history: Who speaks for "Indian" pasts? *Representations, 32*, 1–26.

D'Costa, J. (1983). *The West Indian novelist and language: A search for a literary medium*. Studies in Caribbean Language. Society for Caribbean Linguistics.

D'Costa, J. (1984). Expression and communication: Literary challenges to the Caribbean polydialectical writers. *Journal of Commonwealth Literature, 19*(1), 1984.

Diop, C. A. (1974). *The African origin of civilization* (C. Mercer, Trans., Ed.). Lawrence Hill.

Gosse, E. (1891, January 31). Letter to G. A. Armour. Reprinted in P. Maxiner (Ed.) *Robert Louis Stevenson: The critical heritage*. Routledge.

Harris, W. (1970). History, fable and myth in the Caribbean and the Guianas. In H. Maes-Jelinek (Ed.), *Explorations: A selection of talks and articles 1966–81*. Dangaroo Press. 1981.

Le Page, R. (1969). Dialect in West Indian literature. *Journal of Commonwealth Literature*, 7.

Le Page, R., & DeCamp, D. (1960). *Jamaican Creole*. Macmillan.

Macaulay, T. B. (1835). Minute on Indian education. In G.M. Young (Ed.), *Speeches*. OUP. AMS Edition. 1979.

Malouf, D. (1993). *Remembering Babylon*. Chatto & Windus.

Mbembe, A. (2002). On the power of the false. *Public Culture*, 14.

Muecke, S. (2004). 'I don't think they invented the wheel': The case for Indigenous modernity. *Angelaki: Journal of the Theoretical Humanities*, 9(2), 155–163.

Nandy, A. (1995). History's bles. *History and Theory*, 34(2), 44–66.

Okri, B. (1991). *The famished road*. Jonathan Cape.

Okri, B. (1998). *Infinite riches*. Phoenix House.

Said, E. (1983). *The world the text and the critic*. Vintage.

Scully, P. (2012). Indigeneity, agency and modernity. *Cultural and Social History*, 9(4), 589–592.

Selinker, L. (1972). Interlanguage. *IRAL. International Review of Applied Linguistics*, 10.

Sheppard, E., & McMaster, R. B. (Eds.). (2004). Introduction: Scale and geographic inquiry. In *Scale and geographic inquiry: Nature, society and method*. Blackwell.

Tutuola, A. (1952). *The palm-wine drinkard*. Faber.

Viswanathan, G. (1987). The beginnings of English literary study in British India. *Oxford Literary Review*, 9, 1–2.

White, H. (1982). The politics of historical interpretation: Discipline and desublimation. *Critical Inquiry*, 9.

Yunipingu, G. (1980). *Aboriginal land rights*. Murdoch University.

CHAPTER 32

Transformative Learning as a Passageway to Social Justice in Higher Education: An Asian American and Pacific Islander (AAPI) Perspective on Anti-Bullyist Practice in a North American Context

Mitsunori Misawa

INTRODUCTION

Diversity, inclusion, and equity are important elements in contemporary society at large. While researchers and practitioners in multiculturalism or social justice have provided critical examinations of the cultural melting pot in American culture where many cultures of minority populations based on race, gender, class, sexual orientation, and other sociocultural positions and identities melt into the macro or majority culture that consists of White, upper-middle class, and heterosexual men and women

M. Misawa (✉)
University of Tenneessee, Knoxville, TN, USA
e-mail: mmisawa@utk.edu

© The Author(s), under exclusive license to Springer Nature Switzerland AG 2022
A. Nicolaides et al. (eds.), *The Palgrave Handbook of Learning for Transformation*, https://doi.org/10.1007/978-3-030-84694-7_32

571

(Bonilla-Silva, 2018), there is an increasing understanding of demographics of American populations where people with diverse backgrounds and positionalities coexist and have their own unique sociocultural perspectives.

Similarly, higher education is a microcosm of this society where diverse populations bring their own sociocultural and socioeconomic statuses with them. Although historical perspectives of higher education have been dominated by mostly White (heterosexual) men from the field's establishment over 250 years ago at Harvard University (Twale & De Luca, 2008), traditionally underrepresented groups like women and people of color have an increasing presence in contemporary higher education than ever before (Johnson-Bailey & Cervero, 2018). Because of the demographic shift in the population of higher education, conventional ways of educating learners and conventional thoughts in academic fields are not necessarily applicable to populations who are not White heterosexual men. Implementing an innovative and more diverse perspective has become an important element of contemporary higher education, one that continuously produces new knowledge and disseminates it to communities to make society at large better through this knowledge.

While contemporary higher education has strived to create a diverse and more inclusive culture and environment, it has been faced with the issue of bullying. Bullying in adulthood is pervasive and ingrained in contemporary society, and it is a critical global problem. Bullying impacts the physical and psychological health of all who are involved in a bullying incident, including the targets/victims/survivors, perpetrators/bullies, and bystanders. The Workplace Bullying Institute (2021) reported in their most recent study that close to 80 million adult workers are affected by bullying and that about 49 million Americans are bullied at work, and that 49% of them were affected by abusive conduct at work, 30% suffered abusive conduct at work, and 19% witnessed it. Adult bullying at work involves many factors such as intentionality of negative conduct toward targets/victims.

Scholars and practitioners have explored how bullying influences people's lives and how it transforms people's lives and perceptions due to the experience of it (Misawa & Rowland, 2015). For example, adult bullying influences the physiological health of people who are involved in adult bullying situations, affecting cardiovascular disease, musculoskeletal pain, morbidity, high blood pressure, and diabetes (Khubchandani &

Price, 2015), and the psychological health of people including depression, posttraumatic stress disorder, and suicide (Field, 1996; MacIntosh, 2012; Misawa et al., 2019). There is now an increasing understanding that bullying affects how people live and how they navigate their lives in society, and an understanding that it is a lifelong phenomenon. Some scholars who research bullying among adults have already determined that bullying can happen to anyone in any place at any time, as long as power dynamics exist (Misawa, 2015; Namie & Namie, 2009), and one's positionality shapes and influences bullying situations (Johnson-Bailey, 2015; Misawa et al., 2019). So, bullying can be thought of as a critical, impactful, or disoriented dilemma that targets experience during the coping phase, which shares many similarities to what scholars in adult education call a passageway to transformation.

Due to how bullying was first extensively studied in Scandinavian, Norwegian, and European countries and then brought to the USA, bullying as a phenomenon has been described generically from a Western or Eurocentric perspective with a homogenous or one-size-fits-all perspective which is assumed to be applicable to anyone; however, it does not consider or include others like AAPIs and non-Western populations.

A similar thing can be said about transformative learning. Traditionally, transformative learning has been utilized to depict how White heterosexual individuals change their perspectives from their life experiences or their disorienting dilemmas through critical self-reflective processes (Mezirow, 2000), and the theory has then explored a collective perspective transformation from individuality to White heterosexual groups, communities, and society at large (Cranton, 2016). The Mezirownian perspective of transformative learning has dominated academia including the field of transformative learning where the majority of work has been White or Eurocentric, and such work has been widely disseminated and has become more visible and appreciated as the norm of the field (Johnson-Bailey & Cervero, 2018). From that perspective, the pathway of transformation still seems to be predominantly White or Eurocentric where the perspectives of the others like non-Western or non-Eurocentric perspectives are excluded or unconsidered when transformative learning is applied to exploring the lives of adults.

Since having an increasingly better understanding of conventional Mezirownian and Western and Eurocentric transformative learning in the field is important for its progression and expansion in the future, the field also needs to be aware of, and more inclusive of, the other non-Western

574 M. MISAWA

or non-Eurocentric perspectives, including the perspectives of AAPIs. By so doing the field can develop a passageway for those who possess unconventional ways of knowing. This chapter will focus on uncovering the kinds of transformation that are unconsidered or underexplored in the field of transformative learning by providing a deeper understanding of the AAPI perspective, and by exploring how AAPI perspectives manifest in the passageway of transformation and transformative learning. It will do this by exploring bullyism toward AAPIs in academia and an anti-bullyist practice, deeply rooted in social justice, for AAPIs in American higher education. This chapter will address how AAPI faculty deal with bullying based on the author's previous research on adult bullying in higher education, and will explore the experiences of bullying in higher education among faculty of AAPI men in Western and Eurocentric contexts. The following research question will guide this chapter: How do faculty of AAPI ethnicity experience bullying in higher education?

As stated above, although the field of transformative learning in adult education has contributed to knowledge production in theory and practice, such knowledge production from Asian Americans and Pacific and Islander perspectives has not been widely included, explored, or disseminated. The following sections of this chapter will focus on AAPI perspectives on bullying and transformative learning in higher education, including reviews of the relevant literature such as stereotypes, assumptions, and implicit biases about AAPIs from Critical Race Theory and AsianCrit. In addition, this chapter will explore how those stereotypes and assumptions influenced professors of AAPI who are men with regard to bullying in higher education and how they processed that through transformative learning processes. This chapter also addresses non-Western ways of knowing and how that epistemological perspective facilitates or challenges the transformative learning process for AAPI faculty who have experienced situations where bullying took place. Discussion and implications for AAPIs on transformative learning as a passageway to social justice that is anti-bullyist in practice will be provided.

Relevant Literature

Social justice including diversity, equity, and inclusion has become an important topic in contemporary society, especially in education from K–12 to adult, higher, and lifelong education. However, social justice is not a new topic. In fact, the field of adult education was established from a social justice perspective (Bierema, 2010) and included ideas of equity for people regarding gender, social class, and race (and later on sexual orientation, disability, other social identities). The field has always promoted social justice through formal, informal, and non-formal education (Merriam & Baumgartner, 2020). However, there is a tendency among people to make their own assumptions and hold on to implicit biases about others based on their appearance or physical characteristics (Sue, 2010). Although race is a social construct that is pervasive across all settings and all nations, racial justice and anti-racism matters (Misawa & Johnson-Bailey, 2018). Elements like these are pivotal parts of education because they lead to a better understanding of sociocultural and socioeconomic divisions among diverse groups of people in society. In particular, the race has become a significant factor that divides people into different groups all the while troubling various intersections among racially diverse groups of people.

Race, Racism, and Hate Crimes in the United States

In the United States, race is one of the major sociocultural (or often sociopolitical and socioeconomic) markers to categorize and group people. Race is utilized as one of the social indicators to survey US populations through the US Census, which is conducted every ten years by the federal government to record the demographic information about US populations. Race is also used in medical records and even in college admission applications (Matsuda, 1993). While grouping people into boxes seems to be one of the ways to understand how demographics have changed over time and how the social status of each racial group has grown, race matters particularly when it is used to discriminate and marginalize people who belong to certain racial groups (Delgado & Stefancic, 2017; Johnson-Bailey & Cervero, 2018; Lee, 2010).

As history reveals, race in the United States has negative connotations with negative historical events affecting a myriad of racial minorities, including slavery of African Americans, the internment camps during World War II for Japanese Americans, and many more highly racialized historical events and practices (Chang, 1993; Delgado & Stefancic, 2017; Matsuda, 1993), and each racial minority group has its own historical events with regard to their race and culture (Lee, 2010). Racism, as such, continues to be a critical social issue across the United States. However, in recent years, diversity, equity, and inclusion have gained extensive attention by society at large, both nationally and globally. The US has even begun to start reclaiming racial justice for people of color, due to multiple race-based incidents and hate crimes directed toward them in recent years, although scholars and researchers in Critical Race Theory (CRT) have raised that point about racism and racial perspectives since the late 1960s. Since race can also function as a socially constructed indicator of one's quality of life related to one's success, CRT has constructed the notion of social inquiry based on the different racial groups in the United States (Misawa, 2010). Even so, when discussing race and racism, the perspectives of AAPIs have often been ignored or overlooked by scholars who specialize in race and racism, because AAPIs have historically been treated as invisible or ambiguous racial and ethnic groups.

While racism and hate crimes toward racial minorities have existed for a long time and have been ubiquitous in the US culture, modern racism and hate crimes toward AAPIs have only just started coming to the surface after the recent surge in hate crimes targeting AAPIs across the United States. Until recently AAPIs have not usually been addressed in racial discourse in the United States because they, particularly East Asian descendants, have been thought of as "model minorities," which is a myth or assumption or implicit bias from the White majority group that Asians work hard and are obedient, and that they are able to assimilate into or melt into the White American culture (Delgado & Stefancic, 2017; Lee, 2010). According to Lee (2010), the model minority is a myth about AAPIs that "prevails and has led educators in higher and adult education to stereotype Asians and to develop classes that fail to fully recognize the contributions of Asians in America" (p. 299). The typical grand narrative about Asians is that they are high achievers in education and successful in society so they don't need additional support or resources. That is not true because the myth of the model minority assumes that AAPIs are homogenous populations where AAPIs all have the same experiences. However, AAPI populations are diverse, and, in fact, they are heterogeneous, presenting various ethnic groups and nationalities from different countries. Asia is a vast region, and moreover the term "Asian and Pacific Islanders" is a huge umbrella representing various distinct ethnicities and cultures. So, if we categorize AAPIs as a homogenous group, then the heterogeneous or diverse racial and ethnic perspectives among them get lost in translation.

The prevalence of the myth of the model minority has also led educators and practitioners to perpetuate stereotypes of AAPIs and fail to recognize the actual needs of those who desperately need educational support among AAPIs. The myth could be positive because it seems that AAPIs are more likely to have a smooth assimilation process and therefore they are good citizens; however, it continuously oppresses AAPIs if they do not fit in the model minority myth. This notion implies AAPIs are permanent foreigners, outsiders, or the others, and reminds us of how Sue (2010) describes Asians as "alien in one's own land" (p. 37). Sue (2010) explained that AAPIs are asked where they were from more often than other racial groups, and that they are assumed to be from other countries even if they were born and raised in the United States. So, the mainstream culture in the United States perpetuates the myth of model minorities to label AAPIs "as 'the other,' a non-English-speaking foreigner, or at best, an immigrant" (Lee, 2010, p. 295) even if they were born and raised in the United States.

AAPIs also experience invisibility because the myth of the model minorities implies conventional discourses on race in the United States have been Black-White perspectives where AAPIs are not included, especially in policy matters (Delgado & Stefancic, 2017); due to implicit biases and presumptions made by non-AAPI populations, AAPIs are perceived as successful, not in need of extra support, and already assimilated into US society. These implicit biases and presumptions have caused AAPIs to be invisible in racial discourses about diversity and multicultural education where racial issues are treated as a binary spectrum of Black-White. When there is a space for AAPIs to discuss their racial matters, their voices are suppressed by other racial groups and they become quiet and hard to reach because, as the grand narrative about AAPIs goes, there is no impact of racism toward AAPIs because they are doing well and are the model minorities (Lee, 2010). This type of implicit bias makes AAPIs more invisible and has a negative impact on AAPIs when they go through their own racial development (Bonilla-Silva, 2018).

Bullyism in Academia

This notion of the otherness or alienation or invisibility based on implicit biases toward AAPIs is similar to what the scholars and practitioners say about bullying in adulthood. Namie and Namie (2009) stated that even though bullying has become a serious problem in contemporary society

578   M. MISAWA

and gained a lot of attention from general public and popular media, it has existed for a long time and has become a ubiquitous sociocultural and behavioral problem. Bullying is deeply ingrained in society and is a serious issue for everyone, not only children but also adults, and not only targets or victims but also bullies or perpetrators and bystanders (Misawa, 2015; Randall, 2001). Although bullying was originally associated with a developmental and behavioral issue among children and was thought to decrease and disappear when children entered into adulthood, bullying does not stop at the end of one's childhood (Randall, 2001). It also manifests in adulthood from early adulthood to late adulthood.

Bullying was originally examined in children's group behavior in schooling by early scholars (Olweus, 1993, 2010) to describe how a group of students in school targeted a student who was perceived as less powerful, mostly physically so. Such group behavior was originally described as *mobbing* in Sweden in the late 1960s to early 1970s; the term was introduced by a school physician Heinemann who borrowed the term from Konrad Lorenz, a well-known ethologist in Austria, to describe "a collective attack by a group of animals on an animal of another species....[M]obbing was also used to characterize the action of a school class or a group of soldiers ganging up against a deviating individual" (Olweus, 2010, p. 9). Such group-oriented childhood behavior was originally observed by teachers in school and was understood as a childhood developmental issue.

As bullying became the focus of childhood research, it was mostly examined by the researchers and scholars of students in P–12 settings who were involved in such bullying incidents. Because research in bullying began in schools, it has been thought of as a childhood developmental behavior problem (Randall, 2001) which might disappear when children enter adulthood. However, that realistically does not happen since people develop their behavior over their lifetime (Misawa, 2015; Namie & Namie, 2009; Randall, 2001). So, child bullies can be adult bullies, and, similarly, child victims or survivors can be adult victims or survivors of bullying (Misawa, 2015; Twale & De Luca, 2008). Bullying is a lifelong developmental issue that impacts not only victims or survivors but also perpetrators and bystanders.

Higher education is no exception. Bullying does in fact exist in higher education (Keashly & Neuman, 2010; Misawa, 2015; Twale & De Luca, 2008). Higher education is a unique space that contains both academic and workplace settings, and is a context where people from diverse backgrounds and positionalities cohabitate (Misawa, 2015). Some people can be learners, and others can be workers. And some are both learners and workers. Oftentimes, diverse backgrounds such as sociocultural identities, socioeconomic status, and organizational positions can be elements that create differences among populations in a context where multiple systems and multi-layered positional structures form power differences. In such a complex context, there are multiple power differences within the population in higher education, and when a power imbalance arises, bullying incidents can occur. As such, it is important to understand how positionality influences bullying situations.

There are multiple definitions of bullying in existing literature; however, there is a common understanding of what bullying means and what bullying consists of. Based on literature on bullying, here is a definition of bullying in higher education, which is an operational definition for this work:

> An incident of bullying involves a victim who is somehow less powerful in terms of physical, psychological, or sociocultural positions than the bully or who fits the bully's stereotype, and a perpetuated recurrent or singular; unwanted or unwarranted; intimidating, humiliating, offensive, threatening or excluding intentional conduct on the part of the bully that sustains the bully's position of power and destroys the victim's well-being, dignity, and safety or is significant enough to cause the victim physical and/or psychological harm. (Adapted from Misawa, 2015, p. 8)

Since bullying deals with power dynamics and a power imbalance between a victim and a perpetrator or perpetrators, it is important to understand positionality. Fox and Stallworth (2005) specified racial/ethnic bullying as a bullying behavior that "attacks the target explicitly based on race or ethnicity" (p. 439); they discussed how race could be a significant factor of bullying and reported that although racial minorities more likely experienced bullying, Asians and African Americans responded to bullying experiences with regard to race and ethnic perspectives. In addition, Misawa (2015) discussed how racist and homophobic bullying manifested in higher education from gay faculty men of color and reported that gay faculty men of color typically experienced a combination of racist and homophobic bullying depending on the context in higher education. It was described as a double-edged sword that gay

580   M. MISAWA

faculty men of color could not escape from bullying incidents because they are racially and sexually minoritized by society and culture (Misawa, 2015).

In addition, existing literature on academic bullying in adulthood provides an understanding of how bullying becomes a critical incident and a transformative experience. The general understanding of a transformative experience is that it occurs from a disorienting dilemma and that through self-critical reflection people can have a perspective transformation (Cranton, 2016; Mezirow, 2000). Bullying can be a disorienting dilemma that physiologically and psychologically impacts victims, targets, or survivors. While transformative learning traditionally focuses on one's change of their perspective through a disorienting dilemma, it does not focus much on how a disorienting dilemma shapes one's emotional state.

The effect of emotional and psychological perspectives on a person going through a transformative learning process have not been extensively explored by scholars in transformative learning in the field of adult education. However, existing literature on bullying and transformative learning does provide some potential insight. For instance, some people go through transformative learning processes as a cognitive aspect of transformation, which often leaves emotional or psychological perspectives behind (Dirkx, 2008; Mälkki & Green, 2014; Misawa & Johnson-Bailey, 2018). That means their emotional or psychological status may be stuck in the disorienting dilemma, or in between the disorienting dilemma and transformation, and although they are able to see how their ways of thinking have transformed through their disorienting dilemmas, they are not able to see their transformation from their emotional or psychological perspectives. Also, one can develop negative perspectives on the transformation by going through a transformative experience. That means positive experiences in a context can be changed to negative through transformative learning processes, which is the reverse of how people go through transformation. Transformative learning and bullying have some commonalities in this way, and the subsequent sections will focus on the intersectionality of transformative learning and racist bullying in academia.

METHODS

This chapter focuses on bullyism in higher education experienced by a group of AAPI faculty men, revealed in one of the author's larger studies on bullying in higher education. The original study was conducted to understand how racist and homophobic bullying influenced gay male faculty of color in higher education, by considering their narrative. Nineteen self-identified gay male faculty of color were recruited through the snowball sampling technique in the narrative inquiry. A semi-structured interview guide, a mix of more—and less-structured questions, was utilized to elicit the experiences of the research participants regarding demographics and in-class and on-campus experiences in higher education. All the interviews were recorded digitally and transcribed by the author. After that, the author conducted a thematic analysis to look for commonalities across all interview transcriptions and to come up with codes, categories, and themes. Participants are identified by pseudonyms. The following narratives illustrate how AAPI male faculty experienced academic bullying.

THREE STORIES ON RACIST BULLYING IN HIGHER EDUCATION

The following short stories are snapshots of the author's original study. This section will focus on how AAPI men in higher education made sense of their experiences of bullying in higher education by examining the narratives from three male Asian faculty.

The story from Professor Pat Freeman, an Asian assistant professor, was an example of positional bullying. He expressed that passive forms of discouragement rather than overt or aggressive discouragement had restricted him in terms of what he could do in academia:

> I think for [sexual] orientation. It depends on how you got into your position. Because I chose another field that was not LGBT or Asian Pacific Islanders (API), in this case is gerontology and geriatrics,... my evaluation is not necessarily based on LGBT work or API focused research. Instead, for me it's been kind of difficult to try to do more research in LGBT or API because either my department or my boss don't view it as important, or they don't view it as this is the area of inquiry that they expected from me.... So, a lot of API and LGBT work that I'm trying to do are always on a top of what I'm doing and so it becomes an add-on.... So, I ended up not being able to focus more on LGBT and API work. But I think it has to do with more inconveniences that because of my boss and my department don't really prioritize LGBT work or API work specifically that inconveniences that I have to do my other work on top of what I want to do sometimes, LGBT and API work. I don't know if discourage

is the right word because discourage sounds a little more active. But, a little more passive than that where if you say, "I did this, and I did that." They're kind of, "Oh, that's nice." So, it's very passive kind of, "That's nice"...but it's never encouraged. So, then you kind of read between the lines and kind of know, "Okay, that's not something that they don't really care about," you know? No one ever said don't do it. Or no one else said it is not very important. They all say, "That's nice." But, it's never a priority.

Positional bullying also appeared when the AAPI male faculty members in this study tried to collaborate with their colleagues and instead race and sexual orientation became significant factors. Professor Pat Freeman described how he was trapped by a stereotyping of Asians and was framed as a typical Asian scholar by his colleagues:

> I think as an Asian person in the academic world. I think that there is a certain assumption that you would be quantitative person, so you will be the analyst. So, I think that that's also assumed work ethics that comes with being Asian. In the field that I'm in, Public Health, I think that's very interdisciplinary so every project is involved more than two or three people in general.... I think sometimes as an Asian and as a junior faculty, there is an assumption that you will automatically do your part in the project.... So, I think a lot of the times, I feel like... I would be asked to be a collaborator.... Because I am seen as the analyst and I am seen as the collaborator, but not seen as the principal investigator.... So, I will kind of play on everybody's projects that will be a part of everyone's projects because I'm hard worker, you know, I'm an analyst and know what I'm doing, and which is not a bad thing, you know. It is not a bad thing. But, sometimes it can go a little overboard. You kind of have to fight this reverse stereotype, I think.

The AAPI faculty members in this study also reported that White and/or heterosexual professors in their graduate studies courses had frequently manifested their racist and/or heterosexist assumptions in class. In this study, the AAPIs who experienced such places felt that their professors did not see them in the same way as they saw the rest of their students. In other words, the AAPIs were outsiders (to White heterosexual scholars). Since they were perceived as outsiders in the White heterosexist academia, they were practically ignored by the White and/or heterosexual professors. The professors even frequently confused students of color through their inability to make individual distinctions. While all AAPI faculty members offered examples of this phenomenon, one example of that appeared in a story from Professor Brian Lee, an Asian adjunct professor and administrator offered as representative:

> White professors, both male and female, got always confused about the Asian American male students. You become [a] blur. Like even though you don't look quite the same as others, [they're] just unable to get it. Sometimes it was hilarious how you know they would call different people, like Mr. Wong, Mrs. Chin, and Mr. Lao. It's like everyone looks the same to them. I would definitely say that there could be different classroom dynamics as a student of color. I guess again that I'm talking about five Asian guys in the class [of] over 100. That's kind of sad that the White professor both males and females, old White professor, because it could be age or vision, could not figure out who we were, but they could easily figure out the White students. So again, we defined it kind of problematic that you know you have seventy plus, 30 plus White male students that you knew who they were, why can't they figure out the [five] Asians... I know for the fact that some of the African American male students were kind of sad....As a dynamic that, you know, you can create visibility or the same, there's opposite some sort of a, take away from when a professor cannot figure out who the different students of color are, male students particular.

The story from Professor Mathew Smith, an Asian Pacific Islander tenured associate professor, was one of the common experiences among AAPI male faculty members in the study; one that illustrated the myth of model minorities and invisibility in diversity, equity, and diversity in higher education:

> My current institution recently started becoming very active on DEI (diversity, equity, and inclusion) because the institution has some reputations about not [being] inclusive of underrepresented minorities. Since my scholarship include[s] race, LGBTQ +, and gender issues, higher administrators contacted me to ask to serve on one of the DEI taskforces. It was a taskforce that consisted of faculty members across the campus. I felt that I was recognized and appreciated [for] my work by the campus leaders. So, I was very excited about the great opportunity to contribute to the campus community about DEI. We were scheduled to meet every month. My role as the chair of the taskforce was to facilitate the monthly meetings and provide the members with updates. There were about 20 faculty people from assistant professors to full professors, associate deans, and deans. And

14 of them were Whites, three of them were Blacks, and two of them were Latinas, and one AAPI, which was me. Most of the members were female faculty members. So, demographically, I was minority there. But at the same time, I was in charge of the taskforce. So, I wanted to make sure that everyone had her or his own voice to share in the taskforce meetings. It was very interesting for me to observe how people use their own agenda to push certain things. In particular, it was interesting, but I was shocked by the behaviors of some racially underrepresented minority faculty members whose scholarship consisted of inclusion and social justice. At one of the meetings, I announced that there was going to be an event about invisible labor hosted by one of the administrative offices on campus. Three female faculty members of color suddenly ganged up on me and attacked me why the event was organized and insisted that invisible labor was already studied by them at the institutions. I kind of understood that there were similar events like that in previous years. I also tried to explain that the event was going to be hosted by one of the administrative offices not from us. From my observation at that time, those three female faculty members of color were very territorial and protective of their scholarly areas. But, I thought that no one could own invisible labor or any scholarly area but people could study about it. At the same time, I thought that no one can own DEI. I didn't say that to them. But, anyway, they were becoming angry about my announcement. So, I was going to move on to next topic. But one of those women of color raised her voice and said to me, "What relationship do you have with Blacks?" I was so shocked by being asked that question and could not say anything. I wanted to respond to the questions with so many examples, but I could not say anything. It was shocking to me. And, everyone got quiet for a while. I was upset about it but I could not correctly deal with it. Later on when I had a chance to reflect on that experience, I was depressed and disappointed by it because what she meant was that I was outsider and that I did not have any business talking about invisible labor and DEI issues because of my social positions as male, international, and AAPI.

These three narratives illustrated how AAPIs experience bullying in higher education. In particular, AAPIs in the study told their stories about racial and ethnic aspects of bullying not only from White and/or heterosexual bullies but also from women of color. Bullying influences all agents such as targets/victims, perpetrators/bullies, and bystanders in terms of both their physical and psychological health. The next section will discuss the implications of the study.

Discussion and Implications

This chapter has presented the background of bullyism in higher education based on the narratives from male AAPI faculty. The study participants indicated that bullying had manifested in various settings in higher education. Higher education seems to be an environment where bullying can exist because of its unique institutional cultures and characteristics; higher education has been described as territorial because there are many silo systems and territories as academic disciplines, programs, departments, and colleges where outsiders have difficulty entering and fitting in (Twale, 2018).

Higher education still presents a predominantly White and Eurocentric culture, and if you are not White, then most likely you will have to work harder to fit in and be recognized and appreciated. As illustrated in the narratives above, the AAPI faculty were outsiders and they needed to work harder to deconstruct others' stereotypical assumptions. However, their experiences are not unique to AAPI men but also apply in general to people of color in a White heterosexist society, as Fox and Stallworth (2005) and Lee (2010) discussed. In addition, AAPIs need to live with the myth of model minority and fight against that myth with their invisible status when they are trying to work on racial justice with others collaboratively. AAPIs are still seen as outsiders who are being oppressed by not only Whites but also other racially underrepresented minorities. It can be said that AAPIs are socially and institutionally bullied and oppressed by other racial groups. Professor Matthew Smith was bullied or mobbed by female faculty of color; as a result of that experience he was psychologically and emotionally injured. The myth of model minorities has made AAPIs invisible and made them perceived as weaker and more agreeable, and they find themselves unable to fit in a typical binary of race such as the Black-White binary (Chang, 1993).

The narratives of the participants also illustrated how negative experiences or disorienting dilemmas affected how they should behave or act as AAPIs. Being invisible and unable to place themselves in a social context as AAPIs, in their experiences of transformative learning there seems to be a disconnect between their experiences as victims and survivors of racist bullying and their own developing passages to cognitive and emotional perspective transformation for their development in adulthood. In order for them to be able to successfully process cognitive and emotional perspective transformation from their experiences of being bullied in academia, it is important for them to deconstruct or unpack their own presumptions regarding who they are and to strategize how they are not perpetuating the myth of model minorities through their own critical self-reflective practices. If AAPIs are able to secure their own passageways for their cognitive and emotional perspective transformation, then they should be empowered against racial oppressions and be more visible to others. However, they still need to be able to find those passageways. The relevant literature in this chapter discussed how transformative learning is an educational process for victims and survivors of bullying. As such, educating and training people to process their disorienting dilemmas becomes important for that individual process. Educators and practitioners should ask this question when they want to help their learners: In what ways can educators and practitioners assist their learners in developing a passageway for the transformative learning process that leads to a reduction of bullyism in higher education?

There are many things they can do; however, it is important for them to practice *anti-bullyism* in higher education. Anti-bullyism is a strategy from the social justice perspective that promotes a diversity, equity, and inclusivity perspective in which bullying is unacceptable. One important practice is to create environments where people can have difficult conversations and can self-examine their own biases toward others by deconstructing their own assumptions and reconstructing new ways of being collaborative and respectful with each other.

In addition, educators and practitioners can create a caring space that is empathy-centered in a way that helps bullying victims and targets. These victims and targets of bullying most likely need emotional and psychological support from educators, practitioners, and peers. Showing care and being empathetic are key to an anti-bullyism practice because victims and targets are going through their own developmental process as they try to exit or break the circle of victimization they experience from bullying, which are negative critical incidents or disorienting dilemmas. The ultimate purpose of the anti-bullyist practice is to empower them from their bullying situations and help them transform from victims or targets to survivors.

CONCLUSION

This chapter has addressed how AAPIs experience bullying in higher education from the concept of a passageway and transformative learning.

Educators and practitioners in higher education have an important role in promoting social justice and anti-bullyist practices because they are educating and fostering future scholars in higher education and future citizens in society. In practicing anti-bullyism, educators and practitioners must be sure that learners are civil and respectful to each other. As our society continues to promote diversity, equity, and inclusion in an effort to be a civil society, helping others develop a passageway to process their transformative learning even from negative experiences like bullying through anti-bullyist practice will be one way to achieve that societal value in the future and contribute to social justice for all.

References

Bierema, L. L. (2010). Professional identity. In C. E. Kasworm, A. D. Rose, & J. M. Ross-Gordon (Eds.), *Handbook of adult and continuing education* (pp. 135–145). Sage.

Bonilla-Silva, E. (2018). *Racism without racists: Color-blind racism and the persistence of racial inequality in America* (5th ed.). Roqman& Littlefield.

Chang, R. S. (1993). Toward an Asian American legal scholarship: Critical race theory, post-structuralism, and narrative space. *California Law Review, 81*(5), 1241–1324.

Cranton, P. (2016). *Understanding and promoting transformative learning: A guide to theory and practice* (3rd ed.). Stylus.

Delgado, R., & Stefancic, J. (2017). *Critical race theory: An introduction* (3rd ed.). New York University Press.

Dirkx, J. M. (2008). The meaning and role of emotions in adult learning. *New Directions for Adult and Continuing Education, 120*, 7–18.

Field, T. (1996). *Bully in sight: How to predict, resist, challenge and combat work-place bullying: Overcoming the silence and denial by which abuse thrives.* Success Unlimited.

Fox, S., & Stallworth, L. E. (2005). Racial/ethnic bullying: Exploring links between bullying and racism in the US workplace. *Journal of Vocational Behavior, 66*, 438–456.

Johnson-Bailey, J. (2015). Academic incivility and bullying as a gendered and racialized phenomena. *Adult Learning, 26*(1), 42–47.

Johnson-Bailey, J., & Cervero, R. M. (2018). Different worlds and divergent paths: Academic careers defined by race and gender. *Harvard Education Review, 78*(2), 311–332. https://doi.org/10.17763/haer.78.2.nl53n6704 4365117.

Keashly, L., & Neuman, J. H. (2010). Faculty experiences with bullying in higher education. *Administrative Theory & Praxis, 32*(1), 48–70.

Khubchandani, J., & Price, J. H. (2015). Workplace harassment and morbidity among US adults: Results from the National Health Interview Survey. *Journal of Community Health, 40*, 555–563. https://doi.org/10.1007/s10900-014-9971-2

Lee, M. (2010). Expanding the racialized discourse: An Asian American perspective. In V. Shared, J. Johnson-Bailey, S. A. J. Clin, III., E. Peterson, S. D. Brookfield, & Associates (Eds.), *The handbook of race and adult education: A resource for dialogue on racism* (pp. 295–305). Jossey-Bass.

MacIntosh, J. (2012). Workplace bullying influences women's engagement in the workplace. *Issues in Mental Health Nursing, 33*(11), 762–768.

Mälkki, K., & Green, L. (2014). Navigational aids: The phenomenology of transformative learning. *Journal of Transformative Education, 12*(1), 5–24. https://doi.org/10.1177/1541344614541171

Matsuda, M. J. (1993). Public response to racist speech: Considering the victim's story. In M. J. Matsuda, C. R. Lawrence, III., R. Delgado., & K. W. Crenshaw (Eds.), *Words that wound: Critical race theory, assaultive speech, and the first amendment* (3rd ed., pp. 17–51). Westview Press.

Merriam, S. B., & Baumgartner, L. M. (2020). *Learning in adulthood: A comprehensive guide* (4th ed.). Jossey-Bass.

Mezirow, J. (2000). *Learning as transformation: Critical perspectives on a theory in progress.* Jossey-Bass.

Misawa, M. (2010). Musings on controversial intersections of positionality: A queer crit perspective in adult and continuing education. In V. Shared, J. Johnson-Bailey, S. A. J. Clin, III., E. Peterson, S. D. Brookfield, & Associates (Eds.), *The handbook of race and adult education: A resource for dialogue on racism* (pp. 187–199). Jossey-Bass.

Misawa, M. (2015). Cuts and bruises caused by arrows, sticks, and stones in academia: Theorizing three types of racist and homophobic bullying in adult and higher education. *Adult Learning, 26*(1), 6–13.

Misawa, M., Andrews, J. L., & Jenkins, K. M. (2019). Women's experiences of workplace bullying: A content analysis of peer-reviewed journal articles between 2000 and 2017. *New Horizons in Adult Education & Human Resource Development, 31*(4), 36–50.

Misawa, M., & Johnson-Bailey, J. (2018). *Examining feminist pedagogy from the perspective of transformative learning: Do race and gender matter in feminist classroom?* In Proceedings of the European Society for Research on the Education of Adults (ESREA) Interrogating Transformative Processes in Learning and Education Conference 2018. The University of Milano-Bicocca, Milano, Italy.

Misawa, M., & Rowland, M. L. (2015). Academic bullying and incivility in adult, higher, continuing, and professional education. *Adult Learning, 26*(1), 3–5.

32 TRANSFORMATIVE LEARNING AS A PASSAGEWAY ... 589

Namie, G., & Namie, N. (2009). *The bully at work: What you can do to stop the hurt and reclaim your dignity on the job* (2nd ed.). Sourcebooks, Inc.

Olweus, D. (1993). *Bullying at school: What we know and what we can do.* Blackwell.

Olweus, D. (2010). Understanding and researching bullying. In S. R. Jimerson, S. M. Swearer, & D. L. Espelage (Eds.), *Handbook of bullying in schools: An international perspective* (pp. 9–33). Routledge.

Randall, P. (2001). *Bullying in adulthood: Assessing the bullies and their victims.* Brunner-Routledge.

Sue, D. W. (2010). *Microaggressions in everyday life: Race, gender, and sexual orientation.* Wiley.

Twale, D. J. (2018). *Understanding and preventing faculty-on-faculty bullying: A psycho-social-organizational approach.* Routledge.

Twale, D. J., & De Luca, B. M. (2008). *Faculty incivility: The rise of the academic bullying culture and what to do about it.* Jossey-Bass.

Workplace Bullying Institute. (2021). *2021 WBI U.S. workplace bullying survey.* https://workplacebullying.org/wp-content/uploads/2021/04/2021-Full-Report.pdf.

CHAPTER 33

Informal Transformative Learning Experiences from Humanitarian Emergencies and Other Life Events and Transitions

Paul Akpomuje, Tajudeen Ade Akinsooto, and Olutoyin Mejiuni

INTRODUCTION

We explored the transformational dimensions of the informal learning of persons who had certain iconic experiences, documented in two recent studies in Nigeria (Akinsooto, 2021; Akpomuje, 2021). Transformative learning is often associated with conscious and unconscious informal learning in a variety of contexts (Cranton et al., 2015; Kroth & Cranton, 2014; Mejiuni, 2012). Hoggan (2015) labeled this phenomenon "informal transformative learning." He described it as "engagement in self-directed and/or tacit forms of informal learning that results in significant changes in learners' ways of experiencing, being in, and interacting with the world" (p. 78). We built on this conception.

P. Akpomuje (✉) · T. A. Akinsooto · O. Mejiuni
Department of Adult Education and Lifelong Learning, Obafemi Awolowo University, Ile-Ife, Nigeria

© The Author(s), under exclusive license to Springer Nature Switzerland AG 2022
A. Nicolaides et al. (eds.), *The Palgrave Handbook of Learning for Transformation*, https://doi.org/10.1007/978-3-030-84694-7_33

591

Cranton et al. (2015) wrote that informal learning that occurs within non-formal and formal learning contexts but outside the curriculum in both contexts has transformational potentials. Bishop (2015) and Poirier (2015) accentuated this in their studies. Moreover, as Mejiuni et al. (2015) observed, informal learning is ubiquitous in nature, so it does not take place in educational or formal contexts alone; it takes place in any context where human beings navigate daily living. We explored two important informal learning contexts within the life-course of humankind in this chapter: (1) humanitarian emergencies (HE), and (2) life events and transitions (LETs). We now discuss the potentials they hold for informal transformative learning.

BACKGROUND

The first study (hereafter referred to as Research A [R-A]) through which we explored this phenomenon focused on the specific informal learning experiences of women during and after emergencies (flooding, Boko Haram insurgency, and inter-ethnic conflict)—experiences that resulted in their acquiring new knowledge, skills, values, and change in attitudes, and the connections these had with their coping, survival, and rebuilding strategies during and after the emergencies. The findings of the study revealed that the values and attitudes that participants garnered, and exhibited, or deployed showed that they engaged in the positive interpretation of their deeply negative experiences, which then shaped their meaning making about life, about coping and survival, and about rebuilding and reconstruction, both at individual and community spheres.

The second study (hereafter referred to as Research B [R-B]) explored the specific life events and transitions that older adults who are pensioners in Southern Nigeria identified as impacting their lives meaningfully—experiences which resulted in unconscious informal learning that shaped their current worldview. The experiences which participants shared included demotion and suspension at work, work transfer, financial hardship, training and education, childbirth, retirement, marriage, divorce, and loss of job. Results of the study showed the knowledge, skills, and insight (KSI), and values and attitudes (VAs) from LETs shaped older adults' identities over the life-course—who they are and the beliefs they hold, which serve as frames of reference for what they now do, how and why they do them.

These two studies are connected in two distinct ways. First, they both focused on significant iconic experiences that impacted the lives of adults in specific ways. However, whereas the first study focused on one life event (humanitarian emergencies) that affected women in whole communities, the second study focused on different life events of individual older adults. The second thread that connects both studies is the learning that resulted from participants' iconic experiences; it was mainly informal learning.

For this chapter, we undertook a cross-case analysis of the dimensions of transformative learning in the participants' informal learning experiences. This was with a view to furthering discourses on: (1) The perspective on transformation (mainstream rational or extra rational) that participants' experiences and meaning making point toward; (2) the focus of change and action, that is, the sphere of life impacted, and whether the change is individual or collective; and (3) the impact of the contexts of iconic experiences on (1) and (2). Finally, we attempted to reckon the implications of our contribution for the multi and interdisciplinary perspective on adult learning and change. To achieve these, we have raised the following questions:

1. What were participants' iconic experiences that had transformational impact on their lives?
2. What informal transformative learning (ITL) experiences resulted from these experiences, and what perspective on transformation do they point to?
3. What was the focus of change and action as a result of the ITL?
4. What was the impact of the contexts of life's iconic experiences on ITL and the focus of change?

To begin, we reviewed some literature in relation to life's iconic experiences and informal transformative learning.

SOME ICONIC LIFE EXPERIENCES

Some life experiences, which could be positive or negative, are iconic because they have substantial impact on the experiencers and result in significant changes in their lives. Humanitarian emergencies, family, and work are the contexts of iconic experiences that this chapter explores.

Humanitarian emergencies (HE) pose exceptional and generalized threats to life, health, or subsistence such that there is need for immediate measures to minimize their adverse consequences (Alert, 2010). They could be natural, e.g., flooding, earthquakes, bushfires, and hurricanes, or human-made, e.g., civil unrest, insurgency, militancy, and inter-ethnic conflict/war (Al-Dahash et al., 2016). Some HE can be termed "silent emergencies" because they usually do not result in mass displacement of people, e.g., pandemics such as COVID-19, HIV/AIDS, Ebola, malaria, cholera, and economic crisis (African Development Bank, 2016; Al-Dahash et al., 2016; Shen & Shaw, 2004). The vulnerability in emergencies results in substantial change in the lives of victims.

Familial issues such as marriage, childbirth, divorce, and death of a loved one are iconic experiences impacting people significantly. Work is also an important event in a person's life. For many, work is a source of livelihood and survival, identity, prestige, growth, self-esteem, self-satisfaction, and social recognition. For others, work is meaningful because it gives excitement, creativity, companionship, and opportunity to exercise power (Armstrong, 2009; Kail & Cavanaugh, 2015; Tausig, 2013). Some people see work as a calling because it helps them impact society positively, which in turn brings them happiness (Schwartz, 2015). Work issues that are significant in people's lives include getting a new job, retirement, work hazards, and loss of a job. These contexts are spaces where informal learning can occur, and this learning can result in transformation.

Informal Transformative Learning

Transformative learning is the learning that transforms problematic frames of reference to make them more inclusive, discriminating, reflective, open, and emotionally able to change (Mezirow & Taylor, 2009). It often leads to social/collective and/or individual changes, all of which are determined by the context of the experience (Cranton, 2005; Mejiuni, 2012, 2017). The core elements of transformative learning are experience, disorienting dilemma, critical reflection, and discourse and alternative perspectives (Cranton, 2005; Taylor, 2009). Perspectives on transformation are either rational or extrarational. These have shaped our thoughts about the processes that lead to how people understand their experiences.

Although critical reflection (or rationality), which is an inner journey of reasoning (Cranton, 2005), has gained more attention in the literature as the defining process to understand one's experience (Taylor, 2009), Cranton (2005) indicated that there are other extrarational processes that lead to transformation. The majority of these extrarational processes coincide with the processes of informal learning. Transformative learning often occurs during informal learning processes. Even though formal education spaces are a part of the contexts of transformative learning, and where research on it occurs (Cranton et al., 2015; Mezirow1991), transformative learning is rarely an explicit goal of formal education (Cranton et al., 2015; Taylor & Snyder, 2012). Evidence abounds that there is now a greater understanding that the levels of reflection and differences found in critical reflection are high in life events—which usually occur in informal contexts—when compared with formal and facilitated settings (Taylor, 2017).

Informal learning is a lifelong process through which people acquire knowledge, understanding, skills, and attitude. It is learning from everyday life, related to work, family, and leisure (Akinsooto & Akpomuje, 2018; Jarvis, 2012; Villar & Celdran, 2013). It is non-institutional, experiential, and takes place in all spheres of life (Alenius, 2018; Mejiuni, 2019; Mejiuni & Oyedeji, 2019). The fact that informal learning does not require a designated teacher or facilitator reinforces the position that its processes could be transformative. In addition, from an ethical point of view, learning for transformation cannot be taught (Ettling, 2006; Mezirow, 2012; Taylor & Cranton, 2013). Hoggan et al. (2017) affirmed this by arguing that it is a question of normativity to posit transformative learning as something that can be taught in a formal way. On the contrary, transformative learning is voluntary, and individuals need to be open and willing to engage in the process. Otherwise, it may appear as indoctrination, radicalization, or some other negative outcome (Hoggan et al., 2017, p. 52).

Although many transformative learning scholars have written extensively on its occurrence in informal learning contexts, until Hoggan (2015) explicitly labeled this occurrence as "informal transformative learning," previous authors did not conflate the processes and outcomes of informal learning with those of transformative learning. Whereas Mejiuni et al. (2015) explored the conflation of informal learning with transformative learning by clearly and unambiguously making the meaning and implications of the confluence stronger, it was Hoggan's chapter, which appeared in their edited volume, that provided the framework.

We therefore adopt Hoggan's (2015) use of the term *informal transformative learning* which he described as "experiences wherein people engage in self-directed and/or tacit form of informal learning that result in significant changes in their ways of experiencing being in, and interacting with the world" (p. 69). In building on Hoggan's conception, we include other informal processes by which people make meaning of their lives in ways that shape their worldviews, assumptions, beliefs, and expectations within the contexts of iconic experiences.

METHODS

R-A adopted an exploratory case study design. It sampled 21 women from three locations in Nigeria with experiences of flooding, inter-ethnic conflict, and insurgency that were either recurrent or had long-term consequences. The locations are: Ijora Badia, Lagos State; Ilaje, Ondo State; and an internally displaced persons' camp in Benin City, Edo State. A key informant interview guide and an observation guide were used as instruments for data collection. Data was analyzed using the Interpretive Phenomenological Analysis, which involved coding of each experiential claim; identification of emergent themes; development of dialog, structure, and themes; and analysis of themes in connection with the different contexts of participants' experiences. R-B adopted a narrative design and also sampled 21 participants who were retirees from two states in Nigeria (Edo and Oyo States). An interview guide was used to obtain primary data while secondary sources of data included autobiography, newspaper articles, and a pamphlet written by the retirees' union in one of the states. Data was analyzed using the narrative analysis.

In both studies, participants were asked to share the experiences they encountered within their different sociocultural and economic contexts. They were also asked to share the learning that stemmed from them. The fieldwork for both studies took place in October 2019. There were ethical considerations, and as such, participants were briefed on the nature and purpose of the studies. Persons who were not comfortable in sharing their experiences were excluded from the interviews. In the analysis of data, we explored the themes that emerged from both studies; we focused on the peculiarities of each research, and also the convergencies and divergencies that were relevant to our purpose. We identified participants from R-A as R-A1 to R-21 and those of R-B as R-B1 to R-B21.

RESULTS AND DISCUSSION OF FINDINGS

We present our results by themes and discuss the findings based on the questions we had raised earlier. The themes were generated from the data.

Participants' Iconic Experiences, the Resulting Informal Transformative Learning, Perspectives on Transformation (Rational and Extrarational), and the Focus of Change and Action

In this section, we discuss the experiences that participants described as having had transformational impact on their lives. We also draw from the experiences: the informal transformative learning (ITL), the perspectives on transformation (rational and extrarational), and the focus of change and action. The section answered research questions 1, 2, and 3.

Economic Hardship
Some participants in R-A and R-B shared experiences of the economic hardship they suffered as a result of inter-ethnic conflict and irregular payment of salaries, respectively. R-A1 shared: "My business crumbled. Nothing remained about my business." This economic situation impacted this participant significantly, and resulted in her becoming a philanthropist, a new disposition she embraced after the conflict-induced economic hardship. This impelled her to become generous toward members of her community. She said, "It is easy for me to relate to someone else's suffering because of my experience. I have given some people *5,000* naira cash to start their businesses. I recently gave out 20,000 naira." R-A1 came about this disposition by reflecting on her past experience. Rationality alone may not result in change in disposition; change also requires empathetic viewing (Meijuni, 2009), which is an extrarational perspective. The perspective on transformative learning in this case would be both rational and extrarational.

R-A6 said the inter-ethnic conflict made her abandon her business and run to Lagos, which is about 75 kilometers from her hometown, during which time she became dependent on others for survival. According to her, economic hardship led her to effect a behavioral change regarding savings and investment, things she did not do before the war. She revealed that if she had had savings in the bank, she would have been able to access her money when she fled for safety. This learning came by critical reflection (a rational perspective). As a focus of change, R-A6 avowed that she now always teaches her children the value of savings and investment. Her own informal transformative learning impelled her to foster informal learning for others. This is a form of informal teaching.

R-A5 and R-A7 said the hardship after the inter-ethnic conflict taught them the value of formal education and employment, a position they never considered important because of the commercial nature of their ethnic group, the Ilaje people. The realization that people in formal employment could easily get back to work after the crisis changed their worldview about formal work. This insight came by sensory knowing, because they saw people in this category. Their learning impelled them to turn to formal education to acquire the certificates that could earn them formal employment. This became the focus of change and action that resulted from their learning. R-B2 avowed that nonpayment of salaries during her work life as a teacher impacted her fundamentally so much so that her life-course changed. She learned the value of resourcefulness. As a teacher, it was not expected that she would engage in blue-collar jobs, but she questioned this expectation and engaged in taxi-driving in order to ameliorate her economic condition. As a female, she also questioned another belief that women could not go into commercial taxi-driving. She gained this insight by feeling, a process of emotive knowing which, upon validation, could lead to critical reflection.

Exposure to Literacy and Education
Like R-A5 and R-A7, some participants who experienced the Boko Haram insurgency in northeast Nigeria shared that they had never been to school before; they could neither read, write, nor speak the English language until they were forced into an internally displaced persons' camp (IDP) as a result of the insurgency. It was at the camp that they were interviewed for R-A. Their exposure to literacy and free education for their children in the formal school at the camp was a reorienting connection which resulted in fresh insight about the value of education. This insight came by interaction and connection, an extrarational perspective to transformation. This resulted in fundamental changes in their lives.

Some participants deliberately participated more in literacy classes. One of them graduated to formal secondary school. All the women avowed that they would ensure that their children were educated up to the tertiary level. R-A4 said, "I didn't know how to read before, but as I came here, I went to adult school, and I started learning some words." She added, "One of my sons got admission to a technical school. I encouraged him to further his education. I want all my children educated." A fundamental change and action for R-A2 was a conscious effort to forgive the insurgents, because she realized how her life and those of her children had improved because of education. Forgiveness had the potential for community building/reconstruction after the devastation caused by Boko Haram insurgency, an attitude that could result in collective/social change.

Job Seeking

One participant, R-B3, described how an experience she had in seeking teaching employment in a government establishment transformed her worldview. She was called for interview; it was her first as an adult. She shared, "As soon as I mentioned my name, one of them said he was with my father in the village. Another said, 'Your mother cooked for us.' They all complemented my parents." Although her story did not indicate that she was not qualified for the job, the panelists were kind to her and offered her the job because of her parents' kindness. It was a moment of awe—a reorienting connection for R-B3 in realizing how the generosity of her parents was remembered many years after. This gave her a fresh insight about the principle of "reaping and sowing." This kind of learning came by interacting with the panelists, an extrarational means of knowing. The focus of change and action for her was community service. She started a series of charitable activities for less-privileged people.

Being a Combatant

R-A1, popularly called "woman soldier" in her community in Ilaje, Ondo State, Nigeria, fought in the inter-ethnic conflict reported in this study. She shared that women were not expected to fight in the war. That was a frame of reference she defied. She said, "I no longer had a business. This really annoyed me and it motivated me to go face these people in the war. I could not bear to see my children and aged mother suffer." She had to choose between the two disorienting dilemmas of dying and watching her family die of hunger, or joining in putting an end to the war as a combatant. She said the conflict taught her bravery and courage. Her learning occurred intuitively, which is extrarational; as it is for civilians who take up arms, emotions, and intuition overrun reason. Her experience impelled her to organize and engage in voluntary vigilante and peace-oriented activities in her community after the crisis. This became a focus of change and action for her, which was not just individual, but also collective.

Retirement

When people retire, it is assumed they begin to rest, thereby becoming laid back. One participant, R-B2, revealed how she questioned this assumption on the first day of her retirement. This resulted in fresh insight about what retirement should be. She now holds the view that being a retiree is not a liability. Her learning came by feelings and emotions (emotive knowing), which started off as an extrarational process, and later, critical reflection. R-B2 became a community leader and translated her new view into engaging in and supporting community activities. She leads some groups in her church and organizes women in her community during elections and other civic activities.

Marriage

R-B4 shared an experience about the failure of his first marriage. He said, "The first wife I married gave me a tough time. She was quarrelsome, harsh and destructive." The marriage ended when his wife moved out of the house while he was at work. He said he learned that "character is better than beauty." He had previously held the view that beauty is all that matters in marriage. By reflecting on his experience (rationality), this view changed. Rather than beauty, character is now key in marriage for him. He noted that this has become the focus of his informal teaching about marriage to his children and other young people in his community.

R-B5, who delayed getting married, said it became clear to him that no aspect of life should be taken for granted. He said, "Today, after retirement, late marriage is one of my greatest regrets." R-B5 came to this realization when he saw how grown the children of his peers had become (a form of sensory knowing) whereas his were still in secondary school. This lesson became the focus of his informal teaching about marriage to his children and the young people in his community. R-B6 married an additional wife at a later age. As a retiree, he was still paying school fees for a child. He came to the realization through critical reflection that polygyny is not good. Like R-B4 and R-B5, R-B6 also made this learning the focus of informal teaching to his children and others in his community.

Losses and Forced Displacement

Some participants who experienced inter-ethnic conflict, insurgency, and flooding shared how the loss of loved ones, property, and forced displacement became iconic experiences for them. The majority of them lost their spouses and other relatives. They also lost their belongings such that they moved from being haves to being have-nots; this fundamentally changed their ways of living. For instance, R-A2, a victim of Boko Haram insurgency, said, "My behavior changed. I had a house before. I had a shop. I used to have a lot and now I don't have anything again. So, I am not bothered about anything again in this world." This experience taught her not to envy or covet anyone's possessions. This became a fresh insight about life.

R-A11 expressed, "I stay in a large room with about 14 people and it has thought me patience." R-A3 said she also learned to be patient and detribalized. She saw the way the coordinator of the IDP camp accommodated everyone, irrespective of their ethnic backgrounds. These three participants said their adopting these values came as a result of their intimacy with God (knowing through spirituality). R-A3 learned about being detribalized through observation and the informal mentoring of a pastor. These are extrarational perspectives to transformation. The participants indicated that they teach their children the importance of these values. Hence, informal teaching became the focus of change and action for their transformation.

R-A9 said her experience of inter-ethnic conflict taught her the value of peace, which has become an important worldview for her. From her account, she learned this from what she saw and heard about the adverse impact of conflict on a community. Hence, the process of her learning is sensory knowing (extrarational). She said she did not hesitate to engage in peace and conflict resolution whenever there was tension in the community. R-A10 revealed that on her return to her community after escaping the devastating flood, she observed how the flood had affected her neighborhood and young people. She realized that community was important. From her account, she used to mind her own business until this experience. This resulted in a change of behavior, and also in a social and collective change. First, she personally funded the construction of a road in her community that was destroyed by the flood. A trigger for her transformation was when the government threatened to evacuate residents of her community without providing alternative shelters. This made her become a community activist. She mobilized the community to file a lawsuit against the government. She also started a free catering training program for young people.

Making the Case for Transformation and Informal Transformative Learning

The iconic experiences that participants in this chapter shared resulted in transformation, and not mere change, because first, connection, interaction, spirituality, critical reflection, and intuition (a form of personal insight), which were identified from our analysis of participants' experiences as learning processes, are themselves integral to what Gilpin-Jackson (2014, p. 8) described as resonance, "a moment of awakening that creates an opportunity for conscious engagement in transformational learning." Second, at different points, participants' stories show their different ways of disclosure to a friend, pastor, or family member. This is also similar to what Gilpin-Jackson (2014) described in her study. For instance, R-A1, who said the inter-ethnic conflict taught her bravery and courage, indicated that before she came to her point of transformation, she opened up to her husband, mother, and her king. According to her, their encouragement reinforced her resolve to fight in the war as a woman. Also, she shared that she had to go through rehabilitation in the post-war period, when she became a philanthropist and community vigilante, an experience she said gave her opportunity for disclosure, healing, and transformation.

Other participants from the community where the war occurred also gave accounts that showed that they had moments of disclosure with government and military personnel whom they had come to trust, an action which eventually resulted in their transformation. Some of the participants revealed that R-A1 (a woman soldier) was one of the persons in the community they opened up to because they could trust her. All the Boko Haram victims shared that, mainly after their relocation from their community, they had moments of disclosure with relatives, friends, and the pastor who coordinated their IDP camp; their accounts revealed that those moments were pivotal to their transformation. Stories that participants in R-B shared also indicated that in the moments before their shift in perspectives, adoption of new dispositions, or gaining of new insights, they had to disclose their experiences to persons they could trust.

Also, the iconic experiences that participants reported were bases for their conscious and unconscious informal learning. The rational and extrarational perspectives on transformation identified from the experiences fit into the types of informal learning that Mejiuni et al. (2015) and Schugurensky (2000) described. The types of informal learning and how ITL perspectives fit into them are described thus: tacit (intuitive, emotive), incidental (critical reflection, sensory knowing, interaction, spirituality, observation), and explicit (empathetic viewing, mentoring). This fit made it easy for us to describe the learning of our participants, which resulted in fundamental changes in their frames of reference, assumptions, beliefs, worldviews, expectations, or a shift in their perspectives on issues, as informal transformative learning. We have presented the iconic experiences, the informal learning, the perspectives on transformation of this learning, and the focus of change and action on Table 33.1, to help show the relationship that our discussion explicates.

The Impact of the Contexts of Experiences on ITL and on the Focus of Change

Contexts are important in any form of informal learning because they help us understand the dynamics of learning. Although the earlier conception of Transformative Learning did not seriously engage the importance of context (Clark & Wilson, 1991; Mezirow, 1991), following the view of Hoggan et al. (2017) and Hoggan (2015), the context of an experience shapes the content, process, premise, and product of the learning that emanates from a transformative experience. This guided our conception of informal transformative learning. The different contexts that undergirded the informal transformative learning experiences that this chapter deals with included economic, conflict, sociocultural, historical, and environmental issues.

Table 33.1 shows the different processes of learning that emerged from our analysis. From the earlier conception of transformative learning, critical reflection (rationality) was the major process of learning. However, given the impact of contexts on the experiences that our participants shared, and from the positions of other scholars (Clark & Wilson, 1991; Hoggan et al., 2017), other perspectives to transformation are possible. For instance, the context of conflict, economic, and sociocultural issues determined the processes of learning for participants who experienced losses, displacement, job seeking, retirement, combat, and marriage. These processes include sensory knowing, observation, spirituality, interaction, emotive knowing, connected knowing, and intuition. Some of the

604   P. AKPOMUJE ET AL.

Table 33.1   Informal transformative learning model: iconic experiences, transformative learning, perspectives on transformation and the focus of change and action

Iconic experiences	Participants	Informal transformative learning (ITL)	Perspectives of transformation (Rational [R] or extrarational [Ex])	Focus of change and action
Economic Hardship	R-A1 R-A6 R-A5 R-A7 R-B2	Philanthropy Saving, investment Importance of formal education/employment Importance of formal education/employment Value of resourcefulness/alternative sources of income	Critical reflection (R) Empathetic viewing (Ex) Critical reflection (R) Sensory knowing (Ex) Critical reflection (R) Sensory knowing (Ex) Critical reflection (R) Intuitive knowing (Ex)	Community charity Informal teaching Acquiring formal certificate Acquiring formal certificate and securing formal employment Additional means of livelihood
Exposure to literacy and education	R-A2 R-A4	Compensational value of education Value for education	Interaction and connection (Ex) Interaction and connection (Ex)	Participation in literacy classes and sending children to formal education Forgiveness for insurgents Participation in literacy classes and sending children to formal education
Job seeking	R-B3	Principle of sewing and reaping	Connected knowing (Ex)	Charity

(continued)

Table 33.1 (continued)

Iconic experiences	Participants	Informal transformative learning (ITL)	Perspectives of transformation (Rational [R] or extrarational [Ex])	Focus of change and action
Being a combatant	R-A1	Bravery and courage	Intuition (Ex)	Voluntary vigilante and peace-oriented activities in the community
Retirement	R-B2	Retirees are not liabilities	Emotive knowing (Ex) Critical reflection (R)	Community leadership
Marriage	R-B4 R-B5	Character is better than beauty	Critical reflection (R)	Informal teaching
	R-B6	Every aspect of human life is important	Critical reflection (R)	Informal teaching
		Polygyny is not good	Sensory knowing (Ex) Critical reflection (CR)	Informal teaching

(continued)

participants' experiences did not entirely give room for critical reflection, yet they averred that the lessons gained resulted in fundamental changes in their lives. These processes of learning were extrarational, as they did not require the participants to exercise their intellect and autonomous decision-making. The extrarational perspectives, often determined by the context of experience, fit into the processes of informal learning which are tacit, incidental, and explicit. This proves the argument that cognition or rationality is not enough to determine how persons could understand their experience; contexts matter too (Clark & Wilson, 1991; Hoggan et al., 2017).

For some participants, the varied contexts of an experience led to a combination of the extrarational and the rational perspectives. As we have shown in Table 33.1, there were participants who moved from the extra-rational to the rational. This fusion helps to understand the position of Clark and Wilson (1991), Taylor (2007), and Christie et al. (2015) about the need to reconceptualize transformative learning in ways that are more

Table 33.1 (continued)

Iconic experiences	Participants	Informal transformative learning (ITL)	Perspectives of transformation (Rational [R] or extrarational [Ex])	Focus of change and action
Loss of loved ones, property and forced displacement	R-A2 R-A3 R-A9 R-A10 R-A11	Contentment Patience Being detribalised Value of peace Community is important Patience	Spirituality (Ex) Observation (Ex) Spirituality (Ex) Mentoring (Ex) Sensory knowing (Ex) Observation (Ex) Spirituality (Ex)	Informal teaching Informal teaching Engaging in peace and conflict resolution in the community Investing in community through community activism and non-formal training for young people Informal teaching

Source Akpomuje (2020) and Akinsooto (2020)

permeable, flexible, and accommodating to multiple processes of learning (which informal learning encourages), which could result in transformation, given the place of possible varied contexts. Our model of ITL might be a good way, going forward.

CONCLUSION

This chapter relied on two empirical studies to advance the concept of informal transformative learning, the confluence of informal learning, and transformative learning. As a way to conclude, we draw attention to the implication of our contribution for the multi and interdisciplinary perspective on adult learning and change. Our model of ITL is a recognition of the dynamic nature of adult learning. There is a need for continuous search for the possible ways theories that explain adult learning can be better understood within different contexts and through evidence-based approaches. The more theories are grounded in data, the better the explanatory power they possess.

REFERENCES

African Development Bank. (2016). *Women's resilience: Integrating gender in the response to Ebola.* African Development Bank.

Akinsooto, T. A. (2021). *Older adults' learning from life events and transitions in Southern Nigeria* (Unpublished doctoral thesis). Obafemi Awolowo University, Ile-Ife, Nigeria.

Akinsooto, T. A., & Akpomuje, P. Y. (2018). Achieving sustainable development goals throughadult informal learning. *Australian Journal of Adult Learning, 58*(3), 426–448.

Akpomuje, P. (2021). *An exploration of women's informal learning experiences in emergency situations in Nigeria (1999–2019)* (Unpublished doctoral thesis). Obafemi Awolowo University, Ile-Ife, Nigeria.

Al-Dahash, H. F., Thayaparan, M., & Kulatunga, U. (2016). Understanding the terminologies: Disaster, crisis and emergency. *Association of Researchers in Construction Management, 2,* 1191–1200.

Alert. (2010). *Humanitarian emergencies and humanitarian Action.* http://www.reliefweb.int/fts

Alenius, P. (2018). Migrants' informal learning and education in transnational family space: The experience of people migrating between Estonia and Finland. *Nordic Journal of Migration Research, 8*(1), 47–55. https://doi.org/10.1515/njmr-2018-0007.

Armstrong, M. (2009). *Armstrong's handbook of human resources management practice* (11th ed.). Kogan Page.

Bishop, E. (2015). Enhancing self-reflective practice and conscious service in the helping profession: The value of informal learning. In O. Mejiuni, P. Cranton, & O. Taiwo (Eds.), *Measuring and analyzing informal learning in the digital age* (pp. 233–249). IGI Global. https://doi.org/10.4018/978-1-4666-8265-8.ch016

Christie, M., Carey, M., Robertson, A., & Grainger, P. (2015). Putting transformative learning theory into practice. *Australian Journal of Adult Learning, 55*(1), 9–30.

Clark, M. C., & Wilson, A. L. (1991). Context and rationality in Mezirow's theory of transformational learning. *Adult Education Quarterly, 41,* 75–91.

Cranton, P. (2005). Transformative learning. In L. M. English (Ed.), *International encyclopaedia of adult education* (pp. 630–637). Palgrave Macmillan.

Cranton, P., Taiwo, O., & Mejiuni, O. (2015). Looking back and looking forward. In O. Mejiuni, P. Cranton, & O. Taiwo (Eds.), *Measuring and*

608 P. AKPOMUJE ET AL.

analyzing informal learning in the digital age (pp. 274–294). IGI Global. https://doi.org/10.4018/978-1-4666-8265-8.ch018

English, L. M. (2015). Adult health learning: A critical approach to informal learning about health. In O. Mejiuni, P. Cranton, & Taiwo, O. (Eds.), *Measuring and analyzing informal learning in the digital age* (pp. 169–179). IGI Global.

Ettling, D. (2006). Ethical demands of transformative learning. In E. W. Taylor (Ed.), *Teaching for change* (pp. 59–68). Jossey-Bass.

Gilpin-Jackson, Y. (2014). Resonance as transformative learning moment: The key to transformation in sociocultural and posttrauma contexts. *Journal of Transformative Education, 12*(1), 1–25. https://doi.org/10.1177/154134 4614541547

Hoggan, C. (2015). Informal transformative learning from a life-threatening illness. In O. Mejiuni, P. Cranton, & O. Taiwo (Eds.), *Measuring and analyzing informal learning in the digital age* (pp. 64–79). IGI Global. https://doi.org/10.4018/978-1-4666-8265-8.ch005

Hoggan, C., Mälkki, K., & Finnegan, F. (2017). Developing the theory of perspective transformation: Continuity, intersubjectivity, and emancipatory praxis. *Adult Education Quarterly, 67*(1), 48–64. https://doi.org/10.1177/0741713616674076

Jarvis, P. (2012). Learning from everyday life. *Human and Social Studies Research and Practice, 1*(1), 1–20.

Kail, R. V., & Cavanaugh, J. C. (2015). *Human development. A lifespan view* (8th ed.). Wadsworth Cengage Learning.

Kroth, M., & Cranton, P. (2014). Stories of transformative learning. *Sense Publishers.* https://doi.org/10.1007/978-94-6209-791-9

Mejiuni, O. (2009). *Potential for transformative mentoring relationships among women in academia in Nigeria.* Paper presented at the Eighth International Transformative Learning Conference. College of Bermuda.

Mejiuni, O. (2012). International and community based transformative learning. In E. Taylor & P. Cranton (Eds.), *Handbook of transformative learning: Theory, research and practice* (pp. 304–319). Jossey-Bass.

Mejiuni, O. (2017). Sustaining collective transformative learning: Informal learning and revisions. In A. Laros, T. Fuhr, & E. Taylor (Eds.), *Transformative learning meets bildung: An international exchange* (pp. 205–216). Sense Publishers V. B.

Mejiuni, O. (2019). Informal learning and the social justice practices of academic leaders as invisible and visible pedagogical inputs in higher education institutions. *Voices in Education: Journal of Bermuda College, 5.*

Mejiuni, O., Cranton, P., & Taiwo, O. (2015). Introduction. In O. Mejiuni, P. Cranton, & O. Taiwo (Eds.), *Measuring and analyzing informal learning in the digital age* (pp. 274–294). IGI Global.

Mejiuni, O., & Oyedeji, O. T. (2019). Golden, gendered and knotty: Early and mid-career persons' learning through the new media in Southwestern Nigeria. In M. Avoseh (Ed.), *Proceedings of the 2019 International Pre-Conference, Commission for International Adult Education of the American Association for Adult and Continuing Education (AAACE)*.

Mezirow, J. (1991). *Transformative dimensions of adult learning*. Jossey-Bass.

Mezirow, J. (2012). Learning to think like an adult: Core concepts of transformation theory. In E. W. Taylor, P. Cranton, & Associates (Eds.), *The handbook of transformative learning: Theory, research, and practice* (pp. 73–95). Jossey-Bass.

Poirier, L. (2015). Stories of breastfeeding advocates: The significance of informal learning. In O. Mejiuni, P. Cranton & O. Taiwo (Eds.), *Measuring and analyzing informal learning in the digital age* (pp. 80–90). IGI Global. https://doi.org/10.4018/978-1-4666-8265-8.ch006

Schugurensky, D. (2000). *The forms of informal learning: Towards a conceptualization of the field*. http://www.nall.ca/res/19formsofinformal.htm

Schwartz, B. (2015). *Why we work*. https://works.swarthmore.edu/fac-psychology/810

Shen, S. Y., & Shaw, M. J. (2004). *Managing coordination in emergency response systems with information technologies*. Americas Conference on Information Systems.

Tausig, M. (2013). The Sociology of work and well-being. In C. S. Aneshensel, J. C. Phelan, & A. Bierman (Eds.), *Handbook of the sociology of mental health* (pp. 433–455). Springer.

Taylor, E. W. (2007). An update of transformative learning theory: A critical review of the empirical research (1999–2005). *International Journal of Lifelong Education, 26*(2), 173–191. https://doi.org/10.1080/02601370701219475.

Taylor, E. W. (2009). Fostering transformative learning. In J. Mezirow, & E. Taylor, & Associates (Eds.), *Transformative learning in practice: Insight from community, workplace and higher education* (pp. 3–17). Jossey-Bass.

Taylor, E. W. (2017). Transformative learning theory. In A. Laros, T. Fuhr, & E. Taylor (Eds.), *Transformative learning meets bildung: An international exchange* (pp. 17–29). Sense Publishers.

Taylor, E. W., & Cranton, P. (2013). A theory in progress? Issues in transformative learning theory. *European Journal for Research on the Education and Learning of Adults, 4*(1), 33–47.

Taylor, E. W., & Snyder, M. J. (2012). A critical review of research on transformative learning theory, 2006–2010. In E. W. Taylor, P. Cranton, & Associates (Eds.), *The handbook of transformative learning: Theory, research, and practice* (pp. 37–55). Jossey-Bass.

Villar, F., & Celdran, M. (2013). Learning in later life: Participation in formal, non-formal and informal activities in a nationally representative Spanish sample. *European Journal of Ageing, 10* (135–144). https://doi.org/10.1007/s10433-012-0257-1

CHAPTER 34

Dialogic and Noncoercive Learning for Transformational Change: A Systems Approach

Fodé Beaudet

INTRODUCTION[1]

What role can institutions play to support transformational change for actors in dire situations, given the complex web of entanglements? The inquiry sets up a dilemma: Institutions who endeavor to engage in meaningful change will inevitably encounter barriers embedded in – status quo and reinforce existing narratives. The chapter is divided into five components. First, it describes the context of the dilemma and defines actors in dire situations caught in a complex web of entanglements. Second,

[1] "This disclaimer informs readers that the views, thoughts, and opinions expressed in the text belong solely to the author, and not necessarily to the author's employer."

F. Beaudet (✉)
Canadian Foreign Service Institute (CFSI), Global Affairs Canada (GAC), Ottawa, ON, Canada
e-mail: fode.beaudet@international.gc.ca

© The Author(s), under exclusive license to Springer Nature Switzerland AG 2022
A. Nicolaides et al. (eds.), *The Palgrave Handbook of Learning for Transformation*, https://doi.org/10.1007/978-3-030-84694-7_34

611

it identifies and situates the features of transformational change. Third, it outlines the relevance of a noncoercive learning stance. Fourth, the chapter positions the Dialogic Mindset and two learning pathways to engage meaningfully with the inquiry. Finally, it underlines a key implication for institutions, that is, to co-design for transformational change to redefine the organizations' functions and roles toward a shared purpose. These components are inspired by my experience working around the world in different capacities, whether with networks for social change, NGOs, or the public sector. Brief vignettes in italics will contextualize the ideas put forth.

THE DILEMMA AND ACTORS IN DIRE SITUATIONS

Over the years, I have become keenly aware of several paradoxes, including the thrust to preserve the world as it is, and the yearning for a different future. The "Grey Zone of Change" encapsulates this tension as the "space between the current state and the emerging future that is undefined and unknowable" (Gilpin-Jackson, 2020, p. 1). This paradox is particularly intense for actors in dire situations when juxtaposed within an ecosystem that serves primarily its own rules. By ecosystem, I refer to the interconnections of various entities that are dependent on each other to preserve the stability of their structures. I stopped counting the number of times I heard: "I know it doesn't make sense, but that's the way it is." I am not writing this from a place of cynicism but of reality: Any system serves its own structure. In other words, the purpose of a system is the system (Beer, 2002). Hence the dilemma: Institutions who endeavor to engage in meaningful change will inevitably encounter barriers embedded in their systems that perpetuate the status quo and reinforce existing narratives. Therefore, technical rationality is limited. When measures of success are anchored in pre-determined outcomes, actors must collude to justify either their investments, or for receiving support based on specific expectations. These expectations are often misaligned with the reality of actors in dire situations. This dynamic leaves a narrow window of opportunity to act upon new insights. This is less a critic of any one organization or sector: It is an inherent dynamic of human systems. A system seeks to achieve coherence and "doesn't care who or what it entangles" (Whittington, 2016, p. 8). That is why the dilemma cannot be "fixed." However, once we recognize this system dynamic, we can shift from blame and seek to understand what these patterns reveal

(Meadows, 2008). I am not discounting technical rationality per se, nor matters of efficiency and effectiveness. The question is, what approach and mindset are most promising for transformational change? And specifically, for actors in dire situations? The latter includes individuals, groups, and communities navigating through four interdependent categories, where (1) the security and safety of learners are at risk, (2) the power dynamics implicitly or explicitly condemns changes to a system, (3) the funding architecture is incompatible with the complexity of the situation, and (4) the change narrative is exploited by maligned actors. These four factors have intricate, complex relationships and self-reinforcing loops.

Implied in transformational change is a quest for justice, fairness, inclusivity, and to challenge systems deemed unjust, unfair, and privileging a few; these aspirations, albeit honorable, are threatening for competing interests, whether ideological, economical, or otherwise. Threats are serious. For example, civil society organizations may be the target of "Physical harassment and intimidation, including threats, injuries and killings, impunity and lack of protection" (Gaventa & Oswald, 2019, p. 6). Maligned actors can exasperate fault lines and polarize even more the division sown by transformational change efforts through disinformation campaigns. Such maligned actors can be State-sponsored groups, lobbies, or ideological organizations among others. This makes mobilizing around common interests informed by a diversity of views difficult at best, dangerous at worst.

> *Supporting a team of facilitators in a country with a contentious government track records to support civil liberties, I am seeking advice from individuals with experience in the country. "Don't expect anything to come up out of the workshop. No one will share ideas that may compromise the government's agenda. If you want to address your objectives, set up conversations before the event. The event is simply a ceremony of what has already been decided". How do you engage with learning and change, when status quo is the implied objective?*

In some instances, the sheer perception of undermining powerful authorities is sufficient to silence or stifle people's aspirations. Even in the case of minimal risks to the safety and security, years of internalized oppression may still permeate the dynamic of change (Freire, 2000). And in contexts where violence and authoritarianism prevailed for years, "internalized norms of fear shape the possibilities and nature of 'voice'.

Despite the creation or existence of formalized mechanisms for citizen engagement citizens may hesitate to challenge authority in public ways" (Gaventa & Oswald, 2019, p. 6). I write about these categories with reservation because of the risk to conjure images of only certain parts of the world. Which is why I purposefully avoid referring to developing countries, the Global South, or Fragile States because the characteristics inherent to the categories are present across the world. Nevertheless, there is an inescapable narrative to address. I am reminded of the poet Derek Walcott (1997): "Pray for a life without a plot, a day without a narrative." Dionne Brand mulls about its meaning:

> I cannot know precisely what he means but I recognized something in it. Or perhaps something in it called me. It described perfectly my desire for relief from persistent trope of colonialism. To be without this story of captivity, to dis-remember it, or to have this story forget me, would be heavenly. But of course in that line too is the indifference, the supplication of prayer. Yet I want to think that perhaps there is also regeneration in its meaning. (Brand, 2001, p. 42)

I am treading with any labels cautiously and putting forward that the agent of change is neither "them," "others," but an all-encompassing "we," which is the essence of transformational change. Both poets speak about legacies of the past, alive today, and the desire to transcend narratives. I am cognizant that categories are a plot which must also be "dis-remembered" to avoid the trap of freezing people into inescapable labels— for instance, where some people are saved, and others are cast as the ones doing the saving. The trap influences our way of seeing the world; of being and relating to each other in the world. If we are oblivious to this narrative, we cannot see that we are part of any given system. We then miss out on the greatest opportunity for lasting change, which arises "when all the players reflect on and shift their own intentions, assumptions, and behavior" (Stroh, 2015, p. 31). Failing to integrate one's own behavior and role is a significant blind spot for institutions. Ensuing efforts imply that others must change. The institutional support then becomes about monitoring and evaluating the performance of others, irrespective of whether institutions have been enablers or barriers for change.

Transformational Change

Transformational change implies an existential undertone; as mentioned, it cannot be limited to matters of efficiency, effectiveness, or technical rationality; transformation must involve a "deep, structural shift in the basic premises of thought, feelings, and actions. It is a shift of consciousness that dramatically alters our way of being in the world" (O'Sullivan, 2012, p. 164). When the shift in consciousness "dramatically alters our way of being in the world," the alteration is not permanent. This is because transformational change inevitably deals with wicked problems, where "any solution is doomed to unforeseen consequences, that are not stable but instead constantly shifting" (Ramalingam, 2013, p. 266). Consequently, we cannot control the resulting interplay of intentions through every other organizations, which eventually leads to emerging patterns (Stacey, 2015). These emerging patterns make it difficult to see the whole system. Efforts to do so are bound to fail, or at least, misses the point, because "systems are not reality; they are ways of thinking that help us to understand the multiple realities that different stakeholders experience" (Burns, 2007, p. 7). And as people engage with these multiple realities, they can "perceive critically the way they exist in the world ... they come to see the world not as a static reality, but as a reality in process, in transformation" (Freire, 2000, p. 83). This transformation is more than simply letting go; we must also navigate our way forward by integrating aspects of the old (Gilpin-Jackson, 2020). When seeking transformational change, there is no "end state," it is rather "an interwoven and nested learning and (un)learning process in which new identities are forged BECAUSE of where we have been" (Gilpin-Jackson, 2020, p. 13). Building on the process leading to these new identities, we can distill at least three questions along the journey of transformational change: What do we keep, what do we let go of, and what do we create? In answering these questions, we may find that transformational change does not always need to be framed with a specific label. In fact, for some situations, promoting publicly a transformational agenda can be counterproductive and sow fear. "Fear means that even where collective action is possible, it has to be carried out cautiously or in 'hidden' ways" (Gaventa & Oswald, 2019, p. 6). An example which features successful approaches is described in a report about lessons for donors, policymakers, and external actors when programming in fragile, conflict and violent affected settings:

616 F. BEAUDET

Evidence from Bangladesh, Nigeria, Egypt and Pakistan shows women mobilizing around land rights, health, education, and workers' rights. They are not necessarily mobilizing under either feminist or religious banners, but around community issues. However, labelling these women activists as feminists in these settings, as is sometimes done by the press or by Western donors, can inadvertently give support to nationalist and fundamentalist agendas of anti-women's rights groups who seek to delegitimize local women's rights movements. (Gaventa & Oswald, 2019, citing Tadros & Khan, 2019, p. 12)

The example above is no less transformative despite the absence of a feminist or religious banner. The question of which model or theory of change to pursue raises the question of who is best served. For example, addressing issues of funding for complexity, the Chief Executive Officer of the Big Lottery Fund is blunt: "Too often, those who hold power—and resources—attempt to dilute these complexities. They have looked to make the challenges come to them, to fit their model and to tick their box, to define their work on the basis of what they want, rather than what's right for the community" (Knight et al., 2017). To address what's right for the community, especially for those in dire situations, institutional bureaucracy must then serve a purpose beyond itself; a noncoercive learning can support this process.

NONCOERCIVE LEARNING

While facilitating a workshop on transformational leadership, the client is steadfast: the goal of developing a theory of change must be co-designed with participants. These participants include deans, vice-deans, farmers, students, CEOs, former educational ministers across multiple African countries. Among conversations, there is the question of whether they are designing an educational format to replicate how the world is, or how to transform it. By the end of the workshop, the group self-organized into a governance model reflecting their choice. During breakfast, after the workshop, a dean from a university shares with me over coffee: "I didn't think we could achieve what we did, with so many different groups." I still reflect on what contributed to this. A major factor was the client's stance: Noncoercive learning.

Given our turbulent and unpredictable environment, a corresponding learning process must acknowledge a level of openness to what emerges as people collaborate and learn about change. The concept of noncoercive learning, adapted from Spivak, needs clarification, because "'uncoercive' does not refer to some sort of willing suspension of coercion. It signals the future anterior: whatever you do, even if it looks like your plan succeeded completely, in the end, something (else) will have happened" (Spivak, 2014, p. Chap. 2). Noncoercive learning challenges the linear cause and effect relationship. That is because organizational outcomes are caused by several factors, including the choices and strategies made by groups of people, rather than one group or organization (Stacey, 2015). Noncoercive learning is more akin to a spiral than an elegant circle that neatly wraps up pre-determined stages. Bridging Spivak and Newman's work, noncoercive learning sparks insight. Newman defines insight as a realization, a sudden knowing, both mystical yet a supremely intellectual experience (Newman, 2006). Hence, "There is no gradual fitting together of the pieces one by one in order to reach a conclusion" (Newman, 2006, p. 176).

On one level, noncoercive learning makes sense; how can we predict with certainty what will happen? However, if we consider the dynamic at play for actors in dire situations, an explicit noncoercive learning stance is not simple and can spur anxiety; how do you strategically situate your goals, and position your organization to benefit from institutional support if you are unclear about what will emerge from the process? Any supportive entity, irrespective of its intention, has structures and processes that incentivize certain behaviors. Such behaviors typically reinforce predictability based on pre-determined outcomes. The quest for predictability is alluring. How, then, do we reconcile a noncoercive learning stance with practical and real pressure for certainty? This is where the dialogic mindset is promising.

THE DIALOGIC MINDSET AND LEARNING PATHWAYS

During a sensemaking exercise through a systems network analysis for related to the development, security and humanitarian NEXUS in the Great Lakes, a participant shares: "We need to better understand our mental model models—our theory of change underlying our approaches." The exercise, which provided a visual output of how different stakeholders relate to each other, challenged assumptions about who was connected to whom. The visual output, however, did not provide answers—it merely described connections.

The ensuing dialogue, through participatory methodologies offered meaning behind the connections, thus an example of blending a diagnostic and dialogic approach.

The dialogic mindset serves as a compass to avoid the trap that if all you have is a hammer, then everything looks like nail, and to navigate through the dilemma raised in this chapter. Dialogic Organization Development (Dialogic OD) refers to practices and mindset "anchored in an understanding of human systems as socially constructed; every interaction and conversation is part and parcel of creating the change" (Gilpin-Jackson, 2020, p. 5). The Dialogic OD posture is compatible with noncoercive learning because actions "and outcomes are co-created through inquiry, not enacted by 'experts'" (Gilpin-Jackson, 2020, p. 5). In contrast, the *Diagnostic Mindset* assumes the necessity to correct interpretation of facts through diagnosis and aspires toward change models deemed "healthy," "effective," "high performing," or "world class" (Bushe & Marshak, 2015). The Dialogic Mindset integrates rather than dismisses diagnostic approaches. The mindset is the determining factor for design, specifically "how one thinks about and engages in situations, including selecting and mixing which methods and approaches to use" (Gilpin-Jackson, 2020, p. 5, citing Bushe & Marshak, 2015c, p. 14). With this in mind, two learning pathways are offered; we learn through conversation and we learn by making ourselves available for change.

We Learn Through Conversation

I am opening a folded paper handed to me: "Does it mean we don't always need training?" The scribbled lines are written by a learner in the Horn of Africa, during a workshop on facilitating learning and change. The group had just crafted their own inquiry question, designed a generative dialogue, and were now facilitating their design with other participants in the workshop. The learner was discovering, as did others, that training is not necessarily the response to issues we are facing. Sometimes, it is about understanding what those issues are, discovered through conversation.

Dialogue, when informed by a *beautiful question*, contributes to learning something we do not know. For Southern (2015), a beautiful question "challenges assumptions, considers new possibilities, and serves as a catalyst for action and change" (p. 271). In other words, we do not ask a question for which we already know the answer. Nor do we pursue an inquiry to justify pre-determined outcomes. To do so would fall into the "growing fear that lip-service is being paid to participation simply out of deference to fashion or the current jargon of development aid" (Taylor & Fransman, 2004, p. 1).

In dialogue, new insights are informed by *generativity*, which is "the field of possibility, yet unknown, that is evoked or uncovered when the right conversations take place" (Gilpin-Jackson, 2020, p. 6). Conversation and change are interwoven, as "change occurs through the act of conversation rather than as a result of conversation" (Burns, 2007, p. 33). Moreover, change requires changing the conversations (Bushe & Marshak, 2015).

Dialogue is also noncoercive, provided the host or facilitator of the container does not direct nor impose content. Containers are a nested set of spaces where inquiry, learning, and sensemaking take place; they are characterized by a center for its purpose, and a rim to frame the scope of the task (Corrigan, 2015). A noncoercive dialogue (where what happens cannot be predicted), also sets in motion more honest responses as participants are no longer required to decipher what a sponsor, donor, or other actor wants to hear. Instead, we listen to what wants to be heard. In the UK report on funding for complexity, a commissioner comments about a genuine inquiry-led process:

> It's much less confrontational. Although, ironically, you can be much more confrontational because the atmosphere is not confrontational, if you see what I mean. You can really push, or be pushed about, and it doesn't feel as if you're being attacked. It feels like people are engaging with the ideas, not you the person... (Knight et al., 2017, p. 12)

Privileging the importance of relationship and trust, Lowe and Plimmer (2019) suggest that the "ambition is not to create an environment in which everyone agrees on everything, but one that enables everyone to have a voice, and trust each other enough to disagree and debate" (p. 37). And Spivak demystifies that being nice doesn't equal being noncoercive and that shoving and pushing are necessary for education on psychological ground (Spivak, 2014). The quality and rigor of the container enable honesty. Shoving and pushing can be otherwise counterproductive.

In dialogue, participants are neither instructed to think differently nor lectured about how to think; it is not a transfer of knowledge or skills,

620 F. BEAUDET

but a process toward shared understanding of diverse views. Stating that people's voice will be heard or encouraging everyone to speak is insufficient. Participants in a dialogue must experience hearing their voice by design choice. Whether physically or virtually, this involves a blend of small and large group discussions, genuine agency for co-creating inquiries and involvement in the collective sensemaking. Are people given the opportunity to set their principles of interaction? A dialogue is not a panel of experts presenting findings or opinions followed by a question-and-answer period (although such process may nevertheless be called dialogue). Importantly, dialogue gains from a design unfolding over time (de Guerre & Taylor, 2004).

While often perceived as soft, dialogue is hard, both as a process and as a strategic fit for client systems. For those who prefer to predict outcomes, genuine dialogue creates anxiety; will people come up with what we want to hear? From an organizational standpoint, dialogue can also be a difficult fit administratively. As Gordezky (2015) points out: "The training and development department that employed me did not know how to bill for such work. The director only knew how to earn the department's place in the organization by filling classrooms" (p. 305).

Finally, dialogue helps to navigate through the dilemma raised in this chapter, because an inquiry-led pathway does not presume an answer: Rather it allows for possibility-centric conversations that advance multi-actor interest and engagement. For actors in dire situations, a genuine conversation about questions for which no one has the answer alleviates toing-the-line, provided institutions are genuinely part of the conversation through a noncoercive learning stance. In situations where discretion is necessary, an inquiry can also subtly strip contentious ideological references. With that said, a process honoring generativity will often make clearer the next pathway.

We Learn by Making Ourselves Available for Change

At the conclusion of a train-the-trainer in the Middle East, a man addresses the group in the circle. He points to a woman across the room, with whom he co-designed and co-facilitated a session based on shared interests: "Before coming here, I didn't think women could lead. Not only were you a leader, working with two men, but I have two daughters and I hope someday they will be like you."

> *During a workshop on facilitating multi-stakeholder collaboration, a participant addresses the plenary during reflective practice: "I came here to learn to deal with people with high conflict. And I realize that I am the one that sometimes contributes to conflict."*
>
> *Near Myanmar, I listen to the founder of an organization promoting human rights: "We don't only report on human rights abuse. We purposefully train people from different ethnicities. Because when the Junta will fall, like all dictatorships, factions will fight each other. We must prepare."*

As discussed, noncoercive learning leads to unexpected insights. This means to be humble about claiming "to know (...) how such systems work, and what evidence is telling us. It is not that evidence is unimportant, but that the answers it gives us are only ever partial" (Knight et al., 2017, p. 7). If we cannot control, nor predict, then what becomes of learning for the context of this chapter? The complexity inherent to transformational change does not bode well with easy solutions and is certainly not aligned with quarterly, yearly or long-term strategic plans. Once we let go of the need to solve what cannot be fixed, we may turn to Poland: "Transformation Is Not Something We Make Happen. It Is Something We Make Ourselves Available for[2]" (Poland, 2020, p. 386).

So perhaps how we learn represents a shift from assessing and evaluating whether our preliminary objectives were achieved, to include what emerges from dialogical processes: What new forms of relationships and interrelationships have taken place? How do these inform the behavior of a system? Gradually, we become less enthralled by our own attribution, and more curious about our collective contribution.

IMPLICATIONS FOR INSTITUTIONS SUPPORTING ACTORS IN DIRE SITUATIONS

In this section, I explore how institutions can move beyond the traditional role of predetermining a theory of change based on a diagnosis, setting objectives, implementation, and monitoring performance. Without discounting these steps, the focus proposed is to co-design for transformational change where stakeholders are active participants in the co-creation of knowledge. This echoes Freire's invitation for revolutionary leadership where teachers and students

---

[2] The capital letters reflect the original text.

co-intent on reality, are both Subjects, not only in the task of unveiling that reality, and thereby coming to know it critically, but in the task of re-creating that knowledge. As they attain this knowledge of reality through common reflection and action, they discover themselves as its permanent re-creators. (Freire, 2000, p. 69)

However, when it comes to practical work systems, these are not designed in a vacuum (Selsky et al., 2013). For, "just as objective social reality exists not by chance, but as the product of human action, so it is not transformed by chance ... then transforming that reality is a historical task, a task for humanity" (Freire, 2000, p. 51). Such task is the creation of a new value constellation whereby stakeholders are co-producers of change and redefine their field, not just their function within it (Selsky et al., 2013). Value constellation stems from the work of Selsky et al. (2013) and Ramirez and Mannervik (2016) and is loosely applied here. What is suggested is to go beyond collaborating with others to serve primarily institutional goals or to coordinate what has already been planned. The ambition is to reframe what value can be created as a result of the local interactions in a given social field. How can these elements interact to produce a different purpose through self-reinforcing loops? Given our turbulent environment, Ramirez and Mannervik (2016) propose a socio-ecological approach to strategy. For instance, moving away from the assumption and the models of an industrial economy where "every company occupies a position on a value chain" (Ramirez & Mannervik, 2016, p. 31) and where strategists focus on maximizing profits "rather than on changes or indeed uncertainties beyond its imme-diate industry" (Ramirez & Mannervik, 2016, p. 37). The shift in strategy is an invitation "not only to rethink organizational structures and manage-rial arrangements for value creation, but also rethink value creation itself" (p. 56).

How does this value creation relate to actors in dire situations? First, by setting an "an opportunity to redefine and redistribute roles among many actors [so] that each can play multiple roles that cannot be neatly decomposed into dyadic relationships without affecting the relations with others..." (Ramirez & Mannervik, 2016, p. 85). A parallel can be drawn by invoking once again the Funding and Commissioning work for Complexity: "A number of funders highlighted the role they play as conveners of conversations and facilitators of dialogue across and between actors in a system—we are 'deliberately trying to create collaborative networks and create movements'" (Knight et al., 2017, p. 13). This puts emphasis on relational capital, such that "the locus of capability building shifts from intra-organizational relations to inter-organizational field relations (see Selsky et al., 2007; Pascal et al. 2012)."

One route is to build networks and nurture a movement for actors in dire situation to practice dialogic processes by providing agency for those involved in change to define their role and function, rather than having these prescribed. In my experience, when groups are given an opportunity to join platforms promoting participatory methodologies and inquiry-led dialogue, something opens from within, rather than being imposed from outside. This leads to a predisposition for change and to explore questions that had been held back (for all stakeholders). In other words, transformative practices can be a path toward transformational change, albeit not in a linear fashion. Because when we expect transformative practices (e.g., training, workshops, learning platforms) to immediately contribute to transformational change, we miss an important point: Change is the result of connecting disparate networks contributing to the emergence of a new ecosystem—and such ecosystems require an intentional design among diverse stakeholders. Over time.

CONCLUSION

The historical task of transformational change rises from deep-rooted disorienting dilemmas and complex entanglements. These dilemmas do not stem from a sudden crisis, irrespective of current events; they grow from a "steady accumulation of a thousand slights, a thousand indignities, a thousand unremembered moments" (Parks Daloz, 2000, citing Mandela, 1994, p. 95). This accumulation of indignities and unremembered moments are multiplied over time, positioning transformational change as a task beyond operational plans or quarterly review. Yet, our social identity and institutional ecosystems are designed for technical rationality and incentivize procedural adherence, leaving little space for consideration of the relational and systemic dynamics that drive human behavior. This will not change. We will neither solve nor fix this dilemma: Transformational change will always compete with the desire to preserve ecosystems as they are. Actors in dire situations will continue to face the wrath of powerful interests. Even though the dilemma cannot be solved, how we approach the dilemma can; by being open to noncoercive learning and by strengthening the capacity for the dialogic mindset.

In doing so, the quality of our conversations, over time, blended with the bravery to change ourselves will contribute to the growth of movements and networks with a predisposition for transformational change. The ability to host and convene these movements will help to design a new and diverse value constellations, albeit, imperfectly. This is a difficult task. It is subversive. There are little immediate incentives. Visionary institutions and leaders who approach the dilemma with curiosity will likely create the conditions for transformational change.

So while we will remain entangled, our ability to see clearly will hopefully shift our attention from a position of blame to a position of learning as the goal, whereby noncoercive learning and learning eventually become synonymous.

Finally, there are promising avenues for further research: How do we create new value constellations, over time, involving actors in dire situations? What practices and processes enable institutions to reframe their function and role in an ecosystem? How can the emergence patterns of noncoercive learning complement technical rationality? In the spirit of this chapter, any research would be served by a multi-disciplinary, multi-stakeholder collaboration where collective contribution reigns over singular attribution. Further research and practice for creating new value constellations and reframing institutional functions in support of people in dire situations remain a field of uncharted territory.

REFERENCES

Beer, S. (2002). What is cybernetics. *Kybernetes, 31*(2), 209–219. https://doi.org/10.1108/03684920210417283

Brand, D. (2001). *A map to the door of no return: Notes to belonging.* Vintage Canada.

Burns, D. (2007). *Systemic action research: A strategy for whole system change.* Policy Press.

Bushe, G. R., & Marshak, R. J. (2015). Introduction to the Dialogic Organization Development mindset. In G. R. Bushe, & R. J. Marshak (Eds.), *Dialogic Organization Development: The theory and practice of transformational change.* Berrett-Koehler Publishers.

Corrigan, C. (2015). Hosting and holding containers. In C. Corrigan, G. R. Bushe, & R. J. Marshak (Eds.), *Dialogic Organization Development: The theory and practice of transformational change.* Berrett-Koehler Publishers.

de Guerre, W. D., & Taylor, M. M. (2004). Graduate leadership education in a socio-ecological perspective: Working at the paradigmatic interface. In V. E.

O'Sullivan & M. M. Taylor (Eds.), *Learning toward an ecological consciousness: Selected transformative practices* (pp. 65–83). Palgrave Macmillan.

Freire, P. (2000). *Pedagogy of the oppressed: 30th anniversary edition*. Continuum.

Gaventa, J., & Oswald, K. (2019). *Empowerement and accountability in difficult settings: What are we learning? Key Messages Emerging from the Action for Empowerment and Accountability Programme*. Brighton: IDS.

Gilpin-Jackson, Y. (2020). *Living, leading and facilitating in: Grey zone change*. Supporting Learning and Development Consulting, Inc.

Gordezky, R. (2015). From them to us: Working with multiple constituents in Dialogic OD. In G. Bushe & R. Marshak (Eds.), *Dialogic organization development* (pp. 305–323). Berrett-Koehler.

Knight, A. D., Lowe, T., Brossard, M., & Wilson, J. (2017). *A whole new world: Funding and commissioning in complexity*. Collaborate.

Lowe, T., & Plimmer, D. (2019). *Exploring the new world: Practical insights for funding, commissioning and managing in complexity*. Collaborate CIC.

Mandela, N. (1994). *Long Walk to Freedom*. Boston: Little Brown.

Meadows, D. H. (2008). *Thinking in systems: A primer* (D. Wright, Ed.). Chelsea Green Publishing.

Newman, M. (2006). *Teaching defiance: Stories and strategies for activists educators*. Jossey-Bass.

O'Sullivan, E. V. (2012). Deep Transformation: Forging a Planetary Worldview. In E. W. Taylor, & P. Cranton and Associates (Eds.), *The Handbook of Transformative Learning: Theory, Research, and Practice* (pp. 162–177). San Francisco: Jossey-Bass.

Parks Daloz, L. A. (2000). Transformative Learning for the Common Good. In J. Mezirow and Associates (Ed.), *Learning as Transformation: Critical Perspectives on a Theory in Progress*. San Francisco: Jossey-Bass

Poland, B. (2020). Coming back to our true nature: What is the inner work that supports transition? In K. Zywert & S. Quilley (Eds.), *Health in the Anthropocene: Living well on a finite planet* (pp. 396–416). University of Toronto Press.

Ramalingam, B. (2013). *Aid on the edge of chaos: Rethinking international cooperation in a complex world*. Oxford University Press.

Ramirez, R., & Mannervik, U. (2016). *Strategy for a networked world*. Imperial College Press.

Ricigliano, R. (2012). *Making peace last*. Paradigm Publications.

Selsky, J. W., Ramirez, R., & Babüroglu, O. (2013). Collaborative Capability Design: Redundancy of Potentialities. *System Practice and Action Research*, 377–395.

Southern, N. (2015). Framing inquiry: The art of engaging great questions. In G. R. Bushe & R. J. Marshak (Eds.), *Dialogic organization development: The theory and practice of transformational change* (pp. 269–289). Berret-Koehler.

Spivak, G. C. (2014). *Readings*. Seagull Books.

Stacey, R. (2015). Understanding organizations as complex responsive processes of relating. In G. R. Bushe & R. J. Marshak (Eds.), *Dialogic organization development: The theory and practice of transformational change* (pp. 151–175). Berrett-Koehler.

Stroh, D. P. (2015). *Systems thinking for social change: A Practical guide to solving complex problems, avoiding unintended consequences, and achieving lasting results*. Chelsea Green Publishing.

Tadros, M., & Khan, A. (2019). Beyond the religious/secular binary trap: Keeping the focus on gender equality. *IDS Policy Briefing 165*. Institute of Development Studies.

Taylor, P., & Fransman, J. (2004). *Learning and teaching participation: Exploring the role of Higher Learning Institutions as agents of development and social change*. IDS.

Walcott, D. (1997). *The Bounty*. Farrar Straus & Giroux.

Whittington, J. (2016). *Systemic coaching and constellations: the principles, practices and application for individuals, teams and groups* (2nd ed.). Kogan Page.

CHAPTER 35

In Service to My Community: Exploring Oppression and Internalized Racism

Taj Johns

I am an elder and wear my crown of graying hair with pride. I am female, childless, a few pounds overweight, and I enjoy every step of my life. Every day of my life, I am African American to many and Black to my friends of color. Any of these portrayals of myself can lead to being viewed as outside of a prescribed norm. The reality of my Blackness never loses the space of consciousness in my world.

I learned this consciousness of being Black from a seemingly infinite number of interactions. At a young age the elders taught us to straighten our hair, speak eloquently (a term used to describe an articulate Black person), and behave in a manner accepted by the dominating culture. Still, I was prejudged, marginalized, made invisible, unheard, shamed, mocked, infantilized, and more. Racism is a small word for the world of struggle and transformative learning potential hidden within it.

Transformative learning is an individual recursive journey that has many disorienting dilemmas, reflections, and actions throughout life. A

T. Johns (✉)
Saint Mary's College of California, Moraga, CA, USA

© The Author(s), under exclusive license to Springer Nature Switzerland AG 2022
A. Nicolaides et al. (eds.), *The Palgrave Handbook of Learning for Transformation*, https://doi.org/10.1007/978-3-030-84694-7_35

627

628   T. JOHNS

disorienting dilemma occurs because an experience does not fit into one's pre-existing frame that previously helped make sense of the world.

In the next few pages, I situate racism in general and internalized racism specifically within the concepts of transformative learning. First, I apply Mezirow's (2000) transformative learning theory to stories of my past. Next, assisted by the work of Kegan (2000), I share my understanding of internalized racism as an unconscious tool of oppression.

In this chapter I interlace my stories of oppression with theory. By using stories, I believe that the concepts of internalized racism, internalized oppression, and internalized white superiority can surface how these concepts influence one's thinking.

I do not want to stop with simply making concepts visible. I want to bring them alive in each reader's lived experience by offering exercises to help explore your assumptions about race.

The exercises are exploratory adventures, a beginning step for examining internalized racism, internalized white superiority, oppression, and racism. Because I want to be in dialogue with readers about your shared humanity, I will sometimes speak directly to you.

By making the invisible visible and the unconscious conscious, we create an opportunity to stop reacting to the world, instead of beginning to live in action with the world.

OPPRESSION

The success of oppression depends on two factors, the oppressor and the oppressed. It is an unequal relationship because the oppressor has the ability to negatively influence the lives of others by creating obstacles. The oppressor has power, which, when unjustly used, promotes fear in another. They practice dominance and control finding ways of perpetuating the subordinate position of others.

Freire's (1970/1993) work lends insight into the duality experienced by the oppressed. "The oppressed suffer from the duality which has established itself into their ... being. They are at one and the same time themselves and the oppressor" (p. 48). Until this internalization is realized, it is difficult for the oppressed to self-author their lives. Freire suggests the oppressed develop a critical consciousness to help see systems of inequality and commit to taking actions against these systems.

Certain characteristics are interpreted as influences of oppression such as self-hatred, self-concealment, feelings of inferiority, resignation, isolation, and powerlessness. The resulting behaviors influence the person's concept of self and the world. The power of oppression is that marginalized groups may begin to perceive themselves from the negative lens of the oppressor.

When I hold the stereotypes and myths the dominating culture believes about me as true and judge myself by these standards, I have internalized that culture's beliefs.

INTERNALIZED RACISM

My objective is not to cry stale tears from the past, nor rekindle old hatreds from past injustices, instead I seek to enlighten my path of today by better understanding where and how the lights were turned out yesterday.
—Na'im Akbar (1996, p. 3)

Internalized racism is taking the stereotypes and racist judgments a dominant culture has about my race and internalizing these beliefs and attitudes. These stereotypes are usually based on negative racist opinions, such as "Black people are inferior" or "Black people are angry and violent." The internalization of the oppressing culture's ideologies creates lesions in my psyche. These lesions influence my attitudes and behaviors toward myself and other Black people. I am in a reinforcing loop where the oppressor no longer needs to worry about keeping me down, or influencing my thinking, because I have learned to perceive myself as worthless and unconsciously behave in a manner that supports this view. This is the way any form of internalized oppression works, be it internalized homophobia, internalized anti-Semitism, ageism, etc.

Without knowledge of the power of internalized racism, its causes, and resulting behaviors, the phenomenon remains an unbreakable, self-destructive element in the life forces of many people. Making internalized racism visible can be paralyzing, an overwhelming endeavor, because it is more than adding information into an already existing way of being. It changes the way we think about our being. I expect my stories of oppression to show one Black woman's approach to the difficult work of meeting and transforming internalized racism.

630   T. JOHNS

HOW I USED MEZIROW
TO UNDERSTAND INTERNALIZED RACISM

A defining condition of being human is our urgent need to understand and order the meaning of our experiences, to integrate it with what we know to avoid the threat of chaos.
—Mezirow (2000)

Jack Mezirow's (2000) theory of transformative learning (TL) offers a process by which we can develop a worldview that is more inclusive, flexible, and reflective. According to Hoggan and Kasl (in print):

> Mezirow's theory begins with the assertion that we make meaning by "filtering" our sense perceptions through a "frame of reference" (1996, p. 163); these frames of reference are comprised of meaning schemes and meaning perspectives. A meaning scheme is a particular way of thinking about something; ... a meaning perspective is more foundational; it is the basis upon which meaning schemes are built. (p. 6)

Mezirow's transformative theory describes a 10-phase process wherein the learner begins to examine their frames of references. I illustrate these phases using three vignettes. In my VISTA (Volunteers in Service to America) story I experience the initial three phases of this theory:

- disorienting dilemma
- self-examination of feelings and guilt
- critical assessment of my assumptions.

Phases three and four are demonstrated in the second vignette in which I began examining my Blackness during my 10-year interracial marriage.

- Recognize my discontent and
- explore new roles, relationships and actions.

The next four phases of TL theory are illustrated in a vignette describing my work with a group of African Americans:

- plan a course of action

- acquired knowledge and skills to implement a plan
- tried new roles and Built confidence in my new roles, and relationships.

Phase 10 is the final step of Mezirow's theory. During this phase I offer the reader an integration exercise.

- Reintegration into one's life on conditions dictated by one's perspective.

I expect my stories of oppression to show one Black woman's approach to the difficult work of meeting and transforming internalized racism.

Volunteers in Service to America 1966

It was three decades before I was exposed to Mezirow's (1991) transformative learning theory by which time I had experienced several disorienting dilemmas. In my middle years of school my parents moved to a white neighborhood that tolerated my family's presence. The move ripped me from a caring Black community; those relationships could not be sustained, and I felt abandoned.

After graduating high school, I joined VISTA, Volunteers in Service to America, a national service program to alleviate poverty. I traveled from California to Texas and entered an all-Black neighborhood called the Bottoms. This unexpected cultural shift delivered a major disorienting dilemma. I was probably one of the first northern Black women who came to assist in this community.

We were required to live in the community where much of the housing consisted of dilapidated shacks. The house I rented gave me fewer roaches and more mice. The mice did not get into my bed or bite as the roaches did. Two white female VISTA volunteers resided in the house next door. We met daily to decide what areas of the community needed our attention. There were many needs to address such as getting milk for a family, finding transportation for a resident's visit to a doctor, and starting a youth center.

My transition to becoming a resource to this community was difficult. First, I felt disheartened when I saw white girls greeted, accepted, and admired instantly. I became increasingly aware of the brainwashing stories I received in the north of white is right, beautiful, and something to be admired. These stories contaminated the minds of even this poor community. I remember the daily walks I took on the oyster shell roads, hoping to make myself known and what I could offer. Often the Black kids threw cans and rocks at me and made derogatory remarks, calling me the n-word. I did not have a name for how the Black people of this community treated me. Years later I learned the term *internalized racism* that explained their behavior and my reactions to them. I knew racism from my life in California and tolerated covert expressions. However, my move to the South amplified my familiarity with racism 1000 times. My VISTA placement in the Texas Bottoms provided one of my first lessons on internalized racism as well as several disorienting dilemmas. Fifty years later I remember the horror on the faces of white residents when I jumped into a swimming pool where only white people swam. The white people screamed, "No! No! Don't get in here!" Their eyes were full of fear as they screamed, "Your color is going to come off and get on us. Don't!" and they jumped out of the pool.

I remember being refused service and once I was detained by the police for walking with a white man. They assumed I was a prostitute because of my skin color. How are people expected to survive, not to mention thrive, surrounded by a dominant community that despises them based on their skin color? These were among my first significant disorienting dilemmas that required many years to understand. These overt racist acts colored my two-year stay in the South.

I was between two worlds—and both worlds despised me because of my skin color. Forty years would pass before I came to understand how I was belittled and diminished. I agreed to a loss of dignity by acquiescing to the dominant power's demands. This is how I expressed and experienced my internalized racism.

Incremental Learning

Mezirow (2000) says, "Transformation in habit of mind may be epochal, a sudden dramatic reorienting insight, or incremental, involving a progressive series of related transformations that culminate in a transformation of habit of mind" (p. 21). While I was living in the south, the racial incidents I experienced were good examples of incremental disorienting dilemmas. I became involved in cycles of internalizing my racism. These cycles of self-denigrating thoughts were subtle. Subtleness is an unfortunate characteristic of oppression, like the subtleness of pollen, until the first sneeze. An oppressive act can leave one feeling confused about what happened without delving into the event. Often with internalized racism there is blaming and shaming, often focused on you. I would take years to shift my way of thinking about myself, racism, and other African Americans.

Becoming Critically Conscious of My Reality

How did I make my self-denigrating behaviors known to myself? I had to become aware of the disorienting events I was facing related to my Blackness. My time in VISTA served as an excellent starting point. My experience with the southern Black community proved more daunting, painful, and confusing than the overt racism I experienced from whites. I found myself making assumptions that were feeding my internal shame: "Black people will disappoint you; they will abandon you; they will talk about you because they talk about each other." I felt guilty for having these feelings and embarrassed for having expectations. Unfulfilled, guilty, and uncomfortable, I was forced to question my assumptions and look compassionately at myself. In transformative learning theory, this was the beginning of my critical reflection about my Blackness, phases two and three.

Exploring Experiences and Questioning Assumptions

Mezirow (2000) tells us that meaning schemes are understood and developed through reflection. Looking deeply and deliberately, we can move through the phases toward transforming those structures that limit us. To pursue this goal, I began to journal some of my experiences as an African American woman. Through journaling I realized that during my time in Texas I felt irritated and mortified by the poor Black community. My feelings were not limited to this southern community. They had generalized to my relationship with all Black communities that did not meet my standard of behavior. Reflection became an important step for sorting out my discontent. Journaling enhanced my understanding.

My collection of journal entries became a list of things I was told, heard or believed about being a Black person and my Black community. Once

634   T. JOHNS

on the list, stereotypes and unconscious assumptions that supported self-doubt became visible and useful. Here is a partial list of the stereotypes I was told, heard or believed:

- Black men are angry and dangerous.
- Anglo facial features, lighter skin color, and fine straight hair are the standard of beauty, not my Black features.
- Whites view people of my culture as inferior.
- All Black women want to be white.
- All Black people ever want to talk about is race.

VISTA is a significant marker in my road to consciousness about my identity as a Black woman. I think of this experience as a triggering event that led me to a lifetime of exploring my internalized racism. But my exploration did not begin right away nor was my VISTA experience the start. Unknowingly my internalized racism was getting stronger. My understanding of this self-denigrating behavior was propelled by writing about my experience.

EXERCISE ONE: JOURNALING TO EXPLORE MEZIROW'S PHASES ONE, TWO, AND THREE

We are guided by our narratives. These are stories we make up about our relationships, our learning styles, our parents, our looks, and so on. These stories are internalized, becoming our points of view and habits of mind, in other words, our worldview. What are your stories?

How did we learn these stories? In transformative learning theory, if your response to an event is one of confusion where you become emotionally frozen, shamed, feel distressed and agitation, etc., you may consider that event a disorienting dilemma—step one of Mezirow's 10 steps toward transformation.

In this exercise, you will explore a disorienting racial dilemma, your feelings associated with that dilemma, and take a critical look at your assumptions about race. There are two explorations in this exercise, both using a Free Write method of learning.

Preparation: Set aside 10 minutes for uninterrupted, nonjudgmental writing for each of these writing prompts. Keep your hands moving and don't worry about spelling and grammar. This is a form of heart felt brainstorming using the pen and paper.

- The first exploration is to help you make visible your racial assumptions. Review the list above and identify one or two stereotypical thoughts you believe or were told about people of African ancestry. If you do not see one that works for you, see what you can discover for yourself concerning racial stereotypes.
- Create your own list of things you have been told, heard or believe about people of your culture, gender, status, or social class. This is an exploration of your internalized thoughts.

Take this time to critically reflect and explore your assumptions.

Can I Marry Dignity?

I had more narratives to deconstruct including my selections of romantic partners. As my feelings of unease continued to nip at my esteem, I decided to assuage these mounting emotions of diminished dignity by being in a romantic relationship with a European-American. I used personal characteristics that our culture privileges—youth and heterosexuality—to gain entry into a world that historically minimized and marginalized my existence. I had hoped that this union would grant me some recognition, privilege by proxy, and the possibility of love. After a few months, I realized that marriage to a white man was a significant change, causing me to address mounting discontent with who I was. I began looking for others who had similar experiences, developing new relationships and searching for a new way of being.

Before my partnership, I found it easier to blame others for what was happening to me. Racism was disabling me, and internalized racism was the constant variable in this equation of self-love versus self-doubt, the feeling of being "good enough" versus a battle with my sense of unworthiness. My choice to marry a white man did not support my worldview, or did it? Why did I make this choice and what did it mean for my self-acceptance as a Black woman? My marriage contributed to my ambivalence about my relationship with the Black community. In this period, I began to rid myself of the superfluous baggage I now call internalized racism.

636   T. JOHNS

Shifting Internalized Racism and Oppression from Subject to Object

Robert Kegan (2000), a constructive-developmental psychologist, "believes our meaning making systems, change and grow over time" (Garvey-Berger, 2012, p. 181). Kegan's work combines two ideologies, constructivism and developmental theory.

Constructivists suggest we create our world by the meaning we assign to our experiences. Developmental theory proposes human beings enter different cognitive phases as we grow. Kegan (2000) combines these two concepts advancing the idea that knowing involves a subject and object relationship. Kegan explains:

> That which is 'object' we can look at, take responsibility for, reflect upon, experience control over, integrate with some other way of knowing. That which is 'subject' we are run by, identified with, fused with, at the effect of .... What is 'object' in our knowing describes the thoughts and feelings we say we have; what is 'subject' describes the thoughts and feelings that has [sic] us. We have object and we are subject. (p. 53)

As we grow and expand our ways of knowing, what was once "subject" in one's reality, becomes "object."

Kegan identified five orders of consciousness each having a developmental task that involves a subject and object relational shift. Each order consists of three lines of development on the cognitive, interpersonal, and intrapersonal levels. Below, I offer subject descriptions, how we identify ourselves, in each order which, upon reflection and integration, becomes the object in the subsequent order.

- First order, ages 2–6, one perceives and respond to the world by impulse and emotions.
- Second order, ages 6–10, is motivated by needs and preferences. A person begins to understand consequences.
- Third order is older adolescent and majority of population. This period is known as the socialized mind or traditional mind. One is subject to role consciousness and self-consciousness.
- Fourth order is called the self-authoring mind, where we begin to see systems. During this period, we are subject to autonomy and multiple role consciousness. This order supports Frier's (1970) cultural consciousness theory for exploring one's oppression.

- Fifth order is called the self-transforming mind where one begins to hold multiple perspectives, living with paradox and connection with others.

Before I questioned my internalized racism, I was functioning in what Kegan calls the second order of mind. Racism was a part of me because I had assumptions about the way the world worked and that dictated how I would be in this community and with my Blackness.

I contend internalized racism as well as internalized oppression is a socialized, traditional mind, and considered a third Order of Mind. In this order one has "internalized the feelings and emotions of others and are guided by those people and institutions" (Garvey-Berger, 2012, p. 184). In addition, in the third order, one's "esteem is entirely reliant on others because the person is made up of those around them" (Garvey-Berger, 2012, p. 185).

Kegan (1998) suggests becoming self-guided and self-motivated, one needs to move to the fourth order of mind. In the fourth order there is ownership of one's life, as the individual learns self-identity and autonomy.

In the third order, one would begin to explore their assumptions about internalized racism that leads to self-denigrating behaviors. In the fourth order, one begins to develop an understanding about individualization and being self-regulating.

How does one bring to awareness or surface the subject of internalized oppression in order to transform our connections to the oppressor? We are all involved in this work of unmasking our internalized oppression. As we move forward remember internalized oppression can happen to anyone, internalized racism usually impacts people of color.

Exercise Two: Soul Collage

The last narrative about my interracial marriage illustrates how I chose to address my low self-esteem from a third order of mind. I now invite you to reflect on choices you too have made to ease the pain and discomfort of oppression or internalized racism. Remember, the working definition of these concepts is we are taking the judgments and stereotypes of the dominant culture, internalizing these values as our own, and evaluating ourselves using their yardstick.

For recovery from internalized oppression, we have to move those feelings associated with oppression outside of ourselves. We must begin to realize, what we did to survive racism and oppression was okay.

This next exercise lets you practice moving oppression from subject to object. Reread my story of partnership with a European-American male. Pause, breathe, and make notes about choices you have made to ease the pain and discomfort of your oppression or internalized racism. This next exercise is inspired by Seena Frost (2010), the creator of Soul Collage. Frost uses collage as a way of exploring aspects of yourself, both known and unknown.

Preparation: You will need three cards or pieces of cardboard cut to 7.5 by 5.5 inches, glue, and magazine images.

- Create a collage on the card that represents your intuitive vision of what your oppression looks like. What does internalized racism look like to you?
- Create another collage card that represent ways you act out your internalized oppression or internalized racism.
- Create a third collage card that represents what the world looks like when you are self-authoring your life.

Once you have created your three cards, sit with them, meditate on them, carry the cards with you for a few days. Imagine these cards have answers to these questions:

- Internalized racism or oppression, where did you come from?
- What feelings do I associate with internalized racism or oppression? Shame, numbness, alarm, surprised, unsettled, anxious, mistrustful or frightened? This list is endless.
- How do you (internalized oppression and racism) serve me?
- What can you tell me about ways I am reacting to this world?
- What are my assumptions about
  - my body
  - my social status
  - my race, and gender

Your list of assumptions will expand once you begin to live in the questions. This process is subject reframing. The intention of this exercise is to shift what is subject—oppression and internalized racism—to object, identifying attitudes and beliefs that influence my behaviors. Placing the identities of internalized racism on a card gives you something to focus on outside of yourself. You can begin to critically reflect on the assumptions associated with the things that "got you."

Returning to the steps of Mezirow's (2000) theory of transformation, another important step in transforming one's habits of mind is to make public the dimensions of our dilemmas.

Finding ways to have conversations about or deepen your understanding of internalized racism, is a necessary step for one to develop their own internal governing system, a fourth order of mind. Finding others for creating dialogue circles is a good approach for addressing this step of Mezirow's theory. Remember addressing internalized racism, oppression and racism can be paralyzing. You are asking yourself to acknowledge your discontent and changing your way of knowing, behaving, and feeling.

TELLING MY STORY TO OTHERS AND PLANNING A COURSE OF ACTION

If you want to go quickly go alone; If you want to go far go together.
—African Proverb

Transformative learning theorists agree that sharing personal concerns and process with others is an important part of transformation. In the final vignette I share ways I rebuilt my connection to the African American Community. This connection was reorienting and the impetus for the epochal change in my way of thinking and being.

During the time I was feeling a mounting discontent concerning my relationship with myself and the Black community, I joined four other Black women to grapple with racism's impact on our self-worth. We learned ways of not falling prey to racism's changing disguises. We wanted to understand how internalized racism had been an unseen demon on our shoulders causing us uncertainty. In this group I planned a course of action, acquired new knowledge to implement my plan, tried new roles and built self-confidence. These are phases four through eight of Mezirow's theory.

We designed an environment that supported a way for us to safely explore the impacts of racism. We agreed to meet monthly for two hours at an established place; we developed group guidelines, such as being honest and compassionate with ourselves and each other. We felt, "being honest without compassion could be cruel" (personal journal, 2004). Our process became a road map for 36 other African Americans to begin the journey of understanding ways internalized racism distorted our meaning schemes.

This group of five Black women worked together for many years. During my first months, I questioned my relationship with my European-American partner. I came to understand that nothing was wrong with our union except my motives for being with him. I addressed the shame and guilt I felt for assimilating into a dominant culture. I began to talk about my embarrassment of being assigned lower track classes during my middle school years. I held this shame close to me, influencing my desire to pursue a law degree, because I knew I was flawed. I eventually understood there was nothing wrong with me or the other Black students in the lower track classes. We were victims of an all-white school system that ignored us contributing to our beliefs of being stupid and defected. My school experience was an example of institutional racism, an unfortunate encounter for many people of color.

Through this Black women's group, I began to embrace a different standard of beauty. We wrote poems and meditations honoring our noses, tightly woven hair, our thighs, our lips, and other parts of our bodies that once brought us disgrace. My voice was now important, my experiences were no longer secrets that mortified, but meaning schemes for expanding my worldview. I was important and my community was important; we all learned how to be vulnerable and connect. My supreme takeaway from this group was learning: "There are as many ways of being Black as there are Black people" (personal journal, 2007). I no longer fear being called "not black enough or too black." My Blackness was once defined by a white culture, whose limited view of me I internalized. This internalized view offered a limited definition of who I was and who I could become.

Exercise Three: Begin an Inquiry into Your Bias

Begin to Study Your Oppression or Internalized Racism

Take an Implicit Bias test. This test is often suggested for exploring your hidden bias. Place the name, Implicit Bias Test, in your search engine and take a free test. The implicit bias test results plus exercises one and two in this chapter are good talking points if you decide to work with others to expose your racism, internalized racism and oppression. When I began my work, I preferred whites over Blacks; now I do not have a preference for one or the other. Kegan (2000) might suggest that I have moved to the fifth order of mind.

If you decide to internally explore this subject alone, the Implicit Bias Test can be another Free Write exercise. For example:

- I was surprised by my results because I always thought of myself as
- I have limited my connections to others because
- I am ashamed of my results because

Additional Writing: Shame to Gratitude

Review some podcasts on shame. Understanding your source of shame is a great starting point for understanding your internalized racism, internalized white superiority and oppression. I learned from my years of study, "Internalized racism involves two levels of shame: the shame associated with our African-ness, as a result of slavery and racism, and the shame of being shamed" (Watts-Jones, 2002, p. 593). This is the shame some Blacks carry. What about you as a white person, what shame do you carry? Shame is a powerful tool often used to control one's behavior.

- Write a letter of gratitude to yourself.
- Read it aloud often. You can even make a collage card that represents your self-love.

CONCLUSION

The history of the United States of America is laden with stories of several ethnicities being subjugated to discrimination. To alleviate the discomfort, people assimilated adapting and internalizing both the positive and negative ideas of the dominant culture. This is internalized oppression and internalized racism.

Oppression is a method of social assimilation that influences our ways of thinking from an early age. Our parents did not intend to impose a way of being that could limit our thinking today, yet it was necessary for us to learn these rules to become socialized human beings. Mezirow

(2000) identified what we learned at a young age was habits of mind that becomes our foundation.

As we grew older, our habits of mind became unchallenged assumptions about our lives. Part of these unchallenged assumptions can be about our worthiness. What we were told, heard or believed to be true, can become internalized and restrictive. These internalized norms can create self-doubt, angst, fears, and humiliation, as well as motivation, esteem, happiness, and assurance. I contend unless we look at our habits of mind, they can oppress our expression of life.

I've taken you on a journey to "turn the lights on." This is for you to see your joy and happiness more clearly. First, we needed a better understanding of where and how the lights were turned out. Mezirow (2000) suggests that after we explore our disorienting dilemma, we begin to look at new roles, plan a course of action, build self-confidence and competence in our new roles. The final exercise in this chapter offers a way to integrate new roles and perspectives into your life.

EXERCISE FOUR: MANDALA.
A REINTEGRATION INTO LIFE AS MY AUTHOR

Exploring our experience with a critical mind can be done harshly or gently. I have selected the mandala as the final exercise because I believe it provides a helpful frame for exploring your inner self through a deep and gentle process. Circles and mandalas are reminders of our relationships and sacred connections, thus they represent the infinite and can take us on a profound journey.

Drawing and coloring can be a helpful way to make the images behind the emotion more visible. Drawing can result in whole person learning, through the inclusion of affect, imagination, spirit, and sensation. Working with images helps us connect the knowable world to the unknowable or the unconscious mind.

Preparation:

- Create your own mandala. Find one on the internet or purchase a mandala coloring book.
- Use whatever colorful materials you desire such as watercolors, crayons or paints and pastels. A combination of all might be enjoyable.

- Find a quiet, peaceful place to work.
- Play some music, light a candle, or burn incense if you wish.

As you work:

- Think about bringing together all the parts of yourself into a new role.
- Notice the patterns you choose and colors enticing you.
- Remember the process is nurturing. The product is only for you.

Reflect:

- Take a picture of your finished mandala and keep it with you.
- Your mandala can be your grounding shield, a reminder of a time you felt whole, self-authoring and connected to your inner wellbeing.

These were the beginning steps in your exploration of racism, internalized racism, and internalized oppression. My hope and dream is for you to try these exercises with people who look like you and later with an even more diverse group. Remember that the journey's goal is to seek to enlighten the path of today by better understanding where and how the lights were turned out yesterday. Let there be light!

References

Akbar, N. (1996). *Breaking the chains of psychological slavery.* Mind Productions & Associates.

Freire, P. (1970/1993). *Pedagogy of the oppressed.* Continuum International Publishing Group.

Frost, S. (2010). *Soul collage evolving: An intuitive collage process for self-discovery & community.* Hanford Mead Publishers, Inc.

Garvey-Berger, J. (2012). *Changing on the job: Developing leaders for a complex world.* Stanford University Press.

Hoggan, C. & Kasl, E. (in press). Transformative Learning. In A. Belzer & B. Dashew (Eds.), *Understanding the Adult Learner: Perspectives and practices.* Stylus Publishing.

Kegan, R. (1998) *In over our heads: Mental demands of modern life.* Harvard University Press.

644 T. JOHNS

Kegan, R. (2000). What "form" transforms? A constructive-developmental approach to transformative learning. In J. Mezirow (Ed.), *Learning as transformation: Critical perspective on a theory in progress* (pp. 35–69). Jossey-Bass.

Mezirow, J. M. (1991). *Transformative dimensions of adult learning.* Jossey-Bass.

Mezirow, J. M. (2000). *Learning as transformation: Critical perspectives on a theory in progress.* Jossey-Bass.

Pennebaker, J., & Smyth, J. (2016). *Open it up by writing it down: How expressive writing improved health and ease emotional pain* (3rd ed.). The Guilford Press.

Watts-Jones, D. (2002). Healing internalized racism: The role of a within-group sanctuary among people of African descent. *Family Process, 41*(4), 591–601.

CHAPTER 36

Imaginative Perspectives on Transformative Learning

Randee Lipson Lawrence

IMAGINING NEW REALITIES

Imagination means singing to a wide invisible audience. It means receptivity to the creative unconscious, the macrocosmic mind, artistic mind. It makes erotic philosophers of us, as we imagine the world in images that make whole. To imagine is to give birth to—to embody the Spirit in word and picture and behavior. The world will change when we can imagine it different and, like artists, do the work of creating new social forms.
—Richards (1996, p. 119)

The metamorphosis of the caterpillar to butterfly has long been a metaphor for transformation. And yet, most transformation rarely happens in such a predictable pattern. Surely cocooning needs to happen

---

R. L. Lawrence (✉)
Teachers College Columbia University, New York, NY, USA
e-mail: rlawrence@nl.edu

National Louis University, Chicago, IL, USA

© The Author(s), under exclusive license to Springer Nature   645
Switzerland AG 2022
A. Nicolaides et al. (eds.), *The Palgrave Handbook of Learning for Transformation*, https://doi.org/10.1007/978-3-030-84694-7_36

but what one looks like at the other end of the transformation cannot be known. In these days of coronavirus (a disorienting dilemma to be sure!) many of us are cocooning or going inward. It seems we are ripe for individual and global transformation but what form will this take?

These uncertain times call for imaginative thinking and envisioning new realities. As Maxine Greene (1995, p. 7) emphasized: "It is through the imagination that we are often able to conceive of a reality different from the one we are currently experiencing." We have already seen it happening. Dance and yoga classes are being zoomed into our living rooms. Food shortages in stores are causing us to come up with creative recipes with what we have on hand. We are experiencing virtual meetings, classes, and even weddings and funerals. Artistic expression (Lawrence, 2012) helps us get in touch with our emotions and embodied knowledge and can complement and/or provide alternative pathways to the critical reflection and rational discourse introduced by Mezirow (1991) as tools for transformative learning. These approaches not only help to raise awareness of the unconscious, but they can also give voice to those that have been silenced, providing avenues to begin to have critical conversations about painful and difficult topics.

TEACHING WITH SOUL

As of this writing, K-12 education and university teaching is in flux in the United States due to the global pandemic. It is uncertain when face-to-face teaching will resume. We need to reimagine and transform pedagogy to address students at a distance. What might this look like? Long before this current crisis in education, Cranton (2008) suggested, and I concur, that education was losing its soul. "Where is the joy in learning? Where is the imagination? The heart? The soul?" (Cranton, 2008, p. 125). Institutional constraints, school mandates, and prescribed curricula have created norms for learning that leave little room for imagination. I have been teaching graduate students in adult education for most of my career. While the principles of adult education include self-direction, critical thinking, and emancipation, prior schooling has turned students into "consumers" rather producers of education, as my professor Phyllis Cunningham used to say. They want to be taught. I'm sure I frustrated many students when I would not tell them how many pages were required and what exactly I wanted them to do. I prefer the word "creators" rather than producers of education. When students are given freedom to co-create their educational experiences using imaginative perspectives, the soul is restored and transformative learning becomes possible.

Embracing the Unknown

There is wisdom in not knowing. Frankel (2017) believes that doubt and uncertainty are necessary for growth and change. It is necessary to let go of the known, so that the unexpected can occur, making transformation possible. "When we cannot make sense of our experience at our current level of understanding, we must find a way to enter another world where new meaning and new perspectives emerge" (p. 131).

Transformative learning occurs when we began to re-examine our taken for granted assumptions (Mezirow, 1991). These assumptions often take the form of judgments of self and others about the way things ought to be. Releasing our assumptions (what we perceive to be known reality) can be unsettling, creating a disorienting dilemma (Mezirow, 1991) that can be a catalyst for change (Lawrence & Cranton, 2015) as we discover a reimagined reality.

Working with Images from the Unconscious: Metaphor, Symbol, and Dreams

Transformative learning involves becoming conscious of unconscious knowledge. Much of what is unknown at a consciousness level may be buried in the unconscious. Dirkx (2006) believes that extra-rational processes such as imagination, emotions, myths, and fantasies (what he refers to as soul work) are important ways to engage with the unconscious dimensions of the self. One way to do this is to "take note of our reaction to particular metaphors, symbols or images- what our attention is drawn to—and our emotional reaction to these images" (p. 35). Spear (2014) uses Jacobi's term "conscious cooperation." The ego (conscious self) needs to relinquish control and cooperate with the unconscious in order for individuation to occur. Individuation (Jung, 1964) is further explained as a process of integrating who we are in the inner and outer worlds. For Spear, this is the "first vital step in transformative learning" (p. 226). There are many ways to integrate these images from the inner world of our unconscious with our everyday conscious world. These processes will be discussed in the remainder of this chapter.

Metaphor

Metaphors are useful to help us build bridges between what we know and what we are hoping to understand. The bridge is itself a metaphor. A bridge is a mechanism that creates a safe pathway to cross from one place into another. So too, we can create a bridge between the known and unknown.

Campbell, Parr, and Richardson remind us that "Metaphors allow us to connect the inner and outer, to make the implicit explicit, so that we can better understand, more deeply experience, and more eloquently express who we are and what we do" (2009, p. 211). A metaphor can be an idea or concept but it is mostly accessed through symbol or imagery. While we can conceptualize a metaphor in our heads, I have found that artistic expression through drawing, poetry, photography, or embodiment is useful to translate the image into tangible form. As one student described:

> I think my metaphors tend to be multisensory, and poetry helps me to capture fully. I think this comes from how I experience the world and reflect on my position in it. It allows me to mix areas of my life—sensations, observations, thoughts, feelings—and see what happens when they are rearranged.

Transformative learning is a concept that is initially hard for students to grasp. They have difficulty differentiating transformative learning from other forms of learning. Many of them have had transformative experiences in their pasts without having had the language to name them as such. Asking students to create a metaphor to describe their experience is good first step. Many of the metaphors take on visual or poetic form. For example, one student described her experience as a Jackson Pollack painting:

> I have an abundance of enthusiasm but sometimes lack clarity or feel scattered in many directions. It was only when I did a workshop last summer and used psychodrama to act out the 'cast of characters' within me that I began to understand my struggle. I found that when I externalized my inner dialogue, the 'voices' that once seemed to clash had moments of harmony with one another. I saw an order within the chaos and began to recognize all the various aspects of my being.

Another student came up with the metaphor of making popcorn—taking the seeds, adding oil and heat and then carefully monitoring the process to make sure the kernels transformed into popcorn and did not burn from too much heat. This makes more sense to me than the caterpillar-butterfly metaphor that seems overly simplistic. After all, transformation is not an automatic cyclical process. Patricia Cranton and I (Lawrence & Cranton, 2015) found that people rarely transform in isolation. Relationships are important to encourage transformation. At the same time, relationships can negatively influence, causing the transformation to be delayed or even prevented. We used the metaphor of gardening to describe the process of transformation. "A catalyst can be looked at as a seed that holds the potential for transformation... some seeds germinate within a few days, while others take longer and some do not germinate at all" (p. 63). The growth of the plant or transformative growth depends upon the climatic conditions as well as the attention or lack of attention by the gardener. The creation of this metaphor and the graphic presentation that accompanied it (Lawrence & Cranton, 2015, p. 62) helped us to derive further meaning from the themes of our research.

Dreams

I have long been fascinated by dreams. Dream symbols are always expressed in metaphor and according to Jung (1964) are messages from our unconscious that assist in the process of individuation. Working with our dreams can help us to better understand these unconscious messages. For example, dreams of being pregnant, giving birth, or dreams with babies in them, rarely signify that a baby is in one's future. Rather they represent new ideas or new projects that the dreamer wants to "give birth" to. "Paying attention to the images that present themselves is a way of connecting inner self to the outer world" (Lawrence, 2005, p. 309). Dreams can suggest alternative realities that can lead to trying out new roles or identities; one of the "steps" Mezirow (1991) suggests as part of the transformative learning process.

Psychologist and dream expert Robert Johnson (1986, p. 21) stated: "Dreaming and imagination have one special quality in common: their power to convert the invisible forms of the unconscious into images that are perceptible to the conscious mind." Johnson advocates a 4-step approach to working with our dreams including: Making associations of our dream images to our waking life, connecting these dream images to our inner selves, finding meaning through interpretation, and creating rituals to concretize what was learned from the dream.

While we can learn a lot by paying attention to dreams on our own, such as keeping a dream journal, looking for patterns, and following Johnson's steps, working with dreams in groups can help us to further understand the meaning of our dream symbols. I was part of a dream circle for a number of years. We would each share a current dream and others would suggest possible connections. We can't tell others what their dreams mean but we can suggest ideas such as "if it were my dream I might consider the deep water as ...," or "I noticed the number 4 came up three times. I wonder if that has any meaning for you in your waking life ..." Most people are fascinated by dreams. Giving students permission to include their dreams as another "text" for transformative learning can lead to new understandings of their unconscious processes.

Evoking Imagination in Transformative Learning Through Artistic Expression

In previous writing, I talked about the power of the arts to "get us out of our heads" and explore transformative learning through our emotions and intuitive sensibilities (Lawrence, 2012). In this section I elaborate on several artistic processes including visual, written, and performative arts such as music, dance, and drama.

Visual Arts

Many of us are visual learners. We connect to pictures. Photojournalism, for example, is a way to deliberately wake us up by stirring our emotions and raising awareness of injustice. The images from the Black Lives Matter movement have been particularly provocative in highlighting the problem of systemic racism and police brutality. We can be moved toward transformation through the powerful art of others. We can also create art to represent or assist with our own transformative process.

Lawrence and Cranton (2009) used photography as a metaphor for breaking out of habitual ways of seeing the world by looking for contradictions and creating images to express those contradictions, thus moving "beyond the rational and cognitive into imaginal, symbolic and emotional ways of understanding" (p. 313). The world is full of images. Using a camera is one way to express one's thoughts and emotions through the creation of images.

Photovoice, a participatory action research method, is often used to allow silenced voices a form of expression. For example, Holtby et al. (2015) used photovoice with a group of queer and transgender youth. They distributed cameras to the participants and asked them to take photos of their experiences. This enabled the young people to be seen as they saw themselves rather than being labeled by others.

Painting, drawing, textiles, and mixed media artwork can have similar effects. Mandalas are a form of symbolic imagery expressed as visual art. Carr (2016) used mandalas to explore his own transformative process through his doctoral program at the "intersection of the subconscious and conscious" (p.1 52). He was particularly interested in pre-linguistic images or knowledge that comes to us in pictures rather than words. Mandala is the Sanskrit word for circle. According to Cornell (1994, p. 3), "The sacred circle mirrors an illuminated state of consciousness through a symbolic pattern- making the invisible visible."

While many artists start out with an intention of what they want to create and are even able to visualize the finished product, art can also be an intuitive process of surfacing unconscious knowledge. Creating mandalas is a deliberate way to do this. One can also approach drawing or painting or even collage making in an intuitive way without pre-planning the project, allowing images and ideas to bubble up from the unconscious. An analysis of the colors, shapes, and images in the artwork can often lead to new insights into the artist's worldview.

Fiction and Creative Writing

Transformative learning can be explored through reading or writing fiction, creative prose, and poetry. Novelists rely on their experiences and their knowledge of people to create fictional characters. In other words, fictional characters are based, at least in part, on real people or composites of real people. We can benefit from the experience and expertise of novelists by analyzing their descriptions of their characters. Lawrence and Cranton (2015) read and analyzed the experiences of fictional characters who had appeared to have experienced transformative learning. These fictional characters became research participants. As it did not seem congruent to express our research findings in a traditional way, Patricia and I created imagined dialogues with the fictional characters to explore the themes of the research in a virtual focus group called the "Butterfly Café."

Students in my classes have used the imagined dialogue process by taking on the persona of a fictional character to explore the nuances of transformative learning. Recent characters have included: Darth Vader from *Star Wars*, Hermione Granger from *Harry Potter*, and Elphaba from *Wicked*. Lawrence, Dashew, and Grossman (2018) expanded on the imagined dialogue process by writing dialogues with real people and creating their own fictional characters. They also explored the application of imagined dialogues between people on opposite sides of the political spectrum (Dashew, et al., 2020).

Creative writing is another form of expression that holds the opportunity to surface hidden knowledge. Free writing is a way to let go of self-judgment and the need to "get it right." One writes for 10–15 minutes about whatever comes to mind without lifting the pen (or hand from keyboard). This is another opportunity to get out of our heads by not thinking about what we want to say or editing along the way. Often, one is surprised about what comes up in the writing. Hunt (2009) intentionally used "Creative Writing as a Tool for Transformative Learning" with her students in Sussex England. She asked them to engage in self-reflection using fictional autobiography and poetry. As Hunt's students got in touch with their emotions through the embodied process of writing, their identities began to shift as they saw themselves as writers.

I often use journal writing as a way for students to reflect on what they are learning. Whether as an academic exercise or a self-directed process, journaling is a great way to make sense of that which seems to be incomprehensible. In my class during the spring of 2020, students were grappling with the global pandemic. It seemed as if the world had suddenly become a very different place and nothing made sense anymore. Poetry writing was an outlet to help them express their fear and uncertainty. One student wrote the following poem:

> What do we do?
> Nose is runny, mind is running.
> Thoughts wander, crossing the line.
> The world is fragile, so is the skin I'm in.
> My bones, this flesh.
> The fleshy emotions of grief and wonder
> Small hope untamed.

It's why I can still feel the cadence of my running rhythm.
What do we do?
Thinking of love, as my heart's yearn for love ages.
Internet offers connection, sure, but I wonder...
have I ever gone 1, 4, 7, 9,........... 16 days without a hug?
I don't mean to take it personal, but we're untouchable.
I'm untouchable, is what I said in the race, but how it means something different, I couldn't prepare.
I inhale, I exhale. I wiggle my toes, I taste the lingering notes of a very rich red wine,
There is still a quiet groan in waiting. She purrs, but I don't let her.
I cross the line in feelings.
I hear my friend's new song as she asks, "What do we do?"
Released @ midnight, I beam with pride.
Respect and adoration for art needing to still be art for us.
"Floodgates" are open.
"It's always bitter when I'm away from you"
Just as my head begins to lean --
to rest my face in my hand -
I notice I am afraid to touch my own self.
I am not supposed to touch my face.
I slide it into my hair instead and stretch a spiral curl to what appears to be its limit.
But I know shrinkage, I stretch it and watch it recoil.
I know shrinkage.
I know it superficially, but I know it in my spirit.
The memory of playing small in the world, the reality of playing small in my home.
I begin to remember the world is big enough for my incongruences - the large leaps of knowing more than one thing can be true.
I feel incredibly significant and yet still so small.
I cross the line. I sip. I let the song play again.
I feel the possibility of beginning -
to take up more space even as I stay home.
What can we do but take it hour by hour?

—Shanae Burch (Used with permission)

I have previously written about artistic expression as a way to promote transformation and healing (Lawrence, 2012). For Shanae, poetry was a means to surface unconscious affective knowledge and give to voice to her feelings of helplessness and loneliness. As Hunt's students discovered, creative writing was a way to get in touch with one's "spontaneous

654   R. L. LAWRENCE

bodily-felt and emotional experience" (Hunt, 2009 p. 177). Poetry writing provides an alternative pathway to transformative learning to the cognitive-rational approach suggested by Mezirow (1991).

Writing, like other art forms, takes on additional meaning when shared with an audience who has the opportunity to develop their own interpretation of the work. When Shanae shared her poem with the class, many of the students felt that she had expressed what they were feeling inside but had not yet put it into words. As they discussed the poem, the meaning was extended in deeper ways. While this greater level of conscious awareness may or may not lead to transformative learning, the opportunities are greater than had these feelings remained buried.

Music

Music is a powerful way of connecting people and provoking strong emotions. While not everyone is moved by the same music, almost everyone connects to some form of music, often the music that was popular when they were teenagers. A remarkable documentary *Alive Inside* (Rossato-Bennett, 2014) tells the story of Dan Cohen, a music therapist who created a non-profit organization that gave iPods to Alzheimer's patients, loaded with their favorite music. People who appeared to be out of touch with reality and had not communicated in years suddenly "woke up" and began singing along to their favorite tunes. While most of us enjoy listening to music, few are willing to sing in public. Similar to free writing and intuitive painting, vocal improvisation is one way to encourage people who believe they cannot sing, to make sounds.

Troester (2014) believes the skills involved in vocal improvisation with others mirrors the skills of transformative learning. Practicing vocal improvisation requires deep listening and willingness to break from habitual ways of doing something (in this case singing) in order to create something new with others. Using the skills taught by Rhiannon (www.rhi anonmusic.com) she connects the practice of vocal improvisation to transformative learning. "Vocal improvisation is an interactive musical practice that can teach us to break out of habitual, behavioral patterns and provide a space where we can transform" (p. 316).

Many of us avoid singing in public because we see ourselves as unable to sing or we have come to believe that singing is only for those with musical training. Mezirow (1991, p. 138) would see this as an example of a "psychological premise distortion." Vocal improvisation is an opportunity for those who do not see themselves as singers to challenge this assumption, and to test out new behaviors in a safe environment. Unlike singing songs, vocal improvisation focuses on making sounds. Many of those who practiced vocal improvisation experienced an identity shift as they saw themselves in new ways (Troester, 2014).

Wiessner (2009) also believes that one not need be a musician to benefit from the transformative potential of music. She uses the term "critical creativity" to explain how music can be a way to "foster creative insight in ways that can lead to new thinking and acting, new knowledge construction and social action" (p. 107). In addition to the individual transformation that is fostered, music has the potential for collective transformation when it is experienced in collaboration with others. Music had been the cornerstone of many educational and social movements. For example, the Highlander Folk School used music to mobilize people toward civil rights (Horton, 1998).

Embodied Arts: Theater and Dance

We often store trauma and anxiety in our bodies. This may be experienced as a heaviness we cannot explain, a nervous stomach or muscle aches. Sometimes these bodily sensations result from traumas too painful to talk about or we may not even be conscious of them. Embodied activities are ways to surface these unconscious emotions and give voice to the voiceless. Miller (2018) discusses *Theatre of Witness*: "the work brings people together across divides of difference to bear witness to each other's life experiences" through sharing stories and creating theater experiences. She believes that these practices can help to heal trauma. They can also be transformative as they help to create empathy and build bridges. Similarly, *Theatre of the Oppressed* (Boal, 2019) takes the stance that people have within them the capacity to solve their own problems. In *Forum Theatre* for example, participants rehearse alternative solutions to oppressive situations until they arrive at a satisfactory outcome. While some situations may still exist, it is empowering for people to feel in control of their emotions and responses.

Motter and Baldwin (2018) introduce another process called "dialogic embodiment" as a way to explore identity construction and reconstruction through somatic and embodied practices. One way to experience

656   R. L. LAWRENCE

dialogic embodiment is through autoethnographic dance, a way of reflection on one's own life through embodied process, thus bringing unconscious knowledge to the surface. These dance and theater activities, often surface hidden emotions (Dirkx, 2006), finally allowing for conversations that could not previously have taken place.

These embodied activities are examples of what Yorks and Kasl (2006, p. 43) refer to as "expressive ways of knowing." Expressive ways of knowing can lead to individual transformation and can also impact group learning by forging empathic connections with others. "The pathway between critical discourse and the field of empathic connection deepens a group's capacity to engage one another's worldviews at profound levels of mutual respect, trust, and authentic understanding" (p. 61).

CONCLUDING THOUGHTS

In an interview with the Saturday Evening Post, Albert Einstein said: "Imagination is more important than knowledge. For knowledge is limited, whereas imagination embraces the entire world, stimulating progress, giving birth to evolution" (Viereck, 1929). The term "imagination" comes from the Latin word *imaginari* meaning to picture oneself. We do this by forming images of what could be.

In this chapter I have attempted to illustrate the importance of imagination to help us to envision new realities that are critical for transformative learning. Imagination requires us to leave the comfort of our known worlds to venture into the unknown and uncertain. One way to do this is to tap into our unconscious knowledge through symbolic engagement with our dreams. We can also create symbols and metaphors that help us to build bridges between what we know and what is yet unknown. Artistic expressive processes like visual art, photography, music, creative writing, fictional analysis, dance, and drama can help us to surface images from our unconscious that illuminate what we have always known but have been unable to express in words. Working with these methods in educational settings can help students to reclaim the soul in teaching and learning (Cranton, 2008).

In today's world there is a sense of urgency to create positive change. The global pandemic has created fear and uncertainty, leaving people feeling helpless and pessimistic about the future. Now, more than ever we need to find ways to think outside of the box, to use the power of our imagination to envision and take action to create a world where we can live in harmony and peace.

REFERENCES

Boal, A. (2019). *Theatre of the oppressed* (3rd ed.). London: Pluto Press.

Campbell, T., Parr, M., & Richardson, C. (2009). From implicit to exquisite expression: Finding metaphors for who we are and what we do. *Journal of Transformative Education, 7*(3), 209–229.

Carr, P. T. (2016). *Exploring the intersection of the subconscious and conscious through the use of mandalas.* Proceedings of the 12th International transformative learning conference (pp. 152–160). Pacific Lutheran University, Tacoma, WA.

Cornell, J. (1994). *Mandala: Luminous symbols for healing.* Quest Books.

Cranton, P. (2008). The resilience of soul. In T. Leonard & P. Willis (Eds.), *Pedagogies of the imagination.* Springer.

Cranton, P. (2016). *Understanding and promoting transformative learning.* Stylus Publishing LLC.

Dashew, B., Grossman, K., & Lawrence, R. L. (2020). Listening to the voices of dissent: Bridging political polarization through imagined dialogues. *Reflective Practice: International and Multidisciplinary Practices, 21*(6).

Dirkx, J. M. (2006). Authenticity and imagination. In P. Cranton (Ed.), *Authenticity in teaching: New directions for adult and continuing education, no. 111* (pp. 27–39). Jossey-Bass.

Dirkx, J. (2012). Nurturing soul work: A Jungian approach to transformative learning. In E. W. Taylor & P. Cranton (Eds.), *The handbook of transformative learning* (pp. 116–131). Jossey-Bass.

Frankel, E. (2017). *The Wisdom of not knowing: Discovering a life of wonder by embracing uncertainty.* Hambhala.

Greene, M. (1995). *Releasing the imagination.* Jossey-Bass.

Holtby, A., Klein, K., Cook, K., & Travers, R. (2015). To be seen or not to be seen: Photovoice, queer and trans youth, and the dilemma of representation. *Action Research, 13*(4), 317–335.

Horton, M. (1998). *The long haul: An autobiography.* Teachers College Press.

Hunt, C. (2009). *Creative writing as a tool for transformative learning.* Proceedings of the 8th International Transformative Learning Conference (pp. 172–177). Hamilton, Bermuda.

Johnson, R. A. (1986). *Inner work: Using dreams & active imagination for personal growth.* HarperCollins.

Jung, C. G. (1964). Approaching the unconscious in C. G. Jung (Ed.), *Man and his symbols.* Dell.

658 R. L. LAWRENCE

Lawrence, R. L. (2005). *Hidden dimensions of transformative learning: Dream-work, imagery, metaphor and affect expressed through experiential painting.* Proceedings of the 6th International Transformative Learning Conference (pp. 309–313). Michigan State University, East Lansing Michigan.

Lawrence, R. L., & Cranton, P. (2015). *A novel idea: Researching transformative learning in fiction.* Sense Publishers.

Lawrence, R. L., Dashew, B., & Grossman, K. (2018). *Restoring the possibility for critical, reflective discourse: Using imagined dialogues to rebuild connections across political divides.* Proceedings of the 13th Annual International Transformative Learning Conference. New York, NY.

Lawrence, R. L. (2012). Transformative learning through artistic expression: Getting out of our heads. In E. W. Taylor & P. Cranton (Eds.), *The handbook of transformative learning* (pp. 471–485). Jossey-Bass.

Lawrence, R. L., & Cranton, P. (2009). What you see depends upon how you look: A photographic journey of transformative learning. *Journal of Transformative Education, 7*(4), 312–331.

Mezirow, J. (1991). *Transformative dimensions of adult learning.* Jossey-Bass.

Miller, J. B. (2018). The transformative and healing power of theatre of witness. *Canadian Journal for the Study of Adult Education, 30*(2), 47–56.

Motter, A. E., & Baldwin, C. K. (2018). *A model of dialogic embodiment: Transformative autoethnographic dance.* Proceedings of the 13th International Transformative Learning Conference (pp. 493–499). New York, Columbia Teacher's College.

Richards, M. C. (1996). *Opening our moral eye: Essays, talks & poems embracing creativity & community.* Lindisfarne Press.

Rossato-Bennett, M. (Director). (2014). *Alive Inside: A Story of Music and Memory* [Film]. Projector Media.

Spear, S. B. (2014). Conscious cooperation with the individuating adult learner. *Journal of Transformative Education, 12*(3), 226–247.

Troester, E. (2014). *"Listen to what music needs": Vocal improvisation as trans-formative learning.* Proceedings of the 11th International Transformative Learning Conference (pp. 312–317). New York, Columbia Teacher's College.

Viereck, G. S. (1929, October 26). *What life means to Einstein.* Saturday Evening Post. http://www.saturdayeveningpost.com/wp-content/uploads/satevepost/einstein.pdf

Wiessner, C. (2009). Noting the potential for transformation: Creative expression through music. In C. Hoggan, S. Simpson, & H. Stuckey (Eds.), *Creative expression in transformative learning* (pp. 103–128). Krieger Publishing Company.

Yorks, L., & Kasl, E. (2006). I know more than I can say: A taxonomy for utilizing expressive ways of knowing to foster transformative learning. *Journal of Transformative Education, 4*(1), 43–64.

CHAPTER 37

Perspective Transformation in Interfaith Dialogue: A Six-Step Process

Elizabeth M. Pope

Commonly, scholars examine transformation as an individual (1st person) or collective (3rd person) experience. It is less common for researchers to study transformation as a relational experience (through a 2nd person lens). Yet, a prime condition for transformation is good relationships with others (Gunnlaugson, 2007; Heron, 1996; Jarvis, 2009; Kegan, 1982; Kegan & Lahey, 2009; O'Keefe, 2010; Pope & Nicolaides, 2021). Transformation is a process that often occurs by encountering others with differing beliefs and worldviews. This encounter can be disorienting and hard to reconcile. The mental and emotional stress that encountering a different belief system can have on an individual necessitates good relationships with others if the outcome is to be a transformation of perspective involving a change in worldview regarding individuals

---

E. M. Pope (✉)
Department of Leadership, Research, and School Improvement, University of West Georgia, Carrollton, GA, USA
e-mail: epope@westga.edu

© The Author(s), under exclusive license to Springer Nature Switzerland AG 2022
A. Nicolaides et al. (eds.), *The Palgrave Handbook of Learning for Transformation*, https://doi.org/10.1007/978-3-030-84694-7_37

660 E. M. POPE

or cultures different from oneself (O'Keefe, 2010; Pope & Nicolaides, 2021).

Interfaith dialogue is one setting in which individuals encounter persons of different worldviews. Having good, safe, and generative relationships with individuals of different religious views is a foundational element for transformation within this setting. In what follows, I first present interfaith dialogue as a context through which transformation can occur. Second, I present six steps of transformation leading to *I-Thou* relationships (Buber, 1958) that can occur during interfaith dialogue with excerpts from interview data to illustrate the concepts. Third, I interrogate the nature of the *I-Thou* relationship as perspective transformation. Finally, I conclude with a discussion of how understanding transformation in this way furthers both practice and scholarship and offers possible avenues for the continued study of relationships and their role in generating transformation.

CONTEXT: INTERFAITH DIALOGUE

Interfaith dialogue offers scholars an understanding of how transformation can occur through interactions between persons of different worldviews. According to Swidler (2006), dialogue occurs when two or more participants with alternative viewpoints discuss the same subject to learn from one another. In this chapter, I use the definition of interfaith dialogue provided by Agrawal and Barratt (2014), "an *intentional* encounter between individuals who adhere to differing religious beliefs and practices in an effort to foster [understanding], respect, and cooperation among these groups through organized dialogue" (pp. 571–572; emphasis in original). This definition explains that dialogue requires participants to engage with one another in an attempt to relate to the other's religious traditions and understand what is meaningful or sacred within them (Takim, 2004).

Within this context, the *I-Thou* relationship (described below) is integral to transformation. To understand the process of transformation through interfaith dialogue, this chapter is based on data I generated during a qualitative case study (Simons, 2009) with an interfaith dialogue group located in the Southeastern U.S. (Pope, 2017). I refer to this group as the Trialogue to hold true to the term the members used. They derived the name from their membership of Jewish, Christian, and Muslim adults.

At the time of this writing, the Trialogue is an active organization and has been meeting approximately monthly since 2001.

I generated data through participant observation (Spradley, 1980), individual interviews (Roulston, 2010; Seidman, 2019), focus groups (Kleiber, 2004), and the collection of documents (McCulloch, 2004). I base the analysis within this chapter on interview data. Over the course of four months, I conducted a series of three interviews with nine participants of the Trialogue (Seidman, 2019). These interviews asked participants to provide information about their background, their experience within the Trialogue, and their reflections on the meaning of that experience. At the time of the interviews, participants had been members of the Trialogue between four and 15 years. I conducted interviews either face-to-face or over the phone through Skype, depending on the preference of the interviewee. I interviewed two Jewish members, four Christian members, and three Muslim members of the Trialogue.

I had the audio recordings of the interviews transcribed. I de-identified all transcriptions by using pseudonyms for proper nouns. I have used pseudonyms for all participants in this chapter. I used ATLAS.ti v7 (Windows) to conduct thematic analysis (Braun & Clarke, 2006). With ATLAS.ti I was able to conduct a more efficient and effective analysis including coding, memoing, and building semantic networks to determine relationships between major concepts to create themes.

The Trialogue has created a conversational space that welcomes and supports religious diversity. Within this dialogical space, they have built *I-Thou* relationships founded on mutual trust and respect. Participants' lengthy dedication cultivated these relationships. I merge Buber's (1958) work on *I-Thou* and *I-It* relationships with the concept of transformation to offer scholarship a unique and vital way to understand the process of transformation during dialogic meetings. I equate transformation with the creation *I-Thou* relationships.

According to Buber, *I-It* relationships are those between people with specific purposes and expectations. These relationships are most common. By contrast, it is the *I-Thou* relationship that, "establishes the world of relation" and people are embraced for who they are (p. 6). *I-Thou* relationships are relationships of mutual and holistic existence between two entities (Morgan & Guilherme, 2012). Buber (1958) explained that *I-Thou* relationships, as compared with *I-It* relationships, are those that "can be spoken only with the whole being" (p. 11). Mankind does not stay solely within one type of relationship, but moves between

662   E. M. POPE

them, continually establishing and ending each depending on time, place, and experience. True to Buber's (1958) work on dialogue, members in the Trialogue oscillated between *I-Thou* and *I-It* relationships. Both are necessary for transformation, which can be understood as moving through this continuum of relational space. Next, I present the process of transformation as the creation of *I-Thou* relationships.

TRANSFORMATION: A 6-STEP PROCESS

Buber's (1958) philosophy of dialogue focuses on interpersonal relationships between members of a dialogue. Indeed, true dialogue is dependent upon relationships. A dialogic relationship requires more than mere conversation. Rather, dialogue occurs when two individuals share meaning intersubjectively. It is "an ontological phenomenon—a meeting of one whole being with another whole being" (Gordon, 2011, p. 208). Participants in the case study repeatedly stressed the importance of the deep relationships between them. In harmony with Buber's (1958) description of dialogic relationships, the learning process within interfaith dialogue is dynamic and continually developing. Particularly meaningful moments between members spurred the process of transformation. Interview participants described feeling appreciated and accepted for who they were, wholly. In turn, they described embracing the other in the same way.

I identified six steps to the process of transformation (i.e., developing *I-Thou* relationships), within the context of interfaith dialogue. Figure 37.1 visually represents the steps in this process of transformation. While I show it here as a cycle with individual phases, it is not necessarily a linear process with such mutually exclusive phases. Some of the steps described below may occur out of the indicated order. Additionally, Fig. 37.1 presents transformation as an orderly cycle, yet progression through the phases should be thought of as more flexible, with movement back and forth along a continuum. Due to the challenging nature of both interfaith dialogue and transformation, participants may end up sliding back into previous steps rather than moving forward. Participants must practice critical reflection and develop self-awareness to progress. As this process is built upon interpersonal relationships, members move back and forth between the steps together, supporting each other and making this process one that is fluid, generative, and dynamic. The explanation

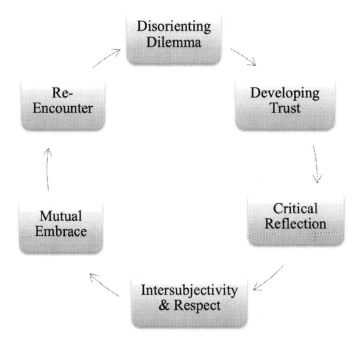

Fig. 37.1 The process of transformation within interfaith dialogue

and model below are an attempt to present a clear, collective, and organized picture of an experience that is at times unorganized, individualistic, and hard to grasp.

Finally, a vital characteristic of this process is that transformation involves prolonged interaction with the religious other. Isaiah, a Jewish participant, explained that it takes time to "put a face on the issue" and people in the Trialogue learn through prolonged engagement. In what follows, I detail each step of this process ending with a discussion of its major outcomes.

Step 1: The Disorienting Dilemma

Transformation in interfaith dialogue begins with a moment of disorientation (Mezirow, 2012). A jarring experience with someone of another religion causes disorientation in this context. These moments are monumental in some way, watershed moments that change the course of participants' interactions with each other. Interview participants noted learning about similarities as disorienting. Similarities included those of practice, theology, faith and belief, or personal behaviors and preferences. Isaiah said learning that Muslims, similar to Jews, pray directly to God rather than through an earthly intermediary such Christian clergy, as "really surprising. I didn't expect it … when I heard that I was just stunned." This revelation shook his assumption that Judaism and Christianity had more in common than Judaism and Islam.

Other disorienting moments come from learning about similarities and differences in scripture and scriptural interpretation. Luke, a Christian participant, explained how following a model of scriptural reasoning (*Scriptural Reasoning*, n.d.) brought both similarities and differences to light in shocking ways. It can shake the foundation of someone's assumptions about another faith to see something they hold as sacred reflected back at them.

Similarities between members not based on faith can also be disorienting. For Khadija, a Muslim participant, learning about fears shared by both the Jewish and Muslim communities during the 2016 Presidential Election was "eye-opening" and "really struck" her, rocking her assumptions of the experience of the Jewish community as a minority in the U.S. These disorienting moments begin the process of transforming what interfaith dialogue participants assume they knew about another religion and its adherents. Whatever disorientation these moments caused, participants in these data sought to make meaning from them, leading them down the pathway to the next steps in the cycle.

Step 2: Developing Trust

By working through disorienting moments, participants in the Trialogue began to trust one another more. Trust is a foundational element of Buber's *I-Thou* relationship. Difficult moments challenge budding trust. Participants may even feel required to reflect on the wisdom of their choice to trust the other. Upon a satisfactory outcome of the disorienting dilemma, interviewees reported stronger trust with individuals of other faiths and at times extended this trust to the other faith community. Daniel explained that a suicide bombing by a Muslim terrorist in Israel "put [him] in a tailspin" and he began to "wonder if it was all just bull-shit." He was, "really, really, really, deeply, deeply conflicted and angry, and suspected the worst." He did not know how to trust. After deep discussion with Muslim participants, he explained, "my real growth with them and my building up of trust with them emerged." His experience illustrates the tenuous nature of relationship building in interfaith groups. Not only do experiences within group engagement impact developing trust, but current events and the political climate do as well.

Moments where interfaith dialogue members begin to trust or when they begin to feel trusted are integral to the transformation process. To build trust, interfaith dialogue groups need clear goals and expectations of conduct. A lack of clear goals causes discord and distrust between partic-ipants (Ibrahim, 1998). When members agree upon and adhere to these goals, they can trust that others are participating with similar mindsets. This confidence allows them to risk and be honest in discussion. Inter-view participants from the Trialogue explained that trust and honesty were indications of genuine discussion.

Trust and honesty do not necessitate agreement of belief. Interfaith dialogue is not meant to be a time of such agreement. It should include respectful disagreement and the confidence to question others (O'Keefe, 2009). This is true of Buber's dialogue as well. True dialogue occurs when individuals listen, not to agree with one another, but to understand other viewpoints and to be authentic in bringing them to the conversation (Froeyman, 2014; Gordon, 2011; Jons, 2014). Being authentic requires trust in others so one is comfortable discussing both what one is assured of and what one struggles with in their own tradition, the latter being a vulnerable position. In the interviews with Trialogue participants, many described meetings as a place to admit that no one has all the answers all the time and to be willing to discuss sometimes difficult questions with one another.

While the impact of trust in honest engagement does not directly correspond to the traditional steps of transformation, it is integral to this transformation process and in building *I-Thou* relationships. Trust underscores an individual's ability to "encounter" another (Buber, 1958). For Buber, the encounter is a moment when an individual experiences another during dialogue and their own beliefs are "completely suspended, hidden, or forgotten" to avoid offense or promote understanding (Prop-erzi, 2011, p. 253). This is a key aspect to the *I-Thou* relationship. Interviewees noted moments of suspending their own beliefs and listening

666   E. M. POPE

to others speak in an attempt to support the inclusion of beliefs not of their own in the dialogue. Thus, the encounter in interfaith dialogue also means listening and contributing to the discussion in a way that is generative rather than closed and exclusive.

Step 3: Critical Reflection

Step 3 in this cycle corresponds to the self-examination and critical reflection phases in the process of transformation. Self-examination and critical reflection are integral to learning through dialogue, communicative learning, and changing frames of reference. In communicative learning "it becomes essential for learners to become critically reflective of the assumptions underlying intentions, values, beliefs, and feelings" (Mezirow, 1997, p. 6). Disorienting dilemmas and feelings of support generated by trusting other members of dialogue allow interfaith dialogue participants to practice critical reflection.

Phoebe, a Christian participant, illustrated how interfaith dialogue participants need to practice critical reflection of their beliefs and assumptions about their own religion and that of others. When a Muslim participant said the Trinity "sounds like Hinduism" and seemed polytheistic, Phoebe was shocked and not sure how to answer. She described this as a particularly challenging moment. She said she needed to "go home and think this thing through," as she was unsure of how to explain the concept she had always just accepted. As a foundational tenet of her monotheistic faith, it was upsetting to her to need to explain how it was not polytheistic. But through critical reflection of her own beliefs and reactions to this statement, Phoebe was able to do so at a subsequent meeting.

Moments of deep reflection, inquiry, and introspection can lead interfaith dialogue participants to a better understanding their own beliefs. During transformation, Mezirow (1997) explained that critical reflection and self-examination come when members focus on the assumptions and biases they bring with them. As Isaiah explained, "I recognize that I have my biases, that I've not always been fair in my thinking. I've also learned I've been naïve and I've learned I need to learn a lot more." Matthew, a Christian participant, stressed the dangers of not challenging preconceptions and assumptions. He explained it is necessary to branch out and associate with people who hold different worldviews because otherwise "you can't understand where they're coming from" and then "you're ignorant. And when you're ignorant, you make assumptions."

Matthew's statement exemplifies the need for individuals to be able to transform their biases, assumptions, and preconceptions of the religious other, particularly in turbulent times. By attempting to understand, develop trust, and reflect on current frames of reference, conflict resolution between peoples of different worldviews can happen in individual communities and across nations. Additionally, appreciating religious diversity is a key outcome of this step. Interfaith dialogue members may learn that differences between faiths should be respected and learned from. When participants make new meaning after critical reflection, they can be reoriented with the budding of a broader, more inclusive mindset of alternative religions. The willingness to be confronted with and accept different, difficult, and disorienting information is integral to the process of building *I-Thou* relationships.

Step 4: The Intersubjective Move Toward Thou-ness

After dialogue members reflect on their own values, beliefs, and assumptions, they can become more self-aware and confident in their own positions and subjectivities. It is here they begin the "turn toward the Other," described by Avakian (2015) as "understanding and transformation of one's own faith-tradition" and "an unrestrained acknowledgement of the Other" (pp. 80–81). This phase is when intersubjectivity between dialogue participants can blossom, which strengthens relationships through mutual respect and shared understandings.

In this turn toward their religious other, mutual respect develops when participants see the other holistically, fully becoming *Thou* rather than *It*. Yusuf, a Muslim participant, described members of the Trialogue as "willing to understand, tolerate, and respect one another." Phoebe said building this respect has been difficult, but respect and intersubjectivity have taught her that "we're really just kindred spirits." Isaiah explained the need for respect of other belief systems by saying, "If I don't respect them, how can I talk about them with an open mind?"

This step can have dramatic effects. Through the previous phase of critical reflection and self-examination, members confronted their own assumptions and misconceptions. With intersubjectivity and respect comes the ability to challenge misconceptions of one's own and other religions (Swidler, 2006). In the Trialogue, interview participants described

668   E. M. POPE

numerous experiences when the group confronted stereotypes and ill-informed assumptions of the religions, both during dialogue and outside it. Luke said:

I've become a little bolder in countering stereotypes... I'm inspired to be more courageous in saying no when someone's talking about why all Muslims are filled with hate. I can't be quiet when I hear such things said.

By confronting stereotypes and misconceptions, interfaith dialogue groups allow participants to explore new roles and plan how to implement these roles in the group and community around them, two traditional phases of transformation (Mezirow, 2012). Feeling secure with one another through *I-Thou* relationships makes this possible and participants develop new courses of action together (Mezirow, 2012). Daniel described meetings as challenging for new attendees because of how meetings confront individuals' assumptions and preconceptions. He said that an individual's initial view of other traditions, understood through their own lens:

Is now going to be shaken. Because now... you're hearing it from somebody that lives it every day. And you may find [your religion] has had an impact on people in ways that you would not have predicted.

This "shaking" of someone's foundational viewpoints is a keen description of the disorientation interfaith learning experiences can create, Step 1 of this transformation process. Once that constructed view of the religious other is disrupted, the opportunity for a different conception becomes available. Interfaith dialogue members work together to create shared understandings of the other leading to more porous worldviews. At times, these new viewpoints incorporate a narrative counter to the "mainstream" rhetoric, one that is often more accurate regarding other faiths. The counter-narrative incorporates informed understandings of religious difference, is co-created through intersubjectivity, and strengthens *I-Thou* relationships, which leads to a willingness to embrace the religious other.

Step 5: Mutual Embrace

Intersubjectivity and respect support interpersonal bonds and Buber's "embrace." Harun, a Muslim participant, explained that he feels comfortable expressing his beliefs in the Trialogue as others are open minded and no one says, "my way or the highway." Interfaith dialogue participants begin to not just tolerate each other, but to fully accept each other during which they are embraced and understood. Gordon (2011) explained Buber's embrace as "the act of identifying with someone else's position and lived situation while simultaneously maintaining a clear sense of self" (p. 212). Here, one accepts others' beliefs as valid while holding on to their own at the same time, an important characteristic of transformation in interfaith dialogue (Abu-Nimer, 2002; Boys & Lee, 1996; Pope, 2020). As Claudia, a Christian participant, said, "No one from the mosque says you have to be Muslim to me. No one tells me I have to be Jewish." They can be wholly themselves in the *I-Thou* relationship, being the whole "I" and receiving the other as "Thou" in their wholeness. In these data, this embrace extended from individuals to entire faith communities.

Through learning from the religious other, members of interfaith dialogue gain the knowledge and experience needed to proceed in this new relationship. Step 4 and Step 5 of this transformation process correspond to more traditional stages of exploring new roles, trying out new courses of action, acquiring knowledge needed to implement one's plans, and building competence and confidence in one's new relationships (Nohl, 2015). In Step 5, the nuances of each faith tradition are embraced and individuals are not seen as the epitome of the entire faith community. No one person can exemplify the diversity of an entire religion. The expectation that they do is a heavy and unfair dialogic responsibility that Daniel described as a "burden." By embracing the individual, interfaith dialogue members can accept others as, Khadija explained, "unique" individuals within their community of faith. As such, they are now seen to be small examples of their faith communities, not representations of the entire community. Thus, this step shows a triumph over this challenging aspect of interfaith dialogue.

The mutual embrace allows interfaith dialogue participants to feel comfortable learning about and leaving stronger in their own faith, a goal of interfaith dialogue (Fernandez & Coyle, 2019). In the Trialogue, each interviewee indicated stronger faith to be a vital outcome of their participation. Matthew's words help demonstrate this point:

I'll say they've helped me with my own faith... it has reinforced my faith... It helps you to be a good witness to your faith and it helps you grow in your faith.

With stronger faith, embracing religious diversity, and fully formed *I-Thou* relationships, members enter the final step in the process of transformation.

670 E. M. POPE

Step 6: Re-encountering with New Frames of Reference

The final step of transformation during interfaith dialogue is re-encountering the religious other with a new perspective. Claudia explained that participation in the Trialogue has allowed her to "trust people that in the past I would have been very suspicious of." Daniel noted he feels a change in his "relationships with the Muslim community" and "that change is really profound." Luke reported a change in his "appreciation and understanding of my neighbor in these two other faith's traditions... it's expanded my understanding and openness to learning new things about God." The transformation process in interfaith dialogue encourages members to create new frames of reference and meaning schemes, which deeply influence perceptions and interactions with the religious other.

This transformation leads to new action, specifically the confidence to express and live their new mindset outside of dialogue sessions. Trialogue members indicated that they are more likely to advocate, support, or speak up for members of other faiths to their peers and family. Phoebe described disseminating what she's learned to others, "I feel like I can be a bridge for our religious traditions coming together, of listening, of respect." This new action is an example of the transformed mindsets and perspectives of the religious other that can occur through interfaith dialogue.

THE *I-THOU* RELATIONSHIP AS PERSPECTIVE TRANSFORMATION

The process of transformation described above illustrates how perspective transformation in interfaith dialogue is both a rational and an extra-rational process, i.e., an experience of both mind and soul (Charaniya, 2012; Dirkx, 1997; Dirkx & Mezirow, 2006). According to Mezirow (1978), meaning perspectives are "the structure[s] of cultural assumptions within which new experience is assimilated to—and transformed by—one's past experience. It is a personal paradigm for understanding ourselves and our new relationships" (p. 101). The relationships people have with others influence meaning perspectives and they define opinions and understandings of others. A change in perspective is often a goal of interfaith dialogue (Abu-Nimer, 2002; Boys & Lee, 1996;

Swidler, 2006). Dialogue has the potential to not only add to an individual's knowledge and understanding of the world but also transform perspectives and lead to social action (Abu-Nimer, 2002; Smock, 2002).

To achieve perspective transformation, interfaith dialogue should be organized so that ambiguity and disorientation are allowed to encourage participants to express doubts and beliefs, reflecting on both themselves and their own traditions (Abu-Nimer, 2002; Boys & Lee, 1996; Properzi, 2011). When an individual moves toward more mature perspectives, their former perspectives are transformed into new ones more appropriate for their new relationships. The mental and emotional complexity involved in interfaith dialogue necessitates that relationships between participants be *I-Thou*, rather than an *I-It*, relationships for real perspective transformation.

Thus, perspective transformation in interfaith dialogue can be best understood by its equation with the *I-Thou* relationship. Building an *I-Thou* relationship allows the process of transformation to begin and a fully formed *I-Thou* relationship supports a changed perspective. Combined, these two theoretical positions provide a way to conceptualize perspective transformation of the other by situating it within a framework of: (1) an individual and relational experience, and (2) a rational and extra-rational experience. Understanding the *I-Thou* relationship provides a view of perspective transformation in which it is more than an individual, rational experience; it is an intersubjective, emotional one where the nature of relationships with the other help define the meaning perspectives that make up a person's worldview.

CONCLUSION

Framing transformation as an *I-Thou* relationship in a dialogical context on difficult topics can significantly impact both practice and scholarship concerning transformation. Learning and transformation are invaluable tools in the practice of conflict resolution, sorely needed in the current U.S. and international climate. For religious conflict particularly, correctly facilitated interfaith dialogue can be a powerful solution. Much of the insight gained from these data is integral for interideological dialogue of any kind, such as religious, political, or cultural. The U.S. is increasingly becoming ideologically polarized.

672   E. M. POPE

An understanding of how individuals can develop more tolerant and inclusive worldviews could better allow for the facilitation of peacemaking and conflict resolution. Considering the nature of transformation, dialogue sessions should occur in a series, giving participants time to get to know one another, develop deep relationships, and become comfortable with each other while learning to dialogue (O'Keefe, 2009). Dialogue sessions should occur over a period of time, with enough time in between sessions for participants to reflect on and make meaning of their experiences. Finally, facilitators should take time throughout the dialogic series to encourage relationships and trust building.

This research offers new insight for the scholarship on transformation in which stagnancy is a threat (Taylor & Cranton, 2013). This chapter highlights the vitality of interpersonal relationships in transformation, particularly in challenging contexts. Here, we see how interpersonal relationships and intersubjectivity in both meaning making and dialogical expectations enhance and serve as a foundation for transformation (Pope & Nicolaides, 2021). In examining transformation and *I-Thou* relationships within the context of interfaith dialogue, this research also keeps in mind the important role context and society play (Tennant, 1993). A key contribution of this chapter to scholarship on transformation is the use of Buber's *I-Thou* relationships to more deeply understand the process. Looking at the phenomenon of interfaith dialogue in this way enhances understandings of transformation and shines a light on the importance of having relationships characterized as *I-Thou* in the context of transformation.

Finally, this research offers new steps in the process of transformation during exchanges across ideological boundaries. Such additions offer nuance to the theory of transformation and open new doors for future research for both expansion and new detail. Further research on the intersections, enhancement, and contradictions between the theory of transformation and Buber's (1958) philosophy of dialogue is needed. Specifically, future research should more deeply examine the role of trust in transformation as a relational process and how the transformation described above plays out in practice.

REFERENCES

Abu-Nimer, M. (2002). The miracles of transformation through interfaith dialogue: Are you a believer? In D. S. Smock (Ed.), *Interfaith dialogue and peacebuilding* (pp. 15–32). United States Institute of Peace Press.

Agrawal, S., & Barratt, C. (2014). Does proximity matter in promoting interfaith dialogue? *International Migration and Integration, 15*(3), 567–587. https://doi.org/10.1007/s12134-013-0295-3

Avakian, S. (2015). The turn to the other: Reflections on contemporary Middle Eastern theological contributions to Christian-Muslim dialogue. *Theology Today, 72*(1), 77–83. https://doi.org/10.1177/0040573614563528

Boys, M. C., & Lee, S. S. (1996). The Catholic-Jewish Colloquium: An experiment in interreligious learning. *Religious Education, 91*(4), 420–466. http://www.religiouseducation.net/

Braun, V., & Clarke, V. (2006). Using thematic analysis in psychology. *Qualitative Research in Psychology, 3*(2), 77–101. https://doi.org/10.1191/1478088706qp063oa

Buber, M. (1958). *I and Thou* (R. G. Smith, Trans.) Scribner. (Original work published in 1923).

Cambridge Inter-Faith Programme. (n.d.). *Scriptural reasoning.* University of Cambridge. https://www.interfaith.cam.ac.uk/sr

Charaniya, N. K. (2012). Cultural-spiritual perspective of transformative learning. In E. Taylor & P. Cranton (Eds.), *The handbook of transformative learning: Theory, research, and practice* (pp. 231–244). Jossey-Bass.

Dirkx, J. M. (1997). Nurturing soul in adult learning. *New Directions for Adult and Continuing Education, 1997*(74), 79–88. https://doi.org/10.1002/ace.7409

Dirkx, J. M., & Mezirow, J. (2006). Musings and reflections on the meaning, context, and process of transformative learning: A dialogue between John M. Dirkx and Jack Mezirow. *Journal of Transformative Education, 4*(2), 132–139. https://doi.org/10.1177/1541344606287503

Fernandez, E. F., & Coyle, A. (2019). Sensitive issues, complex categories, and sharing festivals: Malay Muslim students' perspectives on interfaith engagement in Malaysia. *Political Psychology, 40*(1), 37–53. https://doi.org/10.1111/pops.12501

Froeyman, A. (2014). Hermeneutics, life and dialogue: A sketch of a Buberian dialogue with the past. *Journal of the Philosophy of History, 8*(3), 407–425. https://doi.org/10.1163/18722636-12341282

Gordon, M. (2011). Listening as embracing the other: Martin Buber's philosophy of dialogue. *Educational Theory, 61*(2), 207–220. https://doi.org/10.1111/j.1741-5446.2011.00400

Gunnlaugson, O. (2007). Shedding light on the underlying forms of transformative learning theory: Introducing three distinct categories of consciousness.

674 E. M. POPE

Journal of Transformative Education, 5(2), 134–151. https://doi.org/10. 1177/1541344607303526

Heron, J. (1996). *Cooperative inquiry: Research into the human condition.* Sage.

Ibrahim, I. (1998). Islamic-Christian dialogue: A Muslim view. In M. D. Bryant & S. A. Ali (Eds.), *Muslim-Christian dialogue: Promise and problems* (pp. 15–27). Paragon House.

Jarvis, P. (2009). Learning to be a person in society: Learning to be me. In K. Illeris (Ed.), *Contemporary theories of learning* (pp. 21–34). Routledge.

Jons, L. (2014). Learning as calling and responding. *Studies in Philosophy and Education, 33*(5), 481–493. https://doi.org/10.1007/s11217-013-9398-8

Kegan, R. (1982). *The evolving self: Problems and process in human development.* Harvard University Press.

Kegan, R., & Lahey, L. L. (2009). *Immunity to change: How to overcome it and unlock the potential in yourself and your organization.* Harvard Business School Press.

Kleiber, P. B. (2004). Focus groups: More than a method of qualitative inquiry. In K. deMarrais & S. Lapan (Eds.), *Foundations for research: Methods of inquiry in education and the social sciences* (pp. 87–102). Routledge.

McCulloch, G. (2004). *Documentary research: In education, history, and the social sciences.* Routledge.

Mezirow, J. (1978). Perspective transformation. *Adult Education, 28*(2), 100–110. https://doi.org/10.1177/074171367802800202

Mezirow, J. (1997). Transformative learning: Theory to practice. *New Directions for Adult and Continuing Education, 1997*(74), 5–12. https://doi.org/10. 1002/ace.7401

Mezirow, J. (2012). Learning to think like an adult: Core concepts of transformation theory. In E. Taylor & P. Cranton (Eds.), *The handbook of transformative learning: Theory, research, and practice* (pp. 73–95). Jossey-Bass.

Morgan, W. J., & Guilherme, A. (2012). I and Thou: The educational lessons of Martin Buber's dialogue with the conflicts of his times. *Educational Philosophy and Theory, 44*(9), 979–996. https://doi.org/10.1111/j.1469-5812.2010. 00681.x

Nohl, A. (2015). Typical phases of transformative learning: A practice-based model. *Adult Education Quarterly, 65*(1), 35–49. https://doi.org/10.1177/ 0741713614558582

O'Keefe, T. (2009). Learning to talk: Conversation across religious differences. *Religious Education, 104*(2), 197–213. https://doi.org/10.1080/003440 80902794665

O'Keefe, T. (2010). Relationships across the divide: An instigator of transformation. *Studies in Christian-Jewish Relations, 5*(1), 1–22. http://escholarship. bc.edu/scjr/vol5

Pope, E. M. (2017). *This is a head, hearts, and hands enterprise: Interfaith dialogue and perspective transformation* [Doctoral dissertation, The University of Georgia]. The University of Georgia Libraries. http://getd.libs.uga.edu/pdfs/pope_elizabeth_m_201708_phd.pdf

Pope, E. M. (2020). "This is a head, hearts, and hands enterprise": Adult learning in interfaith dialogue. *Adult Education Quarterly, 70*(3), 205–222. https://doi.org/10.1177/0741713619888632

Pope, E. M., & Nicolaides, A. (2021). Becoming Thou as transformation in interfaith dialogue. *International Journal of Lifelong Education.* Advance online publication. https://doi.org/10.1080/02601370.2021.1882596

Properzi, M. (2011). Looking for balance between identity and encounter: Buber's relations and interreligious dialogue. *Journal of Ecumenical Studies, 46*(2), 251–258. https://dialogueinstitute.org/jes-volume-46-2011

Roulston, K. J. (2010). *Reflective interviewing: A guide to theory and practice.* Sage.

Seidman, I. (2019). *Interviewing as qualitative research: A guide for researchers in education and the social sciences* (5th ed.). Teachers College Press.

Simons, H. (2009). *Case study research in practice.* Sage.

Smock, D. R. (2002). Introduction. In D. R. Smock (Ed.), *Interfaith dialogue and peacebuilding* (pp. 3–11). United States Institute of Peace Press.

Spradley, J. P. (1980). *Participant observation.* Thompson Learning, Inc.

Swidler, L. J. (2006). The dialogue decalogue: Ground rules for interreligious, interideological dialogue. *International Journal of Buddhist Thought & Culture, 7*, 158–159. ftp://www.buruna.org/Publications/IABTC/Vol07_08_Swidler.pdf (Original Work Published in 1983).

Takim, L. (2004). From conversion to conversation: Interfaith dialogue in post 9-11 America. *The Muslim World, 94*(3), 343–355. https://doi.org/10.1111/j.1478-1913.2004.00058.x

Taylor, E. W., & Cranton, P. (2013). A theory in progress? Issues in transformative learning theory. *European Journal for Research on the Education and Learning of Adults, 4*(1), 33–47. https://doi.org/10.3384/rela.2000-7426.rela5000

Tennant, M. C. (1993). Perspective transformation and adult development. *Adult Education Quarterly, 44*(1), 34–42. https://doi.org/10.1177/0741713693044001003

CHAPTER 38

The Interpenetration of Individual and Collective Transformation: A Framework for Development, Collective Intelligence, and Emergence

Abigail Lynam, Geoff Fitch, Tamara Androsoff, and John Wood

INTRODUCTION

We are one, after all, you and I. Together we suffer, together exist, and forever will recreate each other.
—Pierre Teilhard de Chardin

A. Lynam (✉)
School for Leadership Studies, Fielding Graduate University, Santa Barbara, CA, USA
e-mail: abigail@pacificintegral.com; alynam@fielding.edu

A. Lynam · G. Fitch · T. Androsoff · J. Wood
Pacific Integral, Seattle, WA, USA
e-mail: geoff@pacificintegral.com

© The Author(s), under exclusive license to Springer Nature Switzerland AG 2022
A. Nicolaides et al. (eds.), *The Palgrave Handbook of Learning for Transformation*, https://doi.org/10.1007/978-3-030-84694-7_38

677

This chapter focuses on the relationship between individual and collective development and how to support this development in transformative learning communities. We describe a framework that arose out of 16 years of practice and research in the Generating Transformative Change (GTC) program. The framework guides the curriculum and maps the principles and practices we engage with to support participants' and cohorts' development. It supports the development of capacities for what we call "subtle community," which is founded in contextual and systemic understanding, personal self-awareness, interpersonal differentiation and skills, and, eventually, access to transpersonal states and stages of consciousness.

GTC is a 9-month, developmentally informed leadership program offered by Pacific Integral. It consists of four residential retreats, as well as inter-session learning, coaching, and application. It has been delivered on three continents (North America, Oceania, and Africa), with 30 cohorts and over 350 graduates. GTC is a multi-disciplinary, action-learning program which focuses on transformative approaches to leadership and human development. Rooted in integral psychology and whole person learning, GTC helps participants grow the inner capacities necessary for effective leadership in complex and demanding contexts.

To support transformation within GTC, we start with the principle that individuals grow and develop in the context of relationships and groups, and vice versa. By integrating intrapersonal, interpersonal, and collective development, all can be reciprocally deepened. Another primary orienting principle that informs and guides transformation in the program is adult stage development (Cook-Greuter, 2013; O'Fallon, 2016). In GTC, we attend, as constructive developmental theorist Robert Kegan puts it, to the form that transforms (Kegan, 2000).

As we delivered and evolved GTC, we engaged in inquiry around the questions: How do people develop or transform? What is the relationship between the individual and the collective's development? How are the two interdependent? These inquiries developed into an ongoing longitudinal research project in adult development. They resulted in our theory

---

T. Androsoff
e-mail: tamara@integralsolutions.co.nz

J. Wood
e-mail: john@leadershipsolutions.com.au

and practice of Causal Leadership (Ramirez et al., 2013) as well as the STAGES model, a new integral theory of development, articulated by Terri O'Fallon (2016). The STAGES model was developed based on the discoveries we made about how people conceive of and relate to "I" and "We" as they evolve, how they engage in collectives, how they connect and make sense together from diverse perspectives, and what supports healthy growth in both.

Through our observations of the interpenetration of I and We (individuals and collectives), we began to see the implications for transformative change. *Interpenetration* refers to a move beyond both/and toward a recognition of "one within the other" (O'Fallon & Barta, 2018). For example, because no one is truly independent of the collectives in which they are a part, they cannot truly change without a change in their relationships; likewise, no social system can transform without a transformation of the individuals involved (Fitch & Lynam, 2019). This perspective eventually includes an understanding of unity beyond distinctions.

GTC and Transformative Development

Our approach to transformative change is based in and informed by integral theory and adult development theory. Transformative learning is distinguished from other forms of learning by describing a more profound and long-lasting shift in worldview, perspective, or consciousness. O'Sullivan et al. describes transformation as "a deep, structural shift in the basic premises of thought, feelings, and actions. It is a shift of consciousness that dramatically and permanently alters our way of being in the world" (O'Sullivan et al., 2002, p. 11). In GTC we work with adult development theory as a map to guide these deep structural shifts in individuals and collectives and as a method to assess the development.

However, we view transformation as something that does not only happen along a single dimension such as a particular ego development stage shift. We view transformational shifts in consciousness as complex, multidimensional, and multi-leveled, with a movement toward greater wholeness, health, and justice. Given our developmental orientation, we mark these shifts in multiple ways, including movements within a developmental stage along a particular line of growth and as a reorganization of a system at a higher order of complexity.

Given the multiple perspectives we hold on development, transformative change occurs in different ways for different people and groups. For example, for one individual it might involve a significant shift in ego development, and for another the healing of a long-standing trauma with a corresponding shift in self-conception. However, similar to O'Sullivan and many others in the field of transformative learning, change is conceptualized and experienced as involving a significant and lasting shift in form or perspective.

The epistemological and ontological orientation of our approach is most closely aligned with integral methodological pluralism (Esbjörn-Hargens, 2010; Wilber, 2006). We account for transformative change as phenomena in which multiple perspectives and methods are continuously revealing (and enacting) aspects of what are complex and potentially multiple objects. Also, following Barad (2007), we include an understanding that this enactment is innately ethically founded, as how we see and engage reality is deeply intertwined with the justness of our outcomes.

The principles that guide the design of GTC are that it be integral (encompassing as much of reality as possible), developmental (not merely asserting a single worldview, but situated in an ongoing, evolutionary trajectory of perspective-taking capacity), and motivated by universal compassion (serving to reduce suffering and increase fulfillment and justice in the largest span and depth imaginable). Key theoretical underpinnings and areas of learning include: adult development theory and practice (Cook-Greuter, 2013; O'Fallon, 2016); Theory U and Presencing (Scharmer, 2018); integral theory (Wilber, 2006); integral polarity practice (Kesler, 2014); awareness and somatic practices (Brown, 2006; Pierrakos, 2005; Porges, 2011); developmental action inquiry (Torbert et al., 2004); complex systems and paradoxes of group life (Smith & Berg, 1997); collective evolution (Gunnlaugson & Brabant, 2016); communication, truthfulness, and intimacy practices (Golabuk, 2012; Richo, 2014); and individual and collective trauma-informed shadow work (Hubl & Avritt, 2020; Masters, 2018; Menakem, 2017).

STAGES of Adult Development

Our approach to transformative change and specifically the notions of subtle community and the interpenetration of I and We are based on key aspects of the STAGES model of adult development. Building on the ego development lineage of Loevinger and Cook-Greuter, the STAGES model identifies underlying repeating patterns in development and adds two additional later-level stages (Cook-Greuter, 2013; O'Fallon, 2016). It reveals a natural sequence of deep "vertical" structures, as well as iterating, wave-like patterns in the development or transformation of individuals (Fig. 38.1).

There are three tiers of development in the STAGES model: the Concrete, Subtle, and MetAware tiers. Each tier includes two shifts in a core perspective-taking view (called "person perspective"), such as the 1st- and 2nd- person perspectives in the Concrete tier. Each of these person perspectives has two stages (for instance, 1.0 Impulsive and 1.5 Egocentric for 1st-person perspective), for a total of 4 stages per tier. The

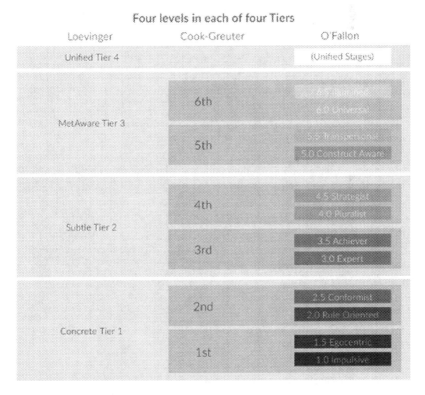

Fig. 38.1 STAGES model (O'Fallon & Barta, 2018)

first stage of each person perspective is more receptive to the new dimensions and awareness of the self and the second is more active with the capacities. In each tier, the first of the person perspectives is individually oriented and the second is collectively oriented (i.e., 1st-person perspective is individually oriented and 2nd-person perspective is collectively oriented).

In the Concrete tier, we engage and understand with the physical world perceived through our senses and more basic emotions. The first-person perspective, which includes the 1.0 and 1.5 stages, is "all about me"; there is no understanding yet of a "We." The second-person perspective (2.0 Rule-Oriented and 2.5 Conformist stages) includes the recognition of others and is the beginning of the social self. These stages are all about group norms, fitting in, rules, and negotiating for fairness.

In the Subtle tier, we understand and engage with the world of ideas, thoughts, subtle feelings, abstractions, contexts, systems, and self-awareness. The 3.0 Expert and 3.5 Achiever are individually oriented stages and give rise to the subtle "I," where a person realizes they have a self beyond the body: the thoughts and emotions independent of rational consciousness. The collective for these stages is still the concrete collective: relationship, family, organization, country, etc. The pattern continues as the 4.0 Pluralist and 4.5 Strategist are collectively oriented stages and bring in the subtle awareness of contexts—how individuals and groups are shaped by culture, identity, values, and systems, etc.

People in the MetAware tier are oriented to awareness of awareness itself, the witness self, and transpersonal wholeness. Individuals first awaken (in the 5.0 Construct Aware and 5.5 Transpersonal stages) to their ever-present awareness beyond the ordinary subtle self, as the ground of their being. The "I," however, is the MetAware self, the limitless open horizon of awareness that we paradoxically seem to share with everyone and everything. The collective remains the subtle community that develops from the post-conventional 4th-person perspective. After the 5th-person perspective, later MetAware collective stages develop. MetAware collectives complexify to embrace all that is—the Concrete, Subtle, and the Kosmos.

I/We Model

Principles and Features

Our life is an apprenticeship to the truth that around every circle another can be drawn; that there is no end in nature, but every end is a beginning, and under every deep, a lower deep opens.
—Ralph Waldo Emerson

The I/We model was developed out of our work with GTC cohorts. It reflects our learning from supporting the transformative development of individuals and collectives (Lynam et al., 2020). The I/We model (distinct from the STAGES model although it integrates it) describes (and then guides) how individuals and collectives form and in-form each other's experience and development. We distinguish individual and collective emergence because doing so reveals the capacities of each that supports their development. But this does not mean that we see the individual-collective as a dichotomy. Both are in a constant process of co-evolving, with and as each other. They interpenetrate and are distinguished from a prior unity: a whole in which individual and collective occupy the same space (Kesler, 2014; Smith & Berg, 1997). Similarly, we distinguish the process of development, in which one stage (way of being and meaning making) builds on the next, and yet we do not view this as a linear step-by-step process. We see it as a dynamic cycle of becoming or unfolding for both individuals and collectives. As one changes so does the other, and vice versa. It is hard to tell which comes first.

The cycle of becoming described by the I/We model builds on a process of differentiation and integration and is refined into four phases (see Fig. 38.2). As the function of a phase is completed, the next phase in the cycle becomes available. This can, however, be a multi-directional process, as prior phases sometimes need to be revisited to address gaps, or for further integration. As individuals or collectives move from one phase to another, there are often transitional disorientations. These are included in the descriptions that follow.

- **Differentiation.** Forming of identity (individual or collective) distinct from its environment or constituent parts, stably sustaining that identity in the face of challenges and change. Transitioning

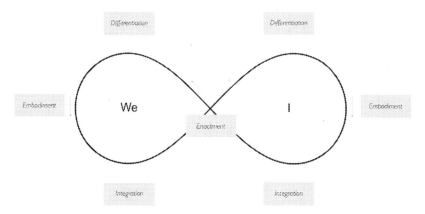

Fig. 38.2 I/We model: four phases

out of differentiation requires developing confidence in the newly formed identity, including daring to give it voice.
- **Embodiment.** Bringing that identity fully into form in a variety of contexts, and making it visible through body, speech, and mind. Transitioning out of embodiment involves opening the boundaries of the identity—having enough confidence to hold it lightly while inter-relating with the world.
- **Integration.** Embracing, attuning to, and dynamically collaborating with one's environment and constituent parts, while stably sustaining a flow of movement and information, toward becoming. The transitional disorientation here is to risk the attainment of a degree of happiness or intimacy for a deeper accomplishment or creativity.
- **Enactment.** Realizing one's purpose (individually and collectively) and expressing it in the world. As this completes a cycle of becoming, the transitional disorientation of this stage is the completion or dissolution of identity, setting up the potential for differentiation of a new form.

MetAwareness and Subtle Collectives

While we theorize that the phases described in this model pertain to all stages of development, our application of the framework is focused primarily on the 4th- and 5th-person perspective stages. Individually, the

I/We model highlights the development of capacities at these stages, the transition into the MetAware tier, and the maturation of the 5th-person perspective stages. Collectively, the focus is on the development of subtle community, which is the collective territory of these stages.

The subtle We consists of the perception of being situated in and arising out of a plurality of contexts. The We is not then a specific group of people, but is a relational space, a quality brought to relationships, or a relational field. For example, in a particular form of dialogical inquiry, there may be a certain quality of depth and intimacy. It is the practice itself that creates the conditions for the particular quality of relationships. Therefore, one can engage this practice with different individuals or groups and encounter a similar relational field. The quality of the connection is not wholly dependent on who the participants are; at the same time, it is shaped and influenced by the individuals' uniqueness. The relational field of subtle collectives is shaped by outer manifestations, such as the room; the systems in which the collective is embedded; the cultural contexts; and also inner manifestations, such as the attitudes, beliefs, assumptions, states of awareness, and ontological dispositions individuals bring to the moment. It is at these stages of development (4.0 Pluralist, 4.5 Strategist, 5.0 Construct Aware, and 5.5 Transpersonal) that the notions of we-space, collective intelligence, transformative change for individuals and collectives, and collective evolution begin to be of interest (Fitch, 2016; Ramirez et al., 2013).

At the 5th-person perspective, the beginning of the MetAware tier, individuals awaken to their ever-present awareness and begin to identify with a new self, one that is both empty and full, transcendent, and immanent. In these stages (5.0 and 5.5), the I is foregrounded, but the subtle We remains as a context for this I. Knowing that even deeper subtle we-spaces are possible (deeper than is generated from the 4th-person perspective), individuals in these MetAware stages often want to experience them, collaborate within them, and act from them. This experience in a group is often described as having some of the following qualities: spacious (including more silence), creative, easeful, adaptive, flowing, less effort, more shared and shifting leadership, less ego or attachment to particular ideas or people, greater ease in addressing and resolving conflict, integrating body, mind, and spirit, and generative.

Now we turn to the four phases of the I/We model and describe the foundations, experiences, and practices of each: Differentiation, Embodiment, Integration, and Enactment.

DIFFERENTIATION

The phase of differentiation supports the emergence of a mature identity of the individual and the collective, that is stable and able to sustain challenges while remaining open and fluid.

Engaging with Shadow and Trauma

The interaction between the I and the We offers the opportunity to work with shadow material. Shadow is what has been repressed, hidden, denied, or disowned in an individual or a collective. In GTC, as participants deepen their individual and collective growth, they learn to become more intimately engaged with shadow as a normal part of being human. In this intimacy, there can be healing (a movement toward wholeness), which provides a deeper sense of aliveness and engagement with all of life.

Shadow can take the form of maps or concepts of self and group that are taken in, or introjected, from early life experiences, often in the relational context in the concrete stages of development. These maps help us navigate how to belong and be safe in a group. Our culture and families are like an "ecosystem," to which we adapt. They shape our sense of self and, in turn, our nervous systems. What is and is not allowed by the standards of the culture and family are repressed, disowned, or hidden, to not disturb the attachment we have to our caregivers and community. These disowned parts may be projected on others and the outer world. What is disowned is also patterned in the nervous system as something that is dangerous and therefore triggers our fight/freeze/flight response (Porges, 2011). These formative experiences shape the initial ways we relate in a group, how safe it feels to reveal what we authentically think and feel, and how able we are to self-regulate our interior processes in the face of different perspectives, challenges, and conflict.

In this phase of differentiation, individuals can learn, heal, and expand their capacities to be autonomous while being emotionally connected to the group. Likewise, groups can learn to form, deepen, and adapt, in the face of a diversity of individual perspectives, intentions, and energies. As they work with the unconscious shadow, individuals begin to heal, integrate, and regulate their nervous systems in ways that provide more embodiment, capacity, and space. As one individual learns to regulate their nervous system, they can help others to begin to do the same (Porges, 2011).

Developing the capacity to rest in the awareness of awareness provides a spacious and still presence that is energetically coherent. The nervous system is calm in this state, which offers to others who are not calm the space to feel what it is like to be witnessed, which can help them find their regulation. It offers the freedom to be more curious rather than judgmental, and to be more open rather than closed. As this capacity is deepened, it is easier to let shadow material emerge without triggering a reactive response, or if triggered, knowing what to do to regulate, calm down, allow, and re-engage. As individuals become adept at this, the collective field is deepened, which in turn can tolerate and explore more shadow. It is a dance that is always in service of healing and growth, collectively and individually (Fitch, 2016; Siegel, 2012).

It is in this rich, subtle collective that habit patterns, once in shadow, can be observed internally and externally, and individually and collectively. These patterns include trauma that has been held inside our bodies and nervous systems, and passed from one generation to the next, and throughout history (Hubl & Avritt, 2020; Menakem, 2017).

We support this phase of differentiation through personal and interpersonal and collective practices, including authentic communication, expressions of truthfulness and vulnerability, individual and collective shadow processes, awareness practices, working with habit patterns as they form in the group, and attending to the developmental patterns of individuals and the collective. We endeavor to hold all of this in a field grounded in trust, love, honesty, and awareness.

Surrendering into the Self and Collective

Engaging with shadow work opens the doorway to deeply embrace one's limitations and gifts as a whole human being and to reside in one's truth, moment to moment. This movement paradoxically also frees one up to take more responsibility for one's limitations and impact on others. This deeper, existential self-acceptance becomes the ground from which relaxing into the collective is possible, which in turn allows the collective to form and accept itself in light of its members. The need to control and defend oneself from the collective is replaced with openness and more agile and permeable boundaries. One can then truly surrender to an expanded sense of I and We—the expansive subtle field infused with boundless meta-awareness—the mature subtle collective. One can have a sense of surrender to life itself as this moment. Concurrently, the We allows itself to exist with its limitations and gifts. Here the interpenetration of I and We can be experienced as the collective and its unique set of individuals reside as a coherent subtle field experienced through a boundless meta-awareness.

EMBODIMENT

The phase of embodiment supports the individual and collective to fully inhabit themselves and to express themselves in their truth: clearly, vibrantly, and wholeheartedly.

The Embodiment of the True Self and the Collective Field

As differentiation supports the individual to relax into the collective as their true self, they can more freely and fully express themselves through their body, speech, and mind. This is a process of deepening, supported in GTC through an invitation to use the space of the program as a territory to experiment with new ways of being and doing. We endeavor to invite, support, and reflect the true expression of each participant and of the collective itself. We practice noticing and releasing the assumptions and projections we hold. We also engage in practices such as movement, dance, and play that support opening habitual ways of being. These practices support individual embodiment as well as collective cohesion and expression.

As embodiment deepens in a collective field that is subtle and informed by an awareness of awareness, a shift in both listening and participation in the collective can develop. A felt sense that the collective is a system that has its own intelligence beyond the self and yet completely includes the self can emerge. From a MetAware perspective, the collective may be seen as a fractal of the larger system of intelligence that comprises all systems, including human and more than human systems. The self can be experienced both as part of, and yet distinct from, the whole. From this place it is possible to have a felt sense of speaking from a place that is personal and true—deeply embodied, authentic, and yet beyond the habitual patterns of the self that occur just through the ego. One can experience that everyone in the collective is a voice for the intelligence that moves through all of life, a piece of the puzzle necessary for the emergence and for collective intelligence.

Speaking and Listening from the Self and Collective

When we engage in a practice of the interpenetration of I and We, speaking for the self and for the collective are not merely seen to coexist but are experienced as interdependent and co-emerging. Even expressions that seem to contradict the collective intention, such as "I don't want to be part of this!" if held from an interpenetrative perspective, paradoxically reinforce the collective cohesion. We understand that intent can only exist with its contradiction, and we welcome it with humor (Smith & Berg, 1997). The expression of both the individual's unique voice and the collective's cohesion, intelligence, and intention is allowed to move more freely.

This interpenetration of the I and the We in a deep subtle collective, informed and supported by MetAware capacities, is the embodied potential that we work toward in GTC. It is an ever-unfolding practice to access these moments of grace. And it is a journey that we are on together, ever falling short, and ever aspiring toward. It is not about the attainment as much as it is attending to the practice of "walking each other home" (Dass & Bush, 2018).

INTEGRATION

The phase of integration supports the deepening of the dynamic collaboration with and attunement to one's environment and constituent parts while sustaining a flow of movement and information toward becoming.

Supporting Self and We-Space from the Meta-Awareness

The work of differentiation and embodiment of the prior phases deepens in the process of integration. As attention is given to shadows, blocks, and unwanted patterns, as well as emergent potentials, experiences can be engaged with from the deeper ground of awareness and a differentiated self.

Supporting the self from meta-awareness allows us to see ourselves through the spaciousness of witnessing awareness, rather than solely identifying with the contents of awareness (such as body sensations, thoughts, and feelings). We do not ignore or bypass these, but instead include them, so that awareness, mind, and body are an integrated whole. Grounded in awareness of awareness, we are freer of our patterns but also able to directly see them as they arise. We can support the self and collective through this conscious awareness by engaging with work to open and shift these patterns, in support of individual and collective learning and growth. Ultimately, this may support us to notice patterns of the mind perceiving and constructing and support the gradual unfolding of the structures of self that open identity into an experience beyond the ordinary boundaries we impose on reality.

Similarly, as a collective, we can experience this awareness as shared in our subtle field. In a sense, it is the same in all things. Just as with self-awareness, through meta-awareness and meta sense-making at the collective level, we can develop a kind of in-the-moment witnessing that supports the emergence of new insight and potentials. We can notice the subtle collective patterns, such as group formation and identity, dynamics that may evolve into cultural forms, collective shadows, and the influence of past and present trauma. We witness what the collective is aware or not aware of, and where the collective is placing its attention. We may ultimately see that the collective is an expression of a larger We that includes the broader, global socio-cultural-economic consciousness, and forces that exist now, in the past, and are yet to be.

Attuning and Freeing Energy and Perspectives

From this awareness, we can learn to track the energetic felt sense and practice to free the energetic movement of the I and We. Individual members of the collective can begin to have a felt sense of release, stillness, and truth when one person speaks as the whole. When this occurs, both the individual and collective become embodied as a more profound truth and whole. What earlier might have been seen as grounds for contradiction or conflict now gets resolved in a deeper order and experienced in a spacious coherence. The capacity of the collective to hold and engage problems this way can allow for the emergence of novel solutions, as well as new ways of being and doing together. Practices we engage with to support this process include awareness and somatic practices to move energy, improv, spontaneous leadership, identifying and shifting habitual roles, and emergent creative processes.

ENACTMENT

The phase of enactment has the individuals and collectives engaging and directing their identity and energy in the world, through an authentic impulse toward a future that is calling.

Individual/Collective Presencing

We draw on Scharmer's Theory U (2018) in GTC as a map for the depth of change one can go through in a transformative process. The term *presencing* refers to the deepest and most profound form of change where novelty emerges from source or ground of being. Before presencing, the process involves examining, encountering, and letting go of what has been. Through willingness and surrender into a deeper source or ground of being, the collective can perceive a sense of the future that wants to emerge. In the I/We model, enactment begins as individuals and collectives emerge into a process of sensing and bringing their future into form in the world.

As one opens to this deeper form of change, we can come to more fully encounter "what is," which in itself can also be transformative. We observe non-judgmentally with meta-awareness and open our hearts to enter into an intimate and committed inter-relatedness with what is—the truth of how things are rather than how we want them to be. The next step is to allow ourselves to let go of fear and trust the deeper unfolding of change, which prompts us to let go more deeply into the ground of being, through the doorway of the boundless silence of meta-awareness. This releasing into presencing is not an act of will, but rather of willingness. It occurs in its own time and allows us to become receptive to the promptings of a future that wants to emerge into the present (Fitch & Lynam, 2019).

This part of the process is chaotic, not in the ordinary sense of being undesirably confusing or disordered, but rather in the original understanding: "the primordial state that precedes Creation. Chaos is an emptiness, but a fertile emptiness, a nothingness that contains the mysterious seeds of all that is, a vast and formless potential capable of bringing forth all form into expression" (Golabuk, 2012). This space of presencing is unpredictable but inevitably gives rise to insight, sensing, and a calling toward an emergent and transformative future.

This process of presencing occurs individually and collectively. The world that wants to emerge is a world of both I and We. We can engage deliberately in presencing for the self and the collective by allowing ourselves to be receptive to their futures and give them voice. Ultimately, these futures are one, so in the complexity that emerges from the presencing, it is important to hold these emergent futures sincerely but lightly as they take shape and cohere.

In the evolution of transformative change in individual/collectives, this phase emerges into the mature form of a system, which has cohered into a new order and begins to live and act in the world from this place. We co-enact the emerging ontology, by taking as real the future that wants to emerge: speaking, thinking, feeling, and working from it. This requires a sincere and vulnerable caring for that nascent future while being in relationship with the realities of the present. We practice to sustain a connection to the ground of being that is birthing this future, without becoming cynical or pessimistic, and while creatively engaging it.

Initially, it is helpful to engage in prototyping and experimentation and to continue the transformative exploration of this future (Scharmer, 2018). Through this process, we revisit and deepen all elements of the work to differentiate, embody, integrate, and enact. Presencing and enactment prompt us to engage with the emergent future creatively, and we can experience individual and collective dimensions of this. Conflict can arise as our passions toward this future take form. We may need to revisit the work of generative conflict, intimacy, shadow, self-acceptance, allowing coherence and flow, and so on. While creatively engaging our work together, the whole of the emergence depends on and develops strength to move into the world with its impulses.

Our deeper purpose or plan unfolds through the I and We and is expressed and offered in the broader context of life and history. The process of presencing depends on developing a greater trust in the self, the world, and in each other, so that our creation will be received and valued. We not only embody our new work in the world, as Scharmer puts it, but also need to participate in creating a new world to receive that work—one that is whole and friendly to the future that wants to emerge (Fig. 38.3).

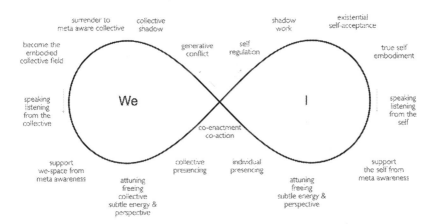

Fig. 38.3 I/We model

Conclusion

Through the process of differentiation, embodiment, integration, and enactment, we continue to deepen our learning about the transformative co-evolution of the I and the We. Realizing the interpenetration of the I and We and their ultimate unity in a deeper ground of awareness makes possible a form of healing and coming home to our true nature that is life-affirming and life-giving. Identification with a self and collective beyond the personal allows for the emergence of novel futures, and fluid, creative engagement in service of a greater whole. This approach also helps to work with and integrate polarities including cultural tendencies to be more individually oriented or more collectively oriented; in developmental orientations toward the individual or the collective; in political leanings between liberal and conservative; in divides between the personal and the transpersonal; the ecological and the social, and the spiritual and the secular. It also reveals how conflict and shadow work and how other forms of working with patterns of differentiation can also serve a greater whole.

We seek to develop capacities for mature subtle community, founded in contextual and systemic understanding, personal self-awareness, interpersonal differentiation and skills, and access to transpersonal states and stages of consciousness. This engagement can also help to realize the promise and potential of subtle capacities—to be with each other in our uniqueness, differences, and similarities, and aware of how internal and external contexts shape how we relate to and understand one another. It makes possible a deeper form of inter-relating, self-regulation, and transformative change. The spaciousness and ground that meta-awareness brings can also support the capacities to work with shadow and conflict in creative and generative ways. It can also enhance collaboration, collective intelligence, and develop new forms of leadership and systemic change so needed in a world of complex and interconnected global challenges.

MetAware subtle collectives also have the potential to reach into the past to heal personal and collective trauma. We can reach toward the future with new forms and ways of being together. And yet, these are potentials that are challenging to realize. We carry with us the harms of the past and the present. We need to cultivate these capacities for new ways of being human together. We may, at times, fail. Yet it is by turning toward our so-called failures with more honesty, compassion, and responsibility, that we can begin to enact new futures, new stories, new potentials as individuals and collectives. We also come to realize the perfection that exists in our being and becoming. We see this in the essence of our being that is not implicated by these challenges: the boundless ground of awareness itself.

References

Barad, K. (2007). *Meeting the universe halfway: Quantum physics and the entanglement of matter and meaning*. Duke University Press.

Brown, D. (2006). *Pointing out the great way: The stages of meditation in the Mahamudra tradition*. Wisdom Publications.

Cook-Greuter, S. (2013). *Ego development: Nine levels of increasing embrace* (Unpublished manuscript). http://www.cook-greuter.com/Cook-Greuter%209%20levels%20paper%20new%201.1%2714%2097p%5B1%5D.pdf

Dass, R. R., & Bush, M. (2018). *Walking each other home: Conversations on loving and dying*. Sounds True.

Esbjörn-Hargens, S. (2010). An ontology of climate change. *Journal of Integral Theory and Practice, 5*(1), 143–174.

Fitch, G. (2016). In, as, and towards the Kosmic we. In O. Gunnlaugson & M. Brabant (Eds.), *Cohering the integral we space: Engaging collective emergence, wisdom and healing in groups*. Integral Publishing House.

Fitch, G., & Lynam, A. (2019). An interpenetrative application of theory U. In O. Gunnlaugson & W. Brendel (Eds.), *Advances in presencing* (pp. 79–104). Trifoss Business Press.

38 THE INTERPENETRATION OF INDIVIDUAL AND COLLECTIVE ...   695

Golabuk, P. (2012). *Field and fate workshop* (Unpublished manuscript).

Gunnlaugson, O., & Brabant, M. (2016). *Cohering the integral we space: Engaging collective emergence, wisdom and healing in groups.* Integral Publishing House.

Hubl, T., & Avritt, J. (2020). *Healing collective trauma: A process for integrating our intergenerational and cultural wounds.* Sounds True

Kegan, R. (2000). What "form" transforms? A constructive- developmental approach to transformative learning. In J. Mezirow (Ed.) & Associates, *Learning as transformation* (pp. 3–34). Jossey-Bass

Kesler, J. (2014). *Introduction to integral polarity practice: An awareness and life practice* (Unpublished manuscript). The IPP Institute.

Lynam, A., Fitch, G., & O'Fallon, T. (2020). The aware leader: Supporting post-autonomous leadership development. In J. Reams (Ed.), *Maturing leadership: How adult development impacts leadership.* Emerald Publishing.

Masters, R. A. (2018). *Bringing your shadow out of the dark: Breaking free from the hidden forces that drive you.* Sounds True.

Menakem, R. (2017). *My grandmother's hands: Racialized trauma and the pathway to mending our hearts and bodies.* Central Recovery Press.

O'Fallon, T. (2016). STAGES: Growing up is waking up—Interpenetrating quadrants, states and structures. *Stages International.* https://www.stagesinternational.com/the-evolution-of-the-human-soul-2/

O'Fallon, T., & Barta, K. (2018). *The STAGES matrix roadmap: A contemporary model of development perspectives* (Unpublished manuscript). STAGES International.

O'Sullivan, E. Morrell, A., & O'Connor, M. A. (Eds.). (2002). *Expanding the boundaries of transformative learning: Essays on theory and praxis.* Palgrave Macmillan.

Pierrakos, J. C. (2005). *Core energetics: Developing the capacity to love and heal.* Core Evolution.

Porges, S. W. (2011). *The polyvagal theory: Neurophysiological foundations of emotions, attachment, communication, and self-regulation.* W. W. Norton.

Ramirez, V., Fitch, G., & O'Fallon T. (2013). *Causal leadership: A natural emergence from later stages of awareness* (Paper presentation). Integral Theory Conference, San Francisco, CA.

Richo, D. (2014). *How to be an adult in love.* Shambhala Publications.

Scharmer, O. (2018) *The essentials of theory U: Core principles and applications.* Berrett-Koehler Publishers.

Siegel, D. J. (2012). *Pocket guide to interpersonal neurobiology: An integrative handbook of the mind.* W. W. Norton.

Smith, K., & Berg, D. (1997). *Paradoxes of group life.* Jossey-Bass.

Torbert, B., Cook-Greuter, S., Fisher, D., Foldy, E., Gauthier, A., Keeley, J., Rooke, D., Ross, S., Royce, C., Rudolph, J., Taylor, S., & Tran, M.

(2004). *Action inquiry: The secret of timely and transforming leadership.* Berrett-Koehler.

Wilber, K. (2006). *Integral spirituality: A startling new role for religion in the modern and postmodern world.* Shambhala.

PART IV

Provocation 4 : Challenges and Emerging Future of Transformation

CHAPTER 39

Power of Questions: Transformation in Complex Systems

Glenda H. Eoyang

The COVID-19 pandemic that began in 2019 has challenged habits of thought and action for individuals, organizations, and communities around the world. For the first time in history, people faced the same global microscopic challenge. Regardless of wealth, language, religion, privilege, culture, or political structure, everyone was faced with fundamental, existential problems. This situation set conditions for radical change at every level of human interaction. The rules were changed, and people had to play a new game to survive. Whether this is labeled "transformational change" or simply "good learning" (Newman, 2012), people and institutions changed their understanding, attitudes, and behaviors radically and quickly.

Change in such extraordinary times is considered to be complex because it is unpredictable and episodic. Individuals and communities find themselves adapting daily to changes they can neither predict nor

G. H. Eoyang (✉)
Human Systems Dynamics Institute, Circle Pines, MN, USA
e-mail: geoyang@hsdinstitute.org

© The Author(s), under exclusive license to Springer Nature   699
Switzerland AG 2022
A. Nicolaides et al. (eds.), *The Palgrave Handbook of Learning for Transformation*, https://doi.org/10.1007/978-3-030-84694-7_39

control. In response to this challenge, the human systems dynamics (HSD) community drew on its decades-long practice of supporting complex change. We introduced a practice to set conditions for individual and collective transformation. In 20-minute online engagements, people brought their most wicked challenges for group exploration. Their challenges give a sense of the people and the problems that were brought to the community.

> I am a physical therapist. The first week of COVID-19 lock down I am distraught. They tell me not to touch my most vulnerable patients, but those are the ones who need me most. What can I do? —Helene, Geneva, Switzerland
>
> My 10-year-old daughter's school has chosen a terrible online training system that is driving us all to tears of failure and frustration. I teach in the same district, but the system isn't required for my classes. How can I balance my child's education and welfare under these circumstances? —Hope, North Texas, USA
>
> What should I do when I wake up one morning, and it looks like my city has turned into a police state? I see helicopters and hear sirens and smell smoke from burning businesses. Yesterday it seemed like peaceful protest, and today the world looks very different. —Sam, Bay Area, USA
>
> In the midst of isolation due to COVID-19, our faith community realizes we won't be able to hold funerals or care for our grieving members the way we have in the past. What can we do instead? —Laura, St. Paul, USA
>
> I am the principal of a 1,500-student high school. I worked all summer to prepare for at least one semester of totally online learning. August 1, two weeks before school was to open, the school board decided we should be 'in school.' It is impossible. What am I supposed to do? —Elizabeth, Nashville, USA
>
> My manufacturing company adapted fairly well to lockdown. A small group of workers kept the factory going, and the rest of us worked from home. The problem came when we went back to working on site. Essential workers had enjoyed the freedom from oversight. They found innovative solutions to cut corners and meet demand. They were proud of their ingenuity and unwilling to go back to the old ways. Office workers, accustomed to being in charge, did not understand their new roles. Besides that, they were still afraid of infection, so they avoided each other. Our coherent culture is gone. Will it ever come back? —Maria, Northern Italy
>
> Our health system adapted quickly to COVID-19 because we had one thing to worry about, and we had few choices to make. As we move

into recovery, we must incorporate the old with the new. My most urgent question now is how to manage both COVID-free and COVID-focused care at the same time and in the same facility? —Paul, National Health Service, U.K.

These are real problems of real people that have emerged from the complex environment of a global pandemic. They challenge assumptions about who we are and what we can do as individuals and communities, and as parents, citizens, and professionals.

Such extreme circumstances invite us to break through our comfortable and familiar worldviews. We have the opportunity for transformational change in this moment. We can shift our perspectives and create a better tomorrow, but that is not always easy. We might reject the invitation and hold onto delusion and disbelief. We could long for what should be, hoping that things will "get back to normal." Those stability-seeking choices will lock us into maladaptive behaviors. In time, the patterns may create individual and collective trauma.

The hopeful and healthy alternative is the kind of learning that can be called transformational. If we break through the expectations and constraints of yesterday, we will move into a new paradigm. The challenges of today set the conditions for a metamorphosis that has the potential to carry us into new habits of thought and action.

Since March of 2020, the Human Systems Dynamics (HSD) Institute and our global community of change agents have set conditions for individuals, organizations, and communities to transform to meet the extraordinary challenges of global pandemic. Over the past 30 years, we have developed a complexity-inspired theory and practice that sets conditions for transformational change (Eoyang & Holladay, 2013). This chapter will outline the theory of change that informs our work: introduce a simple, powerful facilitation process we have used to encourage in-the-moment transformation; and share the stories of people who transcended the habits of thought and action that had them stuck in the COVID-19 reality.

TRANSFORMATIONAL CHANGE AS SELF-ORGANIZED CRITICALITY

Over the last 30 years, complexity science has influenced theory and practice in every physical and social science discipline (Aron, 2020; Bogg,

2007b; Davis & Sumara, 2014; Gershenson, 2010). All complexity-inspired approaches share some of the same concepts: sensitive dependence on initial conditions (butterfly effects), open boundaries, uncertainty, fractal structures, tipping point, path dependence, and unpredictable boundary conditions (Bogg, 2007a). Each field has developed a unique approach of focus, language, theory of change, models, and methods to respond to its traditional questions and challenges. HSD draws from a range of sciences to find concepts and tools that are useful for people who face challenging dilemmas in today's complex reality (Eoyang, 2009). Our primary theory of change comes from the mechanical engineering and materials sciences of Per Bak's "self-organized criticality" (Bak, 1999).

Traditional Newtonian causality depends on objects interacting in space and time. The magnitude and direction of force initiate the change and determine its speed and direction. Change is measured in terms of mass, distance, and time. These assumptions about change have dominated Western thought since the seventeenth century (Prigogine et al., 2017). Many of our metaphors for change and learning in human systems derive from this worldview. We talk about developmental stages, pathways, milestones, objectives, and replication across children and contexts. In organizational change, we say "We have to overcome cultural inertia." "External pressure moves a system forward." "A plan has predictable milestones and a single endpoint." In both learning and organizational change, such a perspective leads us to push past resistance and enforce predictable stages and consistent performance criteria. All of these metaphors draw from the Newtonian theory of change, where momentum and impact determine the pathways of change.

Self-organized criticality in complex adaptive systems offers an alternative worldview. In this view of systems, change is pattern based. Change comes from relationships within a system, rather than forces from beyond. Interdependencies within the system, at many different scales of interaction, hold systemic patterns in place or allow them to shift. Relationships between and among components of the system define degrees of freedom. They determine how quickly and in what way patterns will shift. They determine how much and what kind of potential for change is held within a pattern at a given situation and time. Differences in the system hold tensions, and those tensions define the potential for change. Over time, differences and their tensions intensify. Interactions within the system begin to respond to the tensions and connections are stressed. When the stress reaches a threshold level, the connections shift, the tensions are released, and the pattern changes in extreme and unpredictable ways. It is transformed (Kelso & Engstrøm, 2008).

For example, you can think of employee engagement as a pattern of relationships between and among executives, middle managers, supervisors, and front-line workers. As a whole, those relationships generate a systemic pattern that is recognized as engagement. The local patterns interact to generate system-wide patterns, but the whole is different than the sum of the parts. Any single relationship might be great, but dysfunction above or below can block engagement and create even more cynicism and frustration. In another system, the behavior of one bad manager may be overridden by a preponderance of effective leaders. This theory of change is pattern based. Inside the pattern, differences cause the accumulation of tension within or between leadership levels. Over time, that tension accumulates. When the tension is released, the pattern shifts. The new pattern may be better or worse, but its function is to release accumulated tension and make the overall system more stable.

Any pattern may be stable, if the conditions are strong enough to hold tension as it accumulates over time. For example, in our example of engagement above, an engaged workforce can absorb a single instance of disagreement or hurt feelings without significantly shifting the pattern of engagement. As tensions accumulate over time, however, systemic conditions may no longer be sufficient to hold the pattern in place. In one moment—the moment of self-organized criticality—the system can shift radically and unpredictably. Conditions adjust to find a new, relatively stable pattern. At that moment, when the pattern shifts, the state of the system is permanently transformed. In our engagement example, unresolved tensions can accumulate until they surpass the system's capacity to support them. Some seemingly minor incident may add enough tension to tip the system and generate a persistent pattern of disengagement. Although that single event is a trigger, it is not the cause of the shift. The cause lies in the robustness of the system-wide infrastructure of connections and the history of unresolved and accumulating tensions (Eoyang, 2001).

The principles of self-organized criticality affect change in all scales and facets of human interaction. Piaget represents learning as assimilation and accommodation, as the lattice of rationality shifts to align with new experience and information (Chandler, 2009). Crowds turn into mobs when a moment of self-organized criticality is reached, and the pattern of the whole becomes more powerful than the rationality of the parts (Templeton et al., 2020). Recession turns to depression in an economic system when the fundamentals respond to accumulating tension. Acute illness becomes chronic when physiological patterns break down and are no longer able to regenerate. Innovation, domestic violence, artistic catharsis, divorce, laughter, religious conversion, bankruptcy, individual infection, and pandemic are all examples of self-organized criticality serving as a mechanism for transformative change (Stollenwerk, 2005).

SETTING CONDITIONS FOR TRANSFORMATIONAL CHANGE

When we understand transformational change as self-organized criticality, we see the job of the change agent in a new light. The agents do not cause change. They do not solve a problem. They do not push for change. They do not engage with senior leaders to make change. They do not teach content and skills. Instead, change agents observe current conditions and how they hold tensions in this moment. They assess the resilience, fragility, or rigidity of those current conditions. They explore relevant differences in the system, sources of tension, and means of natural tension release. Change agents observe patterns as they emerge in the systems. They shift conditions within their control as they watch what happens. Perhaps they seek to relieve or release the naturally emerging tensions. Perhaps they introduce new, generative tensions in an effort to stabilize or destabilize current patterns. Perhaps they strengthen or break old connections or create new ones to build an infrastructure for positive, healthy patterns to emerge. They do what they can, they watch the results, and then they collect new information to begin again (Eoyang & Holladay, 2013).

In the Human Systems Dynamics Institute, we have applied this understanding of transformational change in a variety of client contexts, including innovation, collaboration, violent conflict, and trauma-informed care. In all of these contexts, the accumulation of tension leads, ultimately, to a moment of radical, unpredictable, transformational change.

Perhaps the most poignant context in which we have applied these principles has been in teaching and learning. We develop and implement *deep learning ecologies*, in which learner questions, rich stores of resources, and open inquiry focus on differences, amplify tensions, and focus creative release to support learning for teachers and students. In this way, we set conditions for generative and adaptive learning. From early childhood through postsecondary education and adult training and development, we set conditions for individuals and groups to improve their adaptive capacity to respond to the uncertainty and turbulence of complex environments (Patterson & Holladay, 2018).

Our practice of self-organizing, transformational change in all of these complex and emergent applications depends on three basic competencies: Inquiry, Pattern Logic, and Adaptive Action.

Inquiry

Traditional Newtonian change was assumed to be predictable and controllable. If you knew enough about the system and its context, then you should be able to predict the path and outcomes of any change process. Complexity, on the other hand, acknowledges that some systems are, by nature, unpredictable. The future of a complex adaptive system is unknowable, but responsible action is still required from leaders and change agents. Answers are useful only in limited space and over a short period of time. Questions, on the other hand, lead to understanding and action in this world of turbulence and emergent change. Certainty will never be possible, so it must be replaced with inquiry. We practice and teach four simple rules for inquiry to help us operationalize our curiosity: Turn judgment into curiosity; turn conflict into shared exploration; turn defensiveness into self-reflection; and turn assumptions into questions.

These practices set conditions that challenge current and encourage new ways of thinking, feeling, and acting. These rules by themselves cannot cause transformational change, but they are one of the significant factors that set conditions for self-organized criticality in human systems at all scales.

Pattern Logic

We described above how the complex-systems sciences move beyond an object-interaction understanding of change and into one that is pattern based. Such a pattern-oriented approach is derived from the work of complexity scientists, including Prigogine et al. (2017) and Bak (1999), as well as Reynolds (1987), Mandelbrot (1993), and Lorenz (Elgin & Sarkar, 1984). Each of them, in their respective disciplines, revealed a natural world driven by relations among patterns, not objects. The nature of change, then, lies in the ways patterns shift over time. Effective action inside that understanding of the nature of change depends on the ability to see, understand, and influence patterns and how they change over time.

For practical purposes, we define a pattern in terms of the conditions that hold it in place. Those same conditions give information about what a pattern is in the moment and what it might become in the future. We focus on three conditions that influence the speed, path, and outcomes of self-organizing: Container, Difference, and Exchange.

Container (C) refers to any feature of the system that bounds it. Containers may be physical, social, conceptual, or emotional. Many exist at the same time in human systems, and they are massively entangled. For example, an employee is simultaneously a member of a team, a department, a professional group, and a family. Within each of these containers, they participate in meaningful and semi-stable patterns of interactions. A change in one can influence a change in any or all of the others.

Difference (D) focuses on the variations within Containers, including any imaginable characteristic. Different colors, heights, learning styles, ages, races, power, gender, and so on. Each difference has the potential to hold tension or to release the tension in the form of energy and change. In any given situation there are more and fewer relevant differences. Some hold more tension than others, depending on the history, purpose, or focus of the group in the moment.

Exchanges (E) are the connections that transfer information, energy, and/or resources across differences. An exchange can be a verbal expression, a physical contact, transfer of funds, or anything that flows across the system. The Exchange converts the potential energy in the differences into actual change in the system.

Together these three systemic features determine the speed, path, and outcome of self-organized criticality. They also define the pattern of a current state, so they allow you to see the system clearly, understand its dynamics, and take action to influence it by changing any of the features. The three constitute the Eoyang CDE Model of self-organizing in human systems (Eoyang, 2011).

The ability to see, understand, and influence these three conditions we call Pattern Logic. When we are able to see reality in terms of patterns and their potential for change through our possible influence, we become conscious participants in the process of transformational change. Pattern

Logic allows us to approach transformational change through intentional action, without assuming we can predict when or control how the transformational change might emerge (Eoyang, 2001).

Adaptive Action

Simple change is represented as a one-way street, from problem definition to successful implementation. Complex, self-organizing change cannot follow such a linear path because it depends on patterns forming, shifting, and reforming again at many scales simultaneously. As an alternative to linear problem-solving, we rely on Adaptive Action. It is a simple, three-step learning and action cycle, consisting of three questions: *What? So what?* and *Now what?* This simple process moves individuals and groups through data collection (*What?*), meaning making (*So what?*), and action (*Now what?*). It also establishes an ongoing adaptive process because it is iterative. In a complex system, driven by self-organized criticality, any action has the potential to shift system-wide patterns in unpredictable ways. For this reason, Adaptive Action follows every action with a new observation. Each *Now what?* sets conditions for the next *What?*, and the process continues. Each cycle holds the potential for one transformation and sets conditions for the next.

An Adaptive Action cycle can be quick or slow, solo or collective, isolated or interdependent, local or global. Many different Adaptive Action cycles can take place at the same time, or the whole system may be focused on a single cycle.

We have used Adaptive Action to support transformative learning as kindergartners teach each other to read. The same processes support strategic transformational change for communities and institutions. We are not the first to use such a cycle to support learning, research, and Adaptive Action. These three steps are used widely—implicitly and explicitly—to support both incremental and transformational change. Our understanding of transformative learning as self-organizing change depends, as well, on the two other principles of practice: Inquiry and Pattern Logic.

All three of these competencies—Inquiry, Pattern Logic, and Adaptive Action—have been at the center of our response to the COVID-19 pandemic and the complex adaptive responses it demanded. One method, which brings all of these competencies into a simple process, has been particularly useful.

The differences between ordinary and transformative learning is not the focus of this chapter. We are concerned with understanding and supporting learning, in all its various guises. The discontinuity, unpredictability, and irreversibility of self-organized criticality correlate to the most common characteristics attributed to transformative learning. This correlation can provide specific guidance for those who wish to set conditions for learning that is experienced and/or observed to be transformative.

POWER OF QUESTIONS

All the models and methods of human systems dynamics support and enhance our three core competencies. They are embedded in Adaptive Action; they help groups see and shift patterns; and they suggest generative pathways of inquiry into action. All of these approaches have been useful in the current COVID disruption, and we have entered our own Adaptive Action to create approaches that are particularly useful in these extraordinary times.

Four factors encouraged us to assess old and explore new ways of interacting to support learning and transformational change in 2020. First, we, like others, found ourselves online. Although our practice had included online engagement for years, the expanding need stretched us into inquiry and innovation. Second, our clients had little time to devote to learning and intentional change. We were working primarily with health-care, governmental, and educational organizations. Because they were at the center of the COVID-19 response, working with us was not their highest priority. Third, our global network came together as one community. In the online world of global pandemic, everyone shared similar challenges. In addition, we were able to enter the same space at the same time, so our approaches became more global and less geographically and culturally specific. Fourth, personal, community, institution, and regulatory realities were changing quickly and in unpredictable ways. As the rules changed, our colleagues and clients were overwhelmed with the demands and emotions of uncertainty.

In this ever-changing and unpredictable context, we realized how we and our clients were facing problems that were intractable, systemic, and massively entangled. In the literature, such complex challenges are referred to as wicked issues (Stein, 2018). Wicked issues have many stakeholders, no root causes, and no possibility of solution. Classic examples include poverty and social justice. We now add global pandemic to the long list of persistent and pervasive wicked issues.

To address the wicked issues we and our community faced in this emerging environment, we drew on and adapted a method we had found helpful when we were face to face in simpler circumstances. This method merges Adaptive Action, Pattern Logic, and Inquiry into a simple facilitation process to invite transformative learning and address the wicked issues people face in times of COVID-19 adaptation.

The Power of Questions process lasts 20 minutes and can include any number of participants. It begins with one person naming a wicked issue. They do this in a short statement—no longer than three to five sentences. We found that little context was required, as each person in the group was able to see the issue and set it in context that was most useful to them.

Next, the group asks questions, but no one is allowed to give answers. The person who brought the wicked issue simply listens to the questions without responding. This sets conditions for reflection and encourages transformative learning for both the questioners and the listener.

Questioners are encouraged, and sometimes coached, to ask questions that are open-ended, expansive, and not disguised advice. Without instruction, the automatic reaction is to move into expert stance and give unwanted and inappropriate advice in response to the wicked issue. In this exercise, people are challenged to step outside their own assumptions and expectations to explore new patterns and options for inquiry. In this way, the process sets conditions for the questioners to move toward the self-organized critical point and transformative learning. One person commented, "I see your wicked issue in my own life. When I ask you questions it shines a light on new ways for me to see and act."

As the listener receives the questions, their relationship to the wicked issue shifts. At first, they want to answer the questions from their old worldview and defensive stance. When they are not allowed to respond, the patterns of their understanding begin to shift, and they see the issue differently. The patterns that held the problem in place are put under stress, tensions accumulate until patterns shift in unpredictable ways, and new insights and opportunities emerge. Participants describe the experience in many ways. "It was like an upside-down funnel. At first, I saw the problem through a narrow lens. As I heard the questions, the space opened up for me."

In the final step of the process, the person who presented the wicked issue is invited to reflect on their experience. What did they see? What did

710   G. H. EOYANG

they learn? Which questions were most provocative or useful? Finally, and most important, what will they do differently, given their new perspective and understandings?

Transformation of Thought and Action

We hosted 178 Power of Questions sessions between March 15 and September 1, 2020. Participants included leaders from health care, public health, education, government, philanthropy, education, international development, strategic consulting, software engineering, organization development, and social services. They have come from organizations and communities around the world and across multiple cultural boundaries. They have dealt with wicked issues that are personal and professional, urgent and important, individual and systemic. Each engagement has set conditions for participants to challenge the worldviews and assumptions that keep them stuck. As underlying mental models are challenged, the conditions that hold conceptual and behavioral patterns in place shift. Containers expand or contract. Differences are seen in surprising and inspiring ways. New exchanges are imagined, or old ones become less relevant. In the process, what appears to be an intractable wicked problem is converted into a pattern of possibility.

Transformative Learning

Each 20-minute Power of Questions session focuses a group on the locked-in patterns of one wicked issue. The inquiry challenges the assumptions and worldviews that constrict options for seeing and acting differently. In this process of transformational change, a narrow problem space is expanded to include new possibility of a solution space with more freedom and less constraint. Every session held the possibility for everyone who attended to experience unpredictable and significant change in understanding, attitude, and/or action. Even those who listened without asking questions reported seeing old problems in new ways and coming away with new options for action. At the beginning of the chapter, we shared wicked issue statements from participants in the Power of Questions sessions. We summarize the results of their inquiry experiences here.

Helene, the physical therapist from Basil, realized in the questioning that most of her patients were in physical contact with someone, even if it was not her. She began a training program to prepare clients' family members and friends to provide therapeutic and emotional support, when professional contact was impossible. She also realized that her colleagues must be facing the same challenge, so she started a regular discussion group for them to share ideas, empathy, and stories. In this way, she created an additional opportunity for change in another container and at another scale. Systemic, cross-scale change is a common characteristic of self-organized criticality and of transformative learning.

Hope, the teacher in Texas, redefined educational and lifetime success for her daughter and herself. As a result, she brought other parents together to share concerns and opportunities. Ultimately, they wrote a group letter to the school board listing their concerns and offering alternatives. She experienced a transformational change from helplessness and passivity into focused, collaborative action.

Sam engaged with the ambiguities of protest and privilege. He began to come to terms with the balance between peaceful and violent protest. He became more sensitive to what motivated the marchers. He also was sensitized to how others could feel threatened by the dynamics among protesters, counter-protesters, and police. He stepped outside of the need to judge either side. He paid more attention to what happens in parts of the world many recognize as true police states. He started becoming more sensitive to racial dynamics and the Black experience. At the same time, he shared the feeling of having one's property violated by looting. He began to understand the fear such conditions engender and the paranoid environment those conditions create. During the process, Sam's transformative learning shifted him from conceptual analysis of his complex situation toward a more nuanced and emotionally intelligent level of insight and action.

Laura's church established a series of reflection circles that encouraged people to drop in and connect with one another. She hosted a series of Power of Questions sessions with the group. The inquiry session prompted their realization that connecting with more people more often would enable them to know who might be grieving a loss and add the benefit of more ongoing support. Through Laura's intervention, the group shifted its focus from rescuing individual mourners to raising their environmental awareness for the whole community.

Elizabeth, the school principal, realized she might partner with community to solve her wicked problem of safe and effective on-site schooling. Churches and businesses in her neighborhood offered space and Internet access to accommodate the needs of her students and teachers. Her insights revolutionized her community's understanding of "educational institution."

As an entrepreneur, Maria engaged her employees to address their divided culture and fears of engagement. She conducted Power of Question sessions with staff, allowing them to voice and find possibility in the wicked issues they shared. This level of engagement with her staff was new to Maria. It challenged her leadership practice in ways she could not have predicted.

Paul found his green-hospital solution under his own roof. He realized there were already areas in hospitals that managed a variety of sterile environments. Operating rooms, for example, have policies and practices that isolate and also allow for interactions. He sent his team to interview surgeons and their teams to find out what they did and how they did it. Paul's intervention didn't just solve his problem, it also broke down organizational silos that had stifled transformational change for decades.

Transformative Practice

As these stories demonstrate, Power of Questions sets conditions for transformational change. It is an innovative approach to transformative learning for a variety of reasons. First, it is simple. Many approaches to transformational change or transformative learning are complicated, time consuming, and expensive. Power of Questions is none of those things. Second, one simple intervention sets conditions for multiple, unpredictable transformational changes. The transformations are many and varied because they depend on the tensions and patterns participants bring with them into the room. The process sets conditions, and the changes emerge from the current state of the system. Third, the Power of Questions serves as either a group or an individual practice. Participants quickly learned to apply the protocol to challenges in their personal and family situations.

Besides making progress on specific wicked issues, participants took the practices of inquiry into other contexts with teams, families, personal relationships, strategy development, and decision-making. They also noticed that they asked more useful questions, and went into inquiry more often, in their day-to-day practices. Finally, people expressed the freedom and hope they felt when they were able to move from feeling stuck, through transformative learning, and into a place of more generative possibilities.

In each of these cases, an issue was wicked because a pattern seemed to be locked in place by context and external forces. Through the process of inquiry, people were able to transcend their own habits of thought and action. They learned. They experienced transformation, at least they reported this outcome. They developed the capacity to set conditions for transformative learning, to tame a wicked issue, and to build confidence to face wicked issues that are sure to arise in the future.

Theoretical Transformation

In addition to the practical applications and implications of Power of Questions, this approach to transformative learning addresses a persistent theoretical challenge. Some argue that transformative learning is simply learning because all learning is summative. This leads to the theoretical distinction between transformative learning as different in degree and/or different in kind from run-of-the-mill learning. This distinction disappears in the world of self-organized criticality, where small changes do not add up to large changes. Rather, each change shifts the systemic pattern in unpredictable ways. Every change adds to the accumulating tension in the system to prepare it for changes to come. Through this lens, normal learning sets conditions for transformative learning, and transformative learning sets the stage for normal learning. The two are mutually dependent, but the distinction is critical to the practice of teaching and learning. Context and unpredictable, systemic results distinguish the one from the other. The system's readiness for transformational change or the learner's readiness for transformative learning determines whether or not transformation occurs. In this complexity-informed world view, transformation is in the mind of the transformed. The role of the leader, trainer, or change agent is to set conditions that might increase the direction and likelihood of transformational change when the system is ready for it (Patterson & Holladay, 2018).

The COVID-19 Power of Questions series has been quite useful in exploring this emergent nature of change and learning. Over time, patterns have begun to emerge among questions and across wicked issues. They have become a rich data source for exploring transformational change for individuals, institutions, and communities as well as transformative learning for individuals and organizations. Various research projects are currently using the DE Model to analyze how the issues and questions that emerge in the sessions relate to learning and change in

714   G. H. EOYANG

medical education, organizational change, public health practices, literacy, leadership development, American democracy, educational systems' adaptation to the pandemic, and educational leadership in these times. In all these contexts, the learning continues to be transformative.

Ongoing Inquiry

We have practiced power of individual and shared inquiry in a variety of settings over the past decade. It has always been useful to help people see and solve challenges that keep them stuck. In the extraordinary context of COVID-19, we have found new power and expanding relevance in this simple process, Power of Questions. At a time when transformational change was most needed, and its opportunities most constrained, this simple process set conditions for the tiny, but significant, changes that make a difference in peoples' lives today. It also built adaptive capacity that will serve participants well over the uncertainty and turbulence that is sure to emerge in the months and years to come.

We will continue to experiment with this process and to track where, how, and for whom it is most useful. In our own Adaptive Action cycle, as we practice Pattern Logic and Inquiry for ourselves, we are holding our next round of questions about transformational change and transformative learning.

- What patterns emerge among the wicked issues we have addressed? Is there a taxonomy or some standard definitions that can generalize the impact of Power of Questions beyond individual groups and their inquiry experiences?
- What are categories of questions that are most provocative and most likely to set conditions for transformative learning?
- How do individuals and groups develop inquiry skills over time?
- What are possible risks of the Power of Questions process? Where might it be contraindicated?
- What facilitation skills are needed to successful guide a Power of Question session?

We invite others to join us in this inquiry. The process is simple, and we have many recordings of live sessions you can review and analyze. As with all the HSD work, you are welcome to use it without further permission, but we ask that you cite our Web site (www.hsdinstitute.org) as the source and share back into the community what you learn from your own applications and inquiries. We look forward to an ongoing dialogue about the nature of self-organized criticality and transformational change for individuals and their institutions.

REFERENCES

Aron, D. C. (2020). Complex systems in medicine: A hedgehog's tale of complexity in clinical practice, research, education, and management. *Springer*. https://doi.org/10.1007/978-3-030-24593-1

Bak, P. (1999). How nature works: The science of self-organized criticality. *Copernicus*. https://doi.org/10.1007/978-1-4757-5426-1

Bogg, J. (2007a). Social theory and complexity. In J. Bogg & R. Geyer (Eds.), *Complexity, science and society* (pp. 149–164). CRC Press. https://doi.org/10.1201/9781315383132-10

Bogg, J. (with Willis, M.). (2007b). Art and complexity: Complexity from the outside. In J. Bogg & R. Geyer (Eds.), *Complexity, science and society* (pp. 5–10). CRC Press. https://doi.org/10.1201/9781315383132-2

Chandler, M. J. (2009). Piaget on Piaget. *British Journal of Psychology, 100*(S1), 225–228. https://doi.org/10.1348/000712609x414169

Davis, B., & Sumara, D. J. (2014). Complexity and education: Inquiries into learning, teaching, and research. *Routledge*. https://doi.org/10.4324/9780203764015

Elgin, J. N., & Sarkar, S. (1984). Quantum fluctuations and the Lorenz strange attractor. *Physical Review Letters, 52*(14), 1215–1217. https://doi.org/10.1103/physrevlett.52.1215

Eoyang, G. H. (2001). *Conditions for self-organizing in human systems* [Unpublished doctoral dissertation]. Union Institute and University.

Eoyang, G. H. (2009). *Coping with chaos: 7 simple tools* (2nd ed.). Human Systems Dynamics Institute.

Eoyang, G. H. (2011). Complexity and the dynamics of organizational change. In P. Allen, S. Maguire, & B. McKelvey (Eds.), *The Sage handbook of complexity and management* (pp. 319–334). Sage.

Eoyang, G. H., & Holladay, R. J. (2013). Adaptive action: Leveraging uncertainty in your organization. *Stanford Business Books*. https://doi.org/10.1515/9780804785402

Gershenson, C. (2010). Complexity at large. *Complexity, 16*(3), 1–5. https://doi.org/10.1002/cplx.20362

716 G. H. EOYANG

Human Systems Dynamics Institute. (2020). *Inquiry is the answer: COVID-19.* https://www.hsdinstitute.org/resources/inquiry-is-the-answer-covid-19-recordings.html

Kelso, J. A. S., & Engstrøm, D. A. (2008). *The complementary nature.* MIT Press.

Mandelbrot, B. B. (1993). *Fractal geometry in physics.* Yale University. https://doi.org/10.21236/ada273271

Newman, M. (2012). Calling transformative learning into question: Some mutinous thoughts. *Adult Education Quarterly, 62*(1), 36–55. https://doi.org/10.1177/0741713610392768

Patterson, L., & Holladay, R. (2018). *Deep learning ecologies: An invitation to complex teaching and learning.* Human Systems Dynamics Institute

Prigogine, I., Stengers, I., & Toffler, A. (2017). *Order out of chaos: Man's new dialogue with nature.* Verso.

Reynolds, C. W. (1987). Flocks, herds and schools: A distributed behavioral model. *ACM SIGGRAPH Computer Graphics, 21*(4). https://doi.org/10.1145/37401.37406

Stein, J. (with Rittel, H. W., & Webber, M. M.). (2018). Dilemmas in a general theory of planning. *Classic readings in urban planning* (pp. 52–63). https://doi.org/10.4324/9781351179522-6

Stollenwerk, N. (2005). Self-organized criticality in human epidemiology. *AIP Conference Proceedings, 779*(1), 191–194. https://doi.org/10.1063/1.2008613

Templeton, A., Drury, J., & Philippides, A. (2020). Placing large group relations into pedestrian dynamics: Psychological crowds in counterflow. *Collective Dynamics, 4.* https://doi.org/10.17815/cd.2019.23

CHAPTER 40

Emotions, Affective Neuroscience, and Changing One's Mind

Kathleen Taylor and Catherine Marienau

INTRODUCTION

Jack Mezirow's profound contributions to the still-evolving theory of transformative learning need no elucidation here. His well-known definition of transformative learning is "Learning that transforms problematic frames of reference to make them more inclusive, discriminating, reflective, open, and emotionally able to change" (Mezirow, 2009, p. 22). Although this definition could encompass cognitive and affective domains, Mezirow has been criticized for being overly focused on critical reflection and insufficiently attentive to emotions and feelings; thus, implicitly and in practice, emphasizing reason over emotion.

K. Taylor
Saint Mary's College of California, Moraga, CA, USA
e-mail: ktaylor@stmarys-ca.edu

C. Marienau (✉)
DePaul University, Oak Park, IL, USA
e-mail: cmariena@depaul.edu

© The Author(s), under exclusive license to Springer Nature   717
Switzerland AG 2022
A. Nicolaides et al. (eds.), *The Palgrave Handbook of Learning for Transformation*, https://doi.org/10.1007/978-3-030-84694-7_40

Mezirow (2000) located emotion, in passing, as occurring during self-examination, the second of ten phases of the transformative learning process. He later acknowledged that "transformation is often a difficult, highly emotional passage" (2009, p. 28) and invited others to explore what for him was new territory: how emotion, imagination, and intuition align with transformative learning.

Adult educators are responding to his invitation by paying increased attention to these elements. Topics such as "soul work" and "embodied narrative" appear in *The Handbook of Transformative Learning* (Taylor et al., 2012). In synthesizing various perspectives on transformative learning, Merriam and Baumgartner (2020), refer to emotions in embodied learning, noting that the body has been largely ignored as an integral part of the knowing system (p. 204).

In light of new neuroscientific discoveries, we focus first on the essential roles of emotions and the body-brain in transformative learning, and then briefly review findings of affective neuroscience with respect to the influence of emotions on thinking, learning, and decision-making. Three student vignettes illustrate how caring attention to the emotional states of adult learners can encourage learning that transforms. Finally, for adult educators seeking to apply the emerging science of emotion in their transformative practices, we feature John Heron's model of facilitating learning, which embodies key principles of affective neuroscience.

AFFECTIVE NEUROSCIENCE AND EMOTION-BASED LEARNING

What has been historically considered *mind* is essentially a complex system of neural pathways enabling the functions of the embodied brain. To illustrate, we first explore the role of the neuron.

A neuron is a passageway in the brain along the route of memory and perception, toward intention and action. It is the substrate of all human flourishing, ranging from simplest physical movement to most complex and abstract analysis, and from technical creativity to spiritual experience. As noted neuroscientist Eric Kandel (2007) observed: "The cellular mechanisms of learning and memory reside not in the special properties of the neuron itself, but in the connections it receives and makes with other cells in the neuronal circuit to which it belongs" (p. 142). As neural pathways are continually constructed and reconstructed, the (human) organism is drawn toward greater complexity of mind.

Though commonly associated with the brain, these neural networks traverse the entire body. Antonio Damasio (1999) explains, "Certain regions of the brain, which are *part of a largely pre-set neural system related to emotions*, send commands to other regions of the brain and to most everywhere in the body proper" (emphasis added, p. 67), triggering responses throughout. Thus, affective neuroscience refutes 400 years of Cartesian mind–body dualism, which sharply differentiates between the two. Descartes' philosophical declaration, "I think, therefore I am," stemmed from his mistrust of emotions prompted by the body's senses (for example, hunger or pain) as potentially misinforming and misdirecting what he regarded as the mind's higher cognitive functions, including thinking and rationality. Damasio (1994) not only identifies Descartes' fundamental error as "the separation of the most refined operations of mind from the structure and operation of a biological organism" (p. 250); he also finds that "mind is probably not conceivable without some sort of embodiment" (p. 234).

Affective Neuroscience Elaborates on This Connection:

Emotions, and the more biologically primitive drives that undergird them, such as hunger and sex, are action programs that have evolved as extensions of survival mechanisms. Put simply, emotions have evolved to keep us alive ....[They] are central to managing life [which] means managing not just our physical survival but our social life and intellectual life ... the emotions that regulate our sociocultural and intellectual lives appear to have co-opted the same neural systems that manage our survival in the most basic sense. (Immordino-Yang, 2016, pp. 18–19)

"We Feel, Therefore We Learn"

The consequences of these overlapping neural systems became evident as Damasio (1994) observed a neurosurgery patient, Elliott. Removing Elliott's tumor had required excising tissue that, it turned out, altered communications involving the limbic system, the so-called emotional brain. Not long after Elliott's apparently successful post-surgical recovery, unexpected problems emerged in his personal and professional relationships. He divorced and remarried twice in quick succession and was no longer an effective or dependable employee.

720   K. TAYLOR AND C. MARIENAU

Extensive psychological tests and assessments of perception, memory, and learning found no abnormalities. Intelligence and cognitive functioning remained above average. But, though Elliott could correctly categorize informational elements of a problem, he could not establish a values system that would lead toward problem-solving. He could understand and accurately describe the content of complex documents at work, but without access to the emotional centers of his brain he could not construct an organizing principle that would enable him arrive at a meaningful judgment. Damasio's evocative summary: "Elliott's predicament [w]as *to know but not to feel*" (original emphasis, 1994, p. 45).

Eagleman (2015) cites the comparable case of Tammy, a former engineer whose brain was damaged in a motorcycle accident. The affected region normally assures that the "brain is in constant feedback with the body" (p. 120). However, Tammy's traumatic brain injury left her unable to receive these embodied signals.

> Although she can describe all the pros and cons of a choice in front of her, even the simplest situations leave her mired in indecision. Because she can no longer read her body's emotional summaries, decisions become incredibly difficult for her. Now, no choice is tangibly different from another. (p. 120)

These examples illustrate that "Emotions are, in essence, the rudder that steers thinking" (Damasio & Immordino-Yang, 2007, p. 28), thus, we add, substantive meaning making. While cognitive function is possible without emotion, effective application of the embodied system—real world decision-making followed by appropriate action—is impossible without emotions. Emphasizing the interdependence of cognition and emotions, Immordino-Yang (2016) notes, "It is literally neurobiologically impossible to build memories, engage complex thoughts, or make meaningful decisions without emotions" (p. 18).

With regard to learning, affective neuroscience specifies that "we feel, therefore we learn" (Damasio & Immordino-Yang, 2007). This is in stark contrast to the conventional, early cognitive science view that emotions impair learning by muddying rational thinking. It has become clear that "Cognition is embodied ... you think with your body, not just your brain" (Kahneman, 2011, p. 51).

Though the person doing the thinking is unaware of it, between initial experience and ultimate awareness, the embodied brain organizes, connects, and reconstructs a lifetime of analogical memory traces—which includes associated body-states (Taylor & Marienau, 2016). In this way, we eventually arrive at what appears to us as thought. But as David Gelertner (1994), a leading figure in artificial intelligence, observes, people have to stop thinking they can separate emotional from rational: "Emotions are not ... an additional cognitive bonus, [they] are *fundamental* to thought" (p. 47).

It is now widely accepted among cognitive scientists that "the body plays a constituent role in in cognition, that is, cognition depends directly on the body as a functional whole and not just the brain" (Thompson, 2017, p. xxvi). Thus, affective neuroscience confirms that without emotion, our embodied brains cannot accomplish their most meaningful functions.

Adult Learners' Stories of Transformation

The findings of affective neuroscience may make Mezirow's (1991) aims for transformative learning more achievable by offering adult educators deeper understanding of the central role emotions play in changing one's mind.

Carrie's Story

Carrie, a white woman in her early fifties, moved successfully through her graduate studies when focusing on her professional expertise, sales training. But she hit the proverbial wall over one program requirement—to *engage in reflective practice*; that is, to make her own experience the focus of inquiry. Carrie's instructor for the required reflective practice seminars tried various discussion and essay prompts designed to help students self-reflect.

Even so, Carrie confided that the prospect of having to write about herself made her feel jittery, sick to her stomach, and overwhelmed. In response to a critical incident assignment she felt "My mind just shuts down. I can't think of anything." In an evocative image assignment, Carrie chose a picture of a woman on a tightrope above a deep crevasse, yet could not write down her feelings about that image or what it meant to her. Carrie sometimes shared her frustration with classmates: "I can't get my own voice to tune in!" She felt upset, ashamed, and emotionally exhausted and struggled with the urge to "run away," meaning drop out of the program.

Carrie's problem perplexed her peers, instructors, and mentor, and also herself. In classes, she was known as an articulate speaker: eager to voice her perspectives and share insightful stories about her experiences as a salesperson in the field. She could also write intelligently about leadership models and sales techniques, but not about how this content might relate to knowing herself or informing her practice.

Carrie's mentor chose to relax the written requirement for reflective essays and to focus on her demonstrated ability to speak her mind. Carrie began tape-recording her responses to critical incidents at work as they occurred. Initially, Carrie and her mentor listened together for Carrie's reflections within these descriptions. Soon, Carrie could identify the most salient moments and reflect on their meaning. She was ultimately able to compose an impressive portfolio of her learning journey and also came to appreciate her capacity for reflecting on her practice.

Shirley's Story

An African-American woman in her late forties when she returned to college, Shirley had grown up in what she described as a "strict Bible-teaching and -adhering household." As the AIDS crisis made headlines in the San Francisco Bay Area where she then lived, the Minister of her church increasingly denounced gay people as sinful and deserving of eternal damnation. Then, unexpectedly, a White male friend from work—someone who had emotionally supported Shirley through a painful divorce—revealed to her that he was gay and dying of AIDS. Shirley's initial reactions had included horror and disbelief.

Shirley remembered herself questioning *how this could be?*—that a man she trusted unreservedly, whose inherent kindness and goodness were beyond question, was also rejected and reviled by her church? It was impossible that this gentle, nurturing man was inherently evil and destined for hell. Now, for a course assignment that required reflection on meaningful shifts in one's self-understanding, Shirley wrote about having come to a gut-wrenching decision: "it was up to me [not the church] to decide what my beliefs were or not." She also described how that had led to the "exhilarating and liberating [discovery] that something I struggled with so desperately because of my love for God, would ultimately draw me closer to... the essence of Jesus and his teachings."

Instructor feedback helped Shirley consider how these significant changes in her feelings may have affected other areas of her life. Ultimately, this led to the more comprehensive awareness that African-Americans' feelings of being excluded, considered "less than," or in some cases being blatantly discriminated against in a racist society, were parallel to those of her gay friend in a homophobic society.

Jim's Story

For Jim, a Latino, returning to college in his early forties to complete a bachelor's degree was a highly emotional decision. He described growing up in the barrio in difficult circumstances, and an adolescence that included gang membership and run-ins with the law. If not for the intercession of a kindly priest, he might have spent years in prison or perhaps not have made it to adulthood. Now married with three children, he had become a counselor to young gang members and remained devoted to the church and its teachings that had guided him to this nearly miraculous outcome.

Although Jim's academic record clearly demonstrated his scholastic abilities, being back in school caused him great anxiety. In an early assignment, an educational autobiography, Jim explained: "I had heard that upper-level education could threaten my belief system and cause me to doubt my established truths. This was a major concern to me as my entire being revolves around my Creator." Fortunately, when Jim wrote about this apprehension, his instructor reassured him in a marginal comment: "God can handle it."

As the course progressed, and with consistent emotional reassurance from his peers and instructor, something began to shift for Jim. He found himself able to work through his own reactions to issues that had earlier seemed too threatening to consider. For example, though he saw that the church had saved him by instilling in him a new moral compass, he found himself willing to define and assert his own moral compass. "I don't want to believe in God because someone else told me that I should," he wrote. "I want to believe in God because *I* believe in Him...The point is that I am searching for myself, not my created self that is based on others' perceptions."

Summary

These emotion-laden stories illuminate aspects of Mezirow's second phase in the transformational process, following the disorienting dilemma: "self-examination with feelings of fear, anger, guilt, or shame" (2000, p. 22). Each adult was dismayed by experiences or expectations that seemed to call into question aspects of who they knew themselves to be. As is often the case, some also had to contend with socio-historical surrounds that act powerfully to maintain distorted perspectives.

As the vignettes also illustrate, such anxieties can be assuaged both by instructors and mentors who actively acknowledge the emotional upheaval and by a peer group that accepts and encourages each member's viewpoints (Janik, 2005). "The social process of perspective transformation... [including testing] new perspectives on friends, peers, and mentors... can be vitally important in making transformation possible" (Mezirow, 1991, p. 185). Ultimately, being able to change their minds meant seeing themselves and the world around them differently.

TRANSFORMATIVE LEARNING AND HERON'S MODEL

As we now turn to focus on how practitioners can use emotional awareness to facilitate adult learners' transformative experiences, we consider the work of John Heron. In emphasizing the foundational importance of emotion and imagination in learning, he anticipated the findings of modern affective neuroscience and built a philosophy and practice that align with what twenty-first century brain science continues to discover.

The Genius of John Heron

The definitional characteristic of *genius* is originality and brilliance that leads to new ways of seeing and understanding; essentially, to paradigm shift. Over the decades that John Heron (1992, 1999) put forward a new philosophical approach to psychology and human inquiry, the prevailing paradigms for understanding and explaining how the brain works were first, behaviorism, then cognitive science and the computational-processing philosophy of mind: "The dominant model of the brain in early cognitive science was that of a stimulus-driven, sequential processing computer" (Thompson, 2017, p. xix).

Heron proposed a theory and practice based on a different premise: one in which affective experience—and by extension, an embodied brain—is the foundation of knowing. When cognitive science caught up with this reality, emotions were no longer relegated to the fringes of research and considered distractions from the brain's highly valued cognitive activities and capacities, such as learning, problem-solving, and decision-making. These realizations sparked the current expansion of the field of affective neuroscience.

Even before this, Heron continued to refine his philosophical and psychological theories about the essentiality of emotion (1992) and detailed myriad applications that practitioners could understand and use effectively (1999). His overarching purpose continues to be creating learning environments that support and encourage human flourishing: helping people grow and thrive while contributing to the well-being of others (Heron & Reason, 1997).

The Extended Epistemology

As defined by the ancient Greeks, classical epistemology focuses on knowing (*episteme*) through reason (*logos*). In Heron's framework, rather than relying predominantly on the conceptual, intellectual approach, the extended epistemology integrates four ways of knowing that are "manifest in a whole array of skills and competencies—spiritual, psychic, aesthetic, intellectual, political, interpersonal, emotional, technical, clinical, etc." (Heron, 2002, n.p.).

Taken as a whole, these honor the fact that all body-brains exist within sociocultural, physical, and psychic environments that inform aspects of cognition. Furthermore, the brain is fundamentally an organ of *direction*—encouraging movement toward whatever is life-sustaining and away from that which is life-threatening. To discern the difference, the body-brain relies on memory traces created during emotional arousal. The resulting neural networks record body changes that the experience elicited, such as rapid heartbeat, shallow breathing, rush of hormones, and so on—what neuroscientists define as emotion (Damasio, 1999). How we identify these emotions—if we become conscious of them as feelings— depends on the continuous feedback loop of current and prior embodied experience, each informing and adjusting to the other.

For example, rapid heartbeat, shallow breathing, and a rush of hormones may be associated with an automobile accident. They may also be associated with a romantic experience. Each of these experiences includes other embodied associations: the smell and sounds of screeching tires; the smell and sounds of a soft summer evening. Countless neural networks are involved; what happens next depends on emotional arousal and valence: How strong is the association? Does it signal *toward* or *away*? This complex series of interactions operates continuously, as they are essential to the body-brain's primary purpose of self-preservation. However, in most learning environments, the elicited feelings go unnoticed during the conscious process of meaning making. Given what is now understood about the interdependence of emotion and meaning, we explore Heron's extended epistemology.

Adult educators are likely familiar with three of Heron's four ways of knowing: *experiential, propositional*, and *practical*. We focus here on *presentational* and the philosophical implications of Heron's framework as a whole: "this integral account of learning puts an end to the Aristotelian doctrine of intellectual excellence as the supreme educational end" (Heron, 2002, n.p.).

Heron's (1999) tree metaphor (Fig. 40.1) illustrates how his *up*-hierarchy differs from the traditional down-hierarchy, where higher positions control and, in effect, rule those below. The up-hierarchy "works from below upwards, like a tree with roots, a trunk, branches and fruit... [with] the higher branching and flowering out of, and bearing

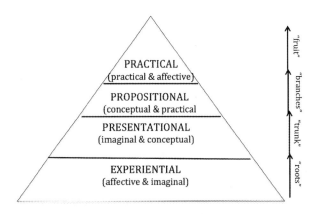

Fig. 40.1 Adapted from Kasl and Yorks (2012, p. 508) and Heron (1999, p. 46)

the fruit of, the lower" (p. 46). The lowest and broadest level—experiential knowing—is the foundation from which everything else emerges. For the brain, experience is not merely something happened. It immediately explores *how is this experience like other experiences?* Neuroscience now affirms Heron's insight that affective traces are *first* routed through networks in which the body-brain relies on "the imaginal mind going through metaphorical drift and [symbolic] association" (p. 81).

What happens next in terms of learning depends on the nature of the experiential prompt and how the adult is directed to attend to the experience. As Iain McGilchrist (2019) notes, the brain's built-in hemispherical differences are a major factor in that response; furthermore, "attention is the basis of our experience of the world....[and] the type of attention we pay determines *what it is we see*" (italics original, p. 16). Though the left and right hemispheres (LH and RH) always work together, their collaboration is limited by the distinct attitudes and approaches each brings to the task.

The RH attends first to the unfamiliar, such as whatever is symbolic, non-literal, and inferential. It concentrates on images, feelings, sensations, and inductive reasoning and is highly attuned to big picture and context. The LH attends quickly to whatever is already known. Alerted to the familiar, it concentrates on literal meaning, logic, and reductive reasoning, and focuses on detail. In essence, the RH imagines possible associations and the LH categorizes them, limited by what it has the syntactic language to articulate.

Presentational Knowing in Practice

When the educator begins with verbal and analytical experiential prompts, she engages the adult's LH semantic networks, which by default direct the adult's associative process toward rational, verbal interpretation (Giannoti, 2014). Thus, the LH will quickly hone in on established neural elements of the experience while missing related but unfamiliar aspects of the whole. Having done so, the self-referential LH will also tend to ignore further RH input, because its narrower perspective is not able to grasp the broader relevance; it is therefore "disinclined to change its mind" (McGilchrist, 2019, p. 21).

By contrast, an educator who uses symbolic or imaginal prompts to activate an adult's experience preferentially engages the RH's affinity for what is not yet known. If the adult's attention is also explicitly directed to non-verbal presentation of the feelings the experience evoked, the RH will have time to pursue unexpected—perhaps deeper and more creative—associations before the more dogmatic LH takes over. McGilchrist (2019) notes that putting emotion, imagination, and intuition in the center of the learning process gives the brain more opportunity to understand different ways "of being in the world [rather than merely]" "thinking about the world" (p. 23).

Heron's presentational knowing specifically foregrounds emotion, imagination, and intuition and provides a channel for exploration of such symbolic meanings. Yorks and Kasl (2002) underscore the

> pivotal role of presentational knowing—the intuitive grasp of the significance of imaginal patterns as expressed in graphic, plastic, moving, musical, and verbal art forms. Presentational knowing provides a bridge between the extralinguistic nature of felt experience, which an individual cannot directly communicate, and the ideas communicated through propositional knowing which is the mode of discourse. (p. 187)

Thus, presentational knowing offers a passageway to otherwise hidden associations that enrich the subsequent emergence of conceptual (discourse) and practical (action-oriented) knowing. The experience of a symbolic prompt "provides a useful focus for the grounding of conceptual learning in the multivalent processes of symbolism, metaphor and analogy, in the deeper imagination" (Heron, 1996, p. 81).

For example, a practitioner might use a symbolic prompt to directly engage the adult's affective and imaginal responses to a concept, issue, or topic. This may include an artifact, or evocative images such as abstract or metaphorical visual representations (Taylor & Marienau, 2016). We generally use images gathered from print sources, such as magazines, or virtual online images. We avoid easily identifiable people, intention-directing words, and obvious connections, such as pictures of classrooms when the focus is learning. General purpose images include nature, animals, geography, design, people in ambiguous attitudes or settings, as well as ambiguous and abstract illustrations. Affective, imaginal responses may also be evoked by non-semantic verbal representations, such as poems, fables, and allegories.

Alternatively, rather than provide a prompt, an educator might ask adults to spontaneously create their own visual (or physical) representation of their feelings related to the topic question. Either option offers a springboard to presentational knowing. Moreover, this symbolic approach need not be limited to initial explorations. It also supports breakthrough with groups that have reached an impasse or may otherwise benefit from being reenergized by tapping into the rich and deep affective well.

In conclusion, as noted earlier, Mezirow's still-evolving theory of transformational learning has been criticized for being overly dependent on critical thinking—the cognitive dimension—and for minimizing the role of feelings. However, he also acknowledged that "most of the process of learning occurs outside of awareness and may include emotional, intuitive, symbolic, imaginistic, and/or contemplative modes of learning" (Cranton, 2006, p. 124).

Affective neuroscience supports such potentially transformational approaches as are embodied in Heron's work. Furthermore, especially with the goal of transformative learning in mind, educators will no longer view adults' "emotions as 'baggage' or 'barriers' to learning ... [as issues] to 'vent'... so they can get back to the 'business of learning'" (Dirkx, 2001, p. 67).

As our understanding of affective neuroscience has grown and we have more intentionally applied Heron's work to our practice, we have come to challenge the metaphor of *emotion-laden*, which suggests bowed down by a weight. We now reimagine emotion as a *reservoir* that can sustain life and growth, especially in times of drought.

Heron intends that, rather than an end unto itself, intellectual capacity be understood as only one aspect of a "self-generating culture, a society whose members are in a continuous process of learning and development, and whose forms are consciously adopted, periodically reviewed and altered in light of experience and deeper vision" (Heron, 1999, p. 317).

We find echoes of this in Mezirow's (2000) description of learning to think like an adult in terms of creating and sustaining democratic societies. He calls on educators to foster learning environments that encourage greater openness to others' beliefs and experiences, the capacity to change one's mind, and actions more informed by deeper self-understanding. These outcomes, he suggests, are more likely to meet the goals of transformative adult education.

References

Cranton, P. (2006). *Musings and reflection on the meaning, context, and process of transformative learning: A dialogue between John M. Dirkx and Jack Mezirow*, 4(2), 123–139. Sage.

Damasio, A. (1999). *The feeling of what happens: Body and emotion in the making of consciousness*. Harcourt Brace.

Damasio, A. (1994/2005). *Descartes' error: Emotion, reason, and the human brain*. Penguin.

Damasio, A., & Immordino-Yang, M. H. (2007). We feel, therefore we learn: The relevance of affective and social neuroscience to education. *Brain, Mind and Education*, 1(1), 3–10. Wiley. https://doi.org/10.1111/j.1751-228X.2007.00004.x

Dirkx, J. (2001, Spring). The power of feelings: Emotion, imagination, and the construction of meaning in adult learning. In S. Merriam (Ed.), *The New Update on Adult Learning Theory, 2001*(89), 63–72. Jossey-Bass. https://doi.org/10.1002/ace.9

Eagleman, D. (2015). *The brain: The story of you*. Pantheon Books.

Gelertner, D. (1994). *The muse in the machine*. Free Press.

Gianotti, G. (2014). Why are the right and left hemisphere conceptual representations different? *Behavioural Neurology*. https://doi.org/10.1155/2014/603134

Heron, J. (1992). *Feeling and personhood: Psychology in another key*. Sage.

Heron, J. (1996). Helping whole people learn. In D. Boud & N. Miller (Eds.), *Working with experience: Animating learning*. Taylor & Francis.

Heron, J. (1999). *The complete facilitator's handbook*. Kogan Page. https://www.educacionymedioscolaborativos.org/sites/default/files/complete_facilitators_handbook.pdf

Heron, J. (2002, July 22–24). *Our process in this place* [Keynote speech on July 24]. International Conference on Organisational Spirituality: "Living Spirit—New Dimensions in Work and Learning," University of Surrey. http://www.human-inquiry.com/Keynote2.htm

Heron, J., & Reason, P. (1997). A participatory inquiry paradigm. *Qualitative Inquiry*, 3(3), 274–294.

Immordino-Yang, M. H. (2016). *Emotions, learning, and the brain: Exploring the educational implications of affective neuroscience*. W.W. Norton & Co.

Janik, D. (2005). *Unlock the genius within: Neurobiological trauma, teaching, and transformative learning*. Rowman & Littlefield.

Kahneman. D. (2011). *Thinking fast and slow*. Farrar, Straus, and Giroux.

Kandel, E. (2007). *In search of memory: The emergence of a new science of mind*. W.W. Norton & Co.

Kasl, E., & Yorks, L. (2012). Learning to be what we know: The pivotal role of presentational knowing in transformative learning. In E. Taylor, P. Cranton &

Associates (Eds.), *The handbook of transformative learning: Theory, research, and practice*. Jossey-Bass.

McGilchrist, I. (2019). *Ways of attending: How our divided brain constructs the world*. Routledge.

Merriam, S., & Baumgartner, L. (2020). *Learning in adulthood: A comprehensive guide* (4th ed.) Jossey-Bass.

Mezirow, J. (2000). Learning to think like an adult: Core concepts of transformation theory. In J. Mezirow & Assoc. (Eds.), *Learning as transformation: Critical perspectives on a theory in progress* (pp. 3–33). Jossey-Bass.

Mezirow, J. (1991). *Transformative dimensions of adult learning*. Jossey-Bass.

Mezirow, J. (2002). *Transformative learning: Theory into practice*. Jossey-Bass.

Mezirow, J. (2009). Transformative learning theory. In J. Mezirow, E. Taylor & Associates (Eds.), *Transformative Learning in Practice*. Jossey-Bass.

Taylor, E., Cranton, P., et al. (2012). *The handbook of transformative learning: Theory, research and practice*. Jossey-Bass.

Taylor, K., & Marienau, C. (in press). Minding the brain: The emotional foundations of adult learning. In A. Belzer & B. Dashew (Eds.), *Meeting adult learning needs: Learning contexts, adult learners, and instructional approaches*. Stylus.

Taylor, K., & Marienau, C. (2016). *Facilitating learning with the adult brain in mind: A conceptual and practical guide*. Wiley.

Thompson, E. (2017). Introduction. In F. Varela, E. Thompson, E. Rosch & J. Kabat-Zinn (Eds.), *The embodied mind, revised edition: Cognitive science and human experience*. MIT Press.

Yorks, L., & Kasl, E. (2002). Toward and theory and practice of whole person learning: Reconceptualizing experience and the role of affect. *Adult Education Quarterly, 52*(3), 176–192.

CHAPTER 41

Living Transformation: The Alchemy of Change in an Epochal Shift

Elizabeth A. Lange

TRANSFORMATIVE LEARNING IN AN EPOCHAL SHIFT

Ideas of transformation are as old as humanity. Acknowledging the preceding giants who helped theorize Western concepts of transformative learning, we need to advance our thinking and perceiving further, expanding attention beyond epistemological transformation, to rise to the challenges of the global epochal shift before us.

This epochal shift is now visible on multiple fronts: The Occupy movement addressing class divisions and massive accumulation of wealth by a few; the #MeToo movement addressing gender disparity and harm; the Black Lives Matter movement addressing racial inequity; the Climate Strikes and other environmental movements giving voice to climate change and environmental despoliation; and the Global Indigenous Rights movements such as Idle No More, Standing Rock, Water Defenders and Amazon Defenders all addressing ongoing colonization in

---

E. A. Lange (✉)
University of Technology Sydney, Ultimo, Australia
e-mail: info@elizabethlange.ca

© The Author(s), under exclusive license to Springer Nature   733
Switzerland AG 2022
A. Nicolaides et al. (eds.), *The Palgrave Handbook of Learning for Transformation*, https://doi.org/10.1007/978-3-030-84694-7_41

734   E. A. LANGE

the global dispute over land access to "resources" that literally fuels the old Industrial Era.

(Re)emerging relational theories from quantum science, posthumanist social science, as well as Ancient, Indigenous, and non-Western philosophies all have substantial implications for the transformative learning field. This paper recaps key findings from quantum science, as part of the Relational Turn, and then turns to alchemy and Indigenous rites of passage, as ancient arts of transformation. Then, data from a transformative sustainability education process will be re-examined for new insights into transformative learning.

Relational Reality

Transformative learning from within a relational ontology is the organic confluence of many thought streams about the nature of reality—quantum physics, living systems theory, consciousness theory, process philosophy, complexity theory, transdisciplinarity, posthumanism, and post-anthropocentrism. Called the Relational Turn, there is a revolution occurring in multiple fields that is reshaping our Western cosmology (understanding of the universe), ontology (way of being), epistemology (way of knowing), and axiology (values and ethics) (Barad, 2007; Spretnak, 2011; Thayer-Bacon, 2003, 2017).

The term relationality is not referring to social relationships, as commonly used. Rather, it refers to a relational understanding of existence, as demonstrated by quantum physics and living systems theory (Capra & Luisi, 2014). In contrast, the current Newtonian ontology sees separation and mechanism as the basis of reality, seeing "independent objects with inherent boundaries and properties," part of reductionism (Barad, 2007, p. 333).

Quantum science fundamentally challenges many of the taken-for-granted understandings and dichotomies that have shaped the trajectory of modern thinking (Zohar, 1990). Quantum scientists experienced an existential disorientation as these findings upended what they knew. As Niels Bohr said, "Anyone who is not shocked by quantum theory has not understood it" (in Wheatley, 2006). David Bohm (1980) explains this challenge,

Being guided by a fragmentary self-world view, humans then act in such a way as to break themselves and the world up, so that all seems to correspond to this way of thinking. We overlook the fact that ... this mode of thought ... has brought about the fragmentation that now seems to have an autonomous existence, independent of human will and desire, ... defeating our deepest urges toward wholeness and integrity. (p. 3; revised for inclusive language)

Relationality means we understand reality as related at all levels, from the micro-quantum level to the macro-cosmos level. This is a dramatic perceptual shift in understanding the nature of reality, which is only now percolating into common understanding, after 100 years. Drawing simultaneously from David Bohm (1980), Danah Zohar (1990), Karen Barad (2007), Christian de Quincey (2010), and Fritjof Capra and Pier Luigi Luisi (2014), the key shifts have been:

- from understanding the universe as a void of separately existing objects with mechanical movements, to the unbroken wholeness of the universe as a complex network of flowing energy fields;
- from exploring the smallest material building blocks of the universe to interchangeability and impermanence, where electrons can show up either as material particles and/or as energy waves or both, dependent on and inseparable from the observer;
- from studying "things" to relations and processes;
- from the primacy of cause and effect, toward inseparability of observer and observed within a participative universe;
- from the certainty and measurability of the Newtonian universe, to uncertainty and approximations of likely behavior;
- from predictability, to constant change given constantly vibrating particles and fluctuating energy;
- from measuring objects in normal space–time, to quantum jumps, where objects appear in another place without traveling through space and time as normally conceived;
- from meaning as a human-based notion, to meaning as performed, where the intelligibility of the world intra-acts with human intelligibility;
- from separation of the parts, to nonlocality of connection where quasi-instant communication among parts of the whole does not adhere to time and space as normally conceived;

- from human exceptionalism whereby humans alone have consciousness, to consciousness all the way down to the smallest particle;
- from the perceived separation of Earth's organic and inorganic elements, to Earth as an integrated self-organizing and self-regulating system that provides optimal conditions for life to persist; and
- from understanding individual parts then extrapolating to the whole, to emergence where certain properties only emerge at higher levels of organization.

These scientific findings also confirm strands of ancient and Indigenous thought, opening up unforeseen possibilities for the retheorizing of transformative learning from multiple angles. One key intersection point is that transformation is a natural and continual part of Earth's existence and of human life, as perpetual self-renewal, not as an unusual occurrence.

Educational Relationality

Rooted in some posthumanist and post-anthropocentric theories, relationality in education departs from many commonly accepted assumptions. It does not start with the Newtonian notion of separate selves and isolated minds (Bache, 2008). It does not start with learners as the subject of individual transformation. It does not even start with subjects having a relation, as this is still subject-centered thinking. It does not start with the "didactical triad of student/teacher/content" (Ceder, 2015, p. 144), who meet in an educational space with the goal of knowledge accumulation or perhaps personal transformation. It also does not start from a certain kind of relation, i.e., an empathetic provocateur, as the desired outcome is still entity-based. It is also not about learning and behavior as causal, where a teacher causes student learning. Learning is not the "processes occurring inside the learning individual" (Ceder, 2015, p. 25). Each of these understandings is based on separation thinking.

Rather, "relationality … is the point of departure" (Ceder, 2015, p. 20). In relationality thinking, the "relations *are* the very condition for education" (p. 27, my emphasis; Barad, 2007). In a posthuman understanding, relations include humans and nonhumans, both with agency. Relations are not instruments, or to be used instrumentally, but relations are foundational for continual human becoming. In other words, all human and nonhuman relations are constantly making us.

In New Science, humans are "temporary constructs of relational flows … constantly moving" (Barad, 2007, p. 100). This is how we are entangled with the world. Decentering any subject or object as the starting point of education, the world becomes the starting point. "We are *of* the universe—there is no inside, no outside. There is only intra-acting from within and as part of the world in its becoming" (Barad, 2007, p. 396). In this view, learning is inherent in the becoming of humans and nonhumans, not the result of a technique or instrument.

Education, then, is not a goal, space, place, technique, or relation between people. Rather education is located within happenings and activities, as beings and things intra-acting back and forth; in every engagement involving people, nature, situations, physical objects, and media. For instance, when we meet in an educational space, we are communicating before anything is said: we are breathing together, we are touching chairs and tables and they are touching us, we are watching each other or looking out the window, and we are sensing the energy in the room. We are feeling a variety of emotions, perhaps drinking a beverage for our physical needs; all responses to the situation at a variety of embodied, conscious, and unconscious levels. Agency is not the aegis of the teacher or even of the student, but in where "things are happening" (Ceder, 2015, p. 123). We are already becoming in these relations, in a certain way, along a conscious-unconscious continuum.

Typically, a teacher intends to help students learn about pre-designed curriculum. Learning, as normally conceived, is where a change is said to have occurred if something was learned, demonstrated through measurement. Ceder (2015) suggests that in posthumanism, educational intention—or an idea with purpose—flows within a matrix of porous *natureculture*—our bodies, thoughts, feelings, what we just ate or drank, air quality, air temperature, memories, textbooks, and the trees through the window.

Ceder reframes learning as intelligibility, where we learn within the intelligibility of all that is around us in an ongoing, reciprocal way. Epistemology then is emergent; engaging in an educational activity with an openness to reciprocity—we affect and are affected. Within the science of a living universe, we can approach the classroom as living, within "a larger cosmic order" (p. 13). From within educational planning, we remain open to the substrate of the universe "waiting for an opportunity to manifest itself" (Bache, 2008, p. 12).

Prior to the Industrial era, learning happened alongside parents, extended family, and village members. Learning happened in the middle of an activity, which we now overlook as "only" informal learning. Learning is intra-acting intelligibility: such as the berry bush's intelligibility through a growth response after berries are picked; deer habits and the deer's choice to give when asked for human need; the aliveness and responsiveness of soil to hoeing, seeding, and weeding; and the meaning of a story told within preparations for a traditional feast. The relationing imparts its own intention and direction to the moment, when the deer escapes or the soil is hard clay, to which we then respond. Barad calls this a shift toward "matters of practices/doings/actions" (2007, p. 802).

If learning is the world's intelligibility, then education is a learning engagement that unveils this intelligibility. Knowing as intelligibility, already implies a responsibility, as reciprocal touching is a matter of response. In this view, ethics is not applied but is already embedded in our response-abilities. As Barad (2012) summarizes,

> in a breathtakingly intimate view, touching and sensing is what matter is doing, or rather, what matter is: matter as condensations of response-ability. Each of "us" is constantly constituted in response-ability, responsible for the other while touching the other. (p. 215)

In transformative learning, these concepts question not only what we consider to be the starting point and the locus of knowing, but our notions of causality and ethics. As Barad explains, "there are no singular causes. And there are no individual agents of change. Responsibility is not ours alone. Responsibility entails an ongoing responsiveness to the entanglements of self and other, here and there, now and then" (p. 394). As Barad implies (2007), the past is never done ... which brings us to alchemy.

ALCHEMY AND TRANSFORMATION

Stories, art, and writings from the Ancient and Classical worlds all illustrate the fascination with which humans have regarded the processes of transformation. One of the historical forerunners of transformation processes is alchemy. Alchemy has been a main current within Eastern and Western esotericism. The older origins of Western alchemy are situated in the mystery cults and their rituals, from the Mithraic mysteries in Persia and later in Rome, to the Egyptian mysteries, and then the Eleusian mysteries in Greece. Paracelsus, writing during the Renaissance, suggests that alchemy is the art of separating what is useful from what is not, by transforming it into ultimate matter and essence, both a material and spiritual process.

Jungian scholar Marie-Louise von Franz explains that Western alchemy emerged from both pre-Socratic and pre-Christian Classical Greek philosophy. Later, it would become the province of Christian scholars, such as Saint Germain (1985), where God was the great alchemist. Typically, alchemy included fostering the highest of human qualities including wisdom and purity of purpose, as part of spiritual chemistry (St. Germain, 1985). Kingsley (2020) explains that early science was originally conceived as emanating from mystical knowing, not rationalism, by learning in a state of stillness "achieved 'during deep meditation, ecstasies, or dreams'" (p. 45). Good research still involves such spaciousness and intuitive knowing, as evident in the stories of Einstein, Watson and Crick, and McClintock.

Von Franz (1979/1997) summarizes, "The really great and creative scientists have the same motivation as the alchemists: to find out more about that spirit or divine substance or whatever you may call it, which lies behind all existence" (p. 13). Early scientists understood that "the mystery of the structure of the universe, [is reflected] in themselves, in their own bodies and in that part of their personality which we call the unconscious," a unified view of reality (p. 10). This is captured in the alchemical axiom: As above, so below. Thus, science, philosophy, psychology, and spirituality were all seeking the same understandings. When science limited itself to the objective, material world, the others developed into siloed disciplines (Marshall, 1995).

Alchemy was rejuvenated in the modern age by Jung who identified two kinds of alchemy, the extraverted and introverted. Extraverted or outer alchemy evolved into chemistry, engaging the transformation of metals such as gold from lead, medicine, and pharmacology. Yet, Jung considered the true alchemy to be the introverted or inner alchemy, the "transformation of the alchemist" (von Franz, p. 37). As alchemists claimed, if you involve yourself with transformative processes, be prepared to be transformed, as were the quantum scientists. Von Franz says, "the true searchers among the alchemists, said:... I am seeking a higher gold, the true gold ....[they] wanted to discover in themselves, as in matter, the mystery of transformation" (p. 19).

740   E. A. LANGE

Briefly, there are several principles present in Western and Eastern alchemy that cohere with quantum science. The first is that the universe is part of a whole or what is now called a unified field. The second is that transformation at one level resonates at other levels of reality. The third is that there is a liminal or chaos stage in the transformation process as well as a dying of one form, even in metals, before another emerges. The fourth is that reality is constant change, and that there is a force or energy that flows through all things.

So, what we are about follows a long, rich, and mysterious history, with these early understandings forgotten in the privileging of Western rationality. It is time to move past separation and mechanist thinking as it manifests in our theorizing, to reengage such earlier insights.

Indigenous Rites of Passage and Transformation

Another source of knowledge about transformation is held among Indigenous people. While much knowledge was brutally eradicated during colonization, fragments still exist and are being reclaimed. Indigenous people have long understood the energetic fabric of the universe and the plasticity of time, space, and matter (Allen, 1992).

Indigenous rites of passage, notably from adolescent to adult, have two purposes. Not only are individuals integrated into adult roles, it is transformation as a type of second birth. It involves continually moving toward a higher level of human character and learning to walk in a sacred manner, coming to understand the spirit world and material world as one reality (Cajete, 1999). This process is less a Mezirowean series of linear, epistemological developments, than movements in a complex, spiraling process of wholistic becoming.

In the context of initiation, transformation is ritualized according to the ancient death/rebirth archetype. Drawing partially from McWhinney and Markos (2003) and Waters (1950) regarding Navajo healing rituals, as well as other Indigenous teachers, there is a spiraling of change until one breaks through into the next cycle. A person begins another transformation process, perhaps addressing a different life facet or occurring at a different time of life. This nonlinear process generally includes these elements:

- Crisis—similar to the disorienting dilemma, crisis entails some form of loss, and establishes conditions which can foster an expansion of awareness;
- Disassembly—a ritual death process involving a retreat from daily life (physical separation), suspension of habitual patterns (psychic separation), and a cleansing process of identities and negative forces (emotional separation);
- Digestion/Metabolism—the passage into a liminal zone or womb of rebirth, in an alchemical process of breaking down and digesting what does not work and metabolizing it into something more life-giving; such a ritual may include a quest or challenging journey under the guidance of a mentor(s); and
- Reconstitution, Rebirth, and Integration—a reconstituting or coagulating of one or more facets—the emotionbody, energybody, physicalbody, psychebody, and cognitivebody—rebirthed into a different form; then prepared for reentry where the new form is toughened for the rigors of daily society.

Similar to quantum science, McWhinney and Markos (2003) assert, "This is the ultimate goal of transformative education: to live in perpetual self-renewal" (p. 30), embracing a process of dynamic change. This is far more wholistic, relational, and process-oriented than Mezirow theorized.

Importantly, the alchemy of the digestion/metabolism/ reconstitution process involves the energetic level. As biologist James Oschman states, "Energy is the currency in which all transactions in nature are conducted" (in Church, 2018, p. 11). Our mind, body, and skin are permeable boundaries in which energy and information flow back and forth in relation to all other beings and elements. In other words,

> consciousness—directed by intention, working through energy fields—can produce radical changes in matter ... [from] atoms and molecules. Scaling up, it can change matter at the level of cells, organs, and bodies. Getting bigger still, it can change social groups and even whole countries .... When you change your mind [thought structures which organize perception], sending new signals through the neural pathways of your brain, altering the energy fields all around you, interacting with the fields of others, you have no idea how far the effect might travel. (in Church, 2018, pp. 22, 23, 27)

742   E. A. LANGE

Generally, your body's electromagnetic field extends about five yards or meters from your body. Persons within that range are interacting with your field. Even saying nothing, your energy fields are shaping each other in an invisible dance of communication (Frey, 1993 in Church, 2018, p. 12). Further, Bache (2008) suggests that there is a field of consciousness resonating in a classroom. De Quincey (2005) explains, the rational search for truth can block the educator's attunement to this field.

Thus, the transformative process goes far beyond the cognitive domain, as an embodied, spiritual, psychic, social, and energetic process, which Mezirow intuited at times but did not theorize. Complexity theory and systems biology (Gleick, 1987) describe the change process as reaching a threshold of critical instability, or tipping point, where the system bifurcates, either completely breaking down or achieving a breakthrough, reaching a higher level of development, called emergence, as a higher level of self-organizing. This is not inevitable, as the organism can break down, continue in a broken state, or stay in perennial liminality. How might this look in education?

LEARNING RELATIONALITY, *LIVING* TRANSFORMATION

In the early 2000s, when I first gathered empirical data with 50 adult learners over several years—all participants in a transformative sustainability education course—I did not have adequate theoretical explanations for some aspects (Lange, 2001). Building from the multiple passageways described above, there is now a more adequate framework, briefly described below.

Crisis and intuitions of wholeness

All the study participants expressed arriving at a crossroad, prior to the course, often from simultaneous pressure points. Natalie described her divorce, mother's death, and an overwhelming new job causing her to rethink why she was living the way she was. Dan, undergoing a divorce, became the primary caregiver to his two children. With stretched finances, he was reassessing his cherished White picket fence principles and the societal norms of worthiness based on income. Kate arrived at a point where achieving personal independence, professional recognition, and material accumulation had lost purpose, often called a midlife crisis, just as her mother died of Alzheimer's disease. Sally was frustrated with the menial nature of her job in a status conscious society, the overwhelming household tasks in a traditional marriage, and burnout manifesting a life-threatening illness. Garth was asked to be complicit in unethical workplace practices, which felt like selling his soul; then, his daughter almost died in a car crash. Most of these adults were wrestling with realities that perforated personal and social illusions, prompting questions of: What is my purpose here? Why am I living like this? and Where am I going? They came into the learning space already in crisis, the conditions for a transformative learning opportunity.

Another challenge they expressed was being "seven different people" pulled in all different directions; trying to fit it all in; constant interruption never completing a task; guilt and sense of failure in attending to some things and not others; and the sense that one is never enough. This whirlwind of daily activity prevented any meaningful rest or focus, and the heavy workload led to profound exhaustion or burnout. Carrying feelings of frustration, anger, sense of exploitation, lack of reward, disillusionment, as well as sensing a lack of efficacy, had an emotional and body spillover effect. Sally echoed many, "How can I come away alive?" (p. 151). From this point, we explored how industrial society creates this fragmentation, with its machine metaphor of reality. It also made sense that participants unanimously expressed a yearning for balance.

The extent to which participants discussed wholeness was astonishing. When describing the texture of their lives, they wanted no disjuncture between who they were at home, at work, or anywhere else. They described that their whole being was not with them in their job, that they had to set aside parts of themselves to perform their work. They also intuited that mindfulness, stress relief, and other quick fix practices did not go deep enough. Workplace rhetoric about smarter work, task organization, or time management rang hollow. As Kay said, "I am a spiritual person, but ... it's got to be more an integrated process, that is beyond just prayer and meditation, but is part of just how your whole life goes" (p. 201). Intuitively, they were pointing to the whole.

They imagined a life not compartmentalized, where their identity was consistent with a sense of overarching purposefulness. They were indirectly identifying the impacts of separation thinking, dividing up life into work lives, home lives, volunteer lives, all with multiple identities and roles. They were also pointing to the mechanistic structures in society, where one must use the force of their will to hammer all the parts of individual and family life into a well-oiled, efficient machine. Rather than developing toward autonomy or rugged individualism, they were yearning for cosmological and ontological coherence—a place in the cosmos that provided meaning for being-in-the-world.

I realized that these were not random musings. Bohm (1980) writes,

> It is instructive to consider that the word 'health' in English is based on an Anglo-Saxon word 'hale' meaning 'whole'... roughly the equivalent of the Hebrew 'shalom' [and] the English 'holy'. ... All of this indicates that [humans] sense always that wholeness or integrity is an absolute necessity to make life worth living. ... [our] deepest urges [are] toward wholeness and integrity (p. 3).

That health, wholeness, and spirituality are profoundly linked is ancient wisdom. This intuition, carried in our DNA as an embodied memory, comes from a time when people lived in small, geographically rooted communities where a collective spirituality brought purpose to the smallest details of living.

So, in class, we started with the whole of relations. Largely through art, such as collage and paper sculpture, I asked them to describe all the entanglements of their many relations, feelings, and behaviors within this Western way of being. In a complementary task, they described ideas about how their way of being might be, using imaginal knowing which gave freedom for the collective unconscious to emerge. In this way, we all began sensing that we are part of a larger body-world. The curriculum emerged as we identified our messy complex of relations.

Disassembly—Death of illusions

Learners really struggled with "what society expects," including physical, material, and emotional independence, all symbolized by a house, car, well-paying job, mate, and perhaps kids. Yet many of them did not conform to this image. Disillusionment, as the ground between the ideal and real, had crept into the nooks and crannies of their lives. They were disillusioned with: doing a good job which was not recognized or rewarded; feeling the inability to make a difference; constant violation of personal ethics by big business operating principles; the importance of work which overtakes private time and energy; trade-offs which put personal and work values into conflict; material things which do not bring any lasting satisfaction but lots of debt and upkeep; and public life where they believed in voluntarism but had no life space for it or had a felt lack of efficacy to effect social change.

The word *illusion*, from the Latin *illudere*, means either to mock or deceive with a misleading image. The vision of Western life was becoming disenchanted. Many felt they had exchanged their soul for security, one of many trade-offs in adult life, thus losing power over one's essence and moral force. Many felt they had dedicated their intelligence, spirit, and desires toward a goal not of their own making, violating their own principles, and losing a sense of self.

Their desire to make a difference was not accompanied by any sense of agency. They struggled with the common equations: doing a good job equals rewards of salary, status, and sense of accomplishment; doing the right thing equals being valued; climbing the career ladder equals increasing autonomy; being a high performer equals respect; a job equals a site for self-expression; white picket fence image of family equals happiness, stability and material comfort; possessions equal wealth; and financial worth equals being a good person. They had assumed that by conforming to these messages they would be spared troubles.

Webster (1979) defines burnout as a situation in which "a tool or instrument is worn out by excessive or improper use so that its usefulness is exhausted, and it ceases to operate" (p. 325). The participants began to sense they were instruments in a Machine Era, continually being used up. They sensed that separation thinking divided up their lives and one person from another. Numerous participants indicated they would no longer persist in this "martyrdom" and all the physical and emotional pain it entailed. Surfacing and naming the illusions reduced suppression, allowing energy to re-emerge and disrupt, particularly in conversations with friends and family. Importantly, it freed up energy for change.

They moved into a soul-searching process, which is a ritual death, in questioning and cleansing habitual patterns of thought and behaviors which are no longer useful. This was augmented by class visits to people who lived by Earth-based values. In comparing these ways of living with their own illusions, they were activated to overcome fragmentation, including the roles they play and the masks they wear. Class participants started to breakthrough the hypnotism of cultural messages, including the notions of mastering relationships, executing life with efficiency, and filling daily life with incessant activity. They slowed their lives down and paid more attention to all relationships, strengthening some, distancing from others.

They began restorying their lives, finding more encompassing explanations that made sense of their chaos, frustration, and sense of obligation. Through deep listening to each other, they began finding a thread of a deeper purpose at work that they could not see earlier, deeper rhythms operating without conscious knowledge. Some began to redefine the principles corrupted by society, and others redefined materialistic lifestyles not as success but as theft from the Earth and participation in human exploitation. Seeing other individuals living with conviction and with conscious principles increased not only their own courage but their horizons of the possible. They began to construct a different way of looking at the world, including what balance and integrity might look like.

This process was not bloodless however … it was filled with angst, fear, anger, and even chaos, some directed at myself. There were constant challenges negotiating desired changes with loved ones, which we discussed, with more conscious enaction every week. There was much grieving for old understandings and behavior patterns, which kept reasserting themselves. There was a looming sense of disaster if they stepped out to make change. But, slowly, over the weeks, a synergy was created that began to breakthrough walls of resistance.

Digestion—Process Learning and the Natureculture Matrix

In process learning, knowledge and knowing are not static but always moving and revealing. Ideas are always circulating and emerging out of the implicate order, says Bohm. When you let go of emotional identifications associated with old patterns and become open and curious, boundaries become more permeable and new ideas do emerge. This is process learning, not knowledge acquisition. In this way, knowing and being are not separate, but lived and emergent; knowing is ontological as well as epistemological.

The learners examined the very patterns of their thinking, bequeathed to them by families and society. By doing less rational analysis and allowing for flow, flashes of insight, and intuitive leaps, learners went past habitual patterns toward deepest intentions.

Process learning is also the province of synchronicity as discussed by Jung, where there is "a coincidence in time of two or more causally unrelated events which have the same or similar meaning" (in de Quincey, 2005, p. 103). Learners often talked about improbable occurrences that had a meaningful connection and sense of hidden order. Dreams and visualization activities connected with powerful symbols and archetypes, from the Virgin Mary (Divine Feminine) to the dissolving of houses (boundaries of self) to wild birds (the wild self) and water crossings (transformation). This is evidence of the psyche digesting illusions and reforming them into something new.

Esteva and Prakash (1998) talk about communal individuality or re-rooting ourselves back into our social and natural relations. As Barad (2012) describes it, the ethics of responsibility and reciprocity already exist within the relation, we just need to recognize it. To do this, activities were undertaken that assisted adults in mapping their relations—from the origin of their drinking water, the origin of their food and clothing, to their ancestral relations. Sitting in the forest and breathing, feeling their way with bare feet on the Earth, laying in the tall prairie grass watching clouds, or blindfolded to hear the language of trees and leaves, all was immersive learning. They responded back and forth with coyotes in the evening air, participating in the language of a living universe. They felt their lived connections to all beings and elemental forces at various levels—mindbody, energybody, emotionbody, spiritbody as well as physical body. Dependence on the complex web of life was clear as it was embodied through various activities in the forest, not abstracted. Feelings of abundance, gratitude, and empathy spontaneously arose when re-embodiment within organic relations is felt. This is what is meant by radical relatedness—a sense of belonging to self, significant others, the natural world, and the larger human community (Lange, 2001).

They tried to imagine how they could use biomimicry in their working and living. Learners thought through all the ethical conflicts and where ethical efficacy could be enacted. This is what I call restorative learning—restoring a consciousness of relationality and restoring a sense of power within relationality. They began to reframe their meanings of financial security, success, working hard, stability, status, comfort of consumption, professional ideals, vocation, and spiritual growth. Kate said, "I guess ... I need to give myself time to 'heal' from my addictive habits," alongside experiences merging into meaningful new patterns.

Reconstitution, Rebirth, and Integration—Participative Engagement and Emergence

As they moved toward breakthrough, there was a rush of energy and excitement. They felt hopeful. They felt courage. Many talked about letting go, letting in, emblematic language of ritual death and rebirth. Some talked about being fired up and others just radiated energy and animation. Lost vitality began to return. They had experienced wholeness as whole being and knew the direction to walk. They talked about the class as a container where they could examine things and practice new steps, small steps. Some of them talked about this as a staging time where they were creating the foundation for a full transition, outside course bounds. Purposefulness trumped fear.

The sense of embeddedness led to voluntary simplicity and decluttering—materially, psychologically, and spiritually. They refocused on social wealth and material adequacy, rather than material wealth and social adequacy. They engaged their relations from a sense of inner centeredness. Over time, they reworked their work lives and/or jobs so that they intentionally and significantly reduced the unintended harm to themselves, their families, communities, or the ecosphere.

They began to hear new labels assigned to them—radical, flaky, and rebel. Rather than feel labeled, they grew strength from this, from each other, and from new convictions. They were able to hold a witness position and ponder these responses as well as how to frame that form of thinking. They also joined like-minded groups that reinforced new thinking and ways of being. This was evidence of emergence into a higher level of self-organization where they knew they did not end at their skin but felt a deep sense of belonging within the universe. They talked about a greater sense of fluidity in responding to challenges, understanding an ebb and flow that they could dance forward with.

ALCHEMISTS OF TRANSFORMATION

All of life is ongoing transformation. Some of the participants talked about their lives as being part of one large transformation. There are countless ways in which we can foster this experience of the unfolding, enfolding universe (Bohm, 1980), and the dance of life (Sahtouris, 1989). The ongoing creativeness of the universe in which humans have a unique place situates our existence in a much larger context. Together, these give us glimpses of the sacred, or implicate order, beyond all thought, time, space, measure, and division. This dance of life has everything to do with transformation, learning, and response-ability. Through these reciprocal ways of learning, we pick up the historical threads and become alchemists of transformation, cooperating with the living cosmos ...anticipating a new epoch.

REFERENCES

Allen, P. G. (1992). *The sacred hoop*. Beacon Press.
Bache, C. (2008). *The living classroom*. SUNY.
Barad, K. (2007). *Meeting the universe halfway*. Duke University Press.
Barad, K. (2012). On touching–The inhuman that therefore I am. *Differences: A Journal of Feminist Cultural Studies, 23*(3), 206–223.
Bohm, D. (1980). *Wholeness and the implicate order*. Routledge.
Cajete, G. (1999). *A people's ecology*. Clear Light Publishing.
Capra, F., & Luisi, P. L. (2014). *The systems view of life*. Cambridge University Press.
Ceder, S. (2015). *Cutting through water: Towards a posthuman theory of educational relationality*. Lund University.
Church, D. (2018). *Mind to matter*. Hay House.
De Quincey, C. (2005). *Radical knowing*. Park Street Press.
De Quincey, C. (2010). *Radical Nature. Rochester*. VM: Park Street Press.
Esteva, G., & Prakash, M. S. (1998). *Grassroots post-modernism*. ZED Books.
Gleick, J. (1987). *Chaos*. Penguin Books.
Lange, E. (2001). *Living transformation* [Unpublished doctoral dissertation]. University of Alberta.
Kingsley, P. (2020). *Reality*. Catafalque Press.
Marshall, J. P. (1995). Alchemy and science. In G. Samuel (Ed.), *Western science and its alternatives*. University of Newcastle Department of Sociology and Anthropology Occasional Papers Series.
McWhinney, W., & Markos, L. (2003). Transformative education: Across the Threshold. *Journal of Transformative Education, 1*(1), 16–37.
Sahtouris, E. (1989). *Gaia: The human journey from chaos to cosmos*. Pocket Books.
Spretnak, C. (2011). *Relational reality*. Green Horizon Books.
St. Germain. (1985). *St Germain on alchemy*. Summit University Press.
Thayer-Bacon, B. (2003). *Relational "(e)pistemologies."* Peter Lang.
Thayer-Bacon, B. (2017). *Relational Ontologies*. Peter Lang.
Von Franz, M. -L. (1979/1997). *Alchemical Active Imagination*. Shambala.
Waters, F. (1950). *Masked gods: Navaho and Pueblo ceremonialism*. The Swallow Press Inc.
Webster's New Collegiate Dictionary (1979). G. & C. Merriam Company.
Wheatley, M. (2006). *Leadership and the new science*. Barrett-Koehler Publishers.
Zohar, D. (1990). *The quantum self*. Quill/William Morrow.

CHAPTER 42

Learning, Experience and the Societal Unconscious: Combining a Materialistic Theory and a Dialectic Methodology

Henning Salling Olesen

INTRODUCTION

We might reserve the term *transformation* for those more comprehensive social changes in which learning plays a significant role—in response to the book title *Learning for Transformation*. This chapter will present a psycho-societal approach to theorizing learning. It will conceptualize individual and collective learning as a potential dimension of social practice, and outline a methodology for empirically tracing learning in everyday life. Change and transformation are first of all *conditio humana*—the individual's life world and ontogenetic development is interwoven with and forcefully accelerated by societal changes seen as permanent aspects of social life—sometimes obvious, sometimes in-transparent—but not generally initiated by learning. More often it is the other way round,

H. Salling Olesen (✉)
Roskilde University, Roskilde, Denmark
e-mail: hso@ruc.dk

© The Author(s), under exclusive license to Springer Nature   751
Switzerland AG 2022
A. Nicolaides et al. (eds.), *The Palgrave Handbook of Learning for Transformation*, https://doi.org/10.1007/978-3-030-84694-7_42

752   H. SALLING OLESEN

learning being forced by change. Having stated that, the relation between changes that deserve the term transformation and subjective processes of learning and reorientation is extremely interesting, both because of scholarly centrality and because of political perspective. Doing that the focus of interest is on the role of learning in its material context and the object-subject-object-dialectic of social practice and consciousness building in which learning may occur. The psycho-societal approach is a theoretical and methodological answer to this interest. Ontologically it is a materialist approach that sees cognitive and emotional dimensions of learning and other subjective processes as embodied in the social practice of concrete living bodies. Epistemologically it is committed to a dialectical analysis that both recognizes historical, material reality and traces endogenous potentials for social dynamics.

The chapter does not focus specifically on educational practice but addresses learning in a wider societal context. I know the theory of transformative learning coined by Jack Mezirow and developed by numerous others and have noticed some of the interesting discussion within the tradition (Alhadeff-Jones, 2012; Brookfield, 2017; Illeris, 2014). But the theoretical background in this chapter is quite different.

SUBJECTIVITY, EXPERIENCE, AND SOCIETY

The most fundamental assumption in the following is that learning is a ubiquitous dimension of all social life. People learn by dealing with the world—about the world, about being in the world, and about acting in the world. The aim is to theorize learning in general, and adult informal learning in particular, as an aspect of social life (Salling Olesen, 2007b). A general concept for the relation of the subject to the world is the concept "Experience" coming from German critical social science *Erfahrung*. With this concept the immediate and situated experience of everyday life is seen as a subjective soup cube, condensing individual life experience and the entire collective and cultural orientation in the world—which is also the framework through which it is perceived (Salling Olesen, 1989; p. 8). The psycho-societal approach to learning aims at understanding the potentials in this soup cube, including contents that are not conscious for the individual, or are even societally unconscious. It draws theoretically on Marxism as well as on psychodynamic theory and combines them into a psycho-social empirical methodology for studying specific learning situations and/or life historical processes of learning (learning trajectories) with the aim of discovering the potentials in the soup cube.

Everyday life in no way automatically entails substantial learning, mostly practice just involves adaptation within a stable world view and life perspective. But it may at the same time build surplus social experience which is not immediately enacted, and this is important for learning from future experiences. Learning is related to, and to some extent dependent on, changing practices. Not all changes are social transformations, but some are and we want to understand the dynamics of learning in those cases.

Theorizing Learning

Knowledge is not an attribute of individuals, and also not an entity that can be extracted, transferred, and possessed. Learning is social and practical. A general theory of learning must be based on understanding the dependence of learning processes on and significance for the dialectic between societal conditions and individual development. In a logical sense, one can speak of an internal relationship between the one and the other part, and between the whole and the part(s). Everyday language and the organization of scientific discourses generally tend to dichotomize the relationship: It is assumed that "society" constitutes external conditions, independent variables, which set the framework for individual agency. And on the other hand, the individual subject is constructed as a free and rational subject who has the opportunity to think independently, recognize objective conditions (including societal frameworks) and within these act according to completely individual preferences and in his own interest. This is exactly the dichotomy I would like to overcome. When individuals in their life courses meet with societal conditions, they sometimes adapt and learn, other times they resist, for reasons to explore. A psycho-societal approach is a framework of understanding these specific cases and individual processes concretely, without losing sight of their societal nature.

At the same time, it is a framework of understanding that is aware of how subjective conditions and individual choices have societal effects. Theoretically, learning can explain the central dynamic in this subject-object dialectic—understanding subjectivity as socially produced and at the same time potential source of social change (the political perspective). Eventually, this theoretical mode of defining learning should also contribute to a theoretical bridge-building between the social sciences and the humanities (the metascientific perspective). I think that the theorizing of learning may also contribute to discussions about agency and democracy in a globalizing capitalism, and about the role of knowledge in a late modern society, with a broader resonance to social theory, politics, and epistemology than can be discussed here (Leledakis, 1995; Salling Olesen, 2002).

This way of thinking is for me embedded in a broader materialistic understanding of society (and thus also of individuals), seeing the current capitalist social formation as the preliminary end stage of an evolutionary and civilization history that includes both conflictual reorganization of materiality and extensive learning processes. Such a position also implies a recognition of the natural basis of sociality—both in terms of the ecological dependence of the planet we inhabit, and in terms of human beings themselves whose social life is mediated through individual bodily lives. The German philosophers and social scientists Oskar Negt and Alexander Kluge have formulated a materialist framework by combining a holistic historical perspective on evolution and civilization with current details (Negt & Kluge, 2014). It is a Marxism that builds on the critical social theory of the Frankfurt School but at the same time points to an ecological perspective on humanity's way of dealing with itself as nature and with the planet we inhabit. The pivotal connection between the critique of capitalism and the ecological perspective in their analysis is the work as a life activity and the basis of sociality (Negt & Kluge, 1972, 2016; Salling Olesen, 2009). I will come back to the implications of this later.

Originally this concept saw learning as a process of connecting experiences from everyday life and cultural/societal knowledge and saw individual learning as entangled in collective learning—with a debt to Wright Mill's idea of sociological imagination. Many educators adopted Negt's ideas as mainly didactic tools for political education (which they also were [Zeuner, 2013]). But eventually, they paved a way for a scholarly development of an alternative (to) didactic thinking (Salling Olesen, 1989, 2007b). The core of this alternative is to think of individuals' learning, specific learning motives and—resistances in the context of their life world and life experiences—past, present, and future.

Individual Learning in Societal Transformation

In order to make the complex and multilayered notion of experience sensitive to subjective specificity (every human subject is a unique result of socialization) and also to the specific context and area of reality in question, we adopted a life history methodology for studying learning as an aspect of subjective participation in social life. I shall give an example.

Quite often (adult) learning is taking place under the coercive conditions of changes in work life. Most of this learning is unintended personal experience. Educational initiatives are often narrowly instrumental attempts to adapt the labor force employability. The following refers to a major Danish government intervention, consisting of vocational training of very marginalized unemployed and unskilled female workers. For foreigners I should note that the all dominant situation in Denmark since 1960s–1970s is that married women also have paid employment, and children are in childcare institutions. But this actual group has had long periods of unemployment and no stable affiliation with a company or just a business area. We conducted a qualitative study of a sample of these women's work career, in order to understand their approach to training and their learning and general life experiences, enabled by narrative interviews. Within societal conditions that were structurally alike—marginal labor position, gender discrimination, precarious work in low paid and unstable jobs, often in cleaning, services, and industrial manufacturing—many suffered low self-esteem. Their identification with wage labor was low and primarily related to the income and/or the need for social contact. But interviews also showed an abundance of life experiences. Many of them had children and had established an everyday life as stay-at-home moms. Traces of a traditional gender role seemed to be subjectively available for many as an idea of a satisfactory life organization once they were made redundant.

What did they learn from training? There were differences depending on their actual internships during the training and on subsequent employment success. But one observation turned out very clearly: A substantial raise in self-esteem for almost all, including a confidence in having relevant skills and employability. Of course, this had to do with course design and social organization of the training, but our analysis primarily observed that objective success (employment and particularly employment in skills demanding jobs) was closely connected with subjective developments

756 H. SALLING OLESEN

along the training process (new awareness of gender relations, identification with specific work experiences, increasing self-confidence) (Larsen, 1992; Salling Olesen, 1994, 2004).

When we analyze these observations within the context of a subject-object dialectic we can see both their situation and their learning outcome as a societal transformation of gender. These women are caught in the crossing between traditional women's roles and wage labor. The training was at the same time acquisition of real/recognized skills, a challenge of gender role, and an (work) identity process. The training option had quite different significance for each of them. Their relation with the world and their view of themselves changed differently, but for many also ambiguously. Although the purpose of these training programs was to improve employability, many of the women actually were ambivalent and skeptical about the meaningfulness of learning. But during the training they seem to discover new social opportunities—and have the opportunity to try out dimensions of themselves that have had no realistic realization before and maybe were entirely suppressed—in a protected space. In spite of a shared socioeconomic destiny, our analysis reveals both interindividual differences but also intraindividual ambivalences and dynamics. In spite of the structural coercive aspects we can see that many, but not all, of them went through a personal transition which aligns with the gender relations transformation, gaining a new work identity as skilled labor. The concept of "double societalization" of women, coined by one of the feminists in critical theory, helps us see how subjective experiences reflect societal contradictions, but also that subjectivity has its own dynamics so that the subject-object dialectic is in dual, interconnected motion (Becker-Schmidt, 2002; Weber, 2020).

A PSYCHO-SOCIETAL CONCEPT OF SUBJECTIVITY

The data used in the first life history research projects were as point of departure language-based methods, mostly narrative interviews. From this followed very practical methodological questions about data production techniques, interpreting data, and validating interpretations, but also more methodological and theoretical discussions around the linguistic turn in social sciences, centering around the theorizing of subjectivity and subjects (Salling Olesen, 2016; Weber & Salling Olesen, 2002). In interpretation methods, we took inspiration from a "depth hermeneutic" (Lorenzer & König, 1986; Salling Olesen & Weber, 2012). Depth hermeneutic interprets cultural phenomena (primarily "fine art") as expressions of not only immediately understandable social meanings but also dimensions of meaning that have been societally repressed or do not have a clear social articulation. In an international research group, we have transposed this type of hermeneutic interpretation to the investigation of social interaction in everyday life and individual mundane agency and meaning making, working with empirical material from work life research, organization studies, education and learning careers, professional experiences—and many more (Salling Olesen & Leithäuser, 2018). The interpretation method is a general intensive qualitative interpretation, building on interview transcripts, field diaries, interaction protocols, etc. This interpretation is immediately a regular hermeneutic procedure, but it pays specific attention to unconscious dimensions in the material as well as in the interpretation process itself. In this respect, it is inspired by and borrows interpretational attitude from a psychoanalytic interpretation, from where Alfred Lorenzer, originally a psychiatrist, had borrowed it. And like any hermeneutic approach it also takes notice of, and benefits from, the involvement of the interpreter subject, but again with a psychodynamic attention—using the concepts of transfer and counter transfer (Devereux, 1967).

Although borrowing the attitude and attention from psychoanalytic interpretation, we have a different objective. Instead of the individual psychic history per se, in the therapeutic interest, the objective here is to trace meanings which are supposed to reveal supra-individual cultural meanings—and again, with a particular interest in those that have been societally repressed or distorted. These interpretations study open and hidden cultural meanings from the way they appear in individuals' language use, agency and in social interaction, symbolic phenomena etc. (Salling Olesen, 2012, 2020). We have adopted the term *psychosocietal interpretation* in order to avoid a (too) narrow identification with psychoanalysis, and also in order to indicate the practical challenge involved, namely to combine what is normally divided: Psychic and societal analytical frameworks.

A key to understanding this methodological strategy is the theoretical question about the nature of the subject. Instead of getting stuck in a too deterministic theory of classical psychoanalysis, or falling in a culturalistic relativism like many post-structuralists do, this methodology refers to a materialistic theory of socialization, the process in which "the individual enters society and society enters the individual body and psyche."

In the social reinterpretation of psychoanalysis, the biological drive theory is reconstructed into an interactional theory according to which the individual psychodynamics is strongly influenced by the early life interaction experiences. The deterministic stereotype in many perceptions of psychoanalysis is overcome by an assumption and empirical validation of an embodied learning of culture from social interaction between mother (primary caregiver) and child (Hollway, 2019; Lorenzer, 1972; Stern, 1985). The individual builds a social world experience in the form of interaction forms, starting early in a prelinguistic phase but continuing all along the life trajectory (Salling Olesen, 2012). With language acquisition and the ability to symbolize the child becomes emotionally more independent of the here and now and gains access to connect individual sensory experiences with a social world, mediated by language, but the interaction forms remain active. If and when the connection of symbolization gets broken or blocked because of problematic/painful relational experiences and/or because of societal taboos that are present in the child's immediate life world, it leaves a non-integrated piece of emotional experience that cannot be articulated very well but may nevertheless be of immense importance for the individual. It may also leave language use without emotional resonance. Such a breach can be seriously damaging to the subject (Lorenzer was originally psychiatrist). But we use it here for understanding that individual life experiences include a latent unconscious level beyond immediate articulation, and also that this level is reflecting meanings that are not articulated in social language but form a societal unconscious. The individual mind may reconfigure these relational experiences throughout the entire life, conceptualized in psychodynamic theory as "deferred action" (Becker-Schmidt, 1993; Weber, 2020). For learning theory, this helps us to understand the psychic (emotional) dimension of the interplay between conscious and unconscious but also reminds us to recognize that this interplay is an individual and situated process. For the purpose of learning theory, it is important to remember that although studying individual life histories, the methodology is primarily suited to reveal societal relations and meanings. The individual is a unique embodiment of a society and a position within it—and what we usually characterize sociologically as e.g., class, gender, ethnicity is in reality in principle an embodied individual and unique version of social experience.

The theory of language acquisition and symbolization, the ability to connect individual sensory experiences (bodily social experiences), and the participation in cultural meaning making (using Wittgenstein's concept of language games) is of pivotal significance for learning, and especially learning regarding basic world views and self-image (Lorenzer, 1972; Salling Olesen & Weber, 2012). In a wider learning perspective, the difficult questions about relation between intellectual and bodily learning may possibly be reconceptualized, with great perspectives for the understanding of professional knowledge, tacit knowledge, and intuitive judgment ("gut feeling") (Salling Olesen, 2007a, 2014). This is one of the important reasons for adopting a materialist (bodily) perspective on learning.

Learning for Transformation—The Societal Level

The premise of the previous theorizing of subjectivity is a materialistic ontology: man as a social animal. Conversely, this materialistic ontology implies that societal dynamics are endogenous, and depends on the dynamics of our embodied world experience. Allow me to quote from a recent book presenting the psycho-societal approach:

> With this material theory of the subject the methodology is a preliminary—procedural—opposition to an exclusively or primarily cultural understanding of the societal nature of subjectivity as we know it from the linguistic turn in the social sciences, in positioning theory, and in discourse analytical criticisms; each of these approaches problematizes the modern understanding of the subject without taking the step out of Cartesian idealism. It is a core aspect of this opposition that the materiality in terms of bodily life, dependence, historical temporality and social practice precedes the culture of the idea and language both in individual life and social development (Negt & Kluge, 2014). But it is not an 'undialectical materialism' (unfortunately the corresponding positive concept is so politically compromised that it can hardly be used to express the opposite). The optimistic experience is that the socially unconscious in a given society contains resources for a dynamics that is not easily predictable, c.f. #metoo. On the societal level, one does not understand revolutions until they have happened, but they could not have happened without unfolding unconscious psychodynamics and social agency that was not transparent at the time. On the individual level, learning processes and identity development take place in unpredictable directions and leaps. Therefore, understanding the socially unconscious must have the nature of a negative theory and a methodology fit for carving out the future of mundane present everyday life. (Salling Olesen, 2020)

The individual is an embodied version of society, with a version of experience of its social order and culture, its contradictions, opportunities, and taboos. Learning means a motion in the subject-object-relation which may be a result of objective conditions as well as subjective dynamics. The subject increases its insights and capability but it happens in practices in the objective world. From birth onwards, it is often objective dynamics (biological development; societal changes) which brings the relation in motion. When the subject produces ideas, phantasies, and desires for changing practices which translate into changes in practice—as experiments which are immediately in dialogue with an entire social life world—these ideas and desires have an experiential base which is material. Theorizing an inner dynamic consequently, including the unconscious, as an embodiment of social experience enables us to understand the potential for eruptive changes in learning processes without voluntarist assumptions. Emerging subjective impulses may be influenced by, but it may also reconfigure, the unconscious dimension of individual life experience depending on social interaction. What was societally unconscious—repressed or not culturally articulated—may emerge in the subject's conscious relation to the world, and it may transcend conscious culture and societal structure. This is not good or bad in itself. That is an empirical and political question. The recent Trump era in the United States certainly mobilized subjective forces that were societally unconscious but gained societal impact as an alternative societal reality—potentially restoring racism and xenophobia, for the benefit of already wealthy and powerful people. In this case, social learning would mean a collective recognition across the dual reality of the United States of those until recently societally repressed frustrations and challenges that Trump manage(d) to mobilize. But apart from the outrageous practical challenges that are handled in political processes, this case also conceals an intricate theoretical question how to distinguish different types of subjective dynamics. Can they be distinguished simply by their sense of reality: fed by fake or realistic information? Or can they be distinguished by their psychodynamic nature: regressive and projective or social and integrative? Or by their outcome: aggressivity or social recognition?

With the perspective of this very complicated and not yet researched and fully reflected process, I will return to work life. I will sketchily show how critical materialistic learning research could trace potentials for transformations which may be emerging from or submerged in work life reality, and may be recognized by means of theoretical awareness.

Learning and Work Life Transformation

The societal organization of work is the immediate determinant for survival and well-being and the most important factor of societal relations in modern societies (in premodern societies violent and mythological power relations ensured the elites' control over the work of others). Researching work and learning is fascinating because it enables insight into micro-processes, in the immediate life world, that instantly shape demands and opportunities, and at the same time points to their perspectives for historical change processes—the possible transformation of capitalist work life—and ultimately for human life conditions, the ecological relationships between society and the natural basis for human life.

Very often, but not exclusively, major transitions that appear in the individual life world are changes and conflicts related to work and employment. They include situations of technological shifts, new forms of work organization and management, or of redundancy (or not obtaining access to the labor market at all). But also the specific types of pressure and workload in everyday life which hardly can be noticed—the intensification, alienation, the double work for women, environmental problems, etc.—are part of it. There is an intense interrelation between these social conditions and subjective processes, each of them having its own logic, but they are ultimately part of a societal order. However, most recent research of work life and work related learning is confined to the concrete work processes. Either in the affirmative sense of trying to work out what is needed for adapting human labor to the changing requirements of the work process, and how these competences can be acquired—researchers may produce sophisticated analyses that take the societal development of work for granted as an independent variable (Nicoll & Olesen, 2013; Salling Olesen, 2013). Or, more interesting in this context: The study of how learning takes place in the interaction with the workplace, and the affordances of concrete work situations. In this type of engagement, you may theorize learning as a more comprehensive and interactive process of adaptation, a subjective process of identity building and negotiation. One important paradigm of workplace learning research is based in a combination of an anthropological concept of cultural transmission and a cultural psychology inherited from Russian psychology (Lave & Wenger, 1991; Wenger, 1998). These approaches give valuable insights in the interactions and relations that facilitate the learning and the (dynamic) reproduction of work processes and culture around work. But they tend to be conservative, or affirmative in relation to the overarching societal work organization. They fail to raise the question of how endogenous dynamics like learning and political articulation of interests may be precursors for fundamental transformation of work. And conversely, they neglect or downplay how external societal dynamics shape the workplace, affecting the living workers and their relations.

A critical research must analyze the concrete phenomena (*in casu*: the work process) with a view to its historical nature, reflecting contextual origins as well as imagining its possible future. A psycho-societal approach to work related learning aims at relating the concrete and specific life world, including the subjective dynamics in the living work, with the central characteristics of the societal order. Its most important aim is to establish a realistic recognition of the dynamics in the field which may enable transformations of work and reflect the wider political and ethical significance of such potential transformations.

In doing so, researchers must invest not only theoretical concepts but also our context knowledge and subjective desires as epistemic tools—directing the attention in empirical investigation, but always confronting findings and interpretations with reality. The idea of transformation as an endogenous process also means that theory must sensitize to this reality. From Marxist theory, we learn to explore the inherent contradictions in capitalist societal organization. But there is an obvious gap in Marxist thinking about the subjective aspects of basic societal relations. This has both implications for understanding the concrete relations in work life—and for political thinking about what a "revolutionary" change might mean. A contemporary concept of revolution is about social learning. Our minds, rationality, and desires are shaped by capitalism in variable forms of competitive individualism, submissive authoritarianism and desire for growth and material wealth, which corresponds very well with the classical industrial society. But the capitalist modernity has also fostered obvious resources, more or less conscious: self-consciousness, desire for recognition, solidarity, social empathy, sense of product quality and usefulness, caring for nature and local community. Such resources that are socially learned may have more or less space in different forms of work life, and also in family and intimate life. *Learning for Transformation* should seek to reconfigure these ideas to a new reality of work, and particularly it should be open to contemporary ongoing and future formation of themes and directions of policy. Departing from the reality of everyday life, the issue of interest would be exploring the potential learning processes departing from the traces of the character masks formed by capitalism to something that would include the classical Marxism notion of class consciousness. This would now be something new, yet unknown form of collective autonomy and solidarity.

Actual developments in capitalist work, formed by technology and societal forces, may well lend more space—and the challenge for learning will be how far this humanizing of work can elude a capitalist control. This will be a matter of political struggle on many levels. There is no systemic transformation which does not include minds.

But there are also within capitalist societal formation work domains which are only partly influenced by capitalist organization. Generally, we are aware of the politically organized domain of the state, for instance, in the discussion about disembedding (Polanyi, 1968). But I would also point out self-organized forms of work organization which transgresses limitations, injustices, and ecological damages of capitalism, and unfold human autonomy and democratic control in the form of cooperatives of different types, nonprofit enterprises and social enterprises with alternative criteria for growth and usefulness. Experiences from cooperative work organizations and autonomous work organizations can be seen as learning arenas for societal transformation (Salling Olesen & Fragoso, 2017). They are extremely diverse, only a minority of them has a direct mission of overcoming capitalism, but they are based in noncapitalist interests, and they produce experiences of other ways of organizing work. But the learning is not only about adapting to the requirements of work, or learning how to run a work organization, but rather the gradual recognition of irrationalities built in the present economic regulation of work, and forming of imaginations for different developments.

It will take us too far to discuss in terms of political economy how the relation between capital ownership, political governance, and human learning within a capitalist political economy may develop potentials for transformation into a different political economy. There are several terms to indicate alternatives—social economy, solidarity economy—I have from an early phase used the term "a political economy of working people" (Salling Olesen & Forrester, 1999), referring to the fundamental dialectic between exchange value and use value by Marx and defining the political economy of working people as an economic organization in which workers' sense of use values direct the production.

The joint underlying point is that a transformation of capitalism must develop from inside and is first and foremost dependent on learning, and there is no fixed destination of such learning from experience. Personally, I see the most essential challenge in the contradiction related to economic growth and the inequalities of the world. On the one hand, some 50 years delayed recognition of "Limits to growth," the title of one of the first alerts about the contradiction between (capitalist) economic growth and natural environment. On the other hand, a growing recognition of the contradictions in the nature of wealth which is obtained on the cost of overload of workers and destruction of social relations. That is the material dependency on nature planet and nature man.

Ernst Bloch, one of the philosophers of the Frankfurt School, who became known for emphasizing the necessity of hope, argued that utopian imaginations of a different reality could only emerge from unconscious or not yet conscious presentiments. He maintains that the dialectic between material reality and alternative imagination is based in a potentiality in material reality itself.

I think we could translate this theoretical idea into an empirical attention to learning processes in and in relation to work, looking for their utopian or just transcending potential. The transformation that we can abstractly describe as a transition from a political economy of capital to a socially and environmentally sustainable political economy is non-determined learning which eventually manifests itself in new practices. From this point of view, a psycho-social theorizing of learning should enable an explorative investigation of the open question of what a Marxist vision for sustainability could actually be today.

Outlook to the Wider Society

The sketchy comments above are based in comprehensive theoretical and empirical research. Contemporary experiences of social change in work seem to indicate major societal and historical change. The development of a post-industrial and service producing society is relativizing the old lines of dispute in work life and has changed workers' relations to work. It does not mean that the defense of working conditions, unionizing etc., has become obsolete, but many workers in the most developed and rich parts of the world have overcome alienated positions of paid labor and relate to work as a subjective meaningful activity. The consciousness of environmental issues and limits to growth have opened a Pandora's box of dilemmas between wealth, employment, and sustainability. In the many forms of social enterprises (many more than we mostly assume) are illustrations of the complicated learning process of making a liveli-hood without profitability as a driver. We need to understand the everyday work life and work identity of a majority of workers and trace the ongoing and potential learning processes taking place. Especially, the overall recog-nized climate change and the necessities for a green transition will depend on what we might term a collective learning process which is full of conflicts and open questions.

However, work life is not the only domain that displays fundamental societal issues and conflicts in everyday life, and in every individual body. The #MeToo movement has exposed how a widespread gender experi-ence, submitted to patriarchal structures and practices, and for long time kept in mainly women's bodies as a submerged suffering under sexist repression and discrimination, can break through and in a flashing process illuminate the demand and the possibility for new gender relations. For the moment it has the nature of a tsunami and it will be a learning process for all (!) genders to sort out the muddy stream of sexual harassment, gender discrimination, and power exercise. It is no coincidence that this breakthrough comes as a subjective reorientation tailing societal changes in socio-material basis for gender relations. But a transformation with new practices, culture and institutions based in (more) equal and respectful gender relations will require a long and conflictual learning process for all.

REFERENCES

Alhadeff-Jones, M. (2012). Transformative learning and the challenges of complexity. In E. W. Taylor & P. Cranton (Eds.), *Handbook of transformative learning: Theory, research and practice* (pp. 178–194). Jossey-Bass.

Becker-Schmidt, R. (1993). Ambivalenz und Nachträglichkeit. Perspektiven einer feministischen Biographieforschung. In M. Krüger (Ed.), *Was heisst hier eigentlich feministisch? Zur theoretischen Diskussion in der Geistes- und Sozialwissenscheaften.* Donat Verlag.

Becker-Schmidt, R. (2002). Theorizing gender arrangements. In R. Becker-Schmidt (Ed.), *Gender and work in transition: Globalization in Western, Middle and Eastern Europe* (pp. 25–48). Opladen.

Brookfield, S. (2017). Critical adult education theory: Traditions and influence. In *The Palgrave International handbook on adult and lifelong education and learning* (pp. 53–74). Palgrave MacMillan.

Devereux, G. (1967). *From anxiety to method in the social sciences.* Mouton.

Hollway, W. (2019). *Knowing mothers.* Palgrave MacMillan.

766   H. SALLING OLESEN

Illeris, K. (2014). Transformative learning and identity. *Journal of Transformative Education.* https://doi.org/10.1177/1541344614548423

Larsen, K. (1992). *Een uddannelse - tre historier.* Roskilde University.

Lave, J., & Wenger, E. (1991). *Situated learning: Legitimate peripheral participation.* Cambridge University Press.

Leledakis, K. (1995). *Society and psyche.* Berg Publishers.

Lorenzer, A. (1972). *Zur Begründung einer materialistischen Sozialisationstheorie.* Suhrkamp-Verlag.

Lorenzer, A., & König, H.-D. (1986). Tiefenhermeneutische Kulturanalyse. In *Kultur-analysen* (Vol. 7334, pp. 11–98). Fischer Taschenbuch Verlag.

Negt, O., & Kluge, A. (1972). *Öffentlichkeit und Erfahrung. Zur Organisationsanalyse von bürgerlicher und proletarischer Öffentlichkeit.* Frankfurt.

Negt, O., & Kluge, A. (2014). *History and obstinacy.* Zone Books.

Negt, O., & Kluge, A. (2016). *Public sphere and experience toward an analysis of the bourgeois and proletarian public Sphere.* Verso.

Nicoll, K., & Olesen, H. S. (2013). Editorial: What's new in a new competence regime? *European Journal for Research on the Education and Learning of Adults, 4,* 103–109. https://doi.org/10.3384/rela.2000-7426.relae7

Polanyi, K. (1968). The economy as instituted process. In E. LeClair & H. Schneider (Eds.), *Economic anthropology.* Holt, Rinehart and Winston.

Salling Olesen, H. (1989). *Adult education and everyday life.* Roskilde University.

Salling Olesen, H. (1994). Qualifying adult women for employment. In T. V. Klenovšek & H. S. Salling Olesen (Eds.), *Adult education and the labour market.* Slovene Adult Education Centre.

Salling Olesen, H., & Forrester, K. (eds). (1999). Political economy of labour - or: Die (Selbst?)Aufhebung des Proletariats als kollektiver Lernprozess. In K. Salling Olesen, Henning; Forrester (Ed.), *Adult education and the labour market V* (pp. 11–24). Roskilde University Press.

Salling Olesen, H. (2002). *Experience language and subjectivity in life history approaches—biography research as a bridge between the humanities and the social sciences?* Roskilde University: Adult Education Research Group.

Salling Olesen, H. (2004). The learning subject in life history—A Qualitative research approach to learning. In M. H. Menne Abrahaõ Barreto (Ed.), *A Aventura (Auto)biografico. Theoria & Empiria.* (pp. 419–464). EDIPUCRS.

Salling Olesen, H. (2007a). Be(com)ing a general practitioner: Professional identities, subjectivity and learning. In L. West (Ed.), *Using biographical and life history approaches in the study of adult and lifelong learning: European perspectives.* P. Lang.

Salling Olesen, H. (2007). Theorising learning in life history: A psychosocietal approach. *Studies in the Education of Adults, 39*(1), 38–53.

Salling Olesen, H. (2009). *Oskar Negt and a few other Germans* [Video]. http://www.youtube.com/watch?v=IQrlcFXYgcQ&feature=youtu.be

Salling Olesen, H. (2012). The societal nature of subjectivity: An interdisciplinary methodological challenge. *Forum Qualitative Sozialforschung/Forum: Qualitative Social Research, 13*(3).

Salling Olesen, H. (2013). Beyond the current political economy of competence development. *RELA European Journal for Research on the Education and Learning of Adults, 4*(2). http://www.rela.ep.liu.se/issues/10.3384_r ela.2000-7426.201342/rela9013/rela9013.pdf

Salling Olesen, H. (2014). Learning and the psycho-societal nature of social practice: Tracing the invisible social dimension in work and learning. *Forum Oswiatowe, 52*(2), 11–27. http://forumoswiatowe.pl/index.php/cza sopismo/article/view/159

Salling Olesen, H. (2016). A psycho-societal approach to life histories. In I. Goodson, A. Antikainen, P. Sikes, & M. Andrews (Eds.), *The Routledge International handbook on narrative and life history* (pp. 214–125). Routledge.

Salling Olesen, H. (2020). The societal unconscious. In H. Salling Olesen (Ed.), *Psychosocial perspectives on adult learning.* https://doi.org/10.1163/978900 4420274

Salling Olesen, H., & Fragoso, A. (2017). Social economy and learning for a political economy of solidarity. *RELA European Journal for Research on the Education and Learning of Adults, 8*(2).

Salling Olesen, H., & Leithäuser, T. (2018). Psycho-societal interpretation of the unconscious dimensions in everyday life. In K. Stamenova & R. D. Hinshelwood (Eds.), *Methods of research into the unconscious: Applying pscyhoanalytic Ideas to Social Science* (pp. 70–86). Routledge.

Salling Olesen, H., & Weber, K. (2012). Socialization, language, and scenic understanding. Alfred Lorenzer's contribution to a psycho-societal methodology. *Forum: Qualitative Social Research Sozialforschung, 13*(3), Art. 22.

Stern, D. N. (1985). *The interpersonal world of the infant: A view from psychoanalysis and developmental psychology.* Basic Books.

Weber, K. (2020). Ambivalence and experience. Un-conscious dimensions of working women's social learning women's lives and experiences. In H. Salling Olesen (Ed.), *The societal unconscious.* Brill/Sense.

Weber, K., & Salling Olesen, H. (2002). Chasing potentials for adult learning: Lifelong learning in a life history perspective. *In Zeitschrift fur Qualitative Bildungs-, Beratungs- und Sozialforschung* (pp. 283–300).

Wenger, E. (1998). *Communities of practice learning, meaning, and identity.* Cambridge University Press.

Zeuner, C. (2013). From workers education to societal competencies: Approaches to a critical, emancipatory education for democracy. *European Journal for Research on the Education and Learning of Adults.* https://doi. org/10.3384/rela.2000-7426.rela9011

CHAPTER 43

Transformative Learning and Microradicalization

Dante Caramellino, Claudio Melacarne, and Benjamin Ducol

INTRODUCTION

In just a few years, the term *radicalization* has become a "catch-all concept" (Coolsaet, 2011, p. 261). Often pointed out as an essentially contested concept (Gallie, 1955), this notion of radicalization (and by extension violent radicalization) is today the subject of various debates both in academia and in the public sphere. While some have questioned

---

D. Caramellino (✉) · C. Melacarne
University of Siena, Viale Cittadini, Italy
e-mail: dante.caramellino@unisi.it

C. Melacarne
e-mail: claudio.melacarne@unisi.it

B. Ducol
Centre for the Prevention of Radicalization Leading To Violence, Montréal, Canada
e-mail: bducol@cprmv.org

© The Author(s), under exclusive license to Springer Nature Switzerland AG 2022
A. Nicolaides et al. (eds.), *The Palgrave Handbook of Learning for Transformation*, https://doi.org/10.1007/978-3-030-84694-7_43

769

the precise meaning to be attributed to this word, others have criticized its scientific use (Richards, 2011) or its negative social effects (Kundnani, 2012). Criticized as an empty shell by some, the fact remains that the idea of (violent) radicalization has become a key debated notion in social sciences and public debates.

This chapter intends to focus on the topic of educational challenges related to radicalization processes that can arise and develop in many contexts of everyday life. The basic assumption of this contribution is that it is possible to understand radicalization processes within the theoretical frameworks of adult learning, and in particular within the framework of the transformative learning theory (Mezirow, 1991), a process that can be described as one of perspective transformation.

Transformative learning theory was born within the field of adult education as a theory and method to develop inclusive thinking, through the valorization of experience and the validation of previous learning or the construction of new ones, able to face new situations. Our perspective is to frame radicalization as a form of precritical thought (Mezirow, 2003).

The theories of adult learning in fact allow us to de-ideologize the use of the term radicalization and develop a reflection on the possibilities, to prevent the deviations of this process in terms of extremist or even terrorist violence through a preventive educational approach.

In this sense, radicalization will not be understood as defined by French scholar Fahad Khosrokhavar (2014) as "the process whereby an individual or group adopts a violent form of action, directly related to a politically, socially or religiously motivated extremist ideology that challenges the established political, social or cultural order" (pp. 8–9). Indeed, a definition of radicalization should not necessarily incorporate the idea that a subject performs a violent act, or that the radical position assumed may be connoted a priori as negative or dangerous. Radicalization might be better understood as an evolutionary process, not as a state, the result of a sedimentation process of meaning perspectives that become rigid and impermeable to debate, dialectics and confrontation over time (Adams et al., 2008). Violence can be an expression of this cognitive rigidification, but it is neither intrinsic nor teleological.

For this reason, it appears interesting to think about radicalization from an educational perspective. Indeed, developing a theoretical look at radicalization from the lens of learning processes and the adult learning point of view is important for many reasons. Firstly, because radicalization has certainly generated historical disasters but also great emancipatory and transformative movements in human societies. Secondly, radicalization has been an implicit issue discussed in many ways in the tradition of adult learning without being explicitly discussed as a topic of interest. Finally, framing radicalization from an educational perspective might drive researchers and educators to explore the limits of transformation and its cultural and ethical implications (Davis, 2018; Zeiger & Aly, 2015).

WHY REDUCING RADICALIZATION TO ITS VIOLENT DIMENSION IS PROBLEMATIC

Widespread uses and abuses of the term radicalization have appeared in the media and more broadly in the public sphere. Those have created confusion around the various meanings of the term and led to the delegitimization of the role that some forms of radicalism, for centuries, have had in promoting democracy and social justice throughout history. It is therefore important to reaffirm the distinction between violent radicalization and nonviolent radicalization (Schmid, 2011). People firmly convinced of their ideas might adopt positions that, although considered radical with respect to the social or collective norm, are not necessarily extremist or contrary to democratic norms and values. Radicalization can, according to some authors, also lead to legitimate but different forms of democratic coexistence, while questioning some social norms historically rooted in a context (Brookfield & Holst, 2011).

Following a careful review of the literature, Schmid notes that even within the scholarly and public debates not all the uses of political violence are all-terrorist or all-extremist, nor is political violence, although illegal under national law, always illegitimate, especially in the context of popular resistance against highly repressive undemocratic regimes (Schmid, 2011).

The debates around radicalization have led to a restrictive apprehension of this notion, leading to an automatic association between radicality and violence. However, people can develop radical ideas and opinions without supporting or practicing violence (Hafez & Mullins, 2015; Khalil, 2014). Indeed, in some areas of our lives, each one of us can develop personal, political, religious, or ethical perspectives that could be considered extreme, at least from the point of view of others (Neumann, 2015). Moreover, "what is radical in a social, cultural and in a certain historical period cannot be considered so in another" (Winter & Feixas, 2019, p. 2). Some nonviolent radical people have played an extremely positive role in their communities, as well as in a wider political context. They have generated forms of political action based on communication or groups of consciousness that grow through dialectics or critical reflection (Freire, 2007). Much of the progress in democratic societies and civil rights has been the result of some form of radical thinking, not a form of radicalization with regard to the status quo. Radicalization might even have a positive connotation in certain contexts (Neumann, 2013). Martin Luther King, Gandhi, and even Nelson Mandela were all considered radical within their historical context. Accordingly, the term radicalization initially refers to a "rejection of the status quo" and the shift from moderate to less consensual views, without necessarily leading to violence (Bartlett & Miller, 2012).

Radical views only become problematic when they legitimize, encourage, or validate violence or forms of extremist behaviors, including terrorism and acts of hatred, intended to promote a particular cause, ideology, or worldview. Individuals who are going through a process of radicalization can encourage, assist, or committing violence in the name of a specific system of beliefs because they are convinced that their assumptions are absolute and exclusive and not framed within a personal or social history that can be reread and renegotiated (Stephens et al., 2019).

FRAMING RADICALIZATION AS MICRO-RADICALIZATION

Today there is no single unified theory of why and how a person develops a radicalized belief system. Each one uses the word radical to indicate something different, and different factors have been explored to identify the predictive factors of violent radicalization.

For example, Clark McCauley and Sophia Moskalenko have identified twelve mechanisms that aggregate into individual and collective factors leading to radicalization (McCauley & Moskalenko, 2011). In the same line, many scholars have tried to capture the essence of radicalization through theoretical frameworks. For example, Borum (2015) defined a model that divides the process of radicalization of an individual into four basic phases, while Moghadam (2009), conceived a staircase model underlining the gradual process of radicalization.

Scientific literature supports a view of the radicalization process toward extremism as a multifactorial process (Klausen, 2015). There is no common pattern of activation and progression, but rather there is a kaleidoscope of factors that may or may not occur, with greater or lesser intensity, in a single subject, and contributing to the progression of radicalization. In sum, the process of radicalization leading to violence must be seen as complex, emergent, as well as a nonlinear and dynamic micro-social phenomenon.

ADULT EDUCATION AND RADICALIZATION

Purified of political, ideological, or social connotations, the process of radicalization can be observed and understood as one of the many learning processes that can generate as much emancipation as closures and limitations. Dewey himself in his more political writings uses the term radicalism to emphasize the need for an authentic reading of liberalism as a social dynamic, as "if radicalism is defined as the perception of the need for radical change, then today any liberalism which is not also radicalism is irrelevant and doomed" (Dewey, 1935, p. 41).

In a more ecological and oriented perspective, O'Sullivan (2012), studying the practices of implementation of transformative theory does not use the term radicalization but suggests how transformative processes must incorporate a perspective of radical change as "we are interested in the generation of energy for radical vision, action, and new ways of being" (O'Sullivan, 2012, p. 187). Dirkx writes that transformative learning experiences foster radical shifts in one's consciousness, in one's ways of being (Dirkx, 2006). A similar position is expressed by Willis when he expresses the idea that "from an existential perspective, transformative learning refers to radical learning choices by which a person orients her- or himself wisely and authentically within the forces of these dialectics" (Willis, 2012, p. 229).

Radicalization is therefore a theoretical category that can be understood within the field of theories of adult education and learning. The relation, between adult education and radicalization, has been present in the scientific debate for many years. For example, Brookfield and Holst have conducted numerous researches to understand how and why people develop exclusive/radical thought or behavior (Brookfield & Holst, 2011). From another perspective, Hill (2008) has used Michel Foucault's theory on postmodern time to explain how radicalism was becoming a movement of movements from 1980, while Ross-Gordon et al. (2017) have explored the idea of "radical education" into "radical philosophy and critical social theory" (p. 365).

774   D. CARAMELLINO ET AL.

More recently, Wilner and Dubouloz have tried to connect the theories of adult learning, and in particular the theory of Mezirow, also to the study of the processes of radicalization, of formation of those personal and community factors that make a constructive dialectic between divergent positions more difficult. Wilner and Dubouloz (2015) use the construct of "violent transformations" (p. 420) to argue that adult learning theory can help explain radicalization, political violence, and in some cases even the processes leading to terrorism. In a recent edition of the Conference on Transformative Learning (2011), the two scholars presented one of the first pieces of research on this topic, connecting the theoretical construct of radicalization with that of transformative learning.

Whatever direction the learning process takes, toward a critical emancipatory or narrow and stereotyped perspective, it takes the form of a radical position, firm and powerful, able to fight and assert itself within a dialectical process.

This reading allows us to avoid essentialist interpretations of phenomena, for example, those that emphasize how the structures of ideology or religion incorporate the seeds of radicalism or, in other cases, how they try to explain how a part of the community does not fight in depth the emerging phenomena of radicalization. Transformative theory brings us back to the negotiating nature with which people produce meaning and allows us to consider radicalization as a manifestation of a transformation of the perspectives of meaning in an exclusive, rigid, and defensive sense. The concept of transformation refers to the process and conditions that can facilitate the development of more inclusive perspectives, open and critical, describing learning as that process in which the adult uses a previous interpretation to build a new interpretation of his experience, to be able to drive and self-direct it (Mezirow, 1991).

Radicalization then becomes a phenomenon much more connected to daily life practices, to the experiences of separation and discrimination that we witness, and in which we are sometimes immersed in the concrete contexts of life and work. For example, it is the theories on adult learning that are redefining this field of study, shifting the focus from macro-readings of the processes of political, cultural, and religious radicalization to the study of contextual situations and micro.

Preventing Radicalization Leading to Violence Through Education

In recent years, several initiatives, projects, and experiences aiming at preventing and countering violent extremism[1] have emerged internationally. These initiatives vary widely both in their form (organizational structure, actors involved, etc.) and their substance (prevention philosophy, preferred intervention approach, type of partnerships between the actors involved, etc.). Overall, two main categories of P/CVE initiatives can be identified.

The first category of prevention initiatives refers to the ones led by the police or national security authorities. Predominantly, these initiatives have extended an already existing community policing approach and have adopted a multi-agency model as a way of approaching the prevention of radicalization and violent extremism. Such P/CVE initiatives have been widely implemented in Northern European countries such as Denmark, the Netherlands, and the United Kingdom (Koehler, 2016). The multi-agency model of P/CVE is structured around the close collaboration between various national security actors (police and intelligence services) and a network of societal actors (schools, social services, and community organizations) that may be in contact with vulnerable individuals or those at risk of radicalization. The objective of this multi-agency model is to deal with potential radicalization situations at an early stage by involving a diversity of actors who can assess each situation and mobilize the relevant resources to deal with them. Accordingly, prevention work led by the police or national security authorities is divided between community awareness activities aimed at raising public awareness of radicalization, and violent extremism issues (conferences, workshops, participation in community activities, etc.) and the identification of vulnerable persons or persons at risk of radicalization, to be able to intervene early and implement the resources (parental, educational, social or health resources) relevant to the situation in question.

The second category refers to local prevention initiatives led by civil society. At present, these initiatives remain few. Usually, they come from community groups, including, for example, Muslim community groups, but also from groups of individuals who may have been affected by

---

[1] We use in this chapter the acronym *P/CVE* to refer to "preventing and countering violent extremism.".

situations of radicalization, such as parents or families of young people engaged in radicalization and violent extremism. Here again, there is a diversity of models and practices, including programs aimed at community awareness or religious education, platforms for the care and support of individuals in a situation or at risk of radicalization or their loved ones, and more traditional youth initiatives. Despite some success, these initiatives are often characterized by a low degree of institutionalization, often due to a lack of recurrent funding, an absence of full-time qualified staff, and a lack of in-depth expertise in working to prevent radicalization leading to violence.

Therefore, is there a model for the prevention of violent extremism between initiatives led by law enforcement authorities and those led by community actors? In Québec, the Centre for the Prevention of Radicalization Leading to Violence (CPRLV) occupies a unique place in the field of P/CVE, both within the Canadian context and internationally.

Preventing Radicalization and Violent Extremism: The Centre for the Prevention of Radicalization Leading to Violence's Experience

Founded in March 2015 by the City of Montreal and the government of Quebec, the CPRLV is a unique experience of P/CVE that intends to ensure a proper balance between public safety and prevention.

Above all, the CPRLV is distinguishing itself by its very own institutional nature. While many P/CVE initiatives are either state/police-led or strictly community-based, the CPRLV has chosen to build itself as a nonprofit organization, strategically and operationally autonomous, enabling it to ensure the implementation of its prevention activities throughout Quebec. Anchored in societal culture of crime and psychosocial prevention (e.g., drug addiction, suicide, crime, prostitution, etc.), the CPRLV's model intends to offer a third path in terms of P/CVE that differs from the other two categories of initiatives already mentioned above.

First of all, it moves away from prevention initiatives emanating from police services or based on the multi-agency model. This mechanism allows the general public to call upon the services of CPRLV professionals in complete confidentiality.

Another unique feature of the CPRLV model is the willingness to bring together the areas of activity, which are in the majority of P/CVE initiatives traditionally compartmentalized.

Preventing Radicalization and Extremism: A Continuum from the Individual to Society and Vice Versa

From a theoretical point of view, CPRLV's approach is based on the idea that radicalization and violence should be understood holistically. As with many social issues, it would be unrealistic to believe that the problem of radicalization leading to violence can be limited exclusively to the individual or rejected at the societal level. CPRLV's approach is based on a theoretical view that considers radicalization and violent extremism as a continuum from the individual to society (Bhui et al., 2012).

This philosophy of prevention considers the phenomena of radicalization and violent extremism as a whole. It promotes a holistic approach that simultaneously addresses the multiple factors associated with radicalization and violent extremism and works on multiple fronts to build individual and collective resilience (Harris-Hogan et al., 2016). From an operational point of view, the CPRLV structures its action around four interconnected areas: (1) research, (2) training and skills development, (3) prevention and community awareness, and (4) intervention and community support.

From Scientific Knowledge to the Implementation of Informed Prevention Practices

A key element of the CPRLV model is its willingness to ensure a continuity that extends from the production of scientific knowledge on the phenomena of radicalization and violent extremism to the implementation of prevention and intervention strategies. Accordingly, CPRLV's first area of activity is research, which aims not only to produce expertise on the issues of radicalization and violent extremism in the Quebec context, but also to ensure a link between academic knowledge on these issues and practical needs in the field. This perspective of research in the field of practice thus contributes to the mobilization of scientific knowledge to ensure the implementation of informed prevention practices based on scientific findings and evidence.

No Prevention Without Training Professional and Frontline Workers

CPRLV's second area of activity aims to provide training and knowledge for professionals and frontline workers (educators, psychologists, social workers, etc.) about radicalization leading to violent extremism (understanding and distinguishing this phenomenon from other social phenomena such as religious fundamentalism or mental health behaviors), its manifestations (break-up and cutting-tie behaviors), as well as the intervention practices to be adopted in a range of situations and contexts.

In terms of training programs, the CPRLV targets the most relevant societal actors for P/CVE including education, health, justice, and public safety front liners, among others. Training workshops offered by CPRLV are also aimed at community leaders and institutional actors. For example, the "behavior barometer" or "Hexagon" are two practical tools that have been created by the CPRLV to recognize behaviors that could indicate that an individual slowly engaging in a radicalization process, while at the same time encouraging individuals to think about such a situation through a holistic frame. Accordingly, radicalization should not be seen just as an individualized issue, but as a multilevel phenomenon involving a person and their various life spheres. In promoting this type of understanding, CPRLV intends to allow for the adoption by professionals and front liners of benevolent responses, beyond the strict security-oriented mindset (Melacarne & Nicolaides, 2019).

Prevention Beyond Professionals: Raising Awareness and Mobilizing the Community

To be effective, prevention cannot be the unique responsibility of professionals. Accordingly, awareness and community mobilization are key in ensuring that the general public and more targeted audiences (such as young people) are aware of the various dimensions associated with radicalization and violent extremism. To raise awareness about those phenomena, CPRLV has chosen to engage through an indirect approach by developing prevention activities that are not directly dealing with radicalization and violent extremism per se, but with proximate issues such identity issues, critical thinking, digital literacy, etc. The CPRLV's awareness campaign, *What If I Was Wrong? I talk, I learn,* launched in September 2017, is an example of this prevention model. The CPRLV also offers a range of activities in schools that focus on raising awareness and sensitizing them to issues related to radicalization leading to violence and hate crimes and incidents.

Because prevention should be understood as the total sum of the efforts of our society as whole community mobilization, community mobilization is key in the CPRLV approach. Public and participatory events among various communities to raise awareness and deconstruct myths about violent extremism have been an important aspect of CPRLV's community mobilization work.

Support and Intervention: A Multidisciplinary, Individualized, and Humanist Philosophy of Social Reintegration

CPRLV's fourth and last area of activity is support and intervention for individuals who might be engaged in violent extremism or who are in the process of becoming radicalized, as well as for families and loved ones. This area of activity is closely linked to the Info-Radical helpline and platform that the CPRLV operates throughout Quebec, a gateway for assistance requests coming from individuals or professionals faced with potential situations of radicalization.

CPRLV's philosophy of intervention focuses on the social reintegration of radicalized individuals to promote a more nuanced return to life, by helping them leave radical environments while helping them evolve in an appropriate social environment. Here, the social reintegration approach replaces what has often been described elsewhere as de-radicalization. Radicalization leading to violence is a process that takes place over a period that can be long. It is nevertheless reversible. A window of opportunity between radical thinking and violent action exists and deserves to be exploited while bringing together all the elements necessary for social reintegration without violent radical thinking. By working positively with the person and their entourage, it becomes possible, on the one hand, to eliminate certain elements that could cause the person to turn violent. On the other hand, it strengthens the person's protective factors, making it easier for him to resist extremist indoctrination.

CPRLV's professionals and experts are there to provide a reassuring and special presence for people who might face the radicalization of a close one.

A social reintegration approach can be divided into five main objectives through a tailor-made care process. First, and if the person is willing to condone the violence, the goal is to make the violence unjustifiable by disengaging the person from the violence. Secondly, it is necessary to develop moral empathy in the individual and to make him/her retreat from ideological extremism. It is in fact disengagement from extremism or a distancing from the extremist discourse that must take place. Third, the person's beliefs should be moderated (i.e., develop a nuanced expression of personal beliefs). Fourth, it is important to gain acceptance of a plurality of beliefs, viewpoints, and opinions (diversification of beliefs) in the person being rehabilitated. Finally, we want the person to reintegrate into society, to have a desire for social inclusion, and to participate in living together by identifying as a stakeholder in the society in which they live.

CONCLUSION

Transformative learning theory can be mobilized as an interesting lens of analysis to understand radicalization phenomena. It incorporates the idea that radicalization can sometimes be interpreted as a form of distortion of thought, as an expression of rigid thinking, unable to transform. But radicalization can also take the form of an emancipatory process of thought when it opens the doors to constructive criticism and coexistence. Transformative theory spoke indirectly of radicalization. Mezirow reported positive examples related to women's empowerment or professional development, describing how transformation produced a reframing of personal assumptions regarding the relationship between women and their professional identities. We always turn to a radicalization account when our perspective becomes impermeable. Therefore, the passage that leads a person to have deep convictions, to absolutize and criticize the rules of his society, to move toward violent actions, and in some cases carry out terrorist acts, assumes a transformative value, although it cannot be regarded as a desirable manifestation.

Transformative theory also allows us to see radicalization as a phenomenon that belongs to everyday life. It allows us to deal with the radical thoughts that we develop during our life journey as an adult. The transformation/radicalization connection helps us as educators to work with people who, by developing a radical thought, risk turning it into violent actions. Radicalization is not a propriety of the person (ontology) and it is not a characteristic of an environment (structuralism or culturalism). It is an emerging phenomenon from an education or learning process.

In this sense, transformative theory, but more generally the theories of adult learning, allow delineating a new object of investigation definable as microradicalization (Bailey & Edwards, 2016). The microradicalization is not necessarily generated by an ideology or a meta-representation;

it starts when a disorienting dilemma does not give rise to a question of learning, but instead a stigmatized, intimidating, or pseudo-rational answer. So, a new goal could be to support adult educational research to study the process of microradicalization as a way to understand why and how people create relational boundaries in daily life, interrupting interactions and polarizing the point of view.

The last point of potential development and interest is the challenge that the radicalization construct poses to the transformative theory in the ethical sense. What is a good and bad transformation? All we have to do is say that if it is self-destructive, it is a desirable educational objective, or we have to go into the direction that the process must take. Radicalization stresses the direction that the learning process could follow. Being radical can be a transformational event, for individuals and society, but can be a dangerous journey also. Transformative learning could be explored more strictly in its relationship with values and rights as an expression of microradicalizational processes.

REFERENCES

Adams, D., Tibbitt, J., Doyle, L., & Welsh, P. (Eds.). (2008). *Building stronger communities: Connecting research, policy and practice.* National Institute of Adult Continuing Education.

Bailey, G., & Edwards, P. (2016). Rethinking radicalisation: Microradicalisations and reciprocal radicalisation as an intertwined process. *Journal for Deradicalisation, 10,* 255–281.

Bartlett, J., & Miller, C. (2012). The edge of violence: Towards telling the difference between violent and non-violent radicalization. *Terrorism and Political Violence, 24*(1), 1–21. https://doi.org/10.1080/09546553.2011.594923

Bhui, K. S., Hicks, M. H., Lashley, M., & Jones, E. (2012). A public health approach to understanding and preventing violent radicalization. *BMC Medicine, 10*(1), 10–16. https://doi.org/10.1186/1741-7015-10-16

Borum, R. (2015). Understanding terrorists. In C. A. Pietz & C. A. Mattson (Eds.), *Violent offenders: Understanding and assessment* (pp. 310–326). Oxford University Press.

Brookfield, S. D., & Holst, J. D. (2011). *Radicalizing learning: Adult education for a just world.* Jossey-Bass.

Coolsaet R. (Ed.) (2011). *Jihadi terrorism and radicalisation challenge: European and American experiences.* Ashgate.

Davis, L. (2018). *Review of educational initiatives in counter-extremism internationally: What works? (Report 5).* The Segerstedt Institute.

Dewey, J. (1935). Liberalism and social action. In J. A. Boydston (Ed.). *The later works of John Dewey, 1925–1953* (vol. 11). Carbondale: Southern Illinois University Press.

Dirkx, J. (2006). Engaging emotions in adult learning: A Jungian perspective on emotion and transformative learning. *New Directions for Adult and Continuing Education, 109*, 15–26. https://doi.org/10.1002/ace.204

Freire, P. (2007). *Pedagogy of the oppressed*. Continuum.

Gallie, W. B. (1955). Essentially contested concepts. *Proceedings of the Aristotelian Society, 56*, 167–198. https://doi.org/10.1093/aristotelian/56.1.167

Hafez, M., & Mullins, C. (2015). The radicalization puzzle: A theoretical synthesis of empirical approaches to homegrown extremism. *Studies in Conflict & Terrorism, 38*(11), 958–975. https://doi.org/10.1080/1057610X.2015.1051375

Harris-Hogan, S., Barrelle, K., & Zammit, A. (2016). What is countering violent extremism? Exploring CVE policy and practice in Australia. *Behavioral Sciences of Terrorism and Political Aggression, 8*(1), 6–24. https://doi.org/10.1080/19434472.2015.1104710

Hill, R. J. (2008). Troubling adult learning in the present time. In S. Merriam (Ed.). *The third update on adult learning theory*. New directions for adult and continuing education, 119 (pp. 83–92). San Francisco: Jossey-Bass.

Koehler, D. (2016). *Understanding deradicalization: Methods, tools and programs for countering violent extremism*. New York: Taylor & Francis.

Khalil, J. (2014). Radical beliefs and violent actions are not synonymous: How to place the key disjuncture between attitudes and behaviors at the heart of our research into political violence. *Studies in Conflict & Terrorism, 37*(2), 198–211. https://doi.org/10.1080/1057610X.2014.862902

Khosrokhavar, F. (2014). *Radicalisation*. Maison des Sciences de l'Homme.

Klausen, J. (2015). Tweeting the Jihad: Social media networks of western foreign fighters in Syria and Iraq. *Studies in Conflict & Terrorism, 38*(1), 1–22. https://doi.org/10.1080/1057610X.2014.974948

Kundnani, A. (2012). Radicalisation: The journey of a concept. *Race & Class, 54*(2), 3–25. https://doi.org/10.1177/0306396812454984

McCauley, C., & Moskalenko, S. (2011). *Friction: How radicalisation happens to them and us*. Oxford University Press.

Melacarne, C., & Nicolaides, A. (2019). Developing professional capability: Growing capacity and competencies to meet complex workplace demands. *New Directions for Adult and Continuing Education, 2019*, 37–51. https://doi.org/10.1002/ace.20340

Mezirow, J. (1991). *Transformative dimensions of adult learning*. Jossey-Bass.

Mezirow, J. (2003). Transformative learning as discourse. *Journal of Transformative Education, 1*(1), 58–63.

Moghadam, F. M. (2009). De-radicalisation and the staircase from terrorism. In D. Canter (Ed.), *The faces of terrorism: Multidisciplinary perspective* (pp. 278–279). Wiley. doi: https://doi.org/10.1002/9780470744499.ch16

Neumann, P. R. (2013). The trouble with radicalization. *International Affairs, 89*(4), 873–893. https://doi.org/10.1111/1468-2346.12049

Neumann, P. R. (2015). *Radicalisation: Major works collection.* Routledge.

O'Sullivan, E. (2012). Deep transformation: Forging a planetary worldview. In E. Taylor & P. Cranton (Eds.), *The handbook of transformative learning: Theory, research and practice* (pp. 162–177). Jossey-Bass.

Richards, A. (2011). The problem with "radicalization": The remit of "Prevent" and the need to refocus on terrorism in the UK. *International Affairs, 87*(1), 143–152. https://doi.org/10.1111/j.1468-2346.2011.00964.x

Ross-Gordon J. M., Rose A. D., & Kasworm, C. E. (2017). *Foundation of adult and continuing education.* Jossey Bass.

Schmid, A.P. (Ed.). (2011). *The Routledge handbook of terrorism research.* Routledge.

Stephens, W., Sieckelinck, S., & Boutellier, H. (2019). Preventing violent extremism: A review of the literature. *Studies in Conflict & Terrorism, 40,* 1–16. https://doi.org/10.1080/1057610X.2018.1543144

Willis, P. (2012). An existential approach to transformative learning. In E. W. Taylor & P. Cranton (Eds.), *The handbook of transformative learning: Theory, research and practice* (pp. 212–227). Jossey-Bass.

Wilner, A., & Dubouloz, C. J. (2015). Homegrown terrorism and transformative learning: An interdisciplinary approach to understanding radicalization. *Global Change, Peace, and Security, 22*(1), 33–51. https://doi.org/10.1080/14781150903487956

Winter, D. A., & Feixas, G. (2019). Toward a constructivist model of radicalization and deradicalization: A Conceptual and methodological proposal. *Frontiers in Psychology, 10*(412). doi: https://doi.org/10.3389/fpsyg.2019.00412

Zeiger, S., & Aly, A. (2015). *Countering violent extremism: Developing an evidence base for policy and practice.* Hedayah/Curtin University.

CHAPTER 44

Evaluation as a Pathway to Transformation
Lessons from Sustainable Development

Scott G. Chaplowe, Adam Hejnowicz,
and Marlene Laeubli Loud

INTRODUCTION

We commit to evaluations that help us learn, understand and support the transformational and systemic changes needed in our countries and the world, as agreed upon in the 2030 Agenda for Sustainable Development. A sustainable balance between the social, economic and environmental domains is crucial in light of the existential threats of the climate crisis,

---

S. G. Chaplowe (✉)
International Evaluation Academy, Barcelona, Spain

A. Hejnowicz
Newcastle University, Newcastle upon Tyne, UK
e-mail: adam.hejnowicz@newcastle.ac.uk

M. Laeubli Loud
Lauco Evaluation & Training, Fribourg, Switzerland
e-mail: marlene.laeubli@bluewin.ch

© The Author(s), under exclusive license to Springer Nature Switzerland AG 2022
A. Nicolaides et al. (eds.), *The Palgrave Handbook of Learning for Transformation*, https://doi.org/10.1007/978-3-030-84694-7_44

mass extinction of species, growing local and global inequity, and ultimately unsustainable use of the resources of the planet.
—IDEAS, 2019, p. 1

Whilst change is inevitable, progress is not. The large-scale, complex and interdependent global environmental and social challenges we confront today require radical solutions if we are to be around the next century. The call for transformation is a call for profound progress. The above quote is taken from the Prague Declaration on Evaluation for Transformational Change, adopted at the Third International Conference of the International Development Evaluation Association (IDEAS, 2019). It reflects the growing attention to transformation in the evaluation of sustainable development (henceforth, "development evaluation"[1]) following the adoption by the UN General Assembly of the landmark *Transforming our World: The 2030 Agenda for Sustainable Development* (henceforth "2030 Agenda") and the Paris Agreement on Climate Change in 2015.

In this chapter, we explore the potential role evaluation can play in transformational learning and change (TLC) in sustainable development, an industry tasked with securing the future of humanity and the resources that sustain it. We first define what we mean by TLC and frame its relevance at the global scale. We then provide an overview of the relatively young but booming field of evaluation, followed by an examination of the uptake and influence of complex systems thinking in development evaluation. This is then followed by a more detailed discussion of evaluation's transformational pathway, highlighting both potholes (obstacles) and bridges (enablers). We end by summarizing key drivers of success for transformational evaluation and promising trends to monitor. We conclude that evaluation's potential for TLC depends on its ability to transform from within. While our focus is primarily on sustainable development evaluation, we hope learning from this chapter resonates with other transformational pursuits, whether in evaluation, or any niche in the global system. We also acknowledge that transformation is an unfolding,

---

[1] Distinguished from Developmental Evaluation, which is one of many evaluation methodologies that can be used in but is not specific to the area of development evaluation (see methodological description at https://www.betterevaluation.org/en/plan/app roach/developmental_evaluation).

open-ended process; therefore, we approach the topic heuristically rather than dogmatically.

Our motivation in writing this chapter is the urgent transformations needed to address the effects of the Anthropocene, the Fourth Industrial Revolution, unbridled capitalism and over-consumption, massive inequalities within and between countries, increasing poverty worldwide in the aftermath of the COVID-19 pandemic, the accelerating destruction of natural ecosystems, and growing geopolitical tensions as power and resources shift. Significant changes are needed to support sustainable, equitable development that focuses on harmony within and between societies, and between humanity and nature. Against this background, we ask: How can evaluation, a profession in the business of assessing and problem solving, inform and accelerate transformation? As we shall see, as a field that straddles both theory and practice, evaluation is uniquely positioned as a passageway for TLC.

But first, let us clarify some of the key concepts we examine. For the purpose of this chapter, our use of *sustainable development* returns to its original conceptualization proposed by the Brundtland Report (WCED, 1987, p. 43): "[D]evelopment that meets the needs of the present without compromising the ability of future generations to meet their own needs". We also include equitable social development and inclusion per the more expansive interpretation of sustainable development adopted 25 years later by the UN General Assembly (UN General Assembly, 2012, p. 1).

Given the international scope of sustainable development, we use *transformation* to refer to deep, rapid, and radical global systems change required to achieve the aspirations of the UN 2030 Agenda's Sustainable Development Goals (SDGs). This definition is often contrasted with incrementalism, reform, or transition to convey the magnitude of required change:

> Unlike a "transition," which implies moving from one place or state to another, "transformation" is more about completely reinventing shape or form—like the metamorphosis of a caterpillar to a butterfly.
> —Waddock et al., 2020, p. 4

It follows that we define *transformational learning* as the process whereby knowledge is created that contributes to transformational

788   S. G. CHAPLOWE ET AL.

change, and *transformational evaluation*[2] to refer to evaluation that supports transformational learning and change.

"Evaluation"—A Bird's Eye View

As a field and discipline, evaluation is relatively young, less than 100 years old, rising in prominence with the growth in public spending and programming throughout the twentieth century (Nielsen et al., 2018; Shadish & Luellen, 2005). Today, evaluation is all around us, an institution in society (Dahler-Larsen, 2011). From education, health care, and policing to business and foreign aid, evaluation has become so ubiquitous in our lives that we often take it for granted. It has become an established administrative protocol associated with a host of interrelated processes, including accountability, transparency, and quality assurance.

The pursuit and institutionalization of evaluation as a field are highly idiosyncratic, contested, and evolving. There is no consensus on evaluation's definition, but the most quoted definition comes from evaluation pioneer Michael Scriven (1991, p. 235), where evaluation is defined as, "the process to determining the merit, worth, and value of things". Evaluation is intentional and involves making a judgement, which are important distinctions from related pursuits. For instance, audits traditionally focus on verification of compliance with established requirements, whereas evaluations judge performance and impact (among many other things).

Evaluation takes many shapes and forms, ranging from project, program, policy, and strategy evaluation to personnel, product, and student evaluation. Evaluations can be conducted prior to an intervention (ex-ante), during its implementation (formative), at its completion (summative), and/or years afterwards (ex-post). Evaluations can also be independent, internal, participatory, or jointly conducted. The technical focus ranges from impact, outcome, and process evaluations to a host of evaluations defined by their methodological approach (e.g. Utilization, Realist, and Empowerment evaluation). Evaluators often engage in a range of related activities, such as program design (e.g. theory of change),

---

[2] Distinguished from *transformative evaluation*, an established theoretical framework developed by Donna Mertens (2009) for conducting research and evaluation in a way that contributes to social justice.

baseline studies, evidence reviews, organizational assessment, and policy analysis.[3]

Importantly, for transformational learning and change, evaluation is a transdiscipline, deeply embedded in and essential to all other fields to make evaluative distinctions—"in the methodological toolbox of every other discipline" (Scriven, 2016, p. 27). From this perch, evaluation is in a useful position to support the integration required for transformation to a more sustainable and equitable future (Patton, 2020).

However, as a form of applied research, evaluation's ascent to thriving industry has not been without difficulties. Evaluation is embedded in the marketplace, and therefore subject to the same forces that shape the political economy of its evaluand (object of evaluation),[4] such as sustainable development. This can clash with some core elements of evaluation, such as independence, legitimacy, and the pursuit of objective, value-free knowledge production (Nielsen et al., 2018). Additionally, the marketplace can consign evaluation to a descriptive, tick-box, accounting exercise that steers clear of judgement rather than judgement to steer decision making (House, 2014; Schwandt, 2015). Such "valuephobia" is ironic in that it undermines evaluation's very value proposition (Scriven, 2016). We shall revisit these challenges later in this chapter.

So, how well suited is evaluative practice today to foster transformation in response to the ever more complex problems society is having to confront? The remainder of this chapter will help us consider this question.

THE ASCENDENCY OF COMPLEXITY AND SYSTEMS THINKING IN EVALUATION

Relative to other fields, evaluation has been slow to embrace complexity and systems thinking (Befani et al., 2015; Williams et al., 2016). But this is changing in the world of international development in response to the persistence of intractable, complex problems and the appropriation of systems and complexity-adaptive approaches to solve them.

---

[3] To learn about different types and approaches to evaluation, we highly recommend the open, online resource, BetterEvalaution (2020).

[4] Evaluand is a generic term to refer to any object of an evaluation, whether it be a person, program, idea, policy, product, object, performance, or any other entity being evaluated (Mathison, 2005, p. 139).

Experts may differ on the details, but they converge on the global scale and the complexity of today's problems. In the field of evaluation, the term *wicked problem* is often used to refer to complex problems, characterized by emergent, nonlinear, and uncertain consequences that defy traditional analysis and solutions (Hopson & Cram, 2018; Williams & van t'Hoff, 2016). Increasingly, *super-wicked problem* is being used for the hyper-complex challenges at the global scale, such as mirrored by the SDGs, characterized by multiple interacting systems, levels of change (e.g. local, regional, and global), and intersecting interventions and actors.

Sustainable development is especially fertile ground for super-wicked problems. Collectively, and individually, the 17 SDGs and their 169 targets and 232 indicators that comprise the 2030 Agenda mirror highly complex problems, from chronic malnutrition and infectious disease to global warming and biodiversity loss. Nested into this complexity is an assortment of actors ranging from bilateral and multilateral aid organizations, philanthropic foundations, and private donors to civil society organizations, the national public sector, and local populations. Evaluation in such contexts involves understanding multiple perspectives with varying priorities, agendas, and resource flows that fluctuate in a global economy where recession, political change, and natural forces result in a high degree of uncertainty.

For example, the convergence of pandemic, climate change, and social unrest aptly illustrates the complex interactions of a super-wicked problem. COVID-19 is a zoonotic disease (from animals) and illustrates how the steady encroachment on, and neglect of, the environment spills over to negatively impact the human system. In the United States, where the median wealth of Black households is a tenth that of Whites, the burden of the pandemic has been disproportionate for Black people at three times the rate of White people (Davis, 2020). Compounded with the viral video of the tragic murder of George Floyd at the hand of law enforcement, as well as incompetent and divisive national leadership, the social tensions spilled over into unrest and protests.

The urgency and persistence of wicked problems have played an important role in the uptake of complexity theory and systems thinking in evaluation. Systems thinking provides a heuristic for navigating complexity, stressing that interventions occur in a broader context that requires understanding interrelationships, engaging with multiple perspectives, and reflecting on where boundaries are drawn in terms of those interrelationships and perspectives (Williams & Hummelbrunner, 2010).

The adoption of the 2030 Agenda, as well as the Paris Agreement on Climate Change, further propelled the recognition and practice of complexity theory and systems thinking in the field of development evaluation (Bamberger et al., 2016). Notably, the SDGs provide a more comprehensive, complexity-adaptive framework for global development than the narrower UN Millennium Development Goals (MDGs) adopted fifteen years earlier (Bamberger et al., 2016, p. 15)[5] (See Fig. 44.1).

While transformation is not explicitly defined in the 2030 Agenda, it encompasses three primary dimensions: economic, environmental, and social (UNRISD, 2016). In other words, transformational change is a change that is far greater than the sum of its parts (politically, economically, socially, technologically, and environmentally), and fundamentally different from the way things are now (Schwandt et al., 2016).

A good example of transformational policy and change at the global level is the landmark Montreal Protocol to regulate the production and consumption of nearly 100 man-made ozone depleting substances (ODS). Agreed on in 1987 and implemented in 1989, the Protocol is to date the only UN treaty ratified by every country on Earth (all 197 UN Member States). It has gone beyond policy into action and change, phasing out 98% of the ODS to reduce the size of the ozone hole to the smallest on record, and saving an estimated two million people annually from skin cancer (UNEP, 2019).

To date, the 2030 Agenda is the largest collaboration for collective welfare, adopted by and premised on the interdependent welfare of all UN Member States. Its authors are explicit about its "supremely ambitious and transformational vision" (UN General Assembly, 2015, p. 3). As a framework, the 17 SDGs may not be perfect, but then any conceptual model is only an approximation of reality. What the framework has going for it is international recognition and credibility, and its acknowledgement that the challenges of our times require TLC.

---

[5] While the MDGs focused primarily on poverty and health, the SDGs also cover the environment, human rights, and gender equality, among other new goals.

Fig. 44.1 Illustrative mapping of SDG interconnectedness (Courtesy of Eurostat, 2019)

Evaluation's Transformatioinal Potential: Potholes and Bridges

The ascendancy of complexity thinking in development work is central to evaluation's transformative potential, akin to a Kuhnian paradigm shift in how we package, deliver, and evaluate development. However, there is also much resistance, implicit and explicit, and habits are hard to change, especially when institutionalized in a mammoth industry like sustainable

44 EVALUATION AS A PATHWAY TO TRANSFORMATION ... 793

development. This perhaps explains why, relative to other fields, evaluation has been slow to fully embrace systems and complexity thinking (Befani et al., 2015). Paradigm shifts, especially in science, advance "One Funeral at a Time" (Azoulay et al., 2019).

In this section, we examine what needs to be transformed if development evaluation is to be transformational. Each of the "potholes" in evaluation's pathway to transformation also carries the kernel of its solution, pointing towards bridges to overcome these traps. We have categorized these obstacles into four groupings, but they are far from exhaustive, and true to any complex system, they and their solutions are very much interrelated and overlap.

Accountability for TLC, Not Evidence-Mania

(T)hose development programs that are most precisely and easily measured are the least transformational, and those programs that are the most transformational are the least measurable.
— Natsios, 2010, p. 4

It is often asserted that "What gets measured gets done". However, another witticism reminds us that "Not everything that can be counted counts, and not everything that counts can be counted".[6] Reality cannot be counted; it is not a binary concept that can be wrapped up into neat, quantitative boxes from which key performance indicators (KPIs) verify whether funded interventions achieve impact. The same attributes that make systems complex make systems change initiatives hard to measure.

However, there is an Obsessive Measurement Disorder (OMD) in the development industry where the production of evidence-based data undermines the very interventions they are supposed to support (Natsios, 2010). The fixation on quantitative measurement and accountability for predetermined, measurable goals limits the range of learning and possibilities to whether something is done "right" versus whether the "right" thing is being done in the first place (Roche & Madvig, 2016, p. 32). Perversely, "the snake of accountability eats its own tail" (Mueller, 2018,

---

[6] Often wrongly attributed to Albert Einstein, the origin of the quote is from Cameron (1963, p. 17).

p. 154). This is at odds with the complexity thinking and innovation required for TLC (Fig. 44.2).

To a large extent, the current fixation on accountability reflects a pervasive legacy from the neoliberalism of Reaganomics and Thatcherism in the 1980s, advocating the creation of marketlike conditions and the use of performance metrics to determine reward and punishment to uphold accountability (Verdung, 2010). Today, it remains dominant in development, epitomized by approaches such as results-based management, value-for-money, payment for results, and return on investment.

A troubling characteristic of this pursuit of accountability, especially for evaluation, is that it seeks to replace judgement with standardized measurement. Reliance on quantitative metrics can side-track decision makers from the very accountability they seek by releasing them from the responsibility of making hard judgement calls based on subject matter expertise, experience, and systems analysis, and instead causing them to make decisions under the allure and implication of numbers.

Certainly, evidence is a valuable source for TLC, and assessing individual and organizational performance serves intervention implementation. But problems arise with the cumulative creep to a tyranny of

Fig. 44.2 Cartoon by Julie Smith (Courtesy of the IFRC, 2011, p. 26)

metrics resulting in excessive bureaucratization and "proceduralization" (Anderson et al., 2012, p. 67; Mueller, 2018). In development, an industry fraught with political/economic agendas that often supersede the collective good, donor monitoring, evaluation, and reporting requirements can distract civil society organizations (CSOs) such that they become more attuned and accountable to the donors' needs than the people they are meant to represent and serve (Chaplowe & Engo- Tjéga, 2007). This exemplifies what House (1995, p. 29) identifies as "clientism" where evaluation mistakenly assumes that whatever benefits the clients' interests is ethically correct.

For fulfilling the transformational aspirations of the SDGs, accountability needs to be foremost for the planet—not discrete interventions and the people who implement them, which is our next topic to examine.

Evaluate Outside the Box

> Critically examining how we got into this situation, evaluation emerges as part of the problem, too often focused only on projects and programs that function within larger systems – but examining those larger system connections and implications would be outside the 'scope' of the evaluator's terms of reference.
> —Patton, 2020, p. 188

Transformational development requires, among other things, a much-needed shift from siloed interventions and funding streams to more holistic, integrated approaches at all levels in the global system. Interventions in the arena of sustainable development have largely been dominated by single, clearly defined projects and programmes provided by single agencies and funded by single donors. These interventions are typically treated as closed systems—boxes—with linear theories of change that overlook the broader context and complex interactions and interdependencies in which they are unpacked. Narrow piecemeal approaches do not connect the dots required for more sustainable development, and risk overlooking important spill-over and side-effects, whether they are synergistic or crippling (Patton, 2020).

By design, the 17 SDGs offer a framework that fittingly illustrates the fundamental interdependence between different but interrelated dimensions and sectors of sustainable development: "Understanding the range of positive and negative interactions among SDGs is key to unlocking their full potential at any scale, as well as to ensuring that progress made in some areas is not made at the expense of progress in others" (ICSU, 2017, p. 7).

For example, Fig. 44.3 illustrates the interactions between SDG 2 (Zero Hunger), SDG 3 (Health and Wellbeing), SDG 7 (Affordable Clean Energy), and SDG 14 (Life Below Water). It is part of a study that identified 316 target-level interactions for these four SDGs collectively on all 17 SDGs, of which 238 are positive, 66 negative, and 12

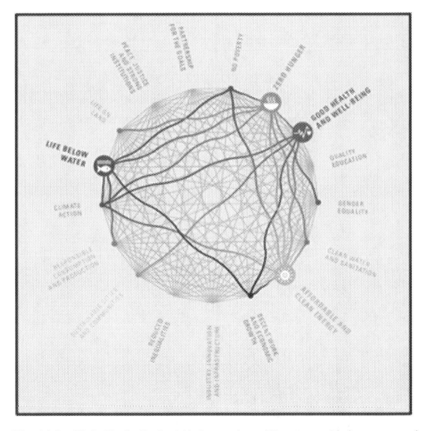

Fig. 44.3 SDG (2, 3, 7, & 14) Interactions (Figure provided courtesy of International Council for Science, 2017)

neutral (ICSU, 2017). For instance, SDG 14 (Life Below Water) critically intersects with land-based pollution, climate change-induced warming and sea-level rise, ocean acidification, and over-exploitation of marine resources; this, in turn, has a multiplier effect on nutrition, livelihoods, and economic growth, especially for coastal communities. Subsequently, these and all SDGs intersect with and are heavily impact by the policy options and strategies governments pursue (SDGs 16 and 17).

Transformation, especially in relation to super-wicked problems, happens in open systems that transcend time and place, ecological niches and biomes, and political borders and specialized interests. Thus, we need to look beyond interventions as the main agent of change and instead consider them as one of and relative to many interacting factors that affect sustainability (Garcia & Zazueta, 2015). Evaluation can support this transformative and holistic perspective by responding to the growing need to design and assess multi-sector and multi-actor coalitions glocally (at all levels of engagement, locally and globally).

Casual Models, Not Straightjackets

Evaluators widely use conceptual models or frameworks to identify the causal linkages that will lead to desired results, which can then be used to assess performance or achievement of these results. In other words, models steer the evaluative questions that evaluators examine—which, in turn, steers the learning and its potential to be transformational. However, the conceptual models used to design international development and guide evaluation typically employ linear casual analysis. This makes measurement and accountability for the intervention more doable, but it is not a good recipe for TLC.

There is no industry standard for the models used to design development interventions, but the more common ones include logical frameworks (and logframes), results frameworks, and Theories of Change (TOC). In addition to specifying hierarchy of desired results, these frameworks typically include SMART[7] indicators to measure progress towards intended results, as well as any assumptions to monitor risks that can affect achievement of the results. In Fig. 44.4, the central green line of inputs, activities, outputs, outcomes, and impact reflects the linear design logic

---

[7] Specific, Measurable, Achievable, Relevant, and Time-bound.

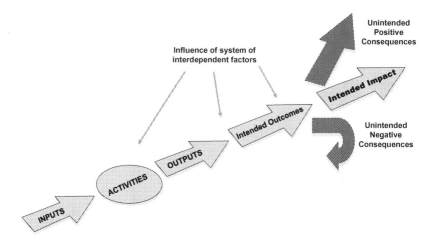

Fig. 44.4 Linear Intervention Design (Figure courtesy of Chaplowe, 2017)

of these models, whereas the red arrows illustrate influence and change typically not captured by these models (discussed later, below).

Predetermined, linear models lead to reductionist planning and analysis that reinforce siloed thinking on an intervention's intended results (e.g. project) while overlooking or downplaying other critical factors (the red aspects depicted in Fig. 44.4). In essence, conceptual models are only theories of what people think will happen, but these maps often become the reality. Such boilerplate approaches risk forcing development into narrow confines of accountability to the exclusion of TLC:

> Impact at scale requires transformational processes that may be composed of multiple pathways going in different directions. As the intervention's TOC is likely to direct the attention of the evaluator to the expected causal links, it can also act as a blinder to chains of causality that had not been contemplated in the intervention design, and are rarely apparent by project completion.
> —(Garcia & Zazueta, 2015, p. 41)

The above summary is not absolute, and increasingly there are examples of more dynamic modelling of causal relationships, such as interlinked logic models or TOC with multiple branches and feedback loops that better model complex interventions. However, if we are to achieve global systems transformation, we need to switch out theories of change (TOC) for theories of transformation (TOT) that transcend programmes and projects (Patton, 2020).[8]

Such transformational models require adaptive, open theories of transformational change with attention to unintended consequences, trade-offs, and future forecasting. Just because it may not be possible to establish direct causation and net results from an intervention does not mean the intervention does not contribute to transformation (Garcia & Zazueta, 2015). There is increased attention on goal-free evaluations that is highly critical of evaluation fixated on goal achievement (Scriven, 1991, 2016; Youkeer et al., 2014), and on the efficacy of accepting and learning from failure (e.g. *Fail Forward.org* and *Admitting Failure.org*). Both trends are promising steps for evaluation's pathway to support TLC.

Real-Time and "Over-Time" Evaluation

Just as transformational evaluation must cut across spatial scales, it is also critical that it encompasses different temporal scales. As we have seen, real-world development, especially sustainable development, is messy and does not fit well with predefined timeframes and funding cycles. Ultimately, we want systems to change over time, which is why we intervene. The problem is that complex systems do not behave the way we would like them, and changes, (whether incremental or transformative), do not necessarily mirror the intervention logic presented in models. Instead, there is a myriad of emergent, intervening variables that can affect the intended intervention logic.

Mechanistic casual models evoke static predictability, order, and timing that exclude emergent unintended, indirect, and secondary impacts that typify complex operating environments. Reflecting back upon the red arrows in Fig. 44.4, there are a multiplicity of factors that can lead to positive and negative outcomes that were unanticipated at the design phase of the intervention. For example, consider the impact of any of the following on the operation of TOCs of organizations working on social equity or environmental conservation: COVID-19, the 2008 Great

---

[8] This is a relatively nascent area in development, but examples of integrating theories that can inform TOTs include theory knitting, layering theories, theory ladders, network theory, innovation theory, the Hage Hypothesis, and Blue Marble Evaluation Theory, to name a few (Patton, 2020, pp. 156–169).

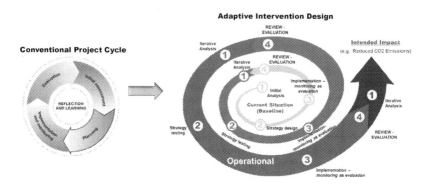

Fig. 44.5 Complexity adaptive intervention design (Figure courtesy of IFRC, 2010; Chaplowe, 2017)

Recession, and the election of political leaders like US President Trump and Brazil's President Bolsonaro.

Therefore, evaluation needs to move away from homing in on the predetermined timeframes of purposive theories of change, and instead adopt more real-time evaluation (monitoring *as* evaluation) that provides immediate and ongoing feedback that allows interventions to be nimbler and receptive to change.[9] Figure 44.5 illustrates this by contrasting a more conventional project cycle with a more complexity-adaptive intervention design. Rather than eventful evaluations, such as baseline, midterm and final evaluations complemented with monitoring data on a more regular basis, this version of formative evaluation is structured to be iterative and ongoing, informing course-correction that is more responsive to complex operating environments and supports emergent transformative learning.

Specific adaptive approaches will vary according to operational context, budget, and other resources. For instance, one author commissioned an evaluation of a climate change investment using light strategy-testing exercises (1 to 2 days) conducted collaboratively by the evaluators with program teams on a quarterly basis. This approach had the added advantage of utilizing a "developmental" approach where evaluators not only

---

[9] Real-time evaluation is often reserved for humanitarian contexts, but it can also be used for broader uses of evaluation in real time.

assess but also engage to support innovation to guide adaptation (Patton, 2010).

Another temporal concern is the degree to which evaluations assess longer-term impacts beyond the stated end of an intervention. While transformation stresses radical, rapid change, what contributes to reaching this tipping point may require time. However, conventional summative (final) evaluations are typically commissioned with an endpoint or exit/transition strategy in mind, which narrows assessment to the short- and midterm outcomes. Meanwhile, follow-up with ex-post evaluation (one to several years later) is rare, meaning that assessment of higher-level results and longer-term consequences are left unevaluated (Zivetz et al., 2017). Yet, for transformational learning and change, this is particularly important because it leaves aside any evaluation of the possible (even probable) future, unintended consequences occurring within the wider system. For instance, for a livelihoods program introducing chemical fertilizers and pesticides for household farming, a final evaluation may focus narrowly on the measurable results, such as increased crop yield and household income. However, this short-term focus excludes considering and capturing downstream costs on the local ecosystem due to introduced chemicals that erode topsoil, pollute groundwater, and decrease biodiversity. In turn, these environmental costs result in economic and health costs for the larger population that far outweigh measured benefits in targeted farmer households.

Looking Forward

A gradual, yet revolutionary, transformation has begun regarding what evaluation should examine; what kind of questions it should address; how these questions should be structured; how answers should be sought; and how the results should be interpreted. Indeed, such an evolution is imperative to help post-modern societies overcome the existential threats of the Anthropocene age.
—Picciotto, 2020, p. 59

Given our premise that complexity and systems thinking—which emphasize iterative and unfolding processes—are essential ingredients for transformational evaluation, we would be amiss to provide a specific recipe or approach for how and the degree to which transformational

802   S. G. CHAPLOWE ET AL.

evaluation will unfold in the remainder of this century. The politically correct mantra in evaluation is adopting mixed-method approaches, especially as interventions become larger and more complex and thus beyond any one method to assess the different dimensions of complexity (Bamberger et al., 2016). However, the reality, especially as we have described in development evaluation, is still predominantly a strong lean towards quantitative, experimental, and purportedly objective methods for accountability.

Nevertheless, as discussed in this chapter, the potholes of conventional evaluation are becoming increasingly apparent, as are the solutions that support bridging evaluation towards realizing a transformational evaluation agenda. These potholes and bridges are summarized in Table 44.1. As these drivers reflect, for evaluation to realize its potential to support systems transformation, it needs to transform from within through a self-critical learning process. Given the immensely complex undertaking of evaluation in complex contexts and processes in which it is pursued, it is important to note that the table is heuristic; as such, it is illustrative and not absolute nor exhaustive, nor black and white as there is much grey and overlap between both columns.

Where and how this TCL within evaluation will emerge, like flowers in the pavement cracks, is to be seen. One critical hurdle to overcome is the political-economic reality of formal commissioning processes for evaluations both in the private and civil sectors, but especially in the public sector. Influencing the mindsets of those that commission evaluations, especially of large-scale public policy programmes and interventions, to promote a cultural shift away from the linear tick-box accountability exercises or stringent quantitative straightjackets towards transformational evaluations is key.

Fortunately, there are some promising signs for transformative evaluation, such as the increase in complexity and systems-savvy scholarly research, publications, and methodological approaches in the evaluation field[10] where, for example, academics and practitioners are partnering with evaluation teams in the public policy sphere to co-create new learning and develop capacity in complex systems analysis. While the

---

[10] For further reading and additional resources on the topic, we recommend: CEACAN's website, https://www.cecan.ac.uk/eppns; the Blue Marble Evaluation website, https://bluemarbleevaluation.org; Zenda Ofir's website, https://zendaofir.com/; and Scott G. Chaplowe's website, https://scottchaplowe.com.

44 EVALUATION AS A PATHWAY TO TRANSFORMATION ... 803

Table 44.1 Illustrative conventional vs. transformational practices

Conventual (Potholes)	*Transformational (Bridges)*
1. Purpose—Accountability for intervention goals; performance reporting to funders	**1. Purpose**—Accountability for the planet; learning for innovation and transformational change
2. Perspective—reductionist, mechanistic	**2. Perspective**—holistic, comprehensive
3. Overarching principles—market driven, human-centric, separation from living systems, scarcity, and tragedy of the commons	**3. Overarching principles**—cooperation, sustainability, regenerative, abundance, and prosperity of the commons
4. Primary User—donor/funder	**4. Primary User**—implementing team/s + key partners
5. Engagement—external, independent evaluation team	**5. Engagement**—multiple actors/levels/perspectives
6. Scale/evaluand—micro focus on intervention	**6. Scale/evaluand**—macro focus beyond intervention
7. Design/modelling—Predetermined, linear intervention logic, e.g. logic models and theories of change	**7. Design/modelling**—Complexity-adaptive, systems-savvy models and theories of transformation
8. Data collection methods—preference for quantitative metrics to support counterfactual analysis	**8. Data collection methods**—mixed methods
9. Measurement—quantitative focus on predetermined goals, KPIs and targets	**9. Measurement**—mixed methods alert for emergent, unintended consequences/outcomes
10. Analytical framework—positivist objectivity; experimental designs and failure adverse	**10. Analytical framework**—systems and complexity thinking; experimentation and failure tolerant
11. Evaluation Timeframe—eventful, limited to intervention implementation, culminating in summative evaluation	**11. Evaluation Timeframe**—real-time, iterative, and ex-post evaluation beyond intervention

Ivory Tower might not institutionalize transformation in itself, thought leadership is an important companion on evaluation's pathway to transformation.

Two notable initiatives geared towards capacity building for TLC in the field of evaluation are the Blue Marble Evaluation (http://www.bluemarbleevaluation.org) and The Centre for the Evaluation of Complexity Across the Nexus (cecan.ac.uk). Named after Michael Quinn Patton's seminal book (2020), Blue Marble Evaluation is a global initiative focused on training the next generation of evaluators to think, act, and evaluate globally, connecting evaluators with others from a variety of disciplines

804   S. G. CHAPLOWE ET AL.

and practices working on transformational change to confront the challenges mirrored in the SDGs. CECAN, hosted by the University of Surrey (UK), has a vision to transform the practice of policy evaluation so it is fit for a complex world by pioneering, testing, and promoting innovative policy evaluation approaches and methods across domains such as food, energy, water, and the environment, through a series of "real life" case study projects in collaboration with co-funders.

We end our chapter identifying two key influences we believe especially relevant for transformational evaluation, coming from both ends of the historical continuum. First is the renewed interest in traditional Indigenous and Aboriginal worldviews that offer alternative paradigms to support TLC in how we practice evaluation (e.g. Chouinard, & Cousins, 2007; OHCHR, 2017; Rowe et al., 2019; Smith, 1999). Many Indigenous peoples throughout the world have accumulated valuable knowledge systems about the relationship between nature and sustainable practices, founded on the belief that everything is equal (land, plants, human beings, stars, water, air, etc.). While paradoxically these traditional paradigms are now unorthodox, they are beginning to seep into and influence the field of evaluation, as evidenced by, for example, the active multi-stakeholder partnership, "EvalIndigenous" at evalpartners.org.

Second, is the incredible revolution in data science, notably the potential (and drawbacks) of big data for TLC (World Bank, 2016; York & Bamberger, 2020). *Big data* refers to huge, diverse sets of data, often generated continuously over long periods of time, from multiple sources, including satellite and remote sensor images, digital financial transaction data, social media streams, internet searches, GPS location data, and pdf data files. The data amassed and the data analytics it offers were unimaginable at the start of this decade. Big data offers new possibilities for more sophisticated types of analysis, including predictive modelling, machine learning and artificial intelligence, and the integration of multiple data sets for the analysis of complex systems.

Yet despite these and other potential benefits, the use of big data and computer modelling circles back to some of the transformational potholes to remind us that evaluation's pathway to transformation is not a given. Inspired by the misuse of mathematical modelling in the response to the COVID-19 pandemic, 22 authors recently published a manifesto cautioning:

Mathematical models are a great way to explore questions. They are also a dangerous way to assert answers. Asking models for certainty or consensus is more a sign of the difficulties in making controversial decisions than it is a solution and can invite ritualistic use of quantification.
——Saltelli et al., 2020, p. 484

In conclusion, we have seen that while evaluation is uniquely positioned as a passageway for the TLC, this potential depends largely on its ability to transform from within. We hope this chapter helps to both frame and foster this transformation so that evaluation can better support sustainable development that secures the future of humanity during these existentially uncertain times.

REFERENCES

Anderson, M. B., Brown, D., & Jean, I. (2012). *Time to listen: Hearing people on the receiving end of international aid*. CDA Collaborative Learning Projects Publication.

Azoulay, P., Fons-Rosen, C., & Zivin, J. (2019). Does science advance one funeral at a time? *The American Economic Review, 109*(8), 2889–2920.

Bamberger, M., Vaessen, J., & Raimondo, E. (2016). *Dealing with complexity in development Evaluation—A practical approach*. Sage.

BetterEvaluation. (2020). https://www.betterevaluation.org/.

Befani, B., Ramalingam, B., & Stern, E. (2015). Introduction—Towards systemic approaches to evaluation and impact. *Institute of Development Studies Bulletin, 46*(1).

Cameron, W. B. (1963). *Informal sociology: A casual introduction to sociological thinking*. Random House.

Chaplowe, S. (2017). *Monitoring & evaluation training slides*. Geneva.

Chaplowe, S., & Engo-Tjéga, R. B. (2007). Civil society organizations and evaluation: Lessons from Africa. *Evaluation, 13*(2), 257–274.

Chouinard, J. A., & Cousins, J. B. (2007). Culturally competent evaluation for Aboriginal communities—A review of the empirical literature. *Journal of MultiDisciplinary Evaluation, 4*(8), 40–57.

Dahler-Larsen, P. (2011). *The evaluation society*. Stanford University Press.

Davis, W. (2020). The unravelling of America. *Rolling Stone*. https://www.rollingstone.com/politics/political-commentary/covid-19-end-of-american-era-wade-davis-1038206/?fbclid=IwAR1bliCU2EAMQ2oEEambYMGhtOCd7ULi6gigR4saSZfFmb_SzOvks-QhORg

Eurostat (2019). *Multi-purpose indicators within the EU SDG indicator set.gif*. https://ec.europa.eu/eurostat/statistics-explained/index.php?title=File:

Multi-purpose_indicators_within_the_EU_SDG_indicator_set.gif&oldid=437034.

Garcia, J. R., & Zazueta, A. (2015). Going beyond mixed methods to mixed approaches: A systems perspective to asking the right questions. *Institute of Development Studies Bulletin, 46*(1), 30–43. https://doi.org/10.1111/1759-5436.12119

Hopson, R., & Cram, F. (Eds.) (2018). *Tackling wicked problems in complex ecologies: The role of evaluation.* Stanford University Press.

House, E. R. (2014). *Evaluating: Values, biases, and practical wisdom (evaluation and society).* Information Age Publishing.

ICSU. (2017). *A guide to SDG interactions: From science to implementation.* International Council for Science.

IDEAS. (2019, October 4). *Prague declaration on evaluation for transformational change.* Adopted by the International Development Evaluation Association (IDEAS).

IFRC. (2010). *Project/programme monitoring and evaluation (M&E) guide.* International Federation of Red Cross and Red Crescent Societies.

IFRC. (2011). *Project/programme monitoring and evaluation (M&E) guide.* International Federation of Red Cross and Red Crescent Societies.

Mathison, S. (Ed.). (2005). *Evaluand.* Sage.

Mertens, D. (2009). *Transformative research and evaluation.* Guilford Press.

Mueller, J. Z. (2018). *The tyranny of metrics.* Princeton University Press.

Natsios, A. (2010). *The clash of the counter-bureaucracy and development.* Center for Global Development. www.cgdev.org/content/publications/detail/1424271.

Nielsen, S. B., Lemire, S., & Christie, C. A. (Eds.). (2018). The evaluation marketplace: Exploring the evaluation industry. *New Directions for Evaluation, 160*, 13–28. Wiley.

OHCHR. (2017). *Indigenous people's rights and the 2030a agenda.* Briefing Note for the Office of the High Commission for Human Rights (OHCHR) and the Secretariat of the Permanent Forum on Indigenous Issues, Division for Social Policy and Development, United Nations Department of Economic and Social Affairs.

Patton, M. Q. (2010). *Developmental evaluation: Applying complexity concepts to enhance innovation and use.* Guilford Press.

Patton, M. Q. (2015). *Qualitative evaluation & research methods.* Sage.

Patton, M.Q. (2020). *Blue marble evaluation: Premises and principles.* Guildford Press.

Picciotto, R. (2020). Evaluation and the big data challenge. *American Journal of Evaluation, 4*(2), 166–181. https://doi.org/10.1177/1098214019850334

Roche, C., & Madvig, A. (2016). *Working towards transformational development and the sustainable development goals* [Working Paper] La Trobe University, Australia. https://doi.org/10.13140/RG.2.2.27601.53606.

Rowe, M. D., Anderson, E. J., Beletsky, D., Stow, C. A., Moegling, S. D., Chaffin, J. D., May, J. C., Collingsworth, P. D., Jabbari, A., & Ackerman, J. D. (2019). Coastal upwelling influences hypoxia spatial patterns and nearshore dynamics in Lake Erie. *JGR Oceans, 124*(8), 6154–6175.

Saltelli, A., Bammer, G., Bruno, I., Charters, E., Di Fore, M., Didier, E., Espeland, W. N., Kay, J., La Piano, S., Mayo, D., Pielke Jr. R., Portaluri, T., Porter, T. M., Puy, A., Rafols, I., Ravetz, J. R., Reinert, E., Sarewitz, D., Startk, P. B., ...Vienos, P. (2020). Five ways to ensure that models serve society: A manifesto. *Nature, 582,* 482–484. https://doi.org/10.1038/d41 586-020-01812-9.

Schwandt, T. A., Ofir, Z., Lucks, D., El-Saddic, K., & D'Errico, S. (2016). Evaluation: A crucial ingredient for SDG success. *An International Institute for Economic Development (IIED) Briefing.* https://pubs.iied.org/17357I IED/#:~:text=The%202030%20Agenda%20for%20Sustainable,especially% 20at%20the%20national%20level.

Schwandt, T. A. (2015). *Evaluation foundations revisited: Cultivating a life of the mind for practice.* Stanford University Press.

Scriven, M. (2016). Roadblocks to recognition and revolution. *American Journal of Evaluation, 37,* 27–44. https://doi.org/10.1177/1098214015617847.

Scriven, M. (1991). *Evaluation thesaurus.* Sage.

Shadish, W. R., & J. K. Luellen. (2005). History of evaluation. In S. Mathison (Ed.), *Encyclopedia of evaluation* (pp. 183–186).

Smith, L. T. (1999). *Decolonizing methodologies: Research and indigenous peoples.* Zed Books.

UNEP. (2019). *Thirty years on, what is the Montreal Protocol doing to protect the ozone?* United Nations Environment Programme News and Stories.

UN General Assembly. (2012, July 27). *The future we want.* A/RES/66/288. New York.

UN General Assembly. (2015, October 21). *Transforming our world: The 2030 agenda for sustainable development.* A/RES/70/1. New York.

UNRISD. (2016). *Policy innovations for transformative change: Implementing the 2030 agenda for sustainable development.* United Nations Research Institute for Social Development.

Vedung, E. (2010). Four waves of evaluation diffusion. *Evaluation, 16*(3), 263–277.

Waddock, S., Waddell, S., Goldstein, B., Linner, B., Schapke, N., & Vogel, C. (2020). Transformation: How to spur radical change. In A. Scrutton (Ed.), *Future Earth: Our future on earth report* (pp. 82–90).

WCED—World Commission on Environment and Development. (1987). *Our common future*. Oxford University Press.

Williams, B., & Sjon van 't Hof. (2016). *Wicked solutions. A systems approach to complex problems* (2nd ed.). https://www.lulu.com/shop/bob-williams-and-sjon-van-t-hof/wicked-solutions-a-systems-approach-to-complex-problems/paperback/product-22562407.html.

Williams, B., & Hummelbrunner, R. (2010). *Systems concepts in action: A Practitioner's toolkit*. Stanford University Press.

World Bank. (2016). *World development report 2016: Digital dividends*. The World Bank.

York, P., & Bamberger, M. (2020). *Measuring results and impact in the age of big data: The nexus of evaluation, analytics, and digital technology*. The Rockefeller Foundation. https://www.rockefellerfoundation.org/wp-content/uploads/Measuring-results-and-impact-in-the-age-of-big-data-by-York-and-Bamberger-March-2020.pdf.

Youkeer, B. W., Ingraham, A., & Bayer, N. (2014). An assessment of goal-free evaluation: Case studies of four goal-free evaluations. *Evaluation and Program Planning, 46*, 10–16. https://doi.org/10.1016/j.evalprogplan.2014.05.002.

Zivetz, L., Cekan, J., & Robbins, K. (2017). *Building the evidence base for post project evaluation*. Valuing Voices publication.

CHAPTER 45

Restoring the Transformative Bridge: Remembering and Regenerating Our Western Transformative Ancient Traditions to Solve the Riddle of Our Existential Crisis

Petra T. Buergelt and Douglas Paton

INTRODUCTION

Instead of stepping forwards and looking into the future for solutions we have to walk backwards into the place inside us all where the answers already lie and have always been waiting.
—Kingsley (2018, p. 195)
Most of us have been displaced from those cultures of origin, a global diaspora of refugees severed not only from land, but from the sheer genius that comes from belonging in a symbiotic relation to it. ... Perhaps we

---

P. T. Buergelt (✉) · D. Paton
University of Canberra, Canberra, ACT, Australia
e-mail: petra.buergelt@canberra.edu.au

D. Paton
e-mail: douglas.paton@cdu.edu.au

© The Author(s), under exclusive license to Springer Nature Switzerland AG 2022
A. Nicolaides et al. (eds.), *The Palgrave Handbook of Learning for Transformation*, https://doi.org/10.1007/978-3-030-84694-7_45

809

need to revisit the brilliant thought paths of our Palaeolithic Ancestors and recover enough cognitive function to correct the impossible messes civilization has created.
—Yunkaporta (2019, pp. 2–3)

Increasingly frequent, severe, cascading, and compounding levels of disease, "natural" disasters, pandemics, food and water shortages, climate change, and environmental destruction highlight how we are living through an apocalyptic and challenging era of cultural transition that could threaten all of existence on earth (Buergelt et al., 2017; Kingsley, 2018; O'Sullivan, 2002). In parallel, we have become progressively less able to comprehend the extent of nor how to resolve the problem (Buergelt et al., 2017; Griffith, 2014; Kingsley, 2018; Yunkaporta, 2019). Consequently, if we want to live and want our children to thrive, we must urgently address this situation. As many, including Einstein and Carl Jung, pointed out, it is impossible for the mindset that created the crisis to resolve it; a paradigm shift, a transformation of our fundamental cosmological, ontological, and epistemological beliefs, is necessary (Buergelt et al., 2017; Kingsley, 2018).

We suggest that this existential crisis is a blessing in disguise—it creates what Mezirow (1991) calls disorienting dilemmas that can spark individual and collective transformation. The etymology of apocalypse supports this interpretation. While apocalypse has come to mean universal destruction or disaster, the ancient Greek word for apocalypse ἀποκάλυψις means "an uncovering" of prophetic revelations of ancient or Indigenous knowledges that can enable humanity to engage in the transformative journey required for creating a new culture that restores harmony/balance. This resonates with literature showing how ancient and Indigenous knowledges offer ways to facilitate cultural transformations that culminate in sustainable and more functional cultures (Buergelt et al., 2017). For instance, Yunkaporta (2019, pp. 78–79) says that diverse Indigenous tribes across Australia "have stories of past Armageddons, warning against the behaviors that make these difficult to survive and offering a blueprint for transitional ways of being, so that

---

D. Paton
College of Health and Human Sciences, Charles Darwin University, Darwin, NT, Australia

our custodial species can continue to keep creation in motion." Consequently, inquiring into ancient and Indigenous knowledges can identify sources of our existential crisis, what needs transforming and how these transformations could be best accomplished.

Building upon our work in the disaster risk reduction space (e.g., Buergelt et al., 2017; Buergelt et al., in press; Paton & Buergelt, 2019; Paton et al., 2017), we start this inquiry by weaving together knowledges from three diverse award-winning, transdisciplinary, and visionary scholar-practitioners of transformation: Peter Kingsley, Jay Griffith, and Tyson Yunkaporta. Peter Kingsley (PhD) is an historian and philosopher who is internationally recognized for his ground-breaking transformative work which complements Carl Jung's work. Jay Griffith is an astute researcher, writer, and author who weaves together eloquently vast and diverse knowledges spanning her own extensive, in-depth experience of living with Indigenous peoples around the world, Indigenous and scientific knowledges, and literary works across deep time. Tyson Yunkaporta (PhD) belongs to the Australian Apalech clan and is an academic, artist, and author who is bridging worldviews, knowledges, and practices from Indigenous culture and Western knowledges to transform thinking in ways that heal and enable sustainable, harmonious living for all creatures. The thinking of these scholar-practitioners developed independently, but each individuals knowledge corroborates and complements the others in ways that create a more comprehensive and compelling story. Thus, we meld their perspectives into a single narrative. To avoid constant citations distracting, we will only provide citation when an idea is particular to just one of them.

The synergy we offer supports transformative learning literature reaching beyond the rational discourse advocated by Mezirow to more holistic and extra-rational ways of being and knowing, particularly through nature, creative arts, and soul work/individuation; it further expands and connects these passageways. We aspire to show that the holistic, extra-rational approach can be understood more fully in the context of an extant Indigenous paradigm that still exists in some world cultures but also preceded the emergence of the western paradigm. We hope that exploring the Western and ancient/Indigenous paradigms in relation to transformative learning will enhance awareness of how their contrasting fundamental philosophical beliefs about the origin and development of the cosmos/universe (cosmology) and the nature of reality and knowledge (ontology and epistemology) influence us and how we live. This enhanced awareness may facilitate new opportunities for scholars and practitioners to theorize transformative pedagogy and improve transformative practices. We start our inquiry with exploring the sources of our existential crisis to uncover what needs transforming and discussing Indigenous ways of being-knowing-living to reveal what we have lost. We then utilize this knowledge to delve into how the required transformations could be achieved.

WHAT ARE THE SOURCES FOR OUR EXISTENTIAL CRISIS? WHAT NEEDS TRANSFORMING AND WHY?

All three authors agree that resolving our existential crisis requires identifying the source. Kingsley (2018) argues that doing so requires our going back in time. Mounting evidence suggests that our crisis developed gradually over millennia, with its origins deriving from Plato and Aristotle using reason to force our mind to separate from the psyche, and orthodox Christianity suppressing the wisdom of our pre-Socratic ancestors. The emergent Western philosophical worldview created a culture that gradually domesticated us and conditioned us into ways of thinking and living that disconnected us from our ancestors and ancient universal laws—our true natural, primordial sacred/divine nature and the sacred, invisible, feminine, spiritual realm. That means, the source of our existential crisis is essentially spiritual. Consequently, to rectify the consequences of abandoning our ancestors and their knowledges, it is of great value to ask: who are our ancestors, what does their ancient knowledge say, what is our true nature and how did we lose it all. This knowledge will lead us ultimately to what needs transforming.

The roots of our Western culture are ancient and precede the pre-Socratic Greek philosophers such as Empedocles and Parmenides who lived over 2,500 years ego (Kingsley, 2018). Rather than being primitive rationalists, which history made them out to be to hide the path back to our innate power from us, they possessed great ancient wisdom. They followed the orally transmitted lineage of mystics and healers that traces back to those in the Gnostics or Hermetic tradition who acquired extensive knowledge; were able to shift/transform into states of consciousness that enabled their accessing the invisible, spiritual realm, and to bring from this realm wisdom into our physical world; and could invoke and interpret divine guidance offered through visions and dreams. The Greek word knôsikos, meaning "having knowledge or insight," points to Gnostics being able to not only see outwardly into the physical world (sight) but also directly inwardly and experience their divine nature (insight). The Gnostics are our intimate spiritual family. Their teachings are the real source of Christianity, but they have been suppressed to serve religious interests.

Gnostic wisdom, like any other ancient/Indigenous culture across the world, holds that all creatures originate from the same universal consciousness of the essential creative life force, that all matter is alive and conscious, and that there exist two intertwined worlds that create each other: an outer, masculine, visible physical world that can be known via the body's eye and an inner, feminine, invisible spiritual world that can be known to the mind's eye via insight. The spirit world is the deeper true reality of the realms of our ancestors, gods, or the dead, and mirrors our authentic nature, psyche, or soul. Our natural ancient laws say that we exist in a dialectical relationship with the ancestors/gods/dead in which we co-create the world and universe/cosmos with them; they create us, we create them, and together we create the universe/cosmos. If that co-creative relationship is interrupted, as it was in the Western culture, the universe/cosmos and ourselves collapse.

These beliefs are reflected in our ancient Greek ancestors calling us *Anthropos*, meaning both women and men being "made in the image of God," with God being a synonym for ancestors/dead (Kingsley, 2018). This meaning reminds us that our true primordial nature is sacred/divine and that we have a boundless inner potential. Our true nature or self has been called many names including cosmic force, psyche, soul, daemon, passion, calling, muse, stream of lava, or divine *métis*, internal fire or flame. The Latin word *psyche* means "breath of life, soul or spirit" and is symbolized as a butterfly. The Greek goddess *psykhê* symbolizes the archetype of the Goddess of the Soul, who represents feminine spiritual and psychological growth or maturation. The soul, *Sophia* in Greek and *Sapientia* in Latin, is symbolized as an ambiguous, extraordinary, mysterious feminine being. Carl Jung called the archetype of the inner feminine as *anima* (Kingsley, 2018).

Our psyche-soul is our instinctive, inner, infinite heightened alertness which enables us to adapt to the constantly subtly changing existence and to transform (shape shift) between the physical and spiritual realities. Our psyche-soul contains detailed guidance for living, compels us to seek our destiny within ourselves, and steers us toward wisdom, expressing our unique gifts and experiencing true happiness. The Greek word for happiness is *eudaimonia* with *eu* representing "good, pleased," and *daimonia* referring to daemon/daimōn meaning "guardian, genius" suggests that to find happiness, we need to hear and follow our inner daemons (Griffith, 2014). When we find our daemon, we experience a eureka moment, indicating that transformation is needed to access our true nature.

The pre-Socratic mystics used ancient transformative techniques of alchemy/magic to carry us over into another state of consciousness that silenced our rational thoughts to enable us accessing and becoming conscious of the sacred, ambiguous spiritual realms of the ancestors/gods/dead, our true nature and the primordial, aboriginal sacred law (Kingsley, 2018). When we experienced the sacred reality, we realized that we no longer belonged to and lived for ourselves but became a source of life for others. Living according to the ancient law meant learning to live harmoniously with our nature and nature.

However, Plato introducing rationality started us stopping to identify with our primordial, archetypical nature and forgetting the purpose of our lives (Griffith, 2014; Kingsley, 2018; Yunkaporta, 2019). Over the next centuries, the ensuing Western culture's troika of patriarchy, capitalism, and Christian church continued to hinder us from connecting with our unique genius and ancient ways of knowing by deliberately suppressing us from accessing and transforming into our innate nature. This troika used diverse interdependent strategies to destroy the conditions that are, according to Indigenous cultures and Western science alike, vital for transformation and the maturing of our both soul/psyche/spirit and mind. These strategies, which we will explore later in detail, create the spiritual crisis that is at the core of our existential crisis, indicating that one key access to turning the tide lies in us becoming present to these strategies and remembering, reviving, and living according to our true nature and ancient/Indigenous Laws.

To start this process, we invite you to join us on a journey back in time to offer deeper glimpses into the worldviews, knowledges, and ways of living of our Western ancestors that relate to transformation, how our Western culture suppressed and exploited us over millennia, and the impact this Western culture had on us. Drawing on common key aspects of contemporary Indigenous worldviews, knowledges, and practices that corroborate the Gnostic wisdom, we outline how such knowledges to complement and add to understanding how transformation was and is at the heart of and in all aspects of our lives.

Our Ancient/Indigenous Ways
of Being-Knowing-Living

Like other Indigenous cultures around the world, we had an ageless need to find the wisdom of the ancients within us via accessing our true nature, psyche, or soul (Griffith, 2014). Finding the ancient wisdom demands embarking on a physical, psychological, and spiritual quest. During the quest, we transformed from children to adults because the challenges forced us to draw out[1] the qualities of the psyche and the ancient wisdom. Freely interacting with nature provided us with the challenges, accidents, and failures required for developing our competence and capabilities that kept us safe and enabled us to respond to the irregularity and unpredictability of nature. The quest entailed going alone into the wild woods; to transform into being adults we needed to reach beyond our limits, and journeying through the woods alone required learning to find and rely on ourselves in ways that opened possibilities for our seeing things differently and making new connections, and enabling us to find our path through life.

Intimately discovering our true self required solitude in wild undefined, infinite places that allowed reflecting on own undefined selves (Griffith, 2014). These places are in nature and nature reflects our self. We used primal ways to create scared spaces (fire, water, food) which allowed us to spin a cocoon for our emerging psyche where we could, like butterflies, facilitate the transformation of our psyche in its own time by reflecting on and transforming our lessons. The fully developed adult butterfly stage is called an imago—an imagination and magic incarnate—reflecting our true nature. Simultaneously, being in nature infused us with the diverse ways of knowing contained within nature. The quest developed our capacity to be with ambiguity, heightened our awareness, and cultivated deeply listening to everything that might guide us, especially messages and signs from the ancients and the imagination. Without going on this transformative quest, we are lost, experience illness, and engage in damaging behavior.

Similar to other Earth-based original cultures, we believed control was against the ancient law of nature; that nature, including human nature, was good; that every creature needed to be respected; that adults were not superior to children; and that people needed to be governed by

---

[1] Note the parallel to the etymological meaning of education deriving from the Latin *educare*, "to draw out, bring up," and *ducere*, "to lead."

themselves and nature as the will was the life force—we allowed and facilitated everybody to be their true self to express their spirits/soul/daemon (Griffith, 2014). We knew that only when were self-willed could we be true to ourselves. To prevent people from following their will selfishly and harming others, we socialized them into cultivating their insight and nature knowledge; both taught them to be aware and respectful of the will of others and to consciously regulate their own will to maintain good relations and ensure the health, safety, and wealth of both individuals and the community. We knew people experiencing their will being valued and respected led to them valuing and respecting the will of others.

We were able to fulfill our custodial role through thinking holistically and understanding complex systems and seeing reality or creation as an open, infinitely complex, interconnected, self-organizing, dynamic, subjective, and self-renewing system of life (Yunkaporta, 2019). We believed in being integral to this system and in being the designated custodial species of this reality whose role is to sustain creation by caring for and looking after all of creation. We knew that all entities, including ourselves, interacted in reciprocal relationships and thus each interaction impacted the whole system. Hence, ancient/Indigenous law perfectly continuously balanced the needs of all parts of the system. We knew that complex systems were composed of equal parts—members carried the intelligence of the whole, were autonomous yet interdependently connected, and were interacting freely within complex heterarchical patterns of relatedness and communal obligation. We understood that systems, and their parts, were self-organizing, patterned, and adaptive in ways that maintained the balance/harmony of the system and members and that to ensure the balance of the entire system, the patterns must emerge organically.

To allow creation to emerge through the free movement of all systems parts, we created governance processes that surrendered control, respectfully observed, and interacted in non-intrusive ways with diverse systems in ways that enabled autonomous self-organizing and adapting in ways that maintained balance (Yunkaporta, 2019). Thus, our governance systems were participatory, distributed, and monitored collectively. We finely honed our holistic thinking by examining things from many points of view, especially those opposed to our own, and through deliberately interacting with people who held different viewpoints.

This process was sustained by knowledge keepers who maintained and enacted processes culminating in attaining higher knowledge in ways that ensured that each member expressed themselves as fully as possible (Yunkaporta, 2019). Knowledge was living because we continually created knowledge through our everyday two-way interactions among and between spirit-ancestors, land-place, people, and groups of peoples. The resulting complex ecosystems of practice were transformative and innovative open systems which were constantly naturally adapting. We knew that "any attempt to control the system from a fixed viewpoint outside is misaligned intervention that will fail. [...] Creation is in a constant state of motion, and we must move with it as the custodial species or we will damage the system and doom ourselves. [...] you have to move and adapt within a system that is in a constant state of movement and adaptation" (Yunkaporta, 2019, pp. 45–46, 49). Consequently, our emergent holistic thinking enabled us to create and maintain diverse, interacting open systems to fulfill our role as custodial species such as our kinship system.

Like in other ancient/Indigenous cultures, our ancient kinship systems were designed so that everybody was related to everybody within and across generations, regardless of our genetic relationships (Griffith, 2014; Yunkaporta, 2019). Our kinship system naturally constantly reinforced and intertwined the past, present and future, ensuring cultural consistency and adapting; this led to transformative education being embedded in every interaction in ways that sustained the cumulative wisdom of our ancestors knowledges and the essential life energies. We balanced feminine and masculine energies in every aspect of life in sophisticated ways (Yunkaporta, 2019). Our women and men were equal partners with complex and layered independent, interdependent, and complementary identities, roles, and relationships involving both friction-conflict and union-cooperating. Friction-conflict is being the force/fire that continuously creates the universe; union-cooperating is continuously keeping the generative force/fire burning. Our ancient law provided our women and men with knowledge of which behaviors supported them fulfilling their roles and which did not, the consequence of destructive behaviors, and how to grow beyond and keep in check these destructive behaviors.

Time in our ancient culture was sacred, mythic, subtle, ambiguous, and merging past-resent-future (Griffith, 2014). Time was alive (changed in the reciprocal interactions among and between us and other creatures); existed within the land and nature's processes; was cyclical; and was diverse (many times). The quality of time mattered. Time connected us to nature and its wisdom. Our language constantly connected us to nature time. Because time was mirroring both nature and our psyche/soul, by learning about wild time we learned about both, leading to our growing up more self-reliant, less obedient, and less malleable to outside forces. Following our inner nature, time also created the space for reverie. Doing nothing, daydreaming, and imagining were crucial for our spirit/soul to breathe, reflect, and self-fertilize. Reverie was our natural wild or undomesticated state during which our mind became highly active in brain areas associated with creativity and complex problem-solving. Reverie created the space for us experiencing epiphanies during which we access our true nature, our daemons, that guide us.

As in other Indigenous cultures, education, reflecting its Latin roots *educare*, "to draw out, bring up" and *ducere*, "to lead," cultivated both our spiritual and physical faculties and virtues. Hence, education's purpose was to "lead a child into the world and educe from the child its own wisdom [...] to draw out what is in the child, the immortal spirit" (Griffith, 2014, p. 234). Our education was about understanding life in all its expressions, holistically and in-depth, and was aligned with how the mind learned naturally. We understood the importance of nature for us to mature, and used nature, along with metaphors and arts (stories, dance, song, ceremony), to continuously access deeper layers of the spiritual, invisible world (Griffith, 2014). We saw nature as our teacher and university. Anthropomorphism, shapeshifting, and metamorphosis, for instance, opened dialogue with nature and increased our sensitivities and knowledge of nature. We saw the transformations during shapeshifting as the "ur-metaphor" (Griffith, 2014, p. 87). Animal metaphors facilitated our mirroring nature; each animal taught us diverse characteristics and skills, expanding our repertoire. Interacting with animals increased our imagination, empathy, sensitivities, diversity of viewpoints, self-esteem, self-control, and autonomy. Fully developing our psyche required interacting with many different animals directly or through ceremonies, song, dance, and music. Western science increasingly confirms this; interacting with nature facilitates our realizing who we truly are, greater self-confidence, independence, and self-belief, increases awareness and social skills, helps focusing and concentrating, encourages positive attitudes toward learning, enhances physical stamina and coordination, and leads to greater insight into and greater respect for nature (Buergelt et al., 2017).

We also saw free play in nature as being at the core of our human nature and learning (Griffith, 2014). We knew that play was vital for the growth of our spirit and mind, health, and well-being because it was engaging the deepest creative energy and was elemental for us to discover our uniqueness and inner abundance. We saw the imagination involved in free play as crucial for us learning to control our emotions and behavior which were critical for the functioning of us as individuals and our entire society. We believed that play was connected to art and knew that art was rooted in true knowledge. We referred to arts as the knowledge of the ancestors or inner wisdom. The Latin *artus* means "joints and connecting the parts," pointing to ability of arts to connect ideas holistically and to carry them across. Kunst, the German word for art, has its source in kennen, "to know, knowledge" and *können*, "to know how, to be able." Thus, like other ancient/Indigenous cultures, we embedded arts in diverse forms, including telling stories, painting, singing, and dancing, in all aspects of our everyday life, to encode and carry over the spiritual, ecological, and ethical knowledges critical for our spiritual and physical survival.

One form of art we used was fairy tales[2] for they mirrored the true but invisible, spiritual world. The Latin word for fairy and feärie is *fata*, meaning "the fates." Fairies symbolize and impart an imaginative, metaphoric mindset full of inner meaning. Feäries are metaphors that are true to, and provide an access to, the psyche/soul. Metaphors reflect our true nature, give life to the mysterious realm, and nurture curiosity, wisdom, and empathy. Metaphor is how the human mind thinks; it weaves together and exchanges facts-physical world and feäries-spiritual world. Metaphor is a metaphor for imagination, which can only be found within our psyche/soul by transforming the physical reality. Metaphors also enabled us to easily carry meaning from something we knew to something new, assisting us to adapt effortlessly. We were masterful in thinking in, understanding, expressing, and applying metaphors naturally.

We used fairy tales to encode and implicitly teach ancient knowledges including the origins of the universe and the nature of reality and knowledge. Fairy tales encoded in our ancient law reminded us to live in harmony with nature; explained how to live in connected, harmonious relationships; and reminded us that each action has consequences. Fairy tales also taught us the importance of seeking knowledges, emphasized the importance of nature, and instilled the understanding of nature as

---

[2] Fairy tales are also called folk tales, legends, sagas, or myths in other ancient/Indigenous cultures.

indefinitely complex ecological system. Because we were an oral culture, we co-created fairy tales together with the storyteller, enabling us to adjust fairy tales to psyche and situation, and to refine them to incorporate new knowledges in accordance with changes in our environment.

However, the inner power associated with our ancient/Indigenous knowledges and ways of thinking threatened the existence of the Western culture; it thus tried for centuries to maintain the status quo by suppressing and invalidating our true primordial nature and ancient wisdom. This domestication and oppression process started according to with the founding father of our Western culture, Plato (Griffith, 2014; Kingsley, 2018; Yunkaporta, 2019). It is to a discussion of this process we turn now.

The Domestication and Oppression of Our True, Primordial Self and Ancient Knowledges

Plato took the ancient knowledges from the Pythagoreans and systematically altered, excluded, and concealed the ancient teaching that letting oneself be carried into the most feminine, most unconscious depths of our selves gave access to the sacred wisdom, and replaced the sacred ancient laws with human reason (Kingsley, 2018). Plato created the scientific method, which promotes rationality and reduces interconnected complexity to separate parts. He banished wildness/nature, arts, metaphors, and emotions, and advanced the view that ancient knowledge be extinguished by schools, focusing instead on the rational, literal, and measurable (Griffith, 2014). He promoted breaking children's wills and affinity with nature, and introduced hierarchy, control, obedience, and violence to create a passive and disciplined workforce to further imperialism and class-division.

By pushing our surrendering to reasoning, Plato eroded our caring for our gods/ancestors and contributed to our forgetting the sacred purpose of our culture, and that our culture needed to be cultivated according to nature laws to fulfill its purpose (Kingsley, 2018; Yunkaporta, 2019). Rationality blocked our access to direct experience of our divine nature and undermined holistic and extra-rational thinking (Griffith, 2014). The greatest ancient pre-Socratic western philosophers and mystics perceived people breaking up reality into pieces as being blind and deaf (Kingsley, 2018). They also believed that reasoning crushed ambiguities, leaving control to reign unchecked. Plato's rationalism was then championed by other Western rationalists and through the Christian church, agriculture and capitalism, creating a culture that suppressed and domesticated us.

In the fifteenth and sixteenth centuries, the wealthy perpetuated the divide between people and nature by privatizing and fencing common land, to control the land and its resources to make us work every day (Griffith, 2014). These enclosures extended the loss of our intimate and reciprocal relationships with nature and hampered our coming into knowledge about our true nature and ancient law and knowledge. Without experiencing this kinship and education, our souls became sick and nature became unsafe. The abolishment of the commons seized our communities, stole our homes and our independence as we could not maintain ourselves any more. Our memory of what it was like growing up and living in nature has been deliberately suppressed over centuries. How we grow up now, and living separated from nature enclosed indoors occurs was unthinkable just a few generations ago.

To support capitalism, the Western culture disconnected us from nature time and our nature, and created exact time measurement to control us (Griffith, 2014). Universal time that is linear and abstract and could be quantified and measured was created and constantly reinforced. Our lives became ruled by clocks that connected us to linear time that created a fear of the future. By controlling our time, the Western lifestyle is overriding and eroding our true nature and power as relentless speed, inputs, and demands suffocate the psyche/soul, exhausts us and create a sense of failure, low self-esteem, distress, and depression. Our Western languages, especially English, veil the ancient truth of reality and who we are and perpetuate the Western worldview and thinking (Kingsley, 2018; Yunkaporta, 2019).

The Western culture also realized that to keep itself alive it needed to maintain the Western paradigm by creating a workforce that was easily controllable yet capable of keeping the economy running (Griffith, 2014; Yunkaporta, 2019). This process was reinforced by developments in public education. In the fifteenth century, church schools deliberately and systemically humiliated, dominated, and oppressed our children until their wills were completely broken. Schools were designed to imitate factories, and education was designed to instill subservience (Yunkaporta, 2019). Our development was limited to "safe" levels; enough to enable us to breed and work, yet low enough to see hierarchy, obedience, discipline, control, and competition as natural. To keep these closed systems alive, the past was manipulated and alternative worldviews, knowledges, and practices—such as those of nature, ancient/Indigenous, women, children, diverse cultures—were suppressed. While more humanistic in orientation, contemporary Western mainstream schooling retains a focus on creating a workforce and consumers, perpetuating imperialist histories and corporate colonialism, and cloaking the source and nature of the problems we experience (Griffith, 2014; Yunkaporta, 2019). Our predominant reductionist education separates and reduces life into subjects and focuses on what can be measured and ignores what cannot be measured, which is not inhibiting us fully developing and maturing into adults, robbing us of our innate knowledges, suppresses embodied ancient knowledges and undermines holistic thinking.

The combined forces of rationalism, reformation, Protestantism and Catholicism, capitalism, and the industrial revolution further eroded our belief in and ability to access the invisible, spiritual world (Griffith, 2014). They further perpetuated the Western worldview that held that only physically visible things are true and that the world needed to be interpreted literally. Literalism is against our nature and hence paralyzes our mind. These forces severely repressed free play and arts to force us to engage in productive work and commodified play to profit (Griffith, 2014). They changed the meaning of arts around the eighteenth century to narrowly mean artistic activity of humans, and to be contrary to nature, and weakened the value of arts and artists. They changed the meaning of daemon to mean something evil and belittled feäries to subdue our inherent power.

Over the course of a several hundred years, we, especially women, have been cheated out of the inheritance of fairy tales, and thus of ancient knowledges, for many oral fairy tales have been rewritten to pave the way for and maintain the current misogynist and patriarchal Western worldview (Griffith, 2014). The original oral version of Little Red Riding Hood, for instance, is a story of a courageous, smart girl who defends herself against attempted rape, providing guidance on how to recognize and respond to rape. Our ancient fairy tales were replaced with literal and predefined images to suppress our pathways to the metaphoric. Over centuries, the disconnection from nature, oppression of play and arts, and public education gradually domesticated us, deteriorated our minds and capabilities, and conditioned us to think in reductionist and objective ways (Yunkaporta, 2019). Western science increasingly evidences our genetic, physical, and mental deterioration over millennia (Hood, 2014).

Importantly, research shows a decline in people in Western cultures being able to move beyond concrete operational thinking. For example, only about 11% of British high school students attained formal and post-formal operational thinking in 2007, which was a drastic decline from about 21% 30 years earlier (Shayer & Ginsburg, 2009). That is, increasingly less people can see the invisible, spiritual reality; can think holistically and see relationships between aspects; perceive the world as process integrating past-present-future; can take others' perspectives and view things from multiple perspectives; engage in both inductive and deductive reasoning; can think hypothetically and critically question information; are receptive to new and contradictory ideas; can understand symbolism; and reflect.

This Western culture is also sustaining itself by creating a closed system via hierarchical, concentrated, and centrally organized patriarchal power and governance structures that suppress two-way feedback loops and consensus; nations with borders; religion being institutionalized, cutting people of from their direct experience of the divine and missionizing people into the Christian and Western worldview; violence creating fear, and Western education and science generally enforcing the Western worldview being right (Griffith, 2014; O'Sullivan, 2002; Yunkaporta, 2019). These diverse colonizing practices have, and still do, created the conditions that have created and intensified our existential planetary crisis (O'Sullivan, 2002) and eroded all aspects that facilitate our individual and collective health/well-being, resilience, and adaptive capacities (Griffith, 2014; Kingsley, 2018; Yunkaporta, 2019). Our being separated from our nature, each other, and nature means we are cut from the source of our power and health/well-being and thus have no power nor security (O'Sullivan, 2002).

However, the domesticating, conditioning, fading memories of the past and oppressing of different perspectives make it difficult for us to realize what has happened and is happening. Gradually, our reality has become distorted and we have slipped away from living in harmony with the ancient laws and our true nature without noticing it. We have largely become obedient, individual workers with specialized knowledge and little shared understanding who are, unable to realize what we lost and to connect to join forces to challenge the system and reclaim our power. We don't question what is happening, and we have lost the capacity to understand the connections required to regenerate our well-being. Now, we even don't remember who we are and the ancient ways. That is, the

Western culture both contributed to creating our existential crisis and undermining us understanding the crisis to perpetuate the status quo (Griffith, 2014; Kingsley, 2018; O'Sullivan, 2002; Yunkaporta, 2019).

When we lost our connection to our inner sacred nature, we also lost our inner life force and guidance system which led to us individually and collectively losing the sacred, invisible, feminine, spiritual reality that exists in virtually every other culture, especially in ancient/Indigenous cultures (Kingsley, 2018). This loss within us is the source of all disasters outside us. If we continue to disregard the ancient/Indigenous law, we will continue to oppress the natural cyclical and reciprocal processes designed to support the renewing and balancing of life. This will lead to the systems supporting us increasingly breaking down, creating disharmony, crisis, disasters, and disease, exacerbating our existential crisis, and leading ultimately to our extinction (O'Sullivan, 2002; Yunkaporta, 2019). Given our knowledge that transformation was central to our ancient worldviews, knowledges, and harmonious living, they might also point us to how to best use the transformative opportunity the crisis entails. In the next section, we explore that possibility.

WHAT ARE TRANSFORMATIVE WAYS OUT OF OUR EXISTENTIAL CRISIS?

For all three scholar-practitioners, recovering our power as custodial species by remembering and reviving our ancient spiritual practices, reconnecting with our true primordial nature, and living in harmony with our nature and with nature is the solution to our existential crisis. However, for reasons introduced above, this solution is not recognized in Western cultures, which only seek rational solutions in the physical world and prevent seeing alternative perspectives. Yet, rational solutions have proven ineffective, and people are increasingly searching for alternatives. Transformative learning is one such alternative that could play a vital role in facilitating people in Western cultures expanding their narrow rational and reductionistic philosophical worldview to an extra-rational and holistic ancient/Indigenous philosophical worldview.

Our exploration indicates that achieving this transformation would require facilitating Western peoples engaging in a transformative journey that comprises two interconnected transformative processes parallel: (a) reflecting, uncovering, acknowledging, and deconstructing our current Western worldview and its sources and impacts; as well as (b) rebirthing, remembering, reviving, and strengthening the ancient-Indigenous world-view and creating a paradigm that transcends both paradigms. Interestingly, a cultural transformation is consistent with our ancient knowledge.

Gnostic wisdom says that when cultures evolve from one age to another, they go through a natural death-rebirth transformative process. According to all three scholar-practitioners, we are in the midst of such a cultural transformation. And, as Kingsley (2018) points out, because our current Western culture has become dysfunctional and is dying to rebirth more functional worldviews and ways of living, it would be not only be pointless but damaging to keep our Western culture alive. Consistent with O'Sullivan (2002), he suggests that to bring a new culture into being, it would be of value to first consciously collectively experience, mark, and honor the passing of our Western culture and rational self by completing lose ends, letting go, grieving, and celebrating the ending.

Kingsley (2018) emphasizes that successfully transitioning between ages requires carrying over the ancient wisdom, unbroken, to connect the past and future to ensure cultural continuity and learning of the lessons of the previous age fully. Building upon Jung, Kingsley (2018) advocates for our collectively looking back and into ourselves by deliberately getting to know our real ancient Western culture and to come to terms with the truth of our divine, sacred nature that we lost, why we lost it, and how this impacted us. Jung and Kingsley (2018) suggest that recognizing that we are conditioned into and undermined by the Western worldview is critical, as is finding ways to shield against it. Both propose that the essential task of people in Western cultures is to give up reasoning and rationalizing and take on valuing, accessing, and living in accordance with our own unique nature and truth; reviving the ancient Western practice of respecting, honoring, and caring for our ancestors and elders; and following and protecting the ancient law and passing it on. This task is achieved by allowing being transformed inside to rebirth our ancient true nature in our current era. The vital question is how we can facilitate this individual and collective transformative transition between ages.

All three authors suggest that a feasible pathway to facilitate this transformation is to remember the ancient/Indigenous knowledge; we did not lose the knowledge, we just lost access to it. Regarding how to regain access, the teachings and practices of our ancestral, mystical pre-Socratic Gnostic and Hermetic tradition of current Indigenous Elders provide trustworthy access to the wisdom capable of facilitating the transformation of our unconscious (Kingsley, 2018). We can restore this bridge to the past by going straight to Jung's *Red Book*, which was finally published in 2009, as it contains the ancient mystical Gnostic and Hermetic knowledge (that has become institutionalized and lost in translation within a few years).

Reacquiring the ancient knowledge is about the process of becoming and being one's true self/psych/soul, which Jung called individuation (Kingsley, 2018). Individuation is a transformative process during which people unlock their Gnostic inward experience of vision or insight so they can directly experience their true original primordial nature, listen to the voice of the divine/sacred/ancestors speaking within them, and care for the divine. Individuation entails encountering and integrating all inner faculties and the sacred, spiritual, feminine reality consciously inside oneself. Finding one's truth requires facing and completely shedding one's personal self.

Individuated—or true—humans are connected to and consciously relate to their own divine reality/awareness deep inside us without any inflation or identification (Kingsley, 2018). They are freed from the physical reality, and internally balanced/harmonious and grounded. They experience the interdependent, synchronous co-existence of the outside and inside (union). They follow their own authentic paths as guided inwardly by their souls or daemons regardless of the consequences.

Consciously living this archetypical life is the life that we are meant to live and which leads us to experience harmony, health, and well-being. This way of being and living remains the way of being in Indigenous cultures (Griffith, 2014, 2015; Yunkaporta, 2019). According to Kingsley (2018), Jung asserted that we either engage in this transformative journey to mature collectively and become adults, or we continue living meaningless lives and stay on the unconscious path of struggling, suffering, and destroying ourselves and all of creation. Recognizing individuation as a key transformational pathway in the wider context of remembering and reviving ancient Gnostic knowledges to reconnect with our true nature to address our existential crisis adds further weight to the work of transformative learning scholars engaged with expanding the spiritual passageway led by Dirkx's (2012) work on soul or inner work including individuation.

Restoring nature as teacher and diverse forms of creative arts as essential aspects of formal and informal education, indeed of everyday life, will be critical for extending awareness (Buergelt et al., in press; Griffith, 2014). These two transformative pathways are consistent with transformative learning scholars developing the transformative learning passageways of nature (e.g., Lange, 2012; O'Sullivan et al., 2002) and creative arts (e.g., Kokkos, 2021; Lawrence, 2012) as holistic, symbolic, imaginative, creative, and emotional ways of experiencing and knowing that transform, individually and collectively, rational knowing. Transformative learning scholars and practitioners connecting with and utilizing transformative, healing, decolonizing, emancipatory, participatory, critical social constructionist paradigms that emerged in the Western culture as well as Indigenous paradigms would also support people in Western cultures expanding their worldviews (Denzin et al., 2008; O'Sullivan et al., 2002).

Given that thinking and language create each other, being able to remember and access our ancient wisdom will be greatly facilitated if we shift our language by using the original languages of our Western culture, such as Greek and Latin (Kingsley, 2018). Transforming universal, linear clock time will be supported by (re)connecting with nature time (Griffith, 2000). Governance systems based on ecological principles that facilitate us self-organizing as open systems and which thus create the conditions for individual and collective transformations to occur will be central for expanding our worldview. Sociocracy seems to fit this bill (Buergelt et al., in press).

Finally, given the commonalities of the ancient roots of our Western culture and those of Indigenous peoples, our genuinely and respectfully engaging in equal, reciprocal learning with Indigenous peoples and braiding our respective worldviews, knowledges, and practices would facilitate our remembering and coming into ancient/Indigenous knowledges (Buergelt et al., 2017; Yunkaporta, 2019). These cross-paradigm interactions also hold great potential for creating transformations that can illuminate new passageways for transitioning into sustainable ways of living.

Conclusion

In essence, the synergy of knowledges from Griffith (2014), Kingsley (2018), and Yunkaporta (2019) argues that our existential crisis is spiritual in nature and is a consequence of centuries-long Western cultural domestication and colonization which disconnected us from our true nature and ancient laws and wisdom. This process domesticated and conditioned into a patriarchal, totalitarian, rational, reductionistic, and objective worldview for several centuries starting with Plato, and is sustained by patriarchy, the Christian church, and capitalism. As a result, we have been living disconnected from our true divine, sacred nature, and from nature, which has created disharmony, ill-health, and destruction. This suggests that the survival of all life on Earth will depend on people in the Western culture transforming their current fundamental cosmological, ontological, and epistemological beliefs toward matriarchal, metaphysical, holistic, spiritual, ecological, equal, and subjective beliefs individually and collectively by remembering, cultivating, and living according to our true sacred nature, our ancestors and the ancestral laws. Our existential crisis creates opportunities for deeply and critically reflecting and inquiring into the origins of this existential crisis and transforming the source.

Accessing our true, primordial nature and our ancient Gnostic and Hermetic knowledges can be accomplished by engaging several interconnected transformative pathways: going on a quest or individuation journey and then listening to and following our psyche/soul/daemon/flame; interacting with and learning from nature, the land belonging to all (commons), and caring for country; playing; immersing ourselves in diverse forms of arts; uncovering our original fairies; learning our ancient languages; restoring nature time; and engaging with Indigenous peoples in equal, reciprocal ways. This set of transformative practices is consistent with and strengthens the turn of transformative learning theorizing toward extra-rational, spiritual knowledges, and practices. Synergizing this set of extra-rational, spiritual transformative practices and connecting it so that it can be collectively utilized to facilitate people in Western cultures expanding their narrow rational worldview to the holistic, spiritual worldview; in so doing we can resolve our existential crisis and fulfill our role as designated custodial species of this reality.

We hope that this journey has been transformative for you and that it inspires you and/or strengthens you to courageously be a transformative agent (Yunkaporta, 2019) or "contrary" (Kingsley, 2018) who, because they remember and can see what others don't yet notice, turn everything upside down, bring up what nobody wants to see, make people question everything on a deeper level, and embody a sacred/divine force others are not aware of. We are the ones who we have been waiting for, and it is high time for us to courageously step into being transformative agents (Yunkaporta, 2019) or contraries (Kingsley, 2018) who wake people up. As Kingsley (2018, p. 444) says, "It's the time for learning our primordial or original instructions, as Native Americans have referred to them for centuries, all over again; the time to turn around and face our ancestors

... its only be shedding everything, including ourselves, that we sow the seeds of the future."

REFERENCES

Buergelt, P. T., Paton, D., Sithole, B., Sangha, K., Campion, O. B., & Campion, J. (2017). Living in harmony with our environment: A paradigm shift. In D. Paton & D. Johnston (Eds.), *Disaster resilience: An integrated approach* (2nd ed., pp. 289–307). Charles C. Thomas.

Buergelt, P., & Paton, D. (in press). Facilitating effective DRR education and human survival: Intentionally engaging the transformation education-paradigm shift spiral. In H. James, R. Shaw, V. Sharma, & A. Lukasiewicz (Eds.), *Risk, resilience and reconstruction: Science and governance for effective disaster risk reduction and recovery in Australia and the Asia Pacific*. Palgrave Macmillan/Springer.

Denzin, N., Lincoln, Y., & Smith, L. T. (Eds.). (2008). *Handbook of critical and Indigenous methodologies*. Sage.

Dirkx, J. M. (2012). Nurturing soul work: A Jungian approach to transformative learning. In E. W. Taylor & P. Cranton (Eds.), *The handbook of transformative learning: Theory, research, and practice* (pp. 116–130). Jossey-Bass.

Griffith, J. (1999). *Pip pip: A sideways look at time*. Harper.

Griffith, J. (2014). *A country called childhood: Children in the exuberant world*. Counterpoint Berkeley.

Griffith, J. (2015). *Savage grace: A journey in wildness*. Counterpoint Berkeley.

Hood, B. (2014). *The domesticated brain*. Penguin.

Jung, C. (2009). *The red book*. W. W. Norton.

Kingsley, P. (2018). *Catafalque: Carl Jung and the end of humanity* (Vol. 1). Catafalque.

Kokkos, A. (2021). *Exploring art for perspective transformation*. Brill.

Lange, E. A. (2012). Transforming transformative learning through sustainability and the new science. In E. W. Taylor & P. Cranton (Eds.), *The handbook of transformative learning: Theory, research, and practice* (pp. 195–211). Jossey-Bass.

Lawrence, R. L. (2012). Transformative learning through artistic expression: Getting out of our heads. In E. W. Taylor & P. Cranton (Eds.), *The handbook of transformative learning: Theory, research, and practice* (pp. 471–485). Wiley.

Mezirow, J. (1991). *Transformative dimensions of adult learning*. Jossey-Bass.

O'Sullivan, E. (2002). The project and vision of transformative education: Integral transformative learning. In E. O'Sullivan, A. Morrell, & A. O'Conner (Eds.), *Expanding the boundaries of transformative learning* (pp. 1–12). Palgrave.

O'Sullivan, E. (2012). Deep transformation: Forging a planetary worldview. In E. W. Taylor & P. Cranton (Eds.), *The handbook of transformative learning: Theory, research, and practice* (pp. 471–485). Wiley.

O'Sullivan, E., Morell, A., & O'Conner, A. (2002). *Expanding the boundaries of transformative learning*. Palgrave.

Paton, D., & Buergelt, P. (2019). Risk, transformation and adaptation: Ideas for reframing approaches to disaster risk reduction. *International Journal of Environmental Research and Public Health, 16*, 2594. https://doi.org/10.3390/ijerph16142594

Paton, D., Michaloudis, I., Pavavaljung, E., Clark, K., Buergelt, P. T., Jang, L., & Kuo, G. (2017). Art and disaster resilience: Perspectives from the visual and performing arts. In D. Paton & D. M. Johnston (Eds.), *Disaster resilience: An integrated approach* (2nd ed.) (pp. 212–235). Charles C. Thomas.

Shayer, M., & Ginsburg, D. (2009). Thirty years on - a large anti-Flynn effect? 11:13- and 14-year olds. Piagetian tests of formal operations norms 1976–2006/7. *British Journal of Educational Psychology, 79*, 409–418.

Yunkaporta, T. (2019). *Sand talk: How Indigenous thinking can save the world.* Text Publishing.

CHAPTER 46

The Embodying of Transformative Learning

Christina Schlattner

PROLOGUE: A PERSONAL STORY OF TRANSFORMATIVE LEARNING

I was lying face up, eyes shut, waiting for him to attack. I knew it was coming and I felt stuck to the ground, paralyzed with fear. I could feel my heart pounding through my back against the floor, the sound of blood filling my ears. For a moment it was the only sound. Smack! He slapped the ground beside my head. My eyes snapped open and then squeezed tight to shut out the fear. He was talking to me now. What was he saying? The words seemed to swim in the air as I struggled to stay present. I felt his hands roughly pin my wrists to the ground. This brought my awareness out of my internal experience and into the room. I breathed deeply. I remembered my training and slowly raised my knee, planting my foot on the ground. I did not struggle. My awareness drifted inside again, and I pulled it back. I knew I would have to fight, and I breathed in to gather my energy, waiting for the right moment.

He let go of one of my wrists. My coach shouted, "Eyes!!" It was my opening and I exploded into action. I jabbed upwards at his eyes as I

C. Schlattner (✉)
New Alchemy Communications Ltd., Sooke, Canada
e-mail: christina@newalchemycommunications.com

© The Author(s), under exclusive license to Springer Nature Switzerland AG 2022 831
A. Nicolaides et al. (eds.), *The Palgrave Handbook of Learning for Transformation*, https://doi.org/10.1007/978-3-030-84694-7_46

832   C. SCHLATTNER

pushed with my planted foot, snapping my hip up, taking him off balance. He was off me. I rammed my knee into his crotch and scuttled around so my feet were facing toward his head. He was moving in to grab me and I kicked him in the face once, twice, maybe more. He was still coming and my kicks were getting weaker as fear sapped the strength out of my body. Time had slowed to an impossible crawl and my choices came into sharp relief. I was so tired. I wanted to just give up. Quit. But this meant giving up on myself. Shame washed over me that all too often I was willing to do this.

I realized my coach was speaking to me and my attention shifted. "You can do this," she reminded me. "I can do this," I thought. Then she shouted—"Kick!" My vision focused on my attacker, and suddenly a surge of power animated my body. Two more kicks aimed at his head and he was knocked out. I heard the other women in the class cheering wildly for me. My coach blew her whistle to signal the end of the simulated fight. My "attacker" was lying face up, arms by his head to signal a knock out. I shakily got up, went to his head and shouted "Look"—I looked around the room for any potential threats. "Assess"—I looked down at him to make sure he was neutralized. "No!"—I ran to a line of women who received me, and together we yelled "911."

This is a description of what I experienced in a self-defense workshop called Model Mugging, where participants fight against a padded "Mugger" to achieve a knockout victory, and more often than not, experience a transformational shift in self-concept.

This experience seemed to closely reflect what Jack Mezirow described in *Transformative Dimensions of Adult Learning* (1991). With "perspective transformation," Mezirow described a fundamental shift in the constructed meanings around self. His description of the phases which characterize perspective transformation (Mezirow, 1991, pp. 168–169) resonated with my experience—I had been through a disorienting crisis; went through a process of self-examination accompanied by intense feelings; questioned many of my previously unconscious assumptions; recognized that others had been through similar processes; explored new roles; planned new action; acquired skills and knowledge to implement these plans; tried the new roles; built self-confidence in my new self-concept; and reconciled my life with my new perspective. However, the more fully I explored my interest in transformative learning, the more I began to experience a lack in Mezirow's theoretical conceptualization. Something didn't feel right.

Introduction: An Evolving Theory of Transformative Learning

Mezirow defined transformative learning primarily as the process of becoming critically aware of how and why our assumptions have come to constrain the way we perceive, understand, and feel about our world; changing these structures of habitual expectation to make possible a more inclusive, discriminating, and integrative perspective; and making choices or otherwise acting upon these new understandings (Mezirow, 1991, p. 167). In later writings, while allowing transformative learning is a theory in progress, Mezirow continued to assert rationality as the defining factor of transformative learning. "Transformative learning is understood as a uniquely adult form of metacognitive reasoning. Reasoning is the process of advancing and assessing reasons, especially those that provide arguments supporting beliefs resulting in decisions to act" (Mezirow, 2003, p. 58).

An evolution of the theory arose from a critique of Mezirow's emphasis on rationality in transformative learning. Cranton (2016) labels "extrarational" other elements of meaning making such as emotion, intuition, and spirituality. Even defining these important elements of learning in opposition to rationality creates a false dualism. In contrast, O'Sullivan (2012) places rationality on a co-equal footing with movement and emotion, describing the experience of transformative learning as "...a deep, structural shift in the basic premises of thought, feelings, and actions" (p. 175). The March 2020 issue of *The Journal of Transformative Education* showcased articles focused on "transformative learning's collective and embodied dimensions" with the editor asserting, "Within transformative education research, we now have a well-elaborated, integrated social, cultural, and biological conception of cognition as an embodied process" (Finnegan, March 2020, p. 84). This signals a growing movement within adult education to recognize and define the embodied nature of transformative learning.

Drawing from Lakoff and Johnson's (1980) work on of embodied knowledge, this chapter seeks to demonstrate ways in which transformative learning is fundamentally embodied through a case illustration of the transformative potential of a particular, full-force self-defense program. Prior research on this program demonstrates how it can facilitate a shift in self-concept—a fundamental element of transformative learning. A case illustration from my own experience, first as a student and then director

834   C. SCHLATTNER

of a Model Mugging programs, provides the connection between the transformative learning phenomenon and the body.

EMBODIED MEANING MAKING

An embodied conception of transformative learning recognizes the inseparability of rationality, movement, emotion, and other related conceptions such as spirituality, creativity, or intuition. This is in contrast with attempts to incorporate emotion, movement, and other aspects of knowing, into the theory of transformative learning, while still defining it as ultimately a practice of rational metacognition. "Experience doesn't separate itself into emotional versus rational components; rather our rationality is at once embodied and emotional, full of eros" (Johnson, 2017, p. 99). It's not a stretch to imagine how emotions are embodied because we "feel" them as sensations in our bodies. Emotions arise from our embodied experiences and can be recalled in a felt sense through memory. When we move in certain ways, we can elicit emotional states. The emotional states of others can be guessed at through body language. What is more difficult to fathom is that rationality likewise is embodied. We don't feel our rational thoughts. But Johnson and Lakoff's exploration of embodied meaning making (1980) elaborates on how meaning is grounded in the acquisition and use of a conceptual system, structured through metaphor. Rationality itself is inherently embodied through metaphors permeating our thoughts and communication. Metaphors are the embodied structures we use to describe concepts and ideas.

Based on linguistic evidence and cognitive science, Johnson and Lakoff (1980) found most conceptual systems are understood through metaphorical representations. Metaphors structure how we understand concepts—sometimes in very basic ways. We are rarely consciously aware of this. Metaphors link embodied experience to abstract thought. Lakoff and Johnson extensively document how the use of metaphor is integral to thought, feeling, and action. Our spatial orientations give rise to orientational metaphors which ascribe "up" and "down" metaphors to concepts—e.g., happy is up, sad is down. Experiences with physical objects (especially our own bodies) provide the basis for a wide variety of ontological metaphors—ways of viewing events, activities, emotions, ideas, etc., as entities and substances. The list of ontological metaphors is enormous and demonstrates how we characterize abstractions as having a physical reality. For example, common expressions related to mental strength use masculine metaphors—"man up," "have some balls." Conversely, expressions signifying mental weakness use feminine metaphors—"don't be a pussy," "like a little girl." Socio-culturally, in language and thought, we are mired in metaphor. These and our own embodied experiences form the basis of embodied self-concept.

Embodied Self-Concept

Goleman (1995), from whom Mezirow borrowed his psychological understanding, called the self the "most basic grouping of schemas" (p. 96). Mezirow credited psychological meaning perspectives about oneself as the most significant meaning scheme to transform. "The most significant learning involves critical premise reflection of premises about oneself" (Mezirow, 1994, p. 224). Cranton (2016) considered transformed self-concept as an integral part of any transformative learning experience. "By definition, transformative learning leads to a changed self-perception" (p. 7).[1] The opposite may also be true: changed self-concept, as an essential part of transformative learning, stimulates critical reflection of socio-linguistic and epistemic meaning perspectives. Some of what can be called self-concept may be consciously known and transformed, but transformation may also occur without critical reflection on one's meaning perspectives. It's possible the changed self-concept may never be apparent to us, or may become so only later on. Regardless, self-concept has an important connection to other meaning schemes and how we approach the opportunity to transform them.

Self-concept is embodied through experience. We come to define ourselves through experience, from the time we can sense (Goleman, 1995, p. 96), through our interactions with our families, communities, and political and cultural artifacts. We hear messages about who we are expected to be. Our construction of self is a combination of how we sense ourselves in our bodies, who we think ourselves to be, embodied metaphors, our actions, and how we feel emotionally (p. 96).

For a woman, a part of self-concept is in relation to gender-based violence which may shape how we hold our bodies, inform our beliefs, affect our emotions, and in other ways teach us who we are. Violence

---

[1] While Cranton used "self-perception" here we use "self-concept" to differentiate the meaning schemes we have about ourselves from the psychological theory of self-perception.

against women continues to be endemic, with 1 out of every 6 American women having been the victim of an attempted or completed rape in her lifetime. This does not include non-penetrative sexual assault, domestic violence, or child sexual abuse. Taken together, the pervasiveness of gender-based violence is enormous (RAINN.org, NCADV.org). Women who have been raped or battered suffer the long-term psychological consequences of that loss of power. Women who have not directly experienced violence also suffer the impact the threat of violence holds (Gordon & Riger, 1989). Most women know someone who has been raped. While not every woman directly experiences gender-based violence, most women experience some form of sexual harassment. Just the awareness of gender-based violence gives virtually all women a sense of their own vulnerability in a way most men in Western societies do not routinely experience. In addition, a large part of social discourse revolves around women's bodies, affecting self-concept. We learn how to hold and move ourselves through media images and the shaping influence of loving arms holding us, or angry fists bruising us. The impact on self-concept can be unconscious—physical, emotional, and metaphorical.

In this context, barriers to women fighting back against an attack are established in childhood and reinforced in adulthood. In my experience, many women are not emotionally prepared to defend themselves against violence. Studies of what actually works against attempted rape indicate that aggressive physical and verbal resistance is the most effective defense (Frost, 1991). However, "it appears that simply teaching physical self-defense techniques is insufficient to counter the teachings of socialization" (Frost, 1991, p. 31). What's required instead is an integrated approach that recognizes the mental, emotional, and physical barriers women face and provides required emotional support as women struggle to overcome deep conditioning. When a fierce response, requiring a willingness to hurt another is required, deep conditioning from childhood, including disempowering self-concept, can prevent this life-preserving response. Yet the ability to be fierce and aggressive is within every woman as part of the survival instinct. Women who take Model Mugging learn more than self-defense moves. By arriving at a willingness and ability to fully and forcefully fight back through simulations, many women undergo a reformation of their self-concept in marked contrast to the everyday social discourse around femininity and power.

Description of the Model Mugging Program

The family of self-defense workshops Model Mugging belongs to is also known locally as KidPower, Empower Training, Worth Defending, and others. Model Mugging and these related programs use scenarios which verbally and physically simulate an actual attack—with many added guard rails to protect against physical or psychological harm. The class is typically led by one female instructor/coach and one male instructor/mugger and is assisted by graduates of the program who provide logistical support for the instructors and emotional support for participants.

Program lengths vary from between 3 to 5 days and are held in a private room with wrestling or gymnastic mats. Circles are facilitated by the female instructor/coach at the beginning and end of each session to consider ideas, tell stories, and share experiences. During teaching sessions, participants typically stand to watch demonstrations and engage in simulated conflicts. During the simulations, participants come to the center of the room one by one and stand with the female instructor/coach. After offering some encouraging words, the coach loudly proclaims—"*Name .... is ready!*" This cues the simulation to begin. The other participants watch quietly as the simulation unfolds, until the woman on the mat makes her first defensive move. Then they join her in yelling the names of the strike zones and cheer for their classmate. When the simulation is over, each participant is received back into the line of cheering women. At the beginning and end of a set of simulations, the participants, female instructor/coach, and assistants, circle up, arms around each other, to get encouragement and feel physically and emotionally supported.

The male instructor/mugger wears full body armor protecting his groin, ribs, arms, shins, feet, shoulders, and head. The armor is designed to allow participants to engage full force in their defensive strikes, especially on the most vulnerable and large targets of the groin and head. Throughout the program, the male instructor/mugger gives feedback with his helmet off and engages participants in simulations with his helmet on. When wearing his helmet, the mugger is always regarded only as a mugger. When the male instructor removes his helmet, he becomes a supportive instructor. This separation of identity of the mugger/instructor reinforces that "man" and "mugger" are separate. The female instructor gives direction to the class, models fights, teaches verbal

838 C. SCHLATTNER

and physical techniques, provides emotional support, coaches the simulations, and collaborates with the other staff to monitor participant progress and make necessary adjustments.

Participants learn to set boundaries and fight back as they would in a real-life scenario. First, they are given instruction in body language and verbal boundary-setting. The female instructor models affect, words, and actions appropriate to the task of preventing and repelling an attack. Participants engage in simulated conflicts with the mugger who could be a stranger or acquaintance attempting to harass, rob, rape, or attack in some way. These scenarios begin as mild, increasing in intensity in order to gradually develop the skills and confidence necessary to stay calm and respond assertively. Next, the women are taught basic self-defense moves which are first practiced in a matter-of-fact manner. When the physical moves are mastered, they are paired with boundary-setting in attack scenarios. At first the attacks are emotionally and physically low-key. Participants build competencies in their physical responses, while shifting their emotional responses to be more controlled and effective. As skills are mastered, the intensity builds until all of the attacks become highly dynamic and forceful. The female instructor coaches participants during their fights with positive feedback and direction on specific actions.

RESEARCH ON MODEL MUGGING'S TRANSFORMATIVE POTENTIAL

Research on Model Mugging illustrates its potentially transformative effect on self-concept and the resulting agency. Gaddis (1990) explored the concept of empowerment in a phenomenological study, asking six women what they experienced as empowering in their Model Mugging training, and how the resulting shifts became apparent in their lives. "The research suggest that this program's impact on the sample of participants generalized into more positive self-perceptions and self-determined social behaviors" (p. i). Frost (1991) studied women's willingness to demonstrate assertive behavior; performance self-esteem; an emotional sense of their physical competence; perceived interpersonal and self-defense self-efficacy; prevalence of feelings of fear, helplessness, and anger; perceived right to resist; and likelihood to resist attack. She found Model Mugging training made a subjective difference in 9 of the 11 measures, up to the three-month post-test. "Anecdotal evidence from Model Mugging graduates is that the impact of the course pervades many areas of their lives, and standardized questionnaires do not reap the rich information that is available to speak to this phenomenon" (Frost, 1991, p. 88).

Ozer and Bandura (1990) studied 43 women to find Model Mugging enhanced perceived coping and cognitive control self-efficacy. The women also reported an increase in the ability to distinguish between safe and risky situations, and a decrease in their perceived vulnerability to sexual assault, anxiety, and restrictions on their behavior. They felt more confident and better able to set limits when necessary. The authors conclude that "empowering people with the means to exercise control over social threats to their personal safety serves to both protect and liberate them" (p. 485).

Gaddis (1990) identifies that in Model Mugging, crisis seems to carry with it the opportunity for intense learning. This aligns with Mezirow's identification of disorienting dilemma as the first phase of transformative learning. Gaddis identifies two implications arising from his study. "The first relates to the nature of change and the second is optimal learning. It seems that these subjects are two sides of the same coin, and that bodily experience ties them together" (p. 203). He concludes, "Change, it would seem is a result, almost a mutation, occurring through 'in situ' learning experiences where the desire for survival, either physical or social, causes the person to 'be here now' and to take responsibility for her choices" (p. 205). This seems to indicate the phenomenon of a fully embodied transformative learning.

My own research, conducted in 1993, picked up the challenge posed by Frost and Gaddis; to conduct a qualitative study on how this program can facilitate transformative learning through embodied experience. I thought it would be hard to find a better case study to illuminate the embodiment of transformative learning than a Model Mugging workshop. It is intensely physical and emotional. The use of intuition is encouraged. It is relational and incorporates discourse on the meaning perspectives that naturally shift throughout the experience. It would not be an exaggeration to say in my seven years facilitating the program, I was among hundreds of women who experienced significant shifts in our self-concept and personal agency. We embodied the creation of new meaning schemes and even meaning perspectives because of the integrated physical and emotional "re-working" of self-concept and personal agency.

POTENTIAL FOR AN EMBODIED TRANSFORMATIVE LEARNING

A number of elements in the program have the effect of creating powerful embodied metaphors, which can transform limiting self-concepts into empowering ones, without rationality, critical thinking, or discourse. Nor are they limited to a transition from "not able to defend myself" to "able to defend myself," as valuable as this is. These elements create the circumstances for embodied metaphors to be formed, which can be available for reference in any situation it in the future.

Through the entire program, participants rely upon each other, class assistants, and their female instructor for unconditional emotional and physical support. The use of voice is particularly important. Participants watch each fight and shout with their fighting classmate the names of her strikes (e.g., "groin!") to connect shouting to the act of striking and validating the action at the same time. Shouting is an empowering use of voice that becomes increasingly natural as the class proceeds. Fighting with the voices of her classmates behind her is designed to be encouraging and validating of the act of fighting back. Classmates cheer for each other when they win their fights, further validating their actions. The use of voice also encourages and reminds watching participants to stay present (to not dissociate) during the fights. Many past participants reported an attack after their training, when they heard my voice say *"Name… is ready!"* The revivification of their coach's voice gave women the confidence to use the skills they learned "in the wild." I also receive many reports of women hearing their classmates cheering for them as they fought off an actual attacker. The program ingrains at a deeply embodied level the validation of self-protection. This is particularly important for women whose self-concept may not have allowed them this basic acts of survival.

One of the primary learning approaches in Model Mugging is to reproduce for participants as realistically as possible the kinesthetic, visual, and auditory sensations of a real-life attack. The words, affect, and physical actions of the "attacker" are realistic and based on studies of what kinds of things have been said and done in actual attacks. The realism of the simulations causes an emotional and physical response close to how a woman would respond during an actual attack. Even though participants rationally know they are in a class and the attacker is one of their teachers, their embodied response is similar to how they would respond if the scenario happened on the street or in their home. This type of training is known as *adrenaline stress conditioning*. The purpose is to condition a new response to an extremely high-stress situation. While in an adrenalized state of fear, participants learn how to control and direct their bodies to take effective action, shifting their emotional response in the process. The experiential context provides an opportunity to learn more appropriate and effective verbal, physical, and emotional responses to harassment or assault. Additionally, each woman experiences each fight emotionally and physically at a deep level, whether it is her fight or someone else's.

The realism is not lost on participants, who may have had doubts about their ability to handle such a high-stress situation. In my experience nearly every one of the hundreds of women I taught, reported fear, and sometimes significant terror, when they began the program. Acting in spite of the fear, and being victorious, becomes a memory of the resourcefulness of body and mind participants experienced through their program. This is a powerful embodied metaphor which most often transformed self-concept, extending the meaning of the program from "being able to fight to defend myself," to "being able to conquer fear and overcome any of life's obstacles."

The primary goal of Model Mugging is to teach effective, realistic self-defense skills. This requires not only physical skill building but also a transformation of mental and emotional responses to a real-life attack. In addition to teaching physical skills, the program also provides space for women to explore thoughts and feelings and to reflect together on how their experiences are transformative. Learning to fight back means confronting the fear of violence. It also means shifting a common self-concept of unworthiness, to that of someone worthy and able to fight back. At one point in the program, a simulation is introduced which is particularly harrowing and continues to the point where the instructors perceive the woman may be ready to give up. At this point, the female instructor gives encouragement meant to elicit a sometimes-buried sense of self-worth. Often these words are personal to the particular participant. Inevitably, the woman gathers strength she didn't know she had and with a burst of energy polishes off the attacker. This moment also becomes a memory of an embodied sense of self-worth, which participants are encouraged to access as a resource state when it may be required to overcome any of life's trials.

On the final day, for their graduation from the program, women invite their support networks to bear witness to their empowerment. When

842 C. SCHLATTNER

participants demonstrate to friends, family, and strangers their skills and personal power, they are also embodying a powerful metaphor for owning their power, being proud of it, and not being afraid to show who they are, thus transforming yet another aspect of self-concept.

One of the metaphors we conventionally use to create coherence of life's events is the "life as story" metaphor. We normally remember events within fixed timelines and give them meaning, which has the potential to shift. It is possible to reframe events to give them a different meaning and doing so usually involves imagination, emotion, and nimble thinking. Being malignly acted upon is often an important event in someone's life story and may have deep impact on self-concept. The negative experience can create a lasting disempowering metaphor for life events to follow. These life events may have nothing to do with the original experience but can still be tainted by the self-concepts it formed.

Through imaginative simulations of how an event would have played out, had participants possessed the skills to respond in their own defense, participants are invited to re-write the story of their lives and create a different metaphor. The simulation plays out the disempowering event in a much more empowering way, creating a different outcome to which a new metaphor can be attached. "New metaphors have the power to create a new reality .... If a new metaphor enters the conceptual system that we base our actions on, it will alter that conceptual system and the perceptions and actions that the system gives rise to" (Lakoff & Johnson, 1980, p. 145). Creating a new metaphorical framework within the life as story metaphor involves connecting imaginatively, emotionally, and physically to a new course of action, to create a new meaning.

Embodiment in Transformative Learning Facilitation

In the *Journal of Transformative Education*, editor Finnegan (2020) asks, "how can we ensure adult learning spaces, and sites of adults learning in institutions ... operate in a way that does justice to the interconnected nature of body and mind?" (p. 83). Mezirow noted that educators make a difference in the world by helping others learn how to be change makers. Below are some thoughts on how educators can use an embodied theory of transformative learning to facilitate change.

Experiential Learning

Dirkx (2012) has emphasized the power of the unconscious in shaping self-concept. By definition, the unconscious is unexamined and unquestioned. Changing meaning perspectives around self-concept often involves changing unconscious structures. Metaphors are powerhouse tools for this work. When we change a metaphor that structures self-concept, we change that self-concept. Because metaphors are embodied structures, physically experiencing a new metaphor is a particularly powerful way to do this. Learning how to fight, when giving up was the only known response is a metaphor that can be accessed in other situations when giving up is a choice. Taking on challenges, experiencing success and the feelings that come with that, and explicitly giving that success a broader meaning is one way to use the power of experiential learning for transformation.

Simulation—Role-Play

Simulation or role-play is a form of experiential learning that brings physical, emotional, mental, and imaginative elements into reshaping meaning. Role-play has the potential to reveal unconscious responses, and if facilitated skillfully, to change them. Etmanski (2007) explores the use of popular theater in the embodiment of transformative learning. She cites Theatre of the Oppressed founder Augusto Boal who said "that the human being is a unity, an indivisible whole. ... all ideas, all mental images, all emotions reveal themselves physically" (cited in Etmanski, 2007, p. 127). Boal uses the question: "what's inside this for you?" to help participants draw connections between their physical sensations, emotions, and rational thoughts. "As people become more aware of their physical sensations and emotions, they can begin to learn from them, not simply experience them at a conscious or unconscious level or react to them without reflection" (Etmanski, 2007, p. 105).

Rationality and Discourse

Understanding that rationality is embodied is important to the facilitation of transformative learning. Encouraging reflection and discourse can bring unconscious shifts which have already emerged into awareness through conscious meaning making and storytelling. We do change our minds,

844   C. SCHLATTNER

but through reference to our embodied experience. Even the expression "change our minds" is itself a metaphor. Embodied learning is a process involving action, emotion, and physiology, which can lead to a critical re-evaluation of assumptions. Critical reflection and discourse can validate and strengthen new self-concepts. This could be described as the conscious mind catching up with an unconscious shift. One way transformative learning occurs is through the generalization of a metaphorical switch into broader meaning perspectives. For example, I often observed students who generalized the felt understanding that they could fight through fear, to mean they could take on a challenge in life unrelated to self-defense. The generalization of any metaphor arrived at through direct experience can be encouraged by asking, "what does this mean for your life?" This is similar to Boal's "what's inside this for you?".

Support

Discourse itself is embodied, both in metaphor and through emotion. The sharing of experience with others is part of the embodiment as we experience ourselves as "part of something," an element in the creation of a meaning gestalt. In supporting others, we also validate and support ourselves. "Support" itself is a metaphor that gives meaning to how we engage in the act of this kind of compassionate discourse. Participants can feel safe to express what may be vulnerabilities, which in turn can bring greater clarity to the meanings being re-evaluated. In Model Mugging, participants support each other physically, validate the raw emotion, cheer for each other, and participate in each other's fights through their attention. The ways women relate to each other during the class is essential to the learning experience. Being part of the social body of the class—which is also a metaphor for self-support—creates a much deeper learning experience than if any woman learned these skills alone. Any facilitation of transformative learning can use the power of relationship to deepen and support the experience.

CONCLUSION

Meaning perspectives are gained through lived, embodied experience—through the metaphors we use, our unconscious representations, our emotional states, how we responded physically, and the actions we take in the moment. The theory of transformative learning is made more accurate by moving beyond rationality and critical thinking as the apex process. In an embodied conception of transformative learning, rationality is an element of learning, not the predominant defining element. It may simply be the one we are trained to predominantly focus on. When we recognize that emotions, concepts, critical thinking, discourse, and the other elements of meaning making are all embodied, none can have a dominant position. All are part of the gestalt of the creation of new meaning, within a body, in an environment. The exploration of embodiment in transformative learning contributes an important facet to what could be considered adult education's most important and consequential area of study. When we can fully appreciate that transformative learning is embodied, we can devote more attention to studying the most effective ways to facilitate empowering meaning making.

References

Cranton, P. (2016). *Understanding and promoting transformative learning.* Jossey-Bass.

Dirkx, J. (2012). Nurturing soul work: A Jungian approach to transformative learning. In E. W. Taylor & P. Cranton (Eds.), *The handbook of transformative learning: Theory, research, and practice* (pp. 116–130). Jossey-Bass.

Etmanski, C. (2007). *Unsettled: Embodying transformative learning and intersectionality in higher education: popular theatre as research with international graduate students* (Doctoral dissertation, University of Victoria). http://hdl.handle.net/1828/233

Finnegan, F. (2020). Editor's notes: Exploring the collective and embodied dimensions of transformative learning. *Journal of Transformative Education, 18*(2), 83–86. https://doi.org/10.1177/1541344620906632

Frost, H. (1991). *Model Mugging: A way to reduce women's victimization* (Doctoral dissertation, University of Kansas). UMI Dissertation Services, 9238641.

Gaddis, J. (1990). *Women's empowerment through Model Mugging: Breaking the cycle of social violence* (Doctoral dissertation, University of California, Santa Barbara). UMI Dissertation Services, 9114756.

Goleman, D. (1995). *Emotional intelligence.* Bantam Books.

Gordon, M., & Riger, S. (1989). *The female fear.* The Free Press.

Iafrate, M. (2018). *The embodied experience and transformative learning: Moving towards a healthy and empowered self* (Masters Thesis, University of Calgary). http://hdl.handle.net/1880/108712

Johnson, M. (2017). *Embodied mind, meaning, and reason: How our bodies give rise to understanding.* The University of Chicago Press.

846   C. SCHLATTNER

Lakoff, G., & Johnson, M. (1980). *Metaphors we live by*. The University of Chicago Press.

Mezirow, J. (1991). *Transformative dimensions of adult learning*. Jossey-Bass.

Mezirow, J. (1994). Understanding transformation theory. *Adult Education Quarterly, 44*(4), 222–232.

Mezirow, J. (2000). Learning to think like an adult. In J. Mezirow & Associates (Eds.), *Learning as transformation: Critical perspectives on a theory in progress* (pp. 3–33). Jossey-Bass.

Mezirow, J. (2003). Transformative learning as discourse. *Journal of Transformative Education, 1*(1), 58–63.

O'Sullivan, E. (2012). Deep transformation: Forging a planetary world view. In E. W. Taylor & P. Cranton (Eds.), *The handbook of transformative learning: Theory, research, and practice* (pp. 162–177). Jossey-Bass.

Ozer, E. M., & Bandura, A. (1990). Mechanisms governing empowerment effects: A self-efficacy analysis. *Journal of Personality and Social Psychology, 58*(3), 472–486.

CHAPTER 47

Transformation and the Language We Use

Linden West

INTRODUCING A TRINITY

This chapter has a strong auto/biographical element and focuses on the words we use about transformation and why we use them. Auto/biography has to do with how we draw on others' stories to make sense of our own, and vice versa. There are constant battles over language and meaning, which include how much our words fulsomely and authentically express some of the complex spirit of learning for transformation. We can witness the same phenomenon in different ways, depending on the perspectives and languages we employ. The Handbook provides an opportunity to think afresh as to how we might bring vibrant insight into processes of profounder change. And to consider what languages we might use in our collective struggle to better illuminate the human search, individually and collectively, for self and societal improvement. Auto/biographically, the chapter encompasses a quest for a language to re-enchant our engagement with learners and learning, beyond a kind

---

L. West (✉)
Faculty of Arts, Humanities and Education, Canterbury Christ Church University, Canterbury, UK
e-mail: linden.west@canterbury.ac.uk

© The Author(s), under exclusive license to Springer Nature Switzerland AG 2022
A. Nicolaides et al. (eds.), *The Palgrave Handbook of Learning for Transformation*, https://doi.org/10.1007/978-3-030-84694-7_47

847

of disembodied, decontextualized rationality, or pervasive commodification. The quest engages with the often-neglected religious dimensions of radical change processes (Formenti & West, 2018; Leopando, 2017; West, 1996, 2001, 2016).

Words matter. They, in speaking and writing, can illuminate and inspire, and provide glimpses of profound truths and meaning in the messiness and mystery of learning lives. Or they fall short, even conspire against the quest for meaning, and lie and seduce us into following false gods. They bring good or fake news, beauty or ugliness. They give glimpses of the sacred and profane. But words create illusions too about what is worthwhile knowledge and legitimate ways of knowing, for example, in traditional forms of positivist science. Here, subjectivity, or the inner world, is regarded as an enemy of a good and satisfying epistemology, indeed of the entire rational Enlightenment project. I want to introduce three languages to help us think afresh about varying perspectives on transformation—from depth psychology, popular education and relatedly, particular literature encompassing the sacred and religious. There can, I suggest, be a damaging dismissal of faith and spirit in secular progressive thought.

Words illuminate our capacity for courage in profounder, transformational learning as well as paradoxically hating the price paid. They reveal, in depth psychology, our resistance to knowledge. Words, at many levels— in politics, ideology, mass and social media, in education, and our intimate relationships—evoke curiosity or conformity, life or death. Powerful forms of politics and ideology close down lives and language. We are seduced by capitalism's enchantments where learning is a product, like any other, or by constraining, authoritarian forms of religion, in which truth is rigid, fixed and pre-determined by the powerful. Racism, classism or sexism can keep us firmly in our place. We experience the dangerous terror of a pandemic and struggle for words and meaning in its presence. Life can be full of existential terrors, combined with oppressive stereotypes of race, gender, sexuality, class, disability, etc. And learning, to repeat, is often about conformity not liberation. If conformity embodies a profound need to belong, it tends to be on other's terms. This is the territory of what Adorno called *Halbildung*, or half education, where we learn to adapt to the established order, whether religious or secular (Formenti & West, 2018). Halbildung involved, in part, the replacement of the hegemony of religion not so much by a liberating science but by capitalism and the market. But science itself, or maybe the ideology of scienticism, can be troubling, often dressed in an omniscient garb. Learning for transformation represents, I suggest, something quite different: a kind of existential quest, sometimes individual, sometimes collective, to create the well-lived life and meaning on more of our own terms.

Words, however, may make us feel anxious or out of our depth in any quest. They make us feel small, unloved, unlovable and inferior. Think the language of slavery or the struggles of Black Lives Matter against the deathly lexicon of racism. A word like transformation is also reduced to an empty signifier, a marketing trope to sell institutions, programmes and even ourselves, using sex, cars and the promise of glittering lives. Learning is easily commodified, presented in nice packaging, with the promise, in exchange for our money, of an easy ride and powerful exchange value. What is sacred, I suggest, is easily profaned. The language of positivistic science can appeal as a satisfying alternative. Truth, according to Huxley, that can neither be demonstrated nor proven is no truth at all. His target was religion. The trouble is that we, and our subjective experience, fall victim to this objectivist dominion (Holland, 2019).

But new words and languages are available in the struggle for some subjective liberation. The first language I introduce is of depth psychology, that of Freud, Jung and Winnicott. It is a language of death as well as life, Eros and Thanatos, logos and mythos, of our capacity for love as well as hate. The second comes from popular education: where dialogue and I/Thou qualities of relationship have been emphasized, but spiritual and important radical religious perspectives can be marginalized in the name of a secular critical rationality. The third language, connected in part with other forms of popular education, is of soul and the sacred, which overlaps with depth psychology. Its genus lies in a questioning religious impulse, in the writings of William Blake, as a prime example, in reaction to the excesses of abstract reason in the French revolution and beyond. This radical language reaches back long before the Enlightenment, to biblical inspiration in the cause of dissent against hegemonies of established Churches, the State and what we might call the moral law or codes of repression and prohibition. The moral law is often determined by the powerful, legitimizing oppression and misery in the here and now for the promise of bliss in the world to come. Biblical inspiration, however, can lie in Christ's solidarity with and love for the poor and marginalized in struggles for justice in the present. These latter perspectives can draw on literature, poetry, painting and illustration and are energized in contemporary language by what we can call the mythopoetic and autoethnographic. Learning for transformation, to paraphrase William Blake, involves seeing a world in a grain of sand, heaven in a wildflower, infinity in a palm of a hand, and new existential possibility in the joy of deeply meaningful communication and profound illumination on a pilgrimage or in a university seminar.

DREAMS OF EMPIRICISM AND DEPTH PSYCHOLOGY

The dream of empiricism and the Enlightenment has inspired the academy, including the study of education, which is often characterized as social science. Here, subjectivity is, or should be, transcended; phenomena are seen more purely in the light of reason, free from superstition, magic and what can be, if not inevitably, the tyranny of top-down religion or other hegemonies. Self and other are kept firmly apart in the struggle for objectivity. Empiricism strove to ensure the perfect representation of everything that can be observed or is visible, free of subjective contamination. It would constitute a linguistic programme of purification following the perversions, distortions and projections of religious wars: eloquence, wrote Thomas Sprat, in his *History of the Royal Society* (1667) is "a thing fatal to Peace and good Manners" (cited in Alison, 2017, p. 96). Sprat rejected amplifications, digressions and swellings of style, seeking brevity in science (Allison, 2017). Empiricism became a revolutionary project, challenging what was perceived as false, magical consciousness.

However, positivistic science can fail to satisfy our longing for meaning and enlightenment in our lives. Sigmund Freud, the father of psychoanalysis, sought to be the good empirical scientist in chronicling mental life and neuroses, including resistance to self-knowledge. Objectivity was psychoanalysis' dream, transcending religious illusions. God was no more than a projection of infantile vulnerability and the need for omnipotent parent substitutes. Psychoanalysis involved what was considered to be transformative liberation from illusion, towards the truth of who we are in Freud's reality principle (Gay, 1988). However, he struggled over words and language. He desired to live the empiricist dream and to create a language to provide a perfect representation of the internal world. He sought to purge himself of the a priori, including of philosophy, the literary and poetic—even of the Greek myths, which he loved, so as to see things fresh and pure. He was well read in literature, history, philosophy and science, in German, French and English but still pursued the empiricist dream in the name of good science and truth (Allison, 2017; Gay, 1988; Symington, 1986).

But he struggled. He believed in the principles of the Enlightenment but was aware that empiricism lacked a sufficient language to explain some of the nuance of mental phenomenon. Science he observed had little or nothing to say about complex sexuality, for instance, towards which, he asserted, not one ray of a hypothesis had penetrated its dark hinterland (Allison, 2017). Freud heroically wrote about this taboo subject, shocking the bourgeois world of his time (Kahr, 2020). Yet he was something of a romantic too and was tempted by the explanatory power of classical and other literary myths to explain clinical phenomenon, famously the Narcissus and Oedipus complexes. How in the former we are caught in our own idealized image, ultimately locked into empty worship of a diminishing self, closed as we become to life, love, others and experience. Freud thought infatuation with one's own person, including one's genitals, was the territory of the Greek myth of the beautiful youth slowly dying and killing a loving object in the form of Echo. The narcissist loves what they are, and were, and would like to be (Freud, 1991; Gay, 1988). In the case of the Oedipus complex, we are trapped in the triangle of traditional parental relationships: captured and enraptured by the mother, for instance, against the father whom we might learn to hate (Freud, 1913). What Freud had in mind (his ideas developed over time) was ubiquitous evidence of sibling rivalry, rivalry between mothers and daughters, fathers and sons, between daughters and parents, and even death wishes against other members of the family. This was the stuff of myth and literary tragedy, as in Shakespeare's *King Lear* or *Hamlet*, which Freud loved. It finds expression in the rivalrous academy, where we may hate our parent/teachers or other students/siblings, and in education, it can fuel our ambivalence towards new knowledge and dependence on others.

Transformation, psychoanalytically, lies in engaging with the unconscious, which includes what is difficult to acknowledge in ourselves—like sexuality or competitiveness—and to release some of the energy consumed by repression and denial. Freud pursued, as he saw it, the truth about humankind and desired a scientific basis and status for his project. But he was forced to admit that his case histories read like short stories, lacking the "serious stamp of science." Notwithstanding, if electrical shock treatment and systematic observation was proper experimental science, it led nowhere in comparison with the detailed description of mental processes "we are accustomed to find in the works of imaginative writers" (Allison, 2017, p. 100).

Moreover, Freud's work evolved towards conceptualizing analysis as a kind of reciprocal relationship between human subjects, mutually shaping each other in the transference and counter-transference. In the transference, we unconsciously perceive the other through powerful influences in our lives—negative figures of authority, for instance—while our own responses, in the counter-transference, offer clues about the state of our own internal life and why we may react strongly to the psychological dynamics of the other. Crucially, what belongs to one or the other becomes relationally difficult to distinguish, which is problematic for empiricism's objectivist desire.

There is a similar problem in auto/biographical case study research, where the ideal, in some traditions, is to minimize the presence of the researcher in gathering life stories. To do any other than this ideal risks jeopardizing the possibility of a singular truth, open to any other researcher to establish as research procedures must minimize intersubjective contamination. On the other hand, especially when working among marginalized peoples, the quality of the researcher's presence, including the capacity for empathy, matters in creating a good enough space for open forms of storytelling. Here storytelling becomes a kind of co-creation. Furthermore, processes of transference and counter-transference operate here too and offer important insights into who the researcher represents for the other and who the other represents for her. The methodology, like psychoanalysis, is more one of reflexive hermeneutics than conventional science (Formenti & West, 2018; Merrill & West, 2009; West, 2014). In fact, the legacy of traditional empiricism has sometimes inhibited an imaginative engagement with learning for transformation in great literature and myth. Shakespeare's *A Winter's Tale* or Ovid's *Metamorphoses* offer profound insights into struggles to transform, including its pain, loss as well as exhilaration (Chapman Hoult, 2012). We miss out in important ways if we restrict ourselves to the observable and traditionally verifiable rather than eclectically embracing literary, poetic and, I want to add, mystical ways of knowing.

Jung, more so than Freud, embraced the language of metaphor and myth—of pilgrimage, encounters with the divine and sublime as well as the unconscious in transformative processes (Formenti & West, 2018). There was in fact an increasingly unresolved tension between the two of them over the nature of sexuality. Jung, over time, sought to widen libido's meaning to encompass not only sexual drives but a more general mental energy or life force. Freud thought Jung suffered from a failure of nerve about the power of sexuality (see Gay, 1988, pp. 225–238, on this debate). On the other hand, Andrew Samuels (2015), a Jungian analyst, thought "Freud spoke for the literal, the instinctual, the causative; Jung for the metaphorical and teleological, asking what is sex really for?" (p. 98). Sex, in these metaphorical terms, can become a kind of symbolic longing for personal regeneration though intimacy with another. For Jung, there was an "instinct" for transformation (an idea given to him by a patient and the subsequently distinguished Russian Jewish analyst Sabina Spielrein, who was murdered by the Nazis) (Formenti & West, 2018). Jung was also enchanted with religious ideas of quest, and the language of divine poetry, as in the work of Dante's *Divine Comedy*.

Jung thought psychology should be an experiential discourse of learning from the soul, rather than learning about it, in a detached empirical way. The soul was far more than the self and contained a faculty of potential connection with the "God-image, or archetype" (Jung, 1963, p. 418). Visionary literature was one means to this soul-fullness, as in Dante's *Divine Comedy*. Here was a blueprint for the soul's journey from purgatorial suffering to the Celestial city of psychological individuation or wholeness. Jung's (2009) own inner journey of death and rebirth was explained in Dantean terms. Erudition and the intellect were simply insufficient for the task, which required archetypes, or visions, guides and teachers, as in Dante's journey. Dante finds guides like Virgil, Beatrice (a Florentine noble woman), the Virgin Mary and the Christ figure on the way towards the relative bliss of the Celestial City. Jung thought archetypes were timeless, inherited imprints, finding expression in culturally and individually specific ways. Their properties reflected common human inheritance. Episodes of earthly love, for instance, were conduits to a larger, divine comedy or poetry of the soul. Transformation lies in paying attention to dreams, visions and apparitions as much as the rational. For Jung, the journey is about aloneness as a basic oneness with something bigger than ego, offering glimpses of divine potential within every one of us.

For John Dirkx (Dirkx et al., 2006), soul work is central to transformative learning. This has to do with individuation, in the spirit of Jung, achieved in part through engaging with the shadow side of who we are, with what we don't like to admit about ourselves. There are several negative archetypal figures, like the trickster, the censor or judge, who pull us up short. Dirkx takes us into various enchanting educational landscapes, where the awesome aesthetic beauty of a text, or the depth of a good idea stirs our soul; or a moment of loving interaction with a soulful other—a teacher, student or other guide—inspires us on our quest. Feelings and unconscious processes matter, as do encounters with beauty and truth. Dirkx draws on a tradition represented, among others, by the American psychotherapist, former monk, and spiritual writer Thomas Moore. Moore (1998) has remarked that soulfulness is often tied to life in all its particulars. "... to good food, satisfying conversation, genuine friends, and experiences that stay in the memory and touch the heart. Soul is revealed in attachment, love, and community as well as retreat on behalf of inner communing and intimacy" (pp. xi–xii). Words like these tend to be absent from the educational and research lexicon leading to a kind of ontological and epistemological sterility.

I have made similar points in my own auto/biographical studies, using psychoanalyst Donald Winnicott as a guide, especially his notion of transitional space (Formenti & West, 2018; West, 1996). A transitional space (it could be a university seminar) is where we negotiate who we are and might be, over time. One struggling, non-traditional older student, who I called Brenda, strongly identified with an abused prostitute when reading Maupassant's short story *Boule de Suif* (*Suet Pudding*) in preparation for a seminar. Both the prostitute and Brenda were abused by men (the novel is set in the Franco-Prussian War of 1870, and two Prussian officers assault the prostitute in a coach). Brenda felt the deepest solidarity with the other woman, through processes of what are called projective identification (in which parts of ourselves are projected into another and can be reinternalized in potentially strengthened ways derived from the others' resilience). The prostitute fought back and kept on keeping on regardless. Brenda suffered her own hell in university seminars as she experienced particular tutors looking straight through her as though she did not exist. She felt, at times, no right to be there, as an "ordinary" older woman. However, one tutor encouraged her to speak about Maupassant, at a crucial moment, and she found words to talk about her insights into the novel. A word like recognition applies to this moment, or even "love," in the intuitive solidarity of the tutor. Brenda claimed space in her quest. The concept of recognition, drawing on Winnicott and the ideas of critical theorist Axel Honneth, is helpful here. Love is foundational in human flourishing, as is the feeling of self-respect when we are recognized as a legitimate member of a creative group. Becoming important to a group builds, in turn, self-esteem, from which we can better recognize others and social solidarities can grow (Formenti & West, 2018). Such depth psychological as well as psychosocial language provides interpretive resources that are often marginal in the academy.

RE-COVERING SOME OF THE ROOTS OF POPULAR EDUCATION

My second example of inspiring language to chronicle the relational depths of transformation comes from the literature of popular education. This literature, however, is often stripped of its spiritual and even religious inspiration, under a banner of secularism, materialism and Marxism. This is true of the patron saint of radical adult education, Paulo Freire, steeped as he was in the power and social commitment of Catholic liberation theology. The influence has tended to be either minimized or reduced to an idiosyncratic, irrelevant aspect of his personality by radical adult educators like Peter Mayo (Leopando, 2017). Collective transformation, some radical educators insisted, lay in critical reason, not faith, in interrogating the material roots of alienation and the importance of challenging how consciousness is constrained by oppressive, controlling relationships in the sphere of making things as well as by poverty. In fact, religion was considered a kind of indulgent self-mystification (Leopando, 2017; Thompson, 1993). Other writers, in turn, have argued that not all religious perspectives are dogmatic and sectarian, but rather focused on the idea of agentic quest, dialogue, spiritual openness and aesthetic power. Denigrating faith of all kinds has been responsible for a kind of spiritual alienation and crisis of meaning (Leopando, 2017).

There are, however, popular education traditions explicitly grounded in a spiritual and religious lexicon, not least, as suggested, the pedagogy of faith of Paulo Freire (Leopando, 2017). Transformation lies in an understanding of the divinity—the mystery and always provisional humanity of every one of us—to be liberated in the quality of our relationship with others, and the symbolic (like Brenda above), in dialogue, in I/Thou dynamics in the existential theology of Martin Buber (McCarraher, 2019). A real community, in Buber's eyes, lay in comradely access to one another, readiness to give to each other, allowing for what we might term psychosocial and spiritual growth in which the whole becomes more than the sum of individual parts (Leopando, 2017). Martin Buber (1937) insisted that we begin in relationship, not as isolated, solipsistic beings. The key to human flourishing lies in having sufficient I/Thou experience of mutual recognition in contrast to dehumanizing I/It objectification. Of being recognized in our infinite human potential by significant others, and thus becoming better able to recognize others in turn. When the other and we are face to face, the distance between the stranger and ourselves recedes, when I meets Thou.

Irwin Leopando (2017) illustrates how Paulo Freire's lifelong pedagogical work was rooted in his Catholicism, although Freire embraced the idea that Marx and Christ could live creatively in solidarity with one another. Freire's motivation derives from a "sacred sense of inviolable dignity, worth and well-being of the person" (Leopando, 2017, p. 215). He strove to create more humanized cultures and person-orientated societies. We can observe his struggle for an I/Thou pedagogy in which a relational transformation is born. Freire was appalled by the estrangement between secular and religious perspectives. For him, the fundamental difference was between sectarian or fundamentalist conviction, and non-sectarian and dialogical relationship. Although influenced by Marxism, it was liberation theology that sustained him in his struggles as an adult educator and activist for social justice (Leopando, 2017). To understand Freire's work without reference to these radical religious beliefs is like reducing the history of socialism to Marxism-Leninism. A cornerstone of Freire's pedagogy was creating an open, loving space for listening and dialogue. Transformation does not lie, for him, primarily at the intellectual or rational level, but when thinking unites with intuition, imagination, aesthetics, culture, values and relationships (Freire, 1998; Leopando, 2017). Freire would have come alongside Brenda, above. He would have intuitively understood her existential struggle to become, in soul work. Moreover, Freire's teaching raises the issue of how critical discourse can lack human empathy and I/Thou qualities. It has been good at argument and debate but can fail to nourish hope in struggles for the good and just (Formenti & West, 2018; Leopando, 2017). The science of society called positivist Marxism, for instance, could lack a human face.

There are similarities between Freire and the praxis of British adult educator R. H. Tawney, despite cultural and religious differences: Tawney, haute bourgeois, high Anglican; Paulo Freire, South American and liberation theologist. Tawney was perceived in earlier decades of the twentieth century to be a great adult educator but suffered, in the 1960s and 1970s the disdain of a generation of secular and Marxist critics. He was dismissed as pious and unscientific, as well as insufficiently theoretical, but his work is undergoing radical reappraisal (Goldman, 2014; West, 2017). His form of adult education could model in microcosm the Kingdom made flesh, a deep experience of communion, given fulsome witness in the testimonies of many worker-students. Tawney's tutorial classes involved 30 ordinary working-class men and women meeting every week, bringing their experiences to bear on aspects of industrial and economic history. A process set within the struggle for a better, more socially just order. The classes represented a social and educational experiment open to the marginalized, with equality of status between students and a culture of listening, tolerance and respect. There was turbulence too, generated when profound difference was encountered as in debates about Marxism. But difference did not, in general, degenerate into I-It objectification; Tawney took care of students who might have been seduced by sectarian dogma. Tea was taken after every class, in someone's home, songs sung, and poetry recited in ways that re-established harmony, dialogue and conviviality. At their best, the classes were communities of imaginative, caring, committed and thoughtful students, in which all were teachers and learners. Here, in Tawney's Christian Socialism lay glimpses of Christ's Kingdom, and a sort of collective transformation (Goldman, 2014; West, 2017).

Other radical social critics and adult educators, like E. P. Thompson, thought dismissals of the religious impulse in social transformation could be profoundly ahistorical. We require, he states, in his study of William Blake (Thompson, 1993), a library ticket to the literatures of radical dissent before the rational or humanist enlightenment. Literature that includes the traditions of the Anabaptists, Ranters, Bunyon and Blake and their antagonism to what they called the moral law. Such law, the law of patriarchs, priests and kings could be in direct contradiction to a gospel of mercy, peace and love. There was a strong autodidactic, antinomian spirit (from the Greek, meaning against the law) among disparate artisans, traders and other ordinary folk in the late eighteenth and nineteenth centuries. They perceived the moral law, deriving from Moses, was in opposition to justification by faith, grounded in Christ's forgiving, all-embracing love. In the eighteenth century, justification by faith was far more than otiose religiosity but considered the key to cultural and social transformation. It presented a radical challenge to the hegemonic ideology of Church and State, and even common sense. The authority of institutions and worldly wisdom was replaced by the individual's inner light of conscience, faith, personal understanding of Scripture and for Blake, a kind of poetic genius, to see beyond hegemony of all kinds. Thompson himself abandoned the authoritarianism and hegemony of the Communist Party after the Soviet tanks directed firepower against the working class, in the name of the proletariat, in Budapest in 1956. He turned in effect to spiritually attuned critiques of capitalism and the struggle for humane alternatives. Something was profoundly missing, he said, in the eventual nightmare of Socialist revolutionary "transformation" or a supposedly transcendental reason; something Blakean. The moral degeneration and spiritual emptiness of Soviet Communism, like capitalism, called for a more poetic vision of self and collective possibility. "There must be some redemption," Thompson (1993) wrote, echoing Blake, in which the "selfish loves" diminish and brotherhood (we should add sisterhood) increases (p. 221). Reason or rationality alone was insufficient without love. Pontius Pilate exercised reason, as do what Blake called the "hirelings" of a genteel, conformist university culture. But something profound, like love, is often absent, then and now: as in Blake's images of Divine suffering, while Hell and the Beast lie in abuses of power and narcissistic, materialist illusion. Transformation required the affirmatives, in Blake's Songs of Innocence and Experience, of "Mercy, Pity, Truth and Love" (Thompson, 1993, p. 221).

RE-SACRALISATION: NEW (AND OLD) LANGUAGE OF THE SACRED IN LEARNING FOR TRANSFORMATION

New forms of soul language are in fact emerging in auto/biographical and autoethnographic enquiry, deepening our understanding of learning for transformation. Here are poetic evocations of beauty, joy, pain, mercy, agony, doubt, pity, vulnerability, ambivalence, soul, life, truth, death, rebirth and wisdom (see Dirkx et al., 2006). Writers like Wilma Fraser (2018) embrace the literary and mythopoetic with enthusiasm. Fraser charts a kind of pilgrimage in seeking wisdom, in the name of Sophia, the Goddess of Wisdom, so neglected in Western epistemology. Fraser encounters Michelangelo's glorious evocation of God bringing the spirit of life to Adam, when visiting the Sistine Chapel in Rome. "Who was the woman?" she asks, framed by God's left arm. Here lay a sacred moment with profound effect on Fraser's writing. Sophia represents the feminine principle in wisdom, a refusal to dissect reality into fragments, but rather to see the whole, which includes the whole human beings in education. Fraser contrasts the corresponding quest for meaning, agency and understanding via literature, the poetic as well as the political with the demon of instrumentalism. What she bears witness to, as a result, is desolation: education hollowed out in the neo-liberal hegemony, instructing people in the ways of the market, consumption and obedience, under a banner of skills for life. Fraser's quest takes her to her own genealogical roots, and she draws on the inspirational poetry of an ancestor, Sorley Maclean, the Gaelic poet. His poetry evokes the brutality and loss of Gaelic communities in the Highland clearances. But Maclean's writing has the power to revive the spirit, to defy barbaric destruction and to inspire action in the here and now. Loss and hope pervade Fraser's multi-layered writing, including losing her own mother to dementia. Transformation requires personal and liberal collective spaces in which issues of climate change, species extinction and the insane belief in consumption at all costs can be interrogated and resisted. Fraser's epistemology is of humility, living with uncertainty and not knowing too; cultivating negative capability, in the English poet Keats' inspiring words, where we are open to what we do not know, and to learning from the other and otherness.

Libby Tisdell (2017) writes in an auto/biographical spirit about pilgrimage, and where wisdom might lie. She brings a Blakean sensibility to language, on her walk towards the shrine of St James at Santiago De Compostela in Northern Spain, completed after a difficult, painful divorce. According to Tisdell, the sacred is experienced when we learn to stand and stare. When the sunflowers turn their faces to the sun, and we experience grace. Potentially empty words, in contemporary secular life, such as blessing our feet, or picking up our bed and walking, take on deeper meaning in pilgrimage. Experiencing pain in blisters, as a prime example, is an inevitable part of the process, and she recalls the miracle story of Jesus healing the paralytic, and the injunction to "pick up your mat and walk." Walking is something I too have done on pilgrimage, which can also serve as a metaphor for getting lost, maybe in life's labyrinths, but also of finding strength to keep on keeping on (Formenti & West, 2018). Tisdell recalled her Catholic Irish roots, the sacred face of her culture, as she frames it, and sang Irish songs in the company of others. She found some healing and new life, which included awareness of the importance of her own religious roots. But the lessons drawn are those of a culturally sensitive and committed non-sectarian feminist, reaching out to the poor, despised and marginalized, deeply aware of what different cultures have to offer us. This includes indigenous peoples in North America and their contribution to a kind of spiritual renewal. Hegemony has little or no part in this reflexive, emotionally attuned, culturally sensitive and eclectic transformative learning.

Conclusion: A Trinity in Motion?

What then of transformation and the languages we use? How much does language encourage openness to and learning from complex experience? We may in fact lack a language to bring meaning to experience and if we do not have the words how can we begin to recognize what they might represent? Language sometimes strangles learning, too, by enmeshing us in the crude reductive words of buying and selling, or skills for life. Capitalism can in fact be considered the religion of modernity, its power and Gods so seductive and pervasive that we hardly recognize their capacity to colonize how we feel, perceive and think. The West, in this view, never gave up on Gods, but rather, as Eugene McCarraher insists, partook of the false God Mammon: of capital accumulation, proprietary rule, narcissistic excess and conspicuous consumption (McCarraher, 2019). Our languaging is also diminished by forms of empiricism in which subjectivity is a problem that needs eradicating and the poetry of soul gets lost. Learning for transformation challenges reductionism, fixedness and conformity from whatever quarter. We are encouraged on a quest of existential freedom, in the company of depth psychologists, radical educators and soul workers; of religious dissenters, autodidacts and diverse others; of those who ascribe to a biblical hermeneutic of a powerless God coming to earth, in redemptive solidarity with the poor and despised. But Freud, in his language of a-theism, reminds us that transformation is difficult and we can become trapped in denial, illusion and repression. Notwithstanding, the quest is worthwhile, if we remember the warning and remain open to languages which liberate rather than domesticate, encompassing therapy and education, inner and outer lives, love and hate, psyche and society, I and Thou, self and otherness, imagination, body and intellect; agency and soul.

References

Allison, E. (2017). Observing the observer: Freud and the limits of empiricism. *British Journal of Psychotherapy, 33*(1), 93–104.

Buber, M. (1937). *I and Thou* (R. G. Smith, Trans.). T. & T. Clark.

Chapman Hoult, C. (2012). *Adult learning and la Recherche Féminine*. Palgrave Macmillan.

Dirkx, J. M., Mezirow, J., & Cranton, P. (2006). Musings and reflections on the meaning, context and process of transformative learning. *Journal of Transformative Learning, 4*, 123–139.

Fraser, W. (2018). *Seeking wisdom in adult teaching and learning*. Palgrave Macmillan.

Freud, S. (1913). *The interpretation of dreams* (3rd ed., A. A. Brill, Trans.). Macmillan.

Freud, S. (1991). *On narcissism: An introduction* (J. Sandler, Ed.). Yale University Press.

Formenti, L., & West, L. (2018). *Transforming perspectives in lifelong learning and adult education: A dialogue*. Palgrave Macmillan.

Freire, P. (1998). *Pedagogy of freedom: Ethics, democracy and civic courage* (P. Clarke, Trans.). Rowman & Littlefield.

Gay, P. (1988). *Freud, a life for our times*. Dent.

Goldman, L. (2014). *The Life of R.H.Tawney. Socialism and history*. Bloomsbury.

Holland, T. (2019). *Dominium: The making of the Western mind*. Little, Brown.

Jung, C. G. (1963/1989). *Memories, dreams, reflections* (A. Jaffé, Ed.). Random House.

Jung, C. G. (2009). *The red book: Liber novus* (S. Shamdasani, Ed.). W. W. Norton.

Kahr, B. (2020, June 19). *How Freud would have handled the coronavirus* (Lecture). Freud Museum Lecture, London.

Leopando, I. (2017). *A pedagogy of faith. The theological vision of Paulo Freire*. Bloomsbury.

McCarraher, E. (2019). *The enchantments of mammon. How capitalism became the religion of modernity*. Harvard University Press.

Merrill, B., & West, L. (2009). *Usng biographical methods in social research*. Sage.

Moore, T. (1998). *Care of the soul: How to add depth and meaning to your everyday life*. Harper Collins.

Samuels, A. (2015). *A new therapy for politics?* Karnac.

Symington, N. (1986). *The analytic experience*. Free Association Books.

Thompson, E. P. (1993). *Witness against the beast*. Cambridge University Press.

Tisdell, E. J. (2017). Transformative pilgrimage learning and spirituality on the Camino de Santiago: Making the way by walking. In A. Laros, T. Fuhr, & E. W. Taylor (Eds.), *Transformative learning meets Bildung: An international exchange* (pp. 341–352). Sense.

West, L. (1996). *Beyond fragments. Adults, motivation and higher education*. Taylor & Francis.

West, L. (2001). *Doctors on the edge. general practitioners, health and learning in the inner city.* Fab Books.

West, L. (2014). *Transformative learning and the form that transforms: Towards a psychosocial theory of recognition using auto/biographical narrrative research. Journal of Transformative Education, 12*(4), 164–179.

West, L. (2016). *Distress in the city.; Racism, fundamentalism and a democratic education.* UCL/IOE Press.

West, L. (2017). Resisting the enormous condescension of posterity: Richard Henry Tawney, Raymond Williams and the long struggle for a democratic education. *International Journal of Lifelong Education, 36*(1–2), 129–144.

CHAPTER 48

Lessons from Utopia: Reflections on *Peak Transformative Experiences* in a University Studio in Auroville, India

Bem Le Hunte, Katie Ross, Suryamayi Clarence-Smith, and Aditi Rosegger

INTRODUCTION

I'm waiting for my students to arrive at my Auroville guest house with trepidation and the thrill of anticipation. The air is pulsing with possibilities. In Auroville it's hard not to feel it, this future unfolding; and like all futures it's emergent, unpredictable. Who knows how the next three weeks will unravel? I have one big expectation and it's the hope that every

---

B. Le Hunte (✉) · K. Ross · A. Rosegger
University of Technology Sydney, Ultimo, SYD, Australia
e-mail: Bem.LeHunte@uts.edu.au

K. Ross
e-mail: Katie.Ross@uts.edu.au

A. Rosegger
e-mail: Aditi.Rosegger@uts.edu.au

S. Clarence-Smith · A. Rosegger
Sri Aurobindo Institute of International Educational Research, Auroville, Tamilnadu, India

© The Author(s), under exclusive license to Springer Nature
Switzerland AG 2022
A. Nicolaides et al. (eds.), *The Palgrave Handbook of Learning for Transformation*, https://doi.org/10.1007/978-3-030-84694-7_48

863

student will "get" Auroville and that they'll be transformed and inspired in the process, as I have been on so many visits. I hope that they won't leave the same as they arrived—that they'll never un-see the possibilities of what they have seen here—and that they'll take everything they've learned back to their homes to transform their worlds and our systems that are so ripe for change. (My personal definition of transformative learning.) No small ambition—and my expectations go far beyond the notion of any assessment task. But I also have a looming fear that they might not leave their cynicism at the door, that they will bring too much of their previous world to bear on this one, complete with its judgements and confines, and that they will lose this opportunity to understand what change is possible and how they might think differently about their futures. I fear that they may feel threatened by Auroville's spirituality (albeit all-inclusive, beyond the notion of any singular religion), and that this might be too large to reconcile with their secular understanding of what a university education should entail. But I also have faith… in them… —Bem

This is an inquiry that sets out to create and observe transformative learning within a three-week global studio in Auroville, an intentional community in India. This global studio is an elective within the fourth year of the Bachelor of Creative Intelligence and Innovation (BCII) at the University of Technology Sydney (Australia).[1] Throughout the BCII degree, we experiment with new ways of learning, working, conducting research, which, most importantly, provide a context for understanding the potential of transformative learning for transforming self and society (Kligyte et al., 2019). What better way to culminate the transformative learnings than to bring BCII students to Auroville, which has been experimenting with spiritualised individual and societal transformation (see Clarence-Smith, 2019) for over 50 years? BCII students study innovation through the lens of systems change, and as Auroville has conducted many successful experiments in social, environmental, educational, and economic practices, it provided the ideal context for immersive global learning, outside the four walls of a classroom.

By taking students from a highly experimental degree (BCII) into an experimental society (Auroville), we witnessed experiences described by

---

e-mail: suryamayi@auroville.org.in

[1] https://www.uts.edu.au/future-students/transdisciplinary-innovation/undergraduate-courses/creative-intelligence-and-innovation.

students, facilitators, and Aurovilians as including an expanded awareness of self, of nature, of their cohort, and of a fresh connection to lived human and beyond-human unity. In this chapter, we define these as *peak transformative experiences*: intense and profound moments of ineffable illuminations and discoveries, sometimes even spiritual or mystical states of consciousness, which, with processes of meaning making and integration, can transform perceptions and enactions of self, identity, intrinsic values, and ways of being in society. We further uncover and synthesise the enabling conditions of these peak transformative experiences, and consider their relevance for transformative learning.

Learning Context: The BCII "Global Studio" in Auroville

BCII is a multi-award-winning transdisciplinary degree that encompasses high-level critical and creative thinking, problem-solving, invention, complexity, innovation, future scenario building, and entrepreneurship/social entrepreneurship.[2] Students study together in a combined, accelerated degree from 25 other core degrees from each faculty at the University of Technology Sydney. Since there is no way we can teach students from diverse disciplines knowledge at any depth, our focus is on developing lifelong learners who can manage uncertainty, work collaboratively and creatively, and learn well beyond the parameters of their discipline. The ultimate goal is that students transform themselves and their society as they progress, a goal that aligns neatly with the philosophy and mission of Auroville. For some leading educators, a focus on "being" (ontology) rather than simply "knowing" (epistemology) (Barnett, 2012)—or a "Curriculum for Being" (Le Hunte, 2019)—is a better way to prepare students for the supercomplexity of our world and an environment where knowledge is more transitional than ever. By privileging being over knowing, we also align with non-Western practices and ways of knowing that intersect elegantly with those fostered in the Auroville context.

---

[2] www.uts.edu.au/future-students/transdisciplinary-innovation/undergraduate-courses/creative-intelligence-and-innovation.

Auroville is the largest and among the oldest intentional communities[3] in the world, with 3,000 people of 60 different nationalities, founded in 1968 in South India. Based on the living philosophy and practice of Integral Yoga, Auroville strives to become a spiritualised society in which "all life is yoga" (Sri Aurobindo, 1999, p. 8). This embodiment of Integral Yoga aspires to gradually bring a higher consciousness into all aspects of life by means of a conscious individual and collective evolution. In the past 50 years, Auroville has envisioned and experimented with this spiritually transformative agenda in a multiplicity of pursuits: commercial and social enterprises, alternative schooling, environmental restoration, participatory governance, and a vibrant artistic and multicultural life. The township has been recognised by UNESCO for its contributions to the advancement of innovative, sustainable, peaceful and harmonious social, cultural and educational development, specifically for its living contribution to the experiential development of lifelong learning (Auroville, 2018).

Auroville is a hive of learning opportunities for people of all ages both within and beyond the community in India and internationally. These opportunities range from new forms of schooling to volunteering opportunities, internships, and training within the community's enterprises, schools, farms, forests, and research centres, to personal development workshops. University student groups, such as from the BCII global studio, regularly visit the community on accredited, immersive field trips and semester programs to use these offerings and the opportunity to experience life within an alternative, experimental society.

A report on educational practices and opportunities for adults in Auroville reveals that an immersion in the Auroville environment facilitates an inner dimension of personal development (Grinnell et al., 2013). This learning orientation is grounded in Auroville's Charter: "Auroville will be the place of an unending education, of constant progress, and a youth that never ages" (Auroville, 2020), and in its ideal of integral education, which strives towards the development and enrichment of all faculties of being and spirit (Auroville, 2016).

The BCII Global Studios in Auroville take place over three weeks. During this period, the students are encouraged to create their own journey of learning within Auroville. This involves developing relationships with the place and people, undertaking a creative residency

---

[3] Alternate terms used are communes, utopian communities, communal utopias, cooperative communities, ecovillages.

or research project, and becoming aware of one's own transformative learning as it is happening.

REVIEW: THE SIGNIFICANCE OF PEAK EXPERIENCES FOR TRANSFORMATIVE LEARNING

Across diverse ecologies of transformative learning, unifying aspects are the concepts of deep change in consciousness, worldview, and self-awareness towards greater openness and inclusion, resulting in changed actions (Lange, 2015; Stuckey et al., 2014; Taylor & Cranton, 2012). Our chapter draws on this understanding of transformative learning, but we explore it through the lens of peak transformative experiences for several reasons.

"Peak experiences" is a term coined by Abraham Maslow to explore the farthest positive potential of humanity (1971). To study peak experiences, Maslow inquired into utopias and individuals becoming the most authentic beings each could be. He believed that peak experiences were fundamental to achieving positive self and societal transformation and should be fostered within learning institutions. Similar to transformative learning, Maslow (1971) saw peak experiences as those which help us listen to our self-identities (pp. 175–177); develop a "cognition of being" guided by intrinsic values (pp. 176–177); strengthen a consciousness of radical interconnectedness and unity (p. 187); and create actions for social improvement (p. 347). As this global studio, with its Curriculum for Being, took place in an experimental society with utopian ideals, the lens of Maslow's peak experience is relevant to and applied in this case study.

In exploring the concept of peak experiences, Maslow was inspired by William James' inquiry into mystical and spiritual states of consciousness (1902). James and Maslow concurred that the spiritual and mystical experiences could lead to transformative insights of self and world important for "growth in being" (James, 1902; Maslow, 1971)—although the context for what they suggested comprised "spiritual" was fascinating and diverse. As this global studio took place in a spiritualised society, Maslow's and James' notions of peak spiritual and mystical states as they contribute to transformative learning are relevant and therefore explored in this case study.

The discussion of spiritual and mystical insights in transformative higher education is growing (Duerr et al., 2003), including in Indigenous (Napan et al., 2020), cultural (Tisdell & Tolliver, 2016), creativity

(Netzer & Rowe, 2010), integral (Gunnlaugson, 2004; Osterhold et al., 2007), sustainability (Lange, 2018), and contemplative courses (Dencev & Collister, 2011; Hart, 2008; Morgan, 2012, 2015), yet these discussions do not use Maslow or James' original markers of peak transformative learning to identify these moments or as a means of reflecting on what might contribute to these peak transformative experiences. This case study contributes the novel application of Maslow and James' characteristics of spiritual states to understand the experiences of the learners.

In addition, the ideas of integral learning are growing within the transformative learning literature as a way to "reconnect education with its transformative and spiritual dimensions in modern academia" (Ferrer et al., 2005) and to develop increasingly comprehensive worldviews (Gunnlaugson, 2005). Sri Aurobindo, the philosopher of Integral Yoga, is recognised as a seminal theorist in integral and contemplative ecologies of transformative learning (Ferrer et al., 2005; Morgan, 2015), and this case study offers a rare exploration of peak transformative learning in the context of the experiences which students of a university course have when immersing themselves in the society founded on Sri Aurobindo's ideals.

Methodology: Towards Identifying Peak Transformative Experiences and Their Enabling Conditions

All four authors have had direct involvement with BCII and Auroville. Bem is the founding director of BCII and leader of the global studio. She first visited Auroville in 1989. Katie is a doctoral researcher in transformative learning at UTS, a staff participant in the BCII degree and mentor of the 2020 BCII global studio in Auroville. Suryamayi and Aditi are native Aurovilians, who have each undertaken doctoral research on the community, and presented modules on Auroville within BCII, during the global studio and at UTS.

To identify peak transformative experiences, we first reflected on students' experiences of the global studio in the light of two existing frameworks: a synthesis of Maslow's characteristics of peak experiences

Table 48.1 Characteristics of peak transformative experiences adopted in this chapter

Characteristic	Explanation of peak transformative experiences
Significance	Intense, profound experiences leading to greater self-awareness; a turning point in life (Privette, 2001)
Fulfillment	Extremely positive, lasting and richly rewarding experiences (Privette, 2001)
Spiritual	Experiences of one-ness and unity—of awe, wonder, ecstasy (Privette, 2001)
Ineffability	Experiences that *defy words* (James, 1902, p. 533)
Noetic quality	Experiences of knowledge, '*illuminations, revelations,* full of significance', which 'carry with them a curious sense of authority' (James, 1902, p. 533)
Transiency	While they '*cannot be sustained for long*', these experiences recur and lead to 'continuous development in what is felt as inner richness and importance' (James, 1902, p. 534)
Passivity	Experiences in which one feels 'grasped and *held by a superior power*' (James, 1902, p. 534)

(concepts offered by Privette, 2001[4]) and James's characteristics of mystical and spiritual states of consciousness (James, 1902) (Table 48.1). After reviewing our own notes and observations of the course through the lens of these criteria, we came together in a dialogic method (Labonté, 2011) to identify examples of these peak experiences we witnessed. In the section below, Bem employs a new ethnographic approach (Goodall, 2000) to share the students' peak transformative experiences. New ethnography can include creative narration of context through scene-setting and reflection of the researchers' personal involvement as well as reflexive examinations of observations of (in this case students') lived experiences (Goodall, 2000). Finally, we again used a dialogic method (Labonté, 2011) to arrive at a synthesis of the enabling conditions that allowed for these experiences to take place (Table 48.1).

---

[4] We recognise that Maslow's characteristics are much more complex and interlinked (see Maslow, 1971, pp. 168–195) than Privette's synthesis of Maslow's work, but we employ Privette's synthesis for the purposes of this chapter as she has honed and condensed these three key features in her 25 years of investigating Maslow's peak experiences.

Peak Transformative Experiences in BCII's Auroville Global Studio

The students arrive, exhausted but excited, in a bus they've hired from Chennai. A good start. They're absorbed in each other—I recognise this. It's necessary to take this leap together, and as much as Auroville is about personal breakthroughs and insights, it's a collective experience. The one giant, optimistic leap into the unknown that's shared. Students bring their own epistemologies and ontologies to individual sense-making, but together we're bigger than this—and we're about to witness many personal revelations about our connectedness. The educational thrill-seeker in me awaits these collective moments when the heat rises for everyone. It's like watching popcorn—moments of being when awareness and discovery are amplified. I'm acutely aware of the fact that you cannot force this "transformation." It happens spontaneously through wonder, gratitude, connection to nature and each other—I call it the "contagion" of learning. Of course, some students come along accidentally speaking of the "holiday" that they're about to take with their peers, but by the end they acknowledge that the inner journey is as profound as the external one.

We all check into shared rooms together, go to get bikes together, and then come our shared outings and activities around Auroville and the bioregion. Learning about permaculture at Solitude Farm. Experiencing a sound bath with facilitators from Auroville's Swaram music factory. Going to the glorious Matrimandir Inner Chamber, Auroville's iconic temple beyond any religion, and introducing students to the 12 meditation "Petal" spaces surrounding the Chamber where they can meditate on 12 "soul qualities" such as sincerity, courage and equality. For the more pragmatic, a visit to the Youth Centre and the Treehouse Community introduces them to peers to broaden out their understanding of utopia in the context of their generation. Our co-author, Suryamayi, takes them for an Awareness Through the Body session, an experience that allows them to ground an unbounded awareness in their physicality. They're also free to go on the numerous classes and workshops run by Aurovilians – for example on the Tamil traditional spiritual practice of kolam …— Bem (Fig. 48.1)

And of course, the students have to do assessments, as per the requirements of our university, but I make sure these are fascinating and fruitful to help facilitate the integration of what they've experienced. Marking these assessments is qualitatively different from any other kind of marking experience common in universities, as student work is intensely personal,

Fig. 48.1 First engagement with "Kolam" practice in an Auroville workshop (Photo K. Ross)

filled with acute observations of self. In keeping with Privette's framework (2001), the assessments are enriched with an awareness of the significance of what they are learning. Many of them speak of the need for radical change in their outlook; one student works with the notion of "applied hope," with increased self-awareness of how a lack of hope, or action in the future, was actually quite debilitating before his moment of epiphany. Fulfilment is another marker that comes through strongly. Their extremely positive experiences are described by students as a feeling of being more centred, connected or inspired—open to expansion. This school receives a 5 out of 5 rating in its anonymous student feedback survey—and students frequently speak about the experience as life-changing. In my feedback to them, I write that the discoveries "were often explosive and overpowering, because they involved a completely new understanding of self and context." A deeper understanding of the meaning of spirituality beyond religion or faith is mentioned repeatedly, along with the realisation that students need to work on themselves. One writes about their initial cynicism of spirituality, and how they arrived at an understanding that a spiritual and pragmatic world has to exist as one. Others explore the feeling of the ecstatic—through poetry, dance, and boundless experiences of self never previously explored. Many students describe their spiritual selves as having been neglected—one speaks of a realisation that they'd only lived a half-life without it. Several students had realisations of our human unity with nature, through close observations of the natural world.

James' framework for peak mystical experiences (1902) is also relevant in many ways. The ineffable is profound. Many students articulate the fact that they simply cannot talk about the deeply rich learning that takes place and do it justice—an explanation of it is considered "futile." One student presents part of an assessment as a sound graph, because of the ineffable quality of their self-discovery. Others use poetry or art—they speak through the Philosophy of Clay. They use symbols to capture their ideas (inspired by the symbols of Auroville). I see the noetic (or revelatory) nature of experience in every assessment. One student writes about herself in the third person—of the previous persona and current person, and the revelation and illumination of the striking difference between the two. The transience of the experience is captured again and again: thoughts of what they might wish to take home with them and how they will sustain the revelations they've had when they leave utopia and return to Sydney. One student wants the red dust of Auroville to stay on her when she returns ... Of James' framework, the only criterion that applies less to student experience in our data seems to be the idea of passivity— that feeling of being held by a higher power. Although this may have been experienced, it is not articulated. (Perhaps because active learning requires our students to seek out opportunities and become agents of change rather than simply passive vessels for transformation?)

48 LESSONS FROM UTOPIA: REFLECTIONS ON ... 873

On our last night, we have a farewell party on the beach under the stars—all of us together, with some Aurovilian friends. We lie down on the sand and one of our students plays a sound bath of recordings from our journey through Auroville. In a circle, a few of us reach for words to describe what we've been through collectively, but the words don't do it justice. Nonetheless, each of us has been touched by the ineffable. For me, the experience is imprinted as a quest—knowing what is possible now. It's a quest that centres around the hope for a better world with transformative learning at its core. And this heartfelt question: if the world really is split up into "peakers" and "non-peakers" as Maslow describes (Maslow, 1964), then how might we help the latter to experience the privilege of this kind of high?—Bem

Enabling Conditions for Peak Transformative Experiences

The *peak transformative experiences* evoked above were enabled by a variety of conditions prompted by the alignment between the design and facilitation of the global studio and Auroville itself.

Alignment of Worldview of Place and Program

A strong resonance exists between the worldviews of the BCII program and the place of Auroville, allowing students to experience similar values in a double-space. Amongst others, both of these settings encourage conscious evolution, boundary-breaking, experimentation, liminality, and both believe in the validity of individual and collective reflexivity, and privilege multiple ways of knowing. Students in the BCII were invited to take and apply everything they learned about creativity and innovation over the past three years into this community. Several students said in conversation that the integration of a Curriculum for Being in a "place of spiritual being" helped them tap into a new understanding of self and their learning to date.

Important to transformative learning is the balancing of brave spaces for learners to step outside of their patterns and habits of comfort, and safe spaces for any disorientations that may happen—in other words, a blend of challenge and support (Gunnlaugson, 2004). The relationship between Auroville and the BCII program enabled a safe and brave space. Auroville offered the space for bravely experiencing and stepping boldly into a place totally outside of the dominant paradigm. The students'

874 B. LE HUNTE ET AL.

past experiences within the BCII program offered a sense of safety. The students have been in the BCII program for three years and had developed an appreciation for learning outside the dominant paradigm and learning from risk-taking. They had developed a trust with Bem for leading them into liminal spaces.

Enabling Processes and Characteristics of the BCII Program

Characteristics and Influences of Facilitator

The lead facilitator, Bem, with the support of other participating mentors, curated and offered diverse enabling conditions to assist with the manifesting and integration of these *peak transformative experiences*. Most importantly, it is imperative for the educator to have deep connection with this type of learning, so that they are able to act as a bridge or guide for the students through the liminality (Ross, 2020). Similarly, travel abroad programs can increase potential for transformative experiences when the facilitator has deep knowledge of and connection to place (Morgan, 2010). Bem offers both. She has a lived and family history with Auroville and India, and has had extended stays in Auroville, as both a visitor and academic. Her extensive and embodied knowledge of Indian and Aurovilian philosophical principles and practices enabled authentic integration with the community for the students. As well, Bem has been meditating for many decades, within the Indian traditions, and has explored these realms of consciousness discussed in Auroville, and thus could model and provide support for the students in these situations.

Bem's embodiment of both typical Aurovilian and Sydney worldviews meant she was an experienced and prepared mediator for students in this liminal space wherever the discussions roamed; for example, helping students compare their preconceived ideas of yoga from a Sydney perspective, verses yoga as a way of being in all that we do towards growing our consciousness and finding connectedness and unity. She also brought in Indian philosophies of consciousness expansion. For example, from the start of the first week, Bem led the students in discussion circles for developing the witness-self. These discussions were prompted with questions such as "How can we observe our own learning as it's happening?" Several students reflected on how developing their witness-self helped as a method of both observation and transformation. Developing a witness-self is a tenant of contemplative, transformative education, particularly as defined through yoga (Morgan, 2012), and this ability for continued meta-awareness is as valuable as the learning (Netzer & Rowe, 2010).

Having gone through these transformative experiences oneself and having a meaningful relationship with the place enabled Bem to teach authentically, and teaching authentically is crucial for transformative learning (Sohn, 2020; Tisdell & Tolliver, 2016). She shared personal stories, joined shared explorations with the students, and helped the students feel comfortable bringing in their own authentic selves.

The Influence of the Students' Mind-Sets

An important principle of transformative learning is that no one is "forced" to have a transformative experience (Moore, 2005), but rather the mind-sets of the learners play a significant role in whether experiences are transformative (Morgan, 2010; Ross, 2019). As the course could only accommodate 20 students, participants were prioritised based on their demonstrated openness to non-judgement, intentionality, and reflexivity for this collective learning opportunity.

Influence of Student Cohort

The closeness of the student cohort can be incredibly profound in terms of enabling transformative learning (Cohen, 2004; Sohn, 2020), which was also witnessed in the global studio. The smaller cohort size enabled comfort in showing vulnerability and getting to deeper levels of conversation of their shared immersion and insights. Together with close contact with the facilitator, the enabling conditions were in place for accelerated interactive realisations.

Learner Identified Praxis for Brave and Creative Self-Discovery

Throughout their time in Auroville, the students were engaged in collective workshops, circle discussions, delicious meals, and inspiring field trips, but an important part of the studio, and transformative learning in general, was for each learner to engage in a praxis of their choice as a form of self-discovery—synthesised in the form of a creative, personal authentic assessment (Dencev & Collister, 2011; Netzer & Rowe, 2010; Sterling et al., 2018). Regardless of the form of praxis chosen by the students, the primary aim as communicated to the students was self-discovery.

To support the students in deciding on what to do for their assessment, students were asked to reflect on their ideal *sadhana* (i.e. work as an offering in Sanskrit) or what their "Bliss-ipline" might be. In designing this assessment, Bem was manifesting her belief that learning should be something that is joyful, lifelong, and life-supporting. This type of freedom (combined with commitment) created profoundly fertile conditions for nourishing *peak transformative experiences*.

Providing Tools for Sense-Making and Integration of Peak Experiences

As the global studio was designed to be open and emergent, allowing for each student to follow their own areas of fascination and curiosity, it was also incredibly important to provide learners with sense-making tools throughout the three weeks (Naor & Mayseless, 2017; Ross, 2019). Reflexivity as a form of sense-making and integration was continually encouraged, in particular in the group circle dialogues—and sage questions were posed as reflection and meaning making—a profound enabler for transformative learning (Duerr et al., 2003; Hart, 2008). The assessments were also designed to support the process of integration, as demonstrated by this introduction to one of the assessments:

> Nearing the end of this Global Studio, we are hoping that you will have had many rich experiences of Auroville, met many fascinating people and understood more about the philosophical, cosmological and spiritual context of this place. Your next task is to map your personal journey / transformation / discovery in any creative format you wish and share it as a story. Note: this is an individual exercise—it's about self-reflection, personal discovery and connection to being and place. As this is an exercise in deep self-observation, when describing your personal journey / experience of Auroville, you may wish to use the integral learning framework as described by Sri Aurobindo, exploring the mental, physical, emotional and spiritual experience of this Global Studio. (What we are privileging here is multiple ways of knowing. You may also like to explore how you might take this experience forward into your professional / social / emotional / spiritual life after BCII.)

Importantly, the assessments were incredibly open; they asked the students to look within to make meaning of the peak experiences without telling them how to do it. They were framed to prompt a deep, personal, unbounded, emergent, intuitive inquiry into one's own meaning making, using "multiple ways of transformative knowing" (Gunnlaugson, 2005; Osterhold et al., 2007). Importantly, students were also encouraged to translate these experiences into ideas for action or change, i.e. another form of integration for peak experiences (Ross, 2019).

Enabling Conditions of Auroville

Auroville's Transformative Worldview
Auroville's reason for being is demonstrating and enabling transformations into a spiritualised society—with an aim of deliberately allowing a unique, deep connection and enquiry into interconnected self, society and consciousness. Students continually described illuminations of self, of experiencing true authenticity in others and seeing other selves. As the notion of transformation is so explicit in Auroville, it provided a shared backdrop and language for students to experience transformation and to reflect on their experiences.

Diversity in Transformative Experiences of Place
As a result of its integral philosophy, Auroville fosters and facilitates a great diversity of transformative experiences. Students were free to engage with this diversity and experience new paradigmatic premises without being constricted to one particular field or aspect. In particular, many of them described peak experiences—such as their first awareness of an energetic body and the energetic bodies of others—during practices of "Awareness Through the Body" (Marti & Sala, 2006), an Integral Yoga practice developed in and by Auroville, which places particular emphasis on the development of the witness-self. Students also described peak experiences in the Matrimandir: some became spell-bound by the quality of its silence, for example, or another with noetic revelations about the need to live life with courage.

Embeddedness in and Engagement with Nature
A core aspect of being in Auroville is the awareness of nature and its role in the Auroville narrative, which describes the transformation of a barren plateau to a flourishing ecosystem (Blanchflower, 2005) replete with sustainability initiatives. The notion of unbounded, undifferentiated self in this context allowed many students to speak about peak spiritual experiences of deep connection to and unity with nature—a kind of "beyond-human unity," which amplified their connection to the planetary challenges we all face. Students mentioned these significant experiences empowered them to take action in their own spheres back home and

were able to gain courage and optimism through the narratives offered by some of Auroville's environmentalists and the ethos they provided.

Conclusion (and a Few Provocations)

> Students are gathered in a circle in Auroville's Botanical Gardens. Bem asks them to share with their neighbour a learning experience they've had before BCII that was transformative of their sense of self and the world. When they finish, she asks the group "Did any of those experiences happen in a classroom at school or university"? Not a single student raises their hand. —Bem

Our case study offers several important contributions to the theory and practice of transformative learning. Based on the work of Abraham Maslow and William James, and our lived experiences of the BCII program, we coin the concept of *peak transformative experiences*. We define *peak transformative experiences* and their impacts as: "moments of profound, perhaps spiritual or mystical insight into self-identities, intrinsic values, and the nature of reality, which are then integrated into deep, lasting changes in worldview, self-understanding, and action." This concept and the *peak transformative experiences* identified contribute to our understandings of mystical and spiritual experience as powerful processes within transformative learning. We identify several enabling conditions for *peak transformative experiences* by offering a rare exploration into how students experienced an experiential university course immersed in a society based on Sri Aurobindo's Integral Yoga, which has informed aspects of transformative learning practice (Ferrer et al., 2005; Morgan, 2015).

We would like to conclude by inviting educators to examine how the enabling conditions described above could be translated into their particular contexts. For example, how could your courses acknowledge and immerse students within alternative ontologies and epistemologies? Where possible, we encourage educators to—ethically and consensually— engage with intentional or Indigenous communities. Additionally, how could your courses integrate a wide range of spiritually-infused field-based activities as learning experiences, and curate diverse, deeply-reflective assessments that facilitate students making sense of their experiences? Importantly, how could you emphasise a witness-self through various methods so that students and faculty develop skills in observing their own transformation and its implications for transforming society?

In this time of such uncertainties, our educational programs have an enormous opportunity to be aligned with transformative agendas by integrating these types of processes. What unites these processes are the conditions they enable for a Curriculum for Being—that is, a curriculum that promotes peak transformational experiences and integrates self, society and consciousness. In the words of Sri Aurobindo: "It is only when we have seen both our self and our nature as a whole, in the depths as well as on the surface, that we can acquire a true basis of knowledge" (1939).

REFERENCES

Auroville. (2016). *A note on unending education in Auroville.* Retrieved July 15, 2020 from https://www.auroville.org/contents/398

Auroville. (2018). *Statements of support—UNESCO.* Retrieved July 15, 2020 from https://www.auroville.org/contents/538

Auroville. (2020). *The Auroville charter: A new vision of power and promise for people choosing another way of life.* Retrieved July 15, 2020 from https://www.auroville.org/contents/1

Barnett, R. (2012). Learning for an unknown future. *Higher Education Research & Development, 31*(1), 65–77.

Blanchflower, P. (2005). Restoration of the tropical dry evergreen forest of Peninsular India. *Biodiversity, 6*(3), 17–24.

Clarence-Smith, S. A. (2019). *Towards a spiritualised society: Auroville, an experiment in prefigurative utopianism* [Doctor of Philosophy in International Development, University of Sussex, England].

Cohen, J. B. (2004). Late for school: Stories of transformation in an adult education program. *Journal of Transformative Education, 2*(3), 242–252.

Dencev, H., & Collister, R. (2011). Authentic ways of knowing, authentic ways of being. *Journal of Transformative Education, 8*(3), 178–196.

Duerr, M., Zajonc, A., & Dana, D. (2003). Survey of transformative and spiritual dimensions of higher education. *Journal of Transformative Education, 1*(3), 177–211.

Ferrer, J., Romero, M., & Albareda, R. (2005). The four seasons of integral education: A participatory proposal. *Journal of Transformative Education, 3*(4).

Grinnell, C., Lung, J., Venet, R., & Pages, D. (2013). *Educational practices & opportunities for adults in Auroville.* SAIIER.

Goodall, H. L. (2000). *Writing the new ethnography.* AltaMira Press.

Gunnlaugson, O. (2004). Toward an integral education for the ecozoic era: A case study in transforming the global learning community of Holma College of Integral Studies, Sweden. *Journal of Transformative Education, 2*(4), 313–335.

Gunnlaugson, O. (2005). Toward integrally informed theories of transformative learning. *Journal of Transformative Education, 3*(4), 331–353.

Hart, T. (2008). Interiority and education: Exploring the neurophenomenology of contemplation and its potential role in learning. *Journal of Transformative Education, 6*(4), 235–250.

James, W. (1902). Lectures XVI and XVII—Mysticism. In W. James (Ed.), *The varieties of religious experience: A study in human nature* (p. 2008). The Floating Press.

Kligyte, G., Baumber, A., van der Bijl-Brouwer, M., Dowd, C., Hazell, N., Le Hunte, B., Newton, M., Roebuck, D., & Pratt, S. (2019). "Stepping in and stepping out": Enabling creative third spaces through transdisciplinary partnerships. *International Journal for Students as Partners, 3*(1), 5–21.

Labonté, R. (2011). Reflections on stories and a story/dialogue method in health research. *International Journal of Social Research Methodology, 14*(2), 153–163.

Lange, E. (2015). The ecology of transformative learning: Transdisciplinary provocations. *Journal of Transformative Learning, 3*(1), 28–34.

Lange, E. (2018). Transforming transformative education through ontologies of relationality. *Journal of Transformative Education, 16*(4), 280–301.

Le Hunte, B. (2019, June 21). *A Curriculum for Being: Creativity for a Complex World*. EC3 Creativity Conference. Marconi Institute of Creativity, Bologna, Italy, Geneva.

Marti, A., & Sala, J. (2006). *Awareness through the body*. SAIIER.

Maslow, A. (1964). *Religions, values and peak experiences*. Ohio State University Press.

Maslow, A. (1971). *The farther reaches of human nature*. The Viking Press.

Moore, J. (2005). Is higher education ready for transformative learning? A question explored in the study of sustainability. *Journal of Transformative Education, 3*(1), 76–91.

Morgan, A. D. (2010). Journeys into transformation: Travel to an "other" place as a vehicle for transformative learning. *Journal of Transformative Education, 8*(4), 246–268.

Morgan, P. F. (2012). Following Contemplative education students' transformation through their "ground-of-being" experiences. *Journal of Transformative Education, 10*(1), 42–60.

Morgan, P. F. (2015). A brief history of the current reemergence of contemplative education. *Journal of Transformative Education, 13*(3), 197–218.

Naor, L., & Mayseless, O. (2017). How personal transformation occurs following a single peak experience in nature: A phenomenological account. *Journal of Humanistic Psychology, 60*(6), 865–888.

Napan, K., Connor, H., & Toki, L. (2020). Cultural pedagogy and transformative learning: Reflections on teaching in a Māori environment in Aotearoa/New Zealand. *Journal of Transformative Education, 18*(1), 59–77.

Netzer, D., & Rowe, N. M. (2010). Inquiry into creative and innovative processes: An experiential, whole-person approach to teaching creativity. *Journal of Transformative Education, 8*(2), 124–145.

Osterhold, H., Rubiano, E. H., & Nicol, D. (2007). Rekindling the fire of transformative education: A participatory case study. *Journal of Transformative Education, 5*(3), 221–245.

Privette, G. (2001). Defining moments of self-actualization: Peak performance and peak experience. In K. J. Schneider, J. F. T. Bugental, & J. F. Pierson (Eds.), *The handbook of humanistic psychology: Leading edges in theory, research, and practice* (pp. 160–181). Sage.

Ross, S. (2019). The making of everyday heroes: Women's experiences with transformation and integration. *Journal of Humanistic Psychology, 59*(4), 499–521.

Ross, K. (2020). *Transforming the ways we create change: experiencing and cultivating transformative sustainability learning* [Doctor of Philosophy in Sustainable Futures, University of Technology Sydney].

Sohn, B. K. (2020). Coming to appreciate diversity: Ontological change through student–student relationships. *Journal of Transformative Education, 19*(1), 50–67.

Sri Aurobindo. (1939). *The life divine.* Sri Aurobindo Ashram.

Sri Aurobindo. (1999). *Complete works of Sri Aurobindo. Vol. 23. The synthesis of Yoga—I.* Sri Aurobindo Ashram.

Sterling, S., Dawson, J., & Warwick, P. (2018). Transforming sustainability education at the creative edge of the mainstream. *Journal of Transformative Education, 16*(4), 323–343.

Stuckey, H., Taylor, E., & Cranton, P. (2014). Developing a survey of transformative learning outcomes and processes based on theoretical principles. *Journal of Transformative Education, 11*(4), 211–228.

Taylor, E., & Cranton, P. (2012). *The handbook of transformative learning: Theory, research and practice.* Jossey-Bass.

Tisdell, E. J., & Tolliver, D. E. (2016). Claiming a sacred face. *Journal of Transformative Education, 1*(4), 368–392.

CHAPTER 49

Could Transformative Learning Involve Youth?

Alexis Kokkos

INTRODUCTION

Theorists involved in studying transformative learning usually associate it with adulthood. Mezirow's view played an important role in shaping this perception, which can be seen even in the titles of his publications. Indicatively, he titled his foundational book *Transformative Dimensions of Adult Learning* (1991), while the title that he selected for his own chapter in the volume that he subsequently edited (Mezirow & Associates, 2000) was *Learning to Think Like an Adult: Core Concepts of Transformation Theory*. Mezirow's basic position was that only adults have the potential to fully engage in transformative learning; this is widely shared by several other theorists (e.g., Baumgartner, 2012; Brookfield, 2000; Tisdell, 2012).

A number of emancipatory scholars, on the other hand, have taken the view that learning for change can occur during youth. Although he

---

A. Kokkos (✉)
Hellenic Open University, Patras, Greece
e-mail: alexiskokkos@eap.gr

© The Author(s), under exclusive license to Springer Nature 883
Switzerland AG 2022
A. Nicolaides et al. (eds.), *The Palgrave Handbook of Learning for Transformation*, https://doi.org/10.1007/978-3-030-84694-7_49

884   A. KOKKOS

was mainly concerned with adult education, Freire, for instance, referred to the need to incorporate an emancipatory pedagogy into schools in various parts of his work (e.g., Freire, 1998; Freire & Macedo, 1987). Greene (2000), as well, regarded school as a key area for the implementation of her ideas of change-oriented learning through art-based education. Larson (2016) examined how adolescents engage in transformative learning from a unique pre-adult perspective. Taylor and Snyder (2012) argued that, through Goulah's research (2007), the transformative learning theory "has expanded to inform the learning of adolescents in a high school classroom" (p. 40).

Along the same lines, Marsick (1998) has maintained that transformative processes may involve school students. Her rationale is grounded in the fact that modern life conditions within the workplace and far beyond it increasingly demand that people think in complex ways, take responsibilities, use their inventiveness, and be self-initiating. However, large segments of organizations are still governed by power relationships and negotiated contracts "that contribute to the owner's bottom line" (p. 130). On the other hand, it is difficult for young people to question the established, taken-for-granted assumptions about how work and public life are organized. Thus, according to Marsick, school students must be strengthened to develop skills that foster critical, independent thinking so that they build the capacity to handle the challenges they may face and achieve their own goals.

Consequently, the issue of whether youth could be effectively involved in transformative learning remains an open question in the literature and poses challenges to current thinking in the field. The present paper attempts to approach the issue by exploring three fundamental prerequisites for taking part in transformative endeavors: cognitive ability, intended engagement, and capacity for critical reflection.

The Cognitive Ability

There is a broad consensus among thinkers that a developed cognitive ability constitutes a sine qua non for critically reviewing and transforming one's problematic assumptions. For instance, Kegan (1994) argues that, in order to reach a state of consciousness in which one may think autonomously, a holistic mental system for organizing experience is required: "not mere skills but a qualitative order of mental complexity" (p. 152). In their dialogue in *Adult Education Quarterly*,

Merriam (2004) and Mezirow (2004) agreed that a certain level of cognitive development is fundamental so as to fully engage in transformative processes.

As far as the development of cognitive ability across different age phases is conserved, Piaget's theory can be considered as a standpoint. Piaget (1954, 1967) suggested four successive stages of cognitive development, each of which is marked by new intellectual capacities and a more complex way of making meaning and constructing knowledge. After the *sensorimotor stage* (birth to age 2) and the *pre-operational stage* (approximately 2–6 years), pre-adolescents normally enter the *concrete operational stage* (approximately 7–11 years) during which they are progressively able to assess various social situations and views, relate them to their experiences, and process alternative practical solutions. Finally, the *formal operational stage*—which begins approximately at the age of eleven and lasts until adulthood—marks the commencement of mature thought. Adolescents may increasingly, over time, think in abstract terms, consider contrary-to-fact questions and alternatives, reflect on the opinions of others, as well as develop hypothetic-deductive reasoning, moving from hypothetical general assumptions to specific implications.

In terms of transformative learning, adolescents within the formal operational stage are potentially able to assess established ideas and values (e.g., justice, ethics, and the notion of truth), as well as the structures of social order, and seek functional ideas and practices on various issues, such as gender differences, social divisions, ethnocentrism, or, in modern times, the ecological crisis and the COVID-19 pandemic.

Nevertheless, Piaget's view of cognitive development has been challenged for a number of reasons. It has been claimed (e.g., Berk, 1997) that his research was framed into a narrow socio-cultural setting (children from European families of high social status) and was based on a small sample; therefore, the outcomes could not be deemed generalizable. Secondly, some scholars (Gardner, 1999; Woolfolk, 2001) consider the rigid Piagetian separation of the stages of development to be unjustified. Finally, Piaget has been rightfully criticized (Illeris, 2017; Stern, 1985) for placing too much emphasis on the cognitive dimension of the learning process and, in turn, underestimating the impact of emotions.

In any case, besides the reasonable critique on Piaget's view, the basic elements of his conception for the stages of cognitive growth are still considered as reliable and enduring (Gardner, 1999; Illeris, 2017; Siegler,

886 A. KOKKOS

1998) and his work is acknowledged as fundamental for understanding the development of human reasoning.

THE PURPOSEFUL ENGAGEMENT

Literature Review

Emancipatory learning theorists seem to be in general agreement that, when it comes to learning for change, having developed the mental structures that are necessary for abstract reasoning is not enough. What is further required is personal readiness and disposition—an intended engagement to undertake an active effort to question one's assumptions. In what follows, various cardinal theoretical views are explored regarding whether young people have this potential.

Dewey (1933/ 1980) highlighted two dimensions, both of which differentiate youth from adulthood. The first dimension is that young people are not likely to possess orderly habits of thought. This is due to the fact that, when compared to adults, they do not necessarily need to efficiently realize goals as professionals, citizens, parents, etc. As such, they do not tend to form a stabilizing and carefully arranged ground for their assumptions, beliefs, and relevant actions. Their way of thinking is characterized by plasticity and lack of consecutiveness and continuity of effort:

> The will of others, his own (the young person's) caprice and circumstances about him tend to produce an isolated momentary act [...] The choice is peculiarly exposed to arbitrary factors, to mere school traditions, to waves of pedagogical fad and fancy, to fluctuating social cross currents. (Dewey, 1933/ 1980, p. 50)

The second dimension pertains to the school environment and, more specifically, to pupils' dependence upon the influence of teachers. Dewey considered that most students tend to adapt to their teachers' requirements and satisfy them, instead of purposely investigating a subject for its own sake:

> His (sic, namely the student's) chief concern is to accommodate himself to what the teacher expects of him, rather than to devote himself energetically to the problems of subject matter. "Is this right?" comes to mean "Will this answer or this process satisfy the teacher?"—instead of meaning "Does

it satisfy the inherent conditions of the problem?" (Dewey, 1933/ 1980, p. 61)

What these two dimensions of pupils' behavior imply is that learners of such age are probably not capable of engaging intentionally and systematically in an in-depth exploration of their own or others' problematic assumptions; in other words, they do not have the individual predisposition to critically examine the aspects and grounds of assumptions, which is a prerequisite for being involved in learning for change.

Erikson's theory of personality development has significantly contributed to a deeper understanding of the issue at hand. Highlighting the difficulties that young people face in constructing their ideas, values, and life choices, Erikson (1968) posited that adolescents experience a conflict between "identity" and "identity confusion." On the one hand, they need to formulate a more coherent self-perception in order to make crucial choices regarding gender roles, occupation, relationships, ideology, and politics. On the other hand, given that the structures of their identity are not yet coherently stabilized, they tend to commit themselves to the values and goals of the persons by which they are affected. Moreover, they "try on" identities and experiment with different views, lifestyles, and ways of behaving.

More recent studies (Arnett, 2007; Nelson et al., 2004) on the ways in which young people conceptualize their lives in industrialized societies have shown that the challenges associated with the formation of identity are prolonged under the present socio-cultural conditions. In this framework, the term *emerging adulthood* is being used to describe the state of 18 to 25-year-old people and perhaps older ones, most of whom never experience conditions that used to constitute the norm a few decades ago, such as stable work, financial independence, marriage or long-term partnerships, and parenthood (Arnett, 2007). Therefore, the transition to adulthood is long and characterized by identity exploration, instability, in-between feelings, and self-focus.

As a result, if we look at the aforementioned ideas in terms of transformative learning, we may conclude that the achievement of a stable identity—which still constitutes a challenge for youth—is a prerequisite for a person to develop a strong sense of commitment to reconsidering his or her way of understanding.

Illeris' Contribution

On the other hand, although sharing the view as regards the fluidity of young people's frame of reference, Illeris (2014, 2017) stresses that they face considerable challenges which need to be critically discussed, as such they may be involved in certain forms of transformative learning.

According to Illeris (2014), during the time frame of youth—which he identifies as the period from early adolescence (11–13 years) to a point of time when "a reasonably stable and coherent identity has been established" (p. 86)—young individuals continue to try out, adjust, or reject various ideas and choices. Illeris actually concurs with Dewey, Erikson, and emerging adulthood theorists:

> (The young persons) perhaps with enthusiasm cling to something, and yet drop it, sometimes from one day to the next, and eventually jump directly to a new identification or start up a new search movement [...] In school it may, for instance, happen that a group of students with great commitment tries to palm a specific position off in their class-mates—for example, in relation to music or sport, to the school or to specific teachers—and this may then perhaps appeal to most of the class for some time and then, typically, slowly fade away to be replaced by something else. (Illeris, 2014, p. 86)

However, as the person grows older, one's identity progressively acquires more fixed qualities, so that assumptions, attitudes, and behaviors tend to take more stable forms. This is not an easy task though, given that youth is besieged daily by a variety of identity challenges that concern, for example, lifestyle, interpersonal relationships, ethical, spiritual, cultural and political dilemmas, professional orientation, and so forth, that contribute to the reproduction of identity confusion. Illeris (2017) explains that within this condition young people are at risk of experiencing symptoms of "pathological narcissism" (p. 132), lack of self-esteem, feelings of emptiness, lack of pleasure in their activities, and a tendency toward routine behavior.

On this basis, Illeris claims that during youth, and especially during late adolescence where identity is intensively formulated—while at the same time one's cognitive capacity for dialectical and critical reflection develops—transformative learning is both necessary and possible to occur.

The Capacity for Critical Reflection

In this section, Mezirow's perspective regarding the understanding of learning processes that adults and non-adults alike may undergo is discussed.

Mezirow (1991) shared the Piagetian conceptualization concerning adolescents' cognitive ability. He considered that they are able to formulate synthetic hypotheses—especially with respect to others' options—and search for reasons to reconsider the validity of claims. Moreover, Mezirow (1991) shared Basseches' view that in late adolescence individuals are able to undertake dialectical cognitive functioning: "He (Basseches) holds that dialectical thinking is an important element in cognitive maturity, which may be achieved in the late adolescent and adult years" (p. 152). Hereby, according to Mezirow (1991), young persons can conceptualize change as a nexus of contradictions within a system leading to a more inclusive alternative system.

Nevertheless, all of Mezirow's work (e.g., 1991, 1998, 2000) is permeated by the perception that young people and adults differ in terms of the extent to which they can validate their potentially problematic assumptions. Young people, for Mezirow, are not capable in challenging the *presuppositions* of the structures of their assumptions, namely their meaning perspectives. Specifically, they cannot embark upon what he referred to as "premise critical self-reflection" on the biographical, cultural, and societal factors that have contributed to shaping the way in which one has come to construct meaning. Accordingly, it can be inferred that young people's inability to engage their sense of self in critical self-reflection on their previously assimilated meaning perspectives deprives them of the possibility to undergo perspective transformation. As Mezirow (1991, p. 110) pointed out, "it is premise reflection that opens the possibility for perspective transformation." This endeavor potentially constitutes a distinct feature of an adult way of reasoning (Mezirow, 1991, 2000).

Perspective transformation, though, is precisely what, in Mezirow's view, constitutes the most significant form of transformative learning:

> *Learning through perspective transformation* is the fourth form that learning may take—becoming aware, through reflection and critique, of specific presuppositions upon which a distorted or incomplete meaning

890   A. KOKKOS

perspective is based and then transforming that perspective through a reorganization of meaning. This is the most significant kind of emancipatory learning. (Mezirow, 1991, p. 94)

From my personal standpoint, this perhaps may explain the reason why Mezirow situated transformative learning within the field of adult education. Given that young people cannot engage in the most important form of transformative learning, that is, the reconsideration of distorted meaning perspectives, then transformative learning, as a construct, should be considered as being addressed to adults.

A crucial question arises at this point: Is it possible for young people to engage in a critical reconsideration of their points of view which, according to Mezirow (1996, 1997), is also a form of transformative learning?

Mezirow has not dealt explicitly with this issue; however, one can draw certain inferences from the whole corpus of his work.

Mezirow (2000) described points of view as clusters of beliefs, feelings, judgments, and consequent behaviors that constitute numerous specific manifestations of a meaning perspective—Mezirow (1996) identified this term as the *habit of mind*. He also argued that the transformation of points of view does not require premise critical self-reflection but just critical reflection on the content of a problem or on the process through which we are addressing it. As a case in point, he (Mezirow, 2000, p. 17) referred to a traditionally oriented woman (habit of mind) who, after her late-afternoon adult education class, thinks that she has to rush home to make dinner for her husband (one of the points of view through which her habit of mind becomes expressed). Mezirow argued that this woman "may engage in transformative learning by becoming critically reflective on her point of view on this topic" (p. 21). It is obvious that this endeavor is much less demanding than attempting to transform a whole habit of mind regarding her role as a woman. According to Mezirow (1994), the transformation of a point of view is an "everyday phenomenon" (p. 224) that can occur "with everyday insights" (Mezirow, 1996, p. 168), namely through the influence of life experiences (ibid.) or feedback from others (Mezirow, 1997) and may happen because "we often merely correct our interpretations" (Mezirow, 1991, p. 167).

Therefore, there are similarities between the way Mezirow identified the process of transformation of points of view and what young people are capable of undertaking with regard to the reassessment of their assumptions. In that sense, the position that young people may be involved in transformation of points of view could be considered as reasonable, provided that this process is tailored to the specific needs and capabilities of each age group. This position is also reinforced by the outcomes of empirical research. Through his study on the transformation of meaning structures of Canadian and Japanese students aged 17–19, Whalley (1995, in Taylor, 2000) found that they did experience a revision of points of view, although not a transformation of habits of mind. Hodgson (2007) and Kerr (2014, in Larson, 2016) described transformative incidents which adolescents had experienced, respectively, during a cultural immersion program and a cultural immersion trip. Rainio and Mälkki (2018) examined, through a micro-interaction analysis, a process of facilitating teenagers to work with their edge-emotions aiming to review assumptions associated with their social givens. A case study discussed by Meerts-Brandsma and Sibthorp (2020) identified that semester schools provide adolescents an environment where they experience stages of transformative learning, although there is not sufficient evidence of how broad or lasting the changes might be.

In conclusion, although it can be deduced from his work, Mezirow did not explicitly state that it is possible for young people to engage in the specific form of transformation of points of view, probably because he was committed to highlighting the most important dimension of transformative learning, namely the transformation of habits of mind, which is not likely to be congruent with the potential of non-adults.

An Example from Practice

In what follows, a transformative learning project that took place in a school setting is presented, as an example. It is drawn from Smith and Neill (2005) and concerns an attempt to reorient students' points of view on ethnic and cultural diversity. Although most students were still in preadolescence, they appeared to engage in processes that include a transformative potential.

School Transformation for Peace

In Northern Ireland in the mid-2000s, there was an acute social division between ethnically defined Protestants and Catholics. As a result of the ubiquitous segregation, most schools were characterized by an intense religious homogeneity among students. Each community of students had internalized extremely negative attitudes toward the community of the other side, while at the same time the "culture of silence" that dominated within the schools discouraged any open discussion that might contribute to reconciliating views.

The starting point of the transformative process was to give students the opportunity to express their voices through poetic peace narratives, aiming at developing their ability to reflect on their problematic situation. Moreover, teachers were urged to interpret the students' assumptions that were emerging from the poems and, accordingly, to design transformative learning strategies.

The outcomes surprised positively the project's creators. Smith and Neil (2005) state: "Across all case study schools, students' understanding of the N. Irish political situation and conflict was found to greatly exceed the expectations of most teachers" (p. 11). Based on these findings, they designed a series of practical suggestions for peace education that aimed to involve students in critical reflection on their taken-for-granted assumptions. Some of these propositions were as follows:

- develop teaching–learning approaches that do not avoid controversial issues and that allow students to engage critically and reflectively with their own background and that of the other main ethnic and cultural group
- develop with schools a personal-communal set of cultural norms rather than rational-bureaucratic
- encourage school improvement approaches that focus as much on learning for change in self and society as much as on narrowly defined attainment targets and performance (Smith & Neil, 2005, p. 29).

Smith and Neil's article does not expand on the results of this process. However, if one judges from what has already been done during the preparatory phase, a transformation of the students' points of view may have possibly emerged.

REFLECTIONS

The dominant perception within the theoretical field of learning for change is that the critical assessment and transformation of dysfunctional assumptions is a goal of adult education. However, the theoretical views that have been explored in this paper, combined with insights from educational practice, can sustain the argument that young people, as they grow older, are potentially able to engage in critical assessment of points of view that need to be questioned.

This does not mean that young people are able to reconsider the very premises of their habits of mind—this is an adult task because it assumes that a person is able to critically evaluate their whole life history, that is to say, the context in which the origins of their meaning perspectives have been shaped. Nor does it mean that a potential transformation of specific young people's points of view could be a durable feature—the continuous trial of ideas, roles, and ways of behavior is a characteristic feature of youth.

However, as long as educators and researchers share the idea that school may not be just a field where knowledge and skills are acquired, but, in addition, an environment where a change of students' problematic, yet taken-for-granted, assumptions can be attempted, then involving students in learning activities toward this direction is a worthwhile endeavor. The reorientation of their points of view may be the result of influence by teachers, or by others, and, therefore, it is likely to be unsteady and provisional. It can, though, create cracks in dysfunctional forms of meaning making that they may have potentially embraced. Furthermore, such a change can be a starting point and create a dynamic process on the basis of which new, more open and viable structures of assumptions could be built. In this sense, school can be considered as a field where it would be possible for students to engage not only in thoughtful learning but also in challenging their own problematic views or those that are communicated to them. Therefore, the transformative learning framework could be significantly expanded to encompass youth. It would provide young people with ideas, dispositions, and skills for them to be able, in adulthood, to undertake more consistent, integral, and self-reflected endeavors of transformative learning. If this process does not begin to take any form before adulthood, then it may be very difficult or too late to materialize.

REFERENCES

Arnett, J. (2007). Emerging adulthood: What is it, and what is it for? *Society for Research in Child Development, 1*(2), 68–73.

Baumgartner, L. (2012). Mezirow's theory of transformative learning from 1975 to present. In E. W. Taylor, P. Cranton, & Associates (Eds.), *The handbook of transformative learning: Theory, research, and practice* (pp. 99–115). Jossey-Bass.

Berk, L. E. (1997). *Child development*. Allyn and Bacon.

Brookfield, S. (2000). Transformative learning as ideology critique. In J. Mezirow & Associates (Eds.), *Learning as transformation: Critical perspectives on a theory in progress* (pp. 125–148). Jossey-Bass.

Dewey, J. (1933/1980). *How we think: A restatement of the relation of reflective thinking to the educative process*. Heath and Co Publishers.

Erikson, E. (1968). *Identity: Youth and crisis*. Norton.

Freire, P. (1998). *Teachers as cultural workers: Letters to those who dare to teach*. Westview Press.

Freire, P., & Macedo, D. (1987). *Literacy: Reading the word and the world*. Routledge and Kegan Paul.

Gardner, H. (1999). *The disciplined mind*. Simon and Schuster.

Greene, M. (2000). *Releasing the imagination. Essays on education, the arts, and social change*. Jossey-Bass.

Hodgson, B.C. (2007). *Experiential approaches to personal transformations: Outward journeys and individual adventures*. [Doctoral dissertation, State University].

Illeris, K. (2014). *Transformative learning and identity*. Routledge.

Illeris, K. (2017). *How we learn: Learning and non-learning in school and beyond*. Routledge.

Kegan, R. (1994). *In over our heads*. Harvard University Press.

Larson, K. T. (2016). *What role does transformative learning play in adolescence?* Proceedings of the 12th International Transformative Learning Conference.

Marsick, V. J. (1998). Transformative learning from experience in the knowledge era. *Daedalus, 12*(4), 119–136.

Meerts-Brandsma, L., & Sibthorp, J. (2020). Considering transformative learning for adolescents enrolled at semester schools. *Journal of Transformative Education, 19*(1), 7–28.

Merriam, S. B. (2004). The role of cognitive development in Mezirow's transformational learning theory. *Adult Education Quarterly, 55*(1), 60–68. https://doi.org/10.1177/0741713604268891

Mezirow, J. (1991). *Transformative dimensions of adult learning*. Jossey – Bass.

Mezirow, J. (1994). Understanding transformation theory. *Adult Education Quarterly, 44*(4), 222–232.

Mezirow, J. (1996). Contemporary paradigms of learning. *Adult Education Quarterly, 46*(3), 158–173.

Mezirow, J. (1997). Transformative learning: Theory to practice. In P. Cranton (Ed.), *Transformative learning in action: Insights from practice* (pp. 5–12). New Directions for Adult and Continuing Education, no. 74. Jossey-Bass.

Mezirow, J. (1998). On critical reflection. *Adult Education Quarterly, 48*, 185–198.

Mezirow, J. (2000). Learning to think like an adult: Core concepts of transformation theory. In J. Mezirow & Associates (Eds.), *Learning as transformation: Critical perspectives on a theory in progress* (pp. 3–33). Jossey-Bass.

Mezirow, J. (2004). Forum comment on Sharan Merriam's "The role of cognitive development in Mezirow's transformational learning theory." *Adult Education Quarterly, 55*(1), 69–70.

Mezirow, J., & Associates (Eds.) (2000). *Learning as transformation: Critical perspectives on a theory in progress.* Jossey-Bass.

Nelson, L., Badger, S., & Wu, B. (2004). The influence of culture in emerging adulthood: Perspectives of Chinese college students. *International Journal of Behavioral Development, 28*, 26–36.

Piaget, J. (1954). *The construction of reality in the child.* Basic Books.

Piaget, J. (1967). *Six psychological studies.* Random House.

Rainio, A. P., & Mälkki, K. (2018). *Micro-interaction analysis of the dilemmatic processes of transformative learning: Ambivalence and edge-emotions in a theatre project with foster care youth.* Proceedings of the Conference "Contemporary dilemmas and learning for transformation". Transformative Processes in Learning and Education Network.

Siegler, R. (1998). *Children's thinking.* Prentice-Hall.

Smith, R., & Neill, J. (2005). Examining the possibilities of school transformation for peace in Northern Ireland from a narrative perspective. *Journal of Transformative Education, 3*(1), 6–32.

Stern, D. (1985). *The interpersonal world of the infant: A view from psychoanalysis and development psychology.* Basic Books.

Taylor, E. W. (2000). Analyzing research on transformative learning theory. In J. Mezirow & Associates (Eds.), *Learning as transformation: Critical perspectives on a theory in progress* (pp. 285–328). Jossey-Bass.

Taylor, E. W., & Snyder, M. (2012). A critical review of research on transformative learning theory, 2006–2012. In E. W. Taylor, P. Cranton, & Associates (Eds.), *The handbook of transformative learning: Theory, research, and practice* (pp. 37–55). Jossey-Bass.

Tisdell, E. (2012). Themes and variations of transformative learning: Interdisciplinary perspectives on forms that transform. In E. W. Taylor, P. Cranton, & Associates (Eds.), *The handbook of transformative learning: Theory, research, and practice* (pp. 21–36). Jossey-Bass.

Woolfolk, A. (2001). *Educational psychology*. Allyn and Bacon.

CHAPTER 50

Between Smoke and Crystal: The Practice of *In-Transformation*

Sarah J. Owusu

FINDING THE WAY

Throughout my career, I have crafted my practice in a multifaceted way; this chapter on transformation praxis tells some of this story. Transformation within organizations and Organization Development (OD) plays a central role, but it is deliberately woven together with wisdom from other fields, as it is this tapestry approach that I believe enables us to respond to the complexity and existential risk of the current, global moment.

I draw from my coaching and consulting experience over the past 10 years within organizations, and from the reflexive practice I have done alongside my work. By sharing my own journey I attempt to animate this chapter through storytelling, a key skill for transformation, and provide a vivid account of transformation in action.

S. J. Owusu (✉)
Cowrie Company, London, UK
e-mail: sarah@cowriecompany.com

© The Author(s), under exclusive license to Springer Nature
Switzerland AG 2022
A. Nicolaides et al. (eds.), *The Palgrave Handbook of Learning for Transformation*, https://doi.org/10.1007/978-3-030-84694-7_50

897

898   S. J. OWUSU

Re-animating Transformation Praxis

I have felt in my work that transformation is often treated as a limited concept used in constrained ways for unhelpful purposes. I consider that it needs re-animating with new ideas. This starts with how we hold ourselves as practitioners. The way we approach transformation is itself transformational, and this chapter gives an account of my own development in working ethically and effectively in the liminal spaces that transformation requires.

To have a hope of moving toward transformation, we need a praxis that works with what I call *in-transformation*, the oscillating balance between "smoke" and "crystal." I introduce these terms (written about by the French bio-physicist and philosopher, Henri Atlan [1979], and gifted to me in the journey described below) to explore transformation praxis in a new way. Crystal is the structured, linear, logical, and certain of making plans and taking action. Smoke is the ambiguous, curious, emergent, and fluid of exploratory discovery and reflection.

Already here, in the attempt to define, we encounter the challenge of remaining in the space of in-transformation—as I crystalize these terms with definitions, we lose some important nuance. For instance, smoke does not preclude action, but instead is inherently linked to action through reflection that generates the impetus to act. But remaining too "smoky" in my descriptions would give us no shared language. I encourage the reader to hold these terms lightly; see them as both a continuum (where over-reliance in either direction becomes pathology) and part of an integrated whole.

The Need for In-Transformation

I suggest that many corporations, fuelled by Western capitalist goals, are more attuned with crystal than smoke, and as such many of our global systems have been constructed on the false comfort of fixity. Narrowly framed challenges lead to deflection, and declarations of success that simply externalize problems, rather than true transformation. The global coronavirus pandemic serves as a clear example of the lack of imagination in our ideas of transformation; this current moment is removing assumed and self-imposed barriers, and inviting us into an abundant opportunity space, but is hampered by a drive to find certainty by crystalizing "the new normal" or look for ways to return to business as usual. Instead, we need to find the way of being and becoming space that in-transformation provides.

This chapter centers my lived experience with transformation in the context of human and organization development, influenced by Dialogic OD, but also more broadly, systems and complexity thinking and Integral Theory (Wilber, 2000).

Beyond organizations, I believe that transformative praxis is an imperative for humanity as a whole. My interest in transformation therefore draws on several schools of thought and contemporary thinkers such as Daniel Schmachtenberger (2017b) who expresses the "existential and catastrophic risks" we face, as well as the urgent need for social change, which he holds "as the central work of this time."

I suggest that the transformation practitioner must powerfully hold the middle way—avoiding the fragmenting effect of too much crystal or the always emerging, never manifesting smoke—to meet the complexity of this moment. As we shall see, they must help organizations find an appropriate position between smoke and crystal, with a practice that leverages dialogue and design. Based on my own work, described in three short vignettes, what follows is my journey discovering and developing a praxis that holds both smoke and crystal lightly, to encounter in-transformation—a praxis that has been personally transforming.

THREE VIGNETTES

Making this tangible is best done by showing it applied, hence my use of a series of vignettes describing three landmark moments in my own practice. These are stories of my growing capacity for in-transformation— learning to work with and between smoke and crystal. Once again I find some resistance in myself as I write this, as the act of documenting is crystallizing and I experience both the constraint and power of this structure. As such, these stories, metaphors, questions, and "generative images" (Bushe & Storch, 2015) are intended to introduce smoke into the structure of the chapter and are an invitation to the reader to populate this trans-disciplinary path with their own experience.

Fighting Crystal

My journey with in-transformation begins explicitly in my first encounter with the brittle structures of a multinational corporation, as I discover and become part of a team labeled Organization Development and Change. Perhaps the journey truly begins long before this, as I trace my intuition for OD back at least a generation; without using the label, my father was always in demand for his ability to make teams and projects more healthy and effective. This story about him only became known to me later in my journey, but there was an embodied knowing when I discovered OD and I was drawn to the work with a sense of remembering.

The terms used to describe the mandate of the team sounded delicious to me: culture, change, systemic, people-centered, transformational. But while the words alluded to what I later came to describe as smoke, they were in fact attempts to fix something elusive in place. For this company, the challenge was to transform the internal culture to "re-orient toward the customer." I have since seen transformation imperatives articulated in a variety of other ways: "becoming more results focused," "embedding innovation in our DNA," "putting people first," "encouraging diversity and inclusion." The reader may recognize some of these deadening corporate transformation taglines.

As I have suggested above, to make these shifts it is necessary to thoughtfully activate both smoke and crystal—to be in-transformation. As it turned out, in this company as in many, crystal was valued over and above the intangibility of smoke. The company operated in a safety critical and highly regulated industry, so the preference was to be expected. But applied to customer service and people and culture change, it resulted in very little space for the movement required to shape shift. The transformation goals were plotted on slides that described the "from-to," a structured narrative was articulated and repeated over and over, behaviors were codified, and service guidelines were documented down to the minutest detail. Transformation was treated as a place to get to, and the destination was defined top-down.

I did not know it at the time, but my role became to gently breathe smoke into the structures. In retrospect, this was also a deep education in how crystal works and when it helps or hinders, which I was later able to integrate into my repertoire. But in the moment, it felt like I was fighting crystal.

The symptoms of over-crystallization fixed transformation into a plan to be rolled out toward a predetermined goal and failed to account for the more emotive quality in the air across the organization among employees: a desire for community and belonging, a hopefulness or fear about the future, a genuine passion for the, an ambition to contribute and be valued. These culture characteristics seemed to me an entry-point for enabling shifts, but the corporate expectations left little room for exploration, and the pressure was on to show tasks ticked off and milestones achieved.

Partly through intuition and naivety, and partly guided by the curiosity of someone at the start of their career, I followed the emotions and whenever I could, created a space to connect personally with anyone who would accept my invitation. The internal campaign that was part of the culture transformation program included the invitation to join the conversation, but these meandering and agenda-less moments of connection that I created were not part of the planned roadmap. Nonetheless, it seemed to me that it was exactly the unplanned nature of the conversations that made them meaningful. I made it my mission to have as many conversations as I could, and with each one, I would disrupt the expectations of structure and answers, with fluidity and questions. The most meaningful conversations happened at the beginnings or ends of days when the headquarters were empty, on walks in operational areas surrounded by buzz and customers, or in small groups tucked away in unused meeting rooms.

Eventually I discovered the book, *Dialogue: The Art of Thinking Together*, that validated my experience that a "conversation with a center, not sides" could transform, or "form a totally new basis from which to think and act" (Isaacs, 1999). Following this thread, I was drawn to action learning and reflective practice (Schön, 1983), and in these conversations, the transformation imperative was held lightly. It seemed right to me that we "must have an empty space where we are not obliged to anything, nor to come to any conclusions, nor to say anything or not say anything. [The conversation is] open and free" (Bohm, 1996). These were conversations that were alive, and this was smoke in practice.

While I was on occasion met with impatience at the lack of structure, at the very least people were intrigued by the smoky intangibility that they experienced. The space enabled sense-making and meaning-making, both for individuals and for groups. Over time, certain parts of the organization invited me to host semi-structured meetings, guided by big, broad questions that their teams cared about. I discovered dialogue technologies such as World Café (Brown & Isaacs, 2005); I borrowed approaches such as the double diamond (Design Council, 2019) from design communities and creative industries. Over time, I found ways to be more intentional with my use of smoke to enable possibilities.

It is no surprise that I found resonance with Dialogic OD (Bushe, 2013; Bushe & Marshak, 2014) that was emerging simultaneously. I had been tasked with taking a diagnostic approach to the transformation, but had gravitated toward the dialogic. I remember the relief of encountering the concepts of "covert processes" and topics that are "under the table" (Marshak, 2006), which seemed to understand my experience. These dialogic pioneers began to give me language for the aspects of the transformation project that I had been unable to articulate, but that I sensed were the real entry-points for transformation.

With this, I began to develop my capacity to work with smoke in a more evidence-based and rigorous way, but I would still alternate between hiding the smoke in order to remain palatable, creating subversive spaces and moments to challenge the norm, or sometimes even dialing up smoke in a contrary attempt to provoke some movement. This stage had a profound influence on me as a practitioner. There was transformative learning, but my discoveries were developed in opposition to the crystal structures of the company and I had not yet gained enough skill to provide what this environment needed to feel safe. Thus, none of the tactics I developed for interpersonal work had the longevity necessary to carry real transformation in the wider connections and relationships that make up an organization of this nature. There was something more to learn.

The Limitations of Smoke

It did not come as a surprise to many when, one Monday afternoon, I decided I would take a sabbatical. When asked why, how, and where to? I would say I didn't know... but in retrospect, I now see that the answer was: "to live like smoke." The journey took me to all the African countries where I had connections, including to Ghana and Botswana to collect the stories of my father, the natural OD practitioner. It was also on these travels that I was gifted the smoke-crystal imagery at the end of a long conversation about my life, work, and travels. It was a roughly drawn sketch, with the two terms laid out at either end of a spectrum, each accompanied with a synonym: smoke = openness, crystal = fixity. It also showed dialogue as my method and placed me in the role of "foreign body."

Seeing this laid out was profound—allowing me to breathe—as it was confirmation of my intuition that smoke was a valid, yet often suppressed dimension of systems change. It gave me the language to describe my preference for smoke over crystal and helped me make sense of feeling like a foreign body within organizations. It resonated with my experience of fighting crystal. I had been an out-of-place irritant—through which I had been able to agitate some movement in the experience of "stuckness" in a system and culture dominated by safety and security, but not transformation.

When this sketch was gifted to me, I was also left with a challenging provocation that I would only come to understand later: What about the potential harm, violence, and ethical implications of smoke, especially for those around the fire starter?

When my travels came to an end I began working as an external consultant, and my first clients were organizations whose entire mission was transformation: world peace, prosperity and economic inclusion, human rights. But while they had charismatic founders, agility, and enough visibility to attract many people to line up behind their purpose, they were fragile endeavors that were at risk of disappearing in a puff of smoke. I was surprised to find myself understanding that what they needed was the fixity of solid organizational infrastructure to contain their highly volatile ways of working. They needed enough smoke to stay open to their expansive aspirations, but enough crystal structure so as to avoid a wildfire. In response to this, I pulled out my box of crystal tools, reluctantly learnt from fighting crystal: project planning, structured conversations that encouraged clear decision-making, rigorous and continuous contracting (Wilde, 2016), and good boundary setting.

During this time, I also began working with a number of social justice organizations, which was another education. What activists within these organizations knew intimately was the need for very robust structure to manage the risks to their personhood and the injury of marginalization as they worked directly to transform oppressive structures. Within movements, there was a need to contain the fear, tension, and emotional impact of dealing with violence. Much like in my corporate experience, the work was also safety critical for the activists. Structure was necessary, but not so much as to throttle the radical transformation they were working in service of, nor could they replicate the structure (and thereby the harms) of the very systems they were working to dismantle.

My work was to support these organizations to re-imagine appropriate and life-affirming structure, and to enable them to direct the destructive, but transformative aspect of fire. It brought to the fore, the critical role of "containment" (Bushe, 2010) provided by the practitioner. From facilitating well-held dialogue, generative questions would emerge such as: How can my fire for change be sustained without me burning out? How do we dismantle and demolish without doing harm? When must we turn up the heat in order to be seen?

I observed and practiced the skill and grace of combining power and passion, resources and radicality, technology and healing (Rankin, 2019). In my own practice, I needed to consider the potential for harm when interventions are not "trauma-informed" (Wilde, 2017) and the need for "psychological safety" (Edmondson, 1999).

The provocation around "the ethical use of smoke" that I had been left with when I was gifted the concepts began to open up for me. I could now hold the possibility that too much smoke might be harmful and that crystal might not be all bad. Smoke, with its origin in fire, had to be used with care and responsibility. It could be violent, erasing all in its path, but it could also be a renewing force.

As I began to design interventions and conversations with more attention to the appropriate level of structure, I found a way to enable openness through fixity, particularly when tackling highly charged subjects such as racism, the invisibility of marginalized voices, and the violence of oppression. I intentionally disrupted structures and re-designed them in order to enable collective sense-making and meaning-making. These generative spaces also began to result in more tangible outputs and I have previously written about "breakthrough environments" where "community-produced enactable insights" emerge (Owusu et al., 2017). I saw that being in-transformation with others generates meaningful insights that uncover in us the desire and ability to act. This marks a move into choice-making and action-taking ... and making transformation manifest.

During this time, I would also deepen my understanding of the purpose of transformation praxis; it was not to merely bring about any transformation (especially not at the smoky whim of a charismatic leader), but to go deeper, challenge initial assumptions, and advocate for transformation that moved us toward a more wholesome way of being in the world.

I was able to reframe crystal: from a limiting force to a liberating one (Lipmanowicz & McCandless, 2014), when applied appropriately. Designing for the right balance of structure and space generates freedom. My role in guiding in-transformation was no longer the reluctant foreign body, but now shifted to the enabling container. A container crystal enough to give shape, but also smoky enough to easily dissipate. And alongside the method of dialogue, I could now add thoughtful design.

Integration

While my official sabbatical travels had ended, at the start of my consulting career I still spent a significant amount of time moving between Africa and Europe, taking on clients in both places and journeying back and forth as required. As a result, this last vignette highlights a personal revolution: from using my European experience as the anchor for my work in the African context, to my experience of working and living in Africa being perceived as a valuable asset, of relevance to the rest of the world.

Once again, there was a sense of remembering (Okonkwo & Owusu, 2016). Of seeing how dialogue, containment, hosting, and creating safe space were, in fact, incredibly close to the surface as I worked across a number of African countries. These were African transformation technologies. I would not suggest any over-simplified accounts of African cultures being more smoky, and Western ones more crystal. What I want to offer is that people everywhere trap themselves, or get trapped, in one or the other. Integration was about leveraging varied praxis and finding a way to bring together smoke and crystal in service of my clients' transformation.

Given the lack of codified or documented African praxis, I will lift up two examples that have been particularly meaningful for me and in my work, both grounded in storytelling. Firstly, Yoruba praise poetry—*Oriki*—applied in a coaching methodology (Okonkwo, 2010) to encourage a rich expression of identity and to support transformative and generative images of self or the group. Secondly, the craft of the *Griot* (the historian, storyteller, and repository of community wisdom in many West African cultures), which animates the We Will Lead Africa project (Gilpin-Jackson et al., 2017) that I co-founded during this time. The project collects, curates, and shares stories of everyday African leaders with the purpose of transforming narratives about African leadership.

These are examples of bringing together smoke and crystal in support of transformation—for both the storyteller and listener, storytelling encourages smoky reflection and imagination as well as crystalized

906   S. J. OWUSU

wisdom and inspiration to act. Stories "shape how we understand the world, our place in it, and our ability to change it" (Saltmarshe, 2018).

This last part about change is critical. Particularly in the context of living and working across African countries, where the urgency and need for taking transformative, future-focused action came to life for me. With the need to radically re-imagine so much of our world, including the way organizations are and behave, the role of the transformation practitioner is not just to contain (enabling us to stand in and navigate in-transformation), but also to be a catalyst (encouraging choice and action for transformation).

More and more, I am drawn to working with startup or small and medium-sized organizations building new practices, and in doing so I am rarely fighting crystal but more frequently trying to see through the smoke. The transformation imperative here is the need to build structure, systems, and processes so that they may contribute fully what they have the potential to give, but without hardening in the way of the corporate world and while maintaining their agility and dynamism. In practice, I have guided organizations in participatory processes to produce their own diagnostic and in response, develop a culture narrative to guide their transformation. I have led design projects where strategies and project plans are constructed through collective sense-making by exploring the questions that are most important to the team. In these examples, I have found the concept of "grey zones" particularly relevant, emphasizing the need for the practitioner to operate on a "continuum in the space between Diagnostic OD and Dialogic OD" (Gilpin-Jackson, 2013). With one pioneering company, I supported them to build storytelling rituals that help them track their social impact, as well as connecting more wholesomely with each other inside the organization. In this work, I see the transformative effect of in-transformation, and integrating smoke and crystal.

A FRAMEWORK FOR TRANSFORMATION

For each vignette, I have reflected on the transformation imperatives of my clients and the personal transformations I experienced that have influenced my rich and trans-disciplinary transformation praxis, drawing from a number of fields, cultures, and experiences. This praxis meets the complexity of the moment and cannot be reduced to a toolkit or extracted checklist as it is built from personal transformations:

- I gained the ability to skillfully apply an appropriate use of smoke and crystal (and manage my own preference for the smoky), backed up with knowing that draws from both poles and the continuum between them;
- I deepened my understanding of and proficiency in the two methods that I see as key for the transformation practitioner: dialogue and design; and
- I shifted from experiencing my own role as an irritant in the system (a foreign body), to the more generative roles of container and catalyst for transformation.

The specifics of my journey may not be the same for you, but it does indicate that the path is one of integrating polarities (on a multi-dimensional continuum) and holding transformation lightly; I can now stand in the not-knowing of being in-transformation while trusting that I do know where to draw from next in order to guide people, groups, and organizations in their/our transformation journeys.

Based on this, I now offer the roughly drawn sketch gifted to me, as a conceptual framework to guide transformation praxis (Fig. 50.1), crystalized for now but likely to come apart and be reformulated as I continue my journey.

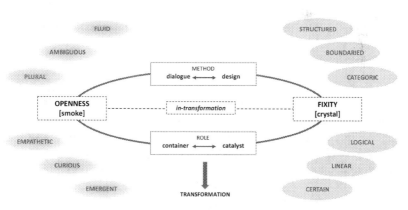

Fig. 50.1 Smoke-crystal conceptual framework for transformation praxis

BEING IN-TRANSFORMATION

The smoke-crystal framework acknowledges the necessary oscillation between smoke and crystal in support of transformation. Only in this way can we hold space for deep sense-making and meaning-making. Only in this way can we encourage transformative choices and actions. This praxis of being in-transformation grows out of my own journey, but is resonant with much existing and emerging OD literature, as well as other leadership and management theory.

With in-transformation, I have sought to address a gap in language when it comes to transformation. We often speak of transformation as a before, during, and an after. This framing is seen in OD approaches such as Kurt Lewin's well-known unfreeze-change-freeze framework for change (Lewin, 1947). This can bring clarity and structure, but is outdated in the face of the complexity we are now experiencing. Our ability to language transformation often remains somewhat linear and static, and suggests a rigidity in our relationship with the concept that will get in our way.

The old story treats transformation as a distant object, usually the remit of a bold, visionary leader. Instead, what is required is an emphasis on the collective, relational, and interdependent to bring about meaningful transformation. See the richness of work by Nora Bateson (2017) who makes clear the need for "warm data," the "transcontextual information about the interrelationships" if we are to meaningfully and appropriately engage with the complexity of systems.

I draw inspiration from the world of innovation and entrepreneurship, with its emphasis on action through the crystal work of prototyping, testing, and validation, yet still holds this with smoky empathy and a deep, almost anthropological understanding of human-centered design. These practices are extremely transferable to transformation work, as we see, for example, in the Theory U methodology of listening, sensing, and co-creating the future (Scharmer, 2009) and the paradigm shifting ideas of "teal organizations" (Laloux, 2014) that emphasize a structure of connection that allows for agency and shared purpose. I have also found resonance with Johnson's (1992), "polarities," and in the concept of "chaordic organizations" (Hock, 1991)—those organizations that can express both chaos and order, and use the two appropriately.

However, I have also felt the limitations of what are mostly Eurocentric approaches that are not always helpful for African organizations, realities, and priorities. While the approaches appear smokier, there would still be something colonial in directly importing these into the African context. In my work, I will continue to center the rich transformative praxis expressed in the traditions and rituals from across the African continent, such as *Oriki* and the *Griot* mentioned above. This praxis stands on its own, and importantly, must not be co-opted by transformation work that is too often the servant of capitalist growth, rather than people, community, and human life.

I offer in-transformation as a subversive alternative to our usual definitions of transformation. The word *transformation* speaks to moving across form, from one form to another; we use it to describe an event (a transformation, the noun) or to indicate a formula to be applied (to transform, the verb). Both have a fragmenting effect on what I see as a rich and fluid concept. I invoke in-transformation as a way of being that shifts us away from rigid expectations for transformation, and toward an as yet unknown form. The commitment to staying in the space between smoke and crystal is a commitment to a life of continuous inquiry, learning, wonder, and expansion—to anchoring profoundly in the present, while simultaneously leaning in to what is always becoming, with both passion and dedication but no attachment to a pre-defined outcome. And for the practitioner, not only enabling transformation but also being transformed in the process. A better description of in-transformation eludes me, but perhaps the profound wisdom of Octavia E. Butler (1993) resonates with the reader: "All that you touch, You change. All that you change, Changes you. The only lasting truth is change. God is change."

The Next Threshold

In writing this, my own thinking about transformation has deepened. It is not lost on me that even this act of crystalizing my story has set off a smoky trail of new discoveries to uncover and I know that the smoke-crystal framework will continue to evolve. New adjacent concepts and imagery have surfaced through this process: smoke and mirrors, the myth of the genie in the bottle whose smoky embodiment is trapped in crystal waiting to be called upon to transform wishes into reality, the magic of fire as it relates to smoke with its "lifecycle" of heat, flames, embers, and ashes. I could go on, but suffice to say that the framework itself may be ready for in-transformation.

As we experience the hope and the fear of this unprecedented moment, we must resist the temptation to capture, lock down, and fix too soon ... but we cannot be paralyzed in non-action or apathy. We need an approach to transformation that can hold and act from the possibility space for the collective, and that honors becoming (not what is, not what will be, but that which is unfolding). We require new imagination, new language, and new praxis. The introduction of the concept in-transformation is my attempt to hold the liminal space and I hope that my story breathes new life into the work of transformation practitioners everywhere.

Being in-transformation is urgent and necessary, but we do not do transformation for the sake of transformation. The praxis must be applied with respect and responsibility to the complex challenges of our time to move the human collective toward not a destination, but a fundamental and meaningful shift. Toward what has been described as "a sustainable, non-self-terminating, thriving, anti-fragile world" (Schmachtenberger, 2017a). The work of the transformation practitioner is to show up boldly, both knowing and not knowing, to hold smoke and crystal lightly, in order to bring the future to life.

References

Atlan, H. (1979). *Entre le cristal et la fumée: Essai sur l'organization de vivant.* Seuil.

Bateson, N. (2017, December 28). *Warm data.* Hackernoon. https://hacker noon.com/warm-data-9f0fcd2a828c

Bohm, D. (1996). *On dialogue.* Routledge.

Brown, J., & Isaacs, D. (2005). *World café: Shaping our futures through conversations that matter.* Berrett-Koehler Publishers.

Bushe, G. R. (2010). Being the container in dialogic OD. *NTL Practicing Social Change* (2). https://b-m-institute.com/wp-content/uploads/2019/11/con tainer.pdf

Bushe, G. R. (2013). Dialogic OD: A theory of practice. *OD Practitioner, 45*(1), 11–17.

Bushe, G. R., & Marshak, R. J. (2014). The dialogic mindset in organization development. *Research in Organizational Change and Development, 22,* 55–97. http://www.gervasebushe.ca/mindset.pdf

Bushe, G. R., & Storch, J. (2015). Generative image: Sourcing novelty. In G. R. Bushe & R. J. Marshak (Eds.), *Dialogic organization development: The theory and practice of transformational change.* Berrett-Koehler. http://www.gervas ebushe.ca/otherdocs/Chap_5.pdf

Butler, O. E. (1993). *Parable of the sower.* Headline Publishing Group.

Design Council. (2019). *What is the framework for innovation?* Design Council. https://www.designcouncil.org.uk/news-opinion/what-framework-innovation-design-councils-evolved-double-diamond

Edmondson, A. (1999). Psychological safety and learning behavior in work teams. *Administrative Science Quarterly, 44*(2), 350–383. http://web.mit.edu/curhan/www/docs/Articles/15341_Readings/Group_Performance/Edmondson%20Psychological%20safety.pdf

Gilpin-Jackson, Y. (2013). Practicing in the grey area between dialogic and diagnostic organization development: Lessons from a healthcare case study. *Organization Development Practitioner, 45*(1), 60–66.

Gilpin-Jackson, Y., Owusu, S. J., & Okonkwo, J. (2017). *We will lead Africa: Volume one.* CreateSpace Independent Publishing Platform.

Hock, D. (1991). Birth of the chaordic age. *The Systems Thinker, 11.* https://thesystemsthinker.com/the-nature-and-creation-of-chaordic-organizations/

Isaacs, W. (1999). *Dialogue and the art of thinking together: A pioneering approach to communicating in business and in life.* Currency.

Johnson, B. (1992). *Polarity management: Identifying and managing unsolvable problems.* HRD Press.

Laloux, F. (2014). *Reinventing organizations: A guide to creating organizations inspired by the next stage of human consciousness.* Nelson Parker.

Lewin, K. (1947). Frontiers in group dynamics: Concept, method and reality in social science, social equilibria and social change. *Human Relations, 1,* 5–41.

Lipmanowicz, H., & McCandless, K. (2014). *The surprising power of liberating structures: Simple rules to unleash a culture of innovation.* Liberating Structures Press.

Marshak, R. J. (2006). *Covert processes at work: Managing the five hidden dimensions of organizational change.* Berrett-Koehler Publishers.

Okonkwo, J. (2010). Coaching using leadership myths and stories: An African perspective. In J. Passmore (Ed.), *Leadership coaching: Working with leaders to develop elite performance.* Kogan.

Okonkwo, J., & Owusu, S. J. (2016). Remembering—The gift of OD. *OD Practitioner, 48*(3), 57–63.

Owusu, S. J., Tuitt, D., & Wilde, J. (2017). Breakthrough environments for inclusive research into race and mental health: Co-creating social justice impact via the #justcare event and social media. *Research for All, 1*(2), 328–350. https://doi.org/10.18546/RFA.01.2.10

Rankin, K. (2019). Queer activism goes online. *Stanford Social Innovation Review* (Summer). https://ssir.org/articles/entry/queer_activism_goes_online

912   S. J. OWUSU

Saltmarshe, E. (2018, February 20). *Using story to change systems*. Stanford Social Innovation Review. https://ssir.org/articles/entry/using_story_to_change_systems

Scharmer, O. (2009). *Theory U: Leading from the future as it emerges*. Berrett-Koehler Publishers.

Schön, D. (1983). *The reflective practitioner: How professionals think in action*. New York.

Schmachtenberger, D. (2017a). *Phase shifting humanity*. Future Thinkers Podcast (#036, February). https://futurethinkers.org/daniel-schmachtenberger-phase-shift/

Schmachtenberger, D. (2017b, October 11). *Solving the generator functions of existential risk*. Civilization Emerging. http://civilizationemerging.com/solving-generator-function/

Wilber, K. (2000). *A theory of everything*. Shambhala Publications.

Wilde, J. (2016). *The social psychology of organizations: Diagnosing toxicity and intervening in the workplace*. Routledge.

Wilde, J. (2017). *When work goes wrong*. Healthandsafetyatwork.com (October edition).

CHAPTER 51

Conclusion Chapter: Propositions at the Threshold of Transformation

Yabome Gilpin-Jackson and Marguerite Welch

I came into this project by invitation. It was the timing, the moment, the audacity to step into a space predominantly filled by white, European, American, men, traditional scholars. So I stepped through and into the opening. And in doing so a portal opened up for a new way to galvanize a group of thoughtful educators, practitioners, researchers, scholars, academics, activists, to imagine a new way to bring more life to an already living theory. The image of passageways embodies movement—a journey beginning when we step into a new space from within living theory. We

---

Y. Gilpin-Jackson (✉)
SLD Consulting, Port Coquitlam, BC, Canada
e-mail: yabome@sldconsulting.org; ykanu@sfu.ca

Simon Fraser University, Burnaby, BC, Canada

M. Welch
Saint Mary's College of California, Moraga, CA, USA
e-mail: mwelch@stmarys-ca.edu; mawelch@tdmsm.com

© The Author(s), under exclusive license to Springer Nature   913
Switzerland AG 2022
A. Nicolaides et al. (eds.), *The Palgrave Handbook of Learning for Transformation*, https://doi.org/10.1007/978-3-030-84694-7_51

ask new questions: How do we move through transformation, and transform? This corpus of work is but a small taste of the luminous possibilities that transformation invokes.

—Aliki

Our editorial team started the journey of this Handbook in 2018, centered on the metaphor of passageways, unaware of the moment in history this work would pass through before coming to fruition and arriving in your hands. As we conclude, we are still in that moment, still living through the threshold of the COVID-19 pandemic. It is a threshold, beckoning us to transformation on the other side of who we are becoming. We are all becoming—the six of us as co-editors, you as scholars and practitioners committed to these ideas of transformation, and all of us as world citizens who are shaping the future by how we choose to live as we address the justice and equity issues of our times.

As the authors of this chapter, we are aligned with transformation, as both process and outcome, that results in a dramatic shift in our thinking, feelings, and actions. We know that when that dramatic shift occurs, our being and worldviews are different—metamorphosis happens—a change in form. It is that experience we pass through when we become a different person or collective, before and after the nemesis events that disrupt our status quo (Taylor & Cranton, 2012). We are therefore using the term threshold in this chapter to define the moment we are standing within, as it aligns with the ideas of transformation and transformative learning embossed in this Handbook. A threshold is the moment before emerging transformations are crystallized. We go to the poetry and prose work of John O'Donohue from the Celtic historical tradition to capture the meaning of threshold we are evoking:

> Like Spring secretly at work within the heart of Winter, below the surface of our lives huge changes are in fermentation. We never suspect a thing. Then when the grip of some long-enduring winter mentality begins to loosen, we find ourselves vulnerable to a flourish of possibility and we are suddenly negotiating the challenges of a threshold ... A threshold is not a simple boundary; it is a frontier that divides two different territories, rhythms, and atmospheres ... At this threshold a great complexity of emotion comes alive: confusion, fear, excitement, sadness, hope ... To acknowledge and cross a new threshold is always a challenge. It demands courage and also a sense of trust in whatever is emerging. This becomes essential when a threshold opens suddenly in front of you, one for which

you had no preparation...No threshold need be a threat, but rather an invitation and a promise. (O'Donohue, 2008, pp. 48–50)

The COVID-19 pandemic was unexpected, and it further illuminated the social justice issues the world was already contending with. For example, the pandemic showed that marginalized communities were being disproportionately impacted by the virus. In addition, movements for racial equity continued to grow around the world during the pandemic. When this context is juxtaposed with the historical and contemporary debates about transformative learning, we sense that we are at a threshold for the transformation of the field. It is possible, through the lens of this moment, to engage the debates of the field differently and to see new ways, new possibilities. It is important to name and mark this threshold, because this chapter gives us a moment for critical reflection. We embrace the opportunity to synthesize what we see emerging and to offer invitations to the choices before us. For, at the crossroad of a threshold, we must choose. In this way, this chapter is not a conclusion, but an invitation to choose a broader framing for fostering and leading transformations into the future, from the breadcrumbs we have collected in the passageways we have come through to arrive at this threshold.

The passageways we have come are firstly the portals of our Handbook Community—the co-editors and contributors to this Handbook, and secondly, our emic-centered analysis of the chapters.[1] These circles of connected passageways led us to the Propositions we offer for what is emerging at the threshold, which we hope will allow this field to step into the promise of transforming itself (Taylor & Cranton, 2013). Just as we started with Provocations, we offer Propositions in this closing invitation. The Provocations we offered for contributors to respond to were:

- Provocation I—The many turns of transformation
- Provocation II—Generating conditions for transformation
- Provocation III—(Un)known discourses of transformation
- Provocation IV—Challenges and emerging future of transformation

---

[1] We wish to acknowledge the support of Ahreum Lim, who was our Research Assistant on the entire Handbook and supported the co-authors of this chapter with our final qualitative analysis—keyword analysis and descriptive statistics—using R software.

916   Y. GILPIN-JACKSON AND M. WELCH

For our Propositions that flow from the chapters, we take inspiration from other works which offer Propositions as a result of reviews of literature and frameworks as a starting point for further research, and practice exploration (Barbuto, 2000).

We base our Propositions on the contents of this Handbook, which have looked both backwards and forwards, thus representing the fullness of the state of the field. We pick up the thread with which we started—to inquire into the visible and invisible realms of transformation from a multidisciplinary perspective. By following this thread, we turn away from efforts to create a unified theory of transformative learning, as well as efforts that have fractured the field or mired it in a sense of stuckness. We hope that our gaze will reinvigorate what is meant to be a living theory and help it find passage into the future. We see this work as a response to the challenge to:

> pay particular attention to voices on the margins—voices of transformative experiences that often are overlooked and inadequately understood. The study of transformative learning in non-Western countries, positionality, and cultural difference holds great promise of offering new understanding of this way of adult learning. (Taylor & Cranton, 2012, p. 572)

We are picking up the torch being entrusted to us as noted in the foreword: "We pass the torch to these exciting new voices of transformative learning who are making sense of new generations of thought and practice in describing our shared Volatile, Uncertain, Complex and Ambiguous (VUCA) world …".

Passageway 1: Portal of the Handbook Community

In keeping with the humanistic, constructivist, and critical social theory roots of the field of transformative learning, we acknowledge that this collection of chapters represents the authors' meaning making in the context of their identity formation and societal intersectionality and positionality (Cranton & Taylor, 2012). As such, it is important to understand the diversity of lenses that informs the meaning making offered in each chapter and across the four Provocations. Because the Handbook represents international contexts and perspectives, we highlight the national, racial/ethnic representation, social identities, and disciplinary perspectives embossed in the collection.

Firstly, our editorial team of six is made up of three members residing in the United States of America and three residing internationally in Canada, Australia, and Germany. However, by ethnic ancestry, the circle of intersectionality expands to include cultural heritage influences from Greece, Palestine, Singapore, Sierra Leone, Germany (including the former East Germany), and Japan. Our disciplinary diversity ranges from direct use of Transformative Learning for teaching in Higher Education to Psychology to Leadership and Human and Organization Development as fields of teaching and practice to adult learners, in organizations, and in communities. By racial and gender identity, we are four White women, one Black woman, and one Asian man. Our sexual orientations include LGBTQ^2+ and heterosexual. We were aware of our non-traditional make-up as an editorial group, as the opening quote points to, and aware that we may be criticized for a lack of gender balance in our editorial lenses. We stepped into the process knowing and accepting this. We saw the importance of claiming space and the potential value our unique editorial gaze from the margins might afford (hooks, 1990). You will find throughout this chapter, quotes from our co-editing team that illuminates our personal experiences through the journey of curating this Handbook. We did not set out to match our reflections with each of the Provocations. Yet, some natural alignments emerged, and we have paired those reflections in the sections they illustrate.

Secondly, the 51 chapters in this volume represent a total of 103 contributors, including our editorial team. 74% of contributors used a preferred pronoun and 26% did not specify a pronoun. From job titles, we infer that 64% identified themselves in the Academy as professor, researcher, or doctoral student, while 36% identified as being a practitioner (consultant, coach, facilitator, trainer, educator, principal, teacher). When assessed by the affiliated country of residence, there are clusters of contributors from the United States of America (36%), Canada (17.5%), Australia and New Zealand (7.8%), and South Africa (6.3%). The remaining quarter represents a spread of geographic locations from Europe (Italy, UK, Denmark, Greece, Norway, Switzerland), Asia (India and Thailand), and Africa (Nigeria, Kenya, Zimbabwe) (Fig. 51.1).

We have international representation in this Handbook from every region of the world, with the notable exception of South America and the Middle East. Although we accepted chapters involving several countries and/or authors from Central and South America, the proposed chapters were not completed in time for this Handbook due to the challenges

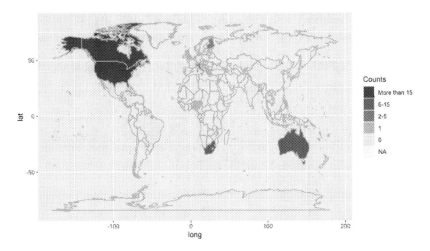

Fig. 51.1 Geographic countries of residence of handbook contributors

of writing in a pandemic era. While we had attrition of other accepted chapters, it is an unfortunate coincidence that we lost all the proposed submissions from South and Central America. In addition, future international works to understand the phenomenon of transformation must include knowledge from the Middle East.

The disciplinary representation ranges widely among 103 authors, with 98 in Arts and Social Sciences fields, including 36% from Education/Learning disciplines, 33% from Leadership/Human and Organization Development (HOD), 9% from Indigenous Studies, and the remaining approximately 22% made of a wide variety of disciplines including Arts and Humanities, English Language and Literature, Health Sciences, Sustainability Education/Sustainable Futures and others (Fig. 51.2).

The multidisciplinary range of the contributors is significant, showing us that new understandings of learning for transformation are coming from within Higher Education, but also beyond. Our propositions reflect this, calling for a future of fostering and leading transformations from a multidisciplinary and transdisciplinary stance. By multidisciplinary, we mean additive knowledge creation from within clear disciplinary lines. By transdisciplinary, we mean:

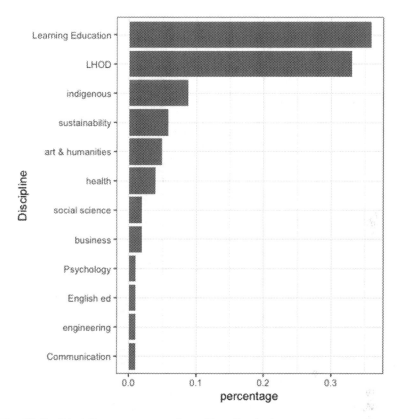

Fig. 51.2 Disciplinary representation of handbook chapters

contributions incorporate a combination of concepts and knowledge not only used by academics and researchers but also other actors in civic society, including representatives of the private sector, public administration and the public. These contributions enable the cross-fertilization of knowledge and experiences from diverse groups of people that can promote an enlarged vision of a subject, as well as new explanatory theories. (Lawrence, 2010, p. 112)

It is essential that we look beyond known discourses of transformative learning if we are to accomplish what we set out to do—to make space for new discourses and language for the field through the phenomenon of transformation. We set out to explore the phenomenon of transformation from a meta-lens of moving among, between, and within disciplines and fields of inquiry. Therefore, one of the calls at our threshold includes actively embracing multidisciplinary and transdisciplinary perspectives to expand and reanimate the scholarship and practice of learning for Transformation.

PASSAGEWAY 2: PORTAL OF EMIC-CENTERED CHAPTER ANALYSIS

The other passageway we went through to arrive at the Propositions you will read next is the emic-centered analytical lens we applied to the collection of chapters. We chose to embrace our position as edgewalkers, both insiders and outsiders, while privileging an emic-orientation to analyzing the chapters from within their own merit (Beals et al., 2020). We focused on what is emerging as opposed to applying existing frameworks of transformation to our analysis. As Beals et al. (2020) note, "the edge is a space that enables bridges to be built and new stories to be told. In a world of emic perspectives, the challenge is to walk and work the edge" (p. 600).

Using standard qualitative coding and categorizing, we sorted the final set of chapters into the four Provocations. Following this sorting, we used R package *ggplot2* (Wickham, 2016) and *tidyverse* (Wickham et al., 2019) to conduct basic keyword, reference network analysis, and topic modeling on each grouping of the chapters per Provocation. Guided by the R software results, we did further immersive qualitative analysis to look for deeper meaning and emerging themes and patterns. The results led us to the Propositions at the threshold of what is emerging for the field.

WHAT IS EMERGING? PROPOSITIONS AT THE THRESHOLD

In this section, we summarize the key takeaways from the chapters within each Provocation and conclude by offering Propositions that can be used as future guidance for the field. The chapters are summarized in the order they appear in the Handbook. This chapter ordering is based on the flow with which chapters build on each other and lead toward the Proposition that emerges. We illustrate each Proposition with a quote from one of the chapters, as is standard in qualitative analysis.

51 CONCLUSION CHAPTER: PROPOSITIONS ... 921

Provocation I: The Many Turns of Transformation: Multiple Perspectives on the Matter of Transformation

The collaborative writing projects I have been part of have all bene-fited from the multiple perspectives of the collaborators. When we came together as an editorial team, we were a collection of individuals who had pre-existing relationships with one or two others. As we were getting to know one another, we were careful with our language and atten-tive to other perspectives. We navigated the complexity of our diversity and the systems in which we were embedded—both institutional and socio-political—with care. Our connections deepened as we met, every two-to-three weeks via Zoom, and an ease in our interactions developed. The boundaries around our perspectives became more permeable as we sought to more deeply understand the perspectives offered. We had a plan to meet in-person for three days prior to a conference in Canada in June of 2020. As it became clear that this wouldn't happen, we carried on virtually. Our work has been personally meaningful to me and I have appreciated the new relationships with colleagues who are now also friends. And, I do wonder how our connections as an editorial team would be different had we been able to meet in person, with time to share meals and tell more stories of our lives.
—Marguerite

The chapters in Provocation I unpack the many turns of transforma-tion. Our analysis confirms that Mezirow's definition of transformative learning appears most frequently. While Mezirow's work focuses on self-change and behavioral change as the evidence of transformation, a number of these chapters extend transformative learning theory into the collective or societal realm.

Four chapters explicitly take up Mezirow's call for a living theory by building on or filling gaps: Ted Fleming (Chapter 2) encourages engage-ment with current critical theorists Habermas, Honneth, and Negt; Peter Levine and Saskia Eschenbauer (Chapter 3) deepen the connection to Habermas' work about the power and value of social movements, and the need to reform society to enable transformative learning; Fergal Finnegan (Chapter 4) draws our attention to critical realism, relational sociology, and social movement studies to further develop the conception of emancipation; Effrosyni Kostara (Chapter 5) advocates for using World Literature to prompt transformative learning.

Chad Hoggan (Chapter 6) seeks to gain insights across the many disparate theories in the literature and offers analytic tools for analysis. Alessandra Romano and colleagues (Chapter 7) examine the contribution that a practice-based view of transformative learning, situated in the frameworks of informal and incidental learning, offers to the study of creativity.

Four chapters seek to integrate theoretical perspectives beyond the field of transformative learning: sustainability education (Heather Burns, Chapter 8); Black Spirituality (Maureen Miller & Karen Watkins, Chapter 9); Actor Network Theory (Claudio Melacarne & Francesca Fabbri, Chapter 10); and Action Research for Transformation (Hillary Bradbury, Chapter 11).

We noticed deep attention to individual transformation and personal engagement in the chapters about pilgrimage (Elizabeth J. Tisdell & Ann Swartz, Chapter 12) and soul work (Janet Ferguson, Chapter 13)—both through lived experience and the creative realm. Brookfield's (Chapter 14) observation about making a transformational shift from thinking about race in individual terms to viewing racism as a structural and systemic reality seems particularly pertinent at this moment in time. Brookfield implores us to go beyond the white lie that life chances result from individual effort and merit alone. He explains:

> Individualism as a dominant ideology in the United States comprises a set of beliefs and practices that help keep a blatantly unequal system in place. It comprises two core beliefs. The first is that we live on a roughly level playing field and that anyone can make what they want of their life by dint of their own perseverance and hard work....The second core belief is that we are in control of our individual destinies, captains of our souls. What we make of our lives is believed to be a result of the personal decisions we take at the significant turning points we all experience... At some deep level, we see ourselves as disconnected from the settings, locations and people that surround us as we choose our particular path....We must move from the personal to the collective, from the individual to the systemic. We must contribute to building movements, commit to furthering institutional and community initiatives that address inequity, and focus our energies on changing policies and structures. People come and go but structures and policies endure unless some collective effort disrupts them. In short, we need to think structurally, not individually.

51 CONCLUSION CHAPTER: PROPOSITIONS ... 923

While Brookfield casts this ideology critique in the context of the United States, we further posit that this colonized thinking permeates the globe where Western capitalist thinking dominates. We propose that it is time to move beyond the oft-debated individual-social dichotomy and how these schools of thought complement each other, to thinking about transformations in the context of structural wholes.

We leave this Provocation, therefore, thinking about the dialectic between individual and collective transformation. There is something about individual transformation that opens one up to collective transformation. And there is something about collective transformation that pulls one into individual transformation. That is to say, the personal is embedded and entangled in the social. We are seeing both right now in the socio-political issues around the world and in the progression of the chapters in this provocation that start with Mezirow, and leave, extend, and integrate other theories that embed the individual in context of the collective on the road to transformation.

Proposition I: Transformation occurs at the nexus of the individual and collective, requiring structural change and collective effort to transform systems. Transformation-in-Context.

Provocation II: Generating Conditions for Transformation

The metaphor of passageways reflects many of the experiences I have had and I will share one of them: In the beginning, I was simply impressed by the other editors, their academic as well as their practical experiences, their successes and skills, which in return meant for me to basically just try and keep up with the pace of learning. The invitation to pass through, to shift my focus and to leave this space of insecurity and enter a new space where I could find myself within this project, both in a personal and professional way, was key to my Handbook journey. The unknown territory ahead of me was one that was filled with an extraordinary sense of community, a space that generated exactly the kind of conditions necessary for development, growth and transformation. While the Handbook was evolving and in progress, our editorial meetings were a constant during the pandemic that I did not want to miss. In the midst of a world in crisis, our work on this Handbook provided not only a sense of community but a safe space for growth, self and professional development. Journeying that path was and still is exciting as we really made the road by walking. This

sense of we, our work together as a group, is an experience to treasure and cultivate.
—Saskia

The chapters grouped in the second Proposition focus on creating the conditions for transformation. These chapters highlight the ways transformation emerges from the relationships among individuals, rather than within an individual. This differs from traditional understanding of transformative learning in the field of adult learning/education where the focus is primarily on individual development. We continued to notice in these chapters, the range of settings and processes used to evoke transformation in response to the complexities of organizational life and the imperative for social change. Transformation happening in context.

The settings include educational settings with students, staff, and teachers; workplaces within a specific organization; group learning events with leaders from various organizations; and group learning events with people drawn to exploring deep engagement across differences. The processes drawn on to facilitate transformation include reorienting connections to attend to self-transcendent emotions; creating holding environments; encouraging deliberately developmental organizations; creating imaginal spaces; coaching; listening; participatory action research; indigenous discussions and strategies; critical reflection focused on meaning structures; and integrative approaches. As you read the brief summaries of the chapters in this provocation, we invite you to notice the role of the dialogic connection between relational spaces and contexts as the site where transformation is sparked.

The set of chapters that are set in educational contexts includes Roz Walker and Rob McPhee's (Chapter 15) description of their experiences, challenges and successes in developing Indigenous discourses and strategies to transform Indigenous education within the complex social and political context of Australia—to offer opportunities for empowerment, self-determination and liberation for Indigenous Peoples. Mark Hathaway (Chapter 16) discusses his work with undergraduate students and the role reorienting connections play in transformative learning and the formation of ecological consciousness. Reorienting connections are not marked by feelings of shame, fear, anger, or guilt, but rather by self-transcendent emotions like love, compassion, wonder, gratitude, and a sense of connection or an expanded self. Kaisu Mälkki and her colleagues (Chapter 17) respond to the problematic nature of reflection in the teacher education field which often limits reflection to concrete teaching practices. Their work revitalizes teacher reflection by developing an understanding of reflection focused on meaning structures rather than on teaching practices. Using a recently developed digital tool called Reflection Facilitator (RF) that is based on the theory of edge emotions, they work with a theory of reflection in the interface between embodied experiencing, societal conditions, and the function of reflection in examining the human condition.

There are chapters that attend to transformation in workplaces. Beth Fisher-Yoshida (Chapter 18) focuses on creating the narrative that will enable women to succeed as they transition into higher positions of leadership and authority, through a coaching engagement. Changkyu Kwon (Chapter 19) describes how Deliberately Developmental Organizations (DDO) create an alternative organizational space for inclusion that cultivates an organizational culture and structure in which employees can form mutual and trustworthy relationships, and safely explore the unknown dimensions of themselves, others, their work, and the system that they are part of on an ongoing basis. Allie Cox and her colleagues (Chapter 20) describe a cohort-based program for women staff in Higher Education designed to enhance the individual capacities necessary for leading through the complexities of higher education. A key element of their process is the creation of "The Collective," a holding environment for women that seeks to create the conditions for support, development, and belonging. Nitasha Ramparsad (Chapter 21) concludes that transformation is largely dependent on the creation of an enabling environment to allow for the workplace to be changed. She uses structural thinking to show how transformations required for gender equality depend on senior management and transformation leaders enabling progressive policy changes.

Two chapters discuss transformation in the context of group learning events. In their work facilitating leadership retreats that draw people from organizations around the world, Mary A. Stacey and Reilly L. Dow (Chapter 22) see the potential of imaginal spaces that awaken and liberate a transformative imagination that is alive at edges, and between things, people, and contexts, and capable of supporting and guiding leadership in times of fragmentation, anxiety, and possibility. Placida V. Gallegos and her colleagues (Chapter 23) design and facilitate group learning events to create the conditions needed for deep engagement across difference, engagement that can lead to transformation in understandings of social identities, and to emergent practices for deconstructing white supremacy and patriarchy. Their integrative model brings together integral theory, including the AQAL model and the notion of We-Space, gestalt group work, and social identity development.

There are chapters that address transformation in multiple contexts. Laurie Anderson-Sathe and colleagues (Chapter 24) describe working with the Transformative Listening Protocol (TLP) they developed. The TLP engages participants in listening and reciprocal storytelling, a re-emerging force for holistic transformation that holds the potential to transform a person's worldview. The TLP responds to a specific gap in the literature, an understanding of the experience of listening through story that creates a third space for transformation in dyads and opens a portal for individual, collective, community, and societal change. Darlene Clover (Chapter 25) describes a feminist multi-media research exhibition. The exhibition was designed as an imaginative, political pedagogical response to persistent problematic representations that have excluded, marginalized, and stereotyped the contributions of Canadian women. She outlines the design and development strategies of the exhibition, illustrates some of its stories and narratives, and describes the transformative learnings experienced by the visitors and herself as the curator.

Maren Seehawer and colleagues (Chapter 26) build on an understanding of transformation that derives from the Southern African paradigm of Ubuntu. They share four South African science teachers' experiences with transformative learning through participatory action research, providing insights into the transformative learning process that involved a gradual shift from focusing on challenges to recognizing a teacher's agency. Transforming the self thus enabled transforming educational practices. They draw insights from the relational aspects of collaborative research that allowed for interacting as "whole persons" by describing how facilitators are embedded in relationships such that in all the cases, there was "transforming through interaction with others, as well as transforming others."

The chapters in this section discuss transformation within the context of groups of people. While there might also be individual transformation that is part of the outcome of these processes, the engagement with others led to new actions and capacities for engaging the larger world.

We are struck that the conditions that enable transformation move beyond the traditional orientations within transformative learning of critical discourse for objective or subjective reflection, or individual embodied experiences. The conditions described in these chapters center relational connection, we-spaces, and a deeply felt collective experience as the passageway to transformation. Our keyword analysis surfaced an interesting finding—that the word ecology was found only in this set of chapters, in close co-occurrence with process and outcome words that denote transformation such as worldview, experience, process. This tells us that the relational ecology and experience between people is a significant condition and portal to transformation.

This phenomenon could not be better captured than through the South African principle of Ubuntu, *I am, because we are*, that is described by Seehawer et al.:

> Ubuntu addresses the core of being human. Conceptualised as "humble togetherness" (Swanson, 2009), it emphasizes communality, caring for, and relating positively to, others. Framed as "humanness" (Ramose, 2009), Ubuntu contains both a dimension of *being human* through humble togetherness and a dimension of *becoming human* through "entering more and more deeply into community with others" (Shutte 2001, in Metz & Gaie, 2010, p. 275). Humanness in the sense of Ubuntu is not anthropocentrism. On the contrary, it emphasizes not only the interconnectedness among human beings, but also among humans and the surrounding environment and the universe, about which humans are just one part (Goduka, 2000; LenkaBula, 2008). Furthermore, interconnectedness has to be understood "in a holistic manner; physically, socially and spiritually. It also focuses on the development of the whole person; physical, mental, spiritual and social" (Mkabela, 2015, p. 287). It is both the infinitive state of *becoming* and "ceaseless unfolding" (Ramose, 2009, p. 308) and the "intertwinement [with others] that makes ubuntu transformative, as there is always more work to do together in shaping our future" (Cornell & Van Marle, 2015, p. 5).

We propose therefore that the conditions for transformation exist in the relational space between people that enables a shift not only in worldview but in relationship to humanity.

Proposition II: The passageway to transformation is the relational ecology (connection, collective engagement) that evokes the interconnected being and becoming of humanity. Transformation-in-Connection.

928 Y. GILPIN-JACKSON AND M. WELCH

Provocation III: (Un)known Discourses of Transformation

Working on this book and with this team has given me meaning as I experienced multiple, cascading, and compounding personal and collective disasters in Australia, which included the 2019–20 Australian bushfires and resulting smoke, a severe hailstorm, and the COVID-19 pandemic. I felt that I contributed to the solution. The tremendous passion, authenticity, care, empathy, appreciation for diverse perspectives, and openness to transform individually and collectively any challenges has repeatedly nurtured, confirmed and strengthened my true self, relit or brightened my flame when I struggled, and filled my hope for humanity to be able to transform. I am proud that we co-created so graciously a transformative handbook that sheds light on transformation from so many diverse cosmological, ontological, epistemological, pedagogical, disciplinary, geographical, gendered and generational angles. This work spans diverse and fluid times in innovative and diverse ways, creating a colorful comprehensive, interconnected and fluid kaleidoscope or symphony of transformation. I am particularly proud that the handbook gives voice to so many contributions of Indigenous scholars and practitioners.
—Petra

The chapters in Provocation III, (Un)known Discourses of Transformation, take us deeper into an exploration of transformation that cannot always be planned with ideal conditions. The explorations described in these chapters focus on unpacking transformation in new/different contexts, from informal learning to international emergencies to postcolonial oppressive/bullyist contexts, to indigenous worldviews and transitional life circumstances. These chapters invite us to explore transformation from the margins, where power, privilege, and both oppression and resistance are at play. These chapters encourage learning at the edge leading to an expansion of knowledge of transformation. The predominance of the role of relationships is noteworthy in these chapters as they address transformation in post-colonial and dire circumstances.

David Newhouse and colleagues (Chapter 27) describe a partnership between indigenous and settler persons to create a transformative education experience for an Indigenous Course Requirement in East-coast Canada, as part of the Canadian national commitment to Truth and Reconciliation. The experience resulted in a deeper understanding of the importance of indigenous education pedagogies in fostering transformation, based on specific behaviors of instructors. They learned that increasing the possibility of creating a transformative learning experience for students centered on four themes: Self as Teacher/Learner, Responsibility to Be Kind, Responsibility to Show Humility, and Stories Matter, Feelings Matter. At the other end of the country on Canada's West coast, Carey Newman and Catherine Etmanski (Chapter 28), an Indigenous master carver and a settler, describe how an individual journey seeded collective transformation. The creation of The Witness Blanket by Carey for an art installation led to legal-structural change, enacted through ceremony, in an innovative stewardship agreement for collective responsibility for The Witness Blanket. The chapter illustrates how bearing witness can promote a sense of responsibility, deep enough to propel individual, collective, and structural change.

Across the globe from South Africa and Zimbabwe, Moyra Keane and colleagues (Chapter 29) share stories grounded in the "right of passage from closed worlds to connected possibilities." Theirs are stories of the expansion of worlds and of becoming, where the sharing of stories facilitates an organic process of growth through, and into, awareness of one's place in the world. Also from the post-colonial context of South Africa, Sal Muthayan (Chapter 30) uses the Art of Facilitation to enable learners to act as agents of transformation. She uses storytelling as decolonizing and empowering methodology and participatory approaches to stimulate the thinking and feeling processes within the learner. She enables the co-creation of the curriculum, through which a passageway is created, linking old ways of knowing to new ways of being, a reclaiming of identity. Muthayan reminds that transformation work grounded in decolonizing methodologies is critical in post-colonial societies where "there is a disjuncture between who we were, who we are and who we can or want to be."

Bill Ashcroft (Chapter 31) discusses the role of colonial writers in actively transforming the discourses and technologies of colonial dominance, primarily through literature. The underlying function of this transformation has been to take hold of representation, and in this process, literary writing becomes a medium of transformation of language and dominant discourses paramount. Following Ashcroft, Mitsunori Misawa (Chapter 32) examines how transformative learning influences social justice that is anti-bullyist in practice. This chapter addresses how some Asian and Asian American faculty deal with bullying and how they cope with their experiences of bullying from the perspective of transformative learning. This chapter addresses non-Western ways of knowing and how that epistemological perspective facilitates or challenges the transformative learning process for some Asian and Asian Americans who experienced situations where bullying took place.

Paul Akpomuje and colleagues (Chapter 33) draw from two studies to advance the conception of informal transformative learning in humanitarian crises circumstances and everyday life transitions, such as retirement. The authors explore how participants in the studies made meaning of their iconic and traumatic experiences through processes of informal learning, which combines the rational and extra-rational perspectives on transformation. They position context as central to shifting perspectives. Likewise, Fodé Beaudet (Chapter 34) describes what it takes to shift our assumptions when supporting learners in dire circumstances. He defines these learners as those in circumstances where: (1) The security and safety of learners are at risk; (2) The power dynamics implicitly or explicitly condemns changes to a system; (3) The funding architecture is incompatible with the complexity of the situation; and (4) The change narrative is exploited by maligned actors. In these circumstances, Beaudet argues that developing a dialogic mindset where co-designing transformational change with learners without the arbitrary mental boundaries of time, with learning framed as a goal instead of a predetermined outcome, creates a new passageway and openness to transformation for learners and facilitators.

We follow Taj Johns (Chapter 35) as she navigates identity as a Black woman in the United States journeying through understanding and transforming oppression and internalized racism using art as a tool for transformation. Johns offers practices for the reader through collage, art, and writing on a journey to "turn the lights on," moving through transformation to integrate new roles and perspectives. Randee Lawrence (Chapter 36) guides us in an odyssey through music, visual arts, theater, dance, writing, and dreams to demonstrate how engaging with the imaginal surfaces unconscious knowledge that can lead to transformative outcomes.

Elizabeth Pope (Chapter 37) illustrates how transformation is reliant upon interpersonal relationships in her study of interfaith dialogues. The chapter shows the importance of humanizing relationships through Buber's seminal I/Thou relationships, to create perspective transformation of another religious tradition. The section ends with Lynam and colleagues' (Chapter 38) description of the relationship between individual and collective development, using the I/We model to examine how individuals and collectives grow and develop, building capacity to navigate the complex challenges that we face today as a human family. They describe how the Generating Transformative Change program, a multidisciplinary, action-learning program delivered on three continents (North America, Oceania, and Africa), focuses on transformative approaches to leadership and human development through Differentiation, Embodiment, Integration, and Enactment. As a result, participants develop the ability for meta-awareness and meta sense-making at the collective level, and the ability to witness the collective in ways that support the emergence of new insight and the transformation of I/We, in the past, present, and for future possibilities.

Through this provocation, the use of language, stories, and storytelling evokes a deep knowing of self and others through imaginal engagement, the power of witness, and joining the other. This deeper exploration of self-in-collective generates the emergence of previously unknown awareness and knowing, a dance at the edge of the (un)known, where actors choose agency in dire circumstances. The unique voices of Indigenous worldviews and post-colonial stories of resistance are evident as validated in the qualitative keyword analysis of the chapters in this provocation.

The power of witnessing to create movement for collective action and transformation is evident in Carey Newman's description of the Witness Blanket (WB) experience.

> As more and more related projects evolve, I have become curious about what it is that empowers those who are moved to action. I believe the answer is connected to the witnessing described above. I have also observed that the impetus to action occurs when a person's understanding moves from intellectual to personal. However, there are other layers related to collective truth (Newman & Etmanski, 2019) and emotional dissonance. ... Collective truth is co-created through these collective memories and in the case of the WB, collective truth is also found in the items from which it is made. Each piece is itself a witness that carries meaning not only through the stories of the person who gave it or the memories of what occurred within the institution it was collected from, but by its own presence, colours, textures and marks of age, contributes a tangible element that anchors the stories and memories. Many Canadians were structurally denied from knowing about the genocide of Canadian colonialism (MacDonald, 2019) and grew up believing in a progressive and just Canada. When the WB shatters that reality by exposing the collective truth

of residential schools, the result can be what I describe as emotional dissonance. ... When looked at as disorientating dilemmas (Mezirow, 1991), or catalysts (Lawrence & Cranton, 2015) these moments of fracture open space for critical reflection and the possibility for transformation. I have started to think of the WB as having its own small orbit, complete with a gravitational pull that draws people, including me, into action.

We propose therefore, that there is power from the margins, where agency in spite of marginal experiences leads to collective transformation.

Proposition III: Imaginal expressions of marginal experiences evoke storytelling and witnessing, sparking personal and collective identity (re)storying and action. Transformation-in-Action.

Provocation IV: Challenges and Emerging Future for Transformation

In summer 2020, I woke up one day to my alarm that was set in time to join our Handbook Editorial team call prior to switching into my first work meeting of the day. After my second snooze that morning though, I still could not move. My blanket seemed to be extra heavy, keeping me locked in place. My fingers knew what to do before my brain began to process the moment. I sent a note to the team that I couldn't join that morning as I needed a break from it all. "It all" was the anti-Black racism ravaging the world and the break I needed was from the experience of aloneness that was creeping into my bones in most of the spaces I occupy, visibly invisible as people in these spaces spoke of the events occurring with incredulity and as a third person experience in my presence, including on the Handbook team. I am still wrestling with the disorientation of the cuts and slights that come with the pervasiveness of systemic anti-Black racism, especially from privileged friends and allies. I wonder what is needed to further awaken the world to the transformations at the door...
    —Yabome

The chapters in Provocation IV explore the phenomenon of transformation from diverse disciplines, sparking new understandings of transformation through engaging the dialectics of theory and practice. They offer insights bridging disciplines and contexts, pointing to global implications and ways of engaging the complex and ever-changing world in which we live.

The study of physical science has flourished for centuries. As we entered the twenty-first century, social scientists looked to complexity science, nonlinear dynamics, and chaos theory, and more recently neuroscience, to better understand change in human systems. The chapters in this section explore understandings of transformation through a lens of complexity.

Glenda Eoyang (Chapter 39) applies a theory of complex change to individual and collective learning and offers a call to action to challenge and expand on complexity-informed theory of transformational change. Kathleen Taylor and Catherine Marineau (Chapter 40) explore how affective neuroscience emphasizes the essential contribution of emotion and the role of an embodied brain in all aspects of cognition, enabling adult educators to approach transformative learning in creative new ways. Elizabeth Lange (Chapter 41) recaps the key findings from New Science, identifies the key elements of the Relational Turn, and discusses the application to transformative learning. She introduces two new streams of thought for consideration in the transformation process—alchemical and indigenous insights—and directs our attention toward what is needed to create a sustainable future.

Four chapters explicitly foreground social change. Henning Salling Olesen (Chapter 42) reserves the term transformation for substantial societal change. He presents a psycho-societal approach that theorizes individual and collective learning, and sees learning and other subjective processes as embodied in the social practice of concrete living people. With attention to learning in everyday life, his studies highlight potential transformations of the societal ecology of work life, with an outlook to wider society. Dante Caramellino and colleagues (Chapter 43) apply transformative learning theory in the areas of radicalization and violent radicalization. Through an example from the Centre for the Prevention of Radicalization Leading to Violence they demonstrate that the prevention of violent behavior connected to radicalization can be faced educationally. Scott G. Chaplowe and colleagues (Chapter 44) examine evaluation's potential as a driver for transformational learning and change. Their chapter is grounded in evaluation's past and potential role in sustainable development. They discuss the uptake and influence of complex systems analysis, and practical as well as political consideration of the potholes (obstacles) and bridges (enablers) for transformational evaluation. Petra T. Buergelt and Douglas Paton (Chapter 45) create a passageway between disaster risk reduction, ancient and Indigenous cultures, and transformative learning. They propose that the crisis is spiritual in nature and that the antidote appears to be the remembering, cultivating, and living according to our sacred nature and the ancestral laws. Accomplishing this requires people in Western cultures to expand their current rational worldview toward a spiritual worldview engaging interconnected extra-rational transformative pathways, specifically individuation, nature, and arts.

Several chapters focus on enhancing transformative learning practices. Christina Schlattner (Chapter 46) connects transformative learning theory and Lakoff and Johnson's work in embodied knowledge, which demonstrates all constructed meaning is embodied, even that which is rationally arrived at. Drawing her lived experience, she demonstrates how embodiment is a key to transformative learning, and how it can enhance transformative learning practices. Linden West (Chapter 47) engages languages from depth psychology, popular education, and soul work to help us in our learning quest. He challenges the neglect of spiritual and liberatory religious insight in our contemporary language, and the danger this brings of ontological sterility, psychological restriction and spiritual alienation. He invites us to consider the possibility of finding a living, more eclectic language doing justice to the depth, richness, vibrancy, and mystery of learning from experience. Bem Le Hunte and colleagues (Chapter 48) describe designing and facilitating transformative experiences. They identify principles of education design for creating peak experiences resulting in provocations for expansion of consciousness and integration of whole being and many ways of knowing.

Alexis Kokkos (Chapter 49) responds to the question in the theoretical field and educational practice, namely the extent to which young people may engage in transformative learning. The chapter explores relevant theoretical views and educational practices and makes the argument that young people are potentially able to be involved in transformation of their problematic points of view, provided that this process is tailored to the specific needs and capabilities of each age group. Involving youth in the transformation of their problematic points of view is an important step in developing capacity for people to respond to our increasingly complex world.

Sarah Owusu (Chapter 50) calls for a new praxis that allows us to engage differently with transformation itself. Like Rorty's call to the ethos of invention and search for new vocabulary, Owusu goes to metaphysics and philosophy to reanimate transformation praxis and language. She offers insight into the oscillating balance that the transformation practitioner must hold—a space she names as being in-transformation—in order to contain and catalyze transformation. Owusu writes:

> To have a hope of transformation we need a praxis that works with what I call in-transformation, the oscillating balance between "smoke" and "crystal". I introduce these terms (written about by the French biophysicist and philosopher, Henri Altan (1979), but gifted to me in the journey I describe in this chapter) to explore transformation praxis in a new way. 'Crystal' is the structured, linear, logical and certain of making plans and taking action. 'Smoke' is the ambiguous, curious, emergent and fluid of exploratory discovery and reflection...Being in-transformation is urgent and necessary, but we do not do transformation for the sake of transformation. The praxis must be applied with respect and responsibility to the complex challenges of our time to move the human collective towards not a destination, but a fundamental and meaningful shift. Towards what has been described as 'a sustainable, non-self-terminating, thriving, anti-fragile world' (Schmachtenberger, 2017a). The work of the transformation practitioner is to show up boldly, both knowing and not knowing, to hold smoke and crystal lightly, in order to bring the future to life.

In essence, Owusu speaks of an emergence of transformation that is fundamentally different in form than what we have known and that we need to leave room for. Her work allows us to think of ourselves as dwelling in the ambiguity of being in-transformation, in the place in-between knowing and not knowing, until a new way emerges.

Our proposition follows this thinking, that by dwelling in-transformation at the intersection of multidisciplinary and transdisciplinary knowing, the unknown starts to emerge and become known.

Proposition IV: It is in dwelling in the unknown spaces between multidisciplinary and transdisciplinary ways of knowing that transformation emerges. In-Transformation.

CLOSING INVITATIONS

I think working with the Handbook editorial team provided me with various occasions to reflect on my journey as a scholar-practitioner and as one of the editorial team members of the Handbook. Our team members

have diverse backgrounds in terms of geographic locations, positionality, and scholarship. I really appreciated their insights, ideas, and plans from the start when we did several brainstorming sessions and then throughout the book development, peer-review, editing and compilation processes. I remember that throughout our collaboration as editors of the handbook, we made our decisions together and moved forward together. It was a wonderful scholarly experience how we consistently moved forward together despite some turbulence such as the global pandemic.
—Mitsu

This Handbook and this chapter bring us here, to an invitation to new passageways into unknown territories that lead to metamorphosis. Sometimes, instrumental or communicative learning is sufficient. However, when we do need new habits of mind and new ways of being, either because the world around us is already changing form or because we find ourselves disrupted, we must choose a transformation journey, or we will inevitably remain mired in stagnation.

As a Handbook community of our editorial team and all the contributors to this volume, we chose to leave our mental home of transformative learning and its disciplinary street of adult learning. We have gone down connected disciplinary roads. We visited sanctuaries and rest stops along the way, where we gained new insights that our transformation depends on each other. We met crossroads leading away from the familiar and the known. We ventured into these unknown streets with new landscapes where the usual rules do not apply. At some dark turns, we met fellow sojourners. We stopped, told stories, witnessed each other, and experienced a deeper call to humanity, where we took action together— transform-in-action. As we learned more, we visited new domains and disciplines and we gave up control, letting ourselves be in-transformation, realizing as noted in Lawrence's chapter that:

> There is wisdom in not knowing. Frankel (2017) believes that doubt and uncertainty are necessary for growth and change. It is necessary to let go of the known, so that the unexpected can occur, making transformation possible. 'When we cannot make sense of our experience at our current level of understanding, we must find a way to enter another world where new meaning and new perspectives emerge' (p. 131).

We have been willing to dance with the unknown. We have accepted the call of our times to individual deep change, where we realize that each of our transformations are bound up in the destinies of the collective (Quinn, 1996). As Ó Tuma (2021) notes on his book jacket for *In the Shelter: Finding a Home in the World:* "it is in the shelter of each other that people live." We try new ways, we operate from Resonance, where we cannot always put words to what is emerging, but we know that we are being ushered into a new way (Gilpin-Jackson, 2020). And so we are here. We have arrived at our next threshold. We invite you to join us and explore these propositions as we invent new language from the living theory of transformative learning, and new passageways into transformation.

Proposition I: Transformation occurs at the nexus of the individual and collective, requiring structural change and collective effort to transform systems.
Transformation-in-Context.
Proposition II: The passageway to transformation is the relational ecology (connection, collective engagement) that evokes the interconnected being and becoming of humanity.
Transformation-in-Connection.
Proposition III: Imaginal expressions of marginal experiences evoke storytelling and witnessing, sparking personal and collective identity (re)storying and action.
Transformation-in-Action.
Proposition IV: It is in dwelling in the unknown spaces between multidisciplinary and transdisciplinary ways of knowing that transformation emerges.
In-Transformation.

References

Barbuto, J. E. (2000). Influence triggers: A framework for understanding follower compliance. *Leadership Quarterly, 11*(3), 365–387. https://doi.org/10.1016/S1048-9843(00)00045-X

Beals, F., Kidman, J., & Funaki, H. (2020). Insider and outsider research: Negotiating self at the edge of the emic/etic divide. *QUAL INQ, 26*(6). https://doi.org/10.1177/1077800419843950

Cranton, P., & Taylor, E. W. (2012). Transformative learning theory: Seeking a more unified theory. In E. W. Taylor & P. Cranton and Associates (Eds.), *Handbook of transformative learning: Theory, research and practice* (pp. 3–20). Wiley.

Gilpin-Jackson, Y. (2020). *Transformation after trauma: The power of resonance.* Peter Lang Publishers.

hooks, b. (1990). Marginality as a site of resistance. In R. Ferguson, M. Gever, T. Minh-ha, & C. West (Eds.), *Out there: Marginalization and contemporary cultures* (pp. 241–243). MIT Press.

Lawrence (2010). Deciphering multidisciplinary and transdisciplinary contributions. *Transdisciplinary Journal of Engineering and Science, 1*(2010), 111–116. https://doi.org/10.22545/2010/0003

O'Donohue, J. (2008). *To bless the space between us: A book of blessings.* Penguin Random House.

Ó Tuma, P. (2021). *In the shelter: Finding a home in the world.* Broadleaf Books

Rorty, R. (1989). *Contingency, irony, and solidarity.* Cambridge University Press.

Taylor, E. W., & Cranton, P. (2012). Reflecting back and looking forward. In E. W. Taylor & P. Cranton and Associates (Eds.), *Handbook of transformative learning: Theory, research and practice.* Wiley.

Taylor, E. W., & Cranton, P. (2013). A theory in progress?: Issues in transformative learning theory. *European Journal for Research on the Education and Learning of Adults, 4*(1), 35–47. https://doi.org/10.3384/rela.2000-7426.rela5000

Quinn, R. E. (1996). *Deep change: Discovering the leader within.* Jossey-Bass.

Wickham, H. (2016). *ggplot2: Elegant graphics for data analysis.* Springer-Verlag. https://ggplot2.tidyverse.org

Wickham, H., Averick, M., Bryan, J., Chang, W., McGowan, L. D., François, R., Grolemund, G., Hayes, A., Henry, L., Hester, J., Kuhn, M., Pedersen, T. L., Miller, E., Bache, S. M., Müller, K., Ooms, J., Robinson, D., Seidel, D. P., Spinu, V., ... Yutani, H. (2019). Welcome to the tidyverse. *Journal of Open Source Software, 4*(43), 1686. https://doi.org/10.21105/joss.01686

INDEX

A

academic bullying, 580, 581

Action Research Transformations (ART), 183, 187, 189, 195, 196, 512

Actor Network Theory (ANT), 165, 170–174, 176–178, 922

Adaptive Action, 707–709, 714

adult bullying, 572, 574

adult development, 153, 168, 181, 186, 187, 189, 191, 194, 351, 367–369, 678–680

affective neuroscience, 718–721, 724, 725, 729, 933

Africa, 227, 471, 532, 561, 566, 618, 678, 905, 917, 931

African, 86, 147–149, 151, 222, 224–226, 228, 233, 234, 382, 384, 469–472, 474, 528–534, 537, 538, 541, 547, 550, 551, 553, 561, 562, 566, 575, 579, 594, 627, 630, 633, 635, 639, 640, 722, 723, 902, 905, 906, 908, 909, 926, 927

agency, 54, 55, 60, 62–64, 66, 68, 70, 71, 112, 132, 188, 225, 262, 264, 273, 286, 338, 344, 349, 384, 451, 463, 465, 473–475, 479, 524, 539, 559, 569, 620, 623, 736, 737, 745, 753, 754, 757, 759, 795, 838, 839, 859, 860, 908, 926, 931, 932

alchemy, 734, 738–741, 814

ancient paradigm, 811, 825

anti-bullyist practice, 574, 586, 587

AQAL, 412, 414, 419–421, 425, 926

art, 36, 78, 79, 81, 113, 134, 148, 295, 397, 400–403, 405, 449–455, 463, 503, 504, 513, 514, 516, 538–540, 549, 552, 553, 560, 564–567, 650, 651, 654, 656, 728, 734, 738, 739, 744, 811, 818–820, 822, 826–828, 918, 929, 930, 934

artifacts, 111, 114, 115, 124, 125, 165, 171, 172, 174, 176, 177, 728, 835

© The Editor(s) (if applicable) and The Author(s), under exclusive license to Springer Nature Switzerland AG 2022

A. Nicolaides et al. (eds.), *The Palgrave Handbook of Learning for Transformation*, https://doi.org/10.1007/978-3-030-84694-7

940 INDEX

artistic expression, 406, 646, 648, 650, 653
arts-based adult education, 448
Asian American and Pacific Islander (AAPI), 573, 574, 576, 577, 580–586
Auroville, 864–866, 868, 872–878
awareness, 9, 13, 29, 38, 78, 79, 111, 132–135, 138, 142, 151, 158, 167, 185, 190, 220, 222, 235, 252, 284, 286, 287, 298, 370, 387, 390, 396, 397, 405, 412, 416, 417, 419, 423–425, 442, 448, 456, 486, 487, 489–492, 496, 499, 526, 532, 534, 538, 543, 552, 637, 646, 650, 654, 680, 682, 685, 687–690, 693, 694, 711, 720, 723, 724, 729, 741, 756, 760, 775–779, 811, 812, 815, 818, 826, 836, 843, 859, 865, 871, 877, 929, 931

B

becoming, 18, 25, 28, 36, 46, 100, 123, 133, 135, 176, 187, 211, 218, 235, 253, 294, 313, 344, 353, 357, 382, 403, 414, 452, 471, 472, 474, 477, 480, 523, 532, 549, 597, 600, 631, 634, 637, 667, 671, 683, 684, 689, 692, 694, 711, 736, 737, 740, 745, 773, 779, 802, 814, 826, 833, 855, 856, 867, 889, 890, 899, 900, 909, 910, 914, 927, 929
being, 3, 6–8, 13, 17, 33, 34, 46, 47, 50–54, 69, 77, 79, 80, 82, 86, 92, 95, 97, 103, 111, 118, 122, 125, 130–133, 142–144, 155, 156, 159, 172, 182, 185, 188, 189, 194, 202, 204, 210, 211, 231, 235, 242–244, 246, 247, 250–253, 260, 269, 280–284, 286–288, 290, 292, 293, 298, 306, 310, 313–315, 317, 319, 321, 333–335, 338–342, 344, 347, 351, 353–355, 358, 366, 389, 391, 396, 399, 402, 406, 413, 417–419, 421, 423, 424, 432, 436, 439–441, 448, 450, 455, 458, 462, 463, 471, 479, 487, 495, 513, 515, 523, 524, 529–531, 533, 541, 542, 544, 545, 547, 548, 550, 553, 558–560, 563–565, 567, 568, 579, 585, 586, 591, 596, 600, 601, 605, 606, 614, 615, 619, 623, 627–630, 632, 633, 635, 637, 639–641, 646, 649, 651, 661, 662, 665, 669, 679, 682, 683, 685, 686, 688, 690–692, 694, 717, 719, 723, 724, 728, 729, 734, 735, 740, 743–746, 748, 752, 771, 773, 780, 781, 789, 790, 793, 810–813, 815–818, 820, 823, 825–828, 841, 842, 844, 856, 865–867, 872–874, 876, 877, 887, 890, 899, 904, 905, 907–910, 914–917, 927, 929, 934–937
bias, 125, 243, 244, 253, 271, 336, 350, 412, 413, 416, 417, 419, 422, 464, 540, 559, 574–577, 586, 640, 641, 666, 667
Black spirituality, 147–149, 155, 157–160, 922
body, 13, 14, 16, 25, 27, 36, 64, 92, 111, 117, 132, 133, 135, 138, 140, 143, 150, 195, 204, 210, 246, 249, 284, 286, 399, 403, 414, 417, 421, 433, 441, 448, 460, 489, 490, 511, 544, 564, 638, 682, 684, 685, 688, 689, 718–721, 725, 741–743, 747,

757, 765, 813, 832, 834, 837, 838, 841, 842, 844, 845, 860, 877, 902, 903, 905, 907
body-brain, 718, 725–727
Buber, M., 660–662, 664, 665, 668, 669, 672, 855, 856, 930
Burren Leadership Retreat (The Retreat), 399

C

case study, 60, 113, 281, 338, 364, 365, 596, 660, 662, 804, 839, 852, 867, 868, 878, 891, 892
CDE Model, 706
Christian, 140, 154, 490, 498, 660, 661, 664, 666, 669, 735, 739, 814, 821, 823, 827, 857
Civic Studies, 54, 55
coaching, 169, 337–339, 341–343, 369, 528, 531, 678, 897, 905, 924, 925
co-create curriculum, 538, 552
cognitive science, 720, 724, 725, 834
collective intelligence, 376, 685, 688, 694
colonization, 50, 52, 260, 270, 272, 488, 490, 496, 553, 563, 566, 733, 740, 827
communicate, 95, 111, 289, 293, 333, 334, 339, 341, 366, 390, 421, 728
community development, 65, 66, 91, 263–266, 540, 541, 550
complexity, 8, 61, 70, 123, 144, 169, 170, 172, 183, 187, 189–191, 196, 209, 217, 259, 262, 263, 270, 352, 364, 367–369, 396, 405, 423, 442, 539, 613, 616, 619, 621, 622, 671, 679, 692, 701, 705, 713, 718, 734, 742, 789–794, 800–803, 820, 865,

884, 897, 899, 906, 908, 914, 921, 924, 925, 930, 933
complex systems analysis, 802, 933
conflict transformation, 187, 191, 195
consciousness, 9, 12, 13, 30, 38, 39, 100, 131, 132, 134, 135, 144, 167, 280, 281, 298, 306, 368, 404, 416, 419, 421, 433, 448, 449, 451, 491, 499, 503, 508, 514, 517, 522, 523, 547, 560, 562, 563, 615, 627, 628, 634, 636, 647, 651, 678, 679, 682, 690, 693, 734, 736, 742, 747, 752, 762–764, 772, 773, 812–814, 850, 855, 865–867, 869, 874, 877, 879, 884, 924, 934
container, 138, 139, 192, 374–376, 418, 423, 440, 441, 542, 543, 545, 619, 706, 710, 711, 748, 905, 907
contemplative practices, 130, 134–137, 140, 144
context, 7, 8, 29, 38, 47, 51, 61, 62, 67, 68, 71, 76, 77, 79–87, 92, 93, 96–98, 101, 102, 104, 105, 112, 113, 115, 118, 124–126, 135, 137, 147–153, 155, 158, 160, 167, 170, 172–176, 178, 183, 184, 188, 192, 193, 200, 202, 218, 220, 223, 226, 228, 233, 234, 258, 259, 261, 262, 264, 267, 282, 303, 304, 306, 311, 313–315, 317, 320, 322–327, 333–337, 341, 348, 352, 353, 355, 366, 373, 374, 397, 399, 403, 413, 423, 425, 429, 431, 433, 434, 436, 438–441, 451, 471, 477–479, 488, 496, 504–506, 510, 515, 522, 530, 532, 533, 538, 539, 542, 544, 546, 547, 550, 552,

942 INDEX

553, 562, 574, 579, 580, 585, 591–596, 603, 605–607, 611, 613, 621, 660, 662, 664, 671, 672, 678, 682, 684–686, 692, 694, 702, 704, 705, 708, 709, 712–714, 727, 740, 748, 752, 754–756, 761, 762, 770–772, 774, 776–778, 790, 795, 800, 802, 811, 826, 836, 841, 864, 865, 867–869, 872, 876–878, 893, 899, 905, 906, 909, 915, 916, 923–926, 928–930, 932

conversation, 3, 14, 125, 130, 139, 182, 214, 248, 251, 252, 268, 344, 345, 359, 371, 374, 413, 414, 421, 422, 430, 433, 434, 439, 441, 443, 459, 470, 474, 476, 498, 526, 544, 586, 618–620, 622, 624, 639, 646, 656, 662, 665, 745, 854, 873, 875, 901–904

coronavirus, 646, 898

creativity, 110, 113, 115–124, 126, 131, 135, 221, 289, 295, 349, 354, 397, 401, 406, 452, 560, 594, 655, 684, 718, 818, 834, 867, 873, 922

critical incident technique (CIT), 152, 153

critical pedagogy, 35, 63, 65, 68, 69

Critical Race, 442, 574, 576

critical realism, 921

critical reflection, 28–30, 33, 34, 37, 39, 52, 61, 63–67, 69–71, 83, 103, 112, 126, 159, 262, 264, 303, 305, 306, 311, 314, 315, 317, 323, 325, 471, 513, 532, 594, 595, 598, 600, 602–605, 633, 646, 662, 666, 667, 717, 772, 835, 844, 884, 888, 890, 892, 915, 924, 932

critical theory, 25–28, 30–35, 40, 48, 50, 53, 61, 66, 756

crystal, 898–900, 902–910, 935

Curriculum for Being, 865, 867, 873, 879

D

defining transformation, 10, 75, 833, 834

Deliberately Developmental Organization (DDO), 348, 350–359, 924, 925

development, 2, 8, 10, 12, 15, 16, 26, 28, 31, 33, 39, 46, 54, 62, 64, 65, 85, 96, 110, 111, 120, 131, 134, 135, 137, 147, 148, 158, 165, 168, 182, 187, 189, 190, 194, 257–260, 262–265, 267, 268, 272, 301–304, 308, 309, 316, 323, 324, 326, 327, 337, 338, 347, 349, 352–359, 364–370, 373–377, 385, 389, 397, 414, 418, 419, 430, 432, 433, 436, 437, 442, 472, 476, 488, 526, 538, 540, 545, 549, 550, 552, 557, 562, 564, 567, 568, 577, 585, 594, 596, 619, 620, 636, 678–681, 683–686, 705, 710, 712, 714, 729, 742, 751, 753, 754, 759, 761, 764, 774, 777, 780, 781, 786, 787, 789, 791–795, 797–799, 802, 811, 821, 866, 877, 885–887, 898, 924–927, 930, 931

dialogic, 430, 612, 617, 618, 623, 655, 656, 661, 662, 669, 672, 869, 902, 924, 930

dialogue, 36, 64, 80, 85, 93, 103, 135, 140, 184, 186, 193–195, 293, 348, 354, 375, 400, 414–416, 423, 432, 436, 438, 477, 532, 596, 618–620, 622,

623, 628, 639, 651, 652, 660, 662, 665–668, 670–672, 715, 760, 818, 849, 855–857, 884, 899, 901, 902, 904, 905, 907
digestion, 741
disassembly, 741, 744
disciplinary power, 250, 252
Disorientation Index, 98, 99
disorienting dilemma, 31, 34, 35, 47, 75, 81, 82, 84, 98, 103, 112, 134, 148, 153, 201, 205, 280, 281, 287, 298, 367, 423, 449, 508, 540, 573, 580, 585, 586, 594, 599, 623, 627, 628, 630–632, 634, 642, 646, 647, 664, 666, 724, 741, 781, 810, 839
diversity, 9, 184, 251, 283, 348–351, 354, 355, 359, 383, 391, 412, 413, 419, 424, 441, 448, 450, 452, 522, 567, 571, 574, 576, 577, 583, 586, 587, 613, 661, 667, 669, 686, 775, 776, 818, 877, 891, 900, 916, 917
dreams, 134, 213, 228, 233, 234, 242, 374, 412, 465, 537, 538, 542, 643, 649, 650, 656, 739, 746, 812, 850, 851, 853, 930

E
edge emotion, 12, 303, 306–309, 311, 315–317, 320, 321, 323–326, 925
education, 2, 5, 9, 12, 13, 16, 17, 27, 35–39, 51, 52, 59–61, 63, 66, 68, 69, 71, 91, 92, 101, 103, 104, 109, 110, 117, 123, 126, 131, 140, 142, 147, 150, 166, 171, 174, 176, 185, 188, 189, 201, 203, 207–210, 218, 231, 259, 260, 267, 273, 301–304, 308, 310, 311, 314, 322, 327,

336, 348, 351, 365, 368, 397, 418, 430, 442, 448, 449, 470, 486–488, 522, 525–527, 529, 530, 532, 533, 539, 540, 549, 552, 557, 573–577, 580, 595, 598, 599, 604, 616, 619, 646, 705, 710, 714, 723, 729, 736–738, 754, 757, 770, 773, 776, 778, 780, 788, 815, 817, 818, 821–823, 826, 833, 845, 848–851, 855, 857, 859, 860, 866, 868, 874, 884, 890, 892, 893, 900, 903, 918, 922, 924, 934
Educational relationality, 736
elder, 129, 213, 252, 453, 489, 491, 492, 497, 499, 534, 627, 825
emancipation, 27, 28, 33, 38, 40, 50, 60–62, 66, 67, 70, 71, 102, 167, 174, 183, 505, 646, 773, 921
emancipatory learning, 28, 35, 59, 76, 886, 890
emancipatory power, 250, 251
embodied/embody, 125, 130, 133, 140–144, 171, 185, 201, 203, 204, 206, 210, 243, 251, 303–307, 312, 317, 319, 320, 325, 327, 388, 413, 433, 438, 442, 494, 504, 507, 564, 645, 646, 652, 655, 656, 688–690, 692, 718, 720, 725, 726, 729, 737, 742, 744, 747, 752, 758–760, 822, 828, 833–835, 839–845, 874, 900, 925, 926, 933, 934
embodied brain, 718, 720, 721, 725, 933
embodied learning, 202, 208–210, 718, 758, 844
Emergence, 77, 170, 219, 281, 359, 397, 565, 567, 623, 624, 683,

688, 690, 692, 693, 728, 736, 742, 748, 811, 931, 935

emotion, 14, 77, 132, 134, 135, 143, 144, 150, 182–184, 186–195, 212, 242, 281, 289, 296, 298, 306, 307, 309–312, 317–321, 323, 324, 391, 401, 405, 440, 441, 451, 489, 490, 495, 496, 542, 545, 599, 600, 635–637, 642, 646, 647, 650–652, 654–656, 682, 708, 717–721, 724–726, 728, 729, 737, 819, 820, 833–835, 842–845, 885, 901, 914, 924, 933

emotion-laden, 724, 729

empathetic viewing, 597, 603, 604

empathy, 29, 87, 104, 143, 144, 281, 290, 373, 401, 405, 415, 416, 430, 431, 438, 440, 442, 545, 546, 586, 655, 711, 747, 762, 779, 818, 819, 852, 856, 908, 928

empiricism, 850–852, 860

empowerment, 67, 99, 133, 257, 262–264, 267, 268, 271, 294, 370, 381, 473, 538, 780, 788, 838, 841, 924

encounter, 33, 53, 64, 81, 86, 202, 219, 235, 281, 289, 403, 404, 406, 441, 494, 525, 529, 548, 566, 611, 612, 640, 659, 660, 665, 666, 685, 691, 852, 854, 858, 898, 899

energy fields, 735, 741, 742

epistemology, 14, 16, 31, 99, 102, 105, 150, 152, 171, 173, 268, 272, 449, 450, 477, 497, 532, 552, 725, 734, 737, 754, 811, 848, 858, 859, 865, 870, 878

epochal shift, 733

equality, 62, 68, 259, 271, 381–391, 462, 495, 516, 791, 857, 925

equity, 354, 383, 385, 388, 412, 413, 419, 420, 422, 430, 431, 442, 532, 571, 574–576, 583, 586, 587, 799, 914, 915

evaluation, 101, 167, 194, 259, 263, 268, 370, 399, 470, 471, 473, 476–478, 785–795, 797, 799–805, 844, 933

exhibition, 448–455, 459–465, 926

experience, 6, 11–14, 26–28, 33–40, 46, 47, 60, 61, 71, 77, 79, 80, 82–87, 93–96, 98–100, 102–105, 111–113, 115, 124–126, 130, 133, 134, 137, 139–142, 144, 147, 148, 150–153, 158–160, 166–169, 173, 174, 176, 177, 185, 190–192, 195, 201–203, 205, 206, 209, 213, 214, 218–221, 225, 233–235, 242, 250–252, 258, 261, 263–265, 272, 280–283, 286, 288–290, 292–296, 303, 304, 306–317, 319–327, 336–338, 350, 351, 353–355, 357–359, 364, 366–368, 370, 373, 375–377, 382–384, 386, 396–402, 404, 406, 413–416, 418–421, 423, 424, 431–434, 436, 437, 439, 440, 447–450, 469, 473, 475, 477, 479, 486, 487, 490, 492, 493, 496, 498, 506–511, 513–515, 522, 524, 526, 528, 532, 534, 540–542, 545–551, 553, 558, 560–563, 572–574, 576, 577, 579–581, 583–587, 592–597, 599–603, 605, 612, 615, 617, 620, 623, 628, 630, 633–636, 640, 642, 647, 648, 651, 654, 655, 659–665, 668–672, 683, 685, 686, 688–690, 692, 703, 709–711,

718, 720–722, 724–729, 747,
748, 752–760, 763–765, 770,
773–776, 794, 811, 813–815,
820, 822, 823, 825, 826,
832–837, 839, 841–844, 848,
849, 851, 854, 856–860, 864,
866–879, 884, 885, 887, 890,
891, 897, 899, 901–903, 905,
906, 910, 914, 916, 917, 919,
922, 924, 926–932, 934, 936,
937
extended epistemology, 725, 726

F

facilitation, 104, 310, 311, 478,
538–540, 549, 552, 553, 672,
701, 709, 714, 843, 844, 873,
929
facilitator, 137, 231, 303, 364, 371,
373, 375, 387, 401, 412, 413,
436, 476, 478, 479, 541, 542,
544, 546, 548, 549, 552, 595,
619, 622, 672, 865, 870, 874,
875, 917, 926, 930
fallback, 187, 188, 190, 192
freedom, 3, 29, 33, 49, 53, 60–63,
65–68, 70, 71, 83, 87, 158–160,
243, 250, 473, 487, 505, 537,
647, 687, 702, 710, 712, 744,
860, 876, 904

G

gestalt, 115, 148, 413, 414, 416,
417, 844, 845, 926

H

Habermas, J., 25–35, 40, 48–54, 66,
167, 183, 921
higher education, 60, 130, 134, 200,
260, 262, 364, 365, 369, 374,

377, 572, 574, 578–581,
583–587, 867, 917, 918, 925
history, 9, 27, 38, 48, 66, 101, 115,
167, 168, 174, 177, 182–184,
186, 194, 203, 209, 212, 218,
219, 223, 231, 232, 250, 258,
266, 268–272, 287, 402, 422,
436, 440, 447, 450, 452, 453,
455, 462, 465, 479, 488–490,
492, 496, 497, 505, 506, 531,
540, 546, 553, 555, 556,
560–562, 568, 575, 641, 687,
692, 699, 703, 706, 740,
754–758, 771, 772, 822, 851,
856, 857, 874, 893, 914
holding environment, 148, 354, 364,
368, 370, 373, 375, 376, 924,
925
holistic, 64, 95, 130–137, 150, 383,
432, 433, 443, 472, 476, 488,
522, 661, 754, 777, 778, 795,
797, 811, 816, 817, 820, 822,
824, 827, 828, 884, 926, 927
horizontal development, 369, 376
human flourishing, 62, 70, 71, 718,
725, 854, 856
humanitarian emergencies (HE),
592–594
Human Systems Dynamics (HSD),
700–702, 704, 708, 715

I

iconic experiences, 591, 593, 594,
596, 601–604
identity, 35, 38, 46, 80, 99, 134,
150, 151, 159, 168, 171, 172,
176, 185, 201, 213, 218, 220,
223, 241–245, 249, 253, 267,
270, 272, 340, 341, 344, 345,
349, 352, 356, 366–369,
371–374, 414–416, 418, 421,
422, 424, 425, 439–441, 450,

493, 504, 505, 524, 525, 529,
540, 542, 544, 545, 547, 553,
559, 562, 563, 571, 579, 592,
594, 615, 634, 639, 649, 652,
655, 682–684, 686, 690, 691,
741, 743, 756, 759, 761, 765,
778, 780, 817, 838, 865, 887,
888, 905, 916, 917, 929, 930,
932, 937
I-It relationship, 661, 662
imaginal space, 399–401, 403, 405,
924, 925
imagination, 35, 38, 39, 67, 76, 77,
79, 92, 119, 120, 123, 229, 282,
289, 290, 395–399, 401,
403–406, 413, 448, 449, 451,
465, 544, 560, 642, 645–647,
649, 656, 657, 718, 724, 728,
754, 763, 764, 815, 818, 819,
842, 856, 860, 898, 905, 910
incidental learning, 109, 922
inclusion, 9, 172, 251, 348–351, 354,
355, 358, 359, 389, 412, 413,
508, 571, 574, 576, 583, 584,
587, 642, 666, 780, 787, 867,
900, 903, 925
Indigenous, 132, 257–269, 272, 273,
450, 453, 458, 461, 470,
472–475, 477, 486–499, 505,
506, 510, 516, 526, 529–532,
541, 547, 551, 553, 564, 565,
567, 568, 734, 736, 740, 804,
810–819, 822, 824–826, 867,
878, 918, 924, 928, 929, 931,
933
Indigenous Course Requirement
(ICR), 488–490, 493, 495, 498,
499, 928
indigenous education, 258–261,
265–267, 272, 488, 924
indigenous education pedagogies,
488, 928

Indigenous knowledge (IK), 2, 131,
257, 261, 265, 266, 272, 273,
470, 472–475, 486, 492, 497,
498, 528–533, 810, 811, 820,
825, 827
Indigenous paradigm, 268, 811, 827
indigenous peoples, 258–262, 264,
266, 267, 272, 273, 473, 486,
488, 490–492, 494, 496, 505,
506, 567, 568, 740, 804, 811,
827, 828, 860, 924
Indigenous rights, 260, 265, 266, 733
Indigenous rites of passage, 734, 740
individualism, 133, 242, 243, 422,
539, 744, 762, 922
individuation, 12, 32, 647, 649, 811,
826, 828, 853, 934
informal learning, 591–596, 598,
602, 603, 605, 606, 738, 752,
928, 930
innovation, 110, 113, 116, 117, 120,
124, 349, 354, 413, 422, 704,
708, 794, 799, 801, 864, 865,
873, 900, 908
inquiry, 2, 13, 15, 16, 18, 26, 55, 69,
112, 113, 117, 119, 120, 124,
135, 182, 183, 185, 186,
191–196, 219, 226, 257, 283,
338, 348, 351, 354, 355, 357,
373, 374, 396, 405, 431, 434,
516, 576, 581, 611, 612,
618–620, 666, 678, 680, 685,
704, 705, 707–715, 721, 724,
811, 812, 864, 867, 876, 909,
920
interdisciplinary, 27, 38, 265, 429,
431, 432, 442, 582, 593, 606
interfaith dialogue, 660, 662–672,
930
internalized oppression, 613, 628,
629, 637, 638, 641, 643

INDEX 947

internalized racism, 416, 628, 629,
631–635, 637–641, 643, 930
interpersonal relationships, 662, 672,
888, 930
in-transformation, 898–900, 904,
906–910, 935–937
intuition, 133, 135, 204, 242, 599,
602, 603, 605, 718, 728, 744,
833, 834, 839, 856, 900–902
intuitive, 13, 29, 295, 399, 406, 413,
603, 604, 638, 650, 651, 654,
728, 729, 739, 746, 759, 854,
876
I/Thou, 849, 855, 856, 930
I-Thou relationship, 660–662, 664,
665, 667–669, 671, 672
I/We model, 683–685, 691, 693, 930

J
Jew, 664
journal writing, 652

K
Kegan, R., 10, 12, 13, 16, 17, 96,
106, 148, 183, 187, 193, 201,
348, 350–353, 355, 367–369,
375, 397, 419, 628, 636, 637,
641, 659, 678, 884

L
language, 2, 4, 6, 10, 14–16, 30, 83,
92, 93, 171, 190, 258, 262, 270,
273, 279, 289, 322, 344, 398,
425, 471, 505, 515, 525, 526,
529, 530, 542, 547, 556–558,
560, 562–564, 566, 568, 598,
648, 699, 702, 735, 747, 748,
753, 756–759, 817, 821, 827,
828, 834, 835, 838, 847–853,
855, 858–860, 877, 898, 902,

903, 908, 910, 918, 919, 921,
929, 931, 934, 937
leadership, 130, 148, 185, 187, 194,
196, 241, 248, 249, 266, 335,
336, 338, 341, 351, 363–377,
388, 396, 397, 399, 403, 404,
406, 407, 415, 460, 478, 551,
605, 616, 621, 678, 679, 685,
690, 694, 703, 712, 714, 722,
790, 803, 905, 908, 917, 918,
925, 931
Leadership for Sustainability
Education (LSE), 130, 131,
137–139
learning, 3, 5, 6, 8–13, 16, 17, 26,
28, 31–40, 45, 46, 48, 50–53,
59–65, 68–70, 76, 92–97, 99,
100, 102–104, 106, 110–113,
117–120, 123–125, 130–144,
148, 150, 151, 153, 154, 160,
166–170, 174, 177, 182–187,
191, 192, 194–196, 201,
203–205, 208–211, 214,
217–219, 221, 231, 242, 244,
253, 261–264, 270, 272, 280,
282, 290, 295, 303, 304, 308,
309, 316, 325–327, 336, 338,
339, 341, 344, 348, 349,
354–356, 358, 359, 364, 366,
369–371, 373, 375–377, 382,
388, 396, 397, 402, 405, 406,
413, 415, 417, 420, 422–425,
432–434, 438, 442, 454, 464,
473, 474, 476, 477, 480,
488–499, 504, 507, 510,
521–525, 528, 530–533,
540–543, 545, 547, 549, 551,
552, 592–596, 598–601, 603,
605–607, 612, 615, 617, 618,
620, 621, 623, 624, 634, 640,
642, 646, 648, 652, 656, 664,
666, 669–672, 678–680, 683,

690, 693, 699, 701–704, 706–708, 713, 714, 717, 718, 720, 722, 724–729, 736–740, 743, 746–748, 751–764, 770, 771, 773, 774, 781, 786, 793, 797, 799, 802, 804, 814, 815, 818, 819, 825, 827, 828, 833, 835, 839, 840, 842–845, 847–850, 852, 853, 858–860, 864, 866, 867, 870–876, 878, 883, 884, 886, 887, 892, 893, 899, 901, 909, 916, 918, 920, 924, 925, 930, 933, 934, 936

learning processes, 31, 39, 51, 68, 111, 117–121, 124, 125, 132, 140, 144, 169–171, 174, 177, 193, 266, 367, 451, 473, 542, 552, 602, 616, 662, 728, 753, 754, 759, 760, 762, 764, 765, 770, 773, 774, 780, 781, 802, 885, 889

legacy, 31, 195, 200, 203, 206, 207, 209, 210, 213, 214, 252, 260, 261, 267, 272, 454, 455, 462, 470, 506, 515, 614, 794, 852

liberate, 3, 46, 53, 252, 399, 405, 413, 839, 860, 925

liberation, 46, 80, 242, 398, 430, 472, 505, 522, 530, 532, 540, 544, 553, 849, 850, 855, 856, 924

life events, 218, 298, 592, 593, 595, 842

lifelong learning, 64, 207–210, 214, 218, 230

listening, 9, 135, 138, 140, 204, 213, 227, 252, 284, 337, 403, 405, 415, 429–434, 436–443, 455, 654, 665, 666, 670, 688, 746, 815, 828, 856, 857, 908, 924, 926

literary works, 75, 77, 83, 85, 87, 558, 811

literature, 12, 15, 39, 54, 61, 76–87, 93, 97, 98, 113, 148, 150, 168, 173, 206, 263, 272, 301, 373, 431, 438, 462, 490, 533, 555–560, 565, 566, 568, 574, 579, 580, 586, 593, 595, 708, 771, 772, 810, 811, 848, 849, 851–853, 855, 857, 859, 868, 884, 908, 916, 918, 922, 926, 929

M

mandala, 642, 643, 651

materialism, 759, 855

meaning making, 148, 151–154, 158, 159, 167, 183, 187, 219, 309, 319, 321, 322, 325, 337, 338, 352, 367, 397, 433, 436, 449, 477, 514, 542, 592, 593, 636, 672, 683, 707, 720, 726, 757, 758, 833, 834, 843, 845, 865, 876, 893, 901, 904, 906, 908, 916

meditation, 135, 138, 140, 141, 184, 202, 207–210, 282–289, 291, 292, 295–297, 400, 640, 739, 743, 870

memory recall, 540, 542, 543, 547, 548

mental exercise, 77, 82

metaphor/metaphorical, 1, 2, 5, 104, 139, 143, 205, 213, 222, 402, 403, 458, 565, 645, 647–650, 656, 702, 726–729, 743, 818–820, 834–836, 840–844, 852, 853, 859, 899, 914, 923

metatheory, 14, 92–94, 96–99, 106, 173

Mezirow, J., 5, 9–14, 16, 17, 25, 26, 28–31, 34, 36, 37, 40, 46–48,

50–53, 60–71, 75, 76, 78–81,
83, 85, 87, 92–94, 102, 103,
106, 110, 111, 115, 116, 124,
133, 148, 151, 159, 165–170,
173, 174, 176, 182, 200, 201,
204–206, 213, 219, 235, 261,
280, 298, 303, 305, 306, 308,
309, 314, 321, 322, 324,
340–342, 347, 367, 375, 397,
423, 433, 448, 449, 464, 471,
487, 513, 539, 573, 580, 594,
595, 603, 628, 630–634, 639,
641, 642, 646, 647, 649, 654,
663, 666, 668, 670, 717, 718,
721, 724, 729, 742, 752, 770,
774, 780, 810, 811, 832, 833,
835, 839, 842, 883, 885,
889–891, 921, 923, 932
mind, 14, 16, 36, 64, 67, 83, 95,
125, 132, 135, 140, 141, 143,
150, 196, 212, 283, 286, 296,
314, 341, 348, 352, 354, 367,
396, 398, 399, 414, 419, 421,
433, 441, 474, 475, 477, 478,
490, 492, 495, 542, 543, 545,
559, 601, 618, 632, 634, 636,
637, 639, 641, 642, 645, 649,
652, 670, 672, 684, 685,
688–690, 713, 718, 719, 721,
722, 727, 729, 741, 758, 801,
812, 814, 818, 819, 822, 841,
844, 851, 890, 891, 893, 936
mindfulness, 100, 102, 135,
138–140, 143, 208, 284, 743
Model Mugging, 832, 834, 836–841,
844
modernity, 7, 8, 49, 221, 229, 347,
555, 560, 563, 565–568, 762,
860
Muslim, 660, 661, 664–670, 775
mystical, 617, 739, 825, 826, 852,
865, 867, 869, 872, 878

N
narrative, 15, 76, 99, 115–117, 137,
149, 152, 157, 173, 193, 209,
218, 220, 221, 223, 225, 245,
283, 335–342, 344, 345, 364,
373, 405, 430, 433, 434,
438–440, 447, 449, 450, 455,
463, 465, 486–488, 490, 492,
493, 496, 506, 521, 524, 532,
534, 541, 553, 560–562, 576,
577, 581, 584, 585, 596,
611–614, 634, 635, 637, 668,
718, 755, 756, 811, 877, 878,
892, 900, 905, 906, 925, 926,
930
nature, 2, 3, 12, 15, 28, 67, 71, 78,
80, 84, 93, 94, 100, 111, 132,
138, 142, 143, 153, 159, 167,
172, 176, 177, 203–205, 207,
208, 210, 214, 243, 253, 262,
281, 284, 286, 288–290, 292,
293, 295, 297–299, 302, 308,
310, 312, 314, 315, 317, 319,
322, 357, 383, 390, 398, 400,
404, 405, 423, 431, 469, 472,
478, 488, 508, 533, 556, 560,
592, 596, 598, 606, 613, 660,
662, 665, 671, 672, 683, 693,
705, 706, 713, 715, 727, 728,
734, 735, 737, 741, 743, 753,
754, 757, 759, 760, 762, 764,
765, 774, 776, 787, 804,
811–828, 833, 839, 842, 853,
865, 870, 872, 877–879, 901,
902, 924, 934
noncoercive, 612, 616–621, 623, 624
normativity, 93, 249, 251, 595
nursing education, 210, 212, 213

O
organization, 8, 35, 36, 46, 106, 122,
170, 178, 333, 334, 336, 339,

342, 343, 348–350, 355–357, 359, 363, 369, 376, 384–389, 391, 392, 496, 563, 612, 617, 620, 621, 654, 661, 679, 682, 736, 743, 748, 753, 755, 757, 761–763, 776, 900–902, 906

organization development (OD), 412, 618, 710, 791, 897, 899, 900, 902, 906, 908

otherness, 79, 84, 577, 859

P

paradigm shift, 173, 351, 442, 534, 540, 724, 792, 793, 810, 908

participatory action research, 15, 469, 651, 924, 926

participatory democracy, 68

Pattern Logic, 705–707, 709, 714

peak transformative experience, 865, 867–869, 874, 876, 878

perspectives, 2, 4, 12, 14, 29, 32, 34, 36, 46, 47, 52–54, 62, 63, 65, 67, 70, 76, 85–87, 92–94, 98, 100, 101, 103, 104, 106, 111, 112, 116, 117, 122, 125, 131, 132, 135, 151–154, 156–159, 165, 167–173, 176–178, 183, 187, 190, 191, 202, 205, 206, 219, 221, 235, 241, 242, 245, 253, 259, 270–272, 284, 290, 294, 303, 305–312, 314–316, 319, 321–325, 338, 341, 342, 345, 348–355, 357–359, 364, 367–372, 375, 377, 387, 391, 396, 398–400, 403, 404, 415, 418–421, 425, 432, 433, 436, 438, 441, 442, 448, 449, 451, 452, 461, 465, 479, 487, 489, 492, 497, 499, 508–510, 514, 517, 522, 524, 532, 535, 540, 561–564, 572–577, 579, 580, 586, 593, 594, 597, 598,

601–603, 605, 606, 631, 637, 642, 647, 659, 670, 671, 679–682, 684–686, 688–690, 701, 702, 710, 722, 724, 727, 752–754, 759–761, 770, 771, 773, 774, 777, 780, 790, 797, 811, 823, 824, 832, 833, 835, 839, 843, 844, 847–849, 855, 856, 874, 884, 889, 890, 893, 916, 920–922, 928–930, 936

perspective transformation, 7, 12, 13, 30, 46–48, 50, 51, 53, 92, 103, 111, 125, 148, 151, 152, 159, 160, 367, 448, 449, 461, 573, 580, 585, 586, 660, 670, 671, 724, 770, 832, 889, 930

philosophical paradigm, 724

pilgrimage, 200–211, 213, 214, 400, 852, 858, 859, 922

place, 7, 8, 10, 18, 65, 84, 96, 98, 105, 119, 133, 139, 153, 157, 172, 183, 190, 194, 203–205, 210, 218, 221, 222, 225, 231, 235, 242, 248, 249, 286, 290, 293, 334, 336, 337, 341, 343, 345, 353, 359, 374, 382, 383, 392, 396, 398, 399, 402–404, 406, 416, 422, 424, 433, 436, 438, 475, 478, 486, 491, 494, 497, 512, 515, 525, 530, 533, 545, 546, 555, 557, 559, 562–565, 568, 573, 574, 582, 585, 592, 595, 596, 606, 612, 619–621, 640, 643, 648, 652, 656, 662, 665, 688, 692, 702, 703, 706, 707, 709, 710, 712, 713, 735, 737, 744, 748, 755, 759, 761, 765, 776, 779, 787, 793, 797, 809, 815, 817, 833, 848, 866, 867, 869, 872–877, 891, 900, 903, 905, 906, 922, 929, 930, 932, 935 post-colonial/postcolonial, 195, 261, 522, 532, 537, 539, 552, 553, 555, 556, 558–563, 566–569, 928, 929, 931

postcolonial transformation, 555, 563, 565, 569

power, 13, 26, 45, 49, 62, 66, 68, 69, 76, 78, 79, 81, 86, 87, 112, 138, 139, 144, 166, 171–174, 178, 182–196, 201–203, 209, 241, 244, 249–252, 259, 261, 267, 270, 271, 280, 289, 298, 348, 349, 353, 374, 381, 385, 392, 403, 404, 412, 414, 416, 418, 419, 422, 424–426, 448, 451, 460, 462, 464, 477–479, 503, 513, 521, 529, 539, 547, 555, 556, 559–561, 563–565, 568, 569, 573, 579, 594, 613, 616, 628, 629, 632, 649, 650, 656, 706, 709–714, 745, 747, 761, 765, 787, 812, 820–824, 832, 836, 837, 842–844, 851, 853, 855, 858–860, 872, 884, 899, 904, 921, 928, 930–932

practice-based approach, 112, 113, 123, 126

practitioner, 2, 68, 92, 99, 101, 114, 116, 117, 119, 121, 122, 124, 134, 184, 231, 262–264, 273, 301, 388, 391, 392, 412, 413, 422, 425, 431, 432, 441, 442, 472, 571, 572, 577, 586, 587, 724, 725, 728, 802, 811, 812, 824, 825, 827, 898, 899, 902, 904, 906, 907, 909, 910, 913, 914, 917, 928, 935

praxis, 37, 149, 153, 158, 194, 303, 856, 875, 897–899, 904–910, 934, 935

propositions, 50, 62, 66, 69, 111, 726, 728, 789, 892, 915, 916, 918, 920, 924, 927, 932, 935, 937

psycho-social, 753, 764

R

racism, 6, 8, 9, 17, 68, 134, 208, 209, 211, 242–245, 250, 252, 253, 412, 417–419, 421, 422, 425, 506, 545, 548, 575–577, 627, 628, 632, 633, 635–641, 643, 650, 760, 848, 849, 904, 922, 932

radical, 53, 66, 68, 69, 176, 210, 249, 259, 348, 353, 413, 415, 422, 563, 699, 704, 741, 747, 748, 770–774, 779–781, 786, 787, 801, 848, 849, 855–857, 860, 867, 871, 903

radicalization, 595, 769–781, 933

reader, 1, 2, 4, 15, 67, 75–87, 97, 386, 387, 402, 413, 430, 431, 433, 441, 504, 505, 507, 557, 562, 611, 628, 631, 898–900, 909, 930

reading, 15, 61, 76–79, 81–85, 87, 97, 103, 142, 154, 172, 173, 176, 177, 203, 247, 249, 284, 289, 333, 413, 414, 455, 504, 508, 517, 531, 651, 773, 774, 802, 854

recognition theory, 27, 33

reconciliation, 236, 270, 485, 489, 491, 492, 499, 504, 506, 512, 514, 516

reflection, 12, 13, 18, 28, 66, 70, 71, 78, 80, 82, 87, 101, 120, 123, 126, 130, 135, 159, 167, 168, 173, 184, 185, 187, 195, 220, 221, 226, 235, 258, 263–267, 270, 272, 280, 282–284, 290, 295, 302–317, 319–327, 336, 345, 354, 358, 366, 369, 370,

952 INDEX

373, 375, 391, 399, 405, 406,
418, 432, 436, 449, 470, 471,
478, 487, 489, 513, 542–546,
553, 580, 595, 604, 605, 622,
627, 633, 636, 652, 656, 661,
666, 705, 709, 711, 722, 770,
835, 843, 869, 876, 889, 890,
898, 905, 917, 924–926, 935
reflexive agency, 60–63, 65–71
reflexivity, 60, 61, 66, 67, 181–183,
185, 191, 192, 195, 196, 373,
873, 875, 876
relational learning, 132, 135–137,
144, 348, 355
relational ontology, 131, 134, 734
religion, 140, 160, 204, 206, 383,
490, 664, 666–669, 699, 774,
823, 848–850, 855, 860, 864,
870, 872
repressive power, 250, 251
resistance, 6, 17, 35, 204, 225, 234,
236, 307, 390, 465, 490,
555–558, 562, 563, 566, 702,
746, 754, 771, 792, 836, 848,
850, 899, 928, 931
responsibility, 101, 141, 151, 192,
193, 199, 200, 207–209, 212,
218, 252, 262, 267, 334, 339,
374, 376, 384, 387, 391,
493–495, 498, 503–505, 507,
508, 510, 514–517, 529, 556,
568, 636, 669, 687, 694, 738,
747, 778, 794, 839, 884, 904,
910, 929, 935
Retreat, 373–376, 399–406, 423,
678, 741, 779, 854, 925

S

science, 39, 131, 132, 134, 176, 184,
209, 265, 397, 469, 470,
472–474, 490, 526, 529–531,
549, 701, 718, 724, 734, 737,

739–741, 752, 793, 804, 814,
818, 822, 823, 848–852, 856,
926, 933
self-compassion, 135, 138, 142–144
self-concept, 46, 367, 499, 680, 832,
834–844
self-defense, 832, 833, 836–838, 841,
844
self-determination, 38, 62, 257, 260,
264, 266, 268, 270, 490, 924
self-organized criticality, 702–708,
711, 713, 715
senior management, 383–385, 388,
389, 392, 925
sensory, 225, 399, 401, 544, 598,
600, 601, 603–606, 758
sensuousness, 79
social change, 10, 12, 27, 33, 35, 52,
54, 64, 69–71, 80, 91, 169, 258,
261–263, 266–268, 273, 442,
556, 599, 612, 745, 751, 754,
764, 899, 924, 933
social determinants, 268, 424, 761
social identity, 412, 414, 418–420,
425, 575, 623, 916, 926
social learning, 34, 183, 760, 762
social movements, 46, 50, 53–55, 61,
62, 64, 69–71, 182, 195, 253,
655, 921
societal unconscious, 758
sociomateriality, 177, 178
Soul Collage, 637, 638
soul work, 647, 718, 811, 853, 856,
860, 922, 934
spiritual/spirituality, 14, 98, 131,
133, 134, 136, 139–141, 147,
150, 151, 153, 157, 159, 160,
169, 201, 202, 204–206, 217,
225, 232, 234, 236, 260, 293,
419, 472, 488, 490, 505, 508,
533, 601–603, 693, 718, 725,
739, 742–744, 747, 748,

812–815, 818, 819, 822–824,
826–828, 833, 834, 849, 854,
855, 858, 860, 864–870, 872,
873, 876–878, 888, 927, 934
STAGES, 189, 679–681, 683
story, 60, 76, 77, 80, 81, 83, 86,
103, 116, 131, 137, 138, 140,
142, 152–154, 156, 201, 202,
204, 207, 213, 217, 219–223,
225, 226, 228, 229, 231,
234–236, 245, 247–251, 268,
270, 281, 282, 286, 288, 290,
293, 294, 335–338, 369, 371,
424, 429–431, 433, 434, 436,
437, 439–442, 447–450,
452–455, 460, 461, 463, 465,
477, 489–497, 504, 506–510,
513–517, 522–525, 533, 534,
541, 542, 546–548, 550–553,
566, 581, 583, 584, 599, 602,
614, 628–632, 634, 638, 641,
654, 655, 694, 701, 711, 712,
722, 724, 738, 739, 810, 811,
819, 822, 837, 842, 847, 851,
852, 854, 859, 875, 876, 897,
899, 900, 902, 905, 906,
908–910, 920, 926, 929, 931,
936
storytelling, 76, 135, 217, 219–221,
223, 225, 337, 430, 431, 433,
434, 436–443, 463, 477, 486,
507, 523, 540–543, 547, 552,
553, 843, 852, 897, 905, 906,
926, 929, 931, 932, 937
structural thinking, 245, 925
subject/object, 12, 26, 30, 31, 38,
78, 102, 111, 112, 114, 115,
117–119, 130, 165–168,
170–174, 176, 177, 183, 191,
193, 209, 229, 253, 280, 283,
286, 289, 292, 307, 319, 351,
353, 358, 359, 368, 376, 419,

451, 453, 459, 475, 486,
504–506, 512, 514, 549, 555,
559, 560, 563, 564, 567, 622,
636–639, 641, 660, 680, 702,
734–737, 752, 753, 755–760,
769, 770, 773, 780, 789, 794,
822, 834, 839, 851, 852, 886,
904, 908, 919

sustainable development, 785–787,
789, 790, 793, 795, 799, 805,
933

sustainable development goals
(SDGs), 787, 790, 791,
795–797, 804

System of Activity, 173, 177, 178

systems, 5, 10, 27, 39, 45, 48–50, 52,
54, 61, 97–99, 102, 123, 125,
130–135, 139, 159, 167, 168,
173, 177, 182, 183, 196, 206,
222, 224, 226, 233, 242, 244,
245, 247–249, 251, 253, 259,
264, 270, 271, 273, 292, 298,
306, 336, 338, 343, 352, 353,
358, 363, 365, 367, 372, 374,
392, 397, 399, 401, 404, 413,
414, 416–420, 424, 425, 470,
478, 499, 506, 530, 532, 534,
538, 544, 548, 553, 564, 568,
579, 585, 612–615, 617, 618,
620–622, 628, 636, 639, 640,
659, 667, 679, 680, 682,
685–688, 692, 700, 702–707,
712, 713, 718–720, 723, 734,
736, 742, 772, 786, 787,
789–791, 793–795, 797, 799,
801, 802, 804, 816, 817, 820,
821, 823, 824, 827, 834, 842,
864, 884, 889, 898, 899, 903,
906–908, 921, 922, 925, 933,
937

954 INDEX

T

tacit, 101, 112, 115, 116, 125, 149, 158, 169, 320, 327, 391, 552, 591, 596, 603, 605, 759

teacher reflection, 301–304, 306, 323, 325, 327, 925

third space, 430, 431, 433, 436, 438, 440, 441, 443, 558, 926

thresholds, 7, 222, 398, 404, 405, 430, 433, 703, 742, 909, 914, 915, 920, 937

training, 85, 87, 117, 126, 134, 159, 176, 253, 368, 384, 417, 506, 526, 538, 540, 542, 547, 549, 586, 592, 602, 606, 618, 620, 623, 654, 700, 705, 711, 721, 755, 756, 777, 778, 803, 831, 837–841, 866

transdisciplinary, 15, 811, 865, 918, 920, 935, 937

transform, 3, 6, 9, 11–15, 17, 18, 46, 52, 54, 55, 81, 94, 95, 102, 111, 166, 167, 169, 171, 178, 201, 213, 257, 261, 267, 269, 270, 272, 280, 304, 326, 345, 367, 398, 404, 433, 443, 450, 465, 475, 479, 486, 492, 495, 499, 503, 504, 524, 538, 539, 555, 557, 558, 564, 568, 569, 572, 586, 594, 616, 637, 646, 649, 667, 671, 678, 679, 701, 717, 718, 780, 786, 802, 804, 805, 811–813, 815, 827, 835, 840, 852, 864, 865, 890, 900, 901, 903, 909, 923, 924, 926, 928, 937

transformational, 5, 8, 54, 76, 77, 93, 94, 99, 113, 126, 140, 178, 217, 221, 342, 344, 368, 416, 450, 463, 489, 494, 499, 513, 591–593, 597, 615, 616, 679, 701, 724, 729, 781, 785, 786, 791, 793, 795, 797–799, 803, 804, 826, 832, 879, 898, 900, 922

transformational change, 100, 611–615, 621, 623, 624, 699, 701, 704–708, 710–715, 786, 788, 791, 799, 804, 930, 933

transformational evaluation, 786, 788, 799, 801, 802, 804, 933

transformational learning, 10, 54, 55, 104, 367, 375, 471, 493–495, 602, 729, 786–789, 801, 848, 929, 933

transformation-in-action, 897, 932, 937

transformation-in-connection, 927, 937

transformation-in-context, 923, 937

transformative, 3, 5, 8, 12, 16, 53, 59, 61, 63, 67, 69, 71, 76, 82, 83, 85, 87, 93, 95–97, 103–106, 116, 130, 132, 133, 135–137, 139, 143, 151, 158, 159, 165, 176, 182, 186, 195, 208, 210, 212, 218, 219, 225, 235, 236, 242, 253, 258, 261–263, 266, 267, 272, 273, 281, 304, 305, 323–327, 364, 369–371, 373, 396, 402, 405, 414, 423, 430, 431, 434, 436, 439, 442, 443, 451, 465, 472, 474, 490, 494, 495, 513, 516, 538, 539, 545, 552, 555, 561, 569, 580, 595, 596, 603, 606, 616, 623, 630, 649–651, 655, 678–680, 683, 685, 691–694, 704, 724, 729, 739, 741, 742, 771, 773, 774, 780, 781, 788, 792, 797, 799, 802, 811, 814, 815, 817, 824–826, 828, 835, 838, 841, 850, 852, 864, 866–868, 873–879, 884, 885, 891, 892,

899, 903, 905, 906, 908, 909, 916, 927, 928, 930, 931

transformative education experience, 486, 928

transformative imagination, 397, 399, 404–406, 925

transformative journey, 211, 258, 259, 479, 516, 810, 824, 826

transformative learning community, 352, 678

transformative learning outcomes, 99, 105

transformative learning (TL), 2–7, 9–17, 25, 26, 28–31, 33–35, 37–40, 46–48, 50–55, 60, 61, 63–65, 67–71, 78–79, 81–85, 92–95, 97–105, 109–113, 116, 119, 124–126, 131, 133, 134, 137, 144, 147, 148, 151–153, 158, 160, 165, 167–170, 173, 174, 176–178, 196, 200–202, 204–206, 209, 213, 219, 234, 235, 257, 263, 267, 280, 281, 298, 303, 306, 336, 341, 347, 348, 354, 356–358, 364, 367–370, 375–377, 397, 406, 414, 416, 430–433, 438, 441–443, 448, 449, 451, 452, 462, 463, 469, 472, 475, 477, 479, 487, 488, 491, 503, 508, 510, 522, 532, 538, 539, 541, 543, 545, 546, 548, 549, 552, 553, 573, 574, 580, 585–587, 591, 593–595, 597, 603, 605, 606, 627, 628, 630, 631, 633, 634, 639, 646–652, 654, 656, 679, 680, 707–709, 711–714, 717, 718, 721, 729, 733, 734, 736, 738, 743, 752, 770, 773, 774, 780, 781, 800, 811, 824, 826–828, 832–835, 839, 842–845, 853, 860, 864, 865, 867, 868, 873, 875, 876, 878, 883–885, 887–893, 902, 914–917, 919, 921, 922, 924, 926, 929, 930, 933, 934, 936, 937

transformative pilgrimage learning (TPL), 200–202, 204–206, 209, 210, 213

transformative sustainability education (TSE), 130–134, 137, 144, 734, 742

transformative teaching and learning, 487, 499

truth, 7, 27, 77–79, 81, 106, 220, 243, 244, 261, 286, 303, 316, 417, 423, 439, 447, 449, 492, 495, 506, 512, 513, 524, 528, 683, 687, 688, 690, 691, 723, 742, 821, 825, 826, 848–852, 854, 858, 885, 909, 931

U

Ubuntu, 471, 472, 476, 477, 479, 480, 528, 531–533, 926, 927

unconscious, 27, 124, 151, 159, 160, 222, 374, 398, 400, 417, 419, 591, 592, 602, 628, 634, 642, 645–647, 649–651, 653, 655, 656, 686, 737, 739, 744, 752, 757–760, 764, 820, 825, 826, 832, 843, 844, 851, 852, 854, 930

utopian, 764, 866, 867

V

vertical development, 367, 373, 376

W

We-Space, 412–415, 419–422, 424, 425, 685, 689, 926, 927

Western paradigm, 811, 821

956 INDEX

white supremacy, 132, 241, 242, 244, 247–253, 412, 418, 422, 425, 926
whole person, 14, 94, 137, 160, 351, 358, 359, 442, 472, 477, 479, 552, 642, 678, 926, 927
Witness Blanket (WB), 503–508, 510–517, 929, 931, 932
women/woman, 46, 51, 83, 85, 86, 104, 151, 153, 185, 188, 201, 207, 212, 217, 224, 225, 231, 232, 245, 246, 251, 283, 293, 334–336, 338, 339, 344, 349, 350, 364–377, 381–383, 385, 387–389, 391, 413, 414, 448–453, 455, 456, 459–465, 472, 491, 516, 525, 527, 548, 551, 571, 572, 584, 592, 593, 596, 598–600, 602, 616, 629, 631, 633, 634, 639, 640, 721, 722, 755, 756, 761, 765, 780, 813, 817, 822, 832, 836–841, 844, 853, 854, 857, 890, 917, 925, 926, 930

women authors, 84, 86
workplace bullying, 572
World Literature, 83–87, 921
worldview, 99, 102, 103, 131, 133, 134, 183, 201, 259, 280, 282, 290, 292, 296, 297, 322, 341, 344, 345, 352, 395, 397, 399, 406, 432, 443, 478, 487, 504, 528, 530, 533, 534, 540, 552, 592, 596, 598, 599, 601, 603, 630, 634, 635, 640, 651, 656, 659, 660, 666–668, 671, 672, 679, 680, 701, 702, 709, 710, 713, 753, 759, 772, 804, 811, 812, 814, 821–825, 827, 828, 867, 868, 873, 874, 878, 914, 926–928, 931, 934

Y
youth, 207, 308, 405, 453, 489, 499, 631, 635, 651, 776, 851, 866, 870, 883, 884, 886–888, 893, 934

Printed in the United States
by Baker & Taylor Publisher Services